W9-BUL-476

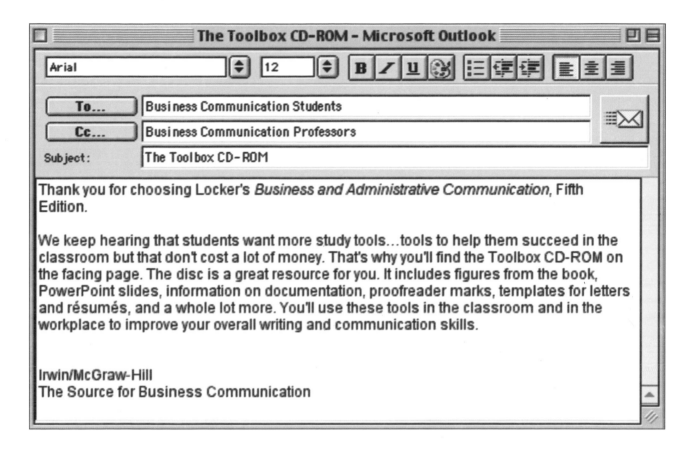

The Toolbox CD-ROM – Microsoft Outlook

Arial | 12 | **B** *I* U

To... | Business Communication Students

Cc... | Business Communication Professors

Subject: | The Toolbox CD-ROM

Thank you for choosing Locker's *Business and Administrative Communication*, Fifth Edition.

We keep hearing that students want more study tools…tools to help them succeed in the classroom but that don't cost a lot of money. That's why you'll find the Toolbox CD-ROM on the facing page. The disc is a great resource for you. It includes figures from the book, PowerPoint slides, information on documentation, proofreader marks, templates for letters and résumés, and a whole lot more. You'll use these tools in the classroom and in the workplace to improve your overall writing and communication skills.

Irwin/McGraw-Hill
The Source for Business Communication

Business and Administrative Communication

Business and Administrative Communication

Fifth Edition

Kitty O. Locker

The Ohio State University

Irwin McGraw-Hill

Boston   Burr Ridge, IL   Dubuque, IA   Madison, WI
New York   San Francisco   St. Louis
Bangkok   Bogotá   Caracas   Lisbon   London   Madrid   Mexico City
Milan   New Delhi   Seoul   Singapore   Sydney   Taipei   Toronto

McGraw-Hill Higher Education

A Division of The McGraw-Hill Companies

BUSINESS AND ADMINISTRATIVE COMMUNICATION

Copyright © 2000, 1998, 1995, 1992, 1989 by The McGraw-Hill Companies, Inc. All rights reserved. Printed in the United States of America. Except as permitted under the United States Copyright Act of 1976, no part of this publication may be reproduced or distributed in any form or by any means, or stored in a database or retrieval system, without the prior written permission of the publisher.

This book is printed on acid-free paper.

domestic   1 2 3 4 5 6 7 8 9 0 VNH/VNH 9 0 9 8 7 6 5 4 3 2 1 0 9
international 1 2 3 4 5 6 7 8 9 0 VNH/VNH 9 0 9 8 7 6 5 4 3 2 1 0 9

ISBN 0-07-229392-6 (book only)
ISBN 0-07-235011-3 (CD-ROM)
ISBN 0-07-235073-3 (text bound with CD-ROM)

Publisher: *Craig S. Beytien*
Development editor: *Sarah Reed*
Marketing manager: *Ellen Cleary*
Senior project manager: *Mary Conzachi*
Manager, new book production: *Melonie Salvati*
Interior designer: *Michael Warrell*
Cover designer: *Z Graphics/Michael Warrell*
Cover illustrations: *Z Graphics*
Photo research coordinator: *Sharon Miller*
Photo researcher: *Charlotte Goldman*
Supplement coordinator: *Betty Hadala*
New media coordinator: *Chet Smith*
Compositor: *Carlisle Communications, Ltd.*
Printer: *Von Hoffmann Press, Inc.*

Library of Congress Cataloging-in-Publication Data

Locker, Kitty O.
    Business and administrative communication / Kitty O. Locker. —
5th ed.
      p. cm.
    Includes bibliographical references and index.
    ISBN 0-07-229392-6
    1. Business communication. 2. Communication in management.
  I. Title. II. Title: Communication.
  HF5718.L63   2000
  651.7—dc21

INTERNATIONAL EDITION   ISBN 0-07-117722-1

Copyright © 2000. Exclusive rights by The McGraw-Hill Companies, Inc. for manufacture and export. This book cannot be re-exported from the country to which it is consigned by McGraw-Hill. The International Edition is not available in North America.

http://www.mhhe.com

To my husband, Bob Mills, with love

Kitty O. Locker is an Associate Professor of English at The Ohio State University in Columbus, Ohio, where she teaches courses in business and technical discourse and in research methods. She has taught as Assistant Professor at Texas A&M University and the University of Illinois.

She has also written *The Irwin Business Communication Handbook: Writing and Speaking in Business Classes* (1993), coauthored *Business Writing Cases and Problems* (1980, 1984, 1987), and co-edited *Conducting Research in Business Communication* (1988). She has twice received the Alpha Kappa Psi award for Distinguished Publication in Business Communication: for her article " 'Sir, This Will Never Do': Model Dunning Letters 1592–1873" and for her article " 'As Per Your Request': A History of Business Jargon." In 1992 she received the Association for Business Communication's Outstanding Researcher Award.

Her research in progress includes work on the effect of commenting styles on student attitudes and performance, collaborative writing in the classroom and the workplace, and the emergence of bureaucratic writing in the correspondence of the British East India Company from 1600 to 1800.

Her consulting work includes conducting tutorials and short courses in business, technical, and administrative writing for employees of URS Greiner, Ross Products Division of Abbott Laboratories, Franklin County, the Ohio Civil Service Employees Association, AT&T, the American Medical Association, Western Electric, the Illinois Department of Central Management Services, the Illinois Department of Transportation, the A. E. Staley Company, Flo-Con, the Police Executive Leadership College, and the Firemen's Institute. She developed a complete writing improvement program for Joseph T. Ryerson, the nation's largest steel materials service center.

She has served as the Interim Editor of *The Bulletin of the Association for Business Communication* and, in 1994–95, as President of the Association for Business Communication (ABC). She is currently editor of ABC's *Journal of Business Communication.*

In 1998, she received ABC's Meada Gibbs Outstanding Teacher Award.

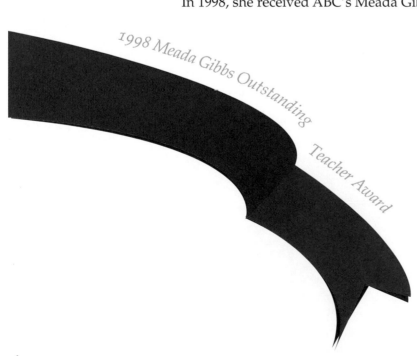

1998 Meada Gibbs Outstanding Teacher Award

BAC Fifth Edition

August 1, 1999

Dear Student:

Business and Administrative Communication (BAC) takes the mystery out of writing and speaking effectively.

As you read,

- Use the Chapter Outline to preview what you'll learn. Check your understanding with the Summary of Key Points at the end of the chapter.

- Note the terms in boldface type and their definitions. In later chapters, the linked chain icon identifies the page where the term is first defined.

- Use items in the lists when you prepare your assignments or review for tests.

- Use the examples, especially the paired examples of effective and ineffective communication, as models to help you draft and revise. Comments in red ink signal problems in an example; comments in blue ink note things done well.

The side columns offer anecdotes and examples that show the principles in the text at work in a variety of business and administrative situations. Some readers like to read all the sidebars first, then come back to read the chapter. Other readers prefer to take a break from the page to read the sidebar. The logos identify the kind of example:

International examples show how to apply or modify the principles when you communicate with international audiences.

Ethical and Legal examples alert you to ethical decisions and legal implications of business and administrative communication.

Technology examples show how technology can help create better messages and how technological changes affect the way people produce, transmit, and interpret business messages.

On-the-Job examples show the principles in the text at work.

Just-for-Fun anecdotes show the lighter side of business communication. Skip them if you're in a hirer read them just for enjoyment.

In addition, gold stars identify sidebar classics. These oldies but goodies are still relevant to today's business world.

When you prepare an assignment,

- Review the analysis questions in Chapter 1. Some assignments have "Hints" to help probe the problem. Some of the longer assignments have preliminary assignments analyzing the audience or developing reader benefits or subject lines. Use these to practice portions of longer documents.

- If you're writing a letter or memo, read the sample problems in Chapters 7, 8, and 9 with a detailed analysis, strong and weak solutions, and a discussion of the solutions to see how to apply the principles in this book to your own writing.

- See the Toolbox CD-Rom for practice exercises (with answers), more sample solutions with evaluations, and templates for letters, memos, and résumés.

- Remember that most problems are open-ended, requiring original, critical thinking. Many of the problems are deliberately written in negative, ineffective language. You'll need to reword sentences, reorganize information, and think through the situation to produce the best possible solution to the business problem.

- Learn as much as you can about what's happening in business. The knowledge will not only help you develop reader benefits and provide examples but also make you an even more impressive candidate in job interviews.

Business and Administrative Communication can help you develop the communication skills required for success in the 21st century. Have a good term—and a good career!

Cordially,

Kitty O. Locker
locker.1@osu.edu

BAC Fifth Edition

August 1, 1999

Dear Professor:

Business and Administrative Communication (BAC) can make your job teaching business communication just a little bit easier.

You'll find that this edition of BAC is as flexible, specific, interesting, comprehensive, and up to date as its predecessors. The features teachers and students find so useful have been retained: the anecdotes and examples, the easy-to-follow lists, the integrated coverage of ethics and international business communication, the analyses of sample problems, the wealth of in-class exercises and out-of-class assignments. But a good thing has become even better. This edition of BAC is the most effective teaching tool yet.

Major Changes in the Fifth Edition

Six major changes make the text even more useful:

- Expanded coverage of ethical issues includes discussion-starters such as Figure 1.6, Ethical Issues in Business Communication, a list of Web sites dealing with ethical issues, and problems with ethical implications, such as analyzing companies' ethics statements and evaluating a prejudiced supervisor.

- Sophisticated Web coverage identifies useful sites for business, personal business, research, ethics, and job hunting. The @ icon identifies where added information can be found on the BAC Web page at www.mhhe.com/locker. Advice about screen design and Web problems in several chapters allow students to play with one of the most enjoyable forms of business communication.

- Enhanced technology coverage in this edition includes actual screen shots of Microsoft Word screens, e-mail screens, and Web screen captures to give students a first-hand look at how their computer will look as they work on different documents and presenta- tions.

- Even more useful coverage of working in groups helps students set ground rules for student groups and troubleshoot group problems.

- A Student Toolbox CD-Rom provides such valuable resources as practice exercises (with answers), format templates, proofreading marks, interview questions and tips, and helpful figures from the book.

- New and revised chapter opening statements by business professionals keep the text up to date.

Features Retained

BAC retains the features that have made it the number one book in business communication:

- **BAC is flexible.** Choose the chapters that best fit your course and your students. Choose from in-class exercises, messages to revise, problems with hints, and cases presented as they'd arise in the workplace. Many problems offer several options: small group discussions, individual writing, group writing, or oral presentations.

- **BAC is specific.** BAC provides specific strategies, specific guidelines, and specific examples. BAC takes the mystery out of creating effective messages.

- **BAC is interesting.** Anecdotes from a variety of fields show business communication at work. The lively side columns from *The Wall Street Journal and* a host of other sources keep students turning pages and provide insights into the workplace that business students demand.

- **BAC is comprehensive.** BAC includes international communication, communicating across cultures in this country, ethics, collaborative writing, organizational cultures, graphs, and technology as well as traditional concerns such as style and organization. Assignments allow students to deal with international audiences or to cope with ethical dilemmas.

- **BAC is up to date.** The fifth edition of BAC incorporates the latest research and practice so that you and your students stay on the cutting edge.

Supplements

The stimulating, user-friendly supplement package has been one of the major reasons that BAC is so popular.

1. The **Instructor's Resource Manual** contains

   - **Answers to all exercises,** an overview and difficulty rating for each problem, and, for several of the problems in the book, a detailed analysis, discussion and quiz questions, and a good solution.

   - **Additional transparency masters with** ready-to-duplicate examples and lecture points.

   - **Additional exercises and cases for** diagnostic and readiness tests, grammar and style, and for letters, memos, and reports.

   - **Lesson plans and class activities for each chapter.** You'll find discussion guides for transparencies, activities to reinforce chapter materials and prepare students for assignments, and handouts for group work, peer editing, and other activities.

   - **Sample syllabi** for courses with different emphases and approaches.

2. The Test **Bank contains** approximately 1,200 test items with answers and a difficulty rating for each.

3. Power Point **presentation** disks are included to enliven your classes.

4. The **Instructor's Presentation CD-Rom** collects many features of the Instructor's Resource Manual, videos, PowerPoint slides, and lecture material in an electronic format and offers a convenient tool that allows you to customize your lectures and presentations.

5. The **Student Toolbox CD-Rom** provides an added study tool for your students in the classroom and in the workplace to help improve their overall writing and communication skills.

6. A **Computerized Test Bank** is available to qualified adopters in both Macintosh and Windows formats, and allows professors to generate and edit their own test questions.

7. A **Video** containing listening and speaking segments is available to give students more information on these important communication skills.

8. You can also get the supplements in an **Instructor's Resource Box,** which contains separate file folders for each chapter so that you can add your own notes and handouts. This box includes

   • The complete Instructor's Resource Manual in loose-leaf format

   • Transparency masters

   • PowerPoint disks
   • Test Bank

   Even if you rarely use an instructor's manual, you may find useful material in the Instructor's Resource Box.

Continuing the Conversation

You can get more information about teaching business communication from the meetings and publications of The Association for Business Communication (ABC). Contact

> Professor Robert J. Myers, Executive Director
> Association for Business Communication
> Baruch College—CUNY
> Department of Speech
> 17 Lexington Avenue
> New York, NY 10010
> Voice:212-387-1340; Fax:212-387-1655; E-mail: MyersABC@compuserve. com

This edition incorporates the feedback I've received from instructors who used earlier editions. Tell me about your own success stories teaching *Business and Administrative Communication.* I look forward to hearing from you!

Cordially,

Kitty O. Locker

Kitty O. Locker
locker. 1@osu. edu

Thanks

All writing is in some sense collaborative. This book in particular builds upon the ideas and advice of teachers, students, and researchers. The people who share their ideas in conferences and publications enrich not only this book but also business communication as a field.

Several people reviewed the fourth edition, suggesting what to change and what to keep. Additional reviewers commented on drafts of the fifth edition, helping me further improve the book. I thank all of these reviewers for their attention to detail and their promptness! The people whose names I have been given are

Randi Meryl Blank, *Indiana University*

Tena Crews, *State University of West Georgia*

Mark DelMaramo, *Thiel College*

Clark Ford, *Middle Tennessee State University*

Barbara Hagler, *Southern Illinois University*

Kathy Harris, *Northwestern State University*

Vincent Hartigan, *New Mexico State University*

Kenneth Hoffman, *Emporia State University*

Elizabeth Hoger, *Western Michigan University*

Donna Kienzler, *Iowa State University*

Gary Kohut, *University of North Carolina, Charlotte*

Luchen Li, *Iowa State University*

Michael Mahler, *Montana State University*

Cheryl Noll, *Eastern Illinois University*

Susan Plutsky, *California State University, Northridge*

Ralph Roberts, *University of West Florida*

Lisa Tyler, *Sinclair Community College*

Catherine Waitinas, *University of Illinois, Champaign-Urbana*

Vicky Waldroupe, *Tusculum College*

Randall Waller, *Baylor University*

The following people commented on specific aspects of the book or helped me with specific needs:

John Cooper, *University of Kentucky*

Susan H. Delagrange, *The Ohio State University*

Paula J. Foster, *The Ohio State University*

Silvia Fuduric, *Wayne State University*

Lisa Klein, *The Ohio State University*

Melissa Ianetta, *The Ohio State University*

Lee Jones, *Shorter College*

Pamela L. Martin, *The Ohio State University*

Brian R. McGee, *Texas Tech University*

Elizabeth Patnoe, *The Ohio State University*

Janet Winter, *Central Missouri State University*

In addition, the book continues to benefit from people who advised me on earlier editions:

Bill Allen, *University of LaVerne*
Vanessa Arnold, *University of Mississippi*
Lynn Ashford, *Alabama State University*
Dennis Barbour, *Purdue University—Calumet*
Jaye Bausser, *The Ohio State University*
Carole Bhakar, *The University of Manitoba*
Sallye Benoit, *Nicholls State University*
Raymond W. Beswick, *formerly of Synerude, Ltd.*
Vincent Brown, *Battelle Memorial Institute*
John Bryan, *University of Cincinnati*
Janice Burke, *South Suburban College of Cook County*
Andrew Cantrell, *University of Illinois*
John Carr, *The Ohio State University*
Brendan G. Coleman, *Mankato State University*
Moira E. W. Dempsy, *Oregon State University*
Gladys DeVane, *Indiana University*
Jose A. Duran, *Riverside Community College*
Dorothy J. Dykman, *Point Loma Nazarene College*
Mary Ann Firmin, *Oregon State University*
W. Clark Ford, *Middle Tennessee State University*
Robert D. Gieselman, *University of Illinois*
Cheryl Glenn, *Pennsylvania State University*
Peter Hadorn, *Virginia Commonwealth University*
Elaine Hage, *Forsythe Technical Community College*
Barbara Hagler, *Southern Illinois University*
Robert Haight, *Kalamazoo Valley Community College*
Les Hanson, *Red River Community College, Canada*
Maxine Hart, *Baylor University*
Mark Harstein, *University of Illinois*
Charles Hebert, *The University of South Carolina*
Paulette Henry, *Howard University*
Carlton Holte, *California State University, Sacramento*
Glenda Hudson, *California State University, Bakersfield*
Elizabeth Huettman, *Cornell University*
Susan Isaacs, *Community College of Philadelphia*
Daphne A. Jameson, *Cornell University*
Elizabeth Jenkins, *Pennsylvania State University*
Paula R. Kaiser, *University of North Carolina at Greensboro*
Joy Kidwell, *Oregon State University*
Susan E. Kiner, *Cornell University*
Keith Kroll, *Kalamazoo Valley Community College*
Milton Kukon, *Southern Vermont College*
Linda M. LaDuc, *University of Massachusetts, Amherst*
Suzanne Lambert, *Broward Community College*
Barry Lawler, *Oregon State University*

Gordon Lee, *University of Tennessee*
Andrea A. Lunsford, *The Ohio State University*
John T. Maguire, *University of Illinois*
Michael D. Mahler, *Montana State University*
Iris Washburn Mauney, *High Point College*
Yvonne Merrill, *University of Arizona*
Jayne Moneysmith, *Kent State University–Stark*
Evelyn Morris, *Mesa Community College*
Frederick K. Moss, *University of Wisconsin–Waukesha*
Frank P. Nemecek, Jr., *Wayne State University*
Jean E. Perry, *University of Southern California*
Florence M. Petrofes, *University of Texas at El Paso*
Virginia Polanski, *Stonehill College*
Kathryn C. Rentz, *University of Cincinnati*
Jeanette Ritzenthaler, *New Hampshire College*
Kelly Searsmith, *University of Illinois*
Sherry Sherrill, *Forsythe Technical Community College*
Frank Smith, *Harper College*
Pamela Smith, *Florida Atlantic University*
Judith A. Swartley, *Lehigh University*
Mel Tarnowski, *Macomb Community College*
Linda Travis, *Ferris State University*
Donna Vasa, *University of Nebraska–Lincoln*
David A. Victor, *Eastern Michigan University*
George Walters, *Emporia State University*
Judy West, *University of Tennessee–Chattanooga*
Rosemary Wilson, *Washtenaw Community College*
Bonnie Thames Yarbrough, *University of North Carolina at Greensboro*
Sherilyn K. Zeigler, *Hawaii Pacific University*

I'm pleased to know that the book has worked so well for so many people and appreciative of suggestions for ways to make it even more useful in this edition. I especially want to thank the students who have allowed me to use their letters and memos, whether or not they allowed me to use their real names in the text.

I am grateful to all the business people who were willing to interrupt busy schedules to write the chapter-opening statements for this book. The companies where I have done research and consulting work have given me insights into the problems and procedures of business and administrative communication. Special acknowledgment is due Joseph T. Ryerson & Son, Inc., which hired me to create the Writing Skills Program that ultimately became the first draft of this book. And I thank the organizations that permitted me to reproduce their documents in this book and in the transparency masters.

Alisha Rohde did library research. She, Sarah Reed, and Andrea Williams made innumerable phone calls to schedule the interviews. Tom Wilk helped with proofreading. The book continues to incorporate the contributions of Bennis Blue, Susan Carlson, Kathy Casto, Jane Greer, Ruth Ann Hendrickson, Gianna Marsella, Scott Miller, Carole Clark Papper, Paula Weston, and Andrea Williams to earlier editions.

My publisher, Irwin/McGraw-Hill, continues to provide strong editorial and staff support. I am particularly grateful to Karen Mellon for her creative problem solving, patience, and encouragement, to Sarah Reed for taking care of necessary details, and to Michael Warrell and Mary Conzachi for the appearance of the book.

And, finally, I thank my husband, Robert S. Mills, who continues to provide a sounding board for ideas, encouragement, and, when deadlines are tight (as they continue to be, even on this fifth edition), weekly or nightly rides to Federal Express.

Part One

The Building Blocks of Effective Messages   1

1   Business Communication, Management, and Success   2
2   Building Goodwill   32
3   Adapting Your Message to Your Audience   58
4   Making Your Writing Easy to Read   82
5   Planning, Composing, and Revising   114
6   Designing Documents, Slides, and Screens   130

Part Two

Letters and Memos   153

7   Informative and Positive Messages   154
8   Negative Messages   190
9   Writing Persuasive Messages   220
10   Handling Difficult Persuasive Situations   258
11   Sales and Fund-Raising Letters   276

Part Three

Interpersonal Communication   311

12   Communicating across Cultures   312
13   Working and Writing in Groups   334

Part Four

Reports   363

14   Planning, Proposing, and Researching Reports   364
15   Analyzing Information and Writing Reports   404
16   Using Graphs and Other Visuals   456
17   Making Oral Presentations   482

Part Five

Job Hunting   503

18   Résumés   504
19   Job Application Letters   536
20   Job Interviews, Follow-Up Letters and Calls, and Job Offers   564

Appendixes   586

A   Formats for Letters, Memos, and E-Mail messages   586
B   Writing Correctly   608
C   Making and Communicating Meaning   632
D   Toulmin Logic   650

Glossary   657
Notes   669
Photo Credits   679
Company Index   681
Organization Index   685
Subject Index   687

Part One

The Building Blocks of
Effective Messages   1

❝ *Leadership relies,
above all else, on
effective
communication
skills.* ❞

**1   Business
Communication,
Management, and
Success   2**

An Inside Perspective: Business
Communication, Management, and
Success   2

Communication Ability =
Promotability   4

"I'll Never Have to Write
Because . . ."   4

The Managerial Functions of
Communication   6

The Cost of Correspondence   8

The Costs of Poor
Correspondence   10

Benefits of Improving
Correspondence   12

Criteria for Effective Messages   12

Trends in Business and
Administrative Communication   12

Understanding and Analyzing
Business Communication
Situations   20

How to Solve Business
Communication Problems   21

Summary of Key Points   25

Exercises and Problems for
Chapter 1   26

2   Building Goodwill   32

An Inside Perspective: Building
Goodwill   33

You-Attitude   34

Positive Emphasis   37

Tone, Power, and Politeness   43

Reducing Bias in Business
Communication   45

Summary of Key Points   51

Exercises and Problems for
Chapter 2   53

**3   Adapting Your
Message to Your
Audience   58**

An Inside Perspective: Adapting Your
Message to Your Audience   59

Identifying Your Audiences   60

Ways to Analyze Your Audience   61

Choosing Channels to Reach Your
Audience   66

Using Audience Analysis to Adapt
Your Message   66

Reader Benefits   72

Writing or Speaking to Multiple
Audiences with Different Needs   77

Summary of Key Points   78

Exercises and Problems for
Chapter 3   79

**4   Making Your Writing
Easy to Read   86**

An Inside Perspective: Making Your
Writing Easy to Read   87

Good Style in Business and
Administrative Writing   88

Half-Truths about Style   91

Evaluating "Rules" about
Writing   92

Building a Better Style   92

Ten Ways to Make Your Writing
Easier to Read   94

Readability Formulas and Good
Style   106

Organizational Preferences for
Style   107

Summary of Key Points   107

Exercises and Problems for
Chapter 4   108

5 Planning, Composing, and Revising 114

An Inside Perspective: Planning, Composing, and Revising 115
The Ways Good Writers Write 116
Activities in the Composing Process 116
Brainstorming, Planning, and Organizing Business Documents 117
Revising, Editing, and Proofreading 119
Getting and Using Feedback 123
Using Boilerplate 124
Overcoming Writer's Block and Procrastination 125
Technology and the Writing Process 126
Summary of Key Points 126
Exercises and Problems for Chapter 5 127

6 Designing Documents, Slides, and Screens 130

An Inside Perspective: Designing Documents, Slides, and Screens 131
Guidelines for Page Design 132
Designing Brochures and Newsletters 138
Designing Presentation Slides 140
Designing Web Pages 141
Testing the Design 142
Document Design as Part of Your Writing Process(es) 143
The Importance of Effective Design 143
Summary of Key Points 143
Exercises and Problems for Chapter 6 145

Part Two

Letters and Memos 153

“*Bad news should be communicated openly and honestly, despite how difficult the news may be for the employees to hear.*”

7 Informative and Positive Messages 154

An Inside Perspective: Informative and Positive Messages 155
Writing Letters and Memos 156
Organizing Informative and Positive Messages 157
Subject Lines for Informative and Positive Messages 159
Using Reader Benefits in Informative and Positive Messages 162
Writing the One-Page Memo 163
Ending Informative and Positive Letters and Memos 163
Writing E-Mail Messages 164
Varieties of Informative and Positive Messages 167
Solving a Sample Problem 171
Summary of Key Points 174
Exercises and Problems for Chapter 7 176

8 Negative Messages 190

An Inside Perspective: Writing Negative Messages 191
Subject Lines for Negative Messages 192
Organizing Negative Letters 193
Organizing Negative Memos 193
The Parts of a Negative Message 196
Tone in Negative Messages 201
Alternate Strategies for Negative Messages 202
Writing Negative E-Mail Messages 202
Varieties of Negative Messages 203
Solving a Sample Problem 203
Summary of Key Points 208
Exercises and Problems for Chapter 8 209

9   Writing Persuasive
    Messages   220

    An Inside Perspective: Writing
    Persuasive Messages   221

    Choosing a Persuasive
    Strategy   222

    Writing Direct Requests   225

    Writing Problem-Solving
    Messages   228

    Tone in Persuasive Messages   234

    Writing Persuasive E-Mail
    Messages   235

    Varieties of Persuasive
    Messages   236

    Solving a Sample Problem   239

    Summary of Key Points   245

    Exercises and Problems for
    Chapter 9   246

10   Handling Difficult
     Persuasive
     Situations   258

    An Inside Perspective: Handling
    Difficult Persuasive Situations   259

    Limiting Your Audience   261

    Bringing Everybody on Board   261

    Involving Your Audience   263

    Convincing the Reader   267

    Summary of Key Points   270

    Exercises and Problems for
    Chapter 10   271

11   Sales and Fund-Raising
     Letters   276

    An Inside Perspective: Sales and
    Fund-Raising Letters   277

    Components of Good Direct
    Mail   278

    Is It "Junk" Mail?   279

    Basic Direct Mail Strategy   280

    How To Organize a Sales or Fund-
    Raising Letter   283

    Strategy in Sales Letters   289

    Strategy in Fund-Raising
    Appeals   290

    Writing Style   297

    Parts of a Direct Mail Package   303

    Summary of Key Points   304

    Exercises and Problems for
    Chapter 11   305

Part Three

Interpersonal
Communication   311

66 *Cultural competence
requires learning to
expect differences
and having a positive
attitude toward
challenges and
change.* 99

12   Communicating Across
     Cultures   312

    An Inside Perspective:
    Communicating Across
    Cultures   313

    The Importance of International
    Business   314

    Diversity in the United States and
    Canada   314

    Ways to Look at Culture   315

    Values, Beliefs, and Practices   315

    Nonverbal Communication   317

    Oral Communication   322

    Writing to International
    Audiences   325

    Learning More about International
    Business Communication   327

    Summary of Key Points   327

    Exercises and Problems for
    Chapter 12   328

13   Working and Writing
     in Groups   334

    An Inside Perspective: Working and
    Writing in Groups   335

    Listening   336

    Group Interactions   338

    Working in Diverse Groups   343

    Conflict Resolution   345

    Effective Meetings   349

    Collaborative Writing   350

    Summary of Key Points   353

    Exercises and Problems for
    Chapter 13   354

Part Four

Reports 363

66 *My purpose and the audience's mix determine the tone and focus of the presentation.* 99

14 Planning, Proposing, and Researching Reports 364

An Inside Perspective: Planning, Proposing, and Researching Reports 365

Varieties of Reports 366

Defining Report Problems 367

Writing Proposals 368

Writing Progress Reports 377

Research Strategies for Reports 380

Using and Documenting Sources 391

Summary of Key Points 397

Exercises and Problems for Chapter 14 398

15 Analyzing Information and Writing Reports 404

An Inside Perspective: Analyzing Data and Writing Reports 405

A Timetable for Writing Reports 406

Analyzing Data and Information for Reports 406

Choosing Information for Reports 411

Organizing Information in Reports 412

Presenting Information Effectively in Reports 421

Writing Formal Reports 425

Summary of Key Points 448

Exercises and Problems for Chapter 15 450

16 Using Graphs and Other Visuals 456

An Inside Perspective: Using Graphs and Other Visuals 457

When to Use Visuals 458

Designing Visuals 459

Integrating Visuals in Your Text 470

Using Visuals in Your Presentation 471

Summary of Key Points 471

Exercises and Problems for Chapter 16 472

17 Making Oral Presentations 482

An Inside Perspective: Making Oral Presentations 483

Purposes in Oral Presentations 484

Comparing Written and Oral Messages 484

Planning a Strategy for Your Presentation 485

Choosing Information to Include in a Presentation 491

Organizing Your Information 492

Delivering an Effective Presentation 493

Handling Questions 497

Making Group Presentations 498

Summary of Key Points 498

Exercises and Problems for Chapter 17 500

Part Five

Job Hunting   503

❝*A good résumé actually helps your interviewer ask questions that showcase your strengths.*❞

18   Résumés   504

An Inside Perspective: Résumés   505

A Time Line for Job Hunting   506

Evaluating Your Strengths and Interests   506

How Employers Use Résumés   507

Guidelines for Résumés   507

Kinds of Résumés   510

What to Include in a Résumé   510

Dealing with Difficulties   523

How an Average Student Produced an Excellent Résumé   525

Online Résumés   526

Summary of Key Points   531

Exercises and Problems for Chapter 18   532

19   Job Application Letters   536

An Inside Perspective: Job Application Letters   537

How Job Letters Differ from Résumés   538

How to Find Out about Employers and Jobs   538

Content and Organization for Job Application Letters   544

E-Mail Application Letters   552

Creating a Professional Image   553

Summary of Key Points   556

Exercises and Problems for Chapter 19   558

20   Job Interviews, Follow-Up Letters and Calls, and Job Offers   564

An Inside Perspective: Job Interviews, Follow-Up Letters and Calls, and Job Offers   564

Interviewing in the Twenty-First Century   566

Developing an Interview Strategy   566

Taking Care of the Details   567

Practicing for the Interview   569

During the Interview   569

Answering Traditional Interview Questions   571

Behavioral and Situational Interviews   576

After the Interview   576

Summary of Key Points   582

Exercises and Problems for Chapter 20   583

A Formats for Letters, Memos, and E-Mail Messages   586

An Inside Perspective: Formats for Letters, Memos, and E-Mail Messages   587

Formats for Letters   588

Alternate Format for Letters That Are Not Individually Typed   597

Typing Envelopes   597

Format for Memos   599

Formats for E-Mail Messages   599

State and Province Abbreviations   603

B Writing Correctly   608

An Inside Perspective: Writing Correctly   609

Using Grammar   610

Understanding Punctuation   614

Punctuating Sentences   614

Punctuation within Sentences   616

Special Punctuation Marks   620

Writing Numbers and Dates   621

Words That Are Often Confused   622

Proofreading Symbols   627

Exercises and Problems for Appendix B   628

C Making and Communicating Meaning   632

An Inside Perspective: Making and Communicating Meaning   633

Communication Channels in Organizations   634

A Model of the Communication Process   634

Principles of Semantics   637

Summary of Key Points   645

Exercises and Problems for Appendix C   646

D Toulmin Logic   650

An Inside Perspective: Toulmin Logic   651

The Toulmin Model   652

How Much of the Full Toulmin Model to Use   653

Summary of Key Points   654

Exercises for Appendix D   655

Glossary   657

Notes   669

Photo Credits   679

Company Index   681

Organization Index   685

Subject Index   687

One

The Building Blocks
of Effective Messages

Chapter One

Business Communication, Management,
and Success   2

Chapter Two

Building Goodwill   32

Chapter Three

Adapting Your Message to Your Audience   58

Chapter Four

Making Your Writing Easy to Read   86

Chapter Five

Effective Strategies for Planning,
Composing, and Revising   114

Chapter Six

Designing Documents, Slides, and Screens   130

1

Business Communication, Management, and Success

Communication Ability = Promotability

"I'll Never Have to Write Because . . ."
- Claim 1: "Secretaries Will Do All My Writing."
- Claim 2: "I'll Use Form Letters When I Need to Write."
- Claim 3: "I'm Being Hired as an Accountant, Not a Writer."
- Claim 4: "I'll Just Pick Up the Phone."

The Managerial Functions of Communication
- The Importance of Listening, Speaking, and Interpersonal Communication
- The Documents That Writers in Organizations Write

The Cost of Correspondence

The Costs of Poor Correspondence
- Wasted Time
- Wasted Efforts
- Lost Goodwill

Benefits of Improving Correspondence

Criteria for Effective Messages

Trends in Business and Administrative Communication
- Focus on Quality and Customers' Needs
- Entrepreneurship and Outsourcing
- Teams
- Diversity
- Globalization
- Technology
- Legal and Ethical Concerns
- Balancing Work and Family
- The End of the Job
- Rapid Rate of Change

Understanding and Analyzing Business Communication Situations

How to Solve Business Communication Problems
- Answer the Six Questions for Analysis.
- Organize Your Information to Fit Your Audiences, Your Purposes, and the Situation.
- Make Your Document Visually Inviting.
- Revise Your Draft to Create a Friendly, Businesslike, Positive Style.
- Edit Your Draft for Standard English; Double-Check Names and Numbers.
- Use the Response You Get to Plan Future Messages.

Summary of Key Points

Business Communication, Management, and Success

Emilia Fonseca Wiener — *Vice President of Capital Management—The MONY Group*

www.mony.com

Emilia Fonseca Wiener heads a group of investment professionals, conducts negotiations, and makes presentations relating to investments in the fixed income securities portfolio of The MONY Group. The companies of The MONY Group provide financial protection and asset accumulation products and services. The primary company is MONY Life Insurance, founded in 1842 as The Mutual Life Insurance Company of New York, which issued the first mutual life insurance policy in the United States in 1843.

Business has become truly global and the electronic age has made possible instantaneous communication. The ability to keep up with these changes and to understand them defines our success as business professionals. But communication is so much more than just the spoken or written word. At its best it is a multifaceted process through which we exchange information with the world around us. We use communication skills in every aspect of our lives: at work, with family and friends, even with ourselves.

66 *Leadership relies, above all else, on effective communication skills.* 99

Quality communication requires intensive listening to the needs and views of those we work with. Sales representatives must listen to their clients, doctors must listen to their patients, and businesses must listen to the changing needs of the marketplaces in which they compete.

Communication is enhanced when it is coupled with an ability to perceive the impact of our actions and words. Great communicators have an interactive style. Armed with clear, well-defined goals for what is to be accomplished, they tailor their communication to the audience or situation at hand. They are able to connect in such a way as to promote true two-way exchanges. Only through this process can we realize the full potential of professional growth and success and fulfill the potential of cultural diversity.

True leadership is not conferred by title or position; it is earned through personal and professional achievements and the ability to motivate those around you. Think of those great teachers you have had and how they really motivated you to learn; think of bosses whom you felt really understood and respected the contributions you made. Leadership relies, above all else, on effective communication skills. This book will walk you through all the tools you need to become great communicators and true leaders. Practice these skills and make them a part of everyday life, and professional success and leadership will surely follow.

Lessons from the Best*

Every year, *Industry Week* recognizes the 10 best manufacturing plants in the United States. Lessons from the 1997 winners were "focus on people, communicate, and have common goals."

"Communication—both formal and informal—is the key to ingraining your company philosophy and goals into each and every employee," points out Darryl Miller, Plant Manager, Aeroquip Corporation, New Haven, IN (air-conditioning components).

"Open . . . lines of communication develop trust, encourage new ideas, eliminate intimidation and skepticism, and aid in building a brighter future for employees and the company," says Steve McGowen, Plant Manager, Halliburton Energy Services, Carrollton, TX (equipment for the oil and gas industries).

"We use group meetings, required readings, a shift newsletter, a monthly newspaper, daily electronic and hard-copy news sheets, all-hands meetings, team meetings, and even public-address announcements to keep people informed. Communication is like dairy farming—you milk the cows but they never stay milked. It has to be a process the organization uses constantly," notes John R. Dew, Manager of Mission Success, Lockheed Martin Utility Services, Paducah, KY (enriched uranium).

*Quotations from Michael A. Verespie, "Lessons from the Best," *Industry Week*, February 2, 1998; INDUSTRYWEEK.COM/Current Articles/asp/articles/asp?ArticleD=262; visited site December 15, 1998.

Business depends on communication. People must communicate to plan products; hire, train, and motivate workers; coordinate manufacturing and delivery; persuade customers to buy; and bill them for the sale. Indeed, for many businesses and nonprofit and government organizations, the "product" is information or services rather than something tangible. Information and services are created and delivered by communication. In every organization, communication is the way people get their points across and get work done.

Communication takes many forms: face-to-face or phone conversations, informal meetings, e-mail messages, letters, memos, and reports. All of these methods are forms of **verbal communication,** or communication that uses words. **Nonverbal communication** does not use words. Pictures, computer graphics, and company logos are nonverbal. Interpersonal nonverbal signals include smiles, who sits where at a meeting, the size of an office, and how long someone keeps a visitor waiting.

Communication Ability = Promotability

Even in your first job, you'll communicate. You'll read information; you'll listen to instructions; you'll ask questions; you may solve problems with other workers in teams. In a manufacturing company, hourly workers travel to a potential customer to make oral sales presentations. In an insurance company, clerks answer customers' letters. Even "entry-level" jobs require high-level skills in reasoning, mathematics, and communicating. As a result, communication ability ranked first among the qualities that employers look for in college graduates.[1]

Many employers complain that nobody who works for them can write a simple paragraph. Paul Goodman, Vice President and Senior Recruiter at Citigroup, says strong writing skills are a "tiebreaker" in deciding whom to hire:

> If I have two job candidates in front of me, equally qualified except that one can write well and the other can't, I'll hire the one who can—every time.[2]

Communication becomes even more important as you advance. Annette Gregorich, Vice President of Human Resources for Multiple Zones International, says,

> I've actually seen people lose promotions because they couldn't write a proposal or stand in front of the management team and make a presentation.[3]

As a result, good writers earn more. Linguist Stephen Reder has found that among people with two- or four-year degrees, workers in the top 20% of writing ability earn, on average, more than three times as much as workers whose writing falls into the worst 20%.[4]

"I'll Never Have to Write Because . . ."

Some students think that a secretary will do their writing, that they can use form letters if they do have to write, that only technical skills matter, or that they'll call rather than write. Each of these claims is fundamentally flawed.

Claim 1: "Secretaries Will Do All My Writing."

Downsizing and voice mail have cut support staffs from 10 to 30% nationwide. Of the secretaries who remain, 71% are administrative assistants whose duties are managerial, not clerical.[5] As a result, most workers in business and government today draft and revise their own letters, memos, and reports at desktop computers or terminals. You'll be responsible for correct spelling, mechanics, and format as well as organization, logic, audience analysis, and tone.

Claim 2: "I'll Use Form Letters When I Need to Write."

A **form letter** is a prewritten fill-in-the-blank letter designed to fit standard situations. The writer can personalize a form letter by having it individually typed with the recipient's name and address. Sometimes form letters have several different paragraphs from which the writer can choose, depending on the circumstances. Using a form letter is OK if it's a good letter, but some of the letters currently in use are dreadful. (See Figure 1.5 later in this chapter for an example of one bad form letter.)

Even good form letters cover only routine situations. The higher you rise in your organization, the more frequently you'll face situations that aren't routine, that demand creative solutions. If you develop the skills necessary for good writing and original thinking, you're far more likely to realize your potential and reach your career goals.

Claim 3: "I'm Being Hired as an Accountant, Not a Writer."

Your technical skill in accounting or computer science or marketing may get you your first job. The ability to speak and write effectively may help you keep it. The inability to write is the main reason that Big Five accounting firms fire new hires.[6] Written communication is crucial to accounting. Dee Castner, Senior Auditor at KPMG, explains,

> We write to clients to communicate the necessities and timeliness of audits. We write to apprise the audit team of internal and external situations. We document in writing the evidence which supports an audit opinion.[7]

Almost every entry-level professional or managerial job requires you to write e-mail messages, speak to small groups, and write some paper documents. Many people in business and government routinely write from 10 pages of letters and memos a week to, in some cases, 20 to 30 pages a day. And that doesn't count the dozens of e-mail messages workers write and receive.[8] The Air Force estimates that it produces 500 million pages of writing a year.[8] First-level supervisors in one manufacturing plant spend 25% of their time writing.[9] Most professionals find that the higher they go, the more they write. Margot Northey found that 80% of the partners in the Big Five accounting firms wrote memos every day; 67% wrote reports or notes to a financial statement and 93% wrote letters to clients *at least* once a week.[10]

Claim 4: "I'll Just Pick Up the Phone."

Most people in organizations say they spend more time talking and listening than they do reading and writing. But no organization depends exclusively on oral communication. People in organizations put things in writing to make themselves visible, to create a record, to convey complex data, to make things convenient for the reader, to save money, and to convey their own messages more effectively.

"If it isn't in writing," says a manager at one company, "it didn't happen." Writing is an essential way to make yourself visible, to let your accomplishments be known.

Written memos and reports document what was said and done and the reasons for decisions. Carefully written memos and reports enable a company to

Legal Implications of Business Writing*

Letters and memos create legal obligations for organizations.

When a lawsuit is filed against an organization, the lawyers for the plaintiffs have the right to subpoena documents written by employees of the organization. These documents may then be used as evidence that an employer fired an employee without adequate notice or that a company knew about a safety defect but did nothing to correct it.

Organizations whose actions are irresponsible or negligent deserve to be condemned by their own words. But a careless writer can create obligations that the writer does not intend and that the organization does not mean to assume.

Careful writers and speakers think about the larger social context in which their words may be read. What might those words mean to other people in your field? What might they mean to a judge and jury?

*Based on Elizabeth A. McCord, "The Business Writer, the Law, and Routine Business Communication: A Legal and Rhetorical Analysis," *Journal of Business and Technical Communication* 5.2 (April 1991): 173–99.

Listening at Pillsbury*

Top managers in some companies are isolated. Pillsbury managers avoid that problem by encouraging anonymous phone calls.

Pillsbury employees can sound off to a recording machine. Another company provides verbatim anonymous transcripts. Pillsbury's CEO gets them all.

Some comments report problems: delayed pension benefits or expense reimbursements.

Many comments suggest ideas or provide genuinely useful knowledge. One caller suggests a new topping for Pillsbury's frozen pizza. Another notes that the time clock in Eden Prairie, Minnesota, was five minutes fast. Still another notes that a certain retail product isn't on the local grocery store shelf.

Some comments support managers' decisions. Dozens of employees phoned in to applaud the action of one manager in shutting down a plant during a snowstorm.

Pillsbury's managers listen. And as a result, in small, important ways, the company is changing the way it does business.

*Based on Thomas Petzinger, Jr., "Two Executives Cook Up Way to Make Pillsbury Listen," *The Wall Street Journal*, September 27, 1996, B1.

use its earlier experience without having to reinvent the wheel every time a new set of people tackles a recurring problem. Written documents also allow individuals and companies to protect themselves. If there is no written record, chaos—and expensive lawsuits—may result.

Written channels (including graphics) are better than oral ones for conveying numbers and complex information. Written channels are less expensive than oral ones for reaching large groups of people or transmitting information over long distances. Writing may also be more convenient for the recipient. To talk, both people must be free at the same time. This is rarely the case in business. Only 12% of business phone calls find the intended receiver in the office on the first try.[11] When you send a letter or memo, the recipient can read it when it's most convenient. Even more important, the reader can proceed at a convenient pace, skimming easier or less important sections and rereading difficult or key sections. Written documents become even more important in international business. Talking on the phone requires immediate comprehension. Reading a fax or e-mail message is easier for a manager doing business in a language other than his or her native language.

Finally, putting a message in writing makes it easier to present your ideas in the most effective way, even in difficult situations. We've all had the experience of fumbling for words, only to think of the perfect words to make a point after it was all over. Writing, because it can be revised, gives us the second chance we may need to achieve the effect we want.

The Managerial Functions of Communication

According to Henry Mintzberg, managers have three basic jobs: to collect and convey information, to make decisions, and to promote interpersonal unity.[12] Every one of those jobs is carried out through communication. Managers collect relevant information from conversations, the grapevine, phone calls, memos, reports, databases, and the Internet. They convey information and decisions to other people inside or outside the organization through meetings, speeches, press releases, videos, memos, letters, and reports. Managers motivate organizational members in speeches, memos, conversations at lunch and over coffee, bulletin boards, and through "management by walking around."

Effective managers are able to use a wide variety of media and strategies to communicate. They know how to interpret comments from informal channels such as the company grapevine; they can speak effectively in small groups and in formal presentations; they write well.

Communication—oral, nonverbal, and written—goes to both internal and external audiences. **Internal audiences** (Figure 1.1) are other people in the same organization: subordinates, superiors, peers. **External audiences** (Figure 1.2) are people outside the organization: customers, suppliers, unions, stockholders, potential employees, government agencies, the press, and the general public.

The Importance of Listening, Speaking, and Interpersonal Communication

Informal listening, speaking, and working in groups are just as important as writing formal documents and giving formal oral presentations. As a newcomer in an organization, you'll need to listen to others both to find out what you're supposed to do and to learn about the organization's values and culture. Informal chitchat, both about yesterday's game and about what's happening at work, connects you to the **grapevine,** an informal source of company information. You may be asked to speak to small groups, either inside or out-

Figure 1.1

The Internal Audiences of the Sales Manager—West

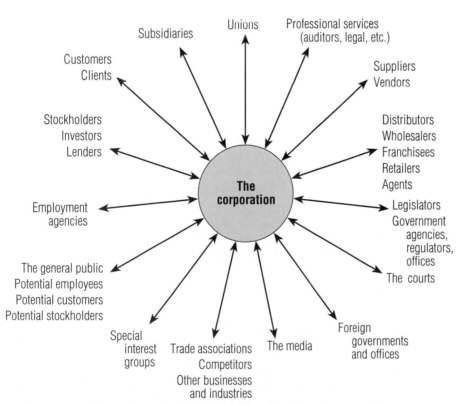

Figure 1.2

The Corporation's External Audiences

Source: Daphne A. Jameson

side your organization.[13] Networking with others in your office and in town and working with others in workgroups will be crucial to your success.

These skills remain important as you climb the corporate ladder. In fact, a study of 15 executives judged good performers by their companies showed that these executives spent most of their time in informal contact with other people. They asked questions; they joked; they schmoozed; they nudged people toward the direction they wanted them to go. These informal discussions and meetings took 76% of these executives' work time. The resulting interactions with thousands of employees and outsiders enabled them to promote their agendas.[14]

The Documents That Writers in Organizations Write

People in organizations produce a large variety of documents. Figures 1.3 and 1.4 list a few of the specific documents produced at Joseph T. Ryerson & Son. Ryerson, a subsidiary of a Fortune 500 company, has 25 plants across the United States; it fabricates and sells steel, aluminum, and plastics to a wide variety of industrial clients.

All of the documents in Figures 1.3 and 1.4 have one or more of the **three basic purposes of organizational writing:** to inform, to request or persuade, and to build goodwill. When you **inform,** you explain something or tell readers something. When you **request or persuade,** you want the reader to act. The word *request* suggests that the action will be easy or routine; *persuade* suggests that you will have to motivate and convince the reader to act. When you **build goodwill,** you create a good image of yourself and of your organization—the kind of image that makes people want to do business with you.

Most messages have multiple purposes. When you answer a question, you're informing, but you also want to build goodwill by suggesting that you're competent and perceptive and that your answer is correct and complete. In a claims adjustment, whether your answer is *yes* or *no,* you want to suggest that the reader's claim has been given careful consideration and that the decision is fair, businesslike, and justified.

Two of the documents listed in Figure 1.4 package the same information in different ways for different audiences. The 10-K report filed with the Securities and Exchange Commission (SEC) and the annual report distributed to stockholders contain essentially the same information, but differing purposes and differing audiences create two distinct documents. The 10-K report is informative, designed merely to show that the company is complying with SEC regulations. The annual report, in contrast, has multiple purposes and audiences. Its primary purpose is to convince stockholders that the company is a good investment and a good corporate citizen. Annual reports will also be read by employees, stockbrokers, potential stockholders, and job applicants, so the firm creates a report that is persuasive and builds goodwill as well as presenting information.

The Cost of Correspondence

Writing costs money. In 1996, according to the Dartnell Institute, a short one-page business letter cost between $13.60 and $20.52, depending on how it was produced.[15] Dartnell's estimates assume that an executive dictates a letter in 10 minutes. But a consultant who surveyed employees in seven industries found that most of them spent 54 minutes planning, composing, and revising a one-page letter.[16] Her respondents, then, each spent over $84 at 1996 prices to create a one-page letter. Dartnell no longer calculates the cost of a business letter, but

Figure 1.3	Internal Documents Produced in One Organization

Document	Description of document	Purpose(s) of document
Transmittal	Memo accompanying document, telling why it's being forwarded to the receiver	Inform; persuade reader to read document; build image and goodwill
Monthly or quarterly report	Report summarizing profitability, productivity, and problems during period. Used to plan activity for next month or quarter	Inform; build image and goodwill (report is accurate, complete; writer understands company)
Policy and procedure bulletin	Statement of company policies and instructions (e.g., how to enter orders, how to run fire drills, etc.)	Inform; build image and goodwill (procedures are reasonable)
Request to deviate from policy and procedure bulletin	Persuasive memo arguing that another approach is better for a specific situation than the standard approach	Persuade; build image and goodwill (request is reasonable; writer seeks good of company)
Performance appraisal	Evaluation of an employee's performance, with recommended areas for improvement or recommendation for promotion	Inform; persuade employee to improve
Memo of congratulations	Congratulations to employees who have won awards, been promoted, or earned community recognition	Build goodwill

Figure 1.4	External Documents Produced in One Organization

Document	Description of document	Purpose(s) of document
Quotation	Letter giving price for a specific product, fabrication, or service	Inform; build goodwill (price is reasonable)
Claims adjustment	Letter granting or denying customer request to be given credit for defective goods	Inform; build goodwill
Job description	Description of qualifications and duties of each job. Used for performance appraisals, setting salaries, and for hiring	Inform; persuade good candidates to apply; build goodwill (job duties match level, pay)
10-K report	Report filed with the Securities and Exchange Commission detailing financial information	Inform
Annual report	Report to stockholders summarizing financial information for year	Inform; persuade stockholders to retain stock and others to buy; build goodwill (company is a good corporate citizen)
Thank-you letter	Letter to suppliers, customers, or other people who have helped individuals or the company	Build goodwill

it seems likely that costs have not fallen. One company in Minneapolis writes 3,000 original letters a day. If each of those letters is written in slightly less than an hour, it spends at least $252,000 a day just on outgoing correspondence.

In many organizations, all external documents must be approved before they go out. A document may **cycle** from writer to superior to writer to another superior to writer again 3 or 4 or even 11 times before it is finally approved. The cycling process increases the cost of correspondence.

The Cost Was Classified*

Fuzzy building instructions have added hundreds of thousands of dollars to building costs. And a single hyphen omitted by a supervisor at a government-run nuclear installation may hold the cost record for punctuation goofs. He ordered rods of radioactive material cut into "10 foot long lengths"; he got 10 pieces, each a foot long, instead of the 10-foot lengths required. The loss was so great it was classified [as secret by the federal government].

*Quoted from William E. Blundell, "Confused, Overstuffed Corporate Writing Often Costs Firms Much Time—and Money," *The Wall Street Journal,* August 21, 1980, 21.

The Value of Clarity Depends on the Culture*

US ads are direct. The Japanese don't like US ads: they prefer subtle messages where the point is not spelled out.

Skilled Japanese managers use ambiguity as a management tool. Instead of criticizing a report, the manager asks for more information. Kazuo Nishiyama points out, "When they say 'I'd like to reflect on your proposal for a while,' when the decision must be [made] soon, it means 'You are dead wrong, and you'd better come up with a better idea very soon. But I don't tell you so, because you should know that yourself!' "

*Based on Christopher A. Amatos, "U.S. Marketing Strategies Fall Flat on Their Faces in Japan," *The Columbus Dispatch,* September 23, 1987, H1; and Kazuo Nishiyama, "Intercultural Problems in Japanese Multinationals," *Communication: The Journal of the Communication Association of the Pacific* 12 (1983): 58.

Longer documents can involve large teams of people and take months to write. An engineering firm that relies on military contracts for its business calculates that it spends $500,000 to put together an average proposal and $1 million to write a large proposal.[17]

Good communication is worth every minute it takes and every penny it costs. In fact, in a survey conducted by the International Association of Business Communicators, CEOs said that communication yielded a 235% return on investment.[18]

The Costs of Poor Correspondence

When writing isn't as good as it could be, you and your organization pay a price in wasted time, wasted efforts, and lost goodwill.

Wasted Time

Bad writing takes longer to read. Studies show that up to 97% of our reading time is taken not in moving our eyes across the page but in trying to understand what we're reading. How quickly we can do this is determined by the difficulty of the subject matter and by the document's organization and writing style.

Second, bad writing may need to be rewritten. Many managers find that a disproportionate amount of their time is taken trying to explain to subordinates how to revise a document.

Third, ineffective writing may obscure ideas so that discussions and decisions are needlessly drawn out. People inside an organization may disagree on the best course, and the various publics with which organizations communicate may have different interests and values. But if a proposal is clear, at least everyone will be talking about the same proposed changes, so that differences can be recognized and resolved more quickly.

Fourth, unclear or incomplete messages may require the reader to ask for more information. A reader who has to supplement the memo with questions interrupts the writer. If the writer is out of the office when the reader stops by or calls, even more time is wasted, for the reader can't act until the answer arrives.

Wasted Efforts

Ineffective messages don't get results. A reader who has to guess what the writer means may guess wrong. A reader who finds a letter or memo unconvincing or insulting simply won't do what the message asks. In 1986, Frank Grazian said that between 15% and 30% of business and government letters and memos were written only because the first document didn't do the job.[19]

One company sent out past-due bills with the following language:

> Per our conversation, enclosed are two copies of the above-mentioned invoice. Please review and advise. Sincerely, . . .

The company wanted money, not advice, but it didn't say so. The company had to write third and fourth reminders. It waited for its money, lost interest on it—and kept writing letters.

Lost Goodwill

Whatever the literal content of the words, every letter, memo, or report serves either to build or to undermine the image the reader has of the writer.

Figure 1.5   *A Form Letter That Annoyed Customers*

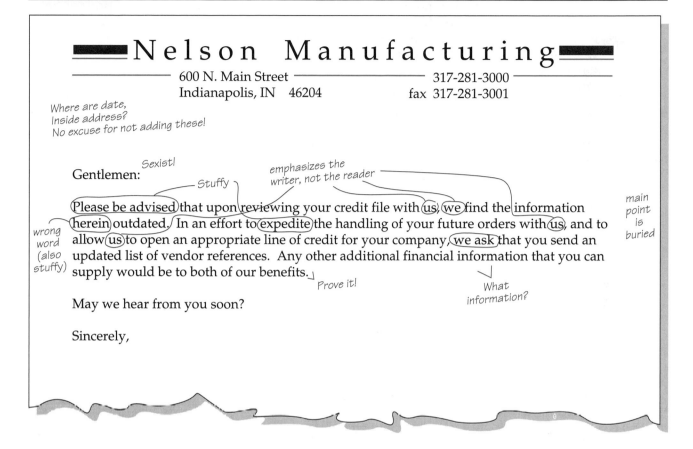

Part of building a good image is taking the time to write correctly. Even organizations that have adopted casual dress still expect writing to appear professional and to be free from typos and grammatical errors.

Messages can also create a poor image because of poor audience analysis and inappropriate style. The form letter printed in Figure 1.5 failed because it was stuffy and selfish. Four different customers called to complain about it. When you think how often you are annoyed by something—a TV commercial, a rude clerk—but how rarely you call or write the company to complain, you can imagine the ill will this letter generated.

As the comments in red show, several things are wrong with the letter in Figure 1.5.

1. **The language is stiff and legalistic.** Note the obsolete (and sexist) "Gentlemen:" "Please be advised," "herein," and "expedite."
2. **The tone is selfish.** The letter is written from the writer's point of view; there are no benefits for the reader. (The writer says there are, but, without a shred of evidence, the claim isn't convincing.)
3. **The main point is buried** in the middle of the long first paragraph. The middle is the least emphatic part of a paragraph.
4. **The request is vague.** How many references does the supplier want? Are only vendor references OK, or would other credit references, like banks, work too? Is the name of the reference enough, or is it necessary also to specify the line of credit, the average balance, the current balance, the years credit has been established, or other information? What "additional

financial information" does the supplier want? Annual reports? Bank balance? Tax returns? The request sounds like an invasion of privacy, not a reasonable business practice.

5. **Words are misused** (*herein* for *therein*), suggesting either an ignorant writer or one who doesn't care enough about the subject and the reader to use the right word.

Benefits of Improving Correspondence

Better writing helps you to

- **Save time.** Reduce reading time, since comprehension is easier. Eliminate the time now taken to rewrite badly written materials. Reduce the time taken asking writers "What did you mean?"
- **Make your efforts more effective.** Increase the number of requests that are answered positively and promptly—on the first request. Present your points—to other people in your organization; to clients, customers, and suppliers; to government agencies; to the public—more forcefully.
- **Communicate your points more clearly.** Reduce the misunderstandings that occur when the reader has to supply missing or unclear information. Make the issues clear, so that disagreements can surface and be resolved more quickly.
- **Build goodwill.** Build a positive image of your organization. Build an image of yourself as a knowledgeable, intelligent, capable person.

Criteria for Effective Messages

Good business and administrative writing meets five basic criteria: it's clear, complete, and correct; it saves the reader's time; and it builds goodwill.

1. **It's clear.** The meaning the reader gets is the meaning the writer intended. The reader doesn't have to guess.
2. **It's complete.** All of the reader's questions are answered. The reader has enough information to evaluate the message and act on it.
3. **It's correct.** All of the information in the message is accurate. The message is free from errors in punctuation, spelling, grammar, word order, and sentence structure.
4. **It saves the reader's time.** The style, organization, and visual impact of the message help the reader to read, understand, and act on the information as quickly as possible.
5. **It builds goodwill.** The message presents a positive image of the writer and his or her organization. It treats the reader as a person, not a number. It cements a good relationship between the writer and the reader.

Whether a message meets these five criteria depends on **the interactions among the writer, the audience, the purposes of the message, and the situation.** No single set of words will work in all possible situations.

Trends in Business and Administrative Communication

Both business and business communication are changing. Ten trends in business, government, and nonprofit organizations affect business and administrative communication: a focus on quality and customers' needs, entrepreneurship and outsourcing, teams, diversity, globalization, technology, legal and ethical concerns, balancing work and family, the end of the job, and the rapid rate of change.

Focus on Quality and Customers' Needs

Successful companies make money by offering high-quality products and services that their customers want. Aladan Corp., founded in 1986 in Dothan, Alabama, has cornered nearly 20% of the world market in latex examination gloves by providing a quality product quickly at a low price.[20] Chris Zane's Cycles has grown 25% a year in New Haven, Connecticut, by offering free lifetime service and a cellular phone with the bicycles Zane sells, gourmet coffee while bikes are serviced, a toll-free number, and 90-day price guarantees.[21]

While flexible, responsive companies have been growing, many of the giant US companies that relied on their large market share for continued profits have gone through painful downsizing. Xerox Corporation, for example, once figured that because the service department earned a profit, it didn't matter that its copiers broke down and had to be serviced. But people wanted copiers that didn't break down and turned to Japanese copiers.[22] Xerox has been able to reinvent itself. Now, more companies are "benchmarking": comparing themselves to the best in their industries. The best companies are working to be even better. Chevron created "process masters" to help spread best practices from one plant to another. A new way of cleaning pipes developed in one refinery now saves $1 million every time a refinery needs cleaning.[23]

Focusing on what customers want may lead a business to redefine itself. Business Interiors sold office furniture in Irving, Texas. The CEO said, "Forget what we sell, let's ask customers what they want and organize ourselves around that." Now the company provides a wide range of products and services—including computer-aided design for offices and office buildings.[24]

Communication is at the center of the focus on quality and customers' needs. Brainstorming and group problem solving are essential to develop more efficient ways to do things. Then the good ideas have to be communicated throughout the company. Innovators need to be recognized. And only by listening to what customers say—and listening to the silences that may accompany their actions—can an organization know what its customers really want.

Entrepreneurship and Outsourcing

In 1995, nearly 13 million Americans were self-employed and working full-time at home.[25] That figure doesn't count the small-business owners whose companies have grown beyond the owner's home or garage. Entrepreneurship

Bumping the Lamp*

"Bumping the lamp" is part of Disney's corporate culture. The phrase refers to a scene in *Roger Rabbit* in which a character bumps into a lamp and makes it shake. The lamp's shadow shakes, too—a touch of excellence that only a few moviegoers will notice. "Bumping the lamp" means achieving a level of excellence—whether or not it's noticed.

The emphasis on customer service continues even when families leave a Disney theme park. Every day, 20,000 guests lock their keys in their cars. Cast members (as employees are called) roam the parking lots to help families get into their cars—no phone call to a locksmith, no waiting, no fee.

*Based on Robert Hiebeler, Thomas B. Kelly, and Charles Ketterman, *Best Practices: Building Your Business with Customer-Focused Solutions* (New York: Simon & Schuster, 1998), 197.

MBNA's success is based on concern for customers. In concrete terms, that means reaching goals—like answering the phone within two rings at least 98.5% of the time. As the computer screen shows, this office is exceeding the goal: 99.7% of calls are answered in two rings or less.

Kelley Dunn created Consider It Dunn, Inc., a corporate concierge service. She's an entrepreneur who includes among her clients several major corporations. These companies offer her services to employees as a benefit. "We looked at it as a good opportunity to help our employees balance their work with their home lives," explains Mike Nordstrom, a Pillsbury vice president.

is so popular that many business schools now offer courses, internships, or whole programs in starting and running a business.

@ For links to Web sites providing information about starting your own company, see the BAC Web site.

Some established companies are trying to match the success and growth rate of start-ups by nurturing an entrepreneurial spirit within their organizations. Innovators who work within organizations are sometimes called **intrapreneurs.** Researchers at 3M can spend 15% of their time working on ideas that don't need management approval; Post-it Notes and the Scotch-Brite Never Rust wool soap pad are two products that came out of 3M's "skunk works." Thermo Electron lets managers "spin out" promising new businesses. Xerox employees write business proposals competing for corporate funds to develop new technologies.[26]

Some businesses have been forced to become entrepreneurial because of outsourcing. **Outsourcing** means going outside the company for products and services that once were made by the company's employees. The people who are now Corsair Communications Inc. were jettisoned in December 1994 by the California-based defense contractor for whom they'd worked most of their professional lives. Instead of automatically getting assignments and pay, they had to propose products and find customers. The company has succeeded—in large part because CEO Mary Ann Byrnes has changed the corporate culture.[27]

Entrepreneurs have to handle all the communication in the organization: hiring, training, motivating, and evaluating employees; responding to customer complaints; drafting surveys; writing business plans; and making presentations to venture capitalists.

Outsourcing makes communication more difficult—and more important—than it was when jobs were done in-house. It's harder to ask questions, since people are no longer down the hall. And it's easier for problems to turn into major ones. Some companies now are creating a "Chief Resource Officer" to monitor contracts with vendors so that lines of communication will be clear.

Teams

To produce quality products while cutting costs and prices, more and more companies are relying on cross-functional teams. A team of 10 middle managers from various departments at the North Island Naval Depot improved the process of manufacturing replacement parts for fighter planes. They cut the time needed to manufacture and deliver a part by 42% and have saved the Navy—and thus taxpayers—$1.7 million in a year and a half.[28] Teams at Dettmers Industries in Stuart, Florida, make a product in 80 hours—down from 140 hours three years ago. Though employees earn more—sometimes much more—than workers in comparable local industries, the company's labor costs have remained steady, while sales are up 50% and profit margins are twice the industry standard.[29]

The prevalence of teams puts a premium on learning to identify and solve problems, to share leadership, to work *with* other people rather than merely delegating work *to* other people, to resolve conflicts constructively, and to motivate everyone to do his or her best job.

Diversity

Teams put a premium on being able to work with other people—even if they come from different backgrounds.

Women, people of color, and immigrants have always been part of the US workforce. But for most of our country's history, they were relegated to clerical, domestic, or menial jobs. Even when men from working-class families began to get college degrees in large numbers after World War II, and large numbers of women and minorities entered the professions in the 1960s and 1970s, only a few made it into management. Now, US businesses realize that barriers to promotion hurt the bottom line as well as individuals. Success depends on using the brains and commitment as well as the hands and muscles of every worker.

In the last decade, we have also become aware of other sources of diversity beyond those of gender and race: age, religion, class, regional differences, sexual orientation, physical disabilities. Helping each worker reach his or her potential requires more flexibility from managers as well as more knowledge about intercultural communication. And it's crucial to help workers from different backgrounds understand each other—especially when continuing layoffs make many workers fear that increased opportunities for someone else will come only at a cost to themselves.

Treating readers with respect has always been a principle of good business and administrative communication. The emphasis on diversity simply makes it an economic mandate as well. To learn more about diversity and the workforce, see the BAC Web site.

Globalization

As Emilia Fonseca Wiener noted at the beginning of this chapter, business has become truly global. The global economy is more than simply importing or exporting products. Instead, more and more companies have factories and offices in several countries. Even small companies send managers on overseas assignments.[30]

For Web sites on doing international business, see the BAC Web site. All the challenges of communicating in one culture and country increase exponentially when people communicate across cultures and countries. Succeeding in a global market requires **intercultural competence,**

Have Customer, Will Travel*

How does a travel agent make a profit when schedules are available free on the Web? Gary Hoover prospers by giving travelers more than just tickets.

At his Travelfest stores in Austin, Texas, customers can pick up visa applications, check the *Hotel and Travel Index*, and buy books, videos, maps, luggage, and water purifiers. A "learning center" offers 20 classes every month, from Spanish to overcoming the fear of flying.

Much of the information is free. The travel supplies bring in about 20% of revenues—but more than 20% of profits. And these goods and services bring in people planning to travel—so that Hoover's 88 employees can sell them tickets, too.

*Based on John Case and Jerry Useem, "Six Characters in Search of a Strategy," *Inc.*, March 1996, 50.

In 1998, Nike introduced into the United States three sport shoes that had proved successful in other countries: a soccer boot designed with and worn by Brazilian national team member Ronaldo; a long distance running shoe designed with the help of Kenyan runners, the Air Rift; and the Air Streak, which had already been sold for a year in Japan.

CompareNet is one of several sites that make it easy for consumers to compare prices and features.

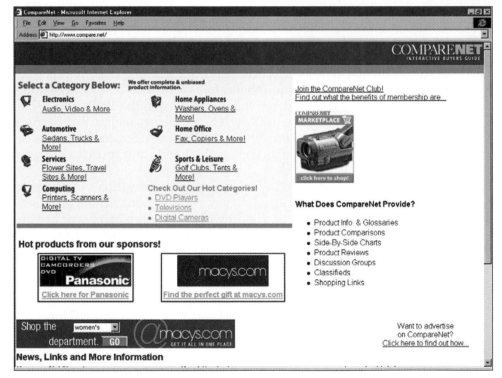

the ability to communicate sensitively with people from other cultures and countries, based on an understanding of cultural differences.

Technology

Changes in technology support and drive changes in other areas. **Intranets**— Web pages just for employees—give everyone in an organization access to information. To save the Waterville, Maine, ballet company, a retired Marine colonel assembled a nationwide board of directors that met every other night on the Internet. Fax, e-mail, pagers, and text typewriter (TTY) telephones enable deaf and other hearing-impaired employees to fill a variety of jobs.[31]

Technology helps organizations save money. FedEx cut the cost of checking on delivery status from $5 a package to only 5 cents by letting customers ask electronically on their own PCs. Total savings are estimated at $2 million a year. Aetna insurance company saves $6 million a year by replacing paper insurance manuals with documents that exist only online. A health insurance company uses desktop publishing to create benefits booklets for its customers. The savings: only 5 days—not 45—are needed to produce new booklets, a huge backlog is eliminated, and the company saves $350,000 in postal costs alone. Fingerhut sends customers with children a birthday flyer advertising toys appropriate for the child's age and sex and a personalized message—complete with the child's name and birth month. Fingerhut's mail order sales have grown every year—up to 14% —even during recessions.[32]

Modems, faxes, and videophones allow employees to work at home rather than commute to a central office. Fax and e-mail make it easy to communicate across oceans and time zones. Teleconferencing makes it possible for people on different continents to have a meeting—complete with visual aids—without leaving their hometowns.

Technological change carries costs. Technology makes it easier for companies to monitor employees—even when they're out of the office. While technology creates new jobs, it eliminates old ones, requiring employees to retrain. Acquiring technology and helping workers master it requires an enormous capital investment. Learning to use new-generation software and improved hardware takes time and may be especially frustrating for people who were perfectly happy with the old software. And the very ease of storing information and sending messages means that managers have more information and more messages to process. **Information overload** occurs when messages arrive faster than the human receiver can handle them. In the information age, time management depends in part on being able to identify which messages are important so that one isn't buried in trivia.

The technology of office communication also affects the way people interpret messages. Readers expect all documents to be well designed and error free—even though not everyone has access to a laser printer or even to a computer. Fax technology leads people to expect documents instantly, even though the work and thinking required to produce the document still take time.

Legal and Ethical Concerns

Legal fees cost US businesses hundreds of thousands of dollars. The price of many simple items, such as ladders, is inflated greatly by the built-in reserve to protect the manufacturer against lawsuits. Companies are finding that clear, open communication can reduce lawsuits by giving all the parties a chance to shape policies and by clarifying exactly what is and isn't being proposed.

For more information about legal issues and links to pages discussing the value of clear legal writing, see the BAC Web site.

Ethical concerns don't carry the same clear dollar cost as legal fees. But over the last 25 years, Clinton's impeachment, Ivan Boesky's insider trading, Beechnut's allowing fake apple juice to be sold in its baby food, Watergate, the savings and loan debacle, and experiments suggesting that many business people and business students were willing to commit fraud[33] have left many consumers with a deep distrust of both business and government. To regain public trust and to avoid further regulation, business and government must both act ethically and convince the public that they are doing so.

To help clients encourage good people to do the right thing, KPMG Peat Marwick, a Big Five accounting firm, offers an "ethics audit" to increase discussion of ethical issues in the workplace and identify places where an organization's system may break down.[34]

How Private Are E-Mail and Voice Mail?*

They aren't private at all.

In 1996, in an e-mail to his boss, a man described another superior as a "back-stabbing bastard." Superiors saw a printout of the message, read all the writer's e-mail, and fired him. A US District Court ruled that the company had the right to read employees' e-mail and act on it.

Both e-mail and voice mail messages can be reproduced and sent (without your knowledge) to audiences you never planned on.

What's the solution? Assume anything you put on e-mail and voice mail can be read and heard by everyone. If you must be indiscreet, do it in person—not on something that will be stored.

*Based on Raju Narisetti, "Work Week," *The Wall Street Journal*, March 19, 1996, A1, and Frances A. McMorris, "Is Voice Mail Private? Don't Bet on It," *The Wall Street Journal*, February 28, 1995, B1.

We Are Whole People*

Sally Mattei supervises 750 EDS employees. She says, "I meet with my direct reports every Monday morning, and we start out listening to a piece of music, generally something calming or reflective. We're silent. We just listen to the music. . . .

"We are whole people, not someone in our private life and someone in our public life. That's what I want in the workplace. . . .

"When something went wrong, I [used to] cut to the quick and say, 'You did this wrong; we need to learn from this. Everybody see this mistake that was made. Now go fix it.'

"All that did was alienate people from me. Yes, the problem got fixed. But my team did it begrudgingly. There were times we didn't do as well as we should have. Now I tell the team: 'I want to talk to you about this. I don't want anyone to feel uncomfortable. I think it would be helpful if we shared about this problem.' "

*Quoted from David Kirkpatrick, "This Tough Guy Wants to Give You a Hug," *Fortune*, October 14, 1996, 176.

In 1997, two-thirds of major US companies monitored their employees electronically.

For links to Web sites showing how some companies work to maintain high ethical standards, see the BAC Web site.

As Figure 1.6 suggests, language, graphics, and document design—basic parts of any business document—can be ethical or manipulative. Persuasion and gaining compliance—activities at the heart of business and organizational life—can be done with respect or contempt for customers, co-workers, and subordinates.

Ethical concerns start with telling the truth and offering good value for money. Organizations must be concerned about broader ethical issues as well: being good environmental citizens, offering a good workplace for their employees, contributing to the needs of the communities in which they operate.

Balancing Work and Family

The Wall Street Journal now runs a regular column on Work and Family. One staff writer notes,

> The whole notion of work has changed. Though America remains a productive and work-oriented society, work is just a part of life. People crave more balance.[35]

Two research studies named a "lack of balance between work and personal life" one of the top six reasons new managers fail and one of the top five reasons relocations fail. In contrast, Xerox and First Tennessee National Corp. are among companies that have found that taking workers' family needs into consideration produces clear gains in productivity and customer service.[36]

Balancing work and family requires using ways other than physical presence to demonstrate one's commitment to and enthusiasm for organizational goals. It may require negotiating conflicts with other workers who have different family situations or who raised children years ago when fewer companies were family-friendly. The downside of this trend is that sometimes work and family life are not so much balanced as blurred. Lori D. Lewis, Hewlett-Packard's Worldwide Reseller Channel Manager for Disk Drives, reports that she has approved prices on a cellular phone on the ski slopes.[37] This flexibility

Figure 1.6	*Ethical Issues in Business Communication*

How the message is conveyed	What the message is	The larger organizational context of the message
Language, Graphics, and Document Design • Is the message audience-friendly? Does it respect the audience? • Do the words balance the organization's right to present its best case with its responsibility to present its message honestly? • Do graphics help the audience understand? Or are graphics used to distract or confuse? • Does the design of the document make reading easy? Does document design attempt to make readers skip key points? **The tactics used to shape response** • Are the arguments logical? • Are the emotional appeals used fairly? Do they supplement logic rather than substituting for it? • Does the organizational pattern lead the audience without undue manipulation? • Are the tactics honest? That is, do they avoid deceiving the audience?	• Is the message that is communicated an ethical one that treats all parties fairly and is sensitive to all stakeholders? • Have interested parties been able to have input into the decision or message? • Does the audience get all the information it needs to make a good decision? • Is information communicated in a timely way, or is information withheld to reduce the audience's power? • Is information communicated in a schema the audience can grasp, or are data "dumped" without any context?	• How does the organization treat its employees? How do employees treat each other? • How sensitive is the organization to stakeholders such as the people who live near its factories, stores, or offices and to the general public? • Does the organization support employees' efforts to be honest, fair, and ethical? • Do the organization's actions in making products, buying supplies, and marketing goods and services stand up to ethical scrutiny? • Is the organization a good corporate citizen, helpful rather than harmful to the community in which it exists? • Are the organization's products or services a good use of scarce resources?

is necessary in an age of downsizing and doing business in many time zones, but it means that she, like many managers, is essentially on call all the time.

For links to Web sites on balancing work and family life, see the BAC Web site.

The End of the Job

In traditional jobs, people did what they were told to do. Now, they do whatever needs to be done. As one man explains,

> [At the old company,] my work could be represented by a small circle labeled "Me" inside of a much larger one labeled "Not Me." At Corsair, a third circle, nearly as large as the first, is inserted between the other two, and it is labeled, "Maybe Me."[38]

With flatter organizations, workers are doing a much wider variety of tasks. Teams of hourly workers at Weyerhaeuser visit customers in the United States and in Japan to see the demands that high-speed printing makes on their newsprint. When they come back from a trip, they make presentations for two or three weeks to co-workers at the plant.[39]

Your parents may have worked for the same company all their lives. You may do that, too, but you have to be prepared to job-hunt—not only when you finish your degree, but also throughout your career. That means continuing to learn—keeping up with new technologies, new economic and political realities, new ways of interacting with people.

Rapid Rate of Change

Rapid change is a constant in business and government today. Change means that what worked yesterday may not work today, let alone tomorrow. But change is stressful. Many people, especially those who have felt battered by changes in the workplace, fear that more change will further erode their positions. Even when change promises improvements, people have to work to learn new skills, new habits, and new attitudes.

Jack Welch, CEO of General Electric, is widely acknowledged as the leading master of corporate change in our time. He says,

> You've got to be on the cutting edge of change. You can't simply maintain the status quo, because somebody's always coming from another country with another product, or consumer tastes change, or the cost structure does, or there's a technology breakthrough. If you're not fast and adaptable, you're vulnerable. This is true for every segment of every business in every country in the world.[40]

Rapid change means that no college course or executive MBA program can teach you everything you need to know for the rest of your working life. You'll need to remain open to new ideas. And you'll need to view situations and options critically, so that you can evaluate new conditions to see whether they demand a new response. But the skills you learn can stand you in good stead for the rest of your life: critical thinking, computer savvy, problem solving, and the ability to write, to speak, and to work well with other people.

Understanding and Analyzing Business Communication Situations

The best communicators are conscious of the context in which they communicate; they're aware of options.

Ask yourself the following questions:

- **What's at stake—to whom?** Think not only about your own needs but also about the concerns your boss and your readers will have. Your message will be most effective if you think of the entire organizational context—and the larger context of shareholders, customers, and regulators. When the stakes are high, you'll need to take into account people's emotional feelings as well as objective facts.
- **Should you send a message?** Sometimes, especially when you're new on the job, silence is the most tactful response. But be alert for opportunities to learn, to influence, to make your case. You can use communication to build your career.
- **What channel should you use?** Paper documents and presentations are formal and give you considerable control over the message. E-mail, phone calls, and stopping by someone's office are less formal. Oral channels are better for group decision making, allow misunderstandings to be cleared up more quickly, and seem more personal. Sometimes you may need more than one message, in more than one channel.
- **What should you say?** Content for a message may not be obvious. How detailed should you be? Should you repeat information that the audience already knows? The answers will depend on the kind of document, your purposes, audiences, and the corporate culture. And you'll have to figure these things out for yourself, without detailed instructions.
- **How should you say it?** How you arrange your ideas—what comes first, second, and last—and the words you use shape the audience's response to what you say.

Just a Deadline. No Directions*

School assignments are spelled out, sometimes even in writing. In the workplace, workers are less likely to get details about what a document should include. The transition can be disorienting. One intern reported, "I was less prepared than I thought. . . . I was so used to professors basically telling you what they want from you that I expected to be, if not taught, then told, what exactly it was that they wanted these brochures to accomplish. . . . They have not taken the time to discuss it—they just put things on my desk with only a short note telling me when they needed it done. No directions or comments were included."

*Intern's quotation from Chris M. Anson and L. Lee Forsberg, "Moving Beyond the Academic Community," *Written Communication* 7, no. 3 (April 1990): 211.

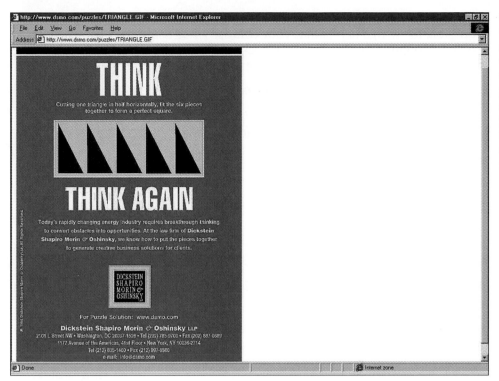

Creative problem solving will help you find good solutions. In this puzzle, fit the six pieces of the cut triangle together to form a perfect square. You'll find the solution at <www.dsmo.com/puzzles/matchsol.htm>. © *Dickstein Shapiro Morin & Oshinsky LLP, 1997.* All rights reserved.

How to Solve Business Communication Problems

When you're faced with a business communication problem, you need to develop a solution that will both **solve the organizational problem and meet the psychological needs of the people involved.** The strategies in this section will help you solve the problems in this book. Almost all of these strategies can also be applied to problems you encounter on the job.

- **Understand the situation.** What are the facts? What can you infer from the information you're given? What additional information might be helpful? Where could you get it?
- **Use the six questions for analysis in Figure 1.7 to analyze your audience, your purposes, and the situation.** Try to imagine yourself in the situation, just as you might use the script of a play to imagine what kind of people the characters are. The fuller an image you can create, the better.
- **Brainstorm solutions.** In all but the very simplest problems, there are *several* possible solutions. The first one you think of may not be best. Consciously develop several solutions. Then measure them against your audience and purposes: Which solution is likely to work best?
- **If you want to add or change information, get permission first.** You can add facts or information to the problems in this book only if the information (1) is realistic, (2) is consistent with the way real organizations work, and (3) does not change the point of the problem. If you have any questions about ideas you want to use, *ask your instructor.* He or she can tell you *before* you write the message.

  Sometimes you may want to use a condition that is neither specified in the problem nor true in the real world. For example, you may want to assume you're sending a letter in April even though you're really writing it in October. Change facts *only with your instructor's approval.*

  When you use this book to create messages on the job, you can't change facts. That is, if it's October, you can't pretend that it's April just because it

Succeeding Against the Odds*

I developed my communication skills as a technique of survival. I was born in poverty and spent two years on the welfare rolls, and I learned early that I had to communicate or die. And so I talked my way out of poverty—I communicated my way to the top. . . .

I read and re-read books on self-improvement, success and communication. The most important lesson I learned from these books is what I call "other focusing." This means, among other things, that if we want to communicate with employees, managers, and even competitors we must ask ourselves not what we want but what they want.

This rule made me a millionaire. For the only way I got to where I am today was by persuading thousands of blacks and whites, some of whom were very prejudiced, that the only way they could get what they wanted was by helping me get what I wanted. All the law and prophecy of communication theory can be found in that formula.

*John H. Johnson, owner and publisher of *Ebony* magazine, quoted in Gloria Gordon, "EXCEL Award Winner John H. Johnson Communicates Success," *IABC Communication World* 6, no. 6 (May 1989): 18–19.

may be easier to think of reader benefits for that time of year. But it may be possible to change habits that your company has fallen into, especially if they no longer serve a purpose. Check with your supervisor to make sure that your departure from company practice is acceptable.

Use this process to create good messages:[41]

Answer the six questions for analysis in Figure 1.7.

Organize your information to fit your audiences, your purposes, and the situation.

Make your document visually inviting.

Revise your draft to create a friendly, businesslike, positive style.

Edit your draft for standard English; double-check names and numbers.

Use the response you get to plan future messages.

Answer the Six Questions for Analysis.

The six questions in Figure 1.7 help you analyze your audience(s), purpose(s), and the organizational context.

1. **Who is (are) your audience(s)? What characteristics are relevant to this particular message? If you are writing or speaking to more than one person, how do the people in your audience differ?**

   How much does your audience know about your topic? How will they respond to your message? Some characteristics of your readers will be irrelevant; focus on ones that matter *for this message*. Whenever you write to several people or to a group (like a memo to all employees), try to identify the economic, cultural, or situational differences that may affect how various subgroups may respond to what you have to say.

2. **What are your purposes in writing?**

   What must this message do to solve the organizational problem? What must it do to meet your own needs? What do you want your readers to do? to think or feel? List all your purposes, major and minor. Specify *exactly* what you want your reader to know or think or do. Specify *exactly* what kind of image of yourself and of your organization you want to project.

   Even in a simple message, you may have several related purposes: to announce a new policy, to make readers aware of the policy's provisions and requirements, and to have them feel that the policy is a good one, that the organization cares about its employees, and that you are a competent writer and manager.

3. **What information must your message include?**

   Make a list of the points that must be included; check your draft to make sure you include them all. If you're not sure whether a particular

---

Figure 1.7	*Questions for Analysis*

1. Who is (are) your audience(s)? What characteristics are relevant to this particular message? If you are writing or speaking to more than one person, how do the people in your audience differ?
2. What are your purposes in writing?
3. What information must your message include?
4. How can you build support for your position? What reasons or reader benefits will your reader find convincing?
5. What objection(s) can you expect your reader(s) to have? What negative elements of your message must you de-emphasize or overcome?
6. What aspects of the total situation may affect reader response? The economy? The time of year? Morale in the organization? The relationship between the reader and writer? Any special circumstances?

fact must be included, ask your instructor or your boss.

To include information without emphasizing it, put it in the middle of a paragraph or document and present it as briefly as possible.

4. **How can you build support for your position? What reasons or reader benefits will your reader find convincing?**

Brainstorm to develop reasons for your decision, the logic behind your argument, and possible benefits to readers if they do as you ask. Reasons and reader benefits do not have to be monetary. Making the reader's job easier or more pleasant is a good reader benefit. In an informative or persuasive message, identify at least five reader benefits. In your message, use those that you can develop most easily and most effectively.

Be sure the benefits are adapted to your reader. Many people do not identify closely with their companies; the fact that the company benefits from a policy will help the reader only if the saving or profit is passed directly on to the employees. That is rarely the case: savings and profits are often eaten up by returns to stockholders, bonuses to executives, and investments in plants and equipment or in research and development.

5. **What objection(s) can you expect your reader(s) to have? What negative elements of your message must you de-emphasize or overcome?**

Some negative elements can only be de-emphasized. Others can be overcome. Be creative: is there any advantage associated with (even though not caused by) the negative? Can you rephrase or redefine the negative to make the reader see it differently?

6. **What aspects of the total situation may affect reader response? The economy? The time of year? Morale in the organization? The relationship between the reader and writer? Any special circumstances?**

Readers may like you or resent you. You may be younger or older than the people you're writing to. The organization may be prosperous or going through hard times; it may have just been reorganized or may be stable. All these different situations will affect what you say and how you say it.

Think about the news, the economy, the weather. Think about the general business and regulatory climate, especially as it affects the organization specified in the problem. Use the real world as much as possible. Think about interest rates, business conditions, and the economy. Is the industry in which the problem is set doing well? Is the government agency in which the problem is set enjoying general support? Think about the time of year. If it's fall when you write, is your business in a seasonal slowdown after a busy summer? Gearing up for the Christmas shopping rush? Or going along at a steady pace unaffected by seasons?

To answer these questions, draw on your experience, your courses, and your common sense. You may want to talk to other students or read *The Wall Street Journal* or look at a company's Web site. Sometimes you may even want to phone a local business person to get information. For instance, if you needed more information to think of reader benefits for a problem set in a bank, you could call a local banker to find out what services it offers customers and what its rates are for loans.

Organize Your Information to Fit Your Audiences, Your Purposes, and the Situation.

You'll learn several different psychological patterns of organization later in this book. For now, remember these three basic principles:

1. Put good news first.

They Needed to Proofread

- One man who dictated his letters found that one letter complained that an office was "eating material improperly." The right word was *E.T.ing* (emergency transferring), not *eating.* But he hadn't told the typist that he wanted capital letters and periods, and the typist didn't understand what he said.

- One woman mailed out a cover letter for a $750,000 contract asking the reader "to take a moment not to read and sign this contract."

- One man mailed a letter to a male friend with the salutation, "Dear Ms. Weeks."

- In 1990, just hours before the graduation ceremony, the head of the U.S. Naval Academy discovered that the 1,600 diplomas conferred degrees from the "U.S. Navel Academy."

2. In general, put the main point or question first. In the subject line or first paragraph, make it clear that you're writing about something that is important to the reader.
3. Disregard point 2 and approach the subject indirectly when you must persuade a reluctant reader.

Make Your Document Visually Inviting.

A well-designed document is easier to read and builds goodwill. To make a document visually attractive

- Use subject lines to orient the reader quickly.
- Use headings to group related ideas.
- Use lists and indented sections to emphasize subpoints and examples.
- Number points that must be followed in sequence.
- Use short paragraphs—usually six typed lines or fewer.

If you plan these design elements before you begin composing, you'll save time and the final document will probably be better.

The best physical form for a document depends on how it will be used. For example, a document that will be updated frequently needs to be in a loose-leaf binder, so the reader can easily throw away old pages and insert new ones.

Revise Your Draft to Create a Friendly, Businesslike, Positive Style.

In addition to being an organizational member or a consumer, your reader has feelings just as you do. Writing that keeps the reader in mind uses **you-attitude.** Read your message over as if you were in your reader's shoes. How would you feel if *you* received it?

Good business and administrative writing is both friendly and businesslike. If you're too stiff, you put extra distance between your reader and yourself. If you try to be too chummy, you'll sound unprofessional. When you write to strangers, use simple, everyday words and make your message as personal and friendly as possible. When you write to friends, remember that your message will be filed and read by people you've never even heard of: avoid slang, clichés, and "in" jokes.

Sometimes you must mention limitations, drawbacks, or other negative elements, but don't dwell on them. People will respond better to you and your organization if you seem confident. Expect success, not failure. If you don't believe that what you're writing about is a good idea, why should they?

You emphasize the positive when you

- Put positive information first, give it more space, or set it off visually in an indented list.
- Eliminate negative words whenever possible.
- Focus on what is possible, not what is impossible.

Edit Your Draft for Standard English; Double-Check Names and Numbers.

Business people care about correctness in spelling, grammar, and punctuation. If your grasp of mechanics is fuzzy, if standard English is not your native dialect, or if English is not your native language, you'll need to memorize rules and perhaps find a good book or a tutor to help you. Even software spelling and grammar checkers require the writer to make decisions. If you know how to write correctly but rarely take the time to do so, now is the time to begin to edit and proofread to eliminate careless errors. Correctness in usage, punctuation, and grammar is covered in Appendix B.

Always proofread your document before you send it out. Double-check the reader's name, any numbers, and the first and last paragraphs.

Use the Response You Get to Plan Future Messages.

Evaluate the **feedback,** or response, you get. The real test of any message is "Did you get what you wanted, when you wanted it?" If the answer is *no,* then the message has failed—even if the grammar is perfect, the words elegant, the approach creative, the document stunningly attractive. If the message fails, you need to find out why.

Analyze your successes, too. You know you've succeeded when you get the results you want, both in terms of objective, concrete actions and in terms of image and goodwill. You want to know *why* your message worked. Often, you'll find that the principles in this book explain the results you get. If your results are different, why? There has to be a reason, and if you can find what it is, you'll be more successful more often.

Summary of Key Points

- Communication helps organizations and the people in them achieve their goals. The ability to write and speak well becomes increasingly important as you rise in an organization.
- People put things in writing to create a record, to convey complex data, to make things convenient for the reader, to save money, and to convey their own messages more effectively.
- **Internal documents** go to people inside the organization. **External documents** go to audiences outside: clients, customers, suppliers, stockholders, the government, the media, and the general public.
- The three basic purposes of business and administrative communication are **to inform, to request or persuade, and to build goodwill.** Most messages have more than one purpose.
- A one-page business letter that took 10 minutes to dictate cost between $13.60 and $20.52 in 1996. Poor writing costs even more since it wastes time, wastes effort, and jeopardizes goodwill.
- Good business and administrative writing meets five basic criteria: it's **clear, complete,** and **correct;** it **saves the reader's time;** and it **builds goodwill.**
- To evaluate a specific document, we must know the interactions among the writer, the reader(s), the purposes of the message, and the situation. No single set of words will work for all readers in all situations.
- Ten trends affecting business and administrative communication are a focus on quality and customers' needs, entrepreneurship and outsourcing, teams, diversity, international competition and opportunities, technology, legal and ethical concerns, balancing work and family, the end of the job, and the rapid rate of change.
- To understand business communication situations, ask the following questions:
  - What's at stake—to whom?
  - Should you send a message?
  - What channel should you use?
  - What should you say?
  - How should you say it?

Can Business Change the World?*

Joseph White, Dean of the University of Michigan Business School, says:

"The most moving experience that I've had in recent years was a meeting with Desmond Tutu in Cape Town. I asked him, 'What are your greatest concerns about the future of South Africa?' He said, 'We have 30 million people living on hope. If the economy and society don't deliver measurable improvements over the next five years, I don't know what's going to happen here.' Now, if you're a 25-year-old student and you're looking for a challenge, then look no further: Archbishop Tutu just delivered it to you.

"That opportunity reflects a fundamental difference between the current generation of business people and the previous generation. . . . If the dream 25 years ago was to join a big company and to pursue a career involving steady advancement, the dream now is to cultivate an economic entity that creates tremendous value, that provides opportunity for others, and that may even change the world."

*Quotation from Polly Labarre, ed., "Unit of One," *Fast Company,* January 1999, 74.

- The following process helps create effective messages:
  - Answer the six numbered questions for analysis below.
  - Organize your information to fit your audiences, your purposes, and the situation.
  - Make your document visually inviting.
  - Revise your draft to create a friendly, businesslike, positive style.
  - Edit your draft for standard English; double-check names and numbers.
  - Use the response you get to plan future messages.
- Use these six questions to analyze business communication problems:
  1. Who is (are) your audience(s)? What characteristics are relevant to this particular message? If you are writing or speaking to more than one person, how do the people in your audience differ?
  2. What are your purposes in writing?
  3. What information must your message include?
  4. How can you build support for your position? What reasons or reader benefits will your reader find convincing?
  5. What objection(s) can you expect your reader(s) to have? What negative elements of your message must you de-emphasize or overcome?
  6. What aspects of the total situation may affect reader response? The economy? The time of year? Morale in the organization? The relationship between the reader and writer? Any special circumstances?
- A solution to a business communication problem must both solve the organizational problem and meet the needs of the writer or speaker, the organization, and the audience.

Chapter 1

Exercises and Problems

Getting Started

1.1   Letters for Discussion—Landscape Plants

Your nursery sells plants not only in your store but also by mail order. Today you've received a letter from Pat Sykes, complaining that the plants (in a $572 order) did not arrive in a satisfactory condition. "All of them were dry and wilted. One came out by the roots when I took it out of the box. Please send me a replacement shipment immediately."

The following letters are possible approaches to answering this complaint. How well does each message meet the needs of the reader, the writer, and the organization? Is the message clear, complete, and correct? Does it save the reader's time? Does it build goodwill?

1.

> Dear Sir:
>
> I checked to see what could have caused the defective shipment you received. After ruling out problems in transit, I discovered that your order was packed by a new worker who didn't understand the need to water plants thoroughly before they are shipped. We have fired the worker, so you can be assured that this will not happen again.
>
> Although it will cost our company several hundred dollars, we will send you a replacement shipment.
>
> Let me know if the new shipment arrives safely. We trust that you will not complain again.

2.

> Dear Pat:
>
> Sorry we screwed up that order. Sending plants across country is a risky business. Some of them just can't take the strain. (Some days I can't take the strain myself!) We'll send you some more plants sometime next week and we'll credit your account for $372.

3.

> Dear Mr. Smith:
>
> I'm sorry you aren't happy with your plants, but it isn't our fault. The box clearly says, "Open and water immediately." If you had done that, the plants would have been fine. And anybody who is going to buy plants should know that a little care is needed. If you pull by the leaves, you will pull the roots out. Since you don't know how to handle plants, I'm sending you a copy of our brochure, "How to Care for Your Plants." Please read it carefully so that you will know how to avoid disappointment in the future.
>
> We look forward to your future orders.

4.

> Dear Ms. Sykes:
>
> Your letter of the 5th has come to the attention of the undersigned.
>
> According to your letter, your invoice #47420 arrived in an unsatisfactory condition. Please be advised that it is our policy to make adjustments as per the Terms and Conditions listed on the reverse side of our Acknowledgment of Order. If you will read that document, you will find the following:
>
> > ". . . if you intend to assert any claim against us on this account, you shall make an exception on your receipt to the carrier and shall, within 30 days after the receipt of any such goods, furnish us detailed written information as to any damage."
>
> Your letter of the 5th does not describe the alleged damage in sufficient detail. Furthermore, the delivery receipt contains no indication of any exception. If you expect to receive an adjustment, you must comply with our terms and see that the necessary documents reach the undersigned by the close of the business day on the 20th of the month.

5.

> Dear Pat Sykes:
>
> You'll get a replacement shipment of the perennials you ordered next week.
>
> Your plants are watered carefully before shipment and packed in specially designed cardboard containers. But if the weather is unusually warm, or if the truck is delayed, small root balls may dry out. Perhaps this happened with your plants. Plants with small root balls are easier to transplant, so they do better in your yard.
>
> The violas, digitalis, aquilegias, and hostas you ordered are long-blooming perennials that will get even prettier each year. Enjoy your garden!

1.2 E-Mail Messages for Discussion—Announcing a Web Page

The Acme Corporation has just posted its first Web page. Ed Zeplin in Management Information Systems (MIS), who has created the page, wants employees to know about it.

The following e-mail messages are possible approaches. How well does each message meet the needs of the reader, the writer, and the organization? Is the message clear, complete, and correct? Does it save the reader's time? Does it build goodwill?

1.

Subject: It's Ready!

I am happy to tell you that my work is done. Two months ago the CEO finally agreed to fund a Web page for Acme, and now the work of designing and coding is done. At last, Acme has joined the 20th century (which is now over).

I wanted all of you to know about Acme's page. (Actually it's over 40 pages.) Now maybe the computerphobes out there will realize that you really do need to learn how to use this stuff. Sign up for the next training session! The job you save may be my own.

If you have questions, please do not hesitate to contact me.

L. Ed Zeplin, MIS

2.

Subject: Web Page

Check out the company Web page at www.server.acme.com/homepage.html

3.

Subject: Visit Our Web Page

Our Web pages are finally operational. The 43 pages take 460 MB on the server and were created using HoT MetaL, a program designed to support HTML creation. Though the graphics are sizable and complex, interlacing and code specifying the pixel size serve to minimize download time. Standard HTML coding is enhanced with forms, Java animation, automatic counters, and tracking packages to ascertain who visits our site.

The site content was determined by conducting a survey of other corporate Web sites to become cognizant of the pages made available by our competitors and other companies. The address of our Web page is www.server/acme/com/homepage.html. It is believed that this site will support and enhance our marketing and advertising efforts, improving our outreach to desirable demographic and psychographic marketing groups.

L. Ed Zeplin, MIS

Voice: 713-555-2879 Fax: 713-555-2880 e-mail: zeplin.1@acme.com

"Only the wired life is worth living."—Anonymous

4.

Subject: Web Page Shows Acme Products to the World, Offers Tips to Consumers, and Tells Prospective
        Employees about Job Possibilities

Since last Friday, Acme's been on the World Wide Web. If you have a computer with Internet access, check out the page at www.server.acme.com/homepage.html. You can't view the page if you don't have a computer or if you're still using a Mac SE or a 286.

I have included pages on our products, tips for consumers, and job openings at Acme in the hope of making our page useful and interesting. Content is the number one thing that brings people back, but I've included some snazzy graphics, too.

When I asked people for ideas for the company pages, almost nobody responded. But if seeing the page inspires you, let me know what else you'd like. I'll try to fit it into my busy schedule.

So check it out. But don't spend too much time on the Web: you need to get your work done, too!

L. Ed Zeplin, MIS
zeplin.1@acme.com
Today's Joke
Fun Links

5.

> Subject: How to Access Acme's Web Page
>
> Tell your customers that Acme is now on the Web:
> www.server.acme.com/homepage.html
>
> Web pages offer another way for us to bring our story to the public. Other companies have found that Web pages increase sales, often reaching customers far from normal sales and distribution channels. Our advertisements and packaging will feature our Web address. And people who check out our Web page can learn even more about our commitment to quality, protecting the environment, and meeting customer needs.
>
> If you'd like to learn more about how to use the Web or how to create Web pages for your unit, sign up for one of our workshops. For details and online registration, see www.server.acme.com/training.
>
> If you have comments on Acme's Web pages or suggestions for making them even better, just let me know.
>
> L. Ed Zeplin
> zeplin.1@acme.com

1.3 Discussing Strengths

Introduce yourself to a small group of other students. Identify three of your strengths that might interest an employer. These can be experience, knowledge, or personality traits (like enthusiasm).

Communicating at Work

1.4 Understanding the Role of Communication in Your Organization

Interview your supervisor to learn about the kinds and purposes of communication in your organization. Your questions could include the following:

- What channels of communication (e.g., memos, e-mail, presentations) are most important in this organization?
- What documents or presentations do you create? Are they designed to inform, to persuade, to build goodwill—or to do all three?
- What documents or presentations do you receive? Are they designed to inform, to persuade, to build goodwill—or to do all three?
- Who are your most important audiences within the organization?
- Who are our most important external audiences?
- What are the challenges of communicating in this organization?
- What kinds of documents and presentations does the organization prefer?

As Your Instructor Directs,
a. Share your results with a small group of students.
b. Present your results in a memo to your instructor.
c. Join with a group of students to make a group presentation to the class.

Memo Assignments

1.5 Introducing Yourself to Your Instructor

Write a memo (at least 1½ pages long) introducing yourself to your instructor. Include the following topics:

Background: Where did you grow up? What have you done in terms of school, extracurricular activities, jobs, and family life?

Interests: What are you interested in? What do you like to do? What do you like to think about and talk about?

Achievements: What achievements have given you the greatest personal satisfaction? List at least five. Include things that gave *you* a real sense of accomplishment and pride, whether or not they're the sort of thing you'd list on a résumé.

Goals: What do you hope to accomplish this term? Where would you like to be professionally and personally five years from now?

Use complete memo format with appropriate headings. (See Appendix A for examples of memo format.) Use a conversational writing style; check your draft to polish the style and edit for mechanical and grammatical correctness. A good memo will enable your instructor to see you as an individual. Use specific details to make your memo vivid and interesting. Remember that one of your purposes is to interest your reader!

1.6   Introducing Yourself to Your Collaborative Writing Group

Write a memo (at least 1½ pages long) introducing yourself to the other students in your collaborative writing group. Include the following topics:

Background: What is your major? What special areas of knowledge do you have? What have you done in terms of school, extracurricular activities, jobs, and family life?

Previous experience in groups: What groups have you worked in before? Are you usually a leader, a follower, or a bit of both? Are you interested in a quality product? In maintaining harmony in the group? In working efficiently? What do you like most about working in groups? What do you like least?

Work and composing style: Do you like to talk out ideas while they're in a rough stage or work them out on paper before you discuss them? Would you rather have a complete outline before you start writing or just a general idea? Do you want to have a detailed schedule of everything that has to be done and who

will do it, or would you rather "go with the flow"? Do you work best under pressure, or do you want to have assignments ready well before the due date?

Areas of expertise: What can you contribute to the group in terms of knowledge and skills? Are you good at brainstorming ideas? Researching? Designing charts? Writing? Editing? Word processing? Managing the flow of work? Maintaining group cohesion?

Goals for collaborative assignments: What do you hope to accomplish this term? Where does this course fit into your priorities?

Use complete memo format with appropriate headings. (See Appendix A for examples of memo format.) Use a conversational writing style; edit your final draft for mechanical and grammatical correctness. A good memo will enable others in your group to see you as an individual. Use details to make your memo vivid and interesting. Remember that one of your purposes is to make your readers look forward to working with you!

1.7   Describing Your Experiences in and Goals for Writing

Write a memo (at least 1½ pages long) to your instructor describing the experiences you've had writing and what you'd like to learn about writing during this course.

Answer several of the following questions:

· What memories do you have of writing? What made writing fun or frightening in the past?

· What have you been taught about writing? List the topics, rules, and advice you remember.

· What kinds of writing have you done in school? How long have the papers been?

· How has your school writing been evaluated? Did the instructor mark or comment on mechanics and grammar? Style? Organization? Logic? Content? Audience analysis and adaptation? Have you gotten extended comments on your papers? Have instructors in different classes had the same standards, or have you changed aspects of your writing for different classes?

· What voluntary writing have you done—journals, poems, stories, essays? Has this writing been just for you, or has some of it been shared or published?

· Have you ever written on a job or in a student or volunteer organization? Have you ever typed other people's writing? What have these experiences led you to think about real-world writing?

· What do you see as your current strengths and weaknesses in writing skills? What skills do you think you'll need in the future? What kinds of writing do you expect to do after you graduate?

Use complete memo format with appropriate headings. (See Appendix A for examples of memo format.) Use a conversational writing style; edit your final draft for mechanical and grammatical correctness.

Chapter

Two

Building
Goodwill

You-Attitude
- How to Create You-Attitude
- You-Attitude beyond the Sentence Level

Positive Emphasis
- How to Create Positive Emphasis
- How to Apologize

Tone, Power, and Politeness

Reducing Bias in Business Communication
- Making Language Nonsexist
- Making Language Nonracist and Nonagist
- Talking about People with Disabilities and Diseases
- Choosing Bias-Free Photos and Illustrations

Summary of Key Points

Building Goodwill

Stephen Hlibok *Assistant Vice President, Merrill Lynch & Co.*

www.ml.com

Stephen Hlibok is a Certified Financial Planner who helps serve more than 4,500 deaf and hard-of-hearing clients. Merrill Lynch, the largest financial service firm in the United States, also provides special services for blind and visually impaired people and for families of children with disabilities.

Revising for you-attitude makes the message more persuasive and builds goodwill. When I helped write a 51-page document proposing that Merrill Lynch create a division to serve investors who were deaf and hard of hearing, we used language and arguments that focused on the company. When I write a letter to an individual investor, you-attitude is one way I present information from the reader's point of view.

" Revising for you-attitude makes the message more persuasive and builds goodwill. "

You-attitude also means respecting the reader. Many potential clients really don't understand finances, so I often need to explain the basics. You-attitude helps me do that in a way that isn't condescending.

As a stockbroker and financial planner, there are times when I can't use positive emphasis. I have to make sure that clients understand the risk of a specific investment. And when news is bad, I give solid facts. If the stock market is down 17%, it would be unprofessional to say, "Your portfolio retains 83% of its value."

Building goodwill also means speaking the client's language. I started my position three months before October 19, 1987—Black Monday—the day the Dow Jones Industrial Average plunged 508 points. On that day, stockbrokers were flooded by calls from worried clients. Due to time constraints, Deaf people found face-to-face appointments hard to come by, and brokers did not have the necessary telecommunications equipment to communicate with people who used American Sign Language.

With determination and guts, I helped build a bridge between Wall Street and the Deaf community. Merrill Lynch recognized the potential untapped community and became the first Wall Street brokerage firm to establish the Deaf and Hard of Hearing Investors' Services Division. The division reflects the company's involvement in a diverse, cross-cultural workforce.

Merrill Lynch's own slogan is "You should know no boundaries." Growing up in a Deaf household, I never thought or believed I couldn't do anything I wanted to because of my deafness. I want to instill the same attitude among other Deaf and disabled people.

The Internet is a revolution for the Deaf community because it helps to solve our communication needs and reduce obstacles. Within five years, videoconferencing should be standard, and there'll be plenty of flying hands!

All Work Is Social*

Establishing good working relationships can help us secure the cooperation of the people we need to accomplish our tasks. If we delay building good relationships until we really need them, it will be too late.

*Quoted from "Be a Social Worker," *Fast Company*, May 1999, 228.

Goodwill smooths the challenges of business and administration. Companies have long been aware that treating customers well pays off in more sales and higher profits. Government organizations now realize that they need citizen support—goodwill—to receive funding. Goodwill is important in internal as well as external documents. More and more organizations are realizing that treating employees well is financially wise as well as ethically sound. Sears Roebuck found that improvements in employee attitudes produced predictable improvements in revenue. Northern Telecom of Toronto, MCI Communications, and Electronic Data Systems have also found that internal goodwill has a measurable effect or   bottom line.[1]

You-attitude, positive emphasis, and bias-free language are three ways to help build goodwill. Writing that shows you-attitude speaks from the reader's point of view, not selfishly from the writer's. Positive emphasis means focusing on the positive rather than the negative aspects of a situation. Bias-free language is language that does not discriminate against people on the basis of sex, physical condition, race, age, or any other category. All three help you achieve your purposes and make your messages friendlier, more persuasive, more professional, and more humane. They suggest that you care not just about money but also about your readers and their needs and interests.

You-Attitude

Putting what you want to say in you-attitude is a crucial step both in thinking about the reader's needs and in communicating your concern to the reader.

How to Create You-Attitude

You-attitude is a style of writing that looks at things from the reader's point of view, emphasizing what the reader wants to know, respecting the reader's intelligence, and protecting the reader's ego.

To apply you-attitude, use the following six techniques:

1. Focus not on what you do for the reader, but on what the reader receives or can do. In positive or neutral situations, stress what the reader wants to know.
2. Refer to the reader's request or order specifically.
3. Don't talk about your own feelings unless you're sure the reader wants to know how you feel.
4. Don't tell readers how they feel or will react.
5. In positive situations, use *you* more often than *I*. Use *we* when it includes the reader.
6. In negative situations, avoid the word *you*. Protect the reader's ego. Use passive verbs and impersonal expressions to avoid assigning blame.

As we look at examples of these techniques, note that many of the you-attitude revisions are *longer* than the sentences lacking you-attitude. You-attitude sentences have *more* information, so they are often longer. They are not wordy. **Wordiness** means having more words than the meaning requires. We can add information and still keep the writing tight.

1. Focus not on what you do for the reader, but on what the reader receives or can do. In positive or neutral situations, stress what the reader wants to know.

Readers want to know how they benefit or are affected. When you provide this information, you make your message more complete and more interesting.

Lacks you-attitude:	I have negotiated an agreement with Apex Rent-a-Car that gives you a discount on rental cars.
You-attitude:	As a Sunstrand employee, you can now get a 20% discount when you rent a car from Apex.

The first sentence focuses on what the writer does, not on what the reader receives. Any sentence that focuses on the writer's work or generosity lacks you-attitude, even if the sentence contains the word *you*. Instead of focusing on what we are giving the reader, focus on what the reader can now do.

Lacks you-attitude:	We are shipping your order of September 21 this afternoon.
You-attitude:	The two dozen Corning Ware starter sets you ordered will be shipped this afternoon and should reach you by September 28.

The reader is less interested in when we shipped the order than in when it will arrive. Note that the phrase "should reach you by" leaves room for variations in delivery schedules. If you can't be exact, give your reader the information you do have: "A UPS shipment from California to Texas normally takes three days." If you have absolutely no idea, give the reader the name of the carrier, so the reader knows whom to contact if the order doesn't arrive promptly.

2. Refer to the reader's request or order specifically.

When you write about the reader's request, order, or policy, refer to it specifically, not as a generic *your order* or *your policy*. If your reader is an individual or a small business, it's friendly to specify the content of the order; if you're writing to a company with which you do a great deal of business, give the invoice or purchase order number.

Lacks you-attitude:	Your order . . .
You-attitude (to individual):	The desk chair you ordered . . .
You-attitude (to a large store):	Your invoice #783329 . . .

3. Don't talk about your own feelings unless you're sure the reader wants to know how you feel.

In most business situations, your feelings are irrelevant and should be omitted.

Lacks you-attitude:	We are happy to extend you a credit line of $5,000.
You-attitude:	You can now charge up to $5,000 on your American Express card.

The reader doesn't care whether you're happy, bored stiff at granting a routine application, or worried about granting so much to someone who barely qualifies. All the reader cares about is the situation from his or her point of view.

It *is* appropriate to talk about your own emotions in a message of congratulations or condolence.

You-attitude:	Congratulations on your promotion to district manager! I was really pleased to read about it.

In internal memos, it may be appropriate to comment that a project has been gratifying or frustrating. In the letter of transmittal that accompanies a report, it is permissible to talk about your feelings about doing the work. But even other readers in your own organization are primarily interested in their own concerns, not in your feelings.

4. Don't tell readers how they feel or will react.

It's distancing to have someone else tell us how we feel—especially if the writer is wrong. Avoid statements about the reader's feelings or reactions.

The Enlightened Manager*

Building goodwill comes from attitudes, not just from words. Enlightened managers assume that workers

- Want to do a good job.
- Can improve.
- Want to be needed, respected, and appreciated.
- Prefer meaningful work.
- Are whole people, with lives outside work.
- Will make good decisions when they have good information.

*Based on "Do You Have What It Takes to Be an Enlightened Manager?" *Inc.*, October 1998, 47–51.

Lacks you-attitude:	You'll be happy to hear that Open Grip Walkway Channels meet OSHA requirements.
You-attitude:	Open Grip Walkway Channels meet OSHA requirements.

Maybe the reader expects that anything you sell would meet government regulations (OSHA—the Occupational Safety and Health Administration—is a federal agency). The reader may even be disappointed if he or she expected higher standards. Simply explain the situation or describe a product's features; don't predict the reader's response.

When you have good news for the reader, simply give the good news.

Lacks you-attitude:	You'll be happy to hear that your scholarship has been renewed.
You-attitude:	Congratulations! Your scholarship has been renewed.

5. In positive situations, use you more often than I. Use we when it includes the reader.

Whenever possible, focus on the reader, not on you or your company.

Lacks you-attitude:	We provide health insurance to all employees.
You-attitude:	You receive health insurance as a full-time Procter & Gamble employee.

Most readers are tolerant of the word *I* in e-mail messages, which seem like conversation. Edit paper documents to use *I* rarely if at all. *I* suggests that you're concerned about personal issues, not about the organization's problems, needs, and opportunities. *We* works well when it includes the reader. Avoid *we* if it excludes the reader (as it would in a letter to a customer or supplier or as it might in a memo about what *we* in management want *you* to do).

6. In negative situations, avoid the word you. Protect the reader's ego. Use passive verbs and impersonal expressions to avoid assigning blame.

In negative situations, the word *you* will attack or insult the reader, so avoid it. One alternative is to use a noun for a group of which the reader is a part instead of *you* so readers don't feel that they're singled out for bad news.

Lacks you-attitude:	You must get approval from the director before you publish any articles or memoirs based on your work in the agency.
You-attitude:	Agency personnel must get approval from the director to publish any articles or memoirs based on their work at the agency.

Two more strategies are to use passive verbs and impersonal expressions to avoid blaming the reader. **Passive verbs** describe the action performed on something, without necessarily saying who did it. (See Chapter 4 for a full discussion of passive verbs.) **Impersonal expressions** omit people and talk only about things.

In most cases, active verbs are better. But when your reader is at fault, passive verbs may be useful to avoid assigning blame.

Normally, writing is most lively when it's about people—and most interesting to readers when it's about them. When you have to report a mistake or bad news, however, you can protect the reader's ego by using an impersonal expression, one in which things, not people, do the acting.

Lacks you-attitude:	You made no allowance for inflation in your estimate.
You-attitude (passive):	No allowance for inflation has been made in this estimate.
You-attitude (impersonal):	This estimate makes no allowance for inflation.

A purist might say that impersonal expressions are illogical: an estimate, for example, is inanimate and can't "make" anything. In the pragmatic world of business writing, however, impersonal expressions often help you convey criticism tactfully.

You-Attitude beyond the Sentence Level

Good messages apply you-attitude beyond the sentence level by using content and organization as well as style to build goodwill.

To create goodwill with content,

- Be complete. When you have lots of information to give, consider putting some details in an appendix, which may be read later.
- Anticipate and answer questions the reader is likely to have.
- When you include information the reader didn't ask for, show why it is important.
- Show readers how the subject of your message affects them.

To organize information to build goodwill,

- Put information readers are most interested in first.
- Arrange information to meet your reader's needs, not yours.
- Use headings and lists so that the reader can find key points quickly.

Consider the letter in Figure 2.1. As the red marginal notes indicate, many individual sentences in this letter lack you-attitude. Fixing individual sentences could improve the letter. However, it really needs to be totally rewritten.

 Figure 2.2 shows a possible revision of this letter. The revision is clearer, easier to read, and friendlier. Check the BAC Web site for another example of a letter revised to improve you-attitude.

Positive Emphasis

Some negatives are necessary. As Stephen Hlibok points out, when you have bad news to give the reader—announcements of layoffs, product defects and recalls, price increases—straightforward negatives build credibility. Sometimes negatives are needed to make people take a problem seriously. Wall Data improved the reliability of its computer programs when it eliminated the term *bugs* and used instead the term *failures*. In some messages, such as disciplinary notices and negative performance appraisals, your purpose is to deliver a rebuke with no alternative. Even here, avoid insults or global attacks on the reader's integrity or sanity. Being honest about the drawbacks of a job reduces turnover. And sometimes negatives create a "reverse psychology" that makes people look favorably at your product. Rent-a-Wreck is thriving. (The cars really don't look so bad.)[2]

But in most situations, it's better to be positive. Annette N. Shelby and N. Lamar Reinsch, Jr., found that business people responded more positively to positive than to negative language and were more likely to say they would act on a positively worded request.[3] Martin Seligman's research for Met Life found that optimistic salespeople sold 37% more insurance than pessimistic colleagues. As a result, Met Life began hiring optimists even when they failed to meet the company's other criteria. These "unqualified" optimists outsold pessimists 21% in their first year and 57% in the next.[4]

How to Create Positive Emphasis

You can de-emphasize negative information by using the following five techniques:

1. Avoid negative words and words with negative connotations.
2. State information positively. Focus on what the reader can do rather than on what you won't or can't let the reader do.

You-Attitude with International Audiences

When you communicate with international audiences, look at the world from their point of view.

The United States is in the middle of most of the maps sold in the United States. It isn't in the middle of maps sold elsewhere in the world.

The United States clings to a measurement system that has been abandoned by most of the world. When you write for international audiences, use the metric system.

Even pronouns and direction words need attention. *We* may not feel inclusive to readers with different assumptions and backgrounds. *Here* won't mean the same thing to a reader in Bonn as it does to one in Boulder.

Figure 2.1   *A Letter Lacking You-Attitude*

450 INDUSTRIAL PARK
CLEVELAND, OH 44120
(216) 555-4670   FAX: (216) 555-4672

December 11, 2000

Ms. Carol McFarland
Rollins Equipment Corporation
18438 East Night Hawk Way
Phoenix, AZ 85043-7800

Dear Ms. McFarland:

Legalistic

Not you- attitude

We are now ready to issue a check to Rollins Equipment in the amount of $14,207.02. To receive said check, you will deliver to me a release of the mechanic's liens in the amount of $14,207.02.   *Sounds dictatorial*

Lacks you-attitude

Focuses on negative

Before we can release the check, we must be satisfied that the release is in the proper form. We must insist that we be provided with a stamped original of the lien indicating the document number in the appropriate district court where it is filed. Also, either the release must be executed by an officer of Rollins Equipment, or we must be provided with a letter from an officer of Rollins Equipment authorizing another individual to execute the release.

Hard to read, remember

Please contact the undersigned so that an appointment can be scheduled for this transaction.   *Jargon*

Sincerely,

Kelly J. Pickett

Kelly J. Pickett

3. Justify negative information by giving a reason or linking it to a reader benefit.
4. If the negative is truly unimportant, omit it.
5. Bury the negative information and present it compactly.

Now, let's see how to apply each of these techniques.

F i g u r e 2.2   *A Letter Revised to Improve You-Attitude*

450 INDUSTRIAL PARK
CLEVELAND, OH 44120
(216) 555-4670   FAX: (216) 555-4672

December 11, 2000

Ms. Carol McFarland
Rollins Equipment Corporation
18438 East Night Hawk Way
Phoenix, AZ 85043-7800

Dear Ms. McFarland:

Starts with main point from the reader's point of view

Let's clear up the lien in the Allen contract.

Focuses on what reader gets

Rollins will receive a check for $14,207.02 when you give us a release for the mechanic's lien of $14,207.02. To assure us that the release is in the proper form,

1. Give us a stamped original of the lien indicating the document's district court number, and

2. Either
   a. Have an officer of Rollins Equipment sign the release
          or
   b. Give us a letter from a Rollins officer authorizing someone else to sign the release.

List makes it easy to see that reader needs to do two things—and that the second can be done in two ways.

Call me to tell me which way is best for you. *Emphasizes reader's choice*

Sincerely,

Kelly J. Pickett

Kelly J. Pickett   *Extension number makes*
Extension 5318   *it easy for reader to phone.*

1. Avoid negative words and words with negative connotations.

Figure 2.3 lists some common negative words. If you find one of these words in a draft, try to substitute a more positive word. When you must use a negative, use the *least negative* term that will convey your meaning.

The Wait from This Point*

Visit Disney World, and you'll stand in line for the most popular rides. Helpful signs tell you how long the wait will be from various points in line. If you're not ready to wait that long, you leave.

If you do stay in line, you'll be pleasantly surprised: the line will move faster than advertised.

The signs deliberately overstate the wait. Recently, the sign at the Indiana Jones Adventure ride advised a wait of 25 minutes. It actually took less than 20.

"It's part of the psychology," says Tony Baxter, Vice President of Conceptual Development at Disney's imagineering unit.

*Based on Jeff Rowe, "Waiting in Line Is All Part of the Amusement at Theme Parks," *The Columbus Dispatch*, June 14, 1996, 1C.

The following examples show how to replace negative words with positive words.

Negative:	We have failed to finish taking inventory.
Better:	We haven't finished taking inventory.
Still better:	We will be finished taking inventory Friday.
Negative:	If you can't understand this explanation, feel free to call me.
Better:	If you have further questions, just call me.
Still better:	Omit the sentence.

If a sentence has two negatives, substitute one positive term.

Negative:	Never fail to back up your disks.
Better:	Always back up your disks.

When you must use a negative term, use the least negative word that is accurate.

Negative:	Your balance of $835 is delinquent.
Better:	Your balance of $835 is past due.

Getting rid of negatives has the added benefit of making what you write easier to understand. Sentences with three or more negatives are very hard to understand.[5]

Beware of **hidden negatives:** words that are not negative in themselves but become negative in context. *But* and *however* indicate a shift, so, after a positive statement, they are negative. *I hope* and *I trust that* suggest that you aren't sure. *Patience* may sound like a virtue, but it is a necessary virtue only when things are slow. Even positives about a service or product may backfire if they suggest that in the past the service or product was bad.

Negative:	I hope this is the information you wanted. [Implication: I'm not sure.]
Better:	Enclosed is a brochure about road repairs scheduled for 2001–2003.
Still better:	The brochure contains a list of all roads and bridges scheduled for repair during 2001–2003. Call Gwen Wong at 555-3245 for specific dates when work will start and stop and for alternate routes.

Figure 2.3

Negative Words to Avoid

afraid	error	lacking	trivial
anxious	except	loss	trouble
avoid	fail	**Some mis- words:**	wait
bad	fault	misfortune	weakness
careless	fear	mistake	worry
damage	hesitate		wrong
delay	ignorant	missing	
delinquent	ignore	neglect	**Many un- words:**
deny	impossible	never	unclear
difficulty		no	unfair
	Many in- words:	not	unfortunate
Some dis- words:	inadequate	objection	unfortunately
disapprove	incomplete	problem	unpleasant
dishonest	inconvenient	reject	unreasonable
dissatisfied	insincere	sorry	unreliable
eliminate	injury	terrible	unsure

Negative:	Please be patient as we switch to the automated system. [Implication: You can expect problems.]
Better:	If you have questions during our transition to the automated system, call Melissa Morgan.
Still better:	You'll be able to get information instantly about any house on the market when the automated system is in place. If you have questions during the transition, call Melissa Morgan.
Negative:	Now Crispy Crunch tastes better. [Implication: it used to taste terrible.]
Better:	Now Crispy Crunch tastes even better.

Removing negatives does not mean being arrogant or pushy.

Negative:	I hope that you are satisfied enough to place future orders.
Arrogant:	I look forward to receiving all of your future business.
Better:	Call Mercury whenever you need transistors.

When you eliminate negative words, be sure to maintain accuracy. Words that are exact opposites will usually not be accurate. Instead, use specifics to be both positive and accurate.

Negative:	The exercycle is not guaranteed for life.
Not true:	The exercycle is guaranteed for life.
True:	The exercycle is guaranteed for 10 years.
Negative:	Customers under 60 are not eligible for the Prime Time discount.
Not true:	You must be over 60 to be eligible for the Prime Time discount.
True:	If you're 60 or older, you can save 10% on all your purchases with RightWay's Prime Time discount.

Legal phrases also have negative connotations for most readers and should be avoided whenever possible. The idea will sound more positive if you use normal English.

| Negative: | If your account is still delinquent, a second, legal notice will be sent to you informing you that cancellation of your policy will occur 30 days after the date of the legal notice if we do not receive your check. |
| Better: | Even if your check is lost in the mail and never reaches us, you still have a 30-day grace period. If you do get a second notice, you will know that your payment hasn't reached us. To keep your account in good standing, stop payment on the first check and send a second one. |

2. State information positively. Focus on what the reader can do rather than on what you won't or can't let the reader do.

Sometimes positive emphasis is a matter of the way you present something: Is the glass half empty or half full? Sometimes it's a matter of eliminating double negatives. When there are limits, or some options are closed, focus on the alternatives that remain.

Negative:	We will not allow you to charge more than $1,500 on your VISA account.
Better:	You can charge $1,500 on your new VISA card.
or:	Your new VISA card gives you $1,500 in credit that you can use at thousands of stores nationwide.

As you focus on what will happen, **check for you-attitude.** In the last example, "We will allow you to charge $1,500" would be positive, but it lacks you-attitude.

A Layoff by Any Other Name*

Companies trying to put a positive spin on layoffs have come up with a variety of euphemisms. They really don't fool anybody, and the companies look foolish at best, dishonest at worst.

Here are some of the terms:

- Bank of America: Release of resources.
- Bell Labs: Involuntary separation from payroll.
- Clifford of Vermont: Career-change opportunity.
- Digital Equipment Corporation: Involuntary severance.
- Harris Bank of Chicago: Right-sizing the bank.
- Newsweek: Reduction in force (RIF).
- Procter & Gamble: Strengthening global effectiveness.
- Stouffer Foods Corp.: Schedule adjustments.
- Wal-Mart: Normal payroll adjustment.

Sometimes, it's better to just be negative.

*Based on William Lutz, "The New Doublespeak," in "Hit the Road, Jack," *Newsweek*, August 12, 1996, 57.

Truth Can Be Spoken in Different Ways*

One Iranian told a fable of an ancient king who had an ominous dream. In the dream the king saw himself aged and afflicted, with decaying and falling teeth. Calling together his court astrologers for an interpretation, the shaken king heard the first say, "Your Majesty, I regret to tell you that the interpretation must be bad. The dream means that you will die within a year." In a rage the king threw the brash astrologer out of his court and turned to the second man.

The second astrologer said, "Your Majesty, it is good news, the very best. It means that all your programs and projects will live on after you, and all your sons and daughters will survive you." The king, who was old and knew he might die soon, nevertheless was pleased with this interpretation and richly rewarded the astrologer.

*Quoted from John P. Fieg and John G. Blair, *There Is a Difference: 12 Intercultural Perspectives* (Washington, DC: Meridian House International, 1975), 83.

When you have a benefit and a requirement the reader must meet to get the benefit, the sentence is usually more positive if you put the benefit first.

Negative: You will not qualify for the student membership rate of $25 a year unless you are a full-time student.

Better: You get all the benefits of membership for only $25 a year if you're a full-time student.

3. Justify negative information by giving a reason or linking it to a reader benefit.

A reason can help your reader see that the information is necessary; a benefit can suggest that the negative aspect is outweighed by positive factors. Be careful, however, to make the logic behind your reason clear and to leave no loopholes.

Negative: We cannot sell computer disks in lots of less than 10.

Loophole: To keep down packaging costs and to help you save on shipping and handling costs, we sell computer disks in lots of 10 or more.

Suppose the customer says, "I'll pay the extra shipping and handling. Send me seven." If you can't or won't sell in lots of less than 10, you need to write:

Better: To keep down packaging costs and to help customers save on shipping and handling costs, we sell computer disks only in lots of 10 or more.

If you link the negative element to a benefit, be sure it is a benefit the reader will acknowledge. Avoid telling people that you're doing things "for their own good." They may have a different notion of what their own good is. You may think you're doing customers a favor by limiting their credit so they don't get in over their heads and go bankrupt. They may think they'd be better off with more credit so they could expand in hopes of making more sales and more profits.

4. If the negative is truly unimportant, omit it.

Omit negatives only when

- The reader does not need the information to make a decision.
- You have already given the reader the information and he or she has access to the previous communication.
- The information is trivial.

The following examples suggest the kind of negatives you can omit:

Negative: A one-year subscription to *PC Magazine* is $49.97. That rate is not as low as the rates charged for some magazines.

Better: A one-year subscription to *PC Magazine* is $49.97.

Still better: A one-year subscription to *PC Magazine* is $49.97. You save 43% off the newsstand price of $87.78.

Negative: If you are not satisfied with Interstate Fidelity Insurance, you do not have to renew your policy.

Better: Omit the sentence.

5. Bury the negative information and present it compactly.

The beginning and end are always positions of emphasis. Use these positions for ideas you want to emphasize. Put negatives in the middle of a paragraph rather than in the first or last sentence and in the middle of the message rather than in the first or last paragraphs.

When a letter or memo runs several pages, remember that the bottom of the first page is also a position of emphasis, even if it is in the middle of a paragraph, because of the extra white space of the bottom margin. (The first page gets more attention because it is on top and the reader's eye may catch lines of the message even when he or she isn't consciously reading it; the tops and bot-

toms of subsequent pages don't get this extra attention.) If possible, avoid placing negative information at the bottom of the first page.

Giving a topic lots of space emphasizes it. Therefore, you can de-emphasize
negative information by giving it as little space as possible. Give negative information only once in your message. Don't list negatives vertically on the
page since lists take space and emphasize material.

How to Apologize

When you are at fault, you may build goodwill by admitting that fact forthrightly.
Apologies are a special kind of negative and call for slightly different rules.

- **No explicit apology is necessary if the error is small and if you are
  correcting the mistake.**

  Negative: I'm sorry the clerk did not credit your account properly.

  Better: Your statement has been corrected to include your payment of $263.75.

- **Do not apologize when you are not at fault.** When you have done
  everything you can and when a delay or problem is due to circumstances
  beyond your control, you aren't at fault and don't need to apologize. It may
  be appropriate to include an explanation so the reader knows you weren't
  negligent. If the news is bad, put the explanation first. If you have good
  news for the reader, put it before your explanation.

  Negative: I'm sorry that I could not answer your question sooner. I had to wait until the sales
                      figures for the second quarter were in.

  Better: We needed the sales figures for the second quarter to answer your question. Now that
  (neutral or   they're in, I can tell you that . . .
  bad news)

  Better: The new advertising campaign is a success. The sales figures for the second quarter
  (good news)   are finally in, and they show that . . .

If the delay or problem is long or large, it is good you-attitude to ask the
reader whether he or she wants to confirm the original plan or make different
arrangements.

  Negative: I'm sorry that the chairs will not be ready by August 25 as promised.

  Better: Due to a strike against the manufacturer, the desk chairs you ordered will not be ready until
                      November. Do you want to keep that order, or would you like to look at the models available
                      from other suppliers?

- **When you apologize, do it early, briefly, and sincerely.** Apologize only
  once, early in the message. Let the reader move on to other, more positive
  information.

  Even if major trouble or inconvenience has resulted from your error, you
  don't need to go on about all the horrible things that happened. The reader
  already knows this negative information, and you can omit it. Instead,
  focus on what you have done to correct the situation.

  If you don't know whether or not any inconvenience has resulted, don't
  raise the issue at all.

  Negative: I'm sorry I didn't answer your letter sooner. I hope that my delay hasn't inconvenienced you.

  Better: I'm sorry I didn't answer your letter sooner.

Tone, Power, and Politeness

Tone is the implied attitude of the writer toward the reader. If the words of
a document seem condescending or rude, tone is a problem. Tone is tricky
because it interacts with power: the words that might seem friendly from a

**A Soft Answer Turneth
Away Lawsuits***

Lawyers usually tell individuals and
companies not to admit liability, lest
the admission become evidence in
a lawsuit for damages. Maybe
that's good advice in major crises
where the CEO has a responsibility
to stockholders to reduce the
company's legal liability.

But one soft drink company found
that sincere apologies satisfied
people, so they didn't sue.

The company had a spate of
complaints about exploding bottles.
But instead of giving people a form
to fill out and saying, "Contact our
risk department," service representatives were told to empathize and
apologize.

The company's liability expenses
went down $2 million in a year.

*Based on Cynthia Crossen, "The Simple
Apology after Poor Service Is in Very
Sorry State," *The Wall Street Journal*,
November 29, 1990, B8; and Lisa Tyler,
"Liability Means Never Being Able to Say
You're Sorry: Corporate Guilt, Legal
Constraints, and Defensiveness in
Corporate Communication," *Manage-
ment Communication Quarterly* 11, no.
1 (August 1997): 51–73.

Positive Emphasis in Canada*

In the United States, ask someone "How are you?" and you'll probably get the standard response: "Fine, thank you" or even "Terrific!" In Canada, the standard response is "Not bad."

The words that create goodwill vary from culture to culture. Canadians—like people in Great Britain, New Zealand, and other Commonwealth countries—tend to understate and downplay. As a result, positive emphasis will be a bit less positive than it would be in the United States.

You-attitude takes precedence over every other principle: use the language that works for your audience.

*Based on Margot Northey, personal communication, October 28, 1993, Montreal, Canada; and Roger Graves, " 'Dear Friend'(?): Culture and Genre in American and Canadian Direct Marketing Letters," *The Journal of Business Communication* 34, no. 3 (July 1997): 235–52.

superior to a subordinate may seem uppity if used by the subordinate to the superior. Norms for politeness are cultural and generational. Language that is acceptable within one group may be unacceptable if used by someone outside the group.

The desirable tone for business writing is businesslike but not stiff, friendly but not phony, confident but not arrogant, polite but not groveling. The following guidelines will help you achieve the tone you want.

- **Use courtesy titles for people outside your organization whom you don't know well.** Most US organizations use first names for everyone, whatever their age or rank. But many people don't like being called by their first names by people they don't know or by someone much younger. When you talk or write to people outside your organization, use first names only if you've established a personal relationship. If you don't know someone well, use a courtesy title:

Dear Mr. Reynolds:

Dear Ms. Lee:

- **Be aware of the power implications of the words you use.** "Thank you for your cooperation" is generous coming from a superior to a subordinate; it's not appropriate in a message to your superior.

Different ways of asking for action carry different levels of politeness.[6]

Order: (lowest politeness)	Turn in your time card by Monday.
Polite order: (midlevel politeness)	Please turn in your time card by Monday.
Indirect request: (higher politeness)	Time cards should be turned in by Monday.
Question: (highest politeness)	Would you be able to turn in your time card by Monday?

Generally, you need less politeness when you're asking for something small, routine, or for the reader's benefit. You need more politeness if you're asking for something that will inconvenience the reader and help you more than the person who does the action.

Higher levels of politeness may be unclear. In some cases, a question may seem like a request for information to which it's acceptable to answer, "No, I can't." In other cases, it will be an order, simply phrased in polite terms.

Generally, requests sound friendliest when they use conversational language.

Poor tone:	Return the draft with any changes by next Tuesday.
Better tone:	Let me know by Tuesday whether you'd like any changes in the draft.

- **When the stakes are low, be straightforward.** Messages that beat around the bush sound pompous and defensive.

Poor tone:	Distribution of the low-fat plain granola may be limited in your area. May we suggest that you discuss this matter with your store manager.
Better tone:	Our low-fat granola is so popular that there isn't enough to go around. We're expanding production to meet the demand. Ask your store manager to keep putting in orders, so that your grocery is on the list of stores that will get supplies when they become available.
or	Store managers decide what to stock. If your store has stopped carrying our low-fat granola, the store manager has stopped ordering it. Talk to the manager. Managers try to meet customer needs, so if you say something you're more likely to get what you want.

- **When you must give bad news, consider hedging your statement.** John Hagge and Charles Kostelnick have shown that auditors' suggestion letters rarely say directly that firms are using unacceptable accounting practices. Instead, they use three strategies to be more diplomatic: specifying the time ("currently, the records are quite informal"), limiting statements ("it appears," "it seems"), and using impersonal statements that do not specify who caused a problem or who will perform an action.[7]

Reducing Bias in Business Communication

Everything we do in good business communication attempts to build goodwill. Bias-free language and bias-free visuals help sustain the goodwill we work so hard to create.

Bias-free language is language that does not discriminate against people on the basis of sex, physical condition, race, age, or any other category. Using bias-free language and visuals is a good idea for at least five reasons. First, organizations that treat people fairly should use language that treats people fairly. A second reason for using bias-free language and visuals is to remove a potential barrier to the images people create of themselves. A steady diet of sexist language encourages women to have low aspirations, to seek jobs rather than careers, to think that middle management is as high as they can go. Pictures in ads, college catalogs, and annual reports that omit people in wheelchairs and people of color make it more difficult for those who have traditionally been pushed to the margins to participate in the center of society. A third reason to use bias-free language and visuals is that the law is increasingly intolerant of biased documents and hostile work environments. The fourth reason is that bias-free language and visuals are profitable. As Stephen Hlibok points out, Merrill Lynch tapped into a new, underserved market when it established its Deaf and Hard of Hearing Investors' Services Division. Treating every group with respect and understanding is essential to win loyalty and business. The fifth reason to use bias-free language and visuals, and perhaps the most important, is that they're fairer and friendlier.

Check to be sure that your language is nonsexist, nonracist, and nonagist. When you talk about people with disabilities or diseases, talk about the people, not the condition. When you produce newsletters or other documents with photos and illustrations, choose a sampling of the whole population, not just part of it.

Making Language Nonsexist

Nonsexist language treats both sexes neutrally. Check to be sure that your writing is free from sexism in four areas: words and phrases, job titles, courtesy titles, and pronouns.

Words and phrases

If you find any of the terms in the first column in Figure 2.4 in your writing or your company's documents, replace them with terms from the second column.

Not every word containing *man* is sexist. For example, *manager* is not sexist. The word comes from the Latin *manus* meaning *hand;* it has nothing to do with maleness.

Avoid terms that assume that everyone is married or is heterosexual.

Biased: You and your husband or wife are cordially invited to the dinner.

Better: You and your guest are cordially invited to the dinner.

Job titles

Use neutral titles which do not imply that a job is held only by men or only by women. Many job titles are already neutral: *accountant, banker, doctor, engineer,*

Figure 2.4

Getting Rid of Sexist Terms and Phrases

Instead of	Use	Because
The girl at the front desk	The woman's name or job title: "Ms. Browning," "Rosa," "the receptionist"	Call female employees *women* just as you call male employees *men.* When you talk about a specific woman, use her name, just as you use a man's name to talk about a specific man.
The ladies on our staff	The women on our staff	Use parallel terms for males and females. Therefore, use *ladies* only if you refer to the males on your staff as *gentlemen.* Few businesses do, since social distinctions are rarely at issue.

Manpower
  Manhours
  Manning
	Personnel
	Hours or worker hours
	Staffing
		The power in business today comes from both women and men. If you have to correspond with the US Department of Labor's Division of Manpower Administration, you are stuck with the term. When you talk about other organizations, however, use nonsexist alternatives.

Managers and their wives	Managers and their guests	Managers may be female; not everyone is married.

inspector, manager, nurse, pilot, secretary, technician, to name a few. Other titles reflect gender stereotypes and need to be changed.

If you need a substitute for a traditional word, check the US Department of Labor's *Job Title Revisions to Eliminate Sex- and Age-Referent Language* from the Dictionary of Occupational Titles, 4th ed., 1991.

Instead of	Use
Businessman	A specific title: executive, accountant, department head, owner of a small business, men and women in business, business person
Chairman	Chair, chairperson, moderator
Foreman	Supervisor (from Job Title Revisions)
Salesman	Salesperson, sales representative
Waitress	Server
Woman lawyer	Lawyer
Workman	Worker, employee. Or use a specific title: crane operator, bricklayer, etc.

Courtesy titles

Memos normally use first and last names without courtesy titles. Letters, however, require courtesy titles in the salutation *unless* you're on a first-name basis with your reader. (See Appendix A for examples of memo and letter formats.)

- When you know your reader's name and gender, use courtesy titles that do not indicate marital status: *Mr.* for men and *Ms.* for women. There are, however, two exceptions:
    1. If the woman has a professional title, use that title if you would use it for a man.
       Dr. Kristen Sorenson is our new company physician.
       The Rev. Elizabeth Townsley gave the invocation.
    2. If the woman prefers to be addressed as *Mrs.* or *Miss,* use the title she prefers rather than *Ms.* (You-attitude takes precedence over nonsexist language: address the reader as she—or he—prefers to be addressed.) To find out if a woman prefers a traditional title,

a. Check the signature block in previous correspondence. If a woman types her name as *(Miss) Elaine Anderson* or *(Mrs.) Kay Royster,* use the title she designates.

b. Notice the title a woman uses in introducing herself on the phone. If she says, "This is Robin Stine," use *Ms.* when you write to her. If she says, "I'm Mrs. Stine," use the title she specifies.

c. Check your company directory. In some organizations, women who prefer traditional titles can list them with their names.

d. When you're writing job letters or crucial correspondence, call the company and ask the receptionist which title your reader prefers.

Ms. is particularly useful when you do not know what a woman's marital status is. However, even when you happen to know that a woman is married or single, **you still use** *Ms.* **unless you know that she prefers another title.**

In addition to using parallel courtesy titles, use parallel forms for names.

Not Parallel	Parallel
Members of the committee will be Mr. Jones, Mr. Yacone, and Lisa.	Members of the committee will be Mr. Jones, Mr. Yacone, and Ms. Melton.
	or
	Members of the committee will be Irving, Ted, and Lisa.

- When you know your reader's name but not the gender, either
  1. Call the company and ask the receptionist, or
  2. Use the reader's full name in the salutation:
     Dear Chris Crowell:
     Dear J. C. Meath:
- When you know neither the reader's name nor gender, you have three options:
  1. Use a letter format that omits the salutation. The AMS Simplified letter format (see Appendix A) includes the inside address and uses a subject line but omits the salutation and complimentary close.
     SUBJECT: RECOMMENDATION FOR BEN WANDELL
  2. Use the reader's position or job title:
     Dear Loan Officer:
     Dear Registrar:
  3. Use a general group to which your reader belongs:
     Dear Investor:
     Dear Admissions Committee:

Terms that are meant to be positive (Dear Careful Shopper: or Dear Concerned Citizen:) may backfire if readers see them as manipulative flattery.

Although many people claim to dislike Dear Friend: as a salutation in a form letter, research shows that letters using it bring in a higher response than letters with no salutation.

Pronouns

When you write about a specific person, use the appropriate gender pronouns:

In his speech, John Jones said that . . .

In her speech, Judy Jones said that . . .

When you are not writing about a specific person, but about anyone who may be in a given job or position, traditional gender pronouns are sexist.

Ms. in Any Language*

Other countries are also developing nonsexist courtesy titles for women.

- United States
  Miss
  Mrs.
  Ms.
- France
  Mademoiselle (Mlle.)
  Madame (Mme.)
  Mad.
- Spain
  Señorita (Srta.)
  Señora (Sra.)
  Sa.
- Denmark
  Frøken
  Fru
  Fr.
- Japan
  San
  San
  San

*Based on Mary Ritchie Key, *Male/Female Language* (Metuchen, NJ: Scarecrow Press, 1975), 50; John C. Condon and Fathi Yousef, *An Introduction to Intercultural Communication* (Indianapolis: Bobbs-Merrill, 1975), 50; and Silvia Fuduric, Letter to the Author, January 19, 1998.

Attempts To Create a Unisex Pronoun*

For 150 years, people have attempted to coin a unisex pronoun. None of the attempts has been successful.

Date	*he* or *she*	*his* or *her*	*him* or *her*
1850	ne	nis	nim
1884	le	lis	lim
1938	se	sim	sis
1970	ve	vis	ver
1977	e	e's	em
1988	ala	alis	alum

*Based on Dennis E. Baron, "The Epicene Pronoun: The Word That Failed," *American Speech* 56 (1981): 83–97; and Ellen Graham, "Business Bulletin," *The Wall Street Journal*, December 29, 1988, A1.

Sexist: a. Each supervisor must certify that the time sheet for his department is correct.

Sexist: b. When the nurse fills out the accident report form, she should send one copy to the Central Division Office.

There are four ways to eliminate sexist generic pronouns: use plurals, use second-person *you,* revise the sentence to omit the pronoun, or use pronoun pairs. Whenever you have a choice of two or more ways to make a phrase or sentence nonsexist, choose the alternative that is the smoothest and least conspicuous.

The following examples use these methods to revise sentences *a* and *b* above.

1. Use plural nouns and pronouns.

    Nonsexist: a. Supervisors must certify that the time sheets for their departments are correct.

    Note: When you use plural nouns and pronouns, other words in the sentence may need to be made plural too. In the example above, plural supervisors have plural time sheets and departments.
    Avoid mixing singular nouns and plural pronouns.

    Nonsexist but lacks agreement: a. Each supervisor must certify that the time sheet for their department is correct.

    Since *supervisor* is singular, it is incorrect to use the plural *their* to refer to it. The resulting lack of agreement is acceptable orally but is not yet acceptable to many readers in writing. Instead, use one of the four grammatically correct ways to make the sentence nonsexist.

2. Use *you.*

    Nonsexist: a. You must certify that the time sheet for your department is correct.

    Nonsexist: b. When you fill out an accident report form, send one copy to the Central Division Office.

    You is particularly good for instructions and statements of the responsibilities of someone in a given position. Using *you* also may shorten sentences, since you write "Send one copy" instead of "You should send one copy." It also makes your writing more direct.

3. Substitute an article (*a, an,* or *the*) for the pronoun, or revise the sentence so that the pronoun is unnecessary.

    Nonsexist: a. The supervisor must certify that the time sheet for the department is correct.

    Nonsexist: b. The nurse will
        1. Fill out the accident report form.
        2. Send one copy of the form to the Central Division Office.

4. When you must focus on the action of an individual, use pronoun pairs.

    Nonsexist: a. The supervisor must certify that the time sheet for his or her department is correct.

    Nonsexist: b. When the nurse fills out the accident report form, he or she should send one copy to the Central Division Office.

Making Language Nonracist and Nonagist

Language is **nonracist** and **nonagist** when it treats all races and ages fairly, avoiding negative stereotypes of any group. Use these guidelines to check for bias in documents you write or edit:

- **Give someone's race or age only if it is relevant to your story.** When you do mention these characteristics, give them for everyone in your story—not just the non-Caucasian, non-young-to-middle-aged adults you mention.
- **Refer to a group by the term it prefers. As preferences change, change your usage.** Fifty years ago, *Negro* was preferred as a more dignified term

You-attitude, positive emphasis, and bias-free language build goodwill with words, just as service, quality, and reliability build goodwill with actions.

than *colored* for African Americans. As times changed, *Black* and *African American* replaced it. Surveys in the mid-1990s showed that almost half of blacks aged 40 and older preferred *Black,* but those 18 to 39 preferred *African American.*[8]

Oriental has now been replaced by *Asian.*

The term *Latino* is the most acceptable group term to refer to Mexican Americans, Cuban Americans, Puerto Ricans, Dominicans, Brazilianos, and other people with Central and Latin American backgrounds. (*Latina* is the term for an individual woman.) Better still is to refer to the precise group. The differences among various Latino groups are at least as great as the differences among Italian Americans, Irish Americans, Armenian Americans, and others descended from various European groups.

Eskimo is a negative label. A better term is *Inuit,* which means *the people.*

Older people and *mature customers* are more generally accepted terms than *Senior Citizens* or *Golden Agers.*

- **Avoid terms that suggest that competent people are unusual.** The statement "She is an intelligent black woman" suggests that the writer expects most black women to be stupid. "He is an asset to his race" suggests that excellence in the race is rare. "He is a spry 70-year-old" suggests that the writer is amazed that anyone that old can still move.

Talking about People with Disabilities and Diseases

A disability is a physical, mental, sensory, or emotional impairment that interferes with the major tasks of daily living. One in six people in the United States has a disability; the number of people with disabilities will rise as the population ages.[9]

Technology helps blind people contribute fully as members of the workforce. This Braille keyboard allows a computer engineer to key in commands and data. Computer programs such as JAWS can read computer screens out loud.

- *People-first* **language focuses on the person, not the condition.**   **People-first language** names the person first, then adds the condition. Use it instead of traditional adjectives used as nouns that imply the condition defines the person.

Instead of	Use	Because
The mentally retarded	People with mental retardation	The condition does not define the person or his or her potential
Cancer patients	People being treated for cancer	

- **Avoid negative terms, unless the audience prefers them.**   You-attitude takes precedence over positive emphasis: use the term a group prefers. People who lost their hearing as infants, children, or young adults often prefer to be called *deaf*, or *Deaf* in recognition of Deafness as a culture. But people who lose their hearing as older adults often prefer to be called *hard of hearing*, even when their hearing loss is just as great as that of someone who identifies him- or herself as part of the Deaf culture.

Just as people in a single ethnic group may prefer different labels based on generational or cultural divides, so differences exist within the disability community. In the late 1990s, many disabled people have rejected such attempts at positive emphasis as "visually impaired" or "mobility challenged." Instead, naming the condition seems more honest and more enabling: blind, crippled. People explain their choices in the video clip on the BAC Web site. Using the right term requires keeping up with changing preferences. If your target audience is smaller than the whole group, use the term preferred by that audience, even if the group as a whole prefers another term. Some negative terms, however, are never appropriate. Negative terms such as afflicted, suffering from, and struck down also suggest an outdated view of any illness as a sign of divine punishment.

Instead of	Use	Because
Confined to a wheelchair	Uses a wheelchair	Wheelchairs enable people to escape confinement.
AIDS victim	Person with AIDS	Someone can have a disease without being victimized by it.
Abnormal	Atypical	People with disabilities are atypical but not necessarily abnormal.

Choosing Bias-Free Photos and Illustrations

When you produce a document with photographs or illustrations, check the visuals for possible bias. Do they show people of both sexes and all races? Is there a sprinkling of various kinds of people (younger and older, people using wheelchairs, etc.)? It's OK to have individual pictures that have just one sex or one race; the photos as a whole do not need to show exactly 50% men and 50% women. But the general impression should suggest that diversity is welcome and normal.

Check relationships and authority figures as well as numbers. If all the men appear in business suits and the women in maids' uniforms, the pictures are sexist even if an equal number of men and women are pictured. If the only blacks and Latinos pictured are factory workers, the photos support racism even when an equal number of people from each race are shown.

In the late 1990s, as Marilyn Dyrud has shown, only 22% of the images of humans in clip art files were women, and most of those showed women in traditional roles. An even smaller percent pictured members of minority groups.[10] Don't use biased clip art or stock photos: create your own bias-free illustrations.

Although this photo includes both men and women and people of different ethnic backgrounds, it could be interpreted as sexist and/or racist. The clothing and arrangement of people suggest that white males are still in charge. When choosing photos, try to convey the message that people of diverse backgrounds are welcome and can rise to power.

Summary of Key Points

- **You-attitude** is a style of writing that looks at things from the reader's point of view, emphasizing what the reader wants to know, respecting the reader's intelligence, and protecting the reader's ego.
  1. Focus not on what you do for the reader, but on what the reader receives or can do. In positive or neutral situations, stress what the reader wants to know.
  2. Refer to the reader's request or order specifically.
  3. Don't talk about your own feelings unless you're sure the reader wants to know how you feel.
  4. Don't tell readers how they feel or will react.

R-E-S-P-E-C-T*

Most major airlines and hotel chains provide disability training to employees. . . . I recognize when someone has been trained—to offer me a Braille menu, use my name when addressing me, or take a moment to orient me to a new environment. What I appreciate even more, though, is . . . simple, common courtesy.

I don't care how many pages in an employee manual somewhere are devoted to . . . the dos and don'ts of interacting with someone who is deaf, blind, or mentally retarded. Among hundreds of experiences in airports and hotels, the one distinction that separates the (mostly) pleasing from the (occasionally) painful in my encounters has been the honest friendliness and respect with which I have or have not been treated.

Ask me where I'd like to sit, whether I need help getting there, and what other kinds of help I need.

Please, assume that I know more about my disability than anyone else ever could.

Respect me as you do any other customer who is paying for the same service, and have the grace to apologize if something does go wrong.

Too many companies, it seems to me, are busy shaking in their boots over the imagined high cost of accommodating people with disabilities when, in many instances, a good old-fashioned refresher course in manners would cover most bases.

*Quoted from Deborah Kendrick, "Disabled Resent Being Patronized," *Columbus Dispatch*, July 21, 1996, 3B.

5. In positive situations, use *you* more often than *I*. Use *we* when it includes the reader.
6. In negative situations, avoid the word *you*. Protect the reader's ego. Use passive verbs and impersonal expressions to avoid assigning blame.

- Apply you-attitude beyond the sentence level by using organization and content as well as style to build goodwill.
- **Positive emphasis** means focusing on the positive rather than the negative aspects of a situation.
    1. Avoid negative words and words with negative connotations.
    2. State information positively. Focus on what the reader can do rather than on what you won't or can't let the reader do.
    3. Justify negative information by giving a reason or linking it to a reader benefit.
    4. If the negative is truly unimportant, omit it.
    5. Bury the negative information and present it compactly.
- The desirable tone for business writing is businesslike but not stiff, friendly but not phony, confident but not arrogant, polite but not groveling. The following guidelines will help you achieve the tone you want.
    - Use courtesy titles for people outside your organization whom you don't know well.
    - Be aware of the power implications of the words you use.
    - When the stakes are low, be straightforward.
    - When you must give bad news, consider hedging your statement.
- Writing should be free from sexism in four areas: words and phrases, job titles, courtesy titles, and pronouns.
- *Ms.* is the nonsexist courtesy title for women. Whether or not you know a woman's marital status, use *Ms. unless* the woman has a professional title or unless you know that she prefers a traditional title.
- Traditional pronouns are sexist when they refer to a class of people, not to specific individuals. Four ways to make the sentence nonsexist are to use plurals, to use *you,* to revise the sentence to omit the pronoun, and to use pronoun pairs.
- Bias-free language is fair and friendly; it complies with the law. It includes all readers; it helps to sustain goodwill.
- Check to be sure that your language is nonsexist, nonracist, and nonagist. When you talk about people with disabilities or diseases, use the term they prefer. When you produce newsletters or other documents with photos and illustrations, picture a sampling of the whole population, not just part of it.

 For a self-test on the concepts in this chapter, visit the BAC Web site.

Chapter 2

Exercises and Problems

Getting Started

2.1   Evaluating the Ethics of Positive Emphasis

The first term in each line below is negative; the second is a positive term that is sometimes substituted for it. Which of the positive terms seem ethical? Which seem unethical? Briefly explain your choices.

junk bonds	high-yield bonds
second mortgage	home equity loan

tax	user fee
nervousness	adrenaline
problem	challenge
price increase	price change
for-profit hospital	tax-paying hospital

2.2   Using Passives and Impersonal Expressions to Improve You-Attitude and Positive Emphasis

Revise each of these sentences to improve you-attitude and positive emphasis, first using a passive verb, then using an impersonal expression (one in which things, not people, do the action). Are both revisions equally good? Why or why not?

1. You did not send us your check.

2. You did not include all the necessary information in your letter.

3. By failing to build a fence around your pool, you have allowed your property to violate city regulations against health hazards.

2.3   Focusing on the Positive

Revise each of the following sentences to focus on the options that remain, not those that are closed off.

1. As a first-year employee, you are not eligible for dental insurance.

2. I will be out of the country October 25 to November 10 and will not be able to meet with you then.

3. You will not get your first magazine for at least four weeks.

2.4   Identifying Hidden Negatives

Identify the hidden negatives in the following sentences and revise to eliminate them. In some cases, you may need to add information to revise the sentence effectively.

1. This publication is designed to explain how your company can start a recycling program.

2. I hope you find the information in this brochure beneficial to you and a valuable reference as you plan your move.

3. In thinking about your role in our group, I remember two occasions where you contributed something.

2.5   Improving You-Attitude and Positive Emphasis

Revise these sentences to improve you-attitude and positive emphasis. Eliminate any awkward phrasing. In some cases, you may need to add information to revise the sentence effectively.

1. Do not fill out and return this form unless you intend to participate in the Dividend Reinvestment Program since this form enrolls you in the program.

2. We are pleased to offer you the ability to sign up for health insurance online on our Intranet.

3. You will be happy to know that you can use your new cell phone number anywhere in the United States; you don't have to use a different number when you travel.

4. I urge you to attend a meeting about HMOs so that we can inform you about your options.

5. If you have further questions, please do not hesitate to contact me.

6. I'm sorry you were worried about your health insurance. It is not too late to sign up for a flexible spending account.

7. You cannot return this item for a full refund if you keep it past 30 days.

(cont.)

8. We have taken a lot of time and trouble to design a Web site that is more than the usual useless fluff.

9. It should be obvious to you that we cannot make an exception in your favor or treat you differently than we treat other clients.

10. We cannot process your application to graduate because you did not supply all of the necessary information.

2.6   Improving You-Attitude and Positive Emphasis

Revise these sentences to improve you-attitude and positive emphasis. Eliminate any awkward phrasing. In some cases, you may need to add information to revise the sentence effectively.

1. When you write a report, do not make claims that you cannot support with evidence.

2. Although I was only an intern and didn't actually make presentations to major clients, I was required to prepare PowerPoint slides for the meetings and to answer some of the clients' questions.

3. You will be happy to learn that we won't charge you anything extra for additional cards for your spouse or child.

4. We have added another employee benefit for you.

5. If you have trouble using our database, I will be happy to try to explain it to you.

6. I'm sorry you were concerned about your account. The missing payment has been found and you no longer have any amount past due.

7. To help us ensure that there are no unnecessary delays in processing your order, please check the form at the end of this letter to see that nothing is omitted or incorrect before you sign the form and return it to us.

8. The employee discount may only be used for purchases for your own use or for gifts; you may not buy items for resale. To prevent any abuse of the discount privilege, you may be asked to justify your purchase.

9. The figures for budget changes made at the meeting may be wrong, since I got lost during John's presentation. Please check the figures and let me know if they need correction.

10. If you mailed a check with your order, as you claim, we failed to receive it.

2.7   Improving You-Attitude and Positive Emphasis

Revise these sentences to improve you-attitude and positive emphasis. Eliminate any awkward phrasing. In some cases, you may need to add information to revise the sentence effectively.

1. We can't mail you a copy of the new directory until it comes back from the printer.

2. We provide all employees (except part-time employees) with health and dental insurance. However, the dental insurance does not begin until you have worked here for three months.

3. I will take the exam for real estate agents in June. I realize that almost everyone who takes it passes, so I guess this statement doesn't mean much, but based on my education and experience I do expect to pass it.

4. You cannot use flextime unless you have the consent of your supervisor.

5. I hope this answers your question. If you still do not understand, do not fail to ask for more information.

6. I'm sorry you were worried about the résumé you e-mailed us. We did not have any problems scanning it into our system.

7. To avoid unnecessary delays, call for an appointment before coming in to the office.

8. I realize that Wednesday at 10 AM is not a convenient time for everyone, but I was unable to arrange a time that is good for everyone.

9. You cannot accept gifts from anyone with whom you, as an employee of the Environmental Protection Agency, deal, because some citizen might suspect that your enforcement decision had been subject to undue influence.

10. If you supplied receipts with your request for reimbursement, as you claim, they have been lost.

2.8   Eliminating Biased Language

Explain the source of bias in each of the following and revise to remove the bias.

1. We recommend hiring Jim Ryan and Elizabeth Shuman. Both were very successful summer interns. Jim drafted the report on using rap music in ads, and Elizabeth really improved the looks of the office.
2. All sales associates and their wives are invited to the picnic.
3. Although he is blind, Mr. Morin is an excellent group leader.
4. Unlike many blacks, Yvonne has extensive experience designing Web pages.
5. Chris Renker
   Pacific Perspectives
   6300 West Coronado Blvd.
   Los Angeles, CA
   Gentlemen:
6. Enrique Torres has very good people skills for a man.
7. *Parenting 2000* shows you how to persuade your husband to do his share of child care chores.
8. Mr. Paez, Mr. O'Connor, and Tonya will represent our office at the convention.
9. Sue Corcoran celebrates her 50th birthday today. Stop by her cubicle at noon to get a piece of cake and to help us sing "The Old Grey Mare Just Ain't What She Used to Be."
10. Because older customers tend to be really picky, we will need to give a lot of details in our ads.

E-Mail Messages

2.9   Advising a Hasty Subordinate

Three days ago, one of your subordinates forwarded to everyone in the office a bit of e-mail humor he'd received from a friend. Titled "You know you're Southern when . . . ," the message poked fun at Southern speech, attitudes, and lifestyles. Today you get this message from your subordinate:

> Subject: Should I Apologize?
>
> I'm getting flamed left and right because of the Southern message. I thought it was funny, but some people just can't take a joke. So far I've tried not to respond to the flames, figuring that would just make things worse. But now I'm wondering if I should apologize. What do you think?

Answer the message.

2.10   Responding to a Complaint

You're Director of Corporate Communications; the employee newsletter is produced by your office. Today you get this e-mail message from Caroline Huber:

> Subject: Complaint about Sexist Language
>
> The article about the "Help Desk" says that Martina Luna and I "are the key customer service representatives 'manning' the desk." I don't MAN anything! I WORK.

Respond to Caroline. And send a message to your staff, reminding them to edit newsletter stories as well as external documents to replace biased language.

Communicating at Work

2.11   Evaluating You-Attitude and Positive Emphasis in Documents That Cross Your Desk

Identify three sentences that use (or should use) you-attitude and positive emphasis. If the sentences are good, write them down or attach a copy of the document(s) marking the sentence(s) in the margin. If the sentences need work, provide both the original sentence and a possible revision.

As Your Instructor Directs,

a. Turn in the sentences and revisions.
b. Share the sentences and revisions with the class in a brief oral presentation.
c. Discuss the sentences and revisions with a group of students. What patterns do you see?

Letter and Memo Assignments

2.12   Evaluating Clip Art

Evaluate the portrayals of people in the clip art available to workers in your office. Does it have the same problems that Marilyn Dyrud found in "An Exploration of Gender Bias in Computer Clip Art," *Business Communication Quarterly* 60, no. 4 (December 1997): 30–51? How are people with color and people with disabilities portrayed? Is the clip art good enough to use in memos, flyers, and the employee newsletter, or would you recommend that workers avoid its depictions of people?

Write a memo to your supervisor.

2.13   Evaluating Access for Deaf and Hard-of-Hearing Customers

Evaluate the access your office, store, or building offers Deaf and hard-of-hearing customers. Do you have enough TTY phone lines (which display the message on a screen and into which a response can be typed)? Do ads give the TTY number as well as the local or 800-number? Do you have people who can sign or interpret for people who are signing? Consider both the access needed for regular business and the access that might be needed during an unusual period, such as the stock market crash Stephen Hlibok discusses on p. 33.

2.14   Revising a Memo

Revise the following memo to improve you-attitude and positive emphasis.

Subject: Status of Building Renovations

We are happy to announce that the renovation of the lobby is not behind schedule. By Monday, October 9, we should be ready to open the west end of the lobby to limited traffic.

The final phase of the renovation will be placing a new marble floor in front of the elevators. This work will not be finished until the end of the month.

We will attempt to schedule most of the work during the evenings so that normal business is not disrupted.

Please exercise caution when moving through the construction area. The floor will be uneven and steps will be at unusual heights. Watch your step to avoid accidental tripping or falling.

2.15   Revising a Form Letter

You've taken a part-time job at a store that sells fine jewelry. In orientation, the manager tells you that the store photographs jewelry it sells or appraises and mails the photo as a goodwill gesture after the transaction. However, when you see the form letter, you know that it doesn't build much goodwill—and you say so. The manager says, "Well, you're in college. Suppose you rewrite it."

Rewrite the letter. Use square brackets for material (like the customer's name) that would have to be inserted in the form letter to vary it for a specific customer. Add information that would help build goodwill.

Dear Customer:

We are most happy to enclose a photo of the jewelry that we recently sold you or appraised for you. We feel that this added service, which we are happy to extend to our fine customers, will be useful should you wish to insure your jewelry or need to identify it should you have the misfortune of suffering a loss.

We trust you will enjoy this additional service. We thank you for the confidence you have shown by coming to our store.

Sincerely,

Your Sales Associate

Adapting Your Message to Your Audience

Identifying Your Audiences

Ways to Analyze Your Audience

- Analyzing Individuals
- Analyzing the Organizational Culture and the Discourse Community
- Analyzing Members of Groups

Choosing Channels to Reach Your Audience

Using Audience Analysis to Adapt Your Message

1. What Will the Reader's Initial Reaction Be to the Message?
2. How Much Information Does the Reader Need?
3. What Obstacles Must You Overcome?
4. What Positive Aspects Can You Emphasize?
5. What Expectations Does the Reader Have about the Appropriate Language, Structure, and Form for Messages?
6. How Will the Reader Use the Document?

Reader Benefits

- Characteristics of Good Reader Benefits
- How to Identify and Develop Reader Benefits
- Why Reader Benefits Work

Writing or Speaking to Multiple Audiences with Different Needs

Summary of Key Points

Adapting Your Message to Your Audience

Cindy V. Casselman

*Executive Technical Assistant to the Senior Vice President
Xerox Research and Technology*

www.xerox.com

Cindy Casselman analyzed a variety of internal audiences to gain approval to create Xerox' Intranet. Xerox provides document solutions that enhance business productivity.

In 1995 it became clear to me that the Internet could be a valuable tool for employee communications at Xerox. Surveys told us that employees wanted timely, relevant, and honest communication. Although the term "Intranet" had not yet been coined, I presented my idea for its use to my manager, Joe Cahalan, Director of Corporate Communications at Xerox. He was intrigued but had several valid concerns about the technology (Was the Internet real and robust?), the cost (How could we design, build, and maintain this new unplanned venture?), and the extra work (Who would feed this beast?). I continued to learn and benchmark other internal Internet sites and soon put together a proposal, answering his questions.

❝Understanding your audiences is the first step to convincing them that your proposal will meet their needs and the needs of the organization.❞

As I analyzed audiences in other Xerox organizations, I realized that I could show them how the Intranet could meet their needs too—which meant that they might help fund this venture. I pointed out to our then-CIO, Pat Wallington, that an internal Web site could provide some of the payoff for our enormous investment in infrastructure, that it could be a place for Xerox people to share information and create a community. I knew that Pat would be motivated to create a knowledge base and a community, both of which could show that our investment was successful.

My efforts continued until we had completely funded the creation, development, and support of the entry point (what is now called the portal) of the Xerox Intranet.

I attribute the success of this effort to our ability to create a powerful vision of what an Intranet could mean and by connecting this vision to other people's organizational objectives. Understanding your audiences is the first step to convincing them that your proposal will meet their needs and the needs of the organization. Everyone wants to do the right thing if you show them how.

Multiple Audiences for an Industry Report*

A consulting company was hired to write a report on how potential changes would affect manufacturing, safety, and cost of a consumer product.

The primary audience was the federal government, which would set the regulations for the product. Within this audience were economists, engineers, and policymakers.

The group of manufacturers that hired the consulting firm was both the initial audience and a gatekeeper. If it didn't like the report, it wouldn't send it on to the federal government.

Secondary audiences included the general public, other manufacturers of the product, and competitors and potential clients of the consulting company.

Industry reviewers emerged as a watchdog audience. They read drafts of the report and commented on it. Although they had no direct power over this report, their goodwill was important for the consulting company's image—and its future contracts. Their comments were the ones that authors took most seriously as they revised their drafts.

*Based on Vincent J. Brown, "Facing Multiple Audiences in Engineering and R&D Writing: The Social Context of a Technical Report," *Journal of Technical Writing and Communication*, 24, no. 1 (1994): 67–75.

Knowing who you're talking to is fundamental to the success of any message. You need to identify your audiences, understand their motivations, and know how to reach them.

Identifying Your Audiences

The first step in analyzing your audience is to decide who your audience is. Organizational messages have multiple audiences:[1]

1. The **initial audience** is the first audience to get your message. Sometimes the initial audience tells you to write the message.

2. A **gatekeeper** has the power to stop your message instead of sending it on to other audiences. The gatekeeper therefore controls whether your message even gets to the primary audience. Sometimes the supervisor who assigns the message is also the gatekeeper; sometimes the gatekeeper is higher in the organization. In some cases, gatekeepers may exist outside the organization.

3. The **primary audience** will decide whether to accept your recommendations or will act on the basis of your message. You must reach the primary audience to fulfill your purposes in any message.

4. The **secondary audience** may be asked to comment on your message or to implement your ideas after they've been approved. Secondary audiences also include lawyers who may use your message—perhaps years later—as evidence of your organization's culture and practices.

5. A **watchdog audience,** though it does not have the power to stop the message and will not act directly on it, has political, social, or economic power. The watchdog pays close attention to the transaction between you and the primary audience and may base future actions on its evaluation of your message.

As the following examples show, one person can be part of two audiences. Frequently, a supervisor is both the initial audience and the gatekeeper. Sometimes the initial audience is also the primary audience who will act on the message.

Dawn is an assistant account executive in an ad agency. Her boss asks her to write a proposal for a marketing plan for a new product the agency's client is introducing. Her **primary audience** is the executive committee of the client company, who will decide whether to adopt the plan. The **secondary audience** includes the marketing staff of the client company, who will be asked for comments on the plan, as well as the artists, writers, and media buyers who will carry out details of the plan if it is adopted. Her boss, who must approve the plan before it is submitted to the client, is both the **initial audience** and the **gatekeeper.**

Joe works in the data processing unit of a bank. He must write a monthly progress report describing his work. This month, he has worked on implementing a centralized system for handling customers' checks. His boss is **both a primary and an initial audience.** His boss will write a performance appraisal evaluating his work, so Joe wants to present his own efforts positively. The boss may also include paragraphs from Joe's progress report in a memo to the president of the bank, who wants to know when the bugs in the system will be worked out. The president is thus also a **primary audience.** The **secondary audience** includes the bank's customer service representatives, who must answer customer questions and deal with complaints about the new system, and sales representatives from the computer company that sold the hardware to the bank, who want to be sure that bank personnel are able to use the equipment effectively.

Before you analyze your audience, analyze yourself—so that you can see what you and your audience share and where you differ. You can find a link to this list of Personality Tests on the WWW on the BAC Web site.

Ways to Analyze Your Audience

The most important tools in audience analysis are common sense and empathy. **Empathy** is the ability to put yourself in someone else's shoes, to feel with that person. Empathy requires that one not be self-centered. In all probability, the audience is *not* just like you. Use what you know about people and about organizations to predict likely responses.

Analyzing Individuals

When you write or speak to people in your own organization and in other organizations you work closely with, you may be able to analyze your audience as individuals. You may already know your audience. It will usually be easy to get additional information by talking to members of your audience, talking to people who know your audience, and observing your audience.

The **Myers-Briggs Type Indicator** uses four dimensions to identify ways that people differ.[2] One of these is well known: introvert-extravert. Introverts get their energy from within; extraverts are energized by interacting with other people. The other three dimensions in the Myers-Briggs scale are sensing-intuitive, thinking-feeling, and perceiving-judging. Sensing-intuitive measures the way someone gets information. Sensing types gather information through their senses. Intuitive types see relationships. Thinking-feeling measures the way someone makes decisions. Thinking types use objective logic to reach decisions. Feeling types make decisions that feel "right," without necessarily being able to define the path they took to make the decision. Judging-perception measures the degree of certainty someone needs. Judging types like closure. Perceptive types like possibilities. (See the BAC Web site for more information.)

My Boss Was an Introvert

I'm sure my former department chair was an introvert. How could I tell? The main clue was that he wrote out the introductory remarks he made at faculty meetings. Clearly, this man didn't like speaking spontaneously; even in this low-stress situation, he wanted to prepare his words.

The clincher was the way he responded to requests. I quickly learned that I should put even simple requests in writing—I was more likely to get what I wanted. If I asked for something orally, he had to say something immediately— and the easiest thing to say was *no*.

The poles on each of these scales represent a preference, just as we have a preference for using either our right or our left hand to write. If necessary, we can use the opposite style, but we have less practice in it and use it less easily.

You can find out your own personality type by taking the Myers-Briggs Type Indicator at your college's counseling center or student services office. Some businesses administer the Myers-Briggs Type Indicator to all employees. Even when you don't have official results, you can often make accurate guesses about someone's type by close observation.

As Figure 3.1 suggests, you'll be most persuasive if you play to your audience's strengths. Indeed, many of the general principles of business communication reflect the types most common among managers. Putting the main point up front satisfies the needs of judging types, and some 75% of US managers are judging. Giving logical reasons satisfies the needs of the nearly 80% of US managers who are thinking types.[3]

Analyzing the Organizational Culture and the Discourse Community

Be sensitive to the culture in which your audiences work and the discourse community of which they are a part. An **organization's culture** is its values, attitudes, and philosophies. An organization's culture is revealed verbally in the organization's myths, stories, and heroes and nonverbally in the allocation of space, money, and power. A **discourse community** is a group of people who share assumptions about what channels, formats, and styles to use for communication, what topics to discuss and how to discuss them, and what constitutes evidence.

See the BAC Web site for sample analyses of specific companies.

In an organization that values equality and individualism, you can write directly to the CEO and address him or her as a colleague. In other

| **Figure 3.1** | *Using Myers-Briggs Types in Persuasive Messages* |

If your audience is	Use this strategy	Because
An introvert	Write a memo and let the reader think about your proposal before responding.	Introverts prefer to think before they speak. Written documents give them the time they need to think through a proposal carefully.
An extravert	Try out your idea orally, in an informal setting.	Extraverts like to think on their feet. They are energized by people; they'd rather talk than write.
A sensing type	Present your reasoning step-by-step. Get all your facts exactly right.	Sensing types usually reach conclusions step-by-step. They want to know why something is important, but they trust their own experience more than someone else's say-so. They're good at facts and expect others to be, too.
An intuitive type	Present the big picture first. Stress the innovative, creative aspects of your proposal.	Intuitive types like solving problems and being creative. They can be impatient with details.
A thinking type	Use logic, not emotion, to persuade. Show that your proposal is fair, even if some people may be hurt by it.	Thinking types make decisions based on logic and abstract principles. They are often uncomfortable with emotion.
A feeling type	Show that your proposal meets the emotional needs of people as well as the dollars-and-cents needs of the organization.	Feeling types are very aware of other people and their feelings. They are sympathetic and like harmony.
A perceiving type	Show that you've considered all the alternatives. Ask for a decision by a specific date.	Perceiving types want to be sure they've considered all the options. They may postpone coming to closure.
A judging type	Present your request quickly.	Judging types are comfortable making quick decisions. They like to come to closure so they can move on to something else.

Source: Based on Isabel Briggs Myers, "Effects of Each Preference in Work Situations," *Introduction to Type* (Palo Alto, CA: Consulting Psychologists Press, 1962, 1980).

companies, you'd be expected to follow a chain of command. Even if you know the name of the real decision maker, you'd be expected to send your message through your boss—and to be deferential to your superiors. Some organizations prize short messages; some expect long, thorough documents. Some cultures expect people to float trial balloons; others prefer that people work out all the details before they propose a change. Messages that are consistent with the organization's culture have a greater chance of succeeding.

Every organization—businesses, government agencies, nonprofit organizations, even colleges—has a culture. An organization's culture is constructed by the people who found the organization and change it.

You can begin to analyze an organization's culture by asking the following questions:

- Is the organization tall or flat? Are there lots of levels between the CEO and the lowest worker, or only a few?
- How do people get ahead? Are the organization's rewards based on seniority, education, being well-liked, making technical discoveries, or serving customers? Are rewards available only to a few top people, or is everyone expected to succeed?
- Does the organization value diversity or homogeneity? Does it value independence and creativity or being a team player and following orders? What stories do people tell? Who are the organization's heroes and villains?
- How important are friendship and sociability? To what extent do workers agree on goals, and how intently do they pursue them?
- How formal are behavior, language, and dress?
- What are the organization's goals? Making money? Serving customers and clients? Advancing knowledge? Contributing to the community?

Two companies in the same field may have very different cultures. In the mid-1980s, researcher Jennifer Chatman found that employees of Touche Ross (now Deloitte & Touche) rated informality as the firm's number one value. At Arthur Andersen, informality was the last of 54 values. More recently, Chatman found that new hires who "fit" the company's culture were more likely to stay with the job, more productive, and more satisfied than those who did not fit the culture.[4]

Organizations, like nations, can have subcultures. For example, manufacturing and marketing may represent different subcultures in the same organization: they may dress differently and have different values.

To analyze an organization's discourse community, ask the following questions:

- What channels, formats, and styles are preferred for communication?
- What do people talk about? What topics are not discussed?
- What kind of and how much evidence is needed to be convincing?

A discourse community may be limited to a few people in an organization. However, some discourse communities span an entire organization or even everyone in the same field in the nation or the world. You will be a member of several overlapping discourse communities. Succeeding in a job—whether it's flipping burgers or balancing books, managing a Fortune 500 company or running a hospital—requires becoming part of a discourse community. In your college courses, you learn what questions to ask about accounting systems or marketing plans; you learn what kinds of evidence you should use to prove that a landscape plan should include perennials or that a company should sell its products in Europe.

Culture Clash*

Kathy Wheeler learned [about corporate culture] the hard way . . . when she left Hewlett-Packard for Apple Computer. . . . Wheeler had felt comfortable with . . . HP culture: collaboration, consensus seeking, rock-solid engineering ability. Those were the qualities HP prized, and Wheeler had them big. At Apple, she says, everything was different. Suddenly she encountered a culture that exalted heroes and admired slick user interfaces. Those who got ahead were not for the most part the most skilled engineers but rather the "evangelists"—brash marketers of Apple products to the outside world. Before long, Wheeler says, she was deeply unhappy. "When you're used to being valued for one set of accomplishments," she says, "and what's actually being valued are accomplishments you either don't feel comfortable with or just aren't able to deliver on, the discomfort is pretty profound." Fourteen months after arriving at Apple, Wheeler returned to HP, notwithstanding Apple's efforts to keep her. "I admire Apple to a large extent," she says. "But I wouldn't work there again because of the cultural issues."

*Quoted from Matt Siegel, "The Perils of Culture Conflict," *Fortune*, November 9, 1998, 257–58.

Micromarketing at Target*

The Target store on Phoenix's eastern edge sells prayer candles, but no child-toting bicycle trailers. The Target store 15 minutes away in Scottsdale, Ariz., sells the trailers but no portable heaters; those can be found 20 minutes south in Mesa. . . .

Target is a master at what retailers call "micromarketing"—a consumer-driven technology-packed strategy to tailor merchandise at each store to the preferences of its patrons. . . .

The watershed event came from Target's success at selling team-logo athletic apparel in the same markets where their fans lived. That business grew from almost nothing in 1991 to $100 million [in 1994]. . . .

The industry adage that "retail is detail" is ever more true in micromarketing. In practice, attending to details for Target means carrying local favorite Jays potato chips in Chicago but stocking Saguaro brand chips in Phoenix. It also means sending more one-piece bathing suits to its stores on Florida's western coast, where the crowd is older, while packing off extra bikinis to the younger patrons of that state's eastern stores.

*Quoted from Gregory A. Patterson, "Different Strokes: Target 'Micromarkets' Its Way to Success; No 2 Stores Are Alike," *The Wall Street Journal*, May 31, 1995, A1, A9.

Different organizations may represent different cultures and different discourse communities, even when they hire people from the same disciplines. Lawyers in one state agency may see the documents they write as dry, factual, and unimportant, with the real emphasis on oral arguments in negotiations or trials. Lawyers at another agency may see themselves writing multipurposed, compelling documents designed not only to carry the weight of litigation but also to enhance the organization's image in the eyes of its various publics.[5] FedEx sales representatives court large customers with frequent phone calls; UPS workers send a bid and let that speak for itself—an approach consistent with UPS's culture of humility and modesty.[6]

Analyzing Members of Groups

In many organizational situations, you'll analyze your audience not as individuals but as members of a group: "taxpayers who must be notified that they owe more income tax," "customers living in the northeast side of the city," or "employees with small children." Focus on what group members have in common. Although generalizations won't be true for all members of the group, generalization is necessary when you must appeal to a large group of people with one message. In some cases, no research is necessary: it's easy to guess the attitudes of people who must be told they owe more taxes. In other cases, databases may yield useful information. In still other cases, you may want to do original research.

If you know where your audience lives, databases enable you to map demographic and psychographic profiles of customers or employees. **Demographic** characteristics are measurable features that can be counted objectively: age, sex, race, religion, education level, income, and so on.

The BAC Web site has links that profile the demographics in your zip code. Sometimes demographic information is irrelevant; sometimes it's important. Does education matter? Well, the fact that the reader has a degree from Eastern State rather than from Harvard probably doesn't matter, but how much the reader knows about accounting may. Does age matter? Sometimes. "Generational marketing" is helping manufacturers design and market products. Ford divides consumers into six generations. Then it develops vehicles to meet the profile of each group.[7] But other marketers are finding that considering age alone is inadequate to sell to the "mature market."[8]

Psychographic characteristics are qualitative rather than quantitative: values, beliefs, goals, and lifestyles. Many marketers use the Values and Life Styles (VALS) profiles developed by the SRI research firm in California. VALS profiles divide US buyers into nine categories, including Believers, the conservative middle class who "have benefited by the rules of the game"; Strivers, conspicuous consumers who don't have lots of money but who want to be in style; Fulfilleds, ambitious, hardworking, comfort-loving people who "control nearly 50% of the buying power" in the United States; and Actualizers, highly educated people who are interested in conservation, the environment, and inner growth.[9] To see where you fit, follow the VALS link from the BAC Web site. Knowing what your audience finds important allows you to organize information in a way that seems natural to your audience and to choose appeals that the audience will find persuasive. For example, Cindy Casselman knew that Xerox had spent an enormous amount of money on infrastructure. So she pointed out that an Intranet would use that infrastructure. She also knew that presenting the Intranet as a way to build a community would appeal to the then-CIO, who was interested in benefits that went beyond dollars and cents.

Market research firm Claritas, Inc., combines demographic and psychographic data to identify the zip codes that are most likely to have one of 62 lifestyle clusters including "Furs and Station Wagons" (wealthy suburbanites with teenagers), "Blue Chip Blues" (upscale blue-collar families), "New Melting Pot" (recent middle-class immigrants and singles), or "Shotguns and Pickups" (rural blue-collar workers and families). Both the catchy names and the drawings are designed by Claritas.

Often it's useful for a company to identify customer segments. Taco Bell identified two groups of high-potential customers: *penny pinchers*, who visit Taco Bell frequently but don't spend much on a visit, and *speed freaks*, who are more interested in convenience than price. To attract these consumers, Taco Bell lowered prices on its core menu items and reengineered its production, cutting wait time by 71%. These changes tripled sales and—even with lower prices—raised profits $20 million.[10]

A Young Manager Adapts to Older Audiences*

When James Ferguson became a manager at the age of 21, he realized he would trigger "conflict right, left and center" if he came on as a young hotshot. . . .

[H]e was . . . supervising a staff of 12, all of them older. He drew on tactics he had learned as head of his college newspaper, where he had to enlist and motivate a staff of volunteers. . . . [I]nstead of trying to assert control, he talked with each of [his subordinates], asking "what are the good and bad things about your job, and what do you want to change[?]" . . .

He incorporated their suggestions into his own plan, which he then sold to upper management. "But my staff owned the plan; they'd been part of the decision-making process," he says. With all employees, but particularly with older ones who are more apt to challenge a younger boss's judgment, "you've got to be a good listener and enroll their thoughts. They're not going to like everything you decide, but at least they'll know you listened."

*Quoted from Carol Hymowitz, "Young Managers Learn How to Bridge the Gap with Older Employees," *The Wall Street Journal*, July 21, 1998, B1.

Choosing Channels to Reach Your Audience

Communication channels vary in speed, accuracy of transmission, cost, number of messages carried, number of people reached, efficiency, and ability to promote goodwill. Depending on the audience, your purposes, and the situation, one channel may be better than another.

A written message makes it easier to

- Present extensive or complex financial data.
- Present many specific details of a law, policy, or procedure.
- Minimize undesirable emotions.

Messages on paper are more formal than e-mail messages. E-mail messages are appropriate for routine interchanges with people you already know. Paper is better for someone to whom you're writing for the first time.

Oral messages make it easier to

- Use emotion to help persuade the audience.
- Focus the audience's attention on specific points.
- Answer questions, resolve conflicts, and build consensus.
- Modify a proposal that may not be acceptable in its original form.
- Get immediate action or response.

Scheduled meetings and oral presentations are more formal than phone calls or stopping someone in the hall.

Important messages should use more formal channels, whether they're oral or written. Oral and written messages have many similarities. In both, you should

- Adapt the message to the specific audience.
- Show the audience how they would benefit from the idea, policy, service, or product.
- Overcome any objections the audience may have.
- Use you-attitude and positive emphasis.
- Use visuals to clarify or emphasize material.
- Specify exactly what the audience should do.

Sometimes your channel choice is determined by the audience. Some organizations still post announcements and job openings on bulletin boards because the mail staff, cleaning people, and some clerical workers don't have computers and so can't check e-mail. Even people who have access to the same channels may prefer different ones. When a university updated its employee benefits manual, the computer scientists and librarians wanted the information online. Faculty wanted to be able to read the information on paper. Maintenance workers and carpenters wanted to get answers on voice mail.[11]

The bigger your audience, the more complicated channel choice becomes, since few channels reach everyone in your target audience. When possible, use multiple channels. For example, print ads and customer service materials should contain not only 800 numbers but also street or e-mail addresses so that people who don't like to make phone calls or who have hearing impairments can contact the company.

Using Audience Analysis to Adapt Your Message

If you know your audience well and if you use words well, much of your audience analysis and adaptation will be unconscious. If you don't know your audience or if the message is very important, take the time to analyze your audience formally and to revise your draft with your analysis in mind.

As you answer these questions for a specific reader, think about the organizational culture in which your reader works. At every point, your reader's reaction is affected not only by his or her personal feelings and preferences but also by the political environment of the organization, the economy, and current events.

1. What Will the Reader's Initial Reaction Be to the Message?

a. Will the reader see this message as highly important?

Readers will read and act on messages they see as important to their own careers; they may ignore messages that seem unimportant to them.

When the reader may see your message as unimportant, you need to

- In a subject line or first paragraph, show your reader that this message is important and relevant.
- Make the action as easy as possible.
- Suggest a realistic deadline for action.
- Keep the message as short as possible.

b. How will the fact that the message is from you affect the reader's reaction to the words you use?

The reader's experience with you, your organization, and the subject you're writing about shapes the way the reader responds to this new message. Someone who thinks well of you and your organization will be prepared to receive your message favorably; someone who thinks poorly of you and the organization will be quick to find fault with what you say and the way you say it.

When you must write to a reader who has negative feelings about your organization, your position, or you personally, you need to

- Make a special effort to avoid phrases that could seem condescending, arrogant, rude, hostile, or uncaring.
- Use positive emphasis (p. 37) to counteract the natural tendency to sound defensive.
- Develop logic and reader benefits fully.

2. How Much Information Does the Reader Need?

a. How much does the reader already know about this subject?

It's easy to overestimate the knowledge an audience has. People outside your own immediate unit may not really know what it is you do. Even people who once worked in your unit may have forgotten specific details now that their daily work is in management. People outside your organization won't know how *your* organization does things.

When some of your information is new to the reader, you need to

- Make a special effort to be clear. Define terms, explain concepts, use examples.
- Link new information to old information that the reader already knows.
- Use paragraphs and headings to break up new information into related chunks, so that the information is easier to digest.
- Test a draft of your document with your reader or a subset of your intended audience to see whether the audience can understand and use what you've written.

How to Find Rich People*

Lots of marketers would like to sell products and services to rich people. But how do you find them?

Tom Stanley looks for business-to-business ads in trade journals. Full-page ads indicate solid companies owned by people who buy cars, insurance, and financial services. Best of all, because the ad is designed to sell, it will have the company's name, address, and phone number.

Rock and Dirt, for example, lists new and used earth-moving and mining equipment. Stanley pointed out a full-page ad selling reconditioned diesel engines. If a sales representative drives to the company, Stanley says, "You will probably visit a plant, and you will probably meet a man who does not wear a suit. He may look like someone that does not have money, but it is likely that this prospect will turn out to be a great client."

*Based on Thomas J. Stanley, *Selling to the Affluent* (Homewood, IL: Business One Irwin, 1991), 55–59.

The Audiences for a CPA Audit Report*

An audit report may be used by at least five different audiences:

The client, who may resent any report that isn't fully favorable.

Bankers, investors, and creditors, who make decisions based on audit reports and who may hold the CPA financially responsible for the report with a "third-party" lawsuit.

Colleagues, who use the reports, but who may have different ethical or theoretical positions.

Attorneys, who will use the reports as evidence for or against the CPA if a suit is filed.

The AICPA (American Institute of Certified Public Accountants), which sets the standards for accounting reports.

Good audit reports meet the needs and overcome the possible objections of all of these audiences.

*Based on Aletha S. Hendrickson, "How to Appear Reliable without Being Liable: C.P.A. Writing in Its Rhetorical Context," *Worlds of Writing: Teaching and Learning in Different Discourse Communities,* ed. Carolyn Matalene (New York: Random House, 1989), 323.

b. Is the reader's knowledge based on reading? Personal experience?

Things we have learned directly, through personal observation and experience, always seem more real and more true than things we've learned indirectly or from books. Other people may see our experience as an exception, an aberration, or a fluke; we see it as the best guide of what to expect in the future.

If you're trying to change a reader's understanding of a policy or organization, you need to

- Acknowledge the reader's initial understanding early in the message.
- Use examples as well as theory or statistics to show the difference between short-term and long-term effects, or to show that the reader's experience is not universal.
- Allow the reader to save face by suggesting that changed circumstances call for new attitudes or action.

c. What aspects of the subject does the reader need to be aware of to appreciate your points?

When the reader must think of background or old information to appreciate your points, you can

- Preface information with "As you know" or "As you may remember" to avoid suggesting that you think the reader does not know what you're saying.
- Put old or obvious information in a subordinate clause.
- If the background information or reminder is long, put it in a separate section with an appropriate heading or in an attachment to your letter or memo.

3. What Obstacles Must You Overcome?

a. Is your reader opposed to what you have to say?

Readers who have already made up their minds are highly resistant to change. When you must write to readers who oppose what you have to say, you need to

- Start your message with any areas of agreement or common ground that you share with your reader.
- Make a special effort to be clear and unambiguous. Points that might be clear to a neutral reader can be misread by someone with a chip on his or her shoulder.
- Make a special effort to avoid statements that will anger the reader.
- Limit your statement or request to the smallest possible area. If parts of your message could be delivered later, postpone them.
- Show that your solution is the best solution currently available, even though it isn't perfect.

b. Will it be easy for the reader to do as you ask?

Everyone has a set of ideas and habits and a mental self-image. If we're asked to do something that violates any of those, we first have to be persuaded to change our attitudes or habits or self-image—a change we're reluctant to make.

When your request is time-consuming, complicated, or physically or psychologically difficult, you need to

Before their redesign, Olathe Lanes East and West looked alike. But East's customers bowl to relax while West's customers bowl to compete. Now a food court with soothing curves is the center of the East facility, with bowling lanes attached. At West, lanes still dominate, decorated with energetic triangles.

- Make the action as easy as possible. Provide a form that can be filled out quickly; provide a stamped, self-addressed envelope if you are writing to someone in another organization.
- Break down actions into a list, so the reader can check off each step as it is completed.
- Show that what you ask is consistent with some aspect of what the reader believes.
- Show how the reader (not just you or your organization) will benefit when the action is completed.

4. What Positive Aspects Can You Emphasize?

a. From the reader's point of view, what are the benefits of what you have to say?

Benefits help persuade the reader that your ideas are good ones. Make the most of the good points inherent in the message you want to convey.

- Put good news in the first paragraph.
- Use reader benefits that go beyond the basic good news of the first paragraph.

b. What experiences, interests, goals, and values do you share with the reader?

A sense of solidarity with someone can be an even more powerful reason to agree than the content of the message itself. Always use all the ethical strategies that are available to win support for your ideas.

When the message will be read by only one reader, or by readers who all share the same experiences, interests, goals, and values, you can

- Consider using a vivid anecdote to remind the reader of what you share. The details of the anecdote should be interesting or new; otherwise, you may seem to be lecturing the reader.
- Make a special effort to make your writing style friendly and informal.
- Use a salutation and close that remind readers of their membership in this formal or informal group.

5. What Expectations Does the Reader Have about the Appropriate Language, Structure, and Form for Messages?

a. What style of writing does the reader prefer?

Good writers adapt their style to suit the reader's preferences. A reader who sees contractions as too informal needs a different style from one who sees traditional business writing as too stuffy. As you write,

- Use what you know about your reader to choose a more or less distant, more or less friendly style.
- Use the reader's first name in the salutation only if you use that name when you talk to him or her in person or on the phone.

b. Are there hot buttons or "red flag" words that may create an immediate negative response?

You don't have time to convince the reader that a term is broader or more neutral than his or her understanding. When you need agreement or approval, you should

- Avoid terms that carry emotional charges for many readers: for example, *criminal, un-American, feminist, fundamentalist, liberal.*
- Use your previous experience with an individual reader to replace any terms that have particular meanings for him or her.

c. How much detail does the reader want?

A message that does not give the reader the amount of or kind of detail he or she wants may fail. When you know your readers, ask them how much detail they want. When you write to readers you do not know well, you can

- Provide all the detail the reader needs to understand and act on your message.
- Group chunks of information under headings so that the reader can go directly to the parts of the message that he or she finds most interesting and relevant.
- Imitate the level of detail in similar documents to the same audience. If they have succeeded, you're probably safe in using the same level of detail that they do.

d. Does the reader prefer a direct or indirect structure?

Individual personality or cultural background may lead a reader to prefer a particular kind of structure. You'll be more effective if you use the structure and organization your reader prefers.

e. Does the reader have expectations about formal elements such as length, visuals, or footnotes?

A document that meets the reader's expectations about length, number of visuals, and footnote format is more likely to succeed. If you can't meet those expectations, you need to

- Revise your document carefully. Be sure that a shorter-than-usual document covers the essential points; be sure that a longer-than-usual document is free from wordiness and repetition.

- Check with the reader to see whether the standards are flexible.
- Pretest the message on a subset of your audience to see if the format enhances or interferes with comprehension and action.

6. How Will the Reader Use the Document?

a. Under what physical conditions will the reader use the document?

Reading a document in a quiet office calls for no special care. But suppose the reader will be reading your message on the train commuting home, or on a ladder as he or she attempts to follow instructions. Then the physical preparation of the document can make it easier or harder to use.

When the reader will use your document outside an office,

- Use lots of white space.
- Make the document small enough to hold in one hand.
- Number items so the reader can find his or her place after an interruption.
- Consider using plastic to protect the document.

b. Will the reader use the document as a general reference? As a specific guide? As the basis for a lawsuit?

Understanding how your audience will use the document will enable you to choose the best pattern of organization and the best level of detail. A great deal of detail is needed in an Environmental Protection Agency inspection report that will be used to determine whether to bring suit against a company for violating pollution control regulations. A memo within a company urging the adoption of pollution control equipment would need less information. Different information would be needed for instructions by the manufacturer of the equipment explaining how to install and maintain it.

If the document will serve as a general reference,

- Use a subject line to aid in filing and retrieval. If the document is online, consider using several key words to make it easy to find the document in a database search program.
- Use headings within the document so that readers can skim it.
- Give the office as well as the person to contact so that the reader can get in touch with the appropriate person some time from now.
- Spell out details that may be obvious now but might be forgotten in six months or a year.

If the document will be a detailed guide or contain instructions,

- Check to be sure that all the steps are in chronological order.
- Number steps or provide check-off boxes so that readers can easily see which steps they've completed.
- Group steps into five to seven subprocesses if there are many individual steps.
- Put any warnings at the beginning of the document; then repeat them just before the specific step to which they apply.

If the document will be used as the basis for a lawsuit,

- Give specific observations with dates and exact measurements as well as any inferences you've drawn from those observations.
- Give a full report with all the information you have. The lawyer can then decide which parts of the information to use in preparing the case.

Rx for Profits*

Mr. Ost owns three of the smallest drugstores you ever saw, all located in the most bombed-out and burned-out section of [Philadelphia]. But he is doing $5 million of business a year, more than twice the average drugstore rate. . . .

[H]e noticed an assistant labeling a prescription by typewriter instead of by computer. She was translating it, she explained, because to many Spanish-speaking customers, English labels were gibberish. Afraid of confusing dosage, some wouldn't take their medicine.

With a few lines of programming code, Mr. Ost expanded a simple commitment to service into a powerful marketing weapon. He loaded some 1,000 common regimens in Spanish, any of which could be printed instead of the English equivalent with a single keystroke. Business took off. . . .

When an Asian influx hit, he leaped forward again, labeling in Vietnamese. Soon he was writing 400 prescriptions a day at his second location—half in English, 30% in Spanish and 20% in Vietnamese.

Quoted from Thomas Petzinger, Jr., "Druggist's Simple Rx: Speak the Language of Your Customers," *The Wall Street Journal*, June 16, 1995, B1.

Different Benefits for Different Audiences*

Fluoride toothpaste sells for its decay prevention benefits in Germany, Holland, and Denmark with the basic US marketing and advertising strategy; but in England, France, and Italy, the cosmetic claims for toothpaste are more important, and the US strategy does not work.

Volvo . . . has emphasized economy, durability, and safety in America; status and leisure in France; performance in Germany; and safety in Switzerland. Price is considered to be a critical variable to Mexican consumers, but quality is of more importance to Venezuelans.

Closing [a $100,000 life insurance sale to a Chinese-American, the sales rep] stressed that Met Life was a venerable 119 years old—a standard pitch to Chinese-Americans. . . . It probably worked better than Snoopy, the "Peanuts" character used in the insurer's mainstream ads. Says Ruben Lopez, Met Life's marketing director for special projects, "The Chinese aren't going to buy life insurance from a dog."

*Quoted from Robert F. Roth, *International Marketing Communications* (Chicago: Crain, 1982), 296–97; David A. Ricks, *Big Business Blunders* (Homewood, IL: Dow Jones–Irwin, 1983), 60; and "Tapping into a Blossoming Asian Market," *Newsweek,* September 7, 1987, 47.

c. Will the document be filed?

In contemporary organizations, everything of importance will be filed. When you know that your message will be filed,

- Use a specific subject line.
- Specify details that may be forgotten six months or a year from now.
- Check both the draft and the final typed copy for accuracy, completeness, and friendliness.

Reader Benefits

Use your analysis of your audience to create effective reader benefits. **Reader benefits** are benefits or advantages that the reader gets by using your services, buying your products, following your policies, or adopting your ideas. In informative messages, reader benefits give reasons to comply with the policies you announce and suggest that the policies are good ones. In persuasive messages, reader benefits give reasons to act and help overcome reader resistance.

Characteristics of Good Reader Benefits

Good reader benefits meet four criteria. Each of these criteria suggests a technique for writing good reader benefits.

1. Adapt reader benefits to the audience.

When you write to different audiences, you may need to stress different reader benefits. Suppose that you manufacture a product and want to persuade dealers to carry it. The features you may cite in ads directed toward customers—stylish colors, sleek lines, convenience, durability, good price—won't convince dealers. Shelf space is at a premium, and no dealer carries all the models of all the brands available for any given product. Why should the dealer stock your product? To be persuasive, talk about the features that are benefits from the dealer's point of view: turnover, profit margin, the national advertising campaign that will build customer awareness and interest, the special store displays you offer that will draw attention to the product.

See the BAC Web site for a link to a page giving lawyers' benefits for communicating clearly by using plain language.

The Wall Street Journal wanted subscribers to renew their subscriptions for two more years rather than just for one. The cost of the second year was 66% of the cost of the first year. The mailing admitted that renewing for two years would tie up the money but presented the cost of the second year as "a 34% tax-free return on your money." The benefit was highly appropriate for an audience concerned about returns on investments and aware of the risk that normally accompanies high returns. *Garbage* magazine urged subscribers to respond to the first renewal notice to save the paper that an additional mailing would take. This logic was appropriate for an audience concerned about the disposal of solid waste.

2. Stress internal as well as external motivators.

Internal motivators come automatically from using a product or doing something. **External motivators** are "added on." Someone in power decides to give them; they do not necessarily come from using the product or doing the action. Figure 3.2 gives examples of external and internal motivators for three activities.

F i g u r e 3.2   *External and Internal Motivators*

Activity	External motivator	Internal motivator
Making a sale	Getting a commission	Pleasure in convincing someone; pride in using your talents to think of a strategy and execute it
Turning in a suggestion to a company suggestion system	Getting a monetary reward when the suggestion is implemented	Solving a problem at work; making the work environment a little more pleasant
Writing a report that solves an organizational problem	Getting praise, a good performance appraisal, and maybe a raise	Pleasure in having an effect on an organization; pride in using your skills to solve problems; solving the problem itself

Internal motivators or benefits are better than external motivators for two reasons:

1. There just aren't enough external motivators for everything you want people to do. You can't give a prize to every customer every time he or she places an order or to every subordinate who does what he or she is supposed to do.
2. Research shows that external motivators may actually make people *less* satisfied with the products they buy or the procedures they follow.

In a groundbreaking study of professional employees, Frederick Herzberg found that the things people said they liked about their jobs were all internal motivators—pride in achievement, an enjoyment of the work itself, responsibility. External motivators—pay, company policy—were sometimes mentioned as things people disliked, but they were never cited as things that motivated or satisfied them. People who made a lot of money still did not mention salary as a good point about the job or the organization.[12] In 1996, 46% of people surveyed in a Harris poll said "success" meant family and/or children, not money.[13] In a 1998 survey of workers all over the United States, Aon Consulting found that the factor most likely to produce employee loyalty and a desire to be productive was management's recognition of employees' personal and family lives. Salary didn't make the top 10. Many family-friendly companies have discovered that a culture of care keeps turnover low. The higher salary that a competitor might pay just doesn't overcome the advantage of working at a supportive, flexible company that values its employees.[14]

Since money is not the only motivator, choose reader benefits that identify internal as well as external motivators for following policies and adopting ideas.

3. Prove reader benefits with clear logic and explain them in adequate detail.

A reader benefit is a claim or assertion that the reader will benefit if he or she does something. Convincing the reader, therefore, involves two steps: making sure that the benefit really will occur, and explaining it to the reader.

If the logic behind a claimed reader benefit is faulty or inaccurate, there's no way to make that particular reader benefit convincing. Revise the benefit to make it logical.

Faulty logic: Using a computer will enable you to write letters, memos, and reports much more quickly.

Analysis: If you've never used a computer, in the short run it will take you *longer* to create a document using a computer than it would to type it. Even after you know how to use a

Reader Benefits for the Tone-Deaf*

The warranty cards returned by new owners of Steinway pianos revealed startling information: 40% of the owners couldn't play the piano. Why, then, had they bought the world's best piano rather than a less expensive one? Probably for the prestige and investment value.

So the company created a direct mail campaign which positioned Steinway as "the sound investment." Copy compared the Steinway not to other pianos but to fine wine, gold, and a Mercedes-Benz. The mailing was "extremely successful."

*Based on Alan Rosenspan, "Which Direct Mail Piece Pulled Best?" *Direct Marketing,* May 1997, 35.

computer and its software, the real time savings comes when a document incorporates parts of previous documents or goes through several revisions. Creating a first draft from scratch will still take planning and careful composing; the time savings may or may not be significant.

Revised reader benefit:	Using a computer allows you to revise and edit a document more easily. It eliminates retyping as a separate step and reduces the time needed to proofread revisions. It allows you to move the text around on the page to create the best layout.

If the logic is sound, making that logic evident to the reader is a matter of providing enough evidence and showing how the evidence proves the claim that there will be a benefit. Always provide enough detail to be vivid and concrete. You'll need more detail in the following situations:

a. The reader may not have thought of the benefit before.

b. The benefit depends on the difference between the long run and the short run.

c. The reader will be hard to persuade, and you need detail to make the benefit vivid and emotionally convincing.

Does the following statement have enough detail?

You'll save money by using our shop-at-home service.

Readers always believe their own experiences. Readers who have never used a shop-at-home service may think, "If somebody else does my shopping for me, I'll have to pay that person. I'll save money by doing it myself." They aren't likely to think of savings from not having to pay for gas and parking, from having less car wear and tear, and from not losing the time it would take to travel to several different stores to get the selection you offer. Readers who already use shop-at-home services may believe you if they compare your items and services with another company's to see that your cost is lower. Even then, you could make saving money seem more forceful and more vivid by telling readers how much they could save and mentioning some of the ways they could use your service.

4. Phrase reader benefits in you-attitude.

If reader benefits aren't in you-attitude (p. 34), they'll sound selfish and won't be as effective as they could be. A Xerox letter selling copiers with strong you-attitude as well as reader benefits got a far bigger response than did an alternate version with reader benefits but no you-attitude.[15] It doesn't matter how you phrase reader benefits while you're brainstorming and developing them, but in your final draft, check to be sure that you've used you-attitude.

Lacks you-attitude:	We have the lowest prices in town.
You-attitude:	At Havlichek Cars, you get the best deal in town.

How to Identify and Develop Reader Benefits

Brainstorm lots of reader benefits—perhaps twice as many as you'll need for the final letter or memo. Then you can choose the ones that are most effective for that audience, or that you can develop most easily. The first benefit you think of may not be the best.

Sometimes reader benefits will be easy to think of and to explain. When they are harder to identify or to develop, use the following steps to identify and then develop good reader benefits.

1. Identify the feelings, fears, and needs that may motivate your reader.
2. Identify the objective features of your product or policy that could meet the needs you've identified.
3. Show how the reader can meet his or her needs with the features of the policy or product.

1. Identify the feelings, fears, and needs that may motivate your reader.

One of the best-known analyses of needs is Abraham H. Maslow's hierarchy of needs.[16] Physiological needs are the most basic, followed by needs for safety and security, for love and a sense of belonging, for esteem and recognition, and finally for self-actualization or self-fulfillment. All of us go back and forth between higher- and lower-level needs. Whenever lower-level needs make themselves felt, they usually take priority.

Maslow's model is a good starting place to identify the feelings, fears, and needs that may motivate your audience. Figure 3.3 shows organizational motivations for each of the levels in Maslow's hierarchy. Often a product or idea can meet needs on several levels. Focus on the ones that audience analysis suggests are most relevant for your audience, but remember that even the best analysis may not reveal all of a reader's needs. For example, a well-paid manager may be worried about security needs if her spouse has lost his job or if the couple is supporting kids in college or an elderly parent.

A Marketer Analyzes Her Audiences*

Analyzing audiences is exactly the same for marketing and writing: you have to identify who the audiences and decision makers are, what motivates them, and how to reach them.

We use both qualitative and quantitative research to learn about our target markets. For example, focus groups showed us that men are increasingly becoming decision makers for food purchases. We also learned that there are distinct differences between northern and southern consumers.

I use my knowledge about the audience to develop a marketing plan. The plan is discussed internally with Glory's national sales manager, sales representatives, and president. Then the plan is presented to Glory Foods' food brokers and retail buyers for their input. Each presentation is based on the audience. What will they want to know? What questions will they have? Does the plan need changes?

*Quoted from a statement by Theresa E. Potter, Director of Marketing, Glory Foods, to Kitty Locker, January 27, 1997.

Figure 3.3   *Organizational Motivations for Maslow's Hierarchy of Needs*

Self-actualization
- Using your talents and abilities.
- Finding solutions to problems.
- Serving humanity.
- Self-respect and pride.
- Being the best you can be.

Esteem, recognition
- Being publicly recognized for achievements.
- Being promoted or gaining authority.
- Having status symbols.
- Having a good personal reputation.
- Having a good corporate reputation.

Love, belonging
- Having friends, working with people you like.
- Cooperating with other people on a project.
- Conforming to a group's norms.
- Feeling needed.
- Being loyal or patriotic.
- Promoting the welfare of a group you identify with or care about.

Safety, security
- Earning enough to afford a comfortable standard of living.
- Having pleasant working conditions.
- Having good health insurance and pension plan.
- Understanding the reasons for actions by supervisors.
- Being treated fairly.
- Saving time and money.
- Conserving human and environmental resources.

Physical
- Earning enough to pay for basic food, clothing, shelter, and medical care.
- Having safe working conditions.

2. Identify the features of your product or policy that could meet the needs you've identified.

Sometimes just listing the reader's needs makes it obvious which feature meets a given need. Sometimes several features together meet the need. Try to think of all of them.

Suppose that you want to persuade people to come to the restaurant you manage. It's true that everybody needs to eat, but telling people they can satisfy their hunger needs won't persuade them to come to your restaurant rather than going somewhere else or eating at home. Depending on what features your restaurant offered, you could appeal to one or more of the following subgroups:

Subgroup	Features to Meet the Subgroup's Needs
People who work outside the home	A quick lunch; a relaxing place to take clients or colleagues
Parents with small children	High chairs, child-size portions, and things to keep the kids entertained while they wait for their order
People who eat out a lot	Variety both in food and in decor
People on tight budgets	Economical food; a place where they don't need to tip (cafeteria or fast-food)
People on special diets	Low-sodium and low-calorie dishes; vegetarian food; kosher food
People to whom eating out is part of an evening's entertainment	Music or a floor show; elegant surroundings; reservations so they can get to a show or event after dinner; late hours so they can come to dinner after a show or game

To develop your benefits, think about the details of each one. If your selling point is your relaxing atmosphere, think about the specific details that make the restaurant relaxing. If your strong point is elegant dining, think about all the details that contribute to that elegance. Sometimes you may think of features that do not meet any particular need but are still good benefits. In a sales letter for a restaurant, you might also want to mention the nonsmoking section, your free coatroom, the fact that you're close to a freeway or offer free parking or a drive-up window, and how fast your service is.

Whenever you're writing to customers or clients about features that are not unique to your organization, it's wise to present both benefits of the features themselves and benefits of dealing with your company. If you talk about the benefits of dining in a relaxed atmosphere but don't mention your own restaurant, people may go somewhere else!

3. Show how the reader can meet his or her needs with the features of the policy or product.

Features alone rarely motivate readers. Instead, link the feature to the readers' needs—and provide details to make the benefit vivid!

Weak: We have placemats with riddles.

Better: Answering all the riddles on Monical's special placemats will keep the kids happy till your pizza comes. If they don't have time to finish (and they may not, since your pizza will be ready so quickly), just take the riddles home—or answer them on your next visit.

Make your reader benefits specific.

Weak: You get quick service.

Better: If you only have an hour for lunch, try our Business Buffet. Within minutes, you can choose from a variety of main dishes, vegetables, and a make-your-own-sandwich-and-salad bar. You'll have a lunch that's as light or filling as you want, with time to enjoy it—and still be back to the office on time.

Why Reader Benefits Work

Reader benefits improve both the attitudes and the behavior of the people you work with and write to. They make people view you more positively; they make it easier for you to accomplish your goals.

Expectancy theory says most people try to do their best only when they believe they can succeed and when they want the rewards that success brings. Reader benefits tell or remind readers that they can do the job and that success will be rewarded.[17] Thus they help overcome two problems that reduce motivation: people may not think of all the possible benefits, and they may not understand the relationships among efforts, performance, and rewards.[18]

Writing or Speaking to Multiple Audiences with Different Needs

Many business and administrative messages go not to a single person but to a larger audience. When the members of your audience share the same interests and the same level of knowledge, you can use the principles outlined above for individual readers or for members of homogenous groups. But often different members of the audience have different needs.

Rachel Spilka has shown that talking to readers both inside and outside the organization helped corporate engineers adapt their documents successfully. Talking to readers and reviewers helped writers involve readers in the planning process, understand the social and political relationships among readers, and negotiate conflicts orally rather than depending solely on the document. These writers were then able to think about content as well as about organization and style, appeal to common grounds (such as reducing waste or increasing productivity) that several readers shared, and reduce the number of revisions needed before documents were approved.[19]

When it is not possible to meet everyone's needs, meet the needs of gatekeepers and decision makers first.

Content and choice of details

- Provide an overview or executive summary for readers who want just the main points.
- In the body of the document, provide enough detail for decision makers and for anyone else who could veto your proposal.
- If the decision makers don't need details that other audiences will want, provide those details in appendixes—statistical tabulations, earlier reports, and so forth.

Organizing the document

- Use headings and a table of contents so readers can turn to the portions that interest them.
- Organize your message based on the decision makers' attitudes toward it.

Level of formality

- Avoid personal pronouns. *You* ceases to have a specific meaning when several different audiences use a document.
- If both internal and external audiences will use a document, use a slightly more formal style than you would in an internal document.
- Use a more formal style when you write to international audiences.

Play to the Primary Audience*

When an architect gave the Worthington City Council its first official look recently at plans for developing 45 acres at the site of the United Methodist Children's Home on High Street, council President John Coleman didn't mince words on which audience the architect should be playing to.

As Rick Morse juggled the plans on an easel, Coleman suggested he move to the other side, because he was blocking the council's view.

"If I stand on the other side, the audience can't see," Morse said.

"They're not going to vote," Coleman said. "You can set your own priorities."

*Quoted from Carol Ann Lease, "Behind the Screens," *The Columbus Dispatch,* July 29, 1987, E1.

They Looked at the Audience and Saw Themselves*

Before a bank took a survey of its customers, employees were asked to describe the bank's typical customer.

The CEO answered: "About 60, upper-income, community leader." The middle managers said: "About 40, with grown children. On the way up; good, solid citizen." The tellers said: "Twenties or thirties, newly married, just starting out. Lots of energy and drive."

According to the survey, the typical customer was in the mid-30s, had been married a few years, earned $20,000 a year, had 1 1/2 cars and 2 children.

People looked at customers but saw only themselves.

*Based on Ray Considine and Murray Raphel, *The Great Brain Robbery* (Pasadena, CA: The Great Brain Robbery, 1981), 68–69.

Use of technical terms and theory

- In the body of the document, assume the degree of knowledge that decision makers will have.
- Put background information and theory under separate headings. Then readers can use the headings and the table of contents to read or skip these sections, as their knowledge dictates.
- If decision makers will have more knowledge than other audiences, provide a glossary of terms. Early in the document, let readers know that the glossary exists.

Summary of Key Points

- The **primary audience** will make a decision or act on the basis of your message. The **secondary audience** may be asked by the primary audience to comment on your message or to implement your ideas after they've been approved. The **initial audience** routes the message to other audiences and may assign the message. A **gatekeeper** controls whether the message gets to the primary audience. A **watchdog audience** has political, social, or economic power and may base future actions on its evaluation of your message.
- Common sense and empathy are crucial to good audience analysis.
- The following questions provide a framework for audience analysis:
  1. What will the reader's initial reaction be to the message?
  2. How much information does the reader need?
  3. What obstacles must you overcome?
  4. What positive aspects can you emphasize?
  5. What expectations does the reader have about the appropriate language, structure, and format for messages?
  6. How will the reader use the document?
- **Reader benefits** are benefits or advantages that the reader gets by using the writer's services, buying the writer's products, following the writer's policies, or adopting the writer's ideas. Reader benefits can exist for policies and ideas as well as for goods and services. Reader benefits tell readers that they can do the job and that success will be rewarded.
- Good reader benefits are adapted to the audience, based on **internal** rather than **external motivators,** supported by clear logic and explained in adequate detail, and phrased in you-attitude. External benefits simply aren't available to reward every desired behavior; further, they reduce the satisfaction in doing something for its own sake.
- To create reader benefits,
  1. Identify the feelings, fears, and needs that may motivate your reader.
  2. Identify the features of your product or policy that could meet the needs you've identified.
  3. Show how the reader can meet his or her needs with the features of the policy or product.
- When you write to multiple audiences, use the primary audience to determine level of detail, organization, level of formality, and use of technical terms and theory.

Exercises and Problems

Getting Started

3.1   Identifying Audiences

In each of the following situations, label the audiences as initial, gatekeeper, primary, secondary, or watchdog.

1. Russell is seeking venture capital so that he can expand his business of offering soccer camps to youngsters. He's met an investment banker whose clients regularly hear presentations from business people seeking capital. The investment banker decides who will get a slot on the program, based on a comprehensive audit of each company's records and business plan.
2. Maria has created a Web page for her travel agency. She hopes to sell tickets for both leisure and business travel.
3. Paul works for the mayor's office in a big city. As part of a citywide cost-cutting measure, a blue-ribbon panel has recommended requiring employees who work more than 40 hours in a week to take compensatory time off rather than being paid overtime. The only exceptions will be the police and fire departments. The mayor asks Paul to prepare a proposal for the city council, which will vote on whether to implement the change. Before they vote, council members will hear from (1) citizens, who will have an opportunity to read the proposal and communicate their opinions to the city council; (2) mayors' offices in other cities, who may be asked about their experiences; (3) union representatives, who may be concerned about the reduction in income that will occur if the proposal is implemented; (4) department heads, whose ability to schedule work might be limited if the proposal passes; and (5) the blue-ribbon panel and good-government lobbying groups. Council members come up for reelection in six months.

3.2   Choosing a Channel to Reach a Specific Audience

Suppose that your business, government agency, or nonprofit group had a product, service, or program targeted for each of the following audiences. What would be the best channel(s) to reach people in that group in your city? Would that channel reach all group members?

a. Renters.
b. African-American owners of small businesses.
c. People who use wheelchairs.
d. Teenagers who work part-time while attending school.
e. Competitive athletes.
f. Parents whose children play soccer.
g. Hispanics.
h. People willing to work part-time.
i. Financial planners.
j. Hunters.

3.3   Identifying and Developing Reader Benefits

Listed here are several things an organization might like its employees to do.

1. Use less paper.
2. Attend a brown-bag lunch to discuss ways to improve products or services.
3. Become more physically fit.
4. Volunteer for community organizations.
5. Ease a new hire's transition into the unit.

As Your Instructor Directs,

a. Identify the motives or needs that might be met by each of the activities.
b. Take each need or motive and develop it as a reader benefit in a full paragraph. Use additional paragraphs for the other needs met by the activity. Remember to use you-attitude!

3.4   Identifying Objections and Reader Benefits

Think of an organization you know something about, and answer the following questions for it.

1. Your organization is thinking of creating a training video. What objections might people have? What benefits could videos offer your organization? Who would be easiest to convince?

2. The advisory council of State College recommends that business faculty members have three-month internships with local organizations to learn material. What objections might people in your organization have to bringing in faculty interns? What benefits might your organization receive? Who would be easiest to convince?

3. Your organization is thinking of expanding or creating a Web site. What fears or objections might people have? What benefits might your organization receive? Who would be easiest to convince?

As Your Instructor Directs,

a. Share your answers orally with a small group of students.

b. Present your answers in an oral presentation to the class.

c. Write a paragraph developing the best reader benefit you identified. Remember to use you-attitude.

3.5   Identifying and Developing Reader Benefits for Different Audiences

Assume that you want to encourage people to do one of the activities listed below.

1. Becoming more physically fit.
   Audiences: College students on the job market.
   Workers whose jobs require heavy lifting.
   Sedentary workers.
   People diagnosed as having high blood pressure.
   Managers who travel frequently on business.
   Older workers.

2. Getting advice about interior decorating.
   Audiences: Young people with little money to spend.
   Parents with small children.
   People upgrading or adding to their furnishings.
   Older people moving from single-family homes into smaller apartments or condominiums.
   Builders furnishing model homes.

3. Getting advice on investment strategies.
   Audiences: New college graduates.
   People earning more than $100,000 annually.
   People responsible for investing funds for a church or synagogue.
   Parents with small children.
   People within 10 years of retirement.

4. Gardening.
   Audiences: People with small children.
   People in apartments.
   People concerned about reducing pesticides.
   People on tight budgets.
   Retirees.
   Teenagers.

5. Buying a laptop computer.
   Audiences: College students.
   Financial planners who visit clients at home.
   Sales representatives who travel constantly.
   People who make PowerPoint presentations.

6. Teaching adults to read.
   Audiences: Retired workers.
   Business people.
   Students who want to become teachers.
   High school and college students.
   People concerned about poverty.

7. Vacationing at a luxury hotel.
   Audiences: Stressed-out people who want to relax.
   Tourists who like to sightsee and absorb the local culture.
   Business people who want to stay in touch with the office even on vacation.
   Parents with small children.
   Weekend athletes who want to have fun.

As Your Instructor Directs,

a. Identify needs that you could meet for the audiences listed here. In addition to needs that several audiences share, identify at least one need that would be particularly important to each group.

b. Identify a product or service that could meet each need.

c. Write a paragraph or two of reader benefits for each product or service. Remember to use you-attitude.

3.6 Understanding Generations*

1. In which age group are people most likely to have moved in the last year?
   a. 20–24
   b. 30–44
   c. 45–64
   d. 65 or older

2. In which age group are people most likely to have moved out of state?
   a. 20–24
   b. 30–44
   c. 45–64
   d. 65 or older

3. Who is most likely to own a gun?
   a. 18–20
   b. 21–29
   c. 30–49
   d. 50 or older

4. Who is most likely to believe that unions are a good influence on the nation?
   a. 20–24
   b. 30–34
   c. 50–64
   d. 65 or older

5. Households headed by people of which age are most likely to include preschoolers?
   a. 20–24
   b. 25–34
   c. 35–39
   d. 40–44

6. Households headed by people of which age are most likely to include three or more children?
   a. 20–24
   b. 25–34
   c. 35–39
   d. 40–44

7. Who is most likely to feel that the influence of religion is declining?
   a. 18–29
   b. 30–49
   c. 50–64
   d. 65 or older

8. Who are the best customers for TVs, radios, and sound equipment?
   a. Under age 25
   b. 25–34
   c. 35–44
   d. 45–54

9. Among full-time, year-round workers, which men (part I) and which women (part II) have the highest median incomes?
   a. 25–34
   b. 35–44
   c. 45–54
   d. 55–64

10. In which age group are people most likely to have a bachelor's degree?
    a. 25–34
    b. 35–44
    c. 45–54
    d. 55–64

Once you know the answers (see the end of the problem section), what generalizations would you draw about different generations? How well do you understand generations other than your own? How could you learn more?

*Source: Susan Mitchell, "The Generations Quiz," *American Demographics*, February 1996, 52–53.

3.7 Announcing an Extension of Health Care Benefits

The Board of Directors of your organization voted at its last meeting to extend health coverage benefits now available to employees with spouses to employees with same-sex domestic partners. (See Problem 7.16.) As Vice President of Human Resources, you need to announce the policy. You want your memo to build support for the policy and for your organization as a good place to work.

Pick a specific organization that you know something about and answer the following questions for it.

1. Approximately how many employees does it have? What age groups are they in? How do their ages affect the kinds of concerns they'll have about health care?

2. How easy is it for the organization to recruit and retain qualified employees?

3. What is the organization's record on tolerance toward homosexuality? For example, is this simply one more progressive step in an organization that fosters diversity in many forms, or is this a turnaround for a company that has not in the past been sympathetic to people outside the mainstream?

4. How tolerant is the general environment in the city and state in which the organization is located?

5. What objections might people have to the program—even people who are not homophobic? How can you respond to those objections?

6. What advantages to the organization does this benefit provide?

3.8   Announcing a Wellness Program

Assume that your organization has decided to implement a wellness program that will give modest rebates to employees who adopt healthy practices. (See Problem 7.17.) As Director of Human Resources, you must explain the program and build support for it. Pick a specific organization that you know something about and answer the following questions about it.

1. What percent of employees currently (a) smoke? (b) drink heavily? (c) are overweight? (d) don't exercise? (e) have high blood pressure or (f) high cholesterol? (g) use seat belts? (h) get annual physicals?
2. Why don't people already follow healthy lifestyles?
3. Do company vending machines, cafeteria, and other facilities make it easy for employees to get low-fat snacks and meals?
4. How much exercise do people get on the job? What work-related injuries are most common?
5. What exactly do people do on the job? Will being healthier help them work more efficiently? Better deal with stress? Have more confidence in interacting with clients and customers?
6. How much do employees know about how much their health insurance costs the organization?
7. What aspects of health and fitness would employees like to know more about? What topics might seem boring or "old hat"?

3.9   Lining up a Consultant to Teach Short Courses in Time Management Skills for Telecommuters

A consultant whom you've hired to teach a short course in time management skills for telecommuters wants to know more about the people she will be working with. (See Problem 7.18.) Choose an organization you know something about and answer these questions about it.

1. Is telecommuting well established at this organization, fairly new, or just about to start?
2. How much experience in telecommuting will the participants have had? Will everyone in the session be at the same stage, or will there be a mixture?
3. What kinds of work are telecommuters likely to do? What time management challenges does this work create?
4. Does the time of year or the organization's competitive position create special challenges?

Communicating at Work

3.10   Analyzing Your Boss

What goals matter most to your boss? What pressures is he or she under? Does your boss want details or just the big picture? What are his or her pet peeves? Is punctuality more important than creativity and thoroughness, or vice versa? If you have a question, would your boss rather answer in person, by e-mail, or in a memo? Is he or she more approachable in the morning or the afternoon?

As Your Instructor Directs,

a. Share your answers orally with a small group of students.
b. Present your answers in an oral presentation to the class.
c. Present your answers in a memo to your instructor.
d. Share your answers with a small group of students and write a joint memo reporting the similarities and differences you found.

3.11   Analyzing Your Co-Workers

What do your co-workers do? What hassles and challenges do they face? To what extent do their lives outside work affect their responses to work situations? What do your co-workers value? What are their pet peeves? How committed are they to organizational goals? How satisfying do they find their jobs? Are the people you work with quite similar to each other, or do they differ from each other? How?

As Your Instructor Directs,

a. Share your answers orally with a small group of students.
b. Present your answers in an oral presentation to the class.
c. Present your answers in a memo to your instructor.
d. Share your answers with a small group of students and write a joint memo reporting the similarities and differences you found.

Memo Assignments

3.12 Analyzing an Organization's Culture

Interview several people about the culture of their organization. Possible organizations include

- Businesses, government agencies, and nonprofit organizations.
- Sports teams.
- Sororities, fraternities, and other social groups.
- Churches, synagogues, and temples.
- Departments in a community college, college, or university.

Questions to ask include those in this chapter and the following:

- Tell me about someone in this organization you admire. Why is he or she successful?

- Tell me about someone who failed in this organization. What did he or she do wrong?
- What ceremonies and rituals does this organization have? Why are they important?
- Why would someone join this group rather than a competitor?

As Your Instructor Directs,

a. Share your results orally with a small group of students.

b. Present your results orally to the class.

c. Present your results in a memo to your instructor.

d. Share your results with a small group of students and write a joint memo reporting the similarities and differences you found.

3.13 Analyzing a Discourse Community

Analyze the way a group you are part of uses language. Possible groups include

- Work teams.
- Sports teams.
- Sororities, fraternities, and other social groups.
- Churches, synagogues, and temples.
- Geographic or ethnic groups.
- Groups of friends.

Questions to ask include the following:

- What specialized terms might not be known to outsiders?
- What topics do members talk or write about? What topics are considered unimportant or improper?
- What channels do members use to convey messages?

- What forms of language do members use to build goodwill? to demonstrate competence or superiority?
- What strategies or kinds of proof are convincing to members?
- What formats, conventions, or rules do members expect messages to follow?

As Your Instructor Directs,

a. Share your results orally with a small group of students.

b. Present your results in an oral presentation to the class.

c. Present your results in a memo to your instructor.

d. Share your results with a small group of students and write a joint memo reporting the similarities and differences you found.

3.6   Answers to Understanding Generations*

1. Answer: a
   The young are the restless. Thirty-five percent of people aged 20 to 24 and 30 percent of those aged 25 to 29 moved between March 1992 and March 1993. Most don't move much farther than a stone's throw, however. Over 60 percent of movers aged 20 to 64 moved to another home in the same country. [*Census Bureau, 1994*]

2. Answer: d
   The young may be the biggest movers, but when the old get going, they are more likely to keep going until they have cleared the state line. While 26 percent of movers aged 65 or older moved to another state, only 17 percent of those aged 20 to 24 got that far. [*Census Bureau, 1994*]

3. Answer: a
   The youngest adults, aged 18 to 20, are the biggest gun-toters. Nearly half (48 percent) own a firearm, up from 34 percent in 1974. In that year, the most-armed group was aged 30 to 49. [*Bureau of Justice Statistics, 1994*]

4. Answer: a
   The generation least likely to belong to a union is the most likely to believe that they are good for the country. Only 6 percent of Xers (aged 16 to 24) are union members, but 70 percent of 18-to-24-year-olds believe unions are a good influence. Older workers are more likely to say that unions are good for them personally, but less likely to say they are good for the nation as a whole. Nearly one-fourth (23 percent) of 45-to-54-year-olds are union members, while 46 percent believe unions are a good influence. [*Bureau of Labor Statistics, 1995; and Times Mirror Center for the People & the Press, 1992*]

5. Answer: b
   The patter of little feet (children under age 6) is most likely to be heard in households headed by people aged 25 to 34. Forty-one percent of their homes include preschoolers. But if you don't care how old the kids are, check out households headed by people aged 35 to 44. Seven in ten include children of any age. [*Census Bureau, 1994*]

6. Answer: c
   They don't make families like they used to, at least when it comes to size. But some boomers are doing their part to keep up population growth. Almost one in four married-couple households headed by boomers aged 35 to 39 has three or more kids under aged 18 at home, as do 20 percent of those headed by 30-to-34-year-olds. [*Census Bureau, 1994*]

7. Answer: b
   Reading all that Nietzsche in college left a lot of baby boomers believing that God is at least in the infirmary. Eighty-three percent of people aged 30 to 49 believe the US is losing its religion. Least likely to agree are teens aged 18 and 19, only 59 percent of whom think the influence of religion is declining. [*The Gallup Poll Monthly, 1994*]

8. Answer: d
   Bet you thought it was young people, heh-heh, heh-heh. Well, Beavis, you're wrong. It takes big bucks to fork out big dough for electronics. Households headed by 45-to-54-year-olds spend 75 percent more than average on TVs, radios, and sound equipment. Everybody else, except for those aged 35 to 44, spends less than average. [*Bureau of Labor Statistics, 1993*]

9. Answer: Part I (c); part II (b)
   On average, people aged 45 to 54 have the highest incomes—but a lot of the people in this group don't work full time. Men aged 45 to 54 with full-time, year-round jobs earn the most of any group, with a 1994 average of $39,700. Among women with full-time jobs, 35-to-44-year-olds have the highest incomes, at $25,300. If you're after women with the biggest bucks, however, you might want to stick with this cohort as time goes on. The age at which women's incomes peak is likely to rise as more career-oriented women replace older women with fewer total years in the work force. [*Census Bureau, 1995*]

10. Answer: b
    Thanks in part to the draft-deferment provision for college students during the Vietnam War, 35-to-44-year-old boomers are most likely to have a college degree. Twenty-seven percent have at least a bachelor's degree, compared with one in four people aged 45 to 54. Younger folks aren't far behind, however. Many Xers aren't finished with their schooling, and they may yet catch up to their elders. All this education is a big reason why consumers are so darn finicky these days. [*Census Bureau, 1994*]

*Source: Quoted from Susan Mitchell, "The Generations Quiz," *American Demographics*, February 1996, 52–53.

4

Making Your Writing Easy to Read

Good Style in Business and Administrative Writing
- Good Report Style
- Good E-Mail Style

Half-Truths about Style
- Half-Truth 1: "Write as You Talk."
- Half-Truth 2: "Never Use *I*."
- Half-Truth 3: "Never Begin a Sentence with *And* or *But*."
- Half-Truth 4: "Never End a Sentence with a Preposition."
- Half-Truth 5: "Big Words Impress People."

Evaluating "Rules" about Writing

Building a Better Style

Ten Ways to Make Your Writing Easier to Read
- As You Choose Words
- As You Write and Revise Sentences
- As You Write and Revise Paragraphs

Readability Formulas and Good Style

Organizational Preferences for Style

Summary of Key Points

Making Your Writing Easy to Read

Dee Castner | *Senior Auditor, KPMG Peat Marwick LLP*

www.kpmg.com

Dee Castner prepares financial statements and audit opinions and documents audit findings for superiors in KPMG. KPMG Peat Marwick is the global leader of the service organizations that provide audit, tax, and consulting services to the international business community.

Good audit writing is
1. Tight.
2. Complete while remaining positive.
3. Easy to understand for all audiences.

" Tight writing is important since working papers and memos go to busy people. "

Tight writing is important since working papers and memos go to busy people. Wordy sentences waste time and paper. Parallel structure in bulleted or numbered lists, like the one above, is often used in working papers to show the different events that have affected an account. Transition words such as *however* and *but* allow the writer to explain multiple fluctuations during the year in a single sentence or paragraph, keeping related ideas together.

I try to be both complete and sensitive to the image my words convey to the client, especially in explaining transactions in complicated or unusual situations. For example, *minimizing taxes* represents a positive, well-managed image of an entity, while *avoiding taxes* sounds illegal. An auditor must be aware of the connotations of the words chosen to describe an event, as certain words may convey the wrong message to the reader.

Our audiences could include other KPMG professionals, employees of the client, or even members of the courts. Since each group has different levels of knowledge about accounting matters, documents should be easy to understand. In external documents, jargon would inhibit the reader's ability to understand. In internal workpapers, however, specialized terms such as PFAW (pass further audit work), P/Minor (pass minor), and PBC (prepared by client) are acceptable since they are commonly understood by auditors. An employee of the client or a member of the court would need to have such terms spelled out.

Good business and administrative writing should sound like a person talking to another person. Unfortunately, much of the writing produced in organizations today seems to have been written by faceless bureaucrats rather than by real people.

Using an easy-to-read style makes the reader respond more positively to your ideas. You can make your writing easier to read in two ways. First, you can make individual sentences and paragraphs easy to read, so that skimming the first paragraph or reading the whole document takes as little work as possible. Second, you can make the document look visually inviting and structure it with signposts to guide readers through the document. This chapter focuses on ways to make words, sentences, and paragraphs easier to read. Chapter 6 will discuss ways to make the document as a whole easier to read.

Good Style in Business and Administrative Writing

Good business and administrative writing is closer to conversation and less formal than the style of writing that has traditionally earned high marks in college essays and term papers. (See Figure 4.1.) However, many business professors also like term papers that are easy to read and use good visual impact.

Most people have several styles of talking, which they vary instinctively depending on the audience. Good writers have several styles, too. A memo to your boss complaining about the delays from a supplier will be informal, perhaps even chatty; a letter to the supplier demanding better service will be more formal.

Keep the following points in mind as you choose a level of formality for a specific document:

- Use a friendly, informal style to someone you've talked with.
- Avoid contractions, slang, and even minor grammatical lapses in paper documents to people you don't know. Abbreviations are OK in e-mail messages if they're part of the group's culture.
- Pay particular attention to your style when you have to write uncomfortable messages: when you write to people you fear or when you must give bad news. Reliance on nouns rather than on verbs and a general deadening of style increase when people are under stress or feel insecure.[1] Confident people are more direct. Edit your writing so that you sound confident, whether you feel that way or not.

Good business style allows for individual variation. Figures 4.2 and 4.3 show the opening paragraphs from the CEO letters in two different annual reports. Jack Welch's hard-hitting style in Figure 4.2 conveys an image of energy and drive. Warren Buffett's wry, self-deprecating style in Figure 4.3 suggests intelligence and total integrity.

Good Report Style

Reports tend to be more formal than letters and memos, since they may be read many years in the future by audiences the writer can barely imagine. In reports, avoid contractions, spell out acronyms and abbreviations the first time you use them, and avoid personal pronouns. Since so many people read reports, *you* doesn't have much meaning. See Chapter 15 for more about report style.

Good E-Mail Style

E-mail is the least formal of all business documents, since it is closest to speech. Nevertheless, readers know that they are reading, not hearing, the message and are likely to apply some of the same standards they use for letters and memos.

To create good e-mail messages, put the most important point in the subject line and the first sentence. Chapters 7, 8, and 9 give advice about subject lines for informative, negative, and persuasive e-mail messages. Keep the message short—to one screen in most cases.

Use these guidelines for e-mail messages:

- Contractions, abbreviations, and jargon are acceptable when you write to people you know well.
- Use regular capitalization. Full capitals look like SHOUTING; all lower-case letters seem childish.
- Write out anything important on your word-processor, reread, and then paste the message into your e-mail screen.
- Most readers will tolerate an occasional typo, but if your message is full of typos and other errors, you'll look unprofessional. If your e-mail system has a spell-checker, use it.
- Be considerate. Not all e-mail systems have the same capabilities. Check with your correspondent before sending attachments, special fonts, and images.
- Be professional. Assume that anything you write can end up in your personnel file. A message criticizing a third person can be forwarded to that person without your knowledge or permission. A message you erase can be retrieved.

 See the BAC Web site for more information on Netiquette.

E-Mail Acronyms

The following abbreviations often show up in e-mail messages:

BTW	By the way
FAQ	Frequently asked questions
IMHO	In my humble opinion
OTOH	On the other hand
TTYL	Talk to you later

Figure 4.1 *Different Levels of Style*

Feature	Conversational style	Good business style	Traditional term paper style
Formality	Highly informal	Conversational; sounds like a real person talking	More formal than conversation would be, but retains a human voice
Use of contractions	Many contractions	OK to use occasional contractions	Few contractions, if any
Pronouns	Uses *I*, first- and second-person pronouns	Uses *I*, first- and second-person pronouns	First- and second-person pronouns kept to a minimum
Level of friendliness	Friendly	Friendly	No effort to make style friendly
How personal	Personal; refers to specific circumstances of conversation	Personal; may refer to reader by name; refers to specific circumstances of readers	Impersonal; may generally refer to *readers* but does not name them or refer to their circumstances
Word choice	Short, simple words; slang	Short, simple words but avoids slang	Many abstract words; scholarly, technical terms
Sentence and paragraph length	Incomplete sentences; no paragraphs	Short sentences and paragraphs	Sentences and paragraphs usually long
Grammar	Can be ungrammatical	Uses standard edited English	Uses standard edited English
Visual impact	Not applicable	Attention to visual impact of document	No particular attention to visual impact

Figure 4.2

Jack Welch's Letter Uses the Standard Business Style

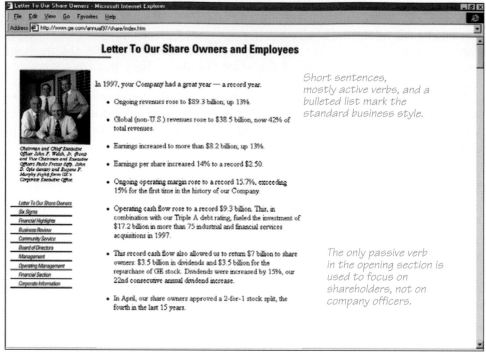

Short sentences, mostly active verbs, and a bulleted list mark the standard business style.

The only passive verb in the opening section is used to focus on shareholders, not on company officers.

[GE] Letter to Our Share Owners and Employees [1997] http://www.ge.com/annual97/share/index.htm

Figure 4.3   *Warren Buffett's Letter Uses a More Individual Style*

Paragraph 1 uses standard business style.

Paragraph 2 shifts to a more individual style.

Homey comparison

Font size here conveys understated humor.

Berkshire Hathaway Inc. 1997 Chairman's Letter. http://berkshirehathaway.com/letters/1997.html.

Half-Truths about Style

Many generalizations about style are half-truths and must be applied selectively, if at all.

Half-Truth 1: "Write as You Talk."

One of the best tests of style is to read what you've written out loud to someone sitting about three feet away. If a passage sounds stiff and overly formal when you read it out loud, revise it; almost certainly it will sound stiff and perhaps even rude to the reader. If you wouldn't say it, don't write it.

However, unless our speech is exceptionally fluent, "writing as we talk" can create awkward, repetitive, and badly organized prose. It's OK to write as you talk to produce your first draft, but edit to create a good written style.

Half-Truth 2: "Never Use *I.*"

Using *I* too often can make your writing sound self-centered; using it unnecessarily will make your ideas seem tentative. However, when you write about things you've done or said or seen, using *I* is both appropriate and smoother than resorting to awkward passives or phrases like *this writer.*

Half-Truth 3: "Never Begin a Sentence with *And* or *But.*"

Beginning a sentence with *and* or *also* makes the idea that follows seem like an afterthought. That's OK when you want the effect of spontaneous speech in a written document, as you may in a sales letter. If you want to sound as though you have thought about what you are saying, put the *also* in the middle of the sentence or use another transition: *moreover, furthermore.*

But tells the reader that you are shifting gears and that the point which follows not only contrasts with but also is more important than the preceding ideas. Presenting such verbal signposts to your reader is important. Beginning a sentence with *but* is fine if doing so makes your paragraph read smoothly.

Half-Truth 4: "Never End a Sentence with a Preposition."

Prepositions are those useful little words that indicate relationships: *with, in, under, at.* The prohibition against ending sentences with them is probably based on two facts: (1) The end of a sentence (like the beginning) is a position of emphasis. A preposition may not be worth emphasizing. (2) When the reader sees a preposition, he or she expects something to follow it. At the end of a sentence, nothing does.

In job application letters, reports, and important presentations, avoid ending sentences with prepositions. Most letters and memos are less formal; it's OK to end an occasional sentence with a preposition. Analyze your audience and the situation, and use the language that you think will get the best results.

Half-Truth 5: "Big Words Impress People."

Learning an academic discipline requires that you master its vocabulary. After you get out of school, however, no one will ask you to write just to prove that you understand something. Instead, you'll be asked to write or speak to people who need the information you have. Sometimes you may want the sense of

Simple Words Save Money and Build Goodwill*

Writing consultant Rosemary Camilleri has a client that administers health care benefits for thousands of companies nationwide. A standard letter explained to patients that part of their claim was "non-certified." People didn't understand, so they phoned or wrote to ask what the letter meant. The company employed nearly 50 nurses to answer the questions.

She helped employees rewrite the form letter.

The manager stopped her in the hall one day to tell her that they now have 25% fewer phone calls to field. People understand the letter and feel they are being treated fairly.

*Based on Rosemary Camilleri, "Re: Adding Value," posting to APCC-L@list-serv.acns.nwu.edu, December 3, 1997.

Words with the right connotations sell products. In focus groups, Iomega learned that computer users either hated or were bored by the idea of data storage. But they liked the idea of getting easier access to their "stuff." So Iomega created an ad campaign for the Zip drive using the friendly, colloquial word.

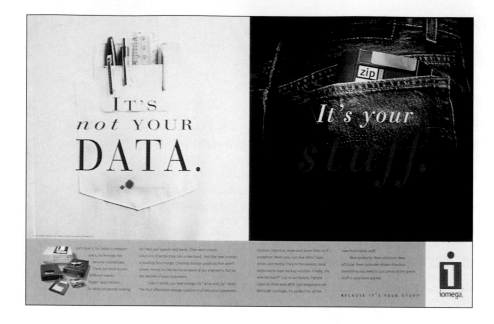

formality or technical expertise that big words create. But much of the time, big words just distance you from your audience and increase the risk of miscommunication. When people misuse big words, they look foolish. If you're going to use big words, make sure you use them correctly.

Evaluating "Rules" about Writing

Some "rules" are grammatical conventions. For example, standard edited English requires that each sentence have a subject and verb, and that the subject and verb agree. Business writing normally demands standard grammar, but exceptions exist. Promotional materials such as brochures, advertisements, and sales and fund-raising letters may use sentence fragments to gain the effect of speech.

Other "rules" may be conventions adopted by an organization so that its documents will be consistent. For example, a company might decide to capitalize job titles (e.g., *Production Manager*) even though grammar doesn't require the capitals, or always to use a comma before *and* in a series, even though a sentence can be grammatical without the comma. A different company might make different choices.

Still other "rules" are attempts to codify "what sounds good." "Never use *I*" and "use big words" are examples of this kind of "rule." To evaluate these "rules," you must consider your audience, the discourse community and organizational culture, (p. 62), your purposes, and the situation. If you want the effect produced by an impersonal style and polysyllabic words, use them. But use them only when you want the distancing they produce.

Building a Better Style

To improve your style,

- Get a clean page or screen, so that you aren't locked into old sentence structures.
- Try WIRMI: *What I Really Mean Is*.[2] Then write the words.

| **Figure 4.4** | *Mutual Fund Prospectuses Revised to Meet the SEC's Plain English Guidelines* |

	Old prospectus	**New prospectus**
John Hancock Sovereign Balanced Fund	The fund utilizes a strategy of investing in those common stocks which have a record of having increased their shareholder dividend in each of the preceding ten years or more.	The fund's stock investments are exclusively in companies that have increased their dividend payout in each of the last ten years.
State Street Research Equity Income Fund	The applicability of the general information and administrative procedures set forth below accordingly will vary depending on the investor and the record-keeping system established for a shareholder's investment in the Fund. Participants in 401(k) and other plans should first consult with appropriate persons at their employer or refer to the plan materials before following any of the procedures below.	If you are investing through a large retirement plan or other special program, follow the instructions in your program materials.
State Street Research Equity Income Fund	The net asset value of the fund's shares will fluctuate as market conditions change.	The fund's shares will rise and fall in value.

Source: Toddi Gutner, "At Last, the Readable Prospectus," *Business Week,* April 13, 1998, 100E10.

See the BAC Web site for the SEC's Guidelines for Plain English for Prospectuses.

Figure 4.5

Ten Ways to Make Your Writing Easier to Read

As you choose words,

1. Use words that are accurate, appropriate, and familiar.
2. Use technical jargon only when it is essential and known to the reader. Eliminate business jargon.

As you write and revise sentences,

3. Use active verbs most of the time.
4. Use strong verbs—not nouns—to carry the weight of your sentence.
5. Tighten your writing.
6. Vary sentence length and sentence structure.
7. Use parallel structure. Use the same grammatical form for ideas that have the same logical function.
8. Put your readers in your sentences.

As you write and revise paragraphs,

9. Begin most paragraphs with topic sentences so that readers know what to expect in the paragraph.
10. Use transitions to link ideas.

- Try reading your draft out loud to someone sitting about three feet away— about as far away as you'd sit in casual conversation. If the words sound stiff, they'll seem stiff to a reader, too.
- Ask someone else to read your draft out loud. Readers stumble because the words on the page aren't what they expect to see. The places where that person stumbles are places where your writing can be better.
- Read widely and write a *lot.*
- Study revised sentences, like those in Figure 4.4.
- Use the 10 techniques in Figure 4.5 to polish your style.

What's in a Name? (1)*

Effective brand names depend on both denotation and connotation.

At Sun Microsystems, Kim Polese called a brainstorming meeting to find a cooler name for Oak software, a product she believed would "wake up the Web." Oak became Java, now the standard for multimedia and animation on Web pages.

*Based on Bradley Johnson, "Java: Kim Polese," *Advertising Age*, June 24, 1996, s20.

Ten Ways to Make Your Writing Easier to Read

Direct, simple writing is easier to read. James Suchan and Robert Colucci tested two versions of a memo report. The "high-impact" version had the "bottom line" (the purpose of the report) in the first paragraph, simple sentences in normal word order, active verbs, concrete language, short paragraphs, headings and lists, and first- and second-person pronouns. The high-impact version took 22% less time to read. Readers said they understood the report better, and tests showed that they really did understand it better.[3] Another study showed that high-impact instructions were more likely to be followed.[4] We'll talk about layout, headings, and lists in Chapter 6.

As You Choose Words

The best word depends on context: the situation, your purposes, your audience, the words you have already used.

1. Use words that are accurate, appropriate, and familiar.

Accurate words mean what you want to say. Appropriate words convey the attitudes you want and fit well with the other words in your document. Familiar words are easy to read and understand.

Meaning arises in context. Many cities use "911" as an easy-to-dial number to get help in an emergency. Microsoft employees use "911" in subject lines of e-mail messages to signal that the message is urgent.[5]

Some meanings have already evolved before we join the conversation. We may learn the meaning of words, of actions, or of office layouts by being alert and observant. We learn some meanings by formal and informal study: the importance of "generally accepted accounting principles," the best strategies for increasing the size of donations in a fund-raising letter, or what the trashcan on a computer screen symbolizes. Some meanings are constrained by the social or work communities in which we move. Some meanings are negotiated as we interact one-on-one with another person, attempting to communicate.

Accurate denotations.   To be accurate, a word's denotation must match the meaning the writer wishes to convey. **Denotation** is a word's literal or dictionary meaning. Most common words in English have more than one denotation. The word *pound*, for example, means, or denotes, a unit of weight, a place where stray animals are kept, a unit of money in the British system, and the verb *to hit*. Coca-Cola spends an estimated $20 million a year to protect its brand names so that *Coke* will denote only that brand and not just any cola drink.

When two people use the same word to mean, or denote, different things, **bypassing** occurs. For example, negotiators for Amoco and for the Environmental Protection Agency (EPA) used *risk* differently. At Amoco, *risk* was an economic term dealing with efficiency; for the EPA, the term "was a four-letter word that meant political peril or health risk."[6] Progress was possible only when they agreed on a meaning.

Problems also arise when writers misuse words.

The western part of Ohio was transferred from Chicago to Cleveland.[7] (Ohio did not move. Instead, a company moved responsibility for sales in western Ohio.)

Three major associations of property-liability companies are poised to strike out in opposite directions.[8] (Three different directions can't be opposite each other.)

Earn a free lunch.[9] (A lunch one earns isn't free.)

Accurate denotations can make it easier to solve problems. In one production line with a high failure rate, the largest category of defects was *missed operations*. At first, the supervisor wondered if the people on the line were lazy or irresponsible. But some checking showed that several different problems were labeled *missed operations*: parts installed backwards, parts that had missing screws or fasteners, parts whose wires weren't connected. Each of these problems had a different solution. Using accurate words redefined the problem and enabled the production line both to improve quality and cut repair costs.[10]

Appropriate connotations.   Words are appropriate when their **connotations,** that is, their emotional associations or colorings, convey the attitude you want. A great many words carry connotations of approval or disapproval, disgust or delight. Words in the first column below suggest approval; words in the second column suggest criticism.

Positive word	Negative word
assume	guess
curious	nosy
negotiate	haggle
cautious	fearful
careful	nit-picking
firm	obstinate
flexible	wishy-washy

A supervisor can "tell the truth" about a subordinate's performance and yet write either a positive or a negative performance appraisal, based on the connotations of the words in the appraisal. Consider an employee who pays close attention to details. A positive appraisal might read, "Terry is a meticulous team member who takes care of details that others sometimes ignore." But the same behavior might be described negatively: "Terry is hung up on trivial details."

Advertisers carefully choose words with positive connotations. Expensive cars are never *used*; instead, they're *pre-owned, experienced,* or even *preloved.* An executive for Rolls-Royce once said, "A Rolls never, never breaks down. Of course," he added, with a twinkle in his eye, "there have been occasions when a car has failed to proceed."[11]

United Technologies found that its international divisions responded negatively to the term *business ethics* and assumed that the US headquarters thought they were unethical. United Technologies changed the term to business *practices,* a term that international workers accepted.[12]

Words may also connote status. Both *salesperson* and *sales representative* are nonsexist job titles. But the first sounds like a clerk in a store; the second suggests someone selling important items to corporate customers.

Although connotations rarely appear in a dictionary, they are not individual or idiosyncratic. The associations a word evokes will be consistent in any one culture but may differ among cultures. One scholar reports that while "the term discussion is connotatively neutral for North Americans, it possesses a negative connotation for Latin Americans, who view it as an attempt to change someone else's mind."[13] Even within a culture, connotations may change over time. The word *charity* had acquired such negative connotations by the 19th century that people began to use the term *welfare* instead. Now, *welfare* has acquired negative associations and we may be ready for another term.

What's in a Name? (2)*

Choosing product names is even more complicated when translation is involved.

When Coca-Cola was introduced in China in the 1920s, a group of Chinese characters were chosen that sounded like the English name. Unfortunately, those characters meant "bite the wax tadpole." Today, the characters used on Coke bottles in China denote "happiness in the mouth."

Mazda sells the Xedos 9 in Europe. Americans didn't like the name, so the company launched the car in the United States as the Millenia [sic].

*Based on David A. Ricks, *Blunders in International Business* (Cambridge, MA: Blackwell, 1993), 34–36; and Joel Achenbach, "Dance of Death Easy to Explain," *The Columbus Dispatch*, July 14, 1996, 3B.

The Ethics of Word Choice*

People can use accurate words to lie.

As a prize for visiting a condominium resort, a woman "won" an all-terrain vehicle. She had to pay $29.95 for "handling, processing, and insurance" to get it.

Then she saw her prize: a lawn chair with four wheels that converts into a wheeled cart.

The company claims it told the truth: "It is a vehicle. It's a four-wheel cart you can take anywhere—to the beach, to the pool. It may not be motorized, but [we] didn't say it was motorized."

The company may be guilty of deceptive trade practices: the courts will have to decide that. But whether or not the practice is illegal, it isn't ethical to use words that most people will misinterpret.

*Based on Carmella M. Padilla, "It's a . . . a . . . a . . . All-Terrain Vehicle, Yeah, That's It, That's the Ticket," *The Wall Street Journal,* July 17, 1987, 17.

Ethical implications of word choice. How positively can we present something and still be ethical? Certainly the words we use can shape response. A *defense budget* sounds essential; a *military budget* sounds less positive. A *nuclear accident* is scary; a *nuclear event* is neutral. We have the right to package our ideas attractively, but we have the responsibility to give the public or our superiors all the information they need to make decisions.

Familiar words. Use familiar words, words that are in almost everyone's vocabulary. Use the word that most exactly conveys your meaning, but whenever you can choose between two words that mean the same thing, use the shorter, more common one. Try to use specific, concrete words. They're easier to understand and remember.[14]

A series of long, learned, abstract terms makes writing less interesting, less forceful, and less memorable. Will big words make you sound more intelligent? Only if they're needed to communicate. Consider this memo, from the superintendent of schools of the Houston School District to "All Administrative Staff:"

> Subject: Sequential Page Numbering of Documents
>
> Please give immediate attention to insure that the pages of all documents prepared for distribution are numbered sequentially and in a place of optimum visibility. This is needed to facilitate our ability to refer to items during meetings.[15]

Impressive? No. Silly? Yes. When you have something simple to say, use simple words.

The following list gives a few examples of short, simple alternatives.

Formal and stuffy	Short and simple
ameliorate	improve
commence	begin
enumerate	list
finalize	finish, complete
prioritize	rank
utilize	use
viable option	choice

There are four exceptions to the general rule that "shorter is better."

1. Use a long word if it is the only word that expresses your meaning exactly.
2. Use a long word if it is more familiar than a short word. *Send out* is better than *emit* and *a word in another language for a geographic place or area* is better than *exonym* because more people know the first item in each pair.
3. Use a long word if its connotations are more appropriate. *Exfoliate* is better than *scrape off dead skin cells.*
4. Use a long word if the discourse community (➤ p. 62) prefers it.

2. Use technical jargon sparingly; eliminate business jargon.

There are two kinds of **jargon.** The first kind of jargon is the specialized terminology of a technical field. *LIFO* and *FIFO* are technical terms in accounting; *byte* and *baud* are computer jargon; *scale-free* and *pickled and oiled* designate specific characteristics of steel. A job application letter is the one occasion when it's desirable to use technical jargon: using the technical terminology of the reader's field helps suggest that you're a peer who also is competent in that field. In other kinds of messages, use technical jargon only when the term is essential and known to the reader.

If a technical term has a "plain English" equivalent, use the simpler term:

Jargon: Foot the average monthly budget column down to Total Variable Costs, Total Management Fixed Costs, Total Sunk Costs, and Grand Total.

Better: Add the figures in the average monthly budget column for each category to determine the Total Variable Costs, the Total Management Fixed Costs, and the Total Sunk Costs. Then add the totals for each category to arrive at the Grand Total.

The revision here is longer but better because it uses simple words. The original will be meaningless to a reader who does not know what *foot* means.

It is especially important to replace jargon with plain English when the specialized meaning of the technical term is not in fact being used. Consider this example:

Jargon: Additional parameters for price exception reporting were established for nonstock labor buy costs.

Better: We decided to include nonstock labor buys of over $_____ in the price exception report.

The word *parameters* means factors that are held constant while other variables change. It is a term that is essential in mathematics and statistics, but it is rarely used properly in general business and administrative writing. As the revision shows, the real meaning here was simple; no technical term was needed.

Terms that have technical meanings but are used in more general senses may be called **business slang.** Business slang includes *bottom line, GIGO, blindsiding,* and *downsize.* Used sparingly, these terms are appropriate in job application letters and in messages for people in your own organization, who are likely to share the vocabulary.

General slang includes words like *cool, diss,* and *going postal.* Slang is sometimes used in business conversations and presentations, but it is too casual for business and administrative writing.

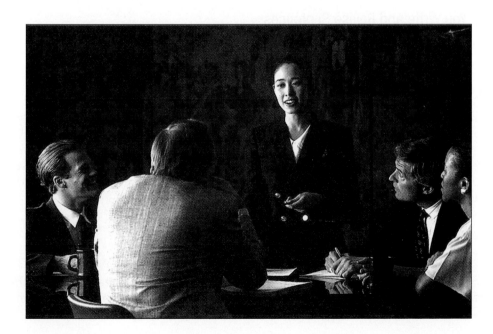

Companies with strong corporate cultures develop their own jargon. At IBM, a *hypo* is a high-potential employee—one destined for management.

Figure 4.6   *Getting Rid of Business Jargon*

Instead of	Use	Because
At your earliest convenience	The date you need a response	If you need it by a deadline, say so. It may never be convenient to respond.
As per your request; 55 miles per hour	As you requested; 55 miles an hour	*Per* is a Latin word for *by* or *for each*. Use *per* only when the meaning is correct; avoid mixing English and Latin.
Enclosed please find	Enclosed is; Here is	An enclosure isn't a treasure hunt. If you put something in the envelope, the reader will find it.
Forward same to this office	Return it to this office	Omit legal jargon.
Hereto, herewith	Omit	Omit legal jargon.
Please be advised; Please be informed	Omit—simply start your response	You don't need a preface. Go ahead and start.
Please do not hesitate	Omit	Omit negative words.
Pursuant to	According to; or omit	*Pursuant* does not mean *after*. Omit legal jargon in any case.
Said order	Your order	Omit legal jargon.
This will acknowledge receipt of your letter.	Omit—start your response	If you answer a letter, the reader knows you got it.
Trusting this is satisfactory, we remain	Omit	Eliminate *-ing* endings. When you are through, stop.

The second kind of jargon is the **businessese** that some writers still use: *as per your request, enclosed please find, please do not hesitate.* None of the words in this second category of jargon are necessary. Indeed, some writers call these terms *deadwood,* since they are no longer living words. Some of these terms, however, seem to float through the air like germs. If any of the terms in the first column of Figure 4.6 show up in your writing, replace them with more modern language.

As You Write and Revise Sentences

At the sentence level, you can do many things to make your writing easy to read.

3. Use active verbs most of the time.

"Who does what" sentences with active verbs make your writing more forceful.

A verb is **active** if the grammatical subject of the sentence does the action the verb describes. A verb is **passive** if the subject is acted upon. Passives are usually made up of a form of the verb *to be* plus a past participle. *Passive* has nothing to do with *past.* Passives can be past, present, or future:

were received   (in the past)
is recommended   (in the present)
will be implemented   (in the future)

To spot a passive, find the verb. If the verb describes something that the grammatical subject is doing, the verb is active. If the verb describes something that is being done to the grammatical subject, the verb is passive.

Active	**Passive**
The customer received 500 widgets.	Five hundred widgets were received by the customer.
I recommend this method.	This method is recommended by me.
The state agencies will implement the program.	The program will be implemented by the state agencies.

Verbs can be changed from active to passive by making the direct object (in the oval) the new subject (in the box). To change a passive verb to an active one, you must make the agent ("by _____" in < >) the new subject. If no agent is specified in the sentence, you must supply one to make the sentence active.

Active	**Passive**
The plant manager approved the request.	The request was approved by the <plant manager.>
The committee will decide next month.	A decision will be made next month. No agent in sentence.
[You] Send the customer a letter informing her about the change.	A letter will be sent informing the customer of the change. No agent in sentence.

If the sentence does not have a direct object in its active form, no passive equivalent exists.

Active	**No passive exists**
I would like to go to the conference.	
The freight charge will be about $1,400.	
The phone rang.	

Passive verbs have at least three disadvantages:

1. If all the information in the original sentence is retained, passive verbs make the sentence longer. Passives take more time to understand.[16]
2. If the agent is omitted, it's not clear who is responsible for doing the action.
3. Using many passive verbs, especially in material that has a lot of big words, can make the writing boring and pompous.

Passive verbs are desirable in these situations:

1. Use passives to emphasize the object receiving the action, not the agent.

   Your order was shipped November 15.

   The customer's order, not the shipping clerk, is important.
2. Use passives to provide coherence within a paragraph. A sentence is easier to read if "old" information comes at the beginning of a sentence. When you have been discussing a topic, use the word again as your subject even if that requires a passive verb.

   The bank made several risky loans in the early 1990s. These loans were written off as "uncollectible" in 1998.

   Using *loans* as the subject of the second sentence provides a link between the two sentences, making the paragraph as a whole easier to read.
3. Use passives to avoid assigning blame.

   The order was damaged during shipment.

   An active verb would require the writer to specify *who* damaged the order. The passive here is more tactful.

What I Really Mean Is . . .*

I wrote asking someone if he could "provide information for" the group he had mentioned on a Web page. He replied that he was too busy to make a submission, and added that he was in full support of the group.

  I got an answer, but a useless one. I had wanted the group's address! I could have avoided confusion (and embarrassment) by simply asking, "Do you have the group's address?"

*Quoted from Margo Metegrano, Letter to the Editor, *Intercom*, May 1996, 2.

4. Use strong verbs—not nouns—to carry the weight of your sentence.

Put the weight of your sentence in the verb. Strong verbs make sentences more forceful and up to 25% easier to read.[17] When the verb is a form of the verb *to be,* revise the sentence to use a more forceful verb.

Weak: The financial advantage of owning this equipment instead of leasing it is 10% after taxes.

Better: Owning this equipment rather than leasing it will save us 10% after taxes.

Nouns ending in *-ment, -ion,* and *-al* often hide verbs.

make an adjustment	adjust
make a payment	pay
make a decision	decide
reach a conclusion	conclude
take into consideration	consider
make a referral	refer
provide assistance	assist

Use verbs to present the information more forcefully.

Weak: We will perform an investigation of the problem.

Better: We will investigate the problem.

Weak: Selection of a program should be based on the client's needs.

Better: Select the program that best fits the client's needs.

5. Tighten your writing.

Writing is **wordy** if the same idea can be expressed in fewer words. Unnecessary words increase typing time, bore your reader, and make your meaning more difficult to follow, since the reader must hold all the extra words in mind while trying to understand your meaning.

  Good writing is tight. Tight writing may be long because it is packed with ideas. In Chapter 2, we saw that revisions to create you-attitude and positive emphasis (➤ pp. 34, 37 resp.) and to develop reader benefits were frequently *longer* than the originals because the revision added information not given in the original.

  Sometimes you may be able to look at a draft and see immediately how to tighten it. When the solution isn't obvious, try the following strategies for tightening your writing.

a. Eliminate words that say nothing.

b. Use gerunds (the *-ing* form of verbs) and infinitives to make sentences shorter and smoother.

c. Combine sentences to eliminate unnecessary words.

d. Put the meaning of your sentence into the subject and verb to cut the number of words.

  The purpose of eliminating unnecessary words is to save the reader's time, not simply to see how few words you can use. You aren't writing a telegram, so keep the little words that make sentences complete. (Incomplete sentences are fine in lists where all the items are incomplete.)

  The following examples show how to use these methods.

a. Eliminate words that say nothing.   Cut words that are already clear from other words in the sentence. Substitute single words for wordy phrases.

Wordy: Keep this information on file for future reference.

Tighter: Keep this information for reference.

or: File this information.

Wordy: Ideally, it would be best to put the billing ticket just below the CRT screen and above the
          keyboard.

Tighter: If possible, put the billing ticket between the CRT screen and the keyboard.

Phrases beginning with *of, which,* and *that* can often be shortened.

Wordy: the question of most importance

Tighter   the most important question

Wordy: the estimate which is enclosed

Tighter: the enclosed estimate

Sentences beginning with *There are* or *It is* can often be tighter.

Wordy: There are three reasons for the success of the project.

Tighter: Three reasons explain the project's success.

Wordy: It is the case that college graduates advance more quickly in the company.

Tighter: College graduates advance more quickly in the company.

Check your draft. If you find these phrases, or any of the unnecessary words shown in Figure 4.7, eliminate them.

b. Use gerunds and infinitives to make sentences shorter and smoother.   A **gerund** is the *-ing* form of a verb; grammatically, it is a verb used as a noun. In the sentence, "Running is my favorite activity," *running* is the subject of the sentence. An **infinitive** is the form of the verb that is preceded by *to: to run* is the infinitive.

In the revision below, a gerund (*purchasing*) and an infinitive (*to transmit*) tighten the revision.

Wordy: A plant suggestion has been made where they would purchase a QWIP machine for the
          purpose of transmitting test reports between plants.

Tighter: The plant suggests purchasing a QWIP machine to transmit test reports between plants.

Even when gerunds and infinitives do not greatly affect length, they often make sentences smoother and more conversational.

c. Combine sentences to eliminate unnecessary words.   In addition to saving words, combining sentences focuses the reader's attention on key points, makes your writing sound more sophisticated, and sharpens the relationship between ideas, thus making your writing more coherent.

Wordy: I conducted this survey by telephone on Sunday, April 21. I questioned two groups of
          upperclassmen—male and female—who, according to the Student Directory, were still
          living in the dorms. The purpose of this survey was to find out why some upperclassmen

Using Your Computer to Improve Style*

Laser copies look so perfect that it can be hard to edit them. But your computer can be an ally, not an enemy, as you revise and edit.

- Use the "search" or "find" command to find potential errors. One student replaces every "is" and "are" with capital letters ("IS" and "ARE") so that he can easily check his draft for weak verbs. Another replaces periods with several asterisks to check sentence integrity.

- Change the font or size. Putting your text in an unusual font or 24-point type can help you really see what you've said. (Just remember to change back to a standard font in a standard size before printing out the final version!)

- Ask a friend to edit, putting changes in all caps, so you can easily find them.

*Based on Todd Taylor, " 'Soft Copy' and the Illusion of Laser-Printed Text," *Technical Communication*, 42 (No. 1), (February 1995): 169–70.

| **Figure 4.7** | *Words to Cut* |

Cut the following words	Cut redundant words	Substitute a single word for a wordy phrase	
quite	a period of three months	at the present time	now
really	during the course of the negotiations	due to the fact that	because
very	during the year of 1996	in the event that	if
	maximum possible	in the near future	soon (or give the date)
	past experience	prior to the start of	before
	plan in advance	on a regular basis	regularly
	refer back		
	the color blue		
	true facts		

The Value of Being Specific*

A survey of car owners revealed complaints about the fit of doors. To correct the problem, the company worked to make the doors more exactly flush with the car body. But a later survey turned up the same complaint. Confused, the company asked several owners to be part of a focus group. It turned out that the owners judged "fit of doors" by how much effort it took to close the door and by the sound the door made when it shut.

*Based on Gerald F. Smith, *Quality Problem Solving* (Milwaukee: ASQ Quality Press, 1998), 57.

continue to live in the dorms even though they are no longer required by the University to do so. I also wanted to find out if there were any differences between male and female upperclassmen in their reasons for choosing to remain in the dorms.

Tighter: On Sunday, April 21, I phoned upperclassmen and women living in the dorms to find out (1) why they continue to live in the dorms even though they are no longer required to do so, and (2) whether men and women had the same reasons for staying in the dorms.

d. Put the meaning of your sentence into the subject and verb to cut the number of words.   Put the core of your meaning into the subject and verb of your main clause. Think about what you *mean* and try saying the same thing in several different ways. Some alternatives will be tighter than others. Choose the tightest one.

Wordy: The reason we are recommending the computerization of this process is because it will reduce the time required to obtain data and will give us more accurate data.

Better: We are recommending the computerization of this process because it will save time and give us more accurate data.

Tight: Computerizing the process will give us more accurate data more quickly.

Wordy: The purpose of this letter is to indicate that if we are unable to mutually benefit from our seller/buyer relationship, with satisfactory material and satisfactory payment, then we have no alternative other than to sever the relationship. In other words, unless the account is handled in 45 days, we will have to change our terms to a permanent COD basis.

Better: A good buyer/seller relationship depends upon satisfactory material and satisfactory payment. You can continue to charge your purchases from us only if you clear your present balance in 45 days.

6. Vary sentence length and sentence structure.

Readable prose mixes sentence lengths and varies sentence structure. A really short sentence (under 10 words) can add punch to your prose. Really long sentences (over 30 or 40 words) are danger signs.

You can vary sentence patterns in several ways. First, you can mix simple, compound, and complex sentences. **Simple sentences** have one main clause:

We will open a new store this month.

Compound sentences have two main clauses joined with *and, but, or,* or another conjunction. Compound sentences work best when the ideas in the two clauses are closely related.

We have hired staff, and they will complete their training next week.

We wanted to have a local radio station broadcast from the store during its grand opening, but the DJs were already booked.

Complex sentences have one main and one subordinate clause; they are good for showing logical relationships.

When the stores open, we will have balloons and specials in every department.

Because we already have a strong customer base in the northwest, we expect the new store to be just as successful as the store in the City Center Mall.

You can also vary sentences by changing the order of elements. Normally the subject comes first.

We will survey customers later in the year to see whether demand warrants a third store on campus.

To create variety, occasionally begin the sentence with some other part of the sentence.

Later in the year, we will survey customers to see whether demand warrants a third store on campus.

To see whether demand warrants a third store on campus, we will survey customers later in the year.

Use these guidelines for sentence length and structure:

- Always edit sentences for tightness. Even a 17-word sentence can be wordy.
- When your subject matter is complicated or full of numbers, make a special effort to keep sentences short.
- Use long sentences
  To show how ideas are linked to each other.
  To avoid a series of short, choppy sentences.
  To reduce repetition.
- Group the words in long and medium-length sentences into chunks that the reader can process quickly.[18]
- When you use a long sentence, keep the subject and verb close together.

Let's see how to apply the last three principles.

- **Use long sentences to show how ideas are linked to each other, to avoid a series of short, choppy sentences, and to reduce repetition.** The following sentence is hard to read not simply because it is long but because it is shapeless. Just cutting it into a series of short, choppy sentences doesn't help. The best revision uses medium-length sentences to show the relationship between ideas.

Too long: It should also be noted in the historical patterns presented in the summary, that though there were delays in January and February which we realized were occurring, we are now back where we were about a year ago, and that we are not off line in our collect receivables as compared to last year at this time, but we do show a considerable over-budget figure because of an ultraconservative goal on the receivable investment.

Choppy: There were delays in January and February. We knew about them at the time. We are now back where we were about a year ago. The summary shows this. Our present collect receivables are in line with last year's. However, they exceed the budget. The reason they exceed the budget is that our goal for receivable investment was very conservative.

Better: As the summary shows, although there were delays in January and February (of which we were aware), we have now regained our position of a year ago. Our present collect receivables are in line with last year's, but they exceed the budget because our goal for receivable investment was very conservative.

- **Group the words in long and medium-length sentences into chunks.** The "better" revision above has seven chunks. In the list below, the chunks starting immediately after the numbers are main clauses. The chunks that are indented are subordinate clauses and parenthetical phrases.

1. As the summary shows,
2. although there were delays in January and February
3. (of which we were aware),
4. we have now regained our position of a year ago.
5. Our present collect receivables are in line with last year's,
6. but they exceed the budget
7. because our goal for receivable investment was very conservative.

The first sentence has four chunks: an introductory phrase (1), a subordinate clause (2) with a parenthetical phrase (3), followed by the main clause of the first sentence (4). The second sentence begins with a main clause (5). The sentence's second main clause (6) is introduced with *but,* showing that it will reverse the first clause. A subordinate clause explaining the reason for the reversal completes the sentence (7). At 27 and 24 words, respectively, these sentences aren't short, but they're readable because no chunk is longer than 10 words.

The Uses of Fuzzy Language*

Specific, concrete words are usually more interesting and more forceful. But fuzzy words may be better to encourage creativity, to promote change, and to create unity.

To encourage creativity, managers should describe the goal vaguely. Santa Fe Southern Railroad wanted to create an upscale space that was flexible enough to use in many ways. Employees came up with many creative alternatives that management hadn't thought of—and that saved the company money.

Fuzzy words are also useful in promoting change. One manufacturer changed to a "cross-functional team-based system"—but let each plant decide just how to structure and implement the teams.

Metaphors and other symbols can create a sense of energy and belonging. But any metaphor is fuzzy. For example, many businesses describe workers as a "family." But many kinds of families exist, and different employees will interpret the metaphor in different ways.

*Based on Gail T. Fairhurst and Robert A. Sarr, *The Art of Framing: Managing the Language of Leadership* (San Francisco: Jossey-Bass, 1996), 36–37.

Death and Taxes*

Connotations can shape attitudes toward proposed laws. US law limits the amount of inheritance that can be passed to beneficiaries tax-free. A sizeable tax (55% at this writing) is assessed on the portion of an inheritance over that amount. This tax is commonly called an "estate tax," because "estate" is the term for the total amount of assets left by someone who dies.

But an "estate" sounds like something only rich people have. In fact, some people who consider themselves middle class—especially owners of small businesses and family farms—will incur the tax. To increase support for this tax cut, Senate Majority Leader Trent Lott calls the tax a "death tax." Everybody dies, so his term makes the tax seem relevant to all voters, not just rich ones. Most of his constituents won't have to pay estate taxes, he admits. "But," he says, "just the idea of a death tax infuriates people."

*Based on Jackie Calmes, "Grave Concern: Washington Is Moving to Alter the Certainty of Death and Taxes," *The Wall Street Journal*, April 28, 1997, A1.

Any sentence pattern will get boring if it is repeated sentence after sentence. Use different sentence patterns—different kinds and lengths of chunks—to keep your prose interesting.

- **Keep the subject and verb close together.** Often you can move the subject and verb closer together if you put the modifying material in a list at the end of the sentence. For maximum readability, present the list vertically.

Hard to read:	Movements resulting from termination, layoffs and leaves, recalls and reinstates, transfers in, transfers out, promotions in, promotions out, and promotions within are presently documented through the Payroll Authorization Form.
Smoother:	The following movements are documented on the Payroll Authorization Form: termination, layoffs and leaves, recalls and reinstates, transfers in and out, and promotions in, out, and within.
Still better:	The following movements are documented on the Payroll Authorization Form:

  - Termination.
  - Layoffs and leaves.
  - Recalls and reinstates.
  - Transfers in and out.
  - Promotions in, out, and within.

Sometimes you will need to change the verb and revise the word order to put the modifying material at the end of the sentence.

Hard to read:	The size sequence code that is currently used for sorting the items in the NOSROP lists and the composite stock lists is not part of the online file.
Smoother:	The online file does not contain the size sequence code that is currently used for sorting the items in the composite stock lists and the NOSROP lists.

7. Use parallel structure.

Parallelism puts words, phrases, or clauses in the same grammatical and logical form. Parallelism is also a powerful device for making your writing smoother and more forceful.

In the following faulty example, *by reviewing* is a gerund, while *note* is an imperative verb. Make the sentence parallel by using both gerunds or both imperatives.

Faulty:	Errors can be checked by reviewing the daily exception report or note the number of errors you uncover when you match the lading copy with the file copy of the invoice.
Parallel:	Errors can be checked by reviewing the daily exception report or by noting the number of errors you uncover when you match the lading copy with the file copy of the invoice.
Also parallel:	To check errors, note 1. The number of items on the daily exception report. 2. The number of errors discovered when the lading copy and the file copy are matched.

Note that a list in parallel structure must fit grammatically into the umbrella sentence that introduces the list.

Words must also be logically parallel. In the following faulty example, *juniors, seniors,* and *athletes* are not three separate groups. The revision groups words into nonoverlapping categories.

Faulty:	I interviewed juniors and seniors and athletes.
Parallel:	I interviewed juniors and seniors. In each rank, I interviewed athletes and nonathletes.

8. Put your readers in your sentences.

Use second-person pronouns (*you*) rather than third-person (*he, she, one*) to give your writing more impact. *You* is both singular and plural; it can refer to a single person or to every member of your organization.

Third-person: Funds in a participating employee's account at the end of each six months will automatically be used to buy more stock unless a "Notice of Election Not to Exercise Purchase Rights" form is received from the employee.

Second-person: Once you begin to participate, funds in your account at the end of each six months will automatically be used to buy more stock unless you turn in a "Notice of Election Not to Exercise Purchase Rights" form.

Be careful to use *you* only when it refers to your reader.

Incorrect: My visit with the outside sales rep showed me that your schedule can change quickly.

Correct: My visit with the outside sales rep showed me that schedules can change quickly.

As You Write and Revise Paragraphs

Paragraphs are visual and logical units. Use them to chunk your sentences.

9. Begin most paragraphs with topic sentences.

A good paragraph has **unity;** that is, it is about only one idea, or topic. The **topic sentence** states the main idea and provides a scaffold to structure your document. Your writing will be easier to read if you make the topic sentence explicit and put it at the beginning of the paragraph.[19]

Hard to read:
(no topic
sentence)

In fiscal 1997, the company filed claims for refund of federal income taxes of $3,199,000 and interest of $969,000 paid as a result of an examination of the company's federal income tax returns by the Internal Revenue Service (IRS) for the years 1993 through 1995. It is uncertain what amount, if any, may ultimately be recovered.

Better: (paragraph
starts with
topic sentence)

The company and the IRS disagree about whether the company is liable for back taxes. In fiscal 1997, the company filed claims for a refund of federal income taxes of $3,199,000 and interest of $969,000 paid as a result of an examination of the company's federal income tax returns by the Internal Revenue Service (IRS) for the years 1993 through 1995. It is uncertain what amount, if any, may ultimately be recovered.

A good topic sentence forecasts the structure and content of the paragraph.

Plan B also has economic advantages.

(Prepares the reader for a discussion of B's economic advantages.)

We had several personnel changes in June.

(Prepares the reader for a list of the month's terminations and hires.)

Employees have complained about one part of our new policy on parental leaves.

(Prepares the reader for a discussion of the problem.)

When the first sentence of a paragraph is not the topic sentence, readers who skim may miss the main point. Move the topic sentence to the beginning of the paragraph. If the paragraph does not have a topic sentence, you will need to write one. If you can't think of a single sentence that serves as an "umbrella" to cover every sentence, the paragraph lacks unity. To solve the problem, either split the paragraph into two or eliminate the sentence that digresses from the main point.

Writing to Be Translated*

When you know that something will be translated into another language, avoid figurative language, images, and humor. They don't translate well.

"Consider the American copywriter who prepared a campaign on snowblowers for the European market without giving a thought to translations. . . . 'Super Snow Hound' [was] the most powerful model. . . . The copywriter wrote the headline: 'Super Snow Hound Blows Up a Storm.' You can imagine the difficulty of retaining the idiom and connotations of 'blows' for snowblower and 'up a storm' for heavy duty performance in a snow storm."

*Paragraph 2 quoted from Robert F. Roth, *International Marketing Communications* (Chicago: Crain, 1982), 139.

The Benefits of Plain English*

Allen-Bradley spent two years converting its manuals to plain English. The work is paying off in five ways. (1) Phone calls asking questions about the products have dropped from 50 a day to only 2 a month. (2) The sales force is selling more systems because people can learn about them more quickly. (3) Distributors spend less time on site teaching customers about products. (4) The clearer documents are easier to translate into Japanese, German, and French for international sales. (5) The tighter documents cost less to print, especially when translated into Arabic and German, which require 125% more space than the same content in English.

*Based on Barry Jereb, "Plain English on the Plant Floor," *Plain Language: Principles and Practice*, ed. Edwin R. Steinberg (Detroit: Wayne State University Press, 1991), 213.

10. Use transitions to link ideas.

Transition words and sentences signal the connections between ideas to the reader. Transitions tell whether the next sentence continues the previous thought or starts a new idea; they can tell whether the idea that comes next is more or less important than the previous thought. Figure 4.8 lists some of the most common transition words and phrases.

Readability Formulas and Good Style

Readability formulas attempt to measure objectively how easy something is to read. However, since they don't take many factors into account, the formulas are at best a very limited guide to good style.

Computer packages that analyze style may give you a readability score. Some states' "plain English" laws require consumer contracts to meet a certain readability score. Some companies require that warranties and other consumer documents meet certain scores.

 See the BAC Web page to see how to calculate the two best known readability formulas: the Gunning Fog Index and the Flesch Reading Ease Scale.

As you can see when you visit the BAC Web page, readability formulas depend heavily on word length and sentence length. But as Janice C. Redish and Jack Selzer have shown,[20] using shorter words and sentences will not necessarily make a passage easy to read. Short words are not always easy to understand, especially if they have technical meanings (e.g., *waive, bear market, liquid*). Short, choppy sentences and sentence fragments are actually harder to understand than well-written medium-length sentences.

No reading formula yet devised takes into account three factors that influence how easy a text is to read: the complexity of the ideas, the organization of the ideas, and the layout and design of the document.

Instead of using readability formulas to measure style, the Document Design Center recommends that you test your draft with the people for whom it is designed. How long does it take them to find the information they need? Do they make mistakes when they try to use the document? Do they think the

---

Figure 4.8   *Transition Words and Phrases*

To show addition or continuation of the same idea	To introduce an example	To show that the contrast is more important than the previous idea	To show time
and	for example (e.g.)	but	after
also	for instance	however	as
first, second, third	indeed	nevertheless	before
in addition	to illustrate	on the contrary	in the future
likewise	namely	**To show cause and effect**	next
similarly	specifically	as a result	then
To introduce the last or most important item	**To contrast**	because	until
finally	in contrast	consequently	when
furthermore	on the other hand	for this reason	while
moreover	or	therefore	**To summarize or end**
finally			in conclusion

document is easy to use? Answers to these questions can give us much more accurate information than any readability score.

Organizational Preferences for Style

Different organizations and bosses may legitimately have different ideas about what constitutes good writing. If the style the company prefers seems reasonable, use it. If the style doesn't seem reasonable—if you work for someone who likes flowery language or wordy paragraphs, for example—you have several choices.

- Go ahead and use the techniques in this chapter. Sometimes seeing good writing changes people's minds about the style they prefer.
- Help your boss learn about writing. Show him or her this book or the research cited in the notes to demonstrate how a clear, crisp style makes documents easier to read.
- Recognize that a style may serve other purposes than communication. An abstract, hard-to-read style may help a group forge its own identity. James Suchan and Ronald Dulek have shown that Navy officers preferred a passive, impersonal style because they saw themselves as followers. An aircraft company's engineers saw wordiness as the verbal equivalent of backup systems. A backup is redundant but essential to safety, because parts and systems do fail.[21] When big words, jargon, and wordiness are central to a group's self-image, change will be difficult, since changing style will mean changing the corporate culture.
- Ask. Often the documents that end up in files aren't especially good; later, other workers may find these and copy them, thinking they represent a corporate standard. Bosses may in fact prefer better writing.

Building a good style takes energy and effort, but it's well worth the work. Good style can make every document more effective; good style can help make you the good writer so valuable to every organization.

Summary of Key Points

- Good style in business and administrative writing is less formal, more friendly, and more personal than the style usually used for term papers.
- To improve your style,
  - Get a clean page or screen, so that you aren't locked into old sentence structures.
  - Try WIRMI: *What I Really Mean Is*. Then write the words.
  - Try reading your draft out loud to someone sitting about three feet away. If the words sound stiff, they'll seem stiff to a reader, too.
  - Ask someone else to read your draft out loud. Readers stumble because the words on the page aren't what they expect to see. The places where that person stumbles are places where your writing can be better.
  - Write a *lot*.
- Use the following techniques to make your writing easier to read: As you choose words,
  1. Use words that are accurate, appropriate, and familiar. **Denotation** is a word's literal meaning; **connotation** is the emotional coloring that a word conveys.

The Boss Won't Let Me Write That Way

When a writing consultant urged them to use *I*, the engineers in Research and Development (R&D) at one firm claimed they couldn't: "Our boss won't let us." The consultant checked with their boss, the vice president for Research and Development. He said, "I don't care what words they use. I just want to be able to understand what they write."

The vice president had a PhD and had once done experiments in R&D himself, but he'd spent several years in management. He no longer knew as many technical details as did his subordinates. Their efforts to impress him backfired: he was annoyed because he couldn't understand their reports and had to tell subordinates to rewrite them.

Moral 1: If you think your boss doesn't want you to use a word, ask. A few bosses do prize formal or flowery language. Most don't.

Moral 2: Even if your boss has the same background you do, he or she won't necessarily understand what you write. Revise your memos and reports so they're clear and easy to read.

Moral 3: What's in the file cabinet isn't necessarily a guide to good writing for your organization.

2. Use technical jargon only when it is essential and known to the reader. Eliminate business jargon.

As you write and revise sentences,

3. Use active verbs most of the time. Active verbs are better because they are shorter, clearer, and more interesting.

4. Use strong verbs—not nouns—to carry the weight of your sentence.

5. Tighten your writing. Writing is **wordy** if the same idea can be expressed in fewer words.

   a. Eliminate words that say nothing.

   b. Use gerunds and infinitives to make sentences shorter and smoother.

   c. Combine sentences to eliminate unnecessary words.

   d. Put the meaning of your sentence into the subject and verb to cut the number of words.

6. Vary sentence length and sentence structure.

7. Use parallel structure. Use the same grammatical form for ideas that have the same logical function.

8. Put your readers in your sentences.

As you write and revise paragraphs,

9. Begin most paragraphs with topic sentences so that readers know what to expect in the paragraph.

10. Use transitions to link ideas.

- Readability formulas are not a sufficient guide to style. They imply that all short words and all short sentences are equally easy to read; they ignore other factors that make a document easy or hard to read: the complexity of the ideas, the organization of the ideas, and the layout and design of the document.

- Different organizations and bosses may legitimately have different ideas about what constitutes good writing.

Chapter 4

Exercises and Problems

4.1   Identifying Words with Multiple Denotations

a. Each of the following words has several denotations. How many can you list without going to a dictionary? How many additional meanings does a good dictionary list?

browser	log
court	table

b. List five words that have multiple denotations.

4.2   Explaining Bypassing

Show how different denotations make bypassing possible in the following examples.

a. France and Associates: Protection from Professionals

b. We were not able to account for the outstanding amount of plastic waste generated each year.

c. I scanned the résumés when I received them.

4.3   Evaluating Connotations

a. Identify the connotations of each of the following metaphors for a multicultural nation.

melting pot
mosaic
tapestry
crazy quilt
garden salad
stew
tributaries

b. Which connotations seem most positive? Why?

4.4   Evaluating the Ethical Implications of Connotations

In each of the following pairs, identify the more favorable term. Is its use justified? Why or why not?

1. wastepaper   recovered fiber
2. feedback   criticism
3. deadline   due date
4. scalper   ticket reseller
5. budget   spending plan

4.5   Correcting Errors in Denotation and Connotation

Identify and correct the errors in denotation or connotation in the following sentences.

1. In our group, we weeded out the best idea each person had thought of.
2. She is a prudent speculator.
3. The three proposals are diametrically opposed to each other.
4. While he researched companies, he was literally glued to the Web.
5. Our backpacks are hand sewn by one of roughly 16 individuals.

4.6   Using Connotations to Shape Response

Write two sentences to describe each of the following situations. In one sentence, use words with positive connotations; in the other, use negative words.

1. Chris doesn't spend time on small talk.
2. Chris often starts work on a new project without being told to do so.
3. As a supervisor, Chris gives very specific instructions to subordinates.

4.7   Choosing Levels of Formality

Identify the more formal word in each pair. Which term is better for most business documents? Why?

1. adapted to   geared to
2. befuddled   confused
3. assistant   helper
4. pilot project   testing the waters
5. cogitate   think

4.8   Eliminating Jargon and Simplifying Language

Revise these sentences to eliminate jargon and to use short, familiar words. In some sentences, you'll need to reword, reorganize, or add information to produce the best revision.

1. Computers can enumerate pages when the appropriate keystroke is implemented.
2. Any alterations must be approved during the 30-day period commencing 60 days prior to the expiration date of the agreement.
3. As per your request, the undersigned has obtained estimates of upgrading our computer system. A copy of the estimated cost is attached hereto.
4. Please be advised that this writer is in considerable need of a new computer.
5. Enclosed please find the proposal for schedule for the training session. In the event that you have alterations which you would like to suggest, forward same to my office at your earliest convenience.

4.9   Changing Verbs from Passive to Active

Identify the passive verbs in the following sentences and convert them to active verbs. In some cases, you may need to add information to do so. You may use different words as long as you retain the basic meaning of the sentence. Remember that imperative verbs are active, too.

1. The business plan was written by Tyrone King.
2. The cost of delivering financial services is being slashed by computers, the Internet, and toll-free phone lines.
3. When the vacation schedule is finalized it is recommended that it be routed to all supervisors for final approval.
4. As stated in my résumé, I have designed Web pages for three student organizations.
5. Material must not be left on trucks outside the warehouse. Either the trucks must be parked inside the warehouse or the material must be unloaded at the time of receiving the truck.

4.10   Using Strong Verbs

Revise each of the following sentences to use stronger verbs.

1. The advantage of using color is that the document is more memorable.
2. Customers who make payments by credit card will receive a 1% rebate on all purchases.
3. When you make an evaluation of media buys, take into consideration the demographics of the group seeing the ad.
4. We provide assistance to clients in the process of reaching a decision about the purchase of hardware and software.
5. We maintain the belief that Web ads are a good investment.

4.11   Reducing Wordiness

1. Eliminate words that say nothing. You may use different words.
   a. There are many businesses that are active in community and service work.
   b. The purchase of a new computer will allow us to produce form letters quickly. In addition, return on investment could be calculated for proposed repairs. Another use is that the computer could check databases to make sure that claims are paid only once.
   c. Our decision to enter the South American market has precedence in the past activities of the company.
2. Use gerunds and infinitives to make these sentences shorter and smoother.
   a. The completion of the project requires the collection and analysis of additional data.
   b. The purchase of laser printers will make possible the in-house production of the newsletter.
   c. The treasurer has the authority for the investment of assets for the gain of higher returns.
3. Combine sentences to show how ideas are related and to eliminate unnecessary words.
   a. Some customers are profitable for companies. Other customers actually cost the company money.
   b. If you are unable to come to the session on HMOs, please call the human resources office. You will be able to schedule another time to ask questions you may have about the various options.
   c. Major Japanese firms often have employees who know English well. US companies negotiating with Japanese companies should bring their own interpreters.

4.12   Improving Parallel Structure

Revise each of the following sentences to create parallelism.

1. The orientation session will cover the following information:

   • Company culture will be discussed.
   • How to use the equipment.
   • You will get an overview of key customers' needs.

2. Five criteria for a good Web page are content that serves the various audiences, attention to details, and originality. It is also important to have effective organization and navigation devices. Finally, provide attention to details such as revision date and the Webmaster's address.

3. When you leave a voice-mail message,

   • Summarize your main point in a sentence or two.
   • The name and phone number should be given slowly and distinctly.
   • The speaker should give enough information so that the recipient can act on the message.
   • Tell when you'll be available to receive the recipient's return call.

4.13   Putting Readers in Your Sentences

Revise each of the following sentences to put readers in them. As you revise, use active verbs and simple words.

1. Mutual funds can be purchased from banks, brokers, financial planners, or from the fund itself.
2. Every employee will receive a copy of the new policy within 60 days after the labor agreement is signed.
3. Another aspect of the university is campus life, with an assortment of activities and student groups to participate in and lectures and sports events to attend.

4.14 Editing Sentences to Improve Style

Revise these sentences to make them smoother, less wordy, and easier to read. Eliminate jargon and repetition. Keep the information; you may reword or reorganize it. If the original is not clear, you may need to add information to write a clear revision.

1. The table provided was unclear due to hard-to-understand headings.
2. By working a co-op or intern position, you may have to be in school an additional year to complete the requirements for graduation, but this extra year is paid for by the income you make in the co-op or intern position.
3. There is a seasonality factor in the workload, with the heaviest being immediately prior to quarterly due dates for estimated tax payments.

4. Informational meetings will be held during next month at different dates and times. These meetings will explain the HMO options. Meeting times are as follows:

   October 17, noon–1 pm.
   October 20, 4–5 pm.
   October 23, 2–3 pm.
5. Listed below are some benefits you get from an HMO:
   1. Routine doctors' visits will charge only a $10 co-payment.
   2. No hassle of prescription reimbursements later. You only pay the co-payment when you fill your prescription.
   3. Hospitalization is covered 100%.

4.15 Using Topic Sentences

Make each of the following paragraphs more readable by opening each paragraph with a topic sentence. You may be able to find a topic sentence in the paragraph and move it to the beginning. In other cases, you'll need to write a new sentence.

1. At Disney World, a lunch put on an expense account is "on the mouse." McDonald's employees "have ketchup in their veins." Business slang flourishes at companies with rich corporate cultures. Memos at Procter & Gamble are called "reco's" because the model P&G memo begins with a recommendation.
2. The first item on the agenda is the hiring for the coming year. George has also asked that we review the

agency goals for the next fiscal year. We should cover this early in the meeting since it may affect our hiring preferences. Finally, we need to announce the deadlines for grant proposals, decide which grants to apply for, and set up a committee to draft each proposal.
3. Separate materials that can be recycled from your regular trash. Pass along old clothing, toys, or appliances to someone else who can use them. When you purchase products, choose those with minimal packaging. If you have a yard, put your yard waste and kitchen scraps (excluding meat and fat) in a compost pile. You can reduce the amount of solid waste your household produces in four ways.

4.16 Revising Paragraphs

Revise each paragraph to make it easier to read. Change, rearrange, or delete words and sentences; add any material necessary.

a. Once a new employee is hired, each one has to be trained for a week by one of our supervisors at a cost of $1,000 each which includes the supervisor's time. This amount also includes half of the new employee's salary, since new hires produce only half the normal production per worker for the week. This summer $24,000 was spent in training 24 new employees. Absenteeism increased in the department on the hottest summer days. For every day each worker is absent we lose $200 in lost production. This past summer there were a total of 56 absentee days taken for a total loss of $11,200 in lost production. Turnover and absenteeism were the

cause of an unnecessary expenditure of over $35,000 this summer.
b. One service is investments. General financial news and alerts about companies in the customer's portfolio are available. Quicken also provides assistance in finding the best mortgage rate and in providing assistance in making the decision whether to refinance a mortgage. Another service from Quicken is advice for the start and management of a small business. Banking services, such as paying bills and applying for loans, have long been available to Quicken subscribers. The taxpayer can be walked through the tax preparation process by Quicken. Someone considering retirement can use Quicken to ascertain whether the amount being set aside for this purpose is sufficient. Quicken's Web site provides seven services.

4.17   Writing Paragraphs

Write a paragraph on each of the following topics.

a. Discuss your ideal job.

b. Summarize a recent article from a business magazine or newspaper.

c. Explain how technology is affecting the field you plan to enter.

d. Explain why you have or have not decided to work while you attend college.

e. Write a profile of someone who is successful in the field you hope to enter.

As Your Instructor Directs,

a. Label topic sentences, active verbs, and parallel structure.

b. Edit a classmate's paragraphs to make the writing even tighter and smoother.

Planning, Composing, and Revising

The Ways Good Writers Write

Activities in the Composing Process

Brainstorming, Planning, and Organizing Business Documents

Revising, Editing, and Proofreading
- What to Look for When You Revise
- What to Look for When You Edit
- How to Catch Typos

Getting and Using Feedback

Using Boilerplate

Overcoming Writer's Block and Procrastination

Technology and the Writing Process

Summary of Key Points

Effective Strategies for Planning, Composing, and Receiving

Robert A. Brullo   *President, Dyneon LLC*

www.dyneon.com

As president of Dyneon, Robert Brullo articulates the company's vision and strategy to employees, customers, shareholders, and alliance partners to help the company achieve its goal of becoming the fluoropolymer industry's supplier of choice. The documents and presentations he creates for a variety of audiences around the world include Dyneon's annual strategic plan, internal "Town Hall" meetings, and executive seminars. Dyneon is a successful global joint venture between the specialty fluoropolymer businesses of 3M and Hoechst, AG.

About 20 years ago I was asked to prepare the business' annual marketing plan. This was a new experience for me and one that forced me to think about what I wanted to say, my audiences, and what they wanted and needed to know. From the beginning I recognized that I needed to explain what our industry was, how we were positioned, what our growth objectives were, and how we were going to reach them.

> 66 *Once I feel basically satisfied with a draft, I go through it page by page for content, flow, and proper grammar.* 99

Writing the first draft of the plan was very daunting; I had many false starts and had to rewrite paragraphs and complete sections. Sometimes when I revisited the text, I realized that points were not clearly stated or that insight was lacking. I ended up abandoning my first plan and instead telling a story about what we had done and what we wanted to do.

This storytelling style proved to be a powerful way to prepare business plans. In fact, a recently retired 3M executive wrote a *Harvard Business Review* article titled "Strategic Stories: How 3M Is Rewriting Business Planning." The plan I prepared for the launch of the Dyneon joint venture is a case study of this "succinct scenario" approach to writing business plans.

I begin business plans—and other documents—by outlining the key elements to include. It's useful to jot down ideas and thoughts without attempting to be grammatically correct. The outline is straightforward, logical, and a great way to organize one's thoughts before starting to compose.

Once I feel basically satisfied with a draft, I go through it page by page for content, flow, and proper grammar. Next, I consult my subordinates to ensure that the draft accurately portrays the key factors that would be useful to the various stakeholders who need to understand, approve, and implement the plan. Not surprisingly, one needs to go through more than one iteration to incorporate editorial comments, reorganize the text, and have it proofed by more than one pair of eyes!

Ethics and the Writing Process*

As you plan a message,

- Brainstorm choices and alternatives. In hard situations, seek allies in your organization and discuss your options with them.

- Check your sources.

- Assume that no document is confidential. Paper documents can be subpoenaed for court cases; e-mail documents can be forwarded and printed out without your knowledge.

As you compose,

- Promise only what you can deliver.

- Warn your readers of dangers or limits in your information.

- Be accurate and complete.

As you revise,

- Use feedback to revise words and visuals that your audience may misunderstand.

*Based on J. C. Mathes and Dwight Stevenson, *Designing Technical Reports*, 2nd ed. (New York: Macmillan, 1991), 469; and John M. Lannon, *Technical Writing*, 5th. ed. (New York: HarperCollins, 1991), 74.

Skilled performances look easy and effortless. In reality, as every dancer, musician, and athlete knows, they're the products of hard work, hours of practice, attention to detail, and intense concentration. Like skilled performances in other arts, writing rests on a base of work.

To get the best results from the time you spend, spend only a third of your time actually "writing." Spend at least one-third of your time analyzing the situation and your audience, gathering information, and organizing what you have to say. Spend another third evaluating what you've said, revising the draft(s) to meet your purposes and the needs of the audience and the organization, editing a late draft to remove any errors in grammar and mechanics, and proofreading the final typed copy.

The Ways Good Writers Write

No single writing process works for all writers all of the time. However, good writers and poor writers seem to use different processes.[1] Good writers are more likely to

- Realize that the first draft will not be perfect.
- Write regularly.
- Break big jobs into small chunks.
- Have clear goals focusing on purpose and audience.
- Have several different strategies to choose from.
- Use rules flexibly.
- Wait to edit until after the draft is complete.

Research shows that experts differ from novices in identifying and analyzing the initial problem more effectively, understanding the task more broadly and deeply, drawing from a wider repertory of strategies, and seeing patterns more clearly. Experts actually composed more slowly than novices, perhaps because they rarely settled for work that was just "OK." Finally, experts were better at evaluating their own work.[2]

Thinking about the writing process and consciously adopting "expert" processes will help you become a more expert writer.

Activities in the Composing Process

Most researchers would agree that writing processes can include eight activities: planning, gathering, writing, evaluating, getting feedback, revising, editing, and proofreading. The activities do not have to come in this order. Not every writing task demands all eight.

Planning includes all the thinking you do. It includes such activities as analyzing the problem, defining your purposes, and analyzing the audience; thinking of ideas; and choosing a pattern of organization or making an outline. Planning includes not only devising strategies for the document as a whole but also generating "mini-plans" that govern sentences or paragraphs.

Gathering includes physically getting the data you need. It can mean simply getting a copy of the letter you're responding to; it can also mean conducting informal and formal research—everything from getting a computer printout or looking something up in a reference book to administering a questionnaire or conducting a focus group.

Writing is the act of putting words on paper or on a screen, or of dictating words to a machine or a secretary. Writing can take the form of lists, fragmentary notes, stream-of-consciousness writing, or formal drafts.

Evaluating means rereading your work and measuring it against your goals and the requirements of the situation and audience. The best evaluation results from *re-seeing* your draft as if someone else had written it. Will your audience understand it? Is it complete? Convincing? Friendly?

You can evaluate *every* activity in the process, not just your draft. Is your view of purposes adequate? Do you have enough information to write? Are your sources believable? Do your revisions go far enough?

Getting feedback means asking someone else to evaluate your work. Again, you could get feedback on every activity, not just your draft. Is your pattern of organization appropriate? Does a revision solve an earlier problem? Are there any typos in the final copy?

Revising means making changes in the draft suggested by your own evaluation or by feedback from someone else: adding, deleting, substituting, or re-arranging. Revision can be changes in single words, but more often it means major additions, deletions, or substitutions as the writer measures (evaluates) the draft against purpose and audience and reshapes the document to make it more effective.

Editing means checking the draft to see that it satisfies the requirements of standard English and the principles of business writing. Here you'd correct spelling and mechanical errors and check word choice and format. Unlike revision, which can produce major changes in meaning, editing focuses on the surface of writing.

Proofreading means checking the final copy to see that it's free from typographical errors.

Note the following points about these eight activities:

- **The activities do not have to come in this order.** Some people may gather data *after* writing a draft when they see that they need more specifics to achieve their purposes.

- **You do not have to finish one activity to start another.** Some writers plan a short section and write it, plan the next short section and write it, and so on through the document. Evaluating what is already written may cause a writer to do more planning or to change the original plan.

- **Most writers do not use all eight activities for all the documents they write.** You'll use more activities when you write a certain kind of document, about a subject, or to an audience that's new to you.

Research about what writers really do has destroyed some of the stereotypes we used to have about the writing process. Consider planning. Traditional advice stressed the importance of planning and sometimes advised writers to make formal outlines for everything they wrote. But we know now that not all good documents are based on outlines.[3] George Jensen and John DiTiberio have found that extroverts do little planning and prefer to work out their ideas as they go along, while introverts prefer to work out their ideas fully before they begin writing.[4] Either method can produce good writing. A study on writer's block found that some ineffective writers spent so much time planning that they left too little time to write the assignment.[5] "Plan!" is too simplistic to be helpful. Instead, we need to talk about how much and what kind of planning for what kind of document.

Brainstorming, Planning, and Organizing Business Documents

Spend at least one-third of your time planning and organizing before you begin to write. The better your ideas are when you start, the fewer drafts you'll need to produce a good document. Start by using the analysis questions from

One Writer's Process for Memos and Reports*

In preparing to write, I spend approximately one-third of my time planning. I feel that analyzing the purpose and audience before beginning to write is one of the most important parts of writing.

I begin by analyzing the purpose of the document . . . persuasion, informative, and so forth.

Secondly, I think about my audiences. It's important to make sure the audience can easily follow a document. The audience may be a group of people. My manager is always an important part of my audience. I write many documents that go to upper management, and I know that being able to write well is crucial so that I can advance to the next level on the corporate ladder. . . .

When beginning a memo or report, I like to outline it. I break the document into the appropriate headings. . . .

Once the document is complete, I go back to revise and edit—tightening up sentences, substituting words, and spell checking. Some documents need just one pass; some require multiple revisions. After revising, I spell check once again. Then I print a hard copy of the document and read it over for typos and grammatical structure. Once this is finished, I ask a colleague to review the document and make comments. If that person can follow the document easily, my audience also should.

*Quoted from Daniel R. Zevchik, statement to Kitty Locker, January 28, 1997.

Writing with Information*

Good writers write with information. Michelle Russo writes reports appraising how much a hotel is worth. Gathering information is a big part of her composing process.

She visits the site. She talks to the general manager. She gets occupancy rates, financial statements, and tax forms. She talks to the tax assessor and all the managers of competing hotels. If it's a convention hotel, she talks to the convention bureau and gets the airlines' passenger traffic counts. Gathering all this information takes about four days. When she gets back to the office, she uses databases for even more information.

*Based on Michelle S. Russo, telephone conversation with the author, December 8, 1993.

Chapter 1 to identify purpose and audience. Use the strategies described in Chapter 3 to analyze audience (✖ p. 60) and identify reader benefits (✖ p. 72). Gather information you can use for your document.

Sometimes your content will be determined by the situation. Sometimes, even when it's up to you to think of reader benefits or topics to include in a report, you'll find it easy to think of ideas. If ideas won't come, try the following techniques.

- Try **brainstorming.** Think of all the ideas you can, without judging them. Consciously try to get at least a dozen different ideas before you stop. Brainstorming helps writers get over the tendency to be overcritical or to develop a mental block after they've thought of one idea or approach. The first idea you have may not be the best.

- Try **freewriting.**[6] Make yourself write, without stopping, for 10 minutes or so, even if you must write "I will think of something soon." At the end of 10 minutes, read what you've written, identify the best point in the draft, then set it aside, and write for another 10 uninterrupted minutes. Read this draft, marking anything that's good and should be kept, and then write again for another 10 minutes. By the third session, you will probably produce several sections that are worth keeping—maybe even a complete draft that's ready to be revised.

- Try **clustering.**[7] Write your topic in the middle of the page and circle it. Write down the ideas the topic suggests, circling them, too. (The circles are designed to tap into the nonlinear half of your brain.) When you've filled the page, look for patterns or repeated ideas. Use different colored pens to group related ideas. Then use these ideas to develop reader benefits in a memo, questions for a survey, or content for the body of a report. Figure 5.1 presents the clusters that one writer created about business communication in the United States and France.

Thinking about the content, layout, or structure of your document can also give you ideas. For long documents, write out the headings you'll use. For anything that's under five pages, less formal notes will probably work. You may want to jot down ideas to use as the basis for a draft. For an oral presentation, a meeting, or a document with lots of visuals, try creating a **storyboard,** with a rectangle representing each page or unit. Draw a box with a visual for each main point. Below the box, write a short caption or label.

Figure 5.2 presents the first draft of a storyboard for a videoconference about business communication between France and the United States. The formless ideas from clustering are starting to take shape. The author still has lots of work to do, but the ideas are now in a form that other people can discuss, criticize, revise, and implement.

Letters and memos will go faster if you choose a basic organizational pattern before you start. Chapters 7, 8, and 9 give detailed patterns of organization for the most common kinds of letters and memos. You may want to customize those patterns with a **planning guide**[8] to help you keep the "big picture" in mind as you write. Figure 5.3 shows planning guides developed for specific kinds of documents.

As you plan your document, pay attention to signals from your boss and the organization's culture. For example, if the organization has a style manual that specifies whether *data* is singular or plural, follow its guidelines. If the organization has an ethics counselor, think about consulting him or her as you decide what to write in a situation with ethical implications. Talk to people in the organization who will be affected by what you are announcing or proposing, to

Figure 5.1   *Clustering Helps Generate Ideas*

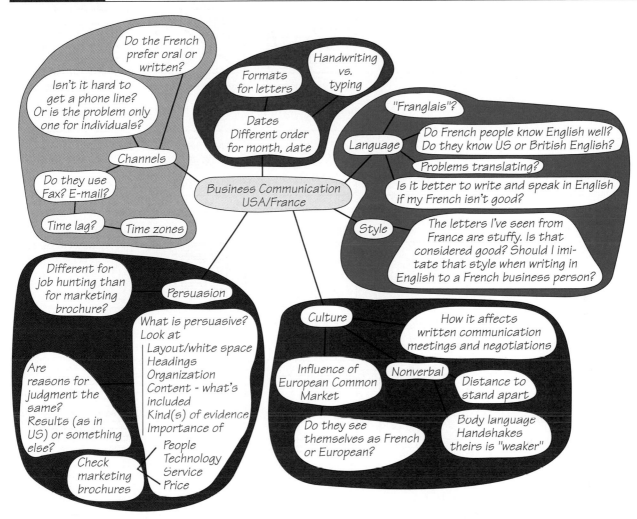

better understand their concerns. In some organizations, your boss may want to see an early planning draft (see Figure 5.6) to see that you're on the right track. In other organizations, you may be expected to do a great deal of revising on your own before anyone else sees the document.

Revising, Editing, and Proofreading

Good writers make their drafts better by judicious revising, editing, and proofreading. **Revising** means making changes that will better satisfy your purposes and your audience. **Editing** means making surface-level changes that make the document grammatically correct. **Proofreading** means checking to be sure the document is free from typographical errors.

What to Look for When You Revise

Every chapter in this book suggests questions you should ask as you revise. When you write to an audience you know well, you may be able to check everything at once. When you're writing to a new audience or have to solve a

Figure 5.2

Storyboards Structure Ideas Visually

Differences in business communication France and the United States

Welcome

Visuals—Importance of international trade

Flags of US / France

Introduce participants

Slide with overview of structure, main points?

Persuasive Techniques
• Organization
• Strategy
• Layout

Close-up of résumé

Person pointing out something

Close-up of letter

People discussing document

Close-up of brochure

Split screen of US / France as people discuss document

Split screen as people ask, answer questions

Shot of group discussion

Summarize/close

Visual to end

particularly difficult problem, plan to revise the draft at least three times. The first time, look for content and clarity. Go back to the analysis questions in Chapter 1 to make sure you've fulfilled all the necessary purposes and have reader benefits for each audience. The second time, check the organization and layout. Finally, check style and tone. Use the information in Chapter 2 to check for you-attitude, positive emphasis, and bias-free language. Use the 10 techniques in Chapter 4 to make sure sentences and paragraphs are tight, smooth, and friendly. Figure 5.4 summarizes the questions you should ask.

Often you'll get the best revision by setting aside your draft, getting a blank page or screen, and redrafting. This strategy takes advantage of the thinking you did on your first draft without locking you into the sentences in it. Use WIRMI (✂ p. 92) to replace awkward phrasing with what you really want to say.

As you revise, be sure to read the document through from start to finish. This is particularly important if you've composed in several sittings or if you've used text from other documents. Researchers have found that such doc-

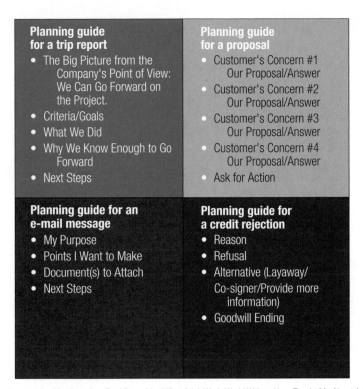

Source: E-mail and proposal guides based on Fred Reynolds, "What Adult Work-World Writers Have Taught Me About Adult Work-World Writing," *Professional Writing in Context: Lessons from Teaching and Consulting in Worlds of Work* (Hillsdale, NJ: Lawrence Erlbaum Associates, 1995), 18, 20.

Figure 5.3

Customized Planning Guides for Specific Documents

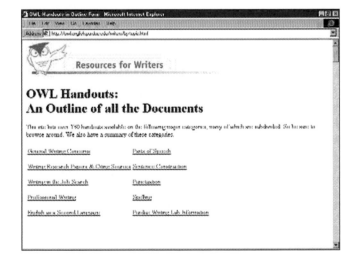

Online Writing Labs (OWLs) offer resources for writers. At Purdue University's OWL, you can find information about revision in business writing as well as information about transitions, grammar, and documenting sources.

uments tend to be well organized but don't flow well.[9] You may need to add transitions, cut repetitive parts, or change words to create a uniform level of formality throughout the document.

If you're really in a time bind, do a light revision, as outlined in Figure 5.5. The quality of the final document may not be as high as with a thorough revision, but even a light revision is better than skipping revision altogether.

Figure 5.4

Thorough Revision Checklist

Content and clarity

☐ Is your view of purposes complete? Does your document meet the needs of the organization and of the reader—and make you look good?

☐ Have you given readers all the information they need to understand and act on your message?

☐ Is all the information accurate?

☐ Is each sentence clear? Is the message free from apparently contradictory statements?

☐ Is the logic clear and convincing? Are generalizations and benefits backed up with adequate supporting detail?

Organization and layout

☐ Is the pattern of organization appropriate for your purposes, audience, and situation?

☐ Are transitions between ideas smooth? Do ideas within paragraphs flow smoothly?

☐ Does the design of the document make it easy for readers to find the information they need? Is the document visually inviting?

☐ Are the points emphasized by layout ones that deserve emphasis?

☐ Are the first and last paragraphs effective?

Style and tone

☐ Is the message easy to read?

☐ Is the message friendly and free from sexist language?

☐ Does the message build goodwill?

Figure 5.5

Light Revision Checklist

☐ Are the first and last paragraphs effective?

☐ Does the design of the document make it easy for readers to find the information they need?

☐ Have you told the reader what to do?

What to Look for When You Edit

Even good writers need to edit, since no one can pay attention to surface correctness while thinking of ideas. Editing should always *follow* revision. There's no point in taking time to fix a grammatical error in a sentence that may be cut when you clarify your meaning or tighten your style. Some writers edit more accurately when they print out a copy of a document and edit the hard copy. But beware: laser printing makes a page look good but does nothing to correct errors.

Check to be sure that the following are accurate:

• Sentence structure.

• Subject–verb and noun–pronoun agreement.

• Punctuation.

• Word usage.

• Spelling—including spelling of names.

• Numbers.

You need to know the rules of grammar and punctuation to edit. Appendix B reviews grammar and punctuation, numbers, and words that are often confused.

See the BAC Web site for links to pages on grammar, punctuation, and editing. Most writers make a small number of errors over and over. If you know that you have trouble with dangling modifiers or subject–verb agreement, for example, specifically look for them in your draft. Also look for any errors that especially bother your boss and correct them.

How to Catch Typos

Proofread every document both with a spell checker and by eye, to catch the errors a spell checker can't find.

To proofread, you must slow your reading speed so you see each individual letter. One way to do that is to read just one line at a time, using a ruler or card to block the text below. Proofreading is hard because writers tend to see what they know should be there rather than what really is there. Since it's always easier to proof something you haven't written, you may want to swap papers with a proofing buddy.

The ideal way to proofread is to have one person read the document aloud, voicing punctuation and spelling out names, while another person follows along the longhand or original typed copy. This way is so slow and so expensive that it is reserved for very important documents or for documents like phone books where it is the only way possible.

An acceptable alternative is to read the document twice. Read once quickly for meaning, to see that nothing has been left out. Read a second time, slowly. When you find an error, correct it and then *reread that line.* Readers tend to become less attentive after they find one error and may miss other errors close to the one they've spotted. Always triple-check numbers, headings, the first and last paragraphs, and the reader's name.

Reading out loud and reading lines backward or pages out of order can help you proofread a document you know well.

Getting and Using Feedback

Getting feedback almost always improves a document. In many organizations, it's required. All external documents must be read and approved before they go out. The process of drafting, getting feedback, revising, and getting more feedback is called **cycling.** Dianna Booker reports that documents in her clients' firms cycled an average of 4.2 times before reaching the intended audience.[10] Susan Kleimann studied a 10-page document whose 20 drafts made a total of 31 stops on the desks of nine reviewers on four different levels.[11] Being asked to revise a document is a fact of life in businesses, government agencies, and nonprofit organizations.

You can improve the quality of the feedback you get by telling people which aspects you'd especially like comments about. For example, when you give a reader the outline or planning draft,[12] you might want to know whether the general approach is appropriate. After your second draft, you might want to know whether reader benefits are well developed. When you reach the polishing draft, you'll be ready for feedback on style and grammar. Figure 5.6 lists questions to ask.

It's easy to feel defensive when someone criticizes your work. If the feedback stings, put it aside until you can read it without feeling defensive. Even if you think that the reader hasn't understood what you were trying to say, the fact that the reader complained usually means the section could be improved. If the reader says "This isn't true" and you know the statement is true, several kinds of revision might make the truth clear to the reader: rephrasing the statement, giving more information or examples, or documenting the source.

Using Spelling and Grammar Checkers

If you use a computer to prepare your documents, use a spell checker to catch typos.

But you still need to proofread by eye.

Spell checkers work by matching words: they will signal any group of letters not listed in their dictionaries. However, they cannot tell that a word is missing or that the meaning demands *of* rather than *or, not* rather than *now,* or *manager* rather than *manger.*

Check numbers and the spelling of names. In international business communication, be sure that you have the right currency symbols: £30 million may be over twice as much as $30 million.

Writers with a good command of grammar and mechanics can do a better job than the computer grammar checkers currently available. Grammar checkers can help a writer whose command of grammar and mechanics is weak. However, since grammar checkers do not catch all errors, it's worth taking the time to master grammar and mechanics so you can edit and proofread yourself.

Review and Revision*

In my most recent experience, $2\frac{1}{2}$ years in a Sales and Marketing Division of a major international corporation, . . . all important writing that is generated by the corporation is reviewed at three or more levels. That means that if a middle manager sends a letter to all or some dealers, the letter will be reviewed by his or her boss (usually a vice president) and a senior vice president. If the contents are sensitive, possibly vulnerable to unfavorable media review, the letter may be reviewed by all senior vice presidents, the legal [staff], and the president/CEO.

If a senior vice president writes a letter, any letter [going] outside the company, it is reviewed by the president *and* by the management level just below him.

All letters going outside the company and written at or below the middle management level are heavily reviewed, sometimes harshly reviewed.

*Quoted from Carol Elizabeth King, Rensselaer Polytechnic Institute, Troy, NY, "Re: Reviews?," posting to bizcom@ebbs.english.vt.edu, January 27, 1998.

Figure 5.6

Questions to Ask Readers

Reading feedback carefully is a good way to understand the culture of your organization. Are you told to give more details or to shorten messages? Does your boss add headings and bullet points? Look for patterns in the comments, and apply what you learn in your next document.

Using Boilerplate

Boilerplate is language—sentences, paragraphs, even pages—from a previous document that a writer includes in a new document. In academic papers, material written by others must be quoted and documented. However, because businesses own the documents their employees write, old text may be included without attribution.

In some cases, boilerplate may have been written years ago. For example, many legal documents, including apartment leases and sales contracts, are almost completely boilerplated. In other cases, writers may use boilerplate they wrote for earlier documents. For example, a section from a proposal describing the background of the problem could also be used in the final report after the proposed work was completed. A section from a progress report describing what the writer had done could be used with only a few changes in the methods section of the final report.

Writers use boilerplate both to save time and energy and to use language that has already been approved by the organization's legal staff. However, as Glenn Broadhead and Richard Freed point out, using boilerplate creates two problems.[13] First, using unrevised boilerplate can create a document with incompatible styles and tones. Second, boilerplate can encourage writers to see as identical, situations and audiences that have subtle differences.

Before you incorporate old language in a new document,

- Check to see that the old section is well written.
- Consciously look for differences between the two situations, audiences, or purposes that may require different content, organization, or wording.
- Read through the whole document at a single sitting to be sure that style, tone, and level of detail are consistent in the old and new sections.

✓ Checklist
Outline or planning draft
☐ Does the plan seem "on the right track"?
☐ What topics should be added? Should any be cut?
☐ Do you have any other general suggestions?
Revising draft
☐ Does the message satisfy all its purposes?
☐ Is the message adapted to the audience(s)?
☐ Is the organization effective?
☐ What parts aren't clear?
☐ What ideas need further development?
☐ Do you have any other suggestions?
Polishing draft
☐ Are there any problems with word choice or sentence structure?
☐ Did you find any inconsistencies?
☐ Did you find any typos?
☐ Is the document's design effective?

Overcoming Writer's Block and Procrastination

Traditional advice about overcoming writer's block focuses on strategies that reduce tension, simplify the writing problem, and "lower the stakes."

- Try to redefine the problem, purpose, or audience. If a fact, constraint, or rule is making it hard for you to write, abandon it—at least for this draft.
- Try brainstorming, freewriting, or clustering.
- Write the part that's easiest to write: the headings, the table that will go in the middle of the report, the history of the problem, whatever you *can* write. The parts of a document don't need to be composed in the order in which they'll appear in the final document.
- Do something you can do without thinking: take a walk, wash the car, fold your laundry. As you work, try "saying" ideas to yourself in your head.
- Try explaining what you mean to a friend. It may be easier to talk to a real audience than to try to imagine your audience as you write.
- Draw a picture or diagram of what you mean. Some people think more easily in pictures rather than words.

To avoid procrastination, modify your behavior by rewarding yourself for activities that *lead* to writing.

- Set a regular time to write. Sit down and stay there for the time you've planned, even if you write nothing usable.
- Develop a ritual for writing. Choose tools—paper, pen, computer, chair— that you find comfortable. Use the same tools in the same place every time you write.
- Try freewriting—writing for 10 minutes without stopping.
- Write down the thoughts and fears you have as you write. If the ideas are negative, try to substitute more positive statements: "I can do this." "I'll keep going and postpone judging." "If I keep working, I'll produce something that's OK."
- Set modest goals (a paragraph, not the whole document) and reward yourself for reaching them.

However, using any single strategy on this list may not be enough. The psychologist who has studied writer's block most thoroughly, Robert Boice, suggests that a combination of five actions works best:[14]

1. Participate actively in the organization and the community. The more you talk to people, the more you interact with some of your audiences, the more you learn about the company, its culture, and its context, the easier it will be to write—and the better your writing will be.
2. Follow a regimen. Practice writing regularly and in moderation.
3. Learn as many strategies as you can. Good writers have a bag of tricks to draw on; they don't have to reinvent the wheel in each new situation. This book suggests many strategies and patterns. Try them out; memorize them; make them your own.
4. Talk positively to yourself: "I can do this." "If I keep working, ideas will come." "It doesn't have to be wonderful; I can always make it better later."
5. Talk about writing to other people. Value the feedback you get from your boss. Talk to your boss about writing. Ask him or her to share particularly good examples—from anyone in the organization. Find colleagues at your own level and talk about the writing you do. Do different bosses value different qualities? What aspects of your own boss's preferences are

Improving the Corporate Writing Process*

A fertilizer company sued several of its competitors, charging that they mislabeled their bags of composted manure. One of the defendants countersued, charging that the original company also mislabeled its bags. All the company's bags contained the same product (compost made of 7% sheep manure, 33% pig manure, and 60% cow manure), but some were called "sheep manure" while others were called "cow manure."

This inconsistency arose from a compartmentalized, linear composing process. Operations filled the bags; marketing wrote the labels. No one noticed that the labels didn't match the contents.

The case was settled out of court after much time and expense. The companies may have lost goodwill by appearing to mislead consumers. By bringing everyone together during the process of writing the labels, these companies could have saved time and money—and written better labels in the first place.

*Based on James E. Porter, "Ideology and Collaboration in the Classroom and in the Corporation," *The Bulletin of the Association for Business Communication* 53, no. 2 (1990): 21.

Spell Checkers' Errors*

The *Dallas Morning News* raised hackles in the computer industry last December when an editor accidentally accepted all of a spell checker's alternate spellings in a technology article that appeared in print—changing chip maker Intel into "Until" and Microsoft into "Microvolts."

*Quoted from Joan E. Rigdon, "Microsoft Word's Spell-Checker Gets Failing Grade in Computerese," *The Wall Street Journal*, November 15, 1995, B1.

individual, and which are part of the discourse community of the organization? Talking to other people expands your repertoire of strategies and helps you understand the discourse community in which you write.

Technology and the Writing Process

Writers using word processing need to pay special attention to revising and proofreading their documents. Since changes are so easy to make with a word processor, some writers plan, revise, edit, and proofread less efficiently.[14] Instead of reading the whole draft through carefully, some writers skim until they reach one error. They fix it, print out the document again, but then find more errors as they read further. Even worse, because documents produced on a good printer look so neat, some writers don't revise or proofread at all. But keying in a document is no more accurate than typing on a traditional typewriter. Editing and proofreading are still necessary.

The widespread use of word processors is raising readers' expectations. Readers are more likely to ask for a revision; they care more about the physical appearance of documents. Because word processing makes it easy to correct typos, change spacing and margins, and insert graphics, readers are less tolerant of badly designed documents and of documents with obvious corrections—even if the document is typed on a manual typewriter.

Summary of Key Points

- Processes that help writers write well include not expecting the first draft to be perfect, writing regularly, modifying the initial task if it's too hard or too easy, having clear goals, knowing many different strategies, using rules as guidelines rather than as absolutes, and waiting to edit until after the draft is complete.
- Writing processes can include eight activities: planning, gathering, writing, evaluating, getting feedback, revising, editing, and proofreading. **Revising** means changing the document to make it better satisfy the writer's purposes and the audience. **Editing** means making surface-level changes that make the document grammatically correct. **Proofreading** means checking to be sure the document is free from typographical errors. The activities do not have to come in any set order. It is not necessary to finish one activity to start another. Most writers use all eight activities only when they write a document whose genre, subject matter, or audience is new to them.
- To think of ideas, try **brainstorming, freewriting** (writing without stopping for 10 minutes or so), and **clustering** (brainstorming with circled words on a page). **Storyboarding** organizes ideas visually, with a rectangle representing each page or unit of a message.
- You can improve the quality of the feedback you get by telling people which aspects of a draft you'd like comments about. If a reader criticizes something, fix the problem. If you think the reader misunderstood you, try to figure out what caused the misunderstanding and revise the draft so that the reader can see what you meant.
- If the writing situation is new or difficult, plan to revise the draft at least three times. The first time, look for content and clarity. The second time, check the organization and layout. Finally, check style and tone.
- **Boilerplate** is language from a previous document that a writer includes in a new document. Using unrevised boilerplate can create a document with

incompatible styles and tones and can encourage writers to see as identical situations and audiences that have subtle differences.

- To overcome writer's block,

    1. Participate actively in the organization and the community.
    2. Follow a regimen. Practice writing regularly and in moderation.
    3. Learn as many strategies as you can.
    4. Talk positively to yourself.
    5. Talk about writing to other people.

Chapter 5

Exercises and Problems

5.1 Interviewing Writers about Their Composing Processes

Interview someone about the composing process(es) he or she uses for on-the-job writing. Questions you could ask include the following:

- What kind of planning do you do before you write? Do you make lists? formal or informal outlines?
- When you need more information, where do you get it?
- How do you compose your drafts? Do you dictate? Draft with pen and paper? Compose on screen? How do you find uninterrupted time to compose?
- When you want advice about style, grammar, and spelling, what source(s) do you consult?
- Does your superior ever read your drafts and make suggestions?
- Do you ever work with other writers to produce a single document? Describe the process you use.

- Describe the process of creating a document where you felt the final document reflected your best work. Describe the process of creating a document you found difficult or frustrating. What sorts of things make writing easier or harder for you?

As Your Instructor Directs,
a. Share your results orally with a small group of students.
b. Present your results in an oral presentation to the class.
c. Present your results in a memo to your instructor.
d. Share your results with a small group of students and write a joint memo reporting the similarities and differences you found.

5.2 Analyzing Your Own Writing Processes

Save your notes and drafts from several assignments so that you can answer the following questions.

- Which practices of good writers do you follow?
- Which of the eight activities discussed in Chapter 5 do you use?
- How much time do you spend on each of the eight activities?
- What kinds of revisions do you make most often?
- Do you use different processes for different documents, or do you have one process that you use most of the time?
- What parts of your process seem most successful? Are there any places in the process that could be improved? How?

- What relation do you see between the process(es) you use and the quality of the final document?

As Your Instructor Directs,
a. Discuss your process with a small group of other students.
b. Write a memo to your instructor analyzing in detail your process for composing one of the papers for this class.
c. Write a memo to your instructor analyzing your process during the term. What parts of your process(es) have stayed the same throughout the term? What parts have changed?

5.3   Checking Spelling and Grammar Checkers

Each of the following paragraphs contains errors in grammar, spelling, and punctuation. Which errors does your spelling or grammar checker catch? Which errors does it miss? Does it flag as errors any words that are correct?

a. Answer to an Inquiry

Enclosed are the tow copies you requested of our pamphlet, "Using the Internet to market Your products. The pamphelt walks you through the steps of planning the Home Page (The first page of the web cite, shows examples of other Web pages we have designed, and provide a questionaire that you can use to analyze audience the audience and pruposes.

b. Performance Appraisal

Most staff accountants complete three audits a month. Ellen has completed 21 audits in this past six months she is our most productive staff accountant. Her technical skills our very good however some clients feel that she could be more tactful in suggesting ways that the clients accounting practices courld be improved.

c. Brochure

Are you finding that being your own boss crates it's own problems? Take the hassle out of working at home with a VoiceMail Answering System. Its almost as good as having your own secratery.

d. Presentation Slides

How to Create a Web résumé

- Omit home adress and phone number
- Use other links only if they help an employer evalaute you.
  - ☐ Be Professional.
  - ☐ Carefully craft and proof read the phrase on the index apage.

How to Create a Scannable Résumé

- Create a 'plain vanilla" document.
- Use include a "Keywords" section. Include personality trait sas well as accomplishments.
- Be specific and quantifyable.

Designing Documents, Slides, and Screens

Guidelines for Page Design
1. Use White Space.
2. Use Headings.
3. Limit the Use of Words Set in All Capital Letters.
4. Limit the Number of Typefaces.
5. Decide Whether to Justify Margins Based on the Situation and the Audience.
6. Put Important Elements in the Top Left and Lower Right Quadrants.
7. Use a Grid to Unify Graphic Elements.
8. Use Highlighting, Decorative Devices, and Color in Moderation.

Designing Brochures and Newsletters

Designing Presentation Slides

Designing Web Pages

Testing the Design

Document Design as Part of Your Writing Process(es)

The Importance of Effective Design

Summary of Key Points

Designing Documents, Slides, and Screens

Susan Kleimann

President, Kleimann Communication Group, LLC

www.beyondwords.org

Susan Kleimann, PhD, works with companies and government agencies to design and test documents that work for their customers. She formerly directed the Document Design Center at the American Institutes for Research in Washington, DC. Kleimann Communication Group, LLC, is a woman-owned small business helping companies understand that clear writing is clear thinking.

Good document design focuses on the reader. Don't just think about your purpose; imagine a particular reader trying to do something with your document.

Think about a credit card statement. What is its purpose? Partly to let you know what you owe, the due date, how much credit you have left. But the most basic purpose is to get you to pay your debt. The "what you owe" line is almost always in the upper-right-hand corner, right next to a place you can write in your payment amount, and surrounded by white space. We're acculturated to expect it in that corner. Document design is not about decoration but rather about guiding the reader through a task.

> *Document design is not about decoration but rather about guiding the reader through a task.*

To test a document, ask people to do something with it, such as fill out a form. Ask them how well it worked; they'll tell you what they understand and what they don't. Observe them; they'll show you when the instructions are unclear or when they can't find the right information. The first kind is cognitive testing, which tells you what readers understand. The second is usability testing, which tells you what readers can do. Both let you know what works.

Good document design is good business. Good design can save time for people who get stuck correcting errors or answering phone calls; they can be freed up to do other work—including providing better customer service. Good design can ensure that important messages get heard. (See the story at the end of this chapter.) Good design shows customers that you care about their time and want to make tasks easier for them. Isn't that the best marketing a company can have?

Standards are still evolving for online documents. Look at www.webpagesthatsuck.com for great examples of what doesn't work and useit.com for great advice on what works now. Just expect things to evolve.

In an age when we all deal with too much information, people have a right to spend as little time as possible with a document or screen and still get the right result. That's what document design is about.

Good document design saves time and money, reduces legal problems, and builds goodwill. A well-designed document looks inviting, friendly, and easy to read. Effective design also groups ideas visually, making the structure of the document more obvious so the document **is** easier to read. Research shows that easy-to-read documents also enhance your credibility and build an image of you as a professional, competent person.[1] Good design is important not only for reports, Web pages, and newsletters but also for announcements and one-page letters and memos.

Guidelines for Page Design

Use the eight guidelines in Figure 6.1 to create visually attractive documents.

1. Use White Space.

White space—the empty space on the page—makes material easier to read by emphasizing the material that it separates from the rest of the text. Normally, margins should be 1 inch. Use bigger margins to line up text with letterhead or other visual elements (see Appendix A). Smaller margins may be acceptable for headers and footers. For example, a page number could be half an inch (0.5") from the top of the page as long as the actual text is surrounded by enough white space. In the body of your document, create white space by varying paragraph lengths and using lists.

Try for a good mix of medium-length, shorter, and very short paragraphs. A page looks easier to read when most of the paragraphs are short (six typed lines or less). First and last paragraphs should be quite short—just three to five typed lines. It's even OK to have a paragraph that's just one sentence. Middle paragraphs should be no longer than seven to eight typed lines.

Use lists to emphasize material. You can use lists for phrases, sentences, or even paragraphs. Lists are normally indented on the left. Since different numbers have different widths in proportional type, use tabs or indents—not spacing—to align items vertically.

- Use numbered lists when the number or sequence of items is exact.
- Use **bullets** (large dots or squares like those in this list) when the number and sequence don't matter.

When you use a list, make sure that all of the items in it are parallel (✖ p. 104) and fit into the structure of the sentence that introduces the list.

Faulty: The following suggestions can help employers avoid bias in job interviews:
1. Base questions on the job description.
2. Questioning techniques.
3. Selection and training of interviewers.

(✖ p. 104)

Figure 6.1	
Guidelines for Page Design	**1.** Use white space to separate and emphasize points.
	2. Use headings to group points and lead the reader through the document.
	3. Limit the use of words set in all capital letters.
	4. Limit the number of typefaces in a single document.
	5. Decide whether to justify margins based on the situation and the audience.
	6. Put important elements in the top left and lower right quadrants of the page.
	7. Use a grid of imaginary columns to unify the elements in a document.
	8. Use highlighting, decorative devices, and color in moderation.

Parallel: The following suggestions can help employers avoid bias in job interviews:
1. Base questions on the job description.
2. Ask the same questions of all applicants.
3. Select and train interviewers carefully.

Also parallel: Employers can avoid bias in job interviews by
1. Basing questions on the job description.
2. Asking the same questions of all applicants.
3. Selecting and training interviewers carefully.

Figure 6.2 shows an original typed document. In Figure 6.3, the same document has been improved by using shorter paragraphs, lists, and headings. These devices take space. When saving space is essential, it's better to cut the text and keep white space and headings. To see how to set up subheadings, see Figure 15.6 in Chapter 15.

2. Use Headings.

As George Miller has shown, our short-term memories can hold only seven plus or minus two bits of information.[2] Only after those bits are processed and

How Big Is Your Short-Term Memory?

One way to test the capacity of your short-term memory is to think about phone numbers. Telephone numbers in the United States are seven digits. If you sometimes forget a phone number while you are dialing it and have to look back at the listing in order to finish dialing, your short-term memory holds only five or six bits of information. If you never have to look back at the book, your memory holds at least seven bits of information.

Figure 6.2   *A Document with Poor Visual Impact*

Full capital letters make title hard to read

MONEY DEDUCTED FROM YOUR WAGES TO PAY CREDITORS

When you buy goods on credit, the store will sometimes ask you to sign a Wage Assignment form allowing it to deduct money from your wages if you do not pay your bill. When you buy on credit, you sign a contract agreeing to pay a certain amount each week or month until you have paid all you owe. The Wage Assignment Form is separate. It must contain the name of your present employer, your social security number, the amount of money loaned, the rate of interest, the date when payments are due, and your signature. The words "Wage Assignment" must be printed at the top of the form and also near the line for your signature. Even if you *Long para-graph is visually uninviting* have signed a Wage Assignment agreement, Roysner will not withhold part of your wages unless all of the following conditions are met: 1. You have to be more than forty days late in payment of what you owe; 2. Roysner has to receive a correct statement of the amount you are in default and a copy of the Wage Assignment form; and 3. You and Roysner must receive a notice from the creditor at least twenty days in advance stating that the creditor plans to make a demand on your wages. This twenty-day notice gives you a chance to correct the problems yourself. If these conditions are all met, Roysner must withhold 15% percent of each paycheck until your bill is paid and give this money to your creditor.

If you think you are not late or that you do not owe the amount stated, you can argue against it by filing a legal document called a "defense." Once you file a defense, Roysner will not withhold any money from you. However, be sure you are right before you file a defense. If you are wrong, you have to pay not only what you owe but also all legal costs for both yourself and the creditor. If you are right, the creditor has to pay all these costs. *Important information is hard to find*

Figure 6.3 *A Document Revised to Improve Visual Impact*

Money Deducted from Your Wages to Pay Creditors

First letter of each main word capitalized— Title split onto two lines

When you buy goods on credit, the store will sometimes ask you to sign a Wage Assignment form allowing it to deduct money from your wages if you do not pay your bill.

Have You Signed a Wage Assignment Form?

Headings divide document into chunks

When you buy on credit, you sign a contract agreeing to pay a certain amount each week or month until you have paid all you owe. The Wage Assignment Form is separate. It must contain

- The name of your present employer,
- Your social security number,
- The amount of money loaned,
- The rate of interest,
- The date when payments are due, and
- Your signature.

List with bullets where order of items doesn't matter

The words "Wage Assignment" must be printed at the top of the form and also near the line for your signature.

When Would Money Be Deducted from Your Wages to Pay a Creditor?

Headings must be parallel.

Here all are questions

Even if you have signed a Wage Assignment agreement, Roysner will not withhold part of your wages unless all of the following conditions are met:

White space between items emphasizes them

1. You have to be more than 40 days late in payment of what you owe;

2. Roysner has to receive a correct statement of the amount you are in default and a copy of the Wage Assignment form; and

Numbered list where number, order of items matter

3. You and Roysner must receive a notice from the creditor at least 20 days in advance stating that the creditor plans to make a demand on your wages. This 20-day notice gives you a chance to correct the problem yourself.

If these conditions are all met, Roysner must withhold fifteen percent (15%) of each paycheck until your bill is paid and give this money to your creditor.

What Should You Do If You Think the Wage Assignment Is Incorrect?

If you think you are not late or that you do not owe the amount stated, you can argue against it by filing a legal document called a "defense." Once you file a defense, Roysner will not withhold any money from you. However, be sure you are right before you file a defense. If you are wrong, you have to pay not only what you owe but also all legal costs for both yourself and the creditor. If you are right, the creditor has to pay all these costs.

Full capitals hide the shape of a word and slow reading 19%.

FULL CAPITALS HIDE THE SHAPE OF A WORD AND SLOW READING 19%.

Figure 6.4

Full Capitals Hide the Shape of a Word

put into long-term memory can we assimilate new information. Large amounts of information will be easier to process if they are grouped into three to seven chunks rather than presented as individual items.

Headings are words, short phrases, or short sentences that group points and divide your letter, memo, or report into sections. Headings enable your reader to see at a glance how the document is organized, to turn quickly to sections of special interest, and to compare and contrast points more easily. Headings also break up the page, making it look less formidable and more interesting.

If you use headings at all, you'll normally have several. Headings should be specific. "Part-Time Personnel in the Dallas Office" is better than "Personnel." Headings must also cover all the material until the next heading. Normally, you will spend at most two or three paragraphs on a subject before you switch your focus—and need a new heading.

Headings can also be complete sentences or questions. Figure 6.3 uses questions for headings. The headings at any one level should be parallel: all noun phrases, for example, or all complete sentences.

In a letter or memo, type main headings even with the left-hand margin in bold. Capitalize the first letters of the first word and of other major words; use lowercase for all other letters. (See Figure 6.3 for an example.) In single-spaced text, triple-space between the previous text and the heading; double-space between the heading and the text that follows.

If you need **subdivisions within a head,** use bold type and put a period after the subhead. Begin the paragraph on the same line. Use subheadings only when you have at least two subdivisions under a given main heading.

In a report, you may need more than two levels of headings. Figure 15.6 in Chapter 15 shows how to set up five levels of headings for reports.

3. Limit the Use of Words Set in All Capital Letters.

We recognize words by their shapes.[3] (See Figure 6.4.) In capitals, all words are rectangular; letters lose the descenders and ascenders that make reading go 19% more quickly.[4] Use full capitals sparingly.

4. Limit the Number of Typefaces.

Typefaces are unified styles of type. Each typeface comes in several sizes and usually in several fonts (bold, italic, etc.). Typewriter typefaces are **fixed;** that is, every letter takes the same space. An *i* takes the same space as a *w*. Courier and Prestige Elite are fixed typefaces. Computers usually offer **proportional** typefaces as well, where wider letters take more space than narrower letters. Times Roman, Palatino, Helvetica, and Arial are proportional typefaces.

Serif typefaces have little extensions, called serifs, from the main strokes. (In Figure 6.5, look at the feet on the *r*'s in New Courier and the flick on the top of the *d* in Lucinda.) New Courier, Elite, Times Roman, Palatino, and Lucinda Calligraphy are serif typefaces. Serif typefaces are easier to read since the serifs help the eyes move from letter to letter. Helvetica, Arial, and Technical are **sans serif** typefaces since they lack serifs (*sans* is French for *without*). Sans serif typefaces are good for titles and tables.

Figure 6.5

This sentence is set in 12-point Times Roman.

This sentence is set in 12-point Arial.

This sentence is set in 12-point New Courier.

This sentence is set in 12-point Lucinda Calligraphy.

This sentence is set in 12-point Broadway.

This sentence is set in 12-point Technical.

Use black type on white paper. White letters on dark paper take longer to read. Shadow or outline fonts are also hard to read; save them for big letters on signs or in ads.

Most business documents use just one typeface—usually Times Roman, Palatino, Helvetica, or Arial. You can create emphasis and levels of headings by using bold, italics, and different sizes. Bold is easier to read than italics, so use bolding if you only need one method to emphasize text. In a complex document, use bigger type for main headings and slightly smaller type for subheadings and text. Avoid Shadow and Outline fonts, which are hard to read. If you combine two typefaces in one document, choose one serif and one sans serif typeface.

Eleven-point Times Roman is ideal for letters, memos, and reports. Twelve-point type is acceptable, especially for readers older than 40. Use 9- or 10-point type to get the effect of a printed book or brochure.

If your material will not fit in the available pages, cut one more time. Putting some sections in tiny type will save space but creates a negative response—a negative response that may extend to the organization that produced the document.

5. Decide Whether to Justify Margins Based on the Situation and the Audience.

Computers often allow you to **justify** margins, so that type on the right side of the page is evenly lined up. This paragraph justifies margins. Justified margins let you get up to 20% more text on the page; they create a finished look. However, use them only with a proportional typeface in a fairly long line (45 characters or so). Justification used with narrow columns or fixed type leaves wide spaces between words. These "rivers" that run down the page are distracting to readers.

Unjustified margins are sometimes called **ragged right margins.** Lines end in different places because words are of different lengths. Anyone using a typewriter will produce ragged right margins. The Sidebar columns in this book use ragged right margins. Ragged right margins are better in narrow lines, since justification would produce "rivers." Ragged right margins are usually less expensive to produce, especially if a document is typeset by a professional compositor. If a change is made in a line of justified type, it affects the spacing for that line and perhaps for the whole page or document. Because ragged right margins are uneven, you probably can change a word or two without affecting other pages. Research suggests that poor readers find unjustified type easier to read than justified type.[5]

Use justified margins when you

- Can use proportional typefaces.
- Want the document to look typeset and professional.
- Want to use as few pages as possible.
- Write to skilled readers.

Use ragged right margins when you

- Do not have proportional typefaces.
- Want an informal look.
- Want to be able to revise an individual page without reprinting the whole document.
- Use very short line lengths.
- Write to poor readers.

6. Put Important Elements in the Top Left and Lower Right Quadrants.

Readers of English start in the upper left-hand corner of the page and read to the right and down. The eye moves in a Z pattern.[6] (See Figure 6.6.) Therefore, as Philip M. Rubens notes, the four quadrants of the page carry different visual weights. The top left quadrant where the eye starts is the most important; the bottom right quadrant where the eye ends is next most important.[7] Titles should always start in the top left; reply coupons or another important element should be in the bottom right.

7. Use a Grid to Unify Graphic Elements.

For years, graphic designers have used a **grid system** to design pages. In its simplest form, a grid imposes two or three imaginary columns on the page. In more complex grids, these columns can be further subdivided. Then all the graphic elements—text indentations, headings, visuals, and so on—are lined up within the columns. The resulting symmetry creates a more pleasing page[8] and unifies long documents.

Figure 6.7 uses grids to organize a page with visuals and a résumé.

8. Use Highlighting, Decorative Devices, and Color in Moderation.

Many word-processing programs have arrows, pointing fingers, and a host of other **dingbats** that you can insert. Clip art packages allow you to insert more and larger images into your text. The Document Design Center used icons as well as better page design when it revised Ford's warranty booklet. (See Figure 6.8.) Used in moderation, highlighting and decorative devices make pages more interesting. However, don't overdo them. A page or screen that uses every possible highlighting device just looks busy and hard to read.

Color works well to highlight points. Use color for overviews and main headings, not for small points. Blue, green, or violet type is most legible for younger readers, but perception of blue diminishes for readers over 50.[9] Red is appropriate for warnings in North America. Since the connotations of colors vary among cultures, check Chapter 12 before you use color with international or multicultural audiences. If a document will be copied on a regular photocopier, avoid color: blue may not be picked up at all, and other colors may be hard to identify.

Cultural Differences in Document Design*

Cultural differences in document design are based on reading practices and experiences with other documents. For example, one laundry detergent company printed ads in the Middle East showing soiled clothes on the left, its box of soap in the middle, and clean clothes on the right. But, because people in that part of the world read not from left to right but from right to left, many people thought the ads meant that the soap actually soiled the clothes.

Different cultures also judge and value aesthetics differently. A Japanese executive explained that the company's annual report was designed to create a visually attractive document which would create a good impression of the company. Visuals, which did not need to be related to the company, were the most important part of the document. US readers of the report were frustrated and found the report "flashy" because they expected visuals to have a direct relationship to the words.

*Based on David A. Ricks, *Blunders in International Business* (Cambridge, MA: Blackwell, 1993), 53; and Kaushiki Maitra and Dixie Goswami, "Responses of American Readers to Visual Aspects of a Mid-Sized Japanese Company's Annual Report: A Case Study," *IEEE Transactions on Professional Communication* 38, no. 4 (December 1995): 197–203.

Figure 6.6

*Put Important Elements in
the Top Left and Bottom
Right Quadrants*

Source: Based on Russel N. Baird,
Arthur T. Turnbull, and Duncan
McDonald, *The Graphics of
Communication: Typography, Layout,
Design, Production,* 5th ed. (New York:
Holt, Rinehart, and Winston, 1987), 37.

Eye movement on the page

Purple quadrants are most important

Figure 6.7   *Examples of Grids to Design Pages*

A page with visuals

Three-column grid.

A newsletter page

Six-column grid.

A résumé page

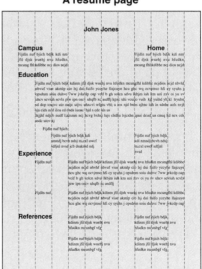

Twelve-column grid.

When you use color,

- Use glossy paper to make colors more vivid.
- Be aware that colors on a computer screen always look brighter than the same colors on paper because the screen sends out light.

Designing Brochures and Newsletters

To design brochures and newsletters, first think about audience and purpose. An "image" brochure designed to promote awareness of your company will have a different look than an "information" brochure telling people how to do something and persuading them to do it.

Start your process by planning content. Create thumbnail sketches (see Figure 5.2) to test various design options. Experiment with different sizes of paper

Figure 6.8	*"Before" and "After" Pages from Ford's Warranty Booklet*

Before

date of first use, whichever occurs first. your warranty coverage are in this booklet.

The warranty begins on the original retail delivery date, or on the date of first use, whichever occurs first.

BASIC COVERAGE

The entire vehicle, except tires, is covered for 12 months or 12,000 miles, whichever occurs first.

The Ford radio or radio/tape components and the factory-installed air conditioning, heater, rear window defogger or de-icer, heated outside rear view mirror systems, and electrically heated windshields are covered for covered for 12 months regardless of mileage.

CORROSION COVERAGE

Repairs to correct perforation from corrosion of any body sheet metal panel are covered to 36 months from the warranty start date, regardless of mileage. (Repair of corrosion due to a defect, without perforation, is covered for 12 months or 12,000 miles, whichever occurs first.)

FORD CONSUMER

If a warranty matter is not handled to your satisfaction, you may want independent third-party review. It is recommended but *not* required ship management and the Ford Parts and Service Division District Cov the Ford Consumer Appeals Board procedure is shown in the Cov detailed information on the Ford Consumer Appeals Boards please tained by calling the Ford Consumer Appeals Board at 1-800-241-1000 peals Board before taking action under the Magnuson-Moss Warranty provided by certain state laws. This dispute handling procedure is a rights which are independent of the Magnuson-Moss Warranty Acc

These warranties give you specific legal rights and you may also have o WARRANTY OF MERCHANTABILITY OR FITNESS FOR A PARTICULAR TIME. INCONVENIENCE, COMMERCIAL LOSS, OR CONSEQUENTIAL

After

Basic coverage

Your warranty begins with a period of basic coverage; here are details about this coverage.

How long does basic coverage last — and what does it cover?

Basic coverage begins at the warranty start date and lasts for 12 months or 12,000 miles, whichever occurs first. Under basic coverage, all parts of your car (except tires) are covered.

The following components and systems are covered for 12 months, regardless of the mileage you put on the cars:

• the Ford radio or radio/tape deck components

and

• these factory-installed systems:
  – air conditioner
  – heater
  – rear window defroster
  – heated outside rear-view mirror
  – electrically heated windshield

Source: Lee L. Gray, "Ford Offers a Readable Warranty Booklet," *Simply Stated . . . in Business*, no. 18 (March 1987): 2.

and layouts. The three-fold brochure shown in Figure 6.9 is the most common, but many other arrangements are possible.

See the BAC Web site for other brochure designs. Use a consistent design for a series of brochures or for issues of a newsletter.

When you design a brochure, think how the reader will get the document. Do you need to leave the back third of the page for a mailing label? Must the brochure compete against many others in a display rack? The best covers usually include a photo or some visual image. Remember that the image needs to work for the audience. A photo of a campus landmark may not mean much to people thinking about coming to your campus for a summer program. Use a central selling point on the cover unless your product or service is very well known.

To make the brochure worth keeping, provide useful information. Make the text candid, believable, and human.

• Answer readers' questions.
• Overcome possible objections.
• Use you-attitude and positive emphasis.
• Be concise.
• Edit carefully to make sure the text is free from typos or other errors.

Figure 6.9   *Three-fold Brochure on 8½-by-11-inch Paper*

Side 1			Side 2			Folded	

Side 1

Inside p. 2	Back cover	**Cover**

Side 2

Inside p. 1	Inside p. 3	Inside p. 4

Folded

Inside p. 3

Inside p. 2

Cover

PaperDirect provides special stationery to use with your laser printer or photocopier to produce brochures and newsletters.

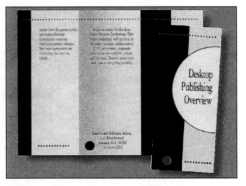

When you design a newsletter,

- Put your strongest image in the top half of the page.
- Arrange small photos in one column of the grid or in the shape of a *C*, a *U*, or a *T*.
- Pull out interesting quotes or statements that summarize a section of a long story. Put these in larger type in the middle of columns to draw the eye to the story.
- Decide how much space to give a story *before* you write it.

In both kinds of documents,

- Keep pictures near the text they illustrate.
- Use small tab indentations when you have small type and narrow columns.
- Justify type and use rules (thin lines) between columns for a more formal look.
- Use bold or italics instead of extensive underlining.
- Provide an e-mail address or phone number for people who want more information.
- Don't put important information on the back of a page or panel that the reader will cut off to fax or mail to you.

 For more information about designing brochures and newsletters, see the BAC Web page.

Designing Presentation Slides

As you design slides for PowerPoint and other presentation programs, keep the following guidelines in mind:

- Use a big font: 44- or 50-point for titles, 32-point for subheads, and 28-point for examples.
- Use bullet-point phrases rather than complete sentences.
- Use clear, concise language.
- Make only three to five points on each slide. If you have more, consider using two slides.
- Customize your slides with the company logo, charts, downloaded Web pages, and scanned-in photos and drawings.

Use clip art only if the art is really appropriate to your points and only if you are able to find nonsexist and nonracist images. (In the late 1990s, Marilyn Dyrud has shown, the major clip art packages were biased.)[10]

Choose a consistent template, or background design, for the entire presentation. Make sure that the template is appropriate for your subject matter. For example, use a globe only if your topic is international business and palm trees only if you're talking about tropical vacations. One problem with PowerPoint is that the basic templates may seem repetitive to people who see lots of presentations made with the program. For a very important presentation, you may want to consider customizing the basic template.

Choose a light background if the lights will be off during the presentation and a dark background if the lights will be on. Slides will be easier to read if you use high contrast between the words and backgrounds. See Figure 6.10 for examples of effective and ineffective color combinations.

Designing Web Pages

Good Web pages have both good content and an interesting design.

Your opening screen is crucial. Jakob Nielsen claims that only 10% of users scroll beyond the first screen.[11] To make it more likely that visitors to your page will scroll down, on the first screen

- Provide an introductory statement or graphic orienting the surfing reader to the organization sponsoring the page.
- Offer an overview of the content of your page, with links to take readers to the parts that interest them.
- Put information that will be most interesting and useful to most readers on the first screen.

Good Document Design Saves Money, I*

- Clearer forms and computer-screen prompts enable Motorola's Corporate Finance department to close its books in 4 days, down from 12. The savings: $20 million a year.

- After rewriting its rules for citizen band radios, the Federal Communications Commission was able to transfer to other jobs five employees who spent all day answering telephone questions about the rules.

- Revised forms cut training time for Citibank employees in half—while improving the accuracy of the information that employees give to customers.

- Simplifying its billing statement reduced customer inquiries at Southern Gas Company and is saving the company an estimated $252,000 a year.

*Based on Karen A. Schriver, "Quality in Document Design: Issues and Controversy," *Technical Communication* 40, no. 2 (1993): 250–51.

Effective

Ineffective

Figure 6.10

Effective and Ineffective Colors for Presentation Slides

Jakob Nielsen's Website of Web page design is one of the most useful pages on the Web. Nielsen provides classic past columns (such as the Top Ten Mistakes of Wed Design) as well as current content and links to other design sites.

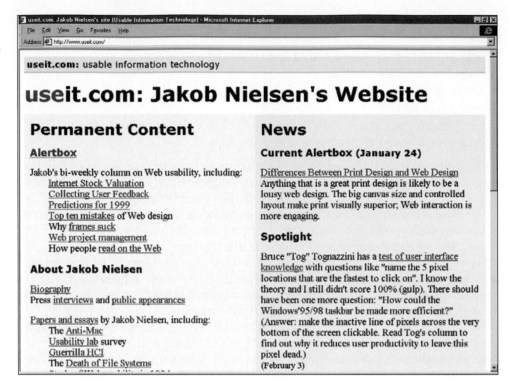

The rest of the page can contain information that only a limited number of readers will want. When a Web document reaches four pages or more, think about dividing it into several documents. Specialized information can go on another page, which readers can click on if they want it.

Make it clear what readers will get if they click on a link.

Ineffective phrasing: Employment. Openings and skills levels are determined by each office.

Better phrasing: Employment. Openings listed by skills level and by location.

As you design pages,

- Keep graphics small. Specify the width and height so that the text can load while the graphics are still coming in.
- Provide visual variety. Use indentations, bulleted or numbered lists, and headings.
- Unify multiple pages with a small banner, graphic, or label so surfers know who sponsors each page.
- On each page, provide a link to the home page, the name and e-mail address of the person who maintains the page, and the date when the page was last revised.

Appropriately enough, the Web has many Web pages on Web page design, as well as technical pages on HTML and Java.

For links to some of the most useful pages, see the BAC Web site.

Testing the Design

A design that looks pretty may or may not work for the audience. To know whether your design is functional, test it with your audience.

For links to Web pages about testing documents for usability, see the BAC Web site.

The best way to test a document is to watch someone as he or she uses the document to do a task. Where does the reader pause, reread, or seem confused? To find out the reader's thought processes, you can (1) ask the reader to "think aloud" while completing the task, (2) interrupt the reader at key points to ask what he or she is thinking, or (3) ask the reader to describe the thought process after completing the document and the task. Learning the reader's thought processes is important, since a reader may get the right answer for the wrong reasons. In such a case, the design still needs work.

If your document will be used by a wide variety of people, test it with those who are most likely to have trouble with it: very old or young readers, people with little education, people who read English as a second language.

Document Design as Part of Your Writing Process(es)

Document design isn't something to "tack on" when you've finished writing. Indeed, the best documents are created when you think about design at each stage of your writing process(es).

- As you plan, think about your audience. Are they skilled readers? Are they busy? Will they read the document straight through or skip around in it?

- As you write, incorporate lists and headings. Use visuals to convey numerical data clearly and forcefully.

- Get feedback from people who will be using your document. What parts of the document do they think are hard to understand? Do they need additional information?

- As you revise, check your draft against the guidelines in this chapter.

For links to stories on the Web about document design, see the BAC Web page.

The Importance of Effective Design

When document design is poor, both organizations and society suffer.

The defect that caused the nuclear accident at Three Mile Island appeared 17 months earlier in a Toledo power plant.[12] At the Toledo plant, workers were able to control damage before a serious problem arose. However, it was clear that a problem existed that might occur again either at that plant or at other locations. A supervisor recommended new guidelines—and put them on the second page of a two-page memo. None of the 12 people on the distribution list for that memo responded. A not-quite-right subject line, ineffective writing, and poor document design caused the memo to be ignored. On March 28, 1979, the same defect led to America's worst nuclear accident to this date—an accident that might have been avoided if writers had been able to design documents that readers could understand and act on.

Summary of Key Points

- An attractive document looks inviting, friendly, and easy to read. The visual grouping of ideas also makes the structure of the document more obvious so it is easier to read.

- Good document design can save time, money, and legal problems.

Good Document Design Saves Money, II*

- The British government began reviewing its forms in 1982. Since then, it has eliminated 27,000 forms, redesigned 41,000, and saved over $28 million.

- Revising the British lost-baggage form for airline passengers cut a 55% error rate to 3%.

- In Australia, rewriting one legal document saved the Victorian government the equivalent of $400,000 a year in staff salaries.

- In the Netherlands, revising the form for educational grants reduced by two-thirds the number of forms applicants filled out incompletely or incorrectly. The government saved time and money; the applicants got decisions more quickly.

*Based on Karen A. Schriver, "Quality in Document Design: Issues and Controversy," *Technical Communication* 40, no. 2 (1993): 250–51.

Designing Documents for Mutual Funds*

Putnam Investments manages over $150 billion in mutual fund and retirement assets. Says its CEO, Lawrence Lasser, "Visually, we started with two objectives: First, we wanted to differentiate ourselves. . . . We wanted to break through the clutter . . . to get both the intermediary's and the investor's attention.

"Our second objective was to simplify. We wanted to simplify the language by getting rid of jargon, and make our literature visually inviting and user-friendly. In this industry, companies typically jam as much as they can into every piece, thinking more is better. We took the opposite approach, saying let's give people something they can comprehend and absorb. We used vivid colors and icons. . . . We added white space, . . . and key messages were highlighted, so that if you just read the headlines and subheads you got a story. . . .

"Design has provided a major way for us to communicate clearly and convincingly what is sometimes pretty archaic stuff."

*Quoted from "Putnam's Lawrence J. Lasser on Design," *@ Issue* 2, no. 2 (Fall 1996): 1–5.

- Eight guidelines help writers create visually attractive documents:
  1. Use white space.
  2. Use headings.
  3. Limit the use of words set in all capital letters.
  4. Limit the number of typefaces.
  5. Decide whether to justify margins based on the situation and the audience.
  6. Put important elements in the top left and lower right quadrants.
  7. Use a grid to unify graphic elements.
  8. Use highlighting, decorative devices, and color in moderation.
- To design brochures and newsletters, first think about audience and purpose. Use a consistent design for a series of brochures or for issues of a newsletter.
- As you design slides for PowerPoint and other presentation programs,
  - Use a big font.
  - Use bullet-point phrases.
  - Make only three to five points on each slide.
  - Customize your slides.
- Good Web pages have both good content and an interesting design.
  - Orient the surfing reader to the organization sponsoring the page.
  - Offer an overview of the content of your page, with links to take readers to the parts that interest them.
  - Make it clear what readers will get if they click on a link.
  - Keep graphics small.
  - Provide visual variety.
- The best documents are created when you think about design at each stage of the writing process.
  - As you plan, think about the needs of your audience.
  - As you write, incorporate lists, headings, and visuals.
  - Get feedback from people who will be using your document.
  - As you revise, check your draft against the guidelines in this chapter.
- To test a document, observe readers, ask them to "think aloud" while completing the task, interrupt them at key points to ask what they are thinking, or ask them to describe the thought process after completing the document and the task.

Chapter 6

Exercises and Problems

Getting Started

6.1   Evaluating Page Designs

Use the guidelines in Chapter 6 to evaluate each of the following page designs. What are their strong points? What could be improved?

a.

Source: Diane Burns and S. Venit, "What's Wrong with This Paper," *PC Magazine* 6, no. 17 (October 13, 1987): 174–75.

b. ☞ RESIST the TEMPTATION to use **all the fonts** available on your COMPUTER. *Too many* fonts **create** *visual* clutter ☹ and **make a document HARD** to read!! **FONTS** that call *attention* to **themselves** are NOT *appropriate* for **BUSINESS** letters, memos, and reports. ✣ *Even* in a **standard font,** avoid ~~shadows~~, **outlines,** and *OVERUSE* OF **bold** and *italics.* ∞

c.

Grainger
invites you to
explore our world.
It's a world that's
rich in opportunity
for a diverse range
of qualified
suppliers.

At Grainger, supplier diversity helps make our world go round. It shapes both our business and our business relationships. And it's the reason we're reaching out to you. As America's leading industrial distributor of maintenance, repair, and operating products, we have many opportunities for qualified suppliers. So whether you supply our company with the products and services we need, or supply us with the products that we distribute to our customers, Grainger can supply your business with the visibility it deserves.

To learn more about Grainger's Supplier Diversity Program, call 1-800-473-3473, ext. 1877 today.

Grainger is a proud, active member of the National Minority Supplier Development Council and the Women's Business Development Center.

GRAINGER
Industrial and Commercial Supply

http://www.grainger.com

Source: Grainger advertisement.

d.

KINKO'S. ALL THE BRIGHTENING POWER YOU NEED.
Are you embarrassed by dull, dingy business materials? Don't be. Come to Kinko's instead, for vibrant colors that dazzle and delight. With our color technology, Kinko's has all the tools you need to get your brochures and banners their brightest. So you'll always look your best.

kinko's
The new way to office.™
www.kinkos.com

Source: Kinko's advertisement.

e.

Less flower.

More power.

Drivers wanted ⓥ

Source: Volkswagen advertisement.

6.2   Evaluating PowerPoint Slides

Evaluate the following drafts of PowerPoint slides.

· Is the slides' background appropriate for the topic?

· Do the slides use words or phrases rather than complete sentences?

· Is the font big enough to read from a distance?

· Is the art relevant and appropriate?

· Is each slide free from errors?

6.3   Recognizing Typefaces

Some companies commission a unique typeface, or wordmark, for their logos. Other companies use a standard font. When a logo is used consistently and frequently, it becomes associated with the organization.

Can you name the brands that go with each letter of the alphabet below?

Source: "Alphabet Soup," *@Issue: The Journal of Business and Design* 3 no. 2 (Fall 1997): 24–25.

@ISSUE:

Alphabet Soup You don't always need to see the whole word to recognize the name of the brand. One letter will do. Used effectively, a distinctive logotype becomes the corporate signature. That is why many companies commission the design of a unique typeface, or wordmark, that incorporates clues to their line of business or operating philosophy. Other companies have adopted an off-the-shelf typeface that they have made their own through the use of designated corporate colors, upper or lower case styling, condensed or expanded leading and other techniques. As with any branding tool, a logotype must be used consistently and frequently to work. Test your familiarity with some of the best-known logotypes by naming the brand that goes with each letter in this alphabet.

AUDI, BALL JARS, CHICAGO CUBS, DHL, ETHAN ALLEN, GOODYEAR, HOLIDAY INN, IBM, JOHNSON & JOHNSON, CIRCLE K, LEGO, MAYTAG, NASA, OREO, PERRIER, REUTERS, SEARS, TWA, UNILEVER, VIRGIN, WESTINGHOUSE, XEROX, YMCA, ZENITH.

6.4   Evaluating the Ethics of Design Choices

Indicate whether you consider each of the following actions ethical, unethical, or a gray area. Which of the actions would you do? Which would you feel uncomfortable doing? Which would you refuse to do?

1. Putting the advantages of a proposal in a bulleted list, while discussing the disadvantages in a paragraph.
2. Using a bigger type size so that a résumé visually fills a whole page.
3. Putting reasons to buy a product in the upper left and lower right quadrants, and the price in a part of the page that will get less emphasis.
4. Using a line at the bottom of the first page so it appears that the document is finished, and then putting the price and limitations on the back of that page.
5. Putting the services that are not covered by your health plan in full caps to make it less likely that people will read the page.

6.5   Using Headings

Reorganize the items in each of the following lists, using appropriate headings. Use bulleted or numbered lists as appropriate.

a. Rules and Procedures for a Tuition Reimbursement Plan

1. You are eligible to be reimbursed if you have been a full-time employee for at least three months.
2. You must apply before the first class meeting.
3. You must earn a "C" or better in the course.
4. You must submit a copy of the approved application, an official grade report, and a receipt for tuition paid to be reimbursed.
5. You can be reimbursed for courses related to your current position or another position in the company, or for courses which are part of a degree related to a current or possible job.
6. Your supervisor must sign the application form.
7. Courses may be at any appropriate level (high school, college, or graduate school).

b. Activities in Starting a New Business

- Getting a loan or venture capital
- Getting any necessary city or state licenses
- Determining what you will make, do, or sell
- Identifying the market for your products or services
- Pricing your products or services
- Choosing a location
- Checking zoning laws that may affect the location
- Identifying government and university programs for small business development
- Figuring cash flow
- Ordering equipment and supplies
- Selling
- Advertising and marketing

Communicating at Work

6.6   Analyzing Documents at Work

1. Collect several documents: letters and memos, newsletters, ads and flyers, and reports. Use the guidelines in Chapter 6 to evaluate each of them.
2. Compare documents or pages produced by your competitors to those produced by your own organization in a specific category (for example, brochures, instructions, Web pages). Which documents are more effective? Why?

As Your Instructor Directs,
a. Discuss the documents with a small group of classmates.
b. Write a memo to your instructor evaluating three or more of the documents. Include originals or photocopies of the documents you discuss as an appendix to your memo.
c. Write a memo to your supervisor recommending ways the organization can improve its documents.
d. In an oral presentation to the class, explain what makes one document good and another one weak. If possible, use transparencies so that classmates can see the documents as you evaluate them.

Document Assignments

6.7   Evaluating Page Designs

Collect several documents that you receive as a consumer or a student: forms, letters, newsletters, announcements, ads, and flyers. Use the guidelines in Chapter 6 to evaluate each of them.

As Your Instructor Directs,
a. Discuss the documents with a small group of classmates.
b. Write a memo to your instructor evaluating three or more of the documents. Include originals or photocopies of the documents you discuss as an appendix to your memo.
c. Write a letter to an organization recommending ways it can improve the design of the documents.
d. In an oral presentation to the class, explain what makes one document good and another one weak. If possible, use transparencies so that classmates can see the documents as you evaluate them.

6.8   Evaluating Web Pages

Compare three Web pages in the same category (for example, helping the homeless, organizations, car companies, university departments, sports information). Which page(s) are most effective? Why? What weaknesses do the pages have?

As Your Instructor Directs,
a. Discuss the pages with a small group of classmates.

b. Write a memo to your instructor evaluating the pages. Include URLs of the pages in your memo.
c. In an oral presentation to the class, explain what makes one page good and another one weak. If possible, put the pages on screen so that classmates can see the pages as you evaluate them.

6.9   Creating a Brochure

Create a brochure for a campus, nonprofit, government, or business organization. Write a memo to your instructor explaining your choices for content and design.

6.10   Creating a Web Page

Create a Web page for an organization that does not yet have one. Write a memo to your instructor explaining your choices for content and design.

6.11   Testing a Document

Ask someone to follow a set of instructions or to fill out a form. (Consider consumer instructions, forms for financial aid, and so forth.)

· Time the person. How long does it take? Is the person able to complete the task?
· Observe the person. Where does he or she pause, reread, seem confused?
· Interview the person. What parts of the document were confusing?

As Your Instructor Directs,
a. Discuss the changes needed with a small group of classmates.

b. Write a memo to your instructor evaluating the document and explaining the changes that are needed. Include the document as an appendix to your memo.
c. Write to the organization that produced the document recommending necessary improvements.
d. In an oral presentation to the class, evaluate the document and explain what changes are needed. If possible, use a transparency of the document so that classmates can see it.

6.12   Improving a Financial Aid Form

You've just joined the financial aid office at your school. The director gives you the following form and asks you to redesign it. The director says:

> We need this form to see whether parents have other students in college besides the one requesting aid. Parents are supposed to list all family members that the parents support—themselves, the person here, any other kids in college, and any younger dependent kids.
>
> Half of these forms are filled out incorrectly. Most people just list the student going here; they leave out everyone else.
>
> If something is missing, the computer sends out a letter and a second copy of this form. The whole process starts over. Sometimes we send this form back two or three times before it's right. In the meantime, students' financial aid is delayed—maybe for months. Sometimes things are so late that they can't register for classes, or they have to pay tuition themselves and get reimbursed later.

> If so many people are filling out the form wrong, the form itself must be the problem. See what you can do with it. But keep it to a page.

As Your Instructor Directs,
a. Analyze the current form and identify its problems.
b. Revise the form. Add necessary information; reorder information; change the chart to make it easier to fill out.

Hints:
· Where are people supposed to send the form? What is the phone number of the financial aid office? Should they need to call the office if the form is clear?
· Does the definition of *half-time* apply to all students or just those taking courses beyond high school?

- Should capital or lowercase letters be used?
- Are the lines big enough to write in?
- What headings or subdivisions within the form would remind people to list all family members whom they support?

- How can you encourage people to return the form promptly?

Please complete the chart below by listing all family members for whom you (the parents) will provide more than half support during the academic year (July 1 through June 30). Include yourselves (the parents), the student, and your dependent children, even if they are not attending college.

EDUCATIONAL INFORMATION, 200_ - 200_						
FULL NAME OF FAMILY MEMBER	AGE	RELATIONSHIP OF FAMILY MEMBER TO STUDENT	NAME OF SCHOOL OR COLLEGE THIS SCHOOL YEAR	FULL-TIME	HALF-TIME* OR MORE	LESS THAN HALF-TIME
STUDENT APPLICANT						

*Half-time is defined as 6 credit hours or 12 clock hours a term.

When the information requested is received by our office, processing of your financial aid application will resume.

Please sign and mail this form to the above address as soon as possible. Your signature certifies that this information and the information on the FAF is true and complete to the best of your knowledge. If you have any questions, please contact a member of the need analysis staff.

_____   _____
Signature of Parent(s)   Date

Two

Letters and Memos

Chapter Seven

Informative and Positive Messages   154

Chapter Eight

Negative Messages   198

Chapter Nine

Writing Persuasive Messages   220

Chapter Ten

Handling Difficult Persuasive Situations   258

Chapter Eleven

Sales and Fund-Raising Letters   276

7

Informative and Positive Messages

Writing Letters and Memos

Organizing Informative and Positive Messages

Subject Lines for Informative and Positive Messages
- Making Subject Lines Specific
- Making Subject Lines Concise
- Making Subject Lines Appropriate for the Pattern of Organization

Using Reader Benefits in Informative and Positive Messages

Writing the One-Page Memo

Ending Informative and Positive Letters and Memos

Writing E-Mail Messages
- Subject Lines for E-Mail
- Format for E-Mail Messages
- E-Mail Etiquette
- Using E-Mail Effectively

Varieties of Informative and Positive Messages
- Transmittals
- Confirmations
- Summaries
- Thank-You and Congratulatory Notes
- Adjustments and Responses to Complaints

Solving a Sample Problem
- Problem
- Analysis of the Problem
- Discussion of the Sample Solutions

Summary of Key Points

Informative and Positive Messages

Diana Sun   *Vice President of Corporate Communications, Capital One*

capitalone.com

As the head of Corporate Communications, Diana Sun manages Capital One's external and internal communications. Using a proprietary Information-Based Strategy, Capital one has quickly become one of the world's largest issuers of credit cards, a direct marketer of consumer lending products, and a pioneer in the direct marketing of wireless phone service.

As one of the nation's fastest-growing companies, we attribute our success to our proprietary Information-Based Strategy, which is enormously complex to execute. It's critical that our more than 10,000 associates around the world have a good understanding of our company's business strategies. And that's where our intensive internal communications come in.

> *Remember that your communication has a lot of competition out there.*

We "layer" our communications, sending messages through a variety of channels: our intranet ("The One Place") and electronic newsletters for speedy delivery; printed materials for more in-depth discussions; and events to celebrate successes. For example, we recently announced a new expansion into the Seattle area. We arranged for free Starbucks coffee in the lobbies of each of our 30-some buildings worldwide. Posters celebrated the announcement and the cups proclaimed, "Caution: This Company is Hot!" It was a really fun way to celebrate that important news.

Another big part of our culture is the incredible access that our associates have to senior management, including our CEO and our President. We organize dozens of major events throughout the year in which associates can engage these executives in two-way dialogues.

We always keep in mind that it is vital that we listen to our associates. By using continual feedback loops, we're able to make sure we're delivering the right information to the right person at the right time, using the right channels. Our twice-yearly survey of all associates tells the story: associates' satisfaction with communications far exceeds industry benchmarks. For example, 93% of Capital One associates agree that our communications are "useful," compared with a 64% benchmark, and 82% agree that communications are "complete," compared with a 44% benchmark.

Remember that your communication has a lot of competition out there. People forget two-thirds of what they've heard or read in 24 hours and 98% in 30 days! So build your communication around the two or three points you want folks to remember. Research tells us that most people can remember no more than three different points. You want to select which three they remember!

The Power of Good Writing*

Darlene was an entry-level auditor for a state government auditing bureau that audited organizations that provided services to citizens of the state. Her audit reports were noticeably superior to those written by everyone else in the bureau. She thought about the multiple audiences for the reports, questioned organizational norms that seemed counterproductive, and chose words consciously to achieve the multiple purposes that even simple reports had.

As a result of her good writing, Darlene was promoted. In her new position, she changed the composing process for reports and the ways that managers worked with staff auditors. She created a database of the various providers and identified whom the bureau was—and was not—auditing. This information will enable the bureau to conduct more and more focused audits.

In her new position, Darlene had less travel and more power. She was allowed to choose and define her own projects. At the end of her first year in the organization, she had gained real power in it.

*Based on Susan M. Katz, "A Newcomer Gains Power: An Analysis of the Role of Rhetorical Expertise," *The Journal of Business Communication* 35, no. 4 (October 1998): 419–42.

Business messages must meet the needs of the writer (and the writer's organization), be sensitive to the audience, and accurately reflect the topic being written about. Informative and positive messages are the bread-and-butter correspondence in organizations.

When we need to convey information to which the reader's basic reaction will be neutral, the message is **informative.** If we convey information to which the reader's reaction will be positive, the message is a **positive** or **good news message.** Neither message immediately asks the reader to do anything. You usually do want to build positive attitudes toward the information you are presenting, so in that sense, even an informative message has a persuasive element. Chapter 8 will discuss messages where the reader will respond negatively; Chapters 9, 10, and 11 discuss messages where you want the reader to act.

Informative and positive messages include acceptances; positive answers to reader requests; information about procedures, products, services, or options; announcements of policy changes that are neutral or positive; and changes that are to the reader's advantage.

Even a simple informative or good news message usually has several purposes:

Primary purposes:

To give information or good news to the reader or to reassure the reader.

To have the reader read the message, understand it, and view the information positively.

To deemphasize any negative elements.

Secondary purposes:

To build a good image of the writer.

To build a good image of the writer's organization.

To cement a good relationship between the writer and reader.

To reduce or eliminate future correspondence on the same subject so the message doesn't create more work for the writer.

Informative and positive messages are not necessarily short. Instead, the length of a message depends on your purposes, the audience's needs, and the complexity of the situation. A public health inspector got a lot of teasing from his colleagues because he wrote 10-page inspection reports; the other inspectors rarely wrote more than 4 pages. He got the last laugh, however, when the lawyers in the enforcement division complimented him on his reports. For the first time, they were getting enough information to win cases against companies and individuals charged with violating the public health statutes. The shorter reports didn't give enough information.

Writing Letters and Memos

Letters go to someone outside your organization; memos go to someone in your own organization.

In large organizations where each unit is autonomous, the organization's culture determines whether people in different units send letters or memos to each other. In some universities, for example, faculty send letters if they need to write to faculty in other departments.

Letters and memos use different formats. The most common formats are illustrated in Appendix A. The AMS Simplified letter format is very similar to memo format: it uses a subject line and omits the salutation and the complimentary close. Thus, it is a good choice when you don't know the reader's name.

The differences in audience and format are the only differences between letters and memos. Both kinds of messages can be long or short, depending on how much you have to say and how complicated the situation is. Both kinds of messages can be informal when you write to someone you know well, or more formal when you write to someone you don't know, to several audiences, or for the record. Both kinds of messages can be simple responses that you can dash off in 15 minutes; both can take hours of analysis and revision when you've never faced that situation before or when the stakes are high.

Organizing Informative and Positive Messages

The patterns of organization in this chapter and the chapters that follow will work for 70 to 90% of the writing situations most people in business and government face. Using the appropriate pattern can help you compose more quickly and create a better final product.

- Be sure you understand the rationale behind each pattern so that you can modify the pattern if necessary. (For example, if you write instructions, any warnings should go up front, not in the middle of the message.)
- Not every message that uses the basic pattern will have all the elements listed. The elements you do have will go in the order presented in the pattern.
- Sometimes you can present several elements in one paragraph. Sometimes you'll need several paragraphs for just one element.

In real life, writing problems don't come with labels that tell you which pattern to use. Chapters 7 through 11 offer advice about when to use each pattern. Figure 7.1 shows how to organize informative and positive messages. Figures 7.2 and 7.3 illustrate two ways that the basic pattern can be applied. The letter in 7.2 authorizes a one-year appointment that the reader and writer have already discussed and describes the organization's priorities. Since the writer knows that the reader wants to accept the job, the letter doesn't need to persuade. The opportunity for the professor to study records that aren't

Good News, Good Business*

In 1995, an industrial fire destroyed Malden Mills' factory in Lawrence, Massachusetts. Owner, president, and CEO Aaron Feuerstein pledged to rebuild—and to pay his more than 1,000 employees full salaries until the new factory was ready for them to work in.

Was he foolish to spend $15 million on employees who couldn't work? *Fortune* reporter Thomas Teal doesn't think so. From 1982 to 1995, general US productivity increased just over 1% a year. At Malden Mills in the same period, revenues in constant dollars tripled—while the workforce barely doubled. Feuerstein has always valued having superior employees. And the employees produce superior products. Malden is best known for its lightweight, thermal, wool-like fabrics sold under the brand names Polarfleece and Polartec by Lands' End, L. L. Bean, Patagonia, Eddie Bauer, and a dozen more upscale companies.

The factory is now rebuilt, and the company is back in business and doing well. At a European trade show in Brussels in September 1996, buyers snapped up Malden Mills' broad new line of high-end upholstery fabrics.

*Based on Thomas Teal, "Not a Fool, Not a Saint," *Fortune*, November 11, 1996, 201–4.

Figure 7.1   *How to Organize Informative and Positive Messages*

1. **Give any good news and summarize the main points.** Include the date policies begin, the percent of a discount, etc. If the reader has already raised the issue, make it clear that you're responding.

   Share good news immediately.

2. **Give details, clarification, background.** Don't repeat information you've already given. Do answer all the questions your reader is likely to have; provide all the information necessary to achieve your purposes. Present details in the order of importance to the reader.

3. **Present any negative elements—as positively as possible.** A policy may have limits; information may be incomplete; the reader may have to satisfy requirements to get a discount or benefit. Make these negatives clear, but present them as positively as possible.

4. **Explain any reader benefits.** Most informative memos need reader benefits. Show that the policy or procedure helps readers, not just the company. Give enough detail to make the benefits clear and convincing. In letters, you may want to give benefits of dealing with your company as well as benefits of the product or policy.

   In a good news message, it's often possible to combine a short reader benefit with a goodwill ending in the last paragraph.

5. **Use a goodwill ending: positive, personal, and forward-looking.** Shifting your emphasis away from the message to the specific reader suggests that serving the reader is your real concern.

Figure 7.2   *A Positive Letter*

**INTERSTATE
FIDELITY
INSURANCE COMPANY**

*100 Interstate Plaza
Atlanta, GA 30301
404-555-5000
Fax: 404-555-5270*

March 8, 2000

Professor Adrienne Prinz
Department of History
Duke University
Durham, North Carolina 27000

Dear Professor Prinz:

Good news   Your appointment as archivist for Interstate Fidelity Insurance has been approved. When you
were in Atlanta in December, you said that you could begin work June 1. We'd like you to start
then if that date is still good for you.   *Tactful*

The Board has outlined the following priorities for your work: *Assumes reader's primary
interest is the job*

*Negative
about lighting
and security
presented
impersonally*

1. Organize and catalogue the archives. You'll have the basement of the Palmer Building for
the archives and can requisition the supplies you need. You'll be able to control heat and
humidity; the budget doesn't allow special lighting or security measures.

Details

2. Prepare materials for a 4-hour training session in October for senior-level managers. We'd
like you to cover how to decide what to send to the archives. If your first four months of
research uncover any pragmatic uses for our archives (like Wells Fargo's use of archives to
teach managers about past pitfalls), include those in the session.

3. Write an article each month for the employee newsletter describing the uses of the archives. When we're cutting costs in other departments, it's important to justify committing
funds to start an archive program.

4. Study the IFI archives to compile information that (a) can help solve current management
problems, (b) could be included in a history of the company, and (c) might be useful to
scholars of business history.

*These
provisions
will appeal
to the
reader*

5. Begin work on a corporate history of IFI. IFI will help you find a publisher and support
the book financially. You'll have full control over the content.   *Salary is
deemphasized
to avoid*

*Negative
that reader
will have to
reapply
presented
as normal
procedure*

Your salary will be $23,000 for six months; your contract can be renewed twice for a total of 18   *implying*
months. You're authorized to hire a full-time research assistant for $8,000 for six months; you'll *that reader*
need to go through the normal personnel request process to request that that money be continued *is "just*
next year. A file clerk will be assigned full-time to your project. You'll report to me. At least for *taking the*
the rest of this calendar year, the budget for the Archives Project will come from my department. *job for the
money"*

Figure 7.2 *A Positive Letter (continued)*

Professor Adrienne Prinz
March 8, 2000
Page 2

IFI offices are equipped with Pentium computers with FoxPro, WordPerfect, and Excel. Is there any software that we should buy for cataloguing or research? Are there any office supplies that we need to have on hand June 1 so that you can work efficiently?

In the meantime,

Goodwill ending

1. Please send your written acceptance right away.

2. Let me know if you need any software or supplies.

3. Send me the name, address, and Social Security number of your research assistant by May 1 so that I can process his or her employment papers.

4. If you'd like help finding a house or apartment in Atlanta, let me know. I can give you the name of a real estate agent.

On June 1, you'll spend the morning in Personnel. Stop by my office at noon. We'll go out for lunch and then I'll take you to the office you'll have while you're at IFI.

Welcome to IFI!

Cordially,

Cynthia Yen

Cynthia Yen
Director of Education and Training

available to the public is an implicit reader benefit; the concern for the reader's needs builds goodwill.

The memo in Figure 7.3 announces a new employee benefit. The first paragraph summarizes the policy. Paragraphs 2–5 give details. Negative elements are in paragraphs 3–5, stated as positively as possible. The last section of the memo gives reader benefits and shows that everyone—even part-timers who are not eligible for reimbursement—will benefit from the new program.

Subject Lines for Informative and Positive Messages

A **subject line** is the title of a document. It aids in filing and retrieving the document, tells readers why they need to read the document, and provides a framework in which to set what you're about to say.

Subject lines are standard in memos. Letters are not required to have subject lines (see Appendix A, Formats for Letters, Memos, and E-mail Messages). However, a survey of business people in the southwest United States found that 68% of them considered a subject line in a letter to be important, very important, or essential; only 32% considered subject lines to be unimportant or only somewhat important.[1]

Figure 7.3 *A Positive Memo*

Memo

January 26, 2000

To: All Crossroads Counselling Center Employees

From: Darlene Bonifas, Director of Human Resources   *DB*

Subject: New Tuition Reimbursement Program   *Good news in subject line and first paragraph*

Starting February 1st, full-time employees who have worked at Crossroads three months or more can be reimbursed for up to $3500 a year for tuition and fees when you take courses related to your current position (including courses needed to keep your licenses), courses that would prepare you for another position you might someday hold at Crossroads, or courses required for a job-related degree program.

You can take the courses at any level: high school, college, or graduate school. You can find a selection of catalogs from nearby schools and colleges in the Office of Human Resources.

How to Apply for the Program   *Headings chunk material and provide good visual impact*

To apply, pick up an application form in the Office of Human Resources, fill it out, and have it signed by your immediate supervisor. Return it to the Office of Human Resources at least two weeks before classes start: your application must be approved before classes start.

How to Get Reimbursed   *Negatives presented as positively as possible*

You'll be reimbursed when you earn a "C" grade or better in the course. Just bring the following documents to the Office of Human Resources:
   1. A copy of the approved application.
   2. An official grade report.
   3. A statement of the tuition and fees paid.

If you are eligible for other financial aid (scholarships, grants, or veterans' benefits), you will be reimbursed for the tuition and fees not covered by that aid, up to $3500 during one calendar year. Reimbursements for undergraduate and basic education programs are currently tax-free.

Goals of the Program

This program will help us stay on top of developments in our field. For example, we're

| **Figure 7.3** | *A Positive Memo (continued)* |

All Employees—New Tuition Reimbursement Program
January 26, 2000
Page 2

*page 2 of memo
doesn't use
letterhead*

working with more and more people who have tested HIV-positive. Some counselors might want to take courses on medical treatments for AIDS. The more we understand about the physical pressures our clients are under, the better we can help them cope with their emotional challenges. Knowing that AIDS leaves patients exhausted may help us understand why someone needs a little extra time or tolerance during an appointment.

Courses about anxiety and stress could help us deal with the increasing number of clients who fear that their jobs will disappear. Perhaps someone would like to take a course in money management or career counseling so that we could offer practical as well as psychological advice. Counselors may want to become registered to administer the MBTI or learn how to use computers to score the MMPI.

Jargon appropriate for the audience

Reader Benefits

Counselors can use this program to earn their doctorates so that they can be the primary psychologist seeing a patient. Having more certified counselors would enable us to enlarge our practice.

Including Benefits for people who are not eligible to participate

But courses don't have to relate to psychology and counselling. Maybe someone would like to learn how to use advanced features in WordPerfect, Access, or Excel. (Could someone learn how to improve our database or chart our client profiles?) Management courses might help us run a tighter ship. And interpersonal courses might sharpen our skills so that we do an even better job of working together to solve problems.

In spite of cutbacks by some insurance providers last fall, Crossroads continues to be financially as well as professionally strong. This program gives us the opportunity to build on our strength as we prepare to help people in Columbus face the challenges of the new millennium.

Goodwill ending

A good subject line meets three criteria: it is specific, concise, and appropriate to the kind of message (positive, negative, persuasive).

Making Subject Lines Specific

The subject line needs to be specific enough to differentiate that message from others on the same subject, but broad enough to cover everything in the message.

Too General:	Training Sessions
Better:	Dates for 2004 Training Sessions
or:	Evaluation of Training Sessions on Conducting Interviews
or:	Should We Schedule a Short Course on Proposal Writing?

Data, Data*

454   Number of documents added to Lexis-Nexis each minute . . .

50%   Percentage of U.S. professionals who repeatedly receive messages that say the same thing . . .

190   Number of messages in all media sent and received daily by the average *Fortune* 1000 office worker

80%   Percentage of information that is filed but never used

150   Hours that the average person spends looking for lost information each year

71%   Percentage of workers who say their main job is tracking down information . . .

7,349,000   Projected increase in the number of URLs between 1997 and 2002

$25,000   Amount that an executive earning $60,000 a year is being paid just to read

*Quoted from "Data, Data," *Inc.*, January 1999, 70.

Making Subject Lines Concise

Most subject lines are relatively short—usually no more than 10 words, often only 3 to 7 words.[2]

Wordy: Survey of Student Preferences in Regards to Various Pizza Factors

Better: Students' Pizza Preferences

or: The Feasibility of a Cassano's Branch on Campus

or: What Students Like and Dislike about Giovanni Pizza

If you can't make the subject both specific and short, be specific.

Making Subject Lines Appropriate for the Pattern of Organization

Since your subject line introduces your reader to your message, it must satisfy the psychological demands of the situation; it must be appropriate to your purposes and to the immediate response you expect from your reader. In general, do the same thing in your subject line that you would do in the first paragraph.

When you have good news for the reader, build goodwill by highlighting it in the subject line. When your information is neutral, summarize it concisely for the subject line.

> Subject: Discount on Rental Cars Effective January 2
>
> Starting January 2, as an employee of Amalgamated Industries you can get a 15% discount on cars you rent for business or personal use from Roadway Rent-a-Car.

> Subject: Update on Arrangements for Videoconference with France
>
> In the last month, we have chosen the participants and developed a tentative agenda for the videoconference with France scheduled for March 21.

Using Reader Benefits in Informative and Positive Messages

Not all informative and positive messages need reader benefits (➤ p. 72).
    You don't need reader benefits when

- You're presenting factual information only.
- The reader's attitude toward the information doesn't matter.
- Stressing benefits may make the reader sound selfish.
- The benefits are so obvious that to restate them insults the reader's intelligence.

    You do need reader benefits when

- You are presenting policies.
- You want to shape readers' attitudes toward the information or toward your organization.
- Stressing benefits presents readers' motives positively.
- Some of the benefits may not be obvious to readers.

Messages to customers or potential customers sometimes include a sales paragraph promoting products or services you offer in addition to the product or service that the reader has asked about. Sales promotion in an informative or positive message should be low-key, not "hard sell."

Reader benefits are hardest to develop when you are announcing policies. The organization probably decided to adopt the policy because it appeared to help the organization; the people who made the decision may not have thought at all about whether it would help or hurt employees. Yet reader benefits are most essential in this kind of message so readers see the reason for the change and support it.

When you present reader benefits, be sure to present advantages *to the reader.* Most new policies help the organization in some way, but few workers will see their own interests as identical with the organization's. Even if the organization saves money or increases its profits, workers will benefit directly only if they own stock in the company, if they're high up enough to receive bonuses, if the savings enables a failing company to avoid layoffs, or if all of the savings goes directly to employee benefits. In many companies, any money saved will go to executive bonuses, shareholder profits, or research and development.

To develop reader benefits for informative and positive messages, use the steps suggested in Chapter 2. Be sure to think about benefits that come from the activity or policy itself, apart from any financial benefits. Does a policy improve the eight hours people spend at work?

Writing the One-Page Memo

Some organizations force writers to be concise by requiring or encouraging one-page memos. In simple situations, a page may be more than you need. Sometimes, careful revising and editing may enable you to cut your memo to a page. When you can't get everything on one page even with careful revision, put the key points on one well-designed page and attach appendices for readers who need more information.

Ending Informative and Positive Letters and Memos

Ending a letter or memo gracefully can be a problem in short informative and positive messages. In a one-page memo where you have omitted details and proof, you can tell readers where to get more information. In long messages, you can summarize your basic point. In persuasive messages, as you'll learn in Chapter 9, you can tell readers what you want them to do. In a short message containing all the information readers need, either write a goodwill paragraph that refers directly to the reader or the reader's organization, or just stop.

Goodwill endings should focus on the business relationship you share with your reader rather than on the reader's hobbies, family, or personal life. When you write to one person, a good last paragraph fits that person so specifically that it would not work if you sent the same basic message to someone else or to a person with the same title in another organization. When you write to someone who represents an organization, the last paragraph can refer to your company's relationship to the reader's organization. When you write to a group (for example, to "All Employees") your ending should apply to the whole group.

Use a paragraph that shows you see your reader as an individual. Possibilities include complimenting the reader for a job well done, describing a reader benefit, or looking forward to something positive that relates to the subject of the message.

**That Reminds Me
of a Story***

The most effective way to give information may be to tell a story.

Sharing stories can guide employees by strengthening the corporate culture. Teresa Lever-Pollary, CEO of the Nightime Pediatrics Clinic in Salt Lake City, asked a consultant to gather stories of employees who went out of their way. The stories, such as one about the nurse who drove a young mother and her sick child home one snowy night, were published as *Nightime Stories*. The stories, Lever-Pollary says, help "people remember what's special about us. My staff now has examples to follow. I think patients are getting better service."

Stories can also communicate complex ideas. Xerox has found that the best way to tap into the expert knowledge of experienced technical repair people is to have them tell stories about their experiences. IBM reassembles global sales teams so that people can respond to, interrupt, and correct each other as they remember how the multiyear deals evolved. Video cameras roll so that later teams can learn about how the process feels when it's going well and what can derail it.

*Based on Thomas A. Stewart, "The Cunning Plots of Leadership," *Fortune,* September 7, 1998, 165.

It's News to Me*

Sometimes, information that's old to you can be new to someone else. During a company retreat of senior executives, Boeing's new chief financial officer, Deborah Hopkins, went to the blackboard to explain some financial basics: profit margins, return on net assets, and inventory turnover. Afterwards, she got dozens of compliments. Some of the senior executives said it was the first time they had understood the concepts.

*Based on Jeff Cole, "New Boeing CFO's Assignment: Signal a Turnaround," *The Wall Street Journal*, January 26, 1999, B1.

In the following examples, a letter answers the question, "When a patient leaves the hospital and returns, should we count it as a new stay?" For one company the answer was that if a patient was gone from the hospital overnight or longer, the hospital should start a new claim when the patient was readmitted.

Weak closing paragraph:	Should you have any questions regarding this matter, please feel free to call me.
Goodwill paragraph:	Many employee-patients appreciate the freedom to leave the hospital for a few hours. It's nice working with a hospital which is flexible enough to offer that option.
Also acceptable:	Omit the paragraph; stop after the explanation.

Some writers end every message with a standard invitation:

If you have questions, please do not hesitate to ask.

That sentence lacks positive emphasis. But revising it to say "feel free to call" is rarely a good idea. Most of the time, the writer should omit the sentence entirely.

Inviting readers to call suggests that you have not answered the question fully. In very complicated situations, it may be simpler to let people call with individual questions. But in simple situations, you can answer the question clearly.

A state agency sent out a memo explaining when the state would pay for the cost of lunch that was included in a conference registration fee. The state would pay for lunch if the conference was out of town. If the conference was in the same town as the employee's office, the employee had to pay for lunch. Either the conference is in the same town or a different town. The answer is simple; no further explanation is necessary.

One of the reasons you write is to save the time needed to tell everyone individually. People in business aren't shrinking violets; they will call if they need help. Don't make more work for yourself by inviting calls to clarify simple messages.

Writing E-Mail Messages

E-mail is an essential tool for millions of workers. Readers read and reply to e-mail quite rapidly. Dealing with 80 to 100 messages in 20 or 30 minutes is normal. Write messages so that readers can deal with them quickly.

As you use e-mail, keep these guidelines in mind:

- Although e-mail feels informal, it is not private, as a conversation might be. Your employer may legally check your messages. And a message sent to one person can be printed out or forwarded to others without your knowledge or consent. Don't be indiscreet on e-mail.

- All the principles of good business writing still apply with e-mail. Remember you-attitude and positive emphasis. Use reader benefits when they're appropriate. Use the pattern of organization that fits the purpose of the message.

- Because e-mail feels like talking, some writers give less attention to spelling, grammar, and proofreading. Many e-mail programs have spell checkers; use them. Check your message for grammatical correctness and to be sure that you've included all the necessary information.

- Reread and proofread your message before sending it out.

E-mail allows you to be a bit playful in language, as Figure 7.4 shows.

Voice Mail Information

Before you make a phone call, think of the information you'll need if you must leave a voice mail message.

- Summarize the purpose of your message in a sentence or two.

- Give your name and phone number early in the message. Speak slowly and distinctly.

- Give the recipient enough information to act.

- Tell when you'll be at your desk to receive a return call.

Subject Lines for E-Mail

Subject lines in e-mail are even more important than those in letters and memos. Subject lines must be specific, concise, and catchy. Some e-mail users get so many messages that they don't bother reading messages if they don't recognize the sender or if the subject doesn't catch their interest. If you have good news to convey, put it in the subject line. Be as brief as you can. The following subject lines would be acceptable for informative and good news e-mail messages:

> Travel Plans for Sales Meeting
> Your Proposal Accepted
> Reduced Prices During February
> Your Funding Request Approved

When you reply to a message, the e-mail system automatically creates a subject line "Re: [subject line of message to which you are responding]." If the subject line is good, that's fine. If it isn't, you may want to create a new subject line. And if a series of messages arises, create a new subject line. "Re: Re: Re: Re: Question" is not an effective subject line.

Format for E-Mail Messages

Most e-mail systems start by asking you to indicate to whom you are sending the message and what the subject line is. The computer puts in the date, time of day, and your name and address automatically. Send yourself an e-mail message so you can see the relationship between what appears on the screen and what the recipient receives.

Putting the reader's name at the beginning of the message isn't necessary, but some people like to do it to make the message more friendly.

You don't need a close such as "Sincerely." But do put your name after your message, since some e-mail systems strip out the automatic header. If you're sending the message through a listserv, put your e-mail address as well, since the header will print the listserv's address, not the address of the individual sender (see Figure 7.4).

E-Mail Etiquette

Follow these guidelines to be a good "netizen":

- Use full caps only to emphasize a single word or two. Putting the whole message in caps is considered as rude as shouting.
- Never send angry messages by e-mail. If you have a conflict with someone, work it out face-to-face, not electronically.
- Send people only messages they need. Send copies to your boss or CEO only if he or she has asked you to.
- Find out how your recipient's system works and adapt your messages to it. Most people would rather get a separate short message on each of several topics, so that the messages can be stored in different mailboxes. But people who pay a fee to download each message may prefer longer messages that deal with several topics.
- When you respond to a message, include only the part of the original message that is essential so that the reader understands your posting.

The Robot Writes*

Good Web sites allow browsers to e-mail someone at the organization. But that can result in hundreds of e-mails a day—all from people who expect fast responses.

A growing number of "robot" programs will generate answers automatically, without any human intervention. The programs look for keywords and can respond to questions written in a conversational style.

Some programs go even further, providing a virtual customer service representative. "Andrette" at Big Science can not only answer questions about the company but also politely say *no* if asked for a date.

*Based on Richard A. Shaffer, "Handling Customer Service on the Web," *Fortune*, March 1, 1999, 204.

Figure 7.4   *A Positive E-Mail Message*

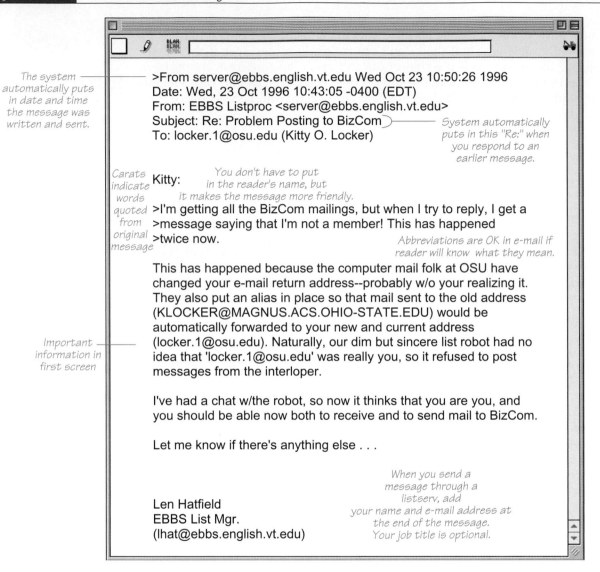

The system automatically puts in date and time the message was written and sent.

>From server@ebbs.english.vt.edu Wed Oct 23 10:50:26 1996
Date: Wed, 23 Oct 1996 10:43:05 -0400 (EDT)
From: EBBS Listproc <server@ebbs.english.vt.edu>
Subject: Re: Problem Posting to BizCom
To: locker.1@osu.edu (Kitty O. Locker)

System automatically puts in this "Re:" when you respond to an earlier message.

Carats indicate words quoted from original message

Kitty:

You don't have to put in the reader's name, but it makes the message more friendly.

>I'm getting all the BizCom mailings, but when I try to reply, I get a
>message saying that I'm not a member! This has happened
>twice now.

Abbreviations are OK in e-mail if reader will know what they mean.

This has happened because the computer mail folk at OSU have changed your e-mail return address--probably w/o your realizing it. They also put an alias in place so that mail sent to the old address (KLOCKER@MAGNUS.ACS.OHIO-STATE.EDU) would be automatically forwarded to your new and current address (locker.1@osu.edu). Naturally, our dim but sincere list robot had no idea that 'locker.1@osu.edu' was really you, so it refused to post messages from the interloper.

Important information in first screen

I've had a chat w/the robot, so now it thinks that you are you, and you should be able now both to receive and to send mail to BizCom.

Let me know if there's anything else . . .

When you send a message through a listserv, add your name and e-mail address at the end of the message. Your job title is optional.

Len Hatfield
EBBS List Mgr.
(lhat@ebbs.english.vt.edu)

Delete the rest. If the quoted material is long, put your response first, then the original material.

- When you compose a message in your word processor and call it up in e-mail, use short line lengths (set the right margin at 2.5 or 3 inches).

 See the BAC Web site for links to sites on e-mail etiquette.

Using E-Mail Effectively

To get the most out of e-mail, learn to use your system's advanced features, such as setting up nicknames or aliases for people you write frequently, creating mailboxes to store messages on various topics, and using attachments to send documents with formatting. Most colleges and universities offer workshops on using e-mail programs.

Electronic greeting cards are fun to send and receive; they build goodwill.
www.hallmarkconnections.com

Varieties of Informative and Positive Messages

Many messages can be informative, negative, or persuasive depending on what you have to say. A transmittal, for example, can be positive when you're sending glowing sales figures or persuasive when you want the reader to act on the information. A performance appraisal is positive when you evaluate someone who's doing superbly, negative when you want to compile a record to justify firing someone, and persuasive when you want to motivate a satisfactory worker to continue to improve. A collection letter is persuasive; it becomes negative in the last stage when you threaten legal action. Each of these messages is discussed in the chapter of the pattern it uses most frequently. However, in some cases you will need to use a pattern from a different chapter.

Transmittals

When you send someone something in an organization, attach a memo or letter of transmittal explaining what you're sending. A transmittal can be as simple as a small yellow Post-it™ note with "FYI"("for your information") written on it, or it can be a separate typed document.

Organize a memo or letter of transmittal in this order:

1. Tell the reader what you're sending.
2. Summarize the main point(s) of the document.
3. Indicate any special circumstances or information that would help the reader understand the document. Is it a draft? Is it a partial document that will be completed later?
4. Tell the reader what will happen next. Will you do something? Do you want a response? If you do want the reader to act, specify exactly what you want the reader to do and give a deadline.

Figure 7.5   *A Transmittal*

100 Barkley Plaza • Denver, CO 80210 • 303.555.4783 • Fax 303.555.4784

October 8, 2000

Mr. Charles Gibney
Personnel Manager
Roydon Interiors
146 East State Street
Denver, CO 80202

Dear Mr. Gibney:

Paragraph one tells reader what is enclosed and summarizes main points.

Here is a copy of the brief we intend to file with the Tenth Circuit Court in support of our position that the sex discrimination charge against Roydon Interiors should be dropped.

Will you please examine it carefully to make sure that the facts it contains are correct? If you have changes to suggest, please call my office by October 22nd, so that we can file the brief by October 24th.

Sincerely,

Last paragraph asks for action by a specific date.

Diana Drew

Diana Drew

Frequently transmittals have important secondary purposes. Consider the writer's purpose in Figure 7.5, a transmittal from a lawyer to her client. The primary purpose of this transmittal is to give the client a chance to affirm that his story and the lawyer's understanding of it are correct. If there's anything wrong, the lawyer wants to know *before* she files the brief. But an important secondary purpose is to build goodwill: "I'm working on your case; I'm earning my fee." The greatest number of complaints officially lodged against lawyers are for the lawyer's neglect—or what the client perceives as neglect—of the client's case.

Confirmations

Many informative messages record oral conversations. These messages are generally short and give only the information shared orally; they go to the other party in the conversation. Start the message by indicating that it is a confirmation, not a new message:

> As we discussed on the phone today, . . .

> As I told you yesterday, . . .

> Attached is the meeting schedule we discussed earlier today.

Be sure to avoid dangling modifiers.

Dangling modifier: Confirming our conversation, your Hot Springs Hot Tub Spa is scheduled for delivery April 12.
(This sentence says that the Spa is doing the confirming.)

Correct: As I told you yesterday, your Hot Springs Hot Tub Spa is scheduled for delivery April 12.

Summaries

You may be asked to summarize a conversation, document, or an outside meeting for colleagues or superiors. (Minutes of an internal meeting are usually more detailed. See Chapter 13 for advice on writing minutes of meetings.)

In a summary of a conversation for internal use, identify the people who were present, the topic of discussion, decisions made, and who does what next.

To summarize a document, start with the main point. Then go on to give supporting evidence or details. In some cases, your audience may also want you to evaluate the document. Should others in the company read this book? Should someone in the company write a letter to the editor responding to this newspaper article?

When you visit a client or go to a conference, you may be asked to share your findings and impressions with other people in your organization. Chronological accounts are the easiest to write but the least useful for the reader. Your company doesn't need a blow-by-blow account of what you did; it needs to know what *it* should do as a result of the meeting.

Summarize a visit with a client or customer in this way:

1. Put the main point from your organization's point of view—the action to be taken, the perceptions to be changed—in the first paragraph.
2. Provide an **umbrella paragraph** to cover and foreshadow the points you will make in the report.
3. Provide necessary detail to support your conclusions and cover each point. Use lists and headings to make the structure of the document clear.

Saving Money Answering Customer Complaints*

Ed Hurston of Wonderwood Corp. says he used to spend an average of $50,000 annually addressing customers' complaints. Then he started asking grumblers this simple question: "How would you like us to handle the situation?" "It's unbelievable what happened when we put it in their hands," says Hurston, the president of the $12 million wood-products manufacturer. "They always tell us something that costs far less than what we'd do." Here's an example: After Wonderwood spent $2,000 replacing an entire picket fence twice for an unhappy customer, the customer still wasn't satisfied. When he was finally asked how he'd like the situation handled, he suggested a $100 solution. Hurston estimates that the company, based in Deland, Fla., now spends less than $2,000 a year addressing customers' complaints.

*Quoted from Stephanie Gruner, "Can We Reduce the Cost of Handling Customers' Complaints?" Inc., December 1997, 148.

In the following example, the revised first paragraph summarizes the sales representative's conclusions after a call on a prospective client:

Original:

On October 10th, Rick Patel and I made a joint call on Consolidated Tool Works. The discussion was held in a conference room, with the following people present:
1. Kyle McCloskey (Vice President and General Manager)
2. Bill Petrakis (Manufacturing Engineer)
3. Garett Lee (Process Engineering Supervisor)
4. Courtney Mansor-Green (Project Engineer)

Revised:

Consolidated Tool Works is an excellent prospect for purchasing a Matrix-Churchill grinding machine. To get the order, we should
1. Set up a visit for CTW personnel to see the Matrix-Churchill machine in Kansas City;
2. Guarantee 60-day delivery if the order is placed by the end of the quarter; and
3. Extend credit terms to CTW.

Thank-You and Congratulatory Notes

Sending a **thank-you note** will make people more willing to help you again in the future. Thank-you letters can be short but must be prompt. They need to be specific to sound sincere.

Congratulating someone can cement good feelings between you and the reader and enhance your own visibility. Again, specifics help.

Avoid language that may seem condescending or patronizing. A journalism professor was offended when a former student wrote to congratulate her for a feature article that appeared in a major newspaper. As the journalist pointed out, the letter's language implied that the writer has more status than the person being praised. The praiser was "quite impressed," congratulated the writer on reaching a conclusion that she had already reached, and assumed that the journalist would have wanted to discuss matters with the praiser. To the reader, "Keep up the good work!" implied that the one cheering her on had been waiting for ages at the finish line.[3]

Adjustments and Responses to Complaints

A study sponsored by Travelers Insurance showed that when people had gripes but didn't complain, only 9% would buy from the company again. But when people did complain—and their problems were resolved quickly—82% would buy again.[4]

When you grant a customer's request for an adjusted price, discount, replacement, or other benefit to resolve a complaint, do so in the very first sentence.

Your Visa bill for a night's lodging has been adjusted to $63. Next month a credit of $37 will appear on your bill to reimburse you for the extra amount you were originally asked to pay.

Thank-you notes can be written on standard business stationery, using standard formats. But one student noticed that his advisor really liked cats and had pictures of them in her office. So he found a cat card for his thank-you note.

Don't talk about your own process in making the decision. Don't say anything that sounds grudging. Give the reason for the original mistake only if it reflects credit on the company. (In most cases, it doesn't, so the reason should be omitted.)

Solving a Sample Problem

Real-life problems are richer and less well defined than textbook problems and cases. But even textbook problems require analysis before you begin to write. Before you tackle the assignments for this chapter, examine the following problem. See how the analysis questions probe the basic points required for a solution. Study the two sample solutions to see what makes one unacceptable and the other one good. Note the recommendations for revision that could make the good solution excellent.[5] The checklist at the end of the chapter (p. 175) can help you evaluate a draft.

Problem

Interstate Fidelity Insurance (IFI) uses computers to handle its payments and billings. There is often a time lag between receiving a payment from a customer and recording it on the computer. Sometimes, while the payment is in line to be processed, the computer sends out additional notices: past-due notices, collection letters, even threats to sue. Customers are frightened or angry and write asking for an explanation. In most cases, if they just waited a little while, the situation would be straightened out. But policyholders are afraid that they'll be without insurance because the company thinks the bill has not been paid.

IFI doesn't have the time to check each individual situation to see if the check did arrive and has been processed. It wants you to write a letter that will persuade customers to wait. If something is wrong and the payment never reached IFI, IFI would send a legal notice to that effect saying the policy would be canceled by a certain date (which the notice would specify) at least 30 days after the date on the original premium bill. Continuing customers always

The Political Uses of Memos*

How the memo is routed is at least as important as what it says. . . . For example, if I put my immediate supervisor's name AND the vice president's name on the top, it means that . . . I have direct access to the VP. If I give the VP a copy but don't indicate that on the supervisor's memo, I am withholding information from my supervisor and asserting that my "real" boss is the vice president. If I want to cooperate with my immediate supervisor, I address the memo to him and allow him to route it—he or she, thereby, gets credit for my activities. . . .

If you author a memo, then you are putting yourself up one or one down with respect to the receivers.

For example, I recently won an award. A peer sent me a memo saying, "Congratulations . . . keep up the fine work," to position himself as a superior. Very irritating. Very effective. He has been promoted. . . .

The simplest way to take credit [for an idea] is to attach your memo ("the attached may be of interest to you") to someone else's work. A slightly more sophisticated technique is to write a memo attaching your name to the idea of someone else or, more honestly, write a memo attaching your name to your own idea before somebody else pirates it.

*Quoted from Carla Butenhoff, "Bad Writing Can Be Good Business," ABCA Bulletin 40, no. 2 (June 1977): 12–13.

get this legal notice as a third chance (after the original bill and the past-due notice).

Prepare a form letter that can go out to every policyholder who claims to have paid a premium for automobile insurance and resents getting a past-due notice. The letter should reassure readers and build goodwill for IFI.

Analysis of the Problem

1. Who is (are) your audience(s)? What characteristics are relevant to this particular message? If you are writing to more than one reader, how do the readers differ?

   Automobile insurance customers who say they've paid but have still received a past-due notice. They're afraid they're no longer insured. Since it's a form letter, different readers will have different situations: in some cases payments did arrive late, in some cases the company made a mistake, in some the reader never paid (check was lost in mail, unsigned, bounced, etc.)

2. What are your purposes in writing?

   To reassure readers: they're covered for 30 days. To inform them they can assume everything is OK *unless* they receive a second notice. To avoid further correspondence on this subject. To build goodwill for IFI: (a) we don't want to suggest IFI is error-prone or too cheap to hire enough people to do the necessary work; (b) we don't want readers to switch companies; (c) we do want readers to buy from IFI when they're ready for more insurance.

3. What information must your message include?

   Readers are still insured. We cannot say whether their checks have now been processed (company doesn't want to check individual accounts). Their insurance will be canceled if they do not pay after receiving the second past-due notice (the legal notice).

4. How can you build support for your position? What reasons or reader benefits will your reader find convincing?

   Computers help us provide personal service to policyholders. We offer policies to meet all their needs. Both of these points would need specifics to be interesting and convincing.

5. What objection(s) can you expect your reader(s) to have? What negative elements of your message must you deemphasize or overcome?

   Computers appear to cause errors. We don't know if the checks have been processed. We will cancel policies if their checks don't arrive.

6. What aspects of the total situation may affect reader response? The economy? The time of year? Morale in the organization? The relationship between the reader and writer? Any special circumstances?

   The insurance business is highly competitive—other companies offer similar rates and policies. The customer could get a similar policy for about the same money from someone else. Most people find that money is tight, so they'll want to keep insurance costs low. Yet the fact that prices are steady or rising means that the value of what they own is higher—they need insurance more than ever.

   Many insurance companies are refusing to renew policies (car, liability, malpractice insurance). These refusals to renew have gotten lots of publicity, and many people have heard horror stories about companies and individuals whose insurance has been canceled or not renewed after a small number of claims. Readers don't feel very kindly toward insurance companies.

People need car insurance. If they have an accident and aren't covered, they not only have to bear the costs of that accident alone but also (depending on state law) may need to place as much as $50,000 in a state escrow account to cover future accidents. They have a legitimate worry.

Discussion of the Sample Solutions

The solution in Figure 7.6 is unacceptable. The red marginal comments show problem spots. Since this is a form letter, we cannot tell customers we have their checks; in some cases, we may not. The letter is far too negative. The explanation in paragraph 2 makes IFI look irresponsible and uncaring. Paragraph 3 is far too negative. Paragraph 4 is too vague; there are no reader benefits; the ending sounds selfish. A major weakness with the solution is that it lifts phrases straight out of the problem; the writer does not seem to have thought about the problem or about the words he or she is using. Measuring the draft against the answers to the questions for analysis suggests that this writer should start over.

The solution in Figure 7.7 is much better. The blue marginal comments show the letter's strong points. The message opens with the good news that is true for all readers. (Whenever possible, one should use the good news pattern of organization.) Paragraph 2 explains IFI's policy. It avoids assigning blame and ends on a positive note. The negative information is buried in paragraph 3 and is presented positively: the notice is information, not a threat; the 30-day extension is a "grace period." Telling the reader now what to do if a second notice arrives eliminates the need for a second exchange of letters. Paragraph 4 offers benefits for using computers, since some readers may blame the notice on computers, and offers benefits for being insured by IFI. Paragraph 5 promotes other policies the company sells and prepares for the last paragraph.

Good Communication Leads to Corporate Success*

Emerson Electronics is a world-class competitor. One way it achieved that status was using effective communication to outline corporate economic goals for employees and to explain why those goals affect jobs, salaries, and survival. Sharing information and shaping attitudes toward it enabled Emerson to excel.

Martin Marietta Government Electronic Systems, a union shop, speeded up information so that changes were communicated within 48 hours of any decision. Once everyone knew what was going on at all times, grievances dropped from 281 a year to just 12. Information creates openness and a sense of trust.

*Based on James L. Gibson, John M. Ivancevich, and James H. Donnelly, *Organizations: Behavior, Structure, Processes* (Burr Ridge, IL: Richard D. Irwin, 1995), 408.

| **Figure 7.6** | *An Unacceptable Solution to the Sample Problem* |

Need date

Dear Customer:

This explanation makes company look bad.

Relax. We got your check.

Not necessarily true. Reread problem.

There is always a time lag between the time payments come in and the time they are processed. While payments are waiting to be processed, the computer with super-human quickness is sending out past-due notices and threats of cancellation.

Too negative

Need to present this positively

Cancellation is not something you should worry about. No policy would be canceled without a legal notice to that effect giving a specific date for cancellation which would be at least 30 days after the date on the original premium notice.

If you want to buy more insurance, just contact your local Interstate Fidelity agent. We will be happy to help you.

This paragraph isn't specific enough to work as a reader benefit. It lacks you-attitude and positive emphasis.

Sincerely,

| **F i g u r e 7.7** | *A Good Solution to the Sample Problem* |

Need date

Dear Customer: *Better: use computer to personalize. Put in name and address of a specific reader*

Your auto insurance is still in effect.   *Good ¶ 1. True for all readers*

Good to treat notice as information, tell reader what to do if it arrives   Past-due notices are mailed out if the payment has not been processed within three days after the due date. This may happen if a check is delayed in the mail or arrives without a signature or account number. When your check arrives with all the necessary information, it is promptly credited to your account.   *Good you-attitude*

Even if a check is lost in the mail and never reaches us, you still have a 30-day grace period. If you do get a second notice, you'll know that we still have not received your check. To keep your insurance in force, just stop payment on the first check and send a second one.

Benefits of using computers   Computer processing of your account guarantees that you get any discounts you're eligible for: multicar, accident-free record, good student. If you have a claim, your agent uses computer tracking to find matching parts quickly, whatever car you drive. You get a check quickly—usually within 3 working days—without having to visit dealer after dealer for time-consuming estimates.   *Better to put in agent's name, phone number*
                                                         Too negative

Need to add benefits of insuring with IFI   Today, your home and possessions are worth more than ever. You can protect them with Interstate Fidelity's homeowners' and renters' policies. Let your local agent show you how easy it is to give yourself full protection. If you need a special rider to insure a personal computer, a coin or gun collection, or a fine antique, you can get that from IFI, too.   *Good specifics*

Whatever your insurance needs—auto, home, life, or health—one call to IFI can do it all.   *Acceptable ending*

Sincerely,

As the red comments indicate, this good solution could be improved by personalizing the salutation and by including the name and number of the local agent. Computers could make both of those insertions easily. This good letter could be made excellent by revising paragraph 4 so that it doesn't end on a negative note and by using more reader benefits. For instance, do computers help agents advise clients of the best policies for them? Does IFI offer good service— quick, friendly, nonpressured—that could be stressed? Are agents well trained? All of these might yield ideas for additional reader benefits.

Summary of Key Points

- Informative and positive messages normally use the following pattern of organization:
  1. Give any good news and summarize the main points.
  2. Give details, clarification, background.
  3. Present any negative elements—as positively as possible.
  4. Explain any reader benefits.
  5. Use a goodwill ending: positive, personal, and forward-looking.

| Checklist | *Checklist for Informative and Positive Messages* |

☐ In positive messages, does the subject line give the good news? In either message, is the subject line specific enough to differentiate this message from others on the same subject?

☐ Does the first paragraph summarize the information or good news? If the information is too complex to fit into a single paragraph, does the paragraph list basic parts of the policy or information in the order in which the memo discusses them?

☐ Is all the information given in the message? [What information is needed will vary depending on the message, but information about dates, places, times, and anything related to money usually needs to be included. When in doubt, ask!]

☐ In messages announcing policies, is there at least one reader benefit for each segment of the audience? Are all reader benefits ones that seem likely to occur in this organization?

☐ Is each reader benefit developed, showing that the benefit will come from the policy and why the benefit matters to this organization? Do the benefits build on the job duties of people at this organization and the specific circumstances of the organization?

☐ Does the message end with a positive paragraph—preferably one that is specific to the readers, not a general one that could fit any organization or policy?

And, for all messages, not just informative and positive ones,

☐ Does the message use you-attitude and positive emphasis?

☐ Is the style easy to read and friendly?

☐ Is the visual design of the message inviting?

☐ Is the format correct?

☐ Does the message use standard grammar? Is it free from typos?

Originality in a positive or informative message may come from

- Creating good headings, lists, and visual impact.
- Developing reader benefits.
- Thinking about readers and giving details that answer their questions and make it easier for them to understand and follow the policy.

- **Letters** go to people in other organizations. **Memos** go to people within your own organization.
- A **subject line** is the title of a document. A good subject line meets three criteria: it's specific; it's reasonably short; and it's adapted to the kind of message (positive, negative, persuasive). If you can't make the subject both specific and short, be specific.
- The subject line for an informative or positive message should highlight any good news and summarize the information concisely.
- Use reader benefits in informative and positive messages when
  - You are presenting policies.
  - You want to shape readers' attitudes toward the information or toward your organization.
  - Stressing benefits presents readers' motives positively.
  - Some of the benefits may not be obvious to readers.
- **Goodwill endings** should focus on the business relationship you share with your reader or the reader's organization. The last paragraph of a message to a group should apply to the whole group.
- Use the analysis questions listed in Chapter 1 to probe the basic points needed for successful informative and positive messages.

Chapter 7

Exercises and Problems

Getting Started

7.1   Memos for Discussion—Introducing a Suggestion System

Your organization has decided to institute a suggestion system. Employees on hourly pay scales will be asked to submit suggestions. (Managers and other employees on salary are not eligible for this program; they are supposed to be continually suggesting ways to improve things as part of their regular jobs.) If the evaluating committee thinks that the suggestion would save money, the employee will receive 10% of the first year's estimated annual savings. If the suggestion won't save money but will improve work conditions, service, or morale, the employee will get a check for $50.

The following memos are possible approaches. How well does each message meet the criteria in the checklist for informative and positive messages?

1.

Subject: Suggestion System (SS)

I want to introduce you to the Suggestion System (SS). This program enables the production worker to offer ideas about improving his job description, working conditions, and general company procedures. The plan can operate as a finely tuned machine, with great ideas as its product.

Operation will begin November 1. Once a week, a designate of SS will collect the ideas and turn them over to the SS Committee. This committee will evaluate and judge the proposed changes.

Only employees listed as factory workers are eligible. This excludes foremen and the rest of supervisory personnel. Awards are as follows:

1. $50 awards will be given to those ideas judged operational. These are awarded monthly.

2. There will be grand prizes given for the best suggestions over the six-month span.

Ideas are judged on feasibility, originality, operational simplicity, and degree of benefit to the worker and company. Evaluation made by the SS Committee is final. Your questions should be channeled to my office.

2.

Subject: Establishment of Suggestion System

We announce the establishment of a Suggestion System. This new program is designed to provide a means for hourly employees to submit suggestions to company management concerning operations and safety. The program will also provide an award system to compensate nonmanagement employees for implemented suggestions.

Here is how the program will work: beginning October 1, suggestions can be submitted by hourly workers to the company on Form 292, which will be furnished to all plants and their departments by October 1st. On the form, the submitting employee should include the suggestion, his or her name, and the department number. The form can be deposited in a suggestion drop box, which will be located near the personnel office in each plant.

Any suggestion dealing with the improvement of operations, safety, working conditions, or morale is eligible for consideration. The award structure for the program will be as follows:

1. For an implemented suggestion which improves safety or efficiency with no associated monetary benefits or cost reduction: $50.00.

2. For an implemented suggestion which makes or saves the company money: 10% of the first year's estimated annual savings or additional revenue.

It is hoped that we will have a good initial and good continuous response from all hourly employees. This year, we are out to try to cut production costs, and this program may be the vehicle through which we will realize new savings and increased revenues. New ideas which can truly increase operational efficiency or cut safety programs will make the company a nicer place for all employees. A safer work environment is a better work environment. If department operations can be made more efficient, this will eventually make everyone's job just a little easier, and give that department and its employees a sense of pride.

3.

Subject: New Employee Suggestion System

Beginning October 1, all of you who are hourly employees of Video Adventures will be able to get cash awards when your suggestions for improving the company are implemented.

Ideas about any aspect of Video Adventures are eligible: streamlining behind-the-counter operations, handling schedule problems, increasing the life of videotapes.

• If your idea cuts costs or increases income (e.g., increasing membership sales, increasing the number of movie rentals per customer), you'll receive 10% of the first year's estimated annual savings.

• If the idea doesn't save money but does improve service, work conditions, or morale, you'll receive a check for $50.

To submit a suggestion, just pick up a form from your manager. On the form, explain your suggestion, describe briefly how it could be implemented, and show how it will affect Video Adventures. Return the completed form in the new suggestion box behind the back counter. Suggestions will be evaluated at the end of each month. Turn in as many ideas as you like!

Think about ways to solve the problems you face every day. Can we speed up the check-in process? Cut paperwork? Give customers faster service? Increase the percentage of customers who bring back their tapes on time? As you serve people at the counter, ask them what they'd like to see at Video Adventures.

Your ideas will keep Video Adventures competitive. Ten years ago, Video Adventures was the only video store on the west side of town. Now there are six other video stores within a two-mile radius, and even the grocery stores rent videotapes. Efficiency, creativity, and service can keep Video Adventures ahead.

Employees whose ideas are implemented will be recognized in the regional Video Adventures newsletter. The award will also be a nice accomplishment to add to any college application or résumé. By suggesting ways to improve Video Adventures, you'll demonstrate your creativity and problem-solving abilities. And you'll be able to share the credit for keeping Video Adventures' reputation as the best video store in town.

7.2   E-Mails for Discussion—Saying Yes to a Subordinate

Today, you get this request from a subordinate.

> Subject: Request for Leave
>
> You know that I've been feeling burned out. I've decided that I want to take a three-month leave of absence this summer to travel abroad. I've got five weeks of vacation time saved up; I would take the rest as unpaid leave. Just guarantee that my job will be waiting when I come back!

You decide to grant the request. The following messages are possible responses. How well does each message meet the criteria in the checklist for informative and positive messages?

1.
> Subject: Re: Request for Leave
>
> I highly recommend Italy. Spend a full week in Florence, if you can. Be sure to visit the Brancacci Chapel—it's been restored, and the frescoes are breathtaking. And I can give you the names of some great restaurants. You may never want to come back!

2.
> Subject: Your Request for Leave
>
> As you know, we are in a very competitive position right now. Your job is important, and there is no one who can easily replace you. However, because you are a valued employee, I will permit you to take the leave you request, as long as you train a replacement before you leave.

3.
> Subject: Your Request for Leave Granted
>
> Yes, you may take a three-month leave of absence next summer using your five weeks of accumulated vacation time and taking the rest as unpaid leave. And yes, your job will be waiting for you when you return!
>
> I'm appointing Garrick to take over your duties while you're gone. Talk with him to determine how much training time he'll need, and let me know when the training is scheduled.
>
> Have a great summer! Let us know every now and then how you're doing!

7.3 Revising a Letter

Your assistant gives you the following letter to sign:

Dear Ms. Hebbar:

I received your request to send a speaker to participate in "Career Day" at King Elementary School next month. I am pleased to be able to send Audrey Lindstrom to speak at your school about her job at the child care center.

Audrey has been working in the child care center for over five years. She trains contracted center personnel on policies and procedures of the department.

Another commitment later that day will make it impossible for her to spend the whole day at your school. She will be happy to spend two hours with your class participating in the event.

Call Audrey to coordinate the time of the program, the expected content, and the age group of the audience.

Your students will see the importance of trained day care providers in our neighborhoods.
Thank you for asking our agency to be part of your school's special event. Our future lies in the hands of today's students.

Sincerely,

This draft definitely needs some work. It lacks you-attitude and positive emphasis, it isn't well organized, and it doesn't have enough details. Though employees in your office call each other by their first names, in a letter to another group, "Ms. Lindstrom" would be more professional than "Audrey." And more information is needed. Exactly when should she show up? Will she be giving a speech (how long?), speaking as a member of a panel, or sitting at a table to answer questions? Will all grade levels be together, or will she be speaking to specific grades? Will all students hear each speaker, or will there be several concurrent speakers from which to choose?

As Your Instructor Directs,

a. Write a memo to your subordinate, explaining what revisions are necessary.

b. Revise the letter.

E-Mail Messages

7.4 Calming an Angry Co-Worker

You're a member of a self-managed team on a factory assembly line. When you check the team's e-mail, you find this message from the factory's Quality Assurance Manager:

Subject: Holes in Your Heads?

Yesterday in the scrap bin I found a casting with three times too many holes in it. How could a machinist make such a mistake? What's going on?

The answer is simple. The extra holes come not from crazy machinists but from crafty ones. Your team uses old machines that aren't computerized. When you make a part on those machines, you have to drill a test piece first to be sure that the alignment and size of the holes are correct. This testing has to be done every time you set up for a new run. Your team has figured out that you can use less material by reusing the test piece until it resembles Swiss cheese, rather than throwing it away after a single testing. Your team is one of the most efficient in the plant, thanks to creative moves like this one.

Write an e-mail response.

7.5   Responding to a Supervisor's Request

You've received this e-mail message from your supervisor:

Subject: Need "Best Practices"

Please describe something our unit does well—ideally something which could be copied by or at least applied to other units. Our organization is putting together something on "Best Practices" so that good ideas can be shared as widely as possible.

Be specific. For example, don't just say "serve customers"—explain exactly what you do and how you do it to be effective. Anecdotes and examples would be helpful.

Also indicate whether a document, a videotape, or some other format would be the best way to share your practice. We may use more than one format, depending on the response.

I need your answer ASAP so that I can send it on to my boss.

Answer the message, describing something that you or others in your unit do well.

7.6   Making Personal Time More Flexible

You're manager of Human Resources at your company. Two weeks ago, you got this e-mail message.

Subject: Flexibility Needed

Higher-up people routinely take time off from work to play golf, coach soccer, or go to school plays. We peons have to fight to stay home with a sick child. It isn't fair. Can you do something about it?

Yesterday, the Executive Committee voted that a change was in order. As long as people tell their supervisors, get their own work done, and aren't out of the office more than a couple of hours a day a couple of times a week, requests for time off will be granted and will be "free"—that is, they won't be deducted from personal or vacation time. But someone who is going to be out all day does have to use sick, personal, or vacation time.

Write an e-mail message to all employees, telling them about the new policy.

7.7   Accepting Suggestions

For years, businesses have asked employees to suggest ways to save money. Your city government has adopted the same program, asking city employees to suggest ways to help balance the city budget. The suggestion committee, which you chair, has voted to adopt five money-saving suggestions.

1. Increase insulation and add weatherstripping around doors and windows to reduce utility bills. Suggested by Lorrie Williams, in Administration.
2. Charge nearby towns and suburbs for sending their police candidates through the city Police Academy. Suggested by Rashad Reed, in Police.
3. Buy a copy machine that does double-sided copies to reduce the amount of paper used. Suggested by Joiwind Ho, in Taxes and Revenue.
4. Cross-train employees so that they can cover for each other during vacations and sick days, reducing the need to hire temporary employees. Suggested by Pat McHenry, in Buildings and Grounds.
5. Use a better grade of paint so that interiors and exteriors need painting less frequently. Suggested by Jason Penn, in Buildings and Grounds.

Each suggester gets $100. The Accounting Department will cut checks the first Monday of next month; checks should reach people in interoffice mail a few days later.

As Your Instructor Directs,

a. Write to one of the suggesters, giving the good news.
b. Write to all employees, announcing the award winners.

Web Pages

7.8   Creating a Human Resources Web Page

As firms attempt to help employees balance work and family life (and as employers become aware that personal and family stresses affect performance at work), Human Resource departments sponsor an array of programs and provide information on myriad subjects. However, some people might be uncomfortable asking for help, either because the problem is embarrassing (who wants to admit needing help to deal with drug or spouse abuse or addiction to gambling?) or because focusing on nonwork issues (e.g., child care) might lead others to think they aren't serious about their jobs. The World Wide Web allows organizations to post information that employees can access privately—even from home.

Create a Web page that could be posted by Human Resources to help employees with one of the challenges they face. Possible topics include

- Appreciating an ethnic heritage.
- Buying a house.
- Caring for dependents: child care, helping a child learn to read, living with teenagers, elder care, and so forth.
- Dealing with a health issue: exercising, having a healthy diet, and so forth.
- Dealing with a health problem: alcoholism, cancer, diabetes, heart disease, obesity, and so forth.
- Dressing for success or dressing for casual days.
- Financial management: basic budgeting, deciding how much to save, choosing investments, and so forth.
- Nourishing the spirit: meditation, religion.
- Getting out of debt.
- Planning for retirement.
- Planning vacations.

- Reducing stress.
- Resolving conflicts on the job or in families.

Assume that this page can be accessed from another of the organization's pages. Offer at least seven links. (More is better.) You may offer information as well as links to other pages with information. At the top of the page, offer an overview of what the page covers. At the bottom of the page, put the creation/update date and your name and e-mail address.

As Your Instructor Directs,

a. Turn in two laser copies of your page(s). On another page, give the URLs for each link.

b. Turn in one laser copy of your page(s) and a disk with the HTML code and .gif files.

c. Write a memo to your instructor identifying the audience for which the page is designed and explaining (a) the search strategies you used to find material on this topic, (b) why you chose the pages and information you've included, and (c) why you chose the layout and graphics you've used.

d. Present your page orally to the class.

Hints:

- Pick a topic you know something about.
- Realize that audience members will have different needs. You could explain the basics of choosing day care or stocks, but don't recommend a specific day care center or a specific stock.
- If you have more than nine links, chunk them in small groups under headings.
- Create a good image of the organization.

Communicating at Work

7.9   Praising Work Done Well

Write a memo to a co-worker (with a copy to the person's supervisor) thanking him or her for helping you or complimenting him or her on a job well done.

7.10   Giving Good News

Write to a customer or client, to a vendor or supplier, or to your boss announcing good news. Possibilities include a product improvement, a price cut or special, an addition to your management team, a new contract, and so forth.

7.11   Recording Information for Other Workers

You have a lot of information in your head. Perhaps you've figured out a machine's quirks; you know a customer's idiosyncrasies; you understand the history of a situation. Write a memo that could be used by a vacation replacement or a new hire who might be asked to fill in for you.

7.12   Easing New Hires' Transition into Your Unit

Prepare a document to help new hires adjust quickly to your unit. You may want to focus solely on work proce-dures; you may also want to discuss aspects of the cor-porate culture.

Letter and Memo Assignments

7.13   Correcting a Misconception

As the Executive Director for a local charity, you've re-ceived an angry letter from a donor:

> According to the *Suburban News*, 89% of the money you raise goes to administrative expenses. Is that true? I always thought you did good work, but now I wonder.
>
> Sincerely,
>
> *Eva Corey*
>
> (Mrs.) Eva Corey

The paper had a major misprint: 89% of the money you raise goes to the work you do; only 11% goes to fund-raising and administrative costs.

As Your Instructor Directs,

a. Write a letter to Mrs. Corey, reassuring her that her donations to your organization indeed go to do good work.

b. Write a letter to the editor of the *Suburban News*, correcting the story.

Hints:

- Pick an organization you know something about.
- Use specifics about what the money supports.

7.14   Reminding Guests about the Time Change

Twice a year in the United States, cities switch to day-light saving time and back again. The time change can be disruptive for hotel guests, who may lose track of the date, forget to change the clocks in their rooms, and miss appointments as a result.

Prepare a form letter to leave in each hotel room re-minding guests of the impending time change. What should guests do?

Write the letter.

Hints:

- Use an attention-getting page layout so readers don't ignore the message.

- Pick a specific hotel or motel chain you know something about.
- Use the letter to build goodwill for your hotel or motel chain. Use specific references to services or features the hotel offers, focusing not on what the hotel does for the reader, but on what the reader can do at the hotel.

7.15   Announcing a 360-Degree Feedback System

Following in the footsteps of Chase Manhattan Bank, Pitney Bowes, and Du Pont, your organization has de-cided to implement a 360-degree feedback system. (See Brian O'Reilly, "360 Feedback Can Change Your Life," *Fortune*, October 17, 1994, 93–100.) Under this system, supervisors and managers will be evaluated not only by their own supervisors (as has always been the case) but also by their peers and subordinates. Everyone will fill out a lengthy, anonymous questionnaire (Are you crisp, clear, and articulate? Abrasive? Spreading yourself too thin? Trustworthy?), including the person being evalu-ated. A computer will tally and graph the results. Then someone from Human Resources will meet with each supervisor or manager to explain how the person's own opinion of himself or herself is or isn't shared by subor-dinates, peer group, and boss. The Human Resources officer will help the employee identify ways to work on two or three of the major shortcomings.

The purpose of this system is to enable people to be more effective supervisors and managers. The system will not replace the existing system of performance evaluations; the results will not be placed in official personnel files.

Companies that use the system find that only one-third of managers produce self-assessments that match the judgments of their co-workers. (One-third rank themselves higher than do their subordinates; one-third rank themselves lower.) Many managers are surprised to find out that they're perceived to be cold and uncaring. Sometimes miscommunication has resulted from different conversational styles; sometimes a behavior that may have worked in earlier circumstances no longer works when the person is a supervisor.

The evaluation focuses on the ways people relate to each other. Companies that use the system report that it improves teamwork and management planning; it does not affect creativity or inventing new products.

As Vice President for Human Resources, write a memo to all employees explaining the system and building support for it.

Hints:

- Pick a business, nonprofit, or government organization you know something about. What does the organization do? How big is it? Has it recently gotten larger or smaller?
- Identify the proportion of people who are supervisors and managers.
- Identify the pressures that supervisors and managers are under. Have these changed recently?
- Identify the concerns that each of the following groups might have:
  a. People who will receive feedback from this system.
  b. Subordinates who will evaluate their superiors.
  c. Superiors who will still need to do performance reviews and recommend raises.
- How does this system relate to the organization's values and culture?
- What external pressures must the organization deal with? How will this system help?

7.16 Announcing an Extension of Health Care Benefits

The Board of Directors of your organization voted at its last meeting to extend health coverage benefits now available to employees with spouses to employees with long-term same-sex partners. (Employees with opposite-sex partners must still marry in order for the partner to receive benefits.)

Currently basic health insurance is $30 a month to cover one additional person and $50 a month to cover two or more additional people. (The employee's own health insurance is currently free.) Optional dental insurance is $10 a month per person (including the employee); an employee must work in the organization for 12 months before the employee or family members are eligible to sign up for dental insurance. Vision insurance is also optional and is $6 a person a month (the employee must pay to be insured, as well as for family members). The fees are subject to change. All three policies have deductibles; some have limits (e.g., the vision insurance pays the first $60 for one pair of glasses or contact lenses every two years). To learn exactly what is and isn't covered, employees can pick up brochures in the Office of Human Resources.

To be eligible, an employee must sign an affidavit in the Office of Human Resources stating that he or she lives with the partner, they intend to stay together, and are responsible for one another. If the relationship ends, the employee is responsible for notifying the Office of Human Resources within 30 days of the date that the partners cease to live together.

As Vice President for Human Resources, write a memo to all employees telling them about the extended benefits. Build support for the policy and for your organization as a good place to work.

Hints:

- Pick an organization you know something about. What does it do? What is its competitive position?
- How many employees does it have? What are their ages? How do their ages affect the kinds of concerns they'll have about health care?
- How easy is it for the organization to recruit qualified employees?
- What is the organization's record on tolerance? In other words, is this simply one more progressive step for an organization that fosters diversity in many forms, or is this a turnaround for a company that has not in the past been sympathetic to people outside the mainstream?
- How tolerant is the general environment in the city or state in which the organization is located?
- What objections might people have to the program—even people who are not homophobic? How can you respond to those objections?
- What advantages to the organization does this benefit provide?
- What advantages to individuals does this benefit provide? (Include individuals whose benefits are not changed!)

7.17   Introducing a Wellness Program

The very best way for a company to save money on health insurance costs is to have healthy employees. Studies show that people who smoke, who are moderate or heavy drinkers, who are overweight, and who do not exercise regularly have significantly higher health care costs: they visit doctors more often, need more prescription drugs, and are hospitalized more often and for longer periods of time. In addition, health costs are also higher for people who do not use seat belts, who indulge in dangerous hobbies like skydiving, and for babies whose mothers do not get adequate prenatal care.

Your company has decided to launch a comprehensive wellness program in an effort to get employees to adopt healthier lifestyles. Employees in your organization pay about 40% of the cost of their health insurance; the organization pays the rest. On January 1 (or July 1) rates are going up, as they have every year for the last nine years. Singles will pay $65 a month; people who also insure a spouse or partner pay $140 a month; the cost for the employee and one child is $130 a month; the family rate is $225 a month.

People who follow good health practices can get several rebates. You'll give a $100 rebate (annually) to each employee who doesn't smoke or use chewing tobacco. An employee who doesn't drink to excess (more than an average of at least 6 ounces of beer or 3 ounces of wine or 1.5 ounces of hard liquor a day) can also get a rebate of $100, as can those who don't use illegal drugs and those whose cholesterol isn't over 150. Employees who exercise at least 30 minutes a day, three times a week will get rebates of $50. Exercise doesn't have to be difficult: walking and gardening count. Other employee rebates are for (1) a waist-to-hip ratio not over 0.8 for women or 0.95 for men: $50; (2) using a seat belt: $25; (3) getting an annual physical: $25. Rebates will not be available until the end of each year. (Spouses and partners get half the rebate amount in each category. There are no discounts for children.)

As part of the wellness program, the company cafeteria and vending machines will offer healthier foods and the company will offer a monthly informational health fair on some aspect of wellness. These parts of the program will begin next month.

Write a memo to all employees informing them about the wellness program and the rates for insurance.

Hints:

- Pick an organization you know something about to use for this message.
- Use your analyses from problems 3.8 and 3.11.
- Much of the program is described negatively. How can you present it positively?
- Specify the date, time, place, and topic of the first health fair and when the new rates start. If the financial program's start is several months away, suggest that people begin to change habits now.
- Is the organization self-insured, or does it buy insurance?
- If the organization saves money, will employees benefit?
- Why don't people already follow healthy practices? What can you do to overcome these objections?
- Saving money may not motivate everyone. Offer benefits that come from following a healthy lifestyle.

7.18   Lining Up a Consultant to Teach Short Courses in Time Management Skills for Telecommuters

As Director of Education and Training you oversee all in-house training programs. Five weeks ago, Diana Hernandez, Vice President for Human Resources, asked you to set up a training course on time management skills for telecommuters. "I'm concerned that working at home presents a whole new set of challenges in managing time. After all, people are supposed to be *working*, not just reading the paper or playing with their kids." After making some phone calls, you tracked down Holly Katona, a management communication professor at a nearby college.

"Yes, I do short courses on time management," she told you on the phone. "The best way to do it is to have three 4-hour sessions, each a week or two apart, so that people can practice skills between sessions and we can work on the obstacles that each participant faces. Each person needs a planning calendar; those run about $50 each. Tuesdays are best for me. I'm willing to work with up to 20 people at a time. Give me some background on the participants. My fee is $300 an hour; I don't charge separately for preparation time."

You told her that you thought three 4-hour sessions would be feasible, but you'd have to get back to her after you got budget approval. You wrote a quick e-mail message to Diana explaining the situation and asking about what the session should cover.

In response, you received this e-mail.

Yes, I'll approve $3,600 for three 4-hour sessions plus $1,000 to cover the cost of the planning calendars plus up to $500 for any other expenses. Remind her to keep all receipts and turn in an itemized list of expenses; we cannot reimburse her if she does not have receipts.

It probably makes sense to start with general time management skills but to focus on dealing with the distractions that working at home presents.

I don't want someone to lecture. I don't want some ivory-tower theorist. We need practical exercises that can help us practice skills that we can put into effect immediately.

Here is a list of 18 people who can attend sessions at 1–5 p.m. for the first three Tuesdays of next month. We've got a good mix of people. If the session goes well, I may want you to schedule additional sessions.

Now you need to write to Professor Katona, giving her the dates and the background on the participants she wants, specifying the financial arrangements, and asking for the information you need. Is she going to buy the planning calendars and bring them with her, or does she want you to order them? If you're buying them, you need ordering information and a Web address or phone number so that you can buy the planners right away.

You also need explain the mechanics of the session. You'll meet in the Conference Room, which has a screen and flip charts. You have an overhead projector, a slide projector, and a laptop computer for showing Power-Point presentations, but you need to reserve these if she wants to use them.

Write to Professor Katona. You don't have to persuade her to come since she's already informally agreed, but you do want her to look forward to the job and to do her best work.

Hints:

· Choose an organization you know something about. Is telecommuting well established at this organization, fairly new, or just about to start?
· How much experience in telecommuting will the participants have had? Will everyone in the session be at the same stage, or will there be a mixture?
· What kinds of work are telecommuters likely to do? What time-management challenges does this work create?
· Check the calendar to get the dates.

7.19 Lining Up a Consultant to Help Workers Deal with Diversity

As Director of Education and Training you oversee all in-house training programs. Five weeks ago, Cameron Jones, Director of Human Resources, asked you to set up a training course on dealing more effectively with fellow workers of the opposite sex and from different cultural, racial, and ethnic backgrounds. After making some phone calls, you tracked down Roberta Lyons, a professor of business communication at a nearby college.

"Yes, I'd be willing to do a session for you," she told you on the phone. "I would want two days with the participants—three would be better. They need time to practice the skills they'll be learning. And they should read the first 60 pages of my book, *Difference as a Source*

of Strength. I'm free Mondays and Tuesdays; I might be able to free up a Wednesday if I had enough notice. I'm willing to work with a group of up to 30 people. Tell me what kinds of groups they work in, what they already know, and what kinds of things you want me to emphasize. My fee is $2,400 a day. Of course, you'd reimburse me for expenses."

You told her you thought a two-day session would be feasible, but you'd have to get back to her after you got budget approval. You wrote a quick memo to Cameron explaining the situation and asking about what the session should cover.

Two weeks ago, you received this memo from him.

I've asked the Veep for budget approval for $4,800 for a two-day session plus no more than $750 for all expenses. I don't think there will be a problem.

You know that many of the women and minorities in our office are at lower levels. We're doing a good job of hiring a diverse workforce, but we may not do an adequate job mentoring people. Some people claim that we have miscommunication between men and women, between blacks and whites, and between recent immigrants and people whose families have been here for a hundred years. All the predictions call for an even more diverse workforce in the coming years.

We do not need someone to preach at us. We know we need to be egalitarian—people here are not consciously prejudiced. But we need to realize that what we say and do could be misinterpreted by people from different backgrounds.

Don't get some ivory-tower theorist. We need practical exercises that can help us practice skills that we can put into effect immediately.

Attached is a list of 28 people who are free Monday and Tuesday of the second week of next month. We've got a good mix of people from different levels and different departments. If the session goes well, I may want you to schedule additional sessions.

Today, you got approval from the vice president to schedule the session and pay Professor Lyons the fee and reimburse her for expenses to a maximum of $750. She will have to keep all receipts and turn in an itemized list of expenses to be reimbursed; you cannot reimburse her if she does not have receipts.

You also need to explain the mechanics of the session. You always have the sessions at a downtown hotel; you've tentatively reserved the Lakota Room, which can be divided into smaller rooms for small group exercises. It has a screen and overhead projector; if she wants anything else, you can provide it but you'll need to know what she needs. You can't get the book to participants in time unless she gives you a phone number to call to order 28 copies quickly.

Write to Professor Lyons. You don't have to persuade her to come since she's already informally agreed, but you do want her to look forward to the job and to do her best work.

Hints:

- Choose an organization you know something about.
- What different racial, ethnic, and cultural groups do its employees come from?
- Does the organization have a long record of helping employees communicate and cooperate with each other, or will Professor Lyons have to overcome a good deal of resistance?
- Why is it especially important for people in this organization to communicate well with each other? Why is it important that both sexes and all groups be given an equal opportunity to excel?
- Check the calendar to get the dates. If there's any ambiguity about what "the second week of next month" is, call Cameron to check.

7.20   Answering an International Inquiry

Your business, government, or nonprofit organization has received the following inquiries from international correspondents. (You choose the country the inquiry is from.)

1. Please tell us about a new product, service, or trend so that we can decide whether we want to buy, license, or imitate it in our country.

2. We have heard about a problem [technical, social, political, or ethical] that occurred in your organization. Could you please tell us what really happened and estimate how it is likely to affect the long-term success of the organization?

3. Please tell us about college programs in this field. We are interested in sending some of our managers to your country to complete a college degree.

4. We are considering setting up a plant in your city. We have already received adequate business information. However, we would also like to know how comfortable our nationals will feel. Do people in your city speak our language? How many? What opportunities exist for our nationals to improve their English? Does your town already have people from a wide mix of nations? Which are the largest groups?

5. Our organization would like to subscribe to an English-language trade journal. Which one would you recommend? Why? How much does it cost? How can we order it?

As Your Instructor Directs,

a. Answer one or more of the inquiries. Assume that your reader either reads English or can have your message translated.

b. Write a memo to your instructor explaining how you've adapted the message for your audience.

Hints:

· Even though you can write in English, English may not be your reader's native language. Write a letter that can be translated easily.

· In some cases, you may need to spell out background information that might not be clear to someone from another country.

7.21 Responding to a Customer Complaint

As a customer service representative for Gerber Products, you've been asked to write a form letter that can be sent to parents who write asking that sugar and starch be taken out of baby foods. You've already removed sugar and starch from 42 kinds of baby foods; when the change is complete, 121 of your 190 products will be free of added starch and sugar.

Gerber is working to make sure that the new formulations still taste good. For example, your researchers learned that hand-peeling bananas and removing the bitter strings on the fruit makes a sweeter mash that babies like even without added sugar.

Write a form letter. Assume that your computer program will put in the reader's name and inside address and print each letter individually.

Source: Based on "Gerber Bows to Moms' Pleas," *Business Week*, July 8, 1996, 42.

7.22 Announcing a Premium Holiday

Rather than paying fees to an insurer, your company is self-insured. That is, you set aside corporate funds to pay for medical bills. If claims are light, the company saves money.

Employees pay a monthly fee for part of the amount of their health insurance. However, with one month to go in the fiscal year, you have more than enough set aside to cover possible costs. You're going to pass along some of the savings to employees (who, by staying healthy, have kept medical costs down). Next month will be a "premium holiday." You will not deduct the monthly premium from employees' checks. As a result, they will have a slightly higher take-home pay next month. The holiday is just for one month; after it, the premium for health insurance will again be deducted each month.

Write a memo to all employees.

7.23 Announcing a Center for Sick Children

Your company has subsidized an on-site day care center for children from infants to age six for several years. However, until now, this center, like most day care centers, has not accepted sick children. A national survey showed that 82% of working parents said they missed days at work, were late, left early, or used work time to deal with child care problems.

So that parents don't have to stay home when their children are sick, your company-subsidized day care center will open a "Sniffles and Snuggles" room for mildly sick children 12 and under. A student nurse or pediatrician will staff the room. The program will begin on the 15th of next month. Any worker can use the service, even if the child is not enrolled in the day care center. Sick children will stay in bed, watch videos, or play quiet games. No more than six sick children will be accepted on any one day.

Parents whose children already attend the center will pay no additional fee if the child is ill. Parents whose children do not attend the center must preregister to use this service and pay $20 a day (the fee includes meals and snacks).

On days when there are no sick children, the sickroom caregivers will work with children in the regular day care program.

Write a memo to all employees, announcing the change.

Hints:

· What proportion of your employees have small children? How can you make people without small children see this as a good use of company funds?

· Why do people need to be at their desks, even if a child is ill?

7.24 Sending Tapes to a Customer

Two months ago, your business school sponsored a colloquium with many local and out-of-town business people. A highlight of the colloquium was small group discussions. The discussions were taped, and people could order tapes and transcripts.

Some of the tapes turned out well: "Ethics in Small Business," "How the Internet Is Changing Business," and "When Your Business Partner Is Your Spouse." But the audiotapes of "Valuing Diversity" and "Small Businesses Can Be Exporters Too" didn't turn out well. You haven't been able to transcribe them, and the quality isn't good enough to distribute.

Write to Paul Cambiaso. You're enclosing the tape on the Internet that he ordered. But he also ordered the tape on diversity. Since it isn't available, you're sending him a check of $12.62 to reimburse him. He's one of several people you have to write. He has a local address, but you don't know him.

7.25   Summarizing *The Wall Street Journal*

Today, your in-basket contains this message from your boss:

> As you know, I'm leaving tomorrow for a vacation in Egypt. While I'm gone, will you please scan *The Wall Street Journal* every day and summarize any articles that are relevant to our business? I'd like your summary in hard copy on my desk when I return.

As Your Instructor Directs,

a. Scan *The Wall Street Journal* for one week, two weeks, or until you find three to five relevant articles for the company you have chosen.

b. Summarize the articles in a memo.

c. Compare summaries with a small group of students. Do summaries of the same article for different organizations focus on different points?

d. Present one of your summaries to the class.

Hints:

· Pick an organization you know something about. If the organization is large, focus on one division or department.

· Provide an overview to let your boss know whether the articles you've summarized are on a single topic or on several topics.

· Show how each article relates to the organization.

· Give the full citation (see Chapter 14) so that it's easy to track down articles if the boss wants to see the original.

7.26   Evaluating Web Pages

Today you get this e-mail from your boss:

> Subject: Evaluating Our Web Page
>
> Our CEO wants to know how our Web page compares to those of our competitors. I'd like you to do this in two steps. First, send me a list of your criteria. Then give me an evaluation of two of our competitors' and of our own pages. I'll combine your memo with others on other Web pages to put together a comprehensive evaluation for the next Executive Meeting.

As Your Instructor Directs,

a. List the generic criteria for evaluating a Web page. Think about the various audiences for the page and the content that will keep them coming back, the way the page is organized, how easy it is to find something, the visual design, and the details, such as a creation/update date.

b. List criteria for pages of specific kinds of organizations. For example, a nonprofit organization might want information for potential and current donors, volunteers, and clients. A financial institution might want to project an image both of trustworthiness and as a good place to work.

c. Evaluate three Web pages of similar organizations. Which is best? Why?

7.27   Writing a Thank-You Letter

Write a thank-you letter to someone who has helped you achieve your goals.

As Your Instructor Directs,

a. Turn in a copy of the letter.

b. Mail the letter to the person who helped you.

c. Write a memo to your instructor explaining the choices you made in writing the thank-you letter.

7.28   Evaluating Your Supervisor

Your organization uses 360-degree evaluation (see problem 7.15), and you must write an evaluation of your department head, Jon Miller. You've been on the job only two months, and you haven't dealt much with Jon directly. But you have had three memorable contacts with him.

- You reported to your first day of work with three other new hires. It happened that the four of you included both sexes and four different races. When Jon welcomed you to the department, his first words were, "Well, HR must have won the diversity sweepstakes!"
- Three weeks ago, an aunt to whom you were very close died. Even though you hadn't yet accumulated any personal or vacation time, Jon let you take off the time you needed with pay.
- At the last department meeting, Jon asked Carole Swales, a young woman with blonde hair, to read a document to the group. The document turned out to be a list of dumb-blonde jokes. Carole seemed

embarrassed but read the jokes. Everyone in the group seemed uncomfortable, but no one said anything directly. People did show resistance by saying the punch lines (the jokes were old) and not laughing. Jon, however, seemed to think the whole thing was hilarious. This was the first item in an hour-long meeting (for which there was no agenda); the meeting never really recovered, and from your admittedly novice position, little seemed to be accomplished.

You are assured that the evaluation will be anonymous; managers will get a summary of what was said, perhaps with quotations from evaluations but with no evaluation quoted in its entirety. The materials that explain the process stress that it is important to identify both strong areas and areas that need improvement.

As Your Instructor Directs,

a. Write the evaluation.
b. Write a memo to your instructor explaining the ethical choices you made.

7.29   Writing a Job Description

Your unit has more business than it can handle, and you're authorized to hire additional staff. Previous searches at advanced levels have rarely been successful, but you've had good luck bringing in entry-level people and teaching them what they need to know. Three groups in your town have higher-than-average unemployment: Russian immigrants, African Americans, and Hispanics. The Russian immigrants are quite recent; few of them speak English. But their sponsors say that they are very willing to learn. The unemployed African Americans and Hispanics may not have had experience with computers. You could write the job description so that members of all three of these groups could compete equally, and people in all three groups need jobs. You also know some specific individuals you'd like to hire: Last summer you had two excellent interns, both of

whom have good communication skills and both of whom (after a summer of training) have relevant computer experience. And you know that your supervisor's nephew is finishing college and looking for a job. He's majored in marketing and has been a member of the school's basketball team. Interviews on TV and in the local paper suggest he isn't articulate. Your supervisor hasn't put any explicit pressure on you to hire him, but you do get regular updates on his job hunt when you see your supervisor.

As Your Instructor Directs,

a. Write a job description for an entry-level job. Pick an organization you know something about.
b. Write a memo to your instructor explaining the ethical choices you made.

7.30   Announcing a Corporate Chaplain

To provide emotional support to employees, your company has hired a part-time corporate chaplain. Elizabeth Singleton is an ordained Methodist minister, but her work will be nondenominational. She'll come to your company four afternoons a week to be available to talk with employees about personal and professional problems. She will offer caring and confidentiality; nothing anyone says to her will be passed on to anyone else in the company without explicit permission. Employees will not have to pay for conversations with her.

Write a memo to all employees.

Hints:

- Choose an organization you know something about.

- Think about the ages of your employees and the kinds of problems they're likely to face.
- What percentage of your employees participate in organized religion?
- What is the general attitude in the community and in your workplace to personal problems and crises?
- How can you show all employees that this appointment is a good use of company funds?

Source: Problem inspired by Edward O. Welles, "Chaplain for a New Economy," *Inc.*, November 1997, 68–77; and Emma Jean Ghee Leche, "Organizational Spirituality: A New Construct for Organizational Communication," Association for Business Communication Annual Conference, San Antonio, TX, November 11–14, 1998.

8

Negative
Messages

Subject Lines for Negative Messages
Organizing Negative Letters
Organizing Negative Memos
- Giving Bad News to Superiors
- Giving Bad News to Peers and Subordinates

The Parts of a Negative Message
- Buffers
- Reasons
- Refusals
- Alternatives
- Endings

Tone in Negative Messages
Alternate Strategies for Negative Messages
- Recasting the Situation as a Positive Message
- Recasting the Situation as a Persuasive Message
- Humor in Negative Messages

Writing Negative E-Mail Messages
Varieties of Negative Messages
- Rejections and Refusals
- Disciplinary Notices and Negative Performance Appraisals
- Layoffs and Firings

Solving a Sample Problem
- Problem
- Analysis of the Problem
- Discussion of the Sample Solutions

Summary of Key Points

Negative Messages

Rajani J. Kamath

Leadership Consultant, Amex Canada

www.americanexpress.com/canada/index.html

A specialist in Employee Communications, Rajani Kamath leads the employee satisfaction, change management, and communication efforts for the Card Operations business at Amex Canada. Amex Canada Inc., a wholly owned subsidiary of American Express Travel Related Services Company, is a leading provider of travel services in Canada and helps companies manage their business and travel expenses.

D elivering bad news is one of the most difficult tasks a leader may be asked to perform. When employee expectations do not match reality, dysfunctional behavior may result. To reduce the potential for dysfunctional behavior, bad news should be communicated openly and honestly, despite how difficult the news may be for the employees to hear.

Preparation is required to effectively communicate bad news to employees so they understand the reasons for a decision and how it affects them. Be able to answer the following key questions:

- What is the big picture? Why is the change needed?
- What is the purpose of the change?
- How does the bad news relate to corporate/business objectives?
- How will the bad news affect employees, customers, and shareholders?

> ❝ Bad news should be communicated openly and honestly, despite how difficult the news may be for the employees to hear. ❞

In 1998, a decision was made to eliminate the third shift (12 am to 8 am) in one of our departments due to a reduction in workflow. We needed to communicate this information not only to the nearly 80 employees who would be directy affected but also to people who would be indirectly affected. Otherwise, rumors would run rampant. Everyone needed to hear the bad news at about the same time.

The department leaders met face-to-face with the third-shift employees to inform them of the organizational decision. The leaders communicated the bad news openly and honestly. The face-to-face format allowed employees to ask questions and voice their concerns immediately. Whenever possible, third-shift employees were reassigned to positions in other departments.

Management teams in other departments then sent a memo about the reorganization to all other employees.

Well planned, honest communication paid dividends because the employees had a clear understanding for the reasons behind the decision and how the decision would affect them.

Open and honest communication, good or bad, is the key to business integrity and success.

The Necessary Negative*

His five Seattle restaurants were losing money. If he closed his newest restaurant—his biggest money-loser—he'd have to repay immediately the $1 million he'd borrowed to open it. So he decided to eliminate the central office and give individual managers 100% power and responsibility: 100% PAR.

He announced the new program—and the layoffs—on what he called "Just-Do-It-Day." He prepared packets for managers, employees, suppliers, bankers, and the press explaining the restructuring, the new reward structure, and new menus and promotional plans. He drove to every restaurant to explain the plan and left copies for employees. He mailed packets to suppliers, bankers, and the press. And he met with 17 people to tell them that they were losing their jobs.

In each conversation, the owner explained his thinking and offered severance pay. Telling them wasn't easy. But it saved the company. And today, all five restaurants are profitable. The former money-loser—Sharps Fresh Roasting restaurant—is now doing so well that it has been franchised.

*Based on Timothy W. Firnstahl, "The Center-Cut Solution," *Harvard Business Review*, May–June 1993, 62–71.

I n a **negative message,** the basic information we have to convey is negative; we expect the reader to be disappointed or angry.

Negative messages include rejections and refusals, announcements of policy changes that do not benefit customers or consumers, requests the reader will see as insulting or intrusive, negative performance appraisals, disciplinary notices, and product recalls or notices of defects.

A negative message always has several purposes:

Primary purposes:

To give the reader the bad news.

To have the reader read, understand, and accept the message.

To maintain as much goodwill as possible.

Secondary purposes:

To build a good image of the writer.

To build a good image of the writer's organization.

To reduce or eliminate future correspondence on the same subject so the message doesn't create more work for the writer.

In many negative situations, the writer and reader will continue to deal with each other. Even when further interaction is unlikely (for example, when a company rejects a job applicant or refuses to renew a customer's insurance), the firm wants anything the reader may say about the company to be positive or neutral rather than negative.

Some messages that at first appear to be negative can be structured to create a positive feeling. Even when it is not possible to make the reader happy with the news we must convey, we still want readers to feel that

- They have been taken seriously.
- Our decision is fair and reasonable.
- If they were in our shoes, they would make the same decision.

Subject Lines for Negative Messages

When you write to superiors, use a subject line (p. 159) that focuses on solving the problem.

> Subject: Improving Our Subscription Letter

When you write to peers and subordinates, put the topic (but not your action on it) in the subject line.

> Subject: Status of Conversion Table Program
>
> Due to heavy demands on our time, we have not yet been able to write programs for the conversion tables you asked for.

Use a negative subject line in e-mail messages.

Subject: Delay in Converting Tables

Never Say *No**

In some cultures, it's rude to say *no*.

Japanese prefer to avoid direct confrontations. Changing the subject—even to something irrelevant—apologies, and silence are ways to avoid saying *no*.

When Japanese businessmen write rejection letters, they begin with buffers and offer reasons, apologies, and appreciation.

To avoid saying *no*, Czechs and Slovaks may say "We will see."

In Hungary, it is considered impolite to say *no* directly to a social equal or superior. Someone who doesn't want to do something may give a series of excuses, until the other person realizes that he or she should stop asking.

**Based on Shoji Azuma, "Rejection Strategy in Business Japanese," Association for Business Communication Annual Meeting, Orlando, FL, November 1–4, 1995; and Yale Richmond, *From Da to Yes: Understanding the East Europeans* (Yarmouth, ME: Intercultural Press, 1995), 89, 110.

Use a negative subject line in letters when you think readers may ignore what they think is a routine message.

The best subject line for negative e-mail messages depends on whether you're refusing a request or initiating the negative. When you say *no* to an e-mail request, just hit "reply" and use "Re:" plus whatever the original subject line was for your response. When you write a new message, you will have to decide whether to use the negative in the subject line. The subject line should contain the negative when

- The negative is serious. Many people do not read all their e-mail messages. A neutral subject line may lead the reader to ignore the message.
- The reader needs the information to make a decision or act.
- You report your own errors (as opposed to the reader's).

Thus the following would be acceptable subject lines in e-mail messages:

Subject: We Lost McDonald's Account

Subject: Power to Be Out Sunday, March 8

Subject: Error in Survey Data Summary

When you write to people whom you know well, exaggerated subject lines are acceptable:

Subject: Gloom, Despair, and Agony

In other situations, a neutral subject line is acceptable.

Subject: Results of 360° Performance Appraisals

Organizing Negative Letters

The first pattern in Figure 8.1 helps writers maintain goodwill.

Figure 8.2 illustrates how the basic pattern for negative messages can be used. This letter omits the reason, probably because the change benefits the company, not the customer. Putting the bad news first (though pairing it immediately with an alternative) makes it more likely that the recipient will read the letter. If this letter seemed to be just a routine renewal, or if it opened with the good news that the premium was lower, few recipients would read the letter carefully, and many would not read it at all. Then, if they had accidents and found that their coverage was reduced, they'd blame the company for not communicating clearly. Emphasizing the negative here is both good ethics and good business.

Organizing Negative Memos

The best way to organize a negative memo depends on whether you're writing to a superior or to a peer or subordinate and on the severity of the negative information.

Giving Bad News to Superiors

Your superior expects you to solve minor problems by yourself. But sometimes, solving a problem requires more authority or resources than you have. When you give bad news to a superior, also recommend a way to deal with the

Figure 8.1   *How to Organize Negative Messages*

Negative letters	Negative memos to superiors	Negative memos to peers and subordinates
1. **When you have a reason that readers will understand and accept, give the reason before the refusal.** A good reason prepares the reader to expect the refusal.	1. **Describe the problem.** Tell what's wrong, clearly and unemotionally.	1. **Describe the problem.** Tell what's wrong, clearly and unemotionally.
2. **Give the negative information or refusal just once, clearly.** Inconspicuous refusals can be missed altogether, making it necessary to say *no* a second time.	2. **Tell how it happened.** Provide the background. What underlying factors led to this specific problem?	2. **Present an alternative or compromise, if one is available.** An alternative not only gives readers another way to get what they want but also suggests that you care about readers and helping them meet their needs.
3. **Present an alternative or compromise, if one is available.** An alternative not only gives readers another way to get what they want but also suggests that you care about readers and helping them meet their needs.	3. **Describe the options for fixing it.** If one option is clearly best, you may need to discuss only one. But if the reader will think of other options, or if different people will judge the options differently, describe all the options, giving their advantages and disadvantages.	3. **If possible, ask for input or action.** People in the audience may be able to suggest solutions. And workers who help make a decision are far more likely to accept the consequences.
4. **End with a positive, forward-looking statement.**	4. **Recommend a solution and ask for action.** Ask for approval so that you can go ahead to make the necessary changes to fix the problem.	

problem. Turn the negative message into a persuasive one. See the middle column in Figure 8.1.

Giving Bad News to Peers and Subordinates

When you must pass along serious bad news to peers and subordinates, use the variation in the last column in Figure 8.1.

No serious negative (such as being downsized or laid off) should come as a complete surprise. Managers can prepare for possible negatives by giving full information as it becomes available. It is also possible to let the people who will be affected by a decision participate in setting the criteria. Someone who has bought into the criteria for awarding cash for suggestions or retaining workers is more likely to accept decisions using such criteria. And in some cases, the synergism of groups may make possible ideas that management didn't think of or rejected as "unacceptable." Some workplaces, for example, might decide to reduce everyone's pay slightly rather than laying off some individuals. To avoid firing workers, Scherer Brothers Lumber in Minneapolis, Minnesota, saved money by temporarily cutting top officers' pay 25%, eliminating fresh flowers on receptionists' desks, and no longer buying professional sports tickets.[1]

When the bad news is less serious, as in Figure 8.3, use the pattern for negative letters unless your knowledge of the reader(s) suggests that another pattern will be more effective. For example, in some organizations each person takes the Myers-Briggs Personality Inventory and puts a sign up indicating his or her "type." In such an organization, someone sending a negative message to a "feeling type" might want to delay the negative by using a buffer (a neutral or positive sentence) even though the organization's discourse community (**⊃** p. 62) as a whole favored directness.

For memos, the context of communication is crucial. The reader's reaction is influenced by the following factors:

Figure 8.2   *A Negative Letter*

Vickers
Insurance Company

3373 Forbes Avenue
Rosemont, PA 19010
(215) 572-0100

Negative information highlighted so reader won't ignore message

Liability Coverage Is Being Discontinued— Here's How to Replace It!

Negative

Alternative

Dear Policyholder:

Negative

Positive information underlined for emphasis

When your auto insurance is renewed, it will no longer include liability coverage unless you select the new Assurance Plan. Here's why.

Liability coverage is being discontinued. It, and the part of the premium which paid for it, will be dropped from all policies when they are renewed.

This could leave a gap in your protection. But you can replace the old Liability Coverage with Vickers' new Assurance Plan.

No reason is given. The change probably benefits the company rather than the reader, so it is omitted.

Alternative

With the new Assurance Plan, you receive benefits for litigation or awards arising from an accident--regardless of who's at fault. The cost for the Assurance Plan at any level is based on the ages of drivers, where you live, your driving record, and other factors. If these change before your policy is renewed, the cost of your Assurance Plan may also change. The actual cost will be listed in your renewal statement.

To sign up for the Assurance Plan, just check the level of coverage you want on the enclosed form and return it in the postage-paid envelope within 14 days. You'll be assured of the coverage you select.

Forward-looking ending emphasizes reader's choice

Sincerely,

C. J. Morgan

C. J. Morgan
President

Alternative

P.S. The Assurance Plan protects you against possible legal costs arising from an accident. Sign up for the Plan today and receive full coverage from Vickers.

- Do you and the reader have a good relationship?
- Does the organization treat people well?
- Have readers been warned of possible negatives?
- Have readers "bought into" the criteria for the decision?
- Do communications after the negative build goodwill?

Figure 8.3   *A Negative Memo to Subordinates*

Memo

**Board of County Commissioners
Olentangy County, Nebraska**

Date: January 10, 2000

To: All Employees

From: Floyd E. Loer, Dorothy A. Walters, and Stewart Mattson

Subject: Accounting for Work Missed Due to Bad Weather

Reason

As you know, Olentangy County Services are always open for our customers, whatever the weather. Employees who missed work during the snowstorm last week may count the absence as vacation, sick day(s), or personal day(s).

Refusal, stated as positively as possible

Hourly workers who missed less than a day have the option of taking the missed time as vacation, sick, or personal hours or of being paid only for the hours they worked.

One small positive

Approval of vacation or personal days will be automatic; the normal requirement of giving at least 24 hours' notice is waived.

Goodwill ending

Thanks for all the efforts you have made to continue giving our customers the best possible service during one of the snowiest winters on record.

The Parts of a Negative Message

This section provides more information about wording each part of a negative message.

Buffers

Traditionally, textbooks recommended that negative messages open with buffers. A **buffer** is a neutral or positive statement that allows you to delay the negative. Since recent research suggests that buffers do not make readers respond more positively,[2] and since good buffers are very hard to write, the standard patterns for negative messages no longer include them for every message. However, in special situations, you may want to use a buffer.

To be effective, a buffer must put the reader in a good frame of mind, not give the bad news but not imply a positive answer either, and provide a natural transition to the body of the letter. The kinds of statements most often used as buffers are good news, facts and chronologies of events, references to enclosures, thanks, and statements of principle.

1. Start with any good news or positive elements the letter contains.

> Starting Thursday, June 26, you'll have access to your money 24 hours a day at First National Bank.

Letter announcing that the drive-up windows will be closed for two days while automatic teller machines are installed

2. State a fact or provide a chronology of events.

> As a result of the new graduated dues schedule—determined by vote of the Delegate Assembly last December and subsequently endorsed by the Executive Council—members are now asked to establish their own dues rate and to calculate the total amount of their remittance.

Announcement of a new dues structure that will raise most members' dues

3. Refer to enclosures in the letter.

> Enclosed is a new sticker for your car. You may pick up additional ones in the office if needed. Please *destroy* old stickers bearing the signature of "L.S. LaVoie."

Letter announcing increase in parking rental rates

4. Thank the reader for something he or she has done.

> Thank you for scheduling appointments for me with so many senior people at First National Bank. My visit there March 14 was very informative.

Letter refusing a job offer

5. State a general principle.

> Good drivers should pay substantially less for their auto insurance. The Good Driver Plan was created to reward good drivers (those with five-year accident-free records) with our lowest available rates. A change in the plan, effective January 1, will help keep those rates low.

Letter announcing that the company will now count traffic tickets, not just accidents, in calculating insurance rates—a change that will raise many people's premiums

Some readers will feel betrayed by messages whose positive openers delay the central negative point. Therefore, use a buffer only when the reader (individually or culturally) values harmony or when the buffer serves another purpose. For example, when you must thank the reader somewhere in the letter, putting the "thank you" in the first paragraph allows you to start on a positive note.

Buffers are hard to write. Even if you think the reader would prefer to be let down easily, use a buffer only when you can write a good one.

Reasons

Research shows that readers who described themselves as "totally surprised" had much more negative feelings and described their feelings as being stronger

Negative Messages to Customers*

I only use buffers when they mean something. Let's face it, most people see right through buffers. The real reason to use one is to save face, to be nice, or for other cultural reasons—important, but issues of style, not substance.

I'm a firm believer in giving the real reason for doing something, unless the reason is too technical or creates liabilities for the business. Sometimes it's enough to give the facts and let the reader draw the conclusions.

If disclosure creates potential liabilities, or is too complex, or will create a firestorm of negative reaction, you've got to think hard. Fortunately, only the rare negative message falls into those categories. Most negative events are temporary, and very few, if any, mean a meltdown of your business or your career. Most customers and employees know you have a business to run and that you need to make and implement business decisions.

*Quoted from statement by Karl P. Keller, Vice President, First Chicago NBD Investments, to Kitty Locker, April 8, 1997.

The Best Negative Is No Surprise*

In the 1990s, Ford Motor Co. downsized, closing the venerable Thunderbird factory and laying off thousands of workers. Ford was able to do this without union strife—by talking about plans far in advance.

Ford's CEO and the United Auto-workers' vice president met for breakfast every other month. Ford shared sensitive information and sought union input. When the Thunderbird factory closed, the union knew six months ahead of time (not the mere 60 days required by law). The union negotiated a hefty bonus for workers who moved to a Ford truck plant in another state.

According to industry analysts, Ford's honesty about upcoming negatives not only averts costly strikes but also contributes to its workers' high productivity.

*Based on "If Ford Can Do It, Why Can't GM?" *Business Week*, June 29, 1998, p. 36.

than did those who expected the refusal.[3] A clear and convincing reason prepares the reader for the refusal, resulting in readers who find it easier to accept the negative.

The following reason is inadequate.

Weak reason: The goal of the Knoxville CHARGE-ALL Center is to provide our customers faster, more personalized service. Since you now live outside the Knoxville CHARGE-ALL service area, we can no longer offer you the advantages of a local CHARGE-ALL Center.

If the reader says, "I don't care if my bills are slow and impersonal," will the company let the reader keep the card? No. The real reason for the negative is that the bank's franchise allows it to have cardholders only in a given geographical region.

Real reason: Each local CHARGE-ALL center is permitted to offer accounts to customers in a several-state area. The Knoxville CHARGE-ALL center serves customers east of the Mississippi. You can continue to use your current card until it expires. When that happens, you'll need to open an account with a CHARGE-ALL center that serves Texas.

Don't hide behind "company policy": readers will assume the policy is designed to benefit you at their expense. If possible, show how readers benefit from the policy. If they do not benefit, don't mention policy at all.

Weak reason: I cannot write an insurance policy for you because company policy does not allow me to do so.

Better reason: Gorham insures cars only when they are normally garaged at night. Standard insurance policies cover a wider variety of risks and charge higher fees. Limiting the policies we write gives Gorham customers the lowest possible rates for auto insurance.

Avoid saying that you *cannot* do something. Most negative messages exist because the writer or company has chosen certain policies or cutoff points. In the example above, the company could choose to insure a wider variety of customers if it wanted to do so.

Being able to say *no* is a necessary skill in life as well as in business. Some of the techniques offered by Drug Abuse Resistance Education (D.A.R.E.) may be more appropriate for saying *no* to friends than to co-workers or customers. However, even in business, simply not answering—similar to walking away—is one of the most common ways to refuse a request.

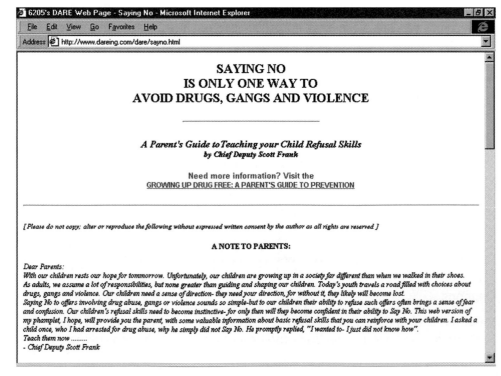

Often you as a middle manager will enforce policies that you did not design and announce decisions that you did not make. Don't pass the buck by saying, "This was a terrible decision." In the first place, carelessly criticizing your superiors is never a good idea. In the second place, if you really think a policy is bad, try to persuade your superiors to change it. If you can't think of convincing reasons to change the policy, maybe it isn't so bad after all.

If you have several reasons for saying *no,* use only those that are strong and watertight. If you give five reasons and readers dismiss two of them, readers may feel that they've won and should get the request.

Weak reason:	You cannot store large bulky items in the dormitory over the summer because moving them into and out of storage would tie up the stairs and the elevators just at the busiest times when people are moving in and out.
Way to dismiss the reason:	We'll move large items before or after the two days when most people are moving in or out.

If you do not have a good reason, omit the reason rather than use a weak one. Even if you have a strong reason, omit it if it makes the company look bad.

Reason that hurts company:	Our company is not hiring at the present time because profits are down. In fact, the downturn has prompted top management to reduce the salaried staff by 5% just this month, with perhaps more reductions to come.
Better:	Our company does not have any openings now.

Refusals

Deemphasize the refusal by putting it in the same paragraph as the reason, rather than in a paragraph by itself.

Sometimes you may be able to imply the refusal rather than stating it directly.

Direct refusal:	You cannot get insurance for just one month.
Implied refusal:	The shortest term for an insurance policy is six months.

Be sure the implication is crystal clear. Any message can be misunderstood, but an optimistic or desperate reader is particularly unlikely to understand a negative message. One of your purposes in a negative message is to close the door on the subject. You do not want to have to write a second letter saying that the real answer is *no.*

Alternatives

Giving the reader an alternative or a compromise, if one is available, is a good idea for several reasons:

- It offers the reader another way to get what he or she wants.
- It suggests that you really care about the reader and about helping to meet his or her needs.
- It enables the reader to reestablish the psychological freedom you limited when you said *no.*
- It allows you to end on a positive note and to present yourself and your organization as positive, friendly, and helpful.

When you give an alternative, give readers all the information they need to act on it, but don't take the necessary steps. Let readers decide whether to try the alternative.

A Profitable Alternative*

Long before Christmas, all of Mattel's holiday-themed Barbie dolls had been sold. But there wasn't time to manufacture more dolls and get them on the shelves.

So Mattel prepared an alternative. It rushed substitute packages to toy stores. Each package contained a framable Barbie poster and an IOU for the holiday doll as soon as it became available.

The alternative meant presents under the tree for Barbie fans— and an additional 300,000 units sold for Mattel.

*Based on "Barbie: Diana Troup," *Advertising Age,* June 24, 1996, S32.

Figure 8.4   *A Refusal with an Alternative*

ROYSNER
Steel Fabrication
"Serving the needs of America since 1890"
1800 Olney Avenue • Philadelphia, PA 19140 • 215•555•7800 • Fax: 215•555•9803

April 27, 2001

Mr. H. J. Moody
Canton Corporation
2407 North Avenue
Kearney, NE 68847

Subject: Bid Number 5853, Part Number D-40040

Dear Mr. Moody:

Buffer   Thank you for requesting our quotation on your Part No. D-40040.

Reason   Your blueprints call for flame-cut rings 1/2" thick A516 grade 70. To use that grade, we'd have to grind down from 1" thick material. However, if you can use A515 grade 70, which we stock in 1/2" thick, you can cut the price by more than half.

Quantity	Description	Gross Weight	Price/Each
75	Rings Drawing D-40040, A516 Grade 70 1" thick x 6" O.D. x 2.8" I.D. ground to .5" thick.	12 lbs.	$15.08
75	Rings Drawing D-40040, A515 Grade 70 1/2" thick x 6" O.D. x 2.8" I.D.	6 lbs.	$6.91

Alternative (Depending on circumstances, different alternatives may exist.)

If you can use A515 grade 70, let me know.   *Leaves decision up to reader to re-establish psychological freedom*

Sincerely,

Valerie Prynne

Valerie Prynne

VP:wc

Negative messages limit the reader's freedom. People may respond to a limitation of freedom by asserting their freedom in some other arena. Jack W. Brehm calls this phenomenon **psychological reactance.**[4] Psychological reactance is at work when a customer who has been denied credit no longer buys even on a cash basis, or a subordinate who has been passed over for a promotion gets back at the company by deliberately doing a poor job.

An alternative allows the reader to react in a way that doesn't hurt you. By letting readers decide for themselves whether they want the alternative, you allow them to reestablish their sense of psychological freedom.

The specific alternative will vary depending on the circumstances. In Figure 8.4, the company is unwilling to quote a price on an item on which it cannot be competitive. In different circumstances, the writer might offer different alternatives.

Endings

If you have a good alternative, refer to it in your ending: "Let me know if you can use A515 grade 70."

The best endings look to the future.

> Wherever you have your account, you'll continue to get all the service you've learned to expect from CHARGE-ALL, and the convenience of charging items at over a million stores, restaurants, and hotels in the United States and abroad—and in Knoxville, too, whenever you come back to visit!

Letter refusing to continue charge account for a customer who has moved

Avoid endings that seem insincere.

> We are happy to have been of service, and should we be able to assist you in the future, please contact us.

This ending lacks you-attitude and would not be good even in a positive message. In a situation where the company has just refused to help, it's likely to sound sarcastic or sadistic.

Tone in Negative Messages

Tone—the implied attitude of the author toward the reader and the subject— is particularly important when you want readers to feel that you have taken their requests seriously. Check your draft carefully for positive emphasis (✖ p. 37) and you-attitude (✖ p. 34), both at the level of individual words and at the level of ideas.

Figure 8.5 lists some of the phrases to avoid in negative messages.

Even the physical appearance and timing of a letter can convey tone. An obvious form rejection letter suggests that the writer has not given much consideration to the reader's application. An immediate negative suggests that the rejection didn't need any thought. A negative delivered just before a major holiday seems especially unfeeling. AT&T was widely criticized for telling a man that he had been fired when he arrived at work with his daughter on "Take Your Daughter to Work" Day. AT&T later found another job for him, but the cost to the company's image was high.

Phrase	Because
I am afraid that we cannot	You aren't fearful. Don't hide behind empty phrases.
I am sorry that we are unable	You probably are *able* to grant the request; you simply choose not to. If you are so sorry about saying *no*, why don't you change your policy and say *yes*?
I am sure you will agree that	Don't assume that you can read the reader's mind.
Unfortunately	*Unfortunately* is negative in itself. It also signals that a refusal is coming.

Workplace Violence*

An increasing number of people respond violently to bad news.

The American Management Association found that nearly a quarter of the companies it surveyed reported that an employee had been killed or attacked. A union steward was killed by an employee who was suspended for refusing a drug test. Eight lawyers were killed by former clients who felt they'd been given bad advice. In several incidents, Postal Service employees who were fired killed co-workers. An employee critically wounded a co-worker at a small California market-research company.

Writing better negative messages, not surprising people, and offering programs in violence prevention can redirect this psychological reactance into less lethal channels.

*Based on "Companies See More Workplace Violence," *The Wall Street Journal*, April 12, 1994, B1; "Waging War in the Workplace," *Newsweek*, July 19, 1993, 30; "It's Murder in the Workplace," *Fortune*, August 9, 1993, 12; and "Preventing On-the-Job Violence," *Inc.*, June 1996, 116.

Figure 8.5

Avoid These Phrases in Negative Messages

Alternate Strategies for Negative Situations

Whenever you face a negative situation, consider recasting it as a positive or persuasive message.

Recasting the Situation as a Positive Message

If the negative information will directly lead to a benefit that you know readers want, use the pattern of organization for informative and positive messages:

Situation:	You're raising parking rates to pay for lot maintenance, ice and snow removal, and signs so renters can have cars towed away that park in their spots—all services renters have asked for.
Negative:	Effective May 1, parking rentals will go up $5 a month.
Positive emphasis:	Effective May 1, if someone parks in your spot, you can have the car towed away. Signs are being put up announcing that all spaces in the lot are rented. Lot maintenance is also being improved. The lot will be resurfaced this summer, and arrangements have been made for ice and snow removal next winter.

Recasting the Situation as a Persuasive Message

Often a negative situation can be recast as a persuasive message. If your organization has a problem, ask readers to help solve it. A solution that workers have created will be much easier to implement.

When the Association for Business Communication raised dues in 1987, the Executive Director wrote a persuasive letter urging members to send in renewals early so they could beat the increase. The letter shared some of the qualities of any persuasive letter: using an attention-getting opener, offsetting the negative by setting it against the benefits of membership, telling the reader what to do, and ending with a picture of the benefit the reader received by acting. More recent increases, however, have been announced directly.

If you are criticizing someone, your real purpose may be to persuade the reader to act differently.[5] Chapter 9 offers patterns for direct requests and problem-solving persuasive messages.

Humor in Negative Messages

Humor can defuse negative messages.

Kathryn McGrath, head of the SEC division of investment management, needed to tell an investment firm that its ad was illegal. The ad showed an index finger pointing up and large bold letters saying that performance was "up," too. Tiny print at the bottom of the page admitted that performance figures hadn't been adjusted to include front-end sales charges. Rather than writing a heavy-handed letter, McGrath sent the firm a photocopy of a thumb pointing down. The ad never ran again.[6]

Humor works best when it's closely related to the specific situation and the message. Humor that seems tacked on is less likely to work. Never use humor that belittles readers.

 See the BAC Web site for more examples of humor—successful and unsuccessful.

Writing Negative E-Mail Messages

Major negatives, like firing someone, should be delivered in person, not by e-mail. But e-mail is appropriate for many less serious negatives.

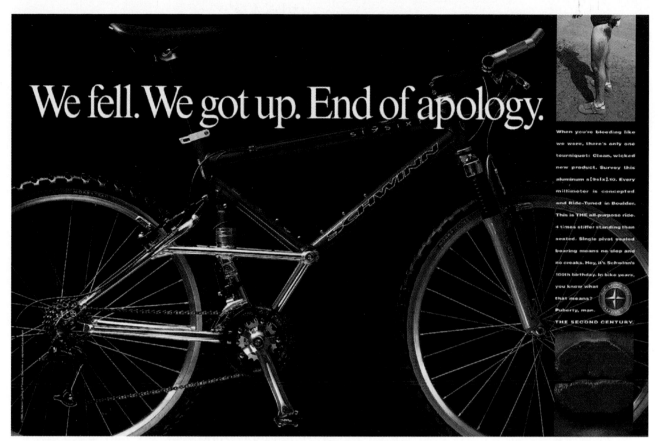

Schwinn needed a new product line to attract sophisticated cyclists. This apology for its old, boring line moves quickly to a discussion of its new technology. By evoking an experience every cyclist has had, the headline also suggests that falling is a minor event.

Never write e-mail messages when you're angry. If a message infuriates you, wait until you're calmer before you reply—and even then, reply only if you must. Flaming does not make you look like a mature, level-headed professional who is a candidate for bigger things. And since employers have the right to read all e-mail, flaming—particularly if directed at co-workers, regulators, suppliers, or customers—may cause an employee to be fired.

Use a friendly, conversational tone. Keep the message short. Edit and proofread your message carefully. An easy way for an angry reader to strike back is to attack typos or other errors.

Remember that e-mail messages, like any other documents, can become documents in lawsuits. When a negative e-mail is hard to write, compose it offline so that you can revise and even get feedback before you send the message.

Varieties of Negative Messages

Three of the most difficult kinds of negative messages to write are rejections and refusals, disciplinary notices and negative performance appraisals, and layoffs and firings.

Rejections and Refusals

When you refuse requests from people outside your organization, try to use a buffer. Give an alternative if one is available. For example, if you are denying credit, it may still be possible for the reader to put an expensive item on layaway.

Legal Layoffs*

Federal law requires that companies with 100 or more workers give
60 days' notice before closing a
plant or laying off two-thirds of the
workers.

Employees cannot be fired on the
basis of race, sex, or age. To with-
stand a lawsuit, a company needs
to be able to show that a fired employee failed to meet objective, uniform standards for performance. A
record of negative performance appraisals is essential to make the
case.

Companies need to follow their
own written guidelines. If they
don't, employees may sue for
wrongful discharge.

*Based on Arthur S. Hayes, "Layoffs
Take Careful Planning to Avoid Losing
the Suits That Are Apt to Follow," *The
Wall Street Journal*, November 2, 1990,
B1.

Politeness and length help. Graduating seniors at a southwestern university preferred rejection letters that addressed them as *Mr./Ms.* rather than calling them by their first names, that said something specific about their good qualities, that phrased the refusal itself indirectly, and that were longer.[7] An experiment using a denial of additional insurance found that subjects preferred a rejection letter that was longer, more tactful, and more personal. The preferred letter started with a buffer, used a good reason for the refusal, and offered sales promotion in the last paragraph. The finding held both for English-speaking US subjects and for Spanish-speaking Mexican subjects.[8]

Double-check the words in the draft to be sure the reason can't backfire if it is applied to other contexts. As Elizabeth McCord has shown, the statement that a plant is "too noisy and dangerous" for a group tour could be used as evidence against the company in a worker's compensation claim.[9]

When you refuse requests within your organization, use your knowledge of the organization's culture and of the specific individual to craft your message. In some organizations, it may be appropriate to use company slogans, offer whatever help already-established departments can give, and refer to the individual's good work (if you indeed know that it is good). In other less personal organizations, a simple negative without embellishment may be more appropriate.

Disciplinary Notices and Negative Performance Appraisals

Performance appraisals are discussed in detail in Chapter 9. Performance appraisals will be positive when they are designed to help a basically good employee improve. But when an employee violates a company rule or fails to improve after repeated negative appraisals, the company may discipline the employee or build a dossier to support firing him or her.

Present disciplinary notices and negative performance appraisals directly, with no buffer. A buffer might encourage the recipient to minimize the message's importance—and might even become evidence in a court case that the employee had not been told to shape up "or else." Cite quantifiable observations of the employee's behavior, rather than generalizations or inferences based on it. If an employee is disciplined by being laid off without pay, specify when the employee is to return.

Layoffs and Firings

If a company is in financial trouble, management needs to communicate the problem clearly. Sharing information and enlisting everyone's help in finding solutions may make it possible to save jobs. Sharing information also means that layoff notices, if they become necessary, will be a formality; they should not be new information to employees.

Before you fire someone, double-check the facts. Give the employee the real reason for the firing. Offering a face-saving reason unrelated to poor performance can create legal liabilities. But avoid broadcasting the reason: to do so can leave the company liable to a defamation suit.[10]

Information about layoffs and firings is normally delivered orally but accompanied by a written statement explaining severance pay or unemployment benefits that may be available.

Solving a Sample Problem

Solving negative problems requires careful analysis. The checklist at the end of the chapter on p. 208 can help you evaluate your draft.

Problem

You're Director of Employee Benefits for a Fortune 500 company. Today, you received the following memo:

> From: Michelle Jagtiani
> Subject: Getting My Retirement Benefits
>
> Next Friday will be my last day here. I am leaving [name of company] to take a position at another firm.
>
> Please process a check for my retirement benefits, including both the deductions from my salary and the company's contributions for the last six and a half years. I would like to receive the check by next Friday if possible.

You have bad news for Michelle. Although the company does contribute an amount to the retirement fund equal to the amount deducted for retirement from the employee's paycheck, employees who leave with less than seven years of employment get only their own contributions. Michelle will get back only the money that has been deducted from her own pay, plus 4½% interest compounded quarterly. Her payments and interest come to just over $17,200; the amount could be higher depending on the amount of her last paycheck, which will include compensation for any unused vacation days and sick leave. Furthermore, since the amounts deducted were not considered taxable income, she will have to pay income tax on the money she will receive.

You cannot process the check until after her resignation is effective, so you will mail it to her. You have her home address on file; if she's moving, she needs to let you know where to send the check. Processing the check may take two to three weeks.

Write a memo to Michelle.

Analysis of the Problem

1. Who is (are) your audience(s)? What characteristics are relevant to this particular message? If you are writing to more than one reader, how do the readers differ?

   Michelle Jagtiani. Unless she's a personal friend, I probably wouldn't know why she's leaving and where she's going.

   There's a lot I don't know. She may or may not know much about taxes; she may or may not be able to take advantage of tax-reduction strategies. I can't assume the answers because I wouldn't have them in real life.

2. What are your purposes in writing?

   To tell her that she will get only her own contributions, plus 4½% interest compounded quarterly; that the check will be mailed to her home address two to three weeks after her last day on the job; and that the money will be taxable as income.

   To build goodwill so that she feels that she has been treated fairly and consistently. To minimize negative feelings she may have.

   To close the door on this subject.

3. What information must your message include?

   When the check will come. The facts that her check will be based on her contributions, not the employer's, and that the money will be taxable income. How lump-sum retirement benefits are calculated. The fact that

The Designated Terminator*

If you're a manager who can't say *you're fired,* you can hire someone to do it for you. In Chicago, George Scharm, a retired police officer, charges $65 an hour to deliver the bad news. "I try to be nice about it." The employee gets the choice of resigning rather than being fired but must do so immediately. Scharm escorts the fired employee out of the building. The manager never has to confront the person he or she is firing.

*Based on "Watch Out If This Professional Terminator Comes Calling," *The Columbus Dispatch* (AP), October 30, 1998, 1G.

Figure 8.6   *An Unacceptable Solution to the Sample Problem*

April 20, 2000

To: Michelle Jagtiani

From   Lisa Niaz   *LN*

Subject   Denial of Matching Funds

Give reason before refusal   You cannot receive a check the last day of work and you will get only your own contributions, not a matching sum from the company, because you have not worked for the company for at least seven full years.

Better to be specific

This is lifted straight from the problem. The language in problems is often negative and stuffy; information is disorganized.   Your payments and interest come to just over $17,200; the amount could be higher depending on the amount of your last paycheck, which will include compensation for any unused vacation days and sick leave. Furthermore, since the amounts deducted were not considered taxable income, you will have to pay income tax on the money you receive.

The check will be sent to your home address. If the address we have on file is incorrect, please correct it so that your check is not delayed. —— *Negative* ——

How will reader know what you have on file? Better to give current address as you have it.

Think about the situation and use your own words to create a satisfactory message.

---

we have her current address on file but need a new address if she's moving.

4. How can you build support for your position? What reasons or reader benefits will your reader find convincing?

   Giving the amount currently in her account may make her feel that she is getting a significant sum of money. Suggesting someone who can give free tax advice (if the company offers this as a fringe benefit) reminds her of the benefits of working with the company. Wishing her luck with her new job is a nice touch.

5. What objection(s) can you expect your reader(s) to have? What negative elements of your message must you deemphasize or overcome?

   She is getting about half the amount she expected, since she gets no matching funds. She might have been able to earn more than 4½% interest if she had invested the money in the stock market. Depending on her personal tax situation she may pay more tax on the money as a lump sum than would have been due had she paid it each year as she earned the money.

Discussion of the Sample Solutions

The solution in Figure 8.6 is not acceptable. The subject line gives a bald negative with no reason or alternative. The first sentence has a condescending tone that is particularly offensive in negative messages. The last sentence focuses on

Figure 8.7   *A Good Solution to the Sample Problem*

April 20, 2000

To: Michelle Jagtiani

From   Lisa Niaz *LN*

Subject   Receiving Employee Contributions from Retirement Accounts

Good to state reason in third-person to deemphasize negative.

Employees who leave the company with at least seven full years of employment are entitled both to the company contributions and the retirement benefit paycheck deductions contributed to retirement accounts. Those employees who leave the company with less than seven years of employment will receive the employee paycheck contributions made to their retirement accounts.

Good to be specific

You now have $17,240.62 in your account which includes 4.5% interest compounded quarterly. The amount you receive could be even higher since you will also receive payment for any unused leave and vacation days.

Good to show how company can help

Because you now have access to the account, the amount you receive will be considered income. Beth Jordan in Employee Financial Services can give you information about possible tax deductions and financial investments which can reduce your income taxes.

Good to be specific

The check will be sent to your home address on May 16. The address we have on file is 2724 Merriman Road, Akron, Ohio 44313. If your address changes, please let us know so you can receive your check promptly.

Positive

Good luck with your new job!

Forward-looking

---

what is being taken away rather than what remains. Paragraph 2 lacks you-attitude and is vague. The memo ends with a negative. There is nothing anywhere in the memo to build goodwill.

The solution in Figure 8.7, in contrast, is very good. The policy serves as a buffer and explanation. The negative is stated clearly but is buried in the paragraph to avoid overemphasizing it. The paragraph ends on a positive note by specifying the amount in the account and the fact that the sum might be even higher.

Paragraph 2 contains the additional negative information that the amount will be taxable but offers the alternative that it may be possible to reduce taxes. The writer builds goodwill by suggesting a specific person the reader could contact.

Paragraph 3 tells the reader what address is in the company files (Michelle may not know whether the files are up to date), asks that she update it if necessary, and ends with the reader's concern: getting her check promptly.

The final paragraph ends on a positive note. This generalized goodwill is appropriate when the writer does not know the reader well.

✓ Checklist   *Negative Messages*

☐ Is the subject line appropriate?

☐ If a buffer is used, does it avoid suggesting either a positive or a negative response?

☐ Is the reason, if it is given, presented before the refusal? Is the reason watertight, with no loopholes?

☐ Is the negative information clear?

☐ Is an alternative given if a good one is available? Does the message provide all the information needed to act on the alternative but leave the choice up to the reader?

☐ Does the last paragraph avoid repeating the negative information?

☐ Is tone acceptable—not defensive, but not cold, preachy, or arrogant either?

And, for all messages, not just negative ones,

☐ Does the message use you-attitude and positive emphasis?

☐ Is the style easy to read and friendly?

☐ Is the visual design of the message inviting?

☐ Is the format correct?

☐ Does the message use standard grammar? Is it free from typos?

Originality in a negative message may come from

• An effective buffer, if one is appropriate.

• A clear, complete statement of the reason for the refusal.

• A good alternative, clearly presented, which shows that you're thinking about what the reader really needs.

• Adding details that show you're thinking about a specific organization and the specific people in that organization.

Summary of Key Points

• In a negative message, the basic information is negative; we expect the reader to be disappointed or angry.

• A good negative message conveys the negative information clearly while maintaining as much goodwill as possible. The goal is to make readers feel that they have been taken seriously, that the decision is fair and reasonable, and that they would have made the same decision. A secondary purpose is to reduce or eliminate future correspondence on the same subject so that the message doesn't create more work for the writer.

• In memos to superiors, the subject line should focus on solving the problem. In memos to peers and subordinates, state the topic but not your action. Use a negative subject line in e-mail messages.

• Organize negative letters in this way:
  1. Give the reason for the refusal before the refusal itself when you have a reason that readers will understand and accept.
  2. Give the negative just once, clearly.
  3. Present an alternative or compromise, if one is available.
  4. End with a positive, forward-looking statement.

• Organize negative memos to superiors in this way:
  1. Describe the problem.
  2. Tell how it happened.
  3. Describe the options for fixing it.
  4. Recommend a solution and ask for action.

• When you must pass along serious bad news to peers and subordinates, use a variation of the pattern to superiors:
  1. Describe the problem.
  2. Present an alternative or compromise, if one is available.
  3. If possible, ask for input or action.

- When the bad news is less serious, use the pattern for negative letters unless your knowledge of the reader(s) suggests that another pattern will be more effective.
- A **buffer** is a neutral or positive statement that allows you to bury the negative message. Buffers must put the reader in a good frame of mind, not give the bad news but not imply a positive answer either, and provide a natural transition to the body of the letter. Use a buffer only when the reader values harmony or when the buffer serves a purpose in addition to simply delaying the negative.
- The kinds of statements most often used as buffers are (1) good news, (2) facts and chronologies of events, (3) references to enclosures, (4) thanks, and (5) statements of principle.
- A good reason must be watertight. Give several reasons only if all are watertight and are of comparable importance. Omit the reason for the refusal entirely if it is weak or if it makes your organization look bad.
- Make the refusal crystal clear.
- Giving the reader an alternative or a compromise
  - Offers the reader another way to get what he or she wants.
  - Suggests that you really care about the reader and about helping to meet his or her needs.
  - Enables the reader to reestablish the psychological freedom you limited when you said *no.*
  - Allows you to end on a positive note and to present yourself and your organization as positive, friendly, and helpful.
- People may respond to limits by striking out in ways that are unacceptable. This effort to reestablish freedom is called **psychological reactance.**
- When you give an alternative, give the reader all the information he or she needs to act on it, but don't take the necessary steps for the reader. Letting the reader decide whether to try the alternative allows the reader to reestablish a sense of psychological freedom.
- Many negative situations can be redefined to use the patterns of organization for informative and positive or for persuasive messages. Humor sometimes works to defuse negative situations.
- Use the analysis questions in Chapter 1 to solve negative problems.

Chapter 8

Exercises and Problems

Getting Started

8.1   Letters for Discussion—Credit Refusal

As director of customer service at C'est Bon, an upscale furniture store, you manage the store's credit. Today you are going to reject an application from Frank Steele. Although his income is fairly high, his last two payments on his college loans were late, and he has three bank credit cards, all charged to the upper limit, on which he's made just the minimum payment for the last three months.

The following letters are possible approaches to giving him the news. How well does each message meet the criteria in the checklist for negative messages?

1.

Dear Mr. Steele:

Your request to have a C'est Bon charge account shows that you are a discriminating shopper. C'est Bon sells the finest merchandise available.

Although your income is acceptable, records indicate that you carry the maximum allowable balances on three bank credit cards. Moreover, two recent payments on your student loans have not been made in a timely fashion. If you were given a C'est Bon charge account, and if you charged a large amount on it, you might have difficulty paying the bill, particularly if you had other unforeseen expenses (car repair, moving, medical emergency) or if your income dropped suddenly. If you were unable to repay, with your other debt you would be in serious difficulty. We would not want you to be in such a situation, nor would you yourself desire it.

Please reapply in six months.

Sincerely,

2.

Dear Frank:

No, you can't have a C'est Bon credit card—at least not right now. Get your financial house in order and try again.

Fortunately for you, there's an alternative. Put what you want on layaway. The furniture you want will be held for you, and paying a bit each week or month will be good self-discipline.

Enjoy your C'est Bon furniture!

Sincerely,

3.

Dear Mr. Steele:

Over the years, we've found that the best credit risks are people who pay their bills promptly. Since two of your student loan payments have been late, we won't extend store credit to you right now. Come back with a record of six months of on-time payments of all bills, and you'll get a different answer.

You might like to put the furniture you want on layaway. A $50 deposit holds any item you want. You have six months to pay, and you save interest charges.

You might also want to take advantage of one of our Saturday Seminars. On the first Saturday of each month at 11 AM, our associates explain one topic related to furniture and interior decorating. Upcoming topics are

How to Wallpaper a Room	February 5
Drapery Options	March 6
Persian Carpets	April 1

Sincerely,

8.2 E-Mails for Discussion—Saying *No* to a Colleague

A colleague in another state agency has e-mailed you asking if you would like to use the payroll software her agency developed. You wouldn't. Switching to a new program would take a lot of time, and what you have works well for you.

The following messages are possible approaches to giving her the news. How well does each message meet the criteria in the checklist for negative messages?

1.
> Subject: Re: Use Our Software?
>
> No.

2.
> Subject: Re: Use Our Software?
>
> Thanks for telling me about the payroll software your team developed. What we have works well for us. Like every other agency, we're operating on a bare-bones budget, and no one here wants to put time (that we really don't have) into learning a new program. So we'll say, no, thanks!

3.
> Subject: Re: Use Our Software?
>
> The payroll software your team developed sounds very good.
>
> I might like to use it, but the people here are computer phobic. They HATE learning new programs. So, being a good little computer support person, I soldier on with the current stuff. (And people wonder why state government is SO INEFFICIENT! Boy, the stories I could tell!)
>
> Anyway, thanks for the offer. Keep me posted on the next development—maybe it will be something so obviously superior that even the Neanderthals here can see its advantages!

8.3 Revising a Negative Message

Rewrite and reorganize the following negative message to make it more positive. Eliminate any sentences that are not needed.

> Dear Client:
>
> A change is needed so that Travel Globe can continue to make a profit. Effective the first of next month, you'll need to pay the cost of overnight delivery if you want tickets sent to you overnight.
>
> If your business has an account with Airborne, FedEx, or United Parcel Service, you may want to give us your account number so that deliveries can be billed directly to you. You'll write fewer checks and, depending on the volume of overnight mail you send, may even be able to get a discount.
>
> Let us know whether you'd like to pay us for deliveries, be billed directly, come in to pick your tickets up, or just have them sent to you by first-class mail.
>
> As you may know, airlines have reduced the commissions they pay travel agents on tickets. We can no longer afford the cost—over $300 a month—of sending your tickets by overnight delivery. As a result, each service must pay for itself. The alternative would be to charge a fee for each transaction, and that doesn't seem fair to customers who do pick up their tickets or for whom regular mail is fast enough.
>
> Sincerely,
>
> *Chris Conrad*
>
> Chris Conrad, President
> Travel Globe

E-Mail Messages

8.4   Closing the Cash Drawer

Employees in your company charge major travel costs (airfare, hotel rooms) directly to the company on corporate American Express cards. For smaller costs that may need to be paid in cash (taxi fares, parking, fast food), they've been able to get cash advances before each trip. These costs can be substantial; most people take at least $100, even for a short trip.

From attending meetings for corporate travel managers and reading trade journals, you know that more and more companies are eliminating cash advances and reimbursing employees after the trip—provided they submit receipts. Companies that have made the change report major savings from three sources: (1) it's no longer necessary to issue, track, and collect cash; (2) the company no longer loses money when an employee doesn't repay an advance or uses it for non-approved expenses; (3) the company is no longer making interest-free loans to employees.

Some parking lots, toll booths, taxis, and fast-food restaurants now take credit cards—usually Visa rather than American Express. People who travel a lot may want to come to your office to apply for a corporate Visa card.

People may not be happy to make this change. And you still want them to travel economically. For example, you want them to pay cash for a cab rather than to rent a car with a credit card. You will make every effort to reimburse people within two weeks of the date they turn in the request with all receipts.

Write a message to all employees.

Hint:

What information must you include?

8.5   Refusing to Provide Graduates' Addresses on Your Web Page

You maintain the Web page for your college or community college department. Today, you get the following e-mail message:

> Subject: Add Graduates' Names?
>
> I really like your Web site. Could you please add the names and addresses (snail and e-mail) of recent graduates? That would help us keep in touch and would be really useful for networking.

You don't want to do this. Probably someone in the college or community college has this information, but you don't know who. You've got enough to do without tracking down the information, posting it on the Web, and updating it as people move. But you don't want to offend the person who asked, since recent graduates are asked to help in many ways (sponsor internships, give money, etc.). So you need to say *no* while maintaining goodwill.

Write the message.

8.6   Telling a Co-Worker that a Workshop Is Full

As Director of Human Resources, you sponsor a variety of workshops for employees. You received this e-mail message today:

> Subject: Re: Diversity Workshops
>
> Please register me for the Workshop on diversity next week. My supervisor has told me I should attend this.

Unfortunately, the workshop is full, and you already have three people on a waiting list to fill vacancies if anyone should cancel. You would repeat the workshop only if you have guarantees for at least 15 participants.

Write the message.

8.7   Rejecting Employees' Suggestions

For years, businesses have had suggestion programs, rewarding employees for money-saving ideas. Now your city government has adopted such a program (see Problem 7.7). But not all of the suggestions are adopted. Today, you need to send messages to the following people. Since their suggestions are being rejected, they will not get any cash award.

1. Marjorie Bartlett, secretary, Accounts Payable. Suggestion: Stop buying Post-its. Reason for rejection: "They don't cost *that* much. If we stop using Post-its, people will use tape—won't that cost just as much? We want to save money, but we also want people to have the supplies they need to do their best work."

2. Manuel Meszaros, Buildings and Grounds. Suggestion: Stop hiring outside consultants to teach courses. Reason for rejection: "We hire outside consultants to teach essential courses: diversity training, effective writing, complying with ADA legislation. These courses help prevent lawsuits and make us work more effectively. In the long run, we think this is money well spent."

3. Toby Huber, Animal Control. Suggestion: Stop allowing people to park free at meters on holidays. Reason for rejection: "If people had to pay, we'd have to have meter readers work on holidays—and pay them overtime. We'd lose money, since not that many people park downtown on most holidays, and we'd lose lots of goodwill."

Write the messages.

8.8   Telling Employees to Remove Personal Web Sites

You're Director of Management and Information Systems (MIS) in your organization. At your monthly briefing for management, a vice president complained that some employees have posted personal Web pages on the company's Web server.

"It looks really unprofessional to have stuff about cats and children and musical instruments. How can people do this?"

You took the question literally. "Well, some people have authorization to post material—price changes, job listings, marketing information. Someone who has authorization could put up anything."

Another manager said, "I don't think it's so terrible—after all, there aren't any links from our official pages to these personal pages."

A third person said, "But we're paying for what's posted—so we pay for server space and connect time. Maybe it's not much right now, but as more and more people become Web-literate, the number of people putting up unauthorized pages could spread. We should put a stop to this now."

The vice president agreed. "The Web site is carefully designed to present an image of our organization. Personal pages are dangerous. Can you imagine the flak we'd get if someone posted links to pornography?"

You said, "I don't think that's very likely. If it did happen, as system administrator, I could remove the page."

The third speaker said, "I think we should remove all the pages. Having any at all suggests that our people have so much extra time that they're playing on the Web. That suggests that our prices are too high and may make some people worry about quality. In fact, I think that we need a new policy prohibiting personal pages on the company's Web server. And any pages that are already up should be removed."

A majority of the managers agreed and told you to write a message to all employees. Create an e-mail message to tell employees that you will remove the personal pages already posted and that no more will be allowed.

Hint:

- Suggest other ways that people can post personal Web pages. Commercial services such as America Online are possibilities. Students at Plugged In (www.pluggedin.org) can also provide Web access for a fee. (Check to be sure that the groups you recommend are still offering Web sites. If possible, get current prices.)

- Give only reasons that are watertight and make the company look good.

8.9   Saying *No* to the Boss

Today, you received this e-mail from your boss.

Subject: Oversee United Way

I'm appointing you to be the company representative to oversee United Way. You've done a good job the last two years, so this year should be a piece of cake!

It's true that you know exactly what to do. The job wouldn't be hard for you. But that's just the problem. You wouldn't learn anything, either. You'd rather have an assignment that would stretch you, teach you new skills, or enable you to interact with new people. Continuing to grow is your insurance of continued employability and mobility. Three upcoming projects in your division might offer growth: creating videos for a "town meeting" for all employees to be held at the beginning of next quarter, creating an Intranet for the company, or serving on the diversity committee. Any of these would be time-consuming, but no more time-consuming than running the United Way campaign.

Write to your boss, asking for something more challenging to do.

Communicating at Work

As Your Instructor Directs in 8.10 through 8.12,

a. Prepare notes for a meeting with or phone call to the person to whom you must give the bad news.

b. Write a paper or e-mail document to achieve the goal.

c. Write a memo to your instructor describing the situation and culture at your workplace and explaining your rhetorical choices (medium, strategy, tone, wording, graphics or document design, and so forth).

d. Examine your organization's files for messages responding to similar situations in the past. Are the messages effective? Why or why not? Write a memo to your instructor analyzing the messages, including copies of them, or make a presentation to the class, using the messages as handouts, transparencies, or slides.

8.10   Telling the Boss about a Problem

In any organization, things sometimes go wrong. Tell your supervisor about a problem in your unit and recommend what should be done.

8.11   Reprimanding a Subordinate

One of a manager's duties is to reprimand subordinates who fail to meet organizational expectations. Think of a situation when someone's performance was below standard. Prepare notes for a meeting with the subordinate, and write a memo documenting your meeting.

8.12   Refusing a Customer Request

The customer isn't always right. Sometimes customers ask for things you're truly unable to provide. Even more frequently, you say *no* because the refusal serves your organization's needs. Think of a situation where a customer asked for something your organization could not provide or felt was unreasonable. Write a response refusing the request.

Letter and Memo Assignments

8.13   Explaining a Pay Mixup

State University has installed a new computer system that is supposed to integrate the 14 different databases formerly in use. Unfortunately, the new system has bugs. The July paychecks that have just been cut include any pay increases that are supposed to start in September. Reissuing the checks would be expensive and would make the checks late, so they're going out with the overpayment. It will be deducted next month. Then in September, people will get the rate they're supposed to get for the new school year.

The paychecks also give more information than did the checks processed under the old system. For example, the number of sick-leave hours appears on the earnings statement attached to the check. Anyone who finds an error or who has questions should contact the fiscal officer for his or her unit.

Not all employees have computers, so write a paper message.

8.14   Announcing a Rent Increase

As manager of an apartment complex, you need to let tenants know that their rent will go up $25 a month when the current lease expires. People who renew the lease for a year will have no additional increases during that year. People who want to rent month-to-month will pay a $30-a-month surcharge and may possibly have other increases as well.

Write a message to put in each mailbox.

As Your Instructor Directs, write messages for one or more of the following situations:

a. There is an oversupply of apartments of the quality and price you offer. Right now your occupancy is only 85%. You think raising rents is a horrible idea, but the owner of the complex has made the decision, and you have to implement it.

b. All of the apartments are rented, and you have a waiting list of people who want apartments.

c. Some of the tenants are especially good ones whom you'd really like to keep. Others, however, you'd be quite happy to see leave.

8.15   Refusing Part of a Guest's Request

As Director of Guest Services for a hotel that is part of a national chain, you've received the following letter:

To Whom It May Concern:

I really don't need to have my room cleaned and made up every day. Every third or fourth day would be fine. That would save you money and reduce the load on the environment (less washing of towels and bedding).

I'll be staying at your hotel when I come to your city next month for a weeklong business trip. What arrangements do I need to make so that my room isn't made up? And how much of a discount from the room rate will I get for the days that no one has to clean my room?

Sincerely,

Rod Bannister

Rod Bannister

Cleaning a room costs about $18 a day ($6 for supplies, $7 for the worker's salary and benefits, and $5 for utilities and other expenses). But your contract with the workers' union guarantees them a certain number of hours a week—if they didn't work, you'd still have to pay them. And the recordkeeping involved—which guests wanted which days—would be a nightmare.

However, to use less water, last summer your hotel started a policy of asking guests to put in the tub towels that need to be replaced. Towels hanging on the towel rack are not replaced, even if they've been used. Each guest decides when a towel needs to be replaced. But you don't keep track of how many towels or washcloths each guest uses, and you don't give a price break to people who use the fewest possible.

Mr. Bannister, you find out, is a member of the "Frequent Guest Club" of the chain, though he hasn't stayed at your hotel for nine months.

Write Mr. Bannister a letter.

8.16   Analyzing Job Rejection Letters

Collect job rejection letters mailed to seniors on your campus. Analyze the letters, answering the following questions:

· What percentage of the letters use a buffer?
· What reasons do the letters give, if any?

· Does the format build goodwill?
· How do the recipients feel about the letters? Which (if any) do they like best?

As Your Instructor Directs,

a. Discuss your findings in a small group.

b. Present your findings orally to the class.

c. Present your findings in a memo to your instructor.

d. Join with other students to write a report based on your findings.

8.17   Refusing a Gift

As the head of a charitable organization, you spend a lot of your time asking for money. But today, you're turning down a gift: a time-share condominium in another state. Time-shares are so difficult to sell that regular real estate agents do not list them. Places that list time-shares frequently charge a nonrefundable up-front fee (not just a commission that is paid if and when the unit sells). If you accepted the gift, your organization would have to pay maintenance fees charged by the home-owners' association and taxes until the unit sold (if it sold). And you'd probably have to hire someone to check on the property occasionally, since the maintenance fee covers general building maintenance, not repairs for a specific unit. You don't want the expense and hassle of something that may or may not ever yield funds for your organization, so you're going to refuse the gift.

Write a letter to the would-be donors, Benjamin and Sarah Mellon, refusing the gift.

As Your Instructor Directs,

Write letters for one or more of the following situations:

a. Yours is a well-known national charity. You have never met the Mellons, but your records show that they have given small gifts (under $100) in three of the last five years.

b. Yours is a local religious organization; the Mellons are prominent members. They don't give much money, but they're active and faithful.

c. Yours is a local charitable organization that struggles to stay open. The Mellons are major contributors. Sarah Mellon served on your board of directors, in a term ending three years ago.

d. Yours is a national charity. No one in the office has ever heard of the Mellons. They haven't contributed in the last three years—your records don't go back further.

Hints:

- Choose a charitable organization you know something about.
- Give the real reason for the refusal. You *would* accept real estate that seemed easy to sell.
- In situations a–c, thank the Mellons for their past support. Be specific about what they've done.
- Use a salutation and complimentary close that are appropriate to the situation.
- In all of the situations, you want to encourage the donor to give other (more liquid) gifts to you in the future. Tell about upcoming opportunities for giving.

8.18   Telling Retirees They Must Switch to HMOs

Your company has traditionally provided health insurance not only to employees but also to retirees who have worked for the company for at least 20 years at the time of retirement. However, the cost of that insurance has been skyrocketing. To cut costs, you have decided to require that retirees switch to health maintenance organizations (HMOs).

Under the current plan, the retiree pays 20% of all costs (up to a yearly ceiling of $10,000 and a lifetime ceiling of $100,000) and you pay 80%. The good news for retirees is that in an HMO, more costs will be covered. Routine doctors' visits, for example, charge only a $10 copayment. Most tests, such as mammograms, X-rays, and blood work, are covered 100%. Hospitalization is covered completely. And there's much less paperwork. By presenting one's card when one fills a prescription, one pays only the copayment, rather than having to pay the entire amount and then filing for partial reimbursement later.

The bad news for retirees is that they have to go to a physician listed with the HMO. If their current physician is not on the list, the retirees will have to switch doctors to retain benefits. Furthermore, the primary care physician must refer the patient to any other health care providers. That is, someone who wants to see a specialist or go to the emergency room must call the primary care physician first. Primary care physicians always approve such referrals whenever they seem medically advisable, but the requirement does limit the patients' freedom. Further, since HMOs are paid a flat fee and therefore have an incentive to give care that costs less than that fee, some people fear that HMOs will be reluctant to prescribe expensive treatments, even when those treatments are essential.

Seven years ago, you cut costs for employee health insurance by switching from open-ended insurance to HMOs. At that time, you kept open-ended insurance for retirees because they wanted to keep their current doctors. But the high cost of that program gives you no choice: to continue to insure retirees, you must hold down costs, and HMOs offer the best way of doing that.

Your company offers a choice of HMOs. Informational meetings will be held next month for retirees (and anyone else who wishes to attend) to explain the various options. Retirees must return a card within two months, indicating which plan they prefer. The card will be enclosed in the mailing. Anyone who does not return a card will be assigned by the company.

As Vice President for Human Resources, write a form letter to all retirees, explaining the change and telling them how to indicate which HMO they prefer.

Hints:

- Choose a business, government, or nonprofit organization that you know something about.
- About how many retirees do you have? What percentage are "young old" (under 80, in reasonably good health)? What percentage are "old old" (80 and

over, sometimes with more serious health problems)?
- How well educated are your retirees? How easy will it be for them to understand the HMO options?
- What times would be convenient for the retirees to come to meetings? Should you have extra times for them, beyond those you've scheduled for employees?
- Specify the date, time, and place of informational meetings.
- Specify the date by which retirees must return the cards indicating their choices.

8.19   Refusing to Grant Credit

You are Credit Director at a major furniture store in town. When people apply for credit, you ask for three references. You've found that the best credit risks are people who own their own homes, who've held the same job for a number of years, and who can furnish good credit references. Your store has a more conservative credit policy than some stores, but as a result, you rarely have to repossess furniture from someone who can't pay.

Today, you have an application from R. B. Geddes that lists only one credit reference: a Visa card that has never been used. The applicant is renting an apartment and has lived at the current address for one month. The application form lists two jobs: server at a local restaurant—again, for one month—and "singer." "Previous occupation" was "college student."

Many new graduates who apply for credit have extensive credit histories, paying back college loans, pay-

ing off credit cards, paying utility bills. It's a bit surprising to deal with someone who has so little credit history.

Six months from now, if this applicant has either a credit history or six months with the same employer (or both), you might be willing to grant credit. But for now, you're going to say *no*.

Write the letter.

Hints:

- How else can people buy furniture at your store besides cash and credit?
- What benefits do you offer that might persuade this applicant to buy from you—even if it means waiting a bit?
- Six months from now, what information would be necessary to convince you to grant credit?

8.20   Turning Down an Internship

Your hard work has turned up several internship leads and two actual offers. Ten days ago, Beverly Dunn called to offer you an internship at Dunn and Associates in another city in your state. You said you were really interested in the job but wanted two weeks to weigh your options. Three days later, Emergent Enterprises called. You accepted the job provisionally, and now the written offer has arrived. EE is your first choice, since it offers the most interesting work and is in your city. It's a very small organization, so you'll get to do a wide variety of things. The internship at Dunn and Associates offers a higher salary but seems more like "go-fer" work. More-

over, the job would require relocating, and the extra money isn't worth having to move and find another place to live for three months.

Though you're turning down Dunn and Associates, you don't want to burn your bridges. The company is a successful midsize organization with good growth prospects. You might be interested in an internship there next summer or a full-time job after you finish your degree.

Write the letter to Beverly Dunn, President. Refuse the internship, but maintain goodwill.

8.21   Rejecting a Would-Be Client

You've just joined Sportstars Inc., a company that represents athletes who want to increase their incomes by doing commercials, making speeches and personal appearances, and endorsing products. Sportstars persuades the sponsor to hire the athlete and helps to negotiate the contract. In addition, a considerable amount of hand-holding is necessary to see the client through

rough times. For these services, Sportstars receives 20% of the fees paid to the athlete.

As part of your orientation, your boss points out what you know already: a well-known athlete can command much higher fees than someone who's less well known; normally, people who win championships net much higher fees than someone who is consistently good but who has not caught the public eye. "The big problem," your boss says, "is what to do about young athletes. We can't afford to represent the also-rans; we'd go broke spending time on them. But some rookies will eventually make it big, and we want to represent them when they get to the top. We've evolved a foolproof way to do this. When an unknown comes to us and asks to hire us as his or her personal representative, we decline but suggest a competing firm that we know does a terrible job representing its clients. Then, when the winner emerges from the pack, we approach that person and offer to represent him or her. We know we'll do a better job—and we can prove it. We've signed everyone we've approached this way."

Today you have a letter from Tyrone Martin, a college basketball player whose team made the NCAA Final Four. He has been drafted by an NBA team and wants a representative to negotiate endorsements. A bit of research shows that while he's a very good player, he isn't yet a star—and may never be. Under Sportstars' policy, you can't grant his request.

As Your Instructor Directs,

a. Write a letter to Tyrone.

b. Write a memo to your boss at Sportstars suggesting that the company's policy be modified.

c. Write a memo to your instructor listing the choices you made and giving the reasons for your choices.

Hints:

- You have no obligation to give a contract to everyone who asks for one, but is it ethical to deliberately recommend the worst of your competitors? At a minimum, you're depriving Tyrone of income, since you know that the competitor doesn't seek commercials and endorsements aggressively for athletes and doesn't get them nearly as favorable terms as Sportstars has been able to do.

- What will happen to you if you disobey your boss and recommend a competent competitor, several competitors, or no competitor at all?

- How can you build goodwill so that Tyrone will have a positive image of Sportstars?

Based on Mark H. McCormack, *What They Don't Teach You at Harvard Business School* (New York: Bantam, 1984).

8.22 Refusing to Participate on a Panel

As a prominent executive, you get many requests to appear before various groups. Today, you've received a request to participate in a panel of three to five professionals who will talk about "Balancing Work and Life." The session will run from 7:30–10 PM on the second Tuesday of next month.

You're trying to cut back on outside commitments. Work continues to take much of your time; you have major obligations in a volunteer organization; and you want some time for yourself and your family. This request does not fit your priorities.

Decline the invitation.

As Your Instructor Directs, assume that the request is from

a. A college business honor society which expects 250 students at the session.

b. The youth group at the church, synagogue, or temple you attend.

c. The Chinese Student Association at the local college or university.

8.23 Saying *No* to a Customer

As a bank vice president, today you receive this letter from one of your customers:

We are not happy with our biweekly mortgage. You withdraw the amount on Thursdays, but my husband and I are paid on Fridays. On two occasions (most recently last week) our account was a little bit short—each time less than $50. Each time you have billed us for a $25 overdraft fee.

However, our paychecks are deposited at midnight Thursday by direct deposit. Our mortgage contract says that you can withdraw the money anytime between Thursday noon and midnight. If you'd just withdraw it at midnight, everything would be OK. Can't you do this? We really don't want to refinance.

Sincerely,

Carla Springer

Carla Springer

You aren't willing to make an exception for the Springers. Rewriting the computer program to extract the money exactly at midnight would be time-consuming and might even require hiring a computer consultant. If the employers' deposits were even 30 seconds late, the account still might not have sufficient funds.

The best solution would be for the Springers to keep more money in their account. They both already work, but maybe they could work more hours; take a second, part-time job; or cut their expenses for a few months so that they aren't living just from paycheck to paycheck. The fact that their account has been only a little bit short suggests that saving just $100 might solve the problem.

Refinancing would enable them to have lower monthly payments. But interest and fees would mean that they would pay out far more money in the long run. Keeping more money in their account would be prudent fiscally.

Write the letter.

Hints:

- What time of year is it? How easy would it be to cut expenses?
- You don't know whether the Springers are overextended financially or whether they just don't understand how banks work. How much do you need to explain? How can you do it without condescending to them?
- Information from the mortgage application will tell you where the Springers work and how much they make. But you still may not know whether they could easily work more hours or take second jobs. In general, how easy is it for people to find work in your area?

8.24 Closing Bill-Payment Offices

For many years, City Gas & Electric had five suburban offices to which people could take their payments. On the first of the month following next month, you're closing these offices. On that date, 100 local merchants, such as grocers, will begin to accept utility payments. Closing the free-standing offices will save your company al-most $3 million a year. Customers will still be able to mail in payments or have them deducted automatically from their paychecks.

Write a notice that can be inserted in utility bills this month and next month.

8.25 Rejecting a Member's Request

All nonsupervisory workers employed by your state government are union members. As a paid staff person for the union, you spend about a third of your time writ-ing and editing the monthly magazine, *Public [Your State] Employee*. You receive this letter:

> Dear Editor:
>
> Every month, we get two copies of the union magazine—one addressed to me, one to my husband. We have different last names, so your computer may not realize that we're connected, but we are, and we don't need two copies. Sending just one copy will save printing and postage costs and reduce environmental waste. My name is Dorothy Livingston; my husband is Eric Beamer. Please combine our listings to send just one copy.
>
> Sincerely,
>
> *Dorothy Livingston*
> Dorothy Livingston

As it happens, a couple of years ago you investigated possible savings of sending just one mailing to couples who both work for the state. Sophisticated computer-ized merge/purge programs to eliminate duplicates are far too expensive for the union's tight budget. And going through the mailing list manually to locate and change duplications would cost more than would be saved in postage. Printing costs wouldn't necessarily drop either, since it actually costs less for each copy to print big runs.

But you want to build goodwill—both to this writer, and for the union in general. Extra copies of the magazine (whether a double mailing or simply a copy someone is finished with) could be given to a nonmember or taken to a doctor's or dentist's waiting room or a barber or beauty shop. Such sharing would help spread public support for the union and state workers.

Write a letter to Ms. Livingston, explaining why you can't combine mailings.

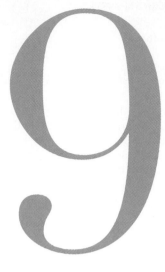

Chapter Nine

Writing Persuasive Messages

Choosing a Persuasive Strategy
1. What Do You Want People to Do?
2. What Objections, If Any, Will the Audience Have?
3. How Strong Is Your Case?
4. What Kind of Persuasion Is Best for the Organization and the Culture?

Writing Direct Requests
- Subject Lines for Direct Requests
- Direct Requests with Multiple Purposes

Writing Problem-Solving Messages
- Subject Lines for Problem-Solving Messages
- Developing a Common Ground
- Dealing with Objections
- Offering a Reason for the Reader to Act Promptly
- Building Emotional Appeal

Tone in Persuasive Messages

Writing Persuasive E-Mail Messages

Varieties of Persuasive Messages
- Collection Letters
- Performance Appraisals
- Letters of Recommendation

Solving a Sample Problem
- Problem
- Analysis of the Problem
- Discussion of the Sample Solutions

Summary of Key Points

Writing Persuasive Messages

James Davis, CEO

Davis Safety Supply Inc.

1-800-622-7133

James Davis founded Davis Safety Supply with an initial investment of $500 in 1993. In six years, the company was worth $3 million. Davis Safety provides safety and environmental equipment to Fortune 500 and smaller businesses.

I built my business by persuading customers to buy equipment that they need to comply with OSHA regulations, protect their employees, and prevent or clean up environmental problems. For me, the most important parts of persuasion are logical reasons, emotional appeal, and credibility.

Most of my customers were already buying the supplies I sell (such as goggles, boots, and gloves) from someone else. I had to give them a reason to change. I decided to offer free shipping—even for next-day or same-day delivery out-of-state. So saving money offers a logical reason for the customer to buy from us.

> 66 *The most important parts of persuasion are logical reasons, emotional appeal, and credibility.* 99

I build relationships with my customers. Even on a first visit, I get to know people. I look around in their offices. If I see pictures of racing cars or baseball players, I can pick up on the customer's interests. That's one way to build a common foundation.

You have to overcome objections. When I started my business, I learned that many people didn't want to deal with a black business owner. I said, I've got to think of another way. So I went in as a sales representative for the company rather than CEO—and made sales. Prejudice is an obstacle that you have to overcome like any other objection.

Credibility is very important. Look the customer in the eye and tell what you can provide. Then deliver what you've promised! Knowledge is another way to build credibility. I know the regulations, so I can tell a customer ways to use products more efficiently to save money. For example, Marriott was using expensive solvent gloves for washing dishes. These gloves are used when working with gasoline; a less expensive glove is fine for washing dishes. Helping customers solve their problems builds my credibility, builds our relationship, and gives them another reason to buy from me.

Persuasion and Emotional Intelligence*

Emotional intelligence is the new buzzword for what enables people to succeed in the workplace. Psychologist Daniel Goleman studied 181 jobs in 121 companies worldwide. He separated technical skills from emotional competencies. The latter were twice as important: "The abilities considered vital for success were emotional competencies like trustworthiness, adaptability, and a talent for collaboration."

For high-level executive jobs, says Goleman, perhaps the most important characteristic is "How persuasive are you? Can you get 'buy-in' for your ideas from the people around you? . . . [Can you] articulat[e] a mission or a goal and . . . bring everyone on board to get it accomplished [?] Can you take the pulse of a group, understand its unspoken currents of thought and concerns, and communicate with people in terms they can understand and embrace? That is great leadership. And it takes huge social intelligence, including a strongly developed sense of empathy."

*Based on and quotations taken from Anne Fisher, "Success Secret: A High Emotional IQ," *Fortune,* October 26, 1998, 293–94.

Persuasion depends on talking to people in their own language, literally and figuratively. Whether you're selling safety equipment or ideas, effective persuasion is based on accurate logic, effective emotional appeal, and credibility or trust. Reasons have to be reasons the audience finds important; emotional appeal is based on values the audience cares about; credibility is in the eye of the beholder.

Persuasive messages include orders and requests, proposals and recommendations, sales and fund-raising letters, job application letters, and efforts to change people's behavior, such as collection letters, criticisms or performance appraisals where you want the subordinate to improve behavior, and public-service ads designed to reduce drunk driving, drug use, and so on. Reports are persuasive messages if they recommend action.

This chapter gives general guidelines for persuasive messages. Chapter 10 discusses situations where the audience is quite resistant. Chapter 11 covers sales and fund-raising letters. Chapter 14 discusses grants and proposals; reports are the subject of Chapter 15. Chapter 19 covers job application letters.

All persuasive messages have several purposes:

Primary purposes:

To have the reader act.

To provide enough information so that the reader knows exactly what to do.

To overcome any objections that might prevent or delay action.

Secondary purposes:

To build a good image of the writer.

To build a good image of the writer's organization.

To cement a good relationship between the writer and reader.

To reduce or eliminate future correspondence on the same subject so the message doesn't create more work for the writer.

Choosing a Persuasive Strategy

Choose a persuasive strategy based on your answers to four questions:

1. What do you want people to do?
2. What objections, if any, will the audience have?
3. How strong a case can you make?
4. What kind of persuasion is best for the organization and the culture?

1. What Do You Want People to Do?

Identify the specific action you want and the person who has the power to do it. If your goal requires several steps, specify what you want your audience to do *now.* For instance, your immediate goal may be to have people come to a meeting or let you make a presentation, even though your long-term goal is a major sale or a change in policy.

2. What Objections, If Any, Will the Audience Have?

If you're asking for something that requires little time, money, or physical effort and for an action that's part of the person's regular duties, the audience is likely to have few objections. For example, when you order a product, the firm is happy to supply it.

Often, however, you'll encounter some resistance. People may be busy and have what they feel are more important things to do. They may have other uses for their time and money. To be persuasive, you need to show your audience that your proposal meets their needs; you need to overcome any objections.

The easiest way to learn about objections your audience may have is to ask. Particularly when you want to persuade people in your own organization or your own town, talk to knowledgeable people. Phrase your questions nondefensively, in a way that doesn't lock people into taking a stand on an issue: "What concerns would you have about a proposal to do x?" "Who makes a decision about y?" "What do you like best about [the supplier or practice you want to change]?" Ask follow-up questions to be sure you understand: "Would you be likely to stay with your current supplier if you could get a lower price from someone else? Why?"

People are likely to be most aware of and willing to share objective concerns such as time and money. They will be less willing to tell you that their real objection is emotional. Readers have a **vested interest** in something if they benefit directly from keeping things as they are. People who are in power have a vested interest in retaining the system that gives them their power. Someone who designed a system has a vested interest in protecting that system from criticism. To admit that the system has faults is to admit that the designer made mistakes. In such cases, you'll need to probe to find out what the real reasons are.

Both individuals and organizations have self-images. It's easier for readers to say *yes* when you ask for something that is consistent with that self-image. For example, a marine biologist used a financial argument to persuade Phillips Petroleum to let him harvest the mussels that grow on oil platforms: "I hear you've just written a check for $100,000 to a hydro-blasting company. I could remove those mussels for free." (The biologist sells the mussels to restaurants.)[1] Aramis persuaded men to buy its over-the-counter skin peel, Lift Off, by linking it to shaving: men who exfoliated with the product could reduce their shaving time by one-third.[2]

3. How Strong Is Your Case?

The strength of your case is based on three aspects of persuasion: argument, credibility, and emotional appeal.

Argument refers to the reasons or logic you offer. Sometimes you may be able to prove conclusively that your solution is best. Sometimes your reasons may not be as strong, the benefits may not be as certain, and obstacles may be difficult or impossible to overcome. For example, suppose that you wanted to persuade your organization to offer a tuition reimbursement plan for employees. You'd have a strong argument if you could show that tuition reimbursement would improve the performance of marginal workers or that reimbursement would be an attractive recruiting tool in a tight job market. However, if dozens of fully qualified workers apply for every opening you have, your argument would be weaker. The program might be nice for workers, but you'd have a hard job proving that it would help the company.

A survey suggests that being ethical builds credibility. See the BAC Web site for the numbers.

Credibility is the audience's response to you as the source of the message. People are more easily persuaded by someone they see as expert, powerful, attractive, or trustworthy. A sexual abstinence program in Atlanta was effective in large part because the lessons on how to say *no* without hurting the other person's feelings were presented by teenagers slightly older than the students in the program. Adults would have been much less credible.[3]

What Do Lawyers Want?*

Sales at Tom Carns's PDQ Printing in Las Vegas are 19 times the average for small print shops. He succeeds by analyzing his audience, identifying decision makers, and meeting their needs.

To enter the market for law-firm photocopying, Tom identified the head of the professional association of paralegals in Las Vegas. He met with her for two hours twice a month for three months to learn about the market, paying $500 for each consultation.

The meetings taught him that price didn't really matter when a legal firm needed photocopying. Quality, timeliness, and confidentiality were crucial. So he made some small changes in his procedures to meet those needs and then advertised the changes in a brochure with "Confidential" on the cover in bright red letters. Inside, his employees promised to treat documents confidentially and to shred any flawed copies. PDQ Printing itself would be liable for any breach of confidentiality.

In the first year of the promotion, law-firm copying generated $600,000 in revenues.

*Based on Edward O. Welles, "Quick Study," *Inc.*, April 1992, 67–76.

By offering a big selection of quality shoes at competitive prices, Larry's Shoes in Fort Worth, Texas, gives customers logical reasons to buy. Emotional appeal is created by complimentary cappuccino, foot massages, and displays of celebrities' shoes, like this pair Clark Gable wore. Credibility comes both from salespeople's knowledge about shoes and from the quality of the brands the store carries.

When you don't yet have the credibility that comes from being an expert or being powerful, build credibility by the language and strategy you use:

- **Be factual.** Don't exaggerate.
- **Be specific.** If you say "X is better," show in detail *how* it is better. Show the reader exactly where the savings or other benefits come from so that it's clear that the proposal really is as good as you say it is.
- **Be reliable.** If you suspect that a project will take longer to complete, cost more money, or be less effective than you originally thought, tell your audience *immediately.* Negotiate a new schedule that you can meet.

Emotional appeal means making the reader *want* to do what you ask. People don't make decisions—even business decisions—based on logic alone. J. C. Mathes and Dwight W. Stevenson cite the following example. During his summer job, an engineering student who was asked to evaluate his company's waste treatment system saw a way that the system could be redesigned to save the company over $200,000 a year. He wrote a report recommending the change and gave it to his boss. Nothing happened. Why not? His supervisor wasn't about to send up a report that would require him to explain why *he'd* been wasting over $200,000 a year of the company's money.[4]

4. What Kind of Persuasion Is Best for the Organization and the Culture?

A strategy that works in one organization may not work somewhere else. James Suchan and Ron Dulek point out that DEC's corporate culture values no-holds-barred aggressiveness. "Even if opposition is expected, a subordinate should write a proposal in a forceful, direct manner."[5] In another organization with different cultural values, an employee who used a hard-sell strategy for a request antagonized the boss.[6]

Corporate culture (✖ p. 62) isn't written down; it's learned by imitation and observation. What style do high-level people in your organization use? When you show a draft to your boss, are you told to tone down your statements or to make them stronger? Role models and advice are two ways organizations communicate their culture to newcomers.

Different cultures also have different preferences for gaining compliance. In one study, students who were native speakers of American English judged di-

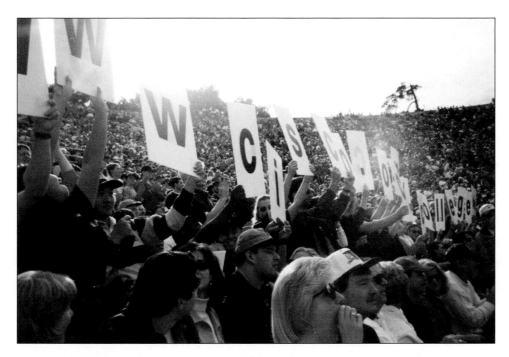

Choose the channel that best gets your persuasive message to the audience you want to reach. In the late 1990s, Cisco Systems added up to 1,200 new employees each quarter. How did it find them? One method was to seat Cisco employees in the end zones at the Stanford-Berkeley football game. Whenever a team scored, employees held up placards. Hits on Cisco's Web site rose 10% in the days after the game.

rect statements ("Do this"; "I want you to do this") clearer and more effective than questions ("Could you do this?") or hints ("This is needed"). Students who were native speakers of Korean, in contrast, judged direct statements to be *least* effective. In the Korean culture, the clearer a request is, the ruder and therefore less effective it is.[7]

Writing Direct Requests

When you expect quick agreement, save the reader's time by presenting the request directly. Also use the direct request pattern for busy people who do not read all the messages they receive and in organizations whose cultures favor putting the request first.

1. **Consider asking immediately for the information or service you want.**
   Delay the request if it seems too abrupt or if you have several purposes in the message.

2. **Give readers all the information they will need to act on your request.**
   Number your questions or set them off with bullets so the reader can check to see that all of them have been answered.

   In a claim (where a product is under warranty or a shipment was defective), explain the circumstances so that the reader knows what happened. Be sure to include all the relevant details: date of purchase, model or invoice number, and so on.

   In more complicated direct requests, anticipate possible responses. Suppose you're asking for information about equipment meeting certain specifications. Explain which criteria are most important so that the reader can recommend an alternative if no single product meets all your needs. You may also want to tell the reader what your price constraints are and ask whether the item is in stock or must be special-ordered.

3. **Ask for the action you want.** Do you want a check? A replacement? A catalog? Answers to your questions? If you need an answer by a certain time, say so. If possible, show the reader why the time limit is necessary.

Direct Requests Don't Translate*

Making a direct request may not be the most direct way to get what you want in all cultures.

In Saudi Arabia, it's rude to say to a taxi driver, "Take me to the airport." Instead say that a ride to the airport might be pleasant. Instead of ordering, suggest.

If you have a problem in China, start by thanking your hosts for all the things that make the experience a good one, praising the people, the accommodations and food, and even the scenery. Only after that should you mention "one little problem." Express confidence that your hosts will fix it. Instead of asking for immediate action, indicate that you'll check back in a few days. And leave behind a small gift.

*Based on Myron W. Lustig and Jolene Koester, *Intercultural Competence* (New York: HarperCollins, 1993), 228; and Iris Varner and Linda Beamer, *International Business Communication* (Chicago: Richard D. Irwin, 1995), 123–24.

Figure 9.1   *A Direct Request*

 Interoffice Memo
Keep each message to one topic.

Date: May 15, 2000

To: Michael Antonucci

From: David Anthony, Chair, BCS Suggestion Committee   *DA*

Subject: Suggestion #97204   *Topic of request in subject line*

Please evaluate the attached suggestion by May 29.   *Put request in ¶ 1.*

Spell out subquestions
- Should BCS adopt it? Why or why not?
- Will it save the company money? If so, how much a year?
- If the suggestion is adopted, how large an award should be given?

Make action easy
You may put your answers and brief reasons for them at the bottom of this page or send them to me by e-mail (anthony.37@bcs.com). Please get your response   *Ask for the action you want.*
in by May 29 as the suggestion committee is meeting on May 30.

Thanks!   *Reason to act promptly*

Figure 9.1 illustrates a direct request. Note that a direct request does not contain reader benefits and does not need to overcome objections: it simply asks for what is needed.

Direct requests should be direct. Don't make the reader guess what you want.

Indirect request: Is there a newer version of the 1995 *Accounting Reference Manual?*

Direct request: If there is a newer version of the 1995 *Accounting Reference Manual*, please send it to me.

Subject Lines for Direct Requests

In a direct request, put the request, the topic of the request, or a question in the subject line.

Subject: Request for Updated Software

My copy of HomeNet does not accept the nicknames for Eudora accounts.

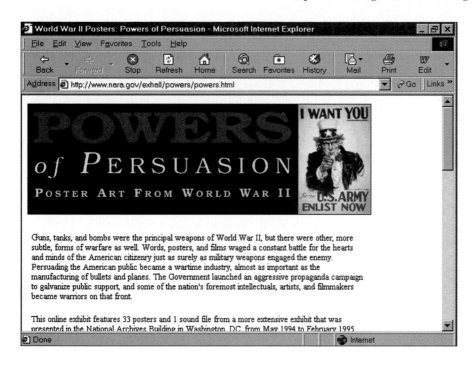

Persuasion can be based on positive or negative appeals. Part I of this exhibition of World War II poster art presents positive appeals focusing on confidence, patriotism, and strength. Part II presents negative appeals: suspicion, fear, and hate.

Subject: Status of Account #3548-003

Please get me the following information about account #3548-003.

Subject: Do We Need an Additional Training Session in October?

The two training sessions scheduled for October will accommodate 40 people. Last month, you said that 57 new staff accountants had been hired. Should we schedule an additional training session in October? Or can the new hires wait until the next regularly scheduled session in February?

Direct Requests with Multiple Purposes

In some direct requests, your combination of purposes may suggest a different pattern of organization. For example, in a letter asking an employer to reimburse you for expenses after a job interview, you'd want to thank your hosts for their hospitality and cement the good impression you made at the interview. To do that, you'd spend the first several paragraphs talking about the trip and the interview. Only in the last third of the letter (or even in the P.S.) would you put your request for reimbursement.

Similarly, in a letter asking about transferring to a four-year school or entering a graduate program, a major purpose might be to build a good image of yourself so that your application for financial aid would be viewed positively. To achieve that goal, provide information about your qualifications and interest in the field as well as asking questions.

Here's How You Benefit*

To create an Intranet for Xerox, Cindy Casselman (see p. 59) needed support from a variety of divisions. She had to persuade her own supervisor to let her work on the project. He said "yes," but told her she had to raise the $250,000 herself. She got the money and the programming talent she needed by showing other managers how they would benefit from the proposed Intranet. The CIO cared about the enormous financial investment the company had already made in its computer infrastructure. She told him that the Intranet would put content there. The director of education and training cared about learning at Xerox. Cindy pointed out that the Intranet would provide a place for learning to happen. She raised the $250,000 by showing people how her idea would benefit the aspects of the company they cared most about.

*Based on Michael Warshaw, "The Good Guy's and Gal's Guide to Office Politics," *Fast Company*, April–May 1998, 156–78.

Writing Problem-Solving Messages

Use an indirect approach and the problem-solving pattern of organization when you expect resistance from your reader but can show that doing what you want will solve a problem you and your reader share. This pattern allows you to disarm opposition by showing all the reasons in favor of your position before you give your readers a chance to say *no*.

1. **Catch the reader's interest by mentioning a common ground.** Show that your message will be interesting or beneficial. You may want to catch attention with a negative (which you will go on to show can be solved).
2. **Define the problem you both share (which your request will solve).** Present the problem objectively: don't assign blame or mention personalities. Be specific about the cost in money, time, lost goodwill, and so on. You have to convince readers that *something* has to be done before you can convince them that your solution is the best one.
3. **Explain the solution to the problem.** If you know that the reader will favor another solution, start with that solution and show why it won't work before you present your solution.

   Present your solution without using the words *I* or *my*. Don't let personalities enter the picture; don't let the reader think he or she should say *no* just because you've had other requests accepted recently.
4. **Show that any negative elements (cost, time, etc.) are outweighed by the advantages.**
5. **Summarize any additional benefits of the solution.** The main benefit—solving the problem—can be presented briefly since you described the problem in detail. However, if there are any additional benefits, mention them.
6. **Ask for the action you want.** Often your reader will authorize or approve something; other people will implement the action. Give your reader a reason to act promptly, perhaps offering a new reader benefit. ("By buying now, we can avoid the next quarter's price hikes.")

Figure 9.2 uses the problem-solving pattern of organization. Reader benefits can be brief in this kind of message since the biggest benefit comes from solving the problem.

Subject Lines for Problem-Solving Messages

When you have a reluctant reader, putting the request in the subject line just gets a quick *no* before you've had a chance to give all your arguments. One option is to use a **directed subject line** that makes your stance on the issue clear.[8] In the following examples, the first is the most neutral. The remaining two increasingly reveal the writer's preference.

Subject: A Proposal to Change the Formula for Calculating Retirees' Benefits

Subject: Arguments for Expanding the Marysville Plant

Subject: Why Cassano's Should Close Its West Side Store

Another option is to use common ground or a reader benefit—something that shows readers that this message will help them.

Subject: Reducing Energy Costs in the New Orleans Office

Energy costs in our New Orleans office have risen 12% in the last three years, even though the cost of gas has fallen and the cost of electricity has risen only 5%.

Figure 9.2   *A Problem-Solving Persuasive Message*

Memorandum

February 16, 2001

To: All Staff Members

From: Melissa J. Gutridge *MJG*

Subject: Why We Are Implementing a New Sign-Out System

Directed subject line indicates writer's position

Common ground

Problem

Successfully mainstreaming our clients into the community is very important and daily interaction with the public is necessary. Our clients enjoy the times they get to go to the mall or out to lunch instead of remaining here all day.   Recently, however, clients have been taken out on activities without a staff member's knowing where the client is and whom the client is with.

Specific example of problem

We need to know where all clients are at all times because social workers, psychologists, and relatives constantly stop by unannounced. Last week Janet's father stopped by to pick her up for a doctor's appointment and she was not here. No one knew where she was or whom she was with. Naturally her father was very upset and wanted to know what kind of program we were running. Staff members' not knowing where our clients are and whom they are with is damaging to the good reputation of our staff and program.

Solution presented impersonally

Additional reader benefit

Starting Monday, February 26, a sign-out board will be located by Betty's desk. Please write down where you and the client are going and when you expect to be back. When signing out, help clients sign themselves out. We can turn this into a learning experience for our clients. Then when a social worker stops by to see someone who isn't here, we can simply look at the sign-out board to tell where the client is and when he or she will return.

Tells reader what to do

Please help keep up the superb reputation you have helped Weststar earn as a quality center for adults with handicaps. Sign out yourself and clients at all times.

Although your first paragraph may be negative in a problem-solving message, your subject line should be neutral or positive.

Both directed subject lines and benefit subject lines can also be used as report titles.

Developing a Common Ground

A common ground avoids the me-against-you of some persuasive situations and suggests that both you and your audience have a mutual interest in solving the problems you face. To find a common ground, we analyze the audience, understand their biases, objections, and needs, and identify with them so that we can make them identify with us. This analysis can be carried out in a cold, manipulative way. It can also be based on a respect for and sensitivity to the audience's position.

Say What?*

The following "benefits" appeared in classified ads. Did the writers think readers are that gullible? Or did they just not realize what they were really saying?

- The Macon County Humane Society offers free spaying/neutering to senior citizens if they adopt an animal out of the animal shelter.

- Remember, you get what you pay for. And at Hub Furniture Store, you pay less.

- Home, $199,500. Great location. . . . Built the way they used to. Won't last.

- Try our cough syrup. You will never get any better.

- Artie's Restaurant and Yogurt Parlor: "An Alternative to Good Eating."

- FOR SALE: Braille dictionary. Must see to appreciate.

- Now you can borrow enough money to get completely out of debt.

*Examples quoted from Richard Lederer, *More Anguished English* (New York: Delacorte, 1993), 107–12.

Readers are highly sensitive to manipulation. No matter how much you disagree with your audience, respect their intelligence. Try to understand why they believe or do something and why they may object to your position. If you can understand your readers' initial positions, you'll be more effective—and you won't alienate your readers by talking down to them.

The best common grounds are specific. Often a negative—a problem the reader will want to solve—makes a good common ground.

Weak common ground:	This program has had some difficulty finding enough individuals to volunteer their services for the children. As a result, we are sometimes unable to provide the one-on-one mentoring that is our goal.
Improved common ground:	On five Sundays in the last three months, we've had too few volunteers to provide one-on-one mentoring. Last Sunday, we had just two college students to take eight children to the Museum of Science and Industry.

Generalizations are likely to bore the reader. Instead, use the idea behind the generalization to focus on something the reader cares about.

Weak common ground:	We all want this plant to be profitable.
Improved common ground:	We forfeited a possible $186,000 in profits last summer due to a 17% drop in productivity.

In your common ground, emphasize the parts of your proposal that fit with what your audience already does or believes. An employee of 3M wanted to develop laser disks. He realized that 3M's previous products were thin and flat: Scotch tape, Post-it Notes, magnetic tape. When he made his presentation to the group that chose new products for development, he held his prototype disk horizontally, so his audience saw a flat, thin object rather than a large, round, recordlike object. Making his project fit with the audience's previous experience was a subtle and effective emotional tool to make it easier for the audience to say *yes*.[9]

Use audience analysis to evaluate possible common grounds. Suppose you want to install a system to play background music in a factory. To persuade management to pay for the system, a possible common ground would be increasing productivity. However, to persuade the union to pay for the system, you'd need a different common ground. Workers would see productivity as a way to get them to do more work for the same pay. A better common ground would be that the music would make the factory environment more pleasant.

Dealing with Objections

If you know that your readers will hear other points of view, or if your audience's initial position is negative, you have to deal with their objections to persuade them. The stronger the objection is, the earlier in your message you should deal with it.

The best way to deal with an objection is to eliminate it. James Davis keeps frequently ordered items in stock to eliminate the objection "I don't want to wait." To sell Jeep Cherokees in Japan, Mitsuru Sato convinced Chrysler to put the driver's seat on the right side, to make an extra preshipment quality check, and to rewrite the instruction booklet in Japanese style, with big diagrams and cartoons.[10]

If an objection is false and is based on misinformation, give the response to the objection without naming the objection. In a brochure, you can present responses with a "question/answer" format. When objections have already been voiced, you may want to name the objection so that your audience realizes that you are responding to that specific objection. However, to avoid solidifying the opposition, don't attribute the objection to your audience. Instead, use a less

The best way to overcome an objection is to remove it entirely. In 1993, Denny's lost a $54 million class action lawsuit for racial discrimination. Since then, the company has worked hard to change its corporate culture. Perhaps the most dramatic evidence of its success is increasing black ownership. Akin Olajuwon (brother of the basketball star) bought 63 restaurants in 1998, with an agreement to raise the number to 100 by 2002.

personal attribution: "Some people wonder . . ."; "Some citizens are afraid that. . . ."

If real objections remain, try one or more of the following strategies to counter objections:

1. Specify how much time and/or money is required—it may not be as much as the reader fears.

> Distributing flyers to each house or apartment in your neighborhood will probably take two afternoons.

2. Put the time and/or money in the context of the benefits they bring.

> The additional $152,500 will (1) allow the Open Shelter to remain open 24 rather than 16 hours a day, (2) pay for three social workers to help men find work and homes, and (3) keep the Neighborhood Bank open, so that men don't have to cash Social Security checks in bars and so that they can save up the $800 they need to have up front to rent an apartment.

3. Show that money spent now will save money in the long run.

> By buying a $100 safety product, you can save $500 in OSHA fines.

4. Show that doing as you ask will benefit some group or cause the reader supports, even though the action may not help the reader directly. This is the strategy used in fund-raising letters, discussed in detail in Chapter 11.

> By being a Big Brother or a Big Sister, you'll give a child the adult attention he or she needs to become a well-adjusted, productive adult.

5. Show the reader that the sacrifice is necessary to achieve a larger, more important goal to which he or she is committed.

Are You Doing the Right Thing?*

Pressures of business sometimes create an environment where people think that anything goes. To be sure that you're doing the right thing, ask the following questions:

- Whom will your action hurt?
- Can you discuss the problem with the people who will be affected before you act?
- How would you define the problem if you stood on the other side of the fence?
- How would you feel if your action were known to your boss, your CEO, your family, or society as a whole?
- What symbolic message will people get if they understand your action? If they misunderstand it?

*Based on Laura L. Nash, "Ethics without the Sermon," *Executive Success: Making It in Management*, ed. Eliza G. Collins (New York: John Wiley & Sons, 1983), 497.

**Creative Response
to an Objection, I***

To cut costs, banks want customers to use ATM machines rather than expensive tellers. But older customers prefer talking to a person. And retirees want their errands to provide social contact.

Canada's second-largest bank, CIBC, hires greeters to train people how to use the ATM machines and to provide human contact at tellerless branches.

And humor helps. Victoria Brink Guillot, manager of a Citibank branch in San Mateo, California, tells her mature customers, "ATMs are just like slot machines, only you never lose."

*Based on Paco Underhill, "Seniors in Stores," *American Demographics*, April 1996, 48.

> These changes will mean more work for all of us. But we've got to cut our costs 25% to keep the plant open and to keep our jobs.

6. Show that the advantages as a group outnumber or outweigh the disadvantages as a group.

> None of the locations is perfect. But the Backbay location gives us the most advantages and the fewest disadvantages.

7. Turn a disadvantage into an opportunity.

> With the hiring freeze, every department will need more lead time to complete its own work. By hiring another person, the Planning Department could provide that lead time.

Offering a Reason for the Reader to Act Promptly

The longer people delay, the less likely they are to carry through with the action they had decided to take. In addition, you want a fast response so you can go ahead with your own plans.

Just asking for prompt action can help speed a response. Request action by a specific date. Try to give people at least a week or two: they have other things to do besides respond to your requests. Set deadlines in the middle of the month, if possible. If you say, "Please return this by March 1," people will think, "I don't need to do this till March." Ask for the response by February 28 instead. If you can use a response even after the deadline, say so. Otherwise, people who can't make the deadline may not respond at all.

Readers may ignore deadlines that seem arbitrary. Show why you need a quick response:

- **Show that the time limit is real.** Perhaps you need information quickly to use it in a report that has a due date. Perhaps a decision must be made by a certain date to catch the start of the school year, the Christmas selling season, or an election campaign. Perhaps you need to be ready for a visit from out-of-town or international colleagues.
- **Show that acting now will save time or money.** If business is slow and your industry isn't doing well, then your company needs to act now (to economize, to better serve customers) in order to be competitive. If business is booming and everyone is making a profit, then your company needs to act now to get its fair share of the available profits.
- **Show the cost of delaying action.** Will labor or material costs be higher in the future? Will delay mean more money spent on repairing something that will still need to be replaced?

Building Emotional Appeal

Stories and psychological description are effective ways of building emotional appeal. Emotional appeal works best when people want to be persuaded.

Even when you need to provide statistics or numbers to convince the careful reader that your anecdote is a representative example, telling a story first makes your message more persuasive. Experiments with both high school teachers and quantitatively trained MBA students show that people are more likely to believe a point and more likely to be committed to it when points were made by examples, stories, and case studies. Stories alone were more effective than a combination of stories and statistics; the combination was more effective than statistics alone. In another experiment, attitude changes lasted longer when the audience had read stories than when they had only read numbers. Recent research suggests that stories are more persuasive because people remember them.[11]

Sense impressions—what the reader sees, hears, smells, tastes, feels—evoke a strong emotional response. **Psychological description** means creating a scenario rich with sense impressions so readers can picture themselves using your product or service and enjoying its benefits. You can also use psychological description to describe the problem your product will solve. Psychological description works best early in the message to catch readers' attention.

Feature:	Snooze alarm
Benefit:	If the snooze button is pressed, the alarm goes off and comes on again nine minutes later.
Psychological description:	Some mornings, you really want to stay in bed just a few more minutes. With the Sleepytime Snooze Alarm, you can snuggle under the covers for a few extra winks, secure in the knowledge that the alarm will come on again to get you up for that breakfast meeting with an important client. If you don't have to be anywhere soon, you can keep hitting the snooze alarm for up to an additional 63 minutes of sleep. With Sleepytime, you're in control of your mornings.
Feature:	Tilt windows
Benefit:	Easier to clean
Psychological description:	It's no wonder so many cleaners "don't do windows." Balancing precariously on a rickety ladder to clean upper-story windows . . . shivering outside in the winter winds and broiling in the summer sun as you scrub away . . . running inside, then outside, then inside again to try to get the spot that always seems to be on the other side. Cleaning traditional windows really is awful.
	In contrast, cleaning is a breeze with Tilt-in Windows. Just pull the inner window down and pull the bottom toward you. The whole window lifts out! Repeat for the outer window. Clean them inside in comfort (sitting down or even watching TV if you choose). Then replace the top of the outer window in its track, slide up, and repeat with the inner window. Presto! Clean windows!

Someone who's already looking for a product may need only the feature or the benefit. Good psychological description uses vivid details and sensory imagery to motivate uncommitted readers. The flyer for a university's food services in Figure 9.3 gets your gastric juices flowing.

In psychological description, you're putting your reader in a picture. If the reader doesn't feel that the picture fits him or her, the technique backfires. To prevent this, psychological description often uses subjunctive verbs ("if you like . . . " "if you were . . . ") or the words *maybe* and *perhaps*.

You're hungry but you don't want to bother with cooking. Perhaps you have guests to take to dinner. Or it's 12 noon and you only have an hour for lunch. Whatever the situation, the Illini Union has a food service to fit your needs. If you want convenience, we have it. If it's atmosphere you're seeking, it's here too. And if you're concerned about the price, don't be. When you're looking for a great meal, the Illini Union is the place to find it.

Illini Union brochure

Creative Response to an Objection, II*

Jim Young sold apples by direct mail order. One year, a hailstorm just before the harvest bruised the apples.

At first, the obstacle appeared insurmountable. For years, his selling point had been that his apples looked as good as they tasted.

But Jim was able to turn the disadvantage into an advantage.

He knew that cold weather (partially responsible for the hailstorm) improves the flavor of ripening apples. So he filled the orders, inserting a note in each box:

Note the hail marks which have caused minor skin blemishes in some of these apples. They are proof of their growth at a high mountain altitude where the sudden chills from hailstorms help firm the flesh, develop the natural sugars, and give these apples their incomparable flavor.

Not one customer asked for a refund. In fact, the next year, some people wrote on their orders, "Send the hail-marked apples if possible."

*Based on Ray Considine and Murray Raphael, *The Great Brain Robbery* (Pasadena, CA: The Great Brain Robbery, 1981), 95–96.

Figure 9.3   *Using Psychological Description to Develop Reader Benefits*

You–attitude psychological description

The Colonial Room

When you dine in the Illini Union Colonial Room, it's easy to imagine yourself a guest in a fine Virginian mansion. Light from the gleaming chandeliers reflects from a hand-carved mirror hanging over the dark, polished buffet. Here you can dine in quiet elegance amid furnishings adapted from 18th century Williamsburg and the Georgian homes of the James River Valley in Virginia.

Perhaps you'd like a dinner of stuffed rainbow trout. Or the pork fricassee. The menu features a variety of complete meals which are changed daily, as well as the regular a la carte service. Whatever your choice, you'll enjoy an evening of fine dining at very reasonable prices.

The Illini Union Colonial Room is located on the northeast corner of the first floor. Dinners are served Monday through Friday from 5:30 to 7:30 p.m. Please call 333-0690 for reservations, and enjoy the flavor of the Colonies tonight.

Visual details

Details appeal to sight, taste, smell

Emphasis on reader's choice— Not every reader will want the same thing

The Cafeteria

In the Illini Union Cafeteria, you start out with an empty tray and silverware. Then comes the food, several yards of it, all yours for the choosing. By the time you've finished, your empty tray has become a delicious meal.

In the morning, the warm aroma of breakfast fills the air. Feast your eyes and then your appetite on the array of eggs, bacon, pancakes, toast, sausage, rolls, juices, and coffee . . . They're all waiting to wake you up with good taste. Have a hearty breakfast or make it quick and tasty. The warm, freshly baked sweet rolls and coffeecakes practically beg to be smothered in butter and savored with a cup of hot coffee.

By 11 a.m. the breakfast menu has made way for lunch. Here come the plump Reuben sandwiches and the toasty grilled cheese. Soups and salads make their appearance. A variety of vegetables are dressed up to entice you and several main dishes lead the luncheon parade. Any number of complete meals can take shape as you move along.

What? Back for dinner? Well, no wonder! The Cafeteria sets out a wide selection of entrees and side dishes. Veal parmigiana steams for your attention but the roast beef right next to it is rough competition. Tomorrow the fried chicken might be up for selection. Choose the dinner combination that best fits your appetite and your pocket.

The newly remodeled Cafeteria is on the ground floor and is open for breakfast from 7 to 11 a.m. Monday through Saturday and 8 to 11 a.m. on Sunday. Lunch is served from 11 a.m. to 1:15 p.m. Monday through Saturday and 11 a.m. to 2 p.m. on Sunday. Dinner is served from 4:45 to 7 p.m. Monday through Friday.

A meal in a restaurant is expensive. A meal at home is a chore. But a meal at the Cafeteria combines good food and reasonable prices to make dining a pleasure.

Tone in Persuasive Messages

The best phrasing depends on your relationship to the reader. When you ask for action from people who report directly to you, orders ("Get me the Ervin file") and questions ("Do we have the third-quarter numbers yet?") will work. When you need action from co-workers, superiors, or people outside the organization, you need to be more forceful but also more polite.

How you ask for action affects whether you build or destroy positive relationships with other employees, customers, and suppliers. Professor and consultant Dan Dieterich notes that the calls to action in many messages are

- Buried somewhere deep in the middle of the correspondence.
- Disguised as either statements or questions.
- Insulting because they use "parental language."

Such messages, Dieterich points out, "lower productivity within the organization and reduce or eliminate the goodwill customers have toward the organization. . . . [T]hose two things . . . can put the organization out of business."[12]

Avoiding messages that sound parental or preachy is often a matter of tone. Saying "Please" is a nice touch, especially to people on your level or outside the organization. Tone will also be better when you give reasons for your request or reasons to act promptly.

Parental: Everyone is expected to comply with these regulations. I'm sure you can see that they are commonsense rules needed for our business.

Better: Even on casual days, visitors expect us to be professional. So leave the gym clothes at home!

When you write to people you know well, humor can work. Just make sure that the message isn't insulting to anyone who doesn't find the humor funny.

Writing to superiors is trickier. You may want to tone down your request by using subjunctive verbs and explicit disclaimers that show you aren't taking a *yes* for granted.

Arrogant: Based on this evidence, I expect you to give me a new computer.

Better: If department funds permit, I would like a new computer.

Passive verbs and jargon sound stuffy. Use active imperatives—perhaps with "Please" to create a friendlier tone.

Stuffy: It is requested that you approve the above-mentioned action.

Better: Please authorize us to create a new subscription letter.

Writing Persuasive E-Mail Messages

It can be particularly tricky to control tone in e-mail messages, which always tend to sound less friendly than paper documents or conversations. For important requests, it's worth taking the time to compose your message offline and revise it carefully before you send it.

Paper messages can work up to the request since readers will normally skim the first page. But e-mail messages have to catch the reader's eye in the subject line. If the message is longer than one screen, the first screen must interest the reader enough to make him or her continue. E-mail messages to people who report directly to you are easy, since people will read anything from their supervisors. But writing to people who are not in a direct reporting relationship or to people outside your unit or organization takes more care.

The subject line of a persuasive e-mail message should make it clear that you're asking for something. If you're sure that the reader will read the message, something as vague as "Request" may work. Most of the time, it's better to be more specific.

Subject: Move Meeting to Tuesday?

Subject: Need Your Advice

Subject: Provide Story for Newsletter?

Subject: Want You for United Way Campaign

Try to keep the subject line short. If that's difficult, put the most important part into the first few words since many e-mail programs only show the first 28 characters of the subject line.

Creative Response to a Problem, III*

While an Ernst & Young team was preparing a proposal to undertake a fixed fee project for a client, the client asked bidders to enlarge the scope of the project. The team immediately said yes, then set about determining how to meet the client's request. But because the request came late in the proposal process, Ernst & Young didn't have enough time to properly figure out how much the additional work would cost. Asking too little would result in a loss for the firm; asking too much might mean losing the bid entirely. So the team suggested to the client that they work together for 30 days as part of the project to determine the value and scope of the project. This flexibility and ability to respond to change resulted in Ernst & Young's winning not only the original project but also even larger work later.

*Based on statement from James Lane to Kitty Locker, March 8, 1999.

**Creative Response
to an Objection, IV***

WearGuard Corporation in Norwell, Massachusetts, makes uniforms and rugged work clothes. Orders are heaviest in the fall, when the company needs 400 more workers than it needs the rest of the year. Training costs soar; quality falls.

Managers didn't like any of the conventional solutions. Lisa Zankman, Vice President for Human Resources, said, "Wouldn't it be great if we could find a company with a different peak season?" They did. Cross Country Motor Club takes distress calls from car owners who need towing. Its workload is busiest summer and winter. Employees at each company learn to take calls for the other; telephone switches carry the calls.

Each company gets trained workers in its busy season, with no need to lay off people when calls are lighter.

Based on "Lisa Zankman Solved Her Staffing Woes with a Wacky Plan," *The Wall Street Journal*, June 21, 1996, B1.

When you ask for something small or for something that it is part of the reader's job duties to provide, your request can be straightforward. In the body of the message, give people all the information they need to act. At the end of the message, ask for the action you want. Make the action as easy as possible, and specify when you need a response. You may want an immediate response now ("Let me know ASAP whether you can write a story for the newsletter so that I can save the space") and a fuller one later ("We'll need the text by March 4").

When you ask for something big or something which is not a regular part of that person's duties, the first paragraph must not only specify the request but also make the reader view it positively. Use the second paragraph to provide an overview of the evidence that the rest of the message will provide: "Here's why we should do this." "Let me describe the project. Then, if you're willing to be part of it, I'll send you a copy of the proposal." Use audience analysis to find a reason to do as you ask that the reader will find convincing. Everyone is busy, so you need to make the reader *want* to do as you ask. Be sure to provide complete information that the reader will need to act on your request. Ask for the action you want.

Major requests that require changes in values, culture, or lifestyles should not be made in e-mail messages.

Varieties of Persuasive Messages

Collection letters, performance appraisals, and letters of recommendation are among the most common varieties of persuasive messages.

Collection Letters

Most businesses find that phoning rather than writing results in faster payment. But as more and more companies install voice mail systems, you will need to write letters when leaving messages doesn't work.

Collection letters ask customers to pay (as they have already agreed to do) for the goods and services they have already received. Instead of sending one letter, or repeated copies of the same letter, good credit departments send a **series** of letters. Letters in the series should be only a week apart. Waiting a month between letters implies that you're prepared to wait a long time—and the reader will be happy to oblige you!

Early letters are gentle, assuming that the reader intends to pay but has forgotten or has met with temporary reverses. Early letters can be obvious form letters or even just a second copy of the bill with the words "Second Notice" or "Past Due" stamped on it.

A student who had not yet been reimbursed by a company for a visit to the company's office put the second request in the P.S. of a letter refusing a job offer:

> P.S. The check to cover my expenses when I visited your office in March hasn't come yet. Could you check to see whether you can find a record of it? The amount was $490 (airfare $290, hotel room $185, taxi $15).

Early collection letters sometimes use humor to defuse negative feelings and to set themselves apart from other mail. Since readers' senses of humor differ, the real test of a collection letter using humor should be: Does it enrage readers who think they have already paid? Does it make the request seem trivial, as though the bill is a joke? If the answer to either of these questions is *yes*, don't use the humor.

If one or two early letters don't result in payment, call the customer to ask if your company has created a problem. It's possible that you shipped something the customer didn't want or sent the wrong quantity. It's possible that the invoice arrived before the product and was filed and forgotten. It's possible that the invoice document is poorly designed, so customers set it aside until they could figure it out. If any of these situations apply, you'll build goodwill by solving the problem rather than arrogantly asking for payment.[13]

Middle letters are more assertive in asking for payment. Figure 9.4 gives an example of a middle letter. This form letter is merged with database information about the customer's name, the amount due, and the magazine the customer is receiving. Other middle letters offer to negotiate a schedule for repayment if the reader is not able to pay the whole bill immediately, may remind the reader of the importance of a good credit rating (which will be endangered if the bill remains unpaid), educate the reader about credit, and explain why the creditor must have prompt payment.

Unless you have firm evidence to the contrary, middle letters should assume that readers have some legitimate reason for not yet paying. Perhaps they've been out of town. Perhaps their checks were lost in the mail. Perhaps they're waiting to receive payments due them so that they can pay their own creditors. Even people who are "juggling" payments because they do not have enough money to pay all their bills or people who will put payment off as long as possible will respond more quickly if you do not accuse them. If a reader is offended by your assumption that he or she is dishonest, that anger can become an excuse to continue delaying payment.

Late letters threaten legal action if the bill is not paid. Under federal law, the writer cannot threaten legal action unless he or she actually intends to sue. Other regulations also spell out what a writer may and may not do in a late letter.

Many small businesses find that establishing personal relationships with customers is the best way to speed payment.

Performance Appraisals

At regular intervals, supervisors evaluate, or appraise, the performance of their subordinates. In most organizations, employees have access to their files; sometimes they must sign the appraisal to show that they've read it. The superior normally meets with the subordinate to discuss the appraisal.

As a subordinate, you should prepare for the appraisal interview by listing your achievements and goals. Where do you want to be in a year or five years? What training and experience do you need to reach your goals? Also think about any weaknesses. If you need training, advice, or support from the organization to improve, the appraisal interview is a good time to ask for this help.

Appraisals need to both protect the organization and motivate the employee. These two purposes conflict. Most of us will see a candid appraisal as negative; we need praise and reassurance to believe that we're valued and can do better. But the praise that motivates someone to improve can come back to haunt the company if the person does not eventually do acceptable work. An organization is in trouble if it tries to fire someone whose evaluations never mention mistakes.

Avoid labels (*wrong, bad*) and inferences. Instead, cite specific observations that describe behavior.

Speedier Collections*

Art Allen, the CEO of Allen Systems Groups, a software manufacturer in Naples, Florida, cut his average collection time from 61 days to 45 days with a combination of computerized "tickler" files and low-tech phone calls.

Before invoices go out, accounts receivable staffers call clients to ask how long payment typically takes and to make certain that the computer information (address, etc.) is correct.

A few days after invoices are mailed, a staffer calls to make sure the bill arrived. If it didn't, a copy of the invoice is faxed.

If the payment doesn't arrive on the expected payment date (based on information about typical payment times), staffers call to find out what went wrong.

Because he's now paid more quickly, Allen has been able to pay off his corporate debt.

*Based on "Speedier Collection," *Inc.*, June 1995, 93.

Getting Action with Voice Mail

If your action is small and easy, you can ask for it in a voice mail message: "Please fax me a copy of your price list."

When you want something more complicated or that the other person may be less willing to give, prepare a 30-second summary of your request, including the benefit to the person whose action you want. Put energy into your voice, so that you sound interesting to talk to.

As in any voice mail message, state your name and phone number slowly and clearly. If you want something sent by e-mail, fax, or mail, give the appropriate number or address clearly. Specify when you'll be available to take return calls. If possible, give the person several options.

Inference:	Sam is an alcoholic.
Vague observation:	Sam calls in sick a lot. Subordinates complain about his behavior.
Specific observation:	Sam called in sick a total of 12 days in the last two months. After a business lunch with a customer last week, Sam was walking unsteadily. Two of his subordinates have said that they would prefer not to make sales trips with him because they find his behavior embarrassing.

Sam might be an alcoholic. He might also be having a reaction to a physician-prescribed drug; he might have a mental illness; he might be showing symptoms of a physical illness other than alcoholism. A supervisor who jumps to conclusions creates ill will, closes the door to solving the problem, and may provide grounds for legal action against the organization.

Be specific in an appraisal.

Too vague:	Sue does not manage her time as well as she could.
Specific:	Sue's first three weekly sales reports have been three, two, and four days late, respectively; the last weekly sales report for the month is not yet in.

Without specifics, Sue won't know that her boss objects to late reports. She may think that she is being criticized for spending too much time on sales calls or for not working 80 hours a week. Without specifics, she might change the wrong things in a futile effort to please her boss.

Good supervisors try not only to identify the specific problems in subordinates' behavior but also in conversation to discover the causes of the problem. Does the employee need more training? Perhaps a training course or a mentor will help. Does he or she need to work harder? Then the supervisor needs to motivate the worker and help him or her manage distractions. Is a difficult situation causing the problem? Perhaps the situation can be changed. If it can't be changed, the supervisor and the company should realize that the worker is not at fault.

Figure 9.4

A Middle Collection Letter

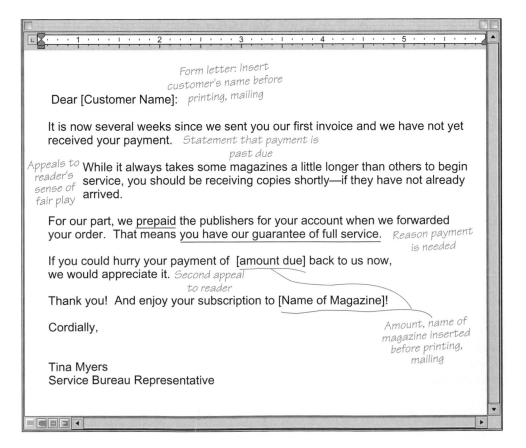

Sometimes a performance appraisal reflects mostly the month or week right before the appraisal, even though it is supposed to cover six months or a year. Many managers record specific observations of subordinates' behavior two or three times a month. These notes jog the memory so that the appraisal doesn't focus unduly on recent behavior.

Appraisals are more useful to subordinates if they make clear which areas are most important and contain specific recommendations for improvement. No one can improve 17 weaknesses at once. Which two should the employee work on this month? Is getting in reports on time more important than increasing sales?

Phrase goals in specific, concrete terms. The subordinate may think that "considerable progress toward completing" a report may mean that the project should be 15% finished. The boss may think that "considerable progress" means 50% or 85% of the total work.

Figure 9.5 shows a performance appraisal for a member of a collaborative business communication group.

 See the BAC Web site for links on performance appraisals.

Letters of Recommendation

In an effort to protect themselves against lawsuits, some companies state only how long they employed someone and the position that person held. Such bare-bones letters have themselves been the target of lawsuits when employers did not reveal relevant negatives. Whatever the legal climate, there may be times when you want to recommend someone for an award or for a job.

Letters of recommendation must be specific. General positives that are not backed up with specific examples and evidence are seen as weak recommendations. Letters of recommendation that focus on minor points also suggest that the person is weak.

Either in the first or the last paragraph, summarize your overall evaluation of the person. Early in the letter, perhaps in the first paragraph, show how well and how long you've known the person. In the middle of the letter, offer specific details about the person's performance. At the end of the letter, indicate whether you would be willing to rehire the person and repeat your overall evaluation. Figure A.3 in Appendix A shows a sample letter of recommendation.

Experts are divided on whether you should include negatives. Some people feel that any negative weakens the letter. Other people feel that presenting but not emphasizing honest negatives makes the letter more convincing.

In many discourse communities, the words "Call me if you need more information" in a letter of recommendation mean "I have negative information that I am unwilling to put on paper. Call me and I'll tell you what I really think."

Solving a Sample Problem[14]

Problem

In one room in the production department of Nakamura Electronics Company, employees work on TV picture tubes under conditions that are scarcely bearable due to the heat. Even when the temperature outside is only 75°, it is over 100° in the "tube room." In June, July, and August, 24 out of 36 workers quit because they couldn't stand the heat. This turnover happens every summer.

On the Road*

A 401(k) program is one of the best ways to save for retirement. The money an employee invests is deducted from taxable income (perhaps bringing one into a lower tax bracket) and grows tax-free until it is withdrawn in retirement.

Persuading eligible people to invest requires education. One of the most effective programs combined education with humor and astute channel choice.

About 80% of J. B. Hunt Transport Services' employees are drivers. So the company created a "Road to Retirement" campaign, putting financial information on the "Super Driver" audiocassette it gives its truckers. Factual material on the benefits of savings shares space with country-and-western songs and tongue-in-cheek romantic advice ("Don't play 'You Can't Always Get What You Want' on your wedding night"). Truckers loved the tape, and participation in J. B. Hunt's 401(k) program rose from 45% to almost 70% in three months.

*Based on Bethany McLean, "How Your 401(k) Stacks Up," *Fortune*, August 19, 1996, 130.

February 13, 2001

To: Barbara Buchanan

From: Brittany Papper *BAP*

Subject line indicates that memo is a performance appraisal

Subject: Your Performance Thus Far in Our Collaborative Group

Overall evaluation

You have been a big asset to our group. Overall, our business communication group has been one of the best groups I have ever worked with, and I think that only minor improvements are needed to make our group even better.

What You're Doing Well

Specific observations provide dates, details of performance

You demonstrated flexibility and compatibility at our last meeting before we turned in our proposal on February 12 by offering to type the proposal since I had to study for an exam in one of my other classes. I really appreciated this because I really did not have the time to do it. I will definitely remember this if you are ever too busy with your other classes and cannot type the final report.

Another positive critical incident occurred February 5. We had discussed researching the topic of sexual discrimination in hiring and promotion at Midstate Insurance. As we read more about what we had to do, we became uneasy about reporting the information from our source who works at Midstate. I called you later that evening to talk about changing our topic to a less personal one. You were very understanding and said that you agreed that the original topic was a touchy one. You offered suggestions for other topics and had a positive attitude about the adjustment. Your suggestions ended my worries and made me realize that you are a positive and supportive person.

Other strengths

Your ideas are a strength that you definitely contribute to our group. You're good at brainstorming ideas, yet you're willing to go with whatever the group decides. That's a nice combination of creativity and flexibility.

Areas for Improvement

Two minor improvements could make you an even better member.

Specific recommendations for improvement

The first improvement is to be more punctual to meetings. On February 5 and February 8 you were about 10 minutes late. This makes the meetings last longer. Your ideas are valuable to the group, and the sooner you arrive the sooner we can share in your suggestions.

Specific behavior to be changed

The second suggestion is one we all need to work on. We need to keep our meetings positive and productive. I think that our negative attitudes were worst at our first group meeting February 5. We spent about half an hour complaining about all the work we had to do and about our busy schedules in other classes. In the future if this happens, maybe you could offer some positive things about the assignment to get the group motivated again.

Overall Compatibility

Positive, forward-looking ending

I feel that this group has gotten along very well together. You have been very flexible in finding times to meet and have always been willing to do your share of the work. I have never had this kind of luck with a group in the past and you have been a welcome breath of fresh air. I don't hate doing group projects any more!

In a far corner of the room sits a quality control inspector in front of a small fan (the only one in the room). The production workers, in contrast, are carrying 20-pound TV tubes. As Production Supervisor, you tried to get air-conditioning two years ago, before Nakamura acquired the company, but management was horrified at the idea of spending $300,000 to insulate and air-condition the warehouse (it is impractical to air-condition the tube room alone).

Inflation has pushed the price of insulation and air-conditioning up to $500,000, but with such high turnover, you're losing money every summer. Write a memo to Jennifer M. Kirkland, Operations Vice President, renewing your request.

Analysis of the Problem

1. Who is (are) your audience(s)? What characteristics are relevant to this particular message? If you are writing to more than one reader, how do the readers differ?

   The Operations Vice President will be concerned about keeping costs low and keeping production running smoothly. Kirkland may know that the request was denied two years ago, but another person was Vice President then; Kirkland wasn't the one who said *no.*

2. What are your purposes in writing?

   To persuade Kirkland to authorize insulation and air-conditioning. To build a good image of myself.

3. What information must your message include?

   The cost of the proposal. The effects of the present situation.

4. How can you build support for your position? What reasons or reader benefits will your reader find convincing?

   Cutting turnover may save money and keep the assembly line running smoothly. Experienced employees may produce higher-quality parts. Putting in air-conditioning would relieve one of the workers' main complaints; it might make the union happier.

5. What objection(s) can you expect your reader(s) to have? What negative elements of your message must you deemphasize or overcome?

   The cost. The time operations will be shut down while installation is taking place.

6. What aspects of the total situation may affect reader response? The economy? The time of year? Morale in the organization? The relationship between the reader and writer? Any special circumstances?

   The electronics industry is having a shakeout; money is tight; the company will be reluctant to make a major expenditure. Filling vacancies in the tube room is hard—we are getting a reputation as a bad place to work. Summer is over, and the problem is over until next year.

Discussion of the Sample Solutions

Solution 1, shown in Figure 9.6, is unacceptable. By making the request in the subject line and the first paragraph, the writer invites a *no* before giving all the arguments. The writer does nothing to counter the objections that any manager will have to spending a great deal of money. By presenting the issue in terms of fairness, the writer produces defensiveness rather than creating a common ground. The writer doesn't use details or emotional appeal to show that the problem is indeed serious. The writer asks for fast action but doesn't show why

Credit Collection and the Law*

The Fair Debt Collection Practices Act (15 U.S.C. § 1601 and following) limits the actions of attorneys and debt collectors.

Collectors are **not** allowed to

- Harass debtors on the phone or in person, threaten violence, use obscenities or profanity, or publish a list of debtors.
- Call debtors at work or late at night.
- Misrepresent the legal status of the debt, the creditor's actual intent to take legal action, or the consequences of not paying.

Collectors are **required** to

- Specify the amount of the debt and the name of the creditor.
- Specify that the debtor has 30 days to dispute the validity of the debt.
- Offer to provide the name and address of the original creditor, if the debtor asks for it, and if the collector is not the original creditor.

*Based on Fredric A. Kannensohn, "Attorney Beware: Fair Debt Collection Practices Act," and Gregory L. Karam, "Drafting a Demand Letter in Compliance with the Fair Debt Collection Practices Act," both in *Ohio State Bar Association Report* 60, no. 30 (July 20, 1987): 1236–44.

F i g u r e   9.6   *An Unacceptable Solution to the Sample Problem*

Date: October 12, 2000

To: Jennifer M. Kirkland, Operations Vice President

From: Arnold M. Morgan, Production Supervisor *AMM*

Subject: Request for Air-Conditioning the Tube Room   *Request in subject line stiffens resistance when reader is reluctant*

Please put air-conditioning in the tube room. This past summer, 2/3 of our employees quit because it was so hot. It's (not fair) that they should work in unbearable temperatures when management sits in air-conditioned comfort.   *attacks reader*

Inappropriate emphasis on writer   (I) propose that we solve this problem by air-conditioning the tube room to bring down the temperature to 78°.

Insulating and air-conditioning the tube room would cost $500,000.   *Cost sounds enormous without a context*

Please approve this request promptly.

Memo sounds arrogant.
Logic isn't developed.
This attacks reader instead of enlisting reader's support.

the reader should act now to solve a problem that won't occur again for eight months.

Solution 2, shown in Figure 9.7, is an effective persuasive message. The writer chooses a positive subject line. The opening sentence is negative, catching the reader's attention. However, the paragraph makes it clear that the memo offers a solution to the problem. The problem is spelled out in detail. Emotional impact is created by taking the reader through the day as the temperature rises. The solution is presented impersonally. There are no *I*'s in the memo.

The memo stresses reader benefits: the savings that will result once the investment is recovered. The last paragraph tells the reader exactly what to do and links prompt action to a reader benefit. The memo ends with a positive picture of the problem solved.

Figures 9.8 and 9.9 provide checklists for direct requests and problem-solving persuasive messages.

Figure 9.7 *A Good Solution to the Sample Problem*

Date: October 12, 2000

To: Jennifer M. Kirkland, Operations Vice President

From: Arnold M. Morgan, Production Supervisor *AMM*

Subject: Improving Summer Productivity

Reader benefit in subject line

Problem creates a common ground

Nakamura forfeited a possible $186,000 in profits last summer due to a 17% drop in productivity. That's not unusual: Nakamura has a history of low summer productivity. But we can reverse the trend and bring summer productivity in line with the rest of the year's.

Good to show problem can be resolved

Cause of problem

The problem starts in the tube room. Due to high turnover and reduced efficiency from workers who are on the job, we just don't make as many TV tubes as we do during the rest of the year. And when we don't have tubes, we can't make TV sets.

Additional reason to solve problem

Both the high turnover and reduced efficiency are due to the unbearable heat in the tube room. Temperatures in the tube room average 25° over the outside temperature. During the summer, when work starts at 8, it's already 85° in the tube room. By 11:30, it's at least 105°. On six days last summer, it hit 120°. When the temperatures are that high, we may be violating OSHA regulations.

Production workers are always standing, moving, or carrying 20-lb. TV tubes. When temperatures hit 90°, they slow down. When no relief is in sight, many of them quit.

We replaced 24 of the 36 employees in the tube room this summer. When someone quits, it takes an average of five days to find and train a replacement; during that time, the trainee produces nothing. For another five days, the new person can work at only half speed. And even "full speed" in the summer is only 90% of what we expect the rest of the year.

More details about problem

Here's where our losses come from:

Normal production = 50 units a person each day (upd)

Loss due to turnover:
loss of 24 workers for 5 days =	6,000 units
24 at ¹/₂ pace for 5 days =	3,000 units
Total loss due to turnover =	9,000 units

Shows detail— Set up like an arithmetic problem

Loss due to reduced efficiency:
loss of 5 upd x 12 workers x 10 days =	600 units
loss of 5 upd x 36 x 50 days =	9,000 units
Total loss due to reduced efficiency =	9,600 units

Total Loss =	18,600 units

(continued)

Figure 9.7   *A Good Solution to the Sample Problem (concluded)*

Jennifer M. Kirkland   2   October 12, 2000

According to the accounting department, Nakamura makes a net profit of $10 on every TV set we sell. And, as you know, with the boom in TV sales, we sell every set we make. Those 18,600 units we don't produce are costing us $186,000 a year.

Shows where numbers in paragraph 1 come from

Bringing down the temperature to 78° (the minimum allowed under federal guidelines) from the present summer average of 112° will require an investment of $500,000 to insulate and air-condition the tube room. Extra energy costs for the air-conditioning will run about $30,000 a year. We'll get our investment back in less than three years. Once the investment is recouped, we'll be making an additional $150,000 a year—all without buying additional equipment or hiring additional workers.

Additional benefit

By installing the insulation and air-conditioning this fall, we can take advantage of lower off-season rates. Please authorize the Purchasing Department to request bids for the system. Then, next summer, our productivity can be at an all-time high.

Tells reader what to do

Reason to act promptly

Ends on positive note of problem solved, reader enjoying benefit

Figure 9.8

✓ Checklist   *Checklist for Direct Requests*

☐ If the message is a memo, does the subject line indicate the request? Is the subject line specific enough to differentiate this message from others on the same subject?

☐ Does the first paragraph summarize the request or the specific topic of the message?

☐ Does the message give all of the relevant information? Is there enough detail?

☐ Does the message answer questions or overcome objections that readers may have without introducing unnecessary negatives?

☐ Does the last paragraph tell the reader exactly what to do? Does it give a deadline if one exists and a reason for acting promptly?

And, for all messages, not just direct requests,

☐ Does the message use you-attitude and positive emphasis?

☐ Is the style easy to read and friendly?

☐ Is the visual design of the message inviting?

☐ Is the format correct?

☐ Does the message use standard grammar? Is it free from typos?

Originality in a direct request may come from

• Good lists and visual impact.

• Thinking about readers and giving details that answer their questions, overcome any objections, and make it easier for them to do as you ask.

• Adding details that show you're thinking about a specific organization and the specific people in that organization.

☐ If the message is a memo, does the subject line indicate the writer's purpose or offer a reader benefit? Does the subject line avoid making the request?

☐ Does the first sentence interest the reader?

☐ Is the problem presented as a joint problem both writer and reader have an interest in solving, rather than as something the reader is being asked to do for the writer?

☐ Does the message give all of the relevant information? Is there enough detail?

☐ Does the message overcome objections that readers may have?

☐ Does the message avoid phrases that sound dictatorial, condescending, or arrogant?

☐ Does the last paragraph tell the reader exactly what to do? Does it give a deadline if one exists and a reason for acting promptly?

And, for all messages, not just persuasive ones,

☐ Does the message use you-attitude and positive emphasis?

☐ Is the style easy to read and friendly?

☐ Is the visual design of the message inviting?

☐ Is the format correct?

☐ Does the message use standard grammar? Is it free from typos?

Originality in a problem-solving persuasive message may come from

• A good subject line and common ground.

• A clear and convincing description of the problem.

• Thinking about readers and giving details that answer their questions, overcome objections, and make it easier for them to do as you ask.

• Adding details that show you're thinking about a specific organization and the specific people in that organization.

Summary of Key Points

• The primary purposes in a persuasive message are to have the reader act, to provide enough information so that the reader knows exactly what to do, and to overcome any objections that might prevent or delay action. Secondary purposes are to build a good image of the writer and the writer's organization, to cement a good relationship between the writer and reader, and to reduce or eliminate future correspondence on the same subject.

• Readers have a vested interest in something if they benefit directly from keeping things as they are.

• **Credibility** is the audience's response to you as the source of the message. You can build credibility by being factual, specific, and reliable.

• Use the persuasive strategy your organization prefers.

• Use the **direct request pattern** when the audience will do as you ask without any resistance. Also use the direct request pattern for busy readers in your own organization who do not read all the messages they receive.

• Use the **problem-solving pattern** when the audience may resist doing what you ask and you expect logic to be more important than emotion in the decision.

• In a direct request, consider asking in the first paragraph for the information or service you want. Give readers all the information they will need to act on your request. In the last paragraph, ask for the action you want.

Responding to Criticism*

By definition, your boss criticizes you during a performance appraisal. Criticism often feels like an attack, and when we are attacked, most of us try to defend ourselves. But doing that in a performance appraisal just makes us look like we can't take criticism.

Fernando Flores, former Chilean minister of finance and current consultant, recommends the following script to respond to criticism: "[Name,] thank you for your assessment. I appreciate your sincerity. I would like to have further conversations with you about the topic."

This script does three things. First it is nondefensive and avoids escalating the conflict. Second, it recognizes that the boss means what he or she says (whether or not the criticism is on target). Third, it asks for further discussion. This discussion might involve probing the meaning of the criticism more fully or discussing ways to improve or even discussing competing agendas that create a double bind for you.

*Based on Harriet Rubin, "The Power of Words," *Fast Company*, January 1999, 144.

- Organize a problem-solving persuasive message in this way:
  1. Catch the reader's interest by mentioning a common ground.
  2. Define the problem you both share (which your request will solve).
  3. Explain the solution to the problem.
  4. Show that any negative elements (cost, time, etc.) are outweighed by the advantages.
  5. Summarize any additional benefits of the solution.
  6. Ask for the action you want.
- In a direct request, put the request, the topic of the request, or a question in the subject line. Do not put the request in the subject line of a problem-solving persuasive message. Instead, use a **directed subject line** that reveals your position on the issue or a reader benefit. Use a positive or neutral subject line even when the first paragraph will be negative.
- Use one or more of the following strategies to counter objections that you cannot eliminate:
  - Specify how much time and/or money is required.
  - Put the time and/or money in the context of the benefits they bring.
  - Show that money spent now will save money in the long run.
  - Show that doing as you ask will benefit some group the reader identifies with or some cause the reader supports.
  - Show the reader that the sacrifice is necessary to achieve a larger, more important goal to which he or she is committed.
  - Show that the advantages as a group outnumber or outweigh the disadvantages as a group.
  - Turn the disadvantage into an opportunity.
- To encourage readers to act promptly, set a deadline. Show that the time limit is real, that acting now will save time or money, or that delaying action will cost more.
- Build emotional appeal with stories and psychological description.
- Performance appraisals should cite specific observations, not inferences. They should contain specific suggestions for improvement and identify the two or three areas that the worker should emphasize in the next month or quarter.
- Letters of recommendation must be specific and tell how well and how long you've known the person.
- Early in the collection series, remind the reader about the debt matter-of-factly. In middle letters, be more assertive. Try to negotiate for partial payment if the reader is not able to pay the full amount.
- Use the analysis questions from Chapter 1 to analyze persuasive situations.

Chapter 9

Exercises and Problems

Getting Started

9.1 Writing Psychological Description

For one or more of the following groups, write two or three paragraphs of psychological description that could be used in a brochure, news release, or direct mail letter directed to members of that group.

1. Having a personal trainer.
   Audiences: Professional athletes.
   Busy managers.
   Someone trying to lose weight.
   Someone making a major lifestyle change after a heart attack.
2. Buying a cellular phone.
   Audiences: People who do a lot of big-city driving.
   People who do a lot of driving in rural areas.
   People who do a lot of flying.
3. Buying a laptop computer.
   Audiences: College students.
   Financial planners who visit clients at home.
   Sales representatives who travel constantly.
   People who make PowerPoint presentations.

4. Attending a fantasy sports camp (you pick the sport), playing with and against retired players who provide coaching and advice.
5. Attending a health spa where clients get low-fat and low-calorie meals, massages, beauty treatments, and guidance in nutrition and exercise.

Hints:
- For this assignment, you can combine benefits or programs as if a single source offered them all.
- Add specific details about particular sports, activities, and so on, as material for your description.
- Be sure to move beyond reader benefits to vivid details and sense impressions.
- Put your benefits in you-attitude.

9.2 Evaluating Subject Lines

Evaluate the following subject lines. Is one subject line in each group clearly best? Or does the "best" line depend on company culture, whether the message is a paper memo or an e-mail message, or on some other factor?

a. Subject: Request
   Subject: Why I Need a New Computer
   Subject: Increasing My Productivity
b. Subject: Who Wants Extra Hours?
   Subject: Holiday Work Schedule
   Subject: Working Extra Hours During the Holiday Season

c. Subject: Student Mentors
   Subject: Can You Be an E-Mail Mentor?
   Subject: Volunteers Needed
d. Subject: More Wine and Cheese
   Subject: Today's Reception for Japanese Visitors
   Subject: Reminder
e. Subject: Reducing Absenteeism
   Subject: Opening a Day Care Center for Sick Children of Employees
   Subject: Why We Need Expanded Day Care Facilities

9.3 Brainstorming Reasons to Act Promptly

Brainstorm one or more reasons that readers should act promptly in each of the following situations:

1. Persuading CPAs to take a continuing education course about changes in the tax law
   a. In May.
   b. In October.
   c. In December.
2. Persuading customers to install storm windows and insulation

a. In March.
b. In June.
c. In October.

3. Persuading your office to make a major change in its computer hardware and software
   a. Just before the end of the fiscal year.
   b. Right before the busiest season of the year.
   c. During the least busy time of the year.

9.4 Identifying Observations

Susan has taken the following notes about her group's meetings. Which of the following are specific observations that she could use in a performance appraisal of group members? If she had it to do over again, what kinds of details would turn the inferences into observations?

1. Feb. 22: Today was very frustrating. Sam was totally out of it—I wonder if he's on something. Jim was dictatorial. I argued, but nobody backed me up. Masayo might just as well have stayed home. We didn't get anything done. Two hours, totally wasted.

2. February 24: Jim seems to be making a real effort to be less domineering. Today he asked Sam and me for our opinions before proposing his own. And he noticed that Masayo wasn't talking much and brought her into the conversation. She suggested some good ideas.

3. February 28: Today's meeting was OK. I thought Masayo wasn't really focusing on the work at hand. She needs to work on communicating her ideas to others. Sam was doing some active listening, but he needs to work at being on time. Jim was involved in the project. He has strong leadership skills. There were some tense moments, but we got a lot done, and we all contributed. I got to say what I wanted to say, and the group decided to use my idea for the report.

4. March 5: This week most of us had midterms, and Masayo had an out-of-town gymnastics trip. We couldn't find a time to meet. So we did stuff by e-mail. Sam and Jim found some great stuff at the library and on the Web. Jim created a tentative schedule which he sent to all of us and then revised. I wrote up a draft of the description of the problem. Then Masayo and I put everything together. I sent my draft to her; she suggested revisions (in full caps so I could find them in the e-mail message). Then I sent the message to everyone. Masayo and Jim both suggested changes, which I made before we handed the draft in.

5. March 15: We were revising the proposal, using Prof. Jones's comments. When we thought we were basically done, Masayo noticed that we had not responded to all of the specific comments about our introductory paragraph. We then went back and thought of some examples to use. This made our proposal better and more complete.

9.5   Revising a Form Memo

You've been hired as a staff accountant; one of your major duties will be processing expense reimbursements. Going through the files, you find this form memo:

Subject: Reimbursements

Enclosed are either receipts that we could not match with the items in your request for reimbursement or a list of items for which we found no receipts or both. Please be advised that the Accounting Department issues reimbursement checks only with full documentation. You cannot be reimbursed until you give us a receipt for each item for which you desire reimbursement. We must ask that you provide this information. This process may be easier if you use the Expense Report Form which is available in your department.

Thank you for your attention to this matter. Please do not hesitate to contact us with questions.

You know this memo is horrible. In addition to wordiness, a total lack of positive emphasis and you-attitude, and a vague subject line, the document design and organization of information bury the request.

Create a new memo that could be sent to people who do not provide all the documentation they need in order to be reimbursed.

E-Mail Messages

9.6   Asking a Question

You're Director of Management Information Systems for your organization. This morning at the Budget Committee meeting, you presented a proposal to buy new laptop computers. One person asked whether it would be cheaper to stop buying desktop computers and buy only laptops. "Today's laptops are really powerful," one person said. "This way no one would need two computers," someone else added. The committee tabled your proposal, asking you to investigate the idea and report back at the next meeting in two weeks.

There's some merit in the idea, though desktop computers, which can be big, are much less expensive than laptops with the same features. And laptops are much more likely to be dropped, have coffee spilled on them, or be stolen.

As you think about the report you'll need to make in two weeks, you realize it isn't just a matter of comparing dollars and cents. You really need information about how people *use* their computers. Maybe some people need both. Maybe others could use just one or the other—especially if there were a few "loaner" laptops for people who don't travel much and a few "community" desktop machines for people in the office. Do the laptops need to be full-featured? Are people using multimedia and CD-ROMs on the road? Do they need big hard drives and good screens to show graphics?

Or would a stripped down (and cheaper) machine do the job?

Write an e-mail message to all employees, asking them about their computer use and preferences. You need responses early enough to put together your own recommendation and support for the Budget Committee.

9.7 Asking for Something for Your Unit

You've received this e-mail message from the Chief Financial Officer (CFO) of your organization:

Subject: RFP for New Money

Nearly $100,000 in new capital has become available. Argue for an item you need, up to $15,000. E-mail your request, a ballpark price, and the justification by Friday. We'll notify winners within two weeks.

Write the message.

Hints:

· Pick an organization you know well (for example, a college computer lab, your workplace, an

organization where you volunteer). Ask for something that's really needed.

· Show how the item will enable your unit to contribute to the organization's mission.

9.8 Asking for More Time and/or Resources

Today, this message shows up in your e-mail inbox from your boss:

Subject: Want Climate Report

This request has come down from the CEO. I'm delegating it to you. See me a couple of days before the board meeting—the 4th of next month—so we can go over your presentation.

I want a report on the climate for underrepresented groups in our organization. A presentation at the last board of directors' meeting showed that while we do a good job of hiring women and minorities, few of them rise to the top. The directors suspect that our climate may not be supportive and want information on it. Please prepare a presentation for the next meeting. You'll have 15 minutes.

Making a presentation to the company's board of directors can really help your career. But preparing a good presentation and report will take time. You can look at exit reports filed by Human Resources when people leave the company, but you'll also need to interview people—lots of people. And you're already working 60

hours a week on three major projects, one of which is behind schedule. Can one of the projects wait? Can someone else take one of the projects? Can you get some help? Should you do just enough to get by? Ask your boss for advice—in a way that makes you look like a committed employee, not a shirker.

9.9 Persuading People to Come to a Session

Several months ago, your organization brought in a consultant to recommend ways your organization could improve and become a "learning organization." One of the recommendations was that regular seminar sessions be held to acquaint people with the "best practices" in each unit, so that they could spread more quickly. You were put in charge of scheduling these sessions. The first few went well, but attendance has fallen.

As a result, it's harder to persuade people to present: with a small audience, they don't feel like taking the time to create a polished presentation.

Perhaps the usefulness of the sessions has run its course. But when you tried tactfully to suggest that maybe it was time to end the sessions, your manager, Earl Stanwyk, vetoed the idea.

From: Earl Stanwyk

Subject: Re: Continue Best Practices Sessions?

Of course we should continue them. So far, we've heard from fewer than half the areas in the organization.

You may need to tinker with the time or format to get people to come to them. I'll authorize payment for modest refreshments. And if you're having a hard time getting speakers, ask Alodie. She developed our Web pages, which have been getting a very good response. Tell her I told you to ask her.

The Director likes this program. It's your job to make it succeed.

Write an e-mail message to Alodie Sun, asking her to give a presentation six weeks from now. Assume that she says *yes,* and send an e-mail message to everyone in the organization, persuading them to attend the talk.

Hints:

· Pick an organization you know something about and pick a time and format that will attract people. What kind of refreshments should you have? What time of day is best? Would people prefer a session with more discussion? Would a plain presentation or one with slick graphics be more successful?

· Pick a subject line that will attract people without misleading them. "Free donuts" will backfire when people find out they have to come to a session to get them.

· How busy are people going to be when this presentation is scheduled? If it's crunch time, how can you make them want to come? What kind of presentation (in terms of content or involvement) could Alodie give that will be easy for you to sell?

9.10   Recommending a Change in Policy

You're a Sales Representative for a computer manufacturer that sells computers directly by phone and over the Web. Each computer is assembled for the individual customer. You've just ended a phone call with a very angry customer.

Five weeks ago, Jane Boles ordered an expensive high-end laptop. The configuration she wanted was back-ordered; you told her that to get it as soon as it came in, she'd have to send a check immediately. She did. Ms. Boles has called every week since then; the configuration she wants is still not available. Today, she asked what you do have in stock. When she learned that you could assemble the laptop without a CD-ROM drive in only a week, she changed her order.

The new configuration will cost $150 less than the original configuration she ordered. She asked that you

send her a check immediately. But under company policy you can't. When a price drops, you send a refund check only when the order is filled and shipped to the customer. Ms. Boles was furious. "You've had my money for a month; I feel you were deceptive when you said the parts would arrive 'any day now.' I want my money *now.*" Finally you said you'd see what you could do.

As Your Instructor Directs,

a. Write an e-mail message to your superior asking that a check for $150 be cut immediately and mailed to Ms. Boles.

b. Write a message which your superior can forward to the Vice President for Sales recommending that the company's policy be changed.

9.11   Changing the Office Envelopes

You've just joined a Fortune 500 company and are amazed to find out that the manila interoffice envelopes say "Mr. _____"—with a line to fill in the name of the recipient. In small print at the bottom of the envelope you find "1967"; it seems likely that the envelopes haven't been changed since then, though surely the company has had to reorder envelopes from time to time.

As Your Instructor Directs,

a. Write an e-mail message to your supervisor to find out whom you should contact to recommend that the envelopes be changed.

b. Write an e-mail message to the appropriate person recommending that the envelopes be changed.

Hints:

- Pick a Fortune 500 company that you know something about.
- How is the firm doing financially? Can it afford to recycle the old envelopes immediately? Or should it use them till they wear out?

- What is the firm's record on promoting women? What is the organization's culture? Are the envelopes consistent with that culture?
- You're new in the organization and don't yet have any power. What tone is most appropriate?

9.12   Asking for Volunteers

You have an executive position with one of the major employers in town. (Pick a business, nonprofit organization, or government office you know something about.) Two years ago, your company "adopted" a local school. You've provided computers and paid for Internet access; a small number of workers have signed up to be mentors. Today you get a call from the school's principal, a friend of yours.

Principal: I'd like to talk to you about the mentoring program. You're providing some mentors, and we're grateful for them, but we need ten times that number.

You: [You wince. This program has not been one of your successes.] I know that part of the program hasn't worked out as well as we hoped it would. But people are really busy here. Not all that many people have two or three hours a week to spend with a kid.

Principal: So you think the time it takes is really the problem.

You: [Maybe your friend will appreciate that you can't force people to do this.] Pretty much.

Principal: Do you think people would be willing to be mentors if we could find a way for it to take less time?

You: Maybe. [You sense that a hook is coming, and you're wary.]

Principal: Your people spend a lot of time on e-mail, don't they?

You: Yes. Two to three hours a day, for most of them.

Principal: What if we created a new mentoring structure, where people just e-mailed their

mentees instead of meeting with them? That way they could still provide advice and support, but they could do it at any time of the day. And it wouldn't have to take long.

You: [This sounds interesting.] So people would just have e-mail conversations. That would be a lot easier, and we'd get more people. But can they really have a relationship if they don't meet the kids?

Principal: Maybe we could have a picnic or go to a game a couple of times a year so people could meet face-to-face.

You: And all the kids have computers?

Principal: Not necessarily at home. But they all have access to e-mail at school. Writing e-mail to professionals will also give them more practice and more confidence. People like to get e-mail.

You: Not when they get 200 messages a day, they don't.

Principal: Well, our kids aren't in that category. What do you say?

You: I think it will work. Let's try it.

Principal: Great. Just send me a list of the people who are willing to do this, and we'll match them up with the kids. We'd like to get this started as soon as possible.

Write an e-mail message to all employees asking them to volunteer, while you're thinking about it right now.

@   Check the BAC Web site to learn more about e-mail mentoring.

9.13   Persuading the CEO to Attend Orientation

As the Director of Education and Training of your organization, you run orientation sessions for new hires. You're planning next quarter's session (new quarters start in January, April, July, and October) for a big group of new college graduates. You'd really like the organization's president and CEO to come in and talk to the group for at least 15 minutes. Probably most of the employees have seen the CEO, but they haven't had any direct contact. The CEO could come any time during the three-day session. Speaking just before or after lunch

would be ideal, because then the CEO could also come to lunch and talk informally with at least a few people. Next best would be speaking just before or after the midmorning or midafternoon breaks. But the CEO is busy, and you'll take what you can get.

As Your Instructor Directs,

a. Assume that your instructor is your CEO, and send an e-mail message persuading him or her to come to orientation.

b. Send an e-mail message to your instructor, asking him or her to address new members of a campus organization.

c. Address the CEO of your college or your workplace, asking him or her to speak to new employees.

Communicating at Work

As Your Instructor Directs,
In 9.14 through 9.18,

a. Create a document or presentation to achieve the goal.

b. Write a memo to your instructor describing the situation at your workplace and explaining your rhetorical choices (medium, strategy, tone, wording, graphics or document design, and so forth).

9.14   Writing a Performance Appraisal

Write an appraisal of someone with whom you work. You may appraise a subordinate, or you may assume

that your organization uses 360° appraisals (see problem 7.15) and appraise a peer or a superior.

9.15   Recommending a Co-Worker for a Bonus or an Award

Recommend someone at your workplace for a bonus or an award. The award can be something bestowed by the organization itself ("Employee of the Month," "Dealer-

ship of the Year," and so forth), or it can be a community or campus award ("Business Person of the Year," "Volunteer of the Year," an honorary degree, and so forth).

9.16   Justifying Your Position

Organizations facing downsizing have to decide which positions to keep and which to cut. Imagine that your organization is facing financial problems and that your supervisor, who wants to keep you, has asked you to draft something explaining why your position should be retained and why you are the best person to keep in the position. Create a memo or presentation to do the job.

Hints:

· Show how you contribute to the unit's and the organization's goals.
· Write your memo in the third person, so that your supervisor can send it upward without having to revise it.

9.17   Requesting Information from a Co-Worker

Often, you need information from other people to do your own work. Write to a co-worker, asking for the information you need.

9.18   Asking to Take a Course or Attend a Conference

Write to your supervisor, asking to take a course or attend a conference (at the organization's expense) that will help you do your job better.

Hints:

· How much does your supervisor know about this course or conference? Have others in your unit taken or attended it, or are you the first?

· How will your work be covered while you're away?
· Include the cost of registration, materials, travel, and lodging so that your supervisor knows what you're asking for.

Memo and Letter Assignments

9.19 Persuading a Magazine to Change Its Subscription Letter

You're Director of Customer Service for a new magazine named *Parenting 2000.* (Actually, you're the whole customer service department, but you negotiated the higher title when you took the job six weeks ago.) Much of your work is routine, but you also respond to customer complaints. In the last three weeks, you've received 36 letters complaining about a direct mail letter soliciting new subscriptions. The complaints fall into three categories:

1. The largest category, with 19 complaints. Here's a sample:

> You claim your magazine will "help you persuade your husband to do his share of the parenting, whether it's changing diapers or helping enforce curfews." This implies that most men have to be "persuaded" to "help"—as if raising kids were really the wife's job. We, like many couples we know, are both actively involved in our children's care and have been from the very beginning. Your letter insults men and parents.

2. The next biggest category, with 14 complaints. Here's a sample:

> Your letter assumes that every mother has a husband who can share the work of raising a child. It's really odd that a magazine that claims to be about parenting in the new millennium doesn't seem to realize that there are a lot of single parents out there, doing the best we can. Why exclude us? And why should I subscribe to a magazine that isn't for me?

3. A category with three complaints. Here's one of them:

> Many of the examples in your letter (how to choose a nanny, should your child be in a private school) suggest that your magazine is really for rich, conservative, white families. You don't mention any concerns of parents of color or of people who are trying to prepare their children to be good citizens in a multiracial world. Shame on you!

From your training and experience in customer service, you know that few people take the time to write letters of complaint, even when they are disappointed or angered by a product, service, or ad. So these three dozen letters likely represent a much larger sample of recipients who didn't like the subscription letter. Even worse, judging from these complaints, the subscription letter misrepresented the magazine: the issues you've seen (in print and in preparation) have useful information for all parents, whatever their politics, marital status, ethnicity, or income level.

You told the editor, Lance Dittrich, about the problem and that the letter needed to be changed. He said that he didn't have anything to do with the letter. "That's all done by the parent company. Actually, they probably hired some freelancer to write the letter, and the person just wasn't very sensitive. But if the results are poor, they'll change the letter. Companies keep using the same letter only if it works."

You think this letter needs to be changed immediately, whether it "works" or not. And people at the magazine should get a chance to comment on drafts before a final letter is mailed out. If you or other staffers had seen the letter, you could have recommended changes in wording and examples to create a more balanced picture of the magazine.

As Your Instructor Directs,

- Write to the CEO of the publishing group, Lana Salazar, urging that this subscription letter be replaced and that future letters come to your office for comments before they go out.

- Read Chapter 11 and write a new subscription letter for the magazine.

9.20 Persuading Guests to Allow Extra Time for Checkout

Your hotel has been the headquarters for a convention, and on Sunday morning you're expecting 5,000 people to check out before noon. You're staffing the checkout desk to capacity, but if everyone waits till 11:30 to check out, things will be a disaster.

So you want to encourage people to allow extra time. And they don't have to stand in line at all: by 4 AM, you'll put a statement of current charges under each guest's door. If that statement is correct and the guest is leaving the bill on the credit card used at check-in, the guest can just leave the key in the room and leave. You'll mail a copy of the final bill together with any morning charges by the end of the week.

Write a one-page message that can be put on pillows when the rooms are made up Friday and Saturday night.

9.21   Asking for Sick-Child Care

Day care is a fact of life for working parents in the United States. But day care centers won't accept sick children. So when their kids are sick, parents may have to call in sick themselves. The problem wreaks havoc on schedules for production, travel, meetings, and presentations.

Write a memo to the upper management of your organization, urging that it provide sick care service. One model is to create a site in a central area. An organization big enough to need a site just for its employees' children may be able to create one on-site. Small companies will want to team up with several other small businesses and split the cost. Another option is to have a visiting caregiver stay with the child in the employee's home.

Hints:

- Pick a business, government office, nonprofit agency, or educational institution that you know something about.
- Use your analysis from problems 3.11 and 3.12. How will this program help individuals? And how will that help the organization?
- Will your organization be more persuaded by a dollars-and-cents comparison showing how much this benefit could save the company? Or would stories be more persuasive?

9.22   Persuading Disability Services to Increase the Handivan's Hours

Assume that your college has a "Handivan" that takes students in wheelchairs from their residences or apartments to campus locations and back again. But the van stops at 6 PM (even though there are evening classes, lectures, and events). And it doesn't take people to off-campus restaurants, movies, grocery stores, or shopping centers. Write to the Director of Disability Services, urging that the Handivan's services be increased.

9.23   Persuading Your Campus to Keep Computer Labs Open Longer Hours

Only a few of the computer labs on your campus are open 24 hours a day. From midterms on, there always seems to be a waiting line for the computers in those labs.

Identify the person(s) with the authority and power to determine lab hours, and write a message that will persuade him, her, or them to keep more labs open longer.

Hints:

- Use your college, community college, or university.
- Do all the labs need to be kept open 24 hours a day all term? If not, what hours in which labs at what points in the term would be most helpful?

- How much would it cost (in terms of hiring people to staff the labs, paying for electricity and building safety) to keep the labs open longer? Where could this money come from?
- Administrators may not know a lot about students' lives and schedules. How can you persuade readers that students will indeed come in to use the labs?
- Revise, edit, and proofread carefully. Mistakes weaken your credibility.

9.24   Recommending Investments

Recommend whether your instructor should invest in a specific stock, piece of real estate, or other investment. As your instructor directs, assume that your instructor has $1,000, $10,000, or $100,000 to invest.

Hints:

- Pick a stock, property, or other investment that you can research easily.
- What are your instructor's goals? Is he or she saving for a house? for retirement? for kids' college

expenses? to pay off his or her own student loans? When will the money from the investment be needed?
- How much risk is your instructor comfortable with?
- Is your instructor willing to put time into the investment (as managing a rental house would require)?

Based on an assignment created by Cathy Ryan, The Ohio State University.

9.25 Handling a Sticky Recommendation

As a supervisor in a state agency, you have a dilemma.
You received this e-mail message today:

> From: John Inoye, Director of Personnel, Department of Taxation
>
> Subject: Need Recommendation for Peggy Chafez
>
> Peggy Chafez has applied for a position in the Department of Taxation. On the basis of her application and interview, she is the leading candidate. However, before I offer the job to her, I need a letter of recommendation from her current supervisor.
>
> Could you please let me have your evaluation within a week? We want to fill the position as quickly as possible.

Peggy has worked in your office for 10 years. She designed, writes, and edits a monthly statewide newsletter that your office puts out; she designed and maintains the department Web site. Her designs are creative; she's a very hard worker; she seems to know a lot about computers.

However, Peggy is in many ways an unsatisfactory staff member. Her standards are so high that most people find her intimidating. Some find her abrasive. People have complained to you that she's only interested in her own work; she seems to resent requests to help other people with projects. And yet both the newsletter and the Web page are projects that need frequent interaction. She's out of the office a lot. Some of that is required by her job (she takes the newsletters to the post office, for example), but some people don't like the fact that she's out of the office so much. They also complain that she doesn't return voice mail and e-mail messages.

You think managing your office would be a lot smoother if Peggy weren't there. You can't fire her: state employees' jobs are secure once they get past the initial six-month probationary period. Because of budget constraints, you can hire new employees only if vacancies are created by resignations. You feel that it would be pretty easy to find someone better.

If you recommend that John Inoye hire Peggy, you will be able to hire someone you want. If you recommend that John hire someone else, you may be stuck with Peggy for a long time.

As Your Instructor Directs,

a. Write an e-mail message to John Inoye.

b. Write a memo to your instructor listing the choices you've made and justifying your approach.

Hints:

· Polarization may make this dilemma more difficult than it needs to be. What are your options? Consciously look for more than two.

· Is it possible to select facts or to use connotations so that you are truthful but still encourage John to hire Peggy? Is it ethical? Is it certain that John would find Peggy's work as unsatisfactory as you do? If you write a strong recommendation and Peggy doesn't do well at the new job, will your credibility suffer? Why is your credibility important?

9.26 Persuading Employees to Join the Company Volleyball Team

Your company has decided to start a company volleyball team to play in the city recreation league. Now, you need to get people to sign up for the team. Ideally, you'd like to have several teams to involve as many people as possible and build company loyalty. If you have enough teams, they can play each other once a week in a round-robin company tournament.

Write a memo to all employees persuading them to sign up.

Hints:

· How young and how athletic are your employees? How busy are they? Will this be an easy or a difficult thing to persuade them to do?

· Some people may be reluctant to join because their skills are rusty. How can you persuade people that you want everyone to participate even if they're not athletic?

· Will the people who sign up have to pay anything or buy uniforms?

· How do people sign up? Is there a deadline?

9.27 Persuading Your Company to Change Its Collection Practices

You've been hired in the credit department of a major retail chain. In your third week on the job, you get this note from your boss:

> Here's a list of customers with open accounts. All of them passed our credit requirements at one time, but now they're late. As is our practice, when they didn't pay their bills we sent a second bill a month later and a third bill the month after that. Now it's time for a letter. Since the list is long, write a form letter, but make it sound like an individual letter. Merge the letter with this list of names and addresses and sign each one individually.

As Your Instructor Directs,

a. Write a form letter, putting in the name, address, and amount owed of one customer.

b. Write a memo to your boss recommending that the company policy be changed to send a second bill a week or two after the due date for the first and to send a first letter one month—rather than three months—after the original due date if the bill still hasn't been paid.

9.28 Getting Permission from Parents for a School Project

As part of a community cleanup program, all public-school students will spend the afternoon of the second Friday of April picking up trash. Younger students will pick up trash on school grounds, in parks, and in parking lots; older students will pick up trash downtown. Schoolteachers will supervise the students; where necessary, school buses will transport them. After students are finished, they'll return to their school's playground, where they'll be supervised until the end of the school day. Each school will maintain a study hall for any students whose parents do not give them permission to participate. Trash bags and snacks have been donated by local merchants.

Write a one-page cover letter that students can take home to their parents telling them about the project and persuading them to sign the necessary permission form. You do *not* need to create the permission form, but do refer to it in your letter.

Hints:

- What objections may parents have? How can you overcome these?
- Where should parents who drive their kids to school pick them up?
- Should students wear their normal school clothing?
- When must the form be returned? Who gets it? Whom can parents call if they have questions before they sign the form?

9.29 Asking an Instructor for a Letter of Recommendation

You're ready for the job market, transfer to a four-year college, or graduate school, and you need letters of recommendation.

As Your Instructor Directs,

a. Assume that you've orally asked an instructor for a recommendation, and he or she has agreed to write one. "Why don't you write up something to remind me of what you've done in the class? Tell me what else you've done, too. And tell me what they're looking for. Be sure to tell me when the letter needs to be in and whom it goes to."

b. Assume that you've been unable to talk with the instructor whose recommendation you want. When you call, no one answers the phone; you stopped by once and no one was in. Write asking for a letter of recommendation.

c. Assume that the instructor is no longer on campus. Write him or her a letter asking for a recommendation.

Hints:

- Be detailed about the points you'd like the instructor to mention.
- How well will this instructor remember you? How much detail about your performance in his or her class do you need to provide?
- Specify the name and address of the person to whom the letter should be written; specify when the letter is due. If there's an intermediate due date (for example, if you must sign the outside of the envelope to submit the recommendation to law school), say so.

9.30 Writing a Performance Appraisal for a Member of a Collaborative Group

During your collaborative writing group meetings, keep a log of events. Record specific observations of both effective and ineffective things that group members do. Then evaluate the performance of the other members in your group. (If there are two or more other people, write a separate appraisal for each of them.)

In your first paragraph, summarize your evaluation. Then in the body of your memo, give the specific details that led to your evaluation by answering the following questions:

· What specifically did the person do in terms of the task? Brainstorm ideas? Analyze the information? Draft the text? Suggest revisions in parts drafted by others? Format the document or create visuals? Revise? Edit? Proofread? (In most cases, several people will have done each of these activities together. Don't overstate what any one person did.) What was the quality of the person's work?

· What did the person contribute to the group process? Did he or she help schedule the work? Raise or resolve conflicts? Make other group members feel valued and included? Promote group cohesion? What roles did the person play in the group?

Support your generalizations with specific observations. The more observations you have and the more detailed they are, the better your appraisal will be.

As Your Instructor Directs,

a. Write a midterm performance appraisal for one or more members of your collaborative group. In each appraisal, identify the two or three things the person should try to improve during the second half of the term.

b. Write a performance appraisal for one or more members of your collaborative group at the end of the term. Identify and justify the grade you think each person should receive for the portion of the grade based on group process.

c. Give a copy of your appraisal to the person about whom it is written.

10

Handling Difficult Persuasive Situations

Limiting Your Audience

Bringing Everybody on Board
- Why Threats Are Less Effective than Persuasion
- How to Develop a Persuasive Strategy

Involving Your Audience

Building Your Credibility

Building Emotional Appeal

Convincing the Reader

Summary of Key Points

Handling Difficult Persuasive Situations

Scott Zimmerman

Chief Information Officer
CenterPoint Properties Trust

www.CenterPoint-Prop.com

Scott Zimmerman is responsible for all computer systems and processes at CenterPoint Properties Trust. CenterPoint is the largest and leading industrial property company in North America's largest and most diverse industrial property market: Greater Chicago. CenterPoint adds value to its tenants through the intense management, development, and redevelopment of warehouse, distribution, light manufacturing, and airfreight buildings.

CenterPoint Properties recently reengineered our business processes to improve efficiencies and increase tenant satisfaction. Our small, "departmental" computer systems made things hard on everyone. Tenants were frustrated because it took so long to answer their questions. Property managers disliked having to learn several different systems to do the same thing. Therefore, CenterPoint decided to consolidate information in a single computer system.

> *Most difficult cases can be solved if you step back and look at the situation from the other person's point of view.*

The existing systems had occasional data inconsistencies. Before migrating to the new system, someone would need to reconcile this information and then enter it by hand. This monumental task could only be performed by the property managers. Thus the classic conflict arose: Many property managers felt that their day-to-day jobs left no time to review and enter that much data. Experience told us that if we didn't have buy-in from the core users the system was doomed.

After speaking with several people, we did four things to persuade our audience:

- First, we convinced them that the long-term benefits would make their lives easier.
- Second, we sat down with each one of them and laid out a detailed project plan with plenty of short-term milestones. We listened to their concerns and modified the plan based on their suggestions. One by one we convinced them that they could maintain day-to-day activities and also complete this project.
- Third, we created rewards for each milestone: a small bonus here, a baseball game there.
- Finally, we convinced their immediate supervisors to reschedule low-priority tasks to free up some time. We also convinced senior managers to go out of their way to encourage these efforts and publicly thank the property managers at a company-wide meeting.

Due to the success of the project, other managers have adopted this approach to difficult situations. Most difficult cases can be solved if you step back and look at the situation from the other person's point of view. Try to see what is standing in the way and then work together to move past the problem. Once you are both working as a team you have already overcome the biggest obstacle.

Negotiating a Raise*

- Seek assignments where you can implement ideas and be accountable for results. Tangible accomplishments increase your worth.

- Be able to show how your work helps the whole organization, not just your own unit.

- Know what your job is worth. See www.wageweb.com, www.execunet.com, and jobsmart.org/tools/salary/index.htm for salary information.

- Prepare your boss for the discussion. Perhaps even write out a proposal explaining what comparable jobs pay, what you want, and why you think you deserve a raise. Base your argument not on what you need the money for, but on your contribution to the organization's bottom line.

- Consider alternatives. If a raise isn't possible, what about an extra week of vacation?

*Based on Michael O'Malley, "How to Get the Raise You Deserve," *Fortune,* September 7, 1998, 169–70; Hal Lancaster, "Managing Your Career," *The Wall Street Journal,* September 1, 1998, B1; and *American Demographics,* "For the Bookmark," November 1998, 21.

As we enter the 21st century, businesses and other administrative agencies depend more and more on persuasion and "buy-in" to get quality work done. You can command people to make widgets. You can't command people to be creative. And even if you're making widgets, just going through the motions isn't enough. You want people to make high-quality widgets, while reducing scrap and other costs. Internal commitment is needed to make that happen.

External motivation doesn't last. Some people will buy a certain brand of pizza if they have a "2 for the price of 1" coupon. But if the coupon expires, or if another company offers the same deal, customers may leave. In contrast, if customers like your pizza better, if they are motivated internally to choose it, then you may keep your customers even if another company comes in with a lower price.

Some persuasive situations are very difficult. Perhaps your audience's initial position is negative; they may be highly committed to their position; doing as you ask raises fears about their comfort, security, and self-images. However, if you understand the situation and your audience, and if you use tight logic and control your tone, you can sometimes find a common meeting ground.

Three sample situations show how difficult persuasion can be:

- People tune out messages they don't want to hear.

    An apartment manager urges residents to pay their rent on time, to take their trash out to the dumpster, and to obey the "no pets" rules. The manager tries everything from pleading to insults, but nothing works.

    Because the apartment manager's messages are unpleasant and limit their freedom, most residents ignore them. That way, they can do what they want without disturbing their images of themselves as reasonable people.

- People are reluctant to say *yes* if doing so requires them to admit they've been wrong all along.

    A Traffic Manager finds that buying trucks rather than continuing to lease them would save his company $10 million over the first three years and an additional $1 million a year after that.

    This isn't an open-and-shut case because the Traffic Manager must convince a reader who has decided every year to lease. Yet the reader will simply become defensive if the Traffic Manager says, "You should have made this change years ago."

- People deny realities that are too much for them to cope with.

    A lab worker becomes infected with the AIDS virus. A government report shows that if lab workers follow safety procedures—if they wear gowns and gloves, and perhaps masks and goggles—they'll be safe. But workers don't follow the procedures.

    When the risk is so great, why don't workers protect themselves? Perhaps because the thought of contracting AIDS is too scary. Many people who deal every day with something life-threatening practice **denial:** they persuade themselves that "nothing will happen" to them. Taking precautions seems to make the risk too real.

Fortunately, even a brief view of history shows that societies, organizations, and people can change. Societies can reject racism and sexism. Companies can abandon unprofitable products and follow the market into new ventures. People can change their minds even about such deeply held beliefs as sexual behavior and how to raise their children. Conversions—both religious and secular—do happen.

When you want readers to do something specific,

1. Limit your audience. Go with the people you can persuade and forget about the rest.
2. Try to bring everyone on board.

Major changes may take months or years and a series of formal and informal messages. These changes will be most successful if you use a third strategy:

3. Involve the audience. Let them find the solution.

Limiting Your Audience

Sometimes you don't need everyone. A political candidate, for example, needs to persuade only enough people to win the election. A shelter for runaway teens doesn't need money from everyone—just enough money to meet the budget.

Figure 10.1 shows a letter that resulted when a company couldn't persuade everyone to respond to a request. Combustion Engineering had decided, as a matter of policy, to favor minority suppliers. Most suppliers ignored its request to let it know their demographic makeup. Suppliers that qualified were happy to respond, but there just weren't reader benefits for those who didn't qualify. But it didn't matter if many—perhaps most—companies didn't respond. Combustion Engineering just needed to hear from the companies it wanted to buy from.

Bringing Everybody on Board

Some changes, such as motivating people in your organization to save money or to adopt diversity goals, will succeed only if most people cooperate. To change people's minds, you need to offer reasons.

Sometimes people think they will be able to mandate change by ordering or threatening subordinates. Real managers disagree. Research shows that managers use threats only for obligatory duties such as coming to work on time. For more creative duties—like being part of a team or thinking of ways to save the company money—managers give reasons.[1] A survey showed that sales representatives were motivated by selling a good product; getting backup, support, training, and commissions; and being affiliated with a good company. Threats ("perform or else") were rated dead last, with 86% saying threats offered little or no motivation.[2] And threats are even less effective in trying to persuade people whose salaries you don't pay.

Why Threats Are Less Effective than Persuasion

A **threat** is a statement—explicit or implied—that someone will be punished if he or she does (or doesn't do) something. Six reasons explain why punishment and threats don't work:[3]

1. **Threats don't produce permanent change.** Many people obey the speed limit only when a marked police car is in sight.
2. **Threats won't necessarily produce the action you want.** If you embarrass or punish people who take too many felt-tip pens or too much paper, they might write fewer reports—hardly the response you'd want!
3. **Threats may make people abandon an action—even in situations where it would be appropriate.** Criticizing workers for talking about

Working Together*

Procter & Gamble and Wal-Mart turned a win–lose way of doing business into a win–win relationship. At one time, P&G tried to sell its products to Wal-Mart for as much money as possible, while Wal-Mart tried to pay as little as possible.

Today, P&G and Wal-Mart work together instead of at cross-purposes. Wal-Mart sends continuous sales data to P&G by satellite. P&G figures out what products and sizes are needed and ships directly from the factory to Wal-Mart. Wal-Mart has a smaller inventory but also fewer stockouts. P&G gets paid more quickly. As a result, sales and profits are higher for both companies.

*Based on "Two Tough Companies Learn to Dance Together," *Harvard Business Review*, November–December 1996, 102.

Figure 10.1   *A Request to Persuade Only Those Who Will Directly Benefit*

COMBUSTION ENGINEERING

Is at Least 50%
of Your Business
Owned by Women
or Minorities?

*Question catches attention,
takes visual place of inside
address, salutation
(See Figure A.9.)*

If it is, we want to try to use you as a supplier.

*Question,
paragraph 1
limit audience*

You qualify for this favorable treatment if one of the following situations applies:

*List
creates
visual
interest*

a.   50% of the business or 51% of the stock is owned by women.

b.   50% of the business or 51% of the stock is owned by minority group members: Blacks, Asian Americans, Native Americans, or Hispanic Americans.

Combustion Engineering is committed to affirmative action programs to prevent discrimination based on race, color, creed, sex, age, or national origin. We believe that the pursuit of profit and the pursuit of social goals are compatible. We try to act affirmatively in hiring and promoting employees. We also try to act affirmatively in choosing suppliers.

*Asks for
action by a
specific date*

If at least 50% of your company is owned by women or minorities, please send us written evidence by May 15.

If we don't hear from you, we'll assume that you're not a minority business.

Sincerely,

J.R. Tran

*Reminds readers that they
must reply to get favorable
treatment*

J. R. Tran
Director, Purchasing

Process Automation Business
Combustion Engineering, Inc.

650 Ackerman Road
Post Office Box 02650
Columbus, Ohio 43202-1502

Tel: (614) 261-2000
Fax: (614) 261-2172
Telex: 246675

nonbusiness topics such as sports may reduce communication about business topics as well.

4. **Threats produce tension.** People who feel threatened put their energies into ego defense rather than into productive work.

5. **People dislike and avoid anyone who threatens them.** A supervisor who is disliked will find it harder to enlist cooperation and support on the next issue that arises.

6. **Threats can provoke counteraggression.** Getting back at a boss can run the gamut from complaints to work slowdowns to sabotage.

How to Develop a Persuasive Strategy

Use the following five analysis steps in difficult persuasive situations:

1. **Find out why your audience members resist what you want them to do.** Sit down one-on-one with people and listen. Don't try to persuade them; just try to understand.

2. **Try to find a win–win solution.** People will be much more readily persuaded if they see benefits for themselves. Sometimes your original proposal may have benefits that the audience had not thought of, and explaining the benefits will help. Sometimes you'll need to modify your original proposal to find a solution that solves the real problem and meets everyone's needs. Chapter 13 has more information about solving the real problem.

3. **Let your audience save face.** Don't ask people to admit that they have been wrong all along. If possible, admit that the behavior may have been appropriate in the past. Whether you can do that or not, always show how changed circumstances or new data call for new action.

4. **Ask for something small.** When you face great resistance, you won't get everything at once. Ask for a month's trial. Ask for one step that will move toward your larger goal. For example, if your ultimate goal is to eliminate prejudice in your organization, a step toward that goal might be to convince managers to make a special effort for one month to recognize the contributions of women or members of minorities in group meetings.

5. **Present your arguments from your audience's point of view.** Offer benefits that help the reader, not just you. Take special care to avoid words that attack or belittle readers. Present yourself as someone helping readers achieve their goals, not someone criticizing or giving orders from above.

The draft in Figure 10.2 makes the mistake of attacking readers in a negative message. Making the memo less accusatory would help, but the message doesn't need to be negative at all. Instead, the writer can take the information in paragraph 3 and use it as the attention-getter and common ground for a problem-solving persuasive message. Figure 10.3 shows a possible revision.

Involving Your Audience

Organizational changes work best when the audience buys into the solution. And that happens most easily when they themselves find it. Management can

1. Help people see and own the problem.
2. Identify values and cultures that need to change.
3. Let people discover solutions.
4. Support change tangibly and symbolically.

Vision Engineering*

Bridgestone/Firestone faced a major decision: should it spend $100 million on a new information system? Gemini Consulting used a process it calls "vision engineering" to help the company decide.

Top executives came into a room to find stacks of cards, each with a single fact. Some facts were general (Americans save less than 5% of their personal income; work schedules are more flexible). Other facts were industry-specific.

Everyone studied the cards, then combined sets of them under a headline representing a change or trend. After small groups debated, edited, and perhaps combined the headlines, the group agreed on 6 to 10 of them. Because leaders had come up with the ideas themselves, they were less likely to say "yes, but."

Bridgestone/Firestone used this process to get past the split between Japanese and Americans, manufacturing and marketing. While the list of 10 business influences is confidential, in general people decided that technology will change how companies market tires, share information with buyers, and forecast and schedule production. Technology—even with a big price tag—was thus even more important than the company had realized. With that understanding, deciding to spend $100 million was an easier call.

*Based on Thomas A. Stewart, "A Refreshing Change: Vision Statements That Make Sense," *Fortune*, September 30, 1996, 195.

F i g u r e   10.2   *Original Unprofessional Memo Attacking Readers*

Inter-office Memorandum

October 25, 2000

Accusatory tone makes this writer look unprofessional

To: Todd Neumann

From: Heather Johnson

Subject: Problems with Instrument Lab Results
          Negative   *Makes reader feel incompetent*

Accusatory tone

The Instrument Technicians Lab again (seems to believe) that if a result is printed out, it is the correct answer. (It doesn't seem to matter) that the chromatogram is terribly noisy, the calibration standards are over a month old, or the area of the internal standards is about half what it should be. What does it matter if the correction factor is 1286 and at the very minimum it should be 1300? That's an average of two results—so what if the calibration standard is six weeks old? I'm *Lacks YA* aware that the conditions in the lab have contributed to the discouraged atmosphere, but I don't feel it's an excuse for the shape of the lab and the equipment. The G.C. columns are in bad shape just from abuse. I've lost count of the number of 10 ml. syringes the lab has buried (at least $20 each) mainly because they were not properly rinsed and the plungers were lost trying to push through dried protein material. When was the last time the glass insert in the B column was changed or even looked at? Has anyone checked the filter on the Autolab I?

Attacks reader

Insults and attacks reader

Lacks YA

During the last six months, I have either reminded the technician of such things or written reminders in the log book. Isn't it time for our responsible lab technicians to take on this responsibility? Shouldn't they have fresh standards made up, especially when they know a run is coming? Granted, we've had many false starts, but I am still uncomfortable that the technicians will be ready when the time comes.

Lacks YA

Problem presented as reader's fault, not a common problem that both share

I don't feel that I should have to go over the chromatograms, printouts, and G.C. book every time we submit samples for analysis. However, just two weeks ago I sent out results without doing this and immediately received a call that the results were impossible—and they were because unacceptable KF was used, the result of an old calibration standard.

Lacks YA

One other item bothers me. I don't know how to get the technicians interested in the way the Autolab integrates each peak when they don't seem to look at anything other than the answer. I feel it's very important they learn this so they will know when a peak has been incorrectly integrated.

Attacks and insults reader

I think it's time they either take hold and run the lab themselves or they be treated as if they were *Whole ¶* children and told what to do which means they'll need a baby-sitter. I also would like to see them *lacks YA* read the Autolab I Instruction Manual and take the tape courses on the gas chromatograph and the Autolab I. I really think the above should be a mandatory part of their training.

The overall attitude and morale of the lab must be raised and a step in that direction is to give them the responsibility which they were supposed to have in the first place and expect them to accept it. These people are being called technicians but they are actually classed as chemists and should be assuming more initative and responsibility.

Attacks reader

Figure 10.3   *Revised Memo Creating a Common Ground and a Professional Image*

Inter-office Memorandum

Straightforward problem-solving approach is the mark of a professional manager

October 25, 2000

To: Todd Neumann

From: Heather Johnson

Subject: Cutting Requests for Re-Work   *Positive Subject Line*

Problem writer and reader share

Two weeks ago a customer called to tell me that the results we'd sent out were impossible. I checked, and the results were wrong because we'd used an old calibration standard.

Redoing work for outside customers and for in-house projects doubles our workload. Yet because people don't trust our results, we're getting an increasing number of requests for re-work.

Writer shows understanding of reader's problems

Part of the problem is that we've had so many false starts. Customers and especially in-house engineers say they'll need a run but then don't have the materials for another day or even a week. Paul Liu has told me that these schedule glitches are inevitable. We'll just have to prepare fresh calibration standards every time a run is scheduled—and prepare them again when the run actually is ready.

You've told me that the equipment in the lab is unreliable. The Capital Expenditures Request includes a line item for G.C. columns and a new gas chromatograph. We'll be able to be more persuasive at the Board meeting if we can show that we're taking good care of the equipment we have. Please remind your staff to

- Rinse the 10-ml. syringes every day.

- Check the glass insert in the B column every week.   *List emphasizes what reader needs to do*

- Check the filter on the Autolab I every week.

Treats reader as an equal who can help solve the problem

Do workers find the Autolab I instruction manual and the tape courses on the gas chromatograph and the Autolab I helpful? If the manual is hard to use or the tape course is boring, perhaps we should ask the manufacturer to redo them and, in the meantime, to send a service worker to offer a short course for our workers. What do you think would be the best way to increase the technical expertise of our staff?

By getting our results right the first time, we can eliminate the re-work and give both customers and in-house clients better service.

Links desired action to benefit and picture of the problem being solved

Difficult situations arise when multiple stakeholders in an issue have different— perhaps contradictory— points of view. This Web site, created by faculty and graduate students at Rice University, presents documents, maps, and reports that led to a successful resolution.

Simply admitting that a serious problem exists is difficult. Videotapes of customer complaints, a visit to a Japanese factory with a more efficient production process, or evidence that the current source of revenue is drying up may help people see the problem. But the tendency is just to keep doing the same thing (perhaps a bit more efficiently). People need to realize that the system is at fault.

For KPMG Netherlands, moving from auditing and tax preparation into new growth areas required recognizing that the company's culture inhibited change. KPMG named 100 of its professionals to work on 14 task forces. Choosing people from different levels in the organization and asking them to work with people from different areas was itself an important symbolic change in a company that was based on hierarchy and fiefdoms. The project manager helped task force members compare the culture they wanted to the culture they actually had and eventually to see how they would have to change to create the new culture. The process wasn't easy. It required formal meetings and one-on-one dialogs. People had to learn to confront conflict openly and resolve it. One strategy that the company developed was to distribute yellow cards like those used by soccer referees to call "foul" when someone refused to listen to coworkers. Over time, the company changed its culture. The task forces identified $50 to $60 million worth of new business opportunities in helping firms create and shape corporate visions and develop learning organizations.[4]

Symbolism makes it easier for people to change, but symbols alone aren't enough. Tangible rewards in performance appraisals, raises, and promotions must support organizational change if it is to succeed.[5]

Building Your Credibility

Credibility in the workplace has three sources: knowledge, image, and relationships.[6] Especially when you face difficult persuasion, it's worth taking the time to learn about all of the issues involved. Citing experts can make your argument more credible. Knowledge and image are intertwined: an outside consultant may have more credibility than someone from within the organization. In some organizations, workers build credibility by getting assigned to high-profile teams. You build credibility by your track record. The more reliable you've been in the past, the more likely people are to trust you now.

We are also more likely to trust people we know. That's one reason that new CEOs make a point of visiting as many branch offices as they can. Building a relationship with someone—even if the relationship is based on an outside interest, like sports or children—makes it easier for that person to see you as an individual and to trust you.

Building Emotional Appeal

In difficult persuasion, logic alone isn't enough. You need to answer fears that may be too deep to articulate. Stories and anecdotes have the power to create emotional appeal. Sometimes a visual image communicates even more powerfully than words. Don Winkler was managing a Citibank branch in Italy when a change in the tax law seemed to threaten bank deposits. To forestall a run of people withdrawing their money, Winkler took all the cash out of the vaults and piled it high at every teller station. The visual message that the bank had plenty of money was so strong that deposits actually grew.[7]

 Difficult situations sometimes have ethical implications. Figure 10.4 lists some of the Web resources that deal with business ethics. You can find links to these sites on the BAC Web page.

Convincing the Reader

Any argument has a better chance if it is logically sound and well presented. Tight logic is crucial when you face a hostile audience hoping to defeat you by picking holes in your logic. To make your logic convincing,

- Give evidence and specific supporting details.
- Connect the parts of your argument.
- Respond to possible objections.
- Limit your claim to make it more persuasive.

By comparing an argument to the Toulmin model (see Appendix D), you can see what kind of statements you need to make an argument convincing. Each of the examples on the next page is unconvincing, but the solutions differ.

• **Business ethics resources on the Internet** library.fgcu.edu/Textsite/Subjects/Business/begen.htm	• **Ethics in International Business** library.lib.binghamton.edu/subjects/business/intbuseth.html
• **Defense Industry Initiative on Business Ethics and Conduct** www.dii.org	• **Ethics of Web Sites (***New York Times*** article)** www.saja.org/stories/ethics.html
• **DePaul University's Institute for Business and Professional Ethics** www.depaul.edu/ethics/contents.html	• **KPMG's business ethics Web site** usserve.us.kpmg.com/ethics/
• **Ethics Effectiveness Quick Test** www.ethics.org/quicktest/quicktest.cfm	• **Various codes of conduct** www.depaul.edu/ethics/codes1.html

 See the BAC Web site for links to these sites.

Let the Audience Find a Solution*

When Carol Roberts joined International Paper as Vice President of People Development, she quickly realized that people were not in fact being developed. How could someone new talk about a major problem?

She realized that she needed to win top managers' hearts and minds to make a change. She scheduled a two-day off-site meeting (led by an outside consultant to build credibility). During the meeting, the managers themselves saw that a problem existed.

The managers came up with some solutions, but they needed backing from the top to implement them. After the off-site meeting, Roberts met with top management to get the needed support.

Less than a year later, the company had a new policy of twice-yearly meetings between employees and managers to discuss career development and "people champions" to make sure that workers got the help they needed to grow.

*Based on Michael Warshaw, "Open Mouth, Close Career?" *Fast Company,* December 1998, 241–51.

F i g u r e 10.4

Business Ethics Resources on the Web

Why Students Sign Organ Donor Cards*

What makes healthy young adults sign organ donor cards? Research shows that college students who have signed cards are knowledgeable, altruistic, and unafraid.

Students who said they intended to sign donor cards but had not done so had less knowledge and more fears. Some mistakenly believed that a card had to be filed with the federal government. Many didn't know that most religious groups support the concept of organ donation and that it is considered unethical for the same doctor to care for both the organ donor and the organ recipient.

Students who said they were unlikely to sign donor cards had even less knowledge and more fears. Some didn't know about the need for organ donors. People in this group weren't altruistic but did care about the opinions of others. Encouraging them to talk about organ donation with family and friends may make them more likely to consider donation.

Different messages are needed for people who view organ donation positively and negatively. For the latter group, a series of messages will be necessary.

*Based on Jenifer E. Kopfman and Sandi W. Smith, "Understanding the Audiences of a Health Communication Campaign: A Discriminant Analysis of Potential Organ Donors Based on Intent to Donate," *Journal of Applied Communication Research*, 24 (1996), 33–49.

Argument 1	By using XTROCUT tubing, you can cut production time and reduce scrap loss.
Problem with argument	This argument needs evidence to support each of its claims.
Revised argument	Because XTROCUT comes in the lengths and shapes you use most often, you spend less time cutting down longer tubes. Since you can order just the length you want, you don't waste 2 feet every time you need a 10-foot tube.
Argument 2	The workers I talked to were split 50/50. The workers at our plant don't agree whether the benefits package is adequate.
Problem with argument	No bridge shows that the "workers I talked to" were a representative or sufficiently large sample. The audience may also wonder whether things have changed since the date of the poll.
Revised argument	I talked to a random sample of 60 workers. They were split 50/50. Last week, the workers didn't agree whether the benefits package is adequate.
Argument 3	Our national advertising campaign will run during the most popular TV shows this month. This ad campaign will increase our sales dramatically.
Problem with argument	Such a claim cannot be made with certainty: too many variables affect sales.
Revised argument	Our national advertising campaign will run during the most popular TV shows this month. This ad campaign will support our sales reps' efforts to increase sales 5% over last month's.

Specific supporting details show that you've thought through your argument. For example, Kris McKnight handed her boss 16 pages of supporting documentation to argue that she could be more effective working out of her home and on the road rather than in the organization's regional office. Part of her reason for wanting to telecommute was personal. But her proposal emphasized the benefits to the organization.[8] Anne Fisher advises including specific details about how you'll spend your time ("8 AM to 9 AM: Read and answer e-mail. Reply to voice mail. Check in with secretary.")[9] A small request—to telecommute one day a week for two months—gives you a chance to prove your claims with the strongest proof of all: personal experience.

In a job application letter, the major claim is "I can do the job." That major claim rests on several smaller claims: "I have the necessary technical skills," "I work well with people," and "I have relevant experience." But each of these smaller claims needs support before it is convincing in supporting the major claim. For example, to prove that she had relevant experience, a student might describe the cost accounting system she developed for a small business, enabling it to save money. She could support that claim by giving details (evidence) about her contribution (to rebut the counterargument that she only used an already-written software package) and by being specific about how the system saved money and how much money it saved. The amount of money limits the claim and makes it more convincing. How specific the applicant needs to be—whether a statement can stand on its own as evidence or whether it first needs to be treated as a claim and proved—depends on how critically the reader will scrutinize the logic. If people who can do cost accounting are in short supply, the simple claim "I can do it" may net an interview. But if the job market is tight, proof will be necessary.

Figure 10.5 is a problem-solving persuasive message (p. 269) written to persuade employees not to make personal calls on office phones. The comments in the margins identify the words, phrases, sentences, or paragraphs that

1. Build a common ground.
2. Offer evidence of the problem.
3. Prove that the problem hurts the organization.

F i g u r e   10.5   *A Problem-Solving Memo*

Inter-office Memorandum

Date: February 19, 2001

From: James Christopher Smith *JCS*

Subject: Improving Service of Customers' Phone Orders   *Common ground as subject line*

To: All Sales Representatives

Writer as problem solver

Common ground (All of you have told me) that your customers are experiencing difficulties in placing orders because all the phone lines are tied up, and that some customers are ordering from other wholesalers as a result. This is causing you a loss in sales commissions.

Evidence The recent opening of the Johnson Wholesale House in Decatur has made competition in our field of wholesale drugs even keener. With the addition of this new warehouse, Johnson can service customers in all our sales areas almost as quickly as we can, and for approximately the same price. This new availability makes it even easier for our customers to call Johnson's instead of us. In fact, Glenn and Jack report that Walgreen's has increased its business with Johnson's from a sixth to a third of its total drug business. Sue and Jerry also say that several of the small independent drug stores in central Illinois, such as the ones in Effingham and Tuscola, have switched to Johnson's from us. With competition as fierce as this, we must make ordering from us a quick and easy operation.

Rebuttal of counter-claim Most orders are phoned in between 9:30 and 11:30 in the morning and 1:00 and 2:00 in the afternoon, according to the times indicated on the order forms from last month. Computer records of our phone use, however, show that the lines are tied up throughout the day, usually by calls from the sales department. In order to relieve congestion, then, it is necessary to reduce phone activity in the sales department.

Solution presented impersonally This reduction can be made by using the pay phones for personal calls during the peak ordering hours. Calls on company business should be made during non-peak hours too, if possible. This will enable us to keep more lines open during the peak ordering hours without spending money on costly new lines.

Additional reader benefits With the lines open to incoming calls, customers will find that they can place their orders quickly and easily. This will encourage them to keep calling us instead of our competitors, which can mean greater sales for you. In addition, good service helps build goodwill which may enable you to get a bigger share of your customers' business. The easy phone ordering service will also serve you as an additional selling point for new customers.

Links action to solution of problem In order to improve customer relations and realize greater sales, then, use the pay phones for personal calls between the peak hours of 9:30-11:30 and 1:00-2:00, and make outgoing business calls during non-peak hours.

Asks for action; tells readers exactly what to do

One Step at a Time*

If your readers have a stake in what you are arguing against, you . . . must resist your impulse to change their beliefs. You have to set your sights much lower. The best you can hope for—and it is hoping for a great deal—is to get your readers just to *understand* your point of view even while not changing theirs in the slightest. . . .

In short, stop trying to persuade the enemy and settle for planting a seed. . . .

What does this mean in practice? . . . [I]f I were writing a short article or leaflet to readers with a stake in what I'm trying to refute, I wouldn't say, "Here's why *you* should believe nuclear power is bad." How can I get them to invest themselves in words which translate "Here's why you've been bad or stupid"? I would take an approach which said, "Here are the reasons and experiences that have made *me* believe nuclear power is bad. Please try to understand them for a moment."

*Quoted from Peter Elbow, *Writing with Power: Techniques for Mastering the Writing Process* (New York: Oxford University Press, 1981), 203–4.

4. Rebut the counterclaim that phones are tied up on business, not personal, calls.
5. Present the solution to the problem in general terms.
6. Present the complete solution in specific terms.
7. Picture the problem being solved.
8. Limit the claims about additional reader benefits that may arise from the solution but are not certain to occur.
9. Ask for action.
10. Create a win–win solution and build an image of the writer as someone who's on the same side as readers, helping them to solve their problems and achieve their goals.

Summary of Key Points

- Persuasion is often difficult because
  - People tune out messages they don't want to hear.
  - People are reluctant to say *yes* if doing so requires them to admit that they've been on the wrong side all along.
  - People deny realities that are too much for them to cope with.
- When you need action quickly, you have two choices:
  1. Limit your audience to the people you can persuade.
  2. Try to bring everyone on board.
- For a major change,
  3. Involve the audience. Let them find the solution.
- If you don't need everyone's cooperation, use a direct request to get action from the people who already agree with you.
- Threats don't produce permanent change; they won't necessarily produce the action you want; they may make people abandon an action entirely—even in situations where it would be appropriate; they produce tension. People dislike and avoid anyone who threatens them. Threats can provoke counteraggression.
- Base persuasion in difficult persuasive situations on the following five analysis steps:
  1. Find out why your audience members resist what you want them to do.
  2. Try to find a win–win solution.
  3. Find a way to let your audience save face.
  4. Ask for something small.
  5. Present your arguments from your audience's point of view.
- When you want people to change their behavior, don't criticize them. Instead, show that you're on their side, that you and they have a mutual interest in solving a problem.
- To make your logic convincing,
  - Give evidence and specific supporting details.
  - Connect the parts of your argument.
  - Respond to possible objections.
  - Limit your claim to make it more persuasive.

Exercises and Problems

Getting Started

10.1 Analyzing Corporate Statements on Ethics

Analyze at least three of the codes of ethics online at www.depaul.edu/ethics/codes1.html. Which codes seem most helpful in making decisions? Why? Which codes do most to protect employees?

As Your Instructor Directs,

a. Write a memo to your instructor, evaluating the three codes.

b. Write a memo to the CEO of the least effective code, urging that it be revised.

c. Share your results orally with a small group of students.

d. Write a group report with a small group of students.

10.2 Evaluating Logic

Miswording creates logical errors in the following sentences. Explain what's wrong in each sentence and revise so that it makes logical sense. (If the sentence is ambiguous, pick one logical meaning.)

1. My parents believe students should speak a foreign language. Therefore I spent a summer in France and another summer in Mexico.

2. We do not issue building keys to employees because we want to keep security to a minimum.

3. If you need to reach me, I'll be at 555-1234 all day Thursday.

4. At an annual subscription price of only US$799 the *Asian Markets Monitor* is no doubt the least costly investment you will make this year. It will also certainly prove to be the most vital and useful.

5. As a result of the questionnaire, many students felt that more computers were needed on campus.

10.3 Responding to Objections

Brainstorm a way to respond to each of the counterclaims to the following goal that a writer might have.

1. Using less paper
   a. If paper costs more, we'll just pass the cost on to customers or deduct it as a business cost on our taxes.
   b. Sure, paper is expensive. But good documents are crucial to our business. Using less paper will cut the quality of our work. We'll lose goodwill, reputation, and, ultimately, income.
   c. Reformatting documents to get them on one page and waiting till the printer cools to print on both sides takes time. We just can't afford the

   time it will take to comply with these "cost-saving" measures.
   d. Reusing scraps of paper is incompatible with our image as a successful organization.

2. Increasing flextime
   a. It will be too hard to hold staff meetings if everyone works different hours.
   b. Managers won't be able to supervise people they can't see.
   c. Representatives will be out of the office when their clients call.
   d. If people get the hours they want, at some times there will be no one in the office at all.

E-Mail Messages

10.4 Persuading People to Use Better Passwords

Your computer system requires each employee to change his or her password every three months. But many people choose passwords that are easy to guess. According to Deloitte & Touche's fraud unit, the 10

most commonly used passwords are (1) the employee's name or child's name, (2) "secret," (3) stress-related words ("deadline," "work"), (4) sports teams or terms, (5) "payday," (6) "bonkers," (7) the current season ("autumn," "spring"), (8) the employee's ethnic group, (9) repeated characters ("AAAAA"), (10) obscenities and sexual terms ("Hackers' Delight," *Business Week*, February 10, 1997, 4).

As Director of Management Information Systems (MIS), you want employees to choose passwords that hackers can't guess based on knowing an employee's background. The best passwords contain numbers as well as letters, use more characters (at least five; eight possible), and aren't real words.

Write an e-mail message to all employees, urging them to choose better passwords.

10.5   Asking for Something Different for Secretary's Day

Your clerical job gives you the flexibility you need while you're in school. Secretary's Day is approaching, and you really don't want flowers or a free lunch. You'd much rather have a bonus or at least time off to attend an educational seminar (whose cost the company should bear). You'd be willing to go to a seminar that would make you even more useful to the company—perhaps learning advanced features of a computer program, for example.

Write an e-mail to the person who supervises clerical workers in your unit, asking that Secretary's Day give you something useful.

Hints:

- Assume that you work in an organization you know something about.

- Specify one or more seminars you'd like to attend.
- Some seminars may cost a lot more than flowers or lunch; some may cost less. How much financial flexibility does the organization have?
- Are there other clerical workers? Would they also like bonuses or seminars, or do some prefer flowers or lunch?
- How well does the person who will make the decision know you? How positively does he or she view you and any other clerical workers?

10.6   Not Doing What the Boss Asked

Today, you get this e-mail message:

To:	All Unit Managers
Subject:	Cutting Costs

Please submit five ideas for cutting costs in your unit. I will choose the best ideas and implement them immediately.

You think your boss's strategy is wrong. Cutting costs will be easier if people "buy into" the decision rather than being handed orders. Instead of gathering ideas by e-mail, the boss should call a meeting so that people can brainstorm, teaching each other why specific strategies will or won't be easy for their units to implement.

Reply to your boss's e-mail request. Instead of suggesting specific ways to cut costs, persuade the boss to have a meeting where everyone can have input and be part of the decision.

Communicating at Work

As Your Instructor Directs in 10.7 through 10.9,

a. Create a document or presentation to achieve the goal.
b. Write a memo to your instructor describing the situation at your workplace and explaining your rhetorical choices (medium, strategy, tone, wording, graphics, document design, and so forth).

10.7   Motivating Workers

Motivate workers in your unit to do their best work.

10.8   Changing What's Wrong

No workplace is perfect. Pick one of the things you'd like to change about your workplace, identify the decision maker(s), and create a memo or presentation to start the persuasion process.

10.9   Asking for More Resources for Your Unit

Write a memo or prepare a presentation to persuade your organization to give more resources to your unit.

Hints:

· Who in the organization decides the level of resources your unit receives? What are the values of that person or group?

· How much do the decision makers know about your unit? How much evidence do you need to provide about your contribution to organization goals?

· What kind of evidence is most persuasive in your organization? Should you talk about customers or clients? About internal clients? Give numbers?

· Will you be more persuasive if you ask for funds to take on new tasks, or argue that additional resources will help you do current tasks better?

Memo and Letter Assignments

10.10   Persuading Payees to Sign Up for Direct Deposit

Most payees who receive regular checks from your organization have them directly deposited to their bank accounts. But 20–40% don't. So you have to cut and process paper checks. Write a letter (to accompany the next check) to this minority, persuading them to sign up for direct deposit.

As Your Instructor Directs,

a. Assume that you work for a major employer in town. Persuade everyone you pay to sign up for direct deposit.

b. Assume that you work for the Social Security Administration. Persuade people who get monthly Social Security checks to sign up for direct deposit.

Hints:

· Can you assume that all members of your audience have bank accounts? How easy would it be for people without bank accounts to get them?

· How can you overcome people's fears that electronic deposits may go wrong?

· What benefits would the payee receive from direct deposit?

10.11   Persuading Employees to Use Less Paper

Your office uses lots of paper. Environmentalists have always felt that the office should reduce its paper use, but now that the cost of paper is skyrocketing, fiscal policy also mandates restraint.

Write a memo to all employees urging them to use less paper, while still producing high-quality work.

Hints:

· Pick an organization you know well. Think about the documents—internal and external—it creates.

· Brainstorm ways that people could use less paper without changing their documents, such as single-spacing all documents and printing on both sides of the page. People who are now double-spacing may not know how to create good visual impact with a single-spaced document, so explain the basics. Also tell people how to print double-sided on laser printers designed for single-side printing.

· Brainstorm ways that people could use less paper: using discards and the backs of documents for notes

and drafts, cutting documents so they fit on fewer pages, using proportional type with justified margins, using a smaller font (11 point rather than 12), making fewer copies of documents, making more revisions on screen before printing out a new draft, and so forth.

· Remind people to use paper only for work—not to print out flyers for kids or clubs. (Or, if you allow personal use, raise the cost per page you charge.)

· Show people how to recycle the paper they discard.

· Allow readers to save face. What changes in the external environment make it necessary to change behavior?

· Rebut the counterarguments from 10.3 (1).

· Present yourself as a problem solver who's on the reader's side, not an authoritarian figure who's on the other side.

10.12 Persuading an Organization to Expand Flextime

County government offices are open 9 to 5. Employees have limited flextime: they can come in and leave half an hour early or half an hour late. But employees want much more flexible hours. Some people want to start at 6 AM so they can leave at 2 PM; others want to work 11 AM to 7 PM.

When the idea has been proposed, supervisors have been very negative. "How will we hold staff meetings? How can we supervise people if everyone works different hours? We have to be here for the public, and we won't be if people work whatever hours they please."

But conversations with co-workers and a bit of research show that there are solutions. Many firms that use flextime require everyone to be at work (or at lunch) between 10 and 2 or 11 and 2, so that staff meetings can be scheduled. Right now, when clients call, a representative is frequently on the phone and has to call back. Voice mail and better message forms could solve the problem. And flextime might actually let offices stay open longer hours—say 8 to 6, which would be helpful for taxpayers who themselves work 9 to 5 and now can come in only on their own lunch hours.

Write a memo to the County Commissioners, persuading them to approve a change in work hours.

Hints:

- Assume that this situation is happening in your own county government. What services does the county offer?
- Use any facts about your county that are helpful (for example, being especially busy right now, having high turnover, whether tax issues have been voted up or down).
- Use what you know about managing to allay managers' fears.
- Rebut the counterarguments from 10.3 (2).

10.13 Retrieving Your Image

As Dean of State University's School of Business, you get this letter from Sharon Davis, a member of your college advisory board and a major donor:

My bank received this letter from one of your soon-to-be graduates. It seems as though a closer look at writing skills is warranted.

To Whom It May Concern:

This is in reference to the loan soliciation that I received in the mail. This is the second offer that I am now inquiring about. The first offer sent to my previous address I did not respond. But aftersome careful thought and consideration I think it wise to consolidate my bills. Therefore I hope the information provided is sufficient to complete a successful application. I think the main purpose of this loan is to enable me to repair my credit history. I have had problems in the past because of job status as part-time and being a student. I will be graduating in June and now I do have a full-time job. I think I just need a chance to mend the past credit problems that I have had.

As for previous job information beyong three years of employment changes, i had been employed at the Student Financial Aid

[The next two inches of the letter are blocked out, and both the signature and typed name are crossed out so that they cannot be read.]

As Your Instructor Directs, write to

a. The faculty who teach business communication, reminding them that the quality of student writing may affect fund-raising efforts.

b. Ms. Davis, convincing her that indeed your school does make every effort to graduate students who can write.

10.14 Persuading Tenants to Pay the Rent on Time

As resident manager of a large apartment complex, you receive free rent in return for collecting rents, doing simple maintenance, and enforcing the complex's rules. You find the following notice in the files:

ATTENTION! DERELICTS

If you are a rent derelict (and you know if you are) *this communique is directed to you!*

RENT IS DUE THE 5TH OF EACH MONTH AT THE LATEST!

LEASE HAS A 5-DAY GRACE PERIOD UNTIL THE 5TH OF THE MONTH NOT THE 15TH.

If rent is not paid *in total* by the 5th, you will pay the $25.00 late charge. You will pay the $25.00 late charge when you pay your late rent or your rent will not be accepted.

Half of you people don't even know how much you pay a month. Please read your lease instead of calling up to waste our time finding out what you owe per month! Let's get with the program so I can spend my time streamlining and organizing maintenance requests. My job is maintenance only.

RENT PAYMENT IS YOUR JOB!

If you can show up for a test on time, why can't you make it to the rental office on time or just mail it.

P.S. We don't take cash any longer due to a major theft.

This message is terrible. It lacks you-attitude and may even encourage people who are now paying on the 1st to wait until the 5th. Write a message to go to people who have been slow to pay in the past.

10.15 Persuading Your Campus to Make a Change

Persuade your campus to make some change.

As Your Instructor Directs,

a. Write a memo to the person or office with the authority to make the change.

b. Join with a small group of students to write a memo about a change all of you want.

c. Make an oral presentation to the class urging this change.

Hints:

• Find out who would have the authority to make the decision. How difficult would it be to make the change, assuming that you convinced your audience?

• What is your campus's mission? Can you show that the change you want will make it easier to meet those goals?

• Will your change create extra work for already-burdened administrators, instructors, or workers? Could you minimize this work?

• How much emotional investment does the audience have in this issue? How can you phrase your request so that you don't sound as though you're criticizing the people you're trying to persuade?

• Is the audience more likely to be persuaded by a short, snappy message or a longer persuasive memo packed with details?

11

Sales and Fund-Raising Letters

Components of Good Direct Mail

Is It "Junk" Mail?

Basic Direct Mail Strategy

1. Understand Your Product, Service, or Organization.
2. Identify and Analyze Your Target Audience.
3. Choose a Central Selling Point.

How to Organize a Sales or Fund-Raising Letter

- Opener (Star)
- Body (Chain)
- Action Close (Knot)
- Using a P.S.

Strategy in Sales Letters

- Dealing with Price
- Sample Sales Letter

Strategy in Fund-Raising Appeals

- Deciding How Much to Ask For
- Logical Proof in Fund-Raising Letters
- Emotional Appeal in Fund-Raising Letters
- Sample Fund-Raising Letter

Writing Style

1. Make Your Writing Interesting.
2. Use Sound Patterns to Emphasize Words.
3. Use Psychological Description.
4. Make Your Letter Sound Like a Letter, Not an Ad.

Parts of a Direct Mail Package

Summary of Key Points

Sales and Fund-Raising Letters

Ray Jutkins ROCKINGHAM*JUTKINS*marketing

rayjutkins.com

Direct marketing expert Ray Jutkins explains techniques that work in the real world in *Power Direct Marketing*. His company ROCKINGHAM*JUTKINS*marketing provides "Spend a Day with Ray" seminars for business-to-business and consumer clients throughout the United States, Canada, Mexico, the Asia/Pacific region, South America, the Middle East, and Europe.

1. Direct mail works because it is "conversation in writing." No matter what you have heard, read, or believe, most people look forward to receiving and reading their mail.

2. Have something to say . . . and say it in a way that's understandable by your audience.

> " Direct mail works because it is "conversation in writing." "

This may seem silly to have to say. But, frequently I receive direct mail that doesn't really say anything. When you beat around the bush or the message roams or rambles, the reader is never quite sure what the point is. Make sure you have something very specific to say—and then present it in such a way that the audience can read it and understand it.

Look at your audience and decide if a few more pages of larger type might be worth it. There is a reason most of the world wears glasses.

3. Keep the opening paragraph of a direct mail letter short—absolutely no more than 17 words!

When you follow this simple principle, you'll be more likely to be read. And understood. The second paragraph is equally important . . . a max of 50 words. If you get your readers to read 50 words, you will get them to read 500.

4. Whenever you go to a second page in a letter, split the last sentence in half. Begin it at the bottom of the first page; end it at the top of the next page. Why? To pulllll the reader with you and "make" them turn the page.

5. Write about benefits. Not the features that you offer . . . but the benefits that readers gain from these features.

6. Of your first-time readers, 79%—almost 4 out of 5—will read the P.S. in your letter first, *before* they read your letter. The P.S. is a repeat of earlier key benefits, opportunities, offers, how to respond.

7. Never, but never tell a lie. Tell funny stories. Be entertaining. Weave a scene. Make a point. Be dramatic. Share a case history. Include testimonials. But never exaggerate. Always be true.

E-Mail: The Ultimate Direct Mail?*

At least once a week, . . . sales assistant [Janniece Martin] signs on to find "reminders" from software vendor Parsons Technology Inc. urging her to buy a new label maker or clip art program. . . . "If I'm not ready to make a purchase, all I have to do is delete the E-mail," she says. . . . She frequently spends up to $100 on supplies after receiving an E-mail nudge. . . .

Although users of E-mail have long complained about unwanted direct marketing—commonly called Spam—that hasn't stopped companies from looking for new and improved ways to exploit E-mail as a marketing tool. Now, by using sophisticated data-mining techniques to develop far more tailored messages, marketers may well be succeeding. Lured by the speed, cost savings, and personalized pitches that are possible online, companies such as 1-800-Flowers, Amazon.com, and Macy's are testing the tactic. . . .

Order a *Star Trek* book one month [from Amazon.com] and a *Lost in Space* volume the next, and you can expect to receive an E-mail containing recommendations for similar sci-fi fare. Amazon.com customers also receive E-mail updates if a favorite author is conducting an online chat or has published new work.

*Quoted from "Spam That You Might Not Delete," *Business Week*, June 15, 1998, 115.

Time-Life Books, Buick, FedEx—these are only a few of the companies that use letters to persuade customers to buy their products, visit their showrooms, and use their services. The American Cancer Society, the Republican National Committee, Gallaudet University—these are only a few of the organizations that use letters to persuade people to donate time or money to their causes.

Sales and fund-raising letters may be even more useful for local charities or small businesses with small advertising budgets. The Country Charm store in a Detroit suburb sent two types of letters to its customers: letters announcing special promotions and thank-you letters with gift certificates based on the customer's past purchases. As a result, within five years the store's sales multiplied eight times and it had hired 14 employees. The store grew so big that it had to move. Another established business gladly moved into Country Charm's old location, thinking the location was great. But that store didn't send letters, and it didn't get much traffic. It closed in a year.[1]

Sales and fund-raising letters are a special category of persuasive messages. They are known as **direct mail** because they ask for an order, inquiry, or contribution directly from the reader. Direct mail is one form of direct marketing. **Direct marketing** also includes catalog sales, space ads in magazines and newspapers that have reply cards so that the reader can buy or contribute directly, telemarketing (telephone sales), and TV direct response ads, where the viewer calls an 800 number to place an order. In 1997, direct mail sold almost $255 billion worth of products in the United States and raised nearly $64 billion for charities.[2]

Fortune 500 companies and well-endowed charitable or political organizations hire professionals to write their direct mail. Professionals charge $3,000 to $25,000 to create a package. And that's just the creative cost: you still have to pay for printing and postage. If you own your own business, you can save money by doing your firm's own direct mail. If you are active in a local group that needs to raise money, writing the letter yourself is likely to be the only way your group can afford to use direct mail. The principles in this chapter will help you write solid, serviceable letters that will build your business and help fund your group.

Sales and fund-raising letters have several purposes.

Primary purposes:

To motivate the reader to read the message.

To have the reader act (order the product, schedule a demonstration, send a donation).

To provide enough information so that the reader knows exactly what to do (even if he or she keeps only the reply coupon).

To overcome any objections that might prevent or delay action.

Secondary purpose:

To build a good image of the writer's organization (to strengthen the commitment of readers who act, and make readers who do not act more likely to respond positively next time).

Components of Good Direct Mail

Good direct mail has three components: a good product, service, or cause; a good mailing list; and a good appeal. A **good product** appeals to a specific segment of people, can be mailed, and provides an adequate profit margin. A **good**

service or cause fills an identifiable need. A **good mailing list** has accurate addresses and is a good match to the product. Most professional direct mailers rent their lists from companies that specialize in compiling and maintaining lists. Small businesses and charities can use in-house lists of their customers or members and can compile lists of prospects from city directories or other local sources. A **good appeal** offers a believable description of benefits, links the benefits of the product or service to a need or desire that motivates the reader, makes the reader want to read the letter, and motivates the reader to act. The appeal is made up of the words in the letter, the pictures in the brochure, and all the parts of the package, from outer envelope to reply card.

All three elements are crucial: the best letter in the world won't persuade someone who doesn't have room for a garden to buy a Rototiller. However, this chapter will examine only the elements of a good appeal: how to create a message that will motivate a reader to act, assuming that you already have a good product to sell or a worthy cause to raise funds for, and that you already have a good list of people who might be interested in that product or organization.

Industry wisdom is that a **cold list**—a list of people with no prior connection to your group—will have a 2% response rate. Good timing, a good list, and a good appeal can double or even triple that percentage.

You can raise the response rate 1% or 2% by including an 800 number as another way for people to respond. Following up the mailing with a phone call 24 to 72 hours after the reader receives the mailing can bring in another 2% to 14%. If people on your list have some connection with your organization (e.g., have been patients at the hospital or have visited the museum you're raising money for), you can expect a higher response rate. From a list of people who have bought from or given *to your organization* before, the response rate can be well over 50% and for some groups can approach 90%.[3]

Is It "Junk" Mail?

Almost everyone claims to dislike "junk" mail.

Junk e-mail is called **spam.** Hormel Foods, which makes the canned meat product called Spam, discusses the term. Visit the BAC Web site for the link.

However, people do like to get mail that interests them: ads for products they want to buy, information about groups they like, letters about subjects they care about. One study found that 75% of the people who got political direct mail read the letters.[4]

To reduce the amount of direct mail you get, write to the Mail Preference Service, Direct Marketing Association, PO Box 9008, Farmingdale, NY 11735-9008. If you want mail only from certain organizations, ask them not to rent your name to other organizations. Many companies have a box on the reply card that you can check to indicate this. American Express reports that only 7% of its cardholders say they don't want "bonus" mail.

Much direct mail is bundled by the mailer for each carrier route in the nation, so that the post office does not have to sort it. (If your mailing label carries the letters CAR-RT SORT, it has been "carrier route sorted.")

The quality of the direct mail written today varies widely. A great deal of research has been done about what works in direct mail, but unlike academic research, this research is not generally available. To learn about direct mail, talk to someone who is experienced in the field, join the Direct Marketing Association and read its publications, or read a book like this one.

Lists, Lists, and More Lists*

Nearly 40,000 mailing lists are available commercially. Among the lists available from one company are

130,310	Women accountants
3,953	Owners of balloon aircraft
171,983	High school athletic directors
6,195,311	Dog owners
263,877	Republican contributors
59,641	Highest salaried executives (home addresses)
2,450	Rabbis
4,600,000	Hispanic families
204,443	Heads of households ages 18–34 in Utah
2,046	Yacht owners in Illinois
62,301	Californians with annual income over $100,000

*Based on Best Mailing Lists, Inc., *1996 Catalog.*

Web pages that sell merchandise are most successful if they have interesting or useful information, so that the target audience is motivated to check the site even when they aren't planning to buy anything. The Camping/Hiking page on the REI site allows hikers to find a partner, announce hikes, and trade tips.

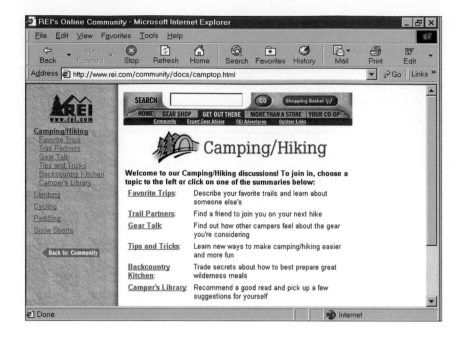

Web pages for charitable organizations should provide information for potential and current donors, volunteers, and clients, as does this page for Habitat for Humanity.

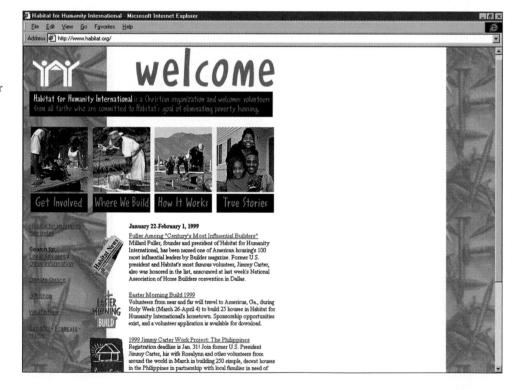

Basic Direct Mail Strategy

Direct mail strategies start with three basic steps: (1) learn about the product, service, or organization; (2) choose and analyze the target audience; and (3) choose a central selling point. These steps interact. An understanding of your target audience may suggest questions to ask about your product. Information you find in researching the product may suggest an idea for a possible central selling point.

1. Understand Your Product, Service, or Organization.

Try to use the product or service. Talk to volunteers who work for your charitable organization; if possible, visit the site where the good work is done.
For a sales letter, ask

- What needs does the product meet? What benefits does it provide? What problems does it remove?
- What are the product's objective features? Size? Color? Materials? How does it work? What options are available?
- How much does it cost? What does the buyer get for the money?
- How is it different from or better than competing products? (If the *details* of differences or superiority are interesting, jot them down. They may work well in a letter.)
- How easy is it to install? To use? To maintain?

For a fund-raising letter, ask

- What is the problem your group is helping to solve? (If possible, collect examples to illustrate the need.)
- How, specifically, is your group helping? (Collect stories about specific people who have been helped, specific gains that have been achieved. Also get overall figures.)
- What support does your group already get from tax dollars, user fees, ticket sales, and so on? Why are private funds necessary?
- What are the group's immediate goals? How much will it cost to achieve them? (Try to get costs for some of the specific subgoals as well as the total budget needed.)

If you're writing a letter for a local organization, visit its office or center and talk to the people who work there, or visit its Web site. If you're writing a letter for a national group, check the phone book to see if there's a local chapter where you can get brochures, flyers, and information. The library may also have information. For fund-raising letters, you can learn about the problem the group is working to solve by checking *The Reader's Guide to Periodical Literature* or the *Business Periodicals Index.* Magazine articles about the problem may have anecdotes and specifics you can use. Also check the Web.

2. Identify and Analyze Your Target Audience.

The **target audience** is all of the people who are likely to be interested in buying the product, using the service, or contributing to the cause. In direct mail, you do not try to sell a subscription to *Sports Illustrated* to someone who loathes sports; you do not ask Republicans to contribute to a Democratic candidate's campaign. In the latter case you might, however, include Independents or people who had never indicated a party preference. In addition to the small number of people who are already interested in your product or committed to your cause, the audience always includes people who could be persuaded if you gave them enough evidence.

As Chapter 3 explains, you can analyze your audience in terms of demographics (p. 64)—objective, measurable features: "This letter is going to homeowners who have children between the ages of 4 and 10." You can also use **psychographic characteristics** (p. 64)—values, beliefs, goals, and lifestyles: "I'm writing to people who care about protecting the environment." Often a combination of demographic and psychographic characteristics works best: 21-year-old college students may have different reasons for using a health

The Name Change*

If you have a sizable customer file, you can bet that at least 10% of the names are incorrect. As the U.S. becomes more multicultural, this percentage is beginning to veer in the direction of 15%. For centuries now (it seems) I've been suggesting that direct marketers prominently display a self-correction device anytime they send out direct mail, particularly to customers: "If your name or any other information is incorrect, please call 1-800-123-4567 and we'll fix things immediately."

*Quoted from James R. Rosenfield, "Personalization and Authenticity," *Direct Marketing*, July 1998, 40.

Recruiting Students*

Sending mail to prospective students helps strengthen their interest in enrolling in a college or university. In the early 1990s, the University of Detroit Mercy was able to print out only one or two letters for each prospective student. Most of these letters were mailed without a signature—hardly a way to build goodwill.

In the mid-1990s, the university installed a system that allows it to create personalized letters triggered by database information. A series of letters could now go out from the admissions counselor, the dean of the college the prospective student might enter, the director of financial aid, and the director of the cooperative education program. Best of all, signatures could be saved as graphic images and printed automatically with the appropriate letter.

By 1997, the university was mailing 250,000 personalized letters a year. The admissions office credits the letters for a 25% increase in enrollment in five years, during a period when the pool of college-age students was growing smaller.

*Based on Janet Kuras, "Personalized Correspondence Contributes to 25% Increase in Student Enrollment at University of Detroit Mercy," *Direct Marketing*, October 1997, 62–63.

club than do 45-year-old executives, even though both groups want to look good and deal with stress. Commercial lists for direct mail can be based on demographics, psychographics, or both.

Whenever possible, think of specific people you know while you write the letter. What do they care about? What would motivate *them*?

3. Choose a Central Selling Point.

Since even a well-defined audience will have people with different motivations and different objections to buying or giving, a direct mail letter needs several selling points. To unify the letter, use a central selling point. A **central selling point** is a reader benefit which by itself could motivate your readers to act and which can serve as an umbrella under which all the other benefits can fit.

Suppose you want to sell copies of a book that explains how to grow vegetables in home gardens. Whenever you try to sell a book or magazine by mail, you are really selling the activity; the book helps readers do the activity successfully. Any of the following statements could be used as central selling points:

- Fresh vegetables from your own garden taste better than store-bought vegetables that are ripened with chemicals.
- Vegetables from your own garden are healthier. You control the chemicals you put on them; you can avoid any insecticides and wax that you don't want.
- It's cheaper to grow your own vegetables than to buy them in a grocery store.
- Growing vegetables is fun for the whole family. Children will be fascinated by growing plants.
- Growing your own vegetables is a way to get back to nature, to have a simpler, more natural lifestyle.

A professional direct mailer might test two or more different approaches with samples of the target market, then send the best letter to the whole list. When you can't run a test, how do you choose? First, eliminate any central selling points that don't fit your target audience. Next, use your own understanding of people to decide whether to stress taste or health or economy or fun or working with nature. If two or more appeals seem equally effective, try writing each of them. In your assignment, use the one that you can develop most effectively.

In a fund-raising letter, you must also choose the appeal that will be most powerful for the target audience. A fund-raising letter to college alumni could use nostalgia, the obligation to repay the college, the feeling of making an investment in young people, or a sense of social responsibility. To create a sense of nostalgia, refer to events that happened when readers were in school. (Check back issues of the college newspaper or yearbook for ideas.) If you're writing to members of a sorority or fraternity, refer to events the house is proud of, and use a salutation and complimentary close that will remind readers of their membership. If you are writing to a group that sees the Bible as an authority, use appropriate biblical quotes and allusions.

When you hope to raise funds from two different target audiences, you may need two separate mailing pieces with different central selling points. Ducks Unlimited can appeal to both hunters and nonhunting environmentalists. Its letters remind hunters that preserving wetlands is essential to maintain the duck populations that hunters need. Environmentalists will be interested in saving the wetlands because of the importance of wetlands as ecosystems.

> 1. Open your letter with a *star* designed to catch the reader's attention.
> 2. In the body, provide a *chain* of reasons and logic.
> 3. End by telling the reader what to do and providing a reason to act promptly. Tie up (*knot*) the motivation you have created and turn it into action.

F i g u r e   11.1

How to Organize a Sales or Fund-Raising Letter

How to Organize a Sales or Fund-Raising Letter

Use the star-chain-knot pattern[5] to organize your letter (see Figure 11.1).

Opener (Star)

The **opener** of your letter gives you 30 to 60 seconds to motivate readers to read the rest of the letter. If the opener fails to do that, your letter will be thrown away.

A good star opener will make readers want to read the letter and provide a reasonable transition to the body of the letter. A very successful subscription letter for *Psychology Today* started out,

> Do you still close the bathroom door when there's no one in the house?

The question is both intriguing in itself and a good transition into the content of *Psychology Today:* practical psychology applied to the quirks and questions we come across in everyday life.

It's essential that the opener not only get the reader's attention but also be something that can be linked logically to the body of the letter. A sales letter started,

> Can You Use $50 This Week?

Certainly that gets attention. But the letter only offered the reader the chance to save $50 on a product. Readers may feel disappointed or even cheated when they learn that instead of getting $50, they have to spend money to save $50.

It's hard to write a brilliant opener the minute you sit down. Two reliable strategies are (1) write four or five openers, and pick the best; (2) just start writing. A good opener may in fact appear on your second or third page; sometimes you can throw away much of the prose that preceded it.

To brainstorm possible openers, use the four basic modes: **questions, narration, startling statements,** and **quotations.**

1. Questions

> Dear Writer:
>
> What is the best way to start writing?

This letter selling subscriptions to *Writer's Digest* goes on to discuss Hemingway's strategy for getting started on his novels and short stories. *Writer's Digest* offers practical advice to writers who want to be published. The information in

Ethics and Direct Mail, I

Deception in direct mail is all too easy to find.

Some mailers have sent "checks" to readers. But the "check" can only be applied toward the purchase of the item the letter is selling.

Some mailings now have yellow Post-it notes with "handwritten" notes signed with initials or a first name only—to suggest that the mailing is from a personal friend.

One letter offers a "free" membership "valued at $675" (note the passive—who's doing the valuing?) but charges—up front—$157 for "maintenance fees."

Such deception has no place in well-written direct mail.

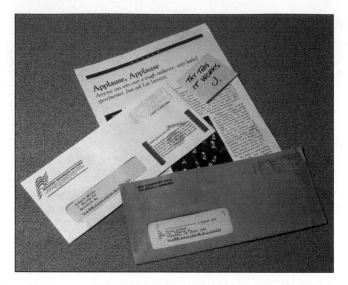

These three documents are unethical attempts to mislead the reader. The top contains a page apparently torn out of a magazine with a personalized Post-it: "Try this. It works." Almost everyone knows someone whose name starts with "J," and people may not realize that this is a scam. The middle document says "Important Documents Enclosed," repeats in small print the US Postal Service statute about tampering with mail, and in the lower right-hand corner has an imprint designed to look like a registered mail sticker. (If you read it, you'll see that it is only fluff, saying nothing.) The bottom envelope is designed to look like an official check. In fact it can be cashed only as a "discount" on a product the mailer is trying to sell.

the letter is useful to any writer, so the recipient keeps reading; the information also helps to prove the claim that the magazine will be useful.

Good questions challenge but don't threaten the reader. They're interesting enough that readers want the answers, so they read the letter.

Poor question: Do you want information about investments?

Better question: Can you still make money investing in land?

A series of questions (as in Figure 11.2 later in the chapter) can be an effective opener.

2. Narration, stories, anecdotes

Dear Reader:

She hoisted herself up noiselessly so as not to disturb the rattlesnakes snoozing there in the sun.

To her left, the high desert of New Mexico. Indian country. To her right, the rock carvings she had photographed the day before. Stick people. Primitive animals.

Up ahead, three sandstone slabs stood stacked against the face of the cliff. In their shadow, another carving. A spiral consisting of rings. Curious, the young woman drew closer. Instinctively, she glanced at her watch. It was almost noon. Then just at that moment, a most unusual thing happened.

Suddenly, as if out of nowhere, an eerie dagger of light appeared to stab at the topmost ring of the spiral. It next began to plunge downwards—shimmering, laser-like.

It pierced the eighth ring. The seventh. The sixth. It punctured the innermost and last. Then just as suddenly as it had appeared, the dagger of light was gone. The young woman glanced at her watch again. Exactly twelve minutes had elapsed.

Coincidence? Accident? Fluke? No. What she may have stumbled across that midsummer morning three years ago is an ancient solar calendar. . . .

This subscription letter for *Science84* argues that it reports interesting and significant discoveries in all fields of science—all in far more detail than do other media. The opener both builds suspense so that the reader reads the subscription letter and suggests that the magazine will be as interesting as the letter and as easy to read.

3. Startling statements

> Dear Membership Candidate:
>
>   I'm writing to offer you a job.
>   It's not a permanent job, understand. You'll be working for only as much time as you find it rewarding and fun.
>   It's not even a paying job. On the contrary, it will cost *you* money.

This fund-raising letter from Earthwatch invites readers to participate in its expeditions, subscribe to its journal, and donate to its programs. Earthwatch's volunteers help scientists and scholars dig for ruins, count bighorns, and monitor changes in water; they can work as long as they like; they pay their own (tax-deductible) expenses.

Variations of this mode include special opportunities, twists, and challenges.

4. Quotations

> "I never tell my partner that my ankle is sore or my back hurts. You can't give in to pain and still perform."
>
> —Jill Murphy
> Soloist

The series of which this letter is a part sells season tickets to the Atlanta Ballet by focusing on the people who work to create the season. Each letter quotes a different member of the company. The opening quote is used on the envelope over a picture of the ballerina and as an opener for the letter. The letters encourage readers to see the artists as individuals, to appreciate their hard work, and to share their excitement about each performance.

Body (Chain)

The *chain* is the **body** of the letter. It provides the logical and emotional links that move readers from their first flicker of interest to the action that is wanted. A good chain answers readers' questions, overcomes their objections, and involves them emotionally.

All this takes space. One of the industry truisms is "The more you tell, the more you sell." Tests show that longer letters bring in more new customers or new donors than do shorter letters. A four-page letter is considered ideal for mailings to new customers or donors. Why?

Direct mail expert Alan Rosenspan admits that the "vast majority" of people won't read long letters.

> However, the two or three in 100 who are interested, who want more information, who may have a need for your product or service, will practically [pore] over every word. After all, you're promising to solve their problems or provide a much-needed benefit. For them it's not long copy. It's just complete.[6]

Long, Longer, Longest

Some tests show that six- or even eight-page letters outpull shorter letters. Many political fund-raising letters are six pages (particularly during the primary seasons when candidates are not yet well known).

Long letters are especially good for publications, high-involvement categories like health and investing, or expensive items. Liberty Mint used an eight-page letter to sell 100 castings of Remington's "The Bronco Buster" made of pure silver for $25,000 each.

Even long letters should look easy to read. Many long letters use short paragraphs (just a sentence or two), headings, and highlighted or underlined sections to encourage skimming.

To get that length, some letters use large type and margins. Expensive mailings sometimes use one uncut, folded 11-by-17-inch sheet, printed on the first and third sides, to give a two-page letter the psychological weight of four pages. And many letters now use bullet points or graphics to make the page easy to read.

Can short letters work? Yes, when you're writing to old customers or when the mailing is supported by other media. One study showed that a one-page letter was just as effective as a two-page letter in persuading recent purchasers of a product to buy a service contract.[7] The shortest letter on record may be the two-word postcard that a fishing lake resort sent its customers: "They're biting!"

Content for the body of the letter can include

- Information readers will find useful even if they do not buy or give.
- Stories about how the product was developed or what the organization has done.
- Stories about people who have used the product or who need the organization's help.
- Word pictures of readers using the product and enjoying its benefits.

Action Close (Knot)

The **action close** in the letter must do four things:

1. **Tell the reader what to do:** respond. Avoid *if* ("If you'd like to try . . .") and *why not* ("Why not send in a check?"). They lack positive emphasis and encourage your reader to say *no.*
2. **Make the action sound easy:** fill in the information on the reply card, sign the card (for credit sales), put the card and check (if payment is to accompany the order) in the envelope, and mail the envelope. If you provide an envelope and pay postage, stress those facts.
3. **Offer a reason for acting promptly.** Readers who think they are convinced but wait to act are less likely to buy or contribute. Reasons for acting promptly are easy to identify when a product is seasonal or there is a genuine limit on the offer—time limit, price rise scheduled, limited supply, and so on. Sometimes you can offer a premium or a discount if the reader acts quickly. When these conditions do not exist, remind readers that the sooner they get the product, the sooner they can benefit from it; the sooner they contribute funds, the sooner their dollars can go to work to solve the problem.
4. **End with a positive picture** of the reader enjoying the product (in a sales letter) or of the reader's money working to solve the problem (in a fund-raising letter). The last sentence should never be a selfish request for money.

The action close can also remind readers of the central selling point, stress the guarantee, and mention when the customer will get the product.

Using a P.S.

Studies of eye movement show that people often look to see who a letter is from before they read the letter. Ray Jutkins cites a study showing that 79% of the people who open direct mail read the P.S. first.[8] Therefore, direct mail often uses a deliberate P.S. after the signature block. It may restate the central selling point or some other point the letter makes, preferably in different words so that it won't sound repetitive when the reader reads the letter through from start to finish.

workers like Li Ki are finding hope through one of Laubach Literacy's international partners.

The Surabaya project is working with 30 women like Li Ki to help them improve the conditions of their lives through literacy and skill training, as well as income-generating activities that produce foods or goods for sale.

Classes are held in the housing sites where female factory workers live. Sessions are conducted at night to accommodate the day-shift workers. This combination of literacy and practical application is wonderfully effective in improving the situations of these factory workers.

And a small grant — just $3,000 — is all they need to continue.

In Indonesia, just $35 will purchase instructional materials for 20 women...or racks for a new cooperative bakery project.

Your gift now will make such a difference!

And not just in Indonesia — grant requests — often for just a few hundred dollars — have arrived on my desk from all over the world. I'm excited by the opportunities they represent.

But we'll only be able to meet these requests with the help of friends like you.

Just look at some of the Partner Programs you have the opportunity to support:

KENYA –
Rangwe Literacy and Community Development Project.

Grant Request — $1,000

In rural Kenya, literacy volunteers hope to expand adult literacy classes that reach ninety women.

Plus, they hope to begin a small chicken-raising business that will supply their village with much-needed protein and a source of income. A gift of as little as $110 will provide enough seed and barbed-wire fencing (to keep wild animals out) to help ninety village women.

Laubach Literacy breaks up the text with photos. Note that the text still uses a typewriter typeface. The largest headlines even use a font imitating the uneven filled-in letters of a manual typewriter. This four-page letter is printed on an 11-by-17-inch sheet. Shown here are the two middle pages.

(continued)

HAITI — Buteau Laubach Literacy of Haiti.

Grant Request — $4,000

Just outside of the capital city of Port-au-Prince, Laubach Partners are using literacy to teach Haitians how to renew their poverty-ravaged land.

Recent deforestation has reduced once-lush tropical rainforests to barren deserts. As participants gain literacy skills, they also become involved in cooperative efforts that lift their families out of poverty. In Haiti, a gift of only $94 will buy 14 blackboards for literacy volunteers.

MALI — Ouelessebougou Alliance.

In the villages of Mali, celebrations and classes are held under the barra ("public") tree.

The heart of the community, the spectacular barra tree lends both shade and significance to the learning taking place beneath its branches. Literacy learners practice writing words in their native Bambara language with sticks in the dirt, taking turns writing on the single chalkboard suspended from a tree limb. A gift of $15 provides a lantern which can be hung from the barra tree to give light for night classe

Grant Request — $4,500

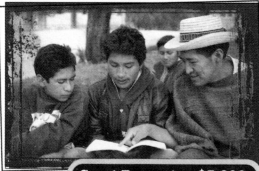

Grant Request — $5,000

COLOMBIA — Pitayo/Paez Bilingual Project.

In the steep mountain valleys tucked in the cordilleros of the Andes, the Paez people support themselves through subsistence farming.

Our partners have requested a grant to expand the basic literacy skills of the people of Pitayo so they can improve their farming techniques. Plus, with literacy comes better record-keeping, management, and organization skills, so urgently needed in producing and marketing their renowned cheese. A gift of $75 will buy school supplies for one village, including benches, chalk boards, notebooks, and pencils.

Here are four of the many kinds of effective P.S.'s.

- Reason to act promptly:

> P.S. Once I finish the limited harvest, that's it! I do not store any SpringSweet Onions for late orders. I will ship all orders on a first-come, first-served basis and when they are gone they are gone. Drop your order in the mail today . . . or give me a call toll free at 800-531-7470! (In Texas: 800-292-5437)

Sales letter for Frank Lewis Alamo Fruit

- Description of a premium the reader receives for giving:

> P.S. And . . . we'll be pleased to send you—as a *new* member—the exquisite, full-color 2000 Sierra Club Wilderness Calendar. It's our gift . . . absolutely FREE to you . . . to show our thanks for your membership at this critical time.

Fund-raising letter for Sierra Club

- Reference to another part of the package:

> P.S. Photographs may be better than words, but they still don't do justice to this model. Please keep in mind as you review the enclosed brochure that your SSJ will look even better when you can see it firsthand in your own home.

Sales letter for the Danbury Mint's model of the Duesenberg SSJ

- Restatement of central selling point:

> P.S. It is not easy to be a hungry child in the Third World. If your parents' crops fail or if your parents cannot find work, there are no food stamps . . . no free government-provided cafeteria lunches. Millions of hungry schoolchildren will be depending on CARE this fall. Your gift today will ensure that we will be there—that CARE won't let them down.

Fund-raising letter for CARE

Strategy in Sales Letters

The basic strategy in sales letters is satisfying a need. People buy to get something or to get rid of something. Your letter must remind people of the need your product meets, prove that the product will satisfy that need, show why your product is better than similar products, and make readers *want* to have the product. Use psychological description (p. 233) to show readers how the product will help them. Testimonials from other buyers can help persuade them that the product works; details about how the product is made can carry the message of quality.

The Better Business Bureau's Web site helps consumers avoid fraudulent companies and get good service. Check it out on the BAC Web site.

Gimmicks and Gadgets in Business-to-Business Sales*

Direct mail letters to business customers often use enclosures to get the attention of busy executives.

To catch attention for its business loans, CIT Group sent baseballs autographed by Willie Mays, Stan Musial, and Mickey Mantle. Of the 98 executives who received the first package, 89 responded. The campaign cost $17,664; it brought in sales of over $120 million.

Taking the term *cold call* literally, James Productions, a corporate events producer, sent Coleman coolers to 75 local human resource directors. On the ice inside was a sealed bag with the letter: "I'll bring some soft drinks for you and your staff to enjoy during our presentation meeting. . . . Let's get together before the ice melts." The campaign netted 15 new accounts.

Phoneworks introduced its interactive marketing system, Smart-Spiffs, by FedExing 100 ad agency heads wallets, each containing $3, an ID card with the agency head's name, and a note: "I found your wallet." Most of the items in the wallet promoted SmartSpiffs: a *Wall Street Journal* article, a to-do reminder to learn more about the system, a matchbook with Smart-Spiffs' 800 number. The mailing cost $5,340 and brought in sales of nearly $5 million in the first eight months.

*Based on "CIT Group Scores Big Points," *Direct Marketing*, November 1992, 38; Wingfield Hughes, "Promotional Products Can *Boost* Direct Mail Responses," *Direct Marketing*, July 1996, 30–31; "Caples Awards," *Direct Marketing*, May 1998, 36; and Josh Inch, "'Quest for Denali' Uncovers DMA's Echo Diamond Award," *Advertising Age*, October 12, 1998, 56.

Talking about Taxes*

Even if your group is not required to pay taxes, contributions may not be tax-deductible. Such groups with incomes over $100,000 a year must "state conspicuously" in all fund-raising solicitations, including phone calls, that the gift is not tax-deductible.

Stressing what the group will achieve with the money can make donors feel that the gift it still worth giving:

> Your dues and gifts to the Sierra Club support our effective citizen-based advocacy and lobbying programs, and therefore are not tax-deductible.

Sometimes, particularly in December, people will give because a gift is tax-deductible. However, you should never suggest that that is the *reason* people would give. In your letter, mention that gifts are tax-deductible (if they are), but subordinate that fact to the work of the organization that the reader's gift makes possible.

*Based on "Tax Report," *The Wall Street Journal*, February 3, 1988, 1; and Sierra Club reply card.

Dealing with Price

Many sales letters make the offer early in the letter—even on the envelope. The exact price, however, is not mentioned until the last fourth of the letter, after the copy makes the reader *want* the product. The only exception is when you're selling something that has a reputation for being expensive (a luxury car, *Encyclopaedia Britannica*). Then you may want to deal with the price issue early in the letter, especially if your readers want the product but think they can't afford it.

You can make the price more palatable with the following techniques:

1. **Link the price to the benefit the product provides.** "Your piece of history is just $39.95."
2. **Show how much the product costs each day, each week, or each month.** "You can have all this for less than the cost of a cup of coffee a day." Make sure that the amount seems small and that you've convinced people that they'll use this product all year long.
3. **Allow customers to charge sales or pay in installments.** Your bookkeeping costs will rise, and some sales may be uncollectible, but the total number of sales will increase.

Always offer a guarantee, usually right after the price. The best guarantees are short, convincing, and positive.

Negative: If the magazine fails to meet your expectations, you can cancel at any time and receive a refund on any unmailed copies.

Better: You'll be satisfied or we'll refund your money. I guarantee that.

You can increase the number of orders simply by repeating your message. A repeat copy of the original sales letter, mailed about three weeks later, will bring in about 70% of the original response rate.[9]

Sample Sales Letter

The sample letter in Figure 11.2 is a subscription letter for *3-2-1 Contact*, a magazine for children ages 8–14. The letter uses an elite typeface on white paper with color in the logo, the "ABSOLUTELY FREE!" and the signature. The folded, uncut 11-by-17-inch paper is printed on four sides.

The letter opens with its central selling point: *3-2-1 Contact* educates kids in a fun way. Since the letter is addressed to parents, the opening questions are designed to be ones that will interest adults so that they'll read to find the answers. The body of the letter builds credibility by pointing out that the magazine is published by a nonprofit group. Material from the magazine itself helps to prove the claim that it teaches in an interesting way. The action close asks the reader to send in the reply card to subscribe.

See the BAC Web site for additional sales letters.

Strategy in Fund-Raising Appeals

In a fund-raising letter, the basic emotional strategy is **vicarious participation.** By donating money, readers participate vicariously in work they are not able to do personally. This strategy affects the pronouns you use. Throughout the letter, use *we* to talk about your group. However, at the end, talk about what *you* the reader will be doing. End positively, with a picture of the reader's dollars helping to solve the problem.

Figure 11.2   *A Magazine Subscription Letter*

PL-CN1

Children's Television Workshop ▪ One Lincoln Plaza, New York, NY 10023

*   *   *   *   *   *   *   *   *   *   *

This letter is not for everyone. But if you're the parent of a youngster between the ages of 8 and 14 . . .

Identifies target audience

. . . then I invite you to send for a free copy of 3-2-1 CONTACT, the <u>award-winning</u> magazine of science, nature and math for the middle grades.

Statement of central selling point

Like the other Children's Television Workshop publications -- <u>Sesame Street</u> and <u>Kid City</u> -- 3-2-1 CONTACT is so spirited, so entertaining, so amusing that its readers seldom notice the fact that it's "educational."

Yet every issue is chock-full of mind-stretching puzzles, mazes, games and mysteries . . . amazing facts . . . and articles and features that promote analytical thinking, encourage patience and concentration, and generally help prepare your child for the world of tomorrow.

Keeps door open for reluctant reader

Don't worry -- I'm not asking you to <u>subscribe</u> to this magazine, at least not yet. All I'm asking is your permission to send an issue of 3-2-1 CONTACT to your home,

ABSOLUTELY FREE!

Repeats powerful word "Free"

*   *   *   *   *   *   *   *   *   *   *

Dear Fellow Parent,

"Why is the ocean salty?"

Attention-getting questions

    "When you take an aspirin, how does it know where you hurt?"

        "What are eyelashes for?"

            "How does a magnifying glass work?"

                                (over, please . . .)

(continued)

"Why is my image upside down when I see myself in a spoon?"

"How do fireworks work?"

"Why do some objects glow in the dark?"

"Why is the sky blue?"

                         *   *   *   *   *   *

Good you-attitude— avoids making reader feel inferior

I don't know about you, but I'm often stumped by the science questions my kids throw at me. I have no trouble helping them with spelling, or simple arithmetic, or even state capitals . . . but when it comes to explaining why teeth chatter, or how roosters know what time it is -- I guess I'm not as well-educated as I should be!

    And yet our children are growing up into a world that is more technological than ever . . .

    . . . a world where familiarity with computers is becoming essential, not just for scientists but for office workers, farmers, teachers, doctors, librarians, almost everyone . . .

Paragraphs indented for emphasis, visual appeal

    . . . a world in which many of the most interesting, most challenging career opportunities call for a background in science and technology.

That's why I'm pleased that my children read 3-2-1 CONTACT, a magazine for 3rd through 8th graders that does for them what <u>Sesame Street</u> does for younger children: It educates without tears, using cartoons, games, jokes, and the attention-getting tricks of television to stimulate, enrich, and enlighten.

3-2-1 CONTACT is published by the non-profit Children's Television Workshop. It is a glossy, colorful magazine, loosely based on the television show of the same name. Like the show, the magazine has high production values: lively graphics, good writing, clear, full-color photographs and amusing illustrations throughout. Issue after issue, your youngsters will be entertained and challenged by such features as . . .

Builds credibility

    <u>EXTRA!</u> The puzzles-and-games pages of the magazine, and the section most readers turn to first. Perhaps there'll be a "what's wrong with this picture" game, designed to promote logic and attention to detail. Sometimes there's a maze to get through, or a simple hands-on experiment, or a word-search puzzle.

    There's often something to write away for -- for example, a free booklet from Kodak on how to make a pin-hole camera. Sometimes there's a riddle your child can solve by doing a series of math problems. (Can you imagine? Fun math!)

    <u>TNT: Tomorrow's News Today</u> -- is a popular monthly column that brings our readers interesting news, often before their parents know of it. Have you heard about pop rice? (It tastes like pop corn, but is made from rice.) Did you know that the planet Pluto is a lot smaller than previously thought, and may be downgraded to a "minor planet"? Have

Figure 11.2   *A Magazine Subscription Letter (continued)*

you heard about the plans for a two-mile-long elevated freeway in Los
Angeles -- for bicycles only? Do you know about the new aerosol spray
that protects against poison ivy? 3-2-1 CONTACT readers know about
all these, and more!

The famous magician Blackstone is a contributor to 3-2-1 CONTACT, usually with
a remarkable math trick, such as this one:

> Using a calculator, punch in any three-digit
> number. (Example: 627.) Then punch it in again,
> so you have a six-digit number. (Example: 627,627.)
> Then divide the six-digit number by seven, divide
> the answer by 11, and divide that answer by 13.
> Amazingly, you'll always end up with the original
> three-digit number! Try it!

Example of material in magazine — helps to prove claims

THE TIME TEAM is another popular feature of 3-2-1 CONTACT. In each
month's story, two teenagers -- with the help of a science fair
project gone awry -- travel into the past or the future. Transported
to different eras and cultures, the heroes become caught up in
exciting historical moments, and have adventures with people both
famous and ordinary. In one episode, set in the 1920s, they use their
mental agility to help Walt Disney solve a mystery involving the
original Mickey Mouse cartoon. In another, they find themselves in
the middle of the Civil War. An entertaining blend of fact and
fiction, the stories make history and science come alive!

FACTOIDS, too, is a popular monthly column, one that provides our
readers with curious little facts which they can share with their
friends. For example, did you know that . . .

Facts to interest parents as well as kids

*   In one day, Americans eat enough pizza to cover 75 football
    fields.

*   A codfish lays up to four million eggs at one time, but on
    average only two will become fish.

*   Lions sleep about 18 hours a day.

*   One hundred years ago, the average 9-year-old was about six
    inches shorter than a 9-year-old today.

*   In one year, your heart beats about 36,000,000 times.

And of course, every issue of 3-2-1 CONTACT contains several major articles
spanning the depth and breadth of science today. For example, recently we had
a special issue on Water, with articles on Rescuing a Coral Reef . . . River
Rafting Catches On . . . and Are We Running Out of Water?

We've also had cover stories on Why Baby Animals Are Cute (in some species,
it's what makes adults take care of their young!) . . . on Finding Homes for
Wild Horses . . . and on Memory, including an article on how memory works,
with tricks and techniques for greatly improving your own memory!

                    *   *   *   *   *   *

Figure 11.2   *A Magazine Subscription Letter (concluded)*

Need to improve positive emphasis here

If these examples of what you'll find in 3-2-1 CONTACT have convinced you to subscribe for your family, then indicate "I ACCEPT" on the enclosed Free Issue Request Card. Send no money now -- we'll send you your first issue, enter your subscription, and bill you later.

Lacks you-attitude

If you'd like to see the magazine before making up your mind, indicate "I'M NOT SURE" on the Free Issue Request Card. We'll send you an issue at no cost and with no obligation to subscribe.

When you receive your first issue, show it to your children. Look through it together, and decide if becoming a subscriber is a good idea for you.

Action close

If not, write "cancel" on our invoice, return it, and owe nothing. The first issue will be yours to keep, free. But if you like 3-2-1 CONTACT -- the only children's magazine ever to receive the National Magazine Award for General Excellence -- and wish to continue receiving it, we'll send you 9 more issues (10 issues in all) for the low price of $1.59 per issue.

Should use you-attitude

There's really nothing to lose -- and the exciting world of science and technology to gain. Say "I ACCEPT" or "I'M NOT SURE," but please -- return your Free Issue Card today!

                    Sincerely,

                    Nina B. Link

                    Nina B. Link
                    Publisher
                    3-2-1 CONTACT

Lacks you-attitude

P.S.   If yours is one of the first fifty request cards to be processed, we'll send you -- absolutely FREE -- a NINTENDO Entertainment System Control Deck. The system includes the Control Deck and two precision-engineered controls designed for instant reflex action! You can play the complete library of NINTENDO games on this system. And its exclusive microchips give you brilliant color, 3-D images and actual shadows -- the most advanced graphics ever! To be considered for this state-of-the-art home entertainment system, remove the "FREE NINTENDO" sticker from the outer envelope and affix it to the postpaid reply envelope provided. Then enclose your request card and mail it immediately!

Split long P.S. into two paragraphs for better visual impact

As part of our promotion, we're giving away fifty (50) NINTENDO™ Entertainment System Control Decks, with a retail value of $100.00 each, to the first 50 people who respond to our offer. To assure equal opportunity for all, one system will be awarded to each of the first fifty respondents on a geographical basis proportionate to the geographical distribution of this offer. No purchase necessary. One entry per person. Only entries received by First Class mail are eligible. If you are a winner, you will be notified by mail. For a list of the winners, please send a self-addressed stamped envelope to: Children's Television Workshop, One Lincoln Plaza, New York, NY 10023. Attn: Magazine Circulation Department. Employees of Children's Television Workshop and its suppliers are not eligible. Void where prohibited by law. LIMIT—ONE SYSTEM PER HOUSEHOLD.

To achieve both your primary and secondary purposes in fund-raising letters, you must give a great deal of information. This information (1) helps to persuade readers; (2) gives supporters evidence to use in conversations with others; and (3) gives readers who are not yet supporters evidence that may make them see the group as worthwhile, even if they do not give money now.

Your appeal must compete against many others. The number of nonprofit organizations in the United States rose 19% in the 10 years from 1987 to 1996. But the proportion of households giving to charity has actually dropped. And the people who do give are giving a smaller proportion of their income. One of the several reasons people give for not contributing is that a gift of $25 or $100 seems too small to matter. It's not. Small gifts are important both in themselves and to establish a habit of giving. Some of the people who can only give $25 or even $5 today will someday have more money.[10]

In your close, in addition to asking for money, suggest other ways the reader can help: doing volunteer work, scheduling a meeting on the subject, writing letters to Congress or the leaders of other countries, and so on. By suggesting other ways to participate, you not only involve readers but also avoid one of the traps of fund-raising letters: sounding as though you are selfish, only interested in readers for the money they can give.

Deciding How Much to Ask For

Most letters to new donors suggest a range of amounts, from $25 or $50 (for employed people) up to perhaps double what you *really* expect to get from a single donor. A second strategy is to ask for a small, set amount that nearly everyone can afford ($10 or $15).

You can increase the size of gifts by using the following techniques:

1. **Suggest amounts in descending order.** Both in your close and on the reply card, say "$100, $50, $25, or whatever amount you prefer" rather than starting with the smallest and going up.
2. **Ask for gifts slightly higher than the normal cut-off points.** Most people think in terms of a gift of $10, $25, $50, and so on, even though they could afford to give slightly more. You can increase the average gift by asking for $12, $30, $60, and so on.
3. **Link the gift to what it will buy.** Tell how much money it costs to buy a brick, a hymnal, or a stained glass window for a church; a book or journal subscription for a college library; a meal for a hungry child. Linking amounts to specific gifts helps readers feel involved and often motivates them to give more: instead of saying, "I'll write a check for $25," the reader may say, "I'd like to give a _____" and write a check to cover it.
4. **Offer a premium for giving.** Public TV and radio stations have used this ploy with great success, offering books, umbrellas, and carryall bags for gifts at a certain level. The best premiums are things that people both want and will use or display, so that the organization will get further publicity when other people see the premium.
5. **Ask for a monthly pledge.** People on tight budgets could give $5 or $10 a month; more prosperous people could give $50 a month or more. These repeat gifts not only bring in more money than the donors could give in a single check but also become part of the base of loyal supporters which is essential to the continued success of any organization that raises funds.

Annual letters to past donors often use the amount of the last donation as the lowest suggested gift, with other gifts 25%, 50%, or even 100% higher.

Enclosures in Fund-Raising Letters

Fund-raising letters sometimes use inexpensive enclosures to add interest and help carry the message.

Brochures are inexpensive, particularly if you photocopy them. Mailings to alumni have included "Why I Teach at Earlham" (featuring three professors) and letters from students who have received scholarships.

Seeds don't cost much. Mailings from both Care and the New Forests Fund include four or five seeds of the leucaena, a subtropical tree that can grow 20 feet in a year. Its leaves feed cattle; its wood provides firewood or building materials; its roots reduce soil erosion. (Indeed, the enclosure easily becomes the theme for the letter.)

Reprints of newspaper or magazine articles about the organization or the problem it is working to solve add interest and credibility. Pictures of people the organization is helping build emotional appeal.

School songs and sports broadcasts on thin vinyl records or audiocassettes motivate people to give to a university and its athletic program.

Major campaigns may budget for enclosures: pictures of buildings, tapes of oral history interviews, even sea shells and Mason jars.

Always send a thank-you letter to people who respond to your letter, whatever the size of their gifts. By telling about the group's recent work, a thank-you letter can help reinforce donors' commitment to your cause.

See the BAC Web site for thank-you letters and for letters to non-donors, encouraging them to give.

Logical Proof in Fund-Raising Letters

The body of a fund-raising letter must prove that (1) the problem deserves the reader's attention, (2) the problem can be solved or at least alleviated, (3) your organization is helping to solve it, (4) private funds are needed, and (5) your organization will use the funds wisely.

1. The problem deserves the reader's attention.

No reader can support every cause. Show why the reader should care about solving this problem.

If your problem is life-threatening, give some statistics: you cannot count on everyone's knowing how many people are killed in the United States every year by drunk drivers, or how many children in the world go to bed hungry every night. Also tell about one individual who is affected.

If your problem is not life-threatening, show that the problem threatens some goal or principle your readers find important. For example, a fund-raising letter to boosters of a high school swim team showed that team members' chances of setting records were reduced because timers relied on stopwatches. The letter showed that automatic timing equipment was accurate and produced faster times, since the timer's reaction time was no longer included in the time recorded.

2. The problem can be solved or alleviated.

People will not give money if they see the problem as hopeless: why throw money away? Sometimes you can reason by analogy. Cures have been found for other deadly diseases, so it's reasonable to hope that research can find a cure for cancer and AIDS. Sometimes you can show that short-term or partial solutions exist. For example, a UNICEF letter showed that four simple changes could save the lives of millions of children: oral rehydration, immunization, promoting breast feeding, and giving mothers cardboard growth charts so they'll know if their children are malnourished. Those solutions don't affect the underlying causes of poverty, but they do keep children alive while we work on long-term solutions.

3. Your organization is helping to solve or alleviate the problem.

Prove that your organization is effective. Be specific. Talk about your successes in the past. Your past success helps readers believe that you can accomplish your goals.

4. Private funds are needed to accomplish your group's goals.

We all have the tendency to think that taxes, or foundations, or church collections yield enough to pay for medical research or basic human aid. If your group does get some tax or foundation money, show why more money is needed. If the organization helps people who might be expected to pay for the service, show why they cannot pay, or why they cannot pay enough to cover the full cost. If some of the funds have been raised by the people who will benefit, make that clear.

5. Your organization will use the funds wisely.

Prove that the money goes to the cause, not just to the cost of fund-raising.

The National Charities Information Bureau grades more than 400 charities. You'll find a link to its Web site on the BAC site.

Emotional Appeal in Fund-Raising Letters

Emotional appeal is needed to make people pull out their checkbooks. How strong should emotional appeal be? A mild appeal is unlikely to sway any reader who is not already committed, but readers will feel manipulated by appeals they find too strong and reject them. Audience analysis may help you decide how much emotional appeal to use. If you don't know your audience well, use the strongest emotional appeal *you* feel comfortable with.

Emotional appeal is created by specifics. It is hard to care about, or even to imagine, a million people; it is easier to care about one specific person. Details and quotes help us see that person as real. A letter for a New York hospital talked about four people who owed their lives to the hospital: a baby, a young girl, a businessman, and an elderly woman. The letter brought in a greater response than previous mailings that simply used statistics.[11]

Sample Fund-Raising Letter

The letter from The Gorilla Foundation shown in Figure 11.3 uses interesting details and color photos to lead the reader through the document.

The letter is printed in Courier on an 11-by-17-inch page folded into 8½ by 11 inches. The letter is a bit text-heavy. Using bigger margins, bigger paragraph indentations, and an occasional list would provide visual variety.

The opening paragraph is weak. The second paragraph offers several possibilities: "Sign language isn't just for Deaf people. A gorilla named Koko can use it too." However, the photo draws the reader's eye down the page. The letter would benefit from more specific supporting details. Much of the appeal of this letter is its novelty: this isn't the standard environmental fund-raising letter. The poster of Koko and her kitten included in the package is cute and involves the reader with the package.

Writing Style

Direct mail is the one kind of business writing where elegance and beauty of language matter; in every other kind, elegance is welcome but efficiency is all that finally counts. Direct mail imitates the word choice and rhythm of conversation. The best sales and fund-raising writing is closer to the language of poetry than to that of academia: it shimmers with images, it echoes with sound, it vibrates with energy.

Many of the things that make writing vivid and entertaining *add* words because they add specifics or evoke an emotional response. Individual sentences should flow smoothly. The passage as a whole may be fun to read precisely because of the details and images that "could have been left out."

1. Make Your Writing Interesting.

If the style is long-winded and boring, the reader will stop reading. Eliminating wordiness (✂ p. 100) is crucial. You've already seen ways to tighten your writing in Chapter 4. Direct mail goes further, breaking some of the rules of grammar. In the following examples, note how sentence fragments and ellipses (spaced dots) are used in parallel structure to move the reader along:

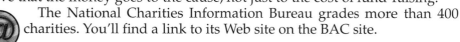

Canadian Culture and Direct Mail*

In the United States, direct mail letters to total strangers often begin "Dear Friend." Canadian letters, in contrast, are more formal and less likely to imply any relationship other than business to be transacted.

US letters often offer some external reward for responding: a cash rebate, a credit on a bank card, a tote bag. Canadian letters avoid such rewards, perhaps because they suggest that if the product itself is not worth purchasing, the cause is not worth supporting.

*Based on Roger Graves, " 'Dear Friend' (?): Culture and Genre in American and Canadian Direct Marketing Letters," *The Journal of Business Communication* 34, no. 3 (July 1997), 235–52.

Figure 11.3 *A Fund-Raising Letter*

Photos break up the text and provide visual interest.

THE GORILLA FOUNDATION

BOX 620-640 WOODSIDE, CA 94062

INTERNET SITE: www.gorilla.org

Dear Friend of Animals,

First paragraph is weak. It isn't really news (as paragraph 3 admits); the allusion to a "myth" doesn't work; the paragraph lacks specifics.

Not you-attitude (I'm writing) to share with you an astonishing breakthrough in our understanding of the world. The news is that a very remarkable gorilla named Koko has changed myth into fact ... by speaking to humans!

Underlining is meant to look as though person had marked key points

Slightly revised, this ¶ would make an acceptable opener

It's true. After years of dedicated teaching, Koko has learned to use sign language--the gestural language used by the deaf. With her newfound vocabulary, Koko is now providing us with an astounding wealth of knowledge about the way animals view the world. *A detail would be nice.*

Builds credibility

If you read magazines such as *National Geographic, People,* and *Life,* or watch television programs like "I Witness Video, Day One and 20/20," then you already know about Koko and the fascinating things she is telling us. Through the media, more than 40 million Americans have discovered what this young female gorilla can teach you and me about *homo sapiens'* closest living relatives.

Builds credibility

My name is Penny Patterson, and I have been Koko's teacher since 1972. In this letter Koko and I would like to share with you what we are learning together. And, perhaps most importantly, we'd like to invite you to become a member of the amazing world of speaking with animals by joining the Gorilla Foundation as part of Koko's extended family.

Emotional appeal

Dangerous to assume reader's reaction

As you read this, I think you'll be astonished at what more than two decades of study here at the Gorilla Foundation have revealed. By using sign language, Koko has confirmed humanity's timeless intuitions about the nature of animal intelligence.

Indeed, I constantly marvel at the complex and all-encompassing spectrum of this gentle animal's emotions: joy and grief, hope and

Talking about your own responses, however, is OK.

Figure 11.3 *A Fund-Raising Letter (continued)*

despair, patience and frustration, greed and generosity, guilt and remorse, confidence and fear, pride and shame, empathy and jealousy, love and hate ... all the emotions that you and I experience.

Let me tell you a particularly poignant story to illustrate what I mean.

For years, Koko had expressed an interest in the cats she saw through her windows or in the pages of her magazines. Her dreams came true when she selected a tailless manx kitten from a litter to be her very own.

I was moved by the relationship that developed between the 230-pound gorilla and the roly-poly kitten she named "All Ball." On occasion we would witness the tragicomical scene of Koko pouting when tiny All Ball had bitten or scratched her.

Interesting details keep the reader reading.

But far more frequently the then 13-year-old Koko would tell us how much she adored her tiny kitten. Certainly there's no better example of the old maxim "A picture is worth 1,000 words" than the cover of the January 1985 *National Geographic* that showed Koko softly cradling the diminutive kitten in her arms.

This photo is on the poster included in the package.

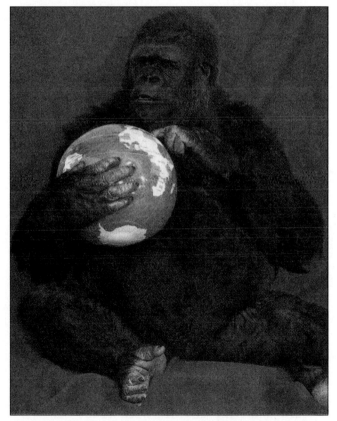

Koko is not alone in teaching us about the remarkable intelligence of these gentle primates. Her gorilla companion Michael has his own stories to tell. Unlike Koko, who was born in the San Francisco Zoo, Michael was orphaned in his birthplace in Cameroon, Africa.

Using sign language, the 400-pound gorilla can relate how he was captured--"big trouble"-- when he was only two years old. He and his mother were "chased" by native gorilla hunters, who then killed his mother. He uses startlingly violent gestures to explain how the men "hit" him and his mother. (There are verified stories of the centuries-old native practice of butchering and eating adult gorillas in front of their young.)

Whether they're telling us about their cats or providing us with a great ape's ideas about life and death, the gorillas are doing something more remarkable and profound than "just" communicating with humans.

Koko and Michael are changing the way we view our world; they're forcing us to reexamine everything we've ever thought about animals.

Figure 11.3 *A Fund-Raising Letter (continued)*

The effects of our studies are nothing less than revolutionary. Just as Copernicus proved that the universe doesn't revolve around the earth, we're proving that all life on this planet doesn't revolve around humans.

Imagine what could happen when people realize that animals have memories ... thought processes ... even hopes and dreams. The fight to end cruelty to animals will gain new momentum; the efforts to preserve animals from extinction will take on even greater importance when humanity realizes what the real stakes are.

links this project to larger environmental concerns

Humans are already reaping the benefits of our work as well. I have received thousands of letters from parents and educators who cite Koko and Michael as inspirations to young children to learn all kinds of skills--from reading to toilet training. (Yes, Koko uses a bathroom just as we do ... and even likes to use that time to leaf through magazines!)

Details are both interesting in themselves and help answer question, "Why does this matter?"

The breakthroughs in non-verbal communication we've pioneered and the teaching methods we've developed with Koko and Michael have exciting and promising applications for reaching autistic children, the severely retarded, and other handicapped people who have difficulty communicating. The possibilities are endless.

More breakthroughs will surely come, for the work we're doing with Koko and Michael is a lifetime project. That's right: A gorilla's life expectancy is over 50 years ... and my colleagues and I have committed the rest of our lives to learning everything these gorillas have to tell us.

This commitment overrides everything else. If we fail, such a long-term project may never happen again.

But our greatest fear--the one grim possibility that lends the greatest urgency to our work--is one simple fact: one day there simply may be no more gorillas.

The fact is that all sub-species of these wonderful animals are in trouble. Only about 600 mountain gorillas survive today in Uganda, Zaire and war-torn Rwanda. It's all too likely that these magnificent primates--all of whom live in a total of 113 square miles--will be extinct within 15 years.

Wouldn't it be tragic if--just as we are learning to talk with these beautiful animals--there were no more to talk with?

general goal
Some day, if you and hundreds of others help us, Koko and Michael will live in a large preserve with other gorillas where they will thrive in a natural setting, communicate with humans, and reproduce future generations.

Specific needs But many obstacles must be overcome before our dream can become reality. Just Koko and Michael's basics--housing, food, and staff to meet their basic needs--require the average income of two adults. And then there are the unique expenses of our revolutionary project: custom

Figure 11.3   *A Fund-Raising Letter (concluded)*

educational tools, a well-trained teaching staff, special data collection and analysis hardware, custom-written computer programs and the weeks of computer time needed to run them, miles of videotape, and thousands of pieces of mail to answer every month from fascinated children and interested colleagues. Add to that the professional administrative support required to keep everything running efficiently and economically, and you can see that our breakthroughs have cost a great deal.

better to continue focus on new need that could be met with contributions

In fact, our work has cost much, much more than we've been able to afford--and so much needs to be done.

That's why we're making this appeal to the general public: We want to invite you to become part of Koko and Michael's extended family as a member of the Gorilla Foundation.

builds emotional appeal

When you do, you'll share in the excitement only "talking gorillas" can generate. As a member, you'll receive special updates on the latest developments in Koko and Michael's education. In addition, we'll send you our special reports--*The Gorilla Foundation Journal*--featuring transcriptions of our conversations with the gorillas; the latest reports on the state of the world's gorillas; and amazing, amusing photographs you'll find nowhere else.

largest amount mentioned is underlined

When I asked Koko "What do gorillas like to do most?" she replied "Gorilla love eat good." Your $50 contribution could buy the approximately 60 pounds of food Koko, Michael and their friend Ndume eat every day.

Good specifics

And you can help establish a sanctuary for gorillas. Your $35 donation could help pay for about two square feet of outdoor habitat in a new tropical preserve.

Amounts are both presented in descending order and linked to what they will buy

A $20 gift could help pay for an hour of videotaped documentation of our research, and $100 will help pay for a mailing to share vital information with every zoo in the world where gorillas are housed.

Highest amount should be first--but linked to something that will seem more important.

You know our work, how we've worked tirelessly for almost two decades to reveal some of nature's greatest secrets. Now we call on your dedication, too: Won't you please join the Gorilla Foundation?

Or, as Koko says, "Love gorilla."

Sincerely,

Penny Patterson

Penny Patterson, Ph.D.
President

Love,

The double signature is a nice touch.

Koko
"Fine Animal Gorilla"

P.S. Please don't put this letter aside with the intention of responding later. We need your help today. Just make your check payable to Koko, and return it in the convenient postage-paid envelope we have enclosed. Our heartfelt thanks.

Political Direct Mail*

Political fund-raising letters entered national politics in 1952. Popular General Dwight Eisenhower had so little political identity that both the Democrats and Republicans asked him to run for them. The successful Republicans didn't know what campaign themes would be best. They chose to test themes by mailing out several letters, each with a different theme. To measure interest, the letter asked the reader to send in $1. The party received enough money to show that fund-raising letters could work.

Republicans are still ahead of Democrats in the fund-raising game and still using direct mail. In 1998, the Republican Party raised 51% of its receipts from responses to fund-raising letters. The Democratic Party received about 40% of its revenues from direct mail.

In addition to raising a significant amount of the money needed to mount a campaign, political direct mail also brings in the largest number of small contributors. And having lots of $100 to $200 donors—from as many states as possible in presidential primary elections—helps convince the big money donors that a candidate is electable and therefore worth supporting.

*Based on Jeanne Cummings, "Democrats Strike Gold Using Direct-Mail Drives Aimed at Small Donors amid Probe of Big Givers," *The Wall Street Journal*, August 20, 1998, A16; and Jeffrey H. Birnbaum, "The Money Chase," *Fortune*, September 7, 1998, 102.

> So tiny, it fits virtually unnoticed in your pocket. So meticulously hand-assembled by unhurried craftsmen in Switzerland, that production may never exceed demand. So everyday useful, that you'll wonder how you ever got along without it.

Letter asking for inquiries about Dictaphone

> Dear Member-elect:
>   If you still believe that there are only nine planets in our solar system . . . that wine doesn't breathe . . . and that you'd recognize a Neanderthal man on sight if one sat next to you on the bus . . .
> . . . check your score. There aren't. It does. You wouldn't.

Subscription letter for *Natural History*

2. Use Sound Patterns to Emphasize Words.

When you repeat sounds, you create patterns that catch the reader's attention, please the ear, and emphasize the words they occur in. **Alliteration** occurs when several syllables begin with the same sound. **Rhyme** is the repetition of the final vowel sounds and, if the words end with consonants, the final consonant sounds. **Rhythm** is the repetition of a pattern of accented and unaccented syllables. The **rule of three** explains that when you have a series of three items that are logically parallel, the last receives the most emphasis.

Alliteration marks the opener-anecdote quoted earlier. The *s* and *z* sounds in the first sentence focus our attention on the snakes. The repetition of *st* in the second indented paragraph emphasizes those words. (Note that these paragraphs also use sentence fragments.)

> She hoisted herself up noiselessly so as not to disturb the rattlesnakes snoozing there in the sun.
>   To her left, the high desert of New Mexico. Indian country. To her right, the rock carvings she had photographed the day before. Stick people. Primitive animals.
>   Up ahead, three sandstone slabs stood stacked against the face of the cliff.

Subscription letter for *Science84*

Rhythm, rhyme, and the rule of three emphasize words in the following example:

> ①   ②   ③   ①   ②
> Nightcalls, pratfalls, and jungle shrieks . . . a scattering of wings, a chattering of monkeys and big, yellow eyes in my headlights! ③

Headline, sales letter for Tom Timmins cigars

This letter goes on to tell the story of a search for tobacco in a tropical jungle—in a style that evokes the feeling of the Bogart-Hepburn movie *The African Queen*.

3. Use Psychological Description.

Psychological description (☞ p. 233) means describing your product or service in terms of reader benefits. In a sales letter, you can use psychological description to create a scenario so the reader can picture himself or herself using your product or service and enjoying its benefits. You can also use psychological description to describe the problem your product will solve.

A *Bon Appétit* subscription letter uses psychological description in its opener and in the P.S., creating a frame for the sales letter:

Ethics and Direct Mail, II

Direct mail letters are rarely written by the people who sign the letter. Al Gore and George W. Bush probably didn't actually draft the fund-raising letters you received. And their signatures were printed, not personally signed.

Sometimes, to create the effect of personal letters, direct mail includes a typo or two.

And one company specializes in producing handwritten letters: letters written by real people (but people whose only connection with the product or cause is that they're being paid as scribes).

Each of these practices is, strictly speaking, misleading. I would argue, however, that these tactics are acceptable. Savvy consumers know that actors and actresses in TV ads are being paid to enthuse about the product. Similarly, ghostwriters (and signers) in direct mail seem acceptable.

*Paragraph 3 based on Bethany McLean, "The Lost Art of Writing Meets the Black Art of Direct Mail," *Fortune*, February 5, 1996, 36.

> Dear Reader:
>
>   First, fill a pitcher with ice.
>   Now pour in a bottle of ordinary red wine, a quarter cup of brandy, and a small bottle of Club soda. Sweeten to taste with a quarter to half cup of sugar, garnish with slices of apple, lemon, and orange. . . .
>   . . . then *move your chair to a warm, sunny spot.* You've just made yourself Sangria—one of the great glories of Spain, and the perfect thing to sit back with and sip while you consider this invitation. . . .
>
>   P.S. One more thing before you finish your Sangria. . . .

It's hard to imagine any reader really stopping to follow the recipe before finishing the letter, but the scenario is so vivid that one can imagine the sunshine even on a cold, gray day.

4. Make Your Letter Sound Like a Letter, Not an Ad.

Maintain the image of one person writing to one other person that is the foundation of all letters. Use an informal style with short words and sentences, and even slang.

You can also create a **persona**—the character who allegedly writes the letter—to make the letter interesting and keep us reading. Use the rhythms of speech, vivid images, and conversational words to create the effect that the author is a "character."

The following opening creates a persona who fits the product:

> Dear Friend:
>
>   There's no use trying. I've tried and tried to tell people about my fish. But I wasn't rigged out to be a letter writer, and I can't do it. I can close-haul a sail with the best of them. I know how to pick out the best fish of the catch, I know just which fish will make the tastiest mouthfuls, but I'll never learn the knack of writing a letter that will tell people why my kind of fish—fresh-caught prime-grades, right off the fishing boats with the deep-sea tang still in it—is lots better than the ordinary store kind.

Sales letter, Frank Davis Fish Company

This letter, with its "Aw, shucks, I can't sell" persona, with language designed to make you see an unassuming fisherman ("rigged out," "close-haul"), was written by a professional advertiser.[12]

Parts of a Direct Mail Package

The letter is the most important part of a **direct mail package,** but several other parts help accomplish your purpose. The package includes the outer envelope and everything that goes in it: the main letter, brochures, samples, secondary letters, reply card, and the reply envelope.

The **envelope** can do more than simply protect the contents during mailing. One test found that an envelope marked "OPEN NOW" produced an 18% higher response rate than a plain envelope (the rest of the package parts were

The Power of Touch*

A classic direct mail package has eight critical surfaces: the front and back of the outer envelope; above the salutation of the letter; the salutation, first line, and first paragraph of the letter; the P.S.; the response device; and the front and back of the brochure. You try to put the right icons on the right surfaces. And you try to build in tactile involvement: the more people handle direct mail, the better the response. Why? Handling the pieces prolongs the time people spend with the package, and subliminally suggests the direct mail transaction, which always involves the hand filling out a form or dialing a phone. Touch, by the way, is processed by the right hemisphere, so it adds a whole brain dimension.

*Quoted from James R. Rosenfield, interview with the author, November 24, 1993.

identical). Words on the envelope are called **teaser copy.** Like openers, teasers must get the reader's attention and have some logical link to the body of the letter.

Brochures give more information about the product or organization and, especially if they have color pictures, can involve the sense of sight and contribute to the package's emotional appeal. Magazines and products relating to food, decorating, scenery, gardening, sports, and history seem especially to lend themselves to good brochures, but you can use a brochure in almost any package.

Samples give the reader something to touch and may help sell your product. Swatches of cloth enable readers to check color and quality of the clothing you're selling; a small packet of seeds may motivate readers to order your book on gardening; a scratch-and-sniff card can help sell perfume or scented soap.

Many packages contain **secondary letters:** letters on small paper to readers who have decided not to accept the offer, letters from people who have benefited from the charity in the past, letters from recognized people corroborating the claims made in the main letter.

The **reply card** can be a separate card, a tear-off stub of the letter or brochure, or even the (large) inside flap of the reply envelope. Make the card easy to fill out. A good reply card not only has space for the reader to fill in mailing and ordering information but also repeats information from the letter such as the central selling point, basic product information, and price. Information from the letter is repeated because readers who plan to order or donate may throw away the letter and just keep the reply card.

If readers will be sending in checks, a separate **reply envelope** is necessary. In sales packages, the postage is normally paid. In fund-raising appeals, even if the postage is paid, the letter often invites the reader to affix a stamp, so that more of the organization's money can go to the cause. A postage-paid reply card, with no envelope, is possible if you are just asking for inquiries or if only credit sales are possible, but be careful—some readers prefer not to make their requests or their credit card numbers public.

Summary of Key Points

- Calling direct mail "junk mail" may cause us to respond to the symbol rather than to the reality.
- The first three steps in writing a sales or fund-raising letter are to (1) learn about the product or service, (2) choose and analyze the target audience, and (3) choose a central selling point. The **target audience** is the group of people one expects to be interested in the product, service, or cause. A **central selling point** is a reader benefit that by itself motivates your readers to act and covers all the other benefits.
- A good **star** (opener) makes readers want to read the letter and provides a reasonable transition to the body of the letter. Four modes for openers are **questions, narration, startling statements,** and **quotations.** A good **chain** (body) answers readers' questions, overcomes their objections, and involves them emotionally. A good **knot** (action close) tells readers what to do, makes the action sound easy, gives them a reason for acting promptly, and ends with a reader benefit or a picture of the reader's money helping to solve the problem.
- Specify price in the last fourth of a sales letter, after you've given your evidence and made the reader *want* the product.
- In a fund-raising letter, the basic strategy is vicarious participation. By donating money, readers participate vicariously in work they are not able to do personally.

- The primary purpose in a fund-raising letter is to get money. An important secondary purpose is to build support for the cause, so that readers who are not persuaded to give will still have favorable attitudes toward the group and will be sympathetic when they hear about it again.
- The body of a fund-raising letter must prove that (1) the problem deserves the reader's attention, (2) the problem can be solved or at least alleviated, (3) your organization is helping to solve it, (4) private funds are needed, and (5) your organization will use the funds wisely.
- To increase the size of gifts, suggest amounts in descending order; ask for gifts slightly higher than the normal cut-off points; link the gift to what it will buy; offer a premium for giving; and ask for a monthly pledge.
- Good writing in direct mail is interesting. It uses sound patterns to emphasize words, uses psychological description, and is specific and conversational.
- A **direct mail package** includes the outer envelope and everything that goes in it: the main letter, brochures, samples, secondary letters, reply card, and the reply envelope.

Chapter 11

Exercises and Problems

Getting Started

11.1 Evaluating Envelope Teasers

In the following examples, the words in square brackets describe the appearance of the envelope or lettering. The name in parentheses is from the return address. If no name is listed, either the return address is a street address only or there is no return address. Unless otherwise noted, the teaser copy appeared on the front (address side) of the envelope.

Would you open the envelope? Why or why not? Do others in the class agree?

1. (National Glaucoma Research) [In blue handwriting above the address window]
   I didn't want to bother you over the phone.
   I hope I made the right decision.
2. (UNICEF) [Oversize 6-by-9-inch envelope. To the right of the address window, a child's color picture of three children. Below the address window, in blue type]
   How good would it feel to know that a piece of your monthly phone bill can now go to children who need it most?

3. [Plain kraft envelope. In a window in the top right-hand corner, three real pennies show through.]
4. (Doctors without Borders. Médecins sans Frontieres) [In large red type to the right of the address window]
   The Enclosed Bracelet
   Is Not a Toy . . .
5. [Large 9-by-12-inch light gray envelope]
   The General figured he had nothing to lose.
   When the brash young man who'd never held a pistol in his life boasted that he could cut training time IN HALF for the United States Army's pistol-shooting program, the General smiled.
   When he vowed that he would raise its success rate at the same time, the General laughed.
   But when the man insisted that he wouldn't take a penny in payment unless he was 100% successful, the General said, "You're on!"
   Using the very same techniques that would make him a millionaire before his 29th birthday
   [continued inside]

11.2 Evaluating P.S.'s

Evaluate the following P.S.'s. Will they motivate readers to read the whole letter if readers turn to them first? Do they create a strong ending for those who have already read the letter?

1. P.S. It only takes <u>one</u> night's stay in a hotel you read about here, <u>one</u> discounted flight, <u>one</u> budget-priced cruise, or <u>one</u> low-cost car

rental to make mailing back your Subscription Certificate well worth it.

P.P.S. About your free gift! Your risk-free subscription to CONSUMER REPORTS TRAVEL LETTER comes with a remarkable 314-page book as a FREE GIFT.

2. P.S. Help spread the tolerance message by using your personalized address labels on all your correspondence. And remember, you will receive a free *Teaching Tolerance* magazine right after your tax-deductible contribution arrives.

3. P.S. Every day brings more requests like that of Mr. Agyrey-Kwakey—for our "miracle seeds." And it's urgent that we respond to the emergency in Malaysia and Indonesia by replanting those forests destroyed by fire. Please send your gift

today and become a partner with us in these innovative projects around the world.

4. P.S. Your FREE GIFT, Editor's Choice Video Clips, is a CD-ROM collection of 250 high-quality AVI videos with sound. You can put these clips on your site with Emblaze VideoPro . . . or just have fun with them. You get action footage of people at work and at play . . . beautiful nature scenes . . . famous places around the world . . . and many other subjects. Editor's Choice Video Clips is worth $99, but it's yours to keep FREE—even if you decide to return Emblaze VideoPro.

5. P.S. Even as you read this letter, a donated load of food waits for the ticket that will move it to America's hungry. Please give today!

11.3   Evaluating Sales and Fund-Raising Letters

Collect the sales and fund-raising letters that come to you, your co-workers, landlord, neighbors, or family. Use the following questions to evaluate each package:

- What mode does the opener use? Is it related to the teaser, if any? Is it related to the rest of the letter? How good is the opener?
- What central selling point or common ground does the letter use?
- What kinds of proof does the letter use? Is the logic valid? What questions or objections are not answered?
- How does the letter create emotional appeal?
- Is the style effective? Where does the letter use sound to emphasize points?
- Does the close tell readers what to do, make action easy, give a reason for acting promptly, and end with a positive picture?
- Does the letter use a P.S.? How good is it?
- Is the letter visually attractive? Why or why not?

- What other items besides the letter are in the package?

As Your Instructor Directs,

a. Share your analysis of one or more letters with a small group of your classmates.

b. Analyze one letter in a presentation to the class. Make overhead transparencies or photocopies of the letter to use as a visual aid in your presentation.

c. Analyze one letter in a memo to your instructor. Provide a copy or photocopy of the letter along with your memo.

d. With several other students, write a group memo or report analyzing one part of the letter (e.g., openers) or one kind of letter (e.g., political letters, organizations fighting hunger, etc.). Use at least 10 letters for your analysis if you look at only one part; use at least six letters if you analyze one kind of letter. Provide copies or photocopies as an appendix to your report.

11.4   Brainstorming Openers for a Magazine Subscription Letter

a. Using at least **two** of the four different modes—question, narration, startling statement, and quotation—write **three** possible openers for a letter urging readers to subscribe to a magazine (you pick the magazine).

b. For each opener indicate (1) what mode it uses and (2) how you would make a transition to the body of

the letter. (You may write out the transition or just describe it, whichever is easier.)

c. Rate the three openers in terms of their effectiveness, and briefly explain the reason for your ratings.

11.5   Evaluating Opener Drafts

The following are the results of a session brainstorming openers for a letter raising funds for a college that has suffered budget cuts. Suggest ways to improve each opener. Which seems the most promising? Why?

1. Do you realize that there are students who are getting a poorer education than you got from the same program you attended?

2. We are in danger of losing our accreditation.

3. Engineering students using dial calipers of only $\frac{1}{10}$ the accuracy needed . . . canceled library subscriptions . . . bigger classes . . . closed courses . . . obsolete equipment. . . . Budget cuts have made it harder for XYZ students to get a good education.

E-Mail Messages

11.6   Raising Money at the Office

A charity you support needs funds.

As Your Instructor Directs,

a. Write an e-mail message to your boss, to find out if it's OK to post fund-raising messages to the entire workforce.

b. Write a fund-raising e-mail message to everyone at your workplace. Be sure to tell where to send cash or checks.

Hints:

· What's the office culture? Does it support volunteer work for and donations to charities?

· How much are people at your workplace likely to know about the organization? What attitudes toward it are they likely to have?

· Do people routinely post nonwork messages on the company e-mail system? If so, how will you differentiate your message from the clutter? In any case, how can you minimize negative feelings from people who don't like nonwork messages?

11.7   Selling Baked Goods at the Office

Your co-workers really appreciate the baked goods you occasionally bring in for office treats. (You may assume that you're the baker or that the baker is your partner, spouse, child, or parent.) Now the baker is planning to start a formal business, called Great Goodies. In addition to putting up posters on the bulletin board designated for nonwork announcements and telling the people you see, you want to announce the venture more widely. And you'd like to send messages to people who've enjoyed the goodies in the past, urging them to consider these goodies for upcoming events.

As Your Instructor Directs,

a. Write an e-mail message to your boss explaining what you're doing. Ask if it's OK to suggest that the organization buy from Great Goodies when it buys sweet rolls or other treats for meetings and receptions. If it is OK, whom do you write to? How could you find out whom to ask?

b. Think of a message that would be appropriate for each month (e.g., December could be Hanukkah, Christmas, Kwanzaa, or finals support). Write messages for three months, urging people to order appropriate treats from Great Goodies.

11.8   Answering an Ethics Question

You're a senior staffer in a charitable organization. Today, you get this message from your boss.

> Subject: Using "Handwritten" Messages
>
> I'd like your feedback on the suggestion from our direct mail consultant to use a mailing with handwritten notes. I understand the argument that this will increase response. But the idea of hiring people who don't have any relation to us to write notes—and implying that the notes are by loyal donors—seems unethical. And frankly, I worry about the image we'd create if our real donors learned that we'd done this.
>
> What do you think?

As Your Instructor Directs,

a. Answer the question, using a charitable organization that you know something about.

b. Answer the question, assuming that it comes from a congressional candidate.

c. Answer the question, assuming that the strategy has been recommended for a sales rather than for a fund-raising letter.

d. Write an e-mail message to your instructor, justifying your answer.

Web Pages

11.9   Creating a Web Page

The World Wide Web enables individuals and companies to sell products and services and organizations, causes, and candidates to raise funds. The cost can be much lower than other forms of marketing, and, because the consumer chooses to go to the page, Web pages may create a more positive response than other forms of marketing.

Create a Web page to sell a product or service or to raise funds for an organization or candidate. At the top of the page, catch the reader's attention, so that he or she is motivated to scroll down. Provide both a "snail mail" address to which funds can be sent and a form on which people can buy or contribute online by entering their credit card numbers. At the bottom of the page, put the creation/update date and your name and e-mail address.

As Your Instructor Directs,

a. Turn in two laser copies of your page(s). On another page, give the URLs for any links.

b. Turn in one laser copy of your page(s) and a disk with the HTML code and .gif files.

c. Write a memo to your instructor (1) identifying the audience for which the page is designed and explaining (2) the search strategies you used to find material on this topic, (3) why you chose the information you've included, and (4) why you chose the layout and graphics you've used.

d. Present your page orally to the class.

Hints:

- Pick a product, service, candidate, or organization you know something about.
- If you have a lot of information, divide it into several pages.
- Interest readers so that they stay with your page(s) as long as possible.
- Use links to pages sponsored by other organizations only if they support your purposes.
- Offer a reason for people to return to the page after their initial visit.

Letter Assignments

11.10 Writing a Magazine Subscription Letter

Write a 2½- to 4-page letter persuading **new subscribers** to subscribe to a magazine of your choice. Assume that your letter would have a reply card and postage-paid envelope. You do NOT have to write these, but DO refer to them in your letter.

Choose a magazine you read or one that deals with a subject or sport you know something about. You may

choose a narrower target audience for this letter than the magazine uses. For example, if the magazine is designed to appeal to women ages 18–35, for this assignment you could write to college women, ages 18–25. If you narrow the target audience, be sure to tell your instructor.

Hints:

- Read several issues of the magazine, looking both at editorial content and at ads, to identify the magazine's target audience. Choose a central selling point that will appeal to that audience.
- Pay special attention to language. To keep your letter moving quickly, consider occasionally using sentence fragments or ellipses. Try to choose vivid, evocative language; try your hand at alliteration or other repetitive patterns.
- Everyone has had the experience of seeing interesting headlines on a magazine cover but then being disappointed by the stories inside. Be sure to prove your claims by giving examples and specifics. You may use material from previous issues of the magazine; you may need to edit or rewrite it for maximum effect. Choose details that will interest your reader.
- Get current figures about subscription rates from the magazine itself. It's OK to offer a free issue, a premium, or a discount, but do not depend on the offer alone to motivate people. Your letter must be fully persuasive even without the special premium.

11.11 Selling a Campus Product or Service

In a marketing class, you and a group of other students have come up with a product or service that you could sell on campus and in your community. It's such a good idea that you decide to get the necessary permissions. Now, you're ready to market it. (Use your own idea for a product or service or pick one of the following: a "smart" [debit] card, creating Web pages, temporary tattoos with the school logo or mascot, reusable bins to collect materials for recycling, an income-tax service, a shopping service.)

As Your Instructor Directs,

a. Write a memo to your instructor describing your target audience and the best central selling point and media for reaching them.

b. Design a one-page flyer that you can post on campus advertising your product or service.
c. Write a letter to students and faculty marketing your product or service.
d. Write a letter to businesses urging them to buy your product or service for employees or clients.
e. Create a brochure for your product or service.
f. Make a 3- to 5-minute presentation persuading people to buy your product or service.

11.12 Selling a Book on Bird Watching

Assume that your state's land-grant college has prepared a paperback book, *Bird Watching in [Your State]*. The book has pictures, descriptions, and a brief statement about the behaviors of 25 birds. It also explains how to attract birds to feeders and plants that birds like. The book is written by a professor of Biology of the land-grant university; the price is $9.95, which includes postage and handling.

Pick a target audience and write a 2½- to 4-page letter persuading them to buy the book.

If your instructor directs, also prepare a reply card.

Hints:

- Give as much information as possible that could be found in the book.
- Use psychological description and sensory details.
- Include benefits for people with kids and for childless people, for people with big yards as well as those in apartments, for those who have already put up feeders and birdbaths as well as for those who may be considering doing so for the first time.

11.13 Writing a Fund-Raising Letter

Write a 2½- to 4-page letter to raise money from **new donors** for an organization you support. You must use a real organization, but it does not actually have to be conducting a fund-raising drive now. Assume that your letter would have a reply card and postage-paid envelope. You do NOT have to write these, but DO refer to them in your letter.

Options for organizations include
- Tax-deductible charitable organizations—churches; synagogues; hospitals; groups working to feed, clothe, and house poor people.

- Lobbying groups—Mothers Against Drunk Driving, the National Abortion Rights Action League, the National Rifle Association, groups working against nuclear weapons, etc.
- Groups raising money to fight a disease or fund research.
- Colleges trying to raise money for endowments, buildings, scholarships, faculty salaries.
- Athletic associations raising money for scholarships, equipment, buildings, facilities.

For this assignment, you may also use groups which do not regularly have fund-raising drives but which may have special needs. Perhaps a school needs new uniforms for its band or an automatic timing device for its swimming pool. Perhaps a sorority or fraternity house needs repairs, remodeling, or expansion.

11.14 Writing a Fund-Raising Letter for a Political Candidate

One of the problems in running for office is financing the campaign. Direct mail is a primary means of raising money. A letter can give far more information about a candidate's views than a TV or radio spot; unlike those media, it can target a specific group of voters. For presidential elections, direct mail is essential: candidates must demonstrate national support to qualify for federal matching funds.

Choose a real candidate and write a letter to raise funds for him or her. Use real information about the candidate's positions and the issues in the race. Let readers know ways to help the campaign instead of or in addition to giving money. Assume that your letter would have a reply card and postage-paid envelope. You do NOT have to write these, but DO refer to them in your letter.

Choose a target audience that would be likely to support this candidate. In a memo to your instructor, describe the audience and explain your decision to personalize or not to personalize the letter with the name and address of a specific voter.

Hints:

- Read newspapers and pick up the candidate's literature to find out where the candidate stands on the issues. The League of Women Voters can help you find each candidate's headquarters.
- Talk to some of the people who live in the district to see what their concerns are. Read material from other candidates so you'll know what you have to combat.

11.15 Attracting People to Your State or Province

Create a brochure or letter to attract people to your state or province. Possible audiences and purposes include the following:

a. Persuade people with high-tech skills to work in your state or province.

b. Persuade growing businesses to move to your state or province.

c. Persuade movie and TV producers to film in your state or province.

d. Persuade retirees to move to your state or province.

Three

Interpersonal
Communication

Chapter Twelve

Communicating across Cultures   312

Chapter Thirteen

Working and Writing in Groups   334

12

Communicating across Cultures

The Importance of Global Business

Diversity in the United States and Canada

Ways to Look at Culture

Values, Beliefs, and Practices

Nonverbal Communication
- Body Language
- Space
- Time
- Other Nonverbal Symbols

Oral Communication
- Understatement and Exaggeration
- Compliments
- Silence
- Voice Qualities

Writing to International Audiences

Learning More about International Business Communication

Summary of Key Points

Communicating across Cultures

Stefania Pinton

Director, International Training and Development, Bata

www.bata.com

Stefania Pinton coordinates and supports the efforts of Bata companies worldwide in selecting, training, and relocating people for international assignments. Bata, a multinational company headquartered in Toronto, operates in 42 countries and is the world's largest manufacturer and marketer of footwear.

Currently, 80% of our General Managers—the people responsible for running our operations around the world—are expatriates. These individuals have worked in an average of six different countries on different continents in 10-20 years. The same is true of many other senior employees. I became an expatriate myself in 1995 when I moved from Italy, my country of origin, to the Bata Limited international office here in Canada. Communicating with managers from all over the world is a daily reality for me.

> *Cultural competence requires learning to expect differences and having a positive attitude toward challenges and change.*

Our management development program, Elixir Vitae, identifies bright, highly motivated, well-educated individuals with an international mindset and education. We put them in a fast-track 12- to 14-month intensive training program and place them in a country of their choice. Our future expatriates visit and work in the host country two or three months before they and their families actually move there to get information about the country, the company environment, and the future job. They are our Bata international managers of the future.

In *The Seven Habits of Highly Effective People,* Stephen R. Covey argues that all our interactions are colored by the amount of *courage* we have to display our feelings and convictions and the amount of *consideration* we have for the feelings and convictions of others. Win/win situations/transactions/international business communication occur only when we adopt a paradigm of both high courage and high consideration. We want such people for international assignments: someone who knows how to demonstrate his/her culture's positive characteristics, but who also knows how to speak positively of the strengths of the other culture, who has the skills to bridge cultural gaps once he/she encounters them, and who knows how to understand and appreciate (or at least accept) differences.

Achieving cultural competence requires more than just memorizing a list of facts about a specific country or learning its language—important though these are. Cultural competence requires learning to expect differences and having a positive attitude toward challenges and change.

Mission Statement*

For more than a century, the Mormons have been sending their young overseas. . . . Some stay on as long-term expatriates, many hail from Utah and return there eventually, and a lot . . . go into business, capitalizing on language skills and contacts developed over the years. . . .

On a hill near the University of Utah, Evans & Sutherland Computer Corp. designs display systems for flight simulators. A cadre of former missionaries can speak Mandarin with the Taiwanese air force, German with German customers, and Hebrew with the Israelis. Nearly 50% of the firm's revenue of $113 million a year is from international sales. . . .

[L]iving abroad in such large numbers has created a better grasp of something important: that large parts of the business world [put] much store in personal relationships. "A lot of US business is blind to relationships," says David Janke, a vice president at Evans & Sutherland, the maker of flight simulator displays. "Everything is very by-the-book. The rest of the world lives on relationships and trust."

*Quoted from "Utah's Economy Goes Global, Thanks in Part to Role of Missionaries," *The Wall Street Journal*, March 28, 1996, A1, A8.

Our values, priorities, and practices are shaped by the culture in which we grow up. Understanding other cultures is crucial if you want to sell your products in other countries, manage an international plant or office, or work in this country for a multinational company headquartered in another country.

This chapter focuses on cultural differences that are linked to national origin. Other kinds of diversity are discussed in Chapter 13.

As Brenda Arbeláez suggests, the successful international communicator is

- Aware that his or her preferred values and behaviors are influenced by culture and are not necessarily "right."
- Flexible and open to change.
- Sensitive to verbal and nonverbal behavior.
- Aware of the values, beliefs, and practices in other cultures.
- Sensitive to differences among individuals within a culture.[1]

The Importance of Global Business

As we saw in Chapter 1, exports are essential both to the success of individual businesses and to a country's economy as a whole. Less technologically advanced countries may offer special opportunities for businesses in mature markets in the United States. For example, the market for buses in Mexico City is greater than the entire bus market in the whole United States.[2]

For links to statistics on international business, see the BAC Web site.

The web of international business is not confined to exports and imports. Many companies—even service businesses—depend on vendors or operations in other countries. The Bombay Furniture Company orders products from more than 30 countries. If you call an 800 number to reserve a hotel room, your call may be taken by a clerk working in a large room equipped with telephones and computers in Montego Bay, Jamaica. Calls to Quarterdeck's customer service line are answered by highly trained, multilingual computer experts in Ireland—who also field questions from Europe.[3]

For executives in global companies, international experience is often essential for career advancement. At Tupperware, each of the nine members of the executive committee speaks two to four languages and has worked outside his or her home country.[4] Robert Staley, Vice Chairman of Emerson Electric, says,

> "If you want to be a senior manager in this company 20 years from now, you'd better get some experience in Asia.[5]

Diversity in the United States and Canada

Even if you never go outside the mainland United States or Canada, you'll deal with people whose background is international.

Bilingual Canada has long compared the diversity of its people to a mosaic. But now immigrants from Italy, Greece, and Hong Kong add their voices to the medley of French, English, and Inuit. Radio station CHIN in Toronto broadcasts in 32 languages.[6] People in the United States increasingly use the metaphor of "a crazy quilt" to describe the country's growing diversity. In the 1990 census, 25% of the people in the United States chose to identify themselves as members of minorities.[7] Forty percent of Californians are African American, Latino, or Asian.[8] The United States now has almost 4 million Muslims, 2 million Buddhists, and a million Hindus.[9] According to one estimate, there may be twice as many Muslims as Episcopalians.[10] People work in Japanese plants in Peterborough, New Hampshire; Marysville, Ohio; and Smyrna,

Tennessee. Employees at 3Com Corporation's modern factory in Chicago come from 65 countries and speak more than 20 languages.[11]

Ways to Look at Culture

Each of us grows up in a **culture** that provides patterns of acceptable behavior and belief. We may not be aware of the most basic features of our own culture until we come into contact with people who do things differently. If we come from a culture where dogs are pets, that interpretation may seem "natural" until we learn that in other cultures, dogs, like chickens, are raised for food.

We can categorize cultures as high-context or low-context. In **high-context cultures,** most of the information is inferred from the context of a message; little is explicitly conveyed. Japanese, Arabic, and Latin American cultures are high-context. In **low-context cultures,** context is less important; most information is explicitly spelled out. German, Scandinavian, and North American cultures are low-context.

As David Victor points out, high- and low-context cultures value different kinds of communication and have different attitudes toward oral and written channels (➤ p. 66).[12] As Figure 12.1 shows, low-context cultures like those of the United States favor direct approaches and may see indirectness as dishonest or manipulative. The written word is seen as more important than oral statements, so contracts are binding but promises may be broken. Details matter. Business communication practices in the United States reflect these low-context preferences.

Values, Beliefs, and Practices

Values and beliefs, often unconscious, affect our response to people and situations. Most North Americans, for example, value "fairness." "You're not playing fair" is a sharp criticism calling for changed behavior. In some countries, however, people expect certain groups to receive preferential treatment. Most North Americans accept competition and believe that it produces better performance. The Japanese, however, believe that competition leads to disharmony. US business people believe that success is based on individual achievement and is open to anyone who excels. In England and in France, success is more obviously linked to social class. And in some countries, people of some castes or races are prohibited by law from full participation in society.

We Are Family*

Who is in your family? Middle-class baby boomers limit "family" to people joined by blood or marriage. Younger whites and people of color have a much more extended sense of family.

Generation Xers include stepparents, adopted and half-siblings, close friends, and live-in lovers.

For US African Americans, "family" may embrace "play kin," the children one played with regularly as a child, and their families. "Family" includes the people who raised one, who may be no blood relationship at all but simply friends who helped out when times were tough.

Similarly, in Hispanic cultures, "family" includes not only people related by blood or marriage but also godparents and the especially close relationship known as the *compadre.*

US businesses normally grant leaves for family emergencies. But the size and extent of the "family" will differ among different subcultures.

*Based on Karen Ritchie, "Marketing to Generation X," *American Demographics,* April 1995, 36; Deneen Shepherd, conversation with the author, July 29, 1993; and H. Ned Seelye and Alan Seelye-James, *Culture Clash* (Lincolnwood, IL: NTC Business Books, 1995), 108–9.

| **Figure 12.1** | *Views of Communication in High- and Low-Context Cultures* |

	High-context (Examples: Japan, United Arab Emirates)	Low-context (Examples: Germany, North America)
Preferred communication strategy	Indirectness, politeness, ambiguity	Directness, confrontation, clarity
Reliance on words to communicate	Low	High
Reliance on nonverbal signs to communicate	High	Low
Importance of written word	Low	High
Agreements made in writing	Not binding	Binding
Agreements made orally	Binding	Not binding
Attention to detail	Low	High

Source: Adapted from David A. Victor, *International Business Communication* (New York: HarperCollins, 1992), 148, 153, 160.

Observing Ramadan*

[Some US companies are making] it
easier for workers who observe the
Islamic holy month, which requires
Muslims to abstain from food, water, cigarettes and sex during day-
light hours. Fort Bragg, N.C., excuses its 165 Muslim soldiers from
physical training. Alaa Shoreibah, a
financial analyst at American International Health Alliance, Washington, D.C., arrives at work an hour
ahead of schedule so he can be
home to break his fast at sundown.

  With an estimated five million
Muslims in the U.S. and their numbers growing, Ramadan is becoming a more common issue for employers. . . .

  Houston Rockets basketball star
Hakeem Olajuwon can't drink water
even during day games. "The thing
is to control your desire," he tells
reporters.

*Quoted from Carl Quintanilla, "Work
Week," *The Wall Street Journal*,
February 4, 1997, A1.

Many people in the United States value individualism. Other countries may value the group. In traditional classrooms, US students are expected to complete assignments alone; if they get much help from anyone else, they're "cheating." In Japan, in contrast, groups routinely work together to solve problems. In US white culture, quiet is a sign that people are working. In Japan people talk to get the work done.[13]

Values and beliefs are influenced by religion. Christianity coexists with a view of the individual as proactive. In some Muslim and Asian countries, however, it is seen as presumptuous to predict the future by promising action by a certain date. The Protestant work ethic legitimizes wealth by seeing it as a sign of divine favor. In other Christian cultures, a simpler lifestyle is considered to be closer to God.

Religion affects what foods may be eaten and on what days businesses are open. For example, Hindus do not eat beef; Muslims consider pork unclean; orthodox Jews eat only kosher meats. In many Muslim countries, Friday, a day of prayer, is an official holiday. During the ninth month of the Muslim lunar calendar, a devout Muslim may be on a pilgrimage to Mecca.[14] An ordinary business day may be a holiday in the country you're visiting. A sampling of international holidays appears in Figure 12.2.

Even everyday practices differ from culture to culture. North Americans and Europeans put the family name last; Asians put it first. North American and European printing moves from top to bottom and from left to right; Arabic reads from right to left, but still from top to bottom. An American carpenter pushes a saw; a Japanese pulls it. Light switches and door knobs turn opposite ways in Japan and in the United States.[15]

Values are more pervasive than we sometimes realize. A US manager whose company was owned by the Japanese was asked to estimate the US sales potential for a piece of construction equipment that is widely used in Japan. The manager believed that the equipment was too small for US construction sites and knew that US builders were happy with the equipment they were using. But smallness is a virtue in crowded Japan, and technological innovation is more important. The manager felt that he had to defer to the values of the parent company in his report. He presented the potential problems of the equipment as mildly as possible and ended his report with a statement that if management decided to sell

Living and working in another country require being sensitive to religious beliefs and practices. Here, thousands of Muslims in India gather to attend a prayer service marking the last day of Islam's holy month of Ramadan.

the equipment in the United States, he would do everything possible to market it. The statement was necessary, the man believed, so that his superiors in Japan would not see him as disloyal and attacking the company.[16]

The Web offers information about almost every country in the world. For links to pages on international news and culture, see the BAC Web site.

Nonverbal Communication

Nonverbal communication—communication that doesn't use words—takes place all the time. Smiles, frowns, who sits where at a meeting, the size of an office, how long someone keeps a visitor waiting—all these communicate pleasure or anger, friendliness or distance, power and status. Most of the time we are no more conscious of interpreting nonverbal signals than we are conscious of breathing.

Yet nonverbal signals can be misinterpreted just as easily as can verbal symbols (words). And the misunderstandings can be harder to clear up because people may not be aware of the nonverbal cues that led them to assume that they aren't liked, respected, or approved. An Arab student assumed that his US roommate disliked him intensely because the US student sat around the room with his feet up on the furniture, soles toward the Arab roommate. Arab culture sees the foot in general and the sole in particular as unclean; showing the sole of the foot is an insult.[17]

Figure 12.2	A Sampling of International Holidays

Holiday	Date	Celebrated in	Commemorates
Chinese New Year (Spring Festival)	January or February (date varies)	Countries with Chinese residents	Beginning of lunar new year
Independence Day	March 6	Ghana	1957 independence from Great Britain
St. Patrick's Day	March 17	Ireland	Ireland's patron saint
Cinco de Mayo	May 5	Mexico	1867 victory over the French
St. Jean-Baptiste Day	June 24	Québec province of Canada	Québec's national holiday
Canada Day	July 1	Canada	1867 proclamation of Canada's status as dominion
Bastille Day	July 14	France	1789 fall of the Bastille prison during the French Revolution
Ramadan	Ninth month of lunar year	Countries with Muslim residents	Atonement; fasting from sunup to sundown
Respect for the Aged Day	September 15	Japan	Respect for elderly relatives and friends
Chun Ben	Last week of September	Cambodia, other Buddhist countries	The dead and actions for one's salvation
Mahatma Ghandi's birthday	October 2	India	Birth of father of Indian independence
Guy Fawkes Day	November 5	England	Capture of Guy Fawkes, who plotted to blow up Parliament
Hanukkah	December (dates vary)	Countries with Jewish residents	Rededication of the temple in Jerusalem
Christmas	December 25	Countries with Christian residents	Birth of Jesus
Boxing Day	December 26	British Commonwealth	Tradition of presenting small boxed gifts to service workers

Getting an International Assignment*

Eric Rosenkranz, executive VP at Grey Advertising International, has three suggestions for anyone trying to get his or her hands on an international assignment: "First, ask to go along with someone else on an overseas trip and use that chance to demonstrate your ability to perform. Become an expert in that country's language, markets, and political situation. Then go on a vacation to that country and use the time to write a detailed report, with recommendations, on a business opportunity." Doing your homework on, say, Asian customs and mores can also help you avoid breaches of etiquette when you do finally get to work there.

*Quoted from Anne Fisher, "Ask Annie: Overseas, U.S. Businesswomen May Have the Edge," *Fortune*, September 28, 1998, 304.

Learning about nonverbal language can help us project the image we want to present and make us more aware of the signals we are interpreting. However, even within a single culture, a nonverbal symbol may have more than one meaning.

Body Language

The Japanese value the ability to sit quietly. They may see the US tendency to fidget and shift as an indication of lack of mental or spiritual balance. Even in North America, interviewers and audiences usually respond negatively to nervous gestures such as fidgeting with a tie or hair or jewelry, tapping a pencil, or swinging a foot.

People from different cultures learn to walk differently. Carmen Judith Nine-Curt observes that Caribbean people move the torso as though it was made up of separable parts, while North American Anglos and Northern Spaniards carry the torso as if it were one piece.[18] People from one culture often react negatively to another culture's walk. The French see the American walk as "uncivilized."[19] Anglo Americans sometimes see the way African American men walk as threatening and the way Latinos walk as sexual, although there is no evidence that these walks carry such meanings in the cultures where people have learned them.

Eye contact

North American whites see **eye contact** as a sign of honesty. But in many cultures, dropped eyes are a sign of appropriate deference to a superior. Puerto Rican children are taught not to meet the eyes of adults.[20] The Japanese are taught to look at the neck.[21] In Korea, prolonged eye contact is considered rude. The lower-ranking person is expected to look down first.[22]

Arab men in laboratory experiments looked at each other more than did two American men or two Englishmen.[23] Eye contact is so important that Arabs dislike talking to someone wearing dark glasses or while walking side by side. It is considered impolite not to face someone directly. In Muslim countries, women and men are not supposed to have eye contact.

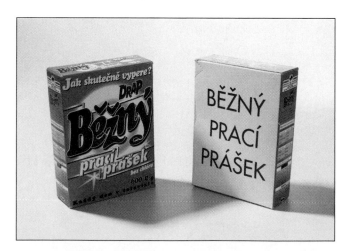

You've seen the laundry detergent cliché: the stern expert in the white coat rebukes the hapless housewife who has been washing her clothes in "ordinary laundry detergent." Now a Czech firm has started selling Ordinary Laundry Detergent, which comes in a box just like the one in the ads. "They talked about Ordinary Laundry Detergent so much on TV that someone had to manufacture it," says Frantisek Cerny, 26, whose tiny detergent manufacturer, Dedra, quickly sold out of the first run. "The mentality of Czechs," says Cerny, "is that when something is put down, they feel sorry for it and they like it. . . . We don't even have to spend any money on advertising. Our detergent is on TV every night."

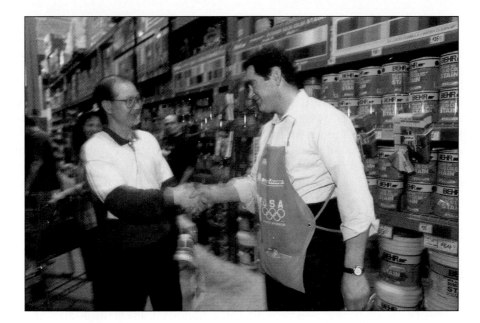

Even if you work in the United States, you'll deal with customers and clients from different cultures. Here, Home Depot employee Robert Purnick speaks Chinese and Greek to lend a hand to non-English-speaking buyers.

Ethics Away from Home*

What should you do in a country that seems to demand bribes, approve of race or sex discrimination, and allow dangerous practices, like dumping unprocessed toxic wastes?

Thomas Donaldson urges businesses to turn down projects that violate the core human values of dignity, basic rights, and good citizenship. If a practice does not violate those values and is necessary to doing business, he sees it as acceptable.

Donaldson also urges moral creativity. Rather than simply "going along with the crowd" or leaving the playing field altogether, it may be possible for a firm to act in a way that is genuinely helpful. Coca-Cola has turned down requests for bribes from Egyptian officials but has gained public trust by planting fruit trees. When Levi Strauss found that two of its Bangladesh suppliers were employing children, just firing the children wouldn't have guaranteed that they went to school. Instead, Levi Strauss forged an agreement that the suppliers would pay the children while they attended school, and that Levi Strauss would pay for tuition, books, and uniforms.

*Based on Thomas Donaldson, "Values in Tension: Ethics Away from Home," *Harvard Business Review*, September–October 1996, 48–62.

These differences can lead to miscommunication in the multicultural workplace. Superiors may feel that subordinates are being disrespectful when the subordinate is being fully respectful—according to the norms of his or her culture.

Smiling

In the United States, smiling varies from region to region. Twenty years ago, Ray Birdwhistell found that "middle-class individuals" from Ohio, Indiana, and Illinois smiled more than did people from Massachusetts, New Hampshire, and Maine, who in turn smiled more than did western New Yorkers. People from cities in southern and border states—Atlanta, Louisville, Memphis, and Nashville—smiled most of all.[24] Some scholars speculate that northeasterners may distrust the sincerity of southerners who smile a lot (like former president Jimmy Carter). Students from other countries who come to US universities may be disconcerted by the American tendency to smile at strangers—until they realize that the smiles don't "mean" anything. In Germany, smiles are reserved for friends.[25] The Japanese smile not only when they are pleased or amused, but also to say "That's none of your business" and to cover embarrassment, sadness, and even anger.[26]

The Japanese learn to control their emotions. In situations of strong emotion, it is considered acceptable to smile or laugh, but not to frown or cry. In some US businesses, it is considered acceptable to frown, swear, and yell, but not to cry. Yet both "anger" and "crying" may be expressions of the same emotion: frustration at not getting what we want.

Gestures

Americans sometimes assume that they can depend on gestures to communicate if language fails. But Birdwhistell reported that "although we have been searching for 15 years [1950–65], we have found no gesture or body motion which has the same meaning in all societies."[27] In Bulgaria, for example, people may nod their heads to signify *no* and shake their heads to signify *yes.*[28]

Gestures that mean approval in the United States may have very different meanings in other countries. The "thumbs up" sign, which means "good

In Hong Kong, a Big Mac Is Bread*

[In Hong Kong,] hamburgers are referred to, in colloquial Cantonese, as *han bou bao*—*han* being a homophone for "ham " and *bou* the common term for stuffed buns or bread rolls. *Bao* are quintessential snacks, and however excellent or nutritious they might be, they do not constitute the basis of a satisfying (i.e., filling) meal. In South China that honor is reserved for culinary arrangements that rest, literally, on a bed of rice (*fan*). Foods that accompany rice are referred to as *sung*, probably best translated as "toppings" (including meat, fish, and vegetables). It is significant that hamburgers are rarely categorized as meat (*yuk*); Hong Kong consumers tend to perceive anything that is served between slices of bread (Big Macs, fish sandwiches, hot dogs) as bread. In American culture, the hamburger is categorized first and foremost as a meat item (with all the attendant worries about fat and cholesterol content), whereas in Hong Kong the same item is thought of primarily as bread.

*Quoted from James L. Watson, "McDonald's in Hong Kong: Consumerism, Dietary Change and the Rise of a Children's Culture," in *Golden Arches East: McDonald's in East Asia*, ed. James L. Watson (Stanford: Stanford University Press, 1997), 84–85.

work" or "go ahead" in the United States and most of Western Europe, is a vulgar insult in Greece. The circle formed with the thumb and first finger that means *OK* in the United States is obscene in Southern Italy and can mean "you're worth nothing" in France and Belgium.[29]

In the question period after a lecture, a man asked the speaker, a Puerto Rican professor, if shaking the hands up and down in front of the chest, as though shaking off water, was "a sign of mental retardation." The professor was horrified: in her culture, the gesture meant "excitement, intense thrill."[30] Studies have found that Spanish-speaking doctors rate the mental abilities of Latino patients much higher than do English-speaking doctors. The language barrier is surely part of the misevaluation of English-speaking doctors. Cultural differences in gestures may contribute to the misevaluation. Similarly, Anglo supervisors in the workplace may underestimate the abilities of Hispanics because gestures differ in the two cultures.

Space

Personal space is the distance someone wants between himself or herself and other people in ordinary, nonintimate interchanges. Observation and limited experimentation show that most North Americans, North Europeans, and Asians want a bigger personal space than do Latin Americans, French, Italians, and Arabs. People who prefer lots of personal space are often forced to accept close contact on a crowded elevator or subway.

Even within a culture, some people like more personal space than do others. One US study found that men took more personal space than women did.[31] In many cultures, people who are of the same age and sex take less personal space than do mixed-age or mixed-sex groups. Latin Americans will stand closer to people of the same sex than North Americans would, but North Americans stand closer to people of the opposite sex.[32] Similarly, Laotians of the same sex sit very close together, almost "on top of each other" according to the space norms of the United States. But people of the opposite sex sit at a distance from each other.[33]

Touch

Repeated studies have shown that babies need to be touched to grow and thrive and that older people are healthier both mentally and physically if they are touched. But some people are more comfortable with touch than others. Each kind of person may misinterpret the other. A person who dislikes touch may seem unfriendly to someone who's used to touching. A toucher may seem overly familiar to someone who dislikes touch. Studies in the United States have shown that touch is interpreted as power: more powerful people touch less powerful people. When the toucher had higher status than the recipient, both men and women liked being touched.[34]

Most parts of North America allow opposite-sex couples to hold hands or walk arm-in-arm in public but frown on the same behavior in same-sex couples. People in Asia, the Middle East, and South America have the opposite expectation: male friends or female friends can hold hands or walk arm-in-arm, but it is slightly shocking for an opposite-sex couple to touch in public. In Iran, even handshakes between men and women are seen as improper.[35]

People who don't know each other well may feel more comfortable with each other if a piece of furniture separates them. For example, a group may work better sitting around a table than just sitting in a circle. In North America, a person sitting at the head of a table is generally assumed to be the group's leader. However, one experiment showed that when a woman sat at the head of a mixed-sex group, observers assumed that one of the men in the group was the leader.[36]

Podiums and desks can be used as barricades to protect oneself from other people. One professor normally walked among his students as he lectured. But if anyone asked a question he was uncomfortable with, he retreated behind the podium before answering it.

Spatial arrangements

In the United States, the size, placement, and privacy of one's office connotes status. Large corner offices have the highest status. An individual office with a door that closes connotes more status than a desk in a common area. Japanese firms, however, see private offices as "inappropriate and inefficient," reports Robert Christopher. Only the very highest executives and directors have private offices in the traditional Japanese company, and even they will also have desks in the common areas.[37]

Time

Differences in time zones complicate international phone calls. But even more important are different views of time and attitudes toward time.

Organizations in the United States—businesses, government, and schools—keep time by the calendar and the clock. Being "on time" is seen as a sign of dependability. Other cultures may keep time by the seasons and the moon, the sun, internal "body clocks," or a personal feeling that "the time is right."

North Americans who believe that "time is money" are often frustrated in negotiations with people who take a much more leisurely approach. Part of the problem is that people in many other cultures want to establish a personal relationship before they decide whether to do business with each other.

The problem is made worse because various cultures mentally measure time differently. Many North Americans measure time in five-minute blocks. Someone who's five minutes late to an appointment or a job interview feels compelled to apologize. If the executive or interviewer is running half an hour late, the caller expects to be told about the likely delay upon arriving. Some people won't be able to wait that long and will need to reschedule their appointments. But in other cultures, 15 minutes or half an hour may be the smallest block of time. To someone who mentally measures time in 15-minute blocks, being 45 minutes late is no worse than being 15 minutes late is to someone who is conscious of smaller units.

Edward T. Hall points out that different cultures have different lead times. In some countries, you need to schedule important meetings at least two weeks in advance. In other countries, not only are people not booked up so far in advance, but a date two weeks into the future may be forgotten. He advises scheduling appointments only three or four days in advance in Arab countries.[38]

Hall also distinguishes between **monochronic cultures,** where one does only one important activity at a time, and **polychronic cultures,** where people do several things at once. The United States has traditionally been considered monochronic, though that may be changing as people close business deals with their cellular phones. But we are expected to focus on other people when we are with them. It is impolite to read a book during a meeting, even if much of the meeting does not directly concern the person reading. When US managers feel offended because a Latin American manager also sees other people during "their" appointments, the two kinds of time are in conflict.

Understanding the Host Nation*

Many US employees have learned, often through costly mistakes, that the key to successful international business relationships lies in a real understanding of the values, priorities, and practices of the counterparts in the host nation.

For example, to do business in Mexico, you need to develop a personal relationship. Tell me about you as a person. That's very important. Then I tell you about me, and we do this sometimes not just one time but several times. Then I will trust you and I will value your qualities. Then I will like to work with you. So that's the first step. In Mexican values, work is number 2, family is number 1. So if something happens, they take off to be there for their families.

Even within the United States, you can learn about other cultures. You can watch Spanish TV channels and listen to Spanish radio. You can buy tapes and cassettes, you have concerts, you have the Hispanic community growing in every single city. The language is incredible, and the culture is here for you to pick up.

*Quoted from Brenda Arbeláez, statement to Kitty Locker, December 12, 1996.

The Bad Guys Wore Black*

Black uniforms make football and hockey players appear—and act—meaner, according to a study by two Cornell University psychologists.

Penalty records of 28 National Football League teams from 1970 to 1986 showed that all five teams that wore predominantly black uniforms were among the 12 most penalized teams. Similarly, the three most penalized teams in the National Hockey League in those 17 years wore black. . . .

This prompted the psychologists to launch a series of experiments on the effects of black uniforms. Groups of football fans and referees were shown either of two videotapes of a staged football play. In one tape the defensive team wore black while in the other tape the defenders wore white. Those who saw the black-uniform team rated the defenders as far more aggressive and "dirty" than those who watched the white-clothed defenders making the same moves. . . .

A black uniform may make others think a person is more aggressive or "mean" and, as a result, the person becomes more aggressive, the psychologists speculate.

*Quoted from Jerry E. Bishop, "Athletes Wearing Black Play More Aggressively," *The Wall Street Journal*, February 29, 1988, 21.

According to some scholars, Europeans schedule fewer events in a comparable period of time than do North Americans. Perhaps as a result, Germans and German Swiss see North Americans as too time-conscious.[39]

Other Nonverbal Symbols

Many other symbols can carry nonverbal meanings: clothing, colors, age, and height, to name a few.

In North America, certain styles and colors of clothing are considered more "professional" and more "credible." In Japan, clothing denotes not only status but also occupational group. Students wear uniforms. Company badges indicate rank within the organization. Workers wear different clothes when they are on strike than they do when they are working.[40]

Colors can also carry meanings in a culture. In the United States, mourners wear black to funerals, while brides wear white. In Japan, white is the color of death. Purple flowers are given to the dead in Mexico. In Korea, red ink is used to record deaths but never to write about living people.[41] In the United States, the first-place winner gets a blue ribbon. In the United Kingdom, the first-place ribbon is usually red.

In the United States, youth is valued. Some men as well as some women color their hair and even have face-lifts to look as youthful as possible. In Japan, younger people defer to older people. Americans attempting to negotiate in Japan are usually taken more seriously if at least one member of the team is noticeably gray-haired.

Height connotes status in many parts of the world. Executive offices are usually on the top floors; the underlings work below. Even being tall can help a person succeed. Studies have shown that employers are more willing to hire men over 6 feet tall than shorter men with the same credentials. Studies of real-world executives and graduates have shown that taller men make more money. In one study, every extra inch of height brought in an extra $1,300 a year.[42] But being too big can be a disadvantage. A tall, brawny football player complained that people found him intimidating off the field and assumed that he "had the brains of a Twinkie."

Oral Communication

Effective oral communication requires cultural understanding. As Figure 12.3 shows, the purpose of and information exchanged in business introductions differs across cultures.

For sites that help you learn foreign languages, see the BAC Web site. Learning at least a little of the language of the country where you hope to do business will help you in several ways. First, learning the language will give you at least a glimpse into the culture. In English, for example, we say that a clock "runs." The French say, "Il marche,"—or, literally, "It is walking." Second, learning some of the language will help you manage the daily necessities of finding food and getting where you need to go while you're there. If you know enough, you'll even be able to sightsee and take advantage of the unique opportunities business travel can provide. Finally, in business negotiations, knowing a little of the language gives you more time to think. You'll catch part of the meaning when you hear your counterpart speak; you can begin thinking even before the translation begins.

If at all possible, take your own translator when you travel abroad on business. Brief him or her with the technical terms you'll be using; explain as much of the context of your negotiations as possible. A good translator can also help you interpret nonverbal behavior and negotiating strategies.

Figure 12.3	*Cultural Contrasts in Business Introductions*		
	United States	**Japan**	**Arab countries**
Purpose of introduction	Establish status and job identity; network	Establish position in group, build harmony	Establish personal rapport
Image of individual	Independent	Member of group	Part of rich culture
Information	Related to business	Related to company	Personal
Use of language	Informal, friendly; use first name	Little talking	Formal; expression of admiration
Values	Openness, directness, action	Harmony, respect, listening	Religious harmony, hospitality, emotional support

Source: Adapted from Farid Elashmawi and Philip R. Harris, *Multicultural Management 2000: Essential Cultural Insights for Global Business Success* (Houston: Gulf, 1998), 113.

Understatement and Exaggeration

To understand someone from another culture, you must understand the speaker's conversational style. The British have a reputation for understatement. Someone good enough to play at Wimbledon may say he or she "plays a little tennis." Many people in the United States exaggerate. An American businessman negotiating with a German said, "I know it's impossible, but can we do it?" The German saw the statement as nonsensical: by definition, something that is impossible cannot be done. The American saw "impossible" as merely a strong way of saying "difficult" and assumed that with enough resources and commitment, the job could in fact be done.[43]

Compliments

The kinds of statements that people interpret as compliments and the socially correct ways to respond to compliments also vary among cultures. The statement "You must be really tired" is a compliment in Japan since it recognizes the other person has worked hard. The correct response is "Thank you, but I'm OK." An American who is complimented on giving a good oral presentation will probably say "Thank you." A Japanese, in contrast, will apologize: "No, it wasn't very good."[44]

Statements that seem complimentary in one context may be inappropriate in another. For example, women in business are usually uncomfortable if male colleagues or superiors compliment them on their appearance: the comments suggest that the women are being treated as visual decoration rather than as contributing workers.

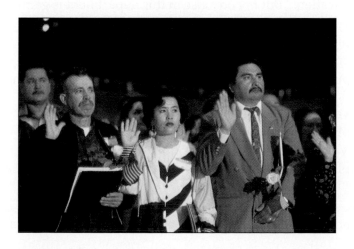

The United States depends upon immigrant labor.

Silence, Please!*

In Japan, silence can mean "I don't like your idea," but it can also mean "I'm thinking." Knowing this is essential for international negotiators. One American businessman offered an apparatus to a Japanese customer for $100,000. The customer sat quietly. After 10 minutes, the American, who couldn't stand the silence any more, lowered his price $10,000.

Reading this through a US lens, you might think that the Japanese customer was happy and perhaps even used silence deliberately. Not so. In fact, he was deeply disappointed by the poor negotiation. Relationships are far more important than price in Japan. How could someone be so impatient?

*Based on J. M. Ulijn, "How Can a Multicultural Workforce of a Company Successfully Communicate in International Trade?" *Acta Universitatis Wratislaviensis*, No. 1774, 264–65.

Silence

Silence also has different meanings in different cultures and subcultures. Muriel Saville-Troike reports that during a period of military tension, Greek traffic controllers responded with silence when Egyptian planes requested permission to land. The Greeks intended silence as a refusal; the Egyptians interpreted silence as consent. Several people were killed when the Greeks fired on the planes as they approached the runway.[45]

Voice Qualities

Tone of voice refers to the rising or falling inflection that tells you whether a group of words is a question or a statement, whether the speaker is uncertain or confident, whether a statement is sincere or sarcastic. Anyone who has written dialog with adverbs ("he said thoughtfully") has tried to indicate tone of voice.

When tone of voice and the meaning of words conflict, people "believe" the tone of voice. Jann Davis reports that one person responded to friends' "How are you?" with the words "Dying, and you?" Most of the friends responded "Fine." Because the tone of voice was cheerful, they didn't hear the content of the words.[46]

Pitch measures whether a voice uses sounds that are low (like the bass notes on a piano) or high. Low-pitched voices are usually perceived as being more authoritative, sexier, and more pleasant to listen to than are high-pitched voices. Most voices go up in pitch when the speaker is angry or excited; some people raise pitch when they increase volume. Women whose normal speaking voices are high may need to practice projecting their voices to avoid becoming shrill when they speak to large groups.

Stress is the emphasis given to one or more words in a sentence. As the following example shows, emphasizing different words can change the meaning.

I'll give you a raise.

[Implication, depending on pitch and speed: "Another supervisor wouldn't" or "I have the power to determine your salary."]

I'll **give** you a raise.

[Implication, depending on pitch and speed: "You haven't **earned** it" or "OK, all right, you win. I'm saying 'yes' to get rid of you, but I don't really agree," or "I've just this instant decided that you deserve a raise."]

I'll give **you** a raise.

[Implication: "But nobody else in this department is getting one."]

I'll give you **a** raise.

[Implication: "But just one."]

I'll give you a **raise.**

[Implication: "But you won't get the promotion or anything else you want."]

I'll give **you** a **raise.**

[Implication: "You deserve it."]

I'll give you a **raise!**

[Implication: "I've just this minute decided to act, and I'm excited about this idea. The raise will please both of us."]

Speakers who use many changes in tone, pitch, and stress as they speak usually seem more enthusiastic; often they also seem more energetic and more intelligent. Someone who speaks in a monotone may seem apathetic or unintelligent. Nonnative speakers whose first language does not use tone, pitch, and stress to convey meaning and attitude may need to practice varying these voice qualities when they give presentations in the United States.

Volume is a measure of loudness or softness. Very soft voices, especially if they are also breathy and high-pitched, give the impression of youth and inexperience. People who do a lot of speaking to large groups need to practice projecting their voices so they can increase their volume without shouting.

In some cultures, it is considered rude to shout; loud voices connote anger and imminent violence. In others, everyday conversations are loud. Edward Hall and William Whyte report that some Arabs discounted "Voice of America" broadcasts because the signal was so "weak."[47] Arab men who are equals speak loudly by North American standards.

Writing to International Audiences

Most cultures are more formal than the United States. When you write to international audiences, use titles, not first names; avoid contractions, slang, and sports metaphors. Do write in English unless you're extremely fluent in your reader's language.

Marcia Sweezey, a manager at Digital Equipment Corporation, offers the following advice for sending e-mail to Japanese recipients.

1. Be clear, but be adult. Don't write in second-grade English.
2. Use complete sentences.
3. Write "Dear Lastname-san" to begin your e-mail: Dear Abo-san. Use this form of address for both men and women. Also use this form to refer to your peers in a formal memo, such as a memo to that person's manager.
4. Tell your peers how to address you. Peers in Japan may write to you "Dear Smith-san" or "Dear Ellen-san." You may wish to invite them to call you by your first name. (The first time you correspond, let them know if you are a man or a woman so they know whether to use "Mr." or "Ms." when they address you formally.)
5. Be honest, friendly, and relaxed.[48]

The patterns of organization that work for North American audiences may need to be modified in international correspondence. For most cultures, buffer negative messages and make requests more indirect. As Figures 12.4 and 12.5 suggest, the style, structure, and strategies that would motivate a US audience may need to be changed for international readers. Make a special effort to avoid phrases that could seem cold and uncaring. Cultural mistakes made orally float away on the air; those made in writing are permanently recorded.

Business people from Europe and Japan who correspond frequently with North America are beginning to adopt US directness and patterns of organization. If you know that your reader understands North American behavior, you can write just as you would to someone in the United States or Canada. If you don't know your reader well, it may be safer to modify your message slightly.

If you're faxing the message, use at least 12-point type. If the transmission has static or if your message is re-faxed to another reader, the larger type will make it easier to read.[50]

In international business correspondence, list the day before the month:

Not: April 8, 2000

But: 8 April 2000

Translators Needed*

As the number of people speaking languages other than English has grown in Los Angeles, so has the need for translators.

Los Angeles businesses put up signs and flyers in Mandarin, Farsi, and Hebrew. Students and their parents in Cupertino elementary schools speak 52 different languages and 12 dialects. Hebrew, Russian, and Farsi are among the 10 most common. Cornish and Carey Real Estate handles about 40 tongues.

Translators have been called upon to translate courtroom testimony, Japanese operating manuals, and Arabic business contracts.

Translation, as always, works best when the translator knows connotations and context as well as the dictionary meaning of words. George Rimalower, president of Interpreting Services International in Van Nuys, California, reports that one church newsletter turned "our Lord in heaven" into "our guy in the sky."

*Based on Jan Lonsdale, "The Real L.A. Speak," *Los Angeles Times Magazine*, June 13, 1993, 8; and "New Companies Fuel Silicon Valley Boom," *The Wall Street Journal*, October 8, 1996, A12.

Extensive information about many countries is available on the Web. This site was created by Professor Archie Kleingartner of UCLA's Anderson School of Management in collaboration with Meikai and Asahi Universities in Japan. It has extensive information about Japanese practices, laws, and culture and has won several prestigious awards.

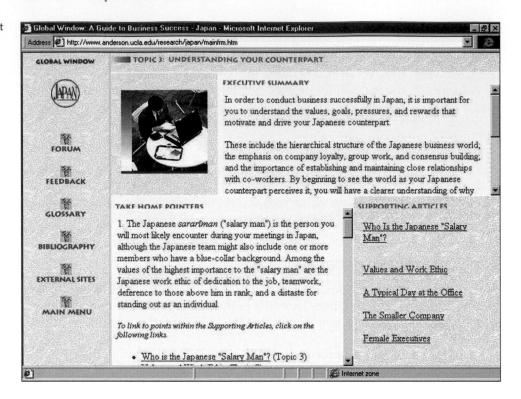

| **Figure 12.4** | *Cultural Contrasts in Written Persuasive Documents* |

	United States	**Japan**	**Arab countries**
Opening	Request action or get reader's attention	Offer thanks; apologize	Offer personal greetings
Way to persuade	Immediate gain or loss of opportunity	Waiting	Personal connections; future opportunity
Style	Short sentences	Modesty, minimize own standing	Elaborate expressions; many signatures
Closing	Specific request	Desire to maintain harmony	Future relationship, personal greeting
Values	Efficiency; directness; action	Politeness; indirectness; relationship	Status; continuation

Source: Adapted from Farid Elashmawi and Philip R. Harris, *Multicultural Management 2000: Essential Cultural Insights for Global Business Success* (Houston: Gulf, 1998), 139.

| **Figure 12.5** | *Cultural Contrasts in Motivation* |

	United States	**Japan**	**Arab countries**
Emotional appeal	Opportunity	Group participation; company success	Religion; nationalism; admiration
Recognition based on	Individual achievement	Group achievement	Individual status; status of class/society
Material rewards	Salary; bonus; profit sharing	Annual bonus; social services; fringe benefits	Gifts for self/family; salary
Threats	Loss of job	Loss of group membership	Demotion, loss of reputation
Values	Competition; risk taking; freedom	Group harmony; belonging	Reputation; family security; religion

Source: Adapted from Farid Elashmawi and Philip R. Harris, *Multicultural Management 2000: Essential Cultural Insights for Global Business Success* (Houston: Gulf, 1998), 169.

Spell out the month to avoid confusion. A US professor wrote to the British library to reserve the books he would need for his visit on April 10th. However, he wrote "4/10" and the British assumed he wanted them on October 4th.

Learning More about International Business Communication

Learning to communicate with people from different backgrounds shouldn't be a matter of learning rules. Instead, use the examples in this chapter to get a sense for the kinds of factors that differ from one culture to another. Test these generalizations against your experience. And when in doubt, ask.

You can deepen your knowledge by reading. Figure 12.6 lists useful sources to check.

You can also learn by seeking out people from other backgrounds and talking with them. Many campuses have centers for international students. Some communities have groups of international business people who meet regularly to discuss their countries. By asking all these people what aspects of the dominant US culture seem strange to them, you'll learn much about what is "right" in their cultures.

Summary of Key Points

- **Culture** provides patterns of acceptable behavior and beliefs.
- The successful intercultural communicator is
  - Aware that his or her preferred values and behaviors are influenced by culture and are not necessarily "right."
  - Flexible and open to change.

Figure 12.6   Print Sources for More Information about International Business

Culturgrams, updated annually, offer 4-page overviews of every country in the world. Write or call:

    Brigham Young University
    The David M. Kennedy Center for International Studies
    P.O. Box 24538
    Provo, UT 84602-4538
    1-800-528-6279

To learn more about a specific country or region, write the embassy for information or consult business magazines and reference books.

- PricewaterhouseCoopers publishes an excellent series of paperbacks titled *Doing Business in [Country]*. Each book covers financial, tax, accounting, and regulatory matters.
- American Society for Quality Control. Assistance in meeting manufacturing standards set by the International Organization for Standardization. 1-800-248-1946.
- Export Legal Assistance Network. Referrals to local attorneys with experience in international trade. 1-202-778-3000.
- Export Opportunity Hot Line. Free information provided by trade experts. Sponsored by the Small Business Foundation of America. 1-800-243-7332. In Washington, DC, call 1-202-223-1104.
- Service Corps of Retired Executives (SCORE). Matches small businesses with one of roughly 500 seasoned exporting counselors. 1-800-634-0245.
- US Commerce Department Hot Line. How to qualify for low tariffs under NAFTA. Free information. 1-800-USA-TRADE.
- US & Foreign Commercial Service. Offices in 68 US cities and in 129 cities in 67 other countries. Offers advice about exports, market research, and sales leads.

Overseas, US Businesswomen May Have the Edge*

[A] growing body of research suggest[s] that American businesswomen abroad may actually enjoy a significant edge over their male counterparts. A study conducted last year by international staffing consultants Cornelius Grove & Associates (www.grovewell.com) concluded that women are often more "nurturing" than men, tend to form close personal connections with colleagues and clients, and are highly respected for it. In China, for example, Cornelius Grove found that a quality called *ren*—which translates loosely as warm-heartedness, benevolence, and a readiness to look out for other people's welfare—is considered essential in business leaders. . . .

"In our interviews with Japanese executives, we find that many of them would much rather work with a woman than a man," [Professor John] Graham writes. Why? "Many American men's conversational style tends toward competitiveness, even aggressiveness, and can get in the way of a free-flowing exchange of information." By contrast, the negotiating style of their female counterparts, emphasizing interpersonal warmth and willingness to listen, are much less disconcerting.

*Quoted from Anne Fisher, "Ask Annie: Overseas, U.S. Businesswomen May Have the Edge," *Fortune,* September 28, 1998, 304.

- Sensitive to verbal and nonverbal behavior.
- Aware of the values, beliefs, and practices in other cultures.
- Sensitive to differences among individuals within a culture.
- In **high-context cultures,** most of the information is inferred from the context of a message; little is explicitly conveyed. In **low-context cultures,** context is less important; most information is explicitly spelled out.
- **Nonverbal communication** is communication that doesn't use words. Nonverbal communication can include voice qualities, body language, space, time, and other miscellaneous matters such as clothing, colors, and age.
- Nonverbal signals can be misinterpreted just as easily as can verbal symbols (words).
- No gesture has a universal meaning across all cultures. Gestures that signify approval in North America may be insults in other countries, and vice versa.
- **Personal space** is the distance someone wants between him or herself and other people in ordinary, nonintimate interchanges.
- North Americans who believe that "time is money" are often frustrated in negotiations with people who want to establish a personal relationship before they decide whether to do business with each other or who measure time in 15- or 30-minute increments rather than the 5-minute intervals North Americans are used to.
- In **monochronic** cultures, people do only one important activity at a time. The United States is monochronic. In **polychronic** cultures, people do several things at once.
- The patterns of organization that work for North American audiences may need to be modified in international correspondence.
- In international correspondence, spell out the month.

Chapter 12

Exercises and Problems

Getting Started

12.1   Identifying Sources of Miscommunication

In each of the following situations, identify one or more ways that cultural differences may be leading to miscommunication.

1. Alan is a US sales representative in Mexico. He makes appointments and is careful to be on time. But the person he's calling on is frequently late. To save time, Alan tries to get right to business. But his hosts want to talk about sightseeing and his family. Even worse, his appointments are interrupted constantly, not only by business phone calls, but also by long conversations with other people and even the customers' children who come into the office. Alan's first progress report is very negative. He hasn't yet made a sale. Perhaps Mexico just isn't the right place to sell his company's products.

2. To help her company establish a presence in Japan, Susan wants to hire a local interpreter who can advise her on business customs. Kana Tomari has superb qualifications on paper. But when Susan tries to probe about her experience, Kana just says, "I will do my best. I will try very hard." She never gives details about any of the previous positions she's held. Susan begins to wonder if the résumé is inflated.

3. Stan wants to negotiate a joint venture with a Chinese company. He asks Tung-Sen Lee if the Chinese people have enough discretionary income to afford his product. Mr. Lee is silent for a time, and then says, "Your product is good. People in the West must like it." Stan smiles, pleased that Mr. Lee

recognizes the quality of his product, and he gives Mr. Lee a contract to sign. Weeks later, Stan still hasn't heard anything. If China is going to be so inefficient, he wonders if he really should try to do business there.

4. Elspeth is very proud of her participatory management style. On assignment in India, she is careful not to give orders but to ask for suggestions. But people rarely suggest anything. Even a formal suggestion system doesn't work. And to make matters worse, she doesn't sense the respect and camaraderie of the plant she managed in the United States. Perhaps, she decides gloomily, people in India just aren't ready for a woman boss.

E-Mail Messages

12.2 Sending a Draft to Japan

You've drafted instructions for a consumer product that will be sold in Japan. Before the text is translated, you want to find out if the pictures will be clear. So you send an e-mail to your Japanese counterpart, Takashi Haneda, asking for a response within a week.

Write an e-mail message; assume that you will send the pictures as an attachment.

12.3 Asking about Travel Arrangements

The CEO is planning a trip to visit colleagues in another country (you pick the country). As Executive Assistant to the CEO of your organization, it's your job to make travel plans. At this stage, you don't know anything except dates and flights. (The CEO will arrive in the country at 7 AM local time on the 28th of next month and stay for three days.) It's your job to find out what the plans are and communicate any of the CEO's requirements.

Write an e-mail message to your contact.

Hints:

- Pick a business, nonprofit organization, or government agency you know something about, making assumptions about the kinds of things its executive would want to do during an international visit.
- How much international traveling does your CEO do? Has he or she ever been to this country before? What questions will he or she want answered?

Communicating at Work

12.4 Studying International Communication at Your Workplace

Does your employer buy from suppliers or sell to customers outside the country? Get a sampling of international messages, or interview managers about the problems they've encountered.

As Your Instructor Directs,

a. Share your results orally with a small group of students.

b. Present your findings orally to the class.

c. Summarize your findings in a memo to your instructor.

d. Join with other students in your class to write a group report.

Web Pages

12.5 Creating a Web Page

Create a Web page for international managers who are planning assignments in other countries or who work in this country for a multinational company headquartered in another country.

Assume that this page can be accessed from another of the organization's pages. Offer at least seven links. (More is better.) You may offer information as well as links to other pages with information. At the top of the page, offer an overview of what the page covers. At the bottom of the page, put the creation/update date and your name and e-mail address.

As Your Instructor Directs,

a. Turn in two laser copies of your page(s). On another page, give the URLs for each link.

b. Turn in one laser copy of your page(s) and a disk with the HTML code and .gif files.

c. Write a memo to your instructor (1) identifying the audience for which the page is designed and explaining (2) the search strategies you used to find material on this topic, (3) why you chose the pages and information you've included, and (4) why you chose the layout and graphics you've used.

d. Present your page orally to the class.

Hints:

· Limit your page to just one country or one part of the world.

· You can include some general information about working abroad and culture, but most of your links should be specific to the country or part of the world you focus on.

· Try to cover as many topics as possible: history, politics, geography, culture, money, living accommodations, transport, weather, business practices, and so forth.

· Chunk your links into small groups under headings.

Memo and Report Assignments

12.6 Requesting Information about a Country

Use one or more of the following ways to get information about a country. Information you might focus on could include

· Business opportunities.
· History and geography.
· Principal exports and imports.
· Dominant religions.
· Holidays.
· School system.
· Political system.

1. Write to the US & Foreign Commercial Service Office in your district. (Your instructor has the addresses in the *Instructor's Manual.*)

2. Check the country's trade office, if there is one in your city.

3. Interview someone from that country or someone who has lived there.

4. Read published materials about the country.

As Your Instructor Directs,

a. Share your findings orally with a small group of students.

b. Summarize your findings in a memo to your instructor.

c. Present your findings to the class.

d. Join with a group of classmates to write a group report on the country.

12.7 Recommending a Candidate for an Overseas Position

Your company sells customized computer systems to businesses large and small around the world. The Executive Committee needs to recommend someone to begin a three-year term as Manager of Eastern European Marketing.

As Your Instructor Directs,

a. Write a memo to each of the candidates, specifying the questions you would like each to answer in a final interview.

b. Assume that it is not possible to interview the candidates. Use the information here to write a memo to the CEO recommending a candidate.

c. Write a memo to the CEO recommending the best way to prepare the person chosen for his or her assignment.

d. Write a memo to the CEO recommending a better way to choose candidates for international assignments.

e. Write a memo to your instructor explaining the assumptions you made about the company and the candidates that influenced your recommendation(s).

Information about the Candidates:
All the candidates have applied for the position and say they are highly interested in it.

1. **Deborah Gere,** 39, white, single. Employed by the company for eight years in the Indianapolis and New York offices. Currently in the New York office as Assistant Marketing Manager, Eastern United States; successful. University of Indiana MBA. Speaks Russian fluently; has translated for business negotiations that led to the setting up of the Moscow office. Good technical knowledge, acceptable managerial skills, excellent communication skills, good interpersonal skills. Excellent health; excellent emotional stability.

Swims. One child, age 12. Lived in the then–Soviet Union for one year as an exchange student in college; business and personal travel in Europe.

2. **Claude Chabot,** 36, French, single. Employed by the company for 11 years in the Paris and London offices. Currently in the Paris office as Assistant Sales Manager for the European Economic Community; successful. No MBA, but degrees from MIT in the United States and l'Ecole Supérieure de Commerce de Paris. Speaks native French; speaks English and Italian fluently; speaks some German. Good technical knowledge, excellent managerial skills, acceptable communication skills, excellent interpersonal skills. Excellent health, good emotional stability. Plays tennis. No children. French citizen; lived in the United States for two years, in London for five years (one year in college, four years in the London office). Extensive business and personal travel in Europe.

3. **Linda Moss,** 35, African American, married. Employed by the company for 10 years in the Atlanta and Toronto offices. Currently Assistant Manager of Canadian Marketing; very successful. Howard University MBA. Speaks some French.

Good technical knowledge, excellent managerial skills, excellent communication skills, excellent interpersonal skills. Excellent health; excellent emotional stability. Does Jazzercize classes. Husband is an executive at a US company in Detroit; he plans to stay in the States with their children, ages 11 and 9. The couple plans to commute every two to six weeks. Has lived in Toronto for five years; business travel in North America; personal travel in Europe and Latin America.

4. **Steven Hsu,** 42, of Asian American descent, married. Employed by the company for 18 years in the Los Angeles office. Currently Marketing Manager, Western United States; very successful. UCLA MBA. Speaks some Korean. Excellent technical knowledge, excellent managerial skills, good communication skills, excellent interpersonal skills. Good health, excellent emotional stability. Plays golf. Wife is an engineer who plans to do consulting work in eastern Europe. Children ages 8, 5, and 2. Has not lived outside the United States; personal travel in Europe and Asia.

Your committee has received this memo from the CEO.

To:	Executive Committee
From:	Ed Conzachi *ERC*
Subject:	Choosing a Manager for the New Eastern European Office

Please write me a memo recommending the best candidate for Manager of East European Marketing. In your memo, tell me whom you're choosing and why; also explain why you have rejected the unsuccessful candidates.

This person will be assuming a three-year appointment, with the possibility of reappointment. The company will pay moving and relocation expenses for the manager and his or her family.

The Eastern European division currently is the smallest of the company's international divisions. However, this area is poised for growth. The new manager will supervise the Moscow office and establish branch offices as needed.

The committee has invited comments from everyone in the company. You've received these memos.

To: Executive Committee

From: Robert Osborne, US Marketing Manager   *RO*

Subject: Recommendation for Steve Hsu

Steve Hsu would be a great choice to head up the new Moscow office. In the past seven years, Steve has increased sales in the Western Region by 15%—in spite of recessions, earthquakes, and fires. He has a low-key, participative style that brings out the best in subordinates. Moreover, Steve is a brilliant computer programmer. He probably understands our products better than any other marketing or salesperson in the company.

Steve is clearly destined for success in headquarters. This assignment will give him the international experience he needs to move up to the next level of executive success.

To: Executive Committee

From: Becky Exter, Affirmative Action Officer   *RRE*

Subject: Hiring the New Manager for East European Marketing

Please be sensitive to affirmative action concerns. The company has a very good record of appointing women and minorities to key positions in the United States and Canada; so far our record in our overseas divisions has been less effective.

In part, perhaps, that may stem from a perception that women and minorities will not be accepted in countries less open than our own. But the experience of several multinational firms has been that even exclusionary countries will accept people who have the full backing of their countries. Another concern may be that it will be harder for women to establish a social support system abroad. However, different individuals have different ways of establishing support. To assume that the best candidate for an international assignment is a male with a stay-at-home wife is discriminatory and may deprive our company of the skills of some of its best people.

We have several qualified women and minority candidates. I urge you to consider their credentials carefully.

To: Executive Committee

From: William E. Dortch, Marketing Manager, European Economic Community   *WED*

Subject: Recommendation for Debbie Gere

Debbie Gere would be my choice to head the new Moscow office. As you know, I recommended in 1996 that Europe be divided and that we establish an Eastern European division. Of all the people from the States who have worked on the creation of the new division, Debbie is the best. The negotiations were often complex. Debbie's knowledge of the language and culture was invaluable. She's done a good job in the New York office and is ready for wider responsibilities. Eastern Europe is a challenging place, but Debbie can handle the pressure and help us gain the foothold we need.

To: Ed Conzachi, President

From: Pierre Garamond, Sales Representative, European Economic Community   *PG*

Subject: Recommendation for Claude Chabot

Claude Chabot would be the best choice for Manager of Eastern European Marketing. He is a superb supervisor, motivating us to the highest level of achievement. He understands the complex legal and cultural nuances of selling our products in Europe as only a native can. He also has the budgeting and managerial skills to oversee the entire marketing effort.

You are aware that the company's record of sending US citizens to head international divisions is not particularly good. European Marketing is an exception, but our records in the Middle East and Japan have been poor. The company would gain stability by appointing Europeans to head European offices, Asians to head Asian offices, and so forth. Such people would do a better job of managing and motivating staffs which will be comprised primarily of nationals in the country where the office is located. Ending the practice of reserving the top jobs for US citizens would also send a message to international employees that we are valued and that we have a future with this company.

To: Executive Committee   *EC*

From: Elaine Crispell, Manager, Canadian Marketing

Subject: Recommendation for Linda Moss

Linda Moss has done well as Assistant Manager for the last two and a half years. She is a creative, flexible problem solver. Her productivity is the highest in the office. Yet though she could be called a "workaholic," she is a warm, caring human being.

As you know, the Canadian division includes French-speaking Montreal and a large Native Canadian population; furthermore, Toronto is an international and intercultural city. Linda has gained intercultural competence both on a personal and professional level.

Linda has the potential to be our first woman CEO fifteen years down the road. She needs more international experience to be competitive at that level. This would be a good opportunity for her, and she would do well for the company.

13

Working and Writing in Groups

Listening

Group Interactions
- Roles in Groups
- Leadership in Groups
- Decision-Making Strategies
- Characteristics of Successful Student Groups
- Peer Pressure and Groupthink

Working in Diverse Groups
- Conversational Style
- Nonverbal Communication

Conflict Resolution
- Steps in Conflict Resolution
- Responding to Criticism
- You-Attitude in Conflict Resolution

Effective Meetings

Collaborative Writing
- Planning the Work and the Document
- Composing the Drafts
- Revising the Document
- Editing and Proofreading the Document
- Making the Group Process Work

Summary of Key Points

Working and Writing in Groups

Lerry Wilson, President | *Wilson McHenry Company*

wmc.com

Wilson McHenry Company is a strategic business communications firm serving high-growth, technology-based businesses in the United States and around the world. Wilson McHenry helps clients establish a distinctive market position and differentiate themselves from their competition by developing communications that reflect the client company's "personality." Lerry Wilson is the "father" of teamwork at Wilson McHenry and leads an orientation class called "The Magic of Teams" for new hires.

Working effectively in groups requires a mix of excellent listening, oral, and written communication skills; a positive problem-solving attitude; and personal self-initiative. The ability to work effectively in groups is a key requirement for achieving success in today's business climate and is perhaps the most critical "soft skill" that individuals can employ.

The success of a group effort is more often than not determined at the first gathering of the individuals. This is the defining moment when the group consciously or unconsciously determines whether it will be a collection of individuals working on a task or a team of individuals seeking a goal. To be truly effective, group members need to discuss goals, expectations, and communication processes. Everyone has to agree on the objective of the program and "buy into" that.

> **66** *Working effectively in groups requires a mix of excellent listening, oral, and written communication skills; a positive problem-solving attitude; and personal self-initiative.* **99**

Technology allows group communication to be instantaneous and dynamic. E-mail, voice mail, and collaborative editing tools allow all team members to add ideas to documents quickly and easily and allow others to be aware of those thoughts immediately. This is the most important aspect of working together—constant communication. Communication drives a sense of "brainstorming" through the process, creating the most creative results possible.

Collaboration also requires an understanding of roles within the group and how each role contributes to the team's success. All the individuals must accept their roles and be committed to excellence in executing them.

At Wilson McHenry Company, we have modified the words of writer Oscar Wilde for our own inspiration. Wilde wrote, "It is personalities, not principles, that move the age." Our corporate ideal reads, "It is personalities and principles that move the age." We believe that communication, collaboration, and creativity help us find the best solution for each client's unique situation.

Teamwork is crucial to success in an organization. Some teams produce products, provide services, or recommend solutions to problems. Other teams—perhaps in addition to providing a service or recommending a solution—also produce documents. **Interpersonal communication** is communication between people. Interpersonal skills such as listening and dealing with conflict are used in one-to-one interchanges, in problem-solving groups, and in writing groups. These skills will make you more successful on the job, in social groups, and in community service and volunteer work. In writing groups, giving careful attention to both group process and writing process (✖ p. 116) improves both the final product and members' satisfaction with the group.

Listening

Listening is crucial to building trust. However, listening on the job may be more difficult than listening in classes. Many classroom lectures are well organized, with signposts and repetition of key points to help hearers follow. But conversations usually wander. A key point about when a report is due may be sandwiched in among statements about other due dates for other projects. Finally, in a classroom you're listening primarily for information. In interchanges with friends and co-workers, you need to listen for feelings, too. Feelings of being rejected or overworked need to be dealt with as they arise. But you can't deal with a feeling unless you are aware of it.

As Appendix C explains, to receive a message, the receiver must first perceive the message, then decode it (that is, translate the symbols into meaning), and then interpret it. In interpersonal communication, **hearing** denotes perceiving sounds. **Listening** means decoding and interpreting them correctly.

Some listening errors happen because the hearer wasn't paying enough attention to a key point. After a meeting with a client, a consultant waited for the client to send her more information, which she would use to draft a formal proposal to do a job for the client. It turned out the client thought the next move was up to the consultant. The consultant and the client had met together, but they hadn't remembered the same facts.

Take notes when you can. In addition,

- As early as possible, make a mental or paper list of the questions you have. When is the project due? What resources do you have? What is the most important aspect of this project, from the other person's point of view? During a conversation, listen for answers to your questions.
- At the end of the conversation, check your understanding with the other person. Especially check who does what next.
- After the conversation, write down key points that affect deadlines or how work will be evaluated.

Many listening errors are errors in interpretation. In 1977 when two Boeing 747 jumbo jets ran into each other on the ground in Tenerife, the pilots seemed to have heard the control tower's instructions. The KLM pilot was told to taxi to the end of the runway, turn around, and wait for clearance. But the KLM pilot didn't interpret the order to wait as an order he needed to follow. The Pan Am pilot interpreted *his* order to turn off at the "third intersection" to mean the third *unblocked* intersection. He didn't count the first blocked ramp, so he was still on the main runway when the KLM pilot ran into his plane at 186 miles an hour. The planes exploded in flames; 576 people died.[1]

To reduce listening errors caused by misinterpretation,

- Don't ignore instructions you think are unnecessary. Before you do something else, check with the order giver to see if there is a reason for the instruction.
- Consider the other person's background and experiences. Why is this point important to the speaker? What might he or she mean by it?
- Paraphrase what the speaker has said, giving him or her a chance to correct your understanding.

Listening to people is an indication that you're taking them seriously. **Acknowledgment responses**—nods, *uh huhs,* smiles, frowns—help carry the message that you're listening. However, listening responses vary in different cultures. Research has found that US whites almost always respond nonverbally when they listen closely, but that African Americans respond with words rather than nonverbal cues (✖ p. 4). This difference in response patterns may explain the fact that some whites think that African Americans do not understand what they are saying. Studies in the mid-1970s showed that white counselors repeated themselves more often to black clients than to white clients.[2] Similarly, black supervisors may miss verbal feedback when they talk to white subordinates who only nod.

In **active listening,** receivers actively demonstrate that they've heard and understood a speaker by feeding back either the literal meaning or the emotional content or both. Other techniques in active listening are asking for more information and stating one's own feelings.

Instead of simply mirroring what the other person says, many of us immediately respond in a way that analyzes or attempts to solve or dismiss the problem. People with problems need first of all to know that we hear that they're having a rough time. Figure 13.1 lists some of the responses that block communication. Ordering and interrogating both tell the other person that the speaker doesn't want to hear what he or she has to say. Preaching attacks the other person. Minimizing the problem suggests the other person's concern is misplaced. Even advising shuts off discussion. Giving a quick answer minimizes the pain the person feels and puts him or her down for not seeing (what is to us) the obvious answer. Even if it is a good answer from an objective point of view, the other person may not be ready to hear it. And sometimes, the off-the-top-of-the-head solution doesn't address the real problem.

Do You Hear What I Hear?*

In Center Harbor, Maine, local legend recalls the day some 10 years ago when Walter Cronkite steered his boat into port. The avid sailor, as it's told, was amused to see in the distance a small crowd of people on shore waving their arms to greet him. He could barely make out their excited shouts of "Hello Walter, Hello Walter."

As his boat sailed closer, the crowd grew larger, still yelling, "Hello Walter, Hello Walter." Pleased at the reception, Cronkite tipped his white captain's hat, waved back, even took a bow.

But before reaching dockside, Cronkite's boat abruptly jammed aground. The crowd stood silent. The veteran news anchor suddenly realized what they'd been shouting: "Low water, low water."

*Quoted from Don Oldenburg, "What You Hear Isn't Always What You Get," *The Columbus Dispatch*, April 12, 1987, 1C.

City Year, a Boston-based, nationwide nonprofit service organization, opens meetings with a show of hands. Smaller groups reach their hands in to form a circle. Larger groups raise their hands high. Conversations stop, all is quiet, and group members are physically engaged in a common action.

Figure 13.1

*Blocking Responses versus
Active Listening*

Blocking response	Possible active response
Ordering, threatening	**Paraphrasing content**
"I don't care how you do it. Just get that report on my desk by Friday."	"You're saying that you don't have time to finish the report by Friday."
Preaching, criticizing	**Mirroring feelings**
"You should know better than to air the department's problems in a general meeting."	"It sounds like the department's problems really bother you."
Interrogating	**Stating one's own feelings**
"Why didn't you *tell* me that you didn't understand the instructions?"	"I'm frustrated that the job isn't completed yet, and I'm worried about getting it done on time."
Minimizing the problem	**Asking for information or clarification**
"You think *that's* bad. You should see what *I* have to do this week."	"What parts of the problem seem most difficult to solve?"
Advising	**Offering to help solve the problem together**
"Well, why don't you try listing everything you have to do and seeing which items are most important?"	"Is there anything I could do that would help?"

Source: The 5 responses that block communication are based on a list of 12 in Thomas Gordon and Judith Gordon Sands, *P.E.T. in Action* (New York: Wyden, 1976), 117–18.

Active listening takes time and energy. Even people who are skilled active listeners can't do it all the time. Furthermore, as Thomas Gordon and Judith Gordon Sands point out, active listening works only if you genuinely accept the other person's ideas and feelings. Active listening can reduce the conflict that results from miscommunication, but it alone cannot reduce the conflict that comes when two people want apparently inconsistent things or when one person wants to change someone else.[3]

Group Interactions

Groups can focus on three different dimensions. **Informational** messages focus on content: the problem, data, and possible solutions. **Procedural** messages focus on method and process. How will the group make decisions? Who will do what? When will assignments be due? **Interpersonal** messages focus on people, promoting friendliness, cooperation, and group loyalty. Different kinds of communication dominate during the four stages of the life of a task group: orientation, formation, coordination, and formalization.[4]

During **orientation,** when members meet and begin to define their task, groups need to develop some sort of social cohesiveness and to develop procedures for meeting and acting. Interpersonal and procedural comments reduce the tension that always exists in a new group. Insistence on information in this first stage can hurt the group's long-term productivity.

Groups are often most effective when they explicitly adopt ground rules. Figure 13.2 lists some of the most common ground rules used by workplace teams.

During **formation,** conflicts almost always arise when the group chooses a leader and defines the problem. Successful leaders make the procedure clear so that each member knows what he or she is supposed to do. Interpersonal communication is needed to resolve the conflict that surfaces during this phase. Successful groups analyze the problem carefully before they begin to search for solutions.

* Start on time; end on time.
* Come to the meeting prepared.
* Focus comments on the issues.
* Avoid personal attacks.
* Listen to and respect members' opinions.
* NOSTUESO (No One Speaks Twice Until Everybody Speaks Once)

* If you have a problem with another person, tell that person, not everyone else.
* Everyone must be 70% comfortable with the decision and 100% committed to implementing it.
* If you agree to do something, do it.
* Communicate immediately if you think you may not be able to fulfill an agreement.

Figure 13.2

Possible Group Ground Rules

Sources: Nancy Schullery and Beth Hoger, "Business Advocacy for Students in Small Groups," Association for Business Communication Annual Convention, San Antonio, November 9–11, 1998; "An Antidote to Chronic Cantankerousness," *Fast Company*, February/March 1998, 176; John Grossmann, "We've Got to Start Meeting Like This," *Inc.*, April 1998, 70; Gary Dessler, *Winning Commitment,* quoted in *Team Management Briefings,* preview issue (September 1998), 5; and 3M Meeting Network, "Groundrules and Agreements," www.3M.com/meetingnetwork/readingroom/meetingguide_grndrules.html (January 30, 1999).

Coordination is the longest phase and the phase during which most of the group's work is done. While procedural and interpersonal comments help maintain direction and friendliness, most of the comments need to deal with information. Good information is essential to a good decision. Conflict occurs as the group debates alternate solutions.

In **formalization,** the group seeks consensus. The success of this phase determines how well the group's decision will be implemented. In this stage, the group seeks to forget earlier conflicts.

Roles in Groups

Individual members can play several roles in groups. These roles can be positive or negative.

Positive roles and actions that help the group achieve its task goals include the following:[5]

* **Seeking information and opinions**—asking questions, identifying gaps in the group's knowledge.
* **Giving information and opinions**—answering questions, providing relevant information.
* **Summarizing**—restating major points, pulling ideas together, summarizing decisions.
* **Evaluating**—comparing group process and products to standards and goals.
* **Coordinating**—planning work, giving directions, and fitting together contributions of group members.

Positive roles and actions that help the group build loyalty, resolve conflicts, and function smoothly include the following:

* **Encouraging participation**—demonstrating openness and acceptance, recognizing the contributions of members, calling on quieter group members.
* **Relieving tensions**—joking and suggesting breaks and fun activities.
* **Checking feelings**—asking members how they feel about group activities and sharing one's own feelings with others.
* **Solving interpersonal problems**—opening discussion of interpersonal problems in the group and suggesting ways to solve them.
* **Listening actively**—showing group members that they have been heard and that their ideas are being taken seriously.

The Power and Peril of Teams*

[Shaunna Sowell at Texas Instruments] was tapped for a product-quality steering committee that was loaded with bosses. She was intimidated at first but her confidence grew with her experience.

"I left one meeting thinking, . . . 'I've ruined my career,' " she recalls. "I'd just told a guy four levels above me he was wrong."

Actually, she impressed an executive on the team who was casting about for a vice president of corporate environmental safety. "You have to be a great individual contributor," she says, "that's how you get picked for the next team." . . .

In leading a team charged with redesigning Boston Gas's distribution operation, [Mary] Kinnear, a human-resources specialist, also knew she risked offending some influential executives whose turf was being threatened. Some had already voiced skepticism about her abilities to do effective work on the team. . . .

When the project ended, however, she was eventually named general manager of one of the eight regional operating divisions created by the project team. Absent the project team, she says she wouldn't have had the experience or the exposure to land her current job.

*Quoted from Hal Lancaster, "That Team Spirit Can Lead Your Career to New Victories," *The Wall Street Journal,* January 14, 1997, B1.

Negative roles and actions that hurt the group's product and process include the following:

- **Blocking**—disagreeing with everything that is proposed.
- **Dominating**—trying to run the group by ordering, shutting out others, and insisting on one's own way.
- **Clowning**—making unproductive jokes and diverting the group from the task.
- **Withdrawing**—being silent in meetings, not contributing, not helping with the work, not attending meetings.

Some actions can be positive or negative depending on how they are used. Criticizing ideas is necessary if the group is to produce the best solution, but criticizing every idea raised without ever suggesting possible solutions blocks a group. Jokes in moderation can defuse tension and make the group more fun. Too many jokes or inappropriate jokes can make the group's work more difficult.

Leadership in Groups

You may have noted that "leader" was not one of the roles listed above. Being a leader does *not* mean doing all the work yourself. Indeed, someone who implies that he or she has the best ideas and can do the best work is likely playing the negative roles of blocking and dominating.

Effective groups balance three kinds of leadership, which parallel the three group dimensions. Providing information leadership (by generating ideas and text) is joined by providing interpersonal leadership (monitoring the group's process, checking people's feelings, and resolving conflicts) and procedural group management (setting an agenda, making sure everyone knows what's due for the next meeting, communicating with absent group members, checking to be sure assignments are carried out). While it's possible for one person to do all of these responsibilities, in many groups, the three kinds of leadership are taken on by three (or more) different people. Some groups formally or informally rotate or share these responsibilities, so that everyone—and no one—is a leader.

Several studies have shown people who talk a lot, listen effectively, and respond nonverbally to other members in the group are considered to be leaders.[6]

Decision-Making Strategies

Probably the least effective decision-making strategy is to let the person who talks first, last, loudest, or most determine the decision.

Voting is quick but may leave people in the minority unhappy with and uncommitted to the majority's plan.

Coming to consensus takes time but results in speedier implementation of ideas.

Two strategies that are often useful in organizational groups are the standard agenda and dot planning.

The **standard agenda** is a seven-step process for solving problems:

1. Understand what the group has to deliver, in what form, by what due date. Identify available resources.
2. Identify the problem. What exactly is wrong? What question(s) is the group trying to answer?
3. Gather information, share it with all group members, and examine it critically.

4. Establish criteria. What would the ideal solution include? Which elements of that solution would be part of a less-than-ideal but still acceptable solution? What legal, financial, moral, or other limitations might keep a solution from being implemented?
5. Generate alternate solutions. Brainstorm and record ideas for the next step.
6. Measure the alternatives against the criteria.
7. Choose the best solution.[7]

Dot planning offers a way for large groups to choose priorities quickly. First, the group brainstorms ideas, recording each on pages that are put on the wall. Then each individual gets two strips of three to five adhesive dots in different colors. One color represents high priority, the other lower priority. People then walk up to the pages and affix dots by the points they care most about. Some groups allow only one dot from one person on any one item; others allow someone who is really passionate about an idea to put all of his or her dots on it. As Figure 13.3 shows, the dots make it easy to see which items the group believes are most important.

Characteristics of Successful Student Groups

A case study of six student groups completing class projects found that students in successful groups were not necessarily more skilled or more experienced than students in less successful groups. Instead, successful and less successful groups communicated differently in three ways.[8]

Figure 13.3 *Dot Planning Allows Groups to Set Priorities Quickly*

Here, green dots mean "high priority;" purple dots mean "low priority." One can see at a glance which items have widespread support, which are controversial, and which are low priority.

Source: "The Color-Coded Priority Setter," *Inc.*, June 1995, 70–71.

Evaluating Teams*

[A]t Con-Way Transportation Services, . . . teams evaluate *themselves* through a process called the Team Improvement Review (TIR). . . .

The TIR process . . . separates feedback sessions from salary reviews. . . .

The TIR also guarantees that feedback takes place in a safe environment. . . . [M]anagers are usually not present. Instead, the groups often bring in a neutral facilitator who leads the discussions.

Last, the TIR has a formal process by which teams offer feedback. The reviews happen about every three months. A week before the TIR meeting, participants rate team performance on a 1-to-5 scale for 31 criteria. During the meeting, people discuss the team's performance as well as individual performance in the context of the team. . . . [T]o keep the discussions focused on performance rather than on personality [, . . . the team uses techniques such as] the Round Robin. Each person creates two columns on a sheet of paper, one labeled "Strengths" and the other "Something to Work On." Then each person lists all the strengths that he or she brings to the team as well as one thing to work on. The papers get passed around the room, and each team member comments on everyone else's forms.

*Quoted from "How Con-Way Reviews Teams," *Fast Company*, September 1998, 152.

First, in the successful groups, the leader set clear deadlines, scheduled frequent meetings, and dealt directly with conflict that emerged in the group. In less successful groups, members had to ask the leader what they were supposed to be doing. The less successful groups met less often, and they tried to pretend that conflicts didn't exist.

Second, the successful groups listened to criticism and made important decisions together. Perhaps as a result, everyone in the group could articulate the group's goals. In the less successful groups, a subgroup made decisions and told other members what had been decided.

Third, the successful groups had a higher proportion of members who worked actively on the project. The successful groups even found ways to use members who didn't like working in groups. For example, one student who didn't want to be a "team player" functioned as a "freelancer" for her group, completing assignments by herself and giving them to the leader. The less successful groups had a much smaller percentage of active members and each had some members who did very little on the final project.

Rebecca Burnett has shown that student groups produce better documents when they disagree over substantive issues of content and document design. The disagreement does not need to be angry: a group member can simply say, "Yes, and here's another way we could do it." Deciding among two (or more) alternatives forces the proposer to explain the rationale for an idea. Even when the group adopts the original idea, considering alternatives rather than quickly accepting the first idea produces better writing.[9]

Kimberly Freeman found that the students who spent the most time meeting with their groups had the highest grades—on their individual as well as on group assignments.[10]

Peer Pressure and Groupthink

Groups that never express conflict may be experiencing groupthink. **Groupthink** is the tendency for groups to put such a high premium on agreement that they directly or indirectly punish dissent.

Many people feel so much reluctance to express open disagreement that they will say they agree even when objective circumstances would suggest the first speaker cannot be right. In a series of experiments in the 1950s, Solomon Asch showed the influence of peer pressure. People sitting around a table were shown a large card with a line and asked to match it to the line of the same length on another card. It's a simple test: people normally match the lines correctly almost 100% of the time. However, in the experiment, all but one of the people in the group had been instructed to give false answers for several of the trials. When the group gave an incorrect answer, the focal person accepted the group's judgment 36.8% of the time. When someone else also gave a different answer—even if it was another wrong answer—the focal person accepted the group's judgment only 9% of the time.[11]

The experimenters varied the differences in line lengths, hoping to create a situation in which even the most conforming subjects would trust their own senses. But some people continued to accept the group's judgment, even when one line was seven inches longer than the other.

Groups that "go along with the crowd" and suppress conflict ignore the full range of alternatives, seek only information that supports the positions they already favor, and fail to prepare contingency plans to cope with foreseeable setbacks. A business suffering from groupthink may launch a new product that senior executives support but for which there is no demand. Student groups suffering from groupthink turn in inferior documents.

The best correctives to groupthink are to consciously search for additional alternatives, to test one's assumptions against those of a range of other people, and to protect the right of people in a group to disagree.

Working in Diverse Groups

In any organization, you'll work with people whose backgrounds differ from yours. Residents of small towns and rural areas have different notions of friendliness than do people from big cities. Californians look, talk, and dress differently from people in the Midwest. Advertising executives and truck drivers have different lifestyles.

Even people who come from the same part of the country and who have the same jobs may differ in personality type. Savvy group members play to each other's strengths and devise strategies for dealing with differences.

In addition, differences arise from gender, class, race and ethnicity, religion, age, sexual orientation, and physical ability. A growing body of literature shows that ethnically diverse teams produce more and higher-quality ideas.[12]

 See the BAC Web page for links to sites for various ethnic groups in the United States. One problem with our awareness of difference, however, is that when someone feels shut out, he or she can attribute the negative interaction to prejudice, when other factors may be responsible. Conversational style and nonverbal communication are two of the areas that may cause miscommunication.

Conversational Style

Deborah Tannen uses the term **conversational style** to denote our conversational patterns and the meaning we give to them: the way we show interest, politeness, appropriateness.[13] Your answers to the following questions reveal your own conversational style:

- How long a pause tells you that it's your turn to speak?
- Do you see interruption as rude? or do you say things while other people are still talking to show that you're interested and to encourage them to say more?
- Do you show interest by asking lots of questions? or do you see questions as intrusive and wait for people to volunteer whatever they have to say?

Tannen concludes that the following features characterize her own conversational style:

> Fast rate of speech.
> Fast rate of turn-taking.
> Persistence—if a turn is not acknowledged, try again.
> Preference for personal stories.
> Tolerance of, preference for simultaneous speech.
> Abrupt topic shifting.

Different conversational styles are not better or worse than each other, but people with different conversational styles may feel uncomfortable without knowing why. A subordinate who talks quickly may be frustrated by a boss who speaks slowly. People who talk more slowly may feel shut out of a conversation with people who talk more quickly. Someone who has learned to make requests directly ("Please pass the salt") may be annoyed by someone who uses indirect requests ("This casserole needs some salt").

"Assertiveness" May Be a Matter of Conversational Style*

Rachel regularly led training groups with a male colleague. He always did all the talking, and she was always angry at him for dominating and not giving her a chance to say anything. . . . He would begin to answer questions from the group while she was still waiting for a slight pause to begin answering. And when she was in the middle of talking, he would jump in—but always when she had paused. So she tried pushing herself to begin answering questions a little sooner than felt polite, and not to leave long pauses when she was talking. The result was that she talked a lot more, and the man was as pleased as she was. Her supervisor complimented her on having become more assertive.

Whether or not Rachel actually became more assertive is debatable. . . . [S]he solved her problem with a simple and slight adjustment of her way of speaking, without soul-searching, self-analysis, external intervention, and—most important—without defining herself as having an emotional problem or a personality defect: unassertiveness.

*Quoted from Deborah Tannen, *That's Not What I Meant!* (New York: William Morrow, 1986), 177–78.

Are Interruptions Impolite?*

In the dominant US culture, interrupting can seem impolite, especially if a lower-status person interrupts a superior.

Simulated negotiations have measured the interruptions by business people in 10 countries. The following list is ordered by decreasing numbers of interruptions:

Korea
Germany
France
China
Brazil
Russia
Taiwan
Japan
United Kingdom
United States

This list does not mean that US business people are more polite, but rather that how people show politeness differs from culture to culture. Chinese and Italians (who also interrupt frequently) use interruptions to offer help, jointly construct a conversation, and show eagerness to do business—all of which are polite.

*Based on Jan M. Ulijn and Xiangling Li, "Is Interrupting Impolite? Some Temporal Aspects of Turn-Taking in Chinese-Western and Other Intercultural Encounters," *Text* 15, no. 4 (1995), 600, 621.

In the workplace, conflicts may arise because of differences in conversational style. Generation Xers often use a rising inflection on statements as well as questions. Xers see this style as gentler and more polite. But baby boomer bosses may see this speech pattern as hesitant, as if the speaker wants advice—which they then proceed to deliver.[14] Thomas Kochman claims that blacks often use direct questions to criticize or accuse.[15] If Kochman is right, a black employee might see a question ("Will that report be ready Friday?") as a criticism of his or her progress. One supervisor might mean the question simply as a request for information. Another supervisor might use the question to mean "I want that report Friday."

Daniel N. Maltz and Ruth A. Borker believe that differences in conversational style (Figure 13.4) may be responsible for the miscommunication that often occurs in male–female conversations. Certainly conversational style is not the same for all men and for all women, but research has found several common patterns in the US cultures studied so far. For example, researchers have found that women are much more likely to nod and to say *yes* or *mm hmm* than men are. Maltz and Borker hypothesize that to women, these symbols mean simply, "I'm listening; go on." Men, on the other hand, may decode these symbols as, "I agree" or at least "I follow what you're saying so far." A man who receives nods and *mm*s from a woman may feel that she is inconsistent and unpredictable if she then disagrees with him. A woman may feel that a man who doesn't provide any feedback isn't listening to her.[16]

Nonverbal Communication

Posture and body movements connote energy and openness. North American **open body positions** include leaning forward with uncrossed arms and legs, with the arms away from the body. **Closed** or **defensive body positions** include leaning back, sometimes with both hands behind the head, arms and legs crossed or close together, or hands in pockets. As the labels imply, open positions suggest that people are accepting and open to new ideas. Closed positions suggest that people are physically or psychologically uncomfortable, that they are defending themselves and shutting other people out.

People who cross their arms or legs often claim that they do so only because the position is more comfortable. But notice your own body the next time you're in a perfectly comfortable discussion with a good friend. You'll probably find that you naturally assume open body positions. The fact that so many people in organizational settings adopt closed positions may indicate that many people feel at least slightly uncomfortable in school and on the job.

As Chapter 12 explains, even within a culture, a nonverbal sign may have more than one meaning. A young woman took a new idea into her boss, who sat there and glared at her, brows together in a frown, as she explained her proposal. The stare and lowered brows symbolized anger to her, and she assumed that he was rejecting her idea. Several months later, she learned that her boss always "frowned" when he was concentrating. The facial expression she had interpreted as anger had not been intended to convey anger at all.

Misunderstandings are even more common when people communicate with people from other cultures or other countries. A white teacher sends two African American students to the principal's office because they're "fighting." US whites consider fighting to have started when loud voices, insults, and posture indicate that violence is likely. But the US African American culture does not assume that those signs will lead to violence: they can be part of nonviolent disagreements.[17]

Knowing something about other cultures may help you realize that a subordinate who doesn't meet your eye may be showing respect rather than dishonesty. But it's impossible to memorize every meaning that every nonverbal sign has in every culture. And in a multicultural workforce, you can't know whether someone retains the meanings of his or her ancestors or has adopted the dominant US meanings. The best solution is to state an observation: "I see you're wearing black." The other person's response will let you know whether the color is a fashion statement or a sign of mourning.

Power Talk*

Conflict Resolution

Conflicts are going to arise in any group of intelligent people who care about the task. Yet many of us feel so uncomfortable with conflict that we pretend it doesn't exist. However, unacknowledged conflicts rarely go away: they fester, making the next interchange more difficult.

Groups can reduce the number of conflicts by making responsibilities and ground rules clear at the beginning, discussing (rather than just accepting) problems as they arise, and realizing that members are not responsible for each other's happiness. Once a conflict arises, groups may need to reopen discussions about responsibilities and confront a troublesome group member.[18]

Figure 13.5 suggests several possible solutions to conflicts that student groups often experience. Often the symptom arises from a feeling of not being respected or appreciated by the group. Therefore, many problems can be averted if people advocate for their ideas in a positive way. As Nancy Schullery and Beth Hogan point out, the best time to advocate for an idea is when the group has not yet identified all possible options, seems dominated by one view, or seems unable to choose among solutions. A tactful way to advocate for the position you favor is to recognize the contributions others have made, to summarize, and then to hypothesize: "What if . . . ?" "Let's look six months down the road." "Let's think about *x*."[19]

 To see how comfortable you are with conflict, take the quiz on the BAC Web site.

A person who feels confident and in control will speak at length, set the agenda for a conversation, stave off interruptions, argue openly, make jokes, and laugh. Such a person is more inclined to make statements, less inclined to ask questions. They are more likely to offer solutions or a program or a plan. . . .

The power deficient drop into conversations, encourage other speakers, ask numerous questions, avoid argument, and rely on gestures such as smiling and nodding that suggest agreement. They tend to offer empathy rather than solutions. They often use unfinished sentences. . . .

The key is figuring out who gets listened to within your corporate culture. That can make you a more savvy user of language. Try to sit in on a meeting as a kind of researcher, observing conversational patterns. . . . Then try to determine who gets noticed and why.

*Quoted from Sarah McGinty, "How You Speak Shows Where You Rank," *Fortune*, February 2, 1998, 156.

Figure 13.4	*Different Conversational Styles*	
	Debating	**Relating**
Interpretation of questions	See questions as requests for information.	See questions as way to keep a conversation flowing.
Relation of new comment to what last speaker said	Do not require new comment to relate explicitly to last speaker's comment. Ignoring previous comment is one strategy for taking control.	Expect new comments to acknowledge the last speaker's comment and relate directly to it.
View of aggressiveness	See aggressiveness as one way to organize the flow of conversation.	See aggressiveness as directed at audience personally, as negative, and as disruptive to a conversation.
How topics are defined and changed	Tend to define topics narrowly and shift topics abruptly. Interpret statements about side issues as effort to change the topic.	Tend to define topics gradually, progressively. Interpret statements about side issues as effort to shape, expand, or limit the topic.
Response to someone who shares a problem	Offer advice, solutions.	Offer solidarity, reassurance. Share troubles to establish sense of community.

Sources: Based on Daniel N. Maltz and Ruth A. Borker, "A Cultural Approach to Male-Female Miscommunication," *Language and Social Identity*, ed. John J. Gumperz (Cambridge: Cambridge University Press, 1982), 213; and Deborah Tannen, *Talking from 9 to 5: Women and Men in the Workplace: Language, Sex and Power* (New York: William Morrow, 1995).

Figure 13.5   *Troubleshooting Group Problems*

Symptom	Possible solutions
We can't find a time to meet that works for all of us.	a. Find out why people can't meet at certain times. Some reasons suggest their own solutions. For example, if someone has to stay home with small children, perhaps the group could meet at that person's home. b. Assign out-of-class work to "committees" to work on parts of the project. c. Use e-mail to share, discuss, and revise drafts.
One person isn't doing his or her fair share.	a. Find out what is going on. Is the person overcommitted? Does he or she feel unappreciated? Those are different problems you'd solve in different ways. b. Early on, do things to build group loyalty. Get to know each other as writers and as people. Sometimes, do something fun together. c. Encourage the person to contribute. "Mary, what do you think?" "Jim, which part of this would you like to draft?" Then find something to praise in the work. "Thanks for getting us started." d. If someone misses a meeting, assign someone else to bring the person up to speed. People who miss meetings for legitimate reasons (job interviews, illness) but don't find out what happened may become less committed to the group. e. Consider whether strict equality is the most important criterion. On a given project, some people may have more knowledge or time than others. Sometimes the best group product results from letting people do different amounts of "work." f. Even if you divide up the work, make all decisions as a group: what to write about, which evidence to include, what graphs to use, what revisions to make. People excluded from decisions become less committed to the group.
I seem to be the only one in the group who cares about quality.	a. Find out why other members "don't care." If they received low grades on early assignments, stress that good ideas and attention to detail can raise grades. Perhaps the group should meet with the instructor to discuss what kinds of work will pay the highest dividends. b. Volunteer to do extra work. Sometimes people settle for something that's just OK because they don't have the time or resources to do excellent work. They might be happy for the work to be done—if they didn't have to do it. c. Be sure that you're respecting what each person can contribute. Group members sometimes withdraw when one person dominates and suggests that he or she is "better" than other members.
People in the group don't seem willing to disagree. We end up going with the first idea suggested.	a. Appoint someone to be a devil's advocate. b. Brainstorm so you have several possibilities to consider. c. After an idea is suggested, have each person in the group suggest a way it could be improved. d. Have each person in the group write a draft. It's likely the drafts will be different, and you'll have several options to mix and match. e. Talk about good ways to offer criticism. Sometimes people don't disagree because they're afraid that other group members won't tolerate disagreement.
One person just criticizes everything.	a. Ask the person to follow up the criticism with a suggestion for improvement. b. Talk about ways to express criticism tactfully. "I think we need to think about x" is more tactful than "You're wrong." c. If the criticism is about ideas and writing (not about people), value it. Ideas and documents need criticism if we are to improve them.

Steps in Conflict Resolution

Dealing successfully with conflict requires both attention to the issues and to people's feelings. This four-step procedure will help you resolve conflicts constructively.

1. Make sure the people involved really disagree.

Sometimes someone who's under a lot of pressure may explode. But the speaker may just be **venting** anger and frustration; he or she may not in fact be angry at the person who receives the explosion. One way to find out if a person is just venting is to ask, "Is there something you'd like me to do?"

2. Check to see that everyone's information is correct.

Sometimes different conversational styles, differing interpretations of symbols, or faulty inferences create apparent conflicts when no real disagreement exists. (See Appendix C for a discussion of symbols and inferences.) During a negotiation between a US businessman and a Balinese businessman, the Balinese man dropped his voice and lowered his eyes when he discussed price. The US man saw the low voice and breaking of eye contact as an indication of dishonesty. But the Balinese believe that it is rude to mention price specifically. He was embarrassed, but he wasn't lying.[20]

Similarly, misunderstanding can arise from faulty assumptions. A US student studying in Colombia quickly learned that only cold water was available for his evening shower. Since his host family washed dinner dishes in cold water, he assumed the family didn't have hot water. They did. Colombians turn off the water heater in the morning after everyone has bathed; washing later in the day is done with cold water. He could have hot water for his showers if he took them in the morning.[21]

3. Discover the needs each person is trying to meet.

Sometimes determining the real needs makes it possible to see a new solution. The **presenting problem** that surfaces as the subject of dissention may or may not be the real problem. For example, a worker who complains about the hours he's putting in may in fact be complaining not about the hours themselves but about not feeling appreciated. A supervisor who complains that the other supervisors don't invite her to meetings may really feel that the other managers don't accept her as a peer. Sometimes people have trouble seeing beyond the presenting problem because they've been taught to suppress their anger, especially toward powerful people. One way to tell whether the presenting problem is the real problem is to ask, "If this were solved, would I be satisfied?" If the answer is *no*, then the problem that presents itself is not the real problem. Solving the presenting problem won't solve the conflict. Keep probing until you get to the real conflict.

4. Search for alternatives.

Sometimes people are locked into conflict because they see too few alternatives. Indeed, they may see only two polarized choices. Robert Moran tells the story of a large US high-technology company that was having trouble in the Japanese market. At a meeting called to discuss the problem, the president wrote two alternatives on the board: "GET OUT" and "MAKE THEM DO WHAT WE WANT." Moran suggested a third alternative: "LEARN TO WORK WITH THE JAPANESE."[22]

Who Does What

Working successfully in a group depends on being open about preferences, constraints, and skills and then using creative problem-solving techniques.

A person who prefers to outline the whole project in advance may be in a group with someone who expects to do the project at the last minute. Someone who likes to talk out ideas before writing may be in a group with someone who wants to work on a draft in silence and revise it before showing it to anyone. By being honest about your preferences, you make it possible for the group to find a creative solution that builds on what each person can offer.

In one group, Rob wanted to wait to start the project because he was busy with other class work. David and Susan, however, wanted to go ahead now because their schedules would get busier later in the term. A creative solution would be for David and Susan to do most of the work on parts of the project that had to be completed first (such as collecting data and writing the proposal) and for Rob to do work that had to be done later (such as revising, editing, and proofreading).

Solve the Real Problem*

Consider the story of two men quarreling in a library. One wants the window open and the other wants it closed. They bicker back and forth about how much to leave it open: a crack, halfway, three quarters of the way. No solution satisfies them both.

Enter the librarian. She asks one why he wants the window open: "To get some fresh air." She asks the other why he wants it closed: "To avoid the draft." After thinking a minute, she opens wide a window in the next room, bringing in fresh air without a draft.

*Quoted from Roger Fisher and William Ury, *Getting to YES: Negotiating Agreement Without Giving In* (Boston: Houghton Mifflin, 1981), 41.

Responding to Criticism

Conflict is particularly difficult to resolve when someone else criticizes or attacks us directly. When we are criticized, our natural reaction is to defend ourselves—perhaps by counterattacking. The counterattack prompts the critic to defend him- or herself. The conflict escalates; feelings are hurt; issues become muddied and more difficult to resolve.

Just as resolving conflict depends upon identifying the needs each person is trying to meet, so dealing with criticism depends upon understanding the real concern of the critic. Constructive ways to respond to criticism and get closer to the real concern include paraphrasing, checking for feelings, checking inferences, and buying time with limited agreement.

Paraphrasing

To **paraphrase,** repeat in your own words the verbal content of the critic's message. The purposes of paraphrasing are (1) to be sure that you have heard the critic accurately, (2) to let the critic know what his or her statement means to you, and (3) to communicate the feeling that you are taking the critic and his or her feelings seriously.

Criticism: You guys are stonewalling my requests for information.

Paraphrase: You think that we don't give you the information you need quickly enough.

Checking for feelings

When you check the critic's feelings, you identify the emotions that the critic seems to be expressing verbally or nonverbally. The purposes of checking feelings are to try to understand (1) the critic's emotions, (2) the importance of the criticism for the critic, and (3) the unspoken ideas and feelings that may actually be more important than the voiced criticism.

Criticism: You guys are stonewalling my requests for information.

Feeling check: You sound pretty angry.

Always *ask* the other person if you are right in your perception. Even the best reader of nonverbal cues is sometimes wrong.

Checking for inferences

When you check the inferences you draw from criticism, you identify the implied meaning of the verbal and nonverbal content of the criticism, taking the statement a step further than the words of the critic to try to understand *why* the critic is bothered by the action or attitude under discussion. The purposes of checking inferences are (1) to identify the real (as opposed to the presenting) problem and (2) to communicate the feeling that you care about resolving the conflict.

Criticism: You guys are stonewalling my requests for information.

Inference: Are you saying that you need more information from our group?

Inferences can be faulty. In the above interchange, the critic might respond, "I don't need *more* information. I just think you should give it to me without my having to file three forms in triplicate every time I want some data."

Buying time with limited agreement

Buying time is a useful strategy for dealing with criticisms that really sting. When you buy time with limited agreement, you avoid escalating the conflict (as an angry statement might do) but also avoid yielding to the critic's point of view. To buy time, restate the part of the criticism you agree to be true. (This is often a fact, rather than the interpretation or evaluation the critic has made of that fact.) *Then let the critic respond, before you say anything else.* The purposes of buying time are (1) to allow you time to think when a criticism really hits home and threatens you, so that you can respond to the criticism rather than simply reacting defensively, and (2) to suggest to the critic that you are trying to hear what he or she is saying.

Criticism:	You guys are stonewalling my requests for information.
Limited agreement:	It's true that the cost projections you asked for last week still aren't ready.

DO NOT go on to justify or explain. A "Yes, but . . ." statement is not a time-buyer.

You-Attitude in Conflict Resolution

You-attitude means looking at things from the audience's point of view, respecting the audience, and protecting the audience's ego. The *you* statements that many people use when they're angry attack the audience; they do not illustrate you-attitude. Instead, substitute statements about your own feelings. In conflict, *I* statements show good you-attitude!

Lacks you-attitude:	You never do your share of the work.
You-attitude:	I feel that I'm doing more than my share of the work on this project.
Lacks you-attitude:	Even you should be able to run the report through a spelling checker.
You-attitude:	I'm not willing to have my name on a report with so many spelling errors. I did lots of the writing, and I don't think I should have to do the proofreading and spell checking, too.

Effective Meetings

Meetings have always taken a large part of the average manager's week. Although e-mail has eliminated some meetings, the increased number of teams means that meetings are even more frequent.

See the BAC Web site for links to pages about meetings and even to play back a virtual meeting.

Formal meetings are run under strict rules, like the rules of parliamentary procedure summarized in *Robert's Rules of Order.* Motions must be made formally before a topic can be debated. Each point is settled by a vote. **Minutes** record each motion and the vote on it. See the BAC Web site for links to minutes posted on the Web. Formal rules help the meeting run smoothly if the group is very large or if the agenda is very long. **Informal meetings,** which are much more common in the workplace, are run more loosely. Votes may not be taken if most people seem to agree. Minutes may not be kept. Informal meetings are better for team-building and problem solving.

Planning the agenda is the foundation of a good meeting. A good agenda indicates

- Whether each item is presented for information, for discussion, or for a decision.
- Who is sponsoring or introducing each item.
- How much time is allotted for each item.

Many groups put first routine items on which agreement will be easy. If there's a long list of routine items, save them till the end or dispense with them in an omnibus motion. An **omnibus motion** allows a group to approve many

Being Taken Seriously*

It's frustrating to speak in a meeting and have people ignore what you say. Here are some tips for being taken seriously:

- Link your comment to the comment of a powerful person. Even if logic suffers a bit, present your comment as an addition, not a challenge. For example, say, "John is saying that we should focus on excellence, AND I think we can become stronger by encouraging diversity."

- Show that you've done your homework. Laura Sloate, who is blind, establishes authority by making sure her first question is highly technical: "In footnote three of the 10K, you indicate. . . ."

- Find an ally in the organization and agree ahead of time to acknowledge each other's contributions to the meeting, whether you agree or disagree with the point being made. Explicit disagreement signals that the comment is worth taking seriously: "Duane has pointed out . . . , but I think that . . . ."

*Based on Joan E. Rigdon, "Managing Your Career," *The Wall Street Journal,* December 1, 1993, B1; and Cynthia Crossen, "Spotting Value Takes Smarts, Not Sight, Laura Sloate Shows," *The Wall Street Journal,* December 10, 1987, A1, A14.

Let's See What We Said*

[O]rganizations from Allstate to McKinsey & Co. have begun to use computers as a medium to manage their meetings. A personal computer is hooked up to an overhead projector and as the participants talk their comments are typed by a designated scribe for all to see. People literally see themselves being heard. Related comments are identified, linked and edited on screen. The digressions and tangents quickly become apparent. Instead of simply swapping ideas, participants are actively collaborating to produce a document—whether it be a spreadsheet, a production manual or a strategic plan. The results are often posted on internal corporate networks for comments and suggestions. These technologies effectively encourage new forms of interaction.

*Quoted from Michael Schrage, "Meetings Don't Have to Be Dull," *The Wall Street Journal*, April 29, 1996, A12.

items together rather than voting on each separately. A single omnibus motion might cover multiple changes to operational guidelines, or a whole slate of candidates for various offices, or various budget recommendations. It's important to schedule controversial items early in the meeting, when people's energy level is high, and to allow enough time for full discussion. Giving a controversial item only half an hour at the end of the day or evening makes people suspect that the leaders are trying to manipulate them.

Pay attention to people and process as well as to the task at hand. At informal meetings, a good leader observes nonverbal feedback and invites everyone to participate. If conflict seems to be getting out of hand, a leader may want to focus attention on the group process and ways that it could deal with conflict, before getting back to the substantive issues.

If the group doesn't formally vote, the leader should summarize the group's consensus after each point. At the end of the meeting, the leader must summarize all decisions and remind the group who is responsible for implementing or following up on each item. If no other notes are taken, someone should record the decisions and assignments. Long minutes will be most helpful if assignments are set off visually from the narrative.

If you're planning a long meeting, for example, a training session or a conference, recognize that networking is part of the value of the meeting. Allow short breaks at least every two hours and generous breaks twice a day so participants can talk informally to each other. If participants will be strangers, include some social functions so they can get to know each other. If they will have different interests or different levels of knowledge, plan concurrent sessions on different topics or for people with different levels of expertise.

Collaborative Writing

Whatever your career, it is likely that some of the documents you produce will be written with a group. Lisa Ede and Andrea Lunsford found that 87% of the 700 professionals in seven fields who responded to their survey sometimes

See 3M's Meeting Network for guides to running better face-to-face and virtual meetings.

www.3M.com

wrote as members of a team or a group.[23] Collaboration is often prompted by one of the following situations:

1. The task is too big or the time is too short for one person to do all the work.
2. No one person has all the knowledge required to do the task.
3. A group representing different perspectives must reach a consensus.
4. The stakes for the task are so high that the organization wants the best efforts of as many people as possible; no one person wants the sole responsibility for the success or failure of the document.

Collaborative writing can be done by two people or by a much larger group. The group can be democratic or run by a leader who makes decisions alone. The group may share or divide responsibility for each of the eight stages in the writing process. The following patterns illustrate three of the many possibilities:

- A group plans the document and divides the work. Individuals gather the necessary material for their parts and each writes a section. The entire group evaluates and revises the document. (Democratic teams in business and students assigned group projects in business classes often organize their work this way.)
- One person plans the work and divides it. Each member of the group carries out his or her assignments. The parts are put together, and the whole group or one person revises it. (Team projects in business may be run this way when the group leader is also the supervisor of the group members.)
- A group gathers information and discusses the topic. A single writer plans and writes a document to reflect the group's position. The group evaluates the document and may suggest possible revisions. The writer revises the document until the group feels it is acceptable. (Many committee reports are written this way.)

Research in collaborative writing is beginning to tell us about the strategies that produce the best writing. Rebecca Burnett found that student groups that voiced disagreements as they analyzed, planned, and wrote a document produced significantly better documents than those that suppressed disagreement, going along with whatever was first proposed.[24] A case study of two collaborative writing teams in a state agency found that the successful group distributed power in an egalitarian way, worked to soothe hurt feelings, and was careful to involve all group members. In terms of writing process, the successful group understood the task as a response to a rhetorical situation, planned revisions as a group, saw supervisors' comments as legitimate, and had a positive attitude toward revision.[25] Ede and Lunsford's detailed case studies of collaborative teams in business, government, and science create an "emerging profile of effective collaborative writers": "They are flexible; respectful of others; attentive and analytical listeners; able to speak and write clearly and articulately; dependable and able to meet deadlines; able to designate and share responsibility, to lead and to follow; open to criticism but confident in their own abilities; ready to engage in creative conflict."[26]

Planning the Work and the Document

Collaborative writing is most successful when the group articulates its understanding of the document's purposes and audiences and explicitly discusses the best way to achieve these rhetorical goals. Businesses schedule formal planning sessions for large projects to set up a time line specifying intermediate

The Integrative Approach*

I have had the opportunity to write in groups . . . in my MBA program at the University of Chicago. The most effective writing process was a truly integrative approach. Our group wrote a paper on leadership that combined six hour-long interviews. The final paper was clear and well organized and read like a single document.

One of the worst ways I have approached group writing is the divide-and-conquer model. . . . On the day before the paper is due, everyone slams the parts together. When you read a paper like this, you realize the problems cut-and-paste writing causes. . . . Simply pasting sections together makes it painfully obvious that there is no continuous style in the document, and that detracts from the content. Had we done this with our leadership paper, it would have been simply six summations of interviews without any comparison of our leaders' styles and experiences.

As we worked, we shared drafts among the six group members by e-mail. This allowed us to revise and edit the document quickly and efficiently. You simply cannot do this with a faxed copy. One person, usually the strongest writer in the group, should complete the final edit of the document to standardize its look and feel.

*Quoted from George Fogel, statement to Kitty Locker, February 18, 1997.

The Importance of Planning, I*

Chris Higgins, . . . [BankAmerica's senior vice president responsible for national currency services] says, spend less time "doing" and more time "planning." Higgins warns that teams are often too quick to act and too slow to think. "If you spend enough time planning, he says, "execution time can be very short. If you work on the fly, you do things fast. But you may do the wrong things, and that slows down the project."

Recently, for example, Higgins led a 500-person team that had one year to develop a system for BankAmerica to accept deposits across state lines. Everyone was eager to "get to work." But Higgins insisted that the team devote six months to planning the system, evaluating business implications, and anticipating technical challenges—all before it wrote a single line of code. After writing the code, the team spent three months testing and refining it. "My approach is 50% planning, 25% doing, and 25% testing and training."

*Quoted from Gina Imperato, "He's Become BankAmerica's 'Mr. Project,' " *Fast Company,* January 1998, 42–44.

and final due dates, meeting dates, who will attend each meeting, and who will do what. Putting the plan in writing reduces misunderstandings during the project.

When you plan a collaborative writing project,

- Make your analysis of the problem, the audience, and your purposes explicit so you know where you agree and where you disagree.
- Plan the organization, format, and style of the document before anyone begins to write to make it easier to blend sections written by different authors.
- Build some leeway into your deadlines. It's harder for a group to finish a document when one person's part is missing than it is for a single writer to finish the last section of a document on which he or she has done all the work.

Composing the Drafts

Most writers find that composing alone is faster than composing in a group. However, composing together may reduce revision time later, since the group examines every choice as it is made.

When you draft a collaborative writing project,

- Use word processing to make it easier to produce the many drafts necessary in a collaborative document.
- If the quality of writing is crucial, have the best writer(s) draft the document after everyone has gathered the necessary information.

Revising the Document

Revising a collaborative document requires attention to content, organization, and style. The following guidelines can make the revision process more effective:

- Evaluate the content and discuss possible revisions as a group. Brainstorm ways to improve each section so the person doing the revisions has some guidance.
- Recognize that different people favor different writing styles. If the style satisfies the demands of standard English and the conventions of business writing, accept it even if you wouldn't say it that way.
- When the group is satisfied with the content of the document, one person—probably the best writer—should make any changes necessary to make the writing style consistent throughout.

Editing and Proofreading the Document

Since writers' mastery of standard English varies, a group report needs careful editing and proofreading.

- Have at least one person check the whole document for correctness in grammar, mechanics, and spelling and for consistency in the way that format elements, names, and numbers are handled.
- Run the document through a spell checker if possible.
- Even if you use a computerized spell checker, at least one human being should proofread the document too.

Making the Group Process Work

All of the information in this chapter can help your collaborative writing group listen effectively, run meetings efficiently, and deal with conflict constructively. The following suggestions apply specifically to writing groups:

- Give yourselves plenty of time to discuss problems and find solutions. Purdue students who are writing group reports spend six to seven hours a week outside class in group meetings—not counting the time they spend gathering information and writing their drafts.[27]
- Take the time to get to know group members and to build group loyalty. Group members will work harder and the final document will be better if the group is important to members.
- Be a responsible group member. Attend all the meetings; carry out your responsibilities.
- Be aware that people have different ways of experiencing reality and of expressing themselves. Use the principles of semantics discussed in Appendix C to reduce miscommunication.
- Because talking is "looser" than writing, people in a group can think they agree when they don't. Don't assume that because the discussion went smoothly, a draft written by one person will necessarily be acceptable.

Summary of Key Points

- **Interpersonal communication** is communication between people.
- In interpersonal communication, **hearing** denotes perceiving sounds. **Listening** means decoding and interpreting them correctly.
- To avoid listening errors caused by inattention,
  - Be conscious of the points you need to know and listen for them.
  - At the end of the conversation, check your understanding with the other person.
  - After the conversation, write down key points that affect deadlines or how work will be evaluated.
- To reduce listening errors caused by misinterpretation,
  - Don't ignore instructions you think are unnecessary.
  - Consider the other person's background and experiences. Why is this point important to the speaker?
  - Paraphrase what the speaker has said, giving him or her a chance to correct your understanding.
- In **active listening,** receivers actively demonstrate that they've heard and understood a speaker by feeding back either the literal meaning or the emotional content or both.
- Effective groups balance information leadership, interpersonal leadership, and procedural group management.
- The **standard agenda** is a seven-step process for solving problems. In **dot planning** the group brainstorms ideas. Then each individual affixes adhesive dots by the points or proposals he or she cares most about.
- A case study of six student groups completing class projects found that students in successful groups had leaders who set clear deadlines, scheduled frequent meetings, and dealt directly with conflict that emerged in the group; an inclusive decision-making style; and a higher proportion of members who worked actively on the project.

The Importance of Planning, II*

Higgins has a second piece of advice: Remember that different projects have lots in common. . . .

Higgins first learned this principle in the army, when he was in charge of supplying a Ranger battalion stationed at Fort Lewis, Washington. He led of unit of 120 people that supported 650 Rangers. Higgins and his team had to supply diverse missions in four different climates: mountain, tropical, desert, and arctic. The goal was to have the support group airborne, headed to meet the Rangers with the right equipment, 18 hours after receiving its orders. Under the previous leader, the . . . best time was 72 hours. Higgins's team eventually did the job in 12 hours.

How? "The previous team always waited until it knew where the mission was headed before assembling gear," Higgins says. "But a lot of what the Rangers need—food, medical supplies, ammunition—is the same no matter where they go." So Higgins and his unit figured out how to prepackage such supplies and how to pack them onto airplanes with maximum efficiency. "Focusing on what's common between projects [has] worked for us time and again."

*Quoted from Gina Imperato, "He's Become BankAmerica's 'Mr. Project,' " *Fast Company*, January 1998, 42–44.

- Students who spent the most time meeting with their groups got the highest grades.
- **Groupthink** is the tendency for groups to put such a high premium on agreement that they directly or indirectly punish dissent. The best correctives to groupthink are to consciously search for additional alternatives, to test one's assumptions against those of a range of other people, and to protect the right of each person in the group to disagree.
- **Conversational style** denotes our conversational patterns and the meaning we give to them: the way we show interest, politeness, and appropriateness.
- To resolve conflicts, first make sure that the people involved really disagree. Next, check to see that everyone's information is correct. Discover the needs each person is trying to meet. The **presenting problem** that surfaces as the subject of dissention may or may not be the real problem. Search for alternatives.
- Constructive ways to respond to criticism include paraphrasing, checking for feelings, checking inferences, and buying time with limited agreement.
- Use statements about your own feelings to own the problem and avoid attacking the audience. In conflict, *I* statements are good you-attitude!
- To make meetings more effective,
  - State the purpose of the meeting at the beginning.
  - Distribute an agenda that indicates whether each item is for information, for discussion, for action, and how long each is expected to take.
  - Allow enough time to discuss controversial issues.
  - Pay attention to people and process as well as to the task at hand.
  - If you don't take formal votes, summarize the group's consensus after each point. At the end of the meeting, summarize all decisions and remind the group who is responsible for implementing or following up on each item.
- **Collaborative writing** means working with other writers to produce a single document. Writers producing a joint document need to pay attention not only to the basic steps in the writing process but also to the processes of group formation and conflict resolution.

C h a p t e r 13

Exercises and Problems

Getting Started

13.1 Making Ethical Choices

Indicate whether you consider each of the following actions ethical, unethical, or a gray area. Which of the actions would you do? Which would you feel uncomfortable doing? Which would you refuse to do?

1. Taking home office supplies (e.g., pens, markers, calculators, etc.) for personal use.
2. Inflating your evaluation of a subordinate because you know that only people ranked *excellent* will get pay raises.
3. Making personal long-distance calls on the company phone.
4. Writing a feasibility report about a new product and de-emphasizing test results that show it could cause cancer.
5. Coming in to the office in the evening to use the company's word processor and computer for personal projects.
6. Designing an ad campaign for a cigarette brand.

7. Working as an accountant for a company that makes or advertises cigarettes.

8. Working as a manager in a company that exploits its nonunionized hourly workers.

9. Writing copy for a company's annual report hiding or minimizing the fact that the company pollutes the environment.

10. "Padding" your expense account by putting on it charges you did not pay for.

11. Writing a subscription letter for a sex magazine that glamorizes rape, violence, and sadism.

12. Doing the taxes of a client who publishes a sex magazine that glamorizes rape, violence, and sadism.

13. Telling a job candidate that the company "usually" grants cost-of-living raises every six months, even though you know that the company is losing money and plans to cancel cost-of-living raises for the next year.

14. Laughing at the racist or sexist jokes a client makes, even though you find them offensive.

15. Reading *The Wall Street Journal* on company time.

13.2   Identifying Responses That Show Active Listening

Which of the following responses show active listening? Which responses block communication?

1. Comment: Whenever I say something, the group just ignores me.

   Responses:

   a. That's because your ideas aren't very good. Do more planning before group meetings.

   b. Nobody listens to me, either.

   c. You're saying that nobody builds on your ideas.

2. Comment: I've done more than my share of work on this project. But the people who have been freeloading are going to get the same grade I've worked so hard to earn.

   Responses:

   a. Yes, we're all going to get the same grade.

   b. Are you afraid we won't do well on the assignment?

   c. It sounds like you feel resentful.

3. Comment: My parents are going to kill me if I don't have a job lined up when I graduate.

   Responses:

   a. You know they're exaggerating. They won't *really* kill you.

   b. Can you blame them? I mean, it's taken you six years to get a degree. Surely you've learned something to make you employable!

   c. If you act the way in interviews that you do in our class, I'm not surprised. Companies want people with good attitudes and good work ethics.

13.3   Practicing Active Listening

Go around the room for this exercise. In turn, let each student complain about something (large or small) that really bothers him or her. Then the next student(s) will

a. Offer a statement of limited agreement that would buy time.

b. Paraphrase the statement.

c. Check for feelings that might lie behind the statement.

d. Offer inferences that might motivate the statement.

13.4   Brainstorming Ways to Resolve Conflicts

Suggest one or more ways that each of the following groups could deal with the conflict(s) it faces.

1. Mike and Takashi both find writing hard. Elise has been getting better grades than either of them, so they offer to do all the research if she'll organize the document and write, revise, edit, and proofread it. Elise thinks that this method would leave her doing a disproportionate share of the work. Moreover, scheduling the work would be difficult, since she wouldn't know how good their research was until the last minute.

2. Because of their class and work schedules, Lars and Andrea want to hold group meetings from 8 to 10 PM, working later if need be. But Juan's wife works the evening shift, and he needs to be home with his children, two of whom have to be in bed before 8. He wants to meet from 8 to 10 AM, but the others don't want to meet that early.

3. Lynn wants to divide up the work exactly equally, with firm due dates. Marcia is trying to get into medical school. She says she'd rather do the lion's share of the work so that she knows it's good. (cont.)

Jessie's father is terminally ill. This group isn't very important in terms of what's going on in her life, and she knows she may have to miss some group meetings.

4. Sherry is aware that she is the person in her group who always points out the logical flaws in arguments: she's the one who reminds the group that they haven't done all the parts of the assignment. She doesn't want her group to turn in a flawed product, but she wonders whether the other group members see her as too critical.

5. Jim's group missed several questions on their group quiz. Talking to Tae-Suk after class, Jim learns that Tae-Suk knew all the answers. "Why didn't you say anything?" Jim asks angrily. Tae-Suk responds quietly, "Todd said that he knew the answers. I did not want to argue with him. We have to work together, and I do not want anyone to lose face."

13.5   Taking Minutes

As Your Instructor Directs, have two or more people take minutes of each class or collaborative group meeting for a week. Compare the accounts of the same meeting.

• To what extent do they agree on what happened?

• Does one contain information missing in other accounts?
• Do any accounts disagree on a specific fact?
• How do you account for the differences you find?

13.6   Keeping a Journal about a Group

As you work in a collaborative writing group, keep a journal after each group meeting.

• What happened?
• What roles did you play in the meeting?

• What conflicts arose? How were they handled?
• What strategies could you use to make the next meeting go smoothly?
• Record one observation about each group member.

E-Mail Messages

In Problems 13.7 through 13.10, assume that your group has been asked to recommend a solution.

As Your Instructor Directs,

• Send e-mail messages to group members laying out your initial point of view on the issue and discussing the various options.

• As a group, answer the message.
• Write a memo to your instructor telling how satisfied you are with
a. The decision your group reached.
b. The process you used to reach it.

13.7   Recommending Ways to Retain Workers

Assume that your small group comprises your organization's Labor-Management Committee. This e-mail arrives from the vice president for human resources:

> Subject: Retaining Workers
>
> As you know, it's a challenge to find employees who have the skills we want. To reduce the need to hire new people, we want to reduce turnover. What could we do to keep people happy? Please divide your recommendations into low-cost and high-cost solutions.

Write a group response recommending ways to retain workers.

Hint:
Agree on an office, factory, store, hospital, or other workplace to use for this problem.

13.8   Recommending a Fair Way to Assign Work around the Holidays

Assume that your small group comprises your organization's Labor-Management Committee. This e-mail arrives from the general manager:

> Subject: Allocating Holiday Hours
>
> As you know, lots of people want to take extra time off around holidays to turn three-day weekends into longer trips. But we do need to stay open. Right now, there are allegations that some supervisors give the time off to their friends. But even "fair" systems, such as giving more senior workers first choice at time off, or requiring that workers with crucial skills work, also create problems. And possibly we need a different system around Christmas, when many people want to take off a week or more, than around lesser holidays, when most people take only an extra day or two.
>
> Please recommend an equitable way to decide how to assign hours.

Write a group response recommending the best way to assign hours.

Hint:
Agree on an office, factory, store, hospital, or other workplace to use for this problem.

13.9   Judging Suggestions

Assume that your small group comprises your organization's Suggestion Committee. Employees submit suggestions that will save money or improve quality, procedures, or morale. Your committee must decide whether to accept, partially accept, or reject each suggestion.

1.
> From: Tresita Red Owl
>
> Subject: Suggestion to Change Sick-Leave Policy
>
> Right now, employees can "cash in" their unused sick-leave days each year, and many people do that. The trouble with that is that people have too few days left if they need to have major surgery or chemotherapy. I recommend that we change the policy to allow people to "cash in" unused sick-leave days only when they retire or quit their jobs.

2.
> From: Doug Williams
>
> Subject: Suggestion—Open Corporate Store
>
> We should have a store. I visited a friend whose company had a store with company-logo clothing, toys, and sundries (mugs, mouse pads, etc.) as well as greeting cards, snacks, and so forth.

3.
> From: Craig De Stephano
>
> Subject: Suggestion: Allow Pets at Work
>
> We should let people bring pets to work. Pets reduce stress and blood pressure. People like Justin's seeing-eye dog.

As Your Instructor Directs,

a. Write minutes summarizing the committee decision and your reason for it.

b. Write a message to the suggestor, informing him or her of your decision.

13.10 Recommending Whether a Mall Should Hire Ethnic Santas

Assume that your small group comprises a committee of store managers elected from all of the managers in a large mall. You get this e-mail from the committee chair:

> Subject: Ethnic Santas?
>
> We've received several complaints that the men we hire to be Santas are always white. Should we change that policy? If so, what to?

Write a group response recommending what the ethnic makeup of people hired to be Santas at the mall should be.

Web Pages

As Your Instructor Directs, in Problems 13.11 through 13.13,

a. Turn in two laser copies of your page(s). On another page, give the URL for each link.
b. Turn in one laser copy of your page(s) and a disk with the HTML code and .gif files.
c. Write a group memo to your instructor (1) identifying the audience for which the page is

designed and explaining (2) the search strategies you used to find material on this topic, (3) why you chose the pages and information you've included, (4) why you chose the layout and graphics you've used, and (5) who did what on the project.
d. Present your page orally to the class.

13.11 Creating a Web Page for a Campus Group

Create a Web page for a campus group that does not yet have one.

13.12 Creating a Web Page for Multicultural Managers and Workers

1. Create a Web page for multicultural managers. What links would help managers better understand the multicultural Workforce 2000?
2. Create a Web page for members of a group that has not traditionally been part of the power structure of US business. (The group could be defined by class, gender, race and ethnicity, religion, physical ability, age, sexual orientation, or education.) What links would provide support to members of this group and help them attain their full potential in their work lives?
3. Create a Web page for a nonprofit, business, or government organization devoted to the advancement of a group that has not traditionally been part of the power structure of US business. (The group could be defined by class, gender, race and ethnicity, religion, physical ability, age, sexual orientation, or education.) You must choose an organization that does not already have a Web page.

13.13 Creating a Web Page on a Topic of Your Choice

Create a Web page on a topic of your choice. Possibilities include

· Information for students new to your campus.
· Study tips for students in your major.
· Links about speakers, bands, or events coming to your town.

· Links to advice about online résumés and to good (and poor) résumés on the Web.
· Information about how to construct a Web page.

Memo and Brochure Assignments

13.14 Answering an Ethics Question

Assume that your small group comprises your organization's Ethics Committee. You receive the following anonymous note:

> People are routinely using the company letterhead to write letters to members of Congress, senators, and even the president stating their positions on various issues. Making their opinions known is of course their right, but doing so on letterhead stationery implies that they are speaking for the company, which they are not.
>
> I think that the use of letterhead for anything other than official company business should be prohibited.

Determine the best solution to the problem. Then write a message to all employees stating your decision and building support for it.

13.15 Answering an Inquiry about Photos

You've just been named Vice President for Diversity, the first person in your organization to hold this position.

Today, you receive this memo from Sheila Lathan, who edits the employee newsletter.

> Subject: Photos in the Employee Newsletter
>
> Please tell me what to do about photos in the monthly employee newsletter. I'm concerned that almost no single issue represents the diversity of employees we have here.
>
> As you know, our layout allows two visuals each month. One of those is always the employee of the month (EM). In the last year, most of those have been male and all but two have been white. What makes it worse is that people want photos that make them look good. You may remember that Ron Olmos was the EM two months ago; in the photo he wanted me to use, you can't tell that he's in a wheelchair. Often the EM is the only photo; the other visual is often a graph of sales or something relating to quality.
>
> Even if the second visual is another photo, it may not look balanced in terms of gender and race. After all, 62% of our employees are men, and 78% are white. Should the pictures try to represent those percentages? The leadership positions (both in management and in the union) are even more heavily male and white. Should we run pictures of people doing important things, and risk continuing the imbalance?
>
> I guess I could use more visuals, but then there wouldn't be room for as many stories—and people really like to see their names in print. Plus, giving people information about company activities and sales is important to maintaining goodwill. A bigger newsletter would be one way to have more visuals and keep the content, but with the cost-cutting measures we're under, that doesn't look likely.
>
> What should I do?

As Your Instructor Directs,

a. Work in a small group with other students to come up with a recommendation for Sheila.

b. Write a memo responding to her.

c. Write an article for the employee newsletter about the photo policy you recommend and how it relates to the company's concern for diversity.

13.16 Writing a Meeting Manual

Create a manual for students next term telling them how to have effective meetings as they work on collaborative projects.

Source: Adapted from Miles McCall, Beth Stewart, and Timothy Clipson, "Teaching Communication Skills for Meeting Management," *1998 Refereed Proceedings*, Association for Business Communication Southwestern United States, ed. Marsha L. Bayless (Nacogdoches, TX), 68.

13.17 Planning a Game

Many companies are using games and contests to solve problems in an enjoyable way. One company promised to give everyone $30 a month extra if they got the error rate below 0.5%. The rate improved immediately. After several successful months, the incentive went to $40 a month for getting it under 0.3% and finally to $50 a month for getting it under 0.2%. Another company offered workers two "well hours" if they got in by 7 AM every day for a month. An accounting and financial-services company divided its employees into two teams. The one that got the most referrals and new accounts received a meal prepared and served by the losing team (the firm paid for the food). Games are best when the people who will play them create them. Games need to make business sense and give rewards to many people, not just a few. Rewards should be small.

Think of a game or contest that could improve productivity or quality in your classroom, on campus, or in a workplace you know well.

As Your Instructor Directs,

a. Write a message to persuade your instructor, boss, or other decision maker to authorize the game or contest.

b. Write a message announcing the game and persuading people to participate in it.

Source: Based on John Case, *The Open-Book Experience: Lessons from Over 100 Companies Who Successfully Transformed Themselves* (Reading, MA: Addison-Wesley, 1998), 129–201.

13.18 Creating Brochures

In a collaborative group, create a series of brochures for an organization and present your design and copy to the class in a group oral presentation. Your brochures should work well as a series but also be capable of standing alone if a reader picks up just one. They should share a common visual design and be appropriate for your purposes and audience. You may use sketches rather than photos or finished drawings. Text, however, should be as it will appear in the final copy.

As you prepare your series, talk to a knowledgeable person in the organization. For this assignment, as long as the person is knowledgeable, he or she does not have to have the power to approve the brochures.

In a manila folder, turn in

1. Two copies of each brochure.
2. A copy of your approved proposal (see Chapter 14).
3. A narrative explaining (a) how you responded to the wishes of the person in the organization who was your contact and (b) five of the choices you made in terms of content, visuals, and design and why you made these choices.

13.19 Interviewing Workers about Listening

Interview someone who works in an organization about his or her on-the-job listening. Possible questions to ask include the following:

· Whom do you listen to as part of your job? Your superior? Subordinates? (How many levels down?) Customers or clients? Who else?
· How much time a day do you spend listening?
· What people do you talk to as part of your job? Do you feel they hear what you say? How do you tell whether or not they're listening?
· Do you know of any problems that came up because someone didn't listen? What happened?

· What do you think prevents people from listening effectively? What advice would you have for someone on how to listen more accurately?

As Your Instructor Directs,

a. Share your information with a small group of students in your class.

b. Present your findings orally to the class.

c. Present your findings in a memo to your instructor.

d. Join with other students to present your findings in a group report.

13.20 Analyzing the Dynamics of a Group

Analyze the dynamics of a task group of which you are a member. Answer the following questions:

1. Who was the group's leader? How did the leader emerge? Were there any changes in or challenges to the original leader?

2. Describe the contribution each member made to the group and the roles each person played.

3. Did any members of the group officially or unofficially drop out? Did anyone join after the group had begun working? How did you deal with the loss or addition of a group member, both in terms of getting the work done and in terms of helping people work together?

4. What planning did your group do at the start of the project? Did you stick to the plan or revise it? How did the group decide that revision was necessary?

5. How did your group make decisions? Did you vote? reach decisions by consensus?

6. What problems or conflicts arose? Did the group deal with them openly? To what extent did they interfere with the group's task?

7. Evaluate your group both in terms of its task and in terms of the satisfaction members felt. How did this group compare with other task groups you've been part of? What made it better or worse?

As you answer the questions,

- Be honest. You won't lose points for reporting that your group had problems or did something "wrong."

- Show your knowledge of good group dynamics. That is, if your group did something wrong, show that you know what *should* have been done. Similarly, if your group worked well, show that you know *why* it worked well.

- Be specific. Give examples or anecdotes to support your claims.

As Your Instructor Directs,

a. Discuss these questions with the other group members.

b. Present your findings orally to the class.

c. Present your findings in an individual memo to your instructor.

d. Join with the other group members to write a collaborative memo to your instructor.

Four

Reports

Chapter Fourteen

Planning, Proposing, and Researching Reports 364

Chapter Fifteen

Analyzing Information and Writing Reports 404

Chapter Sixteen

Using Graphs and Other Visuals 456

Chapter Seventeen

Making Oral Presentations 482

14

Planning, Proposing, and Researching Reports

Varieties of Reports

Defining Report Problems

Writing Proposals
- Proposals for Class Research Projects
- Sales Proposals
- Proposals for Funding
- Figuring the Budget

Writing Progress Reports
- Chronological Progress Reports
- Task Progress Reports
- Recommendation Progress Reports

Research Strategies for Reports
- Finding Information Online and in Print
- Evaluating Web Sources
- Designing Questions for Surveys and Interviews
- Conducting Surveys and Interviews
- Observing Customers and Users

Using and Documenting Sources

Summary of Key Points

Planning, Proposing, and Researching Reports

James B. Lane | *Partner, Ernst & Young LLP*

A specialist in business change management, Jim Lane leads the High Growth/Middle Market sector consulting group in Ernst & Young's Columbus, Ohio, office. One of the Big Five, Ernst & Young is one of the world's leading accounting, tax, and consulting firms, delivering innovative ideas to US and global clients in a wide variety of industries.

A recent competitive bidding process for what I'll call ABC Motors illustrates three key points about sales proposals.

Be Prepared to Work Quickly.

Three days after the request for proposals came out, we met with ABC's CFO. That was a Wednesday. Before the weekend was out, we had established a proposal war room complete with white boards, LAN access, a PC projection system, and a globally accessible Lotus Notes database for sharing proposal work products across the planet. Three weeks after the initial meeting, we presented the winning proposal in a facsimile of ABC's office space complete with desks, computers, graphical posters, and a 3,000-step mural-size work plan outlining the changes we proposed.

> 66 *In order to win consistently, you must listen to the client.* 99

Study Your Audience and the Problem.

In order to win consistently, you must listen to the client. Design your proposal to meet the client's spoken and unspoken needs.

We assembled a team of 15 subject-matter experts to work one-on-one with client personnel in a two-day information-gathering session. We used what we learned to propose eliminating work steps which did not contribute value to the client. Redesigning the work would reduce costs and increase return on investment. This focus on value also enabled us to identify an opportunity related to but not part of the original RFP.

Identify Win Themes.

The written proposal, your oral presentation, your attire, and the staff associated with the sale must all join in a harmonious whole. Focus on a few key messages. Our Win themes included our automotive industry experience, our technical depth in related areas, our program management capabilities, and our knowledge management and reuse processes.

We tailored our themes to competitive information we heard from the client. Key among these was the revelation that the competitor who held the current contract for services had not interacted effectively with ABC's senior executives. To exploit this weakness, we included specific steps in the proposed work plan to assist stakeholders in the company to buy into and support the project.

Summary.

As a result of intense work, audience analysis, and insight, we won a seven-figure contract for the firm.

P roposals and reports depend on research. The research may be as simple as pulling up data with a computer program or as complicated as calling many different people, conducting focus groups and surveys, or even planning and conducting experiments. Care in planning, proposing, and researching reports is needed to produce reliable data.

In writing any report, there are five basic steps:

1. Define the problem.
2. Gather the necessary data and information.
3. Analyze the data and information.
4. Organize the information.
5. Write the report.

After reviewing the varieties of reports, this chapter focuses on the first two steps. Chapter 15 discusses the last three steps.

Varieties of Reports

Many kinds of documents are called *reports*. In some organizations, a report is a long document or a document that contains numerical data. In others, one- and two-page memos are called *reports*. A short report to a client may use letter format. **Formal reports** contain formal elements such as a title page, a transmittal, a table of contents, and a list of illustrations. **Informal reports** may be letters and memos or even computer printouts of production or sales figures. But all reports, whatever their length or degree of formality, provide the information that people in organizations need to make plans and solve problems.

Reports can just provide information, both provide information and analyze it, or provide information and analysis to support a recommendation (see Figure 14.1). Reports can be called **information reports** if they collect data for the reader, **analytical reports** if they interpret data but do not recommend action, and **recommendation reports** if they recommend action or a solution.

The following reports can be information, analytical, or recommendation reports, depending on what they provide:

Figure 14.1

Three Levels of Reports

Reports can provide

Information only

- **Sales reports** (sales figures for the week or month).
- **Quarterly reports** (figures showing a plant's productivity and profits for the quarter).

Information plus analysis

- **Annual reports** (financial data and an organization's accomplishments during the past year).
- **Audit reports** (interpretations of the facts revealed during an audit).
- **Make-good** or **pay-back reports** (calculations of the point at which a new capital investment will pay for itself).

Information plus analysis plus a recommendation

- **Feasibility reports** evaluate two or more alternatives and recommend which alternative the organization should choose.
- **Justification reports** justify the need for a purchase, an investment, a new personnel line, or a change in procedure.
- **Problem-solving reports** identify the causes of an organizational problem and recommend a solution.

- **Accident reports** can simply list the nature and causes of accidents in a factory or office. These reports can also recommend ways to make conditions safer.
- **Credit reports** can simply summarize an applicant's income and other credit obligations. These reports can also evaluate the applicant's collateral and creditworthiness.
- **Progress** and **interim reports** can simply record the work done so far and the work remaining on a project. These reports can also recommend that a project be stopped, continued, or restructured.
- **Trip reports** can simply share what the author learned at a conference or during a visit to a customer or supplier. These reports can also recommend action based on that information.
- **Closure reports** can simply document the causes of a failure or of research that is not economically or technically feasible for new products under current conditions. They can also recommend action to prevent such failures in the future.

Defining Report Problems

Good report problems grow out of real problems: disjunctions between reality and the ideal, choices that must be made. When you write a report as part of your job, the organization may define the topic. To think of problems for class reports, think about problems that face your college or university; housing units on campus; social, religious, and professional groups on campus and in your city; local businesses; and city, county, state, and federal governments and their agencies. Read your campus and local papers and newsmagazines; watch the news on TV or listen to it on National Public Radio.

A good report problem in business or administration meets the following criteria:

1. The problem is
   - Real.
   - Important enough to be worth solving.
   - Narrow but challenging.
2. The audience for the report is
   - Real.
   - Able to implement the recommended action.
3. The data, evidence, and facts are
   - Sufficient to document the severity of the problem.
   - Sufficient to prove that the recommendation will solve the problem.
   - Available to *you*.
   - Comprehensible to *you*.

Often problems need to be narrowed. For example, "improving the college experiences of international students studying in the United States" is far too broad. First, choose one college or university. Second, identify the specific problem. Do you want to increase the social interaction between US and international students? Help international students find housing? Increase the number of ethnic grocery stores and restaurants? Third, identify the specific audience that would have the power to implement your recommendations. Depending on the specific topic, the audience might be the Office of International Studies, the residence hall counselors, a service organization on campus or in town, a store, or a group of investors.

The Questions behind the Question*

Barbara Waugh is Worldwide Personnel Manager at Hewlett Packard Labs. Five years ago, she was asked to investigate the following question: Why wasn't HP labs ranked as the best in the business?

To answer that question, she asked even more basic questions: What does it mean to be the "best" research lab? Having the most Nobel laureates? Filing the most patents? What would it take to become "the best"? Hire more people? Different people? Start different projects? Market current projects better?

A survey asking those questions yielded 800 single-spaced pages of data. She distilled the data into challenges in three areas. *Programs:* HP labs needed clearer priorities and fewer projects. *People:* HP needed to get rid of poor performers more quickly and give good workers more freedom. *Processes:* People needed to share information more effectively.

*Quoted from Katherine Mieszkowski, "I Grew Up Thinking That Change Was Cataclysmic. The Way We've Done It Here Is to Start Slow and Work Small," *Fast Company*, December 1998, 149–50.

Definitions and Problem Solving*

Microscan asked its sales force to identify "customer defectors." At first, salespeople assumed that a "defector" was a former customer who no longer bought anything. By that definition, very few defectors existed.

But then the term was redefined as customers who had stopped buying *some* products and services. By this definition, quite a few defectors existed. And the fact that each of them had turned to a competitor for some of what they used to buy from Microscan showed that improvements—and improved profits—were possible.

*Based on Frederick F. Reichheld, "Learning from Customer Defects," *Harvard Business Review*, March–April 1996, 56–69.

Pick a problem you can solve in the time available. Six months of full-time (and overtime) work and a team of colleagues might allow you to look at all the ways to make a store more profitable. If you're doing a report in 6 to 12 weeks for a class that is only one of your responsibilities, limit the topic. Depending on your interests and knowledge, you could choose to examine the prices and styles of clothes a store carried, its inventory procedures, its overhead costs, its layout and decor, or its advertising budget.

How you define the problem shapes the solutions you find. For example, suppose that a manufacturer of frozen foods isn't making money. If the problem is defined as a marketing problem, the researcher may analyze the product's price, image, advertising, and position in the market. But perhaps the problem is really that overhead costs are too high due to poor inventory management, or that an inadequate distribution system doesn't get the product to its target market. Defining the problem accurately is essential to finding an effective solution.

Once you've defined your problem, you're ready to write a purpose statement. The purpose statement goes both in your proposal and in your final report. A good **purpose statement** makes three things clear:

* The organizational problem or conflict.
* The specific technical questions that must be answered to solve the problem.
* The rhetorical purpose (to explain, to recommend, to request, to propose) the report is designed to achieve.

The following purpose statement has all three elements. The report's audience is the Superintendent of Yellowstone National Park.

> Current management methods keep the elk population within the carrying capacity of the habitat but require frequent human intervention. Both wildlife conservation specialists and the public would prefer methods that controlled the elk population naturally. This report will compare the current short-term management techniques (hunting, trapping and transporting, and winter feeding) with two long-term management techniques, habitat modification and the reintroduction of predators. The purpose of this report is to recommend which techniques or combination of techniques would best satisfy the needs of conservationists, hunters, and the public.

To write a good purpose statement, you must understand the basic problem and have some idea of the questions that your report will answer. Note, however, that you can (and should) write the purpose statement before researching the specific alternatives the report will discuss.

Writing Proposals

Proposals suggest a method for finding information or solving a problem.[1] Finding the information or solving the problem helps an organization decide whether to change, decide how to change, or implement a change that is agreed on. (See Figure 14.2.)

As Donna Kienzler points out, proposals have two goals: to get the project accepted and to get you accepted to do the job. Proposals must stress reader benefits and provide specific supporting details. Attention to details—including good visual impact and proofreading—helps establish your professional image and suggests that you'd give the same care to the project if your proposal is accepted.[2]

Proposals may be competitive or noncompetitive. **Competitive proposals** compete against each other for limited resources. When you collaborate on a group report, each student may propose a topic; only one can be accepted. Similarly, applications for research funding are often very competitive. The National Science Foundation, for example, funds only 12% of the proposals submitted.[3] Many companies will bid for corporate or government contracts, but only one will be accepted. **Noncompetitive proposals** have no real competition. For example, a company could accept all of the internal proposals it thought would save money or improve quality. Similarly, when students write proposals for reports or theses, the proposals compete not against each other but against standards for doing good research. Therefore, all of the proposals can be accepted. And often a company that is satisfied with a vendor asks for a noncompetitive proposal to renew the contract.

To write a good proposal, you need to have a clear view of the problem you hope to solve and the kind of research or other action needed to solve it. A proposal must answer the following questions convincingly:

- **What problem are you going to solve?** Show that you understand the problem and the organization's needs. Define the problem as the audience sees it, even if you believe that the presenting problem is part of a larger problem that must first be solved.

- **How are you going to solve it?** Prove that your methods are feasible. Show that a solution can be found in the time available. Specify the topics you'll investigate. Explain how you'll gather data.

- **What exactly will you provide for us?** Specify the tangible products you'll produce; explain how you'll evaluate them.

- **Can you deliver what you promise?** Show that you have the knowledge, the staff, and the facilities to do what you say you will. Describe your previous work in this area, your other qualifications, and the qualifications of any people who will be helping you.

- **What benefits can you offer?** In a sales proposal, several vendors may be able to supply the equipment needed. Show why the company should hire you. Discuss the benefits—direct and indirect—that your firm can provide.

- **When will you complete the work?** Provide a detailed schedule showing when each phase of the work will be completed.

- **How much will you charge?** Provide a detailed budget that includes costs for materials, salaries, and overhead.

Government agencies and companies often issue Requests for Proposals, known as **RFPs**. Follow the RFP exactly when you respond to a proposal. Competitive proposals are often scored by giving points in each category. Evalua-

Planning a Proposal*

As an Associate Planner for Leo Burnett, I answer key marketing and communication questions to support strategic planning for our clients. . . .

Either the client or someone at the agency asks "Why?" Why do children flip over hamburgers at their favorite restaurants? Why have teens embraced the fashions of the 70s? The questions never end.

Once we identify what we need to know, we usually set up a brainstorming meeting among key agency team members. . . . Here we develop an action plan, which is presented to the client in a written proposal. The proposal outlines the project background (what led to the initiative), the objectives of the project (what we hope to learn), the recommended methods (how and by whom the study will be conducted), the timeline and cost, and any next steps that need to be taken.

*Quoted from Kendra Hatcher to Kitty Locker, March 26, 1997.

Company's current situation	The proposal offers to	The final report will provide
We don't know whether we should change.	Assess whether change is a good idea.	Insight, recommending whether change is desirable.
We need to/want to change, but we don't know exactly what we need to do.	Develop a plan to achieve desired goal.	A plan for achieving the desired change.
We need to/want to change, and we know what to do, but we need help doing it.	Implement the plan, increase (or decrease) measurable outcomes.	A record of the implementation and evaluation process.

Figure 14.2

Relationship among Situation, Proposal, and Final Report

Source: Adapted from Richard C. Freed, Shervin Freed, and Joseph D. Romano, *Writing Winning Proposals: Your Guide to Landing the Client, Making the Sale, Persuading the Boss* (New York: McGraw-Hill, 1995), p. 21.

In-House Proposals*

There is no better way to kick-start a career than acting like an entrepreneur. . . .

That's exactly what P. J. Smoot, head of training and development at International Paper in Chicago, did. When she joined International Paper in 1980, she was in the finance department. "I noticed that there wasn't a lot of career development or training going on, except at the college recruitment level, and I saw a real need for it."

So she wrote a proposal to the HR department, where they liked it so much, they hired her to put her ideas into practice. What started as an 18-month assignment has evolved into a full-fledged companywide training program. Smoot, who oversees the program, has since won six promotions—all because she saw a way to help her company and then acted on it.

*Quoted from Anne Fisher, "Six Ways to Supercharge Your Career," *Fortune,* January 13, 1997, 48.

tors look only under the heads specified in the RFP. If information isn't there, the proposal gets no points in that category.

Proposals for Class Research Projects

You may be asked to submit a proposal for a report that you will write for a class. Even when the report and the assignment are addressed to a real person in a real organization, your instructor is the audience for the proposal. Your instructor wants evidence that your problem is not too big and not too small, that you understand it, that your method will give you the information you need, and that you have the knowledge and resources to collect and analyze the data.

A proposal for a student report usually has the following sections:

1. In your first paragraph (no heading), summarize in a sentence or two the topic and purposes of your report.
2. **Problem.** What organizational problem exists? What is wrong? Why does it need to be solved? Is there a history or background that is relevant?
3. **Feasibility.** Are you sure that a solution can be found in the time available? How do you know?
4. **Audience.** Who in the organization would have the power to implement your recommendation? What secondary audiences might be asked to evaluate your report? What audiences would be affected by your recommendation? Will anyone in the organization serve as a gatekeeper, determining whether your report is sent to decision makers? What watchdog audiences might read the report?

   For each of these audiences and for your initial audience (your instructor), give the person's name, job title, and business address and answer the following questions:

   • What is the audience's major concern or priority? What "hot buttons" must you address with care?

   • What will the audience see as advantages of your proposal? What objections, if any, is the reader likely to have?

   • How interested is the audience in the topic of your report?

   • How much does the audience know about the topic of your report?

   List any terms, concepts, equations, or assumptions that one or more of your audiences may need to have explained. Briefly identify ways in which your audiences may affect the content, organization, or style of the report.

5. **Topics to investigate.** List the questions and subquestions you will answer in your report, the topics or concepts you will explain, the aspects of the problem you will discuss. Indicate how deeply you will examine each of the aspects you plan to treat. Explain your rationale for choosing to discuss some aspects of the problem and not others.
6. **Methods/procedure.** How will you get answers to your questions? Whom will you interview or survey? Provide a draft of your questions. What published sources will you use? Give the full bibliographic references.

   Your METHODS section should clearly indicate how you will get the information needed to answer the questions in the TOPICS TO INVESTIGATE section.

7. **Qualifications/facilities/resources.** Do you have the knowledge and skills needed to conduct this study? Do you have adequate access to the organization? Do you have access to any equipment you will need to conduct your research (computer, books, etc.)? Where will you turn for help if you hit an unexpected snag?

You'll be more convincing if you have already scheduled an interview, checked out books, or printed out online sources.

8. **Work schedule.** List both the total time you plan to spend on and the date when you expect to finish each of the following activities:

    - Gathering information.
    - Analyzing information.
    - Preparing the progress report.
    - Organizing information.
    - Writing the draft.
    - Revising the draft.
    - Preparing the visuals.
    - Editing the draft.
    - Proofreading the report.

    Answer this question either in a chart or in a calendar. A good schedule provides realistic estimates for each activity, allows time for unexpected snags, and shows that you can complete the work on time.

9. **Call to action.** In your final section, indicate that you'd welcome any suggestions your instructor may have for improving the research plan. Ask your instructor to approve your proposal so that you can begin work on your report.

Figure 14.3 shows a student proposal for a long report using survey research.

 For an example of a proposal for a long report based on library research, see the BAC Web site.

Sales Proposals

To sell expensive goods or services, you may be asked to submit a proposal.

Be sure that you understand the buyer's priorities. A phone company lost a $36 million sale to a university because it assumed the university's priority would be cost. Instead, the university wanted a state-of-the-art system. The university accepted a higher bid.

Don't assume that the buyer will understand why your product or system is good. For everything you offer, show the reader benefits (➤ p. 72) of each feature. Be sure to present the benefits using you-attitude (➤ p. 34). Consider using psychological description (➤ p. 233) to make the benefits vivid.

Use language appropriate for your audience. Even if the buyers want a state-of-the-art system, they may not want the level of detail that your staff could provide; they may not understand or appreciate technical jargon (➤ p. 96).

Sales proposals, particularly for complicated systems costing millions of dollars, are often long. Provide a one-page cover letter to present your proposal succinctly. The best organization for this letter is a modified version of the sales pattern in Chapter 11:

1. Catch the reader's attention and summarize up to three major benefits you offer.
2. Discuss each of the major benefits in the order in which you mentioned them in the first paragraph.
3. Deal with any objections or concerns the reader may have.
4. Mention other benefits briefly.
5. Ask the reader to approve your proposal and provide a reason for acting promptly.

Research for a Proposal*

Patti Douglas, Customer Service Representative for Phelps County Bank in Rolla, Missouri, proposed that her bank implement a marketing program for mature adults. To get the information she needed for her proposal, she

- Read articles in trade journals about mature-adult programs.
- Visited local competitors to find out what (if any) programs they offered for mature adults.
- Called the National Center of Health Statistics to find out how long people lived.
- Asked the switchboard operator to track inquiries about a program for mature adults.
- Found out how much free customer checks and other services for mature adults would cost.
- Assembled a group of current customers to find out what benefits would attract mature adults.

*Based on phone interview with Kitty Locker, January 26, 1994.

Figure 14.3 | *Proposal for a Student Report Using Survey Research*

October 15, 2000

To: Kitty O. Locker

From: Natalie M. Rogal *NMR*

In subject line ①indicate that this is a proposal ② specify the kind of report ③ specify the topic.

Subject: Proposal to Write a Report Recommending the Best Summer Internship Program for FFI Health Services

Summarize topic and purposes of report.

Many companies use summer internship programs to recruit and "try out" students who will eventually become permanent employees. FFI Health Services does not have such a program. It is interested in creating a program that will attract quality applicants. Using survey data, materials available on campus and on the Web, and my own experience, I will design an internship program that will meet FFI's needs.

Background on FFI Health Services

Background gives your reader information needed to understand the problem.

FFI Rx Health Services is a small prescription benefit management company based in Macedonia, Ohio. Started five years ago with only two employees, it has experienced explosive growth. It now has 43 employees in the Macedonia office and 7 in Tampa, Florida. Gross profits this year will be approximately $60 million. One of the founders, Mr. Paul Wutz, sees the company as a sort of "niche player" in the health care industry. He recognizes that he cannot compete on equal terms with the largest competitors who are owned as subsidiaries of major pharmaceutical companies. He describes his company as no longer simply providing traditional prescription benefits but rather as being an entrepreneurial marketing company working with pharmacy retailers and manufacturers.

Background on Summer Internships

Not all proposals need background sections.

Student advisors strongly encourage students to pursue co-ops and internships for a variety of reasons, including developing career interests and establishing career goals. The best students aggressively seek internships and use their summer experiences to narrow the field of possible employers. Without an internship program, a company is cutting itself off from some of the most determined and well-rounded undergraduates. Companies can use internship programs to screen permanent hires. Watching a person for three months gives much more information about a person's work ethic and his or her ability to interact with customers or clients than can any interview. Student workers have proven an excellent resource for filling temporary or special needs. They are positively motivated because the work relates to their educational objectives and career interests.

Problem

This problem is unusually simple. Many problems need several paragraphs of explanation.

FFI Rx Health Services does not have an internship program that would help it attract high-potential undergraduate students. Currently the company conducts national searches for managerial positions and runs classified ads in local papers for lower-level jobs. An internship program would enable the company to "grow" its own managers.

If "Problem" section is detailed and well-written, you may be able to use it unchanged in your report.

Proposal to Write a Recommendation Report on Internships
October 15, 2000
Page 2

Feasibility   *Convince your instructor that you have a backup plan if your original proposal proves unworkable.*

I expect that my research will enable me to recommend a program for FFI. However, if FFI is unable to fund the kind of program necessary, or if none of the models I can find will work for FFI, I will recommend that the company delay implementing a program until circumstances change.

Audiences   *Identify the kinds of audiences and the major concerns or priority of each.*

All of my audiences are at least somewhat interested in the topic of my report. None of them are hostile to it, so I will be able to present information straightforwardly. The topic is not particularly technical, so everyone should be able to understand my report easily.

My primary audience is Mr. Paul Wutz, partner of FFI Health Services, Macedonia, Ohio. He has the power to approve my plan. He describes himself as the Human Resources Department and is concerned about the time that would be needed for current staff to train and supervise interns. Still he is open to the idea and currently views an internship program as a kind of philanthropic effort. He also appreciates the fact that I am acting as an outside consultant at no charge to conduct this study for his company.

You are my initial audience. You've told me that you know a moderate amount about internship programs and are interested in them.

Secondary audiences for my report include the workers at FFI who would train and supervise interns, the students who might apply for internships, and the campus placement offices that help students find internships. Most of these people would welcome additional internship programs.

Topics to Investigate   *Indicate what you'll discuss briefly and what you'll discuss in more detail. This list should match your audience's concerns.*

I will investigate the following topics in detail:

1. What do students want from the internship experience?
   - How do students view internships? (a chance to get experience? build a résumé? make connections? a way to get a permanent job?)
   - What do interns want from a summer experience?
   - How willing would Ohio State students be to accept internships at FFI? (interest in managed health care as a field, willingness to spend the summer in Cleveland)

   All items in list must be grammatically parallel. Here, all are questions.

2. What kinds of internship experiences can the company offer?
   - What resources are available to train, mentor, and supervise interns?
   - What interesting, meaningful assignments could the company have interns do?

   If it is well-written, "Topics to Investigate" section will become the "Scope" section of the report —with minor revisions.

3. What models of internships are available?
   - What do interns typically do?
   - What features should a program have?
   - What are common problems and how can FFI avoid them?

I will briefly discuss the advantages to students and the company of summer internships and how interns and internship programs can be evaluated.

Proposal to Write a Recommendation Report on Internships
October 15, 2000
Page 3

Indicate any topics relevant to your report that you choose not to discuss.

I do not plan to discuss how the internship program should be publicized or at what schools the company should focus its recruiting efforts.

If you'll administer a survey or conduct interviews, tell how many subjects you'll have, how you'll choose them, and what you'll ask them.

Methods

If you're writing a report based on library research, list 10-15 sources that look relevant. Give full bibliographic citations.

I expect to get data from three sources: (1) a survey of Ohio State students to learn what features are important to them in an internship; (2) interviews with Mr. Wutz and other workers at FFI to discover the company's needs and resources; and (3) material on internships from the Fisher College of Business Placement Office, the Web, and my own experience coordinating an internship program last summer.

A draft of my survey questions is attached. Ideally, I would like to get a list of business students and send the survey to a random sample of about 200 students (hoping for at least 100 responses). If that is not possible, I will need to use a convenience sample.

Qualifications

Cite knowledge and skills from other classes, jobs, and activities that will will enable you to conduct the research and interpret your data.

As a student in Rhetoric and Composition at Ohio State with a focus in business writing, I have done much research and writing. I am also employed by a large international law firm for which I do administrative and analytical work. Last summer I coordinated and evaluated the summer internship program. I am familiar with strategies involved in organizing and maintaining an internship program.

Work Schedule

The following schedule will enable me to complete the report by the due date.

Activity	Total Time	Completion Date	
Gathering information	25 hours	Nov. 12	
Analyzing information	10 hours	Nov. 19	*Time needed will depend on the length and topic of the report, your knowledge of the topic, and your writing skills.*
Preparing the progress report	3 hours	Oct. 27	
Organizing information	5 hours	Nov. 22	
Writing the draft/Drafting visuals	15 hours	Nov. 29	
Revising draft and visuals	12 hours	Dec. 6	
Editing	7 hours *Allow plenty*	Dec. 8	
Proofreading	3 hours *of time!*	Dec. 10	

Good reports need good revision, editing, and proofreading as well as good research.

Call to Action

Could we set up a conference to discuss my proposal and survey draft? I would welcome any suggestions you may have for improving the research plan or making the report better. Please approve this proposal so that I can begin work on my report.

It's tactful to indicate you'll accept suggestions. End on a positive note.

In your introductory ¶,
① tell how to return the survey
② tell how the information will be used

Survey on Internships

Please answer the following questions and return the completed survey to the person who gave it to you. All information will be confidential and used only for a class project examining the feasibility of establishing an internship program for a particular business.

1. Major _____

2. Rank: First Year _____

Start with   Sophomore _____
easy–to–answer   Junior _____
questions   Senior _____

3. How important it is to you to have one or more internships before you graduate?
   ___ Very important
   ___ Somewhat important   *Put directions in*
   ___ Not important   *parentheses to*
                                    separate them from the
Branch   *question itself.*
questions
allow
reader 4. Did you have an internship last summer?
to skip   ___ Yes   ___ No (Skip to Question 6.)
questions.

5. What were the most beneficial aspects of your internship? (Check all that apply.)
   ___ Work related to my major
   ___ Likely to get a job offer/got a job offer
   ___ Chance to explore my interests
   ___ Made connections
   ___ Worked with clients
   ___ Looks good on my résumé
   ___ Other (Please explain.)

6. How much money did you make last summer? (Approximate hourly rate, before taxes)

Give readers
information   _____
they need to understand your question.
   ❑ Check here if you did not make any
   money last summer.

7. For next summer, could you afford to take an unpaid internship?
   ___ Yes   ___ No

8. For next summer, could you afford to take an internship paying only the minimum wage?
   ___ Yes   ___ No

10. How important is each of the following criteria in choosing whether to accept a specific internship?

These abbreviations are OK when
you survey skilled readers

	Very impt.	Some impt.	Not impt.
a. Money	❑	❑	❑
b. Prestige of company	❑	❑	❑
c. Location near where you live now	❑	❑	❑
d. Quality of mentoring	❑	❑	❑
e. Building connections	❑	❑	❑
f. Chance of getting a job with that company	❑	❑	❑
g. Gaining experience	❑	❑	❑

Make sure to break up the lines. Leaving an extra space makes it more likely that respondent will check the right line.

11. How interested are you in a career in managed care?
    ___ Very interested
    ___ Somewhat interested
    ___ Not interested

12. Could you take a job in Cleveland next summer?
    ___ Definitely
    ___ Maybe
    ___ No

13. Have you heard of FFI Rx Managed Care?
    ___ Yes
    ___ No

14. I invite any other comments you would like to make regarding internships.

Using columns gets the survey on one side, saving money in copying and eliminating the problem of people missing questions on the back. But it leaves almost no room to write in comments.

Thank you for taking the time to answer this survey. Please return to the person who gave it to you.

Repeat where to turn in or mail completed surveys.

375

One of the most useful Web sites on writing proposals is the Foundation Center's *User-Friendly Guide to Funding Research and Resources* (http://fdncenter.org/onlib/ufg).

Proposals for Funding

Proposals for funding include both **business plans** (documents written to raise capital for new business ventures) and proposals submitted to a foundation, a corporation, a government agency, or a religious agency to seek money for public service projects. In a proposal for funding, stress the needs your project will meet and show how your project helps fulfill the goals of the organization you are asking for funds.

See the BAC Web site for advice about writing business plans.

Every funding source has certain priorities; some have detailed lists of the kind of projects they fund. *The Foundation Directory* indexes foundations by state and city and by field of interest. *The Foundation Grants Index Annual* lists grants of $5,000 or more made by the 425 biggest foundations. Check recent awards to discover foundations that may be interested in your project. *Source Book Profiles* describes 1,000 national and regional foundations.

Figuring the Budget

For a class research project, you may not be asked to prepare a budget. However, many proposals do require budgets, and a good budget is crucial to making the winning bid. Ask for everything you need to do a quality job. Asking for too little may backfire, leading the funder to think that you don't understand the scope of the project.

Do some research. Read the RFP to find out what is and isn't fundable. Talk to the program officer and read successful past proposals to find answers to the following questions:

- What size projects will the organization fund in theory?
- Does the funder prefer making a few big grants or many smaller grants?
- Does the funder expect you to provide in-kind or cost-sharing funds from other sources?

Think about exactly what you'll do and who will do it. What will it cost to get that person? What supplies or materials will he or she need? Also think about indirect costs for using office space, about retirement and health benefits as well as salaries, about office supplies, administration, and infrastructure.

Make the basis of your estimates specific.

Weak:	75 hours of transcribing interviews	$1,125
Better:	25 hours of interviews; a skilled transcriber can complete	
	1 hour of interviews in 3 hours; 75 hours @ $15/hour	$1,125

Figure your numbers conservatively. For example, if the going rate for skilled transcribers is $15 an hour, but you think you might be able to train someone and pay only $10 an hour, use the higher figure. Then, even if your grant is cut, you'll still be able to do the project well.

Writing Progress Reports

When you're assigned to a single project that will take a month or more, you'll probably be asked to file one or more progress reports. A progress report reassures the funding agency or employer that you're making progress and allows you and the agency or employer to resolve problems as they arise. Different readers may have different concerns. An instructor may want to know whether you'll have your report in by the due date. A client may be more interested in what you're learning about the problem. Adapt your progress report to the needs of the audience.

Christine Barabas's study of the progress reports in a large research and development organization found that poor writers tended to focus on what they had done and said very little about the value of their work. Good writers, in contrast, spent less space writing about the details of what they'd done but much more space explaining the value of their work for the organization.[4]

Subject lines for progress reports are straightforward. Specify the project on which you are reporting your progress.

> Subject: Progress on Developing a Marketing Plan for TCBY

> Subject: Progress on Group Survey on Campus Parking

If you are submitting weekly or monthly progress reports on a long project, number your progress reports or include the time period in your subject line. Include dates for the work completed since the last report and work to be completed before the next report.

Make your progress report as positive as you honestly can. You'll build a better image of yourself if you show that you can take minor problems in stride and that you're confident of your own abilities.

Negative:	I have not deviated markedly from my schedule, and I feel that I will have very little trouble completing this report by the due date.
Positive:	I am back on schedule and expect to complete my report by the due date.

Progress reports can be organized in three ways: by chronology, by task, and to support a recommendation.

The Political Uses of Progress Reports

Progress reports can do more than just report progress. You can use progress reports to

- Enhance your image. Details about the number of documents you've read, people you've surveyed, or experiments you've conducted create a picture of a hardworking person doing a thorough job.

- Float trial balloons. Explain, "I could continue to do X [what you approved]; I could do Y instead [what I'd like to do now]." The detail in the progress report can help back up your claim. Even if the idea is rejected, you don't lose face because you haven't made a separate issue of the alternative.

- Minimize potential problems. As you do the work, it may become clear that implementing your recommendations will be difficult. In your regular progress reports, you can alert your boss or the funding agency to the challenges that lie ahead, enabling them to prepare psychologically and physically to act on your recommendations.

Chronological Progress Reports

The following pattern of organization focuses on what you have done and what work remains.

1. **Summarize your progress in terms of your goals and your original schedule.** Use measurable statements.

   Poor: My progress has been slow.

   Better: The research for my report is about one-third complete.

2. **Under the heading "Work Completed," describe what you have already done.** Be specific, both to support your claims in the first paragraph and to allow the reader to appreciate your hard work. Acknowledge the people who have helped you. Describe any serious obstacles you've encountered and tell how you've dealt with them.

   Poor: I have found many articles about Procter & Gamble on the Web. I have had a few problems finding how the company keeps employees safe from chemical fumes.

   Better: On the Web, I found Procter & Gamble's home page, its annual report, and mission statement. No one whom I interviewed could tell me about safety programs specifically at P&G. I have found seven articles about ways to protect workers against pollution in factories, but none mentions P&G.

3. **Under the heading "Work to Be Completed," describe the work that remains.** If you're more than three days late (for school projects) or two weeks late (for business projects) submit a new schedule, showing how you will be able to meet the original deadline. You may want to discuss "Observations" or "Preliminary Conclusions" if you want feedback before writing the final report or if your reader has asked for substantive interim reports.

4. **Either express your confidence in having the report ready by the due date or request a conference to discuss extending the due date or limiting the project.** If you are behind your original schedule, show why you think you can still finish the project on time.

   The student progress report in Figure 14.4 uses this pattern of organization.

Task Progress Reports

In a task progress report, organize information under the various tasks you have worked on during the period. For example, a task progress report for a group report project might use the following headings:

> Finding Background Information on the Web and in Print
> Analyzing Our Survey Data
> Working on the Introduction of the Report and the Appendices

Under each heading, the group could discuss the tasks it has completed and those that remain.

Recommendation Progress Reports

Recommendation progress reports recommend action: increasing the funding for a project, changing its direction, canceling a project that isn't working out. When the recommendation will be easy for the reader to accept, use the direct request pattern of organization from Chapter 9 (p. 225). If the recommenda-

Figure 14.4   *A Student Chronological Progress Report*

November 10, 2000

To: Kitty O. Locker

From: David G. Bunnel *DGB*

Subject: Progress on CAD/CAM Software Feasibility Study for the Architecture Firm, Patrick and Associates, Inc.

¶ 1: Summarize results in terms of purpose, schedule.

I have obtained most of the information necessary to recommend whether CADAM or CATIA is better for Patrick and Associates, Inc. (P&A). I am currently analyzing and organizing this information and am on schedule.

Work Completed   *Underline Headings or Bold.*

Be very specific about what you've done.

To learn how computer literate P&A employees are, I interviewed a judgment sample of five employees. My interview with Bruce Ratekin, the director of P&A's Computer-Aided Design (CAD) Department on November 3 enabled me to determine the architectural drafting needs of the firm. Mr. Ratekin also gave me a basic drawing of a building showing both two- and three-dimensional views so that I could replicate the drawing with both software packages.

Show how you've overcome minor problems.

I obtained tutorials for both packages to use as a reference while making the drawings. First I drew the building using CADAM, the package designed primarily for two-dimensional architectural drawings. I encountered problems with the isometric drawing because there was a mistake in the manual I was using; I fixed the problem by trying alternatives and finally getting help from another CADAM user. Next, I used CATIA, the package whose strength is three-dimensional drawings, to construct the drawing. I am in the process of comparing the two packages based on these criteria: quality of drawing, ease of data entry (lines, points, surfaces, etc.) for computer experts and novices, and ease of making changes in the completed drawings. Based on my experience with the packages, I have analyzed the training people with and without experience in CAD would need to learn to use each of these packages.

Indicate changes in purpose, scope, or recommendations. Progress report is a low-risk way to bring the readers on board.

Work to Be Completed

Making the drawings has shown that neither of the packages can do everything that P&A needs. Therefore, I want to investigate the feasibility of P&A's buying both packages.

Specify the work that remains.

As soon as he comes back from an unexpected illness that has kept him out of the office, I will meet with Tom Merrick, the CAD systems programmer for The Ohio State University, to learn about software expansion flexibility for both packages as well as the costs for initial purchase, installation, maintenance, and software updates. After this meeting, I will be ready to begin the first draft of my report.

Whether I am able to meet my deadline will depend on when I am able to meet with Mr. Merrick. Right now, I am on schedule and plan to submit my report by the December 10th deadline.

End on a positive note.

Bermuda *Not* Onion

Searches on the Web can yield hundreds, sometimes thousands, of matches. The computer just matches words. If you enter "Bermuda" as your search term, you'll get articles and pages about Bermuda onions as well as about the cruise market in Bermuda. "Bermuda *and* Travel" limits the search to articles with both the words *Bermuda* and *travel*. But maybe that's too narrow. What if the article uses the word *cruise* or *vacation* instead of *travel?* To capture those variations, use "Bermuda *and* (Cruise* *or* Vacation* *or* Travel)." The parentheses group the "or" items together to flag any one of them with *Bermuda*. The asterisks are wild card endings allowing for plurals and other forms. Some databases use different symbols for wild cards. Specify articles printed in the last two to three years (maybe even more recently, if your topic has been changing quickly). Then read the articles and pages the search finds. When one is relevant, copy or download it so that you can use it in your research.

tion is likely to meet strong resistance, the problem-solving pattern (p. 228) may be more effective.

Research Strategies for Reports

Research for a report may be as simple as getting a computer printout of sales for the last month; it may involve finding published material or surveying or interviewing people. **Secondary research** retrieves information that someone else gathered. Library research and online searches are the best known kinds of secondary research. **Primary research** gathers new information. Surveys, interviews, and observations are common methods for gathering new information for business reports.

Finding Information Online and in Print

You can save time and money by checking online published sources of data before you gather new information. Many college and university libraries provide

- Workshops on research techniques.
- Handouts explaining how to use printed and computer-based sources.
- Free or inexpensive access to computer databases.
- Research librarians who can help you find and use sources.

   Categories of sources that may be useful include

- Specialized encyclopedias for introductions to a topic (for example, *Kodansha Encyclopedia of Japan*).
- Indexes to find articles. Most permit searches by keyword, by author, and often by company name.
- Abstracts for brief descriptions or summaries of articles. Sometimes the abstract will be all you'll need; almost always, you can tell from the abstract whether an article is useful for your needs.
- Citation indexes to find materials that cite previous research. Citation indexes thus enable you to use an older reference to find newer articles on the topic. The *Social Sciences Citation Index* is the most useful for researching business topics.
- Newspapers for information about recent events.
- US Census reports, for a variety of business and demographic information.

   Figures 14.5, 14.6, and 14.7 list a few of the hundreds of online and print sources. More and more resources are going online every month; by the time you read this book, additional online sources will exist. Do a Net search for items in print to see whether they're available.

   To use a computer database efficiently, identify the concepts you're interested in and choose keywords that will help you find relevant sources. **Keywords** or **descriptors** are the terms that the computer searches for. If you're not sure what terms to use, check the **ABI/Inform Thesaurus** for synonyms and the hierarchies in which information is arranged in various databases.

   Specific commands allow you to narrow your search. For example, to study the effect of the minimum wage on employment in the restaurant industry, you might specify the following:

> (minimum wage) *and* (restaurant *or* fast food) *and*
> (employment rate *or* unemployment).

This descriptor would give you the titles of articles that treat all three of the topics in parentheses. Without *and*, you'd get articles that discuss the minimum wage in general, articles about every aspect of *restaurants*, and every article that refers to *unemployment*, even though many of these would not be relevant to your topic. The *or* descriptor calls up articles that use the term *fast food* but not the term *restaurant*. An article that used the phrase *food service industry* would

Figure 14.5

Sources for Electronic Research

These CD-ROM databases are available in many university libraries:

ABI/Inform (indexes and abstracts 800 journals in management and business)

AGRICOLA (CD-ROM version of *Agricultural Index*)

AIDSLINE

BioethicsLine

Biological and Agricultural Index

Black Studies on Disc

CINAHL (nursing and allied health)

ComIndex (indexes and abstracts journals in communication, including *The Journal of Business Communication*)

Congressional Masterfile

Dissertation Abstracts (digital dissertations)

Dun's Million Dollar Disc

EconLit

ERIC (research on education and teaching practices in the United States and other countries)

Ethnic Newswatch

Foreign Trade and Economic Abstracts

GPO on SilverPlatter (government publications)

Handbook of Latin American Studies

Health Planning

HealthSTAR

Index to Legal Periodicals

Legis-Slate

LEXIS/NEXIS Services

A Matter of Fact

MEDLINE

Newspaper Abstracts

PAIS International—Public Affairs Information Service

Peterson's College Database

Peterson's Gradline

PsycINFO

PsycLIT

Social Sciences Index

Social Work Abstracts

Sociofile

SPORT Discus

Statistical Masterfile (statistics collected by the US government)

Telephone Directory (business white pages)

Telephone Directory (residential white pages)

Wilson Business Abstracts

Women's Resources International

Figure 14.6

Sources for Web Research

 Web addresses may change. For links to the current URLs, see the BAC Web site.

Search engines

Alta Vista
   www.altavista.com/

Deja News Research Service (searches Usenet discussion group postings)
   www.dejanews.com

Encyclopedia Britannica's E-Blast
   eblast.com/index.html

Excite
   www.excite.com/

Hotbot
   www.hotbot.com/

LookSmart
   www.looksmart.com/

Infoseek
   www.infoseek.com/

MetaCrawler
   www.metacrawler.com

MetaFind (simultaneously runs Alta Vista, Excite, HotBot, Infoseek, PlanetSearch, and WebCrawler)
   www.metafind.com/

Northern Light
   www.northernlight.com

Savvy Search
   www.savvysearch.com

Search Engine Watch (reviews, tips on using search engines)
   www.searchenginewatch.com/

Yahoo
   www.yahoo.com/

Subject matter directories

AccountingNet
   www.accountingnet.com/

Rutger's Accounting Web (RAW)
   www.rutgers.edu/Accounting/raw.htm

Business sources on the Internet, from University of Strathclyde, Glasgow, Scotland
   www.dis.strath.ac.uk/business/

Education index
   www.educationindex.com/

Resources for economists on the Internet
   econwpa.wustl.edu/EconFAQ/EconFAQ.html

FINWeb
   www.finweb.com/

Human resource management resources on the Internet
   www.nbs.ntu.ac.uk/staff/lyerj/hrm_link.htm

International Business Kiosk
   www.webcom.com/one/world/

International business sources on the WWW
   ciber.bus.msu.edu/busres.htm

Management and entrepreneurship
   www.lib.lsu.edu/bus/managemt.html

The WWW Virtual Library: Marketing

    www.wcupa.edu/library.fhg/marketvl/marketvl.htm

Internet marketing resources

    www.lib.lsu.edu/bus/marketin.html

Links 2000 (marketing resources on the Web)

    www2000.ogsm.vanderbilt.edu/eli/eli.cgi

The WWW Virtual Library

    vlib.stanford.edu/Overview.html

News sites

AJR NewsLink (links to US, Canadian, and international newspapers, magazines, and resources online)

    ajr.newslink.org/menu.html

Business Week Online

    www.businessweek.com/

CNN/CNNFN

    www.cnn.com (news)

    www.cnnfn.com (financial news)

National Public Radio

    www.npr.org

New York Times on the Web

    www.nyt.com

The Wall Street Journal Interactive Edition

    www.wsj.com

Washington Post

    www.WashingtonPost.com

US government information

Congressional Quarterly's Vote Watch (votes by members of Congress)

    www.pathfinder.com/CQ/

EDGAR Online (SEC's online database)

    www.edgar-online.com/

    www.sec.gov/edgarhp.htm

FEDSTATS (links to 70 US government agencies)

    www.fedstats.gov

Statistical Universe (US government statistics back to the 1970s)

    www.cispubs.com

STAT-USA (fast-breaking statistics on US trade and economy)

    www.stat-usa.gov

US Census (including Data FERRET)

    www.census.gov/

US government publications (search databases online)

    www.access.gpo.gov/su_docs/dbsearch.html

US Small Business Administration

    www.sbaonline.sba.gov/

White House Briefing Room (economic issues)

    www.whitehouse.gov/fsbr/esbr.html

White House Briefing Room (social issues)

    www.whitehouse.gov/fsbr/ssbr.html

Figure 14.6

Sources for Web Research (continued)

Figure 14.6

*Sources for Web Research
(concluded)*

Reference collections
Britannica Online
www.eb.com:180/
CEO Express
www.ceoexpress.com/
Hoover's Online (information on more than 13,000 public and private companies worldwide)
www.hoovers.com
Industry Research Desk
www.virtualpet.com/industry/rdindex2.htm
Liszt (mailing lists)
www.liszt.com
My Virtual Reference Desk
www.refdesk.com
Tile.Net's Guide to Listservs
tile.net/lists/

be eliminated unless it also used the term *restaurant.* Alta Vista and some other Web search engines allow you to specify words that cannot appear in a source.

Many words can appear in related forms. To catch all of them, use the database's **wild card** or **truncated code** for shortened terms and root words.

Web search engines are particularly effective for words, people, or phrases that are unlikely to have separate pages devoted to them. For general topics or famous people, directories like E-Blast or Yahoo are more useful, since they yield a smaller number of "hits."

Evaluating Web Sources

Some of the material on the Web is excellent, but some of it is wholly unreliable. With print sources, the editor or publisher serves as a gatekeeper, so you can trust the material in good journals. To put up a Web page, all one needs is access to a server.

Use four criteria to decide whether a Web site is good enough to use for a research project:

1. **Authors.** What person or organization sponsors the site? What credentials do the authors have?
2. **Objectivity.** Does the site give evidence to support its claims? Does it give both sides of controversial issues? Is the tone professional?
3. **Information.** How complete is the information? What is it based on?
4. **Revision date.** When was the site last updated?

Answers to these questions may lead you to discard some of the relevant sites you find. For example, if you find five different Web pages about the cell phones and car accidents that all cite the same Toronto study, you have one source, not five. Choose the most complete for your project.

 For more information on evaluating Web sites, see the BAC Web page.

Designing Questions for Surveys and Interviews

A **survey** questions a large group of people, called **respondents** or **subjects.** The easiest way to ask many questions is to create a **questionnaire,** a written

Indexes:

Accountants' Index

Ageline (physical, psychological, economic, and political aspects of aging)

Business Periodicals Index

Canadian Business Index

Family Resources

Forestry Abstracts

Hospital Literature Index

Personnel Management Abstracts

World Textile Abstracts

Facts, figures, and forecasts (also check the Web):

Almanac of Business and Industrial Financial Ratios

Cost-of-Living Indicators

Moody's Manuals

Predicasts

The Statistical Abstract of the US

Trades and Securities Statistics

The Value Line Investment Survey

US Census reports (also available on the Web):

Census of Population

Census of Manufacturers

Census of Wholesale Trade

Census of Retail Trade

Census of Service Industries

Directories (facts about organizations, including the names of officers and directors; more up-to-date information may be available on the Web):

Directory of American Firms Operating in Foreign Countries

Dun & Bradstreet's *Reference Book of Corporate Managements*

Dun's Employment Opportunities Directory

National Directory of Minority-Owned Business Firms

Poor's Register of Corporations, Directors, and Executives

Thomas' Register of American Manufacturers

International business and government:

Canada Year Book

Dun and Bradstreet's *Principal International Businesses*

European Marketing Data and Statistics

Price, Waterhouse's *Guide to Doing Business in [Name of Country]*

Statistical Yearbook of the United Nations

Who Owns Whom: Continental Europe

Figure 14.7

Print Sources for Research

list of questions that people fill out. An **interview** is a structured conversation with someone who will be able to give you useful information. Surveys and interviews can be useful only if the questions are well designed.

Good questions ask only one thing, are phrased neutrally, avoid making assumptions about the respondent, and mean the same thing to different people.

Phrase questions in a way that won't bias the response. A state representative mailed out a survey to constituents with the question, "Do you think the Legislature should enact a cost-of-living raise for teachers?" He might have gotten a much less positive response if he had asked, "Would you be willing to

Market Research on the Web*

For John Coleman, CEO of VIA Marketing & Design (#287), the Internet is an unequaled business tool. . . .

For example, the Internet is a great place to sample a competitor's marketing strategy, especially when that competitor is several thousand miles away. When Coleman was working on a marketing plan for a client who was introducing a new industrial water-pumping product into markets like Brazil and China, he found valuable information about the marketing strategies of the client's key competitors on their Web sites. . . .

[For another client, Coleman] had to make a pitch to some executives from a New York City financial house, outlining a marketing strategy for its Internet presence. The problem was, Coleman knew next to nothing about on-line marketing for brokerage companies, so he fired up his browser. Stops at *Business-Week Online* (www.businessweek. com), CNNfn (www.cnnfn.com), and other more home-grown brokerage sites provided him with a crash course in on-line trading. . . . VIA Marketing made a successful pitch for the contract.

*Quoted from Shane McLaughlin, "Web Sites We Love," *Inc.*, 1998 Inc. 500, 180–81.

pay higher taxes to fund a cost-of-living raise for teachers?" A *New York Times*/CBS News poll used two different questions about abortion. A majority opposed "a constitutional amendment prohibiting abortions." But about 20% of the sample changed their answer when presented with a more emotionally charged question: "Should there be a constitutional amendment protecting the life of the unborn child?"[5]

Avoid questions that make assumptions about your subjects. The question "Does your wife have a job outside the home?" assumes that your respondent is a married man.

Use words that mean the same thing to you and to the respondents. If a question can be interpreted in more than one way, it will be. Words like *often* and *important* mean different things to different people. Whenever possible, use more objective measures:

Vague: Do you study in the library frequently?

Better: How many hours a week do you study in the library?

Even questions that call for objective information can be confusing. For example, consider the owner of a small business confronted with the question, "How many employees do you have?" Does the number include the owner as well as subordinates? Does it include both full- and part-time employees? Does it include people who have been hired but who haven't yet started work, or someone who is leaving at the end of the month? A better wording would be

How many full-time employees were on your payroll the week of May 16?

Bypassing occurs when two people use the same symbol but interpret it differently. To reduce bypassing,

1. Train your observers. Decide on definitions in advance; do some practice coding to allow observers to apply the definitions.
2. Avoid terms that are likely to mean different things to different people.
3. Pretest your questions with several people who are like those who will fill out the survey to catch questions that can be misunderstood. Even a small pretest with 10 people can help you refine your questions.

Questions can be categorized in several ways.

Closed questions have a limited number of possible responses. **Open questions** do not lock the subject into any sort of response. Figure 14.8 gives examples of closed and open questions. Closed questions are faster for subjects to answer and easier for researchers to score. However, since all answers must fit into prechosen categories, they cannot probe the complexities of a subject. You can improve the quality of closed questions by conducting a pretest with open questions to find categories that matter to respondents.

Use an "Other, Please Specify" category when you want the convenience of a closed question but cannot foresee all the possible responses:

What is the single most important reason that you ride the bus?
_____ I don't have a car.
_____ I don't want to fight rush-hour traffic.
_____ Riding the bus is cheaper than driving my car.
_____ Riding the bus conserves fuel and reduces pollution.
_____ Other (Please specify) _____

| Figure 14.8 | *Closed and Open Questions* |

Closed questions

Are you satisfied with the city bus service? (yes/no)

How good is the city bus service?

  Excellent   5   4   3   2   1   Terrible

Indicate whether you agree or disagree with each of the following statements about city bus service:

  A   D   The schedule is convenient for me.
  A   D   The routes are convenient for me.
  A   D   The drivers are courteous.
  A   D   The buses are clean.

Rate each of the following improvements in the order of their importance to you (1 = most important, 6 = least important)

_____ Buy new buses.
_____ Increase non-rush-hour service on weekdays.
_____ Increase service on weekdays.
_____ Provide earlier and later service on weekdays.
_____ Buy more buses with wheelchair access.
_____ Provide unlimited free transfers.

Open questions

How do you feel about the city bus service?
Tell me about the city bus service.
Why do you ride the bus? (or, Why don't you ride the bus?)
What do you like and dislike about the city bus service?
How could the city bus service be improved?

If People Can Misunderstand the Question, They Will*

Q: Give previous experience with dates.
A: Moderately successful in the past, but I am now happily married!

Q: How many autopsies have you performed on dead people?
A: All my autopsies have been on dead people.

Q: James stood back and shot Tommy Lee?
A: Yes.

Q: And then Tommy Lee pulled out his gun and shot James in the fracas?
A: (After hesitation) No sir, just above it.

Q: What is the country's mortality rate?
A: 100%. Everybody dies.

Q: Give numbers of employees broken down by sex.
A: None. Our problem is booze.

Q: Sex?
A: I feel this is a very personal subject.

*Based on James Hartley, *Designing Instructional Text* (London: Kogan Page, 1978), 109; Richard Lederer, *Anguished English* (New York: Wyrick, 1988); and folklore.

When you use multiple-choice questions, make sure that any one answer fits only in one category. In the following example of overlapping categories, a person who worked for a company with exactly 25 employees could check either *a* or *b*. The resulting data would be unreliable.

Overlapping categories: Indicate the number of full-time employees in your company on May 16:

          ____ a. 0–25
          ____ b. 25–100
          ____ c. 100–500
          ____ d. over 500

Discrete categories: Indicate the number of full-time employees on your payroll on May 16:

          ____ a. 0–25
          ____ b. 26–100
          ____ c. 101–500
          ____ d. more than 500

Giving several options is more important the older your respondents are. Psychologist Cynthia Adams notes that older people are uncomfortable choosing between only two options. When asked "Are discounts important to you," more mature people want to answer, "It depends."[6] A good survey will specify the context or allow the respondent to do so.

Who Tallies That Survey?*

When we think about information and privacy, we usually think about how a company will use the information we've provided. But sometimes the person who tallies the survey puts the respondent at risk.

One woman filled out a questionnaire that promised she'd receive free product samples for her time and answers about products she used. What the instructions didn't say was that prison inmates were hired to enter the data.

The woman got a 12-page letter from a man imprisoned for rape; the letter referred to the magazines she liked, the fact that she was divorced, and her birthday. The letter spun sexual fantasies involving the products she used.

That company says it no longer uses inmates to tally surveys. But inmates in more than a dozen states routinely process data, answer 800 numbers, and even work as telemarketers.

*Based on James P. Miller, "Privacy Issue Raised in Direct-Mail Case," *The Wall Street Journal*, May 6, 1996, B8.

Branching questions direct different respondents to different parts of the questionnaire based on their answers to earlier questions.

> 10. Have you talked to an academic advisor this year?   yes   no
>   (If "no," skip to question 14.)

Use closed multiple-choice questions for potentially embarrassing topics. Seeing their own situation listed as one response can help respondents feel that it is acceptable. However, very sensitive issues are perhaps better asked in an interview, where the interviewer can build trust and reveal information about himself or herself to encourage the interviewee to answer.

Generally, put early in the questionnaire questions that will be easy to answer. Put questions that are harder to answer or that people may be less willing to answer (e.g., age and income) near the end of the questionnaire. Even if people choose not to answer such questions, you'll still have the rest of the survey filled out.

If subjects will fill out the questionnaire themselves, pay careful attention to the physical design of the document. Use indentations and white space effectively; make it easy to mark and score the answers. Include a brief statement of purpose if you (or someone else) will not be available to explain the questionnaire or answer questions. Pretest the questionnaire to make sure the directions are clear. One researcher mailed a two-page questionnaire without pretesting it. Twenty-five respondents didn't answer the questions on the back of the first page.[7]

Conducting Surveys and Interviews

Face-to-face surveys are convenient when you are surveying a fairly small number of people in a specific location. In a face-to-face survey, the interviewer's sex, race, and nonverbal cues can bias results. Most people prefer not to say things they think their audience will find unacceptable. For that reason, women will be more likely to agree that sexual harassment is a problem if the interviewer is also a woman. Members of a minority group are more likely to admit that they suffer discrimination if the interviewer is a member of the same minority.

Telephone surveys are popular because they can be closely supervised. Interviewers can read the questions from a computer screen and key in answers as the respondent gives them. The results can then be available just a few minutes after the last call is completed.

The major limitation of phone surveys is that they reach only people who have phones and thus underrepresent poor people. Other limitations can be avoided with good designs. Since a survey based on a phone book would exclude people with unlisted numbers, professional survey-takers use automatic random-digit dialing. Since women are more likely to answer the phone than men are,[8] decide in advance to whom you want to speak, and ask for that person rather than surveying whoever answers the phone.

To increase the response rate for a phone survey, call at a time respondents will find convenient. Avoid calling between 5 and 7 PM, a time when many families have dinner.

Mail surveys can reach anyone who has an address. Some people may be more willing to fill out an anonymous questionnaire than to give sensitive information to a stranger over the phone. However, mail surveys are not effective for respondents who don't read and write well. Further, it may be more difficult to get a response from someone who is reluctant to participate. Over the phone, the interviewer can try to persuade the subject and overcome his or her objections.

A major concern with any kind of survey is the **response rate,** the percentage of people who respond. A total response rate of 80% or higher is desirable,[9] since people who refuse to answer may differ from those who respond quickly, and you need information from both groups to be able to generalize to the whole population. However, given the current cynicism about surveys, an 80% response rate is impossible to get. Professional pollsters find that about 60% of Americans refuse to answer phone surveys. Mail surveys are better but still get refusal rates of 40%. The Census Bureau projected that 4 in 10 US households wouldn't fill out and return the 2000 census form, even though everyone was required by law to do so.[10] To get as high a response rate as possible, good researchers follow up, contacting nonrespondents at least once and preferably twice to try to persuade them to participate in the survey.

Selecting a sample for surveys and interviews

To keep research costs reasonable, only a sample of the total population is polled. How that sample is chosen and the attempts made to get responses from nonrespondents will determine whether you can infer that what is true of your sample is also true of the population as a whole. The **population** is the group you want to make statements about. Depending on the purpose of your research, your population might be all Fortune 1000 companies, all business students at your college, or all consumers.

A **convenience sample** is a group of subjects who are easy to get: students who walk through the union, people at a shopping mall, workers in your own unit. Convenience samples are useful for a rough pretest of a questionnaire and may be acceptable for some class research projects. However, you cannot generalize from a convenience sample to a larger group.

A **judgment sample** is a group of people whose views seem useful. Someone interested in surveying the kinds of writing done on campus might ask each department for the name of a faculty member who cared about writing, and then send surveys to those people.

In a **random sample,** each person in the population theoretically has an equal chance of being chosen. See the BAC Web page for various ways of taking random samples.

When people say they did something *randomly* they often mean *without conscious bias.* However, unconscious bias exists. Someone passing out surveys in front of the library will be more likely to approach people who seem friendly and less likely to ask people who seem intimidating, in a hurry, much older or younger, or of a different race, class, or sex. True random samples rely on random digit tables, published in statistics texts and books such as *A Million Random Digits.* Computers can also be programmed to generate random numbers. If you take a true random sample, you can generalize your findings to the whole population from which your sample comes. For example, a random phone survey that shows that 65% of the respondents approve of a presidential policy may be accurate $\pm$ 7%. That is, in the population as a whole, between 58% and 72% approve the policy. The accuracy range is based on the size of the sample and the expected variation within the population. Statistics texts tell you how to calculate these figures.

Conducting research interviews

Schedule interviews in advance; tell the interviewee about how long you expect the interview to take. A survey of technical writers (who get much of their information from interviews) found that the best times to interview subject-matter experts are Tuesday, Wednesday, and Thursday mornings.[11]

Affordable Research on Foreign Markets*

A small company interested in exporting products needs inexpensive research. Akihisa Kumayama and Steuart Henderson Britt suggest the following ways to get information cheaply:

- Use foreign nationals in your city. Take a focus group to a good restaurant and let them discuss your proposal there.

- Talk to people in government and journalism in another country about laws, competition, the general readiness for a certain product.

- If you plan to introduce an industrial product in foreign countries, get small samples of knowledgeable people in each country rather than a large sample from only two or three countries.

*Based on Akihisa Kumayama, "Creating a Course Combining Marketing, Language, and Cross-Cultural Communication with Japanese and American Cultures as a Model," Languages and Communication for World Business and the Professions, Sixth Annual Conference, Ann Arbor, MI, May 8–9, 1987, and Steuart Henderson Britt, quoted in Robert A. Roth, *International Marketing Communications* (Chicago: Crain, 1982), 26–27.

Ethical Issues in Interviewing

If you're trying to get sensitive information, interviewees may give useful information when the interview is "over" and the tape recorder has been turned off. Is it ethical to use that information?

If you're interviewing a hostile or very reluctant interviewee, you may get more information if you agree with everything you can legitimately agree to, and keep silent on the rest. Is it ethical to imply acceptance even when you know you'll criticize the interviewee's ideas in your report?

Most people would say that whatever public figures say is fair game: they're supposed to know enough to defend themselves. Many people would say that different rules apply when you'll cite someone by name than when you'll use the information as background or use a pseudonym so that the interviewee cannot be identified.

As a practical matter, if someone feels you've misrepresented him or her, that person will be less willing to talk to you in the future. But quite apart from practical considerations, interview strategies raise ethical issues as well.

Interviews can be structured or unstructured. In a **structured interview,** the interviewer uses a detailed list of questions to guide the interview. Indeed, a structured interview may use a questionnaire just as a survey does. In an **unstructured interview,** the interviewer has three or four main questions. Other questions build on what the interviewee says. To prepare for an unstructured interview, learn as much as possible about the interviewee and the topic. Go into the interview with three or four main topics you want to cover.

Interviewers sometimes use closed questions to start the interview and set the interviewee at ease. The strength of an interview, however, is getting at a person's attitudes, feelings, and experiences. Situational questions let you probe what someone would do in a specific circumstance. Hypothetical questions that ask people to imagine what they would do generally yield less reliable answers than questions about **critical incidents** or key past events.

Hypothetical question:	What would you say if you had to tell an employee that his or her performance was unsatisfactory?
Critical incident question:	You've probably been in a situation where someone who was working with you wasn't carrying his or her share of the work. What did you do the last time that happened?

A **mirror question** paraphrases the content of the last answer: "So you confronted him directly." "You think that this product costs too much." Mirror questions are used both to check that the interviewer understands what the interviewee has said and to prompt the interviewee to continue talking. **Probes** follow up an original question to get at specific aspects of a topic:

Question:	What do you think about the fees for campus parking?
Probes:	Would you be willing to pay more for a reserved space? How much more?
	Should the fines for vehicles parked illegally be increased?
	Do you think fees should be based on income?

Probes are not used in any definite order. Instead, they are used to keep the interviewee talking, to get at aspects of a subject that the interviewee has not yet mentioned, and to probe more deeply into points that the interviewee brings up.

If you read questions to subjects in a structured interview, use fewer options than you might in a written questionnaire.

> I'm going to read a list of factors that someone might look for in choosing a restaurant. After I read each factor, please tell me whether that factor is Very Important to you, Somewhat Important to you, or Not Important to you.

If the interviewee hesitates, reread the scale.

Always tape the interview. Test your equipment ahead of time to make sure it works. If you think your interviewee may be reluctant to speak on tape, take along two tapes and two recorders; offer to give one tape to the interviewee.[12]

Pulitzer Prize–winner Nan Robertson offers the following advice to interviewers:[13]

• Do your homework. Learn about the subject and the person before the interview.

• To set a nervous interviewee at ease, start with nuts-and-bolts questions, even if you already know the answers.

- Save controversial questions for the end. You'll have everything else you need, and the trust built up in the interview makes an answer more likely.
- Go into an interview with three or four major questions. Listen to what the interviewee says and let the conversation flow naturally.
- At the end of the interview, ask for office and home telephone numbers in case you need to ask an additional question when you write up the interview.

Observing Customers and Users

Answers to surveys and interviews may differ from actual behavior—sometimes greatly. To get more accurate consumer information, many marketers observe users.

When she introduced Growing Healthy, a line of frozen baby foods, founder Julia Knight enlisted friends with kids to join her on research shopping trips. She quickly realized that the frozen food section wasn't a good location. Kids didn't like the cold, and parents speeded through as quickly as possible. So she persuaded supermarket managers to place cutaway freezers in the baby food section, and her company succeeded. Her observations also showed Knight why survey and interview data can be so unreliable: "What mother, especially in front of other mothers, would really tell you that she spent more on cat food than on baby food?"[14]

Sometimes the insights from observation are obvious—once the retailer or marketer sees. When Judy George, founder and CEO of Domain furniture stores, watched six hours of videotape of customers in one of her stores, she realized for the first time that almost all shoppers came in couples, and many of the men looked uncomfortable. George knew that people were more likely to buy the longer they stayed in the store. So she's creating entertainment centers in each of her 23 stores with sports on cable TV.[15]

Observation can also be used for in-house research. A custom-machine-parts manufacturer in Danvers, Massachusetts, videotaped tool-setup processes at one milling work center. Management and work teams watched the tape, suggested changes in the processes, and were able to cut setup time 14 to 20% throughout the work center.[16]

Observation is often combined with other techniques to get the most information. **Think-aloud protocols** ask users to voice their thoughts as they use a document or product: "First I'll try. . . ." These protocols are tape-recorded and later analyzed to understand how users approach a document or product. **Interruption interviews** interrupt users to ask them what's happening. For example, a company testing a draft of computer instructions might interrupt a user to ask, "What are you trying to do now? Tell me why you did that." **Discourse-based interviews** ask questions based on documents that the interviewee has written: "You said that the process is too complicated. Tell me what you mean by that."

Using and Documenting Sources

In a good report, sources are cited and documented smoothly and unobtrusively. **Citation** means attributing an idea or fact to its source **in the body of the report.** "According to the 2000 Census. . . ." "Jane Bryant Quinn argues that. . . ." Citing sources demonstrates your honesty and enhances your credibility. **Documentation** means providing the bibliographic information readers

Marketing Bible Bread*

After living in Jerusalem for 25 years, Peter Shamir came back to New York City to study shopping patterns. He was vice president of marketing for an Israeli-based start-up that wanted to sell a wafer-thin cracker called Bible Bread in the United States.

He found that shoppers took "about 10 seconds" to choose crackers in big markets. Clearly, those shelves weren't the place for a new product with a small advertising budget.

Instead, the company distributed the cracker in gourmet, health food, and kosher stores—places where customers are more open to trying new products and where they spend a bit more time looking at what's available.

As a result, the company's US revenues were on track to reach $1 million in 1998.

*Based on Joshua Macht, "The New Market Research," *Inc.*, July 1998, 87–88.

Market Research Creates an Ad Campaign*

[The tiny company that made Boker knives was considering dropping the brand. But before making the decision, executives and ad agency personnel talked to current and potential customers: people who hunt and fish.]

They knew they were onto something when they ran into a longtime Boker customer who told them what he liked about the knife. He said that whenever he wants to make French fries, he just opens his Boker, puts it in the glove box of his four-by-four pickup with a bunch of potatoes, and drives over a rocky road in second gear. He added, "Of course, for hash browns I use third gear."

As they began to collect stories like this, others poured in. The agency ran a print campaign featuring fanciful pictures of old-time Boker users. The title of the ad ran: IN EVERY LIE ABOUT THE BOKER THERE'S A LITTLE BIT OF TRUTH. The ads recounted the tall tales, which guaranteed high readership. Then the ads told the serious part of the Boker message. Within a year, both market share and profits had doubled.

*Quoted from Robert H. Waterman, *The Renewal Factor* (Toronto: Bantam, 1987), 163.

would need to go back to the original source. The two usual means of documentation are notes and lists of references.

Note that citation and documentation are used in addition to quotation marks. If you use the source's exact words, you'll use the name of the person you're citing and quotation marks in the body of the report; you'll indicate the source in parentheses and a list of references or in a footnote or endnote. If you put the source's idea into your own words, or if you condense or synthesize information, you don't need quotation marks, but you still need to tell whose idea it is and where you found it.

Long quotations (four typed lines or more) are used sparingly in business reports. Since many readers skip quotes, always summarize the main point of the quotation in a single sentence before the quotation itself. End the sentence with a colon, not a period, since it introduces the quote. Indent long quotations on the left and right to set them off from your text. Indented quotations do not need quotation marks; the indentation shows the reader that the passage is a quote.

You may want to interrupt a quotation to analyze, clarify, or question it.

To make a quotation fit the grammar of your report, you may need to change one or two words. Sometimes you may want to add a few words to explain something in the longer original. In both cases, use square brackets to indicate words that are your replacements or additions. Omit any words in the original source that are not essential for your purposes. Use ellipses (spaced dots) to indicate where your omissions are.

Document every fact and idea that you take from a source except facts that are common knowledge. Historical dates and facts are considered common knowledge. Generalizations are considered common knowledge ("More and more women are entering the workforce") even though specific statements about the same topic (such as the percentage of women in the workforce in 1975 and in 2000) would require documentation.

The three most widely used formats for footnotes, endnotes, and bibliographies in reports are those of the American Psychological Association (APA), the Modern Language Association (MLA), and the University of Chicago *Manual of Style* format, which this book uses. The APA format uses internal documentation with a list of references; it does not use footnotes or endnotes. **Internal documentation** provides the work and the page number where the reference was found in parentheses in the text. The work may be indicated by the author's last name (if that isn't already in the sentence), or by the last name plus the date of the work (if you're using two or more works by the same author, or if the dates of the works are important). The full bibliographical citation appears in a List of References or Works Cited at the end of the report. Figure 14.9 shows two paragraphs from a report using APA format and the matching part of the Works Cited. See the BAC Web site for this material presented using MLA format. Figure 14.10 shows the APA and MLA formats for books, government documents, journal and newspaper articles, online sources, and interviews.

If you have used many sources that you have not cited, you may want to list both *Works Cited* and *Works Consulted*. Or you can use the term *Bibliography*, which covers all sources on a topic.

If you use a printed source that is not readily available, consider including it as an appendix in your report. For example, you could copy an ad or include an organization's promotional brochure.

Figure 14.9 *Report Paragraphs with APA Documentation*

Author and date in parenthesis.

The main cause of indoor air pollution is inadequate ventilation. The U.S. National Institute of Occupational Safety and Health found that poor ventilation caused problems in 52% of the 450 buildings studied (Moretz, 1988). Health Welfare Canada found that 68% of the 94 buildings it studied had problems with ventilation (Sterling, 1987). Inadequate ventilation can be caused by too little fresh air or by the way the ventilation system recycles air.

All material from citation to parenthesis is from a single source.

During the 1970s, Robert B. Holtom notes, many buildings were built "with sealed windows, over-insulated roofs and closed air-intake ducts" to save energy. "As a result, in many office buildings, air is recirculated without adequate dilution by fresh air" (1990, p. 66). The American Society of Heating, Refrigeration, and Air-Conditioning Engineers recommends that a building's heating, ventilation, and cooling system deliver 20 cubic feet per minute of outside air for each occupant (White, 1990).

Even if a building gets enough outside air, problems may arise from the way the system is used. Systems shut down for the weekend allow microorganisms to grow in the dust and organic matter in filters and ducts. When the system is turned on Monday morning, the microorganisms are, in Sandy Moretz's words, "blown all over the building" (1988, p. 62).

Use page number for quotation.

Square brackets indicate a change from the original.

Stuart E. Salot, a certified industrial hygienist, advises companies not only to improve ventilation, ban smoking, and add plants but also to "[e]mpower complainants" by taking their complaints seriously (Wojcik, 1993, p. 29).

Here, the sense of the paragraph requires a lower-case "e." Since a capital letter was used in the original, brackets are needed.

Includes all works quoted and paraphrased.

References

Holtom, R. B. (1990, Jan.). Underwriting update--Seeking the SBS cure. Best's Review, 64-66, 83.

List source only once, even when used more than once.

Moretz, S. (1988, Feb.). Are your workers safe from sick building syndrome? Occupational Hazards, 58-62.

Sterling, T. D., Collett, C. W., and Sterling, E. M. (1987). Environmental tobacco smoke and indoor air quality in modern office work environments. Journal of Occupational Medicine, 29(1), 57-62.

White, F. A. (1990, Summer). Indoor air quality: What managers can do. Employee Relations Today, 93-101.

Wojcik, J. (1993, Sept.). Indoor air quality causing headaches. Business Insurance, 13, 28-29.

List sources alphabetically.

Figure 14.10 *APA and MLA Formats for Documenting Sources*

@ Documentation formats for electronic sources are evolving. For links to the latest standards, check the BAC Web site.

APA Format

APA internal documentation gives the author's last name and the date of the work in parentheses in the text. A comma separates the author's name from the date (Pagel & Westerfelhaus, 1999). The page number is given only for direct quotations (Katz, 1998, p. 74). If the author's name is used in the sentence, only the date is given in parentheses. (See Figure 14.9.) A list of REFERENCES gives the full bibliographic citation, arranging the entries alphabetically by the author's last name.

Initials only.

Year. Period outside parenthesis.

In titles of books and articles, capitalize only
① first word
② first word of subtitle
③ proper nouns.

Book

Katz, S. M. (1998). *The dynamics of writing review: Opportunities for growth and change in the workplace.* Greenwich, CT: Ablex.

When information is known to you but not printed in document, put in square brackets.

Book or Pamphlet with a Corporate Author

Citibank. (1994). *Indonesia: An investment guide.* [Jakarta]:Author.

Indicates organization authoring document also publishes it.

Indent entries 5 spaces or .4".

Government Document

House Select Committee on Children, Youth, and Families. (1991). *Babies and briefcases: Creating a family-friendly workplace for fathers.* Hearing before the Select Committee on Children, Youth, and Families, House of Representatives, One Hundred Second Congress, first session, hearing held in Washington, DC, June 11, 1991. Washington: Government Printing Office.

No abbreviations.

Editors before book title.

Article in an Edited Book *No quotes around title of Article.*

Just initials for editors' names— But last names last.

Burnett, R. E. (1993). Conflict in collaborative decision-making. In N. R. Blyler & C. Thralls (Eds.), *Professional communication: The social perspective* (pp. 144-162). Newbury Park, CA: Sage.

Give state when city is not well known. *Ampersand*

Article in a Periodical *Comma, even when only two authors.*

In titles of journals, magazines, and newspapers, capitalize all main words.

Pagel S., & Westerfelhaus, R. (1999). Read the book or attend the seminar? Charting ironies in how managers prefer to learn. *The Journal of Business Communication, 36(2),* 163-193.

No "pp." when journal has volume number.

Comma *Volume, issue numbers* *Repeat "1" in "193."*

Petzinger, T., Jr. (1999, April 2). New business leaders find greater profit mixing work, caring. *The Wall Street Journal,* p. B1. *"p." or "pp." for newspapers and magazines without volume number.*

Each author's last name goes first. Put an ampersand before the last author.

Article from an Electronic Database

Atre, T., Auns, K., Badenhausen, K., McAuliffe, K., Nikolov, C., & Ozanian, M. K. (1996, May 20). Sports stocks and bonds. *Financial World,* p. 53 (11). General Reference Center Gold (GPIP). *Name of database.*

Page article begins on. Number of pages in article.

Figure 14.10 *APA and MLA Formats for Documenting Sources (continued)*

Interview Conducted by the Researcher
    [Identify interviews messages in the text as personal communications. Give name of interviewee and as specific a date as possible. Do not list in References.]

E-Mail Message
    [Identify e-mail messages in the text as personal communications. Give name of author and as specific a date as possible. Do not list in References.]

Posting to a Listserv
    [Identify messages on listservs to which one must subscribe in the text as personal communications. Give name of author and as specific a date as possible. Do not list in References.]

World Wide Web Site
    American Express. (1998). Creating an effective business plan. Retrieved April 24, 1999 from the World Wide Web: http://www6.americanexpress.com/ *← Break Web page address at a* smallbusiness/resources/starting/biz_plan/ *slash, period, or hyphen if possible.*

                    No punctuation →

MLA Format

MLA internal documentation gives the author's last name and page number in parentheses in the text. Unlike APA, the year is not given, and no comma separates the name and page number (Katz 74). If the author's name is used in the sentence, only the page number is given in parentheses. A list of WORKS CITED gives the full bibliographic citation, arranging the entries alphabetically by the author's last name.

                    Comma.   Period.
Capitalize Book ↙   ↙
first word   Katz, Susan M. *The Dynamics of Writing Review: Opportunities for Growth and Change in the*
of title,   *Workplace.* Greenwich, CT: Ablex, 1998.
subtitle, and all   *Include state when city is not well known.*
major words.

Book or Pamphlet with a Corporate Author
    Citibank. Indonesia: An Investment Guide. [Jakarta:] Citibank, 1994.

                    Square brackets for ↗
                    information you supply.
Government Document
    United States. House Committee on Interior and Insular Affairs.
        Accident at Three Mile Island Nuclear Powerplant. 2 vols.
        Washington: GPO, 1979.

(continued)

Figure 14.10 *APA and MLA Formats for Documenting Sources (concluded)*

Government Document

Use hanging United States. Cong. Select Committee on Children, Youth, and Families. *Babies and Brief-*
indents. Indent *cases: Creating a Family-Friendly Workplace for Fathers.* *Hearings.* 102nd Cong., 1st sess.
carry-overlines Washington: GPO, 1991.
5 spaces or *Abbreviate "Government Printing Office"* *Abbreviated*
about .4." *and other common words in publisher's name*

Article from an Edited Book

Full name Burnett, Rebecca E. "Conflict in Collaborative Decision-Making." *Professional Communication:*
for editors *The Social Perspective.* Ed. Nancy Roundy Blyler and Charlotte Thralls. Newbury
Park, CA: Sage, 1993. 144-62.
no "pp." *Spelled out*
Omit "1" from "162"

Article in a Periodical

Pagel, Sonya and Robert Westerfelhaus. "Read the Book or Attend the Seminar? Charting
Italicize Ironies in How Managers Prefer to Learn." *The Journal of Business Communication* 36.2
or underline (1999): 163-93. *Volume, issue number*
title of *Colon space page numbers.*
journal, Petzinger, Thomas, Jr. "New Business Leaders Find Greater Profit Mixing Work, Caring."
newspaper, *The Wall Street Journal,* 2 April 1999: B1.
or magazine. *Date before month*

Reverse first last name to alphabetize.
Remaining names go in regular number

Article from an Electronic Database

Atre, Tushar, Kristine Auns, Kurt Badenhausen, Kevin McAuliffe, Christopher Nikolov, and
Michael K. Ozanian. "Sports Stocks and Bonds. " *Financial World,* 20 May 1996, 53 (11).
General Reference Center (GPIP). 30 Mar. 1997.
Date visited. *Date posted* *Starting page* *Number*
number. *of pages*

Interview Conducted by the Researcher

Drysdale, Andrew. Telephone interview. 12 Apr. 1999.
Abbreviate
month

E-Mail Message

Title of e-mail *Recipient of e-mail*
Locker, Kitty O. "Work Remaining on Brochure." E-mail to Stephanie Criner. 15 Apr. 1999.
in Quotations

Posting to a Listserv

Date posted
Bowman, Joel P. "Re: 'They' as Singular." 23 Mar. 1999. Online posting. BizCom.
Name of Listserv.

World Wide Web Site

Date posted *Date visited*
American Express. "Creating an Effective Business Plan." 1998. 24 Apr. 1999.
<http://www6.americanexpress.com/smallbusiness/resources/starting/biz_plan/>.
ULR in angle brackets *Use [n.d.] if no date*
is given on the site.

Summary of Key Points

- **Information reports** collect data for the reader; **analytical reports** present and interpret data; **recommendation reports** recommend action or a solution.
- A good purpose statement must make three things clear:
  - The organizational problem or conflict.
  - The specific technical questions that must be answered to solve the problem.
  - The rhetorical purpose (to explain, to recommend, to request, to propose) that the report is designed to achieve.
- A proposal must answer the following questions:
  - What problem are you going to solve?
  - How are you going to solve it?
  - What exactly will you provide for us?
  - Can you deliver what you promise?
  - When will you complete the work?
  - How much will you charge?
- In a proposal for a class research project, prove that your problem is the right size, that you understand it, that your method will give you the information you need to solve the problem, and that you have the knowledge and resources.
- Use the following pattern of organization for the cover letter for a sales proposal:
  1. Catch the reader's attention and summarize up to three major benefits you offer.
  2. Discuss each of the major benefits in the order in which you mentioned them in the first paragraph.
  3. Deal with any objections or concerns the reader may have.
  4. Mention other benefits briefly.
  5. Ask the reader to approve your proposal and provide a reason for acting promptly.
- In a proposal for funding, stress the needs your project will meet. Show how your project will help fulfill the goals of the organization you are asking for funds.
- Progress reports may be organized chronologically, by task, or to support a recommendation.
- Use positive emphasis in progress reports to create an image of yourself as a capable, confident worker.
- Use indexes and directories to find information about a specific company or topic.
- To decide whether to use a Web site as a source in a research project, evaluate the site's authors, objectivity, information, and revision date.
- A **survey** questions a large group of people, called **respondents** or **subjects.** A **questionnaire** is a written list of questions that people fill out. An **interview** is a structured conversation with someone who will be able to give you useful information.
- Good questions ask just one thing, are phrased neutrally, avoid making assumptions about the respondent, and mean the same thing to different people.
- **Closed questions** have a limited number of possible responses. **Open questions** do not lock the subject into any sort of response. **Branching**

questions direct different respondents to different parts of the questionnaire based on their answers to earlier questions. A **mirror question** paraphrases the content of the last answer. **Probes** follow up an original question to get at specific aspects of a topic.

- Good researchers attempt to reach nonrespondents at least once and preferably twice.
- A **convenience sample** is a group of subjects who are easy to get. A **judgment sample** is a group of people whose views seem useful. In a **random sample,** each person in the population theoretically has an equal chance of being chosen.
- **Citation** means attributing an idea or fact to its source in the body of the report. **Documentation** means providing the bibliographic information readers would need to go back to the original source.

Chapter 14

Exercises and Problems

Getting Started

14.1   Identifying the Weaknesses in Problem Statements

Identify the weaknesses in the following problem statements.

- Is the problem narrow enough?
- Can a solution be found in a semester or quarter?
- What organization could implement any recommendations to solve the problem?
- Could the topic be limited or refocused to yield an acceptable problem statement?

1. One possible report topic I would like to investigate would be the differences in women's intercollegiate sports in our athletic conference.
2. How to market products effectively to college students.
3. Should Web banners be part of a company's advertising?
4. How can US and Canadian students get jobs in Europe?
5. We want to explore ways our company can help raise funds for the Open Shelter. We will investigate whether collecting and recycling glass, aluminum, and paper products will raise enough money to help.
6. How can XYZ university better serve students from traditionally underrepresented groups?
7. What are the best investments for the next year?

14.2   Writing a Preliminary Purpose Statement

Answer the following questions about a topic on which you could write a formal report. (See Problems 15.4, 15.5, 15.6, 15.7, 15.8, 15.9, and 15.10.)

As Your Instructor Directs,

a. Be prepared to answer the questions orally in a conference.
b. Bring written answers to a conference.
c. Submit written answers in class.
d. Give your instructor a photocopy of your statement after it is approved.
1. What problem will you investigate or solve?
   a. What is the name of the organization facing the problem?
   b. What is the technical problem or difficulty?
   c. Why is it important to the organization that this problem be solved?
   d. What solution or action might you recommend to solve the problem?
   e. List the name and title of the person in the organization who would have the power to accept or reject your recommendation.
2. Will this report use information from other classes or from work experiences? If so, give the name and topic of the class and/or briefly describe the job. If you will need additional information (that you have not already gotten from other classes or from a job), how do you expect to find it?

3. List the name, title, and business phone number of a professor who can testify to your ability to handle the expertise needed for this report.

4. List the name, title, and business phone number of someone in the organization who can testify that you have access to enough information about that organization to write this report.

14.3 Choosing Research Strategies

For each of the following reports, indicate the kinds of research that might be useful. If a survey is called for, indicate the most efficient kind of sample to use.

a. How can XYZ store increase sales?

b. What is it like to live and work in [name of country]?

c. Are the signs in our airport adequate for foreign visitors?

d. Is it feasible to start a monthly newsletter for students in your major?

e. How can we best market to mature adults?

f. Can compensation programs increase productivity?

g. What skills are in demand in our area? Of these, which could the local community college offer courses in?

14.4 Identifying Keywords for Computer Searches

As Your Instructor Directs, identify the keyword combinations that you could use in researching one or more of the following topics:

a. Ways to evaluate whether recycling is working.

b. Safety of pension funds.

c. Ethical issues in accounting.

d. Effects of advertising on sales of automobiles.

e. What can be done to increase the privacy of personal data.

f. Retaining royalties on recordings.

g. Advantages and problems of Web advertising.

14.5 Comparing Web Search Engines

Using at least three different search engines, search for sources on a topic on which you could write a formal report. (See Problems 15.5, 15.6, 15.7, 15.8, 15.9, and 15.10.) Compare the top 30 sources. Which sites turn up on all three search engines? Which search engine appears to be most useful for your project?

As Your Instructor Directs,

a. Share your results orally with a small group of students.

b. Present your results to the class.

c. Write a memo to your instructor summarizing your results.

d. With a small group of students, write a report recommending guidelines for using search engines.

14.6 Evaluating Web Sites

Evaluate 10 Web sites related to the topic of your report. For each, consider

- Authors
- Objectivity
- Information
- Revision date.

Based on these criteria, which sites are best for your report? Which are unacceptable? Why?

As Your Instructor Directs,

a. Share your results with a small group of students.

b. Present your results in a memo to your instructor.

c. Present your results to the class in an oral presentation.

14.7 Choosing Samples for Surveys and Interviews

Indicate the best sample(s) to use in surveys and interviews for reports on the following topics.

a. Would XYZ organization raise more money if it sold items besides donuts every morning in [classroom building]?

b. Improving access to computers for students at XYZ College.

c. How can XYZ organization attract more student members?

d. How XYZ restaurant can reduce turnover.

e. Improving communication with international students at XYZ University.

f. Dealing with hate speech at XYZ College.

g. How teaching can be improved in [Department].

14.8   Evaluating Survey Questions

Evaluate each of the following questions. Are they acceptable as they stand? If not, how can they be improved?

a. Survey of clerical workers:
Do you work for the government? ☐
or the private sector? ☐

b. Questionnaire on grocery purchases:
1. Do you *usually* shop at the same grocery store?
   a. Yes
   b. No
2. Do you use credit cards to purchase items at your grocery store?
   a. Yes
   b. No
3. How much is your average grocery bill?
   a. Under $25
   b. $25–50
   c. $50–100
   d. $100–150
   e. Over $150

c. Survey on technology:
1. Would you generally welcome any technological advancement that allowed information to be sent and received more quickly and in greater quantities than ever before?
2. Do you think that all people should have free access to all information, or do you think that information should somehow be regulated and monitored?

d. Survey on job skills:
How important are the following skills for getting and keeping a professional-level job in US business and industry today?

	Low				High
Ability to communicate	1	2	3	4	5
Leadership ability	1	2	3	4	5
Public presentation skills	1	2	3	4	5
Selling ability	1	2	3	4	5
Teamwork capability	1	2	3	4	5
Writing ability	1	2	3	4	5

14.9   Designing Questions for an Interview or Survey

Submit either a one- to three-page questionnaire or questions for a 20- to 30-minute interview AND the information listed below for the method you choose.

Questionnaire
1. Purpose(s), goal(s).
2. Subjects (who, why, how many).
3. How and where to be distributed.
4. Any changes in type size, paper color, etc., from submitted copy.
5. Rationale for order of questions, kinds of questions, wording of questions.
6. References, if building on questionnaires by other authors.

Interview
1. Purpose(s), goal(s).
2. Subjects (who, and why).
3. Proposed site, length of interview.
4. Rationale for order of questions, kinds of questions, wording of questions, choice of branching or follow-up questions.
5. References, if building on questions devised by others.

As Your Instructor Directs,
a. Create questions for a survey on one of the following topics:
   - Survey students on your campus about their knowledge of and interest in the programs and activities sponsored by a student organization.
   - Survey workers at a company about what they like and dislike about their jobs.
   - Survey people in your community about their willingness to pay more to buy products using recycled materials and to buy products that are packaged with a minimum of waste.
   - Survey students and faculty on your campus about whether adequate parking exists.
   - Survey two groups on a topic that interests you.
b. Create questions for an interview on one of the following topics:
   - Interview an international student about the forms of greetings and farewells, topics of small talk, forms of politeness, festivals and holidays, meals at home, size of families, and roles of family members in his or her country.

- Interview a TV producer about what styles and colors work best for people appearing on TV.
- Interview a worker about an ethical dilemma he or she faced on the job, what the worker did and why, and how the company responded.
- Interview the owner of a small business about the problems the business has, what strategies the owner has already used to increase sales and profits and how successful these strategies were, and the owner's attitudes toward possible changes in product line, decor, marketing, hiring, advertising, and money management.
- Interview someone who has information you need for a report you're writing.

14.10 Choosing Subject Lines for Memo Reports

Identify the strengths and weaknesses of each subject line, and choose the best subject line(s) from each group.

1. A proposal to conduct research.
   a. Membership Survey
   b. Proposal to Survey Former Members to Learn Their Reasons for Not Rejoining
   c. Proposal to Investigate Former Members' Reasons for Not Rejoining
2. A survey to find out why former members did not renew their memberships.
   a. 1998 Delinquency Survey
   b. Results of 1998 Former Member Survey
   c. Why Members Did Not Renew Their Memberships in 1998
3. A progress report.
   a. Progress Report
   b. Work Completed, October 15–November 5
   c. Status of the Survey of Former Members

E-Mail Messages

14.11 Writing a Progress Report

As Your Instructor Directs, send an e-mail message
a. To the other members of your group, describing your progress since the last group meeting.
b. To your instructor, describing your progress.
c. To your instructor, asking for help solving a problem you have encountered.

Communicating at Work

As Your Instructor Directs in Problems 14.12 through 14.14,
a. Create a document or presentation to achieve the goal.
b. Write a memo to your instructor describing the situation at your workplace and explaining your rhetorical choices (medium, strategy, tone, wording, graphics or document design, and so forth).

14.12 Proposing a Change

No organization is perfect. Propose a change that would improve your organization. The change can affect only your unit or the whole organization; it can relate to productivity and profits, to quality of life, or to any other aspect your organization can control. Direct your proposal to the person or committee with the power to authorize the change.

14.13 Proposing to Undertake a Research Project

Pick a project you would like to study whose results could be used by your organization. (See Problem 15.4.) Write a proposal to your supervisor requesting time away from other duties to do the research. Show how your research (whatever its outcome) will be useful to the organization.

14.14 Writing a Progress Report to Your Superior

Describe the progress you have made this week or this month on projects you have been assigned. You may describe progress you have made individually, or progress your unit has made as a team.

Memo and Letter Assignments

14.15 Writing a Report Based on a Survey

As Your Instructor Directs,

a. Survey 40 to 50 people on some subject of your choice.

b. Team up with your classmates to conduct a survey and write it up as a group. Survey 50 to 80 people if your group has two members, 75 to 120 people if it has three members, 100 to 150 people if it has four members, and 125 to 200 people if it has five members.

c. Keep a journal during your group meetings and submit it to your instructor.

d. Write a memo to your instructor describing and evaluating your group's process for designing, conducting, and writing up the survey. (See Chapter 13 on working and writing in groups.)

For this assignment, you do **not** have to take a random sample. Do, however, survey at least two different groups so that you can see if they differ in some way. Possible groups are men and women, business majors and English majors, Greeks and independents, first-year students and seniors, students and townspeople.

As you conduct your survey, make careful notes about what you do so that you can use this information when you write up your survey. If you work with a group, record who does what. Use complete memo format. Your subject line should be clear and reasonably complete. Omit unnecessary words such as "Survey of." Your first paragraph serves as an introduction, but it needs no heading. The rest of the body of your memo will be divided into four sections with the following headings: Purpose, Procedure, Results, and Discussion.

In your first paragraph, briefly summarize (not necessarily in this order) who conducted the experiment or survey, when it was conducted, where it was conducted, who the subjects were, what your purpose was, and what you found out. You will discuss all of these topics in more detail in the body of your memo.

In your **Purpose** section, explain why you conducted the survey. What were you trying to learn? What hypothesis were you testing? Why did this subject seem interesting or important?

In your **Procedure** section, describe in detail *exactly* what you did. "The first 50 people who came through the Union on Wed., Feb. 2" is not the same as "The first 50 people who came through the south entrance of the Union on Wed., Feb. 2, and agreed to answer my ques-

tions." Explain any steps you took to overcome possible sources of bias.

In your **Results** section, first tell whether your results supported your hypothesis. Use both visuals and words to explain what your numbers show. (See Chapter 16 on how to design visuals.) Process your raw data in a way that will be useful to your reader.

In your **Discussion** section, evaluate your survey and discuss the implications of your results. Consider these questions:

1. What are the limitations of your survey and your results?

2. Do you think a scientifically valid survey would have produced the same results? Why or why not?

3. Were there any sources of bias either in the way the questions were phrased or in the way the subjects were chosen? If you were running the survey again, what changes would you make to eliminate or reduce these sources of bias?

4. Do you think your subjects answered honestly and completely? What factors may have intruded? Is the fact that you did or didn't know them, were or weren't of the same sex relevant? If your results seem to contradict other evidence, how do you account for the discrepancy? Were your subjects shading the truth? Was your sample's unrepresentativeness the culprit? Or have things changed since earlier data were collected?

5. What causes the phenomenon your results reveal? If several causes together account for the phenomenon, or if it is impossible to be sure of the cause, admit this. Identify possible causes and assess the likelihood of each.

6. What action should be taken?

The discussion section gives you the opportunity to analyze the significance of your survey. Its insight and originality lift the otherwise well-written memo from the ranks of the merely satisfactory to the ranks of the above-average and the excellent.

The whole assignment will be more interesting if you choose a question that interests you. It does not need to be "significant" in terms of major political or philosophic problems; a quirk of human behavior that fascinates you will do nicely.

14.16 Writing a Proposal for a Student Report

Write a proposal to your instructor to do the research for a formal or informal report. (See Problems 15.4, 15.5, 15.6, 15.7, 15.8, 15.9, and 15.10.)

The headings and the questions in the section titled "Proposals for Class Research Projects" are your RFP;

be sure to answer every question and to use the headings exactly as stated in the RFP. Exception: where alternate heads are listed, you may choose one, combine the two ("Qualifications and Facilities"), or treat them as separate headings in separate categories.

14.17 Writing a Proposal for Funding for a Nonprofit Group

Pick a nonprofit group you care about. Examples include professional organizations, a school sports team, a charitable group, a community organization, a religious group, or your own college or university.

As Your Instructor Directs,

a. Check the Web or a directory of foundations to find one that makes grants to groups like yours. Brainstorm a list of businesses that might be willing to give money for specific projects. Check to see whether state or national levels of your organization make grants to local chapters.

b. Write a proposal to obtain funds for a special project your group could undertake if it had the money. Address your proposal to a specific organization.

c. Write a proposal to obtain operating funds or money to buy something your group would like to have. Address your proposal to a specific organization.

14.18 Writing a Sales Proposal

Pick a project that you could do for a local company or government office. Examples include

· Creating a brochure or Web page.
· Revising form letters.
· Conducting a training program.
· Writing a newsletter or an annual report.
· Developing a marketing plan.
· Providing plant care, catering, or janitorial services.

Write a proposal specifying what you could do and providing a detailed budget and work schedule.

As Your Instructor Directs,

a. Phone someone in the organization to talk about its needs and what you could offer.

b. Write an individual proposal.

c. Join with other students in the class to create a group proposal.

d. Present your proposal orally.

14.19 Writing a Progress Report

Write a memo to your instructor summarizing your progress on your report.

In the introductory paragraph, summarize your progress in terms of your schedule and your goals. Under a heading titled *Work Completed,* list what you have already done. (This is a chance to toot your own horn: if you have solved problems creatively, say so! You can also describe obstacles you've encountered that you have not yet solved.) Under *Work to Be Completed,* list what you still have to do. If you are more than two days behind the schedule you submitted with your proposal, include a revised schedule, listing the completion dates for the activities that remain.

In your last paragraph, either indicate your confidence in completing the report by the due date or ask for a conference to resolve the problems you are encountering.

14.20 Writing a Progress Report for a Group Report

Write a memo to your instructor summarizing your group's progress.

In the introductory paragraph, summarize the group's progress in terms of its goals and its schedule, your own progress on the tasks for which you are responsible, and your feelings about the group's work thus far.

Under a heading titled *Work Completed,* list what has already been done. Be most specific about what you yourself have done. Describe briefly the chronology of group activities: number, time, and length of meetings; topics discussed and decisions made at meetings.

If you have solved problems creatively, say so! You can also describe obstacles you've encountered that you have not yet solved. In this section, you can also comment on problems that the group has faced and whether or not they've been solved. You can comment on things that have gone well and have contributed to the smooth functioning of the group.

Under *Work to Be Completed,* list what you personally and other group members still have to do. Indicate the schedule for completing the work.

In your last paragraph, either indicate your confidence in completing the report by the due date or ask for a conference to resolve the problems you are encountering.

15

Analyzing Information and Writing Reports

A Timetable for Writing Reports

Analyzing Data and Information for Reports
- Identifying the Source of the Data
- Analyzing Numbers
- Analyzing Words
- Checking Your Logic

Choosing Information for Reports

Organizing Information in Reports
- Basic Patterns for Organizing Information
- How to Organize Specific Varieties of Reports

Presenting Information Effectively in Reports
1. Say What You Mean.
2. Tighten Your Writing.
3. Introduce Sources and Visuals Gracefully.
4. Use Blueprints, Transitions, Topic Sentences, and Headings.

Writing Formal Reports
- Title Page
- Letter or Memo of Transmittal
- Table of Contents
- List of Illustrations
- Executive Summary
- Introduction
- Background or History
- Conclusions and Recommendations

Summary of Key Points

Analyzing Information and Writing Reports

Diane Kokal

Executive Vice President, Custom Research, Inc.

www.customresearch.com/

Diane has written reports for many of Custom Research, Inc's Fortune 500 clients, including McDonald's, General Mills, Quaker Oats, and Kraft Foods. Custom Research is a market research consulting firm and a recipient of the 1996 Malcolm Baldrige National Quality Award. Diane was a key part of the team that wrote the application.

At Custom Research, Inc. (CRI), our analysis and report writing process begins with the very first conversation we have with a client. We identify objectives up front. Then, *before* any data are collected, we decide what kinds of analysis we will use and create a preliminary outline of the report. Identifying the data needed to answer the objectives ensures that the right data are collected.

> **❝** *A good report offers analysis in an interesting, concise, and error-free document.* **❞**

While there is no one right style for a report, you need to develop *some* style, some viewpoint to give your writing consistency. When parts of a report are written at different times or by different people, make sure that the whole report uses the same style.

To make a report come alive, link the various pieces of information together to create a story or build a case. First *understand* the information, then *organize* it by checking and revising the outline that was created earlier, and then *write* the report. Headings can organize and synthesize information. Instead of just restating the data ("Product A is preferred over Product B by 70% of the people"), use headings that interpret the data ("Product A is a clear winner").

Report format allows varied audiences to find what they need. CRI reports begin with an Executive Summary written for the CEO or Marketing VP. This summary contains a short description of the research and objectives along with key conclusions and recommendations. Giving the basic support for the recommendations here allows executives to understand and approve the basic recommendations without getting bogged down in all the details. Next come the Detailed Findings, written for the marketing or market research manager. This section has detailed information and analysis that can be used to make more specific decisions.

Finally, edit and proofread! Your report should be concise. *And,* it should be error free. Just one wrong number will make the entire report suspect. A good report offers analysis in an interesting, concise, and error-free document.

Reports at Toyota*

Most companies use meetings to hammer out the many decisions and compromises necessary to design a new vehicle. Toyota, in contrast, relies on written reports. When a cross-functional problem arises, the person who identified the problem writes a report identifying the problem, analyzing it, and recommending a solution. These reports focus on a single issue and are brief—often only a page or two long. They may be presented orally as well or supplemented with a phone call. Afterward, the recipient reads the report carefully, then responds in another report.

A couple of rounds of report and response solve most conflicts. If problems remain, the parties meet. At this point, everyone has thought about the issue; the precision that writing demands has focused thinking. So meetings are brief and productive.

*Based on Durward K. Sobek, II, Jeffrey K. Liker, and Allen C. Ward, "Another Look at How Toyota Integrates Product Development," *Harvard Business Review* 76, no. 4 (July/August 1998), 38–40.

Careful analysis, smooth writing, and effective document design work together to make effective reports, whether you're writing a 2½-page memo report or a 250-page formal report complete with all the report components.

Chapter 14 covered the first two steps in writing a report:

1. Define the problem.
2. Gather the necessary data and information.

This chapter covers the last three steps:

3. Analyze the data and information.
4. Organize the information.
5. Write the report.

Other chapters that are especially useful for reports are Chapters 10, 13, 16, and 17. Appendix C, on making and communicating meaning, and Appendix D, on Toulmin Logic, are also helpful.

A Timetable for Writing Reports

To use your time efficiently, think about the parts of the report before you begin writing. Much of the Introduction comes from your proposal with only minor revisions. You can write six sections even before you've finished your research: Purpose, Scope, Assumptions, Methods, Criteria, and Definitions.

The background reading for your proposal can form the first draft of your list of References.

Save a copy of your questionnaire or interview questions to use as an appendix. As you tally and analyze the data, prepare an appendix summarizing all the responses to your questionnaire, your figures and tables, and a complete list of References. You can print appendices before the final report is ready if you number their pages separately. Appendix A pages would be A-1, A-2, and so forth; Appendix B pages would be B-1, B-2, and so forth.

You can write the title page and the transmittal as soon as you know what your recommendation will be.

After you've analyzed your data, write the Executive Summary, the body, and the Conclusions and Recommendations. Prepare a draft of the table of contents and the list of illustrations.

When you write a long report, list all the sections (headings) that your report will have. Mark those that are most important to your reader and your logic, and spend most of your time on them. Write the important sections early. That way, you won't spend all your time on Background or History of the Problem. Instead, you'll get to the meat of your report.

Analyzing Data and Information for Reports

Analyzing the data you have gathered is essential to produce the tight logic needed for a good report.

Identifying the Source of the Data

Check to be sure that your data come from a reliable source. Use the strategies outlined in Chapter 14 to evaluate Web sources (p. 384). When the source has a vested interest (p. 223) in the results, scrutinize them with special care. In 1995, America Online claimed that its subscribers stayed an average of 41 months. But 60% of its customers had joined in the previous nine months.[1] The news release was image advertising, not reliable data. Similarly, to analyze a company's financial prospects, use independent information as well as the company's annual report and press releases.

If your report is based upon secondary data from library and online research, look at the sample, the sample size, and the exact wording of questions to see what the data actually measure. Some studies bias results by limiting the alternatives. Ninety percent of students surveyed by Levi Strauss & Co. said Levi's 501 jeans would be the most popular clothes that year. But the Levi's were the only brand of jeans on the list of choices. Some studies ask biased questions. A poll sponsored by the disposable-diaper industry asked, "It is estimated that disposable diapers account for less than 2% of the trash in today's landfills. In contrast, beverage containers, third-class mail, and yard waste are estimated to account for about 21% of the trash in landfills. Given this, in your opinion, would it be fair to ban disposable diapers?" Not surprisingly, 84% of respondents said *no*.[2]

Identify exactly what the data measure. For example, using a Dun & Bradstreet database, many people claim that only 28% of small businesses survive for eight years. But that database counts a small business as "surviving" only if it remains under the same ownership. Researcher Bruce Kirchoff found that another 26% survive with ownership changes, for a total survival rate of 54%.[3]

Identify the assumptions used in analyzing the data. When studies contradict each other, the explanation sometimes lies in the assumptions. For example, a study that found disposable diapers were better for the environment than cloth diapers assumed that each diaper change used 1.9 or 1.79 diapers and that a cloth diaper lasted for 92.5 uses. A study that found that cloth diapers were better assumed that each diaper change used 1.72 diapers and that each cloth diaper lasted for 167 uses.[4]

Analyzing Numbers

Many reports analyze numbers—either numbers from databases and sources or numbers from a survey you have conducted.

If you've conducted a survey, your first step is to transfer the responses on the survey form into numbers. For some categories, you'll assign numbers arbitrarily. For example, you might record men as 1 and women as 2—or vice versa. Such assignments don't matter, as long as you're consistent throughout your project. In these cases, you can report the number and percentage of men and women who responded to your survey, but you can't do anything else with the numbers.

When you have numbers for salaries or other figures, start by figuring the average, or mean, the median, and the range. The **average** or **mean** is calculated by adding up all the figures and dividing by the number of samples. The **mode** is the number that occurs most often. The **median** is the number that is exactly in the middle. When you have an odd number of observations, the median will be the middle number. When you have an even number, the median will be the average of the two numbers in the center. The **range** is the difference between the high and low figures for that variable. Figure 15.1 shows the raw data that a student recorded in a report evaluating a hospital's emergency room procedures. To analyze the data, we could rearrange them, listing them from low to high (see Figure 15.2). The average waiting time is 26.6 minutes, but the median (the middle number) is only 22.

Quality Analysis*

I regularly write reports to senior management summarizing recent actions of our competitors and recommending what we should do to stay competitive. To make my recommendations meaningful, I cover all of the areas of competitive activity in my report, including pricing, advertising, new product development, financial strength, and strategic alliances. . . .

Quality analysis is based on taking a problem and breaking it down into the questions that must be answered to solve it. (This is "critical thinking.") For instance, you may be asked to write a report explaining why your product sales have stopped growing. To answer this question, you must first answer several other questions: Am I losing market share and, if so, to whom, and why? Is my product the only one whose growth has slowed, or has the entire industry slowed down? Why? Could my product line grow again? What must I do to make that happen? How much investment will it take, and what return on investment should I expect?

*Quoted from Dayton J. D. Semerjian, Statement to Kitty Locker, February 3, 1997.

Figure 15.1

Raw Data from Observations for a Report

Amount of time (rounded off to the nearest minute that patients wait in the emergency room before being examined in triage.

Patient	Wait	Patient	Wait	Patient	Wait
1	12	6	17	11	19
2	17	7	35	12	31
3	15	8	12	13	41
4	22	9	54	14	23
5	35	10	12	15	17

Figure 15.2

Rearranging Data to Find the Average (Mean), Mode, and Median

12, 12
15
17, 17, 17
19
22
23
31
35, 35
41
50
54

Average: 26.6 minutes
Median: 22 minutes
Mode: 17 minutes
Range: 12–54 minutes

Finding the average takes a few more steps when you have different kinds of data. For example, it's common to ask respondents whether they find a feature "very important," "somewhat important," or "not important." You might code "very important" as "3," "somewhat important" as "2," and "not important" as "1." To find the average in this kind of data,

1. For each response, multiply the code by the number of people who gave that response.
2. Add up the figures.
3. Divide by the total number of people responding to the question.

For example, suppose you have the following data after surveying 50 people about the features they want in a proposed apartment complex:

	Very important (coded as "3")	Somewhat important (coded as "2")	Not important (coded as "1")
Party house	26	12	13
Extra parking for guests	26	23	1

Following step 1, to get the average for "party house," multiply $3 \times 26 = 78$; $2 \times 12 = 24$; and $1 \times 13 = 13$. Then add $78 + 24 + 13 = 115$. Divide by the number of people answering the question and you get the average for that factor: 115 divided by $50 = 2.3$. Repeat the process for the next factor, "extra parking": $3 \times 26 = 78$; $2 \times 23 = 46$; $1 \times 1 = 1$. Adding $78 + 46 + 1 = 125$; dividing by 50 $= 2.5$.

The average then gives an easy way to compare various features. If the party house averages 2.3 while extra parking for guests is 2.5, you know that your respondents would find extra parking more important than a party house. You can now arrange the factors in order of importance:

Table 4. "How Important Is Each Factor to You in Choosing an Apartment?"

n = 50; 3 = "Very Important"

Extra parking for guests	2.5
Party room	2.3
Pool	2.2
Convenient to bus line	2.0

Often it's useful to simplify numerical data: rounding it off, combining similar elements. Then you can see that one number is about 2½ times another. Charting it can also help you see patterns in your data. (See Chapter 16 for a full discussion of charts as a way of analyzing and presenting numerical data.) Look at the raw data as well as at percentages. For example, a 50% increase in shoplifting incidents sounds alarming—but an increase from two to three shoplifting incidents sounds well within normal variation.

Yet another way to analyze numerical data is use a **quadrant analysis.** A quadrant analyzes two factors of interest. For example, a company interested in knowing whether it was using its sales representatives effectively might analyze its accounts into more and less profitable and more and less time-consuming. (See Figure 15.3.) The dividing points are arbitrary. A small business might label accounts yielding profits of up to $25,000 a year "less profitable" and accounts yielding $25,000 or more "more profitable." A big company would have a much higher cut-off to divide "less" from "more" profitable.

The ideal situation, from the company's point of view, would be to have lots of highly profitable accounts that needed little time from sales representatives. The next best condition is to spend time on profitable accounts. Figure 15.3 shows how many accounts fall into each of the four possibilities. The highest number of accounts is in the quadrant of "less profit, but lots of time." The sales representatives would better use their time on more accounts that yield more profits.

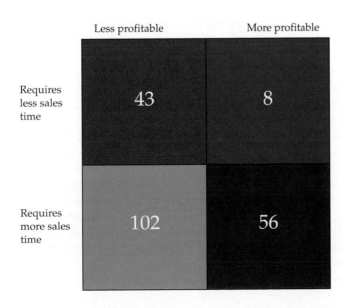

Figure 15.3

A Quadrant Analysis Shows Which Accounts Meet Two Desirable Criteria

Analyzing Words

If your data include words, try to find out what the words mean to the people who said them. Respondents to Whirlpool's survey of 180,000 households said they wanted "clean refrigerators." After asking more questions, Whirlpool found that what people really wanted were refrigerators that *looked* clean, so the company developed models with textured fronts and sides to hide fingerprints.[5] Also try to measure words against numbers. When he researched possible investments, Peter Lynch found that people in mature industries were pessimistic, seeing clouds. People in immature industries saw pie in the sky, even when the numbers weren't great.[6]

Look for patterns. If you have library sources, on which points do experts agree? Which disagreements can be explained by early theories or numbers that have now changed? Which disagreements are the result of different interpretations of the same data? Which are the result of having different values and criteria? In your interviews and surveys, what patterns do you see?

- Have things changed over time?
- Does geography account for differences?
- What similarities do you see?
- What differences do you see?
- What confirms your hunches?
- What surprises you?

Checking Your Logic

State accurately what your data show. For example, suppose that you've asked people who use computers if they could be as productive without them and the overwhelming majority say *no*. This finding shows that people *believe* that computers make them more productive, but it does not prove that they in fact *are* more productive.

Don't confuse causation with correlation. **Causation** means that one thing causes or produces another. **Correlation** means that two things happen at the same time. One might cause the other, but both might be caused by a third. For example, suppose you're considering whether to buy PCs for everyone in your company, and suppose your surveys show that the people who currently have computers are, in general, more productive than people who don't use computers. Does having a computer lead to higher productivity? Perhaps. But perhaps productive people are more likely to push to get computers from company funds, while less productive people are more passive. Perhaps productive people earn more and are more likely to be able to buy their own computers if the organization doesn't provide them. Perhaps some third factor—experience in the company, education, or social background—leads both to increased productivity and to acquiring computers.

Consciously search for at least three possible causes for each phenomenon you've observed and at least three possible solutions for each problem. The more possibilities you brainstorm, the more likely you are to find good options. In your report, mention all of the possibilities; discuss in detail only those that will occur to readers and that you think are the real reasons and the best solutions.

When you have identified patterns that seem to represent the causes of the problem or the best solutions, check these ideas against reality. Can you find support in the quotes or in the numbers? Can you answer counterclaims? If you can, you will be able to present evidence for your argument in a convincing way. See Appendix D for a discussion of Toulmin Logic.

Make the nature of your evidence clear to your reader. Do you have observations that you yourself have made? Or do you have inferences based on observations or data collected by others? Check the principles of semantics in Appendix C. Old data and *either-or* classifications are not good guides to future action. A statement—even one from a computer printout—is never the whole story.

If you can't prove the claim you originally hoped to make, modify your conclusions to fit your data. Even when your market test is a failure or your experiment disproves your hypothesis, you can still write a useful report.

- Identify changes that might yield a different result. For example, selling the product at a lower price might enable the company to sell enough units.
- Divide the discussion to show what part of the test succeeded.
- Discuss circumstances that may have affected the results.
- Summarize your negative findings in progress reports to let readers down gradually and to give them a chance to modify the research design.
- Remember that negative results aren't always disappointing to the audience. For example, the people who commissioned a feasibility report may be relieved to have an impartial outsider confirm their suspicions that a project isn't feasible.[7]

Choosing Information for Reports

Don't put information in reports just because you have it or just because it took you a long time to find it. Instead, choose the information that your reader needs to make a decision.

If you know your readers well, you may know what their priorities are. If you don't know your readers, you may be able to get a sense for what is important by showing them a tentative table of contents (a list of your headings) and asking, "Have I included everything?" When you cannot contact an external audience, show your draft to superiors in your organization.

One report writer was asked to examine a building that had problems with heating, cooling, and air circulation. The client who owned the building wanted quick answers to three questions: Can we do it? What will it cost? When will it pay for itself? The report could have been three pages with a seven-page appendix showing the payback figures.[8]

How much information you need to include depends on whether your audience is likely to be supportive, neutral, or skeptical. As Jeanne Halpern of McKinsey says,

> If the audience is very likely to go along with you, then you can give the message directly and explain how to do it. If you have a message that the people have no conviction about or don't feel happy about, then you have to show the reasons why and explain your thinking in a persuasive way.[9]

You must also decide whether to put information in the body of the report or in appendixes. Put material in the body of the report if it is crucial to your proof or if it is short. (Something less than half a page won't interrupt the reader.)

Anything that a careful reader will want but that is not crucial to your proof can go in an appendix. Appendixes can include

- A copy of a survey questionnaire or interview questions.
- A tally of responses to each question in a survey.
- A copy of responses to open-ended questions in a survey.

What Does the Reader Want? (I)*

What criteria do experienced investors use to read strategic business plans? Researchers Evelyn Pierce, Richard Young, and Thomas Hajduk found that the return on investment and the management team were the most important criteria. Investors didn't really care what product or service the business would provide, and they skipped most of the material in business plans that didn't relate to their criteria.

*Based on Evelyn Pierce, Richard Young, and Thomas Hajduk, "Using Experienced Audience Insights That Reveal How Readers Respond to Business Documents," Southeast Association for Business Communication, Kiawah Island, South Carolina, March 7–9, 1996.

- A transcript of an interview.
- Computer printouts.
- Previous reports on the same subject.

Tell Them a Story*

To persuade people, tell them a story or anecdote that proves your point.

Experiments with both high school teachers and quantitatively trained MBA students show that people are more likely to believe a point and more likely to be committed to it when points were made by examples, stories, and case studies. Stories alone were more effective than a combination of stories and statistics; the combination was more effective than statistics alone. In another experiment, attitude changes lasted longer when the audience had read stories than when they had only read numbers. Recent research suggests that stories are more persuasive because people remember them.

In many cases, you'll need to provide statistics or numbers to convince the careful reader that your anecdote is a representative example. But give the story first. It's more persuasive.

*Based on Daniel J. O'Keefe, *Persuasion* (Newbury Park, CA: Sage Publications, 1990), 168; Joanne Martin and Melanie E. Powers, "Truth or Corporate Propaganda," *Organizational Symbolism*, eds. Louis R. Pondy, Thomas C. Dandridge, Gareth Morgan, and Peter J. Frost (Greenwich, CT: JAI Press 1983), 97–107; and Dean C. Kazoleas, "A Comparison of the Persuasive Effectiveness of Qualitative versus Quantitative Evidence: A Test of Explanatory Hypotheses," *Communication Quarterly* 41, no. 1 (Winter 1993), 40–50.

Organizing Information in Reports

Most sets of data can be organized in several logical ways. Choose the way that makes your information easiest for the reader to understand and use. If you were compiling a directory of all the employees at your plant, for example, alphabetizing by last name would be far more useful than listing people by height, social security number, or length of service with the company, although those organizing principles might make sense in other lists for other purposes.

In one company, a young employee comparing the economics of two proposed manufacturing processes gave his logic and his calculations in full before getting to his conclusion. But his superiors didn't want to wade through eight single-spaced pages; they wanted his recommendation up front.[10]

The following three guidelines will help you choose the arrangement that will be the most useful for your reader:

1. **Process your information before you present it to your reader.** The order in which you became aware of information usually is not the best order to present it to your reader.
2. **When you have lots of information, group it into three to seven categories.** The average person's short-term memory can hold only seven chunks, though the chunks can be of any size.[11] By grouping your information into seven categories (or fewer), you make your report easier to read.
3. **Work with the reader's expectations, not against them.** Introduce ideas in the overview in the order in which you will discuss them.

Basic Patterns for Organizing Information

Seven basic patterns for organizing information are useful in reports:

1. Comparison/contrast.
2. Problem-solution.
3. Elimination of alternatives.
4. General to particular or particular to general.
5. Geographic or spatial.
6. Functional.
7. Chronological.

Any of these patterns can be used for a whole report or for only part of it.

1. Comparison/contrast

Many reports use comparison/contrast sections within a larger report pattern. Comparison/contrast can also be the purpose of the whole report. Feasibility studies usually use this pattern. You can focus either on the alternatives you are evaluating or on the criteria you use. See Figure 15.4 for examples of these two patterns in a report.

Focus on the alternatives when

Focus on alternatives	
Alternative A	Opening a New Store on Campus
Criterion 1	Cost of Renting Space
Criterion 2	Proximity to Target Market
Criterion 3	Competition from Similar Stores
Alternative B	Opening a New Store Downtown
Criterion 1	Cost of Renting Space
Criterion 2	Proximity to Target Market
Criterion 3	Competition from Similar Stores
Alternative C	Opening a New Store in the Suburban Mall
Criterion 1	Cost of Renting Space
Criterion 2	Proximity to Target Market
Criterion 3	Competition from Similar Stores
Focus on criteria	
Criterion 1	Cost of Renting Space for the New Store
Alternative A	Cost of Campus Locations
Alternative B	Cost of Downtown Locations
Alternative C	Cost of Locations in the Suburban Mall
Criterion 2	Proximity to Target Market
Alternative A	Proximity on Campus
Alternative B	Proximity Downtown
Alternative C	Proximity in the Suburban Mall
Criterion 3	Competition from Similar Stores
Alternative A	Competing Stores on Campus
Alternative B	Competing Stores Downtown
Alternative C	Competing Stores in the Suburban Mall

Figure 15.4

Two Ways to Organize a Comparison/Contrast Report.

- One alternative is clearly superior.
- The criteria are hard to separate.
- The reader will intuitively grasp the alternative as a whole rather than as the sum of its parts.

    Focus on the criteria when

- The superiority of one alternative to another depends on the relative weight assigned to various criteria. Perhaps Alternative A is best if we are most concerned about Criterion 1, cost, but worst if we are most concerned about Criterion 2, proximity to target market.
- The criteria are easy to separate.
- The reader wants to compare and contrast the options independently of your recommendation.

    A variation of the divided pattern is the **pro-and-con pattern.** In this pattern, under each specific heading, give the arguments for and against that alternative. A report recommending new plantings for a university quadrangle uses the pro and con pattern:

Advantages of Monocropping
   High Productivity
   Visual Symmetry
Disadvantages of Monocropping
   Danger of Pest Exploitation
   Visual Monotony

Whatever information comes second will carry more psychological weight. This pattern is least effective when you want to de-emphasize the disadvantages of a proposed solution, for it does not permit you to bury the disadvantages between neutral or positive material.

2. Problem-solution

Identify the problem; explain its background or history; discuss its extent and seriousness; identify its causes. Discuss the factors (criteria) that affect the decision. Analyze the advantages and disadvantages of possible solutions. Conclusions and recommendation can go either first or last, depending on the preferences of your reader. This pattern works well when the reader is neutral.

A report recommending ways to eliminate solidification of a granular bleach during production uses the problem-solution pattern:

Recommended Reformulation for Vibe Bleach
Problems in Maintaining Vibe's Granular Structure
   Solidifying during Storage and Transportation
   Customer Complaints about "Blocks" of Vibe in Boxes
Why Vibe Bleach "Cakes"
   Vibe's Formula
   The Manufacturing Process
   The Chemical Process of Solidification
Modifications Needed to Keep Vibe Flowing Freely

3. Elimination of alternatives

After discussing the problem and its causes, discuss the *impractical* solutions first, showing why they will not work. End with the most practical solution. This pattern works well when the solutions the reader is likely to favor will not work, while the solution you recommend is likely to be perceived as expensive, intrusive, or radical.

A report on toy commercials eliminates alternatives:

The Effect of TV Ads on Children
Camera Techniques Used in TV Advertisements
Alternative Solutions to Problems in TV Toy Ads
   Leave Ads Unchanged
   Mandate School Units on Advertising
   Ask the Industry to Regulate Itself
   Give FCC Authority to Regulate TV Ads Directed at Children

4. General to particular or particular to general

General to particular starts with the problem as it affects the organization or as it manifests itself in general and then moves to a discussion of the parts of the problem and solutions to each of these parts. Particular to general starts with the problem as the audience defines it and moves to larger issues of which the problem is a part. Both are good patterns when you need to redefine the reader's perception of the problem to solve it effectively.

The directors of a student volunteer organization, VIP, have defined their problem as "not enough volunteers." After studying the subject, the writer is convinced that problems in training, supervision, and campus awareness are responsible both for a high dropout rate and a low recruitment rate. The general-to-particular pattern helps the audience see the problem in a new way:

> Why VIP Needs More Volunteers
> Why Some VIP Volunteers Drop Out
> > Inadequate Training
> > Inadequate Supervision
> > Feeling That VIP Requires Too Much Time
> > Feeling That the Work Is Too Emotionally Demanding
> Why Some Students Do Not Volunteer
> > Feeling That VIP Requires Too Much Time
> > Feeling That the Work Is Too Emotionally Demanding
> > Preference for Volunteering with Another Organization
> > Lack of Knowledge about VIP Opportunities
> How VIP Volunteers Are Currently Trained and Supervised
> Time Demands on VIP Volunteers
> Emotional Demands on VIP Volunteers
> Ways to Increase Volunteer Commitment and Motivation
> > Improving Training and Supervision
> > Improving the Flexibility of Volunteers' Hours
> > Providing Emotional Support to Volunteers
> > Providing More Information about Community Needs and VIP Services

5. Geographic or spatial

In a geographic or spatial pattern, you discuss problems and solutions by units by their physical arrangement. Move from office to office, building to building, factory to factory, state to state, region to region, etc.

A sales report uses a geographic pattern of organization:

> Sales Have Risen in the European Community
> Sales Are Flat in Eastern Europe
> Sales Have Fallen Sharply in the Middle East
> Sales Are Off to a Strong Start in Africa
> Sales Have Risen Slightly in Asia
> Sales Have Fallen Slightly in South America
> Sales Are Steady in North America

Failure Isn't Final*

Researchers write closure reports when the company decides that the project they're working on isn't feasible. However, a few years later, new technologies, new conditions, or new ideas may make a "failed" idea feasible.

Post-It® notes use a "failed" adhesive because one 3M employee saw the weak adhesive as a solution to a problem:

> I was singing in the choir in my church. . . . I would mark the pages with little pieces of paper normally. And sometimes they would fall out. . . . I thought what I really need is . . . a bookmark that's going to stick to those pages . . . and still not damage the book when I pull them off. . . . I knew that Spence Silver back in our laboratory had just developed an adhesive that would do that. And I made. . . rough samples of the bookmarks. . . . I had also made up some larger sizes and found, hey, these are really handy for notes.

An adhesive that failed in its original application was a spectacular success in a new and highly profitable product.

*Based on John Nathan, *In Search of Excellence* (Waltham, MA: Nathan/Tyler Productions, 1985), 9.

6. Functional

In functional patterns, discuss the problems and solutions of each functional unit. For example, a report on a new plant might divide data into sections on the costs of land and building, on the availability of personnel, on the convenience of raw materials, and so on. A government report might divide data into the different functions an office performed, taking each in turn.

A strategy report for a political party uses a functional pattern of organization:

> Current Makeup of the House and Senate
> Congressional Seats Open in 2004
>   Seats Held by a Democratic Incumbent
>   Races in Which the Incumbent Has a Commanding Lead
>   Races in Which the Incumbent Is Vulnerable
>   Seats Held by a Republican Incumbent
>   Races in Which the Incumbent Has a Commanding Lead
>   Races in Which the Incumbent Is Vulnerable
>   Seats Where No Incumbent Is Running
> Senate Seats Open in 2004
>   Seats Held by a Democratic Incumbent
>   Races in Which the Incumbent Has a Commanding Lead
>   Races in Which the Incumbent Is Vulnerable
>   Seats Held by a Republican Incumbent
>   Races in Which the Incumbent Has a Commanding Lead
>   Races in Which the Incumbent Is Vulnerable
>   Seats Where No Incumbent Is Running

7. Chronological

A chronological report records events in the order in which they happened or are planned to happen. Many progress reports are organized chronologically:

> Work Completed in October
> Work Planned for November

How to Organize Specific Varieties of Reports

Informative, feasibility, and justification reports will be more successful when you work with the readers' expectations for that kind of report.

Informative and closure reports

Informative and **closure reports** summarize completed work or research that does not result in action or recommendation.

Informative reports often include the following elements:

- Introductory paragraph summarizing the problems or successes of the project.
- Purpose and Scope section(s) giving the purpose of the report and indicating what aspects of the topic it covers.
- Chronological account of how the problem was discovered, what was done, and what the results were.

- Concluding paragraph with suggestions for later action. In a recommendation report, the recommendations would be based on proof. In contrast, the suggestions in a closure or recommendation report are not proved in detail.

Figure 15.5 presents this kind of informative closure report.

Closure reports also allow a firm to document the alternatives it has considered before choosing a final design and to prove its right to copyrights and patents. Dwight W. Stevenson has shown that firms challenged in product liability suits need to be able to document in detail the evaluation process that led to the product design.[12] In another kind of case, the Wells Fargo bank fought off a $480 million suit charging that it had misappropriated someone else's idea for a credit card operation. The bank used materials from its archives going back 20 years to prove that it had developed the idea itself.[13]

Feasibility reports

Feasibility reports evaluate several alternatives and recommend one of them. (Doing nothing or delaying action can be one of the alternatives.)

Feasibility reports normally open by explaining the decision to be made, listing the alternatives, and explaining the criteria. In the body of the report, each alternative will be evaluated according to the criteria using one of the two comparison/contrast patterns. Discussing each alternative separately is better when one alternative is clearly superior, when the criteria interact, and when each alternative is indivisible. If the choice depends on the weight given to each criterion, you may want to discuss each alternative under each criterion.

Whether your recommendation should come at the beginning or the end of the report depends on your reader and the culture of your organization. Most readers want the "bottom line" up front. However, if the reader will find your recommendation hard to accept, you may want to delay your recommendation until the end of the report when you have given all your evidence.

Justification reports

Justification reports recommend or justify a purchase, investment, hiring, or change in policy. If your organization has a standard format for justification reports, follow that format. If you can choose your headings and organization, use this pattern when your recommendation will be easy for your reader to suggest:

1. **Indicate what you're asking for and why it's needed.** Since the reader has not asked for the report, you must link your request to the organization's goals.
2. **Briefly give the background of the problem or need.**
3. **Explain each of the possible solutions.** For each, give the cost and the advantages and disadvantages.
4. **Summarize the action needed to implement your recommendation.** If several people will be involved, indicate who will do what and how long each step will take.
5. **Ask for the action you want.**

If the reader will be reluctant to grant your request, use this variation of the problem-solving pattern described in Chapter 9:

1. **Describe the organizational problem (which your request will solve).** Use specific examples to prove the seriousness of the problem.
2. **Show why easier or less expensive solutions will not solve the problem.**
3. **Present your solution impersonally.**

Figure 15.5   *An Informative Memo Report Describing How a Company Solved a Problem*

March 14, 2000

To: Kitty O. Locker

From: Sara A. Ratterman *SAR*   *Informal short reports use*
                                              letter or memo format.

First   Subject: Recycling at Bike Nashbar
paragraph
summarizes
main   Two months ago, Bike Nashbar began recycling its corrugated cardboard boxes. The program
points.   was easy to implement and actually saves the company a little money compared to our previous
             garbage pickup.

Purpose   In this report, I will explain how, why, and by whom Bike Nashbar's program was initiated; how
and scope the program works and what it costs; and why other businesses should consider similar programs.
of report.

                              Bold or underline headings.

The Problem of Too Many Boxes and Not Enough Space in Bike Nashbar

             Every week, Bike Nashbar receives about 40 large cardboard boxes containing bicycles and other
             merchandise. As many boxes as possible would be stuffed into the trash bin behind the building,
Cause of   which also had to accommodate all the other solid waste the shop produces. Boxes that didn't fit
problem.   in the trash bin ended up lying around the shop, blocking doorways, and taking up space needed
             for customers' bikes. The trash bin was only emptied once a week, and by that time, even more
             boxes would have arrived.

                       Triple space before
                              heading.

The Importance of Recycling Cardboard Rather than Throwing It Away

             Arranging for more trash bins or more frequent pickups would have solved the immediate
             problem at Bike Nashbar but would have done nothing to solve the problem created by throwing
             away so much trash in the first place.
                       Double space between paragraphs within heading.

             According to David Crogen, sales representative for Waste Management, Inc., 75% of all solid
             waste in Columbus goes to landfills. The amount of trash the city collects has increased 150% in
Further   the last five years. Columbus's landfill is almost full. In an effort to encourage people and
seriousness businesses to recycle, the cost of dumping trash in the landfill is doubling from $4.90 a cubic yard
of problem. to $9.90 a cubic yard next week. Next January, the price will increase again, to $12.95 a cubic
             yard. Crogen believes that the amount of trash can be reduced by cooperation between the
             landfill and the power plant and by recycling.

                                                      Capitalize first letter of
How Bike Nashbar Started Recycling Cardboard   *major words in heading.*

             Waste Management, Inc., is the country's largest waste processor. After reading an article about
             how committed Waste Management, Inc., is to waste reduction and recycling, I decided to see
Solution. whether Waste Management could recycle our boxes. Corrugated cardboard (which is what Bike
             Nashbar's boxes are made of) is almost 100% recyclable, so we seemed to be a good candidate for
             recycling.

Kitty O. Locker   *Reader's name,*
March 14, 2000   *date,*
Page 2   *page number.*

To get the service started,

1.   I looked up Waste Management's phone number and called the company.

2.   I met with a friendly sales rep, David Crogen, that same afternoon to discuss the service.

Waste Management, Inc., took care of all the details. Two days later, Bike Nashbar was recycling its cardboard.

How the Service Works and What It Costs   *Talking heads tell reader what to expect in each section.*

Details of solution. Waste Management took away our existing 8-cubic-yard garbage bin and replaced it with two 4-yard bins. One of these bins is white and has "cardboard only" printed on the outside; the other is brown and is for all other solid waste. The bins are emptied once a week, with the cardboard being taken to the recycling plant and the solid waste going to the landfill or power plant.

Double space between paragraphs. Since Bike Nashbar was already paying more than $60 a week for garbage pickup, our basic cost stayed the same. (Waste Management can absorb the extra overhead only if the current charge is at least $60 a week.) The cost is divided 80/20 between the two bins: 80% of the cost pays for the bin that goes to the landfill and power plant; 20% covers the cardboard pickup. Bike Nashbar actually receives $5.00 for each ton of cardboard it recycles.

Each employee at Bike Nashbar is responsible for putting all the boxes he or she opens in the recycling bin. Employees must follow these rules:

- The cardboard must have the word "corrugated" printed on it, along with the universal recycling symbol.

Indented lists provide visual variety.
- The boxes must be broken down to their flattest form. If they aren't, they won't all fit in the bin and Waste Management would be picking up air when it could pick up solid cardboard. The more boxes that are picked up, the more money and space that will be made.

- No other waste except corrugated cardboard can be put in the recycling bin. Other materials could break the recycling machinery or contaminate the new cardboard.

- The recycling bin is to be kept locked with a padlock provided by Waste Management so that vagrants don't steal the cardboard and lose money for Waste Management and Bike Nashbar.

Kitty O. Locker
March 14, 2000
Page 3

Dis-
advantages
of
solution.

Minor Problems with Running the Recycling Program

The only problems we've encountered have been minor ones of violating the rules. Sometimes employees at the shop forget to flatten boxes, and air instead of cardboard gets picked up. Sometimes people forget to lock the recycling bin. When the bin is left unlocked, people do steal the cardboard, and plastic cups and other solid waste get dumped in the cardboard bin. I've posted signs where the key to the bin hangs, reminding employees to empty and fold boxes and relock the bin after putting cardboard in it. I hope this will turn things around and these problems will be solved.

Advantages of the Recycling Program

Advantages
of
solution.

The program is a great success. Now when boxes arrive, they are unloaded, broken down, and disposed of quickly. It is a great relief to get the boxes out of our way, and knowing that we are making a contribution to saving our environment builds pride in ourselves and Bike Nashbar.

Our company depends on a clean, safe environment for people to ride their bikes in.   Now we have become part of the solution. By choosing to recycle and reduce the amount of solid waste our company generates, we can save money while gaining a reputation as a socially responsible business.

Why Other Companies Should Adopt Similar Programs

Argues
that her
company's
experience
is relevant
to other
companies.

Businesses and institutions in Franklin County currently recycle less than 4% of the solid waste they produce. David Crogen tells me he has over 8,000 clients in Columbus alone, and he acquires new ones every day. Many of these businesses can recycle a large portion of their solid waste at no additional cost. Depending on what they recycle, they may even get a little money back.

The environmental and economic benefits of recycling as part of a comprehensive waste reduction program are numerous. Recycling helps preserve our environment. We can use the same materials over and over again, saving natural resources such as trees, fuel, and metals and decreasing the amount of solid waste in landfills. By conserving natural resources, recycling helps the U.S. become less dependent on imported raw materials. Crogen predicts that Columbus will be on a 100% recycling system by the year 2020. I strongly hope that his prediction will come true and the future may start to look a little brighter.

4. **Show that the disadvantages of your solution are outweighed by the advantages.**

5. **Summarize the action needed to implement your recommendation.** If several people will be involved, indicate who will do what and how long each step will take.

6. **Ask for the action you want.**

How much detail you need to give in a justification report depends on the corporate culture and on your reader's knowledge of and attitude toward your recommendation. Many organizations expect justification reports to be short—only one or two pages. Other organizations may expect longer reports with much more detailed budgets and a full discussion of the problem and each possible solution.

Presenting Information Effectively in Reports

The advice about style in Chapter 4 also applies to reports, with three exceptions:

1. **Use a fairly formal style, without contractions or slang.**

2. **Avoid the word *you*.** In a document with multiple audiences, it will not be clear who *you* is. Instead, use the company name.

3. **Include in the report all the definitions and documents needed to understand the recommendations.** The multiple audiences for reports include readers who may consult the document months or years from now; they will not share your special knowledge. Explain acronyms and abbreviations the first time they appear. Explain the history or background of the problem. Add as appendixes previous documents on which you are building.

This United Nations report on the state of the global environment is posted on the Web. Companies rarely post reports, but government agencies often do. For links to more reports on the Web, see the BAC Web site.

Who Did What?*

The passive verbs and impersonal constructions in US reports of coal mine disasters ("coal dust was permitted to accumulate" and "an accident occurred") suggest that accidents are inevitable. Who permitted the coal dust to accumulate? What could have been done to prevent the accumulation? Mine disaster reports contain sentences like the following: "The . . . fatality occurred when the victim proceeded into an area . . . before the roof was supported." *Why* did the man who was killed go into the area? Had a supervisor checked to see that the roof was supported? Who ordered what?

British reports of mine disasters, in contrast, focus on people and what they did to limit the damage from the disaster. Perhaps as a result, British mines have a much lower incidence of disasters than do US coal mines.

*Based on Beverly A. Sauer, "Sense and Sensibility in Technical Documentation: How Feminist Interpretation Strategies Can Save Lives in the Nation's Mines," *Journal of Business and Technical Communication* 7 (January 1993), 63–83.

The following points apply to any kind of writing, but they are particularly important in reports:

1. Say what you mean.
2. Tighten your writing.
3. Introduce sources and visuals gracefully.
4. Use blueprints, transitions, topic sentences, and headings to make your organization clear to your reader.

Let's look at each of these principles as they apply to reports.

1. Say What You Mean.

Not-quite-right word choices are particularly damaging in reports, which may be skimmed by readers who know very little about the subject. Occasionally you can simply substitute a word.

Incorrect: With these recommendations, we can overcome the solutions to our problem.

Correct: With these recommendations, we can overcome our problem.

Also correct: With these recommendations, we can solve our problem.

Putting the meaning of your sentence in the verbs will help you say what you mean.

Vague: My report revolves around the checkout lines and the methods used to get price checks when they arise.

Better: My report shows how price checks slow checkout lines and recommends ways to reduce the number of price checks needed.

Sometimes you'll need to completely recast the sentence.

Incorrect: The first problem with the incentive program is that middle managers do not use good interpersonal skills in implementing it. For example, the hotel chef openly ridicules the program. As a result, the kitchen staff fear being mocked if they participate in the program.

Better: The first problem with the incentive program is that some middle managers undercut it. For example, the hotel chef openly ridicules the program. As a result, the kitchen staff fear being mocked if they participate in the program.

2. Tighten Your Writing.

Eliminate unnecessary words, use gerunds and infinitives, combine sentences, and reword sentences to cut the number of words.

Wordy: Campus Jewelers' main objective is to increase sales. Specifically, the objective is to double sales in the next five years by becoming a more successful business.

Better: Campus Jewelers' objective is to double sales in the next five years.

Wordiness in reports may arise from two sources that are less likely to affect shorter messages: writers may deliberately put in extra words to create a longer document, and repetition may occur in different sections that are written at different times.

No reader wants length for the sake of length. Even in a class report, the page requirement is an indication of the complexity of analysis that the instructor expects. If you've chosen an appropriate topic, collected enough data, and analyzed the data thoroughly, you should reach any minimum page requirement easily. (If you suspect that you don't have enough data to yield an adequate report, talk to your instructor well before the due date to revise your topic.)

Some repetition in reports is legitimate. The Conclusion section restates points made in the body of the report; the recommendations appear in the

Transmittal, the Abstract or Executive Summary, and in the Recommendations sections of the report. However, repetitive references to earlier material ("As we have already seen") may indicate that the document needs to be reorganized. Read the document through at a single sitting to make sure that any repetition serves a useful purpose. If the repetition is boring, eliminate it.

3. Introduce Sources and Visuals Gracefully.

The first time you cite an author's work, use his or her full name: "Rosabeth Moss Kanter points out. . . ." In subsequent citations, use only the last name: "Kanter shows. . . ." Use active rather than passive verbs.

The verb you use indicates your attitude toward the source. *Says* and *writes* are neutral. *Points out, shows, suggests, discovers,* and *notes* suggest that you agree with the source. Words such as *claims, argues, contends that, believes,* and *alleges* distance you from the source. At a minimum, they suggest that you know that not everyone agrees with the source; they are also appropriate to report the views of someone with whom you disagree.

Use active verbs to refer to visuals, too:

As Table 1 shows, . . .
See Figure 4.

4. Use Blueprints, Transitions, Topic Sentences, and Headings.

Blueprints are overviews or forecasts that tell the reader what you will discuss in a section or in the entire report. Make your blueprint easy to read by telling the reader how many points there are and numbering them (either with words or figures). In the following example, the first sentence in the revised paragraph tells the reader to look for four points; the numbers separate the four points clearly. This overview paragraph also makes a contract with readers, who now expect to read about tax benefits first and employee benefits last.

Paragraph without numbers:	Employee stock ownership programs (ESOPs) have several advantages. They provide tax benefits for the company. ESOPs also create tax benefits for employees and for lenders. They provide a defense against takeovers. In some organizations, productivity increases because workers now have a financial stake in the company's profits. ESOPs are an attractive employee benefit and help the company hire and retain good employees.
Revised paragraph with numbers:	Employee stock ownership programs (ESOPs) provide four benefits. First, ESOPs provide tax benefits for the company, its employees, and lenders to the plan. Second, ESOPs help create a defense against takeovers. Third, ESOPs may increase productivity by giving workers a financial stake in the company's profits. Fourth, as an attractive employee benefit, ESOPs help the company hire and retain good employees.

Transitions are words, phrases, or sentences that tell the reader whether the discussion is continuing on the same point or shifting points.

There are economic advantages, too.
(Tells the reader that we are still discussing advantages but that we have now moved to economic advantages.)

An alternative to this plan is . . .
(Tells reader that a second option follows.)

The second factor . . .
(Tells reader that the discussion of the first factor is finished.)

These advantages, however, are found only in A, not in B or C.
(Prepares reader for a shift from A to B and C.)

Legal Liability and Report Drafts*

During civil litigation (such as a tort case charging that a product has injured a user), rough drafts may be important to establish the state of mind and intent of a document's drafters.

To protect the company, one lawyer recommends labeling all but the final draft "Preliminary Draft: Subject to Change." That way, if there's ever a lawsuit, the company will be able to argue that only the final report, not the drafts, should be used as evidence.

*Based on Elizabeth McCord, " 'But What You Really Meant Was . . .': Multiple Drafts and Legal Liability," paper presented at the Association for Business Communication Midwest Regional Conference, Akron, OH, April 3–5, 1991.

A **topic sentence** introduces or summarizes the main idea of a sentence. Readers who skim reports can follow your ideas more easily if each paragraph begins with a topic sentence.

Hard to read (no topic sentence):	Another main use of ice is to keep the fish fresh. Each of the seven kinds of fish served at the restaurant requires one gallon twice a day, for a total of 14 gallons. An additional 6 gallons a day are required for the salad bar.
Better (begins with topic sentence):	Twenty gallons of ice a day are needed to keep food fresh. Of this, the biggest portion (14 gallons) is used to keep the fish fresh. Each of the seven kinds of fish served at the restaurant requires one gallon twice a day ($7 \times 2 = 14$). An additional 6 gallons a day are required for the salad bar.

Headings are single words, short phrases, or complete sentences that indicate the topic in each section. A heading must cover all of the material under it until the next heading. For example, *Cost of Tuition* cannot include the cost of books or of room and board. You can have just one paragraph under a heading or several pages. If you do have several pages between headings you may want to consider using subheadings. Use subheadings only when you have two or more divisions within a main heading.

Topic headings focus on the structure of the report. As you can see from the following example, topic headings give very little information.

Topic headings

Recommendation
Problem
    Situation 1
    Situation 2
Causes of the Problem
    Background
    Cause 1
    Cause 2
Recommended Solution

Informative, or **talking, heads,** in contrast, tell the reader what to expect. Informative heads, like those in the examples in this chapter, provide an overview of each section and of the entire report:

Talking heads

Recommended Reformulation for Vibe Bleach
Problems in Maintaining Vibe's Granular Structure
    Solidifying during Storage and Transportation
    Customer Complaints about "Blocks" of Vibe in Boxes
Why Vibe Bleach "Cakes"
    Vibe's Formula
    The Manufacturing Process
    The Chemical Process of Solidification
Modifications Needed to Keep Vibe Flowing Freely

Headings must be **parallel** (p. 104), that is, they must use the same grammatical structure. Subheads must be parallel to each other but do not necessarily have to be parallel to subheads under other headings.

Not parallel: Are Students Aware of VIP?
                       Current Awareness among Undergraduate Students
                       Graduate Students
             Ways to Increase Volunteer Commitment and Motivation
                       We Must Improve Training and Supervision
                       Can We Make Volunteers' Hours More Flexible?
                       Providing Emotional Support to Volunteers
                       Provide More Information about Community Needs and VIP Services

Parallel: Campus Awareness of VIP
                       Current Awareness among Undergraduate Students
                       Current Awareness among Graduate Students
             Ways to Increase Volunteer Commitment and Motivation
                       Improving Training and Supervision
                       Improving the Flexibility of Volunteers' Hours
                       Providing Emotional Support to Volunteers
                       Providing More Information about Community Needs and VIP Services

In a very complicated report, you may need up to five levels of headings. Figure 15.6 illustrates one way to set up headings. When you don't need this many levels, pick the headings you find most attractive. Use a lower level for subheadings.

Figure 15.6 shows only one example of each level of heading. In an actual report, however, you would not use a subheading unless you had at least two subsections under the next higher heading.

Whatever the format for headings, avoid having a subhead come immediately after a heading. Instead, some text should follow the main heading before the subheading. (If you have nothing else to say, give an overview of the division.) Avoid having a heading or subheading all by itself at the bottom of the page. Instead, have at least one line (preferably two) of type. If there isn't room for a line of type under it, put the heading on the next page. Don't use a heading as the antecedent for a pronoun. Instead, repeat the noun.

Writing Formal Reports

Formal reports are distinguished from informal letter and memo reports by their length and by their components. A full formal report may contain the following components:

Cover
Title Page
Letter or Memo of Transmittal
Table of Contents
List of Illustrations
Executive Summary
Report Body
   Introduction (Orients the reader to the report. Usually has subheadings for Purpose and Scope; depending on the situation, may also have Limitations, Assumptions, Methods, Criteria, and Definitions.)
   Background or History of the Problem (Orients the reader to the topic of the report. Serves as a record for later readers of the report.)
   Body (Presents and interprets data in words and visuals. Analyzes causes of the problem and evaluates possible solutions. Specific headings will depend on the topic of the report.)

Quality Packaging*

Quality packaging means that the final report is clear, concise and well organized. . . .

The most critical piece of the final report is the Executive Summary. Why? Because most time-pressed executives never read beyond this section. Therefore the writer should make certain that the key findings, conclusions and recommendation(s) are laid out clearly here. The rest of the report, in all its detail, is attached so the reader may decide whether she or he would like more information on a particular topic.

How much detail should you include? As much as you believe the audience reading the report will want. . . . Put yourself in the reader's shoes. Would you rather read about the problem and solution in 5 pages or in 50 pages? In each of the supporting sections, state the question you answer, your analytic method, findings, and conclusions. Put the raw data in appendices.

The final piece of the process is editing and revising. . . . This step is necessary to "polish" your report and refine your thinking. How well you perform this step is often the difference between a good report and a great report.

*Quoted from Dayton J. D. Semerjian, statement to Kitty Locker, February 3, 1997.

F i g u r e 15.6   *Five Levels of Headings in a Single-Spaced Document*

Center
Bold or underline   **FIRST-LEVEL HEADINGS**   *For titles of short reports,*
Full capital letters   *chapter titles in very long*
                                                             documents

First-level headings are used for the titles of short documents and for chapter titles within long documents. Center them, using full capital letters. You may use bold type or a larger type size if you choose.

This example uses just one heading at each level. However, in a business document use at least two headings at each level.

Center
Bold or underline   **Second-Level Headings**   *Main divisions in a*
Regular capital letters   *medium-length report*

Second-level headings introduce divisions within major points. The first letter of each major word in the heading is capitalized; the heading is either underlined or put in bold type; it is centered on the page. In a single-spaced document, triple-space between the previous text and the heading; double-space between the heading and the text which follows. In a double-spaced document, double-space twice between the previous text and the heading; double-space either once or twice between the heading and the following text.

When you do not need five levels of division, you may use "second-level headings" for the major divisions (Roman numerals in an outline) of the report.

                        Left margin   *Used for subheadings in a medium-*
Third-Level Headings *Bold or underline*   *length report*
                        Regular capitals   *Used for main headings in memos*

Third-level headings are flush with the left-hand margin and are either set in bold or underlined. The first letters of the first word and of other major words are capitalized; all other letters are lowercase. In a single-spaced document, triple-space between the previous text and the heading; in a double-spaced document, double-space twice before the heading. In both, double-space between the heading and the text which follows.

In a report using second-level headings for the Roman numerals, third-level headings would indicate capital letter points. Third-level headings are usually used for the main headings in memos.

Bold or underline
Followed   **Fourth-level headings.** Fourth- and fifth-level headings will appear only in a very long or
by a period complicated report. Fourth-level headings use the normal paragraph indentation, if any, are underlined or set in bold, and are followed by a period. Double-space between previous text and the heading. The paragraph begins on the same line on which the heading is placed.

Bold or underline   *Used only in very long, complex documents*
Part of   **Fifth-level headings** are integral parts of the first sentence of the first paragraph about a
sentence   topic. They are underlined or set in bold. Since they are part of the paragraph, only the first letter of the first word is capitalized and only the normal spacing between paragraphs is used between previous text and the heading.

More formal ←	→ Less formal	
Cover	Title Page	Introduction
Title Page	Table of Contents	Body
Transmittal	Executive Summary	Conclusions
Table of Contents	Body	Recommendations
List of Illustrations	Introduction	
Executive Summary	Body	
Body	Conclusions	
Introduction	Recommendations	
Body		
Conclusions		
Recommendations		
Notes/References		
Appendixes		
Questionnaires		
Interviews		
Computer Printouts		
Related Documents		

Figure 15.7

The Components in a Report Can Vary

Conclusions (Summarizes main points of report.)

Recommendations (Recommends actions to solve the problem. May be combined with Conclusions; may be put at beginning of body rather than at the end.)

Notes, References, or Works Cited (Documents sources cited in the report.)

Appendixes (Provide additional materials that the careful reader may want: transcript of an interview, copies of questionnaires, tallies of all the questions, computer printouts, previous reports.)

As Figure 15.7 shows, not every formal report necessarily has all these components. In addition, some organizations call for additional components or arrange these components in a different order. As you read each section below, you may want to turn to the corresponding pages of the long report in Figure 15.8 to see how the component is set up and how it relates to the total report.

Title Page

The Title Page of a report usually contains four items: the title of the report, whom the report is prepared for, whom it is prepared by, and the release date. Sometimes reports also contain a brief summary or abstract of the contents of the report; some title pages contain decorative artwork.

The title of the report should be as informative as possible. Like subject lines, report titles are straightforward.

Poor title: New Plant Site

Better title: Why Eugene, Oregon, Is the Best Site for the New Kemco Plant

Poor title: Planting for the Quadrangle

Better title: Why Honey Locusts Are the Best Trees for the New Quadrangle

In many cases, the title will state the recommendation in the report: "Why the United Nations Should Establish a Seed Bank." However, the title should omit recommendations when

- The reader will find the recommendations hard to accept.
- Putting all the recommendations in the title would make it too long.
- The report does not offer recommendations.

If the title does not contain the recommendation, it normally indicates what problem the report tries to solve.

Eliminate any unnecessary words:

Wordy: Report of a Study on Ways to Market Life Insurance to Urban Professional People Who Are in Their Mid-40s

Better: Ways to Market Life Insurance to the Mid-40s Urban Professional

The statement of whom the report is prepared for normally includes the name of the person who will make a decision based on the report, his or her job title, the organization's name, and its location (city, state, and zip code). Government reports often omit the person's name and simply give the organization that authorized the report.

If the report is prepared primarily by one person, the *Prepared by* section will have that person's name, his or her title, the organization, and its location (city, state, and zip code). In internal reports, the organization and location are usually omitted if the report writer works at the headquarters office.

If several people write the report, government reports normally list all their names, using a separate sheet of paper if the group working on the report is large. Practices in business differ. In some organizations, all the names are listed; in others, the division to which they belong is listed; in still others, the name of the chair of the group appears.

The **release date,** the date the report will be released to the public, is usually the date the report is scheduled for discussion by the decision makers. The report is due four to six weeks before the release date so that the decision makers can review the report before the meeting.

If you have the facilities and the time, try using different sizes and styles of type, color, and artwork to create a visually attractive and impressive title page. However, a plain typed page is acceptable. The format in Figure 15.8 will enable you to create an acceptable title page by typing it only once.

Letter or Memo of Transmittal

Use a letter of transmittal if you are not a regular employee of the organization for which you prepare the report; use a memo if you are a regular employee. See Appendix A for letter and memo formats.

The transmittal has several purposes: to transmit the report, to orient the reader to the report, and to build a good image of the report and of the writer. An informal writing style is appropriate for a transmittal even when the style in the report is more formal. A professional transmittal helps you create a good image of yourself and enhances your credibility. Personal statements are appropriate in the transmittal, even though they would not be acceptable in the report itself.

Organize the transmittal in this way:

1. **Transmit the report.** Tell when and by whom it was authorized and the purpose it was to fulfill.
2. **Summarize your conclusions and recommendations.** If the recommendations will be easy for the reader to accept, put them early in

the transmittal. If they will be difficult, summarize the findings and conclusions before the recommendations.

3. **Mention any points of special interest in the report. Indicate minor problems you encountered in your investigation and show how you surmounted them. Thank people who helped you.** These optional items can build goodwill and enhance your credibility.

4. **Point out additional research that is necessary, if any.** Sometimes your recommendation cannot be implemented until further work is done. If you'd be interested in doing that research, or if you'd like to implement the recommendations, say so.

5. **Thank the reader for the opportunity to do the work and offer to answer questions.** Even if the report has not been fun to do, expressing satisfaction in doing the project is expected. Saying that you'll answer questions about the report is a way of saying that you won't charge the reader your normal hourly fee to answer questions (one more reason to make the report clear!).

The Letter of Transmittal on page i of Figure 15.8 uses this pattern of organization.

Table of Contents

In the Table of Contents, list the headings exactly as they appear in the body of the report. If the report is less than 25 pages, you'll probably list all the levels of headings. In a very long report, pick a level and put all the headings at that level and above in the Table of Contents.

Page ii of Figure 15.8 shows the Table of Contents.

List of Illustrations

A List of Illustrations enables readers to refer to your visuals.

Report visuals comprise both Tables and Figures. **Tables** are words or numbers arranged in rows and columns. **Figures** are everything else: bar graphs, pie charts, flow charts, maps, drawings, photographs, computer printouts, etc. Tables and figures are numbered independently, so you may have both a Table 1 and a Figure 1. In a report with maps and graphs but no other visuals, the visuals are sometimes called Map 1 and Graph 1. Whatever you call the illustrations, list them in the order in which they appear in the report; give the name of each visual as well as its number.

See Chapter 16 for information about how to design and label visuals.

Executive Summary

An **Executive Summary** or **abstract** tells the reader what the document is about. It summarizes the recommendation of the report and the reasons for the recommendation or describes the topics the report discusses and indicates the depth of the discussion.

A good abstract is easy to read, concise, and clear. Edit your abstract carefully to tighten your writing and eliminate any unnecessary words.

Wordy: The author describes two types of business jargon, *businessese* and *reverse gobbledygook*. He gives many examples of each of these and points out how their use can be harmful.

Tight: The author describes and gives examples of two harmful types of business jargon, *businessese* and *reverse gobbledygook*.

It's OK to use exactly the same words in the abstract and the report. Abstracts generally use a more formal style than other forms of business writing.

Figure 15.8   *A Long Report*

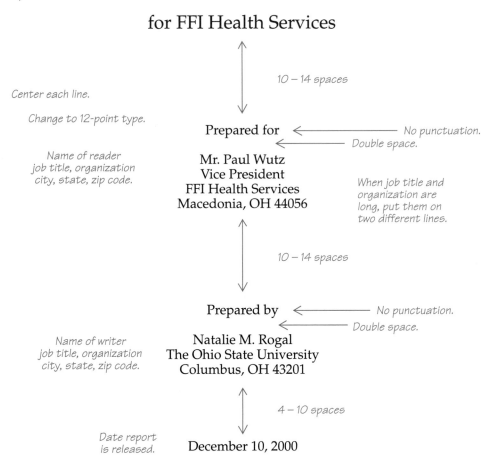

$1\frac{1}{2} - 2''$

Center each line.

Use a large
font. This is
18-point.

A College Internship Program

for FFI Health Services

10 – 14 spaces

Center each line.

Change to 12-point type.

Prepared for   ← *No punctuation.*
   ← *Double space.*

Name of reader
job title, organization
city, state, zip code.

Mr. Paul Wutz
Vice President
FFI Health Services
Macedonia, OH 44056

*When job title and
organization are
long, put them on
two different lines.*

10 – 14 spaces

Prepared by   ← *No punctuation.*
   ← *Double space.*

Name of writer
job title, organization
city, state, zip code.

Natalie M. Rogal
The Ohio State University
Columbus, OH 43201

4 – 10 spaces

Date report
is released.

December 10, 2000

1 1/2 – 2''

Figure 15.8   *A Long Report (continued)*

This letter uses modified block format (see Figure A.5). Block format is also acceptable.

You may also design a letterhead for yourself, especially if you're assuming that you are doing the report as a consultant.

1470 Highland St.
Columbus, OH 43201
December 9, 2000

Mr. Paul Wutz
Vice President
FFI Health Services
8635 Crow Drive, Suite 105
Macedonia, OH 44056

In paragraph 1, release the report. Note when and by whom the report was authorized. Note report's purpose.

Dear Mr. Wutz:

Here is the report you authorized in October exploring the kind of internship program that might be best for FFI.

FFI Health Services can benefit from establishing an internship program while providing a valuable service to students. To establish an internship program, you should

Give recommendations or thesis.

- Use the guidelines suggested by Ohio State's Professional Experience Program.

- Pilot the program, focusing on finance and computer science majors the first summer.

- Set intern salaries at $9-$10 an hour for all majors except computer science. Start computer science majors at at least $15 an hour.

- Survey your staff to find out which employees would like to supervise and mentor interns.

- Publicize the program on the Web as well as in Ohio State's Career Services Center. Conduct further research on the best way to reach computer science majors.

- Conduct further research to identify schools other than Ohio State which would also be good sources of interns.

Thank people who helped you.

The information for this report came from online and print sources, a survey of 150 Ohio State students, and an interview with Mindy Kannard of Career Services at The Fisher College of Business. I especially appreciate the guidance of Ms. Kannard and others involved in the Professional Experience Program.

Thank the reader for the opportunity to do the research.

Thank you for the opportunity to conduct this research. I appreciate the chance to apply my experience helping to run an internship program last summer. If you have any questions about the material in this report, please call me.

Offer to answer questions about the report. Answers would be included in your fee—no extra charge!

Sincerely,

Natalie Rogal

Natalie Rogal

Center page number at the bottom of the page. Use a lower-case Roman numeral.   i

Figure 15.8   *A Long Report (continued)*

Table of Contents

Table of Contents does not list itself.

Use lower-case Roman numerals for front matter.

Letter of Transmittal i

Executive Summary.. iii

Introduction 1
    Purpose 1
    Scope 1
    Assumptions 1
    Methodology.. 2
    Limitations 2
    Criteria 2

Background on FFI Health Services 2

General Benefits of College Internship Programs 3

A Model Internship Program 3
    Intern Duties 3
    Program Features... 4
        Supervising Interns 5
        Evaluating Interns 5
        Setting Salary 5
    Common Problems.. 5

Making Internships Attractive to Ohio State Students 6
    Providing Good Experience 6
    Providing Competitive Pay.. 7
    Finding a Niche for FFI Internships 7

Conclusions and Recommendations 8
    1. Choosing Positions for Interns 8
    2. Setting Intern Salaries 8
    3. Choosing Supervisors and Mentors 8
    4. Publicizing the Program 8
    5. Recruiting Interns 9

References.. 10

Appendix A: Raw Survey Data 11

Appendix B: Responses to Open-Ended Question 12

Indent subheads.

Intro begins on page "1".

Capitalize first letter of each major word in headings.

Some reports have separate sections for "Conclusions" and "Recommendations"

Headings or subheadings must be parallel within a section. Here, headings are nouns and noun (gerund) phrases. Questions and complete sentences can also be used.

Add a "List of Illustrations" at the bottom of the Table of Contents or on a separate page if the report has graphs and other visuals. Omit "List of Illustrations" if you have only tables.

Line up right margin (justify).

ii

Figure 15.8   *A Long Report (continued)*

A College Internship Program
for FFI Health Services

Report
title.

Executive Summary

Start with recommendations or thesis.

FFI Health Services should create a college internship program following the model outlined in Ohio State's Professional Experience Program. Following this program will cover the basics of a sound internship program and will enable FFI to hire interns at The Ohio State University.

Provide brief support for each recommendation

FFI can eventually offer internships in eight areas: accounting, computer science, finance, fulfillment, human resources, marketing, transportation logistics, and Web maintenance. FFI does work in each of these areas and could benefit both from the projects that interns might complete and from the opportunity to make permanent hires in these areas. In its first year, however, the internship program should focus on two or three main areas of employment to pilot the program. Finance and computer science are FFI's areas of greatest need.

Since the best students have several options, FFI should offer interns a competitive wage. The average intern earned between $8 and $9 last summer, so FFI Health Services should set intern pay at $9-$10 an hour for all majors except computer science. To hire the best computer science majors will require starting salaries of at least $15 an hour. Providing housing would make the internships more attractive and would enlarge the pool of applicants.

One person should not attempt to supervise all of the interns, even during the first summer when there may be only two or three interns. FFI will need to conduct internal research to determine how potential supervisors and mentors feel about working closely with interns. Acting as a mentor should be a voluntary position to ensure active and enthusiastic guidance for the intern.

Participating in the Professional Experience Program will mean that FFI's job descriptions will be available to students who come to the Fisher College of Business Career Services Center looking for internships. However, other kinds of publicity are also desirable so that FFI can have the widest pool of applicants from which to choose. Announcing the internships on FFI's Web site is an obvious step and would bring up FFI's internships when students do Web searches for "internships." Many other companies already give information about internships on Web sites. If computer majors remain in such high demand, FFI will need to do something special to attract them. Further research will be needed to determine what kind of niche FFI can develop.

FFI may want to recruit at other schools besides Ohio State. More research needs to be done to determine the optimal places for FFI Health Services to recruit student interns. Since students may not be able to relocate for the summer or may only move if given a substantial pay incentive, recruiting at colleges in Cleveland and in Tampa may make sense. In addition, it would be useful to identify any colleges that offer majors in managed care. Such colleges would be a good source of students who would be interested in the kind of work FFI does.

Language in Executive Summary can come from report. Make sure any repeated language is well-written!

The abstract or executive summary contains the logical skeleton of the report: the recommendation(s) and evidence supporting them.

iii

Figure 15.8   *A Long Report (continued)*

A running header is optional.

Here, the running head and page numbers   *Start with introduction.*
are one point size smaller than the text
used for the body of the report.   **Introduction**   *Center first-level heads. This author*
                                                                                    uses bold (one point larger than body).

Many companies use internship programs to recruit and "try out" students who will eventually become permanent employees. Internships are so popular that they have increased 37% in the last five years (Ferguson, 1998). FFI Health Services is interested in creating a college internship program that will attract quality applicants.

Purpose   *Rhetorical purpose*
                                              /

The purpose of this report is to recommend a college internship program that will meet FFI's needs.

                                  Tell what you discuss and how thoroughly you discuss each topic. Scope section
Scope   *should match report. This section has changed a bit from the proposal because*
                                            of the available information.

In this report, I will focus on three topics: models of internships, what Ohio State students want from internships, and the kinds of internship experiences FFI Health Services can offer. My information about models for internships comes largely from The Fisher College of Business' Professional Experience Program (PEP). PEP suggests activities for interns and outlines the features for an internship program. I also use anecdotal evidence about common internship problems and how FFI can avoid them.

I discuss what Ohio State students want from the internship experience based on a survey of 150 Ohio   *Give*
State students. I discuss how students view internships, what students want from a summer experience, and   *topics*
their willingness to accept internships at FFI. Finally, based on interviews with staff members, especially Paul   *in the*
Wutz, I discuss the kinds of internship experiences FFI can offer.   *order*
                                                                                                                    in which
I will also briefly discuss the general advantages of internships and how the internship program could be *you'll*
publicized.   *discuss*
                              List relevant topics that you will not discuss.   *them.*

I will not discuss the financial feasibility of the program or at what schools the company should focus its recruiting efforts.

Assumptions   *Assumptions cannot be proven. But if they are wrong,*
                                          the report's recommendation may no longer be valid.

These   My recommendations are based on three assumptions:
ideas could
be   • The job market will remain tight, making it difficult to find qualified applicants. The tight job market
presented in   makes an internship program especially desirable. If the job market changed so that there were many
a paragraph.   more applicants than jobs, FFI might be able to hire managers more easily without needed to "grow"
But the   its own managers.
list provides
visual variety
and makes   • FFI's central office will remain in Macedonia, Ohio, making it desirable to recruit students from The
it easier   Ohio State University. If the central office moved, students from other universities might be more
for the reader   desirable than Ohio State students as interns.
to skim
the page.   • Ohio State students' preferences regarding internships are typical of students at other universities.

Figure 15.8	*A Long Report (continued)*

If you use only library and online sources, you do not need a "Methodology" section. Instead, briefly describe your sources in a paragraph under "Purpose."

A College Internship Program for FFI Health Services   Page 2

Even if it focuses on Ohio State students, FFI will hire interns from other universities as well and should investigate preferences at other universities.

Methodology

If you collected original data (surveys, interviews, or observations), tell how you chose whom to study, what kind of a sample you used, and on what date(s) you collected the information.

Information for this report comes from print and online sources, interviews, and a survey of 150 Ohio State University students. I was unable to take a random sample of business students because the Fisher College of Business does not make available a directory of its students. Thus it was necessary for me to use a convenience sample. I chose to survey students on November 20, 2000 at the Ohio Union during a Career Fair. To get the desired number in the sample I asked every student who walked by if he or she had a few minutes to fill out a survey.

Summarize the demographic information about your respondents.

The students who responded represent a wide variety of majors and interests. Two-thirds of the students in my sample were juniors and seniors; 32% had an internship last summer. (See Appendix A for all of the raw data from the survey.) *Refer to your Appendixes in the text of your report.*

Limitations

If your report has limitations, state them.
Giving the number makes it easier for the reader to read the paragraph.

My research has <u>four</u> limitations. First, I surveyed students only at The Ohio State University, and FFI will probably want to recruit from other universities as well. Second, at Ohio State, FFI is probably most interested in interns from the College of Business and of Engineering, where Computer Science is housed. Yet my sample covers a wide variety of colleges and has no Engineering students at all. Third, the fact that my survey is based on a convenience sample means that we cannot generalize from my survey to all Ohio State students. Indeed, respondents' demographics show that the students I surveyed are not representative. The College of Social and Behavioral Sciences has the most undergraduate majors at Ohio State, yet it is not the College with the most students in my sample. Fourth, my survey may have interviewer error, which results from the interviewer answering questions differently for different people. Some respondents asked for clarification on some questions while others did not. I tried to answer consistently but my wording was open to interpretation and may have affected the responses. This source of error probably did not significantly affect the accuracy.

Criteria

Triple-space (2 empty spaces) before new head. Double-space after head before paragraph.

According to Paul Wutz, the two most important criteria for an internship program are that (1) supervising interns take as little time as possible and (2) the program yield permanent promotable workers. A less important criterion is that interns be able to complete some of the projects that full-time FFI personnel have not had time to do.

Background on FFI Health Services

FFI Health Services contracts with companies to manage prescription benefits. FFI enables employers to give employees prescription coverage at a very reasonable price. Employees can order deeply discounted prescription drugs on FFI's Web site.

Figure 15.8   *A Long Report (continued)*

The company is five years old and started with two employees. FFI Health Services has experienced explosive growth. It now employs 50 people in two offices, one in Macedonia, Ohio, and the other in Tampa, Florida. Hiring qualified personnel is a challenge. Current hiring procedures include running classified advertisements or conducting nationwide searches depending on the type of position to be filled. Some specialized positions such as computer programmers are in such high demand that FFI Health Services does not always feel it is getting the best candidates.

Use talking heads. Note how much more informative this is than "Advantages".

General Benefits of College Internship Programs

Begin most paragraphs with topic sentences.

Businesses benefit enormously from hiring interns. Students are good, productive employees who are positively inclined toward work that is related to their career interests. They can serve as temporary staff or provide assistance for ongoing or special projects. Hiring interns also increases access for hiring women and minorities. Students cost less to hire than regular permanent employees and improve morale in the workplace. Furthermore, student employees bring new ideas and technology to the work site (Ohio State, 1998).

Other benefits include recruiting opportunities. When interns become full-time employees, they need less training and orientation into the company. "Research shows that the turnover rate of employees who have had co-op/internship experience with the organization is significantly less than that for those who did not have this type of job-related opportunity" (Ohio State, 1998, "Criteria and Guidelines"). *APA format calls for page numbers when you quote a source. This Web source doesn't have page numbers, but the student gives the subpage from which the quote was taken.*

A Model Internship Program

When starting a new internship program, a company can benefit by following a model. The Director of the Professional Experience Program (PEP) at Ohio State works with employers to design internships that benefit both the company and the student. The PEP Employer Handbook offers extensive, specific guidelines for employers. In addition, several articles suggest general guidelines for successful internships.

Spell out term the first time you use it, with the abbreviation in parentheses. Then you can use the abbreviation by itself.

Intern Duties

Appropriate job duties are at the heart of a successful internship program. Admitting that gofer and grunt work are "ubiquitous" in internships, Martha Stone argues that the best internships provide "planned, hands-on" tasks in the field of the student's major (1998, p. 8). Some companies ask interns to do small projects that no one in the organization has time for, but that the organization wants to have done.

When author's name is in the sentence, use only year and page number in parentheses.

Another option is to give interns the same kinds of jobs that entry-level employees would have. Allegiance Healthcare (Watson, 1998), Micron Technology (King, 1997), and Aetna are three of the many companies that take this approach. Aetna's actuarial interns analyze data, improve processes, and "mak[e] things happen" (1999, "Qualifications and Rewards"). One intern reports,   *Use square brackets for your changes in quoted text.*

Quote when the source is especially credible for the point you want to make.

As an Aetna actuarial intern, I worked closely with the other actuaries in my area. I helped to develop a reserving system and price a new contract. I began contributing to the area on my first day, which really surprised me. I worked side-by-side with the other actuaries in the area, as well as the other non-financial areas. What I did really made a difference. My technical, communication, and analytical skills were appreciated and demanded. (1999, "On the Job with Aetna Actuarial Interns")

This quote comes from the Web and has no page number. Title of subpage makes it easy for reader to find page on which quote appears.

Figure 15.8   *A Long Report (continued)*

A College Internship Program for FFI Health Services   Page 4

The Professional Experience Program requires that the employer submit a one-page job description. Examples of job duties in past internships include the following:

Accounting
- Perform inventory costing and cost accounting
- Prepare monthly and year-end close-outs
- Prepare and produce financial statements for reports
- Implement and audit programs to verify accuracy
- Coordinate procurement and transmittal records for audit
- Use Excel, Lotus 1-2-3 and other business software

Periods could be used to end each line. But since this is part of a quote, give text exactly as it appears in the source.

Finance
- Prepare program management cost estimates for projects
- Perform Capital Investment Analysis—analyze the Net Present Value and Internal Rate of Return   *This line could be tightened—"Analyze Capital Investments."*
- Gather financial and accounting data for financial planning and analysis purposes
- Prepare Cost of Capital Estimates
- Prepare Monthly Cash Budgets

But since this is part of a quote, give it exactly as in the source. If you make changes, put them in square brackets [ ].

Human Resources
- Train employees on writing and supervisory skills
- Redesign clerical salary structures
- Evaluate and track recruiting efforts
- Develop a guide for cooperative education
- Assist with targeted selection recruiting plan
- Conduct grievance and disciplinary interviews (Ohio State, 1998, "Job Descriptions")

Other duties are also possible. For example, the Professional Experience Program guidelines suggest that employers may want to ask interns to present their projects to other managers or to employees within the department, both to inform other employees and to enhance students' communication skills.

As these job descriptions suggest, interns can be assigned the same work that might be given to entry-level employees. One question that a company might have is whether college interns who have not yet graduated can really do the work normally assigned to college graduates. Anecdotal evidence suggests that they can. According to Mindy Kannard, Director of Ohio State's Professional Experience Program, "We have very few problems" (personal communication, November 1, 2000). Testimonials from companies that have hired interns are even more positive. According to Heidi A. Willis, Internship Coordinator for American Backhaulers,

When the source is in the paragraph, the parentheses come before the period at the end of the sentence.

> Implementing a successful internship program was effortless with the help of the Career Services staff. Students from OSU's Fisher College of Business selected to join our internship team have an elevated level of maturity, a hearty appetite for success, and an active desire to convert learned theories into working ideas. (Ohio State, "Testimonials")

Long quotations are indented; no quotation marks necessary.

Note that the source parenthesis goes after the period at the end of the sentence in indented quotes.

Program Features

Employers who work with Ohio State's Professional Experience Program must supervise and evaluate interns. Setting appropriate salaries is also important.

Figure 15.8 *A Long Report (continued)*

Third-level headings have periods even when they are not complete sentences.

Quote when you can't think of any better words than those in the source.

Supervising Interns. Interns must receive supervision that is "on-going, consistent and positive" (Ohio State, 1998, "Criteria & Guidelines." At the beginning of the assignment, orientation should include identifying the "key players," the chain of command, office policy (for example, time sheets, overtime, and sick leave), and the corporate culture (including appropriate dress). Ideally, the supervisor or someone else should mentor the intern, not merely give an assignment and disappear. Students benefit from learning not only what is needed, but also why it's needed—how it fits into the larger picture of the company's goals. Identifying specific learning goals can help interns budget their time and also makes evaluation easier.

Mr. Wutz has assumed that since FFI does not have a Human Resources department, he would have to do all the work of supervising and evaluating interns. However, this work could be done by people in the areas in which the interns are working. Because the mentor provides guidance and acts as a "go-to" person for addressing concerns and questions, a mentor working in the same area as the student is ideal. It is important that each student be matched with an enthusiastic mentor who will take an active role in guiding the student's development and providing career advice.

Evaluating Interns. Interns should be evaluated midway through the work period and again at the end. The evaluation should be based on specific goals established earlier. Areas for evaluation might include quality of work, enthusiasm toward assignments, comprehension and knowledge, organizational skills, and judgment. Objectives set forth at the onset of the internship should be reiterated at the interim evaluation and discussed again before the student returns to school. The supervisor should discuss the evaluation with the student and provide constructive criticism and encouragement.

The Professional Experience Program provides a sample form which the employer can use (www.cob.ohio-state.edu/careers/pep/EmpEvual.htm). Employers can also use another evaluation instrument but must turn in some form of written evaluation to the Fisher College of Business Career Services Center.

Setting Salary. The Professional Experience Program at Ohio State gives useful suggestions for setting interns' salaries. While the initial salary should be high enough to attract quality applicants, it should be low enough so that wages can be raised commensurate with increased responsibilities developed should the student be hired again for another internship or hired as a permanent employee.

Second-level heads are flush with the left margin and bolded. Triple-space before new head; double-space after.

Common Problems

Some of the possible problems, such as not giving interns substantive work assignments, can be prevented by following the guidelines for the Professional Experience Program. Professor Dawn Kalmuth, who teaches a class for interns, reports that most interns experience situations in which they feel uncertain. Discussions among interns are helpful in understanding situations, brainstorming alternatives, and developing strategies for implementing the preferred alternative. Some interns find that their supervisors are not in fact very knowledgeable and that they need to seek information from more active (but busier) people. Some interns have been given huge assignments which require massive overtime. Other interns are asked to pick up a project started by a former intern without adequate documentation about what has been done and why. Still other interns experience problems that might be encountered by full-time employees, including sexual harassment (Dawn Kalmuth, personal communication, November 12, 2000). Telling the intern about company channels for dealing with problems and good communication between the intern and his or her mentor or supervisor is essential.

APA format for phone calls, conversations and other sources which the reader cannot check.

Figure 15.8   *A Long Report (continued)*

A College Internship Program for FFI Health Services

Heading must cover everything under that heading until the next head or subhead at that level.   Page 6

Making Internships Attractive to Ohio State Students

Few of the people I surveyed—only 15%—had heard of FFI Rx Managed Care. Companies with strong internship programs are "overwhelmed with applications" ("Internships," 1997, p. 102), but it will be a while before FFI commands that kind of interest. To get off to a good start, FFI's internship program should be attractive to Ohio State students.

When an article has no author, use the first word of the title to identify it.

Providing Good Experience

In terms of accepting a specific internship, the students I surveyed ranked experience as most important, as Table 1 shows.

Refer to Tables in your text.

Table 1. How Important Are Various Criteria in Accepting a Specific Internship?

Rank	Criterion	Average; N = 150 (3 = Very impt., 2 = Somewhat impt., 1 = Not impt.)
1	Gaining experience	2.99
2	Quality of mentoring	2.92
3	Building connections	2.73
4	Chance of getting a job with that company	2.57
5	Prestige of company	2.43
6	Location where you live now	2.36
7	Money	2.22

Compare Table 1 with the raw data for Question 10 in Appendix A (p. 11 of report). Here, the items have been re-arranged to go from the highest to the lowest score.

This emphasis on gaining experience is consistent with the reports of people who had internships last summer. The top four benefits of their internships, according to the people who had them last summer, were "looks good on my résumé, work related to my major, chance to explore my interests," and "made connections." (See Table 2.) If FFI provides internships that give students experience related to their majors, it can attract interns even though it is not yet well known.

Table 2. What Were the Most Beneficial Aspects of Your Internship?

Rank	Aspect	N = 48 n	%
1	Looks good on my résumé	42	86%
2	Work related to my major	41	85%
3	Chance to explore my interests	35	73%
4	Made connections	34	71%
5	Worked with clients	22	46%
6	Likely to get a job offer/got a job offer	15	31%

"N" is the total number of people responding to the question; "n" is the number of people giving a particular response. Giving percentages makes it easier for readers to understand data.

Surprisingly, as Table 1 shows, "chance of getting a job with that company" ranked only fourth out of seven criteria. Fewer than a third of the students who had internships got or expected to get a job offer from that company (Table 2). This emphasis on experience rather than employment will work to FFI's benefit. Only 13% of the students I surveyed were "very interested" in a career in managed care, with a full 47% "not interested." But since students do not necessarily expect to work permanently at the site of their internships, they probably will be

Quote to give the exact wording of survey questions, so reader can interpret data accurately.

Figure 15.8   *A Long Report (continued)*

willing to accept any internship that gives them good experience. Then, a good internship experience can convince students that FFI is a good employer.

Part of providing good experience is assigning students to a good mentor. Some companies assign interns to otherwise unproductive people (Dawn Kalmuth, personal communication, November 12, 2000). However, this is a mistake. FFI should assign its most effective people as mentors, so that students have the best internship experience possible.

FFI's greatest needs are computer personnel, including a Web weaver, and finance personnel (Paul Wutz, personal communication, November 18, 2000). The company also could offer internships in accounting, fulfillment, human resources, marketing, and transportation logistics. Each of these areas could offer solid experience to college students while meeting FFI's needs.

Providing Competitive Pay

Begin most paragraphs with topic sentences. Numbering your points helps the reader.

My survey indicates three points in regards to pay. First, students who did not have internships last summer made an average of $7.67 per hour. The average wage for students with internships was $8.20. The highest-paid interns seem to be those majoring in Management Information Sciences (MIS): One respondent reported that computer science interns received $2,500 a month plus a bonus. Second, the survey demonstrates that only 20% of the respondents could afford to take an unpaid internship next summer. However, 49% could afford to take an internship paying only the minimum wage next summer. Third, while money is the least important of the seven criteria in choosing whether to accept a specific internship, it is at least "somewhat important" to most students. Therefore, FFI should offer competitive wages to attract the best students.

Here published, online, and survey data are combined.

Some internship programs provide more than just an hourly wage. Micron Technology provides corporate housing (King, 1997). Aetna provides not only housing but also round-trip travel to and from its corporate headquarters (Aetna, 1999). Only 15% of the students I surveyed said they could definitely take a job in Cleveland next summer. These may well be students who live in Cleveland. Providing housing and round-trip transportation could win over many of the students who say they "could not" take a job in Cleveland.

Vary paragraph lengths to provide good visual impact.

Finding a Niche for FFI Internships

Don't need author's name in parenthesis if name is used in the sentence.

Simply announcing the internships may not be enough to get high-demand students such as MIS majors. If FFI develops an image or "niche" it will stand a better chance of attracting the strongest students. Natalie Engler (1998) shows the lengths to which some companies go. Sapient Corporation conducts "Super Saturdays" eight times a year. These team-based exercises are designed not only to test students' skills but, more importantly, to develop a good impression of Sapient. In one exercise, teams of six were asked to design and build a gift made out of Legos for a book-writing marine biologist. Sapient has used these Super Saturdays to attract employees. The company has added 300 people in the last year and has a very low rate of turnover.

Not every idea needs a source. Use your knowledge of people and of business.

Vary sentence length and sentence structure.

What sets Allegiance Healthcare's internships apart is its on-campus "virtual internship" program. Allegiance installed workstations on campus which students used to complete Allegiance projects throughout the school year (Watson, 1998). Thus Allegiance's location was immaterial; students did not need to relocate. An added benefit to Allegiance was that the interns' work could continue year-round.

Since most students don't know about FFI and don't come to the hiring process interested in managed care, it would be useful for FFI to develop some "gimmick" that could set it apart in students' minds.

Figure 15.8   *A Long Report (continued)*

Conclusions repeat points made in the report.
Recommendations are actions the readers should take.

10 pt.   A College Internship Program for FFI Health Services   Page 8

12 pt. **Conclusions and Recommendations**

11 pt.   I recommend that FFI Health Services establish an internship program following the model outlined in the Professional Experience Program. Following this program will cover the basics of a sound internship program and will enable FFI to hire interns at The Ohio State University. Decisions to be made include choosing *List in* which positions to offer interns, deciding how much to pay them, identifying supervisors and mentors within *the order* each department, and determining how to publicize the program and at which colleges to recruit. *in which you'll discuss them.*

Some companies ask for Conclusions and
1. Choosing Positions for Interns   *Recommendations at the beginning of reports.*

FFI should eventually offer internships in eight areas: accounting, computer science, finance, fulfillment, human resources, marketing, transportation logistics, and Web maintenance. FFI does work in each of these areas and could benefit both from the projects that interns might complete and from the opportunity to make permanent hires in these areas.

In its first year I recommend that the internship program focus on two or three main areas of employment. For instance, hiring only finance and computer science majors will give FFI Health Services the opportunity to pilot the program. This strategy will help to ensure that each intern gets the necessary attention and career-related experience. Also, FFI Health Services can detect and correct any flaws in the initial program.

2. Setting Intern Salaries

My survey indicates that only 20% of students could afford to take an unpaid internship, and 51% would not be able to work for minimum wage. Since the best students have several options, FFI should offer interns a competitive wage. Because the average intern earned between $8 and $9 last summer, I recommend that FFI Health Services set intern pay at $9-$10 an hour for all majors except computer science. To hire the best computer science majors will require starting salaries of at least $15 an hour. Providing housing would make the internships more attractive and would enlarge the pool of applicants.

Numbering the issues makes it easy
3. Choosing Supervisors and Mentors   *for readers to discuss them.*

One person should not attempt to supervise all of the interns, even during the first summer when there may be only two or three interns. I suggest conducting internal research to determine how potential supervisors and mentors feel about working closely with interns. Acting as a mentor should be a voluntary position to ensure active and enthusiastic guidance for the intern. Supervisors should be made familiar with assignment and evaluation procedures and should feel comfortable with their role in the internship program. Willing and dedicated supervisors and mentors will make for a more effective program.

4. Publicizing the Program

Participating in the Professional Experience Program will mean that FFI's job descriptions will be available to students who come to the Fisher College of Business Career Services Center looking for internships. However, other kinds of publicity are also desirable so that FFI can have the widest pool of applicants from

Figure 15.8   *A Long Report (continued)*

which to choose. Announcing the internships on FFI's Web site is an obvious step and would bring up FFI's internships when students do Web searches for "internships." Many other companies already give information about internships on Web sites. If computer majors remain in such high demand, FFI will need to do something special to attract them. Further research will be needed to determine what kind of niche FFI can develop.

5. Recruiting Interns

While my research focuses on Ohio State students, FFI may want to recruit at other schools. More research needs to be done to determine the optimal places for FFI Health Services to recruit student interns. Since students may not be able to relocate for the summer or may only move if given a substantial pay incentive, recruiting at colleges in Cleveland and in Tampa may make sense. In addition, it would be useful to identify any colleges that offer majors in managed care. Such colleges would be a good source of students who would be interested in the kind of work FFI does.

Because many readers turn to the "Recommendations"
first, provide a brief rationale for each. The ideas in
this section must be logical extensions of the points
made and supported in the body of the report.

Figure 15.8   *A Long Report (continued)*

A College Internship Program for FFI Health Services   Page 10

Treat short Web
pages like journal articles.   **References**   *APA Format*

Aetna. (1999). Actuarial internships. Retrieved November 4, 1999 from the World Wide Web:
http://www.aetna.com/working/interns.htm   *When you use two sets of*
pages that are part of one Web site,

Engler, N. (1998, March 23). We want you! (Please?!?) *Computerworld*, pp. 72-73.   *combine them in a single entry.*

Ferguson, L. H. (1998, April). Guidelines for a safety internship program in industry. *Professional Safety*,
43(no. 4), 22-25.

Give the page
number(s)   Internships identify promising future employees among college students. (1997, April). *HRMagazine*,
without 42(no. 4), 102.   *Start with the title of the article when no author is given.*
"p." when
you give the   King, J. (1997, February 17). Companies use interns as hiring pool. *Computerworld*, pp. 63, 65.
volume and issue number.   *Use "pp." when you don't have volume and issue number.*

Ohio State University, Fisher College of Business. (1998). *The professional experience program: Employer
handbook.* Retrieved November 4, 1999 from the World Wide Web: http://www.cob.ohio-state.edu/
careers/pep/

Stone, M. L. (1998, June). How to offer successful internships. *Advertising Age's Business Marketing*, p. 8.

Watson, S. (1998, September 21). Changing perceptions. *Computerworld*, pp. C2-C4.

Month or date of   *Underline titles of magazines,*
issue goes after year.   *journals, and books if you don't have*
italics.

List all the printed and online
sources cited in your report. Do not
list sources you used for background
but did not cite. Do not list interviews,
phone calls, or other information to which
the reader has no access.

Figure 15.8   *A Long Report (continued)*

Tell how many people responded.

Appendix A: Raw Survey Data

N = 150. Percentages sometimes total more than 100% due to rounding.

1. Major (Grouped by College)
   Agriculture   *Also give*   7 (5%)
   Arts   *percentages.* 11 (7%)
   Business   35 (23%)
   Human Ecology   15 (10%)
   Humanities   41 (27%)
   Math & Physical Sciences 23 (15%)
   Social & Behav. Sciences 18 (12%)

2. Rank: First-Year   15 (10%)
             Sophomore   34 (23%)
             Junior   47 (31%)
             Senior   54 (36%)

3. How important is it to you to have one or more internships before you graduate?
   80 (53%) Very important
   57 (38%) Somewhat important
   14 (9%)   Not important

4. Did you have an internship last summer?
   48 (32%) Yes
   103 (68%) No (skip to Question 6)

5. What were the most beneficial aspects of your internship? (Check all that apply.)
   41 (85%) Work related to my major
   15 (31%) Likely to get a job offer/ got a job offer
   35 (73%) Chance to explore my interests
   34 (71%) Made connections
   22 (46%) Worked with clients
   42 (93%) Looks good on my résumé

6. How much money did you make last summer? (Approximate hourly rate, before taxes)
   Intern: average $8.20/hr
   Non-intern: average $7.67/hr

   ☐ Check here if you did not make any money last summer.
   3 interns; 9 non-interns

7. For next summer, could you afford to take an unpaid internship?
   30 (20%) Yes   121 (60%) No

8. For next summer, could you afford to take an internship paying only the minimum wage?
   73 (42%) Yes   76 (51%) No

10. How important is each of the following criteria in choosing whether to accept a specific internship?

	Very impt. (3)	Some impt. (2)	Not impt. (1)
			Average
a. Money			2.22
b. Prestige of company			2.43
c. Location near where you live now			2.36
d. Quality of mentoring			2.92
e. Building connections			2.73
f. Chance of getting a job with that company			2.57
g. Gaining experience			2.99

11. How interested are you in a career in managed care?
    19 (13%) Very interested
    63 (42%) Somewhat interested
    71 (47%) Not interested

12. Could you take a job in Cleveland next summer?
    22 (15%) Definitely
    70 (47%) Maybe
    58 (39%) No

13. Have you heard of FFI Rx Managed Care?
    23 (15%) Yes
    122 (81%) No

Include a copy of your survey with the raw data. Here, the format is changed a bit to make room for the data.

Figure 15.8   *A Long Report (concluded)*

Appendix B: Responses to Open-Ended Question

"Whether or not I could take an unpaid internship or one paying minimum wage would depend on the type of internship and how relevant the experience would be."

"I wish internships would pay."

"I might sacrifice money for one summer if the internship was worth it in terms of gaining experience."

"Just as long as it dealt with my career field, I would be interested in taking an internship."

"It was told to me that internships are as important as some classes. Yet students who work themselves through college cannot afford some of these due to pay. Companies need to start making it worth the while for the working student."

— Give responses verbatim—errors and all!

"Another important factor in deciding whether or not to accept a specific internship would be how enjoyable and comfortable the atmosphere is."

"I'll only work where it is warm!"

"Everyone should intern at least one quarter."

"I feel internships are *extremely* important!"

"MIS majors can make $33,000 or $2500 + bonus a month for internships."

"Philosophy students don't do internships, too much like work."

"I think internships are very important."

"Internships give you a taste for what your career will be like and what it's like to work in the 'real world.'"

Provide the text of survey comments so readers get a sense of the flavor of responses.

What Does the Reader Want?*

When she was Director of the Information Design Center in Washington, DC, Susan Kleimann researched reply forms for a hotel. The managers said they didn't want to read a report. So Kleimann limited the "report" to an executive summary with conclusions and recommendations. Everything else went into "appendixes."

*Based on Susan D. Kleimann, "The Need to Test Forms in the Real World," Association for Business Communication Annual Convention, Orlando, FL, November 1–4, 1995.

Avoid contractions. Use second-person *you* only if the article uses second-person; even then, use *you* sparingly.

It is not necessary to follow the organization, wording, or proportions of the original report or article. The abstract usually uses a logical pattern of organization, putting the thesis first, even though the report may use another pattern (a psychological problem-solving pattern, for instance).

Summary abstracts present the logical skeleton of the article: the thesis or recommendation and its proof. Use a summary abstract to give the most useful information in the shortest space.

> To market life insurance to mid-40s urban professionals, Interstate Fidelity Insurance should advertise in upscale publications and use direct mail.
>
> Network TV and radio are not cost-efficient for reaching this market. This group comprises a small percentage of the prime-time network TV audience and a minority of most radio station listeners. They tend to discard newspapers and general-interest magazines quickly, but many of them keep upscale periodicals for months or years. Magazines with high percentages of readers in this group include *Architectural Digest, Bon Appetit, Business Week, Forbes, Golf Digest, Metropolitan Home, Southern Living,* and *Smithsonian.* Most urban professionals in their mid-40s are already used to shopping by mail and respond positively to well-conceived and well-executed direct mail appeals.
>
> Any advertising campaign needs to overcome this group's feeling that they already have the insurance they need. One way to do this would be to encourage them to check the coverage their employers provide and to calculate the cost of their children's expenses through college graduation. Insurance plans that provide savings and tax benefits as well as death benefits might also be appealing.

To write abstracts of business and government reports, conference papers, and published articles, write a sentence outline. A **sentence outline** not only uses complete sentences rather than words or phrases but also contains the thesis sentence or recommendation and the points that prove that point. Combine the sentences into paragraphs, adding transitions if necessary, and you'll have your abstract.

Descriptive abstracts indicate what topics the article covers and how deeply it goes into each topic, but they do not summarize what the article says about each topic. Phrases that describe the paper ("this paper reports," "it includes," "it summarizes," "it concludes") are marks of a descriptive abstract. An additional mark of a descriptive abstract is that the reader can't tell what the article says about the topics it covers.

> This report recommends ways Interstate Fidelity Insurance could market insurance to mid-40s urban professionals. It examines demographic and psychographic profiles of the target market. Survey results are used to show attitudes toward insurance. The report suggests some appeals that might be successful with this market.

A **mixed abstract** is a hybrid: part summary, part description. Mixed abstracts enable you both to comment about the kind of information and present the thesis and its proof.

Introduction

The **Introduction** of the report always contains a statement of purpose and scope and may include all the parts in the following list.

- **Purpose.** The Purpose statement identifies the organizational problem the report addresses, the technical investigations it summarizes, and the rhetorical purpose (to explain, to recommend).

- **Scope.** The Scope statement identifies how broad an area the report surveys. For example, Company XYZ is losing money on its line of radios. Does the report investigate the quality of the radios? The advertising campaign? The cost of manufacturing? The demand for radios? A Scope statement allows the reader to evaluate the report on appropriate grounds. If the person who approved the proposal accepted a focus on advertising, then one cannot fault a report that considers only that factor.

- **Limitations.** Limitations make your recommendations less valid or valid only under certain conditions. Limitations usually arise because time or money constraints haven't permitted full research. For example, a campus pizza restaurant considering expanding its menu may ask for a report but not have enough money to take a random sample of students and townspeople. Without a random sample, the writer cannot generalize from the sample to the larger population.

   Many recommendations are valid only for a limited time. For instance, a campus store wants to know what kinds of clothing will appeal to college men. The recommendations will remain in force only for a short time: three years from now, styles and tastes may have changed, and the clothes that would sell best now may no longer be in demand.

- **Assumptions.** Assumptions in a report are like assumptions in geometry: statements whose truth you assume, and which you use to prove your final point. If they are wrong, the conclusion will be wrong too.

   For example, to plan cars that will be built five years from now, an automobile manufacturer commissions a report on young adults' attitudes toward cars. The recommendations would be based on assumptions both about gas prices and about the economy. If gas prices radically rose or fell, the kinds of cars young adults wanted would change. If there were a major recession, people wouldn't be able to buy new cars.

   Almost all reports require assumptions. A good report spells out its assumptions so that readers can make decisions more confidently.

- **Methods.** If you conducted surveys, focus groups, or interviews, you need to tell how you chose your subjects, and how, when, and where they were interviewed. Reports based on scientific experiments usually put the Methods section in the body of the report, not in the Introduction.

   If your report is based solely on library or online research, omit Methods; simply cite your sources in the text and document them in Notes or References. See Chapter 14 on how to cite and document sources.

- **Criteria** or **Standards.** The Criteria section outlines the factors that you are considering and the relative importance of each. If a company is choosing a city for a new office, is the cost of office space more or less important than the availability of skilled workers? Check with your audience before you write the draft to make sure that your criteria match those of your readers.

- **Definitions.** When you know that some members of your primary, secondary, or immediate audience will not understand technical terms, define them. If you have only a few definitions, you can put them in the Introduction. If you have many terms to define, use a **Glossary** either early in the report or at the end. If the glossary is at the end, refer to it in the Introduction so that readers know that you've provided it.

Background or History

Formal reports usually have a section that gives the background of the situation or the history of the problem. Even though the current audience for the report probably knows the situation, reports are filed and consulted years later. These later audiences will probably not know the background, although it may be crucial for understanding the options that are possible.

In some cases, the History may cover many years. For example, a report recommending that a US hotel chain open hotels in Romania will probably give the history of that country for at least the last hundred years. In other cases, the History is much briefer, covering only a few years or even just the immediate situation.

Conclusions and Recommendations

Conclusions summarize points you have made in the body of the report; **Recommendations** are action items that would solve or ameliorate the problem. These sections are often combined if they are short: *Conclusions and Recommendations.*

The Conclusions section is the most widely read part of the report.[14] No new information should be included in the Conclusions. Conclusions are usually presented in paragraphs, but you could also use a numbered or bulleted list.

Many readers turn to the Recommendations section first; some organizations ask that recommendations be presented early in the report. Number the recommendations to make it easy for people to discuss them. If the recommendations will seem difficult or controversial, give a brief paragraph of rationale after each recommendation. If they'll be easy for the audience to accept, you can simply list them without comments or reasons. The recommendations will also be in the Executive Summary and perhaps in the title and the transmittal.

Summary of Key Points

- **Causation** means that one thing causes or produces another. **Correlation** means that two things happen at the same time. One might cause the other, but both might be caused by a third.
- In **comparison/contrast,** you can focus on alternatives or on criteria. The **pro-and-con pattern** divides the alternatives and discusses the arguments for and against that alternative. A **problem-solving report** identifies the problem, explains its causes, and analyzes the advantages and disadvantages of possible solutions. **Elimination** identifies the problem, explains its causes, and discusses the least practical solutions first, ending with the one the writer favors. **General to particular** begins with the problem as it affects the organization or as it manifests itself in general, then moves to a discussion of the parts of the problem and solutions to each of these parts. **Particular to general** starts with specific aspects of the problem, then moves to a discussion of the larger implications of the problem for the organization. **Geographical or spatial** patterns discuss the problems and solutions by units. **Functional** patterns discuss the problems and solutions of each functional unit.
- Reports use the same style as other business documents, with three exceptions:
  1. Reports use a more formal style than do many letters and memos.
  2. Reports rarely use the word *you.*

3. Reports should be self-explanatory.

- To create good report style,
  1. Say what you mean.
  2. Tighten your writing.
  3. Introduce sources and visuals gracefully.
  4. Use blueprints, transitions, topic sentences, and headings.
- **Headings** are single words, short phrases, or complete sentences that cover all of the material under it until the next heading. **Informative,** or **talking, heads** tell the reader what to expect in each section.
- Headings must use the same grammatical structure. Subheads under a heading must be parallel to each other but do not necessarily have to be parallel to subheads under other headings.
- The Title Page of a report usually contains four items: the title of the report, whom the report is prepared for, whom it is prepared by, and the date.
- The title of a report should contain the recommendations unless
  - The reader will find the recommendations hard to accept.
  - Putting all the recommendations in the title would make it too long.
  - The report does not offer recommendations.
- If the title does not contain the recommendations, it normally indicates what problem the report tries to solve.
- If the report is 25 pages or less, list all the headings in the Table of Contents. In a long report, pick a level and put all the headings at that level and above in the contents.
- Organize the transmittal in this way:
  1. Release the report.
  2. Summarize your conclusions and recommendations.
  3. Mention any points of special interest in the report. Indicate minor problems you encountered in your investigation and show how you surmounted them. Thank people who helped you.
  4. Point out additional research that is necessary, if any.
  5. Thank the reader for the opportunity to do the work and offer to answer questions.
- **Summary abstracts** present the logical skeleton of the article: the thesis or recommendation and its proof. **Descriptive abstracts** indicate what topics the article covers and how deeply it goes into each topic, but do not summarize what the article says about each topic. **Mixed abstracts** have some characteristics of both summary and descriptive abstracts. They may list all of the topics covered in an article and summarize some of the points about some of the topics.
- A summary abstract is based on a sentence outline. A descriptive abstract is based on a topic outline.
- A good abstract or executive summary is easy to read, concise, and clear. A good abstract can be understood by itself, without the original article or reference books.
- The **Introduction** of the report always contains a statement of Purpose and Scope. The **Purpose** statement identifies the organizational problem the report addresses, the technical investigations it summarizes, and the rhetorical purpose (to explain, to recommend). The **Scope** statement identifies how broad an area the report surveys. The Introduction may also include **Limitations,** problems or factors that limit the validity of your recommendations; **Assumptions,** statements whose truth you assume, and

Report Your Way to a Better Job*

Joan was hired by a computer company to find references to the computer industry in current publications. To expand her job description, Joan wrote reports summarizing the data instead of just sending files of clippings. The receivers were delighted because she was saving them time.

Her second step was to meet with the people who got her reports to ask them what sorts of information they needed. Now she was able to target her reports to her readers' needs. People in each unit began to invite her to meetings discussing the projects she was researching.

As a member of the various groups within the company, Joan now had the information she needed to take a third step: drafting the report for decision makers. For example, if the sales department wanted information for a proposal to a client, she presented her information in a sales proposal. If the president wanted material for a speech, she arranged her information in a speech outline.

When the director of business communications resigned, Joan was the obvious choice for the job.

*Based on Janice LaRouche, "I'm Stuck in a Dead-End Job," *Family Circle,* March 24, 1987, 121.

which you use to prove your final point; **Methods,** an explanation of how you gathered your data; **Criteria** or **Standards** used to weigh the factors in the decision; and **Definitions** of terms readers may not know.

- A **Background** or **History** section is included because reports are filed and may be consulted years later.
- **Conclusions** summarize points made in the body of the report; **Recommendations** are action items that would solve or ameliorate the problem. These sections are often combined if they are short.

Chapter 15

Exercises and Problems

Getting Started

15.1   Identifying Assumptions and Limitations

Indicate whether each of the following would be an Assumption or a Limitation in a formal report.

a. Report on Ways to Encourage More Students to Join XYZ Organization
1. I surveyed a judgment sample rather than a random sample.
2. These recommendations are based on the attitudes of current students. Presumably, students in the next several years will have the same attitudes and interests.

b. Report on the Feasibility of Building Hilton Hotels in Vietnam
1. This report is based on the expectation that the country will be politically stable.

2. All of my information is based on library research. The most recent articles were published two months ago; much of the information was published a year ago or more. Therefore some of my information may be out of date.

c. Report on Car-Buying Preferences of Young Adults
1. These recommendations may change if the cost of gasoline increases dramatically or if there is another deep recession.
2. This report is based on a survey of adults ages 20 to 24 in California, Texas, Illinois, Ontario, and Massachusetts.
3. These preferences are based on the cars now available. If a major technical or styling innovation occurs, preferences may change.

15.2   Revising an Executive Summary

The following Executive Summary is poorly organized and too long. Rearrange information to make it more effective. Cut information that does not belong in the summary. You may use different words as you revise.

In this report I will discuss the communication problems which exist at Rolling Meadows Golf Club. The problems discussed will deal with channels of communication. The areas which are causing problems are internal. Radios would solve these internal problems.

Taking a 15-minute drive on a golf cart in order to find the superintendent is a common occurrence. Starters and rangers need to keep in touch with the clubhouse to maintain a smooth flow of players around the course. The rangers have expressed an interest in being able to call the clubhouse for advice and support.

Purchasing two-channel FM radios with private channels would provide three advantages. First, radios would make the golf course safer by providing a means of notifying someone in the event of an emergency. Second, radios would make the staff more efficient by providing a faster channel of communication. Third, radios would enable clubhouse personnel to keep in touch with the superintendent, the rangers, and the starters.

During the week, radios can be carried by the superintendent, the golf pro, and another course worker. On weekends and during tournaments, one radio will be used by the golf professional. The other two will be used by one starter and one ranger. Three radios is the minimum needed to meet basic communication needs. A fourth radio would provide more flexibility for busy weekends and during tournaments.

Tekk T-20 radios can be purchased from Page-Com for $129 each. These radios have the range and options needed for use on the golf course. Radios are durable and easy to service. It is possible that another brand might be even less expensive.

Rolling Meadows Golf Club should purchase four radios. They will cost under $600 and can be paid for from the current equipment budget.

Communicating at Work

As Your Instructor Directs, in Problems 15.3 and 15.4,

a. Create a document or presentation to achieve the goal.
b. Write a memo to your instructor describing the situation at your workplace and explaining your rhetorical choices (medium, strategy, tone, wording, graphics or document design, and so forth).

15.3   Explaining "Best Practices"

Write a report explaining the "best practices" of your unit that could also be adopted by other units in your organization.

15.4   Recommending Action

Write a report recommending an action that your unit or organization should take. Possibilities include

- Buying more equipment for your department.
- Hiring an additional worker for your department.
- Making your organization more family-friendly.

- Making a change that will make the organization more efficient.
- Making changes to improve accessibility for customers or employees with disabilities.

Address your report to the person who would have the power to approve your recommendation.

15.5   Evaluating a Report from Your Workplace

Consider the following aspects of a report from your workplace:

- How much information is included? How is it presented?
- Visuals and layout. Are visuals used effectively? Are they accurate and free from chartjunk? What image do the pictures and visuals create? Are color and white space used effectively? (See Chapter 16 on visuals.)
- Emphasis. What points are emphasized? What points are de-emphasized? What verbal and visual techniques are used to highlight or minimize information?

As Your Instructor Directs,

a. Write a memo to your instructor analyzing the report.
b. Join with a small group of students to compare and contrast several reports. Present your evaluation in an informal group report.
c. Present your evaluation orally to the class.

Report Assignments

15.6   Writing a Feasibility Study

Write a report evaluating the feasibility of two or more alternatives. Possible topics include the following:

1. Is it feasible for a local restaurant to open another branch? Where should it be?
2. Is it feasible to create a program to mentor women and minorities in your organization?
3. Is it feasible to produce a video yearbook in addition to or instead of a paper yearbook at your college, community college, or university?
4. Is it feasible to create or enlarge a day care center for the children of students?
5. Could your college host a regional meeting of the Association for Business Communication on campus or in town?

6. Is it feasible to start a monthly newsletter for students in your major?
7. Is it feasible for local grocery stores to stock (or increase their stock of) carambolas, mamey, longans, lychees, atemoyas, sugar apples, jackfruit, and other exotic Asian and Latin American fruits and vegetables? If so, where should the additional space come from: Less space for traditional fruits and vegetables? Less space for another department? (If so, which one?) Store expansion?

Pick a limited number of alternatives, explain your criteria clearly, evaluate each alternative, and recommend the best course of action.

15.7   Writing an Informative or Closure Report

Write an informative report on one of the following topics.

1. What should a US or Canadian manager know about dealing with workers from _____ [you fill in the country or culture]? What factors do and do not motivate people in this group? How do they show respect and deference? Are they used to a strong hierarchy or to an egalitarian setting? Do they normally do one thing at once or many things? How important is clock time and being on time? What factors lead them to respect someone? Age? Experience? Education? Technical knowledge? Wealth? Or what? What conflicts or miscommunications may arise between workers from this culture and other workers due to cultural differences? Are people from this culture similar in these beliefs and behaviors, or is there lots of variation?
2. Describe an ethical dilemma encountered by workers in a specific organization. What is the background of the situation? What competing

loyalties exist? In the past, how have workers responded? How has the organization responded? Have "whistle-blowers" been rewarded or punished? What could the organization do to foster ethical behavior?
3. Describe a problem or challenge encountered by an organization where you've worked. Describe the problem, show why it needed to be solved, tell who did what to try to solve it, and tell how successful the efforts were. Possibilities include
   - How the organization is implementing work teams, downsizing, or a change in organizational culture.
   - How the organization uses e-mail or voice mail, statistical process control, or telecommuting.
   - How managers deal with stress, make ethical choices, or evaluate subordinates.
   - How the organization is responding to changing US demographics, the Americans with Disabilities Act, or international competition and opportunities.

15.8   Writing a Consultant's Report—Restaurant Tipping

Your consulting company has been asked to conduct a report for Diamond Enterprises, which runs three national chains: FishStix, The Bar-B-Q Pit, and Morrie's. All are medium-priced, family-friendly restaurants. The CEO is thinking of replacing optional tips with a 15% service fee automatically added to bills.

You read articles in trade journals, surveyed a random sample of 200 workers in each of the chains, and conducted an e-mail survey of the 136 restaurant managers. Here are your findings:

1. Trade journals point out that the Internal Revenue Service (IRS) audits restaurants if it thinks that servers underreport tips. Dealing with an audit is time-consuming and often results in the restaurant's having to pay penalties and interest.
2. Only one Morrie's restaurant has actually been audited by the IRS. Management was able to convince the IRS that servers were reporting tips accurately. No penalty was assessed. Management

spent $1,000 on CPA and legal fees and spent over 80 hours of management time gathering data and participating in the audit.

3. Restaurants in Europe already add a service fee (usually 15%) to the bill. Patrons can add more if they choose. Local custom determines whether tips are expected and how much they should be. In Germany, for example, it is more usual to round up the bill (from 27 DM to 30 DM, for example), than to figure a percentage.

4. If the restaurant collected a service fee, it could use the income to raise wages for cooks and hosts and pay for other benefits, such as health insurance, rather than giving all the money to servers and bussers.

5. Morrie's servers tend to be under 25 years of age. FishStix employs more servers over 25, who are doing this for a living. The Bar-B-Q Pit servers are students in college towns.

6. In all three chains, servers oppose the idea. Employees other than servers generally support it.

	Retain tips	Change to service fee added to bill	Don't care
FishStix servers (n = 115)	90%	7%	3%
Bar-B-Q servers (n = 73)	95	0	5
Morrie's servers (n = 93)	85	15	0
Morrie's nonservers (n = 65)	25	20	5
FishStix nonservers (n = 46)	32	32	37
Bar-B-Q nonservers (n = 43)	56	20	25

(Numbers do not add up to 100% due to rounding.)

7. Servers said that it was important to go home with money in their pockets (92%), that their expertise increased food sales and should be rewarded (67%), and that if a service fee replaced tips they would be likely to look for another job (45%). Some (17%) thought that if the manager distributed service-fee income, favoritism rather than the quality of work would govern how much tip income they got. Most (72%) thought that customers would not add anything beyond the 15% service fee, and many (66%) thought that total tip income would decrease and their own portion of that income would decrease (90%).

8. Managers generally support the change.

	Retain tips	Change to service fee added to bill	Don't care
FishStix managers (n = 44)	20%	80%	0%
Bar-B-Q managers (n = 13)	33%	67%	0%
Morrie's managers (n = 58)	55%	45%	0%

9. Comments from managers include: "It isn't fair for a cook with eight years of experience to make only $12 an hour while a server can make $25 an hour in just a couple of months," and "I could have my pick of employees if I offered health insurance."

10. Morale at Bar-B-Q seems low. This is seen in part in the low response rate to the survey.

11. In a tight employment market, some restaurants might lose good servers if they made the change. However, hiring cooks and other nonservers would be easier.

12. The current computer systems in place can handle figuring and recording the service fee. Since bills are printed by computer, an additional line could be added. Allocating the service-fee income could take extra managerial time, especially at first.

15.9   Writing a Library Research Report

Write a library research report.

As Your Instructor Directs,
Turn in the following documents:

a. The approved proposal.

b. Two copies of the report, including
  Cover.
  Title Page.
  Letter or Memo of Transmittal.
  Table of Contents.
  List of Illustrations.
  Executive Summary or Abstract.
  Body (Introduction, all information, recommendations). Your instructor may specify a minimum length, a minimum number or kind of sources, and a minimum number of visuals.
  References or Works Cited.

c. Your notes and rough drafts.

Choose one of the following topics.

1. **Building Baseball Fans.** In the United States, the popularity of baseball has dropped to third place, behind football and basketball. Even more worrisome, fans are fewest in younger demographic groups. Of 12- to 18-year-olds, 67% call themselves baseball fans, while 78% call themselves football fans, and 82% claim to be basketball fans. The gap is even greater for kids who call themselves avid fans. For more on how baseball can build fans—especially the next generation of fans—see Allen St. John, "Who's on Deck?" *American Demographics,* October 1998, 60–69.

As Your Instructor Directs,
Recommend actions to

a. A farm team for one of the major league teams (pick your favorite).
b. A major league team (pick your favorite).
c. Major League Baseball Enterprises.

2. **Retaining Record Royalties.** Your boss is Director of Marketing for a major music label. "We've got a real problem. Labels that let people download music files get a lot more hits on their Web pages than we do. But if we distribute music on the Web, why should anyone buy a CD? As it is, we've got a problem with bootleg recordings that fans post. What can we do?" Start your research with "New Technology Expected to Change Music Industry, Consumer Habits," *The Columbus Dispatch,* December 13, 1998, 8F.

3. **Helping Car Dealerships Adapt.** More and more car buyers are going to Web sites for information about manufacturers' prices or even to close the deal. Some Web pages send buyers to a dealer for a prenegotiated, no-bargaining discount. Will the Web eliminate car dealerships?

As Your Instructor Directs,
Recommend actions to

a. A car dealership thinking of going online.
b. A car dealership interested in remaining in the car business as long as possible.

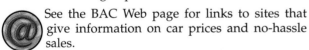 See the BAC Web page for links to sites that give information on car prices and no-hassle sales.

4. **Dealing with "Anti" Web Pages.** The next great challenge for public relations may be dealing with Web sites complaining about a company. Learning that other people have also received defective products or poor service transforms the individual, not-very-powerful consumer into a powerful moral force. If the allegation is true, the company can salvage matters by fixing the problem, as Intel did in 1994 when it finally recalled its defective Pentium chip. But what if the story isn't true—or is true but represents an unusual, perhaps a unique, breakdown in customer service? See "Foiling the Rogues," *Newsweek,* October 27, 1997, 80.

As Your Instructor Directs,
Recommend the best strategies to

a. A public relations firm.
b. A company which denies the stories posted about it (e.g., Nike).
c. A company which contends that the problem, though true, is atypical or unique (e.g., United Airlines).
d. A company that, so far as it knows, does not yet have an "anti" Web site.

 See the BAC Web site for links to a few "anti" pages.

5. **(Re)Saving Social Security.** As an aide to one of your state's senators, you frequently research topics for possible legislation. "I want some research on Social Security. Have we done enough to fix it? Should we privatize it? What if people make poor choices?" Start your research with Steve Stecklow and Sara Calian, "Social Security Switch in U.K. Is Disastrous; A Caution to the U.S.?" *The Wall Street Journal,* August 10, 1998, A1 and A8; and Peter Coy, "Social Security: Let It Be," *Business Week,* November 30, 1998, 34–35.

6. **Evaluating Big Write-Offs.** Your boss at the Securities and Exchange Commission (SEC) wants to know whether big write-offs artificially inflate earnings—and, if they do, whether the problem is serious enough that the SEC should regulate the practice. For background on the problem, see Greg Ip, "Do Big Write-Offs Artificially Inflate Earnings?" *The Wall Street Journal,* July 6, 1998.

7. **Improving the Neighborhood.** You're on the mayor's staff in a major metropolitan city. "We've got some neighborhoods that really need work," the mayor says. "The ideas in this article look promising. Find out what happened—whether these plans worked—and recommend which if any of them we should implement." Start your research with Ron Stodghill, "Bringing Hope Back to the 'Hood," *Business Week,* August 19, 1996, 70–73. (Pick a city you know well. You may need to focus on one part of the problem: public housing, tax policies for individuals or businesses, involving churches or other groups in improving the neighborhood.)

8. **Proposing a "Euro" for South America.** Mercosur is a customs union made up of Brazil, Argentina, Uruguay, and Paraguay. In 1998, Argentine

president Carlos Menem called for a single monetary unit. Just as Europe took many years to develop and implement the euro, the South American countries need to resolve many questions before a single currency is created in Mercosur. Your boss is president of a multinational bank with branches in every country in South America. "Let me know what the current thinking is on a single currency. Will South America face the same problems that Europe faced? Would it be better to keep the project small, or expand it to more—maybe all—of the countries in South America? How would a single currency affect banking?" For an introduction to the topic, see

Kerry Capell, "What a 'Euro' Could Do for the Latins," *Business Week,* April 13, 1998, p. 100.

9. **Evaluating "Phantom Stock."** You work for a privately owned technology company that is considering going public. One of the advantages of selling stock would be to offer stock options to employees. But your boss wonders whether "phantom stock" would be even better and hands you a copy of Shawn Tully's "A Better Taskmaster Than the Market?" *Fortune,* October 26, 1998, pp. 277–86, and says, "Update this research and let me know."

10. With your instructor's permission, choose your own topic.

15.10 Writing a Recommendation Report

Write an individual or a group report.

As Your Instructor Directs,
Turn in the following documents:

1. The approved proposal.
2. Two copies of the report, including
   Cover.
   Title Page.
   Letter or Memo of Transmittal.
   Table of Contents.
   List of Illustrations.
   Executive Summary or Abstract.
   Body (Introduction, all information, recommendations). Your instructor may specify a minimum length, a minimum number or kind of sources, and a minimum number of visuals.
   Appendixes if useful or relevant.
3. Your notes and rough drafts.

Pick one of the following topics.

1. **Evaluating Airport Signs.** When international students or business people arrive in town, can they easily get information in their own languages? What information needs to be on airport signs? In which languages? What information could be on an interactive kiosk? What languages should it include? Address your report to the manager of the airport.

2. **Recommending Courses for the Local Community College.** Businesses want to be able to send workers to local community colleges to upgrade their skills; community colleges want to prepare students to enter the local workforce. What skills are in demand in your community? What courses at what levels should the local community college offer?

3. **Improving Sales and Profits.** Recommend ways a small business in your community can increase sales and profits. Focus on one or more of the following: the products or services it offers, its advertising, its decor, its location, its accounting methods, its cash management, or any other aspect that may be keeping the company from achieving its potential. Address your report to the owner of the business.

4. **Increasing Student Involvement.** How could an organization on campus persuade more of the students who are eligible to join or to become active in its programs? Do students know that it exists? Is it offering programs that interest students? Is it retaining current members? What changes should the organization make? Address your report to the officers of the organization.

5. **Evaluating a Potential Employer.** What training is available to new employees? How soon is the average entry-level person promoted? How much travel and weekend work are expected? Is there a "busy season," or is the workload consistent year-round? What fringe benefits are offered? What is the corporate culture? Is the climate nonracist and nonsexist? How strong is the company economically? How is it likely to be affected by current economic, demographic, and political trends? Address your report to the Placement Office on campus; recommend whether it should encourage students to work at this company.

6. With your instructor's permission, choose your own topic.

16

Using Graphs and Other Visuals

When to Use Visuals

Designing Visuals
- Check the Source of the Data.
- Determine the Story You Want to Tell.
- Choose the Right Visual for the Story.
- Follow the Conventions for Designing Typical Visuals.
- Use Color and Decoration with Restraint.
- Be Sure the Visual Is Accurate and Ethical.

Integrating Visuals in Your Text

Using Visuals in Your Presentation

Summary of Key Points

Using Graphs and Other Visuals

Cindy Huffman

Development Tester, SAS Institute

www.sas.com/

Cindy Huffman tests the functionality of visuals such as bar, pie, and scatter charts and Java applets displaying maps, various graphs, and contour plots. SAS Institute develops, markets, and supports the world's foremost data warehousing and decision support software.

Just as a picture is worth a thousand words, a good visual *replaces* a thousand words (of documentation).

It is important for users to produce high-end graphics that are intuitive and easy to understand. It's even more useful when the user can place these graphics within a Web page, presentation, paper, or even an application.

Data mining—analyzing data for relationships or patterns—plays an important role in producing visualizations. With piles and piles of data available, data mining allows users to find trends and stories in their data.

> *Data mining allows users to find trends and stories in their data.*

For example, a market analysis can find patterns in data identifying which products are commonly purchased together in a grocery store. These items can be easily identified graphically (by the height in a bar chart, or the size of a slice in a pie chart). With this information, the grocery store can place commonly purchased items together for greater success.

Computers give users the ability to generate powerful visuals, but it is up to the user to understand the data and figure out what type of graph represents the data accurately. As one of my Computer Science professors said throughout three semesters of classes, "Computers are dumb machines. They only do what you **tell** them to do."

It is important for graphs to be accurate, because they can be used in very important business decisions (opening a business in an area that matches the demographics portrayed in a graph). It's unethical to use graphics to mislead people with a visual that uses made-up or skewed data to support an agenda (for example, implying that sales are up, when they're not). However, verifying the accuracy can be as difficult as hand–calculating numbers and figures to support what is displayed. One way to validate graphs is to try several different types and determine if the visualizations are similar.

**Showing Trends
and Changes***

Jerry Atkinson gives his clients not only financial statements but also graphs of key trends. Atkinson is managing director of Atkinson and Company, a 62-employee CPA firm in Albuquerque, New Mexico.

Current-month or -year information isn't enough, he says. Clients need to see trends and changes. And graphs offer an easy way to show that.

Atkinson personalizes the graphs by using the colors of the company being profiled.

*Based on John von Brachel, "Interpreting Financial Statements: How One Firm Uses the Language of Graphics," *Journal of Accountancy* 180, no. 2 (August 1995), 42–43.

Visuals help make numbers meaningful and thus help communicate your points in telecasts, oral presentations, memos, letters, reports, and meetings. This chapter shows you how to turn data into graphs and other visuals. See Chapter 6 for a discussion of designing slides for oral presentations and Chapter 17 for a discussion of other aspects of good oral presentations.

Visuals can present numbers dramatically. The Consumer Federation of America crystallized discontent with high interest rates on consumer loans by issuing a simple three-page study with a graph showing that while the prime rate was going down, interest on consumer loans was going up. Dan Rather showed the graph and discussed the report on the evening news; the publicity helped persuade Congress to pass laws requiring fuller disclosure and some caps on interest rates.[1]

Numbers are no more "objective" than words are: both require interpretation and context to have meaning. On November 1, 1990, both *The Wall Street Journal* and *The Columbus Dispatch* carried stories about General Motors' third-quarter loss, which had been announced the day before. *The Dispatch*'s headline was negative: "GM's $2 Billion Quarterly Loss Biggest Ever." *The Wall Street Journal*, in contrast, saw the loss as a positive strategic move: "Smaller Giant: Huge GM Write-Off Positions Automaker to Show New Growth."[2] The two headlines come from and suggest very different ways to view the loss and GM's potential.

The same numbers can be presented in different ways to create very different impressions. In 1999, a pharmaceutical company announced that, in a year-long clinical test, people taking its anti-obesity drug lost 50% more weight than people receiving a placebo. That statement is true but isn't a reason to rush to a doctor to get a prescription. People in the group getting only the placebo lost an average of 13 pounds. People taking the drug lost an extra 6½ pounds—in a year.[3]

When to Use Visuals

The ease of creating visuals by computer may make people use them uncritically. Use a visual only to achieve a specific purpose. Never put in numbers or visuals just because you have them; instead, use them to convey information the audience needs or wants.

In your rough draft, use visuals

- **To see that ideas are presented completely.** A table, for example, can show you whether you've included all the items in a comparison.
- **To find relationships.** For example, charting sales on a map may show that the sales representatives who made quota all have territories on the East or the West Coast. Is the central United States suffering a recession? Is the product one that appeals to coastal lifestyles? Is advertising reaching the coasts but not the central states? Even if you don't use the visual in your final document, creating the map may lead you to questions you wouldn't otherwise ask.

In the final presentation or document, use visuals

- **To make points vivid.** Readers skim memos and reports; a visual catches the eye. The brain processes visuals immediately. Understanding words—written or oral—takes more time.
- **To emphasize material** that might be skipped if it were buried in a paragraph. The beginning and end are places of emphasis. However,

something has to go in the middle, especially in a long document. Visuals allow you to emphasize important material, wherever it logically falls.

- **To present material more compactly and with less repetition** than words alone would require. Words can call attention to the main points of the visual, without repeating all of the visual's information.

The number of visuals you will need depends on your purposes, the kind of information, and the audience. You'll use more visuals when you want to show relationships and to persuade, when the information is complex or contains extensive numerical data, and when the audience values visuals. Some audiences and discourse communities (✕ p. 62) expect oral presentations and reports to use lots of visuals. Other audiences may see visuals as frivolous and time spent making visuals as time wasted. For these audiences, you'd sharply limit the number of visuals you use—but you'd still use them when your own purposes and the information called for them.

Designing Visuals

Use these six steps to create good visuals:

1. Check the source of the data.
2. Determine the story you want to tell.
3. Choose the right visual for the story.
4. Follow the conventions for designing typical visuals.
5. Use color and decoration with restraint.
6. Be sure the visual is accurate and ethical.

Let's discuss each of these briefly.

1. Check the Source of the Data.

Your chart is only as good as the underlying data. Check to be sure that your data come from a reliable source. When the source has a vested interest (✕ p. 223) in the results, scrutinize them with special care. In 1995, America Online claimed that its subscribers stayed an average of 41 months. But 60% of its customers had joined in the previous nine months.[4] The news release was image advertising, not reliable data.

Identify the assumptions used in analyzing the data. When studies contradict each other, the explanation sometimes lies in the assumptions. For example, a study that found disposable diapers were better for the environment than cloth diapers assumed that each diaper change used 1.9 or 1.79 diapers and that a cloth diaper lasted for 92.5 uses. A study that found that cloth diapers were better assumed that each diaper change used 1.72 diapers and that each cloth diaper lasted for 167 uses.[5]

Identify exactly what the data measure. For example, using a Dun & Bradstreet database, many people claim that only 28% of small businesses survive for eight years. But that database counts a small business as "surviving" only if it remains under the same ownership. Researcher Bruce Kirchoff found that another 26% survive with ownership changes, for a total survival rate of 54%.[6]

You may be able to use data based on assumptions and definitions in careful titles or notes: "Under the Fast-Growth Scenario, Sales Will Triple." "Over One-Fourth of Small Businesses Last Eight Years under Original Owners." If the data themselves are unreliable, you're better off not using visuals. The visual picture will be more powerful than verbal disclaimers, and the audience will be misled.

Interpreting Statistics*

In 1982, Stephen Jay Gould, author of *The Panda's Thumb* and other essays on evolution, learned that he had a rare, incurable form of cancer. Patients lived a median of eight months after the disease was discovered.

Gould knew that "lived a median of eight months" meant half the people lived longer. Some of them lived a lot longer.

Furthermore, he knew that the statistics referred to cases treated by conventional means. Gould entered an experimental protocol. He thus had the opportunity to be in a new group with a new median and a new distribution curve.

Gould was young; his disease had been caught early; he had excellent medical care; he wanted to live; and he knew enough about statistics to read the data correctly and avoid despair.

As this book goes to press 17 years after the initial diagnosis, Gould is alive and doing well. And he's still writing essays helping us understand science and statistics.

*Based on Stephen Jay Gould, "The Median Isn't the Message," *Discover*, June 1985, 40–42.

2. Determine the Story You Want to Tell.

Every visual should tell a story. Stories can be expressed in complete sentences that describe something that happens or changes. The sentence also serves as the title of the visual.

Not a story:	US Sales, 1996–2000
Possible stories:	Forty Percent of Our Sales Were to New Customers. Growth Was Highest in the South. Sales Increased from 1996 to 2000. Most Sales Representatives Have 2–5 Years' Experience. Sales Were Highest in the Areas with More Sales Representatives.

Stories that tell us what we already know are rarely interesting. Instead, good stories may

- Support a hunch you have.
- Surprise you or challenge so-called "common knowledge."
- Show trends or changes you didn't know existed.
- Have commercial or social significance.
- Provide information needed for action.
- Be personally relevant to you and the audience.

To find stories,

1. Focus on a topic (purchases of cars, who likes jazz, and so forth).
2. Simplify the data on that topic and convert the numbers to simple, easy-to-understand units.
3. Look for relationships and changes. For example, compare two or more groups: do men and women have the same attitudes? Look for changes over time. Look for items that can be seen as part of the same group. For example, to find stories about entertainers' incomes, you might compare the number of writers, actors, and musicians in three rankings.
4. Process the data to find more stories. Find the average and the median (✖ p. 407). Calculate the percentage change from one year to the next.

When you think you have a story, test it against all the data to be sure it's accurate.

Some stories are simple straight lines: "Sales Increased." But other stories are more complex, with exceptions or outlying cases. Such stories will need more nuanced titles to do justice to the story. And sometimes the best story arises from the juxtaposition of two or more stories. In Figure 16.1, *Business Week* uses four **paired graphs** to tell a complex story. Two of the four stories tell us that growth is slowing : profit margins have peaked (story 1) and foreign demand is sinking (story 2). In story 2, the dramatic word *sinking* is justified by the steep drop. Stories 3 and 4, however, tell us that job growth is healthy and inflation is low—factors that suggest a healthy economy.

Gene Zelazny points out that the audience should be able to *see* what the message *says:*

> [D]oes the chart support the title; and does the title reinforce the chart? So if I *say* in my title that "sales have increased significantly" I want to *see* a trend moving up at a sharp angle. If not, if the trend parallels the baseline, it's an instant clue that the chart needs more thinking.[7]

Almost every data set allows you to tell several stories. You must choose the story you want to tell. Dumps of uninterpreted data confuse and frustrate your audience; they undercut the credibility and goodwill you want to create.

Figure 16.1 *A Complex Story Using Paired Graphs*

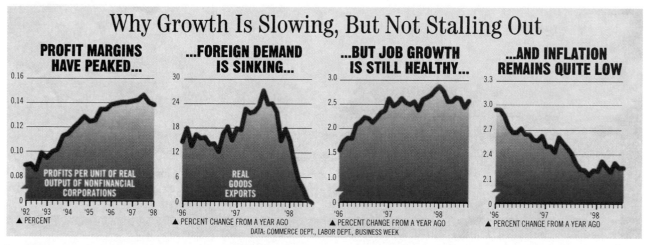

Source: *Business Week*, September 28, 1998, 46.

Sometimes several stories will be important. When that's the case, you'll need a separate visual for each.

3. Choose the Right Visual for the Story.

Visuals are not interchangeable. Good writers choose the visual that best matches the purpose of presenting the data.

- Use **tables** when the reader needs to be able to identify exact values. (See Figure 16.2a.)

- Use a chart or graph when you want the reader to focus on relationships.[8]
  - To compare a part to the whole, use a **pie chart.** (See Figure 16.2b.)
  - To compare one item to another item, use a **bar chart** or a **map.** (See Figure 16.2c.)
  - To compare items over time, use a **bar chart** or a **line graph.** (See Figure 16.2d.)
  - To show frequency or distribution, use a **bar chart** or **line graph.** (See Figure 16.2e.)
  - To show correlations, use a **bar chart,** a **line graph,** or a **dot chart.** (See Figure 16.2f.)

- Use **photographs** to create a sense of authenticity or show the item in use. If the item is especially big or small, include something in the photograph that can serve as a reference point: a dime, a person.
- Use **drawings** to show dimensions or emphasize detail.
- Use **sketches** to show processes in an interesting way.
- Use **maps** to emphasize location.
- Use **Gannt charts** to show timelines for proposals or projects.

4. Follow the Conventions for Designing Typical Visuals.

Every visual should contain six components:

1. A title that tells the story that the visual shows.
2. A clear indication of what the data are. For example, what people *say* they did is not necessarily what they really did. An estimate of what a number

Figure 16.2   *Choose the Visual to Fit the Story*

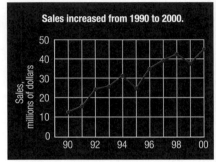

a. Tables show exact values.

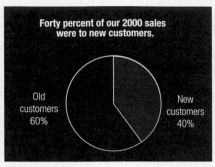

b. Pie charts compare a component
     to the whole.

c. Bar charts compare items or
     show distribution or correlation.

d. Line charts compare items over
     time or show distribution or
     correlation.

e. Bar charts can show frequency.

f. Dot charts show correlation.

will be in the future differs from numbers in the past that have already
been measured.

3. Clearly labeled units.

4. Labels or legends identifying axes, colors, symbols, and so forth.

5. The source of the data, if you created the visual from data someone else
    gathered and compiled.

6. The source of the visual, if you reproduce a visual someone else created.

Formal visuals are divided into tables and figures. **Tables** are numbers or
words arrayed in rows and columns; **figures** are everything else. In a document, formal visuals have both numbers and titles, e.g., "Figure 1. The Falling
Cost of Computer Memory, 1990–2000." In an oral presentation, the title is usually used without the number: "The Falling Cost of Computer Memory,
1990–2000." The title should tell the story so that the audience knows what to
look for in the visual and why it is important. Informal or **spot** visuals are inserted directly into the text; they do not have numbers or titles.

Tables

Use tables only when you want the audience to focus on specific numbers.
Graphs convey less specific information but are always more memorable. Figure 16.3 illustrates the basic structure of tables. The **boxhead** is the variable
whose label is at the top; the **stub** is the variable listed on the side.

* Use common, understandable units. Round off to simplify the data (e.g.,
  35% rather than 35.27%; 34,000 rather than 33,942).

| **F i g u r e   16.3** | *Tables Show Exact Values* |

Table Number – Title

			Boxhead		
Stub					

Table 4.   Half of the 10 largest corporations are headquartered in Japan

1997 Rank	Company (Country)	Market Value, Millions of US Dollars
1	General Motors (US)	$178,174
2	Ford Motor (US)	153,627
3	Mitsui (Japan)	142,688
4	Mitsubishi (Japan)	128,922
5	Royal Dutch/Shell Group (UK, Netherlands)	128,142
6	Itochu (Japan)	126,632
7	Exxon (US)	122,379
8	Wal-Mart Stores (US)	119,299
9	Marubeni (Japan)	111,121
10	Sumitomo (Japan)	102,395

- Provide column and row totals or averages when they're relevant.
- Put the items you want readers to compare in columns rather than in rows to facilitate mental subtraction and division.
- When you have many rows, screen alternate entries or double-space after every five entries to help readers line up items accurately.

Pie charts

Pie charts force the audience to measure area. Research shows that people can judge position or length (which a bar chart uses) much more accurately than they judge area. The data in any pie chart can be put in a bar chart.[9] Therefore, use a pie chart only when you are comparing one segment to the whole. When you are comparing one segment to another segment, use a bar chart, a line graph, or a map—even though the data may be expressed in percentages.

- Start at 12 o'clock with the largest percentage or the percentage you want to focus on. Go clockwise to each smaller percentage or to each percentage in some other logical order.
- Make the chart a perfect circle. Perspective circles distort the data.
- Limit the number of segments to five or seven. If your data have more divisions, combine the smallest or the least important into a single "miscellaneous" or "other" category.
- Label the segments outside the circle. Internal labels are hard to read.

Bar charts

Bar charts are easy to interpret because they ask people to compare distance along a common scale, which most people judge accurately. Bar charts are useful in a variety of situations: to compare one item to another, to compare items over time, and to show correlations. Use horizontal bars when your labels are long; when the labels are short, either horizontal or vertical bars will work.

- Order the bars in a logical or chronological order.
- Put the bars close enough together to make comparison easy.
- Label both horizontal and vertical axes.

F i g u r e   16.4   *Varieties of Bar Charts*

a. Grouped bar charts compare several aspects of each item, or several items over time.

b. Segmented, subdivided, or **stacked bars** sum the components of an item.

c. Deviation bar charts identify positive and negative values.

d. Paired bar charts show the correlation between two items.

e. Histograms or **pictograms** use images to create the bars.

- Put all labels inside the bars or outside them. When some labels are inside and some are outside, the labels carry the visual weight of longer bars, distorting the data.
- Make all the bars the same width.
- Use different colors for different bars only when their meanings are different: estimates as opposed to known numbers, negative as opposed to positive numbers.
- Avoid using perspective. Perspective makes the values harder to read and can make comparison difficult.

  Several varieties of bar charts exist. See Figure 16.4 for examples.

- **Grouped bar charts** allow you to compare several aspects of each item, or several items over time.
- **Segmented, subdivided,** or **stacked bars** sum the components of an item. It's hard to identify the values in specific segments; grouped bar charts are almost always easier to use.
- **Deviation bar charts** identify positive and negative values, or winners and losers.
- **Paired bar charts** show the correlation between two items.
- **Histograms** or **pictograms** use images to create the bars.

Line graphs

Line graphs are also easy to interpret. Use line graphs to compare items over time, to show frequency or distribution, and to show correlations.

- Label both horizontal and vertical axes.
- When time is a variable, put it on the horizontal axis.
- Avoid using more than three different lines on one graph. Even three lines may be too many if they cross each other.
- Avoid using perspective. Perspective makes the values harder to read and can make comparison difficult.

Line graphs with the area below the line filled in are sometimes called **landscape graphs** (Figure 16.1).

Dot charts

Dot charts show correlations or other large data sets.

- Label both horizontal and vertical axes.
- Keep the dots fairly small. If they get too big, they no longer mark data "points"; some of the detail is lost.

Photographs

Photographs convey a sense of authenticity. The photo of a prototype helps convince investors that a product can be manufactured; the photo of a devastated area can suggest the need for government grants or private donations.

You may need to **crop** a photo for best results. If someone else is doing the production, mark the places for cropping in the margins of the photo or attach nonsticky paper. Never write or mark on the photo or the negative.

A growing problem with photos is that they may be edited or staged, purporting to show something as reality which never occurred.

Drawings

The richness of detail in photos makes them less effective than drawings for focusing on details. With a drawing, the artist can provide as much or as little detail as is needed to make the point; different parts of the drawing can show different layers or levels of detail. Drawings are also better for showing structures underground, undersea, or in the atmosphere.

Sketches

Unlike drawings, sketches omit details. In the sketch in Figure 16.5, no attempt is made to draw a specific person; instead, a generic male is shown. Sketches are good to help readers visualize processes. Here, the sketch shows how workers in Mexico get paid in a virtual system that eliminates paychecks and the need to have a bank account.

Maps

Use maps to emphasize location or to compare items in different locations. Several computer software packages now allow users to generate local, state, national, or global maps, adding color or shadings, and labels. (See Figure 16.6.)

- Label states, provinces, or countries if it's important that people be able to identify levels in areas other than their own.
- Avoid using perspective. Perspective makes the values harder to read and can make comparison difficult.

Gannt charts

Gannt charts are bar charts used to show schedules. They're most commonly used in proposals. (See Figure 16.7.)

- Color-code bars to indicate work planned and work completed.
- Use a red outline to indicate **critical activities,** which must be completed on time if the project is to be completed by the due date.
- Use diamonds to indicate progress reports, major achievements, or other accomplishments.

Putting Business on the Map*

Geographic information systems (GIS) software lets you map information on your own PC.

Archadeck in Richmond, Virginia, builds decks. Using a GIS "prospect-finder" called GeoWizard, Archadeck's marketing director identifies homeowners living near new projects. Before construction starts, likely prospects get a soft-sell notice asking them to call Archadeck if there's too much noise. Once construction starts, a second postcard invites people to stop by to take a look. GeoWizard has cut direct mail costs and, by providing better lists, tripled the response rate.

Another company learned that its high-end garden implement stores were saturating some affluent areas—and competing against themselves—while neglecting others. GIS software showed the right population mix for new stores.

*Based on Kazumi Tanaka, "Putting Your Business on the Map," *Inc. Technology* (1996), 94–99.

Figure 16.5

Sketches Can Show Processes

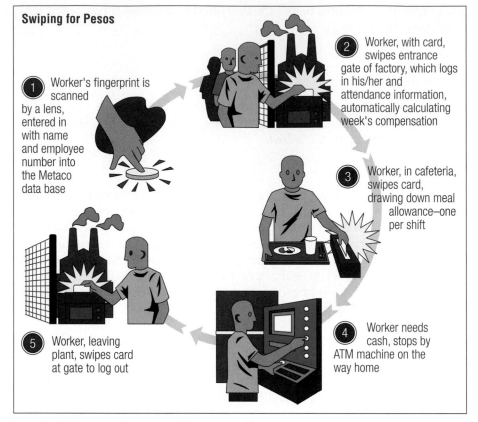

Swiping for Pesos

1. Worker's fingerprint is scanned by a lens, entered in with name and employee number into the Metaco data base

2. Worker, with card, swipes entrance gate of factory, which logs in his/her and attendance information, automatically calculating week's compensation

3. Worker, in cafeteria, swipes card, drawing down meal allowance—one per shift

4. Worker needs cash, stops by ATM machine on the way home

5. Worker, leaving plant, swipes card at gate to log out

Source: *The Wall Street Journal*, November 23, 1998, B1.

Figure 16.6

Maps Show Where Potential Customers Are

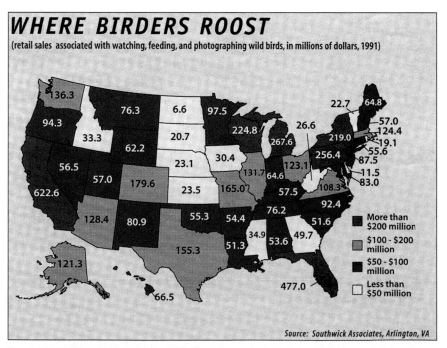

WHERE BIRDERS ROOST

(retail sales associated with watching, feeding, and photographing wild birds, in millions of dollars, 1991)

- More than $200 million
- $100 - $200 million
- $50 - $100 million
- Less than $50 million

Source: Southwick Associates, Arlington, VA

Source: *American Demographics*, December 1996, 49.

Figure 16.7   *Gannt Charts Show the Schedule for Completing a Project*

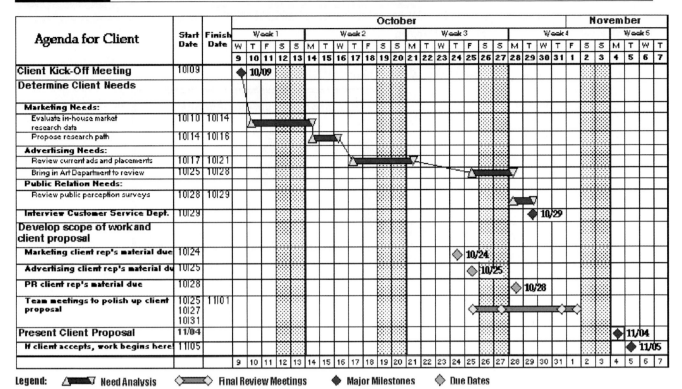

5. Use Color and Decoration with Restraint.

Color makes visuals more dramatic, but it creates at least two problems. First, readers try to interpret color, an interpretation that may not be appropriate. Perhaps the best use of color occurs in the weather maps printed daily in many newspapers. Blue seems to fit cold; red seems to fit hot temperatures. Second, meanings assigned to colors differ depending on the audience's national background and profession.

As we have seen in Chapter 12, connotations for color vary from culture to culture. Blue suggests masculinity in the United States, criminality in France, strength or fertility in Egypt, and villainy in Japan. Red is sometimes used to suggest danger or *stop* in the United States; it means *go* in China and is associated with festivities. Red suggests masculinity or aristocracy in France, death in Korea, blasphemy in some African countries, and luxury in many parts of the world. Yellow suggests caution or cowardice in the United States, prosperity in Egypt, grace in Japan, and femininity in many parts of the world.[10]

These general cultural associations may be superseded by corporate, national, or professional associations. Some people associate blue with IBM or Hewlett Packard and red with Coca-Cola, communism, or Japan. People in specific professions learn other meanings for colors. Blue suggests *reliability* to financial managers, *water* or *coldness* to engineers, and *death* to health care professionals. Red means *losing money* to financial managers, *danger* to engineers, but *healthy* to health care professionals. Green usually means *safe* to engineers, but *infected* to health care professionals.[11]

These various associations suggest that color is safest with a homogenous audience that you know well. In an increasingly multicultural workforce, color may send signals you do not intend.

To see how mapping works, visit the Web site developed by Environmental Systems Research Institute (maps.esri.com/ESRI/map objects/demos.htm). Scroll down to "Make a Thematic Map" and click. Use the boxes to find your state and the variable you want to map: population, rent, and so forth.

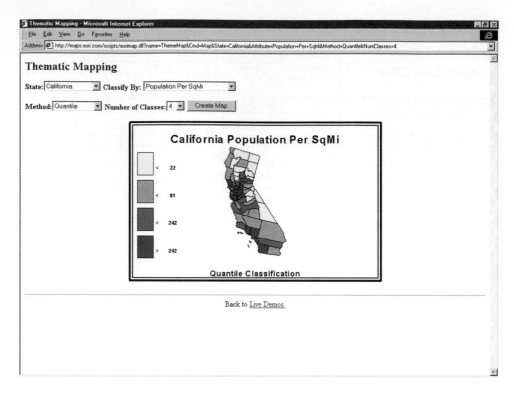

When you do use color in visuals, Thorell and Smith suggest these guidelines:[12]

- Use no more than five colors when colors have meanings.
- Use glossy paper to make colors more vivid.
- Be aware that colors on a computer screen always look brighter than the same colors on paper because the screen sends out light.

In any visual, use as little shading and as few lines as are necessary for clarity. Don't clutter up the visual with extra marks. When you design black and white graphs, use shades of gray rather than stripes, wavy lines, and checks to indicate different segments or items.

Resist the temptation to make your visual "artistic" or "relevant" by turning it into a picture or adding clip art. **Clip art** consists of predrawn images that you can import into your newsletter, sign, or graph. A small drawing of a car in the corner of a line graph showing the number of miles driven is acceptable in an oral presentation, but out of place in a written report. Turning a line graph into a highway to show miles driven makes it harder to read: it's hard to separate the data line from lines that are merely decorative. Edward Tufte uses the term **chartjunk** for decorations that at best are irrelevant to the visual and at worst mislead the reader.[13] If you use clip art, be sure that the images of people show a good mix of both sexes, various races and ages, and various physical conditions.

6. Be Sure the Visual Is Accurate and Ethical.

Always double-check your visuals to be sure the information is accurate. However, many visuals have accurate labels but misleading visual shapes. Visuals communicate quickly; audiences remember the shape, not the labels. If the reader has to study the labels to get the right picture, the visual is unethical even if the labels are accurate.

| **Figure 16.8** | *Chartjunk and Dimensions Distort Data* |

Source: *Fortune*, April 13, 1998, 122.

Figure 16.8 is distorted by chartjunk and dimensionality. In an effort to make "Mouse Power" interesting, the artist used icons rather than simple bars. Admissions to Disney theme parks were not even twice NBA admissions, but the mouse appears to be six or eight times bigger than the basketball player. The Statue of Liberty is twice the height of the White House, reflecting twice the number of admissions. But since we expect the statue to be taller than the White House, the force of the comparison is lost. Two-dimensional figures distort data by multiplying the apparent value by the width as well as by the height—four times for every doubling in value. Perspective graphs are especially hard for readers to interpret and should be avoided.[14]

Even simple bar and line graphs may be misleading if part of the scale is missing, or **truncated.** Truncated graphs are most acceptable when the audience knows the basic data set well. For example, graphs of the stock market almost never start at zero; they are routinely truncated. This omission is acceptable for audiences who follow the market closely.

Since part of the scale is missing in truncated graphs, small changes seem like major ones. The graph in Figure 16.9, from Philadelphia Suburban's *1994 Annual Report*, seems to show a healthy growth. But a close look at the numbers shows a different story. It turns out that the bottom of the glass is 230,000 customers, not zero. The real growth was 6.4%, not the 300% that the visual shows.[15] Another annual report disguised losses by using a negative base.[16] Because readers expect zero to be the base, they're almost certain to misread the visual. Labels may make the visual literally "accurate," but a visual is unethical if someone who looks at it quickly is likely to misinterpret it. For more examples of misleading visuals, see the BAC Web site.

Data can also be distorted when the context is omitted. As Tufte suggests, a drop may be part of a regular cycle, a correction after an atypical increase, or a permanent drop to a new, lower plateau.

To make your visuals more accurate,

- Differentiate between actual and estimated or projected values.
- When you must truncate a scale, do so clearly with a break in the bars or in the background.

Figure 16.9

Truncated Scales Distort Data

Source: *The Wall Street Journal,* May 25, 1995, B1.

- Avoid perspective and three-dimensional graphs.
- Avoid combining graphs with different scales.
- Use images of people carefully in histographs to avoid sexist, racist, or other exclusionary visual statements.

Integrating Visuals in Your Text

Refer to every visual in your text. Normally one gives the table or figure number in the text but not the title. Put the visual as soon after your reference as space and page design permit. If the visual must go on another page, tell the reader where to find it:

As Figure 3 shows (page 10), . . .

(See Table 2 on page 14.)

Summarize the main point of a visual *before* you present the visual itself. Then when readers get to it, they'll see it as confirmation of your point.

Weak: Listed below are the results.

Better: As Figure 4 shows, sales doubled in the last decade.

The weak statement mirrors the thought processes that occur as the writer processes data: one first categorizes the data in a very general way ("results"); one next looks at the data; and one finally decides what the data mean. But when this mental process becomes the writer's organizing pattern, the reader is forced to duplicate the whole process by which the writer reached a conclusion. Most readers, understandably, are unwilling to do work which the writer is supposed to do, so they will skim or skip the data presented in this unsatisfactory fashion. When the writer finally comes to the point, readers may be unconvinced because they haven't recognized the significance of the evidence in the table. Remember that you are writing not to reveal how your own mind works but to explain something to your readers and to convince them that your analysis is correct.

How much discussion a visual needs depends on the audience, the complexity of the visual, and the importance of the point it makes. If the material is new to the audience, you'll need a fuller explanation than if similar material is presented to this audience every week or month. If the visual is complex, you may want to help the reader find key data points in it. If the point is important, you'll want to discuss its implications in some detail. In contrast, one sentence about a visual may be enough when the audience is already familiar with the topic and the data, when the visual is simple and well designed, and when the information in the visual is a minor part of your proof.

When you discuss visuals, spell out numbers that fall at the beginning of a sentence. If spelling out the number or year is cumbersome, revise the sentence so that it does not begin with a number.

Forty-five percent of the cost goes to pay wages and salaries.

The year 1999 marked the introduction of the euro in electronic transfers.

Put numbers in parentheses at the end of the clause or sentence to make the sentence easier to read:

Hard to read: As Table 4 shows, teachers participate (54%) in more community service groups than do members of the other occupations surveyed; dentists (20.8%) participate in more service groups than do members of five of the other occupations.

Better: As Table 4 shows, teachers participate in more community service groups than do members of the other occupations surveyed (54%); dentists participate in more service groups than do five of the other occupations (20.8%).

Using Visuals in Your Presentation

Visuals for presentations need to be simpler than visuals the audience reads on paper. The table in Figure 16.3, for example, is too complex for a slide. Depending on the point you needed to make, you might be able to cut out one of the columns, round off the data even more, or present the material in a chart rather than a table.

Visuals for presentations should have titles but don't need figure numbers. Do know where each visual is so that you can return to one if someone asks about it during the question period. Decorative clip art, even though technically chartjunk, is acceptable in oral presentations as long as it does not obscure the story you're telling with the visual.

Rather than reading the visual to the audience, summarize the story and then elaborate on what it means for the audience. If you have copies of all the visuals for your audience, hand them out at the beginning of the talk.

Summary of Key Points

- Numbers are not "objective." Like words they require interpretation and context to make sense.
- In the rough draft, use visuals to see that ideas are presented completely and to see what relationships exist. In the final report, use visuals to make points vivid, to emphasize material that the reader might skip, and to present material more compactly and with less repetition than words alone would require.
- You'll use more visuals when you want to show relationships and to persuade, when the information is complex or contains extensive numerical data, and when the audience values visuals.
- Pick data to tell a story, to make a point.
- To find stories,
  1. Focus on a topic.
  2. Simplify the data.
  3. Look for relationships and changes.
- **Paired graphs** juxtapose two or more simple stories to create a more powerful story.
- Visuals are not interchangeable. The best visual depends on the kind of data and the point you want to make with the data.

Japanese Children and Statistics*

Japanese children outscore US children on math tests. The difference is not just the result of a longer school year, but of a different national attitude toward numbers.

In Japan, statistics are the subject of a holiday, local and national conventions, award ceremonies and nationwide statistical collections and graph-drawing contests. "This year," said Yoshiharu Takahashi, a Government statistician, "we had almost 30,000 entries. Actually, we had 29,836."

Entries in the [children's] statistical graph contest were screened three times by judges, who gave first prize this year to the work of five 7-year-olds. Their graph creation, titled, "Mom, play with us more often," was the result of a survey of 32 classmates on the frequency that mothers play with their offspring and the reasons given for not doing so. . . . Other children's work examined the frequency of family phone usage and correlated the day's temperature with cicada singing.

*Paragraphs 2 and 3 quoted from Andrew H. Malcolm, "Data-Loving Japanese Rejoice on Statistics Day," *New York Times*, October 28, 1977, A1.

- Tables are numbers or words arrayed in rows and columns; figures are everything else. Formal visuals have both numbers and titles that indicate what to look for in the visual or why the visual is included and is worth examining.
- Visuals must present data accurately, both literally and by implication. **Chartjunk** denotes decorations that at best are irrelevant to the visual and at worst mislead the reader. **Truncated scales** omit part of the scale and visually mislead readers. Perspective graphs and graphs with negative bases mislead readers.
- Summarize the main point of a visual before it appears in the text.
- Visuals for presentations need to be simpler than visuals on paper.
- How much discussion a visual needs depends on the audience, the complexity of the visual, and the importance of the point it makes.

Chapter 16

Exercises and Problems

Getting Started

16.1   Identifying Stories

Of the following, which are stories?

1. Results
2. Computer Use
3. Computer Prices Fall
4. More Single Parents Buy Computers than Do Any Other Group
5. Where Your Tax Dollars Go
6. Sixty Percent of Tax Dollars Pay Entitlements, Interest
7. Percent of Tax Dollars Spent on Entitlements

16.2   Choosing Titles for Stories and Visuals

Which is the best title in each group? Why? Would the other titles ever be acceptable? Why or why not?

1. a. Single Women Are Buying More Computers than Are Single Men.
   b. More Women than Men Will Live Alone with Computers.
   c. What Do Single Women Want? Computers!
2. a. Lawyers in Private Practice Make More than Those in Public Practice.
   b. Lawyers Should Be Private in Choosing Their Salaries.
   c. Private Practice Pays.
3. a. The Poor Give More.
   b. People Making under $11,000 a Year Gave a Larger Percentage of Their Incomes to Churches than Did People Making over $100,000 a Year.
   c. People Making Least Give the Highest Percentage to Church.

16.3   Matching Visuals with Stories

What visual(s) would make it easiest to see each of the following stories?

1. Canada buys 20% of US exports.
2. Undergraduate enrollment rises, but graduate enrollment declines.
3. Population growth will be greatest in the West and South.
4. Open communication ranks Number 1 in reasons to take a job.
5. Companies with fewer than 200 employees created a larger percentage of new jobs than did companies with more than 5,000 employees.
6. Men are more likely than women to see their chances for advancement as good.
7. America's heads of households are getting older.

16.4   Evaluating Visuals

Evaluate each of the following visuals.

- Is visual's message clear?
- Is it the right visual for the story?
- Is the visual designed appropriately? Is color, if any, used appropriately?
- Is the visual free from *chartjunk*?
- Does the visual distort data or mislead the reader in any way?

1.

Source: *Business Week*, April 1, 1996, 57.

2.

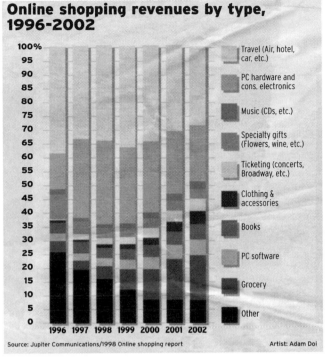

Source: *Ad Age*, October 26, 1998, 514.

3.

How My Time Will Be Used

4.

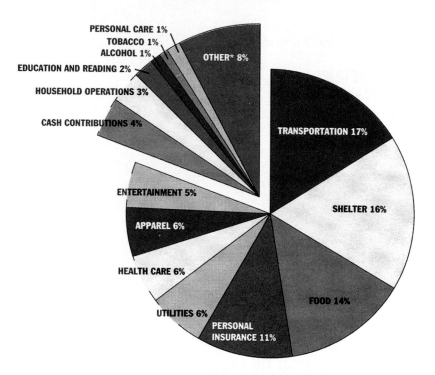

The Spending Pie

The average U.S. metropolitan household devotes half its spending to housing, utilities, transportation, and food.

(percent distribution of estimated average spending by category for households in metropolitan areas, 1993)

- PERSONAL CARE 1%
- TOBACCO 1%
- ALCOHOL 1%
- EDUCATION AND READING 2%
- HOUSEHOLD OPERATIONS 3%
- CASH CONTRIBUTIONS 4%
- ENTERTAINMENT 5%
- APPAREL 6%
- HEALTH CARE 6%
- UTILITIES 6%
- PERSONAL INSURANCE 11%
- FOOD 14%
- SHELTER 16%
- TRANSPORTATION 17%
- OTHER* 8%

* Housekeeping supplies, furnishing and equipment, and miscellaneous fees such as legal and accounting.
Note: Percentages do not sum to 100 due to rounding.

Source: *American Demographics,* January 1996, 22.

5.

Source: *PC Magazine,* February 19, 1997, 28.

6.

These Management Tools Were 1997's Favorites ...

By percent of users

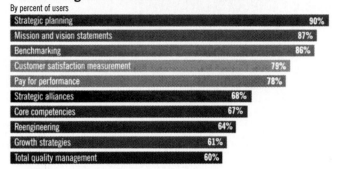

Strategic planning	90%
Mission and vision statements	87%
Benchmarking	86%
Customer satisfaction measurement	79%
Pay for performance	78%
Strategic alliances	68%
Core competencies	67%
Reengineering	64%
Growth strategies	61%
Total quality management	60%

But They Go in and out of Fashion ...

Usage rate

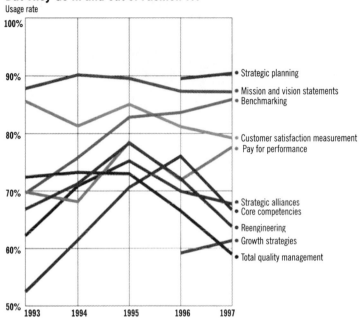

Because Companies Disagree About Their Value

Ranking by percent of extremely satisfied minus dissatisfied users

Source: *Fortune,* September 7, 1998, 163.

7.

Source: *Direct Marketing*, Special Advertising Section, np.

Web Page

16.5   Creating a Web Guide to Graphs

Create a Web page explaining how to create good visuals. Offer general principles and at least seven links to examples of good and poor visuals. (More is better.) At the top of the page, offer an overview of what the page covers. At the bottom of the page, put the creation/update date and your name and e-mail address.

As Your Instructor Directs,

a. Turn in two laser copies of your page(s). On another page, give the URLs for each link.

b. Turn in one laser copy of your page(s) and a disk with the HTML code and .gif files.

c. Write a memo to your instructor (1) identifying the audience for which the page is designed and explaining (2) the search strategies you used to find material on this topic, (3) why you chose the pages and information you've included, and (4) why you chose the layout and graphics you've used.

d. Present your page orally to the class.

Hints:

- Searching for words (*graphs, maps, Gannt charts, data*) will turn up only pages with those words. Also check pages on topics that may use graphs to explain their data: finance, companies' performance, sports, cost of living, exports, and so forth.

- In addition to finding good and bad visuals on the Web, you can also scan in examples you find in newspapers, magazines, and textbooks.

- If you have more than nine links, chunk them in small groups under headings.

Visuals, Memos, and Report Assignments

16.6   Creating Visuals

As Your Instructor Directs,

a. Identify visuals that you might use to help analyze each of the following data sets.

b. Identify and create a visual for one or more of the stories in each set.

c. Identify additional information that would be needed for other stories related to these data sets.

1. Online sales

	1997 sales	2001 estimated sales
Financial services	$1.2 billion	$5 billion
Apparel and footware	$92 million	$514 million
PC hardware and software	$863 million	$3.8 billion
Entertainment	$298 million	$2.7 billion
Travel	$654 million	$7.4 billion
Books and music	$156 million	$1.1 billion
Ticket event sales	$79 million	$2 billion
Business-to-business sales	$8 billion	$183 billion

Source: "Online Sales Are Soaring," *Business Week*, June 22, 1998, 124–25.

2. Women of color in corporate management

Catalyst surveyed 1,700 women (African-American: 54%; Asian-American: 21%; Hispanic: 24%)

Satisfied with content of job: 57% (African-American: 55.2%; Asian-American: 53.4%; Hispanic: 65.8%)

Believe affirmative action helped them get hired and/or promoted (African-American: 54.4%; Asian-American: 29.5%; Hispanic: 42%)

Believe opportunities for advancement have improved: (African-American: 47.9%; Asian-American: 41.8; Hispanic: 50%)

Plan to leave current employer: 21.6% (African-American: 24.5%; Asian-American: 19.3%; Hispanic: 16.7%)

Source: "Hispanic Professional Women Say Opportunities Looking Good," *Hispanic Business*, May 1998, 70.

3. Responses to TV commercials

Exhibit III: Percent of Adults Who Report They Often Respond to Television Commercials in Selected Ways

	TOTAL	FEMALE	MALE
Watch commercials	22%	19%	24%
Turn down the sound	14	13	14
Change channels	27	31	24
Leave television	45	44	47
Get annoyed	51	51	50
Talk to others, ignoring commercials	35	36	34
Talk to others about commercials	14	13	16
Get amused by funny commercials	26	24	29
Pay attention to information on new products and services	10	8	11
Fast forward through commercials when watching a taped program	35	38	32
Learn about products and services of interest	17	14	19

Source: The Roper Organization, 1993

Source: "Special Report," Internet Advertising Bureau, supplement to *Advertising Age*, Spring 1998, 68A.

16.7   Interpreting Data

As Your Instructor Directs,

a. Identify at least seven stories in one or more of the following data sets.

b. Create visuals for three of the stories.

c. Write a memo to your instructor explaining why you chose these stories and why you chose these visuals to display them.

d. Write a memo to some group that might be interested in your findings, presenting your visuals as part of a short report. Possible groups include career counselors, radio stations, advertising agencies, and Mothers Against Drunk Driving.

e. Brainstorm additional stories you could tell with additional data. Specify the kind of data you would need.

1. Attendance rates for various activities by
   demographic factors

ATTENDANCE RATES FOR VARIOUS ACTIVITIES BY DEMOGRAPHIC FACTORS

	U.S. Adult Population (millions)	Jazz	Classical Music	Opera	Musicals	Plays	Ballet	Art Museums	Reading Literature	Sample Size
GRAND MEAN	195.6	11.9%	15.6%	4.7%	24.5%	15.8%	5.9%	34.5%	68.4%	12,376
Gender										
Male	94.1	13.2	14.2	4.0	22.5	14.6	4.1	34.3	60.0	5,250
Female	101.3	10.6	16.1	5.2	26.7	16.8	7.5	35.5	74.7	7,093
Race										
White	142.0	12.1	17.5	5.2	26.4	16.6	6.5	36.1	70.7	9,268
Black	21.5	15.6	9.6	2.1	22.4	16.4	3.9	31.1	65.9	1,110
Age										
18–24	22.3	14.8	16.8	5.5	26.0	20.6	7.1	38.6	72.4	1,047
25–34	38.9	12.9	11.2	3.9	22.8	13.4	4.7	36.5	65.8	2,433
35–44	44.0	14.3	14.3	4.3	25.3	14.6	6.4	37.2	69.1	2,887
45–54	33.3	13.0	20.6	6.2	29.2	19.4	7.1	39.8	72.5	2,147
55–64	20.8	8.8	11.6	4.8	23.5	15.1	4.9	30.4	65.6	1,389
65–74	19.2	8.4	17.9	4.1	24.2	14.3	5.5	28.3	66.9	1,221
75–96	12.6	3.9	14.4	3.7	15.5	12.8	3.9	20.2	66.8	920
Education										
Grade school	13.5	1.8	2.1	0.2	6.0	3.1	1.5	6.0	28.5	516
Some high school	26.6	3.4	3.9	1.5	12.6	7.2	1.8	14.4	49.4	957
High school grad	61.3	4.8	8.3	1.7	15.7	9.1	3.6	24.6	58.8	3,545
Some college	49.9	15.4	18.1	5.2	28.4	18.9	6.5	43.2	74.5	3,527
College grad	24.9	21.3	28.0	10.2	43.6	27.7	10.8	57.7	80.1	2,012
Graduate school	13.5	27.7	44.5	14.3	50.3	37.2	14.4	69.8	86.5	1,653

Source: NEA Survey of Public Participation in the Arts '97

Source of data: *American Demographics,* October 1998, 47.

2. Drinking patterns

WHO DRINKS HOW MUCH HOW OFTEN

PERCENT OF ADULT MALE POPULATION THAT ...	DRINKS AT ALL	DRINKS DAILY	DRINKS 60+ DRINKS A MONTH	DRINKS 5+ DRINKS A DAY AT LEAST ONCE A WEEK	DRINKS 8+ DRINKS A DAY AT LEAST ONCE A WEEK
TOTAL	71%	10%	21%	9%	4%
BY AGE:					
18–29	77%	5%	24%	17%	9%
30–39	73%	9%	19%	7%	2%
40–49	72%	8%	21%	8%	4%
50–59	65%	16%	23%	7%	4%
60 and over	66%	16%	18%	3%	1%
BY EDUCATION:					
Less than high school	65%	13%	23%	15%	6%
High school graduate	70%	7%	21%	10%	5%
Some college	76%	10%	23%	8%	4%
College degree/higher	77%	11%	20%	3%	2%
BY FAMILY INCOME:					
Up to $9,999	68%	9%	30%	19%	10%
$10,000–$19,999	66%	12%	20%	12%	4%
$20,000–$29,999	65%	9%	22%	11%	4%
$30,000–$39,999	72%	8%	18%	7%	5%
$40,000–$59,999	80%	13%	20%	6%	2%
$60,000 and over	79%	10%	26%	6%	3%

Source of data: *Fortune,* March 6, 1995, 168.

3. Projected drinking patterns, 1997–2007

HAPPY HOUR IN AMERICA

(projected thousands of adults who drank any alcoholic beverage in the past six months, by sex and age, 1997, 2000, and 2007, and percent change, 1997–2000, and 1997–2007)

	1997	2000	2007	percent change 1997–2000	percent change 1997–2007
MEN					
Total	54,481	54,472	54,419	0.0%	−0.1%
21 to 24 ..	4,579	4,596	4,685	0.4	2.3
25 to 34 ..	13,446	12,273	11,268	−8.7	−16.2
35 to 44 ..	14,182	14,140	12,287	−0.3	−13.4
45 to 54 ..	10,304	11,201	12,558	8.7	21.9
55 to 64 ..	5,465	5,798	7,088	6.1	29.7
65 and older	6,506	6,465	6,534	−0.6	0.4
WOMEN					
Total	47,637	46,890	44,948	−1.6%	−5.6%
21 to 24 ..	3,649	3,573	3,375	−2.1	−7.5
25 to 34 ..	11,315	10,156	8,864	−10.2	−21.7
35 to 44 ..	12,691	12,531	10,746	−1.3	−15.3
45 to 54 ..	8,838	9,466	10,197	7.1	15.4
55 to 64 ..	5,062	5,348	6,486	5.7	28.1
65 and older	6,083	5,815	5,279	−4.4	−13.2

Source: Mediamark Research, Inc., Census Bureau, and American Demographics

SIPPING IN THE 21ST CENTURY

(projected thousands of men and women who drank alcohol in the past six months, by type of alcohol, 1997 and 2007, and percent change 1997–2007)

	1997	2007	percent change 1997–2007
MEN			
Any	54,481	54,419	−0.1%
Wine	24,972	21,751	−12.9
Beer	46,549	46,547	0.0
White goods .	18,530	16,829	−9.2
Brown goods	22,603	18,745	−17.1
WOMEN			
Any	47,637	44,948	−5.6%
Wine	32,045	29,061	−9.3
Beer	28,071	25,761	−8.2
White goods .	18,410	17,064	−7.3
Brown goods	16,326	10,541	−35.4

Note: White goods are distilled spirits, such as vodka and gin; brown goods include whiskey and cognac.

Source: Mediamark Research Inc, Census Bureau, and American Demographics

Source of data: *American Demographics*, January 1997, 4, 6.

4. Highest-paid entertainers

Income in millions of dollars		
Rank 1998	**1997 and 1996**	**1995 and 1994**
1 Jerry Seinfeld ($225)	Steven Spielberg ('97: $283; '96: $30)	Steven Spielberg ('95: $120; '94: $165)
2 Larry David ($200)	George Lucas ('97: $189; '96: $52)	Oprah Winfrey ('95: $74; '94: $72)
3 Steven Spielberg ($175)	Oprah Winfrey ('97: $104; '96: $97)	Beatles ('95: $100; '94: $30)
4 Oprah Winfrey ($125)	Michael Crichton ('97: $65; '96: $35)	Rolling Stones ('95: $71; '94: $50)
5 James Cameron ($115)	Beatles ('97: $68; '96: $30)	Eagles ('95: $43; '94: $52)
6 Tim Allen ($77)	Jerry Seinfeld ('97: $66; '96: $28)	David Copperfield ('95: $52; '94: $29)
7 Michael Crichton ($65)	David Copperfield ('97: $45; '96: $40)	Pink Floyd ('95: $14; '94: $56)
8 Harrison Ford ($58)	Stephen King ('97: $50; '96: $34)	Michael Jackson ('95: $45; '94: $22)
9 Rolling Stones ($57)	Tom Cruise ('97: $55; '96: $27)	Barbra Streisand ('95: $11; '94: $52)
10 Master P ($56.5)	Arnold Schwarzenegger ('97: $22; '96: $52)	Sylvester Stallone ('95: $34; '94: $24)
11 Robin Williams ($56)	Harrison Ford ('97: $47; '96: $25)	Tom Hanks ('95: $36; '94: $16)
12 Celine Dion ($55.5)	Rolling Stones ('97: $62; '96: $6)	Bill Cosby ('95: $15; '94: $34)
13 Mel Gibson ($55)	Tim Allen ('97: $47; '96: $19)	Andrew Lloyd Webber ('95: $24; '94: $24)
14 Garth Brooks ($54)	John Grisham ('97: $36; '96: $30)	Harrison Ford ('95: $19; '94: $27)
15 Sean (Puffy) Combs ($53.5)	Celine Dion ('97: $34; '96: $31)	Stephen King ('95: $22; '94: $21)
16 Mike Judge ($53)	David Bowie ('97: $57; '96: $6)	Grateful Dead ('95: $18; '94: $94)
17 Greg Daniels ($53)	John Travolta ('97: $39; '96: $22)	Barney ('95: $15; '94: $24)
18 Chris Carter ($52)	Mel Gibson ('97: $42; '96: $17)	Siegfried & Roy ('95: $23; '94: $17)
19 David Copperfield ($49.5)	Siegfried & Roy ('97: $33; '96: $25)	Garth Brooks ('95: $22; '94: $18)
20 Spice Girls ($49)	Sting ('97: $40; '96: $17)	Michael Crichton ('95: $22; '94: $77)
21 Paul Reiser ($48)	Garth Brooks ('97: $26; '96: $29)	Jim Carrey ('95: $29; '94: $10)
22 Eddie Murphy ($47.5)	Roseanne ('97: $34; '96: $21)	Robert Zemeckis ('95: $32; '94: $5)
23 John Travolta ($47)	Michael Jackson ('97: $20; '96: $35)	Charles Schulz ('95: $18; '94: $18)
24 Drew Carey ($45.5)	Ron Howard & Brian Grazer ('97: $37; '96: $17)	Elton John ('95: $15; '94: $20)
25 Bonnie & Terry Turner ($45)	Michael Flatley ('97: $27; '96: $27)	Bruce Willis ('95: $16; '94: $19)

Based on pretax gross income in year earned. Excludes income from sources other than entertainment (e.g., investments). Ranks for 1997 and 1996, and 1995 and 1994 based on income for two years.

Source: Robert La Franco and Ben Pappas, "Star Bucks," *Forbes*, September 21, 1998, 220–37; Robert La Franco, "The Forbes Top 40," *Forbes*, September 22, 1997, 162–76; Robert La Franco, "The Top 40," *Forbes*, September 25, 1995, 136ff.

16.8 Graphing Data from the Web

Find data on the Web about a topic that interests you. Sites with data include the following:

American Demographics Archives
   www.marketingtools.com/search.htm
Catalyst
   www.catalystwomen.org/research
CompareNet
   www.comparenet.com
FEDSTATS (links to 70 US government agencies)
   www.fedstats.gov
Graphic, Visualization, & Usability Center's WWW surveys
   www.gvu.gatech.edu/user_surveys/survey-1998-04/graphs/general/q33.htm
Statistical Universe (US government statistics back to the 1970s)
   www.cispubs.com

White House Briefing Room (economic issues)
   www.whitehouse.gov/fsbr/esbr.html

As Your Instructor Directs,
a. Identify at least seven stories in the data.
b. Create visuals for three of the stories.
c. Write a memo to your instructor explaining why you chose these stories and why you chose these visuals to display them.
d. Write a memo to some group which might be interested in your findings, presenting your visuals as part of a short report.
e. Print out the data and include it with a copy of your memo or report.

17

Making Oral Presentations

Purposes in Oral Presentations

Comparing Written and Oral Messages

Planning a Strategy for Your Presentation
- Choosing the Kind of Presentation
- Adapting Your Ideas to the Audience
- Planning a Strong Opening and Close
- Planning Visuals and Other Devices to Involve the Audience

Choosing Information to Include in a Presentation

Organizing Your Information

Delivering an Effective Presentation
- Dealing with Fear
- Using Eye Contact
- Developing a Good Speaking Voice
- Standing and Gesturing
- Using Notes and Visuals

Handling Questions

Making Group Presentations

Summary of Key Points

Making Oral Presentations

Luis E. Lamela

President and CEO, CAC Medical Centers

www.uhc.com

Luis Lamela makes presentations to a variety of internal and external audiences including medical professionals, providers, clients. CAC Medical Centers, headquartered in Coral Gables, Florida, is a comprehensive medical delivery network comprised of 28 single- and multispecialty medical centers in south Florida. It is a federally qualified health maintenance organization (HMO). Its parent company is United HealthCare Corporation, a national leader in health care management.

The key to a successful oral presentation is to keep things simple. I try to stick to three points. I give an overview of the points, present them to the audience, and summarize them at the end.

My purpose and the audience mix determine the tone and focus of the presentation, the kind of visuals, the number of anecdotes, and the jokes or examples that I use. Most of my presentations are designed to sell, to explain, or to motivate. When I plan the presentation, I think about the audience. Are they professionals or nonprofessionals? Purchasers or sellers? Providers or users? Internal or external?

> 66 *My purpose and the audience mix determine the tone and focus of the presentation.* 99

When I make a presentation, I use the visuals as the outline. I will not use notes. I like to select the kind of visual that not only best supports the message but also best fits the audience and the physical location. PowerPoint, slides, overhead transparencies, and flip charts are the four main kinds of visuals I use.

PowerPoint and slide presentations work well when I am selling a product or an idea to large groups (15 people or more). In this format, I like to use examples and graphs and tables to support my message in a general way.

In small presentations, including one-on-ones and presentations where the audience is part of the actual process, I like transparencies or flip charts. They allow me to be closer to the audience and to be more informal.

I get very, very nervous when I speak in public. I handle my nervousness by just trying to look as if, instead of talking to so many people, I'm walking in and talking to a single person. I don't like to speak behind lecterns. Instead, I like to get out and just be open and portray that openness: "I'm here to tell you a story."

I try not to lecture but to use anecdotes, and I think that people find them interesting and relate better to them. For example, our multispecialty medical centers differ according to the demographics of the area. In Hispanic areas, examination rooms need to be bigger because as Hispanics we bring the concept of the extended family right into the examination room. But if we're going to build a center in an Anglo area, exam rooms will be smaller.

I try very hard for people to enjoy my presentations by showing enthusiasm on the subject and by being sincere. In addition, it helps that I am speaking about something that I very strongly believe in and something that I really, really enjoy doing.

Make Your Message Memorable*

At a beverage conference in Spain, Nick Rosa, then president of The NutraSweet Company, began, "Every time I practice soccer with my sons, aged seven and eight, I am reminded of the generation game. When I consider my area of expertise, my boys represent this new generation perfectly. First, they're young. Second, they're thirsty. Third, they have grown up with diet drinks in the fridge." Then Nick launched into his speech. Six months later he met a conference delegate who greeted him by saying, "How's it going? I haven't seen you since that great speech where you talked about your kids."

By adding a personal touch, Nick helped make his speech memorable.

*Quoted from Elizabeth Urech, *Speaking Globally: Effective Presentations Across International and Cultural Barriers* (Dover, NH: Kogan Page, 1998), 31.

he power to persuade people to care about something you believe in is crucial to business success. Making a good oral presentation is more than just good delivery: it also involves developing a strategy that fits your audience and purpose, having good content, and organizing material effectively. The choices you make in each of these areas are affected by your purposes, the audience, and the situation.

Purposes in Oral Presentations

Oral presentations have the same three basic purposes that written documents have: to inform, to persuade, and to build goodwill. Like written messages, most oral presentations have more than one purpose.

Informative presentations inform or teach the audience. Training sessions in an organization are primarily informative. Secondary purposes may be to persuade new employees to follow organizational procedures, rather than doing something their own way, and to help them appreciate the organizational culture (✖ p. 62).

Persuasive presentations motivate the audience to act or to believe. Giving information and evidence is an important means of persuasion. In addition, the speaker must build goodwill by appearing to be credible and sympathetic to the audience's needs. The goal in many presentations is a favorable vote or decision. For example, speakers making business presentations may try to persuade the audience to approve their proposals, to adopt their ideas, or to buy their products. Sometimes the goal is to change behavior or attitudes or to reinforce existing attitudes. For example, a speaker at a meeting of factory workers may stress the importance of following safety procedures. A speaker at a church meeting may talk about the problem of homelessness in the community and try to build support for community shelters for the homeless.

Goodwill presentations entertain and validate the audience. In an after-dinner speech, the audience wants to be entertained. Presentations at sales meetings may be designed to stroke the audience's egos and to validate their commitment to organizational goals.

Make your purpose as specific as possible.

Weak: The purpose of my presentation is to discuss saving for retirement.

Better: The purpose of my presentation is to persuade my audience to put their 401K funds in stocks and bonds, not in money market accounts and CDs.

or: The purpose of my presentation is to explain how to calculate how much money someone needs to save in order to maintain a specific lifestyle after retirement.

Note that the purpose *is not* the introduction of your talk; it is the principle that guides your choice of strategy and content.

Comparing Written and Oral Messages

Giving a presentation is in many ways very similar to writing a message. All of the chapters up to this point—on using you-attitude and positive emphasis, developing reader benefits, analyzing your audience, designing slides, overcoming objections, doing research, and analyzing data—remain relevant as you plan an oral presentation.

A written message makes it easier to

- Present extensive or complex financial data.
- Present many specific details of a law, policy, or procedure.
- Minimize undesirable emotions.

Oral messages make it easier to

- Use emotion to help persuade the audience.
- Focus the audience's attention on specific points.
- Answer questions, resolve conflicts, and build consensus.
- Modify a proposal that may not be acceptable in its original form.
- Get immediate action or response.

Oral and written messages have many similarities. In both, you should

- Adapt the message to the specific audience.
- Show the audience how they would benefit from the idea, policy, service, or product.
- Overcome any objections the audience may have.
- Use you-attitude and positive emphasis.
- Use visuals to clarify or emphasize material.
- Specify exactly what the audience should do.

Planning a Strategy for Your Presentation

A **strategy** is your plan for reaching your specific goals with a specific audience.

In all oral presentations, simplify what you want to say. Identify the one idea you want the audience to take home. Simplify your supporting detail so it's easy to follow. Simplify visuals so they can be taken in at a glance. Simplify your words and sentences so they're easy to understand.

An oral presentation needs to be simpler than a written message to the same audience. If readers forget a point, they can turn back to it and reread the paragraph. Headings, paragraph indentation, and punctuation provide visual cues to help readers understand the message. Listeners, in contrast, must remember what the speaker says. Whatever they don't remember is lost. Even asking questions requires the audience to remember which points they don't understand.

Analyze your audience for an oral presentation just as you do for a written message. If you'll be speaking to co-workers, talk to them about your topic or proposal to find out what questions or objections they have. For audiences inside the organization, the biggest questions are often practical ones: Will it work? How much will it cost? How long will it take?[1]

Think about the physical conditions in which you'll be speaking. Will the audience be tired at the end of a long day of listening? Sleepy after a big meal? Will the group be large or small? The more you know about your audience, the better you can adapt your message to them.

For example, Matt Hession knew that his audience of pharmacists didn't want to talk to salespeople. So he devised a one-minute presentation which he offers as entertainment—and as a challenge. Figure 17.1 gives his script. He takes off his watch to drive home the point that he really will take only a minute of the pharmacist's time. He starts off with reader benefits (p. 72) and uses psychological description (p. 233) so that the pharmacists can see themselves enjoying those benefits. Because the commission structure is complicated, that goes in a handout rather than in the presentation itself. When he calls the next week, he says, "This is Matt. I did the one-minute presentation. . . . They always remember me." And 90% of them eventually sign contracts.

Choosing the Kind of Presentation

Choose one of three basic kinds of presentations: monologue, guided discussion, or interactive.

What CEOs Learn about Presentations*

Executives preparing to take their companies public make scores of presentations in dozens of towns over a few short weeks. The purpose of this "road show" is to introduce the company to investment professionals—persuading them to buy, or at least to chart, the stock.

To prepare for these crucial presentations, many CEOs take lessons. Four days of intensive training from one expert costs $20,000. Here are some of the lessons three CEOs learned:

- Trip Hawkins, CEO of The 3DO Co. *'I had to suppress my 'ums' and 'ahs'—people don't know how many times they use those in conversation. And I have a tendency to look around too much—my eyes were zigging and zagging around the room.'*
- Scott Cook, Chairman of Intuit *'If I got negative questions, I'd get defensive and put a chill on things. . . . He taught me that when somebody asks a negative question, restate it positively, answer it positively.'*
- Timothy Koogle, CEO of Yahoo! *'He had me . . . loosen up. Get rid of the podium death grip. . . . Connect with the audience physically, with my eyes. Encourage them to drink in a really important slide by having a big pause in my speech.'*

*Quotations quoted from Quentin Hardy, "Meet Jerry Weisman, Acting Coach to CEOs," *The Wall Street Journal,* April 21, 1998, B1.

"When I walk into a store, I spot the clerk closest to the pharmacist. Because the pharmacist is behind the counter, I can't get to him directly. So I speak loudly, and I know he is overhearing what's going on. If I walk in looking like a salesman, the pharmacist immediately thinks, `I don't want to buy anything or talk to you.' I nullify that feeling right off the bat. The pharmacist thinks, `He's entertainment. It's only a minute, and it doesn't cost anything.' I'm not threatening anymore. Customers smile; they want to hear what I have to say. I take off my watch to show that I'm serious."

My name is Matt Hession with Key Medical. I know the pharmacist is real busy. But when he has a moment, I have a one-minute presentation. (Start to take off watch.) **And he can leave his wallet in his pocket.**

"As I walk behind the counter, I try to assess how promising a partner this would be. How busy is the place? Is it handling any medical equipment—like walkers—already? Is the back of the store neat, clean, and well organized? I'm also thinking of anything I can quickly add to personalize the presentation. For example, if there is a pediatrician next door, I'll point out that we handle nebulizers—small machines used by kids with asthma—and that we can get same-day approval on Medicaid. I hold up my watch again to emphasize that I'm serious about this taking only one minute."

(The clerk acknowledges and relays the request. But the pharmacist has overheard the conversation. "I'll be with you in a bit," he says. A couple of minutes later, he motions for me to step behind the counter. As we shake hands, I introduce myself again and hold up the watch.)

"I am telling the pharmacists that this is something the chains do not have. This strikes an immediate note. Independent pharmacists, who are usually also the store owners, complain that chains like Wal-Mart have certain advantages. Now, they think, they will have an edge. They have two questions: How much time will it take? How much will it cost me? I answer those right up front."

We're in the home-medical-equipment business. Our company has developed a program just for independently owned community drugstores. Our program costs you nothing and takes up very little of your time.

Here's how it works: a customer walks into your store and sees one of the signs that we provide to you, indicating that you can get customers any type of home-medical equipment. The customer inquires about a home oxygen system that her father needs. You answer, "Let me get our equipment partner on the phone for you." You dial our 800 number and tell us who you are, the name of your store, and its location. Then you give us your customer's name and her question. We either talk to the customer right there or call her at home—your choice. We see if we can answer her questions and help to meet her needs. If it results in a sale or rental, we deliver the equipment, and we teach the customer how to use it. We do the insurance filing or billing. We service the equipment. The whole nine yards. Your job is to educate your customers that they can obtain home-medical equipment through you.

"It would take longer than a minute, obviously, to explain the commission structure. There are three different scenarios—a sale, a rental, or a lease-to-own option—and I can't cover those in under two minutes. And with customers in earshot, we don't have privacy, anyway. But I will give answers on two questions the pharmacists often ask: Where is your home office, and how do you deliver these things? The details are very clearly spelled out in the material I give them."

Here's a copy of our partnership agreement. It spells out your commission structure as well as other important concerns.

Source: Joshua Hyatt, "The 60-Second Sales Pitch," *Inc.*, October 1994, 88–89.

In a **monologue presentation,** the speaker speaks without interruption; questions are held until the end of the presentation, where the speaker functions as an expert. The speaker plans the presentation in advance and delivers it without deviation. This kind of presentation is the most common in class situations, but it's often boring for the audience. Good delivery skills are crucial, since the audience is comparatively uninvolved.

Linda Driskill suggests that **guided discussions** offer a better way to present material and help an audience find a solution it can "buy into." In a guided discussion, the speaker presents the questions or issues that both speaker and audience have agreed on in advance. Rather than functioning as an expert with all the answers, the speaker serves as a facilitator to help the audience tap its own knowledge. This kind of presentation is excellent for presenting the results of consulting projects, when the speaker has specialized knowledge, but the audience must implement the solution if it is to succeed. Guided discussions need more time than monologue presentations, but produce more audience response, more responses involving analysis, and more commitment to the result.[2]

An **interactive presentation** is a conversation, even if the speaker stands up in front of a group and uses charts and overheads. Most sales presentations are interactive presentations. The sales representative uses questions to determine the buyer's needs, probe objections, and gain provisional and then final commitment to the purchase. Even in a memorized sales presentation, the buyer will talk at least 30% of the time. In a problem-solving sales presentation, top salespeople let the buyer do 70% of the talking up until the action close (✖ p. 286).[3]

Adapting Your Ideas to the Audience

Measure the message you'd like to send against where your audience is now. If your audience is indifferent, skeptical, or hostile, focus on the part of your message the audience will find most interesting and easiest to accept.

Don't seek a major opinion change in a single oral presentation. If the audience has already decided to hire an advertising agency, then a good presentation can convince them that your agency is the one to hire. But if you're talking to a small business that has always done its own ads, limit your purpose. You may be able to prove that an agency can earn its fees by doing things the owner can't do and by freeing the owner's time for other activities. A second presentation may be needed to prove that an ad agency can do a *better* job than the small business could do on its own. Only after the audience is receptive should you try to persuade the audience to hire your agency rather than a competitor.

Make your ideas relevant to your audience by linking what you have to say to their experiences and interests. Showing your audience that the topic affects them directly is the most effective strategy. When you can't do that, at least link the topic to some everyday experience.

> When was the last time you were hungry? Maybe you remember being hungry while you were on a diet, or maybe you had to work late at a lab and didn't get back to the dorm in time for dinner.

Speech about world hunger to an audience of college students

Planning a Strong Opening and Close

The beginning and end of a presentation, like the beginning and end of a written document, are positions of emphasis. Use those key positions to interest the audience and emphasize your key point. You'll sound more natural and more

Adapting the Presentation to the Audience*

When Jerry Stackhouse turned pro, many companies made presentations designed to sign him to represent their products. Fila won, in part because of a presentation and visuals specifically adapted to Mr. Stackhouse.

During his initial presentation to Mr. Stackhouse, Fila executive Howe Burch placed a poster directly across from where Mr. Stackhouse was sitting. It listed the names of 18 NBA Nike endorsers in fuzzy, hard-to-read type. But there was no mistaking the slogan printed in big letters: "Looks like the Swoosh [Nike's logo] is becoming a blur. At Fila, Stackhouse will be a Standout."

Mr. Burch also brought along a prototype of the Stackhouse shoe, a model that was ready to go into production but just needed a name. At a second meeting, Mr. Burch arrived carrying a paper bag that he placed on a side table. Mr. Stackhouse asked, "Is that my shoe in the bag?"

Fila knew right then that it had Mr. Stackhouse in the bag, too.

*Paragraphs 2–4 quoted from Roger Thurow, "A Rookie Guard Scores Big at Marketing," *The Wall Street Journal,* February 9, 1996, A6.

Strategy for a Corporate Speech*

Security directors of the 50 most prominent international banks meet periodically to discuss common problems. BankAmerica's Bob Beck wanted to talk to the group about chemical dependency and BankAmerica's approach to the problem.

Audience's initial position: Resistant. Most favored testing, not treatment.

One point to leave with audience: Treatment is a practical alternative that works.

Adapting message to audience: Used terms from sports, banking, and security to make it easy for audience to identify with message. Backed up points with details and statistics. Explained problems of drug testing. Did not ask for action.

Opener: Hard-hitting statistics on how much chemical dependency costs US businesses— $26 billion a year.

Outline: (1) Chemical dependency as a disease; the size of the problem; testing as the usual response. (2) BankAmerica's treatment approach: policy, program design, and education in the workplace. (3) The business advantages of treatment: protects investment in trained people; confines business losses caused by chemical dependency.

*Based on Robin Welling, *No Frills, No Nonsense, No Secrets* (San Francisco: International Association of Business Communicators, 1988), 290–93.

effective if you talk from notes but write out your opener and close in advance and memorize them. (They'll be short: just a sentence or two.)

Consider using one of the four modes for openers that appeared in Chapter 11: startling statement, narration or anecdote, question, or quotation. The more you can do to personalize your opener for your audience, the better. Recent events are better than things that happened long ago; local events are better than events at a distance; people they know are better than people who are only names.

Startling statement

> Twelve of our customers have canceled orders in the past month.

This presentation to a company's executive committee went on to show that the company's distribution system was inadequate and to recommend a third warehouse located in the Southwest.

Narration or anecdote

> A mother was having difficulty getting her son up for school. He pulled the covers over his head.
> "I'm not going to school," he said. "I'm not ever going again."
> "Are you sick?" his mother asked.
> "No," he answered. "I'm sick of school. They hate me. They call me names. They make fun of me. Why should I go?"
> "I can give you two good reasons," the mother replied. "The first is that you're 42 years old. And the second is *you're the school principal.*"[4]

This speech to a seminar for educators went on to discuss "the three knottiest problems in education today." Educators had to face those problems; they couldn't hide under the covers.

Question

> Are you going to have enough money to do the things you want to when you retire?

This presentation to a group of potential clients discusses the value of using the services of a professional financial planner to achieve one's goals for retirement.

Quotation

> According to Towers Perrin, the profits of Fortune 100 companies would be 25% lower—they'd go down $17 billion—if their earnings statements listed the future costs companies are obligated to pay for retirees' health care.

This presentation on options for health care for retired employees urges executives to start now to investigate options to cut the future costs.

Your opener should interest the audience and establish a rapport with them. Some speakers use humor to achieve those goals. However, an inappropriate joke can turn the audience against the speaker. Never use humor that's directed against the audience. In contrast, speakers who can make fun of themselves almost always succeed:

> It's both a privilege and a pressure to be here.[5]

Humor isn't the only way to set an audience at ease. Smile at your audience before you begin; let them see that you're a real person and a nice one.

The end of your presentation should be as strong as the opener. For your close, you could do one or more of the following: (1) restate your main point; (2) refer to your opener to create a frame for your presentation; (3) end with a vivid, positive picture; (4) tell the audience exactly what to do to solve the problem you've discussed. The following close from a fund-raising speech combines a restatement of the main point with a call for action, telling the audience what to do.

> Plain and simple, we need money to run the foundation, just like you need money to develop new products. We need money to make this work. We need money from you. Pick up that pledge card. Fill it out. Turn it in at the door as you leave. Make it a statement about your commitment . . . make it a big statement.[6]

When you write out your opener and close, be sure to use oral rather than written style. As you can see in the example close above, oral style uses shorter sentences and shorter, simpler words than writing does. Oral style can even sound a bit choppy when it is read by eye. Oral style uses more personal pronouns, a less varied vocabulary, and more repetition.

Planning Visuals and Other Devices to Involve the Audience

Visuals can give your presentation a professional image. As more and more businesses buy computer graphics packages, more and more presentations use slides or overhead transparencies, which, confusingly, are often called *slides*, too. You design the graphics on your computer, then give the disk to a service bureau that produces slides. As color printers become more common, business people will be able to produce color overhead transparencies in-house.

One study showed that presenters using overhead transparencies were perceived as "better prepared, more professional, more persuasive, more credible, and more interesting" than speakers who did not use visuals. They were also more likely to persuade a group to adopt their recommendations.[7] A study comparing the use of different kinds of visuals found that presenters using slides appeared more professional, but presenters using overhead transparencies seemed more interesting. Colored overhead transparencies were most effective in persuading people to act.[8]

Use at least 14-point type for transparencies; 18-point is even better. If possible, use a square area for your text or visual, rather than the whole vertical page, so that your transparency will fit on the screen without your having to move it. For PowerPoint slides, use 44-point type (or larger) for titles and main heads. Your smallest subheading should be no smaller than 28-point type.

Cultural Styles of Presentations*

When you make an international presentation, be sensitive to your host country's cultural preferences for presentations.

In Japan, speak in a modest, personal, conversational style. Look at the whole group; remember that the oldest person is probably the most important. Plan carefully so that your presentation fits in the available time—and remember that interpretation cuts your actual speaking time in half.

In Sweden, don't save points for a question-and-answer session. Swedes consider it rude to ask questions at the end of a presentation: to do so suggests the speaker has not been clear. Instead, include all your material in the body of the presentation. The best close is a well-crafted question that applies the material from the presentation, leaving the audience something to think about.

*Based on Bronwen Jones, *Doing Business in Japan: An ABC for Better Communications* ([Tokyo:] JETRO, 1991), 16; and H. Ned Seelye and Alan Seelye-James, *Culture Clash* (Lincolnwood, IL: NTC Business Books, 1995), 30–31.

F i g u r e 17.2   *PowerPoint Slides for an Informative Presentation*

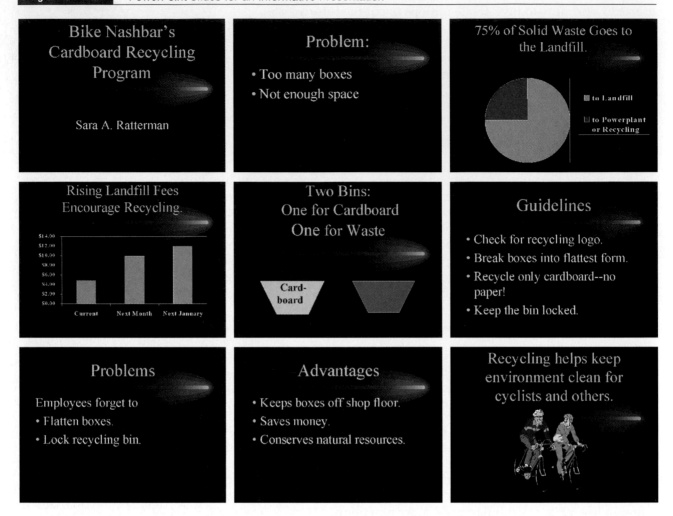

Well-designed visuals can serve as an outline for your talk (see Figure 17.2), eliminating the need for additional notes. Plan at most one visual for every minute of your talk, plus two visuals to serve as title and conclusion. Don't try to put your whole talk on visuals. Visuals should highlight your main points, not give every detail.

Use these guidelines to create and show visuals for presentations:

- Make only one point with each visual. Break a complicated point down into several visuals.
- Give each visual a title that makes a point.
- Limit the amount of information on a visual. Use 35 words or less; use simple graphs, not complex ones.
- Don't put your visual up till you're ready to talk about it. Leave it up until your next point; don't turn the projector or overhead off.

See Chapter 6 for information on designing slides and Chapter 16 for information on how to present numerical data through visuals.

See the BAC Web site for links to sites on how to use advanced Power-Point techniques and for backgrounds, graphics, and MIDIs you can use royalty-free in your presentations.

Visuals work only if the technology they depend on works. When you give presentations in your own office, check the equipment in advance. When you make a presentation in another location or for another organization, arrive early so that you'll have time not only to check the equipment but also to track down a service worker if the equipment isn't working. Be prepared with a backup plan to use if you're unable to show your slides or videotape.

You can also involve the audience in other ways. A student giving a presentation on English-French business communication demonstrated the differences in US and French handshakes by asking a fellow class member to come up to shake hands with her. Another student discussing the need for low-salt products brought in a container of salt, a measuring cup, a measuring spoon, and two plates. As he discussed the body's need for salt, he measured out three teaspoons onto one plate: the amount the body needs in a month. As he discussed the amount of salt the average US diet provides, he continued to measure out salt onto the other plate, stopping only when he had 1¼ pounds of salt—the amount in the average US diet. The demonstration made the discrepancy clear in a way words or even a chart could not have done.[9] To make sure that his employees understood where money went, the CEO of a specialty printing shop in Algoma, Wisconsin, printed up $2 million in play money and handed out big cards to employees marked *Labor, Depreciation, Interest,* and so forth. Then he asked each "category" to come up and take its share of the revenues. The action was more dramatic than a color pie chart could ever have been.[10] Another speaker who was trying to raise funds used the simple act of asking people to stand to involve them, to create emotional appeal, and to make a statistic vivid:

> [A speaker] was talking to a luncheon club about contributing to the relief of an area that had been hit by a tornado. The news report said that 70% of the people had been killed or disabled. The room was set up [with] ten people at each round table. He asked three persons at each table to stand. Then he said, ". . . You people sitting are dead or disabled. You three standing have to take care of the mess. You'd need help, wouldn't you?"[11]

Choosing Information to Include in a Presentation

Choose the information that is most interesting to your audience and that answers the questions your audience will have. Limit your talk to three main points. In a long presentation (20 minutes or more) each main point can have subpoints. Your content will be easier to understand if you clearly show the relationship between each of the main points. Turning your information into a story also helps. For example, a controller might turn charts of financial data into the following story:

> The increase in sales income is offset by an increase in manufacturing costs. Why? Because the cost of material is out of line. Material costs for product #503 tripled last month. An analysis of the three shifts shows that the cost of materials jumped 800% on the second shift. Now, the problem is to find out why the second shift uses so much more material than the other shifts making the same product.[12]

Back up each point with solid support. Statistics and numbers can be convincing if you present them in ways that are easy to hear. Simplify numbers by reducing them to two significant digits.

Get the Story Straight*

How do you persuade investors, bankers, and securities analysts to want to invest in your company? You tell them a story.

Presentation coach Jerry Weissman leads business people through an entire day on identifying the best story. Presentation skills (like building in pauses so listeners can absorb information) come later.

Before coaching, client David Angel described his company like this: "Information Storage Devices provides voice solutions using the company's unique, patented multilevel storage technique. . . ."

After coaching, Angel started his presentation this way: "We make voice chips. They're extremely easy to use. They have unlimited applications. And they last forever."

*Based on Dan Gillmor, "Putting on a Powerful Presentation," *Hemispheres*, March 1996, 31–32.

**An Alternative
to PowerPoint***

[Once Barbara Waugh had analyzed her survey data—p. 367—she had to plan a presentation.] But how could she capture and communicate what she'd learned? How could she share this powerful critique with senior management? The last thing she wanted was to preach through PowerPoint. So instead of creating bullet-point slides, she drew on her experience with street theatre and created a "play" about HP Labs. She worked passages from the surveys into dialogue and then recruited executives to act as staff members, and junior people to act as executives. The troupe performed for 30 senior managers. "At the end of the play, the managers were very quiet," Waugh remembers. "Then they started clapping. It was exciting. They really got it. They finally understood."

*Quoted from Katherine Mieszkowski, "I Grew Up Thinking That Change Was Cataclysmic. The Way We've Done it Here is to Start Slow and Work Small." *Fast Company*, December 1998, p. 152.

Hard to hear:	If the national debt were in pennies, it would take 17,006,802,720 people, each carrying 100 pounds of pennies, to carry all of our debt.
Easier to hear:	If the national debt were in pennies, it would take 17 billion people, each carrying 100 pounds of pennies, to carry all of our debt.[13]

In an informative presentation, link the points you make to the knowledge your audience has. Show the audience members that your information answers their questions, solves their problems, or helps them do their jobs. When you explain the effect of a new law or the techniques for using a new machine, use specific examples that apply to the decisions they make and the work they do. If your content is detailed or complicated, give people a written outline or handouts. The written material both helps the audience keep track of your points during the presentation and serves as a reference after the talk is over.

Quotations work well as long as you cite authorities whom your audience genuinely respects. Often you'll need to paraphrase a quote to put it into simple language that's easy to understand. Be sure to tell whom you're citing: "According to Al Gore," "An article in *Business Week* points out that," and so forth.

Demonstrations can prove your points dramatically and quickly. During the investigation of the space shuttle *Challenger* disaster, the late physicist Richard Feynman asked for a glass of water. When it came, he put a piece of the space shuttle's O-ring into the cold water. After less than a minute, he took it out and pinched it with a small clamp. The material kept the pinched shape when the clamp came off. The material couldn't return to its original shape.[14] A technical explanation could have made the same point: the O-ring couldn't function in the cold. But the demonstration was fast and easy to understand. It didn't require that the audience follow complex chemical or mathematical formulas. In an oral presentation, seeing is believing.

To be convincing, you must answer the audience's questions and objections.

> Some people think that working women are less reliable than men. But the facts show that women take fewer sick days than men do.

However, don't bring up negatives or inconsistencies unless you're sure that the audience will think of them. If you aren't sure, save your evidence for the question phase. If someone does ask, you'll have the answer.

Organizing Your Information

Most presentations use a direct pattern of organization, even when the goal is to persuade a reluctant audience. In a business setting, the audience is in a hurry and knows that you want to persuade them. Be honest about your goal, and then prove that your goal meets the audience's needs too.

In a persuasive presentation, start with your strongest point, your best reason. If time permits, give other reasons as well and respond to possible objections. Put your weakest point in the middle so that you can end on a strong note.

Often one of five standard patterns of organization will work:

- **Chronological.** Start with the past, move to the present, and end by looking ahead.
- **Problem–causes–solution.** Explain the symptoms of the problem, identify its causes, and suggest a solution. This pattern works best when the audience will find your solution easy to accept.

- **Excluding alternatives.** Explain the symptoms of the problem. Explain the obvious solutions first and show why they won't solve the problem. End by discussing a solution that will work. This pattern may be necessary when the audience will find the solution hard to accept.

- **Pro–con.** Give all the reasons in favor of something, then those against it. This pattern works well when you want the audience to see the weaknesses in its position.

- **1-2-3.** Discuss three aspects of a topic. This pattern works well to organize short informative briefings. "Today I'll review our sales, production, and profits for the last quarter."

Make your organization clear to your audience. Written documents can be reread; they can use headings, paragraphs, lists, and indentations to signal levels of detail. In a presentation, you have to provide explicit clues to the structure of your discourse.

Early in your talk—perhaps immediately after your opener—provide an **overview of the main points** you will make.

> First, I'd like to talk about who the homeless in Columbus are. Second, I'll talk about the services The Open Shelter provides. Finally, I'll talk about what you—either individually or as a group—can do to help.

An overview provides a mental peg that hearers can hang each point on. It also can prevent someone from missing what you are saying because he or she wonders why you aren't covering a major point that you've saved for later.[15]

Offer a clear signpost as you come to each new point. A **signpost** is an explicit statement of the point you have reached. Choose wording that fits your style. The following statements are four different ways that a speaker could use to introduce the last of three points:

> Now we come to the third point: what you can do as a group or as individuals to help homeless people in Columbus.

> So much for what we're doing. Now let's talk about what you can do to help.

> You may be wondering, what can I do to help?

> As you can see, the Shelter is trying to do many things. We could do more things with your help.

Delivering an Effective Presentation

Audiences want the sense that you're talking directly to them and that you care that they understand and are interested. They'll forgive you if you get tangled up in a sentence and end it ungrammatically. They won't forgive you if you

Advice from the Pros*

Creation

1. Think of your last summary slide first—then make sure each of those key bullet points are clearly explained in the body of your presentation.

2. Use simple, clear graphics and pictures of familiar people to capture attention and build audience identification.

3. Get someone else to check spellings and the logical flow of your slide show. Another pair of eyes will often pick up an error that you have missed.

Presentation

1. Practice, Practice, Practice. Rehearse several times—aloud and standing up, with the same equipment you will use for your presentation.

2. Make eye contact with more than one audience member during the course of your presentation.

3. Always carry backup disks of your presentation program, your slide show, and any special fonts that were used in its creation.

*Quoted from Shonan Noronha and John Rhodes, "Power Presentations," *Presentations,* special advertising section, n.p.

Being Interviewed by the Press*

Business people and community leaders are often interviewed by the press. To appear your best on camera, on tape, or in a story,

- Try to find out in advance why you're being interviewed and what information the reporter wants.

- Practice answering possible questions in a single sentence. A long answer is likely to be cut for TV or radio news.

- Talk slowly. You'll have time to think, the audience will have more time to understand what you're saying, and a reporter taking notes will record your words more accurately.

- To reduce the possibility of being misquoted, bring along a cassette recorder to tape the interview. Better still, bring two—and offer to give one tape to the interviewer.

*Based on James L. Graham, "What to Do When a Reporter Calls," *IABC Communication World*, April 1985, 15; and Robert A. Papper, conversation with Kitty Locker, March 17, 1991.

seem to have a "canned" talk that you're going to deliver no matter who the audience is or how they respond. You can convey a sense of caring to your audience by making direct eye contact with them and by using a conversational style.

Dealing with Fear

Feeling nervous is normal. But you can harness that nervous energy to help you do your best work. As one student said, you don't need to get rid of your butterflies. All you need to do is make them fly in formation.

To calm your nerves before you give an oral presentation,

- Be prepared. Analyze your audience, organize your thoughts, prepare visual aids, practice your opener and close, check out the arrangements.
- Use only the amount of caffeine you normally use. More or less may make you jumpy.
- Avoid alcoholic beverages.
- Relabel your nerves. Instead of saying, "I'm scared," try saying, "My adrenaline is up." Adrenaline sharpens our reflexes and helps us do our best.

Just before your presentation,

- Consciously contract and then relax your muscles, starting with your feet and calves and going up to your shoulders, arms, and hands.
- Take several deep breaths from your diaphragm.

During your presentation,

- Pause and look at the audience before you begin speaking.
- Concentrate on communicating well.
- Use body energy in strong gestures and movement.

Using Eye Contact

Look directly at the people you're talking to. In one study, speakers who looked more at the audience during a seven-minute informative speech were judged to be better informed, more experienced, more honest, and friendlier than speakers who delivered the same information with less eye contact.[16] An earlier study found that speakers judged sincere looked at the audience 63% of the time, while those judged insincere looked at the audience only 21% of the time.[17]

The point in making eye contact is to establish one-on-one contact with the individual members of your audience. People want to feel that you're talking to them. Looking directly at individuals also enables you to be more conscious of feedback from the audience, so that you can modify your approach if necessary.

Developing a Good Speaking Voice

People will enjoy your presentation more if your voice is easy to listen to. To find out what your voice sounds like, tape-record it. Also tape the voices of people on TV or on campus whose voices you like and imitate them. In a few weeks, tape yourself again.

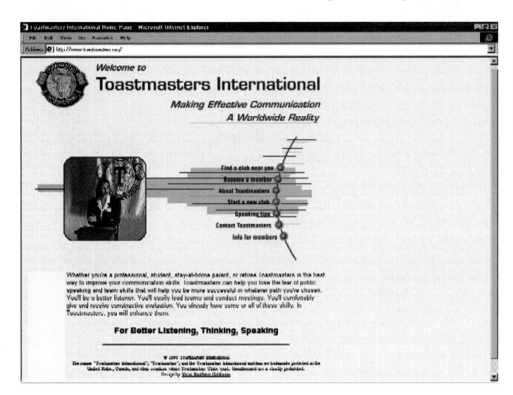

Organizations such as Toastmasters International help members become more effective speakers by providing a good place to practice their skill and receive feedback from their peers.

George Fluharty and Harold Ross suggest three ways to find your best speaking voice:

- Close your ears with your fingers and hum up and down the scale until you find the pitch where the hum sounds loudest or most vibrant to you. This pitch will be near your optimum pitch.
- Sing down the scale as far as you can go without forcing. Call this note *do* and sing up the scale to *sol.* This note will be near your optimum pitch.
- If you have a piano, locate the lowest note you can produce and also your highest falsetto note. Your optimum pitch will be approximately one fourth of the distance from your lowest note.[18]

When you speak to a group, talk loudly enough so that people can hear you easily. If you're using a microphone, adjust your volume so you aren't shouting. When you speak in an unfamiliar location, try to get to the room early so you can check the size of the room and the power of the amplification equipment. If you can't do that, ask early in your talk, "Can you hear me in the back of the room?"

The bigger the group is, the more carefully you need to **enunciate,** that is, voice all the sounds of each word. Words starting or ending with *f, t, k, v,* and *d* are especially hard to hear. "Our informed and competent image" can sound like "Our informed, incompetent image."

To enunciate, use your tongue and lips. Researchers have identified 38 different sounds. Of these, you make 31 with your tongue and 7 with your lips. None are made with the jaw, so how wide you open your mouth really doesn't matter. If the tongue isn't active enough, muscles in the throat try to compensate, producing sore throats and strained voices.[19]

Appearing on Camera*

When you make a presentation on video, be informal and friendly. Look at the camera when you talk to create the effect of making eye contact with the audience.

Since the sound reproduction equipment may deaden voices, make a special effort to vary pitch and expression. Don't interrupt another speaker. Two people talking at the same time on camera produce gibberish.

Dress for the camera.

• Don't wear white. Only very expensive cameras can handle pure white.

• Don't wear bold stripes, checks, plaids, or polka dots.

• Don't wear large accessories.

• Red, blue, and green photograph well. If an entire outfit in red seems too bold, consider wearing a red tie or blouse.

*Based on Robert A. Papper, conversation with Kitty Locker, March 17, 1991.

Tongue twisters can help you exercise your tongue and enunciate more clearly. Stephen Lucas suggests the following:

• Sid said to tell him that Benny hid the penny many years ago.
• Fetch me the finest French-fried freshest fish that Finney fries.
• Three gray geese in the green grass grazed.
• Shy Sarah saw six Swiss wristwatches.
• One year we had a Christmas brunch with Merry Christmas mush to munch. But I don't think you'd care for such. We didn't like to munch mush much.[20]

You can also reduce pressure on your throat by fitting phrases to your ideas. If you cut your sentences into bits, you'll emphasize words beginning with vowels, making the vocal cords hit each other. Instead, run past words beginning with vowels to emphasize later syllables or later words:[21]

Choppiness hurts vocal cords:	*We* must take more responsibility not *O*nly for *O*urselves *A*nd *O*ur families but for *O*ur communities *A*nd *O*ur country.
Smooth phrasing protects throat:	*We* must take more *R*esponsibility *N*ot only for our *S*elves and our *F*amilies but for our *C*ommunities and our *C*ountry.

You can reduce the number of *uhs* you use by practicing your talk several times. Filler sounds aren't signs of nervousness. Instead, say psychologists at Columbia University, they occur when speakers pause searching for the next word. Searching takes longer when people have big vocabularies or talk about topics where a variety of word choices are possible. Practicing your talk makes your word choices automatic, and you'll use fewer *uhs*.[22]

Vary your volume, pitch, and speed. Speakers who speak quickly and who vary their volume during the talk are more likely to be perceived as competent.[23] Sound energetic and enthusiastic. If your ideas don't excite you, why should your audience find them exciting?

Standing and Gesturing

Stand with your feet far enough apart for good balance, with your knees flexed. Unless the presentation is very formal or you're on camera, you can walk if you want to. Some speakers like to come in front of the lectern to remove that barrier between themselves and the audience.

Build on your natural style for gestures. Gestures usually work best when they're big and confident.

Using Notes and Visuals

Unless you're giving a very short presentation, you'll probably want to use notes. Even experts use notes. The more you know about the subject, the greater the temptation to add relevant points that occur to you as you talk. Adding an occasional point can help to clarify something for the audience, but adding too many points will destroy your outline and put you over the time limit.

Put your notes on cards or on sturdy pieces of paper. Most speakers like to use 4-by-6-inch or 5-by-7-inch cards because they hold more information. Your notes need to be complete enough to help you if you go blank, so use long phrases or complete sentences. Under each main point, jot down the evidence or illustration you'll use. Indicate where you'll refer to visuals.

Look at your notes infrequently. Most of your gaze time should be directed to members of the audience. Hold your notes high enough so that your head doesn't bob up and down like a yo-yo as you look from the audience to your notes and back again.

If you have lots of visuals and know your topic well, you won't need notes. If possible, put the screen to the side so that you won't block it. Face the audience, not the screen. With transparencies, you can use colored marking pens to call attention to your points as you talk. Show the entire visual at once: don't cover up part of it. If you don't want the audience to read ahead, prepare several visuals that build up. In your overview, for example, the first visual could list your first point, the second the first and second, and the third all three points.

Keep the room lights on if possible; turning them off makes it easier for people to fall asleep and harder for them to concentrate on you.

Handling Questions

Prepare for questions by listing every fact or opinion you can think of that challenges your position. Treat each objection seriously and try to think of a way to deal with it. If you're talking about a controversial issue, you may want to save one point for the question period, rather than making it during the presentation. Speakers who have visuals to answer questions seem especially well prepared.

During your presentation, tell the audience how you'll handle questions. If you have a choice, save questions for the end. In your talk, answer the questions or objections that you expect your audience to have. Don't exaggerate your claims so that you won't have to back down in response to questions later.

During the question period, don't nod your head to indicate that you understand a question as it is asked. Audiences will interpret nods as signs that you agree with the questioner. Instead, look directly at the questioner. As you answer the question, expand your focus to take in the entire group. Don't say, "That's a good question." That response implies that the other questions have been poor ones.

If the audience may not have heard the question or if you want more time to think, repeat the question before you answer it. Link your answers to the points you made in your presentation. Keep the purpose of your presentation in mind, and select information that advances your goals.

If a question is hostile or biased, rephrase it before you answer it. "You're asking whether. . . ." Or suggest an alternative question: "I think there are problems with both the positions you describe. It seems to me that a third solution which is better than either of them is. . . ."

Occasionally someone will ask a question that is really designed to state the speaker's own position. Respond to the question if you want to. Another option is to say, "I'm not sure what you're asking," or even, "That's a clear statement of your position. Let's move to the next question now." If someone asks about something that you already explained in your presentation, simply answer the question without embarrassing the questioner. No audience will understand and remember 100% of what you say.

Handling Questions*

On behalf of Greenpeace USA, Christopher Childs gives more than 100 presentations a year to schools, colleges, and churches.

"For the question-and-answer period, I try to stay in touch with our campaigners to find out what's most important. But I also try to stay aware of my personal motivations. When I'm very clear about what I want to accomplish, the questions take care of themselves. . . .

"Occasionally I get hostile questions, and while I try to deal on a factual level with the issues, I look to see if I can tell what's going on with the person. Oftentimes they're not hostile at all, but very concerned. When it's workable in a public forum, I might suggest to them what I hear them really saying. Often they really appreciate the effort."

*Quoted from Jess Wells, "Stage Presence: Professional Speakers Share Their Techniques," *Publish*, December 1990, 82.

If you don't know the answer to a question, say so. If your purpose is to inform, write down the question so that you can look up the answer before the next session. If it's a question to which you think there is no answer, ask if anyone in the room knows. When no one does, your "ignorance" is vindicated. If an expert is in the room, you may want to refer questions of fact to him or her. Answer questions of interpretation yourself.

At the end of the question period, take two minutes to summarize your main point once more. (This can be a restatement of your close.) Questions may or may not focus on the key point of your talk. Take advantage of having the floor to repeat your message briefly and forcefully.

Making Group Presentations

Plan carefully to involve as many members of the group as possible in speaking roles.

The easiest way to make a group presentation is to outline the presentation and then divide the topics, giving one to each group member. Another member can be responsible for the opener and the close. During the question period, each member answers questions that relate to his or her topic.

In this kind of divided presentation, be sure to

- Plan transitions.
- Enforce time limits strictly.
- Coordinate your visuals so that the presentation seems a coherent whole.
- Practice the presentation as a group at least once; more is better.

The best group presentations are even more fully integrated: the group writes a very detailed outline, chooses points and examples, and creates visuals together. Then, within each point, voices trade off. See the BAC Web site for links to advice on giving this sophisticated kind of team presentation. This presentation is most effective because each voice speaks only a minute or two before a new voice comes in. However, it works only when all group members know the subject well and when the group plans carefully and practices extensively.

Whatever form of group presentation you use, be sure to introduce each member of the team to the audience and to pay close attention to each other. If other members of the team seem uninterested in the speaker, the audience gets the sense that that speaker isn't worth listening to.

Summary of Key Points

- **Informative presentations** inform or teach the audience. **Persuasive presentations** motivate the audience to act or to believe. **Goodwill presentations** entertain and validate the audience. Most oral presentations have more than one purpose.
- A written message makes it easier to present extensive or complex information and to minimize undesirable emotions. Oral messages make it easier to use emotion, to focus the audience's attention, to answer questions and resolve conflicts quickly, to modify a proposal that may not be acceptable in its original form, and to get immediate action or response.
- In both oral and written messages, you should
  - Adapt the message to the specific audience.
  - Show the audience how they benefit from the idea, policy, service, or product.

- Overcome any objections the audience may have.
- Use you-attitude and positive emphasis.
- Use visuals to clarify or emphasize material.
- Specify exactly what the audience should do.

- An oral presentation needs to be simpler than a written message to the same audience.
- In a **monologue presentation,** the speaker plans the presentation in advance and delivers it without deviation. In a **guided discussion,** the speaker presents the questions or issues that both speaker and audience have agreed on in advance. Rather than functioning as an expert with all the answers, the speaker serves as a facilitator to help the audience tap its own knowledge. An **interactive presentation** is a conversation using questions to determine the buyer's needs, probe objections, and gain provisional and then final commitment to the purchase.
- Adapt your message to your audience's beliefs, experiences, and interests.
- Use the beginning and end of the presentation to interest the audience and emphasize your key point.
- Using visuals makes a speaker seem more prepared, more interesting, and more persuasive.
- Use a direct pattern of organization. Put your strongest reason first.
- Limit your talk to three main points. Early in your talk—perhaps immediately after your opener—provide an **overview of the main points** you will make. Offer a clear signpost as you come to each new point. A **signpost** is an explicit statement of the point you have reached.
- To calm your nerves as you prepare to give an oral presentation,
    - Be prepared. Analyze your audience, organize your thoughts, prepare visual aids, practice your opener and close, check out the arrangements.
    - Use only the amount of caffeine you normally use.
    - Avoid alcoholic beverages.
    - Relabel your nerves. Instead of saying, "I'm scared," try saying, "My adrenaline is up." Adrenaline sharpens our reflexes and helps us do our best.

Just before your presentation,

- Consciously contract and then relax your muscles, starting with your feet and calves and going up to your shoulders, arms, and hands.
- Take several deep breaths from your diaphragm.

During your presentation,

- Pause and look at the audience before you begin speaking.
- Concentrate on communicating well.
- Use body energy in strong gestures and movement.

- Convey a sense of caring to your audience by making direct eye contact with them and by using a conversational style.
- Treat questions as opportunities to give more detailed information than you had time to give in your presentation. Link your answers to the points you made in your presentation.
- Repeat the question before you answer it if the audience may not have heard it or if you want more time to think. Rephrase hostile or biased questions before you answer them.
- The best group presentations result when the group writes a very detailed outline, chooses points and examples, and creates visuals together. Then, within each point, voices trade off.

Cut to the Chase*

When a student took a job at Intel, her first assignment was to present a strategic plan to CEO Andy Grove two weeks later.

Five minutes into her presentation, he interrupted her: "Please flip to page 22. That's what I need to know."

*Based on Evelyn Pierce, Thomas Hadjuk, and Richard Young, "Using Verbal Protocol Research to Determine What Business Audiences Want in Documents," Association for Business Communication Conference, Chicago, IL, November 6–9, 1996.

Chapter 17

Exercises and Problems

Getting Started

17.1 Analyzing Openers and Closes

The following openers and closes came from class presentations on information interviews.

- Does each opener make you interested in hearing the rest of the presentation?
- Does each opener provide a transition to the overview?
- Does the close end the presentation in a satisfying way?

a. Opener: I interviewed Mark Perry at AT&T.
    Close: Well, that's my report.

b. Opener: How many of you know what you want to do when you graduate?
    Close: So, if you like numbers and want to travel, think about being a CPA. Arthur Andersen can take you all over the world.

c. Opener: You don't have to know anything about computer programming to get a job as a technical writer at CompuServe.
    Close: After talking to Raj, I decided technical writing isn't for me. But it is a good career if you work well under pressure and like learning new things all the time.

d. Opener: My report is about what it's like to work in an advertising agency.
    Middle: They keep really tight security; I had to wear a badge and be escorted to Susan's desk.
    Close: Susan gave me samples of the agency's ads and even a sample of a new soft drink she's developing a campaign for. But she didn't let me keep the badge.

Presentation Assignments

17.2 Making a Short Oral Presentation

As Your Instructor Directs,
Make a short (three- to five-minute) presentation, with three to eight PowerPoint slides, on one of the following topics:

a. Explain how what you've learned in classes, in campus activities, or at work will be useful to the employer who hires you after graduation.

b. Profile someone who is successful in the field you hope to enter and explain what makes him or her successful.

c. Describe a specific situation in an organization in which communication was handled well or badly.

d. Make a short presentation based on another problem in this book.

   1.6   Introduce yourself to the class.
   3.10   Analyze your boss.
   3.11   Analyze your co-workers.
   7.5   Explain a "best practice" in your organization.
   7.12   Explain what a new hire in your unit needs to know to be successful.
   8.10   Tell your boss about a problem in your unit.

   9.15   Recommend a co-worker for a bonus or an award.
   10.6   Motivate employees in your unit to do their best work.
   10.9   Ask for more resources for your unit.
   11.11   Make a sales presentation for a product or service.
   13.18   Describe your choices in creating a brochure.
   18.2   Tell the class in detail about one of your accomplishments.
   19.4   Explain one of the challenges (e.g., technology, ethics, international competition) that the field you hope to enter is facing.
   19.5   Profile a company you would like to work for and explain why you think it would be a good employer.
   19.6   Share the results of an information interview.
   20.2   Share the advice of students currently on the job market.
   20.3   Share what you learn when you interview an interviewer.
   20.4   Explain your interview strategy.

17.3   Making a Longer Oral Presentation

As Your Instructor Directs,
Make a 5- to 12-minute presentation on one of the following. Use visuals to make your talk effective.

a. Show why your unit is important to the organization and either should be exempt from downsizing or should receive additional resources.

b. Persuade your supervisor to make a change that will benefit the organization.

c. Persuade your organization to make a change that will improve the organization's image in the community.

d. Persuade classmates to donate time or money to a charitable organization. (Read Chapter 11.)

e. Persuade an employer that you are the best person for the job.

f. Use another problem in this book as the basis for your presentation.

    3.12 Analyze an organization's culture.

3.13 Analyze a discourse community.

5.1   Describe the composing process(es) of a writer you've interviewed.

6.5   Evaluate the page design of one or more documents.

6.6   Evaluate the design of a Web page.

7.8   Present a Web page you have designed.

8.16 Analyze rejection letters students on your campus have received.

10.15 Persuade your campus to make a change.

11.3 Analyze one or more sales or fund-raising letters.

12.4 Analyze international messages that your workplace has created or received.

14.15 Summarize the results of a survey you have conducted.

15.10 Summarize the results of your research.

17.4   Making a Group Oral Presentation

As Your Instructor Directs,
Make a 5- to 12-minute presentation on one of the following. Use visuals to make your talk effective.

1.5   Explain the role of communication in one or more organizations.

12.6 Report on another country.

13.10 Recommend whether a mall should hire ethnic Santas.

13.18 Present brochures you have designed to the class.

13.19 Describe the listening strategies of workers you have interviewed.

17.5   Evaluating Oral Presentations

Evaluate an oral presentation given by a classmate or given by a speaker on your campus. Use the following categories:

Strategy

1. Choosing an effective kind of presentation for the situation.
2. Adapting ideas to audience's beliefs, experiences, and interests.
3. Using a strong opening and close.
4. Using visual aids or other devices to involve audience.

Content

5. Using specific, vivid supporting material and language.
6. Providing rebuttals to counterclaims or objections.

Organization

7. Providing an overview of main points.
8. Signposting main points in body of talk.

9. Providing adequate transitions between points and speakers.

Delivery

10. Making direct eye contact with audience.
11. Using a conversational style.
12. Using voice and gestures effectively.
13. Using notes and visuals effectively.
14. Handling questions effectively.

As Your Instructor Directs,

a. Fill out a form indicating your evaluation in each of the areas.

b. Share your evaluation orally with the speaker.

c. Write a memo to the speaker evaluating the presentation. Send a copy of your memo to your instructor.

17.6   Evaluating Team Presentations

Evaluate team presentations using the following questions:

1. How thoroughly were all group members involved?
2. Did members of the team introduce themselves or each other?
3. Did team members seem interested in what their teammates said?
4. How well was the material organized?
5. How well did the material hold your interest?
6. How clear did the material seem to you?
7. How effective were the visuals?
8. How well did the team handle questions?
9. What could be done to improve the presentation?
10. What were the strong points of the presentation?

As Your Instructor Directs,

a. Fill out a form indicating your evaluation in each of the areas.
b. Share your evaluation orally with the speaker.
c. Write a memo to the speaker evaluating the presentation. Send a copy of your memo to your instructor.

17.7   Evaluating the Way a Speaker Handles Questions

Listen to a speaker talking about a controversial subject. (Go to a talk on campus or in town, or watch a speaker on a TV show like *Face the Nation* or *60 Minutes*.) Observe the way he or she handles questions.

- About how many questions does the speaker answer?
- What is the format for asking and answering questions?
- Are the answers clear? responsive to the question? something that could be quoted without embarrassing the speaker and the organization he or she represents?
- How does the speaker handle hostile questions? Does the speaker avoid getting angry? Does the speaker retain control of the meeting? How?
- If some questions were not answered well, what (if anything) could the speaker have done to leave a better impression?
- Did the answers leave the audience with a more or less positive impression of the speaker? Why?

As Your Instructor Directs,

a. Share your evaluation with a small group of students.
b. Present your evaluation formally to the class.
c. Summarize your evaluation in a memo to your instructor.

Five

Job Hunting

Chapter Eighteen
Résumés   504

Chapter Nineteen
Job Application Letters   536

Chapter Twenty
Job Interviews, Follow-Up Letters and Calls,
and Job Offers   564

18

Résumés

A Time Line for Job Hunting

Evaluating Your Strengths and Interests

How Employers Use Résumés

Guidelines for Résumés
- Length
- Emphasis
- Details
- Writing Style
- Layout, Printing, and Paper

Kinds of Résumés

What to Include in a Résumé
- Name, Address, and Phone Number
- Career Objective
- Education
- Honors and Awards
- Experience
- Activities
- References

Dealing with Difficulties
- "All My Experience Is in My Family's Business."
- "I've Been Out of the Job Market for a While."
- "I Want to Change Fields."
- "I Was Fired."
- "I Don't Have Any Experience."

How an Average Student Created an Excellent Résumé

Online Résumés
- Creating a Web Résumé
- Creating a Scannable Résumé

Summary of Key Points

Résumés

Kevin Slakey

University Relations Representative, Cisco Systems

www.cisco.com

Kevin Slakey builds relationships among Cisco, universities, and students. His many job responsibilities include reviewing résumés and conducting interviews. Cisco Systems, Inc. is the worldwide leader in networking for the Internet.

On average, a recruiter will spend 30 to 60 seconds looking at your résumé. Recruiters look as much for things to disqualify you (like typos, misspellings, and poor grammar) as for things to capture their interest and get them to linger longer over your qualifications. Here's how to capture more "eyeball time" and increase the odds of having your résumé placed in the "interview" stack:

"A good résumé actually helps your interviewer ask questions that showcase your strengths."

- Highlight any relevant internships or co-ops. Provide details about the projects you worked, tools you used, accomplishments you achieved. Spent the summers flipping burgers? Then downplay your work experience and expand upon projects you completed during coursework.

- Provide a short list of the major courses you took, especially if they were the most difficult courses offered at your school in your major.

- Use industry buzzwords and acronyms. Recruiters and hiring managers zero in on them. Remember—anything you put in your résumé is fair game for interview questions. If you state that you have "in-depth" experience with something, you better have it.

- Create different versions of your résumé, including one that can be scanned into a résumé database and one in ASCII to e-mail to appropriate company contacts.

A résumé is only one tool in your career search arsenal. Just as important is developing a good network of contacts in the industry you are targeting. Get as much relevant work experience as you can during summers and the school year. It isn't enough these days to have a sought-after major or high GPA. What increasingly sets candidates apart is work experience gained while in pursuit of their degrees.

A good résumé actually helps your interviewer ask questions that showcase your strengths. Good luck!

A résumé is a persuasive summary of your qualifications for employment. If you're on the job market, having a résumé makes you look well organized and prepared. When you're employed, having an up-to-date résumé makes it easier to take advantage of opportunities that may come up for an even better job. If you're several years away from job hunting, preparing a résumé now will help you become more conscious of what to do in the next two or three years to make yourself an attractive candidate. Writing a résumé is also an ego-building experience: the person who looks so good on paper is **you!**

This chapter covers paper, Web, and scannable résumés. Job application letters (sometimes called "cover letters") are discussed in Chapter 19. Chapter 20 discusses interviews and the communication after the interview. All three chapters focus on job hunting in the United States. Conventions, expectations, and criteria differ from culture to culture: different norms apply in different countries.

All job communications must be tailored to your unique qualifications. Adopt the wording or layout of an example if it's relevant to your own situation, but don't be locked into the forms in this book. You've got different strengths; your résumé will be different, too.

A Time Line for Job Hunting

Informal preparation for job hunting should start soon after you arrive on campus. Join extracurricular organizations on campus and in the community to increase your knowledge and provide a network for learning about jobs. Find a job that gives you experience. Note which courses you like—and why you like them. If you like thinking and learning about a subject, you're more likely to enjoy a job in that field.

Formal preparation for job hunting should begin a full year *before you begin interviewing.* Visit the campus placement office to see what services it provides. Ask friends who are on the job market about their experiences in interviews; find out what kinds of job offers they get. Check into the possibility of getting an internship or a co-op job that will give you relevant experience before you interview.

The year you interview, register with your Placement Office early. If you plan to graduate in the spring, prepare your résumé and plan your interview strategy early in the fall. Initial campus interviews occur from October to February for May or June graduation. In January or February, write to any organization you'd like to work for that hasn't interviewed on campus. From February to April, you're likely to visit one or more offices for a second interview.

Try to have a job offer lined up *before* you get the degree. People who don't need jobs immediately are more confident in interviews and usually get better job offers. If you have to job-hunt after graduation, plan to spend at least 30 hours a week on your job search. The time will pay off in a better job that you find more quickly.

Evaluating Your Strengths and Interests

A self-assessment is the first step in producing a good résumé. Each person could do several jobs happily. Personality and aptitude tests can tell you what your strengths are, but they won't say, "You should be a _____ ." You'll still need to answer questions like these:

- What achievements have given you the most satisfaction? *Why* did you enjoy them?

- Would you rather have firm deadlines or a flexible schedule? Do you prefer working alone or with other people? Do you prefer specific instructions and standards for evaluation or freedom and uncertainty? How comfortable are you with pressure? Are you willing to "pay your dues" for several years before you are promoted? How much challenge do you want?

- Are you willing to take work home? To travel? How important is money to you? Prestige? Time to spend with family and friends?

- Where do you want to live? What features in terms of weather, geography, cultural and social life do you see as ideal?

- Is it important to you that your work achieve certain purposes or values, or do you see work as "just a way to make a living"? Are the organization's culture and ethical standards important to you?

Once you know what is most important to you, analyze the job market to see where you could find what you want. For example, Peter's greatest interest is athletics, but he isn't good enough for the pros. Studying the job market might suggest several alternatives. He could teach sports and physical fitness as a high school coach or a corporate fitness director. He could cover sports for a newspaper, a magazine, or a TV station. He could go into management or sales for a professional sports team, a health club, or a company that sells sports equipment.

What Employers Want*

In a survey conducted by the National Association of Colleges and Employers, the number one thing employers wanted was communication skills.

Interpersonal skills ranked second.

Technical skills, such as knowledge of accounting or fashion merchandising or engineering, came next, followed by experience working in teams and previous work experience.

*Based on Carol Kleiman, "Web Site Occupations Are Growing by the Gigabyte," *The Columbus Dispatch*, February 9, 1997.

How Employers Use Résumés

Understanding how employers use résumés will help you create a résumé that works for you.

1. **Employers use résumés to decide whom to interview.** (The major exceptions are on-campus interviews, where the campus placement office has policies that determine who meets with the interviewer.) Since résumés are used to screen out applicants, omit anything that may create a negative impression.

2. **The search committee skims résumés.** Companies often get 100 or more résumés a day even when they have not advertised positions; a company that advertises an opening may get up to 1,000 applicants for a single position. A résumé gets a quick glance for 8 to 30 seconds. Only the résumés that pass the "skim test" are read more closely. Use layout and visual impact to highlight your credentials.

3. **Employers assume that your letter and résumé represent your best work.** Neatness, accuracy, and freedom from typographical errors are essential.

4. **Interviewers usually reread your résumé before the interview to refresh their memories.** Be ready to offer fuller details about everything on your résumé.

5. **After the search committee has chosen an applicant, it submits the applicant's résumé to people in the organization who must approve the appointment.** These people may have different backgrounds and areas of expertise. Spell out acronyms. Explain Greek-letter honor societies, unusual job titles, or organizations that may be unfamiliar to the reader.

Guidelines for Résumés

Writing a résumé is not an exact science. If your skills are in great demand, you can violate every guideline here and still get a good job. But when you must compete against many applicants, these guidelines will help you look as good on paper as you are in person.

Length

A one-page résumé is sufficient, but do fill the page. Less than a full page suggests that you do not have very much to say for yourself.

The average résumé is now two pages, according to career-planning consultant Marilyn Moats Kennedy. An experiment that mailed one- or two-page résumés to Big Six accounting firms (when there were still six firms) showed that even readers who said they preferred short résumés were more likely to want to interview the candidate with the longer résumé.[1]

If you do use more than one page, the second page should have at least 10 to 12 lines. Use a second sheet and staple it to the first so that readers who skim see the staple and know that there's more. Leave less important information for the second page. Put your name and "Page 2" or "Cont." on the page. If the pages are separated, you want the reader to know who the qualifications belong to and that the second page is not your whole résumé.

Emphasis

Emphasize the things you've done that (a) are most relevant to the position for which you're applying, (b) show your superiority to other applicants, and (c) are recent.

Show that you're qualified by giving details on relevant course projects, activities, and jobs where you've done similar work. Marketing recruiters responded more positively to résumés giving details about course projects, especially when candidates had little relevant work experience.[2] Be brief about low-level jobs that simply show dependability. To prove that you're the best candidate for the job, emphasize items that set you apart from other applicants: promotions, honors and achievements, experience with computers or other relevant equipment, foreign languages, and so on.

You may include high school jobs, activities, and honors to fill the page if you're getting a two- or four-year degree. If you can fill a page without high school activities and honors, omit them. When you're 25 or older, include information about high school only if you need it to show geographical flexibility. Focus on achievements in the last three to five years. Whatever your age at the time you write a résumé, you want to suggest that you are now the best you've ever been.

Include full-time work after high school before you returned to college and work during college to support yourself or to earn expenses. If the jobs you held then were low-level ones, present them briefly or combine them:

1997–99	Part-time and full-time jobs to support family

You can emphasize material by putting it at the top or the bottom of a page, by giving it more space, and by setting it off with white space. The beginning and end—of a document, a page, a list—are positions of emphasis. When you have a choice (e.g., in a list of job duties), put less important material in the middle, not at the end, to avoid the impression of "fading out."

Weak order: Coordinated weekly schedules, assigned projects to five staff members, evaluated their performance, and submitted weekly time sheets.

Emphatic order: Coordinated weekly schedules and submitted weekly time sheets. Assigned projects to five staff members and evaluated their performance.

You can also emphasize material by presenting it in a vertical list, by using a phrase in a heading, and by providing details. For example, rather than presenting your internship work in long paragraphs, use bulleted lists to make your accomplishments stand out.

Details

Details provide evidence to support your claims, convince the reader, and separate you from other applicants. Tell how many people you trained or supervised, how much money you budgeted or raised. Describe the aspects of the job you did.

Too vague: Sales Manager, *The Daily Collegian,* University Park, PA, 1999–2000. Supervised staff; promoted ad sales.

Good details: Sales Manager, *The Daily Collegian,* University Park, PA, 1999–2000. Supervised 22-member sales staff; helped recruit, interview, and select staff; assigned duties and scheduled work; recommended best performers for promotion. Motivated staff to increase paid ad inches 10% over previous year's sales.

Omit details that add nothing to a title, that are less impressive than the title alone, or that suggest a faulty sense of priorities (e.g., listing minor offices in an organization that tries to give everyone something to do). Either use strong details or just give the office or job title without any details.

Writing Style

Without sacrificing content, be as concise as possible.

Wordy: Member, Meat Judging Team, 1997–98
Member, Meat Judging Team, 1998–99
Member, Meat Judging Team, 1999–2000
Captain, Meat Judging Team, 2000–01

Tight: Meat Judging Team, 1997–2001; Captain 2000–01

Wordy: Performed foundation load calculations

Tight: Calculated foundation loads

Résumés normally use phrases and sentence fragments. Complete sentences are acceptable if they are the briefest way to present information. To save space and to avoid sounding arrogant, never use *I* in a résumé. *Me* and *my* are acceptable if they are unavoidable or if using them reduces wordiness.

Verbs or gerunds (the *-ing* form of verbs) create a more dynamic image of you than do nouns, so use them on résumés that will be read by people. (Rules for scannable résumés to be read by computers come later in this chapter.) In the revisions below, nouns, verbs, and gerunds are in bold type.

Nouns: Chair, Income Tax Assistance Committee, Winnipeg, MB, 1998–99. Responsibilities: **recruitment** of volunteers; flyer **design, writing,** and **distribution** for **promotion** of program; **speeches** to various community groups and nursing homes to advertise the service.

Verbs: Chair, Income Tax Assistance Committee, Winnipeg, MB, 1998–99. **Recruited** volunteers for the program. **Designed, wrote,** and **distributed** a flyer to promote the program; **spoke** to various community groups and nursing homes to advertise the service.

Gerunds: Chair, Income Tax Assistance Committee, Winnipeg, MB, 1998–99. Responsibilities included **recruiting** volunteers for the program; **designing, writing,** and **distributing** a flyer to promote the program; and **speaking** to various community groups and nursing homes to advertise the service.

Note that the items in the list must be in parallel structure (⚹ p. 104).

Résumés for the Big Five*

Carl M. Anderson, a Regional Director of Recruiting for Coopers & Lybrand's office in Columbus, Ohio, says,

"[Students should] use the placement office. Researching employers does two things for them. They can learn more specifics about the companies they're going to talk to and truly be more knowledgeable and interested in the job, and then they can make a more enlightened decision about it. Second, to get through the process successfully, I think students have to do fairly thorough self-assessments. They have to sit down with a pad and pencil and list their strengths and weaknesses.

"[On the résumé,] I want to see some evidence of some involvement and some leadership. I'm looking for evidence of taking on some specific responsibilities, putting forth some effort. I'm looking for doers rather than joiners. Just being a member of eight organizations never impresses me. I want to see some phraseology on there that says 'Took responsibility for annual such-and-such drive as chairman, led successful drive'— quantified in these ways."

*Quoted from phone interview with Kitty Locker, January 25, 1994.

A Flexible Marketing Document*

A good resume is a flexible marketing document that can be customized for different situations. . . [E]mployers like to see facts on achievements—such as sales figures or quotas that have been attained—in the resume as long as they're concise. Beyond that, common sense rules. Be brief and clear and tailor the document to each employer['s] needs.

*Quoted from Hal Lancaster, "The Standard Resume Still Has a Role in Job Searches," *The Wall Street Journal*, February 3, 1998, B1.

Layout, Printing, and Paper

Experiment with layout, fonts, and spacing to get an attractive résumé. Consider creating a letterhead that you use for both your résumé and your application letter.

Use enough white space to make your résumé easy to read, but not so much that you look as if you're padding. Even if you pay someone else to produce your résumé, *you* must specify the exact layout: you cannot expect a paid typist to care as much about your résumé as you do.

Print your résumé on a laser printer. Take advantage of different sizes of type and perhaps of rules (thin lines) to make your résumé look professional.

Print your résumé on standard 8½-by-11-inch paper (never legal size). White paper is standard; a very pale color is also acceptable. If you have a two-page résumé, consider having it printed on the front and left-inside page of a folded 11-by-17-inch page, with your application letter on the right-inside page.

Kinds of Résumés

There are two kinds of résumés: chronological and skills. A **chronological résumé** summarizes what you did in a time line (starting with the most recent events, and going backward in **reverse chronology**). It emphasizes degrees, job titles, and dates. It is the traditional résumé format. Figures 18.1 and 18.3 show chronological résumés. Use a chronological résumé when

- Your education and experience are a logical preparation for the position for which you're applying.
- You have impressive job titles, offices, or honors.

A **skills résumé** emphasizes the skills you've used, rather than the job in which or the date when you used them. Figures 18.4 and 18.5 show skills résumés. Use a skills résumé when

- Your education and experience are not the usual route to the position for which you're applying.
- You're changing fields.
- You want to combine experience from paid jobs, activities or volunteer work, and courses to show the extent of your experience in administration, finance, speaking, etc.
- Your recent work history may create the wrong impression (e.g., it has gaps, shows a demotion, shows job-hopping, etc.).

The two kinds differ in what information is included and how that information is organized. You may assume that the advice in this chapter applies to both kinds of résumés unless there is an explicit statement that the two kinds of résumés would handle a category differently.

What to Include in a Résumé

Although the résumé is a factual document, its purpose is to persuade. In a job application form or an application for graduate or professional school, you answer every question even if the answer is not to your credit. In a résumé, you cannot lie, but you can omit anything that does not work in your favor.

Figure 18.1 | *Chronological Résumé*

---

*A vertical line
provides visual variety.*

*Vary font sizes. The name is in 18-point,
the main headings in 12-point,
and the text in 11-point type.*

Jerry A. Jackson

Campus Address   **Permanent Address**
1636½ Highland Street   45 East Mulberry
Columbus, OH 43201   Huntington, NY 11746
(614) 555-5718   (516) 555-7793
jackson.2495@osu.edu
www.fisher.osu/students/jackson.2495/home.htm

If you have a professional Web page, include its URL.

Education
B.S. in Family Financial Management, June 2001, The Ohio State University,
Columbus, OH
"B" Average   *List not only major courses but also others*
Courses Related to Major: *that will enhance your performance*

Accounting I and II	Business and Professional Writing
Finance	Computer Programming
Economics I and II	Statistics
Family Resource Management	Public Speaking
Family and Human Development	Interpersonal Communication

Sports Experience
BAAD (Buckeye Athletes Against Drugs)
Intramural Hockey Team (Division Champions, Winter 2000)
Three-year Varsity Letterman, Ohio State University, Columbus, OH
Men's NCAA Division I Lacrosse   *(The Lacrosse team did poorly,
so he omits its ranking.)*

Experience

Financial Sales Representative, Primerica Company, Columbus, OH,
February 2000–present. Work with clients to plan investment strategies;
recommend specific investments.

Entrepreneur, Huntington, NY, and Columbus, OH, September 1999–January
2000. Created a saleable product, secured financial backing, found a
manufacturer, supervised production, and sold product—12 dozen T-shirts
at a $5.25 profit each—to help pay for school expenses.   *How to handle
self-employment.*

Landscape Maintenance Supervisor, Huntington, NY, Summers 1991–99.
Formed a company to cut lawns, put up fences, fertilize, garden, and paint
houses. Hired, fired, trained, motivated, and paid friends to complete jobs.

Collector and Repairman, ACN Inc., Huntington, NY, Summers 1991–97.
Specify large sums of money. Collected and counted up to $10,000 a day. Worked with technicians
troubleshooting and repairing electronic and coin mechanisms of video and
pinball games, cigarette machines, and jukeboxes. Drove company cars and
trucks throughout New York metro area to collect cash and move and repair
machines.   *Provide details to interest readers,
set you apart from other applicants.*

Honesty in the Résumé

Never lie in a résumé.

It's OK to omit negative information (like a low grade point average). If you were an officer in an organization, it's OK to list the title even if you didn't do much. It's OK to provide details when you did more than the job title indicates, or to give the job title alone if you had an inflated official title (e.g., Assistant Manager) but didn't really do much.

But it isn't OK to lie.

Interviewers will ask you about items in the résumé. If you have to back down, you destroy your credibility. And if lies are discovered after someone is hired, the person is fired.

Résumés commonly contain the following information. The categories marked with an asterisk are essential.

*Name, Address, and Phone Number

Career Objective

*Education

*Experience

Honors

Activities

References

You may choose other titles for these categories and add categories that are relevant for your qualifications: COMPUTER SKILLS, FOREIGN LANGUAGES.

EDUCATION and EXPERIENCE always stand as separate categories, even if you have only one item under each head. Combine other headings so that you have at least two long or three short items under each heading. For example, if you're in one honor society, two social clubs, and on one athletic team, combine them all under ACTIVITIES AND HONORS.

If you have more than seven items under a heading, consider using subheadings. For example, a student who had a great many activities might divide them into STUDENT GOVERNMENT, OTHER CAMPUS ACTIVITIES, and COMMUNITY SERVICE.

Put your strongest categories near the top and at the bottom of the first page. If you have impressive work experience, you might want to put that category first after your name, put EDUCATION in the middle of the page, and put your address at the bottom.

Name, Address, and Phone Number

Use your full name, even if everyone calls you by a nickname. You may use an initial rather than spelling out your first or middle name. Put your name in big type.

If you use only one address, consider centering it under your name. If you use two addresses (office and home, campus and permanent, until _____/ after _____) set them up side by side to balance the page visually. Use a comma after the city before the state. It is OK to use either post office (two-letter, full caps, no period) or traditional abbreviations for the state. Be consistent throughout the résumé.

Urbana, IL 61801

Wheaton, Illinois 60187

Morton, Ill. 61550

If you have an e-mail address, give it too.

Give a complete phone number, including the area code. Either put the area code in parentheses, space, then put the number OR separate the area code by a hyphen.

(217) 555-1212 or 217-555-1212

If you don't have a phone, try to make arrangements with someone to take messages for you—employers usually call to schedule interviews and make job offers.

Omit your age, marital status, race, sex, and health. Questions about these topics are illegal.

Career Objective

CAREER OBJECTIVE statements should sound like the job descriptions an employer might use in a job listing. Keep your statement brief—two or three lines at most. Tell what you want to do, what level of responsibility you want to hold.

Ineffective career objective:	To offer a company my excellent academic foundation in hospital technology and my outstanding skills in oral and written communication
Better career objective:	Hospital and medical sales requiring experience with state-of-the-art equipment

Good CAREER OBJECTIVES are hard to write. If you talk about entry-level work, you won't sound ambitious; if you talk about where you hope to be in 5 or 10 years, you won't sound as though you're willing to do entry-level work. When you're applying for a job that is a natural outgrowth of your education and experience, omit this category and specify the job you want in your cover letter.

Often you can avoid writing a CAREER OBJECTIVE statement by putting the job title or field under your name:

Joan Larson Ooyen	Terence Edward Garvey	David R. Lunde
Marketing	Technical Writer	Corporate Fitness Director

Note that you can use the field you're in even if you're a new college graduate. To use a job title, you should have some relevant work experience.

If you use a separate heading for CAREER OBJECTIVE, put it immediately after your address, before the first major heading.

Education

EDUCATION can be your first major category if you've just earned (or are about to earn) a degree, if you have a degree that is essential or desirable for the position you're seeking, or if you can present the information briefly. Put EDUCATION later if you need all of page 1 for another category or if you lack a degree that other applicants may have (see Figure 18.3).

Under EDUCATION, include information about your undergraduate and graduate degrees. You may set up the information in one of three ways. In all of them, use commas to separate elements:

> Bachelor of Science in Business Administration, May 2002, University of Illinois at Urbana–Champaign
> Options: University of Illinois, Urbana, IL
>   University of Illinois (Urbana, Illinois)

Use the same form for city, state of all schools. If you continue information about education on the same line, put a period after the state. Otherwise, use no punctuation.

> B.S. in Education, June 2000, The Ohio State University, Columbus, OH.
>   Undeclared minor in business.

But . . .

> B.S. in Education, June 2000, The Ohio State University, Columbus, OH

Objectional Objectives*

The following quotations show how bad a poor objective can be.

Objective: Easy work, pleasant surroundings, large expense account, high wages, and close to home.

Objective: To work with real people again.

Objective: To have something to do.

Objective: To get out of a rut.

Objective: Cash for talent.

Objective: A management position in which I can make order out of chaos and evil.

Objective: To have fun and live large.

*Quoted from "Robert Half's Resumania," in Taunee Besson, *The Wall Street Journal National Employment Business Weekly: Resumes* (New York: John Wiley and Sons, 1994), 64; and Web sites that will remain unidentified.

When you're getting a four-year degree, include junior college if it gave you an area of expertise different from the area of your major. Include summer school if you took courses to fit in extra electives or to graduate early but not if you were making up a course you flunked during the year. Include study abroad, even if you didn't earn college credits. If you got a certificate for international study, give the name and explain the significance of the certificate.

To punctuate your degrees, do not space between letters and periods:

A.S. in Office Administration

B.S. in Accountancy

Ed.D. in Business Education

Current usage also permits you to omit the periods.

MBA

PhD in Finance

Highlight proficiency in foreign or computer languages by using a separate category.

Professional certifications can be listed under EDUCATION or in a separate category.

If your GPA is good, include it. Because grade point systems vary, specify what your GPA is based on: "3.4/4.0" means 3.4 on a 4.0 scale. If your GPA is under 3.0 on a 4.0 scale, use words rather than numbers: "B− average." If your GPA isn't impressive, calculate your average in your major and your average for your last 60 hours. If these are higher than your overall GPA, consider using them.

There are two basic options for presenting your educational information. Option I just gives degrees, dates, school, and city; option II also tells about your course work.

Option I: List in reverse chronological order (most recent first) each degree earned, field of study, date, school, city, state of any graduate work, short courses and professional certification courses, college, junior college, or school from which you transferred.

Master of Accounting Science, May 2001, Arizona State University, Tempe, AZ
Bachelor of Arts in Finance, May 1999, New Mexico State University, Las Cruces, NM

Plan to sit for the CPA exam November 2001

BS in Personnel Management, June 2000, Georgia State University, Milledgeville, GA
AS in Office Management, June 1997, Georgia Community College, Atlanta, GA

Option II: After giving the basic information (degree, field of study, date, school, city, state) about your degree, list courses, using short descriptive titles rather than course numbers. Use a subhead like "Courses Related to Major" or "Courses Related to Financial Management" that will allow you to list all the courses (including psychology, speech, and business communication) that will help you in the job for which you're applying. Don't say "Relevant Courses," as that implies your other courses were irrelevant.

Bachelor of Science in Management, May 2001, Illinois State University, Normal, IL
GPA: 3.8/4.0
Courses Related to Management:

Personnel Administration	Business Decision Making
Finance	International Business
Management I and II	Marketing
Accounting I and II	Legal Environment of Business
Business Report Writing	Business Speaking

Salutatorian, Niles Township East High School, June 1997, Niles, IL

Listing courses is an unobtrusive way to fill a page. You may also want to list courses or the number of hours in various subjects if you've taken an unusual combination of courses that uniquely qualify you for the position for which you're applying.

BS in Marketing, May 2002, California State University at Northridge
　　30 hours in marketing
　　15 hours in Spanish
　　　9 hours in Chicano studies

Honors and Awards

It's nice to have the word HONORS in a heading where it will be obvious even when the reader skims the résumé. If you have fewer than three and therefore cannot justify a separate heading, consider a heading ACTIVITIES AND HONORS to get that important word in a position of emphasis.

Include the following kinds of entries in this category:

- Listings in recognition books (e.g., *Who's Who in the Southwest*).
- Academic honor societies. Specify the nature of Greek-letter honor societies so the reader doesn't think they're just social clubs.
- Fellowships and scholarships, including honorary scholarships for which you received no money and fellowships you could not hold because you received another fellowship at the same time.
- Awards given by professional societies.
- Major awards given by civic groups.
- Varsity letters; selection to all-state or all-America teams; finishes in state, national, or Olympic meets. (These could also go under ACTIVITIES but may look more impressive under HONORS. Put them under one category or the other—not both.)

Omit honors like "Miss Congeniality" that work against the professional image you want your résumé to create.

As a new college graduate, try to put HONORS on page 1. In a skills résumé, put HONORS on page 1 if they're major (e.g., Phi Beta Kappa, Phi Kappa Phi). Otherwise, save them till page 2—EXPERIENCE will probably take the whole first page.

Résumé Goofs*

Flunked my CPA exam with high grades.

Typing speed: 756 wpm.

Statistics mayor.

My GPA at night is 3.0.

Cities of preference: Mexico City. Languages Spoken: French.

Exposure to German for two years, but many words are not appropriate for business.

Married girls 16 and 18 years.

Delivered papers at age 12 like many other great Americans. The only difference is that they became great.

I am not smart, but I am not stupid.

I am considered charming. References available.

*Quoted from Robert Half, "Rseume goofs," *Managing Your Career,* Spring 1989, 37, 39; Selwyn Feinstein, "Labor Letter," *The Wall Street Journal,* April 5, 1989, A1; Geoff Martz, *How to Survive without Your Parents' Money: Making It from College to the Real World* (New York, Villard Books, 1993), 112; and Web sites that will remain unidentified.

Experience

You may use other headings if they work better: WORK EXPERIENCE, SUMMER AND PART-TIME JOBS, MILITARY EXPERIENCE, MARKETING EXPERIENCE, ACHIEVEMENTS RELATED TO CAREER OBJECTIVE.

What to include

Under this section, include the following information for each job you list: position or job title, organization, city and state (no zip code), dates of employment, and other details, such as full- or part-time status, job duties, special responsibilities, or the fact that you started at an entry-level position and were promoted. Include unpaid jobs and self-employment if they provided relevant skills (e.g., supervising people, budgeting, planning, persuading).

Normally, go back as far as the summer after high school. Include earlier jobs if you started working someplace before graduating from high school but continued working there after graduation. However, give minimal detail about high school jobs. If you worked full-time after high school, make that clear. Give details of relevant skills, such as those listed in Figure 18.2.

If as an undergraduate you've earned a substantial portion of your college expenses, say so in a separate sentence either under EXPERIENCE or in the section on personal data. (Graduate students are expected to support themselves.)

> These jobs paid 40% of my college expenses.

> Paid for 65% of expenses with jobs, scholarships, and loans.

Note that a complete sentence is acceptable if it does not use *I*.

Formats for setting up EXPERIENCE

There are two basic ways to set up the EXPERIENCE section of your résumé. In **indented format,** items that are logically equivalent begin at the same space, with carryover lines indented three spaces or a quarter of an inch. Indented format emphasizes job titles. Figure 18.3 uses indented format. Use commas to

Figure 18.2

Action Verbs for Résumés

analyzed	directed	led	reviewed
budgeted	earned	managed	revised
built	edited	motivated	saved
chaired	established	negotiated	scheduled
coached	examined	observed	simplified
collected	evaluated	organized	sold
conducted	helped	persuaded	solved
coordinated	hired	planned	spoke
counseled	improved	presented	started
created	increased	produced	supervised
demonstrated	interviewed	recruited	trained
designed	introduced	reported	translated
developed	investigated	researched	wrote

Steven W. Zajano

921 South Seventh Street
Cambridge, Ohio 43725
(614) 555-4715

*Vertical lists of duties
emphasize experience
when reader skims.*

WORK EXPERIENCE

Use present tense when you're doing the job now.

Groundskeeper, Muskingum College, New Concord, Ohio, 1995–present.
   Duties include
   * Maintaining campus grounds, athletic fields, and equipment
   * Performing electrical, plumbing, and carpentry as needed

Crew Leader, Seneca National Fish Hatchery, Senecaville, Ohio, 1992–94.

*How to
present
a job
where
you've
been
promoted.*
   Started as Young Adult Conservation Corps (YACC) member; promoted to crew leader after five months.
   Duties as crew leader included
   *Maintaining hatchery facilities
   *Planning work activities and schedules for 12 YACC workers

*Be specific about number of
people you've supervised.*

*Puts this duty
second so the space
below it emphasizes it.*

Landscaper, R.G.'s Landscaping Service, Canton, Ohio, Summer 1993.
   Duties included
   * Maintaining existing lawns
   * Landscaping and establishing new lawns

Farm Worker, Hanover Stud Horse Farm, Canal Fulton, Ohio, 1991–93.

*Use
parallel
structure
for all
duties.*
   Duties included
   * Maintaining tractors and mending fences
   * Baling hay and straw
   * Caring for thoroughbred racing horses   *Puts most interesting duty
   last where it stands out.*

ACTIVITIES AND INTERESTS
   Boy Scout Troop, Cambridge, Ohio (Leader)
   Bus Ministry, Cambridge United Christian Church
   Hunting, fishing, camping, swimming, hiking

*Some readers may respond
negatively. But this ministry
is an important part of
Steve's life, and he wants to
suggest that he isn't just
interested in outdoor
recreational pursuits.*

EDUCATION
   Associate of Applied Sciences, June 2001, Hocking Technical
      College, Nelsonville, Ohio
      Specialization: Recreation and Wildlife Management

REFERENCES
   James Heidler, Grounds Supervisor, Muskingum College, New Concord,
      Ohio 43725 (614) 555-5024
   Richard Jordet, YACC Program Director, Seneca National Fish Hatchery,
      Bytesville, Ohio 43723 (614) 555-5541
   Gerald Sagan, Professor of Recreation and Wildlife Management,
      Hocking Technical College, Nelsonville, Ohio 43765 (614) 555-3492

But I Haven't Done Anything!*

Some students have trouble coming up with details. "I've never really done anything." That's too negative. *Everybody* has done *something.* How have you spent the last five years?

One woman's only job was as a part-time salesclerk in the lighting department of a department store. Her official duties weren't important. But when she focused on what she'd actually done, she had evidence of skills employers want.

She had done research. To answer customers' questions, she read about lighting, vision, and energy consumption. She visited competitors and noticed their products and displays.

She had demonstrated creativity. In August, she rigged up a mannequin to look like a student— slouched in a chair, holding textbook and pop bottle, surrounded by clothes, a football, and a guitar. On the table was a lamp positioned to provide good study light with a sign, "At least he won't ruin his eyes."

Her display worked. The store sold four times as many lamps that August as it ever had, including the month before Christmas.

A résumé entry could give these details to support claims for experience in research and persuading. And she had increased sales in her unit 400%.

*Based on John L. Munschauer, *Jobs for English Majors and Other Smart People* (Princeton, NJ: Peterson's Guides, 1986), 36–37.

separate items. Put a period after the date, before other details about the job (responsibilities, etc.):

Job title, name of organization, city, state, dates. Other information.

EXPERIENCE

Engineering Assistant, Sohio Chemical Company, Lima, Ohio, Summer 2001. Originally hired as a laboratory technician, Summer 2000; promoted following year. As laboratory technician, tested wastewater effluents for compliance with Federal EPA standards. As engineering assistant, helped chemists design a test to analyze groundwater quality and seepage around landfills. Presented weekly oral and written progress reports to Director of Research and Development.

Animal Caretaker, Animalcare, Worthington, Ohio, June 1997–September 1999. Full-time during summers; part-time during senior year of high school.

Two-margin or **block format** emphasizes *when* you worked. Don't use two-margin format if your work history has gaps. Figure 18.5 uses two-margin format for EXPERIENCE.

EXPERIENCE

Summers, 1998–2000	Repair worker, Bryant Heating and Cooling, Providence, RI.
1999–2000	Library Clerk, Boston University Library, Boston, MA. Part-time during school year.
1997–99	Food Service Worker, Boston University, Boston, MA. Part-time during school year.
Summer, 1998	Delivery person, Domino's Pizza, Providence, RI.

Use a hyphen to join inclusive dates:

March-August, 2000 or write out March to August, 2000
1997–99
'97–'99

If you use numbers for dates, do not space before or after the slash: 10/00–5/01

Choosing headings for skills résumés

In a skills résumé the subheadings under EXPERIENCE will be the *skills* used in or the *aspects* of the job you are applying for, rather than the title or the dates of the jobs you've held (as in a chronological résumé). For entries under each skill, combine experience from paid jobs, unpaid work, classes, activities, and community service.

Use headings that reflect the jargon of the job for which you're applying: *logistics* rather than *planning* for a technical job; *procurement* rather than *purchasing* for a job with the military. Figure 18.4 shows a skills résumé for someone who is changing fields. Marcella suggests that she already knows a lot about the field she hopes to enter by using its jargon for the headings.

A job description can give you ideas for headings. Possible headings and subheadings for skills résumés include

Administration	Communication
Alternates or Subheadings:	Alternates or Subheadings:
Budgeting	Conducting Meetings
Coordinating	Editing
Evaluating	Fund-Raising

Figure 18.4   *A Skills Résumé for Someone Changing Fields*

On the first page of a skills résumé, put skills directly related to job for which you're applying.

Marcella G. Cope

370 Monahan Lane
Dublin, OH 43016
614-555-1997
mcope@postbox.acs.ohio-state.edu

Centered format is eye-catching but can be hard to read. Here, bold headings draw the reader's eye.

Objective

Put company's name in objective.

To help create high-quality CD-ROM products in Metatec's New Media Solutions Division

Editing and Proofreading Experience

Edited a textbook published by Simon and Schuster, revising with attention to format, consistency, coherence, document integrity, and document design.
Proofed training and instructor's manuals, policy statements, student essays and research papers, internal documents, and promotional materials.
Worked with authors in a variety of fields including English, communication, business, marketing, economics, education, history, sociology, biology, agriculture, computer science, law, and medicine to revise their prose and improve their writing skills by giving them oral and written feedback.

Writing Experience

Wrote training and instructor's manuals, professional papers, and letters, memos, and reports.
Co-authored the foreword to a forthcoming textbook (Fall 1999) from NCTE press.
Contributed to a textbook forthcoming (Fall 1999) from Bedford Books/St. Martin's Press.

Computer Experience

Center headings only when you use a large font. Here, 14 pt. is used.

Designed a Web page using Microsoft Front Page
(www.cohums.ohio-state.edu/english/People/Bracken.1/Sedgwick/)
Learned and used a variety of programs on both Macintosh and PC platforms:

Computer experience is crucial for almost every job. Specify the software and hardware you've worked with.

Word Processing and Spreadsheets
Microsoft Project
Front Page
Pagemaker
Aspects (a forum for online synchronous discussion)
Storyspace (a hypertext writing environment)
PowerPoint
E-Mail

Other Business and Management Experience

Developed policies, procedures, and vision statements.
Supervised new staff members in a mentoring program.
Coordinated program and individual schedules, planned work and estimated costs, set goals, and evaluated progress and results.
Member of team that directed the nation's largest first-year writing program.

Figure 18.4   *(concluded)*

Marcella G. Cope

Page 2

Employment History

Graduate Teaching Associate, Department of English, The Ohio State University, September 1995-Present. Taught Intermediate and First-Year Composition.
Writing Consultant, University Writing Center, The Ohio State University, January-April 1998
Program Administrator, First-Year Writing Program, The Ohio State University, September 1996–January 1998

Honors

Phi Kappa Phi Honor Society, inducted 1996. Membership based upon performance in top ten percent of graduate students nationwide.
Letters of Commendation, 1995–1998. Issued by the Director of Graduate Studies in recognition of outstanding achievement.
Dean's List, Northwestern University, Evanston, IL

Education

Master of Arts, June 1997, The Ohio State University, Columbus, OH. Cumulative GPA: 4.0/4.0
Bachelor of Arts, June 1995, Northwestern University, Evanston, IL. Graduated with Honors.

References

Kitty O. Locker
Associate Professor, Business and Administrative Communication
The Ohio State University
421 Denney Hall, 164 W. 17th Ave.
Columbus, OH 43210
614-555-6556
locker.1@osu.edu

Choose references who can speak about your skills for the job for which you're applying.

Marilyn Duffey
Director, Ohio University Writing Program
Ohio University
140 Chubb Hall
Athens, OH 45701
614-555-9443
duffey@ohiou.edu

James Bracken
Associate Professor, English and Library Science
The Ohio State University
224 Main Library, 1858 Neil Avenue Mall
Columbus, OH 43210
614-555-2786
bracken@osu.edu

Administration, cont.

    Implementing

    Negotiating

    Planning

    Keeping Records

    Scheduling

    Solving Problems

    Supervising

Communication, cont.

    Interviewing

    Oral Skills

    Negotiating

    Persuading

    Proposal Writing

    Report Writing

More Résumé Goofs*

Mistakes and errors of judgment continue:

"Accomplishments: Completed 11 years of high school." (Now that's dedication.)

Qualifications: "I have a current passport." (This is a unique achievement.)

"Work Experience: Responsibilities included checking customers out."

"Excellant at people oriented positiaons and organizional problem solving." (But not so good at proofreading.)

"Spent several years in the United States Navel Reserve." (Is this where the oranges remain until they're ripe?)

"1881 1995: Spent my time teaching and going to school for computer science." (That's all in 114 years?)

"Reason for leaving: maturity leave." (An innovative approach to professional growth.)

"Received a plague for Salesperson of the Year." (Get well soon!)

"Wholly responsible for two (2) failed financial institutions." (How proud you must be.)

"Shot at the local gun club." (Next time, you may want to stand behind the bullet-proof glass.)

*Quoted from Robert Half, "Resumania," April–December 1998, <ww.rhic.com/jobsRHIC/jobzone/resumania/archive.html>; nd, <www.wonderlic.com/nlresmna.htm>; and nd, <www2.minnbankcenter.org/mba/resgoofs.htm>.

Many jobs require a mix of skills. Try to include the skills that you know will be needed in the job you want. For example, one study identified the six top communication skills for jobs in finance and in management.[3] Applicants who had experience in some of these areas could list them as well as subject-related skills and knowledge.

Finance

    Listening

    Advising

    Building Relationships

    Exchanging Routine Information

    Giving Feedback

    Persuading

Management

    Listening

    Motivating

    Advising

    Building Relationships

    Persuading

    Instructing

You need at least three subheadings in a skills résumé; six or seven is not uncommon. Give enough detail under each subheading so the reader will know what you did. Put the most important category from the reader's point of view first.

In a skills résumé, list your paid jobs under WORK HISTORY or EMPLOYMENT RECORD near the end of the résumé (see Figure 18.4). List only job title, employer, city, state, and dates. Omit details about what you did, since you will have already used them under EXPERIENCE.

Activities

Employers are very interested in your activities if you're a new college graduate. If you've worked for several years after college or have an advanced degree (MBA, JD), you can omit ACTIVITIES and include PROFESSIONAL ACTIVITIES AND AFFILIATIONS or COMMUNITY AND PUBLIC SERVICE. If you went straight from college to graduate school but have an unusually strong record under ACTIVITIES, include this category even if all the entries are from your undergraduate days.

Include the following kinds of items under ACTIVITIES:

- Volunteer work. Include important committees and leadership roles.
- Membership in organized student activities. Include important subcommittees, leadership roles. Include minor offices only if they're directly related to the job for which you're applying or if they show growing responsibility (you held a minor office one year, a bigger office the following year). Include so-called major offices (e.g., vice president) even if you did very little. Provide descriptive details if (but only if) they help the reader realize how much you did and the importance of your work.
- Membership in professional associations. To find out about the association(s) in your field, ask your professors or check scholarly journals.
- Participation in organized activities that require talent or responsibility (e.g., choir, freshman orientation).

Finding Your Flaws Online*

Ever file a workers' compensation claim? Wrecked a company car? Received a speeding ticket?

Prospective employers can find out if you did. And now, thanks to the Internet, they can do it almost instantly.

Informus Corp. makes a living giving curious employers information such as the names and phone numbers of your neighbors. Besides access to workers' compensation claims, Informus connects employers to credit bureaus and state agencies that store financial and criminal information.

*Quoted from Tawn Nhan, "On-line Service Checks Out Job Applicants," The Columbus Dispatch, May 19, 1996.

- Participation in varsity, intramural, or independent athletics. However, don't list so many sports that you appear not to have had any time to study.
- Social clubs, if you held a major leadership role or if social skills are important for the job for which you're applying.
- Religious organizations if you held a major leadership role or if you're applying for a church-related job.

Major leadership roles may look more impressive if they're listed under EXPERIENCE instead of under ACTIVITIES.

References

Including references anticipates the employer's needs and removes a potential barrier to your getting the job. To make your résumé fit on one page, you can omit this category. However, include REFERENCES if you're having trouble filling the page. Don't say "References Available on Request" since no job applicant is going to refuse to supply references. If you don't want your current employer to know you're job-hunting, omit the category in the résumé and say in the letter, "If I become a finalist for the job, I will supply the names of current references."

When you list references, include at least three, usually no more than five, never more than six. As a college student or a new graduate, include at least one professor and at least one employer or advisor—someone who can comment on your work habits and leadership skills. Don't use relatives or roommates, even if you've worked for them. Omit personal or character references who can say nothing about your work. If you're changing jobs, include your current superior.

Always ask the person's permission to list him or her as a reference. Don't say, "May I list you as a reference?" Instead, say, "Can you speak specifically about my work?" Jog the person's memory by taking along copies of work you did for him or her and a copy of your current résumé. Tell the person what points you'd like him or her to stress in a letter. Keep your list of references up to date. If it's been a year or more since you asked someone, ask again—and tell the person about your recent achievements.

For each reference, list name, title or position, organization, city and state, and phone number. You could also give the full mailing address if you think people are more likely to write than to call. Use courtesy titles (*Dr., Mr., Ms.*) for all or for none. By convention, all faculty with the rank of assistant professor or above may be called *Professor.* If you want to list teaching assistants, omit titles for all references.

References whom the reader knows are by far the most impressive. In a skills résumé, choose references who can testify to your abilities in the most important skills areas.

Include the name and address of your placement office if you have written recommendations on file there.

Ways to set up REFERENCES

To save space, present references in indented line format (see Figures 18.1 and 18.3). If you have slightly more room, double-space between the names of references. (See Figure 18.3.) In indented line format, use a comma to separate lines. Do not put any punctuation after the zip code.

REFERENCES
Thomas Elgee, Professor of Community Health, University of Northern Colorado, Greeley, CO 80639
(302) 351-1111
Elizabeth Tormei, Professor of Women's Studies, University of Northern Colorado, Greeley, CO
80639 (302) 351-2222
Amy Wilson, Director, Rape Crisis Center, Denver, CO 80203 (303) 555-3333
Matthew J. Kohl, Director, Brethren Community Services, Eugene, CO 80689 (302) 726-4444

When you list references vertically, omit punctuation at the end of a line, just as you would in the lines of an address on an envelope. Two-margin format takes up more space and can help you fill a page.

REFERENCES

Thomas Elgee	Elizabeth Tormei
Professor of Community Health	Professor of Women's Studies
University of Northern Colorado	University of Northern Colorado
321 Blevins Building	100 Humanities Building
Greeley, CO 80639	Greeley, CO 80639
(302) 351-1111	(302) 351-2222
Amy Wilson	Matthew J. Kohl
Director	Director
Rape Crisis Center	Brethren Community Services
100 Main Street	4835 Goodale Blvd.
Denver, CO 80203	Eugene, CO 80689
(303) 351-3333	(302) 726-4444

Dealing with Difficulties

Some job hunters face special problems. This section gives advice for five common problems.

"All My Experience Is in My Family's Business."

In your résumé, simply list the company you worked for. For a reference, instead of a family member, list a supervisor, client, or vendor who can talk about your work. Since the reader may wonder whether "Jim Clarke" is any relation to the owner of "Clarke Construction Company," be ready to answer interview questions about why you're looking at other companies. Prepare an answer that stresses the broader opportunities you seek but doesn't criticize your family or the family business.

"I've Been Out of the Job Market for a While."

You need to prove to a potential employer that you're up-to-date and motivated. Carl Quintanilla suggests the following ways to do that:

• Be active in professional organizations. Attend meetings; read trade journals.
• Learn the computer programs that professionals in your field use.

- Find out your prospective employer's immediate priorities. If you can show you'll contribute from day one, you'll have a much easier sell. But to do that, you need to know what skills the employer is looking for, what needs the employer has.
- Show how your at-home experience relates to the workplace. Dealing with unpredictable situations, building consensus, listening, raising money, and making presentations are transferable skills.
- Create a portfolio of your work—even if it's for imaginary clients—to demonstrate your expertise.[4]

"I Want to Change Fields."

Have a good reason for choosing the field in which you're looking for work. "I want a change" or "I need to get out of a bad situation" does not convince an employer that you know what you're doing.

Think about how your experience relates to the job you want. Jack is an older-than-average student who wants to be a pharmaceutical sales representative. He has sold woodstoves, served subpoenas, and worked on an oil rig. A chronological résumé makes his work history look directionless. But a skills résumé could focus on persuasive ability (selling stoves), initiative and persistence (serving subpoenas), and technical knowledge (courses in biology and chemistry).[5]

Learn about the skills needed in the job you want: learn the buzzwords of the industry. (Chapter 19 has suggestions for ways to find these things out.) Figure 18.4 shows a skills résumé of someone changing fields.

"I Was Fired."

First, deal with the emotional baggage. You need to reduce negative feelings to a manageable level before you're ready to job-hunt.

Second, try to learn from the experience. You'll be a much more attractive job candidate if you can show that you've learned from the experience—whether your lesson is improved work habits or that you need to choose a job where you can do work you can point to with pride.

Third, suggests Phil Elder, an interviewer for an insurance company, call the person who fired you and say something like this: "Look, I know you weren't pleased with the job I did at _____ . I'm applying for a job at _____ now and the personnel director may call you to ask about me. Would you be willing to give me the chance to get this job so that I can try to do things right this time?" All but the hardest of heart, says Elder, will give you one more chance. You won't get a glowing reference, but neither will the statement be so damning that no one is willing to hire you.[6]

"I Don't Have Any Experience."

If you have a year or more before you job hunt, you can get experience in several ways:

- Take a fast-food job—and keep it. If you do well, you'll be promoted to a supervisor within a year. Use every opportunity to learn about the management and financial aspects of the business.
- Join a volunteer organization that interests you. If you work hard, you'll quickly get an opportunity to do more: manage a budget, write fund-raising materials, and supervise other volunteers.

- Freelance. Design brochures, create Web pages, do tax returns for small businesses. Use your skills—for free, if you have to at first.
- Write. Create a portfolio of ads, instructions, or whatever documents are relevant for the field you want to enter. Ask a professional—an instructor, a local business person, someone from a professional organization—to critique them. Volunteer your services to local fund-raising organizations and small businesses.

Getting experience is particularly important for students with good grades. Pick something where you interact with other people, so that you can show that you can work well in an organization.

If you're on the job market now, think carefully about what you've really done. Complete sentences using the action verbs in Figure 18.2. Think about what you've done in courses, in volunteer work, in unpaid activities. Especially focus on skills in problem solving, critical thinking, teamwork, and communication. Solving a problem for a hypothetical firm in an accounting class, thinking critically about a report problem in business communication, working with a group in a marketing class, and communicating with people at the senior center where you volunteer are experience, even if no one paid you.

If you're not actually looking for a job but just need to create a résumé for this course, ask your instructor whether you may assume that you're a senior and add the things you hope to do between now and your senior year.

How an Average Student Created an Excellent Résumé

Allyson was convinced that she had nothing to put on her résumé. In a conference, her instructor asked Allyson to describe exactly what she'd done. Allyson's "baby-sitting" was actually house management and child care. But a summer job at Harvard had consisted of changing beds and cleaning rooms for conference guests.

Her five summers of work at a law firm sounded more promising. She went to the library, formulated medical and legal questions, and searched for answers. The information she found helped the firm win a $7 million out-of-court settlement. Not bad for a sophomore in college. But Allyson was in advertising and wanted to go into copywriting, not market research. The experience was certainly worth putting on her résumé, but the kind of thinking she'd done as a law clerk wasn't the kind of thinking she needed to demonstrate to an ad agency.

Some of the items under ACHIEVEMENTS were interesting. The Locker Room was a new restaurant in town where Allyson had had dinner. Its menu said the restaurant "had a long history." In fact, the restaurant was new: the *building* was old. Allyson went up to the owner, told him several of the things that were wrong with the menu, and offered to rewrite it. The owner told her he'd pay her for doing that and also invited her to submit ideas for ads.

The instructor was impressed. The whole anecdote might work in a job application letter, while the résumé could highlight the fact that Allyson had written menu and advertising copy for a real business (not just a class). "What you need," the instructor said, "is a skills résumé."

"Are skills résumés very common?"

"Not as common as chronological résumés. And they're a little harder to write. You can write a chronological résumé just by going through the list and remembering what you've done under EDUCATION, under EXPERIENCE, and so on. You can almost fill in the blanks: the job title, the organization, the city and state, the dates. With a skills résumé, you think about the skills you'd need in the job you want to have, the skills the employer is looking for, and

Privacy and Web Résumés

If you post your résumé on the Web, your current employer may find it—and find out that you're job hunting. If you're changing careers or seeking advancement, you'll want to keep your job hunt quiet until you have an offer you want to accept.

Before you post your résumé on a job site, check to see what its policy is. The best ones ask you whether you want to submit your résumé for a specific job. Less good, but perhaps OK, are sites that send the body of the résumé—without name or address—to potential employers. Depending on your credentials, your current employer may or may not identify you. Avoid sites that send your résumé to employers without your permission.

show how you've used those skills in what you've already done. A skills résumé lets you take things from classes, from paid jobs, from volunteer work and put them all together.

"How do employers feel about skills résumés?"

"There isn't any good research. One survey asked employers which they'd rather get, and more people said 'the traditional résumé.' But that's just because they know where to look for things on the traditional résumé. Nobody's ever done research taking the same qualifications, presenting them in two different ways, and seeing which way got more interviews or more job offers. I know people who've gotten jobs using skills résumés.

"You want a résumé that immediately says 'WOW' to the employer. People always get more résumés than they want to deal with. To survive the cut, a résumé has to stand out. You want the résumé to have the same punch that you have in person."

The next step was to answer two questions: "What do you want to do? What do you think the employer is looking for?" Allyson replied, "I want to get a job as a copywriter in Cleveland. It's the 10th biggest market, and I'd rather work as a copywriter in a smaller market than have to start as a secretary at a New York agency. I think the agencies want someone who shows creativity, who has a strong personality, who isn't afraid to take risks."

"Then your résumé needs to do that. And it can. You're coming across as a self-starter, a problem solver. When you actually write your résumé, use the language of your field. *Problem solver* is a positive term in most fields, but it may or may not be right for advertising. Given what you've done, you could have headings for WRITING EXPERIENCE, CREATING ADS, PLANNING PROMOTIONAL CAMPAIGNS, RESEARCH, and SPEAKING, with a list of items under each one.

"Your résumé is going to make you look qualified. Highly qualified. Other students are going to read it and say, 'But she has done so much. *I* haven't done anything. They're going to feel just the way you felt when you said you hadn't done much in the last four years. But you *have* done a lot. You'll look great in your résumé. Anyone can, who understands the options and who puts in the time and energy."

Allyson still had to tinker with headings, decide what details to use, and experiment with layout and spacing. The final product (Figure 18.5) is worth the work.

Online Résumés

Most large companies scan résumés into an electronic job-applicant tracking system.[7] Creating a Web résumé is optional, but prepare a scannable version of your résumé to send any company that asks for it.

Creating a Web Résumé

Post a résumé on the Web only if you can do so for free and if you already know HTML and Java. The chance of an employer finding your résumé is too low to justify the cost of paying to post or taking the time to learn HTML or Java if you don't already know them.

If you create a Web résumé,

- Include an e-mail link at the top of the résumé under your name.
- Omit your street addresses and phone numbers. (A post office box is OK.) Employers who find your résumé on the Web will have the technology to e-mail you.

Figure 18.5 A Skills Résumé for a Graduate Entering the Job Market

Allyson Karnes

A border creates visual variety.

195 W. Ninth
Columbus, OH 43210
(614) 555-3498
karnes.173@osu.edu

6782 Fenwick Drive
Solon, OH 44121
(216) 555-6182

Career Objective

This really is Allyson's philosophy— and it's one an agency will appreciate.

To write creative headlines and print ads that make people remember the product

Education

She presents herself as a fellow professional.

B.A. in Advertising, June 2000, The Ohio State University, Columbus, OH
  Core courses: Copywriting, promotional strategies, magazine writing, graphics, media planning
  Harvard University Writing Program, Summer 1998, Boston, MA

Experience Creating Ads

Skills résumé allows her to combine experience from classes and life.

Led the team that developed the winning promotional strategy for Max & Erma's Restaurants.
  • Developed idea for theme for a year's campaign of ads.
  • Wrote copy for radio spots, magazine ads, and billboards. One billboard ad had the headline "Multiple Choice" and boxes for burgers, chicken, and salads—with all the boxes checked.
  • Presented creative strategy to Max & Erma's CEO and the Head of Advertising.
  • Strategy won first place from among 17 proposals.

Details, wording demonstrate her creativity.

Wrote more than 15 ads for Copywriting class, including
  • Ad for cordless phone: "Isn't It Time to Cut the Cord?"
  • Slogan for Ohio University's Springfest Jamboree: "In Short, It Jams"
  • Billboard for Columbus Boys' School: "Who Said It's Lonely at the Top?"
Wrote ads and revised menu for The Locker Room (restaurant).

Other Writing Experience

Wrote profile on Charlotte Witkind, part owner of the New York Yankees.
Wrote "Commuter Flights" (humor).
Wrote more than 30 magazine articles as part of courses at Harvard University and Ohio State.
Wrote legal briefs as part of course at Harvard.
Wrote summary of research on $7 million medical malpractice case for Garson and Associates.

Employment History

1999–2000	Child care and house management, Worthington, OH. Part-time daily during school year.
Summer 1999	Mother's Helper, Princeton, NJ. Cared for six-month-old baby; cared for all three children when parents were away on weekends.
Summer 1997	Maid, Harvard Student Agency, Boston, MA. Part-time while attending Harvard University Writing Program.
Summers 1993–97	Law Clerk, Garson and Associates, Cleveland, OH. Did independent case research used by the firm to win $7 million malpractice out-of-court.

Reverse chronology.

A position of emphasis.

Portfolio Available on Request

Résumé Advice on the Web

The best advice on résumés is still in books. If you want to surf, check these sites for information and links.

Archeus: Guide to WWW Resume Writing Resources
   www.golden.net/
   ~archeus/reswri.htm
   Summaries, ratings of, and links to dozens of WWW articles on résumés.
The Career Advisor, by William S. Frank
   www.careerlab.com/
   homeruns.htm
Catapult Job Search Guides
   www.jobweb.org/catapult/
   jsguides.htm
Tips on Writings an Electronic Resume, by Joyce Lain Kennedy
   www.espan.com/does/
   jlkresv.html
How to Write an Exceptional Resume (Rockport Institute)
   www.his.com/~rockport/
   resumes.htm
Kitty Locker's Job Hunting Page
   www.cohums.ohio-state.edu/
   english/People/Locker.1/job.htm
   Current links to these pages and others.
Resume Doctor
   www1.mhv.net/~acorn/Bad.html
   Click on parts of a bad résumé and get an explanation of what's wrong.
Writing a Resume for Susie the Screener
   www.gsia.cmu.edu/afs/
   andrew/gsia/coc/student/
   screener.html

- Consider having links under your name and e-mail address to the various parts of your résumé. Use phrases that give the viewer some idea of what you offer: e.g., *Marketing Experience.*
- Link to other pages that provide more information about you (a list of courses, a document you've written), but not to organizations (your university, an employer) that shift emphasis away from your credentials.
- Don't be cute. Do be professional. Link to other pages you've created only if they convey the same professional image as your résumé.
- Put your strongest qualification immediately after your name and e-mail address. If the first screen doesn't interest readers, they won't scroll through the rest of the résumé.
- Specify the job you want. Recruiters respond negatively to scrolling through an entire résumé only to find that the candidate is in another field.[8]
- Specify city and state for educational institutions and employers.
- Use lists, indentations, and white space to create visual variety.
- Most commercial and many university sites offer lists of applicants, with a short phrase after each name. Craft this phrase to convince the recruiter to click on your résumé.
- Proofread the résumé carefully.

Be prepared during the job interview to create HTML or Java text or provide an in-office writing sample. Firms know that candidates can get help with Web pages and online portfolios and may want confirmation that the skills they represent indeed belong to the candidate.[9]

Creating a Scannable Résumé

Increasingly, large companies such as Bank of America, Ford Motor Company, Walt Disney, and the Clorox Company use electronic job-applicant-tracking systems like Resumix and Res-Track. After paper résumés are scanned in, the systems can search them by keyword to match job descriptions. Advanced systems take care of the paperwork throughout the hiring process, notifying each applicant when the résumé has been scanned in, saving interview notes and results of pre-employment testing, automatically generating an "offer" letter, and updating the candidate's file to "hired" and the job requisition to "filled" after the candidate accepts.

Figure 18.6 is an example of a scannable résumé.
To increase the chances that the résumé is scanned correctly,

- Use a standard typeface. Beverly Nelson, William Gallé, and Donna Luse recommend Helvetica, Futura, Optima, Times Roman, New Century Schoolbook, Courier, Univers, and Bookman.[10]
- Use 12- or 14-point type.
- Use a ragged right margin rather than full justification. Scanners can't always handle the extra spaces between words and letters that full justification creates.
- Don't italicize or underline words—even titles of books or newspapers that grammatically require such treatment.
- Check text in full caps or bold to make sure letters don't touch each other.
- Don't use lines, boxes, script, leader dots, or borders.
- Don't use two-column formats or vertical text.
- Print the résumé using portrait (standard page) rather than landscape orientation.

Figure 18.6 *A Scannable Résumé*

Jerry A. Jackson   *Use 12 or 14-point type in a standard
typeface. Here, Times Roman is used.*

Keywords: family financial management; investment sales; computer modeling;
competitive; self-starter; hard worker; responsible; collegiate athletics; sales
experience   *In keywords, use labels and terms
that employer might include in job listing.*

Campus Address
1636$^1/_2$ Highland Street
Columbus, OH 43201
(614) 555-5718
E-mail address: jackson.2495@osu.edu
Created a Web page on saving for life goals, such as a home, children's education,
and retirement: www.fisher.osu/students/jackson.2495/home.htm

*Give as much information as you like.
The computer doesn't care how long
the document is.*

Permanent Address
45 East Mulberry
Huntington, NY 11746
(516) 555-7793

Education
B.S. in Family Financial Management, June 2001, The Ohio State University,
Columbus, OH
"B" Grade Point Average
Comprehensive courses related to major provide not only the basics of family
financial management but also skills in communication, writing, speaking, small
groups, and computer modeling
Accounting I and II
Business and Professional Writing
Computer Programming
Finance   *Don't use columns. Scanners
can't handle them.*
Economics I and II
Family Resource Management
Family and Human Development
Statistics
Public Speaking
Interpersonal Communication

Sports Experience
BAAD (Buckeye Athletes Against Drugs)
Intramural Hockey Team (Division Champions, Winter 2000)
Three-year Varsity Letterman, Ohio State University, Columbus, OH
Men's NCAA Division I Lacrosse

Experience
Financial Sales Representative, Primerica Company, Columbus, OH, February
2000–present. Work with clients to plan investment strategies; recommend specific
investments, including stocks, bonds, mutual funds, and annuities.

(continues)

Figure 18.6   *A Scannable Résumé (concluded)*

Entrepreneur, Huntington, NY and Columbus OH, September 1999–January 2000. Created a saleable product, secured financial backing, found a manufacturer, supervised production, and sold product—12 dozen T-shirts at a $5.25 profit each—to help pay for school expenses.

Landscape Maintenance Supervisor, Huntington, NY, Summers 1991–99. Formed a company to cut lawns, put up fences, fertilize, garden, and paint houses. Hired, fired, trained, motivated, and paid friends to complete jobs.

Collector and Repairman, ACN Inc., Huntington, NY, Summers 1991–97. Collected and counted up to $10,000 a day. Worked with technicians troubleshooting and repairing electronic and coin mechanisms of video and pinball games, cigarette machines, and jukeboxes. Drove company cars and trucks throughout New York metro area to collect cash and move and repair machines.

Willing to relocate
U.S. citizen

Don't justify margins.
Doing so creates extra spaces
which confuse scanners.

- Put each phone number on a separate line.
- Use plenty of white space.
- Don't fold or staple the pages.
- Don't write anything by hand on your résumé.
- Send a laser copy or a high-quality photocopy. Stray marks defeat scanners.

To increase the number of matches or "hits,"

- Prepare a traditional chronological résumé. Don't be "creative." It doesn't matter where information is: the system can find it anywhere.
- Use a *Keywords* section under your name, address, and phone. In it, put not only degrees, job field or title, and accomplishments but also personality traits and attitude: *dependable, skill in time management, leadership, sense of responsibility.*[11]
- Use industry buzzwords and jargon, even if you're redundant. For example, "Web page design and HTML coding" will "match" either "Web" or "HTML" as a keyword.
- Use conventional terms, even if they're a bit wordy.
- Use nouns. Some systems don't handle verbs well.
- Use common headings such as *Summary of Qualifications, Strengths, Certifications,* and so forth as well as *Education, Experience,* and so on.
- Use as many pages as necessary.
- Mention specific software programs (e.g., *Lotus 1-2-3*) you've used.

- Be specific and quantifiable. "Managed $2 million building materials account" will generate more hits than "manager" or "managerial experience." Listing Microsoft Front Page as a skill won't help as much as "Used Microsoft Front Page to design an interactive Web page for a national fashion retailer, with links to information about style trends, current store promotions, employment opportunities, and an online video fashion show."

- Join honor societies, professional and trade organizations, since they're often used as keywords.[12] Spell out Greek letter societies (the scanner will mangle Greek characters, even if your computer has them): "Pi Sigma Alpha Honor Society." For English words, spell out the organization name; follow it with the abbreviation in parentheses: "College Newspaper Business and Advertising Managers Association (CNBAM)." That way, the résumé will be tagged whether the recruiter searches for the full name or the acronym.

- Put everything in the résumé rather than "saving" some material for the cover letter. While some applicant-tracking systems can search for keywords in cover letters and other application materials, most extract information only from the résumé, even though they store the other papers. The length of the résumé doesn't matter.

Send only one résumé, even if the firm has more than one position for which you qualify. Most recruiters have negative reactions to multiple résumés, and the tracking system allows the applicant to be coded "NH" (never hire), a coding that persists even if the original recruiter leaves the company. Do, however, bring a separate résumé (designed to be read by humans) to the interview.

Experts differ on whether candidates should phone to follow up. Taunee Besson advises phoning the administrator or verifier of the tracking system to ask, "Did you receive my résumé? Was I a match anywhere? Has my résumé been routed? To whom? Which department?" and then calling the manager to whom the résumé has been routed. But Besson admits that some recruiters say that they code "unsolicited phone calls" and see people who make too many as pests.[13]

Summary of Key Points

- Informal preparation for job hunting should start soon after you arrive on campus. Formal preparation for job hunting should begin a full year before you begin interviewing. The year you interview, register with your placement office early.

- Employers skim résumés to decide whom to interview. Employers assume that the letter and résumé represent your best work. Interviewers normally reread the résumé before the interview. After the search committee has chosen an applicant, it submits the résumé to people in the organization who must approve the appointment.

- A résumé must fill at least one page. Use two pages if you have extensive activities and experience.

- Emphasize information that is relevant to the job you want, is recent (last three years), and shows your superiority to other applicants.

- To emphasize key points, put them in headings, list them vertically, and provide details.

- Résumés use sentence fragments punctuated like complete sentences. Items in the résumé must be concise and parallel. Verbs and gerunds create a dynamic image of you.

- A **chronological résumé** summarizes what you did in a time line (starting with the most recent events, and going backward in **reverse chronology**). It emphasizes degrees, job titles, and dates. Use a chronological résumé when
  - Your education and experience are a logical preparation for the position for which you're applying.
  - You have impressive job titles, offices, or honors.
- A **skills résumé** emphasizes the skills you've used, rather than the job in which or the date when you used them. Use a skills résumé when
  - Your education and experience are not the usual route to the position for which you're applying.
  - You're changing fields.
  - You want to combine experience from paid jobs, activities or volunteer work, and courses to show the extent of your experience in administration, finance, speaking, etc.
  - Your recent work history may create the wrong impression (e.g., it has gaps, shows a demotion, shows job-hopping, etc.).
- Résumés commonly contain the applicant's name, address, phone number, education, and experience. Activities, honors, and references should be included if possible.
- To fill the page, list courses or list references vertically.
- Using a laser printer, print your résumé on quality paper.
- To create a scannable résumé, create a "plain vanilla" text using industry jargon, buzzwords, and acronyms.

Chapter 18

Exercises and Problems

Getting Started

18.1 Analyzing Your Accomplishments

List the 10 accomplishments that give you the most personal satisfaction. These could be things that other people wouldn't notice. They can be things you've done recently or things you did years ago.

Answer the following question for each accomplishment:

1. What skills or knowledge did you use?
2. What personal traits did you exhibit?

3. What about this accomplishment makes it personally satisfying to you?

As Your Instructor Directs,

a. Share your answers with a small group of other students.

b. Summarize your answers in a memo to your instructor.

c. Present your answers orally to the class.

18.2 Remembering What You've Done

Use the following list to jog your memory about what you've done. For each, give three or four details as well as a general statement.

Describe a time when you

1. Used facts and figures to gain agreement on an important point.

2. Identified a problem that a group or organization faced and developed a plan for solving the problem.

3. Made a presentation or a speech to a group.

4. Won the goodwill of people whose continued support was necessary for the success of some long-term project or activity.

5. Interested other people in something that was important to you and persuaded them to take the actions you wanted.
6. Helped a group deal constructively with conflict.
7. Demonstrated creativity.

As Your Instructor Directs,

a. Identify which job(s) each detail is relevant for.
b. Identify which details would work well on a résumé.
c. Identify which details, further developed, would work well in a job letter.

18.3   Developing Action Statements

Use 10 of the verbs from Figure 18.2 to write action statements describing what you've done in paid or vol- unteer work, in classes, in extracurricular activities, or in community service.

18.4   Evaluating Career Objective Statements

None of the following career objective statements is ef- fective. What is wrong with each statement as it stands? Which statements could be revised to be satisfactory? Which should be dropped?

1. To use my acquired knowledge of accounting to eventually own my own business.
2. A progressively responsible position as a MARKETING MANAGER where education and ability would have valuable application and lead to advancement.

3. To work with people responsibly and creatively, helping them develop personal and professional skills.
4. A position in international marketing which makes use of my specialization in marketing and my knowledge of foreign markets.
5. To bring Faith, Hope, and Charity to the American workplace.
6. To succeed in sales.
7. To design and maintain Web pages.

18.5   Deciding How Much Detail to Use

In each of the following situations, how detailed should the applicant be? Why?

1. Ron Oliver has been steadily employed for the last six years while getting his college degree, but the jobs have been low-level ones, whose prime benefit was that they paid well and fit around his class schedule.
2. Adrienne Barcus was an assistant department manager at a clothing boutique. As assistant manager, she was authorized to approve checks in the absence of the manager. Her other duties were ringing up sales, cleaning the area, and helping mark items for sales.

3. Lois Heilman has been a clerk-typist in the Alumni Office. As part of her job, she developed a schedule for mailings to alumni, set up a merge system, and wrote two of the letters that go out to alumni. The merge system she set up has cut in half the time needed to produce letters.
4. As a co-op student, Stanley Greene spends every other term in a paid job. He now has six semesters of job experience in television broadcasting. During his last co-op he was the assistant producer for a daily "morning magazine" show.

Résumé Assignments

For problems 18.6 through 18.8, write the kind of ré- sumé (chronological, skills, a combination, or a new cre- ation) that best represents your qualifications.

18.6   Writing a Web Résumé

Create a set of Web pages to present your qualifications to an employer. Provide links to course projects and other documents that support your claims.

18.7   Writing a Paper Résumé

Write a résumé on paper that you could mail to an employer or hand to an interviewer at an interview.

As Your Instructor Directs,

a. Write a résumé for the field in which you hope to find a job.

b. Write two different résumés for two different job paths you are interested in pursuing.

c. Adapt your résumé to a specific company you hope to work for.

18.8   Writing a Scannable Résumé

Take the résumé you like best from problem 18.7, and create a scannable version of it.

19

Job Application Letters

How Job Letters Differ from Résumés

How to Find Out about Employers and Jobs
- Using the Internet in Your Job Search
- Information Interviews
- Tapping into the Hidden Job Market

Content and Organization for Job Application Letters
- How to Organize Solicited Letters
- How to Organize Prospecting Letters
- First Paragraphs of Solicited Letters
- First Paragraphs of Prospecting Letters
- Showing a Knowledge of the Position and the Company
- Showing What Separates You from Other Applicants
- The Last Paragraph

E-Mail Application Letters

Creating a Professional Image
- Writing Style
- Positive Emphasis
- You-Attitude
- Paragraph Length and Unity
- Length

Summary of Key Points

Job Application Letters

Teresa Moburg

Midwest Area Assurance Recruiting Manager
KPMG Peat Marwick LLP

www.us.kpmg.com

Teresa Moburg recruits for all lines of business for KPMG Peat Marwick in 11 states. As one of the Big Five professional services firms, KPMG Peat Marwick LLP specializes in consulting, assurance and tax services, and process management in five lines of business.

You can find information about organizations and career opportunities on Web sites, in career libraries at colleges and universities, and sometimes directly from the organization, especially from the human resources office at the main location. Web sites are a wonderful source of quick and timely information. KPMG's Web site includes information about the firm, job postings, training opportunities, benefits, and key clients just to name a few.

> *For each of the position qualifications, show how your experience and skills meet the employer's needs.*

To create a good application letter, apply for a specific position. Include where you learned of the position (Internet, advertisement, a current employee of the firm). For each of the position qualifications, show how your experience and skills meet the employer's needs. **Include specific but concise examples of your experience and skills that qualify you for the position.** In this era of team building, a good personality fit is important. Learn about the culture of the organization (the Web site can help) and adapt your writing style and content to the organization's style. Do not try to fit where you're not comfortable, though. It is always best to err on the conservative side if you are uncertain.

Send the letter to a specific person—and know the person's name and the correct title and spelling! Proofread your letter carefully, especially if you use a computer to adapt a basic letter to several different companies. I've received letters addressed to me with the content of the letter still bearing a competitor's name.

Remember, recruiters are very busy and see hundreds of applications a week. The easier you make it for them to identify you as a qualified candidate, the greater your chances of being contacted. By adapting the letter to the company, you're showing your knowledge of the business and how you could contribute to its continued success.

This first impression is critical in determining if you make it to the next step. Good luck!

T he purpose of a job application letter is to get an interview. If you get a job through interviews arranged by your campus placement office or through contacts, you may not need to write a letter. However, if you want to work for an organization that isn't interviewing on campus, or later when you change jobs, you will. Writing a letter is also a good preparation for a job interview, since the letter is your first step in showing a specific company what you can do for it.

How Job Letters Differ from Résumés

The job application letter accompanies your résumé. Although the two documents overlap slightly, they differ in several ways:

- A résumé is adapted to a position. As Teresa Moburg notes, the letter is adapted to the needs of a particular organization.
- The résumé summarizes all your qualifications. The letter shows how your qualifications can help the organization meet its needs, how you differ from other applicants, and that you have some knowledge of the organization.
- The résumé uses short, parallel phrases (✖ p. 104) and sentence fragments. The letter uses complete sentences in well-written paragraphs.

How to Find Out about Employers and Jobs

To adapt your letter to a specific organization, you need information both about the employer and about the job itself. You'll need to know

- **The name and address of the person who should receive the letter.** To get this information, check the ad, call the organization, check its Web site, or consult the directories listed in Figure 19.1. An advantage of calling is that you can find out what courtesy title (✖ p. 46) a woman prefers and get current information. A directory that went to press months ago will not include recent promotions.
- **What the organization does, and at least four or five facts about it.** Knowing the organization's larger goals enables you to show how your specific work will help the company meet its goals. Useful facts can include market share, new products or promotions, the kind of computer or manu-

Figure 19.1

Where to Get Addresses and Facts about Companies

General Directories	Specialized Directories and Resource Books
Directory of Corporate Affiliations	*Accounting Firms and Practitioners*
Dun's *Million Dollar Directory*	*California Manufacturers Register*
Standard & Poor's Register of Corporations, Directors, and Executives	*Directory of American Firms Operating in Foreign Countries*
Thomas Register of American Manufacturers	*Directory of Hotel and Motel Systems*
	Directory of Management Consultants
	Directory of New England Manufacturers
	Franchise Annual: Handbook and Directory
	O'Dwyer's Directory of Public Relations Firms
	The Rand McNally Banker's Directory
	Thomas Grocery Register
	Standard Directory of Advertisers ("Red Book")
	Who's Who in Direct Marketing Creative Services
	Television Factbook

facturing equipment it uses, plans for growth or downsizing, competitive position, challenges the organization faces, the corporate culture (✖ p. 62), and so forth.

The directories listed in Figure 19.1 provide information ranging from net worth, market share, and principal products to the names of officers and directors. To get specific financial data (and to see how the organization presents itself to the public), get the company's annual report from your library, the Web, or the company itself. (Note: Only companies whose stock is publicly traded are required to issue annual reports. In this day of mergers and buyouts, many companies are owned by other companies. The parent company may be the only one to issue an annual report.) Recruiting notebooks at your campus placement office may provide information about training programs and career paths for new hires. To learn about new products, plans for growth, or solutions to industry challenges, read business newspapers such as *The Wall Street Journal* or *The Financial Post,* business magazines such as *Fortune, Business Week, Forbes,* and trade journals. Each of these has indexes listing which companies are discussed in a specific issue. A few of the trade journals available are listed in Figure 19.2.

• **What the job itself involves.** Campus placement offices and Web listings often have fuller job descriptions than appear in ads. Talk to friends who have graduated recently to learn what their jobs involve. Conduct information interviews to learn more about opportunities that interest you.

Using the Internet in Your Job Search

Every candidate should check the Internet as part of a job search. As Figure 19.3 shows, many job listings are on the Web. You can click directly to many of these links on the BAC Web page. The Riley Guide and KMPG Campus, listed in Figure 19.3, provide good advice and links to many job-related Web pages.

Even better, the Web can be a fast way to learn about the company you hope to join.

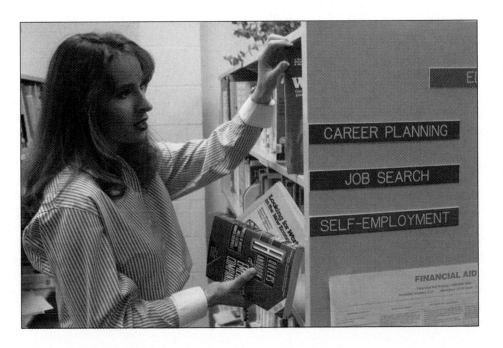

Your campus career center can provide job listings and information about companies, register you for campus interviews, and send your résumé to employers who aren't interviewing on campus. Many career centers offer services to alumni as well as to graduating students, so check the center when you're ready for advancement.

Figure 19.2

Examples of Trade Journals

Advertising Age	Direct Marketing	The Practical Accountant
American Banker	Discount Store News	Sales and Marketing Management
Automotive News	Electric Power Monthly	Software Canada
Aviation Week	Financial Analysts Journal	Television/Radio Age
Beverage Industry	Graphic Arts Monthly	Today's Realtor
Benefits Canada	HR Focus	Training & Development
Cable Communication Magazine	Internal Auditor	Travel Agent
CA Magazine	International Advertiser	Women's Wear Daily
Canadian Business	Logging and Sawmilling Journal	Variety
CPA Practitioner	Nation's Restaurant News	

Check professional listservs and electronic bulletin boards. Employers sometimes post specialized jobs on them, and they're always a good way to get information about the industry you hope to enter.

Information Interviews

In an **information interview** you talk to someone who works in the area you hope to enter to find out what the day-to-day work involves and how you can best prepare to enter that field. An information interview can let you know whether or not you'd like the job, give you specific information that you can use to present yourself effectively in your résumé and application letter, and create a good image of you in the mind of the interviewer. If you present yourself positively, the interviewer may remember you when openings arise.

In an information interview, you might ask the following questions:

- Tell me about the papers on your desk. What are you working on right now?
- How do you spend your typical day?
- Have your duties changed a lot since you first started working here?
- What do you like best about your job? What do you like least?
- What do you think the future holds for this kind of work?
- How did you get this job?
- What courses, activities, or jobs would you recommend to someone who wanted to do this kind of work?

To set up an information interview, you can phone or write a letter like the one in Figure 19.4. If you do write, phone the following week to set up a specific time.

Tapping into the Hidden Job Market

Many jobs are never advertised—and the number rises the higher on the job ladder you go. Over 60% of all new jobs come not from responding to an ad but from networking with personal contacts.[1] Some of these jobs are created especially for a specific person. These unadvertised jobs are called the **hidden job market**. Referral interviews, an organized method of networking, offer the most systematic way to tap into these jobs. **Referral interviews** are interviews you schedule to learn about current job opportunities in your field. Sometimes an interview that starts out as an information interview turns into a referral interview.

The Accidental Job Hunter*

Jennifer Beardsley found her job as Marketing Manager for Starbucks almost by accident. Checking her business school alumni page for news of friends, she found a link to Career Central for MBAs <www.mbacentral.com>. Bored, she typed in her profile one night in about 20 minutes. "I wasn't really looking for a job," she said.

Six weeks later, she got an e-mail asking her if she wanted to send her résumé to Starbucks, where the Web page had found a match. She did, and she got the job.

*Based on "The Accidental Job Seeker," *Fast Company*, August 1998, 198.

Figure 19.3

Career Resources on the Web

Job listings

Career Path Online
www.careerpath.com
Job listings from 71 papers, including the *Boston Globe, Chicago Tribune, Los Angeles Times, New York Times, San Jose Mercury News,* and *Washington Post.*

CareerMosaic
www.careermosaic.com
Searches its own database and Internet newsgroups. Includes jobs in Canada, Europe, and Asia as well as in the United States.

America's Job Bank
www.ajb.dni.us/index.html

CareerMagazine
www.careermag.com

CareerSite
www.careersite.com

CareerWEB
www.cweb.com

Career Resource Center
www.careers.org

Federal Jobs Central
www.fedjobs.com

Job Search Sites on the WWW
www.ups.purdue.edu/Student/jobsites.htm

JobTrak
www.jobtrak.com

Monster Board
www.monster.com

Nonprofit Jobnet
www.philanthropy-journal.org/jobnet/jobs.htm

Ohio State Business Job Finder
www.cob.ohio-state.edu/dept/fin/osujobs.htm

SkillSearch
www.skillsearch.com

World Wide Web Employment Office
www.harbornet.com/biz/office/annex.html

Job-hunting resources

Cost of Living in US Cities
www.z.homefair.com
Lets job applicants see what salaries will actually buy in various cities.

Family-Friendly Employers
www.womenswire.com/work/work.htm

Kitty Locker's Job Hunting Page for BAC
www.mhhe.com/locker
Links to the job sites listed here and more.

KPMG Campus
www.kpmgcampus.com
Walks people through the application process for entry-level jobs at KPMG.

Online Career Center
www.occ.com
One-page profiles of many companies. Not as much information as the company's own home page, but a good starting point. Especially useful for companies that don't yet have their own Web pages.

The Riley Guide: Incorporating the Internet into Your Job Search
www.dbm.com/jobguide/jobsrch.htm
Good information about what to search for and where to look, with links to resources.

Figure 19.4   *Letter Requesting an Information Interview*

72 E. 13th Avenue
Columbus, OH 43210
November 4, 2000

Use the courtesy title the reader prefers.

Mrs. Kam Yuricich
Clary Communications
1372 Grandview Avenue
Suite 230
Columbus, OH 43212

Dear Mrs. Yuricich:

If starting with the request seems too abrupt, work up to it more gradually.

    Could I schedule an information interview with you to learn more about how public relations consultants interact with their clients?

Refer to any previous contact with reader.

    I was very interested in your talk to OSU's PRSSA Chapter last month about the differences between working for a PR firm and being a PR staff person within an organization. Last summer I had the chance to work as an intern at Management Horizons. While many of my assignments were "go-fer" jobs, my supervisor gave me the chance to work on several brochures and to draft two speeches for managers. I enjoyed this variety and would like to learn more about the possibility of working in a PR firm.

Ask about ways to enter the field.

    Perhaps we could also talk about courses that would best prepare me for PR work. I have a year and a half left before I graduate, and I have room for several free electives in my schedule. I'd like to use them as productively as possible.

    I'll call you early next week to set up an appointment. I look forward to your advice as I attempt to find my niche in the workforce.

Mentioning your qualifications and including a sample of your work may help persuade the reader to take time to see you.

Sincerely,

Lee Tan

Lee Tan
555-5932

Even though you shouldn't depend on the reader to call you, it's polite to give your phone number under your name.

Encl.: Marketing Brochure for Riverside Hospitals

    A referral interview should give you information about the opportunities currently available in the town in the area you're interested in, refer you to other people who can tell you about job opportunities, and enable the interviewer to see that you could make a contribution to his or her organization. Therefore, the goal of a referral interview is to put you face-to-face with someone who has the power to hire you: the president of a small company, the division vice president or branch manager of a big company, the director of the local office of a state or federal agency.

    Start by scheduling interviews with people you know who may know something about that field—professors, co-workers, neighbors, friends. Call your alumni office to get the names and phone numbers of alumni who now work where you would like to work. Your purpose in talking to them is (ostensibly) to get advice about improving your résumé and about general job-hunting strategy and (really) to get **referrals** to other people. In fact, go into the interview with the names of people you'd like to talk to. If the interviewee doesn't suggest anyone, say, "Do you think it would be a good idea for me to talk to _____?"

Then, armed with a referral from someone you know, you call Mr. or Ms. Big and say, "So-and-so suggested I talk with you about job-hunting strategy." If the person says, "We aren't hiring," you say, "Oh, I'm not asking *you* for a job. I'd just like some advice from a knowledgeable person about the opportunities in banking [or desktop publishing, or whatever] in this city." If this person doesn't have the power to create a position, you seek more referrals at the end of *this* interview. (You can also polish your résumé, if you get good suggestions.)

Even when you talk to the person who could create a job for you, you *do not ask for a job.* But to give you advice about your résumé, the person has to look at it. When a powerful person focuses on your skills, he or she will naturally think about the problems and needs in that organization. When there's a match between what you can do and what the organization needs, that person has the power to create a position for you.

Some business people are cynical about information and referral interviewing. Prepare as carefully for these interviews as you would for an interview when you know the organization is hiring. Think in advance of good questions; know something about the general field or industry; try to learn at least a little bit about the specific company.

Many Web pages give you all the information you need to write a good job letter. Follow links to "about Intel" to learn about the company's values, work/family programs, and specific job listings. Both the home page and "pressroom" give information about recent achievements. "Investor relations" has financial information.

Be a Successful Job Hunter!*

A study by the Administrative Management Society revealed that successful job hunters were more likely to

- Make lots of contacts; schedule lots of interviews. Increasing the number of contacts and interviews increases the number of job offers.

- Adapt the approach to the individual employer. Many students use the same approach for all potential employers. Adapting the strategy to the employer sets you apart from other applicants and increases the chances of a job offer.

- Take control of the process. Employers prefer motivated, active, aggressive candidates.

- Polish communication and interpersonal skills. These skills are needed both to present your qualifications effectively and to make you competitive for the many jobs that require communicating and working with people in addition to specific technical skills.

- Investigate the hidden job market. Don't rely just on advertised openings. Use the techniques in this chapter to tap into the hidden job market.

*Based on Steven R. Dzubow, "Entering the Job Market," *Journal of College Placement* 45, no. 3 (Spring 1985), 49–50.

Always follow up information and referral interviews with personal thank-you letters. Use specifics to show that you paid attention during the interview, and enclose a copy of your revised résumé.

Content and Organization for Job Application Letters

In your letter, focus on

- Major requirements of the job for which you're applying.
- Points that separate you from other applicants.
- Points that show your knowledge of the organization.
- Qualities that every employer is likely to value: the ability to write and speak effectively, to solve problems, to get along with people.

Two different hiring situations call for two different kinds of application letters. Write a **solicited letter** when you know that the company is hiring: you've seen an ad, you've been advised to apply by a professor or friend, you've read in a trade publication that the company is expanding. This situation is similar to a direct request in persuasion (✖ p. 225): you can indicate immediately that you are applying for the position. Sometimes, however, the advertised positions may not be what you want, or you may want to work for an organization that has not announced openings in your area. Then you write a **prospecting letter.** (The metaphor is drawn from prospecting for gold.) The prospecting letter is like a problem-solving persuasive message (✖ p. 228).

Prospecting letters help you tap into the hidden job market. In some cases, your prospecting letter may arrive at a company that has decided to hire but has not yet announced the job. In other cases, companies create positions to get a good person who is on the market. Even in a hiring freeze, jobs are sometimes created for specific individuals.

In both solicited and prospecting letters you should

- Address the letter to a specific person.
- Indicate the specific position for which you're applying.
- Be specific about your qualifications.
- Show what separates you from other applicants.
- Show a knowledge of the company and the position.
- Refer to your résumé (which you would enclose with the letter).
- Ask for an interview.

The following discussion follows the job letter from beginning to end. The two kinds of letters are discussed separately where they differ and together where they are the same. Letters for internships follow the same patterns: use a solicited letter to apply for an internship that has been advertised and a prospecting letter to create an internship with a company that has not announced one.

How to Organize Solicited Letters

When you know the company is hiring, organize your letter in this way:

1. State that you're applying for the job (phrase the job title as your source phrased it). Tell where you learned about the job (ad, referral, etc.). Include any reference number mentioned in the ad. Briefly show that you have the major qualifications required by the ad: a college degree, professional certification, job experience, and so on. Summarize your other qualifica-

tions briefly in the same order in which you plan to discuss them in the letter. This **summary sentence** or **paragraph** then covers everything you will talk about and serves as an organizing device for your letter.

> I have a good background in standard accounting principles and procedures and a working knowledge of some of the special accounting practices of the oil industry. This working knowledge is based on practical experience in the oil fields: I've pumped, tailed rods, and worked as a roustabout.

> My business experience, experience using DeVilbiss equipment, and communication skills qualify me to be an effective part of the sales staff at DeVilbiss.

> Let me put my creative eye, artistic ability, and experience to work for McLean Design.

2. Develop your major qualifications in detail. Be specific about what you've done; relate your achievements to the work you'd be doing in this new job. Remember that readers know only what you tell them. This is not the place for modesty!
3. Develop your other qualifications, even if the ad doesn't ask for them. (If the ad asks for a lot of qualifications, pick the most important three or four.) Show what separates you from the other applicants who will also answer the ad. Demonstrate your knowledge of the organization.
4. Ask for an interview; tell when you'll be available to be interviewed and to begin work. End on a positive, forward-looking note.

Figure 19.5 is an example of a solicited letter. See the BAC Web site for other solicited letters, including one applying for an internship.

How to Organize Prospecting Letters

When you don't have any evidence that the company is hiring, you cannot use the pattern for solicited letters. Instead, organize your letter this way:

1. Catch the reader's interest.
2. Create a **bridge** between the attention-getter and your qualifications. Focus on what you know and can do. Since the employer is not planning to hire, he or she won't be impressed with the fact that you're graduating. Summarize your qualifications briefly in the same order in which you plan to discuss them in the letter. This **summary sentence** or **paragraph** then covers everything you will talk about and serves as an organizing device for your letter.
3. Develop your strong points in detail. Be specific. Relate what you've done in the past to what you could do for this company. Show that you know something about the company. Identify the specific niche you want to fill.
4. Ask for an interview and tell when you'll be available for interviews. (Don't tell when you can begin work.) End on a positive, forward-looking note.

Figure 19.6 shows a prospecting letter.

Creating a Job for Yourself*

David made friends with Lee's receptionist and secretary. Candidates who keep calling and trying to reach potential employers in a pleasant fashion create an obligation on the part of a conscientious support person to determine a time for the hiring manager and candidate to connect by phone. People who leave numerous, pesty voice mail messages, by contrast, seldom get a return call.

When David got a chance to speak to Lee, he said, "I would just like a chance to meet you; I promise I won't take more than 15 minutes." . . . Few hiring managers want to spend more than a few minutes with a borderline "fit." . . . [People] whose résumés don't fit the job profile or posted requirements must ask for a few minutes—not an interview. . . .

David . . . asked about possible areas [in Lee's company] that could be improved or opportunities that Lee's people hadn't had a chance to pursue. Once Lee began thinking about the areas where he needed help, he realized that David did have skills to offer, and he was hired on a contract contingency basis soon after. David's position has since become permanent.

*Quoted from Jackie Larson, "To Get a Job, Be a Pest," *The Wall Street Journal,* April 17, 1995, A12.

F i g u r e 19.5   *A Solicited Letter from a Graduating Senior*

Tracey has had only course work and one part-time job. But by being specific about what she's done in class and on the job, she creates a positive impression.

1072 Adams Street, Apt. 23
Waltham, MA 02254
April 17, 2000

Mr. Robert H. Catanga, Senior Accountant
IBM Corporation
1717 Central
New York, NY 10021

Modified block format is good for letters of application.

Dear Mr. Catanga:

Tell where you learned about the job. If the job has a number, provide it.

I am applying for the Accounting position announced on IBM's Web site (jof17747). I will receive a Bachelor of Science degree in accountancy from Bentley this August and plan to take the CPA exam in December.

In paragraph 1, show you have the qualifications the ad lists.

These terms come from the job listing.

My courses in the accountancy curriculum at Bentley have given me not only the necessary theoretical background but also extensive practical experience in General Ledgers, Accounts Payable, and Travel Expenses. I have worked many cases and problems using computer data, including preparing simulated accounting records for hypothetical firms.

Many courses provide practice with simulated cases—you may be able to use Tracey's strategy, too.

Referring to her Web page suggests her technological savvy.

These true-to-life cases gave me the opportunity to interpret all sorts of data in order to prepare accurate financial statements. For instance, I've learned the best measures for fixed assets and property controls, how to figure inter/intra-company and travel expenses, and the best methods of matching revenues with expenditures. These I could then analyze and compare to past statements to identify trends and recommend ways that costs could be reduced so that the business could be run even more efficiently.

The ad asked for experience with spreadsheets and computer graphics.

Courses in speech communication and business writing have taught me how to communicate with various business audiences. This means that I would be able to provide reports, financial statements, and visuals to show how accounting information is related to management needs. I can use Excel and create computer graphics to provide the reliable accounting data that IBM needs to continue growing each year. Visit my Web page (www.bentley/business/students/mckenna/report.htm) to see the report I wrote on choosing the best method to accelerate depreciation.

Relates what she has done to what she could do for the company.

Phrase from the CEO's letter in the annual report, which Tracey read on the Web.

My three years of experience working for Allstate Insurance Company have also given me the opportunity to take leadership and show responsibility. Although I was hired merely as a part-time typist, my supervisor frequently asked for my recommendations of ways to get work done more efficiently. In fact, I developed a procedure for making out arbitration reports which saved so much time that I was asked to teach it to the other employees in my department.

She gets a lot of mileage out of her part-time job by being specific.

One way to refer to résumé.

The enclosed résumé summarizes my qualifications. I can come to New York for an interview any Tuesday or Thursday afternoon. I can begin work in September and look forward to discussing with you ways in which I can help IBM carry its tradition of excellence into the new millennium.

Nice allusion to inclusion of IBM in In Search of Excellence.

Sincerely,

Tracey McKenna

Tracey McKenna

Encl.: Résumé

You don't have to note the enclosure, but doing so is a nice touch if you have room at the bottom of the page.

Figure 19.6   *A Prospecting Letter from a Career Changer*

Marcella G. Cope
370 Monahan Lane
Dublin, OH 43016
614-555-1997
mcope@postbox.acs.ohio-state.edu

Marcella creates a "letterhead" that harmonizes with her résumé (see Figure 18.4).

August 23, 1999

Mr. John Harrobin
New Media Solutions
Metatec Corporation
7001 Metatec Boulevard
Dublin, OH 43017

Block format with justified margins lets Marcella get this letter on one page.

Dear Mr. Harrobin:

In a prospecting letter, open with a sentence which (1) will seem interesting and true to the reader and (2) provides a natural bridge to talking about yourself.

One way to refer to the enclosed résumé.

Putting a textbook on a CD-ROM saves paper but does nothing to take advantage of the many possibilities the CD-ROM environment provides. Yet it can be a real challenge to find people who write well, proof carefully, and understand multimedia design. You will see from my enclosed résumé that I have this useful combination of skills.

Shows knowledge of the company.

Rita Haralabidis tells me that Metatec needs people to design and develop high-quality CD-ROM products to meet business and consumer deadlines. Most of the writing and editing that I do is subject to strict standards and even stricter deadlines, and I know information is useful only if it is available when clients need it.

Shows she can meet company needs.

When I toured Metatec this spring, members of the New Media Solutions Group shared some of their work from a series of interactive CD-ROM textbooks they were developing in tandem with Harcourt Brace. This project sparked my interest in Metatec because of my own experience with evaluating, contributing to, and editing college-level textbooks.

Relates what she's done to what she could do for this company.

As a program administrator at The Ohio State University, I examined dozens of textbooks from publishers interested in having their books adopted by the nation's largest First-Year Writing Program. This experience taught me which elements of a textbook--both content and design--were successful, and which failed to generate interest. Often, I worked closely with sales representatives to suggest changes for future editions. My own contributions to two nationally distributed textbooks further familiarized me with production processes and the needs of multiple audiences. My close contact with students convinces me of the need to produce educational materials that excite students, keep their attention, and allow them to learn through words, pictures, and sounds.

All of these terms fit Metatec's production of multi-media educational materials.

My communication and technology skills would enable me to adapt quickly to work with both individual clients and major corporations like CompuServe and The American Medical Association. I am a flexible thinker, a careful editor, a fluent writer, and, most importantly, a quick study. I will call you next week to find a mutually convenient time when we can discuss putting my talents to work for Metatec.

Names specific clients, showing more knowledge of the company.

Sincerely,

Marcella G. Cope

Marcella G. Cope

When you're changing fields, learning quickly is a real plus.

Enclosed: Résumé

Relating What You've Done to the Job*

The letter continued . . .

As I looked into publishing, it occurred to me that of all the things I have done, the one I could most closely relate to the field was, strangely enough, an experience I had as a baby-sitter.

Immediately, he had the editor's full attention. How could baby-sitting fit in with publishing? During the summer of his junior year in college he had taken a job as a sailing instructor, tutor, and companion for the children of a wealthy family. . . . While the parents were on a cruise, the governess suffered a stroke, sending the cook into a tizzy, the maid into tears, and the chauffeur and gardener into the local bar. Only the student could cope, and he took charge and managed the estate for the rest of the summer.

In his letter of application he described the crisis, and subsequent problems he had faced, and told how he had met them. Then he related those experiences to the problems that he had learned editors, advertisers, printers, and others encounter in the publishing industry.

*Quoted from John L. Munschauer, *Jobs for English Majors and Other Smart People* (Princeton, NJ: Peterson's Guides, 1986), 75–76.

First Paragraphs of Solicited Letters

When you know that the firm is hiring, announcing that you are applying for a specific position enables the firm to route your letter to the appropriate person, thus speeding consideration of your application. Identify where you learned about the job: "the position of junior accountant announced in Sunday's *Dispatch*," "William Paquette, our placement director, told me that you are looking for . . ."

Note how the following paragraph picks up several of the characteristics of the ad:

Ad: Business Education Instructor at Shelby Adult Education. Candidate must possess a Bachelor's degree in Business Education. Will be responsible for providing in-house training to business and government leaders. . . . Candidate should have at least six months' office experience. Prior teaching experience not required.

Letter: I am interested in your position in Business Education. I will receive a Bachelor of Science degree from North Carolina A & T University in December. I have two years' experience teaching word processing and computer accounting courses to adults and have developed leadership skills in the North Carolina National Guard.

Good word choices can help set your letter apart from the scores or even hundreds of letters the company is likely to get in response to an ad. The following first paragraph of a letter in response to an ad by Allstate Insurance Company shows a knowledge of the firm's advertising slogan and sets itself apart from the dozens of letters that start with "I would like to apply for . . ."

> The Allstate Insurance Company is famous across the nation for its "Good Hands Policy." I would like to lend a helping hand to many Americans as a financial analyst for Allstate, as advertised in the *Chicago Tribune.* I have a Bachelor of Science degree in Accounting from Iowa State University and I have worked with figures, computers, and people.

Note that the last sentence forecasts the organization of the letter, preparing for paragraphs about the student's academic background and (in this order) experience with "figures, computers, and people."

First Paragraphs of Prospecting Letters

In a prospecting letter, asking for a job in the first paragraph is dangerous: unless the company plans to hire but has not yet announced openings, the reader is likely to throw the letter away. Instead, catch the reader's interest. Then in the second paragraph you can shift the focus to your skills and experience, showing how they can be useful to the employer. Figure 19.6 is an example of a prospecting letter.

Here are some effective first paragraphs and the second paragraphs that provide a transition to the writer's discussion of his or her qualifications:

- First two paragraphs of a letter to the Director of Publications of Standard Oil:

> Americans are so concerned about the preservation of oil reserves that some are even beginning to walk instead of riding. If scarcity of resources makes us use them more carefully, perhaps it would be a good idea to announce that words are in short supply. If people used them more carefully, internal communications specialists like you would have fewer headaches because communications jobs would be done right the first time.

An architecture student's job letter was hand-delivered to the president of the firm he hoped to join. When the box was opened, a cardboard house popped up. The letter started out, "I can design larger buildings, using other materials." Although the firm had not planned to recruit, the student got an interview—and the job.

> I have worked for the last six years improving my communications skills, learning to use words more carefully and effectively. I have taught business communication at a major university, worked for two newspapers, completed a Master's degree in English, and would like to contribute my skills to your internal communications staff.

- First two paragraphs of a letter applying to be a computer programmer for an insurance company:

> Computers alone aren't the answer to demands for higher productivity in the competitive insurance business. Merging a poorly written letter with a database of customers just sends out bad letters more quickly. But you know how hard it is to find people who can both program computers and write well.
>
> My education and training have given me this useful combination. I'd like to put my associate's degree in computer technology and my business experience writing to customers to work in State Farm's service approach to insurance.

- Questions work well only if the answers aren't obvious. One student used the following paragraph in his first draft:

> Do you think that training competent and motivated operating personnel is a serious concern in the nuclear power industry?

If the reader says *yes*, the question will seem dumb. If the reader says *no*, the student has destroyed his common ground. In the next draft, the student revised the first paragraph to read:

> Competent and motivated operating personnel are just as important to the safe and efficient operation of a nuclear power plant as is high-quality equipment.

This paragraph gave him an easy transition into talking about himself as a competent, motivated person.

Showing a Knowledge of the Position and the Company

If you could substitute another inside address and salutation and send out the letter without any further changes, it isn't specific enough. A job application letter is basically a claim that you could do a job. Use your knowledge of the position and the company to choose relevant evidence from what you've done to support your claims that you could help the company. (See Figures 19.5 and 19.6.)

The following paragraphs also use the writer's knowledge of the company.

- A letter to Bendix Home Appliances uses information that the student got from information in the campus placement office about the job duties and market share.

> Coursework in business communication has taught me how to write reports that meet the needs of readers. I can use this knowledge to summarize the trends that show up in the Saturday Night Reports that your dealers submit. . . .
>
> A minor in personnel management plus public-relations study has taught me that trends are manifestations of human motives and human feelings, and not just cold numbers. My attention to this fact will enable me to interpret retailers' reports concretely—to keep that thirty cents of every washing machine dollar clinking into Bendix tills.

- A letter to PricewaterhouseCoopers's Minneapolis office uses information the student learned in a referral interview with a partner in an accounting firm. Because the reader will know that Herr Wollner is a partner in the Berlin office, the student does not need to identify him.

> While I was studying in Berlin last spring, I had the opportunity to discuss accounting methods for multinational clients of PricewaterhouseCoopers with Herr Fritz Wollner. We also talked about communication among PricewaterhouseCoopers's international offices.
>
> Herr Wollner mentioned that the increasing flow of accounting information between the European offices—especially those located in Germany, Switzerland, and Austria—and the US offices of PricewaterhouseCoopers makes accurate translations essential. My fluency in German enables me to translate accurately; and my study of communication problems in Speech Communication, Business and Professional Speaking, and Business and Technical Writing will help me see where messages might be misunderstood and choose words which are more likely to communicate clearly.

- A letter to KMPG uses information the student learned in a summer job.

> As an assistant accountant for Pacific Bell during this past summer, I worked with its computerized billing and record-keeping system, BARK. I had the opportunity to help the controller revise portions of the system, particularly the procedures for handling delinquent accounts. When the KMPG audit team reviewed Pacific Bell's transactions completed for July, I had the opportunity to observe your System 2170. Several courses in computer science allow me to appreciate the simplicity of your system and its objective of reducing audit work, time, and costs.

One or two specific details about the company usually are enough to demonstrate your knowledge. Be sure to use the knowledge, not just repeat it. Never present the information as though it will be news to the reader. After all, the reader works for the company and presumably knows much more about it than you do.

Showing What Separates You from Other Applicants

Your knowledge of the company separates you from other applicants. You can also use coursework, an understanding of the field, and experience in jobs and extracurricular events to show that you're unique. As Teresa Moburg points out, be specific but concise. Usually three to five sentences will enable you to give enough specific supporting details.

- This student uses both coursework and summer jobs to set herself apart from other applicants:

My college courses have taught me the essential accounting skills required to contribute to the growth of Monsanto. Since you recently adopted new accounting methods for fluctuations in foreign currencies, you will need people knowledgeable in foreign currency translation to convert currency exchange rates. In two courses in international accounting, I compiled simulated accounting statements of hypothetical multinational firms in countries experiencing different rates of currency devaluation. Through these classes, I acquired the skills needed to work with the daily fluctuations of exchange rates and at the same time formulate an accurate and favorable representation of Monsanto.

A company as diverse as Monsanto requires extensive record-keeping as well as numerous internal and external communications. Both my summer jobs and my coursework prepare me to do this. As Office Manager for the steamboat *Julia Belle Swain,* I was in charge of most of the bookkeeping and letter writing for the company. I kept accurate records for each workday, and I often entered over 100 transactions in a single day. In business and technical writing I learned how to write persuasive letters and memos and how to present extensive data in reports in a simplified style that is clear and easy to understand.

- This student uses her sorority experience and knowledge of the company to set herself apart from other applicants in a letter applying to be Assistant Personnel Manager of a multinational firm:

As a counselor for sorority rush, I was also able to work behind the scenes as well as with the prospective rushees. I was able to use my leadership and communication skills for group activities for 70 young women by planning numerous activities to make my group a cohesive unit. Helping the women deal with rejection was also part of my job. Not all of the rushees made final cuts, and it was the rush counselor who helped put the rejection into perspective.

This skill could be helpful in speaking to prospective employees wishing to travel to Saudi Arabia. Not all will pass the medical exams or make the visa application deadlines in time, and the Assistant Manager tells these people the news. An even more delicate subject to handle is conveying news of a death of a relative or employee to those concerned. My experience with helping people deal with small losses gives me a foundation to help others deal with more severe losses and deeper grief.

In your résumé, you may list activities, offices, and courses. In your letter, give more detail about what you did and show how that experience will help you contribute to the employer's organization more quickly.

When you discuss your strengths, don't exaggerate. No employer will believe that a new graduate has a "comprehensive" knowledge of a field. Indeed, most employers believe that six months to a year of on-the-job training is necessary before most new hires are really earning their pay. Specifics about what you've done will make your claims about what you can do more believable and ground them in reality.

Getting a Job with an *Inc.* 500 Company*

Paul Moran decided he wanted to work for a small company. So he got the *Inc.* 500 list (the list of the 500 fastest-growing small companies, published each year by *Inc.* magazine). He sent letters to all 17 companies in the Los Angeles area, offering to work for free. "I am confident that any financial rewards will come later."

He included a reply coupon, asking employers to fill in a "preliminary job description" and check one of two boxes:

☐ Yes, we are interested in interviewing you for an UNPAID POSITION.

☐ Sorry, we are not interested in having you work for us WITHOUT PAY.

The coupon noted that Moran would call three finalists to set up interviews.

Paul Moran got a job with Collectech Systems. He's now regional president, and the firm is still on the *Inc.* 500 list.

*Based on George Gendron, "FYI," *Inc.*, October 1995, 13.

The Last Paragraph

In the last paragraph, indicate when you'd be available for an interview. If you're free any time, you can say so. But it's likely that you have responsibilities in class and work. If you'd have to go out of town, there may be only certain days of the week or certain weeks that you could leave town for several days. Use a sentence that fits your situation.

> I could come to Albany for an interview any Wednesday or Friday.

> I'll be attending the Oregon Forestry Association's November meeting and will be available for interviews there.

> I could come to Memphis for an interview March 17–21.

Should you wait for the employer to call you, or should you call the employer to request an interview? In a solicited letter, it's safe to wait to be contacted: you know the employer wants to hire someone, and if your letter and résumé show that you're one of the top applicants, you'll get an interview. In a prospecting letter, call the employer. Because the employer is not planning to hire, you'll get a higher percentage of interviews if you're aggressive.

If you're writing a prospecting letter to a firm that's more than a few hours away by car, say that you'll be in the area the week of such-and-such and could stop by for an interview. Companies pay for follow-up visits, but not for first interviews. A company may be reluctant to ask you to make an expensive trip when it isn't yet sure it wants to hire you.

End the letter on a positive note that suggests you look forward to the interview and that you see yourself as a person who has something to contribute, not as someone who just needs a job.

> I look forward to discussing with you ways in which I could contribute to The Limited's continued growth.

E-Mail Application Letters

Some Web ads give you a street address to submit applications but say "e-mail preferred." Other ads just give an e-mail address.

No research exists on whether e-mail application letters should be shorter than paper ones. Until we know which works better, you have two choices: paste a traditional letter into your e-mail screen, or edit your letter to create a shorter, one-screen letter (see Figure 19.7).

When you submit an e-mail letter with an attached résumé,

- Tell what word-processing program your scannable résumé is saved in.
- Put the job number or title for which you're applying in your subject line and in the first paragraph.

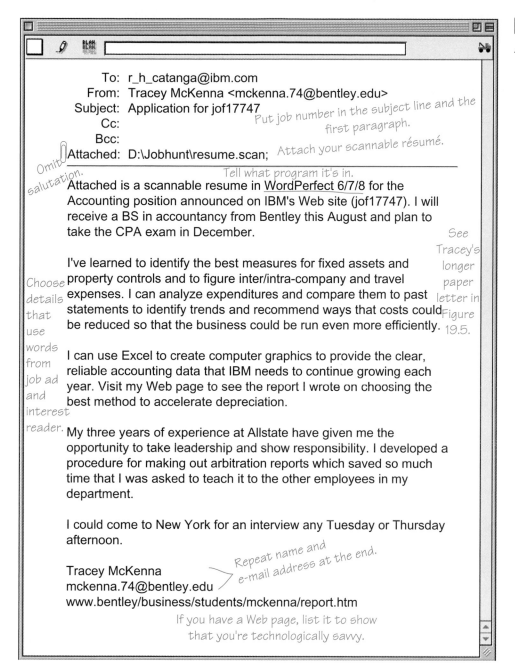

F i g u r e 19.7

An E-Mail Application Letter

- Prepare your letter in a word-processing program with a spell checker to make it easier to edit and proof the document.
- Don't send anything in all capital letters.
- Don't use smiley faces or other emoticons.
- Put your name and e-mail address at the end of the message. Most e-mail programs send along the "sender" information at the top of the screen, but a few don't, and you want the employer to know whose letter this is!

Creating a Professional Image

Every employer wants businesslike employees who understand professionalism. To make your application letter professional,

Getting a Job Overseas*

The Council on International Educational Exchange in New York City can provide information about work permits in Europe. Call 212-822-2600.

Useful books include

- *Directory of Jobs and Careers Abroad* (Peterson's Guides).

- *How to Get a Job in Europe* (Surrey Books).

- *How to Get a Job in the Pacific Rim* (Surrey Books).

*Based on "Ask Annie," *Fortune*, December 9, 1996, 221.

- Create your letter on a computer. Use a standard font (Times Roman, Palatino, or Helvetica) in 11- or 12-point type.
- Address your letter to a specific person. If the reader is a woman, call the office to find out what courtesy title she prefers.
- Don't mention relatives' names. It's OK to use names of other people if the reader knows those people and thinks well of them, if they think well of you and will say good things about you, and if you have permission to use their names.
- Omit personal information not related to the job.
- Unless you're applying for a creative job in advertising, use a conservative style: few contractions, no sentence fragments, clichés, or slang.
- Edit the letter carefully and proof it several times to make sure it's perfect. Errors suggest that you're careless or inept.

Writing Style

Use a smooth, tight writing style (p. 100). Use the technical jargon of the field, but avoid businessese and stuffy words like *utilize, commence,* and *transpire* (for *happen*).

Use a lively, energetic style that makes you sound like a real person.

Avoid words that can be interpreted sexually. A model letter distributed by the placement office at a midwestern university included the following sentence:

> I have been active in campus activities and have enjoyed good relations with my classmates and professors.

One young woman incorporated this sentence in a letter she mailed. The recipient circled the sentence and then passed the letter around the office (and did not invite the woman for an interview). That's not the kind of attention you want your letter to get!

Positive Emphasis

Be positive. Don't plead ("Please give me a chance") or apologize ("I cannot promise that I am substantially different from the lot"). Most negatives should be omitted in the letter.

Avoid word choices with negative connotations (p. 95). Note how the following revisions make the writer sound more confident.

> Negative: I have learned an excessive amount about writing through courses in journalism and advertising.
>
> Positive: Courses in journalism and advertising have taught me to recognize and to write good copy. My profile of a professor was published in the campus newspaper; I earned an "A+" on my direct mail campaign for the American Dental Association to persuade young adults to see their dentist more often.

Excessive suggests that you think the courses covered too much—hardly an opinion likely to endear you to an employer.

> Negative: You can check with my references to verify what I've said.
>
> Positive: Professor Hill can give you more information about the program in Industrial Distribution Management.

Verify suggests that you expect the employer to distrust what you've said.

> Negative: I am anxious to talk with you about the opportunities for employment with Arthur Andersen.
>
> Positive: I look forward to talking with you about opportunities at Arthur Andersen.

Anxious suggests that you're worried about the interview.

You-Attitude

Unsupported claims may sound overconfident, selfish, or arrogant. Create you-attitude (✖ p. 34) by describing exactly what you have done and by showing how that relates to what you could do for this employer.

Lacks you-attitude:	An inventive and improvising individual like me is a necessity in your business.
You-attitude:	Building a summer house-painting business gave me the opportunity to find creative solutions to challenges. At the end of the first summer, for example, I had nearly 10 gallons of exterior latex left, but no more jobs. I contacted the home economics teacher at my high school. She agreed to give course credit to students who were willing to give up two Saturdays to paint a house being renovated by Habitat for Humanity. I donated the paint and supervised the students. I got a charitable deduction for the paint and hired the three best students to work for me the following summer. I could put these skills in problem solving and supervising to work as a personnel manager for Burroughs.
Lacks you-attitude:	A company of your standing could offer the challenging and demanding kind of position in which my abilities could flourish.
You-attitude:	Omit.
Lacks you-attitude:	I want a job with your company.
You-attitude:	I would like to apply for Procter & Gamble's management trainee program.

Remember that the word *you* refers to your reader. Using *you* when you really mean yourself or "all people" can insult your reader by implying that he or she still has a lot to learn about business:

Lacks you-attitude:	Running my own business taught me that you need to learn to manage your time.
You-attitude:	Running my own business taught me to manage my time.

Since you're talking about yourself, you'll use *I* in your letter. Reduce the number of *I*'s by revising some sentences to use *me* or *my*.

Under my presidency, the Agronomy Club . . .

Courses in media and advertising management gave me a chance to . . .

My responsibilities as a summer intern included . . .

In particular, avoid beginning every paragraph with *I*. Begin sentences with prepositional phrases or introductory clauses:

As my résumé shows, I . . .

In my coursework in media and advertising management, I . . .

As a summer intern, I . . .

Paragraph Length and Unity

Keep your first and last paragraphs fairly short—preferably no more than four or five typed lines. Vary paragraph length within the letter; it's OK to have one long paragraph, but don't use a series of eight-line paragraphs.

When you have a long paragraph, check to be sure that it covers only one subject. If it covers two or more subjects, divide it into two or more paragraphs. If a short paragraph covers several subjects, consider adding a topic sentence (✖ p. 105) to provide paragraph unity.

Length

Always use at least a full page. A short letter throws away an opportunity to be persuasive; it may also suggest that you have little to say for yourself or that you aren't very interested in the job.

Application Bloopers*

The following sentences came from separate application letters.

- Thank you for accepting me recent phone call.

- My position has been recently has been eliminated.

- I am seeking a position on the Eat Coast.

- Attached is a one-page summery.

- Please disregard my attached resume as it is woefully out of date.

- My talent is at an inordinately high level and my ability to maintain accurate figures and meet deadlines is unspeakable.

- In closing, let me outline the previous bookkeeping experience I've been able to endure.

- Thank you for your consideration. Hope to hear from you shorty.

- P.S. If you hire me away from this nightmare, you'll also save me thousands in therapy.

*Sentences quoted from Tom Burke, "How Do You Spell Quality?" *The Wall Street Journal*, April 8, 1996, A18; and Robert Half's Resumania, quoted in Taunee Besson, *Cover Letters: Proven Techniques for Writing Letters That Will Help You Get the Job You Want* (New York: John Wiley and Sons, 1995), 96–97, and in Rochelle Sharp, "Labor Letter," *The Wall Street Journal*, March 22, 1994, A1, and "Work Week," *The Wall Street Journal*, February 27, 1996, A1.

Separating Yourself from Other Applicants*

The following will help set you apart from other applicants:

- Computer literacy. Be able to use word processing programs, spreadsheets, and databases. Graphics and page layout programs are a plus.

- Foreign languages and international experience. Be able to speak at least one language other than English fluently. If funds permit, travel or study abroad. Cultivate the international students on your campus to gain experience interacting with people from other cultures.

- Experience. Put your knowledge and skills to work in internships, volunteer work, and campus or community activities. Take a part-time or full-time job that's related to your field—both to earn money for college and to get experience to land a job after graduation.

- The ability to sell yourself. Know about the product (you) and the customer (the employer).

*Based on Joan E. Rigdon, "Glut of Graduates Lets Recruiters Pick Only the Best," *The Wall Street Journal*, May 20, 1993, B1.

Without eliminating content, tighten each sentence (✖ p. 100) to be sure that you're using space as efficiently as possible. If your letter is still a bit over a page, use slightly smaller margins, a type size that's one point smaller, or justified proportional type to get more on the page.

However, if you need more than a page, use it—as long as you have at least 6–12 lines of body text on the second page. The extra space gives you room to be more specific about what you've done and to add details about your experience that will separate you from other applicants. Employers don't *want* longer letters, but they will read them *if* the letter is well written and *if* the applicant establishes early in the letter that he or she has the credentials the company needs.

Summary of Key Points

- Résumés differ from letters of application in the following ways:
  - A résumé is adapted to a position. The letter is adapted to the needs of a particular organization.
  - The résumé summarizes all your qualifications. The letter shows how your qualifications can help the organization meet its needs, how you differ from other applicants, and that you have some knowledge of the organization.
  - The résumé uses short, parallel phrases and sentence fragments. The letter uses complete sentences in well-written paragraphs.
- Use directories, annual reports, recruiting literature, business periodicals, trade journals, and the Web to get information about employers and jobs to use in your letter.
- Information and referral interviews can help you tap into the **hidden job market**—jobs that are not advertised. In an **information interview** you find out what the day-to-day work involves and how you can best prepare to enter that field. **Referral interviews** are interviews you schedule to learn about current job opportunities in your field.
- When you know that a company is hiring, send a **solicited job letter.** When you want a job with a company that has not announced openings, send a **prospecting job letter.** In both letters, you should
  - Address the letter to a specific person.
  - Indicate the specific position for which you're applying.
  - Be specific about your qualifications.
  - Show what separates you from other applicants.
  - Show a knowledge of the company and the position.
  - Refer to your résumé (which you would enclose with the letter).
  - Ask for an interview.
- Organize a solicited letter in this way:
  1. State that you're applying for the job and tell where you learned about the job (ad, referral, etc.). Briefly show that you have the major qualifications required by the ad. Summarize your qualifications in the order in which you plan to discuss them in the letter.
  2. Develop your major qualifications in detail.
  3. Develop your other qualifications. Show what separates you from the other applicants who will also answer the ad. Demonstrate your knowledge of the organization.
  4. Ask for an interview; tell when you'll be available to be interviewed and to begin work. End on a positive, forward-looking note.

- Organize a prospecting letter in this way:
  1. Catch the reader's interest.
  2. Create a bridge between the attention-getter and your qualifications. Summarize your qualifications in the order in which you plan to discuss them in the letter.
  3. Develop your strong points in detail. Relate what you've done in the past to what you could do for this company. Show that you know something about the company. Identify the specific niche you want to fill.
  4. Ask for an interview and tell when you'll be available for interviews. End on a positive, forward-looking note.
- Use your knowledge of the company, your coursework, your understanding of the field, and your experience in jobs and extracurricular activities to show that you're unique.
- Don't repeat information that the reader already knows; don't seem to be lecturing the reader on his or her business.
- Never use relatives' names in a job letter. Using names of other people is OK if the reader knows those people and thinks well of them, if they think well of you and will say good things about you, and if you have permission to use their names.
- Use positive emphasis to sound confident. Use you-attitude by supporting general claims with specific examples and by relating what you've done to what the employer needs.
- Use at least a full page. It's desirable to limit your letter to one page, but use up to two pages if you need them to showcase all your credentials.

Exercises and Problems

Getting Started

19.1   Analyzing First Paragraphs of Prospecting Letters

All of the following are first paragraphs in prospecting letters written by new college graduates. Evaluate the paragraphs on these criteria:

- Is the paragraph likely to interest the reader and motivate him or her to read the rest of the letter?
- Does the paragraph have some content that the student can use to create a transition to talking about his or her qualifications?
- Does the paragraph avoid asking for a job?

1. For the past two and one-half years I have been studying turf management. On August 1, I will graduate from _____ University with a BA in Ornamental Horticulture. The type of job I will seek will deal with golf course maintenance as an assistant superintendent.

2. Ann Gibbs suggested that I contact you.

3. Each year, the Christmas shopping rush makes more work for everyone at Nordstrom's, especially for the Credit Department. While working for Nordstrom's Credit Department for three Christmas and summer vacations, the Christmas sales increase is just one of the credit situations I became aware of.

4. Whether to plate a two-inch eyebolt with cadmium for a tough, brilliant shine or with zinc for a rust-resistant, less expensive finish is a tough question. But similar questions must be answered daily by your salespeople. With my experience in the electro-plating industry, I can contribute greatly to your constant need of getting customers.

5. What a set of tractors! The new 9430 and 9630 diesels are just what is needed by today's farmer with his ever-increasing acreage. John Deere has truly done it again.

6. Prudential Insurance Company did much to help my college career as the sponsor of my National Merit Scholarship. Now I think I can give something back to Prudential. I'd like to put my education, including a B.S. degree in finance from _____ University, to work in your investment department.

7. Since the beginning of Delta Electric Construction Co. in 1993, the size and profits have grown steadily. My father, being a stockholder and vice president, often discusses company dealings with me. Although the company has prospered, I understand there have been a few problems of mismanagement. I feel with my present and future qualifications, I could help ease these problems.

19.2   Improving You-Attitude and Positive Emphasis in Job Letters

Revise each of these sentences to improve you-attitude and positive emphasis. You may need to add information.

1. I understand that your company has had problems due to the mistranslation of documents during international ad campaigns.

2. Included in my résumé are the courses in Finance that earned me a fairly attractive grade average.

3. I am looking for a position that gives me a chance to advance quickly.

4. Although short on experience, I am long on effort and enthusiasm.

5. I have been with the company from its beginning to its present unfortunate state of bankruptcy.

19.3   Evaluating Rough Drafts

Evaluate the following drafts. What parts should be omitted? What needs to be changed or added? What parts would benefit from specific supporting details?

1.
> Dear _____:
>
> There is more to a buyer's job than buying the merchandise. And a clothing buyer in particular has much to consider.
>
> Even though something may be in style, customers may not want to buy it. Buyers should therefore be aware of what customers want and how much they are willing to pay.
>
> In the buying field, request letters, thank-you letters, and persuasive letters are frequently written.
>
> My interest in the retail field inspired me to read The Gap's annual report. I saw that a new store is being built. An interview would give us a chance to discuss how I could contribute to this new store. Please call me to schedule an interview.
>
> Sincerely,

2.
> Dear Sir or Madam:
>
> I am taking the direct approach of a personnel letter. I believe you will under stand my true value in the areas of practical knowledge and promotional capabilities.
>
> I am interested in a staff position with Darden in relation to trying to improve the operations and moral of the Olive Garden Restaurants, which I think that I am capable of doing. Please take a minute not to read my résumé (enclosed) and call to schedule an interview.
>
> Sincerely,

3.
> Dear _____:
>
> I would like to apply for the opening you announced for an Assistant Golf Course Superintendent. I have the qualifications you are asking for.
>
> Every year the Superintendent must go before the greens committee to defend its budget requests. To prepare myself to do this, I took courses in accounting, business and administrative writing, and speech.
>
> I have done the operations necessary to maintain the greens properly.
>
> I look forward to talking with you about this position.
>
> Sincerely,

19.4 Gathering Information about an Industry

Use six recent issues of a trade journal to report on three to five trends, developments, or issues that are important in an industry.

As Your Instructor Directs,

a. Share your findings with a small group of other students.

b. Summarize your findings in a memo to your instructor.

c. Present your findings to the class.

d. Join with a small group of other students to write a report summarizing the results of this research.

19.5   Gathering Information about a Specific Organization

Gather information about a specific organization, using several of the following methods:

- Check the organization's Web site.
- Read the company's annual report.
- Pick up relevant information at the Chamber of Commerce.
- Read articles in trade publications and *The Wall Street Journal* or *The Financial Post* that mention the organization (check the indexes).
- Get the names and addresses of its officers from a directory or the Web.
- Read recruiting literature provided by the company.

As Your Instructor Directs,

a. Share your findings with a small group of other students.
b. Summarize your findings in a memo to your instructor.
c. Present your findings orally to the class.
d. Write a paragraph for a job letter using (directly or indirectly) the information you found.

19.6   Conducting an Information Interview

Interview someone working in a field you're interested in. Use the questions listed on page 540 or the shorter list here:

- How did you get started in this field?
- What do you like about your job?
- What do you dislike about your job?
- Can you give me names of three other people who could also give me information about this job?

As Your Instructor Directs,

a. Share the results of your interview with a small group of other students.
b. Write up your interview in a memo to your instructor.
c. Present the results of your interview orally to the class.
d. Write to the interviewee thanking him or her for taking the time to talk to you.

E-Mail Messages

19.7   Networking

Write to a friend who is already in the workforce, asking about one or more of the following topics:

- Are any jobs in your field available in your friend's organization? If so, what?
- If a job is available, can your friend provide information beyond the job listing that will help you write a more detailed, persuasive letter? (Specify the kind of information you'd like to have.)
- Can your friend suggest people in other organizations who might be useful to you in your job search? (Specify any organizations in which you're especially interested.)

19.8   Applying Electronically

Write a one-screen application letter to accompany a résumé that you submit electronically.

Communicating at Work

As Your Instructor Directs in problems 19.9 and 19.10,

a. Create a document or presentation to achieve the goal.

b. Write a memo to your instructor describing the situation at your workplace and explaining your rhetorical choices (medium, strategy, tone, wording, graphics or document design, and so forth).

19.9   Applying for an Open Position

Many companies post open positions. Apply for one that interests you.

19.10   Creating a Position for Yourself

Identify a need that your employer has, and propose that you be hired (or promoted) to a full-time position working in this area.

Letter Assignments

19.11   Writing a Solicited Letter

Write a letter of application in response to an announced opening for a full-time job (not an internship) which a new college graduate could hold.

Turn in a copy of the listing. If you use option (a), (b), or (d) below, your listing will be a copy. If you choose option (c), you will write the listing and can design your ideal job.

a. Respond to an ad in a newspaper, a professional journal, in the placement office, or on the Web. Use an ad that specifies the company, not a blind ad. Be sure that you are fully qualified for the job.

b. Take a job description and assume that it represents a current opening. Use a directory to get the name of the person to whom the letter should be addressed.

c. If you have already worked somewhere, you may assume that your employer is asking you to apply for full-time work after graduation. Be sure to write a fully persuasive letter.

d. Respond to one of the listings below. Use a directory to get the name and address of the person to whom you should write.

1. Enterprise Rent-A-Car has an immediate opening for an entry-level **staff accountant.** Responsibilities will include but are not limited to A/P, A/R, Bank Recs and journal entries. To qualify you must possess a four-year accounting degree, strong written and oral skills, and a strong desire to succeed.

2. A member of Congress in your state wants an **office manager** for a local office in your state and a **staff member** for the Washington, DC, office. The office manager will answer constituent questions, write press releases, assist with travel appearances, record contributions, and recruit and supervise volunteer staff. Good oral and interpersonal skills a must; political and financial skills helpful. The staff member in Washington will answer mail, help with political research, and draft bills and reports. Good writing and research skills a must; interpersonal skills and political savvy helpful.

3. Arthur Andersen seeks **international human resources trainees** to interact with corporate human resources, payroll, relocation and accounting functions, and the expatriate. Bachelor's degree in an international field a plus. Personal expatriate experience preferred but not required. Must have computer skills. Please refer to job number MMGE-3W7LAY in your correspondence.

4. Roxy Systems (Roxy.com) seeks **Internet Marketing Coordinators** to analyze online campaigns and put together detailed reports, covering ad impressions and click-through rates. Must have basic understanding of marketing; be organized, creative, and detail-oriented; know Microsoft Excel; have excellent communication skills; and be familiar with the Internet. Send letter and resume to mike@roxy.com.

5. Bose Corporation seeks **public relations/communications administrative associate** (Job Code 117BD). Write, edit, and produce the in-house newsletter using desktop publishing software. Represent the company to external contacts (including the press). Provide administrative support to the manager of PR by scheduling meetings, preparing presentations, tabulating and analyzing surveys, and processing financial requests. Excellent organizational, interpersonal, and communication skills (both written and oral) required. Must be proficient in MS Office and Filemaker Pro.

6. The Limited is hiring **executive development program trainees.** After completing 10-week training programs, trainees will become assistant buyers. Prefer people with strong interest and experience in retailing. Apply directly to the store for which you want to work.

7. Winterland, a leading supplier of screen-printed apparel, seeks an **Assistant Account Manager** (HR/AAM) to oversee day-to-day execution and service of client needs. The successful candidate will possess an extremely high degree of attention to detail and problem-solving abilities. Superior communication and interpersonal skills required. Proficiency with both MS Word and Excel an absolute must. Prior experience in the

textile or apparel industry highly desirable. Send correspondence to personnel@winterland.com (no attachments please).

8. A local nonprofit organization seeks a **Coordinator of Volunteer Services.** Responsibilities for this full-time position include coordinating volunteers' schedules, recruiting and training new volunteers, and evaluating existing programs. Excellent listening and communication skills required.

9. Your state wants **assistant international trade managers** for offices in London, Paris, Tokyo, Hong Kong, and Buenos Aires. Duties include promoting state exports, promoting the state as a site for foreign business investment and branch plants, and representing the state to government officials. Candidate should know language and culture of target country.

10. Ogilvie & Mather is hiring **assistant account executives.** You will be assigned to a major client account, and will help develop strategies for marketing and advertising, with specific assignments in one of the following: creative, media, research, or production.

19.12   Writing a Prospecting Letter

Pick a company you'd like to work for and apply for a specific position. The position can be one that already exists or one that you would create if you could to match your unique blend of talents. Give your instructor a copy of the job description with your letter.

Address your letter to the president of a small company, or the area vice president or branch manager of a large company. Use directories to get the name and address of the person with the power to create a job for you.

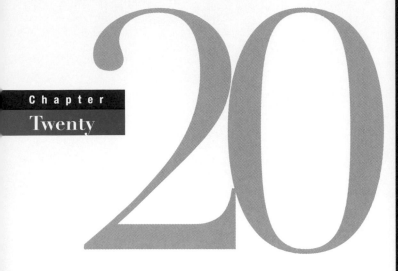

Job Interviews, Follow-Up Letters and Calls, and Job Offers

Interviewing in the 21st Century

Developing an Interview Strategy

Taking Care of the Details
- What to Wear
- What to Bring to the Interview
- Note-Taking

Practicing for the Interview

During the Interview
- How to Act
- Parts of the Interview
- Stress Interviews

Answering Traditional Interview Questions

Behavioral and Situational Interviews

After the Interview
- Follow-Up Phone Calls and Letters
- Negotiating for Salary and Benefits
- Deciding Which Offer to Accept

Summary of Key Points

Job Interviews, Follow-Up Letters and Calls, and Job Offers

Tim R. Moore

Division Manager, Pro Staff

www.prostaff.com

A recruiter since 1991, Tim Moore interviews hundreds of people each year and has helped thousands in their career searches. Pro Staff is a progressive staffing solutions company with more than 200 offices nationwide.

An interview is your opportunity to demonstrate that you're bright and energetic—the kind of person the company wants to hire. Doing a little pre-interview research and paying close attention to details is critical.

I can't tell you how many people I've interviewed over the years who came to my office without a clue about the company or the job they were interviewing for. I often ask, "What was it about our ad that caught your attention or interested you in our company?" The response "Umm, I don't really remember your ad. Could you tell me what it said?" is not the right one.

> *Good interviewing is a series of details that work together.*

Before an interview, research the organization. When was it founded? What is the main line of business? Does it have subsidiaries? What is the annual revenue? Who owns the company? Formulate questions to ask the interviewer about the important issues the company faces.

Be prompt. Make sure that you know exactly where you are going and plan ahead so you'll have plenty of time to get there. Ideally, arrive 15–20 minutes early. Take a couple of paper copies of your résumé, even if you already sent one by fax or e-mail.

Wear a suit. An interview is not the time or place to make a trendy fashion statement. Even if the company is casual, I strongly recommend that you break out your best dark suit for the interview.

Be honest. Answer questions directly and without excessive "spin." Present yourself in the best light possible, but don't set false or unrealistic expectations.

Follow-up. After an interview, send a brief note to the people with whom you met thanking them for their time and reaffirming your interest in the company.

Good interviewing is a series of details that work together to demonstrate that you are a thoughtful, bright, courteous person that the company should talk to more.

Video Interviews*

Two kinds of video interviews exist. In the first, the company sends a list of questions, asking the applicant to tape the responses. The second kind is a live interview using videoconferencing equipment.

If you're asked to prepare a videotape,

- Practice your answers.
- Tape the interview as many times as necessary to get a tape that presents you at your best.
- Be specific. Since the employer can't ask follow-up questions, you need to be detailed about how your credentials could help the employer.

If you have an interview by videoconference,

- Tape yourself so you can make any adjustments in pronunciation, voice qualities, posture, and clothing.
- Keep your answers short. Then say, "Would you like more information?" People are more reluctant to interrupt a speaker in another location, and body language is limited.

*Based on Raju Narisetti, "Work Week," *The Wall Street Journal*, November 21, 1995, A1; Steve Ralston, "Advances in Employment Interviewing Technology," and Jan Harding, Comments, both in Mini-Conference on Emerging Technologies: Focus on the World Wide Web and Its Uses in Business Communication, Columbus, OH, July 28–29, 1995.

J ob interviews are scary, even when you've prepared thoroughly. But when you are prepared, you can harness the adrenaline to work for you, so that you put your best foot forward and get the job you want.

Interviewing in the 21st Century

Interviews are changing as interviewers respond to interviewees who are prepared to answer the standard questions. Today, many employers expect you to

- Be more aggressive. One employer says he deliberately tells the company receptionist to brush off callers who ask about advertised openings. He interviews only those who keep calling and offer the receptionist reasons why they should be interviewed.
- Follow instructions to the letter. The owner of a delivery company tells candidates to phone at a precise hour. Failing to do so means that the person couldn't be trusted to deliver packages on time.[1]
- Participate in many interviews. In 1996, Xerox outsourced preliminary interviews. Applicants went through six interviews with a separate company before they actually met someone from Xerox. High-level jobs may require even more preliminary interviews. A senior vice president in a high-tech company went through 17 interviews before she was offered the job.[2]
- Have one or more interviews by phone, computer, or video.
- Take one or more tests, including drug tests, aptitude tests, computer simulations, and essay exams where you're asked to explain what you'd do in a specific situation.
- Be approved by the team you'll be joining. In companies with self-managed work teams, the team has a say in who is hired.
- Provide—at the interview or right after it—a sample of the work you're applying to do. You may be asked to write a memo or a proposal, calculate a budget on a spreadsheet, or make a presentation.

All the phoning required in 21st-century interviews places a special emphasis on phone skills.

If you speak to a secretary, be nice to him or her. Find out the person's name on your first call and use it on subsequent calls. "Thank you for being so patient. Can you tell me when a better time might be to try to get Mr. or Ms. X? I'll try again on [date]." Sometimes, if you call after 5 PM, executives answer their own phones since clerical staff have gone home.

If you get someone's voice mail, leave a concise message—complete with your name and phone number. Even if you've called 10 times, keep your voice pleasant.

If you get voice mail repeatedly, call the main company number to speak with a receptionist. Ask whether the person you're trying to reach is in the building. If he or she is on the road, ask when the person is due in.

Developing an Interview Strategy

Develop an overall strategy based on your answers to these three questions:

1. **What about yourself do you want the interviewer to know?** Pick two to five points that represent your strengths for that particular job. These facts may be achievements, character traits (such as enthusiasm), experiences that qualify you for the job and separate you from other applicants, the

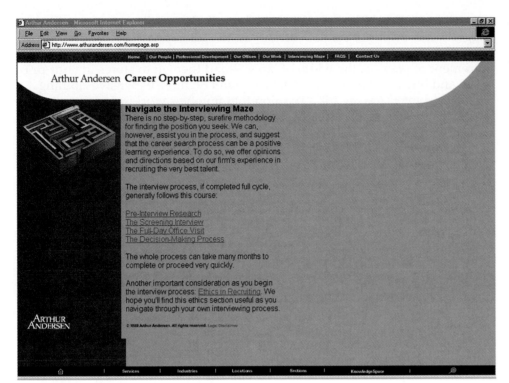

Arthur Andersen's "Interviewing Maze" offers useful information (even if you're not interviewing for Big Five jobs) about the interview process and what to expect.

fact that you really want to work for this company, and so on. For each strength, think of a specific action or accomplishment to support it. For example, be ready to give an example to prove that you're hardworking. Be ready to show how you helped an organization save money or serve customers better.

Then at the interview, listen to every question to see if you could make one of your key points as part of your answer. If the questions don't allow you to make your points, bring them up at the end of the interview.

2. **What disadvantages or weaknesses do you need to minimize?** Expect that you may be asked to explain weaknesses or apparent weaknesses in your record: age, sex, physical disabilities, lack of experience, so-so grades, and gaps in your record.

   Plan how to deal with these issues if they arise. See the suggestions later in this chapter under "Kinds of Interviews" and "Traditional Questions."

3. **What do you need to know about the job and the organization to decide whether or not you want to accept this job if it is offered to you?** Plan *in advance* the criteria on which you will base your decision (you can always change the criteria). Use "Deciding Which Offer to Accept" below to plan questions to elicit the information you'll need to rank each offer.

Taking Care of the Details

Wearing inappropriate clothing or being late can cost you a job. Put enough time into planning details so that you can move on to substantive planning.

What to Wear

If you're interviewing for a management or office job, wear a business suit. What kind of suit? If you've got good taste and a good eye for color, follow your instincts. If fashion isn't your strong point, read John Molloy's *Dress for Success*

Using Your Portfolio in an Interview*

Take a portfolio with examples of your work to a job interview. The best items for a portfolio are documents that could be used in a business (not just school papers). Proof everything to make sure it's perfect.

Add labels that give the purpose and audience for each document. If you have evidence of the document's success, include that.

Let the interviewer turn the pages. When he or she stops to look at a document, give more information about your strategy.

Be sure to take the portfolio home with you. In both New York City and Minneapolis, one-third of the portfolios left at the client site are "lost." Ask interviewers to make copies of documents they want to read carefully, rather than leaving the whole portfolio at the site.

*Based on Pat O'Donnell, "What Recruiters Look for in Marcom Writers," *Impact!*, Vol. 5, no. 3 (Spring 1999), 4.

(men's clothes) and *The New Woman's Dress for Success Book.* Perhaps the best suggestion in Molloy's books is the advice to visit expensive stores, noting details—the exact shade of blue in a suit, the number of buttons on the sleeve, the placement of pockets, the width of lapels—and then go to stores in your price range and buy a suit that has the details found on more expensive clothing.

If you're interviewing for a position that involves working, visiting, or supervising muddy or dirty sites, wear sturdy clothes that suggest you're willing to wear flannel shirts and get your shoes dirty.[3] In this case, looking "good" is less important than looking businesslike.

Consider the corporate culture. A woman who was interviewing for a job at The Gap wore a matching linen skirt and blouse that were similar to Gap clothing. Her clothing was evidence that she'd researched the job.[4]

Choose comfortable shoes. You may do a fair amount of walking during the office visit or plant trip.

Take care of all the details. Check your heels to make sure they aren't run down; make sure your shoes are shined. Have your hair cut or styled conservatively. Jewelry and makeup should be understated. Personal hygiene must be impeccable. Avoid cologne and perfumed aftershave lotions.

What to Bring to the Interview

Bring extra copies of your résumé. If your campus placement office has already given the interviewer a data sheet, present the résumé at the beginning of the interview: "I thought you might like a little more information about me."

Bring something to write on and something to write with. It's OK to bring in a small notepad with the questions you want to ask on it.

Bring copies of your work or a portfolio: an engineering design, a copy of a memo you wrote on a job or in a business writing class, an article you wrote for the campus paper. You don't need to present these unless the interview calls for them, but they can be very effective: "Yes, I have done a media plan. Here's a copy of a plan I put together in my advertising seminar last year. We had a fixed budget and used real figures for cost and rating points, just as I'd do if I joined Foote, Cone & Belding."

Bring the names, addresses, and phone numbers of references if you didn't put them on your résumé. Bring complete details about your work history and education, including dates and street addresses, in case you're asked to fill out an application form.

If you can afford it, buy a briefcase to carry these items. At this point in your life, an inexpensive vinyl briefcase is acceptable.

Note-Taking

During or immediately after the interview, write down

- The name of the interviewer (or all the people you talked to, if it's a group interview or an office visit).
- What the interviewer seemed to like best about you.
- Any negative points or weaknesses that came up that you need to counter in your follow-up letter or phone calls.
- Answers to your questions about the company.
- When you'll hear from the company.

The easiest way to get the interviewer's name is to ask for his or her card. You may be able to make all the notes you need on the back of the card.

Some interviewers say that they respond negatively to applicants who take notes during the interview. However, if you have several interviews back-to-back or if you know your memory is terrible, do take brief notes during the interview. That's better than forgetting which company said you'd be on the road every other week and which interviewer asked that *you* get in touch with him or her.

Practicing for the Interview

Rehearse everything you can: put on the clothes you'll wear and practice entering a room, shaking hands, sitting down, and answering questions. Ask a friend to interview you. Saying answers out loud is surprisingly harder than saying them in your head.

Some campuses have videotaping facilities so that you can watch your own sample interview. Videotaping is more valuable if you can do it at least twice, so you can modify behavior the second time and check the tape to see whether the modification works.

During the Interview

Your interviewing skills will improve with practice. If possible, schedule a few interviews with other companies before your interview with the company that is your first choice. However, even if you're just interviewing for practice, you must still do all the research on that company. If interviewers sense that you aren't interested, they won't take you seriously and you won't learn much from the process.

How to Act

Should you "be yourself"? There's no point in assuming a radically different persona. If you do, you run the risk of getting into a job that you'll hate (though the persona you assumed might have loved it). Furthermore, as interviewers point out, you have to be a pretty good actor to come across convincingly if you try to be someone other than yourself. Yet keep in mind that all of us have several selves: we can be lazy, insensitive, bored, slow-witted, and tongue-tied, but we can also be energetic, perceptive, interested, intelligent, and articulate. Be your best self at the interview.

Interviews can make you feel vulnerable and defensive; to counter this, review your accomplishments—the things you're especially proud of having done. You'll make a better impression if you have a firm sense of your own self-worth.

Every interviewer repeats the advice that your mother probably gave you: sit up straight, don't mumble, look at people when you talk. It's good advice for interviews. Be aware that many people respond negatively to smoking.

Office visits that involve meals and semisocial occasions call for sensible choices. When you order, choose something that's easy and unmessy to eat. Watch your table manners. Eat a light lunch, with no alcohol, so that you'll be alert during the afternoon. At dinner or an evening party, decline alcohol if you don't drink. If you do drink, accept just one drink—you're still being evaluated, and you can't afford to have your guard down. Be aware that some people respond negatively to applicants who drink hard liquor.

Parts of the Interview

Every interview has an opening, a body, and a close.

In the **opening** (two to five minutes), good interviewers will try to set you at ease. Some interviewers will open with easy questions about your major or

Stress Interviews for Salespeople at Dataflex*

Rick Rose, CEO of Dataflex, is "deliberately adversarial" at a first interview. After about five minutes, he tells interviewees they aren't very good—even if they are. He wants applicants who believe in themselves and will try to persuade him that he's wrong.

He challenges canned answers. If an applicant says he or she wants to be in sales "to help people," Rose responds, "You want to help people? Go be a nurse."

Rick tells candidates to call him after the interview. Those who do call back get second interviews with all the current salespeople.

And when all of that goes positively, the interviewee is invited to participate in a week's worth of sales meetings, which start at 7 AM four times a week. The people who do participate—not merely attend—are the people who get hired.

*Based on Richard C. Rose and Echo Montgomery Garrett, "Guerrilla Interviewing," *Inc.*, December 1992, 145–47.

interests. Others open by telling you about the job or the company. If this happens, listen so you can answer questions later to show that you can do the job or contribute to the company that's being described.

The **body** of the interview (10 to 25 minutes) is an all-too-brief time for you to highlight your qualifications and find out what you need to know to decide if you want to accept a plant trip. Expect questions that give you an opportunity to showcase your strong points and questions that probe any weaknesses evident from your résumé. (You were neither in school nor working last fall. What were you doing?) Normally the interviewer will also try to sell you on the company and give you an opportunity to raise questions.

You need to be aware of time so that you can make sure to get in your key points and questions: "We haven't covered it yet, but I want you to know that I . . . ." "I'm aware that it's almost 10:30. I do have some more questions that I'd like to ask about the company."

In the **close** of the interview (two to five minutes), the interviewer will usually tell you what happens next: "We'll be bringing our top candidates to the office in February. You should hear from us in three weeks." One interviewer reports that he gives applicants his card and tells them to call him. "It's a test to see if they are committed, how long it takes for them to call, and whether they even call at all."[5]

Close with an assertive statement. Depending on the circumstances, you could say: "I've certainly enjoyed learning more about General Electric." "I hope I get a chance to visit your Phoenix office. I'd really like to see the new computer system you talked about." "This job seems to be a good match between what you're looking for and what I'd like to do."

Stress Interviews

A **stress interview** deliberately puts the applicant under stress. If the stress is physical (for example, you're given a chair where the light is in your eyes), be assertive: move to another chair or tell the interviewer that the behavior bothers you.

Usually the stress is psychological. A group of interviewers fire rapid questions. A single interviewer probes every weak spot in your record and asks questions that elicit negatives. If you get questions that put you on the defensive, **rephrase** them in less inflammatory terms, if necessary, and then **treat them as requests for information.**

Q: Why did you major in physical education? That sounds like a pretty Mickey Mouse major.

A: You're asking whether I have the academic preparation for this job. I started out in physical education because I've always loved sports. I learned that I couldn't graduate in four years if I officially switched my major to business administration because the requirements were different in the two programs. But I do have 21 hours in business administration and 9 hours in accounting. And my sports experience gives me practical training in teamwork, motivating people, and management.

Respond assertively. The candidates who survive are those who stand up for themselves and who explain why indeed they *are* worth hiring.

Silence can also create stress. One woman walked into her scheduled interview to find a male interviewer with his feet up on the desk. He said, "It's been a long day. I'm tired and I want to go home. You have five minutes to sell yourself." Since she had planned the points she wanted to be sure interviewers knew, she was able to do this. "Your recruiting brochure said that you're looking for someone with a major in accounting and a minor in finance. As you may remember from my résumé, I'm majoring in accountancy and have had 12 hours in finance. I've also served as treasurer of a local campaign committee and have worked as a volunteer tax preparer through the Accounting Club." When she finished, the interviewer told her it was a test: "I wanted to see how you'd handle it."

Increasingly common is the variety of stress interview that asks you to do—on the spot—the kind of thing the job would require. An interviewer for a sales job handed applicants a ballpoint pen and said, "Sell me this pen." (It's OK to ask who the target market is and whether this is a repeat or a new customer.) AT&T asks some applicants to deliver presentations or lead meetings. Massachusetts Mutual Life asked the finalists for a vice presidency to process memos and reports in a two-hour in-basket exercise and participate in several role plays.[6]

Sexist interviews are a special variety of stress interviews. Although questions about marriage and children are illegal, they occasionally are asked. An interview can also be categorized as sexist if the interviewer implies that an applicant can't do the job because she's female: "You're a woman and you're short. You'd be working with tall men in this job. How would you handle them?"

Although you're within your rights to say "I don't think that question is legal," a low-key response is more likely to lead to a job offer. Respond as you would to a stress question: **rephrase the question and treat it as a legitimate request for information.**

Q: Aren't you just looking for a husband?

A: You may be asking whether I'll stay with you long enough to justify the expense of training me as a staff accountant. Well, I'm not promising to work for you the rest of my life, just as you're not promising to employ me for the rest of my life. How long I stay will depend upon whether my assignments continue to be interesting and challenging and whether I can advance.

Sometimes interviewers who do not ask sexist questions still have reservations about offering jobs to women. You may want to set at rest the interviewer's fears by bringing up the subject yourself: "You may have noticed that I'm married. My husband is a dentist and could relocate if the company wanted to transfer me."

Answering Traditional Interview Questions

First interviews seek to screen out less qualified candidates rather than to find someone to hire. Negative information will hurt you less if it comes out in the middle of the interview and is preceded and followed by positive information. If you blow a question near the end of the interview, don't leave until you've said something positive—perhaps restating one of the points you want the interviewer to know about you.

As Figure 20.1 shows, successful applicants use different communication behaviors than do unsuccessful applicants. Successful applicants are more likely to use the company name during the interview, support their claims with specific details, and ask specific questions about the company and the industry. In addition to practicing the content of questions, try to incorporate these tactics.

The following questions frequently come up at interviews. Do some unpressured thinking before the interview so that you'll be able to come up with answers that are responsive, honest, and paint a good picture of you. Choose answers that fit your qualifications and your interview strategy.

Testing the Intangibles*

A growing number of companies, including General Motors and American Express, are no longer satisfied with traditional job interviews.

They are making applicants for many white-collar jobs run a gauntlet of paper-and-pencil tests, role-playing exercises, decision-making simulations, and brain teasers. Others put candidates through a long series of interviews by psychologists or trained interviewers. . . .

[E]mployers want to grade upper-echelon job candidates on intangible qualities. Is she creative and entrepreneurial? Can she lead and coach? Can he work in teams? Is he flexible and capable of learning? Does she have passion and a sense of urgency? How will he function under pressure?

Most important, will the potential recruit fit the corporate culture?

These tests . . . can take from an hour to two days.

*Quoted from Judith H. Dobrzynski, "Applicants Find It Takes More Than a Resume to Land a Job in the '90s," *The Columbus Dispatch*, September 8, 1996, 8I.

Amy's Ice Cream stores sell entertainment. To find creative, zany employees, Amy Miller gives applicants a white paper bag and a week to do something with it. People who produce something unusual are hired.

Figure 20.1   *The Communication Behaviors of Successful Interviewees*

Behavior	Unsuccessful interviewees	Successful interviewees
Statements about the position	Had only vague ideas of what they wanted to do; changed "ideal job" up to six times during the interview.	Specific and consistent about the position they wanted; were able to tell why they wanted the position.
Use of company name	Rarely used the company name.	Referred to the company by name four times as often as unsuccessful interviewees.
Knowledge about company and position	Made it clear that they were using the interview to learn about the company and what it offered.	Made it clear that they had researched the company; referred to specific brochures, journals, or people who had given them information.
Level of interest, enthusiasm	Responded neutrally to interviewer's statements: "OK," "I see." Indicated reservations about company or location.	Expressed approval of information provided by the interviewer nonverbally and verbally; "That's great!" Explicitly indicated desire to work for this particular company.
Picking up on interviewer's cues	Gave vague or negative answers even when a positive answer was clearly desired ("How are your math skills?").	Answered positively and confidently—and backed up the claim with a specific example of "problem solving" or "toughness."
Use of industry terms and technical jargon	Used almost no technical jargon.	Used technical jargon: "point of purchase display," "NCR charge," "two-column approach," "direct mail."
Use of specifics in answers	Gave short answers—10 words or less, sometimes only one word; did not elaborate. Gave general responses: "fairly well."	Supported claims with specific personal experiences, comparisons, statistics, statements of teachers and employers.
Questions asked by interviewee	Asked a small number of general questions.	Asked specific questions based on knowledge of the industry and the company. Personalized questions: "What would my duties be?"
Control of time and topics	Interviewee talked 37% of the interview time, initiated 36% of the comments.	Interviewee talked 55% of the total time, initiated subjects 56% of the time.

Source: Based on research reported by Lois J. Einhorn, "An Inner View of the Job Interview: An Investigation of Successful Communicative Behaviors," *Communication Education* 30 (July 1981), 217–28.

1. Tell me about yourself.

   Don't launch into an autobiography. Instead, state the things about yourself that you want the interviewer to know. Give specifics to prove each of your strengths.

2. What makes you think you're qualified to work for this company? Or, I'm interviewing 120 people for two jobs. Why should I hire you?

   This question may feel like an attack. Use it as an opportunity to state your strong points: your qualifications for the job, the things that separate you from other applicants.

3. What two or three accomplishments have given you the greatest satisfaction?

   Pick accomplishments that you're proud of, that create the image you want to project, and that enable you to share one of the things you want the interviewer to know about you. Focus not just on the end result, but on the problem-solving and thinking skills that made the achievement possible.

4. Why do you want to work for us? What is your ideal job?

   Even if you're interviewing just for practice, make sure you have a good answer—preferably two or three reasons you'd like to work for that company. If you don't seem to be taking the interview seriously, the interviewer won't take you seriously, and you won't even get good practice.

   If your ideal job is very different from the ones the company has available, the interviewer may simply say there isn't a good match and end the interview. If you're interested in this company, do some research so that what you ask for is in the general ballpark of the kind of work the company offers.

5. What college subjects did you like best and least? Why?

   This question may be an icebreaker; it may be designed to discover the kind of applicant they're looking for. If your favorite class was something outside your major, prepare an answer that shows that you have qualities that can help you in the job you're applying for: "My favorite class was a seminar in the American novel. We got a chance to think on our own, rather than just regurgitate facts; we made presentations to the class every week. I found I really like sharing my ideas with other people and presenting reasons for my conclusions about something."

6. What is your class rank? Your grade point? Why are your grades so low?

   If your grades aren't great, be ready with a nondefensive explanation. If possible, show that the cause of low grades now has been solved or isn't relevant to the job you're applying for: "My father almost died last year, and my schoolwork really suffered." "When I started, I didn't have any firm goals. Once I discovered the field that was right for me, my grades have all been B's or better." "I'm not good at multiple-choice tests. But you need someone who can work with people, not someone who can take tests."

7. What have you read recently? What movies have you seen recently?

   These questions may be icebreakers; they may be designed to probe your intellectual depth. The term you're interviewing, read at least one book or magazine (regularly) and see at least one movie that you could discuss at an interview.

8. Show me some samples of your writing.

   Many jobs require the ability to write well. Employers no longer take mastery of basic English for granted, even if the applicant has a degree from a prestigious university.

Persistence Pays Off*

The interview was a disaster. She was awkward and inarticulate. All she could say was that she really wanted to work for the company, but she could not say what she could offer in return. She was turned down flat.

As she interviewed more, she got the hang of it and began to get some job offers, but her first interview gnawed at her. It had been for the job she really wanted. Figuring that she had one zero from that company and that two zeroes would not be worse than one, she called on the employer again, explained that when she had been there before it had been her first interview and that she had really not known how to handle herself. She told the employer that she really felt she had something to offer and asked if she could have another interview.

The employer was impressed. He liked persistence. The fact that the candidate had come back demonstrated a real interest in the company. A second interview was granted, and the young woman got the job.

*Quoted from John L. Munschauer, *Jobs for English Majors and Other Smart People* (Princeton, NJ: Peterson's Guides, 1986), 159–60.

The Same Answer Can Get Different Responses*

One job hunter I knew named O'Brian looked a recruiter straight in the eye and said, "As for my goals, they are to become president of your company in not too many years." The recruiter called him arrogant and told him to see a counselor. That same day O'Brian was asked again about his vocational plans by another recruiter and gave the same self-assured answer. This recruiter was delighted. As he said later, "All day long, I'd been asking students what they wanted to be in our company some day, and I'd been getting evasive or self-effacing answers. Then O'Brian came along. He is smart and knows what he is after. He is the candidate I want."

A friend of mine was once asked the hackneyed old saw, "And where do you expect to be in three years?" The friend, who should have known better (and does now), replied with the also hackneyed but dangerous, "I expect to be sitting in your chair." . . . The interviewer was shocked. His face got white, and he asked my friend, "Where will I be if you get my job?" The guy was dead serious; he planned to be in the job for a long time and had never thought of moving anywhere. We all laughed when we heard the story, but my friend didn't ever hear from them again.

*Quoted from John L. Munschauer, *Jobs for English Majors and Other Smart People* (Princeton, NJ: Peterson's Guides, 1986), 28–29, and William Lareau, *Inside Track: A Successful Job Search Method* (Piscataway, NJ: New Century, 1985), 157.

The year you're interviewing, go through your old papers and select the best ones, retyping them if necessary, so that you'll have samples if you're asked for them. If you don't have samples at the interview, mail them to the interviewer immediately after the interview.

9. **Where do you see yourself in five years?**

Employers ask this question to find out if you are a self-starter or if you passively respond to what happens. You may want to have several scenarios for five years from now to use in different kinds of interviews. Or you may want to say, "Well, my goals may change as opportunities arise. But right now, I want to. . . ."

10. **What are your interests outside work? What campus or community activities have you been involved in?**

While it's desirable to be well-rounded, naming 10 interests is a mistake: the interviewer may wonder when you'll have time to work.

If you mention your fiancé, spouse, or children in response to this question ("Well, my fiancé and I like to go sailing"), it is perfectly legal for the interviewer to ask follow-up questions ("What would you do if your spouse got a job offer in another town?"), even though the same question would be illegal if the interviewer brought up the subject first.

11. **What have you done to learn about this company?**

An employer may ask this to see what you already know about the company (if you've read the recruiting literature, the interviewer doesn't need to repeat it). This question may also be used to see how active a role you're taking in the job search process and how interested you are in this job.

12. **What adjectives would you use to describe yourself?**

Use only positive ones. Be ready to illustrate each with a specific example of something you've done.

13. **What is your greatest strength?**

Employers ask this question to give you a chance to sell yourself and to learn something about your values. Pick a strength related to work, school, or activities: "I'm good at working with people." "I really can sell things." "I'm good at solving problems." "I learn quickly." "I'm reliable. When I say I'll do something, I do it." Be ready to illustrate each with a specific example of something you've done.

14. **What is your greatest weakness?**

Use a work-related negative, even if something in your personal life really is your greatest weakness. Interviewers won't let you get away with a "weakness" like being a workaholic or just not having any experience yet. Instead, use one of the following three strategies:

a. Discuss a weakness that is not related to the job you're being considered for and will not be needed even when you're promoted. (Even if you won't work with people or give speeches in your first job, you'll need those skills later in your career, so don't use them for this question.) End your answer with a positive that *is* related to the job:

[For a creative job in advertising:] I don't like accounting. I know it's important, but I don't like it. I even hire someone to do my taxes. I'm much more interested in being creative and working with people, which is why I find this position interesting.

[For a job in administration:] I don't like selling products. I hated selling cookies when I was a Girl Scout. I'd much rather work with ideas—and I really like selling the ideas that I believe in.

[For a job in architecture:] I hate fund-raising. It always seemed to me if people wanted to give, they would anyway. I'd much rather have something to offer people which will help them solve their own problems and meet their own needs.

   b. Discuss a weakness that you are working to improve:

In the past, I wasn't a good writer. But last term I took a course in business writing that taught me how to organize my ideas and how to revise. I may never win a Pulitzer Prize, but now I'm a lot more confident that I can write effective reports and memos.

   c. Discuss a work-related weakness:

I procrastinate. Fortunately, I work well under pressure, but a couple of times I've really put myself in a bind.

15. Why are you looking for another job?
        Stress what you're looking for in a new job, not why you want to get away from your old one.
        If you were fired, say so. There are three acceptable ways to explain why you were fired:
        a. It wasn't a good match. Add what you now know you need in a job, and ask what the employer can offer in this area.
        b. You and your supervisor had a personality conflict. Make sure you show that this was an isolated incident, and that you normally get along well with people.
        c. You made mistakes, but you've learned from them and are now ready to work well. Be ready to offer a specific anecdote proving that you have indeed changed.

16. What questions do you have?
        This question gives you a chance to cover things the interviewer hasn't brought up; it also gives the interviewer a sense of your priorities and values. Don't focus on salary or fringe benefits. Better questions are
        • What would I be doing on a day-to-day basis?
        • What kind of training program do you have? If, as I'm rotating among departments, I find that I prefer one area, can I specialize in it when the training program is over?
        • How do you evaluate employees? How often do you review them? Where would you expect a new trainee (banker, staff accountant) to be three years from now?
        • What happened to the last person who had this job?
        • How are interest rates (a new product from competitors, imports, demographic trends, government regulations, etc.) affecting your company?

Is There Life after Work?*

Questions about work-life balance—which in the past were saved for the final round of interviews or never asked at all—are surfacing in job candidates' first-round talks with employers.
   A sampling of questions asked by undergraduate recruits . . . :
   1. Do people who work for you have a life off the job?
   2. Do your employees get to see their families?
   3. What support can you offer my significant other?
   4. Do you offer flextime?
   5. If my job requires too much travel, can I change without doing serious damage to my career? . . .
[S]everal [recruiters] say many of the candidates who asked these questions in the past ended up being top performers in their jobs. "The thing I found is that these folks can set their priorities within time limits," says Faye Ambrefe Omasta, who recruits management trainees for GTE. Gordon Welton, placement manager for Principal Financial Group, adds, . . . "They know what's important to them. They're passionate not just about their work, but about themselves."

*Quoted from Sue Shellenbarger, "New Job Hunters Ask Recruiters, 'Is There Life After Work?' " *The Wall Street Journal,* January 29, 1996, B1.

- How would you describe the company's culture?
- This sounds like a great job. What are the drawbacks?

You won't be able to anticipate every question you may get. (One interviewer asked students, "What vegetable would you like to be?" Another asked, "If you were a cookie, what kind of cookie would you be?"[7]) Check with other people at your college or university who have interviewed recently to find out what questions are being asked in your field.

Behavioral and Situational Interviews

Many companies, dissatisfied with hires based on responses to traditional questions, are now using behavioral or situational interviews. **Behavioral interviews** ask the applicant to describe actual behaviors, rather than plans or general principles. Thus instead of asking "How would you motivate people?" the interviewer might ask, "Tell me what happened the last time you wanted to get other people to do something." Follow-up questions might include, "What exactly did you do to handle the situation? How did you feel about the results? How did the other people feel? How did your superior feel about the results?" Since behavioral questions require applicants to tell what they actually did—rather than to say what ought to be done—interviewers feel they offer better insight into how someone will actually function as an employee.

Situational interviews put you in a situation that allows the interviewer to see whether you have the qualities the company is seeking. For example, Southwest Airlines found that 95% of the complaints it received were provoked by only 5% of its personnel. When managers explored further, they found that these 5% of employees were self-centered. To weed out self-centered applicants, Southwest now puts several candidates into a room and asks each to give a five-minute speech on "Why I Want to Work with Southwest Airlines." But the interviewers watch the *audience* to hire the people who are pulling for other speakers to do well, as opposed to those who are only thinking about their own performance.[8]

Situational interviews may also be conducted using traditional questions but evaluating behaviors other than the answers. Greyhound hired applicants for its customer-assistance center who made eye contact with the interviewer and smiled at least five times during a 15-minute interview.[9]

Figure 20.2 shows the poor responses to behavioral interview questions that cost candidates jobs at Gore-Tex. Figure 20.3 shows good responses to questions asked in Motley Fool interviews.

After the Interview

What you do after the interview can determine whether you get the job. One woman wanted to switch from banking, where she was working in corporate relations, to advertising. The ad agency interviewer expressed doubts about her qualifications. Immediately after leaving the agency, she tracked down a particular book the interviewer had mentioned he was looking for but had been unable to find. She presented it to him—and was hired.[10]

Xerox expects applicants for sales and repair positions to follow up within 10 days. If they don't, the company assumes that they wouldn't follow up with clients.[11]

If the employer sends you an e-mail query, answer it promptly. You're being judged not only on what you say but on how quickly you respond.

GORE-TEXT

Carolyn Murray (cmurray@wlgore.com), 37, a savvy recruiter at W.L. Gore & Associates, developers of Gore-Tex, pays little attention to a candidate's carefully scripted responses to her admittedly softball questions. Instead, she listens for a throwaway line that reveals the reality behind an otherwise benign reply. Herewith, Murray delivers a post-game analysis of how three job candidates whiffed during their interviews.

the PITCH	the SWING	the MISS
"Give me an example of a time when you had a conflict with a team member."	" 'Our leader asked me to handle all of the FedExing for our team. I did it, but I thought that FedExing was a waste of my time.' "	"At Gore, we work from a team concept. Her answer shows that she won't exactly jump when one of her team-mates needs help."
"Tell me how you solved a problem that was impeding your project."	" 'One of the engineers on my team wasn't pulling his weight, and we were closing in on a deadline. So I took on some of his work. ' "	"The candidate may have resolved the issue for this particular deadline, but he did nothing to prevent the prob-lem from happening again."
"What's the one thing that you would change about your current position?"	" 'My job as a salesman has become mundane. Now I want the responsibility of managing people.' "	"He's not maximizing his cur-rent position. Selling is never mundane if you go about it in the right way."

Source: *Fast Company,* January 1999, 156.

FOOL'S TOOL

As CEO of Motley Fool, a wildly popular investment Web site, **Erik Rydholm** (erikr@fool.com), 31, has little time for fooling around with undesirable job candidates. To streamline the interview process, he's come up with three questions that quickly separate the fools from the Fools.

FOOLISH question	WISE answer	FOOL'S take-away
" 'What does Foolishness mean to you?' That's a great first question, one that sepa-rates those who get it from those who are clueless."	"One guy emphasized that we give people the power to gather investing information from many sources by visit-ing a single Web site."	"He understood that we're trying to revolutionize the way people lead their finan-cial lives—by putting a lot of power at their disposal."
" 'Should the Motley Fool consider putting its name on mutual funds and selling a line of financial services?' "	"He encouraged us to consid-er whether branding a fund would undercut our integrity and whether it even related to our core competencies."	"He understood that there's integrity to the Motley Fool brand, and he recognized the risk of undercutting that integrity."
" 'How does the Motley Fool succeed?' That gets to the heart of how we can contin-ue to capitalize on our cur-rent market share."	"One candidate argued that the Motley Fool is not a source—it's a service: We guide people through their investment decisions."	"He understood the differ-ence between a 'source' and a 'service'—which made me confident that he could think distinctively for us."

Source: *Fast Company,* January 1999, 157.

Brain-Teaser Interview Questions*

Microsoft is one of many companies that tries to ask questions interviewees haven't anticipated.

Some recent questions:

1. Why are manhole covers round?
2. How many gas stations are there in the United States?
3. Why do many vending machines and jukeboxes have both letters and numbers?

The answers? (1) Round covers can be moved by rolling, and, unlike squares, won't fall through the hole. (2) If you figure 250 million people in the United States and one car for each four people and maybe 500 cars for each gas station, you get 125,000 stations. (3) To have the most different combinations for different products or songs with the fewest possible buttons.

Says Microsoft's director of recruiting, David Pritchard, "We're not looking for a 'right' answer. We're looking for the method, and we want them to talk about it. We want to see what information they ask for. . . . [T]he worst way to answer a question is 'I don't know, and I don't know how to figure it out.' "

*Based on "Can You Pass This Test?" *Newsweek*, February 24, 1992, 65; last paragraph quoted from "Wired for Hiring: Microsoft's Slick Recruiting Machine," *Fortune*, February 5, 1996, 124.

Follow-Up Phone Calls and Letters

After a first interview, make follow-up phone calls to reinforce positives from the first interview, to overcome any negatives, and to get information you can use to persuade the interviewer to hire you. Career coach Kate Weldon suggests asking the following questions:

- "Is there more information I can give you?"
- "I've been giving a lot of thought to your project and have some new ideas. Can we meet to go over them?"
- "Where do I stand? How does my work compare with the work others presented?"[12]

A letter after an office visit is essential to thank your hosts for their hospitality as well as to send in receipts for your expenses. The letter should

- Remind the interviewer of what he or she liked in you.
- Counter any negative impressions that may have come up at the interview.
- Use the jargon of the company and refer to specific things you learned during your interview or saw during your visit.
- Be enthusiastic.
- Refer to the next move, whether you'll wait to hear from the employer or whether you want to call to learn about the status of your application.

Be sure the letter is well written and error-free. One employer reports,

> I often interviewed people whom I liked, . . . but their follow-up letters were filled with misspelled words and names and other inaccuracies. They blew their chance with the follow-up letter.[13]

Figure 20.4 is an example of a follow-up letter after an office visit.

Negotiating for Salary and Benefits

The best time to negotiate for salary and benefits is after you have the job offer. Try to delay discussing salary early in the interview process, when you're still competing against other applicants.

Prepare for salary negotiations by finding out what the going rate is for the kind of work you hope to do. Cultivate friends who are now in the workforce to find out what they're making. Ask the campus placement office for figures on what last year's graduates got. Check trade journals. For example, *Advertising Age* publishes an annual salary survey segmented by agency size and region of the country. The survey gives figures for managers and officers, not entry-level workers, but the numbers still give you an upper limit: you can figure that an entry-level copywriter will make less than the chief copywriter. *Working Woman* publishes a salary survey every July that gives figures for a variety of jobs. Specialized books can also help, such as the annual *Direct Marketing and Telemarketing Guide* or the *Robert Half and Accountemps Salary Guide*.

This research is crucial. One study showed that male BA and MBA candidates expected to start at salaries 16.5% higher than the salaries women BA and MBA candidates expected.[14] Knowing what a job is worth will give you the confidence to negotiate more effectively.

If the interviewer asks you about your salary requirements before a job offer has been made, try this response: "I'm sure your firm can pay me what I'm worth." Then either ask about pay ranges or go back to your qualifications for the job. If the interviewer demands a response, give a range using odd incre-

F i g u r e   20.4   *Follow-Up Letter after an Office Visit*

405 West College, Apt. 201   *Single-space your address, date*
Thibodaux, LA 70301   *when you don't use letterhead.*
April 2, 2000

Mr. Robert Land, Account Manager
Sive Associates
378 Norman Boulevard
Cincinnati, OH 48528

Dear Mr. Land:

After visiting Sive Associates last week, I'm even more sure that writing direct mail is the career for me.

Refers to things she saw and learned during the interview.

I've always been able to brainstorm ideas, but sometimes, when I had to focus on one idea for a class project, I wasn't sure which idea was best. It was fascinating to see how you make direct mail scientific as well as creative by testing each new creative package against the control. I can understand how pleased Linda Hayes was when she learned that her new package for *Smithsonian* beat the control.

Seeing Kelly, Luke, and Gene collaborating on the Sesame Street package gave me some sense of the tight deadlines you're under. As you know, I've learned to meet deadlines, not only for my class assignments, but also in working on Nicholls' newspaper. The award I won for my feature on the primary election suggests that my quality holds up even when the deadline is tight!

Reminds interviewer of her strong points.

Thank you for your hospitality while I was in Cincinnati. You and your wife made my stay very pleasant. I especially appreciate the time the two of you took to help me find information about apartments that are accessible to wheelchairs. Cincinnati seems like a very liveable city.

Be positive, not pushy. She doesn't assume she has the job.

I'm excited about a career in direct mail and about the (possibility) of joining Sive Associates. I look forward to hearing from you soon!

Refers to what will happen next.

Sincerely,

Gina Focasio

Gina Focasio
(504) 555-2948

Writer's phone number.

Puts request for reimbursement in P.S. to de-emphasize it, focuses on the job, not the cost of the trip.

P.S. My expenses totalled $454. Enclosed are receipts for my plane fare from New Orleans to Cincinnati ($367), the taxi to the airport in Cincinnati ($30), and the bus from Thibodaux to New Orleans ($57).

Encl.: Receipts for Expenses

Finding Rewarding Work*

In the last nine years, a group of 22 business school graduates have averaged 4.3 jobs per person, with a few in their seventh job. Eight have had "involuntary departures." Their careers would have been more efficient and less painful if they had known more about themselves and about the world they were entering.

They didn't understand the changing nature of work.

They didn't expect business cycles and politics to affect them.

They didn't know people were irrational, driven by fear, greed, and jealousy.

They hadn't thought about the nonfinancial sources of satisfaction they needed.

They hadn't realized that they had moral values.

The lesson their experience teaches is that the more you know about yourself, about the economy, and about the company you're considering joining, the more likely it is that your job will give you a sense of reward that goes beyond a paycheck.

*Based on Jan Harding, "Closing the Circle: Collaboration with Recent Graduates," Mini-Conference on Accounting and Business Communication, Columbus, OH, July 26–27, 1996.

ments: "I'd expect to make between $32,300 and $36,900." As you say this, *watch the interviewer.* If he or she has that blank look we use to hide dismay, you may have asked for much more than the company was planning to offer. Quickly continue, ". . . depending, of course, on fringe benefits and how quickly I could be promoted. However, salary isn't the most important criterion for me in choosing a job, and I won't necessarily accept the highest offer I get. I'm interested in going somewhere where I can get good experience and use my talents to make a real contribution."

The best way to get more money is to convince the employer that you're worth it. During the interview process, show what you can do that the competition can't. Work to redefine the position in the employer's eyes from a low-level, anybody-could-do-it job to a complex combination of duties that only someone with your particular mix of talents could do.

After you have the offer, you can begin negotiating salary and benefits. You're in the strongest position when (1) you've done your homework and know what the usual salary and benefits are and (2) you can walk away from this offer if it doesn't meet your needs. Again, avoid naming a specific salary. Don't say you can't accept less. Instead, Kate Wendleton suggests, say you "would find it difficult to accept the offer" under the terms first offered.[15]

Remember that you're negotiating a package, not just a starting salary. A company that truly can't pay any more money now might be able to review you for promotion sooner than usual, or pay your moving costs, or give you a better job title. Some companies offer fringe benefits that may compensate for lower taxable income: use of a company car, reimbursements for education, child care or elder care subsidies, or help in finding a job for your spouse or partner. And think about your career, not just the initial salary. Sometimes a low-paying job at a company that will provide superb experience will do more for your career (and your long-term earning prospects) than a high salary now with no room to grow.

Work toward a win–win solution. You want the employer to be happy that you're coming on board and to feel that you've behaved maturely and professionally.

Deciding Which Offer to Accept

The problem with choosing among job offers is that you're comparing apples and oranges. The job with the most interesting work pays peanuts. The job that pays best is in a city where you really don't want to live. It's your life. The secret of professional happiness is taking a job where the positives are things you want and the negatives are things that don't matter much to you.

To choose among job offers, you need to know what is truly important to *you.* Start by answering questions like the following:

- Are you willing to take work home? To travel? How important is money to you? Prestige? Time to spend with family and friends?
- Would you rather have firm deadlines or a flexible schedule? Do you prefer working alone or with other people? Do you prefer specific instructions and standards for evaluation or freedom and uncertainty? How comfortable are you with pressure? How much challenge do you want?
- Where do you want to live? What features in terms of weather, geography, cultural and social life do you see as ideal?
- Is it important to you that your work achieve certain purposes or values, or do you see work as "just a way to make a living"? Are the organization's culture and ethical standards ones you find comfortable?

- Can you picture yourself doing this job 40 hours a week?
- Will you be able to do work you can point to with pride?

After you've done this brainstorming, make a list of *everything you'd like in your ideal job.* Then, to see which points are really important to you, do a forced choice. In a **forced choice,** you compare each item against every other one. Number the items in the order in which they happened to occur to you. Then, using the table of fractions in Figure 20.5, rank each pair. For " ½" compare item 1 and item 2. If you could only have one of the two, which would you prefer? Circle that number. For "⅓," compare item 1 with item 3. Again, circle the item that's more important. Repeat until you've made a choice between each of the possible pairs. Then count the number of times you've chosen each item. The things you've chosen most often are the ones that matter: they're the ones you should look for in your job.

Figure 20.6 is the list that one man produced. The items are numbered in the order in which they occurred to him. To find out what's truly important and what's nice but not necessary, Jim can do a forced choice. If he had to choose between a high income and having time for his family, which would he prefer? Counting up the number of times he chooses each factor will tell him what he really wants.

Some employers offer jobs at the end of the office visit. In other cases, you may wait for weeks or even months to hear. Employers almost always offer jobs orally. You must say something in response immediately, so it's good to plan some strategies in advance.

Figure 20.5   *Forced Choice Chart*

When you're not sure which job to accept, use this table of fractions. See instructions in the first paragraph on this page.

1/2	1/3	1/4	1/5	1/6	1/7	1/8	1/9	1/10	1/11	1/12	1/13	1/14	1/15	1/16	1/17	1/18	1/19	1/20
2/3	2/4	2/5	2/6	2/7	2/8	2/9	2/10	2/11	2/12	2/13	2/14	2/15	2/16	2/17	2/18	2/19	2/20	
3/4	3/5	3/6	3/7	3/8	3/9	3/10	3/11	3/12	3/13	3/14	3/15	3/16	3/17	3/18	3/19	3/20		
4/5	4/6	4/7	4/8	4/9	4/10	4/11	4/12	4/13	4/14	4/15	4/16	4/17	4/18	4/19	4/20			
5/6	5/7	5/8	5/9	5/10	5/11	5/12	5/13	5/14	5/15	5/16	5/17	5/18	5/19	5/20				
6/7	6/8	6/9	6/10	6/11	6/12	6/13	6/14	6/15	6/16	6/17	6/18	6/19	6/20					
7/8	7/9	7/10	7/11	7/12	7/13	7/14	7/15	7/16	7/17	7/18	7/19	7/20						
8/9	8/10	8/11	8/12	8/13	8/14	8/15	8/16	8/17	8/18	8/19	8/20							
9/10	9/11	9/12	9/13	9/14	9/15	9/16	9/17	9/18	9/19	9/20								
10/11	10/12	10/13	10/14	10/15	10/16	10/17	10/18	10/19	10/20									
11/12	11/13	11/14	11/15	11/16	11/17	11/18	11/19	11/20										
12/13	12/14	12/15	12/16	12/17	12/18	12/19	12/20											
13/14	13/15	13/16	13/17	13/18	13/19	13/20												
14/15	14/16	14/17	14/18	14/19	14/20													
15/16	15/17	15/18	15/19	15/20														
16/17	16/18	16/19	16/20															
17/18	17/19	17/20																
18/19	18/20																	
19/20																		

Number of times I've chosen

1 _____	5 _____	9 _____	13 _____	17 _____
2 _____	6 _____	10 _____	14 _____	18 _____
3 _____	7 _____	11 _____	15 _____	19 _____
4 _____	8 _____	12 _____	16 _____	20 _____

Figure 20.6

Jim's List for a Forced Choice

You can list more items or fewer, in any order. Then use the Forced Choice Chart to see which really matter to you.

1. High income
2. Time to spend with my family
3. Near mountains
4. Job opportunities for Linda
5. Opportunity for advancement
6. Nonracist environment
7. Company with other African Americans in leadership roles
8. Socially responsible company
9. Lots of open land near by
10. Challenging work
11. Minimal travel as part of job
12. Good college or pro sports teams in town
13. Cost of living not too high
14. Good schools
15. Town with large African American community
16. Town with parks, civic services
17. Lots of interaction with other people
18. Company that will encourage me to get a master's degree and even pay for it
19. Company with good fringe benefits
20. Not have to work weekends

If your first offer is not from your first choice, express your pleasure at being offered the job, but do not accept it on the phone. "That's great! I assume I have two weeks to let you know?" Then *call* the other companies you're interested in. Explain, "I've just got a job offer, but I'd rather work for you. Can you tell me what the status of my application is?" Nobody will put that information in writing, but almost everyone will tell you over the phone. With this information, you're in a better position to decide whether to accept the original offer.

Companies routinely give applicants two weeks to accept or reject offers. Some students have been successful in getting those two weeks extended to several weeks or even months. Certainly if you cannot decide by the deadline, it is worth asking for more time: the worst the company can do is say *no*. If you do try to keep a company hanging for a long time, be prepared for weekly phone calls asking you if you've decided yet.

Make your acceptance contingent upon a written job offer confirming the terms. That letter should spell out not only salary but also fringe benefits and any special provisions you have negotiated. If something is missing, call the interviewer for clarification: "You said that I'd be reviewed for a promotion and higher salary in six months, but that isn't in the letter." You have more power to resolve misunderstandings now than you will after six months or a year on the job.

When you've accepted one job, let the other places you visited know that you're no longer interested. Then they can go to their second choices. If you're second on someone else's list, you'll appreciate other candidates' removing themselves so the way is clear for you.

Summary of Key Points

- Develop an overall strategy based on your answers to these three questions:
  1. What two to five facts about yourself do you want the interviewer to know?

2. What disadvantages or weaknesses do you need to overcome or minimize?
3. What do you need to know about the job and the organization to decide whether or not you want to accept this job if it is offered to you?

- Wear a conservative business suit to the interview.
- Bring an extra copy of your résumé, something to write on and write with, and copies of your work to the interview.
- Record the name of the interviewer, what the interviewer liked about you, any negative points that came up, answers to your questions about the company, and when you'll hear from the company.
- Rehearse everything you can. Ask a friend to interview you. If your campus has videotaping facilities, watch yourself on tape so that you can evaluate and modify your interview behavior.
- Be your best self at the interview.
- In a **stress interview,** the interviewer deliberately creates physical or psychological stress. Change the conditions that create physical stress. Meet psychological stress by rephrasing questions in less inflammatory terms and treating them as requests for information.
- Successful applicants know what they want to do, use the company name in the interview, have researched the company in advance, back up claims with specifics, use technical jargon, ask specific questions, and talk more of the time.
- As you practice answers to questions you may be asked, choose answers that fit your qualifications and your interview strategy.
- **Behavioral interviews** ask the applicant to describe actual behaviors, rather than plans or general principles. **Situational interviews** put you in a situation that allows the interviewer to see whether you have the qualities the company is seeking.
- Use follow-up phone calls to reinforce positives from the first interview, to overcome any negatives, and to get information you can use to persuade the interviewer to hire you.
- A follow-up letter should
  - Remind the interviewer of what he or she liked in you.
  - Allay any negative impressions that may have come up at the interview.
  - Use the jargon of the company and refer to specific things you learned during your interview or saw during your visit.
  - Be enthusiastic.
  - Refer to the next move you'll make.
- In a **forced choice,** you compare each item against every other one to learn which points are most important to you.
- If your first offer isn't from your first choice, call the other companies you're interested in to ask the status of your application.

Behind the Scenes with a CPA Recruiter*

Every half hour [Don Kipper] will interview a different candidate.... What he looks for is "persistence, self-confidence, verbal skills, an ability to answer questions clearly and concisely. Can you think on your feet?" . . .

He's always on campus, officially and unofficially at the honor societies, cocktail parties and the like. He takes an active interest in student affairs and uses it to scoop his rivals on the best potential executives. Once identified, they are invited straight into the corporate office. . . .

Kipper is active in campus workshops, helping students improve their interviewing skills. . . . One unfortunate recently got Kipper's face three inches from his, demanding, "You were drunk last night. After that, why should I waste my time talking to you?" . . .

His advice? "Get involved with the extracurricular campus activities. That's where you'll get discovered."

*Quoted from Martin John Yate, "The Life of a Recruiter," *The Columbus Dispatch,* November 18, 1986, F1.

Chapter 20

Exercises and Problems

Getting Started

20.1 Making a Forced Choice

On another sheet of paper, list the criteria you'd like in a job. Number each item. Then compare each pair of items.

If you have 20 items or fewer, you can use the Forced Choice Chart in Figure 20.5 to record your preferences.

If you have more than 20 items, make a new chart so that each number will be compared with every other number.

On the chart, mark the number in each pair that corresponds with the item you'd choose if you could have only one of them. Then count how many times you've marked "1," how many times you've marked "2," etc. The items that you mark most often are the features you should try to find in a job.

As Your Instructor Directs,

a. Share your answers with a small group of other students.

b. Summarize your answers in a memo to your instructor.

c. Present your answers orally to the class.

20.2   Interviewing Job Hunters

Talk to students at your school who are interviewing for jobs this term. Possible questions to ask them include

- What field are you in? How good is the job market in that field this year?
- How long is the first interview with a company, usually?
- What questions have you been asked at job interviews? Were you asked any stress or sexist questions? Any really oddball questions?
- What answers seemed to go over well? What answers bombed?
- At an office visit or plant trip, how many people did you talk to? What were their job titles?
- Were you asked to take any tests (skills, physical, drugs)?

- How long did you have to wait after a first interview to learn whether you were being invited for an office visit? How long after an office visit did it take to learn whether you were being offered a job? How much time did the company give you to decide?
- What advice would you have for someone who will be interviewing next term or next year?

As Your Instructor Directs,

a. Summarize your findings in a memo to your instructor.

b. Report your findings orally to the class.

c. Join with a small group of students to write a group report describing the results of your survey.

20.3   Interviewing an Interviewer

Talk to someone who regularly interviews candidates for entry-level jobs. Possible questions to ask include the following:

- How long have you been interviewing for your organization? Does everyone on the management ladder at your company do some interviewing, or do people specialize in it?
- Do you follow a set structure for interviews? What are some of the standard questions you ask?
- What are you looking for? How important are (1) good grades, (2) leadership roles in extracurricular groups, or (3) relevant work experience? What advice would you give to someone who lacks one or more of these?
- What are the things you see students do that create a poor impression? Think about the worst candidate you've interviewed. What did he or she do (or not do) to create such a negative impression?

- What are the things that make a good impression? Recall the best student you've ever interviewed. Why did he or she impress you so much?
- How does your employer evaluate and reward your success as an interviewer?
- What advice would you have for someone who still has a year or so before the job hunt begins?

As Your Instructor Directs,

a. Summarize your findings in a memo to your instructor.

b. Report your findings orally to the class.

c. Join with a small group of students to write a group report describing the results of your survey.

d. Write to the interviewer thanking him or her for taking the time to talk to you.

20.4   Preparing an Interview Strategy

Based on your analysis in problems 18.1, 18.2, and 20.1, prepare an interview strategy.

1. List two to five things about yourself that you want the interviewer to know before you leave the interview.

2. Identify any weaknesses or apparent weaknesses in your record and plan ways to explain them or minimize them.
3. List the points you need to learn about an employer to decide whether to accept an office visit or plant trip.

As Your Instructor Directs,

a. Share your strategy with a small group of other students.
b. Describe your strategy in a memo to your instructor.
c. Present your strategy orally to the class.

20.5 Preparing Questions to Ask Employers

Prepare a list of questions to ask at job interviews.

1. Prepare a list of three to five general questions that apply to most employers in your field.
2. Prepare two to five specific questions for the three companies you are most interested in.

As Your Instructor Directs,

a. Share the questions with a small group of other students.
b. List the questions in a memo to your instructor.
c. Present your questions orally to the class.

20.6 Preparing Answers to Questions You May Be Asked

Prepare answers to each of the interview questions listed in this chapter and to any other questions that you know are likely to be asked of job hunters in your field or on your campus.

As Your Instructor Directs,

a. Write down the answers to your questions and turn them in.
b. Conduct mini-interviews in a small group of students. In the group, let student A be the interviewer and ask five questions from the list. Student B will play the job candidate and answer the questions, using real information about student B's field and qualifications. Student C will evaluate the content of the answer. Student D will observe the nonverbal behavior of the interviewer (A); student E will observe the nonverbal behavior of the interviewee (B).

After the mini-interview, let students C, D, and E share their observations and recommend ways that B could be even more effective. Then switch roles. Let another student be the interviewer and ask five questions of another interviewee, while new observers note content and nonverbal behavior. Continue the process until everyone in the group has had a chance to be "interviewed."

c. Assume that you are an independent behavioral psychologist hired to conduct screening interviews and interview yourself (silently, if you like). Then write a report to the organization considering the applicant, identifying each strength, weakness, and other characteristics. Support each claim with one or more behavioral examples. Write about yourself in the third person.

(Option c based on a problem written by William J. Allen, University of La Verne and University of Phoenix.)

E-Mail and Letter Assignments

20.7 Writing a Follow-Up Letter after an Office Visit or Plant Trip

Write a follow-up e-mail message or letter after an office visit or plant trip. Thank your hosts for their hospitality; relate your strong points to things you learned about the company during the visit; allay any negatives that may remain; be enthusiastic about the company; and submit receipts for your expenses so you can be reimbursed.

20.8 Clarifying the Terms of a Job Offer

Last week, you got a job offer from your first choice company, and you accepted it over the phone. Today, the written confirmation arrived. The letter specifies the starting salary and fringe benefits you had negotiated. However, during the office visit, you were promised a 5% raise in six months. The job offer says nothing about the raise. You do want the job, but you want it on the terms you thought you had negotiated.

Write to your contact at the company, Damon Winters.

A

Formats for Letters, Memos, and E-Mail Messages

Formats for Letters

Alternate Format for Letters That Are Not Individually Typed

Typing Envelopes

Format for Memos

Formats for E-Mail Messages

State and Province Abbreviations

Formats for Letters, Memos, and E-Mail Messages

William A. Anthony, Jr.

Staff Representative, Ohio Civil Service Employees Association

Bill Anthony writes memos and announcements to union members and letters to a variety of audiences, including government officials and political candidates. The Ohio Civil Service Employees Association (OCSEA), headquartered in Columbus, Ohio, is a union representing the majority of the 65,000 employees who work for the state of Ohio.

When I write letters on behalf of OCSEA, I want our readers to perceive us as a professional organization. Using letterhead stationery for the first page of a letter helps create a professional image. Our letterhead tells the reader who we are, gives our address and our 1-800, local phone, and fax numbers. It also lists the names and titles of our officers. The second and subsequent pages use plain paper.

66 Using letterhead stationery for the first page of a letter helps create a professional image 99

In the salutation, I use the name I use in conversation. For example, in a letter summarizing a recent conversation, I used "Dear Sue." It would seem odd to say "Dear Ms. Smith" if I called her "Sue" during the conversation. If I am attempting to build unity and encourage solidarity, I might use "Dear Sister" instead of "Dear Sue."

Even form letters can be personalized. For example, if I'm asking candidates to appear before our screening committee, then I personalize each of those letters by using the computer's merge function to put in the reader's name and even references to something I had talked to that person about.

I use the close "In Solidarity" in my letters to union members in good standing. This close helps solidify the goodwill, unity, and trust union members must have towards each other.

Even though people call me "Bill," I sign my letters "William A. Anthony, Jr." The only exceptions are to close friends and some staff.

We use letterhead for memos, too. (Again, I use a plain sheet of paper if a second page is required.) I have also created a memo format on my computer to use for memos within the office and to members I know very well. I initial memos either "BA" or "WAA." I use "BA" to other staff and friends and "WAA" for everyone else.

L etters normally go to people outside your organization; **memos** go to other people in your organization. In very large organizations, corporate culture determines whether people in different divisions or different locations feel close enough to each other to write memos. Letters and memos do not necessarily differ in length, formality, writing style, or pattern of organization. However, letters and memos do differ in format. The format for e-mail messages is evolving. **Format** means the parts of a document and the way they are arranged on the page.

Formats for Letters

Many organizations adopt a single format that all writers must use. If your organization has a standard format, use it.

Many organizations and writers choose one of three letter formats: **block** (see Figure A.2), **modified block** (see Figure A.3), or the **Administrative Management Society Simplified** format, also called **AMS Simplified** (see Figure A.4). Your organization may make minor changes from the diagrams in margins or spacing.

Figure A.1 shows how the three formats differ.

Use the same level of formality in the **salutation,** or greeting, as you would in talking to someone on the phone: *Dear Glenn* if you're on a first-name basis, *Dear Mr. Helms* if you don't know the reader well enough to use the first name.

Some writers feel that the AMS Simplified format is better since the reader is not *Dear.* Omitting the salutation is particularly good when you do not know the reader's name or do not know which courtesy title (✂ p. 46) to use. (For a full discussion on nonsexist salutations and salutations when you don't know the reader's name, see Chapter 2.) However, readers like to see their names. Since the AMS Simplified omits the reader's name in the salutation, writers who use this format but who also want to be friendly often try to use the reader's name early in the body of the letter.

The Simplified letter format is good in business-to-business mail, or in letters where you are writing to anyone who holds a job (admissions officer, customer service representative) rather than to a specific person. It is too cold and distancing for cultures that place a premium on relationships, such as in Puerto Rico.[1]

Sincerely and *Yours truly* are standard **complimentary closes.** When you are writing to people in special groups or to someone who is a friend as well as a business acquaintance, you may want to use a less formal close. Depending on

| **Figure A.1** | *Comparing and Contrasting Letter Formats* |

	Block	**Modified block**	**AMS Simplified**
Date and signature block	Lined up at left margin	Lined up ½ or ⅔ of the way over to the right	Lined up at left margin
Paragraph indentation	None	Optional	None
Salutation and complimentary close	Yes	Yes	None
Subject line	Optional	Rare	Yes
Lists, if any	Indented	Indented	At left margin
Writer's signature	Yes	Yes	None
Writer's typed name	Upper- and lower-case	Upper- and lower-case	Full capital letters
Paragraph spacing	Single-spaced, double-space between	Single-spaced, double-space between	Single-spaced, double-space between

Figure A.2   *Block Format on Letterhead (mixed punctuation)*

Northwest Hardware Warehouse

100 Freeway Exchange	Provo, UT 84610	(801) 555-4683

Line up everything at left margin

↕ 2–6 spaces depending on length of letter

June 20, 2000

Mr. James E. Murphy, Accounts Payable   *Title could be on a separate line*
Salt Lake Equipment Rentals
5600 Wasatch Boulevard
Salt Lake City, Utah 84121

↔ 1"–1 1/2"

Dear Jim: *Colon in mixed punctuation*

Use first name in salutation if you'd use it on the phone

The following items totaling $393.09 are still open on your account.   *¶ 1 never has a heading*

Invoice #01R-784391 *Bold or underline heading*

After the bill for this invoice arrived on May 14, you wrote saying that the material had not been delivered to you. On May 29, our Claims Department sent you a copy of the delivery receipt signed by an employee of Salt Lake Equipment. You have had proof of delivery for over three weeks, but your payment has not yet arrived.   *5/8" – 1"*

Single-space paragraphs
Double-space between paragraphs

Please send a check for $78.42.

Triple-space before new heading

Voucher #59351

The reference line on your voucher #59351, dated June 11, indicates that it is the gross payment for invoice #01G-002345. However, the voucher was only for $1171.25, while the invoice amount was $1246.37. Please send a check for $75.12 to clear this item.

Do not indent paragraphs

Voucher #55032

Voucher #55032, dated June 15, subtracts a credit for $239.55 from the amount due. Our records do not show that any credit is due on this voucher. Please send either an explanation or a check to cover the $239.55 immediately.

Total Amount Due   *Headings are optional in letters*

Please send a check for $393.09 to cover these three items and to bring your account up to date.

↕ 2–3 spaces
Sincerely,

3–4 spaces   *[signature: Neil Hutchinson]*

Neil Hutchinson
Credit Representative

cc: Joan Stottlemyer, Credit Manager

↕ Leave bottom margin of 3–6 spaces— more if letter is short

Figure A.3   *Modified Block Format on Letterhead (mixed punctuation)*

▣▣ Bay City
▣▣ Information Systems

2–6 spaces

September 14, 2001

*Line up date with signature block
1/2 or 2/3 of the way over to the right*

2–4 spaces

Ms. Mary E. Arcas
Personnel Director
Cyclops Communication Technologies
1050 South Sierra Bonita Avenue
Los Angeles, CA 90019 *Zip code on same line*

1"–1½"

Dear Ms. Arcas: *Colon in mixed punctuation*

5/8" - 1"

*Indenting ¶
is optional
in modified
block*

Let me respond to your request for an evaluation of Colleen Kangas. Colleen was hired as a clerk-typist by Bay City Information Systems on April 4,1998, and was promoted to Administrative Assistant on August 1, 1999. At her review in June, I recommended that she be promoted again. She is an intelligent young woman with good work habits and a good knowledge of computer software.

*Single-space
paragraphs*

As an Adminstrative Assistant, Colleen not only handles routine duties such as processing time cards, ordering supplies, and entering data, but also screens calls for two marketing specialists, answers basic questions about Bay City Information Systems, compiles the statistics I need for my monthly reports, and investigates special assignments for me. In the past eight months, she has investigated freight charges, inventory department hardware, and microfiche files. I need only to give her general directions: she has a knack for tracking down information quickly and summarizing it accurately.

*Double-space
between
paragraphs*

Although the department's workload has increased during the year, Colleen manages her time so that everything gets done on schedule. She is consistently poised and friendly under pressure. Her willingness to work overtime on occasion is particularly remarkable considering that she has been going to college part-time ever since she joined our firm.

At Bay City Information Systems, Colleen uses Microsoft Word and Access software. She tells me that she has also used WordPerfect and PowerPoint in her college classes.

If Colleen were staying in San Francisco, we would want to keep her. She has the potential either to become an Executive Secretary or to move into line or staff work, especially once she completes her degree. I recommend her highly.

2–3 spaces

Sincerely, *Comma in mixed punctuation*

*Headings are
optional in letters*

3–4 spaces

Jeanne Cederlind

Jeanne Cederlind
Vice President, Marketing

Line up signature block with date

2–4 spaces

Encl.: Evaluation Form for Colleen Kangas

*Leave at least 3–6 spaces
at bottom of page—more if
letter is short*

F i g u r e   A.4   *AMS Simplified Format on Letterhead*

McFarlane
Memorial
HOSPITAL

1500 Main Street ◆ Iowa City, IA 52232 ◆ (319) 555-3113

↕ 2 – 4 spaces

*Line up
everything
at left
margin*

August 24, 2001

↕ 2 – 4 spaces

←   1"–1½"   →

Melinda Hamilton
Medical Services Division
Health Management Services, Inc.
4333 Edgewood Road, NE
Cedar Rapids, IA 52401

Triple space   *Subject line in full capital letters*

REQUEST FOR INFORMATION ABOUT COMPUTER SYSTEMS

←   No salutation

We're interested in upgrading our computer system and would like to talk to one of
your marketing representatives to see what would best meet our needs. We will use
the following criteria to choose a system:

1.   Ability to use our current software and data files.   *Double-space between items
                                                                        In list if any items are more
2.   Price, prorated on a three-year expected life.   than one line long*

3.   Ability to provide auxiliary services, e.g., controlling inventory of drugs and
     supplies, monitoring patients' vital signs, and faster processing of insurance
     forms.

4.   Freedom from downtime.

Triple-space between list, next paragraph

*Do not
indent
paragraphs*

McFarlane Memorial Hospital has 50 beds for acute care and 75 beds for long-term
care. In the next five years, we expect the number of beds to remain the same while
outpatient care and emergency room care increase.

Could we meet the first or the third week in September? We are eager to have the
new system installed by Christmas if possible.

Please call me to schedule an appointment.   *Headings are
                                                            optional in letters*
No close. No signature.

HUGH PORTERFIELD   *Writer's name in full capital letters*
Controller

↕ 2–4 spaces

Encl.:   Specifications of Current System
         Databases Currently in Use

cc: Rene Seaburg

*↕ Leave 3–6 spaces at bottom
  of page — more if letter is short*

the circumstances, the following informal closes might be acceptable: *Yours for a better environment, Cordially, Thank you!,* or even *Ciao.*

In **mixed punctuation,** a colon follows the salutation and a comma follows the close. In a sales or fund-raising letter, it is acceptable to use a comma after the salutation to make the letter look like a personal letter rather than like a business letter. In **open punctuation,** omit all punctuation after the salutation and the close. Mixed punctuation is traditional. Open punctuation is faster to type.

A **subject line** tells what the letter is about. Subject lines are required in memos; they are optional in letters. Good subject lines are specific, concise, and appropriate for your purposes and the response you expect from your reader.

- When you have good news, put it in the subject line.
- When your information is neutral, summarize it concisely in the subject line.
- When your information is negative, use a negative subject line if the reader may not read the message or needs the information to act, or if the negative is your error.
- When you have a request that will be easy for the reader to grant, put either the subject of the request or a direct question in the subject line.
- When you must persuade a reluctant reader, use a common ground, a reader benefit, or a directed subject line that makes your stance on the issue clear.

For examples of subject lines in each of these situations, see Chapters 7, 8, and 9.

A **reference line** refers the reader to the number used on the previous correspondence this letter replies to, or the order or invoice number this letter is about. Very large organizations, like the IRS, use numbers on every piece of correspondence they send out so that it is possible to find quickly the earlier document to which an incoming letter refers.

Although not every example uses the same devices to provide visual impact, all three formats can use headings, lists, and indented sections for emphasis.

Each of the three formats has advantages. Both block and AMS Simplified can be typed quickly since everything is lined up at the left margin. Block format is the format most frequently used for business letters; readers expect it. Modified block format creates a visually attractive page by moving the date and signature block over into what would otherwise be empty white space. Modified block is a traditional format; readers are comfortable with it.

The examples of the three formats in Figures A.2–A.4 show one-page letters on company letterhead. **Letterhead** is preprinted stationery with the organization's name, logo, address, and phone number. Figure A.5 shows how to set up modified block format when you do not have letterhead. (It is also acceptable to use block format without letterhead.)

When your letter runs two or more pages, use a heading on the second page to identify it. Using the reader's name helps the writer, who may be printing out many letters at a time, to make sure the right second page gets in the envelope. The two most common formats are shown in Figures A.6, A.7, A.8, and below. Note even when the signature block is on the second page, it is still lined up with the date.

```
Reader's Name
Date
Page Number
```

F i g u r e   A.5   *Modified Block Format without Letterhead (open punctuation)*

6 – 12 spaces

Single space

11408 Brussels Ave. NE
Albuquerque, NM 87111
November 5, 2001

2 – 6 spaces

1"–1½"

Mr. Tom Miller, President
Miller Office Supplies Corporation
P.O. Box 2900
Lincolnshire, IL 60197-2900

Subject: Invoice No. 664907, 10/29/01   *Subject line is optional in block & modified block*

Indenting paragraphs is optional in modified block

Dear Mr. Miller   *No punctuation in open punctuation*

My wife, Caroline Lehman, ordered and received the briefcase listed on page 71 of your catalog (881-CD-L-9Q-4). The catalog said that the Leatherizer, 881-P-4, was free. On the order blank she indicated that she did want the Leatherizer and marked "Free" in the space for price. Nevertheless, the bill charged us for the Leatherizer.   *5/8" – 1"*

Please remove the $3.19 charge for the Leatherizer from our bill. The total bill was for $107.53, and with the $3.19 deducted, I assume the correct amount for the bill should be $104.34. I have enclosed a check for $104.34.

Please confirm that the charge has been removed and that our account for this order is now paid in full.

Sincerely   *No punctuation in open punctuation*

3 - 4 spaces

William T. Mozing

2 – 4 spaces

Encl.: Check for $104.34   *Line up signature block with date*

Figure A.6   *Second Page of a Two-Page Letter, Block Format (mixed punctuation)*

State
University

4300 Gateway Boulevard
Midland, TX

August 10, 2001

← 1"–1 1/2" →

Ms. Stephanie Voght
Stephen F. Austin High School
1200 Southwest Blvd.
San Antonio, TX 78214

↕ *2 – 3 spaces*

Dear Ms. Voght: *Colon in mixed punctuation.*

Enclosed are 100 brochures about State University to distribute to your students. The brochures describe the academic programs and financial aid available. When you need additional brochures, just let me know.

← 5/8" – 1" →

Videotape about State University

You may also want to show your students the videotape "Life at State University."

Plain paper for page 2.

↕ *1/2" – 1"*

Center

Stephanie Voght ← *Reader's name*   2   August 10, 2001

Also OK to line up page number date at left under reader's name.

campus life, including football and basketball games, fraternities and sororities, clubs and organizations, and opportunities for volunteer work. The tape stresses the diversity of the student body and the very different lifestyles that are available at State.

Triple space before each new heading.

Scheduling the Videotape   *Bold or underline headings.*

To schedule your free showing, just fill out the enclosed card with your first, second, and third choices for dates, and return it in the stamped, self-addressed envelope. Dates are reserved in the order that requests arrive. Send in your request early to increase the chances of getting the date you want.

Same margins as p 1.

"Life at State University" will be on its way to give your high school students a preview of the college experience.

Sincerely, *Comma in mixed punctuation.*

Headings are optional in letters.

3 – 4 spaces ↕ *Michael L. Mahler* (signature)

Michael L. Mahler
Director of Admissions

↕ *2 – 4 spaces*

Encl.: Brochures, Reservation Form

cc: R. J. Holland, School Superintendent
      Jose Lavilla, President, PTS Association

Figure A.7 *Second Page of a Two-Page Letter, Modified Block Format (mixed punctuation)*

Glenarvon Carpets

1500 Summit Avenue   (612) 555-1002
Minneapolis, MN   Fax (612) 555-4032

November 8, 2000

Line up date with signature block.

2 – 4 spaces

Mr. Roger B. Castino
Castino Floors and Carpets
418 E. North Street
Brockton, MA 02410

Dear Mr. Castino:

Indenting paragraphs is optional in modified block.

Welcome to the team of Glenarvon Carpet dealers!

Your first shipment of Glenarvon samples should reach you within ten days. The samples include new shades in a variety of weights. With Glenarvon Carpets, your customers can choose matching colors in heavy-duty weights for high-traffic areas and lighter, less expensive weights for less-used rooms.

Plain paper for page 2

1/2" – 1"

Center

Mr. Roger B. Castino   2   November 8, 2000

Reader's name

territory. In addition, as a dealer you receive

   * Sales kit highlighting product features
   * Samples to distribute to customers
   * Advertising copy to run in local newspapers
   * Display units to place in your store.

Indent or center list to emphasize it.

Use same margins as p 1.

    The Annual Sales Meeting each January keeps you up-to-date on new products while you get to know other dealers and Glenarvon executives and relax at a resort hotel.

    Make your reservations now for Monterey January 10-13 for your first Glenarvon Sales Meeting!

Cordially, *Comma in mixed punctuation.*

3 – 4 spaces

Barbara S. Charbonneau
Vice President, Marketing

Line up signature block with date in heading and on p 1.

1 – 4 spaces

Encl.: Organization Chart
       Product List
       National Advertising Campaigns in 2000

1 – 4 spaces

cc: Nancy Magill, Northeast Sales Manager
       Edward Spaulding, Sales Representative

3 – 6 spaces — more if second page isn't a full page.

Figure A.8   *Second Page of a Two-Page Letter, AMS Simplified Format*

♿ptions
for
Living

↕ 2 – 4 spaces

January 20, 2001

↕ 2 – 3 spaces

Gary Sammons, Editor
<u>Southeastern Home</u> Magazine
253 North Lake Street
Newport News, VA 23612

Triple space   *Subject line in full caps*

MATERIAL FOR YOUR STORY ON HOMES FOR PEOPLE WITH DISABILITIES

No salutation

Apartments and houses can easily be designed to accommodate people with disabilities. From the outside, the building is indistinguishable from conventional housing. But the modifications inside permit people who use wheelchairs or whose sight or hearing is impaired to do everyday things like shower, cook, and do laundry.

Plain paper for page 2

↕ 1/2" – 1"

Gary Sammons   *← Reader's name*
January 20, 2001

Page 2

Everything lined up at left margin   in hallways and showers and adjustable cabinets that can be raised or lowered. Cardinal says that the adaptations can run from a few dollars to $5000, depending on what the customer selects.

The Builders Association of South Florida will install many features at no extra cost: 36-inch doorways—eight inches wider than standard—to accommodate wheelchairs and extra wiring for electronic items for people whose sight or hearing is impaired.

Same margins as page 1   If you'd like pictures to accompany your story, just let me know.

No close, no signature

MARILYN TILLOTSON   *Writer's name in full caps*
Executive Director

Encl.: Blueprints for Housing for People with Disabilities

cc: Douglas Stringfellow, President, BASF
     Thomas R. Galliher, President, Cardinal Industries

↕ at least 3 – 6 spaces — more if page 2 is not a full page

or

Reader's Name	Page Number	Date

When a letter runs two or more pages, use letterhead only for page 1. (See Figures A.6, A.7, and A.8.) For the remaining pages, use plain paper that matches the letterhead in weight, texture, and color.

Set side margins of 1 inch to 1½ inches on the left and ⅝ inch to 1 inch on the right. If your letterhead extends all the way across the top of the page, set your margins even with the ends of the letterhead for the most visually pleasing page. The top margin should be three to six lines under the letterhead, or 2 inches down from the top of the page if you aren't using letterhead. If your letter is very short, you may want to use bigger side and top margins so that the letter is centered on the page.

To eliminate typing the reader's name and address on an envelope, some organizations use envelopes with cut-outs or windows so that the **inside address** (the reader's name and address) on the letter shows through and can be used for delivery. If your organization does this, adjust your margins, if necessary, so that the whole inside address is visible.

Many letters are accompanied by other documents. Whatever these documents may be—a multipage report or a two-line note—they are called **enclosures,** since they are enclosed in the envelope. The writer should refer to the enclosures in the body of the letter: "As you can see from my résumé, ..." The enclosure line reminds the person who seals the letter to include the enclosures.

Sometimes you write to one person but send copies of your letter to other people. If you want the reader to know that other people are getting copies, list their names on the last page. The abbreviation *cc* originally meant *carbon copy* but now means *computer copy.* Other acceptable abbreviations include *pc* for *photocopy* or simply *c* for *copy.* You can also send copies to other people without telling the reader. Such copies are called **blind copies.** Blind copies are not mentioned on the original; they are listed on the copy saved for the file with the abbreviation *bc* preceding the names of people getting these copies.

You do not need to indicate that you have shown a letter to your superior or that you are saving a copy of the letter for your own files. These are standard practices.

Alternate Format for Letters That Are Not Individually Typed

Merge functions in word processing programs allow you to put in a reader's name and address even in a form letter. *If you use a specific name in the salutation,* also use the reader's name and address in the inside address.

If you cannot afford to type each reader's name and address individually on the page, you have two options. The first option is to omit the inside address and use a generic salutation: "Dear Voter." The second option is to omit the salutation and use the space where it and the inside address normally go for a benefit or attention-getter. Figure A.9 illustrates this option.

Typing Envelopes

Business envelopes need to put the reader's name and address in the area that is picked up by the Post Office's Optical Character Readers (OCRs). Use side

F i g u r e A.9   *A Form Letter Whose Attention-Getter Mimics an Inside Address*

**COMPUTER
SUPPORT
CORPORATION**

2215 Midway Road
Carrollton, Texas 75006
(214) 661-8960
Telex: 284831 CSCTX UR
Fax: (214) 661-1096

*"Johnson Box" used for emphasis,
visual variety*

```
* * * * * * * * * * *
* Five FREE Libraries *
* Worth Up to $615!   *
* * * * * * * * * * *
```

*Date omitted so letter can be sent
out unchanged
Johnson Box visually substitutes
for date*

*Attention–getter
visually
substitutes
for inside
address,
salutation*

No Other Business
Graphics Software Can
Match the Versatility &
Flexibility of Diagraph!

Let us prove to you that Diagraph is a breakthrough in business
graphics software.

Use Diagraph to turn your ideas, concepts, plans, and data into
organization charts, signs, flow charts, diagrams, forms, and maps.
Diagraph comes with a money-back guarantee. Use it for 30 days and
we're certain that you will have discovered so many uses for
Diagraph that you won't want to part with it.

And now you have two choices: Diagraph/500 for only $99 or
Diagraph/2000 for $395.

Diagraph/500 files are fully compatible with Diagraph/2000 so you
can upgrade to Diagraph/2000 at any time. What's more, the cost of
Diagraph/500 is credited towards your purchase of Diagraph/2000.

See the enclosed data sheet for additional information or call us
today to see how the power of Diagraph can enhance everything you
write!

Sincerely,

4 sp. *Gail McCannon*

Gail McCannon
Director, Customer Services

*Signature block lined up with
Johnson Box*

Initials of writer

Initials of typist

GM:ec

Encl.

P.S. As an added incentive, if you purchase Diagraph/2000 before
November 30, you can select five Diagraph libraries, worth up to
$615, absolutely free. Call for more details.

*Reader benefit saved for a P.S.
People's eyes go to P.S., which they may
read before returning to rest of letter.*

margins of at least 1 inch. Your bottom margin must be at least ⅝ inch but no bigger than 2¼ inches.

Most businesses use envelopes that already have the return address printed in the upper left-hand corner. When you don't have printed envelopes, type your name (optional), your street address, and your city, state, and zip code in the upper left-hand corner. Since the OCR doesn't need this information to route your letter, exact margins don't matter. Use whatever is convenient and looks good to you.

Format for Memos

Memos omit both the salutation and the close entirely. Memos never use indented paragraphs. Subject lines are required; headings are optional. Each heading must cover all the information until the next heading. Never use a separate heading for the first paragraph.

Figure A.10 illustrates the standard memo format typed on a plain sheet of paper. Note that the first letters of the reader's name, the writer's name, and the subject phrase are lined up vertically. Note also that memos are usually initialed by the To/From block. Initialing tells the reader that you have proofread the memo and prevents someone sending out your name on a memo you did not in fact write.

Some organizations have special letterhead for memos. When *Date/To/From/ Subject* are already printed on the form, the date, writer's and reader's names, and subject are set at the main margin to save typing time. (See Figure A.11.)

Some organizations alter the order of items in the Date/To/From/Subject block. Some organizations ask employees to sign memos rather than simply initialing them. The signature goes below the last line of the memo, starting halfway over on the page, and prevents anyone's adding unauthorized information.

If the memo runs two pages or more, set up the second and subsequent pages just as you do for the second page of a letter. When you write frequently to the same people, putting a brief version of the subject line will be more helpful than just using "All Employees." See Figure A.12.

Brief Subject Line
Date
Page Number

or

Brief Subject Line   Page Number   Date

Formats for E-Mail Messages

Most e-mail programs prompt you to supply the various parts of the format. For example, a blank Eudora screen prompts you to supply the name of the person the message goes to and the subject line. See chapters 7, 8, and 9 for information about designing e-mail subject lines. "Cc:" denotes computer copies; the recipient will see that these people are getting the message. "Bcc:" denotes blind computer copies; the recipient does not see the names of these people. Most e-mail programs also allow you to attach documents from other

Figure A.10   *Memo Format (on plain paper)*

Everything lined up at left   *Plain paper*

October 7, 2000

2 – 4 spaces

Line up

To: Annette T. Califero

Double space

From: Kyle B. Abrams **KBA**   *Writer's initials added in ink*

1" – 1½"

Subject: A Low-Cost Way to Reduce Energy Use   *Capitalize first letter of each major word in subject line*

No heading for ¶ 1

As you requested, I've investigated low-cost ways to reduce our energy use. Reducing the building temperature on weekends is a change that we could make immediately, that would cost nothing, and that would cut our energy use by about 6%.

5/8" – 1"

Triple space before each new heading

The Energy Savings from a Lower Weekend Temperature *Bold or underline headings*

Single-space paragraphs; double-space between paragraphs

Lowering the temperature from 68° to 60° from 8 p.m. Friday evening to 4 a.m. Monday morning could cut our total consumption by 6%. It is not feasible to lower the temperature on weeknights because a great many staff members work late; the cleaning crew also is on duty from 6 p.m. to midnight. Turning the temperature down for only four hours would not result in a significant heat saving.

Turning the heat back up at 4 a.m. will allow the building temperature to be back to 68° by 9 a.m. Our furnace already has computerized controls which can be set to automatically lower and raise the temperature.

Triple sp

How a Lower Temperature Would Affect Employees   *Capitalize first letter of each major word of heading*

Do not indent paragraphs

A survey of employees shows that only 7 people use the building every weekend or almost every weekend. Eighteen percent of our staff have worked at least one weekend day in the last two months; 52% say they "occasionally" come in on weekends.

People who come in for an hour or less on weekends could cope with the lower temperature just by wearing warm clothes. However, most people would find 60° too cool for extended work. Employees who work regularly on weekends might want to install space heaters.

Action Needed to Implement the Change

Would you also like me to check into the cost of buying a dozen portable space heaters? Providing them would allow us to choose units that our wiring can handle and would be a nice gesture towards employees who give up their weekends to work. I could have a report to you in two weeks.

We can begin saving energy immediately. Just authorize the lower temperature, and I'll see that the controls are reset for this weekend.

Memos are initialed by To/From/Subject block — no signature

Headings are optional in memos

Figure A.11   *Memo Format (on memo letterhead)*

Kimball, Walls, and Morganstern

Date: March 15, 2001   *Line up horizontally with printed Date/To/From/Subject*

To: Annette T. Califero

From: Kyle B. Abrams *KBA*   *Writer's initials added in ink*   *Capitalize first letter of each major word in subject line*

Subject: The Effectiveness of Reducing Building Temperatures on Weekends

Triple space

Margin lined up with items in To/From/Subject block to save typing time

Reducing the building temperature to 60° on weekends has cut energy use by 4% compared to last year's use from December to February and has saved our firm $22,000.

This savings is particularly remarkable when you consider that this winter has been colder than last year's, so that more heat would be needed to maintain the same temperature.   *5/8" – 1"*

Fewer people have worked weekends during the past three months than during the preceding three months, but snow and bad driving conditions may have had more to do with keeping people home than the fear of being cold. Five of the 12 space heaters we bought have been checked out on an average weekend. On one weekend, all 12 were in use and some people shared their offices so that everyone could be in a room with a space heater.

Fully 92% of our employees support the lower temperature. I recommend that we continue turning down the heat on weekends through the remainder of the heating season and that we resume the practice when the heat is turned on next fall.

Headings are optional in memos

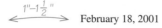
Option 2 for Page 2 of a Memo

$1"-1\frac{1}{2}"$

February 18, 2001

To: Dorothy N. Blasingham

From: Roger L. Trout **R.L.T.**   *Writer's initials added in ink*

Double space

Subject: Request for Third-Quarter Computer Training Sessions   *Capitalize first letter of all major words in subject line*

¶ I never has a heading

Triple space $5/8" - 1"$

Could you please run advanced training sessions on using Lotus 1-2-3 and WordPerfect in April and May and basic training sessions for new hires in June?

Triple-space before a heading

Advanced Sessions on Lotus 1-2-3
Bold or underline headings

Once the tax season is over, Jose Cisneros wants to have his first- and second-year people take your advanced course on Lotus 1-2-3. Plan on about 45-50 people in three sessions. The people in the course already use Lotus 1-2-3 for basic spreadsheets but need to learn the fine points of macros and charting.

Double-space between paragraphs

If possible, it would be most convenient to have the sessions run for four afternoons rather than for two full days.

Plain paper for page 2

$1/2" - 1"$

Dorothy N. Blasingham   *Brief subject line or reader's name*   2 *Page number*   February 18, 2001

Also OK to line up page number, date at left under reader's name

Same margins as p 1.   before the summer vacation season begins.

Orientation for New Hires   *Capitalize first letter of all major words in heading*

With a total of 16 full-time and 34 part-time people being hired either for summer or permanent work, we'll need at least two and perhaps three orientation sessions. We'd like to hold these the first, second, and third weeks in June. By May 1, we should know how many people will be in each training session.

Would you be free to conduct training sessions on how to use our computers on June 8, June 15, and June 22? If we need only two dates, we'll use June 8 and June 15, but please block off the 22nd too in case we need a third session.

Triple-space before a heading

Request for Confirmation

Let me know whether you're free on these dates in June, and which dates you'd prefer for the sessions on Lotus 1-2-3 and WordPerfect. If you'll let me know by February 25, we can get information out to participants in plenty of time for the sessions.

Thanks!

Headings are optional in memos

Memos are initialed by To/From/Subject block

Figure A.13   *A Basic E-Mail Message in Eudora (direct request)*

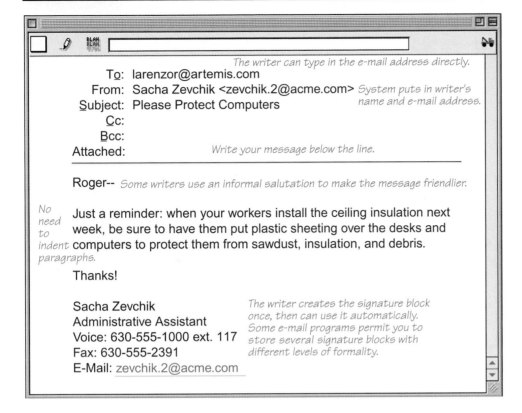

The writer can type in the e-mail address directly.

To: larenzor@artemis.com

From: Sacha Zevchik <zevchik.2@acme.com> *System puts in writer's name and e-mail address.*

Subject: Please Protect Computers

Cc:

Bcc:

Attached: *Write your message below the line.*

Roger-- *Some writers use an informal salutation to make the message friendlier.*

No need to indent paragraphs. Just a reminder: when your workers install the ceiling insulation next week, be sure to have them put plastic sheeting over the desks and computers to protect them from sawdust, insulation, and debris.

Thanks!

Sacha Zevchik
Administrative Assistant
Voice: 630-555-1000 ext. 117
Fax: 630-555-2391
E-Mail: zevchik.2@acme.com

The writer creates the signature block once, then can use it automatically. Some e-mail programs permit you to store several signature blocks with different levels of formality.

programs. Thus you can send someone a document with formatting, drafts of PowerPoint slides, or the design for a brochure cover. The computer program supplies the date and time automatically.

Some aspects of e-mail format are still evolving. In particular, some writers treat e-mail messages as if they were informal letters; some treat them as memos. Even though the e-mail screen has a "To" line (as do memos), some writers still use an informal salutation, as in Figure A.13. The writer in Figure A.13 ends the message with a signature block. You can store a signature block in the e-mail program and set the program to insert the signature block automatically. In contrast, the writer in Figure A.14 omits both the salutation and his name. When you send a message to an individual or a group you have set up, the "From:" line will have your name and e-mail address. If you post a message to a listserv, be sure to give at least your name and e-mail address at the end of your message, as some listservs strip out identifying information when they process messages.

When you hit "reply," the e-mail program automatically uses "Re:" (Latin for *about*) and the previous subject. The original message is set off with carats (see Figure A.15). You may want to change the subject line to make it more appropriate for your message.

Use short line lengths in your e-mail message. If the line lengths are too long, they'll produce awkward line breaks as in Figure A.15.

State and Province Abbreviations

States with names of more than five letters are frequently abbreviated in letters and memos. The Post Office abbreviations use two capital letters with no punctuation. See Figure A.16.

Figure A.14   *An E-Mail Message with an Attachment (direct request)*

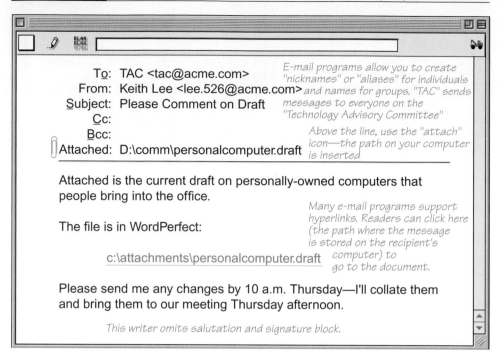

To: TAC <tac@acme.com>
From: Keith Lee <lee.526@acme.com>
Subject: Please Comment on Draft
Cc:
Bcc:
Attached: D:\comm\personalcomputer.draft

E-mail programs allow you to create "nicknames" or "aliases" for individuals and names for groups. "TAC" sends messages to everyone on the "Technology Advisory Committee"

Above the line, use the "attach" icon—the path on your computer is inserted

Attached is the current draft on personally-owned computers that people bring into the office.

The file is in WordPerfect:

c:\attachments\personalcomputer.draft

Many e-mail programs support hyperlinks. Readers can click here (the path where the message is stored on the recipient's computer) to go to the document.

Please send me any changes by 10 a.m. Thursday—I'll collate them and bring them to our meeting Thursday afternoon.

This writer omits salutation and signature block.

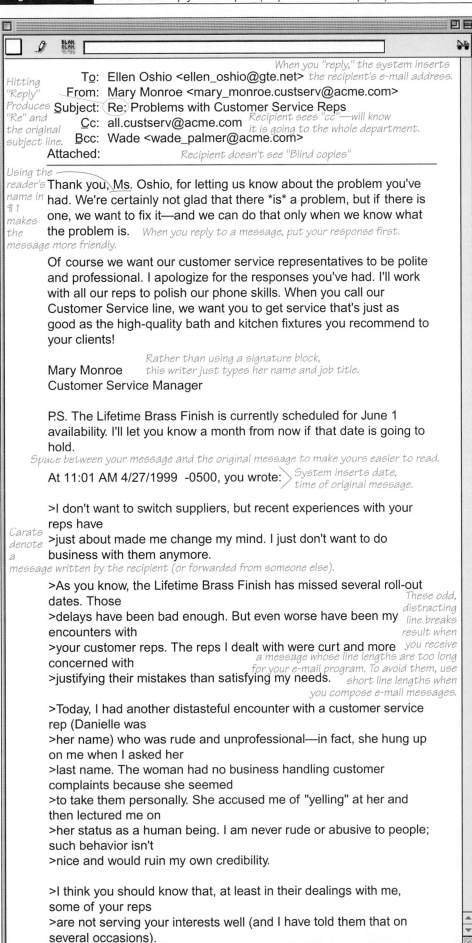

When you "reply," the system inserts

To: Ellen Oshio <ellen_oshio@gte.net> *the recipient's e-mail address.*

Hitting "Reply" Produces "Re" and the original subject line.

From: Mary Monroe <mary_monroe.custserv@acme.com>

Subject: Re: Problems with Customer Service Reps

Cc: all.custserv@acme.com *Recipient sees "cc"—will know it is going to the whole department.*

Bcc: Wade <wade_palmer@acme.com>

Attached: *Recipient doesn't see "Blind copies"*

Using the reader's name in ¶ 1 makes the message more friendly.

Thank you, Ms. Oshio, for letting us know about the problem you've had. We're certainly not glad that there *is* a problem, but if there is one, we want to fix it—and we can do that only when we know what the problem is. *When you reply to a message, put your response first.*

Of course we want our customer service representatives to be polite and professional. I apologize for the responses you've had. I'll work with all our reps to polish our phone skills. When you call our Customer Service line, we want you to get service that's just as good as the high-quality bath and kitchen fixtures you recommend to your clients!

Mary Monroe *Rather than using a signature block, this writer just types her name and job title.*

Customer Service Manager

P.S. The Lifetime Brass Finish is currently scheduled for June 1 availability. I'll let you know a month from now if that date is going to hold.

Space between your message and the original message to make yours easier to read.

At 11:01 AM 4/27/1999 -0500, you wrote: *System inserts date, time of original message.*

>I don't want to switch suppliers, but recent experiences with your reps have

Carats denote a message written by the recipient (or forwarded from someone else).

>just about made me change my mind. I just don't want to do business with them anymore.

>As you know, the Lifetime Brass Finish has missed several roll-out dates. Those

>delays have been bad enough. But even worse have been my encounters with

>your customer reps. The reps I dealt with were curt and more concerned with

>justifying their mistakes than satisfying my needs.

These odd, distracting line breaks result when you receive a message whose line lengths are too long for your e-mail program. To avoid them, use short line lengths when you compose e-mail messages.

>Today, I had another distasteful encounter with a customer service rep (Danielle was

>her name) who was rude and unprofessional—in fact, she hung up on me when I asked her

>last name. The woman had no business handling customer complaints because she seemed

>to take them personally. She accused me of "yelling" at her and then lectured me on

>her status as a human being. I am never rude or abusive to people; such behavior isn't

>nice and would ruin my own credibility.

>I think you should know that, at least in their dealings with me, some of your reps

>are not serving your interests well (and I have told them that on several occasions).

Figure A.16

Post Office Abbreviations for States, Territories, and Provinces

State name	Post office abbreviation	State name	Post office abbreviation
Alabama	AL	Missouri	MO
Alaska	AK	Montana	MT
Arizona	AZ	Nebraska	NE
Arkansas	AR	Nevada	NV
California	CA	New Hampshire	NH
Colorado	CO	New Jersey	NJ
Connecticut	CT	New Mexico	NM
Delaware	DE	New York	NY
District of Columbia	DC	North Carolina	NC
Florida	FL	North Dakota	ND
Georgia	GA	Ohio	OH
Hawaii	HI	Oklahoma	OK
Idaho	ID	Oregon	OR
Illinois	IL	Pennsylvania	PA
Indiana	IN	Rhode Island	RI
Iowa	IA	South Carolina	SC
Kansas	KS	South Dakota	SD
Kentucky	KY	Tennessee	TN
Louisiana	LA	Texas	TX
Maine	ME	Utah	UT
Maryland	MD	Vermont	VT
Massachusetts	MA	Virginia	VA
Michigan	MI	Washington	WA
Minnesota	MN	West Virginia	WV
Mississippi	MS	Wisconsin	WI
		Wyoming	WY

Territory	Post office abbreviation	Province name	Post office abbreviation
Guam	GU	Alberta	AB
Puerto Rico	PR	British Columbia	BC
Virgin Islands	VI	Labrador	LB
		Manitoba	MB
		New Brunswick	NB
		Newfoundland	NF
		Northwest Territories	NT
		Nova Scotia	NS
		Ontario	ON
		Prince Edward Island	PE
		Quebec	PQ
		Saskatchewan	SK
		Yukon Territory	YT

B

Writing Correctly

Using Grammar
- Agreement
- Case
- Dangling Modifier (DM)
- Misplaced Modifier (MM)
- Parallel Structure
- Predication Errors

Understanding Punctuation

Punctuating Sentences
- Comma Splices (CS)
- Run-on Sentences (RO)
- Sentence Fragments (Frag)

Punctuation within Sentences
- Apostrophe
- Colon
- Comma
- Dash
- Hyphen
- Parentheses
- Period
- Semicolon

Special Punctuation Marks
- Quotation Marks
- Square Brackets
- Ellipses
- Underlining and Italics

Writing Numbers and Dates

Words That Are Often Confused

Proofreading Symbols

Writing Correctly

Caroline Sanchez Crozier   *President/CEO, Computer Services & Consulting, Inc.*

Caroline Sanchez Crozier was named "Small Business Person of the Year" in 1993 by the State of Illinois. Computer Services & Consulting, in Chicago, Illinois, provides computer hardware and software sales, services, and support throughout the Midwest. The company's interactive software programs help children and adults improve reading, punctuation and grammar, usage, and spelling.

Communicating clearly with your clients is an important part of any business's success. Effective writing, presentation, and communication skills are essential. These skills are especially important to individuals running their own businesses. Your writing and grammar skills speak volumes about you.

> 66 *Your writing and grammar skills speak volumes about you.* 99

Clients view clear, precise communication skills as a sign of the company being confident, knowledgeable, and caring. A company that takes the time to present well-written material to a customer or client is showing responsibility. A company that presents material filled with grammatical errors looks sloppy. To a consumer, sloppiness denotes a poorly run business. Clients will look instead to a company that takes care of details and can be relied upon to do quality work.

Technology, especially e-mail and the Internet, focuses on writing. Communicating through writing is replacing much of what used to be oral communication. Many employees and students rely on spelling and grammar checkers on their computers. These tools will not always save you. If an employer sees a mistake even after your work has been through a spell checker, you look careless. You did not take the time or did not care enough about your work to read through it.

Our company designs educational software with a focus on children who learn English as their second language (ESL). As an ESL student myself, I understand the importance of learning good grammar skills early on. Students need to overcome their fears of learning grammar. Be committed that you're just going to do it, and find a way to learn. You may want to find someone that you're comfortable with to read your material and critique it. Before you know it, you've improved. Or you may want to take courses on your own, such as the reading or grammar programs that I have. Computer learning is private: it's just between you and the computer.

There is only one way to become a better writer and that is to practice. Students should write often and constantly strive to strengthen their grammar skills.

Look at writing as a way to document the good things you do throughout your job. Keep a diary of your work habits, of your strengths, of the successes that only you know. Then when it's time for a review or time to talk about a promotion, you can provide this information. You are your best spokesperson.

Too much concern for correctness at the wrong stage of the writing process can backfire: writers who worry about grammar and punctuation when they're writing a first or second draft are more likely to get writer's block. Wait till you have your ideas on paper to check your draft for correct grammar, punctuation, typing of numbers and dates, and word use. Use the proofreading symbols at the end of this appendix to indicate changes needed in a typed copy.

Most writers make a small number of grammatical errors repeatedly. Most readers care deeply about only a few grammatical points. Keep track of the feedback you get (from your instructors now, from your supervisor later) and put your energy into correcting the errors that bother the people who read what you write. A command of standard grammar will help you build the credible, professional image you want to create with everything you write.

This appendix begins with a discussion of six grammatical issues: agreement, case, dangling and misplaced modifiers, parallel structure, and predication errors. The section on punctuating sentences shows you how to use periods, semicolons, and commas to avoid comma splices, run-on sentences, and sentence fragments. The section on punctuation within sentences covers apostrophes, colons, commas, dashes, hyphens, parentheses, periods, and semicolons. The section on special punctuation covers marks used to quote material or for emphasis: quotation marks, square brackets, ellipses, and underlining and italics. Next, the appendix defines 50 pairs of words that are often confused and shows how to use them correctly. The last section shows you how to make changes in a typed draft when you proofread.

Using Grammar

With the possible exception of spelling, grammar is the aspect of writing that writers seem to find most troublesome. Faulty grammar is often what executives are objecting to when they complain that college graduates or MBAs "can't write." See the BAC Web site for links that explain grammar.

Agreement

Subjects and verbs agree when they are both singular or both plural.

Incorrect: The accountants who conducted the audit was recommended highly.

Correct: The accountants who conducted the audit were recommended highly.

Subject–verb agreement errors often occur when other words come between the subject and the verb. Edit your draft by finding the subject and the verb of each sentence.

American usage treats company names and the words *company* and *government* as singular nouns. British usage treats them as plural:

Correct (U.S.):   State Farm Insurance trains its agents well.

Correct (Great Britain):   Lloyds of London train their agents well.

Use a plural verb when two or more singular subjects are joined by *and.*

Correct: Larry McGreevy and I are planning to visit the client.

Use a singular verb when two or more singular subjects are joined by *or, nor,* or *but.*

Correct: Either the shipping clerk or the superintendent has to sign the order.

When the sentence begins with *Here* or *There,* make the verb agree with the subject that follows the verb.

Correct: Here is the booklet you asked for.

Correct: There are the blueprints I wanted.

Note that some words that end in *s* are considered to be singular and require singular verbs.

Correct: A series of meetings is planned.

When a situation doesn't seem to fit the rules, or when following a rule produces an awkward sentence, revise the sentence to avoid the problem.

Problematic: The Plant Manager in addition to the sales representative (was, were?) pleased with the new system.

Better: The Plant Manager and the sales representative were pleased with the new system.

Problematic: None of us (is, are?) perfect.

Better: All of us have faults.

Errors in **noun–pronoun agreement** occur if a pronoun is of a different number or person than the word it refers to.

Incorrect: All drivers of leased automobiles are billed $100 if damages to his automobile are caused by a collision.

Correct: All drivers of leased automobiles are billed $100 if damages to their automobiles are caused by collisions.

Incorrect: A manager has only yourself to blame if things go wrong.

Correct: As a manager, you have only yourself to blame if things go wrong.

The following words require a singular pronoun:

everybody	neither
each	nobody
either	a person
everyone	

Correct: Everyone should bring his or her copy of the manual to the next session on changes in the law.

If the pronoun pairs necessary to avoid sexism seem cumbersome, avoid the terms in this list. Instead, use words that take plural pronouns or use second-person *you*.

Each pronoun must refer to a specific word. If a pronoun does not refer to a specific term, add a word to correct the error.

Incorrect: We will open three new stores in the suburbs. This will bring us closer to our customers.

Correct: We will open three new stores in the suburbs. This strategy will bring us closer to our customers.

Hint: Make sure *this* and *it* refer to a specific noun in the previous sentence. If either refers to an idea, add a noun ("this strategy") to make the sentence grammatically correct.

Use *who* and *whom* to refer to people and *which* to refer to objects. *That* can refer to anything: people, animals, organizations, and objects.

Correct: The new Executive Director, who moved here from Boston, is already making friends.

Correct: The information which she wants will be available tomorrow.

Correct: This confirms the price that I quoted you this morning.

Case

Case refers to the grammatical role a noun or pronoun plays in a sentence. Figure B.1 identifies the case of each personal pronoun.

The Errors That Bother People in Organizations*

Professor Maxine Hairston constructed a questionnaire with 65 sentences, each with one grammatical error. The administrators, executives, and business people who responded were most bothered by the following:

- Wrong verb forms ("he brung his secretary with him")
- Double negatives
- Objective pronoun used for subject of sentence ("Him and Richards were the last ones hired.")
- Sentence fragments
- Run-on sentences
- Failure to capitalize proper names
- "Would of" for "would have"
- Lack of subject–verb agreement
- Comma between verb and complement ("Cox cannot predict, that street crime will diminish.")
- Lack of parallelism
- Adverb errors ("He treats his men bad.")
- "Set" for "sit"

They also disliked

- Errors in word meaning
- Dangling modifiers
- "I" as objective pronoun ("The army moved my husband and I")
- Not setting off interrupters (e.g., "However") with commas
- Tense switching
- Plural modifiers with singular nouns.

*Based on Maxine Hairston, "Not All Errors Are Created Equal: Nonacademic Readers in the Professions Respond to Lapses in Usage," *College English* 43, no. 8 (December 1981),794–806.

Figure B.1

The Case of the Personal Pronoun

	Nominative (subject of clause)	Possessive	Objective	Reflexive/ intensive
Singular				
1st person	I	my, mine	me	myself
2nd person	you	your, yours	you	yourself
3rd person	he/she/it	his/her(s)/its	him/her/it	himself/herself/itself
	one/who	one's/whose	one/whom	oneself/(no form)
Plural				
1st person	we	our, ours	us	ourselves
2nd person	you	your, yours	you	yourselves
3rd person	they	their, theirs	them	themselves

Use **nominative** pronouns for the **subject** of a clause.

Correct: Shannon Weaver and I talked to the customer, who was interested in learning more about integrated software.

Use **possessive** pronouns to show who or what something belongs to.

Correct: Microsoft Office 98 will exactly meet her needs.

Use **objective** pronouns as **objects** of verbs or prepositions.

Correct: When you send in the quote, thank her for the courtesy she showed Shannon and me.

Hint: Use *whom* when *him* would fit grammatically in the same place in your sentence.

I am writing this letter to (who/whom?) it may concern.
I am writing this letter to him.
Whom is correct.
Have we decided (who, whom?) will take notes?
Have we decided he will take notes?
Who is correct.

Use **reflexive** and **intensive** pronouns to refer to or emphasize a noun or pronoun that has already appeared in the sentence.

Correct: I myself think the call was a very productive one.

Do not use reflexive pronouns as subjects of clauses or as objects of verbs or propositions.

Incorrect: Elaine and myself will follow up on this order.

Correct: Elaine and I will follow up on this order.

Incorrect: He gave the order to Dan and myself.

Correct: He gave the order to Dan and me.

Note that the first-person pronoun comes after names or pronouns that refer to other people.

Dangling Modifier (DM)

Modifiers are words or phrases that give more information about the subject, verb, or object in a clause. A modifier **dangles** when the word it modifies is not actually in the sentence. The solution is to reword the modifier so that it is grammatically correct.

Incorrect:	Confirming our conversation, the truck will leave Monday. [The speaker is doing the confirming. But the speaker isn't in the sentence.]
Incorrect:	At the age of eight, I began teaching my children about American business. [This sentence says that the author was eight when he or she had children who could understand business.]

Correct a dangling modifier in one of these ways:

- Recast the modifier as a subordinate clause.

Correct:	As I told you, the truck will leave Monday.
Correct:	When they were eight, I began teaching my children about American business.

- Revise the main clause so its subject or object can be modified by the now-dangling phrase.

Correct:	Confirming our conversation, I have scheduled the truck to leave Monday.
Correct:	At the age of eight, my children began learning about American business.

Hint: Whenever you use a verb or adjective that ends in *-ing*, make sure it modifies the grammatical subject of your sentence. If it doesn't, reword the sentence.

Misplaced Modifier (MM)

A **misplaced modifier** appears to modify another element of the sentence than the writer intended.

Incorrect:	Customers who complain often alert us to changes we need to make. [Does the sentence mean that customers must complain frequently to teach us something? Or is the meaning that frequently we learn from complaints?]

Correct a misplaced modifier by moving it closer to the word it modifies or by adding punctuation to clarify your meaning. If a modifier modifies the whole sentence, use it as an introductory phrase or clause; follow it with a comma.

Correct:	Often, customers who complain alert us to changes we need to make.

Parallel Structure

Items in a series or list must have the same grammatical structure.

Not parallel:	In the second month of your internship, you will
	1. Learn how to resolve customers' complaints.
	2. Supervision of desk staff.
	3. Interns will help plan store displays.
Parallel:	In the second month of your internship, you will
	1. Learn how to resolve customers' complaints.
	2. Supervise desk staff.
	3. Plan store displays.
Also parallel:	Duties in the second month of your internship include resolving customers' complaints, supervising desk staff, and planning store displays.

Hint: When you have two or three items in a list (whether the list is horizontal or vertical) make sure the items are in the same grammatical form. Put lists vertically to make them easier to see.

Predication Errors

The predicate of a sentence must fit grammatically and logically with the subject.

In sentences using *is* and other linking verbs, the complement must be a noun, an adjective, or a noun clause.

Anguished English*

Richard Lederer recorded the following howlers:

- CEMETERY ALLOWS PEOPLE TO BE BURIED BY THEIR PETS.
- KICKING BABY CONSIDERED TO BE HEALTHY
- DIRECTOR OF TRUMAN LIBRARY KNOWS NEWSMAN'S PROBLEMS—HE WAS ONE.
- MAN FOUND BEATEN, ROBBED BY POLICE

*Quoted from Richard Lederer, *More Anguished English* (New York: Delacorte Press, 1993), 166–67.

What Bothers Your Boss?

Most bosses care deeply about only a few points of grammar. Find out which errors are your supervisor's pet peeves, and avoid them.

Any living language changes. New usages appear first in speaking. Here are four issues on which experts currently disagree:

1. Plural pronouns to refer to *everybody, everyone,* and *each.* Standard grammar says these words require singular pronouns.

2. Split infinitives. An infinitive is the form of a verb that contains *to: to understand.* An infinitive is **split** when another word separates the *to* from the rest of an infinitive: *to easily understand.*

3. *Hopefully* to mean *I hope that. Hopefully* means "in a hopeful manner." However, a speaker who says "Hopefully, the rain will stop" is talking about the speaker's hope, not the rain's.

4. *Verbal* to mean *oral. Verbal* means "using words." Both writing and speaking are verbal communication. Nonverbal communication (for example, body language) does not use words.

Ask your instructor and your boss whether they are willing to accept the less formal usage. When you write to someone you don't know, use standard grammar and usage.

Incorrect: The reason for this change is because the SEC now requires fuller disclosure.

Correct: The reason for this change is that the SEC now requires fuller disclosure.

Make sure that the verb describes the action done by or done to the subject.

Incorrect: Our goals should begin immediately.

Correct: Implementing our goals should begin immediately.

Understanding Punctuation

Punctuation marks are road signs to help readers predict what comes next. (See Figure B.2.)

When you move from the subject to the verb, you're going in a straight line; no comma is needed. When you end an introductory phrase or clause, the comma tells readers the introduction is over and you're turning to the main clause. When words interrupt the main clause, like this, commas tell the reader when to turn off the main clause for a short side route and when to return.

Some people have been told to put commas where they'd take breaths. That's bad advice. How often you'd take a breath depends on how big your lung capacity is, how fast and how loud you're speaking, and the emphasis you want. Commas aren't breaths. Instead, like other punctuation, they're road signs.

Punctuating Sentences

A **sentence** contains at least one main clause. A **main clause** is a complete statement. A **subordinate** or **dependent clause** contains both a subject and verb but is not a complete statement and cannot stand by itself. A phrase is a group of words that do not contain both a subject and a verb.

Main clauses
    Your order will arrive Thursday.
    He dreaded talking to his supplier.
    I plan to enroll for summer school classes.
Subordinate clauses
    if you place your order by Monday
    because he was afraid the product would be out of stock
    since I want to graduate next spring
Phrases
    With our current schedule
    As a result
    After talking to my advisor

A clause with one of the following words will be subordinate:

after
although, though
because, since

Figure B.2

What Punctuation Tells the Reader

Mark	Tells the reader
Period	We're stopping.
Semicolon	What comes next is closely related to what I just said.
Colon	What comes next is an example of what I just said.
Dash	What comes next is a dramatic example of or a shift from what I just said.
Comma	What comes next is a slight turn, but we're going in the same basic direction.

before, until

if

when, whenever

while, as

Using the correct punctuation will enable you to avoid three major sentence errors: comma splices, run-on sentences, and sentence fragments.

Comma Splices (CS)

A **comma splice** or **comma fault** occurs when two main clauses are joined only by a comma (instead of by a comma and a coordinating conjunction).

Incorrect: The contest will start in June, the date has not been set.

Correct a comma splice in one of the following ways:

- If the ideas are closely related, use a semicolon rather than a comma. If they aren't closely related, start a new sentence.

    Correct: The contest will start in June; the exact date has not been set.

- Add a coordinating conjunction.

    Correct: The contest will start in June, but the exact date has not been set.

- Subordinate one of the clauses.

    Correct: Although the contest will start in June, the date has not been set.

Remember that you cannot use just a comma with the following transitions:

however

therefore

nevertheless

moreover

Instead, use a semicolon to separate the clauses or start a new sentence.

Incorrect: Computerized grammar checkers do not catch every error, however, they may be useful as a first check before an editor reads the material.

Correct: Computerized grammar checkers do not catch every error. However, they may be useful as a first check before an editor reads the material.

Run-on Sentences (RO)

A **run-on sentence** strings together several main clauses using *and, but, or, so,* and *for.* Run-on sentences and comma splices are "mirror faults." A comma splice uses *only* the comma and omits the coordinating conjunction, while a run-on sentence uses *only* the conjunction and omits the comma. Correct a short run-on sentence by adding a comma. Separate a long run-on sentence into two or more sentences. Consider subordinating one or more of the clauses.

Incorrect: We will end up with a much smaller markup but they use a lot of this material so the volume would be high so try to sell them on fast delivery and tell them our quality is very high.

Correct: Although we will end up with a much smaller markup, volume would be high since they use a lot of this material. Try to sell them on fast delivery and high quality.

Sentence Fragments (Frag)

In a **sentence fragment,** a group of words that is not a complete sentence is punctuated as if it were a complete sentence.

The Most Common Errors in First-Year Composition Papers*

A survey of hundreds of student papers found that the following errors were most common:

1. No comma after introductory element
2. Vague pronoun reference
3. No comma in compound sentence
4. Wrong word
5. No comma in nonrestrictive clause
6. Wrong/missing inflected endings
7. Wrong or missing preposition
8. Comma splice
9. Possessive apostrophe error
10. Tense shift
11. Unnecessary shift in person
12. Sentence fragment
13. Wrong tense or verb form
14. Subject–verb agreement error
15. Lack of comma in series
16. Pronoun agreement error
17. Unnecessary comma with restrictive clause
18. Run-on or fused sentence
19. Dangling or misplaced modifier
20. Its/it's error

*Based on Robert J. Connors and Andrea A. Lunsford, "Frequency of Formal Errors in Current College Writing, or Ma and Pa Kettle Do Research," *College Composition and Communication* 39, no. 4 (December 1988), 403.

The Fumblerules of Grammar*

1. Avoid run-on sentences they are hard to read.
2. A writer must not shift your point of view.
3. Verbs has to agree with their subjects.
4. No sentence fragments.
5. Reserve the apostrophe for it's proper use and omit it when its not needed.
6. Proofread carefully to see if you any words out.
7. Avoid commas, that are un-necessary.
8. Steer clear of incorrect forms of verbs that have snuck in the language.
9. In statements involving two word phrases make an all out effort to use hyphens.
10. Last but not least, avoid clichés like the plague; seek viable alternatives.

*Quoted from William Safire, "On Language: The Fumblerules of Grammar," *New York Times Magazine*, November 11, 1979, 16, and "On Language: Fumblerule Follow-up," *New York Times Magazine*, November 25, 1979, 14.

Incorrect: Observing these people, I have learned two things about the program. The time it takes. The rewards it brings.

To fix a sentence fragment, either add whatever parts of the sentence are missing or incorporate the fragment into the sentence before it or after it.

Correct: Observing these people, I have learned that the program is time-consuming but rewarding.

Remember that clauses with the following words are not complete sentences. Join them to a main clause.

after
although, though
because, since
before, until
if
when, whenever
while, as

Incorrect: We need to buy a new computer system. Because our current system is obsolete.

Correct: We need to buy a new computer system because our current system is obsolete.

Punctuation within Sentences

The good business and administrative writer knows how to use the following punctuation marks: apostrophes, colons, commas, dashes, hyphens, parentheses, periods, and semicolons.

Apostrophe

1. Use an apostrophe in a contraction to indicate that a letter has been omitted.

    We're trying to renegotiate the contract.

    The '90s have been years of restructuring for our company.

2. To indicate possession, add an apostrophe and an *s* to the word.

    The corporation's home office is in Houston, Texas.

    Apostrophes to indicate possession are especially essential when one noun in a comparison is omitted.

    This year's sales will be higher than last year's.

    When a word already ends in an *s,* add only an apostrophe to make it possessive.

    The meeting will be held at New Orleans' convention center.

    With many terms, the placement of the apostrophe indicates whether the noun is singular or plural.

    Incorrect: The program should increase the participant's knowledge. [Implies that only one participant is in the program.]

    Correct: The program should increase the participants' knowledge. [Many participants are in the program.]

    Hint: Use "of" in the sentence to see where the apostrophe goes.

    The figures of last year = last year's figures

    The needs of our customers = our customers' needs

Note that possessive pronouns (e.g., *his, ours*) usually do not have apostrophes. The only exception is *one's*.

> The company needs the goodwill of its stockholders.

> His promotion was announced yesterday.

> One's greatest asset is the willingness to work hard.

3. Use an apostrophe to make plurals that could be confused for other words.

> I earned A's in all my business courses.

However, other plurals do not use apostrophes.

Colon

1. Use a colon to separate a main clause and a list that explains the last element in the clause. The items in the list are specific examples of the word that appears immediately before the colon.

> Please order the following supplies:
>
> > Printer ribbons
> >
> > Computer paper (20-lb. white bond)
> >
> > Bond paper (25-lb., white, 25% cotton)
> >
> > Company letterhead
> >
> > Company envelopes

When the list is presented vertically, capitalize the first letter of each item in the list. When the list is run in with the sentence, you don't need to capitalize the first letter after the colon.

> Please order the following supplies: printer ribbons, computer paper (20-lb. white bond), bond paper (25-lb., white, 25% cotton), company letterhead, and company envelopes.

Do not use a colon when the list is grammatically part of the main clause.

> Incorrect: The rooms will have coordinated decors in natural colors such as: eggplant, moss, and mushroom.
>
> Correct: The rooms will have coordinated decors in natural colors such as eggplant, moss, and mushroom.
> > or
>
> Correct: The rooms will have coordinated decors in a variety of natural colors: eggplant, moss, and mushroom.

If the list is presented vertically, some authorities suggest introducing the list with a colon even though the words preceding the colon are not a complete sentence.

2. Use a colon to join two independent clauses when the second clause explains or restates the first clause.

> Selling is simple: give people the service they need, and they'll come back with more orders.

Comma

1. Use commas to separate the main clause from an introductory clause, the reader's name, or words that interrupt the main clause. Note that commas both precede and follow the interrupting information.

> R. J. Garcia, the new Sales Manager, comes to us from the Des Moines office.

The History of Punctuation*

WHENWRITINGBEGAN
THEREWERENOBREAKS
BETWEENWORDS

In inscriptions on monuments in ancient Greece, breaks were chosen to create balance and proportion.

W H E N W R I T I
N G B E G A N T H
E R E W E R E N O
B R E A K S B E T
W E E N W O R D S

In the third century BC, Aristophanes added a dot high in the line (like this ˙), after a complete thought, or *periodos*. For part of a complete thought, or *colon,* he used a dot on the line (like this .). For a comma, or subdivision of a colon, he used a dot halfway up (like this ·).

The monks in the Middle Ages substituted a strong slash for the midway dot. As time went on, the strong slash was shortened and acquired a curl—becoming our comma today.

*Based on Lionel Casson, "howandwhy punctuationevercametobeinvented," *Smithsonian* 19, no. 7 (October 1988), 216.

A **nonessential clause** gives extra information that is not needed to identify the noun it modifies. Because nonessential clauses give extra information, they need extra commas.

> Sue Decker, who wants to advance in the organization, has signed up for the company training program in sales techniques.

Do not use commas to set off information that restricts the meaning of a noun or pronoun. **Essential clauses** give essential, not extra, information.

> Anyone ☐ who wants to advance in the organization ☐ should take advantage of on-the-job training.

Do not use commas to separate the subject from the verb, even if you would take a breath after a long subject.

> Incorrect: Laws requiring anyone collecting $5,000 or more on behalf of another person, apply to schools and private individuals as well to charitable groups and professional fund-raisers.

> Correct: Laws requiring anyone collecting $5,000 or more on behalf of another person ☐ apply to schools and private individuals as well to charitable groups and professional fund-raisers.

2. Use a comma after the first clause in a compound sentence if the clauses are long or if they have different subjects.

> This policy eliminates all sick leave credit of the employee at the time of retirement, and payment will be made only once to any individual.

Do not use commas to join independent clauses without a conjunction. Doing so produces comma splices.

3. Use commas to separate items in a series. Using a comma before the *and* or *or* is not required by some authorities, but using a comma always adds clarity. The comma is essential if any of the items in the series themselves contain the word *and*.

> The company pays the full cost of hospitalization insurance for eligible employees, spouses, and unmarried dependent children under age 23.

Dash

Use dashes to emphasize a break in thought.

> Ryertex comes in 30 grades—each with a special use.

To type a dash, use two hyphens with no space before or after.

Hyphen

1. Use a hyphen to indicate that a word has been divided between two lines.

> Attach the original receipts for lodging, meals, tips, transpor-
> tation, and registration fees.

Divide words at syllable breaks. If you aren't sure where the syllables divide, look up the word in a dictionary. When a word has several syllables, divide it after a vowel or between two consonants. Don't divide words of one syllable (e.g., *used*); don't divide a two-syllable word if one of the syllables is only one letter long (e.g., *acre*).

2. Use hyphens to join two or more words used as a single adjective.

> Order five 10- or 12-foot lengths.

> The computer-prepared Income and Expense statements will be ready next Friday.

The hyphen prevents misreading. In the first example, five lengths are needed, not lengths of 5, 10, or 12 feet. In the second example, without the hyphen, the reader might think that *computer* was the subject and *prepared* was the verb.

Parentheses

1. Use parentheses to set off words, phrases, or sentences used to explain or comment on the main idea.

   > For the thinnest Ryertex (.015″) only a single layer of the base material may be used, while the thickest (10″) may contain over 600 greatly compressed layers of fabric or paper. By varying the fabric used (cotton, asbestos, glass, or nylon) or the type of paper, and by changing the kind of resin (phenolic, melamine, silicone, or epoxy), we can produce 30 different grades.

   Any additional punctuation goes outside the second parenthesis when the punctuation applies to the whole sentence. It goes inside when it applies only to the words in the parentheses.

   > Please check the invoice to see if credit should be issued. (A copy of the invoice is attached.)

2. Use parentheses for the second of two numbers presented both in words and in figures.

   > Construction must be completed within two (2) years of the date of the contract.

Spell Checkers' Errors*

The *Dallas Morning News* raised hackles in the computer industry . . . when an editor accidentally accepted all of a spell-checker's alternate spellings in a technology article that appeared in print—changing chip maker Intel into "Until" and Microsoft into "Microvolts."

*Quoted from Joan E. Rigdon, "Microsoft Word's Spell-Checker Gets Failing Grade in Computerese," *The Wall Street Journal*, November 15, 1995, B1.

Period

1. Use a period at the end of a sentence. Leave two spaces before the next sentence.
2. Use a period after some abbreviations. When a period replaces a person's name, leave one space after the period before the next word. In other abbreviations, no space is necessary.

   > R. J. Teheaux has been named Vice President for Marketing.

   > The U.S. division plans to hire 300 new M.B.A.s in the next year.

   The tendency is to reduce the use of punctuation. It would also be correct to write

   > The US division plans to hire 300 new MBAs in the next year.

Semicolon

1. Use semicolons to join two independent clauses when they are closely related.

   > We'll do our best to fill your order promptly; however, we cannot guarantee a delivery date.

   Using a semicolon suggests that the two ideas are very closely connected. Using a period and a new sentence is also correct but implies nothing about how closely related the two sentences are.

2. Use semicolons to separate items in a series when the items themselves contain commas.

   > The final choices for the new plant are El Paso, Texas; Albuquerque, New Mexico; Salt Lake City, Utah; Eureka, California; and Eugene, Oregon.

   > Hospital benefits are also provided for certain specialized care services such as diagnostic admissions directed toward a definite disease or injury; normal maternity delivery, Caesarean section delivery, or complications of pregnancy; and in-patient admissions for dental procedures necessary to safeguard the patient's life or health.

Hint: A semicolon could be replaced by a period and a capital letter. It has a sentence on both sides.

Special Punctuation Marks

Quotation marks, square brackets, ellipses, and underlining are necessary when you use quoted material.

Quotation Marks

1. Use quotation marks around the names of brochures, pamphlets, and magazine articles.

   Enclosed are 30 copies of our pamphlet "Saving Energy."

   You'll find articles like "How to Improve Your Golf Game" and "Can You Keep Your Eye on the Ball?" in every issue.

   In US punctuation, periods and commas go inside quotation marks. Colons and semicolons go outside. Question marks go inside if they are part of the material being quoted.

2. Use quotation marks around words to indicate that you think the term is misleading.

   These "pro-business" policies actually increase corporate taxes.

3. Use quotation marks around words that you are discussing as words.

   Forty percent of the respondents answered "yes" to the first question.

   Use "Ms." as a courtesy title for a woman unless you know she prefers another title.

   It is also acceptable to underline or italicize words instead of using quotation marks.

4. Use quotation marks around words or sentences that you quote from someone else.

   "The Fog Index," says its inventor, Robert Gunning, is "an effective warning system against drifting into needless complexity."

Square Brackets

Use square brackets to add your own additions to or changes in quoted material.

Senator Smith's statement:	"These measures will increase the deficit."
Your use of Smith's statement:	According to Senator Smith, "These measures [in the new tax bill] will increase the deficit."

The square brackets show that Smith did not say these words; you add them to make the quote make sense in your document.

Ellipses

Ellipses are spaced dots. In typing, use three spaced periods for an ellipsis. When an ellipsis comes at the end of a sentence, use a dot immediately after the last letter of the sentence for a period. Then add three spaced dots. Two spaces follow the last of the four dots.

1. Use ellipses to indicate that one or more words have been omitted in the middle of quoted material. You do not need ellipses at the beginning or end of a quote.

   The Wall Street Journal notes that Japanese magazines and newspapers include advertisements for a "$2.1 million home in New York's posh Riverdale section . . . 185 acres of farmland [and] . . . luxury condos on Manhattan's Upper East Side."

2. In advertising and direct mail, use ellipses to imply the pace of spoken comments.

If you've ever wanted to live on a tropical island . . . cruise to the Bahamas . . . or live in a castle in Spain . . .

. . . you can make your dreams come true with Vacations Extraordinaire.

Underlining and Italics

1. Underline or italicize the names of newspapers, magazines, and books.

   The Wall Street Journal   *The Wall Street Journal*

   Fortune   *Fortune*

   The Wealth of Nations   *The Wealth of Nations*

   Titles of brochures and pamphlets are put in quotation marks.

2. Underline or italicize words to emphasize them.

   Here's a bulletin that gives you, in handy chart form, <u>workable data</u> on over 50 different types of tubing and pipe.

   If you have a printer that has a bold typeface, you may use bold to emphasize words.

Writing Numbers and Dates

Spell out **numbers** from one to nine. Use figures for numbers 10 and over in most cases. Always use figures for amounts of money.

Spell out any number that appears at the beginning of a sentence. If spelling it out is impractical, revise the sentence so that it does not begin with a number.

Fifty students filled out the survey.

The year 1992 marked the official beginning of the European Economic Community.

When two numbers follow each other, spell out the smaller number and figures for the larger number.

In **dates,** use figures for the day and year. The month is normally spelled out. Be sure to spell out the month in international business communication. American usage puts the month first, so that *1/10/99* means *January 10, 1999.* European usage puts the day first, so that *1/10/99* means *October 1, 1999.* Modern punctuation uses a comma before the year only when you give both the month and the day of the month:

May 1, 2000

but

Summers 1997–00

August 1999

Fall 1998

No punctuation is needed in military or European usage, which puts the day of the month first: 13 July 1998. Do not space before or after the slash used to separate parts of the date: 5/97-10/98.

Use a hyphen to join inclusive dates.

March-August 1999 (or write out: March to August 1999)

'98-'99

1996-2000

Note that you do not need to repeat the century in the date that follows the hyphen: 1998-99.

More Anguished English*

- Family Physician. Hours: 10:30-12:20; 3:30-4:45 Monday-Friday. 10:30-11:45 Saturday. Limited Amount of Patience.

- Aunt and Roach Killer—1.29.

- He is recovering from a near-fatal accident that sent him into a comma.

- The board voted by telephone pole.

- I found a liter of pups.

*Quoted from Richard Lederer, *More Anguished English* (New York: Delacorte Press, 1993), 166–67.

Words That Are Often Confused

Here's a list of words that are frequently confused. Master them, and you'll be well on the way to using words correctly.

1. accede/exceed
   accede: to yield
   exceed: to go beyond, surpass
     I accede to your demand that we not exceed the budget.

2. accept/except
   accept: to receive
   except: to leave out or exclude; but
     I accept your proposal except for point 3.

3. access/excess
   access: the right to use; admission to
   excess: surplus
     As supply clerk, he had access to any excess materials.

4. adept/adopt
   adept: skilled
   adopt: to take as one's own
     She was adept at getting people to adopt her ideas.

5. advice/advise
   advice: (noun) counsel
   advise: (verb) to give counsel or advice to someone
     I asked him to advise me but I didn't like the advice I got.

6. affect/effect
   affect: (verb) to influence or modify
   effect: (verb) to produce or cause; (noun) result
     He hoped that his argument would affect his boss's decision, but so far as he could see, it had no effect.
     The tax relief effected some improvement for the citizens whose incomes had been affected by inflation.

7. affluent/effluent
   affluent: (adjective) rich, possessing in abundance
   effluent: (noun) something that flows out
     Affluent companies can afford the cost of removing pollutants from the effluents their factories produce.

8. a lot/allot
   a lot: many (informal)
   allot: divide or give to
     A lot of players signed up for this year's draft. We allotted one first-round draft choice to each team.

9. amount/number
   amount: (use with concepts that cannot be counted individually but can only be measured)
   number: (use when items can be counted individually)
     It's a mistake to try to gauge the amount of interest he has by the number of questions he asks.

10. are/our
    are: (plural linking verb)
    our: belonging to us
      Are we ready to go ahead with our proposal?

11. attributed/contributed
    attributed: was said to be caused by
    contributed: gave something to

The rain probably contributed to the accident, but the police officer attributed the accident to driver error.

12. between/among
    between: (use with only two choices)
    among: (use with more than two choices)
    > This year the differences between the two candidates for president are unusually clear.
    > I don't see any major differences among the candidates for city council.

13. cite/sight/site
    cite: (verb) to quote
    sight: (noun) vision, something to be seen
    site: (noun) location, place where a building is or will be built
    > She cited the old story of the building inspector who was depressed by the very sight of the site for the new factory.

14. complement/compliment
    complement: (verb) to complete, finish; (noun) something that completes
    compliment: (verb) to praise; (noun) praise
    > The compliment she gave me complemented my happiness.

15. compose/comprise
    compose: make up, create
    comprise: consist of, be made up of, be composed of
    > The city council is composed of 12 members. Each district comprises an area 50 blocks square.

16. confuse/complicate/exacerbate
    confuse: to bewilder
    complicate: to make more complex or detailed
    exacerbate: to make worse
    > Because I missed the first 20 minutes of the movie, I didn't understand what was going on. The complicated plot exacerbated my confusion.

17. dependant/dependent
    dependant: (noun) someone for whom one is financially responsible
    dependent: (adjective) relying on someone else
    > IRS regulations don't let us count our 25-year-old son as a dependant, but he is still financially dependent on us.

18. describe/prescribe
    describe: list the features of something, tell what something looks like
    prescribe: specify the features something must contain
    > The law prescribes the priorities for making repairs. This report describes our plans to comply with the law.

19. discreet/discrete
    discreet: tactful, careful not to reveal secrets
    discrete: separate, distinct
    > I have known him to be discreet on two discrete occasions.

20. do/due
    do: (verb) act or make
    due: (adjective) scheduled, caused by
    > The banker said she would do her best to change the due date.
    > Due to the computer system, the payroll can be produced in only two days for all 453 employees.

21. elicit/illicit
    elicit: (verb) to draw out
    illicit: (adjective) not permitted, unlawful
    > The reporter could elicit no information from the senator about his illicit love affair.

The Knead for Approve Reed Her with a Spell Chequer*

Who wood have guest
The Spell Chequer would super seed
The assent of the editor
Who was once a mane figure? . . .
Once, awl sought his council;
Now nun prophet from him.
How suite the job was;
It was all sew fine. . . .
Never once was he board
As he edited each claws,
Going strait to his deer work
Where he'd in cyst on clarity.
Now he's holy unacceptable,
Useless and knot kneaded. . . .
This is know miner issue,
Fore he cannot urn a wage.
Iwo this he takes a fence,
Butt nose naught watt too due.
He's wade each option
Of jobs he mite dew,
But nothing peaks his interest
Like making pros clear.
Sum will see him silly
For being sew upset,
But doesn't good righting
Go beyond the write spelling?

*Quoted from Jeff Lovill, "On the Uselessness of an Editor in the Presents of a Spell Chequer," *Technical Communication* 35, no. 4 (1988), 267; and Edward M. Chilton, "Various Comments on 4Q88," *Technical Communication* 36, no. 2 (1989), 173.

22. eminent/immanent/imminent
    eminent: distinguished
    immanent: dwelling within tangible objects
    imminent: about to happen
       The eminent doctor believed that death was imminent. The eminent
       minister believed that God was immanent.

23. fewer/less
    fewer: (use for objects that can be counted individually)
    less: (use for objects that can be measured but not counted individually)
       There is less sand in this bucket; there are probably fewer grains of
       sand, too.

24. forward/foreword
    forward: ahead
    foreword: preface, introduction
       The author looked forward to writing the foreword to the book.

25. good/well
    good: (adjective, used to modify nouns; as a noun, means something that
    is good)
    well: (adverb, used to modify verbs, adjectives, and other adverbs)
       Her words "Good work!" told him that he was doing well.
       He spent a great deal of time doing volunteer work because he
       believed that doing good was just as important as doing well.

26. i.e./e.g.
    i.e.: (*id est*—that is) introduces a restatement or explanation of the
    preceding word or phrase
    e.g.: (*exempli gratia*—for the sake of an example; for example) introduces
    one or more examples
       Although he had never studied Latin, he rarely made a mistake in
       using Latin abbreviations, e.g., i.e., etc., because he associated each
       with a mnemonic device (i.e., a word or image used to help one
       remember something). He remembered *i.e.* as *in effect,* pretended that
       e.g. meant *example given,* and used *etc.* only when *examples to continue*
       would fit.

27. imply/infer
    imply: suggest, put an idea into someone's head
    infer: deduce, get an idea out from something
       She implied that an announcement would be made soon. I inferred
       from her smile that it would be an announcement of her promotion.

28. it's/its
    it's: it is, it has
    its: belonging to it
       It's clear that a company must satisfy its customers to stay in business.

29. lectern/podium
    lectern: raised stand with a slanted top that holds a manuscript for a
    reader or notes for a speaker
    podium: platform for a speaker or conductor to stand on
       I left my notes on the lectern when I left the podium at the end of my
       talk.

30. lie/lay
    lie: to recline; to tell a falsehood (never takes an object)
    lay: to put an object on something (always takes an object)
       He was laying the papers on the desk when I came in, but they aren't
       lying there now.

31. loose/lose
    loose: not tight
    lose: to have something disappear
    > If I lose weight, this suit will be loose.

32. moral/morale
    moral: (adjective) virtuous, good; (noun: morals) ethics, sense of right and wrong
    morale: (noun) spirit, attitude, mental outlook
    > Studies have shown that coed dormitories improve student morale without harming student morals.

33. objective/rationale
    objective: goal
    rationale: reason, justification
    > The objective of the meeting was to explain the rationale behind the decision.

34. personal/personnel
    personal: individual, to be used by one person
    personnel: staff, employees
    > All personnel will get personal computers by the end of the year.

35. possible/possibly
    possible: (adjective) something that can be done
    possibly: (adverb) perhaps
    > It is possible that we will be able to hire this spring. We can choose from possibly the best graduating class in the past five years.

36. precede/proceed
    precede: (verb) to go before
    proceed: (verb) to continue; (noun: proceeds) money
    > Raising the money must precede spending it. Only after we obtain the funds can we proceed to spend the proceeds.

37. principal/principle
    principal: (adjective) main; (noun) person in charge; money lent out at interest
    principle: (noun) basic truth or rule, code of conduct
    > *The Prince,* Machiavelli's principal work, describes his principles for ruling a state.

38. quiet/quite
    quiet: not noisy
    quite: very
    > It was quite difficult to find a quiet spot anywhere near the floor of the stock exchange.

39. regulate/relegate
    regulate: control
    relegate: put (usually in an inferior position)
    > If the federal government regulates the size of lettering on country road signs, we may as well relegate the current signs to the garbage bin.

40. residence/residents
    residence: home
    residents: people who live in a building
    > The residents had different reactions when they learned that a shopping mall would be built next to their residence.

41. respectfully/respectively
    respectfully: with respect
    respectively: to each in the order listed

Spelling Demons*

The words listed below (in order of increasing difficulty) are among the most frequently misspelled words in English. How many of them do you spell correctly?
1. Grammar
2. Argument
3. Surprise
4. Achieve
5. Definitely
6. Separate
7. Desirable
8. Development
9. Existence
10. Occasion
11. Assistant
12. Repetition
13. Privilege
14. Dependent
15. Consensus
16. Accommodate
17. Occurrence
18. Commitment
19. Allotted
20. Liaison
21. Proceed
22. Harass
23. Dissention
24. Prerogative
25. Inadvertent

*Based on Bruce O. Boston, ed., *Stet!* (Alexandria, VA: Editorial Experts, 1986), 267–68.

When I was introduced to the queen, the prime minister, and the court jester, I bowed respectfully, shook hands politely, and winked, respectively.

42. role/roll
role: part in a play or script, function (in a group)
roll: (noun) list of students, voters, or other members; round piece of bread; (verb) move by turning over and over
While the teacher called the roll, George—in his role as class clown—threw a roll he had saved from lunch.

43. simple/simplistic
simple: not complicated
simplistic: watered down, oversimplified
She was able to explain the proposal in simple terms without making the explanation sound simplistic.

44. stationary/stationery
stationary: not moving, fixed
stationery: paper
During the earthquake, even the stationery was not stationary.

45. their/there/they're
their: belonging to them
there: in that place
they're: they are
There are plans, designed to their specifications, for the house they're building.

46. to/too/two
to: (preposition) function word indicating proximity, purpose, time, etc.
too: (adverb) also, very, excessively
two: (adjective) the number 2
The formula is too secret to entrust to two people.

47. unique/unusual
unique: sole, only, alone
unusual: not common
I believed that I was unique in my ability to memorize long strings of numbers until I consulted the *Guinness Book of World Records* and found that I was merely unusual: someone else had equaled my feat in 1993.

48. verbal/oral
verbal: using words
oral: spoken, not written
His verbal skills were uneven: his oral communication was excellent, but he didn't write well. His sensitivity to nonverbal cues was acute: he could tell what kind of day I had just by looking at my face.
Hint: Oral comes from the Latin word for mouth, **os.** Think of Oral-B Toothbrushes: for the mouth. Verbal comes from the Latin word for word, **verba.** Nonverbal language is language that does not use words (e.g., body language, gestures).

49. whether/weather
whether: (conjunction) used to introduce possible alternatives
weather: (noun) state of the atmosphere: wet or dry, hot or cold, calm or storm
We will have to see what the weather is before we decide whether to hold the picnic indoors or out.

50. your/you're
your: belonging to you
you're: you are
You're the top candidate for promotion in your division.

Proofreading Symbols

Use the proofreading symbols in Figure B.3 to make corrections when you no longer have access to a typewriter. Figure B.4 shows how the symbols can be used to correct a typed text.

✍	delete		⌐	move to left
✍	insert a letter		⌐	move to right
¶	start a new paragraph here		⌐	move up
(stet)	stet (leave as it was before the marked change)		⊔	move down
(tr)	transpose (reverse)		#	leave a space
(lc)	lower case (don't capitalize)		⌒	close up
≡	capitalize		‖	align vertically

Figure B.3

Proofreading Symbols

Figure B.4

Marked Text

We could cut our travel bill by reimbursing employees only for the cost of a budget hotel or motel room.

A recent article from *The Wall Street Journal* suggests that many low-cost hotels and motels are trying to appeal to business travelers. chains that are actively competing for the business market include

Motel 6
Hampton Inns
Fairfield Inns
Econologde
Super 8

Comfort Inn
Travelodge.

To attract business travelers, some budget chains now offer free local phone calls, free in-room movies, free continental breakfasts, and free Computer hookups.

By staying in a budget hotel, the business travelers can save at least $10 to $20 a night--often much more. For a company whose employees travel frequently, the savings can be considerable. Last year Megacorp reimbursed employees for a total of 4,392 nights in hotels. If each employee had stayed in a budget hotel, our expenses for travel would be $44,000 to $88,000 lower. Budget hotels would not be appropriate for sales meetings since they lack photocopying facilities or meeting rooms. However, we could and should use budget hotels and motels for ordinary on-the-road travel.

Appendix B

Exercises and Problems

B.1   Diagnostic Test on Punctuation and Grammar

Identify and correct the errors in the following passages.

a.

> Company's are finding it to their advantage to cultivate their suppliers. Partnerships between a company and it's suppliers can yield hefty payoffs for both company and supplier. One example is Bailey Controls, an Ohio headquartered company. Bailey make control systems for big factories. They treat suppliers almost like departments of their own company. When a Bailey employee passes a laser scanner over a bins bar code the supplier is instantly alerted to send more parts.

b.

> Entrepreneur Trip Hawkins appears in Japanese ads for the video game system his company designed. "It plugs into the future! he says in one ad, in a cameo spliced into shots of U.S kids playing the games. Hawkins is one of several US celebrieties and business people whom plug products on Japanese TV. Jodie Foster, harrison ford, and Charlie Sheen adverstises canned coffee beer and cigarettes respectively.

c.

> Mid size firms employing between 100 and 1000 peopole represent only 4% of companies in the U.S.; but create 33% of all new jobs. One observe attributes their success to their being small enough to take advantage of economic opportunity's agilely, but big enough to have access to credit and to operate on a national or even international scale. The biggest hiring area for midsize company's is wholesale and retail sales (38% of jobs), construction (20% of jobs, manufacturing (19% of jobs), and services (18 of jobs).

B.2   Providing Punctuation

Provide the necessary punctuation in the following sentences. Note that not every box requires punctuation.

1. The system ☐ s ☐ user ☐ friendly design ☐ provides screen displays of work codes ☐ rates ☐ and client information.

2. Many other factors also shape the organization ☐ s ☐ image ☐ advertising ☐ brochures ☐ proposals ☐ stationery ☐ calling cards ☐ etc.

3. Charlotte Ford ☐ author of ☐ Charlotte Ford ☐ s ☐ Book of Modern Manners ☐ ☐ says ☐ ☐ Try to mention specifics of the conversation to fix the interview permanently in the interviewer ☐ s ☐ mind and be sure to mail the letter the same day ☐ before the hiring decision is made ☐ ☐

4. What are your room rates and charges for food service ☐

5. We will need accommodations for 150 people ☐ five meeting rooms ☐ one large room and four small ones ☐ ☐ coffee served during morning and afternoon breaks ☐ and lunches and dinners.

6. The Operational Readiness Inspection ☐ which occurs once every three years ☐ is a realistic exercise ☐ which evaluates the National Guard ☐ s ☐ ability to mobilize ☐ deploy ☐ and fight.

7. Most computer packages will calculate three different sets of percentages ☐ row percentages ☐ column percentages ☐ and table percentages ☐

8. In today ☐ s ☐ economy ☐ it ☐ s almost impossible for a firm to extend credit beyond it ☐ s regular terms.

9. The Department of Transportation does not have statutory authority to grant easements ☐ however ☐ we do have authority to lease unused areas of highway right ☐ of ☐ way.

10. The program has two goals ☐ to identify employees with promise ☐ and to see that they get the training they need to advance.

B.3   Providing Punctuation

Provide the necessary punctuation in the following sentences. Note that not every box requires punctuation.

1. To reduce secretaries ☐ overtime hours ☐ the office should hire part ☐ time secretaries to work from 5 to 9 p.m.
2. Since memberships can begin at any time during the year ☐ all member ☐ s ☐ dues are recognized on a cash basis when they are received.
3. I would be interested in working on the committee ☐ however ☐ I have decided to do less community work so that I have more time to spend with my family.
4. One of the insurance companies ☐ American Family Corp ☐ ☐ Columbus ☐ GA ☐ said it hopes to persuade the FASB to reconsider the rule.
5. The city already has five ☐ two ☐ hundred ☐ bed hospitals.
6. Students run the whole organization ☐ and are advised by a Board of Directors from the community.
7. I suggest putting a bulletin board in the rear hallway with all the interviewer ☐ s ☐ pictures on it.
8. ☐ Most African American businesses just get enough money to open the doors ☐ ☐ says Mr. Quinn ☐ adding ☐ that the $10,000 or so of savings he used to start up simply wasn ☐ enough ☐ ☐
9. Otis Conward, Jr ☐ ☐ who grew up in this area ☐ now heads the Council for Economic development.
10. Volunteers also participate in a one ☐ on ☐ one pal program.

B.4   Editing for Grammar and Usage

Revise these sentences to correct errors in grammar and usage.

1. As one of the students in a good program, our company is interested in interviewing you.
2. By making an early reservation, it will give us more time to coordinate our trucks to better serve your needs.
3. Videoconferencing can be frustrating. Simply because little time is available for casual conversation.
4. Often documents end up in files that aren't especially good.
5. Pay yourself with the Automatic Savings Account, with this account any amount your choose will be transferred automatically from your checking account to your savings account each month.
6. We help clients
   - Manage change
   - Marketing/promotion
   - Developing better billing systems.
7. My education and training has prepared me to contribute to your company.
8. Employees which lack experience in dealing with people from other cultures may benefit from seminars in international business communication.
9. A team of people from marketing, finance, and production are preparing the proposal.
10. A new employee should try to read verbal and nonverbal signals to see which aspects of your job are most important.

B.5   Editing for Grammar and Usage

Revise the following sentences to eliminate errors in grammar and usage.

1. The number of students surveyed that worked more than 20 hours a week was 60%.
2. Not everyone is promoted after six months some people might remain in the training program a year before being moved to a permanent assignment.
3. The present solutions that has been suggested are not adequate.
4. At times while typing and editing, the text on your screen may not look correct.
5. All employees are asked to cut back on energy waste by the manager.
6. The benefits of an on-line catalog are
   1. We will be able to keep records up-to-date;
   2. Broad access to the catalog system from any networked terminal on campus;
   3. The consolidation of the main catalog and the catalogs in the departmental and branch libraries;
   4. Cost savings.
7. You can take advantage of several banking services. Such as automatic withdrawal of a house

or car payment and direct deposit of your pay check.

8. As a freshman, business administration was intriguing to me.

9. Thank you for the help you gave Joanne Jackson and myself.

10. I know from my business experience that good communication among people and departments are essential in running a successful corporation.

B.6   Editing for Grammar and Usage

Revise the following sentences to eliminate errors in grammar and usage.

1. If a group member doesn't complete their assigned work, it slows the whole project down.

2. Our phones are constantly being used. Not only for business calls, but also for personal calls.

3. Todd drew the graphs after him and I discussed the ideas for them.

4. Originally a group of four, a member dropped out after the first meeting due to a death in the family.

5. Our group met seven times outside of class, we would have met even more if we could have found times when we could all get together.

6. There has also been suggestions for improving the airflow in the building.

7. I didn't appreciate him assuming that he would be the group's leader.

8. With people like yourself giving gifts, the 4-H program will be able to survive and grow.

9. Volunteers need a better orientation to Planned Parenthood as a whole, to the overall clinic function, and to the staff there is also a need to clarify volunteer responsibilities.

10. Children are referred to the Big Brother/Big Sister program by their school social workers, often from underprivileged homes.

B.7   Using Plurals and Possessives

Choose the right word for each sentence.

1. Many Canadian (companies, company's) are competing effectively in the global market.

2. We can move your (families, family's) furniture safely and efficiently.

3. The (managers, manager's) ability to listen is just as important as his or her technical knowledge.

4. A (memos, memo's) style can build goodwill.

5. (Social workers, social worker's) should tell clients about services available in the community.

6. The (companies, company's) benefits plan should be checked periodically to make sure it continues to serve the needs of employees.

7. Information about the new community makes the (families, family's) move easier.

8. The (managers, manager's) all have open-door policies.

9. (Memos, memo's) are sent to other workers in the same organization.

10. Burnout affects a (social workers, social worker's) productivity as well as his or her morale.

B.8   Choosing the Right Word

Choose the right word for each sentence.

1. Exercise is (good, well) for patients who have had open-heart surgery.

2. This response is atypical, but it is not (unique, unusual).

3. The personnel department continues its (roll, role) of compiling reports for the federal government.

4. The Accounting Club expects (its, it's) members to come to meetings and participate in activities.

5. Part of the fun of any vacation is (cite, sight, site)-seeing.

6. The (lectern, podium) was too high for the short speaker.

7. The (residence, residents) of the complex have asked for more parking spaces.

8. Please order more letterhead (stationary, stationery).

9. The closing of the plant will (affect, effect) house prices in the area.

10. Better communication (among, between) design and production could enable us to produce products more efficiently.

B.9 Choosing the Right Word

Choose the right word for each sentence.

1. The audit revealed a small (amount, number) of errors.
2. Diet beverages have (fewer, less) calories than regular drinks.
3. In her speech, she (implied, inferred) that the vote would be close.
4. We need to redesign the stand so that the catalog is eye-level instead of (laying, lying) on the desk.
5. (Their, There, They're) is some evidence that (their, there, they're) thinking of changing (their, there, they're) policy.

6. The settlement isn't yet in writing; if one side wanted to back out of the (oral, verbal) agreement, it could.
7. In (affect, effect), we're creating a new department.
8. The firm will be hiring new (personal, personnel) in three departments this year.
9. Several customers have asked that we carry more campus merchandise, (i.e., e.g.,) pillows and mugs with the college seal.
10. We have investigated all of the possible solutions (accept, except) adding a turning lane.

B.10 Choosing the Right Word

Choose the right word for each sentence.

1. The author (cites, sights, sites) four reasons for computer phobia.
2. The error was (do, due) to inexperience.
3. (Your, you're) doing a good job motivating (your, you're) subordinates.
4. One of the basic (principals, principles) of business communication is "Consider the reader."
5. I (implied, inferred) from the article that interest rates would go up.
6. Working papers generally are (composed, comprised) of working trial balance, assembly

sheets, adjusting entries, audit schedules, and audit memos.
7. Eliminating time clocks will improve employee (moral, morale).
8. The (principal, principle) variable is the trigger price mechanism.
9. (Its, It's) (to, too, two) soon (to, too, two) tell whether the conversion (to, too, two) computerized billing will save as much time as we hope.
10. Formal training programs (complement, compliment) on-the-job opportunities for professional growth.

B.11 Tracking Your Own Mechanical Errors

Analyze the mechanical errors (grammar, punctuation, word use, and typos) in each of your papers.

- How many different errors are marked on each paper?
- Which three errors do you make most often?
- Is the number of errors constant in each paper, or does the number increase or decrease during the term?

As Your Instructor Directs,

a. Correct each of the mechanical errors in one or more papers.

b. Deliberately write two new sentences in which you make each of your three most common errors. Then write the correct version of each sentence.
c. Write a memo to your instructor discussing your increasing mastery of mechanical correctness during the semester or quarter.
d. Briefly explain to the class how to avoid one kind of error in grammar, punctuation, or word use.

Making and Communicating Meaning

Communication Channels in Organizations

A Model of the Communication Process

Principles of Semantics

1. Perception Involves the Perceiver as Well as What Is Perceived.
2. Observations, Inferences, and Judgments Are Not the Same Thing.
3. No Two Things Are Ever Exactly Alike.
4. Things Change Significantly with Time.
5. Most *Either-Or* Classifications Are Not Legitimate.
6. A Statement Is Never the Whole Story.
7. Words Are Not Identical to the Objects They Represent.
8. The Symbols Used in Communication Must Stand for Essentially the Same Thing in the Minds of the Sender and the Receiver.

Summary of Key Points

Making and Communicating Meaning

Ruth Ann Hendrickson | *Policy Analyst, Battelle Memorial Institute*

www.battelle.org

Ruth Ann Hendrickson conducts policy analysis and prepares reports for Congress and federal agencies that support public policy development and technology deployment. Headquartered in Columbus, Ohio, Battelle serves industry and government by developing, commercializing, and managing technology.

O ur projects start out as brainstorming around a table. We bring in government representatives, policy analysts, economists, subject-matter experts from Battelle, industry representatives, and state and local planning officials. Everyone has something to say, since the decision will affect their organizations and their lives. Sometimes the same idea comes up from several different perspectives. It's like a game of "telephone." As information goes from one person to another, it can be distorted, lost, or embroidered. Our job is to try to verify and organize what people have said into an objective document that can be reviewed by, for example, the Secretary of the US Department of Transportation. Reports are our products.

> " *The biggest challenge of my job is to ensure that we see the nuances of an issue.* "

The scientific method drives what we do. Policy analysis and development should be based on facts and inferences—which can be verified—not on judgments and opinions. Business people often are very emotional. Sometimes, emotion is wrapped up in money—people want to do things that will benefit them financially. But emotions come from other sources as well. Sometimes someone will argue passionately about a safety or an environmental issue, but the passion is based on emotions, not facts. We define facts as results that can be replicated—so that whoever collects the data, the results stay the same. When the results change, you have a specific observation, perhaps, but not a fact.

Recently we worked on a study that will be used to determine regulations for truck size and weight. The federal government will use the study to support decisions about regulations for highways; some states may also base decisions on the report. These decisions have to be based on factual analysis, not on emotional response. For the study, we prepare estimations from models, compile data, gather information, conduct analysis, verify that the data are reliable, and screen out unsubstantiated opinions and judgments.

The biggest challenge in my job is to ensure that we see the nuances of an issue. It's important that we not polarize an issue, seeing only black and white. Instead, with public policy, it's important to see many possible alternatives and to think outside the box. If you don't do that, policy will never change.

He Sounds Older than He Looks*

Low-tech communication can have advantages. Michael G. Rubin makes most of his deals by phone, thus avoiding questions about his age.

At the age of 13, with $2,500 in bar mitzvah money, he opened a ski-repair shop in the basement of his parents' home. The next year, he opened his first retail store. By the time he was 16, the single store had expanded into a small chain.

When he was 17, he founded KPR Sports International. Within five years, the company was earning $5 million on sales of $50 million. Mr. Rubin was 22.

*Based on Stephanie N. Mehta, "Man in a Hurry: A Mogul in Sporting Goods at Age 22," *The Wall Street Journal*, June 5, 1995, B1.

Many miscommunications arise not because people genuinely disagree but because they use symbols to mean different things and make different assumptions. **Communication theory** attempts to explain what happens when we communicate. **Semantics** is the study of the way our behavior is influenced by the words and other symbols we use to communicate. (Sometimes it is called *general semantics* to distinguish it from more narrow meanings of *semantics*.) Because semantics deals with the way we perceive and process information, conflicts that "are just a matter of semantics" may be serious. Depending on the situation, it may or may not be possible to find words that everyone can endorse.

Communication theory and semantics both show why and where communication can break down. They are most useful for persuasion in difficult situations, working and writing in groups, and writing reports. This appendix suggests what we can do—as writers and speakers—to get more of our meaning across to other people and—as readers and listeners—to more accurately understand the messages that we receive.

Communication Channels in Organizations

Channels vary in speed, accuracy of transmission, cost, number of messages carried, number of people reached, efficiency, and ability to promote goodwill. Depending on the audience, your purposes, and the situation, one channel may be better than another.

Oral channels are better for group decision making, allow misunderstandings to be cleared up more quickly, and seem more personal. Shorter communication channels are more accurate than longer chains. And all-channel patterns, where everyone can communicate with everyone else, produce better group decisions and more satisfaction. Figure C.1 illustrates some of the communication channels that exist in organizations.

Managers choose channels based on their familiarity with the channel and on the situation. Lamar Reinsch and Raymond Beswick found that voice mail was the preferred channel when employees on one shift needed to communicate with those on another. Administrative, professional, and technical workers were less likely to use voice mail for complex or negative messages or for messages that needed to be documented in writing. In fact, for important messages when the cost of miscommunication was high, managers usually used two different channels, for example, talking to someone about a written memo.[1]

Channel choice may also be influenced by organizational culture. At Microsoft, e-mail is the preferred channel, and new employees have to learn to use it effectively.

A Model of the Communication Process

The following model of the communication process drastically simplifies what is perhaps the most complex human activity. However, even a simplified model can give us a sense of the complexity of the communication process. And the model is useful in helping us see where and why miscommunication occurs. Figure C.2 shows the basic process that occurs when one person tries to communicate ideas to someone else.

The process begins when Person A (let's call him Alex) **perceives** some stimulus. Here we are talking about literal perception: the ability to see, to hear, to taste, to smell, to touch. Next, Alex **interprets** what he has perceived. Is it important? Unusual? The next step is for Alex to **choose** or **select** the information

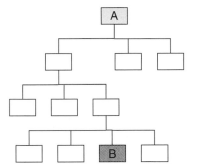

Direct channel from A to B

A must go through other people to get to B.

Figure C.1

Examples of Communication Patterns in Organizations

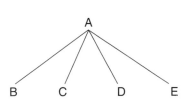

A can send messages to four people simultaneously. They must go through A to send messages to each other.

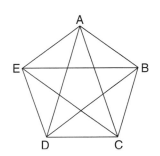

A can send messages to four people simultaneously. They can send messages directly to each other.

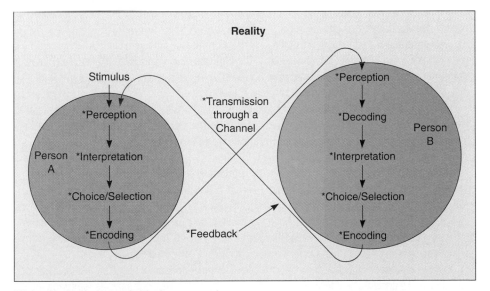

*Noise (and miscommunication) can occur here.

Figure C.2

A Model of Two-Person Communication with Feedback

he wishes to send to Person B (whom we'll call Barbara). Now Alex is ready to put his ideas into words. (Some people argue that we can think only in words and would put this stage before interpretation and choice.) Words are not the only way to convey ideas; gestures, clothing, and pictures can carry meaning nonverbally. The stage of putting ideas into any of these symbols is called **encoding.** Then Alex must **transmit** the message to Barbara using some **channel.** Channels include memos, phone calls, meetings, billboards, TV ads, and e-mail, to name just a few.

To receive the message, Barbara must first **perceive** it. Then she must **decode** it, that is, extract meaning from the symbols. Barbara then repeats the steps Alex has gone through: interpreting the information, choosing a response, and encoding it. The response Barbara sends to Alex is called **feedback.** Feedback may be direct and immediate or indirect and delayed; it may be verbal or nonverbal.

Noise can interfere with every aspect of the communication process. Noise may be physical or psychological. Physical noise could be a phone line with static, a lawn mower roaring outside a classroom, or handwriting that is hard to read. Psychological noise could include not liking a speaker, being concerned about something other than the message, or already having one's mind made up on an issue.

Channel overload occurs when the channel cannot handle all the messages that are being sent. A small business may have only two phone lines; no one else can get through if both lines are in use. **Information overload** occurs when more messages are transmitted than the human receiver can handle. Some receivers process information "first come, first served." Some may try to select the most important messages and ignore others. A third way is to depend on abstracts or summaries prepared by other people. None of these ways is completely satisfactory.

Here's how the process might work in an organizational situation:

Alex is an inspector for a state Department of Public Health. He inspects nursing homes to be sure that they meet state standards. Answering some of the questions on the form calls only for **perception** (Does each resident have a separate bed?). Others depend on **interpretation** as well as perception (Do residents receive appropriate care?). Today Alex is appalled at the condition of the Olde Folks Inne. He must **choose** details to put in his report to document his judgment that Olde Folks violates state standards.

Alex **encodes** his information in words only; he didn't think to bring a camera along, and he doesn't think a drawing or a table is necessary. The **channel** he chooses is the standard format for inspection reports in his office. He **transmits** his report to his boss, who may forward it to the attorney general's office if the violations are sufficiently severe.

Barbara is a lawyer in the attorney general's office. She gets Alex's report about three weeks after he wrote it (the **channel** isn't very fast) but doesn't read the report for another two weeks because she's so busy. Barbara is experiencing **information overload:** she cannot deal with messages as fast as they arrive.

When Barbara finally reads Alex's report, she **perceives** the typed document and **decodes** it. There are some technical terms in the report (Alex has talked about § 302.1.a of the State Code for Nursing Homes), which she understands since she's an expert in this area. She must **interpret** Alex's information. Are the violations severe enough to warrant filing a case against Olde Folks? She thinks they are. Furthermore, the governor made a speech three months ago promising to curb abuses in nursing homes, so clearing up this case will make her and her office look good.

Barbara **chooses** points that she wants to check on; she **encodes** her questions in simple, direct language and **transmits** her message to Alex by a phone call. Her questions serve as **feedback.** Alex learns that his report is on target, but that at several points Barbara needs more information. (It isn't enough to say that residents are *neglected*; Barbara needs measurable, objective data to prove her case.)

The initial communication circuit expands. Barbara makes an appointment to visit the nursing home with Alex to collect the evidence she needs and interview some of the residents. She adds these **perceptions** to the information Alex has already given her. In her office after the visit, Barbara will **interpret** the evidence, **choose** the strongest arguments, and **encode** and **transmit** messages designed to make the nursing home make the necessary improvements voluntarily. She'll try persuasion and negotiation first; if they fail, she'll **encode** and **transmit** the documents necessary to file a suit against the nursing home.

The example above represents successful communication. But things don't always work so well. At every stage, both Alex and Barbara could misperceive, misinterpret, choose badly, encode poorly, and choose inappropriate channels. Miscommunication can also occur because different people have different frames of reference. We always interpret messages in light of our personal experiences, our cultures (➤ p. 315) and subcultures, and even the point in history at which we live.

Principles of Semantics

Semantic principles offer guidelines for improving communication. The basic principles of semantics may be expressed in eight statements. In the list below, the principles are linked to the parts of the communication model they explain.

Perception

1. Perception involves the perceiver as well as what is perceived.

Interpretation

2. Observations, inferences, and judgments are not the same thing.
3. No two things are ever exactly alike.
4. Things change significantly with time.
5. Most *either-or* classifications are not legitimate.

Choice

6. A statement is never the whole story.

Encoding and decoding

7. Words are not identical to the objects they represent.
8. The symbols used in communication must stand for essentially the same thing in the minds of the sender and the receiver.

Let's look at each of these principles.

1. Perception Involves the Perceiver as Well as What Is Perceived.

What we see is conditioned by what we are able to see, what we have seen in the past, what we are prepared to see, and what we want to see.

Our ability to perceive is limited first of all by our senses. Some people cannot distinguish between red and green; some people need glasses to see or hearing aids to hear. Perception is also affected by context. A line may appear longer or shorter depending on arrows at its ends (Figure C.3a). A circle may appear bigger or smaller depending on the circle around it (Figure C.3b). Parallel lines may appear slanted when other lines cross them (Figure C.3c). A symbol may appear to be the letter *S* or the number *5* depending on whether it's part of a word or a number (Figure C.3d).

Perceptions can even shape reality. In one school, a group of researchers gave teachers their students' aptitude scores, telling the teachers that they wanted to see whether high-scoring children really learned more quickly. At the end of the term, the high-aptitude children indeed scored higher on achievement tests than their classmates did. At this point, the researchers revealed the truth: the aptitude scores they had given the teachers had no relation to the students' real scores. The children who learned the most were not the smartest ones, but rather those the teachers *perceived* to be the smartest—those they expected to learn most easily. Evidently, by nonverbal feedback, extra attention, or some other means, the teachers enabled these children to learn more, whether or not they really were "smart."[2]

Freshness Is in the Eye of the Beholder*

Stew Leonard's food store in Norwalk, Connecticut, is one of the most successful supermarkets in the United States. Part of the success comes from listening to customers—and giving them what they ask for.

At a focus group meeting, a woman complained that the store didn't sell fresh fish. The fish sales rep, who was also at the meeting, protested: the fish came fresh every morning, some from the Fulton Fish Market, some from the Boston Piers. But the customer held her ground. To her, fish on a styrofoam plate in plastic wrap didn't look fresh.

What did the Leonards do? "We set up a fish bar with ice in it . . . it's the same price as over in the package. Our packaged fish didn't decrease at all, but we doubled our fish sales. We were doing about 15,000 pounds a week; now we're doing 30,000 pounds a week."

*Based on "In Search of Excellence: The Film," transcript by John Nathan (Waltham, MA: Nathan-Tyler Productions, 1985), 6–8; and Joanne Kaufman, "In the Moo: Shopping at Stew Leonard's," *The Wall Street Journal,* September 17, 1987, 28.

Figure C.3

How Context Affects Perception

a.

b.

c.

d.

Nike's "swoosh" is such a powerful symbol that ads don't need to carry the brand name.

1-800-305-2185

This experiment has implications for supervisors as well as teachers, for it suggests that our own expectations may shape the performances we get from those we evaluate.

Perception is also affected by what we want to see. Most people have a tendency to attribute their own feelings to other people as well; we tend to repress ideas that are unpleasant or threatening. We may tune out messages we think will challenge our own positions; we seek messages that support the positions we have taken. The most avid readers of car ads are people who have just bought that make of car and who want to be reassured that they made the right choice.[3]

Use these correctives to check the accuracy of your perceptions:

1. Recognize that everyone's perception will be in some measure biased; the person who sees only reality does not exist.
2. Recognize that different positions cause us to view reality differently and to make different inferences from what we observe. When you disagree with someone, try to go back to the original observation to see if a difference in perception is at the root of the conflict.
3. If a new idea comes along that does not fit neatly into your worldview, recognize that your worldview, not the challenging idea, may need rethinking.

2. Observations, Inferences, and Judgments Are Not the Same Thing

> Ten minutes before lunchtime, Jan is talking on the phone. Her manager thinks, "I don't believe it! She's talking again. Doesn't she ever work?" Jan is talking to a potential customer; she sees the call as part of her job, since it may eventually lead to a sale. She can't understand why her manager doesn't think she's serious about her career.

Jan's manager sees a woman talking on the phone; he assumes that she's wasting time. He has jumped to the wrong conclusion about the meaning of her behavior. But, as Tim R. V. Davis points out, we are usually less interested in an action than in what we think that action means.[4] And interpretation invariably creates the possibility of error.

Semanticists would say that Jan's boss is confusing observations and inferences. To a semanticist, an **observation** is a statement that you yourself have verified. An **inference** is a statement that you have not personally verified, but whose truth or falsity could be established, either now or in the future. A **judgment** or an **opinion** is a statement that can never be verified, since it includes terms that cannot be measured objectively. Let's look at some examples.

1. The book you are reading is titled *Business and Administrative Communication.*
2. The author teaches at The Ohio State University.
3. The book is the best college text in business communication.

Statement 1 is an observation: you can verify it by checking the cover and title page. Statement 2 is an inference. It seems reasonable, based on what the title page says, but you don't know that of your own knowledge. (Even if the statement was true when the book went to press, is it still true?) However, you could check the truth of the statement if you wanted to take the time and trouble to do so. Statement 3 is a judgment. There is no way to prove that it is true, because people will have different notions of what makes a textbook the "best."

Semanticists claim that only observations are facts. Consider this statement:

Scientists first cloned mammals in 1997.

Is that a fact? Very few people reading this book observed the birth of the cloned sheep in Scotland in person. Most of us saw pictures of the sheep on TV or read about it in newspapers and newsmagazines. We accept statements about the cloning as fact because we trust the TV announcers who reported it

General Inference*

Our battalion reported to the recreation-theater for a briefing by the new general. Among the topics he spoke about was safety. "How many of you wore your seat belts on the way over here?" he asked us. Of the 400 soldiers present, only a few raised their hands.

The general, obviously annoyed, began to berate us for not following regulations. Then his aide leaned over to him. "Excuse me, sir," he whispered. "Their battalion area is across the street, so most of them walked."

*Quoted from "Humor in Uniform," *Reader's Digest,* July 1993, 111.

The Camera Lies*

The truthfulness of photographic images has been vastly overrated. . . . [Cameras] can distort the viewer's interpretation of reality in at least six ways:

- The angle of view is critical, as football fans know well from instant replays. From one angle of view, the receiver is in bounds; from another, it's no catch.

- The framing of an image extracts only a portion of a scene. . . . What lies beyond the edge of the frame could lead to a completely different reading of the situation.

- Timing also removes context, by isolating a fraction of a second in time . . . Was the Congressman truly asleep or just blinking?

- Under- or overexposure can . . . wash out detail in parts of an image, deleting essential information.

- The lens itself modifies perspective. A telephoto lens makes foreground and background objects appear much closer to each other than they really are.

- Reproduction size significantly alters perception of content. . . . [Details can be emphasized by blowing up the photo; patterns can be hidden when the photo doesn't show] "the whole picture."

*Quoted from A. G., "Photographic Truth: Fact or Fiction," *NADTP Journal*, September 1993, 16–18.

then and the books that record it now. But all of us have seen images on TV that were fiction, not fact. Digital imaging allows editors to alter pictures in magazines and books. In the mid-1990s, The Gap removed the cigarettes that jazz trumpeter Miles Davis and actor John Wayne were holding in pictures showing them in khakis.[5] Nor is printed information necessarily true. A widely quoted 1987 report called "Workplace 2000" said that the percentage of non-Hispanic white males entering the US workforce would drop to 15% by the end of the century. A missing word and the word *entering* distorted the meaning: actually, the percentage of white males in the workforce is expected to decline only 3 percentage points, from 41% in 1994 to 38% in 2005.[6]

Usually, we call statements *facts* if nearly everyone in our culture accepts them as true. But something is not necessarily true just because large numbers of people believe it. Before Columbus's discovery of America, nearly everyone believed that the world was flat. If one defines *facts* not as widely shared beliefs but as observations, there are almost no facts. Almost everything we know we take on someone else's authority rather than on our own. Even much of what we know by observation may be inference rather than direct observation. Furthermore, observations vary from person to person, since different people will have verified different things.

In everyday life and in business, you have to make decisions based on inferences ("That driver whose right turn signal is blinking intends to turn right." "I will live long enough to need a retirement fund." "The sales figures I've been given are accurate.") and even on judgments ("We have too much money tied up in long-term investments."). What should you as a reader or writer do?

Both as a reader and writer,

1. Check to see whether a statement is an observation, an inference, or a judgment.

As a reader or listener making decisions based on information you get from other people,

2. Estimate the accuracy of the inference by comparing it to your experiences with the source and with this kind of situation. If the cost of making a mistake is high, try to get more information.

As a writer or speaker trying to persuade people,

3. Use measurable statements, not just statements that contain value terms that will mean different things to different people.

   Not: Buying a slag grinder would be a good investment.

   But: Buying a slag grinder will enable us to save $25,000 on the Moreland order alone.

4. Label your inferences, so that your audience can distinguish between what you know to be the case and what you think, assume, believe, or judge to be true. In the following examples, the italicized words remind readers that the statements are inferences.

He predicts that the stock market *could* move up an additional 10% to 20% during the next 12 to 18 months.

The results of our survey suggest that employees will accept the proposed limits on health care benefits only if benefits for top management are also frozen or cut.

3. No Two Things Are Ever Exactly Alike

We make sense of the world by grouping things into categories. Once we have categories, we do not have to evaluate each new experience independently; instead, we simply assign it to a category and then make the response we find appropriate to that category.

Unfortunately, this convenient lumping can lead to **stereotyping:** putting similar people or events into a single category, even though significant differences exist. A list of the customers whose accounts are overdue, for example, may include several different kinds of people:

- A good customer who is behind on bills because of a temporary setback.
- A marginal risk who won't pay the bill until forced to do so.
- Someone whose record-keeping is poor and who has honestly forgotten to pay.
- Someone who claims that he or she never received the merchandise or that the amount of the bill is in error and who is delaying payment until the dispute is settled.

The approach that would be needed to get a customer in the second category to pay would be unnecessary and even offensive if used with customers in other groups. Different "delinquent" customers need to be treated differently.

Generalizing—faultily—on the basis of experience is a particular problem when our experience is limited to one or two cases. Suppose, for example, that someone has an Asian supervisor who isn't a good boss. If the supervisor is the only Asian boss the employee has ever known, the employee may conclude that Asians don't make good supervisors. If the same employee has an Anglo supervisor who isn't a good boss, he or she is less likely to assume that Anglos can't be good supervisors. Because we see many Anglo supervisors, some of whom are better than others, it is easy to recognize that the weakness of an individual doesn't condemn the whole group.

To guard against stereotyping, you should

1. Recognize significant differences as well as similarities. The members of any one group are not identical.
2. Be sure that any analogy you use to make your point clear is accurate at the point of comparison.

4. Things Change Significantly with Time

If you keep up with the stock market, with commodity prices, or with interest rates, you know that things (especially prices) change significantly with time.

People change too. The sales representative who was once judged too abrasive to make a good supervisor may have mellowed by now; employees who accepted management dictates without question 20 years ago may be more critical; the student who almost flunked out freshman year may have settled down, solved his or her problems, and become an excellent prospect for employment or graduate school.

Someone who does not recognize that prices, situations, and people change is guilty of making a **frozen evaluation.** The following corrections help us remember not to freeze evaluations:

1. Date statements. The price of IBM stock on October 20, 1991, is not the price of IBM stock on January 3, 2001.
2. Provide a frame of reference so your reader has some basis for comparing grades, profits, injuries, percentages, or whatever the relevant criterion may be.

3. Periodically retest your assumptions about people, businesses, products, and services to make sure that your evaluations apply to the present situation.

5. Most *Either-Or* Classifications Are Not Legitimate

A common logical fallacy is **polarization:** trying to force the reader into a position by arguing that there are only two possible positions, one of which is clearly unacceptable:

> Either the supervisor runs this department with a firm hand, or anarchy will take over and the work will never get done.

Very few areas of life allow only two options. Running a department "with a firm hand" is only one of several possible leadership styles; sharing authority with or even transferring it entirely to subordinates need not result in anarchy.

Even people who admit that there are more than two possible positions may still limit the options unnecessarily. Imposing limits that do not exist in reality is called **blindering,** after the blinders that horses wear. Blindering can lead to polarization.

Sometimes blindering is responsible for bad questions in surveys:

> Do you own _____ , rent _____ , or live with your parents _____ ?

At first glance, that may seem to cover the options. But what about someone who lives with a friend or with relatives other than parents? What about a minister who lives in a parsonage or manse furnished by the church as part of the minister's compensation? The minister does not own the house, but neither does he or she rent it. Depending on what the makers of the questionnaire really want to know, better questions would be:

How much is your housing worth a month?
How much do you pay a month for your housing?

Polarization sharpens divisions between people and obscures the common ground on which they could forge a decision that everyone could live with. Blindering prevents our seeing creative solutions to the problems we face. Here are some correctives:

1. Recognize the complexities of a situation. Resist the temptation to oversimplify.
2. Whenever you see only two alternatives, consciously search for a third, and maybe even a fourth or fifth, before you make your decision.
3. Redefine the question or problem to get at the real issue.

   Don't ask: How can I as a manager show that I'm in control?
   Ask: How can we improve productivity in this unit?

6. A Statement Is Never the Whole Story.

It is impossible to know everything; it is impossible to tell someone everything. Thinking that we know everything about a subject or can communicate everything about it that is important is the fallacy semanticists call **allness.** When we

---

But Things Are Different Now*

Conventional wisdom is that US companies can't sell unaltered appliances in Japan: Japanese houses are just too small for them. Conventional wisdom is no longer true.

The Japanese discount chain Kojima sells GE appliances. Between June 1995 and June 1996, GE's share of the Japanese refrigerator market went from 1% to 3%.

Why the change? Two factors seem responsible: more Japanese women continue to work after marriage and can't shop daily for food. And Japan's weak economy has made consumers interested in saving money. A GE refrigerator costs about half as much as a smaller Japanese model.

True, the larger model won't fit in small kitchenettes. Buyers solve that problem by putting the US refrigerators in their living rooms.

*Based on Morihiko Shirouzu, "Flouting 'Rules' Sells GE Fridges in Japan," *The Wall Street Journal*, October 31, 1995, B1.

assume that a statement contains all the important information, or when the context is omitted (deliberately or inadvertently), meanings are inevitably twisted.

For example, you've probably read that US investments suffer because US families save far less than do Japanese families. But, according to several economists, this statement overlooks differences in what counts as savings and as investments. Many US families own their own homes, yet their equity isn't considered "savings." Few Japanese own homes; their "savings" are more likely to be in stocks and bonds. Economist Fumio Hayashi points out that Japanese accounting values depreciation at historical cost figures, thus understating the value of assets and making investments look higher. Furthermore, the US counts government spending—even on schools, roads, and warships—as consumption. The Japanese system considers such expenditures to be investments.[7] When these differences are considered, the alleged gap between the two countries' savings and investment rates disappears.

Since, even with the best intentions, we cannot include everything, what can we do to avoid misstatements by implication?

1. Recognize that the reports you get are filtered; you are not getting all the facts, and you are almost certainly getting inferences as well as observations.
2. Check the correspondence you send out to make sure you have provided the background information the reader needs to interpret your message accurately.

7. Words Are Not Identical to the Objects They Represent.

People perceive objects and think of ideas; they attach labels to those objects and ideas. Other labels could be substituted without changing reality. Indeed, the ability to attach a new label to an object—to attach a different meaning to it—is a key element of creative intelligence. In the **semantic triangle** in Figure C.4, there is no base, no connection between the thing and the word that symbolizes it. People, who name things and use words, provide the only connection.

We often respond to the label rather than to reality. Our degree of distress during a bleak economic period is likely to be as much a product of the label given the period as it is of the rate of unemployment: a *slowdown* doesn't sound as bad as a *recession,* and even that is better than a *depression.* Labeling a book a *best-seller* is sure to increase sales. An album titled "John Denver's Greatest Hits" catapulted Denver to popularity; none of his previous records had been hits. Billy Joel put the song "You're Only Human" on his "Greatest Hits" album before he had even released it as a single.

Because people respond to symbols, organizations choose names carefully. Corporate name changes raise stock prices 2.4% "solely because of name

The Map Is Not the Territory*

Traveling over the United States in a balloon, Huck Finn expects the world to look just like the maps he has seen:

". . . [If] we was going so fast we ought to be past Illinois, oughtn't we?"

"Certainly."

"Well, we ain't."

"What's the reason we ain't?"

"I know by the color. We're right over Illinois yet. And you can see for yourself that Indiana ain't in sight."

"I wonder what's the matter with you, Huck. You know by the *color?*"

"Yes, of course I do."

"What's the color got to do with it?"

"It's got everything to do with it. Illinois is green, Indiana is pink. You show me any pink down here, if you can. No, sir; it's green."

"Indiana *pink?* Why, what a lie!"

"It ain't no lie; I've seen it on the map, and it's pink."

*Quoted from Mark Twain, *Tom Sawyer Abroad,* Chap. 3, *The Family Mark Twain* (New York: Harper, 1935), 1101–02.

Figure C.4

Semantic Triangle

What's in a Name?, (I)*

If you love God, mom or apple pie, you'll adore the US Congress.

Lawmakers this term have been drafting a rich assortment of nifty-sounding legislation. First came the Personal Responsibility Act, then the American Dream Restoration Act; the Freedom and Fairness Act wasn't far behind, along with the Public Health and Safety Protection Act. . . .

But don't cast your "aye" vote based on the name. The Personal Responsibility Act reduces aid to the poor, and the Freedom and Fairness Act would enact a flat tax. The Public Health Act is really a gun-control bill, and the American Dream Restoration Act is a tax credit. Then there is the proposal to cut the capital-gains tax and loosen health and safety regulations: the Job Creation and Wage Enhancement Act.

*Quoted from Dana Milbank, "May We Propose an Act to Salute Editors Who Edited This Story?" *The Wall Street Journal*, February 28, 1996, B1.

changes."[8] In World War II, a Navy ship changed its call signal from SAPWORTH to HELLCAT—with a marked improvement in morale.[9] Eastman Kodak called its division making cameras in the United States the "US Equipment Division" until someone looked at the acronym and pointed out that people might not want to buy USED cameras.[10]

Responding to the symbol rather than to reality, "confusing the map with the territory," is called **intensionalism.** Advertising works in part because we respond intensionally to symbols. A man working at a flea market noticed that garden supplies went quickly, but no one was buying broom handles. He bought the entire supply of broom handles for a dime each, put up a sign in his own booth advertising "Tomato stakes—25¢ each," and sold all 300 in two hours.[11] The characteristics of the wooden poles hadn't changed, but the symbol had, and people responded differently to the new symbol.

Since we must use symbols to communicate, it's hard to avoid treating symbols as if they were reality. Semanticists suggest these correctives:

1. Support general statements and evaluations with specific evidence or examples.
2. Check your own responses to make sure that your decisions are based not on labels but on valid, logical arguments.

8. The Symbols Used in Communication Must Stand for Essentially the Same Thing in the Minds of the Sender and the Receiver.

Communication depends on symbols; if those symbols mean different things to the people who use them, communication will fail. **Bypassing** occurs when two people use the same symbol to mean different things.

Bypassing creates misunderstandings. A factory employee who had been absent frequently notified his supervisor that he would not be at work the next day. The supervisor said "OK," meaning only that he had heard what the worker had said and was acknowledging having heard it. The worker thought the *OK* signified approval, that is, that his absence was acceptable. When he received a written warning notice for poor attendance, he felt he was being treated unfairly and filed a grievance against management.

"Virtual signs" exist in computer feeds to TV screens but not in reality. Fans watching the Philadelphia Phillies on TV see large ads for Coca-Cola or for the team's Web site on the wall behind the batter. But the ads aren't really there. They're generated by computer for the TV audience. Fans at the ball park just see a blank wall.

Symbols have to be learned. New computer users frequently experience by-passing because they don't yet know the computer meaning of various symbols.

> A man called the support line complaining that his computer wasn't working, though he'd followed the directions to the letter. "I inserted the disk into the drive. It said insert the disk into the drive, OK? Then I got up and closed the door to my office. It said close the door."
>
> A computer consultant told a customer to send him a copy of his disk. A photocopy of the disk arrived in the mail the next day.
>
> When the instructor told students to erase their disks, one student took out a pencil eraser and applied it to the oxide.[12]

Until we learn to look into each other's minds, we can't be certain that symbols mean exactly the same things to us as they do to the people with whom we communicate. But there are some measures that will help us avoid bypassing:

1. Be sensitive to contexts.
2. Consider the other person. Given his or her background and situation, what is he or she likely to mean?
3. Mirror what the other person has said by putting it into your own words, and let him or her check it for accuracy. (Note: use different words for the key ideas. If you use exactly the same word, you still won't be able to tell if you and the other person mean the same thing by it.)
4. Ask questions.

Summary of Key Points

- **Communication theory** attempts to explain what happens when we communicate. **Semantics** is the study of the way our behavior is influenced by the words and other symbols we use to communicate. Communication theory and semantics both show why and where communication can break down and what we can do to communicate more effectively.

- Because semantics deals with the way we perceive and process information, conflicts that "are just a matter of semantics" may be serious. Depending on the situation, it may or may not be possible to find words that everyone in the group can endorse.

- The best channel for a message will depend on the audience, the sender's purposes, and the situation. Channel choice may be shaped by the organizational culture.

- **Channel overload** occurs when a channel cannot handle all the messages being sent. **Information overload** occurs when the receiver cannot process all the messages that arrive. Both kinds of overload require some sort of selection to determine which messages will be sent and which ones will be attended to.

- A sender goes through the following steps: **perception, interpretation, choice** or **selection, encoding,** transmitting the message through a **channel.** The receiver perceives the message, **decodes** it, interprets it, chooses a response, encodes the response, and transmits it. The message transmitted to the original sender is called **feedback. Noise** is anything that interferes with communication; it can be both physical and psychological. Miscommunication can occur at every point in the communication process.

What's in a Name? (II)*

Twenty years ago, no one could sell portabella mushrooms. But they weren't called portabellas.

In the 1970s, when exotic cultivated mushrooms became a market segment, growers began to remarket the mature, brown mushrooms that were out of favor. In the 1980s, the name *portabella* emerged.

Now, at the turn of the century, portabellas are featured in chefs' signature dishes. In grocery stores, portabellas cost as much as steak. And growers can't keep up with demand.

It helps to have a beautiful name.

*Based on Kim Pierce, "Meaty Portabella Mushrooms Are Springing Up All Over: Change of Name Promotes Interest in Giant, Unglamorous Fungi," *Columbus Dispatch,* May 31, 1995, 6H.

- Eight principles of semantics will help us avoid errors in perception, interpretation, choice, and encoding and decoding.

Perception

1. Perception involves the perceiver as well as what is perceived.

Interpretation

2. **Observations** are statements you yourself have verified. **Inferences** are statements that have not yet been verified, but which could be. **Judgments** can never be proven, since they depend not on measurable quantities but on values.
3. No two things are ever exactly alike.
4. Things change significantly with time. Violating this principle produces **frozen evaluations.**
5. Most *either-or* classifications are not legitimate. Seeing only two alternatives is called **polarization.** Assuming limits that do not exist is called **blindering.**

Choice

6. A statement is never the whole story. Thinking that one can know or tell everything is called **allness.**

Encoding and Decoding

7. Words are not identical to the objects they represent. The **semantic triangle** shows that the only link between word and object is the person who uses the word.
8. The symbols used in communication must stand for essentially the same thing in the minds of the sender and the receiver. When the sender and the receiver use the same symbol to mean different things, **bypassing** occurs.

Appendix C

Exercises and Problems

C.1   Choosing a Channel to Reach a Specific Audience

Suppose that your business, government agency, or non-profit group had a product, service, or program targeted for each of the following audiences. What would be the best channel(s) to reach people in that group in your city? Would that channel reach all group members?

a. Macintosh users.
b. People who own mutual funds.
c. Teenagers who do the family grocery shopping.
d. People who bowl.
e. Muslims.
f. Parents whose children play team sports.
g. Native Americans/Native Canadians.
h. Lawyers.
i. People who have Web sites.
j. People who use wheelchairs.

C.2   Choosing a Channel to Convey a Specific Message

Assume that you're the campaign manager for a campus, local, or state race. (Pick a real candidate and a real race.) What would be the advantages and disadvantages of each of the following channels as media to carry ads for your side?

a. Ad in the campus newspaper.
b. Posters around campus.
c. Ad in the local newspaper.
d. Ad on a local radio station after midnight.
e. Ad on the local TV station during the local news show.
f. Ads on billboards.
g. Ads on yard signs.
h. Flyers distributed door-to-door.
i. Ad on cable TV.

C.3   Dealing with Channel and Information Overload

In each of the following situations, identify ways that people could deal with the overloads described. What are the consequences of the methods that might be used?

a. When a radio station announces a prize for the ninth caller, dozens of people try to phone in.
b. After Bill Gates's e-mail address is printed in a magazine, he gets 5,000 messages in three days.
c. A car buyer in the United States can choose from 572 makes and models.
d. At State University, every accounting senior with a GPA of "B" or better wants to interview for jobs with the Big Five Accounting firms, but each firm will interview only 34 seniors at the school.
e. A major freeway is closed for repairs.
f. System capacity allows only two of every five calls on cellular phones to get through.
g. A student wants to attend a lecture by a prominent speaker the night before a paper is due.
h. A sales representative's job requires him to be on the road four nights a week, but he wants to spend more time with his family.

C.4   Separating Observations, Inferences, and Judgments

Indicate whether each of the following statements is an observation, an inference, or a judgment.

a. This statement is printed in black ink on a page edged in purple.
b. All the exercises and problems in this book are printed on pages edged in purple.
c. Printing the problems on pages with colored edges makes them easier to find.
d. Five years from now, 90% of the college texts designed for business courses will use at least two colors of ink.
e. Color printing makes textbooks more interesting.

C.5   Separating Observations, Inferences, and Judgments

Indicate whether each of the following statements is an observation, an inference, or a judgment.

a. There is a chair in this room.
b. The Dow Jones Industrial Average closed above 7000 for the first time in February 1997.
c. High stock prices are a sign that the economy is healthy.
d. Accounting majors get good jobs.
e. All the people in this room will be employed three years from today.
f. It's better to be 75% right and 100% on time than 100% right and a week late.
g. This statement is a complete sentence.

C.6   Separating Observations, Inferences, and Judgments

Pick a topic and write a statement of observation, a statement of inference, and a statement of judgment about it.

C.7   Explaining Bypassing

1. Show how the following statements could produce bypassing.
   a. The house needs painting badly.
   b. I made reservations for seven.
   c. If you think our servers are rude, you should see the manager.
2. Bypassing is the basis of many jokes. Find a joke that depends on bypassing and share it with the class.

C.8   Identifying Semantic Errors

Match each of the following statements with the semantic error it represents.

1. Allness
2. Frozen evaluation
3. Intensionalism
4. Polarization
5. Stereotyping
   a. All Australians are cricket maniacs.
   b. We tried that two years ago and it didn't work. There's no point in trying it again.

c. My subordinate isn't looking at me while I talk to him. He must be rebelling against my authority.

d. *The New York Times* prints all the news that's fit to print.

e. Junk mail wastes paper and money.

f. He applied for a job last year, and we hired someone else. There's no reason to consider him for our jobs this year.

g. If we grant pay increases, we will have to raise our cost to customers.

h. I swear to tell the truth, the whole truth, and nothing but the truth.

i. Women are more nurturing than men are.

j. Any man who wears a Brooks Brothers suit will be politically and fiscally conservative.

C.9   Verbal Map-Reality Test

Directions: If a statement is *true under all circumstances,* check the line in the "True" column. If the statement is *ever false* or if its truth *cannot be determined,* put a check in the "False" column.

True	False	
_____	_____	1. A statement is either true or false.
_____	_____	2. 1 + 1 = 2
_____	_____	3. A college education is a good thing to have.
_____	_____	4. A person is dead when he or she has no heartbeat.
_____	_____	5. No one wants to die.
_____	_____	6. Roses are red.
_____	_____	7. The sum of the angles of a triangle is 180 degrees.
_____	_____	8. All people are born equal.
_____	_____	9. Freedom of speech is good.
_____	_____	10. Do unto others as you would have them do unto you.

Source: Adapted from "Advertising as Communication: How To Test Your Semantic I.Q.," Harry E. Maynard, *Printer's Ink*, December 11, 1964, 52.

C.10   Inference-Observation Tests

Directions: You will read a brief story. Assume that all the information in the story is *accurate* and *true.* You will then read statements about the story. Answer them in order. You may reread the story as you answer the questions, but DO NOT go back to fill in answers or change answers once you have marked them.

As you read each statement, determine whether the statement is

"T"—on the basis of the information presented in the story, the statement is definitely true.

"F"—on the basis of the information presented in the story, the statement is definitely false.

"?"—the statement may be true (or false) but on the basis of the information presented in the story one cannot be sure. (Mark "?" if any part of the statement is doubtful.)

Sample Story

The only vehicle parked in front of 619 Oak Street is a blue van. The words "Valley Cable TV Plumber" are spelled in large black letters across the side of the van.

Statements about the Sample Story

1. The color of the van in front of 619 Oak Street is blue.   T   F   ?

2. There is no lettering on the side of the van parked in front of 619 Oak Street.   T   F   ?

3. The people at 619 Oak Street have cable TV.   T   F   ?

4. The blue van parked in front of 619 Oak Street belongs to Valley Cable TV.   T   F   ?

Test Story

Babe Smith has been killed. Police have rounded up six suspects, all of whom are gangsters. All of them are known to have been near the scene of the killing at the approximate time that it occurred. All had substantial motives for wanting Smith killed. However, one of the suspected gangsters, Slinky Sam, has positively been cleared of guilt.

Statements about the Story

1. Slinky Sam is known to have been near the scene of the killing of Babe Smith.   T   F   ?
2. All six of the rounded-up gangsters were known to have been near the scene of the murder.   T   F   ?
3. Only Slinky Sam has been cleared of guilt.   T   F   ?
4. All six of the rounded-up suspects were near the scene of Smith's killing at the approximate time that it took place.   T   F   ?
5. The police do not know who killed Smith.   T   F   ?
6. All six suspects are known to have been near the scene of the foul deed.   T   F   ?
7. Smith's murderer did not confess of his or her own free will.   T   F   ?
8. Slinky Sam was not cleared of guilt.   T   F   ?
9. It is known that the six suspects were in the vicinity of the cold-blooded assassination.   T   F   ?

Source: Test by William Haney, in Harry E. Maynard, "Advertising as Communication: How to Test Your Semantic I.Q.," *Printer's Ink*, December 11, 1964, 53.

C.11 Removing Blinders

To solve the following problems, you may need to remove some "blinders."

a. How can the following be true:
   A = 3
   B = 4
   But A + B = 5

b. How can you drop an egg six feet through the air over a hard surface without breaking the egg?

c. How can you, with one line, turn VII into the number 8?
   How can you, with one line, turn IX into the number 6?

d. Finish the alphabet, putting each letter above or below the line according to the pattern below:

   A   EF   HI.
   ————————————————
     BCD   G   J

e. When men and women are on an elevator and all of them are getting off on the seventh floor, who should get off first?

f. Separate all nine dots into their own individual spaces by drawing two squares.

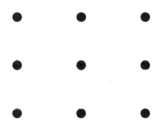

C.12 Identifying Logos

Find four corporate logos. Do all your classmates recognize all the logos? Which logos seem to be especially effective symbols for their organizations? What makes them so effective?

D

Toulmin Logic

The Toulmin Model
How Much of the Full Toulmin Model to Use
Summary of Key Points

Toulmin Logic

Thomas Wilk

Technical Editor, Battelle Memorial Institute

www.battelle.org/

Tom Wilk provides editorial guidance on Battelle Environmental Restoration projects and coordinates document production. Battelle Memorial Institute, headquartered in Columbus, Ohio, serves industry and government by developing, commercializing, and managing technology. Battelle's Environmental Restoration team specializes in engineering-oriented cleanup and remediation solutions.

Battelle's Environmental Restoration (ER) department produces final reports that deliver the results of lengthy research to a wide variety of readers. A report on new technologies for cleaning up hydrocarbon-contaminated sites, for example, might be read by workers in industry and government, by federal and state regulating bodies, by other scientists, by present and future legal teams, and by citizens concerned about the environment. The claims made by these reports must be supported by generally accepted norms of scientific research and also must be made in clear, unambiguous, and (if possible) familiar language.

> *The difference between "support" and "strongly support" can determine whether a client spends more than $500,000.*

In our discourse community, the most common kinds of evidence are measurements and calculations. For example, if writers want to recommend one particular strategy for cleaning up a contaminated site, they can support this claim logically with evidence ranging from tables of raw analytic data and graphics that illustrate geological contours at the site to specific terms for the level of technology development (emerging, conventional, innovative) and estimates of the cost of cleanup.

Limiting claims appropriately is important. For example, one recent exchange between writers centered on whether data tended to "support" or to "strongly support" the final recommendations. At that point, I was able to point out that language in preceding analytic sections more often expressed ambiguity rather than certainty, so the word "strongly" was dropped. The difference between "support" and "strongly support" can determine whether a client spends more than $500,000 to take remedial action at a particular site.

Different audiences (such as federal versus state regulators) may have different standards for proof. In cases like this, we analyze and summarize data using both standards to meet the needs of both audiences or specify that the more "conservative" standard will be applied. When we use one method of analysis or set of regulatory standards rather than another, we give the reasons for the decision, not only to support the strongest claim possible but also to prevent alienating potential readers through the language used to contextualize our recommendations.

Limiting Statements in Accounting Reports*

Accountants carefully limit the claims they make in their reports. The following paragraph from a review contains four limiting phrases:

> Based on our review we are not aware of any material modifications that should be made to the accompanying financial statements in order for them to be in conformity with generally accepted accounting principles.

"Based on our review" and "we are not aware" acknowledge that evidence may exist which the auditors have not seen. To say that "material modifications" are not needed leaves the door open for possible minor improvements. Finally, "generally accepted accounting principles" is itself limited. CPAs are not claiming that these principles are unchanging or that everyone in the world accepts them.

*Based on Aletha S. Hendrickson, "How to Appear Reliable without Being Liable: C.P.A. Writing in Its Rhetorical Context," *Worlds of Writing: Teaching and Learning in Different Discourse Communities*, ed. Carolyn Matalene (New York: Random House, 1989), 308–13.

While any system of logic will help you craft solid arguments, **Toulmin logic,** developed by Stephen Toulmin,[1] is particularly useful for business communication since it can help you both to see whether an argument is valid and to decide how much—or what kind of—evidence you need to provide.

The Toulmin Model

In everyday life, the first part of the argument to emerge is frequently the **claim** we wish to make. When the reader is already on our side, all we have to do is state the claim. But when the reader resists the claim, we must support it with **data** or **evidence.**

Just providing evidence may not be enough in difficult situations. The reader has to see the relationship between the evidence and the claim. If the reader doesn't see the relationship (doesn't know it, agree with it, or happen to think of it at the moment), he or she won't be convinced. Adding more evidence won't help. Instead, we need to spell out the assumption or **bridge** that links the evidence to the claim. (In the old movie, *If Today is Tuesday, This Must Be Belgium,* the bridge is that we're on a whirlwind package trip through Europe that sticks to the itinerary. Without that assumption, there would be no bridge between the evidence that today is Tuesday and a claim about where we are.)

If the audience may disagree with the bridge, we need to prove it. When the proof is made explicit, the statement supporting the bridge is called the **foundation.** Sometimes the reader may accept the bridge but think of a **counterclaim** that negates the claim. If a counterargument exists, we must provide a **rebuttal** to it to be convincing.

Here's an example, labeling the parts of an argument that a college sports team needs to communicate more often with high school athletes it wants to recruit.

Claim:	Better communication will improve our recruiting record.
Evidence:	We are losing recruits to other schools.
Bridge:	Recruits don't necessarily go to the most prestigious school they can. Instead, recruits are more likely to choose schools that communicate with them often during the recruiting process.
Foundation:	Research shows that frequency and quality of communication were key factors in influencing recruits to attend a specific school. Communication strengthened recruits' initial interest and helped overcome objections. Our informal surveys of recruits show that they receive more mail and phone calls from other schools than from us.
Counterclaim:	Our communication might be poor. Frequent communication might hurt rather than help.
Rebuttal:	We will hire a consultant to help our coaches write effective letters.

Many claims cannot be made with 100% certainty. If the claim is only *probably* and not *necessarily* true, we need to **limit** it. You can limit a claim with the words *probably, help,* and *may be* and with explicit disclaimers: "These results are accurate within ± 5.6%." "This projection is based on surveys taken October 28th." Qualifying your claims will build your credibility as a person who promises only what you can deliver.

In a paragraph, the parts of the Toulmin model can come in almost any order; choose the one that makes ideas flow most smoothly. In a longer document—a letter, memo, or report—claims, once you prove them, become data or evidence (now that the reader accepts them) that can be used to support bigger claims. Thus logic becomes a pyramid: small claims support medium-sized claims, which, when proven, in turn support major claims.

How Much of the Full Toulmin Model to Use

It is possible to outline the full Toulmin model for any claim, even simple ones such as "Your order will arrive Thursday." However, it is not always necessary to do so. Decide how much of the model to use by analyzing the reader and the situation.

The following guidelines can help.

1. **Make both the claim and the evidence explicit** unless you are *sure* the reader will accept what you say totally without questions. Present obvious evidence in a subordinate clause beginning with "since" or "because" to avoid giving the impression that this information is new and surprising.

> Since employers prefer job candidates with work experience, we should set up an internship program for our students.

Here the claim "we need an internship program" is supported by evidence in the introductory subordinate clause: "employers prefer candidates with experience."

2. **Include the bridge**
   a. **If it is new information to the reader.**
   b. **If the reader may have heard the bridge but forgotten it.**
   c. **If the reader may disagree with the bridge.**
   d. **If invalid as well as valid bridges exist.**

> All of the money saved in the cost-reduction program will go into salaries and benefits, not into research and development, executive bonuses, or stockholder dividends. Therefore employees will benefit if the company saves money.

The first sentence is a bridge connecting saving money to the claim, "employees will benefit." The bridge is necessary because invalid bridges exist: any money saved might be spent on several things other than salaries and benefits.

3. **Make the foundation explicit**
   a. **If it is new information to the reader.**
   b. **If the reader will disagree with the bridge.**
   c. **If invalid as well as valid foundations exist.**
   d. **If there are arbitrary demands for documentation (e.g., in a term paper or a paper you are submitting for publication, where you must indicate your sources for each fact).**

> XYZ university will have trouble developing a top-20 football team because its academic standards are high. After practicing four hours a day, football players don't have the time or energy to complete complex, lengthy assignments. Long practices are necessary both to reduce the risk of injury and to make the moves automatic.

The implicit bridge here is "good football players can't meet high academic standards." Readers who think of the possible but invalid foundation "Good football players are dumb" will reject the argument.

Giving the valid foundation (the last two sentences) makes the argument more persuasive.

4. **Always offer rebuttals to counterclaims.** Failure to dispose of loopholes is, after failure to provide a valid bridge, probably the most common cause of unconvincing—and unaccepted—recommendations.

> Three of our best customers got busy signals for two straight hours Monday. Business was slow Monday: quotes were down 11%, and the logs compiled by the inside sales reps don't show many outgoing business calls. But the phones were busy, and it seems likely that they were tied up with personal calls.

A reader who accepts the evidence "our phones were tied up" may offer the counterclaim "all the calls were to business customers." If that claim were true, customers would get busy signals even though no one was making personal calls. The middle sentence rebuts that counterclaim by showing that business activity was down. That rebuttal is crucial to making convincing the claim in the last clause: the phones were tied up with personal calls.

5. **Limit any claim whose truth is uncertain or relative.**

> This procedure should produce more accurate results.

The word *should* limits the claim. Without it, we would be promising that the procedure would definitely bring an improvement. But many things could go wrong. Limiting the claim makes it more persuasive because it is now more realistic.

Summary of Key Points

- Toulmin logic is useful in labeling the parts of an argument and showing you how much information you need to include.
- In Toulmin logic, the **claim** is the point we want the audience to accept. **Evidence** is material the audience already accepts. The **bridge** is the assumption that allows us to infer the claim from the evidence. The **foundation** supports (proves) the bridge. **Counterclaims** are statements that invalidate the claim even when the evidence and bridge are sound. The **rebuttal** answers the counterclaim. The **limiter** shows under what circumstances, or with what limitations, the claim is true.
- Use these guidelines to determine how much of the full Toulmin model to use.
  1. Make both the claim and the evidence explicit.
  2. Include the bridge
     a. If it is new information to the reader.
     b. If the reader may have heard the bridge but forgotten it.
     c. If the reader may disagree with the bridge.
     d. If invalid as well as valid bridges exist.
  3. Make the foundation explicit
     a. If the reader will disagree with the bridge.
     b. If invalid as well as valid foundations exist.
     c. If there are arbitrary demands for documentation.
  4. Always offer rebuttals to loopholes the reader may find in the main claim.
  5. Limit any claim whose truth is uncertain or relative.

Exercises and Problems

Getting Started

D.1   Using Toulmin Logic

In each of the following arguments, identify the claim and the evidence (if any). What bridge could link the evidence to the claim? Is it valid? Why or why not?

1. When you work harder, our customers are more satisfied. And that in turn raises the price of the company's stock.
2. Tom majored in accounting and he got five job offers. I should major in accounting, too.
3. I've worked for two large companies and hated both of them. I'd be happier starting my own business.
4. Of all the applicants, Bob got the highest score on the test. He's the person who should get the job.
5. Last month we spent 34% more on paper than we did six months ago. People are either wasting it or stealing it.

6. The vote on whether to move to a four-day work week was 50/50. Our employees can never agree on whether or not a shorter work week would be beneficial.
7. The vote on whether to move to a four-day work week was split 50/50. Our employees don't care whether or not we change the work week.
8. Since profits are falling, we need to downsize.
9. Customers already believe that our microwave meals taste better than other brands. So we should use our new advertising campaign to stress other advantages, such as their convenience or nutrition.
10. This company is a team. And just as every player does what the coach says, so each of you needs to run the game plan that your manager creates.

D.2   Brainstorming Evidence

Brainstorm ways to support each of the following claims. What kinds of evidence could you use? What bridges would be necessary? What counterclaims would you need to refute?

1. Many students are interested in serving as Big Brothers and Big Sisters.
2. I have a solid understanding of accounting principles.

3. Stocks should be part of every retirement plan.
4. Today's cellular phones are too dangerous to use while driving.
5. Our city should provide more support to help people start small businesses.

D.3   Rebutting Counterclaims

The Southwest School System has several computer classrooms for students to use, but teachers do not have individual desktop computers. The School Board is considering a proposal to buy computers and to replace the courier system of hand delivery of documents with e-mail.

Brainstorm ways to answer each of the following counterclaims:

1. "People won't use computers if they have them."
2. "Learning to use the computers will take time. People will spend more time getting mail than they do now."

3. "By the time you buy computers and pay for the energy and maintenance they need and for printer supplies, it won't be any cheaper to use e-mail than to pay people to drive from building to building to deliver inter-system mail."
4. "People will just print out copies of documents, so the cost of paper won't go down. And if we're going to print hundreds of copies of a document, it's more efficient to print copies centrally."

D.4   Analyzing Arguments

Analyze the arguments in one or more of the following kinds of documents. For each, identify the claim and (if present) the evidence, the bridge, the foundation, rebuttals to counterclaims, and limiters. What additional parts (if any) are needed to make the argument convincing?

1. An article in a business periodical or Web site recommending that it is or is not a good idea to buy a particular company's stock.

2. A recruiting brochure or Web page explaining why a company is a good place to work.

3. The CEO's letter in an annual report arguing that the company is well positioned for the coming year.

4. A fund-raising letter arguing that the organization is doing good work and is a deserving candidate for financial gifts.

5. A letter of recommendation recommending a candidate for a job or for a promotion.

6. Material from your city's Chamber of Commerce presenting your city as a good place to live and work.

7. An editorial in *The Wall Street Journal* or *Business Week* recommending economic policy.

A

abstract or **executive summary**   A summary of a report, specifying the recommendations and the reasons for them.

acknowledgment responses   Nods, smiles, frowns, and words that let a speaker know you are listening.

action close   The end of a direct mail letter, which tells the reader what to do, makes action sound easy, gives a reason for acting promptly, and ends with a reader benefit or a picture of the reader's money helping to solve the problem.

active listening   Feeding back the literal meaning or the emotional content or both so that the speaker knows that the listener has heard and understood.

active verb   A verb that describes the action of the grammatical subject of the sentence.

adjustment   The response to a claim letter. If the company agrees to grant a refund, the amount due will be adjusted.

alliteration   A sound pattern occurring when several words begin with the same sound.

allness   The semantic error of assuming it is possible to know or communicate everything that is important about a topic.

alternating pattern   Discussing the alternatives first as they relate to the first criterion, then as they relate to the second criterion, and so on: ABC, ABC, ABC.

AMS Simplified format   A letter format that omits the salutation and complimentary close and lines everything up at the left margin.

analytical report   A report that interprets information.

annual report   A report distributed to stockholders and other audiences summarizing the firm's financial performance and achievements during the year; a document with informative, persuasive, and goodwill purposes.

argument   The reasons or logic offered to persuade the audience.

assumptions   Statements that are not proven in a report, but on which the recommendations are based.

B

bar graph   A visual consisting of parallel bars or rectangles that represent specific sets of data.

behavioral interviews   Job interviews that ask candidates to describe actual behaviors they have used in the past in specific situations.

bias-free language   Language that does not discriminate against people on the basis of sex, physical condition, race, age, or any other category.

bibliography   A list of all the books and articles about a topic.

blind ads   Job listings that do not list the company's name.

blind copies   Copies sent to other recipients that are not listed on the original letter or memo.

blindering   Imposing limits that do not exist in reality.

block format   In letters, a format in which inside address, date, and signature block are lined up at the left margin. In résumés, a format in which dates are listed in one column and job titles and descriptions in another. This format emphasizes work history.

blocking   Disagreeing with every idea that is proposed in a meeting.

body   The main part of a letter, memo, or report.

body language   Nonverbal communication conveyed by posture and movement, eye contact, facial expressions, and gestures.

boilerplate   Language from a previous document that a writer includes in a new document. Writers use boilerplate both to save time and energy and to use language that has already been approved by the organization's legal staff.

boxhead   Used in tables, the boxhead is the variable whose label is at the top.

brainstorming   A method of generating ideas by recording everything people in a group think of, without judging or evaluating the ideas.

branching question   Question that sends respondents who answer differently to different parts of the questionnaire. Allows respondents to answer only those questions that are relevant to their experience.

bridge (in *prospecting job letters*)   A sentence that connects the attention-getter to the body of a letter.

bridge (in *Toulmin logic*)   The general principle that authorizes making the step between the claim and the evidence in an argument.

buffer   A neutral or positive statement designed to allow the writer to bury, or buffer, the negative message.

build goodwill   To create a good image of yourself and of your organization—the kind of image that makes people want to do business with you.

bullets   Large round dots or squares that set off items in a list. When you are giving examples, but the number is not exact and the order does not matter, use bullets to set off items.

business slang   Terms that have technical meaning but are used in more general senses. Used sparingly, these terms are appropriate in job application letters and in messages for people in the same organization, who are likely to share the vocabulary.

businessese   A kind of jargon including unnecessary words. Some words were common 200–300 years ago but are no longer part of spoken English. Some have never been used outside of business writing. All of these terms should be omitted.

buying time with limited agreement Agreeing with the small part of a criticism that one does accept as true.

bypassing Miscommunication that occurs when two people use the same symbol to mean different things.

C

case The grammatical role a noun or pronoun plays in a sentence. The nominative case is used for the subject of a clause, the possessive to show who or what something belongs to, the objective case for the object of a verb or a preposition.

central selling point A super reader benefit, big enough to motivate readers by itself, but also serving as an umbrella to cover other benefits and to unify the message.

chain The body of a direct mail letter, providing the logical and emotional links that move readers from interest to the action the writer wants.

channel The physical means by which a message is sent. Written channels include memos, letters, and billboards. Oral channels include phone calls, speeches, and face-to-face conversations.

channel overload The inability of a channel to carry all the messages that are being sent.

chartjunk Decoration that is irrelevant to a visual and that may be misleading.

checking for feelings Identifying the emotions that the previous speaker seemed to be expressing verbally or nonverbally.

checking for inferences Trying to identify the unspoken content or feelings implied by what the previous speaker has actually said.

choice or **selection** The decision to include or omit information in a message.

chronological résumé A résumé that lists what you did in a time line, starting with the most recent events and going backward in reverse chronology.

citation Attributing a quotation or other idea to a source in the body of the report.

claim The part of an argument that the speaker or writer wants the audience to agree with.

claim letter A letter seeking a replacement or refund.

clear A message whose audience gets the meaning the writer or speaker intended.

clip art Predrawn images that you can import into your newsletter, sign, or graph.

close The ending of a document.

closed or **defensive body position** Keeping the arms and legs crossed and close to the body. Suggests physical and psychological discomfort, defending oneself, and shutting the other person out.

closed question Question with a limited number of possible responses.

closure report A report summarizing completed research that does not result in action or recommendation.

clowning Making unproductive jokes and diverting the group from its task.

clustering A method of thinking up ideas by writing the central topic in the middle of the page, circling it, writing down the ideas that topic suggests, and circling them.

cognitive dissonance A theory which posits that it is psychologically uncomfortable to hold two ideas that are dissonant or conflicting. The theory of cognitive dissonance explains that people will resolve dissonance by deciding that one of the ideas is less important, by rejecting one of the ideas, or by constructing a third idea that has room for both of the conflicting ideas.

cold list A list used in marketing of people with no prior connection to your group.

collaborative writing Working with other writers to produce a single document.

collection letter A letter asking a customer to pay for goods and services received.

collection series A series of letters asking customers to pay for goods and services they have already received. Early letters in the series assume that the reader intends to pay but final letters threaten legal action if the bill is not paid.

comma splice or **comma fault** Using a comma to join two independent clauses. To correct, use a semicolon, subordinate one of the clauses, or use a period and start a new sentence.

common ground Values and goals that the writer and reader share.

communication theory A theory explaining what happens when we communicate and where miscommunication can occur.

complaint letter A letter that challenges a policy or tries to get a decision changed.

complete A message that answers all of the audience's questions. The audience has enough information to evaluate the message and act on it.

complex sentence Sentence with one main clause and one subordinate clause.

complimentary close The words after the body of the letter and before the signature. *Sincerely* and *Cordially* are the most commonly used complimentary closes in business letters.

compound sentence Sentence with two main clauses joined by a conjunction.

conclusions Section of a report that restates the main points.

conflict resolution Strategies for getting at the real issue, keeping discussion open, and minimizing hurt feelings so that people can find a solution that feels good to everyone involved.

connotations The emotional colorings or associations that accompany a word.

convenience sample A group of subjects to whom the researcher has easy access.

conversational style Conversational patterns such as speed and volume of speaking, pauses between speakers, whether questions are direct or indirect. When different speakers assign different meanings to a specific pattern, miscommunication results.

coordinating Planning work, giving directions, fitting together contributions of group members.

coordination The third stage in the life of a task group, when the group finds, organizes, and interprets information and examines alternatives and assumptions. This is the longest of the four stages.

correct Used to describe a message that is accurate and free from errors in punctuation, spelling, grammar, word order, and sentence structure.

counterclaim In Toulmin logic, a statement whose truth would negate the truth of the main claim.

credibility The audience's response to the source of the message.

criteria The standards used to evaluate or weigh the factors in a decision.

critical activities Activities that must be done on time if a project is to be completed by its due date.

critical incident An important event that illustrates a subordinate's behavior.

cropping Cutting a photograph to fit a specific space. Also, photographs are cropped to delete visual information that is unnecessary or unwanted.

culture The unconscious patterns of behavior and beliefs that are common to a people, nation, or organization.

cutaway drawings or **schematic diagrams** Line drawings that depict the hidden or interior portions of an object.

cycling The process of sending a document from writer to superior to writer to yet another superior for several rounds of revisions before the document is approved.

D

dangling modifier A phrase that modifies a word that is not actually in a sentence. To correct a dangling modifier, recast the modifier as a subordinate clause or revise the sentence so its subject or object can be modified by the now-dangling phrase.

data Facts or figures from which conclusions can be drawn.

database A computer program that organizes data in categories the user can then manipulate to get the information he or she needs.

decision trees A branching chart of sequential questions with different paths depending on the answer to each question, designed to allow the user to find the best solution quickly.

decode To extract meaning from symbols.

decorative visual A visual that makes the speaker's points more memorable but that does not convey numerical data.

defensive or **closed body position** Keeping the arms and legs crossed and close to the body. Suggests physical and psychological discomfort, defending oneself, and shutting the other person out.

demographic characteristics Measurable features of an audience that can be counted objectively: age, sex, race, education level, income, etc.

denial A refusal to accept or believe something that is potentially harmful or life-threatening. People deny realities that are too much for them to cope with.

denotation A word's literal or "dictionary" meaning. Most common words in English have more than one denotation. Context usually makes it clear which of several meanings is appropriate.

dependent clause A group of words that contains a subject and a verb but cannot stand by itself as a complete sentence.

descriptive abstract A listing of the topics an article or report covers that tells how thoroughly each topic is treated but does not summarize what is said about each topic.

descriptors Words describing the content of an article. Used to permit computer searches for information on a topic.

desktop publishing The use of powerful desktop computers and laser printers to produce documents that look typeset.

dingbats Small symbols such as arrows, pointing fingers, and so forth that are part of a typeface.

direct mail A form of direct marketing that asks for an order, inquiry, or contribution directly from the reader.

direct mail package The outer envelope of a direct mail letter and everything that goes in it: the letter, brochures, samples, secondary letters, reply card, and reply envelope.

direct marketing All advertisements that ask for an order, inquiry, or contribution directly from the reader. Includes direct mail, catalogs, telemarketing (telephone sales), and newspaper and TV ads with 800 numbers to place an order.

direct request A pattern of organization that makes the request directly in the first and last paragraphs.

directed subject line A subject line that makes clear the writer's stance on the issue.

discourse community A group of people who share assumptions about what channels, formats, and styles to use for communication, what topics to discuss and how to discuss them, and what constitutes evidence.

divided pattern Discussing each alternative completely before going on to the next alternative: AAA, BBB, CCC.

document design The process of writing, organizing, and laying out a document so that it can be easily used by the intended audience.

documentation Providing full bibliographic information so that interested readers can go to the original source of material used in a report.

dominating Trying to run a group by ordering, shutting out others, and insisting on one's own way.

dot charts Dot charts show correlations or other large data sets. Dot charts have labeled horizontal and vertical axes.

E

early letter A collection letter that is gentle. An early letter assumes that the reader intends to pay but has forgotten or has met with temporary reverses.

editing Checking the draft to see that it satisfies the requirements of good English and the principles of business writing. Unlike revision, which can produce major changes in meaning, editing focuses on the surface of writing.

ego-involvement The emotional commitment the audience has to its position.

electronic mail or **e-mail** A mail system that uses computer terminals to bypass paper. Messages are composed on a computer screen; the recipient reads the message on screen.

elimination of alternatives A pattern of organization for reports that discusses the problem and its causes, the impractical solutions and their weaknesses, and finally the solution the writer favors.

emotional appeal Making the audience want to do what the writer or speaker asks.

empathy The ability to put oneself in someone else's shoes, to *feel with* that person.

encode To put ideas into symbols.

enunciate To voice all the sounds of each word while speaking.

evaluating Measuring the draft against your goals and the requirements of the situation and audience. Anything produced during each stage of the writing process can be evaluated, not just the final draft.

evidence Facts or data the audience already accepts.

exaggeration Making something sound bigger or more important than it really is.

executive summary A summary of a report, specifying the recommendations and the reasons for them.

expectancy theory A theory that argues that motivation is based on the expectation of being rewarded for performance and the importance of the reward.

extensionalism Inspecting and responding to reality itself.

external audiences Audiences who are not part of the writer's organization.

external documents Documents that go to people in another organization.

external report Report written by a consultant for an organization of which he or she is not a permanent employee.

extrinsic benefits Benefits that are "added on"; they are not a necessary part of the product or action.

eye contact Looking another person directly in the eye.

F

facsimile or **fax machine** Machine that can send a copy of a document to another location in less than a minute. Fax machines may be stand-alone machines or part of a computer.

feasibility study A report that evaluates two or more possible alternatives and recommends one of them. Doing nothing is always one alternative.

feedback The receiver's response to a message.

figure Any visual that is not a table.

five Ws and H Questions that must be answered early in a press release: who, what, when, where, why, and how.

fixed typeface A typeface in which each letter has the same width on the page. Sometimes called *typewriter typeface.*

flaming Sending out an angry e-mail message before thinking about the implications of venting one's anger.

Flesch "Reading Ease Scale" A readability formula that determines reading ease (measured on a 0 to 100 scale) by subtracting multiples of average words per sentence and average syllables per word from 206.835.

flow chart A chart representing each subprocess and decision point in a process.

focus groups Small groups who come in to talk with a skilled leader about a potential product.

forced choice A choice in which each item is ranked against every other item. Used to discover which of a large number of criteria are crucial.

form letter A letter that is sent unchanged or with only minor modifications to a large number of readers.

formal meetings Meetings run under strict rules, like the rules of parliamentary procedure summarized in *Robert's Rules of Order.*

formal report A report containing formal elements such as a title page, a transmittal, a table of contents, and an abstract.

formalization The fourth and last stage in the life of a task group, when the group makes and formalizes its decision.

format The parts of a document and the way they are arranged on a page.

formation The second stage in the life of a task group, when members choose a leader and define the problem they must solve.

foundation A statement proving the truth of a bridge.

freewriting   A kind of writing uninhibited by any constraints. Freewriting may be useful in overcoming writer's block, among other things.

frozen evaluation   An assessment that does not take into account the possibility of change.

G

Gannt charts   Bar charts used to show schedules. Gannt charts are most commonly used in proposals.

gatekeeper   The audience with the power to decide whether your message is sent on to other audiences. Some gatekeepers are also initial audiences.

gathering   Physically getting the background data you need. It can include informal and formal research or simply getting the letter to which you're responding.

general semantics   The study of the ways behavior is influenced by the words and other symbols used to communicate.

general slang   Words or phrases such as *awesome, smokin'*, or *at the end of my rope* that are sometimes used in conversations and in presentations, but are not appropriate in business and administrative writing since they appear sloppy or imprecise.

gerund   The *-ing* form of a verb; grammatically, it is a verb used as a noun.

getting feedback   Asking someone else to evaluate your work. Feedback is useful at every stage of the writing process, not just during composition of the final draft.

glossary   A list of terms used in a report with their definitions.

good appeal   An appeal in direct marketing that offers believable descriptions of benefits, links the benefits of the product or service to a need or desire that motivates the reader, makes the reader want to read the letter, and motivates the reader to act.

good mailing list   A mailing list used in direct marketing that has accurate addresses and is a good match to the product.

good product   A product that appeals to a specific segment of people, is not readily available in stores, is mailable, and provides an adequate profit margin.

good service or cause   A service or cause that fills an identifiable need.

goodwill   The value of a business beyond its tangible assets, including its reputation and patronage. Also, a favorable condition and overall atmosphere of trust that can be fostered between parties conducting business.

goodwill ending   Shift of emphasis away from the message to the reader. A goodwill ending is positive, personal, and forward-looking and suggests that serving the reader is the real concern.

goodwill presentation   A presentation that entertains and validates the audience.

grammar checker   Software program that flags errors or doubtful usage.

grapevine   The informal informational network in an organization, which carries gossip and rumors as well as accurate information.

grid system   A means of designing layout by imposing columns on a page and lining up graphic elements within the columns.

ground rules   Procedural rules adopted by groups to make meetings run smoothly.

groupthink   The tendency for a group to reward agreement and directly or indirectly punish dissent.

guided discussion   A presentation in which the speaker presents the questions or issues that both speaker and audience have agreed on in advance. Instead of functioning as an expert with all the answers, the speaker serves as a facilitator to help the audience tap its own knowledge.

Gunning "Fog Index"   A readability formula that determines level of education necessary for comprehension by multiplying average words per sentence by percentage of difficult words by .4.

H

hard copy   The paper copy of what is recorded on a word processor.

hardware   The computer and other equipment necessary for computer technology.

headings   Words or short phrases that group points and divide your letter, memo, or report into sections.

hearing   Perceiving sounds.

hidden job market   Jobs that are never advertised but that may be available or may be created for the right candidate.

hidden negatives   Words that are not negative in themselves, but become negative in context.

high-context culture   A culture in which most information is inferred from the context, rather than being spelled out explicitly in words.

histogram   A bar graph using pictures, asterisks, or points to represent a unit of the data.

I

impersonal expression   A sentence that attributes actions to inanimate objects, designed to avoid placing blame on a reader.

indented format   A format for résumés in which items that are logically equivalent begin at the same horizontal space, with carryover lines indented three spaces. Indented format emphasizes job titles.

independent clause   A group of words that can stand by itself as a complete sentence.

inference   A statement that has not yet been verified, but whose truth or falsity could be established, either now or in the future.

infinitive   The form of the verb that is preceded by *to*.

inform   To explain something or tell the audience something.

informal meetings   Loosely run meetings in which votes are not taken on every point.

informal report   A report using letter or memo format.

information interview   An interview in which you talk to someone who works in the area you hope to enter to find out what the day-to-day work involves and how you can best prepare to enter that field.

information overload   The inability of a human receiver to process all the messages he or she receives.

information report   A report that collects data for the reader but does not recommend action.

informational messages   In a group, messages focusing on the problem, data, and possible solutions.

informative message   Message to which the reader's basic reaction will be neutral.

informative presentation   A presentation that informs or teaches the audience.

informative report   A report that provides information.

informative or **talking heads**   Headings that are detailed enough to provide an overview of the material in the sections they introduce.

inside address   The reader's name and address; put below the date and above the salutation in most letter formats.

initial audience   The audience that assigns the message and routes it to other audiences.

instructions   Step-by-step information about how to perform actions that a single person does.

intensionalism   An unconscious response to a symbol rather than reality.

interactive presentation   A conversation in which the seller uses questions to determine the buyer's needs, probe objections, and gain provisional and then final commitment to the purchase.

intercultural competence   The ability to communicate sensitively with people from other cultures and countries, based on an understanding of cultural differences.

internal audiences   Audiences in the writer's organization.

internal document   Document written for other employees in the same organization.

internal documentation   Providing information about a source in the text itself rather than in footnotes or endnotes.

internal report   Reports written by employees for use only in their organization.

interpersonal communication   Communication between people.

interpersonal messages   In a group, messages promoting friendliness, cooperation, and group loyalty.

interpret   To determine the significance or importance of a message.

interview   Structured conversation with someone who is able to give you useful information.

intrapreneurs   Innovators who work within organizations.

intrinsic benefits   Benefits that come automatically from using a product or doing something.

introduction   The part of a report that states the purpose and scope of the report. The introduction may also include limitations, assumptions, methods, criteria, and definitions.

J

jargon   There are two kinds of jargon. The first kind is the specialized terminology of a technical field. The second is businessese, outdated words that do not have technical meanings and are not used in other forms of English.

judgment or **opinion**   A statement that can never be verified, since it includes terms that cannot be measured objectively.

judgment sample   A group of subjects whose views seem useful.

justification report   Report that justifies the need for a purchase, an investment, a new personnel line, or a change in procedure.

justified margins   Margins that end evenly on the right side of the page.

K

keywords or **descriptors**   Words describing the content of an article used to permit computer searches for information on a topic.

knot   The action close of a direct mail letter, which harnesses the motivation you have created and turns it into action.

L

landscape graphs   Line graphs with the area below the line filled in are sometimes called landscape graphs.

laser printer   A computer printer that produces high-resolution, sharp, easy-to-read letters.

late letter   A collection letter that threatens legal action if the bill is not paid.

lead   An attention-getting statement opening a press release.

letter   Short document using block, modified, or AMS simplified letter format that goes to readers outside your organization.

letterhead   Stationery with the organization's name, logo, address, and telephone number printed on the page.

limit   Boundary placed on a claim that cannot be made with 100% certainty.

limitations   Problems or factors that limit the validity of the recommendations of a report.

line graph   A visual consisting of lines that show trends or allow the viewer to interpolate values between the observed values.

listening   Decoding and interpreting sounds correctly.

low-context culture   A culture in which most information is conveyed explicitly in words rather than being inferred from context.

M

mailing list   The list of names and addresses to which a direct mail letter is sent.

main or **independent clause**   A group of words that can stand by itself as a complete sentence.

Maslow's hierarchy of needs   Five levels of human need posited by Abraham H. Maslow. They include physical needs, the need for safety and security, for love and belonging, for esteem and recognition, and for self-actualization.

mean   The average. Found by adding up all the numbers and dividing by the number of numbers.

median   The middle number.

memo   Document using memo format sent to readers in your organization.

methods section   The section of a report or survey describing how the data were gathered.

middle letter   A collection letter that is more assertive than an early letter. Middle letters may offer to negotiate a schedule for repayment if the reader is not able to pay the whole bill immediately, remind the reader of the importance of good credit, educate the reader about credit, or explain why the creditor must have prompt payment.

minutes   Records of a meeting, listing the items discussed, the results of votes, and the persons responsible for carrying out follow-up steps.

mirror question   Question that paraphrases the content of the answer an interviewee gave to the last question.

misplaced modifier   A word or phrase that appears to modify another element of the sentence than the writer intended.

mixed abstract   An abstract that has characteristics of both summary and descriptive abstracts: it contains the thesis or recommendation and proof, but also contains statements about the article or report.

mixed punctuation   Using a colon after the salutation and a comma after the complimentary close in a letter.

mode   The most frequent number.

modified block format   A letter format in which the inside address, date, and signature block are lined up with each other one-half or one-third of the way over on the page.

modifier   A word or phrase giving more information about another word in a sentence.

monochronic culture   Culture in which people do only one important activity at a time.

monologue presentation   A presentation in which the speaker speaks without interruption. The presentation is planned and is delivered without deviation.

multiple graphs   Three or more simple stories juxtaposed to create a more powerful story.

Myers-Briggs Type Indicator   A scale that categorizes people on four dimensions: introvert-extravert; sensing-intuitive; thinking-feeling; and perceiving-judging.

N

negative message   A message in which basic information conveyed is negative; the reader is expected to be disappointed or angry.

news release   Messages that package information about a company and that the writer would like announced in local and national media.

noise   Any physical or psychological interference in a message.

nominative case   The grammatical form used for the subject of a clause. *I, we, he, she,* and *they* are nominative pronouns.

nonagist   Words, images, or behaviors that do not discriminate against people on the basis of age.

nonracist   Words, images, or behaviors that do not discriminate against people on the basis of race.

nonrestrictive clause   A clause giving extra but unessential information about a noun or pronoun. Because the information is extra, commas separate the clause from the word it modifies.

nonsexist language   Language that treats both sexes neutrally, that does not make assumptions about the proper gender for a job, and that does not imply that men are superior to or take precedence over women.

nonverbal communication   Communication that does not use words.

normal interview   A job interview with some questions that the interviewer expects to be easy, some questions that present an opportunity to showcase strong points, and some questions that probe any weaknesses evident from the résumé.

noun–pronoun agreement   Having a pronoun be the same number (singular or plural) and the same person (first, second, or third) as the noun it refers to.

O

objective case   The grammatical form used for the object of a verb or preposition. *Me, us, him, her,* and *them* are objective pronouns.

observation   In semantics, a statement that you yourself have verified.

omnibus motion   A motion that allows a group to vote on several related items in a single vote. Saves time in formal meetings with long agendas.

open body position　Keeping the arms and legs uncrossed and away from the body. Suggests physical and psychological comfort and openness.

open punctuation　Using no punctuation after the salutation and the complimentary close.

open question　Question with an unlimited number of possible responses.

opinion　A statement that can never be verified, since it includes terms that cannot be measured objectively.

organization　The order in which ideas are arranged in a message.

organizational culture　The values, attitudes, and philosophies shared by people in an organization that shape its messages and its reward structure.

orientation　The first stage in the life of a task group, when members meet and begin to define their task.

original or **primary research**　Research that gathers new information.

outpull　To bring in a bigger response than another version of the same direct mailing.

outsourcing　Going outside the company for products and services that once were made by the company's employees.

P

package　The outer envelope and everything that goes in it in a direct mailing.

paired graphs　Two simple stories juxtaposed to create a more powerful story.

parallel structure　Putting words or ideas that share the same role in the sentence's logic in the same grammatical form.

paraphrase　To repeat in your own words the verbal content of what the previous speaker said.

passive verb　A verb that describes action done to the grammatical subject of the sentence.

people-first language　Language that names the person first, then the condition: "people with mental retardation." Used to avoid implying that the condition defines the person's potential.

perception　The ability to see, to hear, to taste, to smell, to touch.

performance appraisals　Supervisors' written evaluations of their subordinates.

persona　The "author" or character who allegedly writes a letter; the voice that a writer assumes in creating a document.

personal space　The distance someone wants between him- or herself and other people in ordinary, nonintimate interchanges.

personalized　A form letter that is adapted to the individual reader by including the reader's name and address and perhaps other information.

persuade　To motivate and convince the audience to act.

persuasive presentation　A presentation that motivates the audience to act or to believe.

pictograph or **histogram**　A bar graph using pictures, asterisks, or points to represent a unit of the data.

pie chart　A circular chart whose sections represent percentages of a given quantity.

pitch　The highness or lowness of a sound. Low-pitched sounds are closer to the bass notes on a piano; high-pitched sounds are closer to the high notes.

planning　All the thinking done about a subject and the means of achieving your purposes. Planning takes place not only when devising strategies for the document as a whole, but also when generating "mini-plans" that govern sentences or paragraphs.

polarization　A logical fallacy that argues there are only two possible positions, one of which is clearly unacceptable.

polychronic culture　Culture in which people do several things at once.

population　The group a researcher wants to make statements about.

positive emphasis　Focusing on the positive rather than the negative aspects of a situation.

positive or **good news message**　Message to which the reader's reaction will be positive.

possessive case　The grammatical form used to indicate possession or ownership. *My, our, his, hers, its,* and *their* are possessive pronouns.

post office abbreviations　Two-letter abbreviations for states and provinces.

prepositions　Words that indicate relationships, for example, *with, in, under, at.*

presenting problem　The problem that surfaces as the subject of disagreement. The presenting problem is often not the real problem.

primary audience　The audience who will make a decision or act on the basis of a message.

primary research　Research that gathers new information.

pro and con pattern　A pattern of organization for reports that presents all the arguments for an alternative and then all the arguments against it.

probe question　A follow-up question designed to get more information about an answer or to get at specific aspects of a topic.

problem-solving persuasion　A pattern of organization that describes a problem that affects the reader before offering a solution to the problem.

procedural messages　Messages focusing on a group's methods: how it makes decisions, who does what, when assignments are due.

procedures　Information about how to perform actions that involve several different people at various stages.

process of writing　What people actually do when they write. Most researchers would agree that the writing process can include eight parts: planning, gathering, writing, evaluating, getting feedback, revising, editing, and proofreading.

product of writing The final written document.

progress report A statement of the work done during a period of time and the work proposed for the next period.

proofreading Checking the final copy to see that it's free from typographical errors.

proportional typeface A typeface in which some letters are wider than other letters (for example, *w* is wider than *i*).

proposal Document that suggests a method for finding information or solving a problem.

prospecting letter A job application letter written to companies that have not announced openings but where you'd like to work.

psychographic data Human characteristics that are qualitative rather than quantitative: values, beliefs, goals, and lifestyles.

psychological description Description of a product or service in terms of reader benefits.

psychological reactance Phenomenon occurring when a reader reacts to a negative message by asserting freedom in some other arena.

purpose statement The statement in a proposal or a report specifying the organizational problem, the technical questions that must be answered to solve the problem, and the rhetorical purpose of the report (to explain, to recommend, to request, to propose).

Q

questionnaire List of questions for people to answer in a survey.

R

ragged right or **unjustified margins** Margins that do not end evenly on the right side of the page.

random cluster sample A random sample of subjects at each of a random sample of locations. This method is faster and cheaper when face-to-face interviews are required.

random sample A sample for which each person of the population theoretically has an equal chance of being chosen.

reader benefits Benefits or advantages that the reader gets by using the writer's services, buying the writer's products, following the writer's policies, or adopting the writer's ideas. Reader benefits can exist for policies and ideas as well as for goods and services.

rebuttal The refutation of a counterargument.

recommendation report A report that recommends action.

recommendations Section of a report that specifies items for action.

reference line A *subject line* that refers the reader to another document (usually a numbered one, such as an invoice).

referral interview Interviews you schedule to learn about current job opportunities in your field and to get referrals to other people who may have the power to create a job for you. Useful for tapping into unadvertised jobs and the hidden job market.

release date Date a report will be made available to the public.

request To ask the audience to take an easy or routine action.

request for proposal (RFP) A statement of the service or product that an agency wants; a bid for proposals to provide that service or product.

reply card A card or form designed to make it easy for the reader to respond to a direct mail letter. A good reply card not only leaves space for the reader to fill in mailing and ordering information but also repeats the central selling point, basic product information, and price.

respondents The people who fill out a questionnaire.

response rate The percentage of subjects receiving a questionnaire who agree to answer the questions.

restrictive clause A clause limiting or restricting the meaning of a noun or pronoun. Because its information is essential, no commas separate the clause from the word it restricts.

résumé A persuasive summary of your qualifications for employment.

reverse chronology Starting with the most recent job or degree and going backward. Pattern of organization used for chronological résumés.

revising Making changes in the draft: adding, deleting, substituting, or rearranging. Revision can be changes in single words, but more often it means major additions, deletions, or substitutions, as the writer measures the draft against purpose and audience and reshapes the document to make it more effective.

RFP See *request for proposal.*

rhetorical purpose The effect the writer or speaker hopes to have on the audience (to inform, to persuade, to build goodwill).

rhyme Repetition of the final vowel sounds, and if the words end with consonants, the final consonant sounds.

rhythm The repetition of a pattern of accented and unaccented syllables.

rival hypotheses Alternate factors that might explain observed results.

roll out To send to the whole list of recipients the version of a direct mail letter that performed better in a test of part of the list.

rule of three The rule explaining that when a series of three items are logically parallel, the last will receive the most emphasis.

run-on sentence A sentence containing several main clauses strung together with *and, but, or, so,* or *for.*

S

salutation The greeting in a letter: "Dear Ms. Smith."

sample The portion of the population a researcher actually studies.

sans serif Literally, *without serifs*. Typeface whose letters lack bases or flicks. Helvetica and Geneva are examples of sans serif typefaces.

saves the reader's time The result of a message whose style, organization, and visual impact help the reader to read, understand, and act on the information as quickly as possible.

scope statement A statement in a proposal or report specifying the subjects the report covers and how broadly or deeply it covers them.

secondary audience The audience affected by the decision or action. These people may be asked by the primary audience to comment on a message or to implement ideas after they've been approved.

secondary letters Additional letters in a direct mail package. Often on smaller paper, these letters may be to readers who have decided not to accept the offer, from people who have benefited from the charity in the past, and from recognized people corroborating the claims made in the main letter.

secondary research Research retrieving data someone else gathered.

semantic triangle A triangle without a base, a graphic portrayal of the idea that people provide the only connection between words and things.

semantics or **general semantics** The study of the ways behavior is influenced by the words and other symbols used to communicate.

sentence fragment A group of words that are not a complete sentence but that are punctuated as if they were a complete sentence.

sentence outline An outline using complete sentences that lists the sentences proving the thesis and the points proving each of those sentences. A sentence outline is the basis for a summary abstract.

serif The little extensions from the main strokes on the *r* and *g* and other letters. Times Roman and Courier are examples of serif typefaces.

sexist interview A stress interview in which questions are biased against one sex. Many sexist questions mask a legitimate concern. The best strategy is to respond as you would to a stress question: rephrase it and treat it as a legitimate request for information.

signpost An explicit statement of the place that a speaker or writer has reached: "Now we come to the third point."

simple random sample A random sample generated by using a list of all members of a population and a random digit table.

simple sentence Sentence with one main clause.

situational interviews Job interviews in which candidates are asked to describe what they would do in specific hypothetical situations.

skills résumé A résumé organized around the skills you've used, rather than the date or the job in which you used them.

software A computer program, usually sold on a disk, that performs a specific task.

solicited letter A job letter written when you know that the company is hiring.

spot visuals Informal visuals that are inserted directly into text. Spot visuals do not have numbers or titles.

star The attention-getting opener of a direct mail letter.

stereotyping Putting similar people or events into a single category, even though significant differences exist.

storyboard A visual representation of the structure of a document, with a rectangle representing each page or unit. An alternative to outlining as a method of organizing material.

strategy A plan for reaching your specific goals with a specific audience.

stratified random sample A sample generated by first dividing the sample into the same proportion of subgroups as exists in the population and then taking a random sample for each subgroup. This method enables a researcher to be sure that all important subgroups are included in the sample.

stress Emphasis given to one or more words in a sentence.

stress interview A job interview that deliberately puts the applicant under stress, physical or psychological. Here it's important to change the conditions that create physical stress and to meet psychological stress by rephrasing questions in less inflammatory terms and treating them as requests for information.

strong verbs Verbs that help to convey information forcefully or more clearly than verb strings or nouns.

structured interview An interview that follows a detailed list of questions prepared in advance.

stub Used in tables, the stub is the variable listed on the side.

subject line The title of the document, used to file and retrieve the document. A subject line tells readers why they need to read the document and provides a framework in which to set what you're about to say.

subjects The people studied in an experiment, focus group, or survey.

subordinate or **dependent clause** A group of words containing a subject and a verb but that cannot stand by itself as a complete sentence.

summarizing Restating and relating major points, pulling ideas together.

summary abstract The logical skeleton of an article or report, containing the thesis or recommendation and its proof.

summary sentence or **paragraph** A sentence or paragraph listing in order the topics that following sentences or paragraphs will discuss.

survey A method of getting information from a large group of people.

systematic random sample A random sample generated by setting up a template for a random entry on a page, choosing a random interval, and then taking the name at that entry on every page at the interval. A systematic random sample is often used when the researcher has a phone book.

T

table   Numbers or words arrayed in rows and columns.

talking heads   Headings that are detailed enough to provide an overview of the material in the sections they introduce.

target audience   The audience one tries to reach with a mailing: people who are likely to be interested in buying the product, using the service, or contributing to the cause.

teaser copy   Words written on the envelope to get the reader's attention and persuade him or her to open the envelope.

teleconferencing   Telephone conference calls among three or more people in different locations and video-conferences where one-way or two-way TV supplements the audio channel.

telephone tag   Making and returning telephone calls repeatedly before the two people are on the line at the same time.

telex   System in which messages are keyed in on a special machine that translates the keystrokes into a code. Incoming messages are decoded by the machine and printed on paper. Telex messages are common in international business communication.

10-K report   A report filed with the Securities and Exchange Commission summarizing the firm's financial performance; an informative document.

thank-you letter   A letter thanking someone for helping you.

threat   A statement, explicit or implied, that someone will be punished if he or she does something.

tone   The implied attitude of the author toward the reader and the subject.

tone of voice   The rising or falling inflection that indicates whether a group of words is a question or a statement, whether the speaker is uncertain or confident, whether a statement is sincere or sarcastic.

topic outline   An outline listing the main points and the subpoints under each main point. A topic outline is the basis for the table of contents of a report.

topic sentence   A sentence that introduces or summarizes the main idea in a paragraph. A topic sentence may be either stated or implied, and it may come anywhere in the paragraph.

Toulmin logic   A model, developed by Stephen Toulmin, useful in planning and in presenting arguments.

transmit   To send a message.

transitions   Words, phrases, or sentences that show the connections between ideas.

transmittal   A memo or letter explaining why something is being sent.

truncated code   Symbols such as asterisks that turn up other forms of a keyword in a computer search.

truncated scales   Graphs with part of the scale missing.

two-margin or **block format**   A format for résumés in which dates are listed in one column and job titles and descriptions in another. This format emphasizes work history.

typeface   A unified style of type. Each typeface has a design for each letter, number, and symbol. A single typeface will be available in many sizes; it may also be available in bold or italic.

U

umbrella sentence or **paragraph**   A sentence or paragraph listing in order the topics that following sentences or paragraphs will discuss.

understatement   Downplaying or minimizing the size or features of something.

unity   Using only one idea or topic in a paragraph or other piece of writing.

unjustified margins   Margins that do not end evenly on the right side of the page.

unstructured interview   An interview based on three or four main questions prepared in advance and other questions that build on what the interviewee says.

V

verbal communication   Communication that uses words; may be either oral or written.

vested interest   The emotional stake readers have in something if they benefit from keeping things just as they are.

vicarious participation   An emotional strategy in fund-raising letters based on the idea that by donating money, readers participate vicariously in work they are not able to do personally.

visual impact   The visual "first impression" you get when you look at a page.

volume   The loudness or softness of a voice or other sound.

W

watchdog audience   An audience that has political, social, or economic power and that may base future actions on its evaluation of your message.

weak verbs   Verbs composed of a form of the verb *to be* plus a noun.

white space   The empty space on the page. White space emphasizes material that it separates from the rest of the text.

wild card or **truncated code**   Symbols such as asterisks that turn up other forms of a keyword in a computer search.

withdrawing   Being silent in meetings, not contributing, not helping with the work, not attending meetings.

wordiness   Taking more words than necessary to express an idea.

works cited   The sources specifically referred to in a report.

works consulted   Sources read during the research for a report but not mentioned specifically in the report.

writing   The act of putting words on paper or on a screen, or of dictating words to a machine or a secretary.

Y

you-attitude   A style of writing that looks at things from the reader's point of view, emphasizes what the reader wants to know, respects the reader's intelligence, and protects the reader's ego. Using *you* probably increases you-attitude in positive situations. In negative situations or conflict, avoid *you* since that word will attack the reader.

Chapter 1

1. W. B. Johnson and A. E. Packer, *Workforce 2000* (Indianapolis: Hudson Institute, 1987), 99; and Albert R. Karr, "Work Week," *The Wall Street Journal,* December 29, 1998, A1.

2. Anne Fisher, "The High Cost of Living and Not Writing Well," *Fortune,* December 7, 1998, 244.

3. Hal Lancaster, "Making the Break from Middle Manager to a Seat at the Top," *The Wall Street Journal,* July 7, 1998, B1.

4. Fisher, 244

5. Elaine Viets, "Voice Mail Converts Boss into a Secretary," *Columbus Dispatch,* August 10, 1995, 3E; Rochelle Sharpe, "Work Week," *The Wall Street Journal,* September 26, 1995, A1.

6. Lynn Griffin and James O'Rourke, discussion during the Mini Conference on Communication in Accounting Curricula, Columbus, OH, July 22–23, 1994.

7. Dee Castner to Kitty Locker, April 21, 1997

8. Nancy G. Wilds, "Writing in the Military: A Different Mission," *Worlds of Writing: Teaching and Learning in Discourse Communities,* ed. Carolyn B. Matalene (New York: Random House, 1989), 189.

9. Mark Mabrito, "Writing on the 'Front Line!': A Study of Workplace Writing," *Business Communication Quarterly,* 60, no. 3 (September 1997): 60.

10. Margot Northey, "The Need for Writing Skill in Accounting Firms," *Management Communication Quarterly,* 3 (1990): 480.

11. "Pagers That Say Who Called," *Inc.,* August 1993, 39.

12. Henry Mintzberg, *The Nature of Managerial Work* (New York: Harper & Row, 1973), 32, 65.

13. Frederick K. Moss, "Perceptions of Communication in the Corporate Community," *Journal of Business and Technical Communication* 9.1 (January 1995): 67.

14. John Kotter, *The General Managers* (1982), summarized in Alan Deutschman, "The CEO's Secret of Managing Time," *Fortune,* June 1, 1992, 140.

15. "1996 Cost of a Business Letter" (Chicago: Dartnell/From 9 to 5, September 30, 1996), 1.

16. Dianna Booher, *Cutting Paperwork in the Corporate Culture* (New York: Facts on File, 1986), 24.

17. Claudia MonPere McIsaac and Mary Ann Aschauer, "Proposal Writing at Atherton Jordan, Inc.: An Ethnographic Study," *Management Communication Quarterly* 3 (1990): 535.

18. Elizabeth Allen, "Excellence in Public Relations & Communication Management," IABC/Dayton Awards Banquet, Dayton, OH, July 12, 1990.

19. Frank Grazian, "Can We Cure Murky Memos?" *Communication Briefings* 5, no. 4 (1986): 3.

20. Teri Lammers, "What's Luck Got to Do with It?" *Inc.,* December 1993, 90, and Michael Selz, "Quick Off the Mark: Small Manufacturers Display the Nimbleness the Times Require," *The Wall Street Journal,* December 29, 1993, A1.

21. Donna Fenn, "Leader of the Pack," *Inc.,* February 1996, 31–36.

22. Joseph M. Juran, "Made in U.S.A.: A Renaissance in Quality," *Harvard Business Review,* July–August 1993, 45.

23 Justin Martin, "Are You as Good as You Think You Are?" *Fortune,* September 30, 1996, 152.

24. Susan Greco, "The Art of Selling," *Inc.,* June 1993, 73.

25. John Case, "The Hype about Home Businesses," *Inc.,* The State of Small Business 1996, 58.

26. L. D. DeSimone, George N. Hatsopoulous, Charles P. Holt, et al., "How Can Big Companies Keep the Entrepreneurial Spirit Alive?" *Harvard Business Review,* November–December 1995, 183–92.

27. Alessandra Bianchi, "Mission Improbable," *Inc.,* September 1996, 68–75.

28. John Hilikirk, "Listening to Workers Pays Off," *USA Today,* April 2, 1993, 1B–2B.

29. "Teams: A Formula for Success," *Inc.,* May 1996, 111.

30. Carl Quintilla, "Work Week," *The Wall Street Journal,* August 18, 1998, A1.

31. John J. Fialka, "Col. Wyly's Corps Uses Military Skills to Rescue a Ballet," *The Wall Street Journal,* September 16, 1996, A1; and Ayumi Wakizaka, "Faxes, E-Mail Help the Deaf Get Office Jobs," *The Wall Street Journal,* October 3, 1995, B1, B5.

32. "Tracking with FedEx," *Selling Power,* September 1996, 72; "Here Comes the IntraNet," *Business Week,* February 26, 1996, 76; William M. Bulkeley, "Advances in Networking and Software Push Firms Closer to Paperless Office," *The Wall Street Journal,* August 5, 1993, B1; Xerox ad, *The Wall Street Journal,* August 11, 1993, A4; and Jim Bessen, "Riding the Marketing Information Wave," *Harvard Business Review,* September–October 1993, 157–58.

33. Dawn Blalock, "Study Shows Many Execs Are Quick to Write Off Ethics," *The Wall Street Journal,* March 26, 1996, C1.

34. Thomas Petzinger, Jr., "The Front Lines: This Auditing Team Wants You to Create a Moral Organization," *The Wall Street Journal,* January 19, 1996, B1.

35. Clare Ansberry, "Shock Absorber: Bob Stadler Has Lived All the Business Trends of the Past 50 Years," July 11, 1996, A1.

36. Sue Shellenbarger, "All Work and No Play Can Make Jack a Dull Manager," *The Wall Street Journal,* January 24, 1996, B1; Sue Shellenbarger, "Family-Friendly Jobs Are the First Step to Efficient Workplace," *The Wall Street Journal,* May 15, 1996, B1; and Keith H. Hammonds, "Balancing Work and Family," *Business Week,* September 16, 1996, 74.

37. Lori Lewis, "Critical Issues in Communications: Applications to Business," Panel, Association for Business Communication Western Regional Conference, Boise, ID, April 12, 1996.

38. Bianci, "Mission Improbable," 75.

39. Rahul Jacob, "Why Some Customers Are More Equal Than Others," *Fortune,* September 19, 1994, 222, 224.

40. "A Master Class in Radical Change," *Fortune,* December 13, 1993, 82–83.

41. This process was inspired by a process developed by Francis W. Weeks, *Principles of Business Communication* (Champaign, IL: Stipes, 1973), 45.

Chapter 2

1. Sue Shellenbarger, "Companies Are Finding It Really Pays to Be Nice to Employees," *The Wall Street Journal,* July 22, 1998, B1.

2. Charles Burck, "Learning from a Master," *Fortune,* December 27, 1993, 144; Kathy Casto, "Assumptions about Audience in Negative Messages," Association for Business Communication Midwest Conference, Kansas City, MO, April 30–May 2, 1987; and John P. Wanous and A. Colella, "Future Directions in Organizational Entry Research," *Research in Personnel/Human Resource Management,* ed. Kenneth Rowland and G. Ferris (Greenwich, CT: JAI Press, 1990).

3. Annette N. Shelby and N. Lamar Reinsch, Jr., "Positive Emphasis and You-Attitude: An Empirical Study," *Journal of Business Communication* 32, no. 4 (October 1995): 303–27.

4. Alan Farnham, "Are You Smart Enough to Keep Your Job?" *Fortune,* January 15, 1996, 42.

5. Mark A. Sherman, "Adjectival Negation and the Comprehension of Multiply Negated Sentences," *Journal of Verbal Learning and Verbal Behavior* 15 (1976): 143–57.

6. Margaret Baker Graham and Carol David, "Power and Politeness: Administrative Writing in an 'Organized Anarchy,' " *Journal of Business and Technical Communication* 10, no. 1 (January 1996): 5–27.

7. John Hagge and Charles Kostelnick, "Linguistic Politeness in Professional Prose: A Discourse Analysis of Auditors' Suggestion Letters, with Implications for Business Communication Pedagogy," *Written Communication* 6, no. 3 (July 1989): 312–39.

8. Brad Edmondson, "What Do You Call a Dark-Skinned Person?" *American Demographics,* October 1993, 9.

9. Lisa Tyler, "Communicating about People with Disabilities: Does the Language We Use Make a Difference?" *The Bulletin of the Association for Business Communication* 53, no. 3 (September 1990): 65.

10. Marilyn A. Dyrud, "An Exploration of Gender Bias in Computer Clip Art," *Business Communication Quarterly* 60, no. 4 (December 1997): 30–51.

Chapter 3

1. Audiences 1, 3, and 4 are based on J. C. Mathes and Dwight Stevenson, *Designing Technical Reports: Writing for Audiences in Organizations,* 2nd ed. (New York: Macmillan, 1991), 40. The fifth audience is suggested by Vincent J. Brown, "Facing Multiple Audiences in Engineering and R&D Writing: The Social Context of a Technical Report," *Journal of Technical Writing and Communication,* 24, no. 1 (1994): 67–75.

2. Isabel Briggs Myers, *Introduction to Type* (Palo Alto, CA: Consulting Psychologists Press, 1980). The material in this section follows Myers's paper.

3. Isabel Briggs Myers and Mary H. McCaulley, *Manual: A Guide to the Development and Use of the Myers-Briggs Type Indicator* (Palo Alto, CA: Consulting Psychologists Press, 1985), 251, 248, respectively.

4. Matt Siegel, "The Perils of Culture Conflict," *Fortune,* November 9, 1998, 258.

5. Kitty O. Locker, "What Makes a Collaborative Writing Team Successful? A Case Study of Lawyers and Social

Service Workers in a State Agency," *New Visions of Collaborative Writing,* ed. Janis Forman (Portsmouth, NH: Boynton/Cook, 1991), 52–54.

6. Daniel Pearl, "UPS Takes On Air-Express Competition," *The Wall Street Journal,* December 20, 1990, A4.

7. Keith Naughton, "How Ford's F-150 Lapped the Competition," *Business Week,* July 29, 1996, 74–76.

8. Gabrielle Sándor, "Attitude (Not Age) Defines the Mature Market," *American Demographics,* January 1994, 18–21.

9. Eric N. Berkowitz, Roger A. Kerin, Steven W. Hartley, and William Rudelius, *Marketing,* 3rd ed. (Homewood, IL: Irwin, 1992), 126; and Carla Marinucci, "Marketers Have Word for You," *San Francisco Examiner,* in *The Columbus Dispatch,* December 23, 1987, B1–B2.

10. Alan W. H. Grant and Leonard A. Schlesinger, "Realize Your Customers' Full Profit Potential," *Harvard Business Review,* September–October 1995, 65–66.

11. Linda Driskill, "Negotiating Differences among Readers and Writers" (Paper presented at the Conference on College Composition and Communication, San Diego, CA, March 31–April 3, 1993).

12. John J. Weger reports Herzberg's research in *Motivating Supervisors* (New York: American Management Association, 1971), 53–54.

13. Glenn Burkins, "Work Week," *The Wall Street Journal,* February 13, 1996.

14. Diane L. Coutu, "Human Resources: The Wages of Stress," *Harvard Business Review,* November–December 1998, 21–24; and Charles Fishman, "Sanity Inc.," *Fast Company,* January 1999, 85–99.

15. Kevin Leo, "Effective Copy and Graphics," DADM/DMEF Direct Marketing Institute for Professors, Northbrook, IL, May 31–June 3, 1983.

16. Abraham H. Maslow, *Motivation and Personality* (New York: Harper & Row, 1954).

17. Cf. Tove Helland Hammer and H. Peter Dachler, "A Test of Some Assumptions Underlying the Path-Goal Model of Supervision: Some Suggested Conceptual Modifications," *Organizational Behavior and Human Performance* 14 (1975): 73.

18. Edward E. Lawler, III, *Motivation in Work Organizations* (Monterey, CA: Brooks/Cole, 1973), p. 59. Lawler also notes a third obstacle: people may settle for performance and rewards that are just OK. Offering reader benefits, however, does nothing to affect this obstacle.

19. Rachel Spilka, "Orality and Literacy in the Workplace: Process- and Text-Based Strategies for Multiple Audience Adaptation," *Journal of Business and Technical Communication* 4, no. 1 (January 1990): 44–67.

Chapter 4

1. Robert L. Brown, Jr., and Carl G. Herndl, "An Ethnographic Study of Corporate Writing: Job Status as Reflected in Written Text," *Functional Approaches to Writing: A Research Perspective,* ed. Barbara Couture (Norwood, NJ: Ablex, 1986), 16–19, 22–23.

2. Linda Flower, *Problem-Solving Strategies for Writing* (New York: Harcourt Brace Jovanovich, 1981), 39.

3. James Suchan and Robert Colucci, "An Analysis of Communication Efficiency between High-Impact and Bureau-

cratic Written Communication," *Management Communication Quarterly* 2, no. 4 (May 1989): 464–73.

4. Hilvard G. Rogers and F. William Brown, "The Impact of Writing Style on Compliance with Instructions." *Journal of Technical Writing and Communication* 23, no. 1 (1993): 53–71.

5. Gloria Pfeif, interview with Kitty Locker, January 26, 1994.

6. Caleb Solomon, "Clearing the Air: EPA–Amoco Study of Refinery Finds Pollution Rules Focusing on Wrong Part of It," *The Wall Street Journal,* March 29, 1993, A6.

7. Interoffice memo in a steel company.

8. Quoted by Emery Hutchison, "Things My Mother Never Taught Me about Writing," *Journal of Organizational Communications,* Winter 1972, 20.

9. Sign in front of a Kentucky Fried Chicken franchise in Bloomington, IN, July 13, 1984.

10. Philip B. Crosby, *Quality Is Free: The Art of Making Quality Certain* (New York: New American Library, 1979), 79–84.

11. *News-Gazette,* Champaign-Urbana, IL, January 16, 1979, C-8.

12. Frank McAlbee, Second Plenary Session, 1995 Second International Conference for Business Leaders, "Building the Ethics of Business in a Global Economy," Columbus, OH, Nov. 8, 1995.

13. D. Rhoads, "Cultural Influences on Negotiations with Latin Americans," cited in Lawrence B. Nadler, Marjorie Keeshan Nadler, and Benjamin J. Broome, "Culture and the Management of Conflict Situations," *Communication, Culture, and Organizational Processes,* ed. William B. Gudykunst, Lea P. Stewart, and Stella Ting-Tommey (Beverly Hills, CA: Sage Publications, 1985), 109.

14. Richard C. Anderson, "Concretization and Sentence Learning," *Journal of Educational Psychology* 66, no. 2 (1974): 179–83.

15. January 31, 1978, quoted in Lynn Ashby, "7, 8, Facilitate," *Houston Post,* February 17, 1978.

16. Harris B. Savin and Ellen Perchonock, "Grammatical Structure and the Immediate Recall of English Sentences," *Journal of Verbal Learning and Verbal Behavior* 4 (1965): 348–53; and Pamela Layton and Adrian J. Simpson, "Deep Structure in Sentence Comprehension," *Journal of Verbal Learning and Verbal Behavior* 14 (1975): 658–64.

17. E. B. Coleman, "The Comprehensibility of Several Grammatical Transformations," *Journal of Applied Psychology* 48, no. 3 (1964): 186–90; and Keith Raynor, "Visual Attention in Reading: Eye Movements Reflect Cognitive Processes," *Memory and Cognition* 5 (1977): 443–48.

18. Arn Tibbetts, "Ten Rules for Writing Readably," *Journal of Business Communication* 18, no. 4 (Fall 1981): 55–59.

19. Thomas N. Huckin, "A Cognitive Approach to Readability," *New Essays in Technical and Scientific Communication: Research, Theory, Practice,* ed. Paul V. Anderson, R. John Brockmann, and Carolyn R. Miller (Farmingdale, NY: Baywood, 1983), 93–98.

20. Janice C. Redish and Jack Selzer, "The Place of Readability Formulas in Technical Communication," *Technical Communication* 32, no. 4 (1985): 46–52.

21. James Suchan and Ronald Dulek, "A Reassessment of Clarity in Written Managerial Communications," *Management Communication Quarterly* 4, no. 1 (August 1990): 93–97.

Chapter 5

1. See especially Linda Flower and John R. Hayes, "The Cognition of Discovery: Defining a Rhetorical Problem," *College Composition and Communication* 31 (February 1980): 21–32; Rose, *Writer's Block;* and the essays in two collections: Charles R. Cooper and Lee Odell, *Research on Composing: Points of Departure* (Urbana, IL: National Council of Teachers of English, 1978), and Mike Rose, ed., *When a Writer Can't Write: Studies in Writer's Block and Other Composing-Process Problems* (New York: Guilford Press, 1985).

2. Rebecca E. Burnett, "Content and Commas: How Attitudes Shape a Communication-Across-the-Curriculum Program," Association for Business Communication Convention, Orlando, FL, November 1–4, 1995.

3. W. Ross Winterowd, *The Contemporary Writer* (New York: Harcourt Brace Jovanovich, 1975), 61.

4. George H. Jensen and John K. DiTiberio, *Personality and the Teaching of Composition* (Norwood, NJ: Ablex Publishing, 1989), 42.

5. Mike Rose, *Writer's Block: The Cognitive Dimension,* published for Conference on College Composition and Communication (Carbondale, IL: Southern Illinois University Press, 1984), 36.

6. Peter Elbow, *Writing with Power: Techniques for Mastering the Writing Process* (New York: Oxford University Press, 1981), 15–20.

7. See Gabriela Lusser Rico, *Writing the Natural Way* (Los Angeles: J. P. Tarcher, 1983), 10.

8. Fred Reynolds, "What Adult Work-World Writers Have Taught Me About Adult Work-World Writing," *Professional Writing in Context: Lessons from Teaching and Consulting in Worlds of Work,* (Hillsdale, NJ: Lawrence Erlbaum Associates, 1995), 18–21.

9. Raymond W. Beswick, "Communicating in the Automated Office," American Business Communication Association International Convention, New Orleans, LA, October 20, 1982.

10. Dianna Booher, *Cutting Paperwork in the Corporate Culture* (New York: Facts on File Publications, 1986), 23.

11. Susan D. Kleimann, "The Complexity of Workplace Review," *Technical Communication* 38, no. 4 (1991): 520–26.

12. This three-step process is modeled on the one suggested by Barbara L. Shwom and Penny L. Hirsch, "Managing the Drafting Process: Creating a New Model for the Workplace," *The Bulletin of the Association for Business Communication,* 57, no. 2 (June 1994): 1–10.

13. Glenn J Broadhead and Richard C. Freed, *The Variables of Composition: Process and Product in a Business Setting,* Conference on College Composition and Communication Studies in Writing and Rhetoric (Carbondale, IL: Southern Illinois University Press, 1986), 57.

14. This list of five actions is adapted from Robert Boice, "Writing Blocks and Tacit Knowledge," *Journal of Higher Education* 64, no. 1 (January/February 1993), 41–43.

15. Christina Haas, "How the Writing Medium Shapes the Writing Process: Effects of Word Processing on Planning," *Research in the Teaching of English* 23, no. 2 (May 1989): 181; and Christina Haas, " 'Seeing It on the Screen Isn't Really Seeing It': Computer Writers' Reading Problems," *Critical Perspectives on Computers and Composition*

Instruction, ed. Gail Hawisher and Cynthia Selfe (New York: Teachers College Press, 1989), 18–23.

Chapter 6

1. Linda Reynolds, "The Legibility of Printed Scientific and Technical Information," *Information Design,* ed. Ronald Easterby and Harm Zwaga (New York: John Wiley & Sons, 1984), 187–208.

2. George A. Miller, "The Magical Number Seven, Plus or Minus Two: Some Limits on Our Capacity for Processing Information," *Psychological Review* 63, no. 2 (March 1956): 81–97.

3. Once we know how to read English, the brain first looks to see whether an array of letters follows the rules of spelling. If it does, the brain then treats the array as a word (even if it isn't one, such as *tweal*). The shape is processed in individual letters only when the shape is not enough to suggest meaning. Jerry E. Bishop, "Word Processing: Research on Stroke Victims Yields Clues to the Brain's Capacity to Create Language," *The Wall Street Journal,* October 12, 1993, A6.

4. David Matis, "The Graphic Design of Text," *Intercom,* February 1996, 23.

5. M. Gregory and E. C. Poulton, "Even versus Uneven Right-Hand Margins and the Rate of Comprehension of Reading," *Ergonomics* 13 (1970): 427–34.

6. Russell N. Baird, Arthur T. Turnbull, and Duncan McDonald, *The Graphics of Communication: Typography, Layout, Design, Production,* 5th ed. (New York: Holt, Rinehart & Winston, 1987), 37.

7. Philip M. Rubens, "A Reader's View of Text and Graphics: Implications for Transactional Text," *Journal of Technical Writing and Communication* 16, nos. 1–2 (1986): 78.

8. M. E. Wrolstad, "Adult Preferences in Typography: Exploring the Function of Design," *Journalism Quarterly* 37 (Winter 1960): 211–23; summarized in Rolf F. Rehe, "Typography: How to Make It Most Legible," Design Research International, Carmel, IN, 57.

9. Elizabeth Keyes, "Typography, Color, and Information Structure," *Technical Communication,* 40, no. 4 (November 1993): 652; and Joseph Koncelik, "Design, Aging, Ethics, and the Law" (Paper presented in Columbus, OH, May 6, 1993).

10. Marilyn A. Dyrud, "An Exploration of Gender Bias in Computer Clip Art," *Business Communication Quarterly* 60, no. 4 (December 1997): 30–51.

11. Jakob Nielsen, "Top Ten Mistakes in Web Design," May 1996, www.useit.com/alertbox/9605.html.

12. For a review of the events and an analysis of the management problems, see J. C. Mathes, "Three Mile Island: The Management Communication Role," *Engineering Management International* 3 (1986): 261–68.

Chapter 7

1. Thomas L. Fernandez and Roger N. Conaway, "Writing Business Letters II: Essential Elements Revisited," *1996 Refereed Proceedings,* Association for Business Communication Southwest Region, ed. Marsha L. Bayless, 65–68.

2. In a study of 483 subject lines written by managers and MBA students, Priscilla S. Rogers found that the average subject line was 5 words; only 10% of the subject lines used 10 or more words ("A Taxonomy for Memorandum

Subject Lines," *Journal of Business and Technical Communication* 4, no. 2 [September 1990]: 28–29).

3. Deborah Tannen, *That's Not What I Meant: How Conversational Style Makes of Breaks Your Relationships with Others* (New York: Morrow, 1986), 108.

4. Richard C. Whitely, *The Customer-Driven Company* (Reading, MA: Addison-Wesley, 1991), 39–40.

5. An earlier version of this problem, the sample solutions, and the discussion appeared in Francis W. Weeks and Kitty O. Locker, *Business Writing Cases and Problems* (Champaign, IL: Stipes, 1980), 40–44.

Chapter 8

1. Kitty O. Locker, "Factors in Reader Responses to Negative Letters: Experimental Evidence for Changing What We Teach," *Journal of Business and Technical Communication,* 13, no. 1 (January 1999): 21.

2. Locker, 25–26.

3. Allan Sloan, "The Hit Men," *Newsweek,* February 26, 1996, 48.

4. Jack W. Brehm, *A Theory of Psychological Reactance* (New York: Academic Press, 1966).

5. Carol David, "Rereading Bad News: Policy and Procedural Memos and Bad News Lore," Association for Business Communication Annual Convention, Montreal, Canada, October 27–30, 1993.

6. Leslie N. Vreeland, "SEC 'Cop' Has Eye on Mutual Funds," *The Columbus Dispatch,* July 21, 1987, 3F.

7. Frederick M. Jablin and Kathleen Krone, "Characteristics of Rejection Letters and Their Effects on Job Applicants," *Written Communication* 1, no. 4 (October 1984): 387–406.

8. John D. Pettit, "An Analysis of the Effects of Various Message Presentations on Communicatee Responses," Ph.D. diss. Louisiana State University, 1969; and Jack D. Eure, "Applicability of American Written Business Communication Principles across Cultural Boundaries in Mexico," *The Journal of Business Communication* 14 (1976): 51–63.

9. Elizabeth A. McCord, "The Business Writer, the Law, and Routine Business Communication: A Legal and Rhetorical Analysis," *Journal of Business and Technical Communication* 5, no. 2 (1991): 183.

10. Gabriella Stern, "Companies Discover That Some Firings Backfire into Costly Defamation Suits," *The Wall Street Journal,* May 5, 1993, B1.

Chapter 9

1. Art Kleiner, "Flexing Their Mussels, *Garbage,* July/August 1992, 50.

2. Alan Farnham, "You're So Vain," *Fortune,* September 9, 1996, 78–80.

3. John D. Hartigan, "Giving Kids Condoms Won't Work," *The Wall Street Journal,* December 19, 1990, A16.

4. J. C. Mathes and Dwight W. Stevenson, *Designing Technical Reports: Writing for Audiences in Organizations* (Indianapolis: Bobbs-Merrill, 1979), 18–19.

5. James Suchan and Ron Dulek, "Toward a Better Understanding of Reader Analysis," *Journal of Business Communication* 25, no. 2 (Spring 1988): 40.

6. Frances Harrington, "Formulaic Patterns versus Pressures of Circumstances: A Rhetoric of Business Situa-

tions," Conference on College Composition and Communication, New Orleans, LA, March 17–19, 1986.

7. Min-Sun Kim and Steven R. Wilson, "A Cross-Cultural Comparison of Implicit Theories of Requesting," *Communication Monographs* 61, no. 3 (September 1994): 210–35.

8. Priscilla S. Rogers, "A Taxonomy for the Composition of Memorandum Subject Lines: Facilitating Writer Choice in Managerial Contexts," *Journal of Business and Technical Communication* 4, no. 2 (September 1990): 21–43.

9. See John Nathan, "In Search of Excellence: The Film" (Waltham, MA: Nathan/Tyler Productions, 1985), 9–14.

10. Karen Lowry Miller and David Woodruff, "The Man Who's Selling Japan on Jeeps," *Business Week,* July 19, 1993, 56–57.

11. Daniel J. O'Keefe, *Persuasion* (Newbury Park, CA: Sage, 1990), 168; Joanne Martin and Melanie E. Powers, "Truth or Corporate Propaganda," *Organizational Symbolism,* ed. Louis R. Pondy, Thomas C. Dandridge, Gareth Morgan, and Peter J. Frost (Greenwich, CT: JAI Press, 1983), 97–107; and Dean C. Kazoleas, "A Comparison of the Persuasive Effectiveness of Qualitative versus Quantitative Evidence: A Test of Explanatory Hypotheses," *Communication Quarterly,* 41, no. 1 (Winter 1993): 40–50.

12. Daniel Dieterich to Kitty Locker, March 24, 1993.

13. "Phoning Slow Payers Pays Off," *Inc.,* July 1996, 95.

14. An earlier draft of this problem and analysis appeared in Francis W. Weeks and Kitty O. Locker, *Business Writing Problems and Cases* (Champaign, IL: Stipes, 1980), 78–81.

Chapter 10

1. Kathleen J. Krone and John T. Ludlum, "An Organizational Perspective on Interpersonal Influence," in *Seeking Compliance: The Production of Personal Influence Messages,* ed. James Price Dillard (Scottsdale, AZ: Gorsuch Scarisbrick, 1990), 123–42.

2. "Sell Prospects by Using Their Motivational Triggers," *Personal Selling Power,* October 1993, 48.

3. Walter R. Nord, "Beyond the Teaching Machine: The Neglected Area of Operant Conditioning in the Theory and Practice of Management," *Organizational Behavior and Human Performance* 4 (1969): 375–401.

4. Ronald A. Heifetz and Donald L. Laurie, "The Work of Leadership," *Harvard Business Review,* January–February 1997, 124–34.

5. Denise Rousseau, "Corporate Culture Isn't Easy to Change," *The Wall Street Journal,* August 12, 1996, A12.

6. The first and the last two are identified by Jay A. Conger, "The Necessary Art of Persuasion," *Harvard Business Review,* May-June 1998, 88.

7. Thomas Petzinger, Jr., "A Banc One Executive Credits His Success to Mastering Dyslexia," *The Wall Street Journal,* April 24, 1998, B1.

8. Diana Kunde, "Many Workers Afraid to Ask Boss for Flextime," *The Columbus Dispatch,* February 15, 1998, 27J.

9. Anne Fisher, "How Do I Persuade My Boss to Let Me Work at Home?" *Fortune,* November 9, 1998, 264.

Chapter 11

1. Murray Raphel, "Reviving the Dying Store," *Direct Marketing,* November 1993, 20–21.

2. "Direct Marketing . . . An Aspect of Total Marketing," *Direct Marketing,* October 1998, 2.

3. Ernan Roman, "More for Your Money," *Inc.,* September 1992, 113; and Con Squires, "Using Personalization to Increase Response," *Fund Raising Management,* August 1993, 51.

4. Larry J. Sabato, "Mailing for Dollars," *Psychology Today,* October 1984, 38.

5. This pattern is an adaptation of the Star-Chain-Hook pattern developed by Cy Frailey in the 1930s.

6. Alan Rosenspan, "My Secret Weapon: Starch Tested Copy," *Direct Marketing,* August 1998, 35.

7. John D. Beard, David L. Williams, and J. Patrick Kelly, "The Long versus the Short Letter: A Large Sample Study of a Direct-Mail Campaign," *Journal of Direct Marketing* 4, no. 12 (Winter 1990): 13–20.

8. Ray Jutkins, "All about Post and Post Post Scripts—A Key Element in Direct Mail," *Direct Marketing,* January 1997, 44.

9. Jack Maguire to Kitty Locker, December 30, 1986.

10. Eileen Daspin, "How to Give More," *The Wall Street Journal,* October 2, 1998, W1, W4.

11. Jane Maas, *Better Brochures, Catalogs and Mailing Pieces* (New York: St. Martin's Press, 1981), 98–99.

12. Maxwell Sackheim, *My First Sixty-Five Years in Advertising* (Blue Ridge Summit, PA: Tab Books, 1975), 97–100.

Chapter 12

1. Brenda Arbeláez, statement to Kitty Locker, December 12, 1996.

2. "All It Takes Is a Little Investigation," *Going Global: Mexico,* brochure published by *Inc.,* October 1993, n.p.

3. Brian O'Reilly, "Your New Global Work Force," *Fortune,* December 14, 1992, 52–66.

4. Joann S. Lublin, "An Overseas Stint Can Be a Ticket to the Top," *The Wall Street Journal,* January 29, 1996, B1.

5. Rob Norton, "Exploding the Myths about Growth," *Fortune,* November 25, 1996, 84.

6. "Amazing Numbers," *Selling Power,* September 1996, 28.

7. "Hispanic Population Up by More than 50%," *The Columbus Dispatch,* March 11, 1991.

8. "Ethnic Mix Gives California Its Youth," *The Wall Street Journal,* July 12, 1990, B1.

9. Mary Rourke, "U.S. Shifts into Religious Melting Pot," *The Columbus Dispatch,* July 3, 1998, 1F.

10. R. Gustav Niebuhr, "Islam is Growing Fast in the U.S., Fighting Fear and Stereotypes," *The Wall Street Journal,* October 5, 1990, A1.

11. Timothy Aeppel, "A 3Com Factory Hires a Lot of Immigrants, Gets Mix of Languages," *The Wall Street Journal,* March 30, 1998, A1, A12.

12. David A. Victor, *International Business Communication* (New York: HarperCollins, 1992), 148–60.

13. Christina Haas and Jeffrey L. Funk, " 'Shared Information': Some Observations of Communication in Japanese Technical Settings," *Technical Communication* 36, no. 4 (November 1989): 365.

14. Mahund S. Hashmi and Kent L. Foutz, "Marketing in the Islamic Context," Sixth Annual Eastern Michigan University Conference on Languages and Communication for

World Business and the Professions, Ann Arbor, MI, May 7–9, 1987.

15. William Ruch, *Corporate Communication: A Comparison of Japanese and American Practices* (Westport, CT: Quorum Books, 1984), 5–6.

16. Paula J. Pomerenke, "Cultural Influences on Formulating Arguments in Marketing Reports," Modern Language Association Convention, Toronto, Canada, December 27–30, 1993.

17. Laray M. Barna, "Stumbling Blocks in Intercultural Communication, in *Intercultural Communication,* ed. Larry A. Samovar and Richard E. Porter (Belmont, CA: Wadsworth, 1985), 331.

18. Carmen Judith Nine-Curt, "Hispanic-Anglo Conflicts in Nonverbal Communication," in *Perspectivas Pedagogicas,* ed. I. Abino et al. (Universidad de Puerto Rico, 1983), 235.

19. Laurence Wylie, *Beaux Gestes: A Guide to French Body Talk* (Cambridge, MA: Undergraduate Press, 1977), xi.

20. Marjorie Fink Vargas, *Louder than Words* (Ames, IA: Iowa State University Press, 1986), 47.

21. Michael Argyle, *Bodily Communication* (New York: International University Press, 1975), 89.

22. Jerrold J. Merchant, "Korean Interpersonal Patterns: Implications for Korean/American Intercultural Communication," *Communication* 9 (October 1980): 65.

23. Argyle, *Bodily Communication,* 92.

24. Ray L. Birdwhistell, *Kinesics and Context: Essays on Body Motion Communication* (Philadelphia: University of Philadelphia Press, 1970), 30–31.

25. Edward T. Hall and Mildred Reed Hall, *Hidden Differences* (Hamburg, West Germany: Stern Magazine, 1983), 47.

26. Jack Seward, *The Japanese* (New York: Morrow, 1972), 37.

27. Birdwhistell, *Kinesics and Context,* 81.

28. Foseco Minsep, *The Business Traveller's Handbook: How to Get Along with People in 100 Countries* (New York: Prentice-Hall, 1983), 30.

29. Paul Ekman, Wallace V. Friesen, and John Bear, "The International Language of Gestures," *Psychology Today* 18, no. 5 (May 1984): 64.

30. Nine-Curt, "Hispanic-Anglo Conflicts," 234.

31. Baxter, 1970, reported in Marianne LaFrance, "Gender Gestures: Sex, Sex-Role, and Nonverbal Communication," in *Gender and Nonverbal Behavior,* ed. Clara Mayo and Nancy M. Henley (New York: Springer-Verlag, 1981), 130.

32. Nine-Curt, "Hispanic-Anglo Conflicts," 238.

33. Khamdi Amnatvong, interview with the author, Columbus, OH, August 1987.

34. Brenda Major, "Gender Patterns in Touching Behavior," in *Gender and Nonverbal Behavior,* ed. Clara Mayo and Nancy M. Henley (New York: Springer-Verlag, 1981), 26, 28.

35. "Iran Going to Great Lengths to Keep Men, Women Apart," *The Columbus Dispatch,* July 28, 1994, 12A.

36. Natalie Porter and Florence Gies, "Women and Nonverbal Leadership Cues: When Seeing Is Not Believing," in *Gender and Nonverbal Behavior,* ed. Clara Mayo and Nancy M. Henley (New York: Springer-Verlag, 1981), 48–49.

37. Robert C. Christopher, *Second to None: American Companies in Japan* (New York: Crown, 1986), 102–03.

38. Edward Twitchell Hall, *Hidden Differences: Doing Business with the Japanese* (Garden City, NY: Anchor-Doubleday, 1987), 25.

39. Lawrence B. Nadler, Marjorie Keeshan Nadler, and Benjamin J. Broome, "Culture and the Management of Conflict Situations," in *Communication, Culture, and Organizational Processes,* ed. William B. Gudykunst, Lea P. Stewart, and Stella Ting-Toomey (Beverly Hills, CA: Sage, 1985), 103.

40. Argyle, *Bodily Communication,* 90.

41. Carl Quintanilla, "Work Week," *The Wall Street Journal,* August 13, 1996, A1; Mary Ritchie Key, *Paralanguage and Kinesics* (Metuchen, NJ: Scarecrow, 1975), 23; Fred Hitzhusen, conversation with Kitty Locker, January 31, 1988; and William Horton, "The Almost Universal Language: Graphics for International Documents," *Technical Communication* 40, no. 4(1993): 687.

42. David Stipp, "Mirror, Mirror on the Wall, Who's the Fairest of Them All?" *Fortune,* September 9, 1996, 87.

43. Vincent O'Neill, "Training the Multi-Cultural Manager," Sixth Annual EMU Conference on Languages and Communication for World Business and the Professions, Ann Arbor, MI, May 7–9, 1987.

44. Akihisa Kumayama, comment during discussion, Sixth Annual EMU Conference on Languages and Communication for World Business and the Professions, Ann Arbor, MI, May 7–9, 1987.

45. Muriel Saville-Troike, "An Integrated Theory of Communication," in *Perspectives on Silence,* ed. Deborah Tannen and Muriel Saville-Troike (Norwood, NJ: Ablex, 1985), 10–11.

46. A. Jann Davis, *Listening and Responding* (St. Louis: Mosby, 1984), 43.

47. Edward T. Hall and William Foote Whyte, "Intercultural Communication: A Guide to Men of Action," *Human Organization* 19, no. 1 (Spring 1960): 7.

48. Marcia Sweezey to BizCom, September 14, 1992.

49. Tim Comerford to Kitty Locker, Akron, OH, April 4, 1991.

Chapter 13

1. For a full account of the accident, see Andrew D. Wolvin and Caroline Gwynn Coakely, *Listening,* 2nd ed. (Dubuque, IA: William C. Brown, 1985), 6.

2. Molefi Asante and Alice Davis, "Black and White Communication: Analyzing Work Place Encounters," *Journal of Black Studies* 16, no. 1 (September 1985): 87–90.

3. Thomas Gordon with Judith Gordon Sands, *P.E.T. in Action* (New York: Wyden, 1976), 83.

4. Thomas J. Knutson, "Communication in Small Decision-Making Groups: In Search of Excellence," *Journal for Specialists in Group Work* 10, no. 1 (March 1985): 28–37. The next four paragraphs summarize Knutson's analysis.

5. For a fuller listing of roles in groups, see David W. Johnson and Frank P. Johnson, *Joining Together: Group Theory and Group Skills* (Englewood Cliffs, NJ: Prentice Hall, 1975), 26–27.

6. Beatrice Schultz, "Argumentativeness: Its Effect in Group Decision-Making and Its Role in Leadership Perception," *Communication Quarterly* 30, no. 4 (Fall 1982): 374–75; Dennis S. Gouran and B. Aubrey Fisher, "The Functions of Human Communication in the Formation, Maintenance, and Performance of Small Groups," in *Handbook of Rhetor-*

ical and Communication Theory, ed. Carroll C. Arnold and John Waite Bowers (Boston: Allyn and Bacon, 1984), 640; Curt Bechler and Scott D. Johnson, "Leadership and Listening: A Study of Member Perceptions," *Small Group Research* 26, no. 1 (February 1995): 77–85; and Scott D. Johnson and Curt Bechler, "Examining the Relationship between Listening Effectiveness and Leadership Emergence: Perceptions, Behaviors, and Recall," *Small Group Research* 29, no. 3 (August 1998): 452–71.

7. H. Lloyd Goodall, Jr., *Small Group Communications in Organizations* (Dubuque, IA: William C. Brown, 1985), 39–40.

8. Nance L. Harper and Lawrence R. Askling, "Group Communication and Quality of Task Solution in a Media Production Organization," *Communication Monographs* 47, no. 2 (June 1980): 77–100.

9. Rebecca E. Burnett, "Conflict in Collaborative Decision-Making," in *Professional Communication: The Social Perspective,* ed. Nancy Roundy Blyler and Charlotte Thralls (Newbury Park, CA: Sage, 1993), 144–62.

10. Kimberly A. Freeman, "Attitudes Toward Work in Project Groups as Predictors of Academic Performance," *Small Group Research* 27, no. 2 (May 1996): 265–82.

11. Solomon F. Asch, "Opinions and Social Pressure," *Scientific American* 193, no. 5 (November 1955): 31–35. For a review of recent literature on groupthink, see Marc D. Street, "Groupthink: An Examination of Theoretical Issues, Implications, and Future Research Suggestions," *Small Group Research* 28 no. 1 (February 1997): 72–93.

12. Poppy Lauretta McLeod, Sharon Alisa Lobel, and Taylor H. Cox, Jr., "Ethnic Diversity and Creativity in Small Groups," *Small Group Research* 27, no. 2 (May 1996): 248–64.

13. Deborah Tannen, *That's Not What I Meant!* (New York: William Morrow, 1986).

14. Karen Ritchie, "Marketing to Generation X," *American Demographics,* April 1995, 34–36.

15. Thomas Kochman, *Black and White Styles in Conflict* (Chicago: University of Chicago Press, 1981), 103.

16. Daniel N. Maltz and Ruth A. Borker, "A Cultural Approach to Male-Female Miscommunication," in *Language and Social Identity,* ed. John J. Gumperz (Cambridge: Cambridge University Press, 1982), 202.

17. Thomas Kochman, *Black and White Styles in Conflict* (Chicago: University of Chicago Press, 1981), 44–45.

18. David S. Jalajas and Robert I. Sutton, "Feuds in Student Groups: Coping with Whiners, Martyrs, Saboteurs, Bullies, and Deadbeats," *Mastering Management Education: Innovations in Teaching Effectiveness,* ed. Charles M. Vance (Newbury Park, CA: Sage, 1993), 217–27.

19. Nancy Schullery and Beth Hoger, "Business Advocacy for Students in Small Groups," Association for Business Communication Annual Convention, San Antonio, TX, November 9–11, 1998.

20. Jeffrey A. Fadiman, "Intercultural Invisibility: Deciphering the 'Subliminal' Marketing Message in Afro-Asian Commerce," Sixth Annual Conference on Languages and Communication for World Business and the Professions, Ann Arbor, MI, May 8–9, 1987.

21. Raymond L. Gordon, *Living in Latin America* (Skokie, IL: National Textbook, 1974), 41.

22. Philip R. Harris and Robert T. Moran, *Managing Cultural Differences,* 3rd. ed. (Houston: Gulf, 1991), 79, 80.

23. Lisa Ede and Andrea Lunsford, *Singular Texts/Plural Authors: Perspectives on Collaborative Writing* (Carbondale, IL: Southern Illinois Press, 1990), 60.

24. Rebecca Burnett, "Characterizing Conflict in Collaborative Relationships: The Nature of Decision-Making During Coauthoring." PhD dissertation, Carnegie-Mellon University, Pittsburgh, PA, 1991.

25. Kitty O. Locker, "What Makes a Collaborative Writing Team Successful? A Case Study of Lawyers and Social Service Workers in a State Agency," in *New Visions in Collaborative Writing,* ed. Janis Forman (Portsmouth, NJ: Boynton, 1991), 37–52.

26. Ede and Lunsford, *Singular Texts/Plural Authors,* 66.

27. Meg Morgan, Nancy Allen, Teresa Moore, Dianne Atkinson, and Craig Snow, "Collaborative Writing in the Classroom," *The Bulletin of the Association for Business Communication* 50, no. 3 (September 1987): 22.

Chapter 14

1. For a useful taxonomy of proposals, see Richard C. Freed and David D. Roberts, "The Nature, Classification, and Generic Structure of Proposals," *Journal of Technical Writing and Communication* 19, no. 4 (1989): 317–51.

2. Donna Kienzler, e-mail to Kitty Locker, November 5, 1998.

3. Dana Milbank, "Scientists Have to Beat the Bushes for Money to Stay in Business," *The Wall Street Journal,* November 7, 1990, A1.

4. Christine Peterson Barabas, *Technical Writing in a Corporate Culture: A Study of the Nature of Information* (Norwood, NJ: Ablex Publishing, 1990), 327.

5. Brock Brower, "The Pernicious Power of the Polls," *Money,* March 1988, 146.

6. David B. Wolfe, "Targeting the Mature Mind," *American Demographics,* March 1994, 34.

7. Janice M. Lauer and J. William Asher, *Composition Research: Empirical Designs* (New York: Oxford University Press, 1986), 66.

8. Irving Crespi, quoted in W. Joseph Campbell, "Phone Surveys Becoming Unreliable, Pollsters Say," *The Columbus Dispatch,* February 21, 1988, 8F.

9. Lauer and Asher, *Composition Research,* 67.

10. "The Wired Bunch," *American Demographics,* June 1997, 10–12.

11. Earl E. McDowell, Bridget Mrolza, and Emmy Reppe, "An Investigation of the Interviewing Practices of Technical Writers in Their World of Work," in Earl E. McDowell, *Interviewing Practices for Technical Writers* (Amityville, NY: Baywood Publishing, 1991), 207.

12. Robert A. Papper to Kitty Locker, March 17, 1991.

13. Thomas Hunter, "Pulitzer Winner Discusses Interviewing," *IABC Communication World,* April 1985, 13–14.

14. Joshua Macht, "The New Market Research," *Inc.,* July 1998, 90–92.

15. Macht, 92–93.

16. Phaedra Hise, "The Camera Doesn't Lie," *Inc.,* October 1993, 35.

Chapter 15

1. Jared Sandberg, "On-Line Services' User Counts Often Aren't What They Seem," *The Wall Street Journal,* October 6, 1995, B1.

2. Cynthia Crossen, "Diaper Debate: A Case Study of Tactical Research," *The Wall Street Journal*, May 17 1994, B8.

3. "The Incredible Shrinking Failure Rate," *Inc.*, October 1993, 58.

4. Cynthia Crossen, "Margin of Error: Studies Galore Support Products and Positions, but Are They Reliable?" *The Wall Street Journal*, November 14, 1991, A1, A7.

5. "Whirlpool: How to Listen to Consumers," *Fortune*, January 11, 1993, 77.

6. Peter Lynch with John Rothchild, *One Up on Wall Street: How to Use What You Already Know to Make Money in the Market* (New York: Simon and Schuster, 1989), 187.

7. Patricia Sullivan, "Reporting Negative Research Results," and Kitty O. Locker to Pat Sullivan, June 8, 1990.

8. Michael L. Keene, conversation with Kitty Locker, May 17, 1988.

9. Jeanne H. Halpern, phone interview with Kitty Locker, January 21, 1994.

10. James Paradis, David Dobrin, and Richard Miller, "Writing at Exxon ITD: Notes on the Writing Environment of an R&D Organization," in *Writing in Nonacademic Settings* (New York: Guilford, 1985), 300–02.

11. George A. Miller, "The Magical Number Seven, Plus or Minus Two: Some Limits on Our Capacity for Processing Information," *Psychological Review* 63, no. 2 (March 1956): 81–97.

12. Dwight W. Stevenson, Business and Technical Writing Teachers' Roundtable, Purdue, West Lafayette, IN, October 19–20, 1986.

13. Frederick Rose, "In Wake of Cost Cuts, Many Firms Sweep Their History Out the Door," *The Wall Street Journal*, December 21, 1987, 21.

14. Thomas E. Pinelli, Virginia M. Cordle, and Raymond F. Vondran, "The Function of Report Components in the Screening and Reading of Technical Reports," *Journal of Technical Writing and Communication* 14, no. 2 (1984): 92.

Chapter 16

1. Barbara Rosewicz, "Consumer Lobbies Gain Ground on Capitol Hill by Parlaying Tactics, Timing on Banking Bills," *The Wall Street Journal*, October 5, 1987, 46.

2. "GM's $2 Billion Quarterly Loss Biggest Ever," AP, *The Columbus Dispatch*, November 1, 1990, 1B; and Joseph B. White and Paul Ingrassia, "Huge GM Write-Off Positions Automaker To Show New Growth," *The Wall Street Journal*, November 1, 1990, A1.

3. Karen Springer, "Finally, the Free Lunch?" *Newsweek*, February 1, 1999, 57.

4. Jared Sandberg, "On-Line Services' User Counts Often Aren't What They Seem," *The Wall Street Journal*, October 6, 1995, B1.

5. Cynthia Crossen, "Diaper Debate: A Case Study of Tactical Research," *The Wall Street Journal*, May 17 1994, B8.

6. "The Incredible Shrinking Failure Rate," *Inc.*, October 1993, 58.

7. Gene Zelazny, *Say It with Charts: The Executive's Guide to Successful Presentations*, 2nd ed. (Homewood, IL: Business One Irwin, 1991), 52.

8. Most of these guidelines are given by Zelazny, *Say It With Charts*.

9. W. S. Cleveland and R. McGill, "Graphical Perception: Theory, Experiments, and Application to the Development of Graphic Methods," *Journal of the American Statistical Association* 79, nos. 3 & 7 (1984): 531–53; cited in Jeffry K. Cochran, Sheri A. Albrecht, and Yvonne A. Greene, "Guidelines for Evaluating Graphical Designs: A Framework Based on Human Perception Skills," *Technical Communication* 36, no. 1 (February 1989): 27.

10. L. G. Thorell and W. J. Smith, *Using Computer Color Effectively: An Illustrated Reference* (Englewood Cliffs, NJ: Prentice Hall, 1990), 12–13; William Horton, "The Almost Universal Language: Graphics for International Documents," *Technical Communication* 40, no. 4 (1993): 687; and Thyra Rauch, "IBM Visual Interface Design," *The STC Usability PIC Newsletter*, January 1996, 3.

11. Thorell and Smith, *Using Computer Color Effectively*, 13.

12. Ibid., 49–51, 214–15.

13. Edward R. Tufte, *The Visual Display of Quantitative Information* (Cheshire, CT: Graphics Press, 1983), 113.

14. Thophilus Addo, "The Effects of Dimensionality in Computer Graphics," *Journal of Business Communication* 31, no. 4 (October 1994): 253–65.

15. Kathleen Deveny, "What's Wrong with This Picture? Utility's Glasses Are Never Empty," *The Wall Street Journal*, May 25, 1995, B1.

16. Day Mines *1974 Annual Report*, 1; reproduced in Tufte, *The Visual Display of Quantitative Information*, 54.

Chapter 17

1. Carol Hymowitz, "When You Tell the Boss, Plain Talk Counts," *The Wall Street Journal*, June 16, 1989, B1.

2. Linda Driskill, "How the Language of Presentations Can Encourage or Discourage Audience Participation," paper presented at the Conference on College Composition and Communication, Cincinnati, OH, March 18–21, 1992.

3. Anne Fisher, "Willy Loman Couldn't Cut It," *Fortune*, November 11, 1996, 210.

4. Ray Alexander, *Power Speech: Why It's Vital to You* (New York: AMACOM, 1986), 156.

5. Robert S. Mills, conversation with Kitty Locker, March 10, 1988.

6. Phil Theibert, "Speechwriters of the World, Get Lost!" *The Wall Street Journal*, August 2, 1993, A10.

7. "A Study of the Effects of the Use of Overhead Transparencies on Business Meetings," Wharton Applied Research Center, reported in Martha Jewett and Rita Margolies, eds., *How to Run Better Business Meetings: A Reference Guide for Managers* (New York: McGraw-Hill, 1987), 109–110.

8. University of Minnesota/3M Study, reported in Martha Jewett and Rita Margolies, eds., *How to Run Better Business Meetings: A Reference Guide for Managers* (New York: McGraw-Hill, 1987), 115.

9. Stephen E. Lucas, *The Art of Public Speaking*, 2nd ed. (New York: Random House, 1986), 248.

10. John Case, "A Company of Businesspeople," *Inc.*, April 1993, 90.

11. Edward J. Hegarty, *Humor and Eloquence in Public Speaking* (West Nyack, NY: Parker, 1976), 204.

12. Based on Jewett and Margolies, *How to Run Better Business Meetings: A Reference Guide for Managers*, 183–85.

13. The comparison is taken from Jim Martin, "National Debt: Pennies to Heaven," *The Wall Street Journal*, February 22, 1988, 18.

14. Andy Rooney, "World Has Lost Mental Magician," Tribune Media Syndicate, *The Columbus Dispatch*, February 22, 1988, 7A.

15. Some studies have shown that previews and reviews increase comprehension; other studies have found no effect. For a summary of the research see Kenneth D. Frandsen and Donald R. Clement, "The Functions of Human Communication in Informing: Communicating and Processing Information," *Handbook of Rhetorical and Communication Theory*, ed. Carroll C. Arnold and John Waite Bowers (Boston: Allyn and Bacon, 1984), 340–41.

16. S. A. Beebe, "Eye Contact: A Nonverbal Determinant of Speaker Credibility," *Speech Teacher* 23 (1974): 21–25; cited in Marjorie Fink Vargas, *Louder than Words* (Ames, IA: Iowa State University Press, 1986), 61–62.

17. J. Wills, "An Empirical Study of the Behavioral Characteristics of Sincere and Insincere Speakers," Ph.D. diss., University of Southern California, 1961; cited in Vargas, *Louder than Words*, 62.

18. George W. Fluharty and Harold R. Ross, *Public Speaking* (New York: Barnes & Noble, 1981), 162–63.

19. Ralph Proodian, "Mind the Tip of Your Tongue," *The Wall Street Journal*, May 4, 1992, A20.

20. Stephen E. Lucas, *The Art of Public Speaking*, 2nd ed. (New York: Random House, 1986), 243.

21. Ralph Proodian, "Raspy Throat? Read This, Mr. President," *The Wall Street Journal*, January 25, 1993, A14.

22. Michael Waldholz, "Lab Notes," *The Wall Street Journal*, March 19, 1991, B1.

23. George B. Ray, "Vocally Cued Personality Prototypes: An Implicit Personality Theory Approach," *Communication Monographs* 53, no. 3 (1986): 266–76.

Chapter 18

1. Timothy D. Schellhardt, "Managing: Pitfalls to Avoid in Drafting a Résumé," *The Wall Street Journal*, November 28, 1990, B1; and Elizabeth Brockman and Kelly Belanger, "One- or Two-Page Résumés: Does It Make a Difference?" Association for Business Communication Midwest Regional Convention, Akron, OH, April 4–5, 1991.

2. Davida H. Charney, Jack Rayman, and Linda Ferreira-Buckley, "How Writing Quality Influences Readers' Judgments of Résumés in Business and Engineering," *Journal of Business and Technical Communication* 6, no. 1 (January 1992): 38–74.

3. Vincent S. Di Salvo and Janet K. Larsen, "A Contingency Approach to Communication Skill Importance: The Impact of Occupation, Direction, and Position," *The Journal of Business Communication* 24, no. 3 (Summer 1987): 13.

4. Carl Quintanilla, "Coming Back," *The Wall Street Journal*, February 22, 1996, R10.

5. LeAne Rutherford, "Five Fatal Résumé Mistakes," *Business Week's Guide to Careers* 4, no. 3 (Spring/Summer 1986): 60–62.

6. Phil Elder, "The Trade Secrets of Employment Interviews," Association for Business Communication Midwest Convention, Kansas City, MO, May 2, 1987.

7. Kitty O. Locker, Gianna M. Marsella, Alisha C. Rohde, and Paula C. Weston, "Electronic Résumés: Lessons from *Fortune* 500, *Inc.* 500, and Big Six CPA Firms," Association for Business Communication Annual Convention, Chicago, IL, November 6–9, 1996.

8. Ibid.

9. T. T. Sekine, "Employment Portfolios in the Nineties," Association for Business Communication Midwest Convention, Indianapolis, IN, April 20–22, 1995.

10. Beverly H. Nelson, William P. Gallé, and Donna W. Luse, "Electronic Job Search and Placement," Association for Business Communication Convention, Orlando, FL, November 1–4, 1995.

11. Resumix, "Preparing the Ideal Scannable Resume," www.resumix.com] October 16, 1996.

12. Taunee Besson, *The Wall Street Journal National Employment Business Weekly: Résumés* (New York: John Wiley and Sons, 1994), 245.

13. Besson, *Résumés*, 245–56.

Chapter 19

1. Walter Kiechel III, "Preparing for Your Outplacement," *Fortune*, November 30, 1992, 153.

Chapter 20

1. Thomas Petzinger, Jr., "Lewis Roland's Knack for Finding Truckers Keeps Firm Rolling," *The Wall Street Journal*, December 1, 1995, B1.

2. Claud Dotson, comment at Association for Business Communication Western Regional Conference, Boise, ID, April 13, 1996; and Julie Amparano Lopez, "Choosy Firms Force Job Seekers to Jump through Many Hoops," *The Wall Street Journal*, October 6, 1993, B4.

3. Judith A. Swartley to Kitty Locker, March 20, 1989.

4. Sherri Eng, "Company Culture Dictates Attire for Interviews," *The Columbus Dispatch*, August 25, 1996, 33J.

5. The Catalyst Staff, *Marketing Yourself* (New York: G. P. Putnam's Sons, 1980), 179.

6. Lopez, "Firms Force Job Seekers to Jump through Hoops," *The Wall Street Journal*, October 6, 1993, B1.

7. Donna Stine Kienzler, letter to Ann Granacki, April 6, 1988.

8. Joel Bowman, "Using NLP to Improve Classroom Communication," Association for Business Communication Regional Conference, Lexington, KY, April 9–11, 1992.

9. Christopher Conte, "Labor Letter," *The Wall Street Journal*, October 19, 1993, A1.

10. *Marketing Yourself*, 101.

11. Claud Dotson, comment at the Association for Business Communication Western Regional Conference, Boise, ID, April 13, 1996.

12. Kate Wendleton, *Through the Brick Wall: How to Job-Hunt in a Tight Market* (New York: Villard Books, 1992), 244.

13. Ray Robinson, quoted by Dick Friedman, "The Interview as Mating Ritual," *Working Woman*, April 1987, 107.

14. Brenda Major and Ellen Konar, "An Investigation of Sex Differences in Pay Expectations and Their Possible Causes," *Academy of Management Journal* 27, no. 4 (1984): 782.

15. Wendleton, *Through the Brick Wall*, 278.

Appendix A

1. Maria Rivera, comment to the author, Association for Business Communication East Regional Convention, San Juan, PR, April 28, 1995.

Appendix C

1. N. L. Reinsch, Jr., and Raymond W. Beswick, "Voice Mail versus Conventional Channels: A Cost Minimization Analysis of Individuals' Preferences," *Academy of Management Journal* 11, no. 4 (1990): 801–16.

2. Robert Rosenthal, *Pygmalion in the Classroom* (New York: Holt, Rinehart, and Winston, 1968).

3. Danuta Ehrlich, Isaiah Guttman, Peter Schonbach, and Judson Mills, "Postdecision Exposure to Relevant Information," *Journal of Abnormal and Social Psychology* 54 (1957): 98–102; summarized in Elliot Aronson, *The Social Animal* (San Francisco: W. H. Freeman, 1972), 101.

4. Tim R. V. Davis, "Managing Culture at the Bottom," in *Gaining Control of the Corporate Culture,* ed. Ralph H. Kilman, Mary J. Saxton, Roy Serpa, and Associates (San Francisco: Jossey-Bass Publishers, 1985), 175.

5. "What's Wrong with This Picture?" *The Columbus Dispatch,* May 9, 1994, 2D.

6. Paulette Thomas, "Work Week," *The Wall Street Journal,* October 29, 1996, B1.

7. Paul Craig Roberts, "America's 'Savings Crisis' Is a Chimera," *Business Week,* February 12, 1990, 20.

8. William M. Bulkeley, "A Firm by Any Other Name Means Likely Rise in Stock, Research Finds," *The Wall Street Journal,* July 10, 1987, 22.

9. Elmo R. Zumwalt, Jr., *On Watch: A Memoir* (New York: Times Books, 1976), 189; cited in Thomas J. Peters and Robert H. Waterman, Jr., *In Search of Excellence: Lessons from America's Best-Run Companies* (New York: Warner, 1992, 263–64.

10. "Kodak Alters Use of Name," Champaign-Urbana *News-Gazette,* April 8, 1983, C–1.

11. Roger Trench, "All in a Day's Work," *Readers' Digest,* September 1989, 138.

12. John C. Dvorak, "Crazy Mistakes, Part 1," *PC Magazine,* March 28, 1989, 71, and "Crazy Mistakes, Part 2" *PC Magazine,* June 13, 1989, 71.

Appendix D

1. See Stephen Toulmin, *The Uses of Argument* (Cambridge: Cambridge University Press, 1958).

P1-1: Un fig 1.2, © Steve Rubin. P1-2: Un fig 1.3, Per Breiehagen. P1-3: Un fig 1.4, Clive Brunskill/Allsport. P1-4: Un fig 1.5, Courtesy CompareNet. P1-5: Un fig 1.6, Copyright © 1999 The Conde Nast Publications Inc. All rights reserved. Reprinted by permission. Photograph by Aaron Caplan. P1-6: Un fig 1.7, Courtesy Dickstein Shapiro Morin & Oshinsky LLP. P2-0, Courtesy Service Intelligence. P2-1: Un fig 2.2, Bill Sikes/AP Wide World Photos. P2-2a: Un fig 2.3a, Jon Feingersh/The Stock Market. P2-2b: Un fig 2.3b, © PhotoDisc, Inc. P3-1, Courtesy Claritas Inc. P3-2a, Courtesy Lifecode®. Photography by Bob Greenspon. P3-2b, Courtesy Lifecode®. Photography by Bob Greenspon. P3-3: Un fig 3.2, Courtesy 2H i Helenelund HB. P4-1: Un fig 4.2, Courtesy Iomega. P4-2: Fig 4.2, Courtesy General Electric. P4-3: Fig 4.3, Copyrighted material used with permission of Warren E. Buffett. P4-4: Un fig 4.3, Lou Jones/The Image Bank. P5-1: Fig 5.4, Copyright (1999) by Purdue Research Foundation, West Lafayette, Indiana 47907. All rights reserved. P5-2, David Young Wolff/Tony Stone Images. P6-1: Un fig 6.2, Courtesy Jakob Nielsen. P6-2: Un fig 6.3a, These designs are trademarks of PaperDirect, Inc. All Rights Reserved. P6-3: Un fig 6.3b, These designs are trademarks of PaperDirect, Inc. All Rights Reserved. P6-4: Ex 6.1c, Courtesy W. W. Grainger, Inc. P6-5: Ex 6.1d, Kinko's is a registered trademark of Kinko's Ventures, Inc. All depictions of Kinko's and its trademarks are used by permission. © 1998-1999 Kinko's Inc. All rights reserved. P6-6: Ex 6.1e, Courtesy Volkswagen of America, Inc. and Arnold Communications, Inc. P6-7: Ex 6.3, Source: "Alphabet Soup," @Issue: The Journal of Business and Design, Vol. 3, No. 2 (Fall 1997): 24-25, Courtesy Corporate Design Foundation. @Issue is sponsored by Potlatch Corporation. P7-1: Un fig 7.2, www.hallmarkconnections.com, Hallmark Cards, Inc. P8-1: Un fig 8.2, Courtesy Schwinn Bicycle. P8-2, Courtesy Chief Deputy Scott A. Frank, Ottawa County (Ohio) Sheriff's Office. P9-1, Courtesy of Direct Marketing Magazine. P9-2, Courtesy Cisco Systems, Inc.

P9-3, Wyatt McSpadden. P9-4: Un fig 9.4, National Archives and Records Administration online exhibit "Powers of Persuasion-Posters from World War II", http://www.nara.gov/exhall/powers/powers.html. P10-1: Un fig 10.2, Used with permission of Rice University. P11-1: Un fig 11.2a, Courtesy of www.rei.com. P11-2: Un fig 11.2b, Courtesy of Habitat for Humanity® International. P11-3: Un fig 11.3, John Thoeming. P11-4: Un fig 11.4a, Courtesy Laubach Literacy. P11-5: Un fig 11.4b, Courtesy Laubach Literacy. P11-6: Fig 11.3, © The Gorilla Foundation/Ronald H. Cohn, www.gorilla.org. P12-1: Un fig 12.2, AP/Wide World Photos. P12-2: Un fig 12.3, © Jessica Wecker 1999. P12-3: Un fig 12.4, Nina Berman/SIPA. P12-4: Un fig 12.5, © Mark Richards. P12-5, Courtesy The Anderson School at UCLA. P13-1: Un fig 13.2, Marnie Crawford Samuelson. P13-2: Un fig 13.3, Courtesy 3M Meeting Network. P14-1: Un fig 14.2a, The Foundation Center © 1995-1999. P14-2: Un fig 14.2b, The Foundation Center © 1995-1999. P15-1: Un fig 15.2, Courtesy of the United Nations Environment Programme, Global Environment Outlook-1, Global State of the Environment Report 1997. P16-1: Un fig 16.2, Selected graphic image supplied courtesy of Environmental Systems Research Institute, Inc. Copyright © 1996, Environmental Research Institute, Inc. P17-1: Un fig 17.2, Courtesy Toastmasters International. P18-1: Un fig 18.2, Courtesy Rockport Institute, Ltd. P19-1: Un fig 19.1, Carl J. Single/The Image Works. P19-2, No credit. P19-3, Reproduced by permission of Intel Corporation. P20-1: Un fig 20.2, © Copyright 1999 Arthur Andersen. All rights reserved. Reprinted with permission. www.arthurandersen.com. P20-2: Un fig 20-3, Copyright © by Danny Turner. All Rights Reserved. PappC-1:Un fig C.2, Reprinted with permission of NIKE, Inc. PappC-2: Un fig C.3a, Courtesy Princeton Video Image (www.pvimage.com). PappC-2: Un fig C.3b, Courtesy Princeton Video Image (www.pvimage.com).

A

Achenbach, Joel, 95
Adams, Cynthia, 388
Allen, Art, 239
Amatos, Christopher A., 10
Anderson, Carl M., 509
Angel, David, 491
Anson, Chris M., 20
Anthony, William A., Jr., 587
Arbeláez, Brenda, 314, 321
Asch, Solomon, 342
Atkinson, Jerry, 458
Azuma, Shojl, 193

B

Baird, Russel N., 138
Barbaras, Christine, 377
Baron, Dennis E., 48
Baxter, Tony, 40
Beamer, Linda, 225
Beardsely, Jennifer, 540
Beck, Bob, 488
Besson, Taunee, 513, 531, 555
Beswick, Raymond, 634
Birdwhistell, Ray, 319
Birnbaum, Jeffrey H., 302
Bishop, Jerry E., 322
Blair, John G., 42
Blundell, William E., 10
Boesky, Ivan, 17
Boice, Robert, 125
Booker, Dianna, 123
Borker, Ruth A., 344, 345
Boston, Bruce O., 626
Brehm, Jack W., 200
Britt, Steuart Henderson, 389
Broadhead, Glenn, 124
Brown, Vincent J., 60
Buffett, Warren, 90
Burch, Howe, 487
Burke, Tom, 555
Burnett, Rebecca, 342
Burns, Diane, 145
Butenhoff, Carla, 172
Byrnes, Mary Ann, 14

C

Calmes, Jackie, 104
Camilleri, Rosemary, 108
Carns, Tom, 223
Carter, Jimmy, 319
Case, John, 15
Casselman, Cindy V., 59, 228
Casson, Lionel, 617
Castner, Dee, 5, 91
Chatman, Jennifer, 63
Childs, Christopher, 497
Chilton, Edward M., 623
Christopher, Robert, 321
Clinton, Bill, 17
Cole, Jeff, 164
Coleman, John, 77, 386
Collins, Eliza G., 231
Colucci, Robert, 94
Condon, John C., 47
Connors, Robert J., 615
Considine, Ray, 78, 233
Cook, Scott, 485
Covey, Stephen R., 313
Cronkite, Walter, 337
Crossen, Cynthia, 43, 349
Crozler, Caroline Sanchez, 609
Cummings, Jeanne, 302

D

Dandridge, Thomas C., 412
Davis, James, 221, 230
Davis, Jann, 324
Davis, Tim R. V., 639
Dessler, Gary, 339
Dew, John R., 4
Dieterich, Dan, 234, 235
DiTiberio, John, 117
Dobrzynski, Judith H, 571
Donaldson, Thomas, 319
Donnelly, James H., 173
Douglas, Patti, 371
Driskill, Linda, 487
Dulek, Ronald, 107, 224
Dunn, Kelley, 14
Dyrud, Marilyn, 51, 141
Dzubow, Steven R., 544

E

Ede, Lisa, 350
Einhorn, Lois J., 572
Eisenhower, Dwight, 302
Elashmawi, Farid, 323, 326
Elbow, Peter, 270

F

Fairhurst, Gail T., 103
Feinstein, Selwyn, 525
Ferguson, James, 66
Feuerstein, Aaron, 157
Fieg, John P., 42
Firnstahl, Timothy W., 192
Fisher, Anne, 222, 318, 327, 370
Fisher, Roger, 348
Flores, Fernando, 246
Fluharty, George, 495
Fogel, George, 351
Forsberg, L. Lee, 20
Frank, William S., 528
Freed, Richard C., 124, 369
Freed, Shervin, 369
Freeman, Kimberly, 342
Frost, Peter J., 412
Fuduric, Silvia, 47

G

Gallé, William, 528
Garrett, Echo Montgomery, 570
Gendron, George, 552
George, Judy, 391
Gibson, James L., 173
Gillmor, Dan, 491
Goleman, Daniel, 222
Goodman, Paul, 4
Gordon, Gloria, 22
Gordon, Thomas, 338
Goswami, Dixie, 137
Gould, Stephen Jay, 459
Graham, Ellen, 48
Graham, James L., 494
Graham, John, 327
Graves, Roger, 297
Gray, Lee L., 139

Grazian, Frank, 10
Greogrich, Annette, 4
Grossman, John, 339
Gruner, Stephanie, 170
Guillot, Victoria Brink, 232
Gumperz, John J., 345
Gutner, Toddi, 93

H

Hadjuk, Thomas, 499
Hagge, John, 44
Hairston, Maxine, 611
Hajduk, Thomas, 411
Half, Robert, 525, 555
Hall, Edward T., 321, 325
Halpern, Jeanne, 411
Harding, Jan, 568, 580
Hardy, Quentin, 485
Harris, Philip R., 323, 326
Hartley, James, 387
Hatcher, Kendra, 369
Hawkins, Trip, 485
Hayashi, Fumio, 643
Hayes, Arthur S., 204
Hendrickson, Aletha S., 68, 652
Hendrickson, Ruth Ann, 633
Herzberg, Frederick, 73
Hession, Matt, 485, 486
Hiebeler, Robert, 13
Higgins, Chris, 352, 353
Hilbok, Stephen, 33
Hogan, Beth, 339, 345
Hoover, Gary, 15
Huffman, Cindy, 457
Hughes, Wingfield, 289
Hurston, Ed, 170
Hyatt, Joshua, 486
Hymowitz, Carol, 66

I

Imperato, Gina, 352, 353
Inch, Josh, 289
Ivancevich, John M., 173

J

Jameson, Daphne A., 7
Janke, David, 314
Jensen, George, 117
Jereb, Barry, 106
Joel, Billy, 643
Johnson, Bradley, 94
Johnson, John H., 22
Jones, Bronwen, 489
Jutkins, Ray, 277, 286

K

Kannensohn, Fredric A., 241
Kanter, Rosabeth Moss, 423

Karam, Gregory L., 241
Katz, Susan M., 156
Kaufman, Joanne, 637
Kazoleas, Dean C., 412
Keller, Karl P., 197
Kelly, Thomas B., 13
Kendrick, Deborah, 52
Kennedy, Marilyn Moats, 508
Ketterman, Charles, 13
Key, Mary Ritchie, 47
Kienzler, Donna, 368
King, Carol Elizabeth, 124
Kinnear, Mary, 340
Kipper, Don, 583
Kirchoff, Bruce, 407, 459
Kirkpatrick, David, 18
Kleiman, Carol, 507
Kleimann, Susan D., 123, 131, 446
Knight, Julia, 391
Kochman, Thomas, 344
Koester, Jolene, 225
Koogle, Timothy, 485
Kopfman, Jennifer E., 268
Kostelnick, Charles, 44
Kumayama, Akihisa, 389
Kuras, Janet, 282

L

La Franco, Robert, 480
Labarre, Polly, 25
Lamela, Luis E., 483
Lancaster, Hal, 260, 340
Lane, James B., 235, 365
Lannon, John M., 126
Lareau, William, 574
LaRouche, Janice, 449
Larson, Jackie, 545
Lasser, Lawrence, 142
Lease, Carol Ann, 77
Leche, Emma Jean Ghee, 189
Lederer, Richard, 230, 387, 613, 622
Leonard, Stew, 637
Lever-Pollary, Teresa, 163
Lewis, Lori D., 18
Liker, Jeffrey K., 406
Lonsdale, Jan, 325
Lopez, Ruben, 72
Lott, Trent, 104
Lovill, Jeff, 623
Lucas, Stephen, 496
Lunsford, Andrea A., 350, 615
Luse, Donna, 528
Lustig, Myron W., 225
Lutz, William, 41
Lynch, Peter, 409

M

McCord, Elizabeth A., 5, 204, 424
McDonald, Duncan, 138

McGinty, Sarah, 345
McGowen, Steve, 4
McGrath, Kathryn, 202
Macht, Joshua, 391
McLaughlin, Shane, 386
McLean, Bethany, 237, 303
McMorris, Frances A., 17
Maitra, Kaushiki, 137
Malcolm, Andrew H., 471
Maltz, Daniel N., 344, 345
Martin, Janniece, 278
Martin, Joanne, 412
Martz, Geoff, 525
Maslow, Abraham H., 75
Matalene, Carolyn, 68, 652
Mathes, J. C., 126, 224
Mattei, Sally, 18
Mehta, Stephanie N., 634
Metegrano, Margo, 100
Mieszkowski, Katherine, 367, 492
Milbank, Dana, 644
Miller, Amy, 572
Miller, Darryl, 4
Miller, George, 133
Miller, James P., 388
Mintzberg, Henry, 6
Moburg, Teresa, 537, 538, 551
Molloy, John, 567
Moore, Tim R., 565
Moran, Paul, 552
Morgan, Gareth, 412
Morse, Rick, 77
Munschauer, John L., 518, 548, 573, 574
Myers, Isabel Briggs, 62

N

Narisetti, Raju, 17, 568
Nash, Laura L., 231
Nathan, John, 416, 637
Nelson, Beverly, 528
Nhan, Tawn, 522
Nine-Curt, Carmen Judith, 318
Nishiyama, Kazuo, 10
Nordstrom, Mike, 14
Noronha, Shonan, 493
Northey, Margot, 5, 44

O

O'Keefe, Daniel J., 412
O'Malley, Michael, 260
Olajuwan, Hakeem, 316
Oldenburg, Don, 337
Omasta, Faye Ambrefe, 575

P

Padilla, Carmella M., 96
Pappas, Ben, 480
Papper, Robert A., 494, 496

Patterson, Gregory A., 64
Petzinger, Thomas, Jr., 6, 71
Pierce, Evelyn, 411
Pierce, Kim, 645
Pinton, Stefania, 313
Polese, Kim, 94
Pondy, Louis R., 412
Porter, James E., 125
Potter, Theresa E., 75
Powers, Melanie E., 412
Pritchard, David, 578

Q

Quinn, Jane Bryant, 391
Quintanilla, Carl, 316, 523

R

Ralston, Steve, 568
Raphael, Murray, 78, 233
Reder, Stephen, 4
Redish, Janice C., 106
Reichheld, Frederick F., 368
Reinsch, N. Lamar, Jr., 37, 634
Reynolds, Fred, 119, 121
Rhodes, John, 493
Richmond, Yale, 193
Ricks, David A., 72, 95, 137
Rigdon, Joan E., 126, 349, 556, 619
Rimalower, George, 325
Ritchie, Karen, 315
Roberts, Carol, 267
Robertson, Nan, 390
Romano, Joseph D., 369
Rosa, Nick, 484
Rose, Richard C., 570
Rosenfield, James R., 281, 304
Rosenkranz, Eric, 318
Rosenpan, Alan, 74, 285
Ross, Harold, 495
Roth, Robert A., 389
Roth, Robert F., 72, 105
Rowe, Jeff, 40
Rubens, Philip M., 137
Rubin, Harriet, 246
Rubin, Michael G., 634
Russo, Michelle, 118

S

Safire, William, 616
Sands, Judith Gordon, 338

Sarr, Robert A., 103
Sato, Mitsuru, 230
Sauer, Beverly A., 422
Saville-Troike, Muriel, 324
Schrage, Michael, 350
Schriver, Karen A., 141, 143
Schullery, Nancy, 339, 345
Seelye, H. Ned, 315, 489
Seelye-James, Alan, 315, 489
Seligman, Martin, 37
Semerjian, Dayton J. D., 407, 425
Shaffer, Richard A., 165
Shamir, Peter, 391
Sharp, Rochelle, 555
Shelby, Annette N., 37
Shellenbarger, Sue, 575
Shepherd, Deneen, 315
Shirouzu, Morihiko, 642
Shoreibah, Alaa, 316
Siegel, Matt, 63
Slakey, Kevin, 505
Slezer, Jack, 106
Smith, Gerald F., 102
Smith, Sandi W., 268
Smoot, P. J., 370
Sobek, Duward K., II, 406
Sowell, Shaunna, 340
Spilka, Rachel, 77
Stackhouse, Jerry, 487
Staley, Robert, 314
Stanley, Thomas J., 67
Steinberg, Edwin R., 106
Stevenson, Dwight W., 126, 224, 417
Stewart, Thomas A., 163, 263
Suchan, James, 94, 107, 224
Sun, Diana, 155
Sweezey, Marcia, 325

T

Takahashi, Yoshiharu, 471
Tanaka, Kazumi, 465
Tannen, Deborah, 343
Taylor, Todd, 101
Teal, Thomas, 157
Thurow, Roger, 487
Toulmin, Stephen, 652
Tufte, Edward, 468, 469
Turnbull, Arthur T., 138
Twain, Mark, 643
Tyler, Lisa, 43

U

Ulijn, Jan M., 324, 344
Underbill, Paco, 232
Urech, Elizabeth, 484
Ury, William, 348
Useem, Jerry, 15

V

Varner, Iris, 225
Venit, S., 145
Verespie, Michael A., 4
Victor, David A., 315
von Brachel, John, 458

W

Ward, Allen C., 406
Warshaw, Michael, 228, 267
Waterman, Robert H., 392
Watson, James L., 320
Waugh, Barbara, 367, 492
Weissman, Jerry, 491
Welch, Jack, 20, 90
Weldon, Kate, 578
Welles, Edward O., 189, 223
Welling, Robin, 488
Wells, Jess, 497
Welton, Gordon, 575
Wheeler, Kathy, 63
White, Joseph, 25
Whyte, William, 325
Wiener, Emilia Fonseca, 3, 15
Wilk, Thomas, 651
Wilson, Lerry, 335
Winkler, Don, 267

X

Xiangling Li, 344

Y

Yate, Martin John, 583
Young, Richard, 411, 499
Yousef, Fathi, 47

Z

Zankman, Lisa, 236
Zelazny, Gene, 460
Zevchik, Daniel R., 117
Zimmerman, Scott, 259

A

Aeroquip Corporation, 4
Aetna Insurance Company, 17
Aladan Corp., 13
Allen Systems Groups, 239
Amazon.com, 278
America Online, 406, 459
American Cancer Society, 278
American Express, 279, 571
Amy's Ice Cream, 572
Archadeck, 465
Arthur Andersen, 63, 567
Artie's Restaurant and Yogurt
    Parlor, 230
AT&T, 201, 571

B

Bank of America, 41, 528
BankAmerica, 352, 488
Bata Limited, 313
Battelle, 633
Battelle Memorial Institute, 651
Beechnut, 17
Bell Labs, 41
Bombay Furniture Company, 314
Bridgestone/Firestone, 263
Buick, 278
Business Interiors, 13

C

CAC Medical Centers, 483
Capital One, 155
Care, 296
CenterPoint Properties Trust, 259
Chevrolet, 95
Chevron, 13
Chris Zane's Cycles, 13
CIBC, 232
Cisco Systems, 505
CIT Group, 289
Citibank, 141, 232
Citigroup, 4
City Year, 337
Claritas, Inc., 65
Clifford of Vermont, 41
Clorox Company, 528
Coca-Cola, 95, 319, 467

Computer Services & Consulting,
    Inc., 609
Con-Way Transportation
    Services, 342
Consider It Dunn, Inc., 14
Consumer Federation
    of America, 458
Cornelius Grove & Associates, 327
Cornish and Carey Real Estate, 325
Corsair Communications Inc., 14
Council on International Educational
    Exchange, 554
Country Charm, 278

D

Datafelx, 570
Davis Safety Supply Inc., 221
Deloitte & Touche, 63
Dettmers Industries, 15
Dickstein Shapiro Morin &
    Oshinksky, 21
Digital Equipment Corporation, 41
Direct Marketing Association, 279
Disney World, 40
Document Design Center, 106
Domain furniture stores, 391
Drug Abuse Resistance Education
    (D.A.R.E), 198

E

Eastman Kodak, 644
Electronic Data Systems, 34
Emerson Electronics, 173, 314
Environmental Systems Research
    Institute, 468
Ernst & Young, 235, 365
Evans & Sutherland Computer
    Corp., 314
Exxon, 463

F

Federal Communications
    Commission, 141
FedEx, 64, 278
Fila, 487
Fingerhut, 17
First Tennessee National Corp., 18

Ford Motor Company, 139, 198,
    463, 528
Foundation Center, 377

G

Gallaudet University, 278
Gap, The, 640
Garbage, 72
General Motors, 458, 463, 471
Gore Tex, 577
Gorilla Foundation, 297-301
Grainger, 146
Grey Advertising International, 318
GTE, 575

H

Habitat for Humanity, 280
Halliburton Energy Services, 4
Harris Bank, 41
Hewlett-Packard, 18, 367, 467
Hormel Foods, 279
Hub Furniture Store, 230

I

IBM, 97, 163, 467
Informus Corp., 522
International Paper, 370
Interpreting Services
    International, 325
Iomega, 92
Itochu, 463

J

J.B. Hunt Transport Services, 237
James Productions, 289
John Hancock Sovereign Balanced
    Fund, 93
Joseph T. Ryerson & Son, 8

K

Kinko's, 146
Kleinmann Communication
    Group, 131
KPMG Netherlands, 266
KPMG Peat Marwick, 17, 537
KPR Sports International, 624

L

Larry's Shoes, 224
Leo Burnett, 369
Levi Strauss & Co., 319, 407
Lockheed Martin Utility Services, 4

M

Macon County Humane Society, 230
Macy's, 278
Malden Mills, 157
Martin Marietta Government
     Electronic Systems, 173
Marubeni, 463
Massachusetts Mutual Life, 571
Mattel's, 199
Mazda, 95
MBNA, 13
MCI Communications, 34
Merrill Lynch & Co., 33
Met Life, 37, 72
Microsoft, 578
Mitsubishi, 463
Mitsui, 463
MONY Group, 3
Motley Fool, 577
Motorola, 141
Multiple Zones International, 4

N

National Charities Information
     Bureau, 297
National Science Foundation, 369
New Forests Fund, 296
Newsweek, 41
Nike, 638
North Island Naval Depot, 15
Northern Telecom, 34

O

Ohio Civil Service Employees
     Association, 587

Olathe Lanes, 69
1-800-FLowers, 278

P

Parsons Technology Inc., 278
PDQ Printing, 223
Phelps County Bank, 371
Phoneworks, 289
Pillsbury, 6
Principal Financial Group, 575
Pro Staff, 565
Procter & Gamble, 41, 261

Q

Quarterdeck, 314

R

REI, 280
Rent-a-Wreck, 37
Republican National Committee, 278
Rice University, 266
ROCKINGHAM*JUTKINS*
     marketing, 277
Royal Dutch/Shell Group, 463

S

Santa Fe Southern Railroad, 103
SAS Institute, 457
Schwinn, 203
Sears Roebuck, 34
Sharps Fresh Roasting
     Restaurant, 192
Southern Gas Company, 141
Southwest Airlines, 576
State Street Research Equity Income
     Fund, 93
Steinway, 74
Stouffer Foods Corp., 41
Sumitomo, 463
Sun Microsystems, 94

T

Taco Bell, 65
Target, 64
Thermo Electron, 14
3Com Corporation, 315
3M, 14, 230, 350, 416
3-2-1 Contact, 290-294
Time-Life Books, 278
Toastmasters International, 495
Toyota, 406
Travelers Insurance, 170
Tupperware, 314

U

United Nations, 421
United Technologies, 95
University of Detroit Mercy, 282
UPS, 64

V

VIA Marketing & Design, 386
Volkswagen, 146
Volvo, 72

W

Wal-Mart, 41, 261, 463
Wall Street Journal, 72
Walt Disney, 528
WearGuard Corporation, 236
Wells Fargo, 417
Whirlpool, 409
Wilson McHenry Company, 335
Wonderwood Corp., 170

X

Xerox Corporation, 13, 18, 59, 163,
     228, 566, 576

A

a lot, allot, 622
ABI/Inform Thesaurus, 384
Abstract, 429, 446
accede, exceed, 622
accept, except, 622
access, excess, 622
Accident reports, 367
Acknowledgment responses, 337
Active listening, 337, 338
Active verbs, 98, 99
Adapting message to audience, 58-84
   analyze the audience, 61-65
   communication channels, 66
   identifying the audience, 60
   multiple audiences, 60, 68, 77, 78
   reader benefits, 72-77
   use audience analysis to adapt
      message, 66-72
adept, adopt, 622
Advertising Age, 578
advice, advise, 622
affect, effect, 622
affluent, effluent, 622
Alliteration, 302
Allness, 643
among, between, 623
amount, number, 622
AMS simplified format, 588, 591, 596
Analytical reports, 366
Annoying letter, 11
Annual reports, 366
APA format, 392-396
Apologies, 43
Apostrophe, 616, 617
are, our, 622
Argument, 223
Assumptions, 447
attributed, contributed, 622
Audience; *see* Adapting message to
   audience
Audit reports, 366
Audit writing, 91
Average, 407

B

Bad news messages; *see* Negative
   messages
Balancing work and family, 18

Bar charts, 462-464
Barbie, 199
Behavioral interviews, 576
Beliefs, 315-317
Benefits of improving
   correspondence, 12
between, among, 623
Bias-free language, 45
Bias-free photos/illustrations, 51
Bibliography, 392-396
Big words, 91, 92
Black uniforms, 322
Blindering, 642
Block format, 588, 589, 594
Blocking responses, 337, 338
Blueprints, 423
Body, 285
Body language, 318-320
Body movements, 344
Boilerplate, 124
Bold, 136
Boxhead, 462
Braille keyboard, 50
Brainstorming, 118
Branching questions, 388
Bridge, 545, 652
Brochures, 138, 139, 304
Budget, 376, 377
Buffers, 196, 197
Building goodwill, 32-57
   bias-free language, 45-51
   disabilities, people with, 49-51
   nonracist/nonagist language, 48, 49
   nonsexist language, 45-48
   positive emphasis, 37-43
   tone/power/politeness, 43-45
   you-attitude, 34-37
Bullets, 132
Business envelopes, 597, 599
Business etiquette; *see also* Ethics
   bias-free language, 45-51
   e-mail, 89, 165
   interruptions, 344
Business introductions, 323
Business Periodicals Index, 281
Business plans, 376
Business slang, 97
Business style, 89
Businesses, 98
Bypassing, 94, 386, 644, 645

C

c, 597
Canada
   diversity, 314, 315
   positive emphasis, 44
CAR-RT SORT, 279
Case, 612, 613
Causation, 410
cc, 597
Central selling point, 282
Channel overload, 636
Chartjunk, 468, 469
Checklists
   direct requests, 244
   information and positive
      messages, 175
   light revision, 122
   negative messages, 208
   persuasive messages, 245
   thorough revision, 122
Chronological progress reports,
   378, 379
Chronological report, 416
Chronological résumé, 510, 511, 517
Citation, 391
cite, sight, site, 623
Claim, 652
Clip art, 137, 141, 468
Close; *see* Endings
Closed body positions, 344
Closed questions, 386, 387
Closure reports, 367, 416, 417
Clothing, 322
Clustering, 118, 119
Cold list, 279
Collaborative writing, 350-353
Collective letters, 236, 237, 241
Colon, 617
Color, 137, 138, 322, 467, 468
Comma, 617, 618
Comma splice, 615
Common ground, 229, 230
Communicating across cultures; *see*
   Cross-cultural communication
Communication channels, 634
Communication process, 634-637
Communication theory, 634
Company badges, 322
CompareNet, 16

Comparison contrast report, 412-414
Competitive proposals, 369
Complaints, 170, 171
complement, compliment, 623
Complex sentences, 102
complicate, exacerbate, confuse, 623
Complimentary close, 588
Compliments, 323
compose, comprise, 623
Composing process, 116, 117
Compound sentences, 102
Conclusions (reports), 448
Confirmations, 169
Conflict resolution, 345-349
confuse, complicate, exacerbate, 623
Congratulatory notes, 170
Connotations, 95
contributed, attributed, 622
Convenience sample, 389
Conversational style, 89, 343-345
Coordination, 339
Corporate culture, 62
　analyzing, 63
　culture clash, 63
　jargon, 97
　persuasive strategy, and, 224
Correlation, 410
Cost of correspondence, 8-10
Costs of poor correspondence, 10-12
Counterclaim, 652
Courtesy titles, 44, 46, 47
Credibility, 223, 224, 266, 267
Credit reports, 367
Criteria section, 447
Critical incidents, 390
Criticism, 246, 345, 349
Cross-cultural communication,
　　312-333
　body language, 318-320
　business introductions, 323
　compliments, 323
　exaggeration, 323
　eye contact, 318
　gestures, 319, 320
　informational sources, 326, 327
　interruptions, 344
　nonverbal communication, 317-322
　oral communication, 322-325
　personal space, 320
　persuasive documents, 326
　silence, 324
　smiling, 319
　space, 320, 321
　spatial arrangements, 321
　time, 321, 322
　touch, 320, 321
　understatement, 323
　voice qualities, 324, 325
　writing to international audiences,
　　325-327

Cultural differences
　direct requests, 225
　document design, 137
　emotional appeal, 326
　persuasive documents, 326
Culture; *see* Corporate culture
Culturgrams, 327
Customer complaints, 170, 171
Customized planning guides, 121

D

Dangling modifiers, 612, 613
Dash, 618
Data, 652
Data mining, 457
Dates, 621
Debating, 345
Decorative devices, 137
Defensive body positions, 344
Definitions (glossary), 447, 657-668
Demographic characteristics, 64
Denotations, 94, 95
dependant, dependent, 623
Dependent clause, 615
describe, prescribe, 623
Descriptive abstracts, 446
Descriptors, 384
Design; *see* Document design
Deviation bar charts, 464
Difficult persuasive situations, 258-
　　275; *see also* Persuasive messages
　bring everybody on board, 261-263
　convince the reader, 267-270
　credibility, 266, 267
　developing a persuasive
　　strategy, 263
　emotional appeal, 267
　ethical issues, 267
　involve the audience, 263-267
　limit the audience, 261
　threats, 261-263
Dingbats, 137
Direct mail, 289; *see also* Sales and
　　fund-raising letters
Direct mail package, 303, 304
Direct Market-Working Woman, 578
Direct marketing, 289; *see also* Sales
　　and fund-raising letters
*Direct Marketing and Telemarketing
　　Guide,* 578
Direct requests, 225-227, 244
Directed subject line, 228
Disabilities, people with, 49-51
Disability, 49
Disciplinary notices, 204
Discourse-based interviews, 391
Discourse community, 61, 62
discreet, discrete, 623
Diversity, 15, 314, 315

do, due, 623
Document design, 130-151
　brochures, 138, 139
　cultural differences, 137
　newsletters, 140
　page design, 132-138
　part of writing process, as, 143
　presentation slides, 140, 141
　testing the design, 142, 143
　Web pages, 141, 142
Documentation, 392
Documenting sources, 391-396
Dot charts, 461, 462
Dot planning, 341
Drawings, 465
Dress for Success (Molloy), 567
due, do, 623

E

E-mail
　acronyms, 89
　effective use of, 166
　etiquette, 89, 165
　format, 165, 599, 603-605
　guidelines, 89, 164
　Japanese recipients, to, 325
　negative message, as, 202, 203
　persuasive message, as, 236
　privacy, and, 17
　subject lines, 165
E-mail application letters, 552, 553
e.g., i.e., 624
Early letters, 236, 237
Editing, 117, 122
effect, affect, 622
Effective messages, 12
effluent, affluent, 622
Either-or classifications, 642
elicit, illicit, 623
Elimination of alternatives, 414
Ellipses, 620
eminent, immanent, imminent, 624
Emotional appeal
　cultural contrasts, 326
　defined, 224
　difficult persuasive situations, 267
　fund-raising letters, 297
　how created, 224, 232
　sense impressions, and, 233
Emotional intelligence, 222
Empathy, 61
Enclosures, 597
Endings
　informative and positive
　　messages, 163, 164
　job interviews, 570
　oral presentations, 489
　negative messages, 201
　sales and fund-raising letters, 286

Entrepreneurship, 13, 14
Enunciate, 495
Envelopes, 303, 597, 599
Essential clause, 618
Ethics, 17, 18
   direct mail, 284, 303
   how message conveyed, 19
   international business, 319
   interviewing, 390
   organizational content, 19
   visuals, 469
   Web sites, 267
   what the message is, 19
   word choice, 96
   writing process, 126
Etiquette; *see* Business etiquette
Evaluating, 117
Evidence, 652
exacerbate, confuse, complicate, 623
Exaggeration, 323
exceed, accede, 622
except, accept, 622
excess, access, 622
Executive summary, 429, 446
Expectancy theory, 77
External audiences, 6, 7
External motivators, 72, 73
Extraverts, 61, 62
Eye contact, 318

F

Face-to-face surveys, 388
Facts, 639, 640
Fair Debt Collection Practices
   Act, 241
Familiar words, 96
Feasibility reports, 366, 417
Feeling type, 61, 62
fewer, less, 624
Figures, 429, 462
Firings, 204
Flaming, 203
Flesch Reading Ease Scale, 106
Fonts, 136
Forced choice, 581
Form letter, 5
Formal meetings, 349
Formal reports, 366, 425, 427
Formalization, 339
Formation, 338
Formats, 586-606
   e-mail messages, 599, 603-605
   envelopes, 597, 599
   letters, 588-597
   memos, 599-602
   state/province abbreviations,
      603, 606
forward, foreword, 624
Foundation, 652

Foundation Directory, The, 376
Foundation Grants Index Annual,
   The, 376
401(k) program, 237
Freewriting, 118
Frozen evaluations, 641
Functional pattern, 416
Fund-raising letters, 290, 295-301;
   see also Sales and fund-raising
   letters
   emotional appeal, 297
   enclosures, 296
   increasing size of gift, 295
   logical proof, 296, 297
   sample letter, 297-301
   tax-deductibility, 290
   vicarious participation, 290
Funding proposals, 376
Fuzzy words, 103

G

Gannt charts, 465, 467
Gatekeeper, 60
Gathering, 116
General slang, 97
General to particular, 415
Generalizations, 230, 392, 641
Geographic information systems
   (GIS), 465
Geographic pattern, 415
Gerund, 101
Gestures, 319, 320
Getting feedback, 117, 123
GIS software, 465
Globalization, 15, 16, 314
Glossary, 447, 657-668
good, well, 624
Good appeal, 279
Good mailing list, 279
Good news message, 156; *see also*
   Informative and positive
   messages
Good product, 278
Good report problems, 367
Good service or cause, 279
Goodwill; *see* Building goodwill
Goodwill endings, 163
Goodwill presentations, 484
Grammar
   agreement, 610, 611
   apostrophe, 616, 617
   case, 612, 613
   colon, 617
   comma, 617, 618
   comma splices, 615
   dangling modifiers, 612, 613
   dash, 618
   dates, 621
   ellipses, 620

   hyphen, 618
   main/subordinate clauses,
      614, 615
   misplaced modifiers, 613
   numbers, 621
   oft-confused words, 622-626
   parallel structure, 613
   parentheses, 619
   period, 619
   phrases, 614
   prediction errors, 613, 614
   proofreading symbols, 627
   quotation marks, 620
   run-on sentences, 615
   semicolon, 619
   sentence fragments, 615, 616
   square brackets, 620
   underlining/italics, 621
Grammar checkers, 123
Grapevine, 6
Graphs; *see* Visuals
Grid system, 137
Group presentations, 498
Grouped bar charts, 464
Groups, 334-361
   collaborative writing, 350-353
   conflict resolution, 345-349
   conversational style, 343-345
   criticism, 348, 349
   decision-making strategies,
      340, 341
   ground rules, 338, 339
   groupthink, 342
   integrative approach, 351
   leadership, 340
   listening, 336-338
   meetings, 349, 350
   negative roles, 340
   nonverbal communication,
      344, 345
   peer pressure, 342
   positive roles, 339
   roles, 339, 340
   stages of life, 338, 339
   student, 341, 342
   troubleshooting, 346
Groupthink, 342
Guided discussions, 487
Gunning Fog Index, 106

H

Headings, 135, 424-426
Hearing, 336
Height, 322
Hidden job market, 540
Hidden negatives, 40
Hierarchy of needs, 75
High-context cultures, 315
Highlighting, 137

Histograms, 464
Holidays, 317
hopefully, 614
Humor, 202
Hyphen, 618

I

I, 91
i.e., e.g., 624
illicit, elicit, 623
immanent, imminent, eminent, 624
Impersonal expressions, 36
imply, infer, 624
infer, imply, 624
Inferences, 348, 639
Infinitive, 101
Informal meetings, 349
Informal reports, 366, 427
Information interviews, 540
Information overload, 17, 636
Information reports, 366
Information sources; *see* Sources
     of information
Informational messages, 338
Informative and positive messages,
     154-189
  checklist, 175
  complaints, responses to, 170, 171
  confirmations, 169
  congratulatory notes, 170
  e-mail; *see* E-mail
  endings, 163, 164
  letters, 588-597
  memos, 163, 599-602
  one-page memo, 163
  organizing, 157-159
  primary purposes, 156
  reader benefits, 162, 163
  sample problem, 171-174
  secondary purposes, 156
  subject lines, 159-162
  summaries, 169, 170
  thank-you notes, 170, 171
  transmittals, 168, 169
Informative heads, 424
Informative presentations, 484
Informative reports, 416, 417
Initial audience, 60
Inside address, 597
Intensionalism, 644
Intensive pronouns, 612
Interactive presentation, 487
Intercultural competence, 15
Interim reports, 367
Internal audiences, 6, 7
Internal documentation, 392
Internal motivators, 72, 73
International audiences; *see*
     Cross-cultural communication

International holidays, 317
Internet; *see also* Web research
     sources
  job-hunting resources, 541
  job listings, 541
  job search, and, 539, 540
  résumés, and, 528
Interpersonal communication, 336
Interpersonal messages, 338
Interruption interviews, 391
Interruptions, 344
Interviewing maze, 567
Interviews
  behavioral, 576
  information, 540
  job; *see* Job interviews
  referral, 540-543
  research, and, 386-391
  sexist, 571
  situational, 576
  stress, 570, 571
Intranets, 16
Introduction (reports), 446, 447
Introverts, 61, 62
Intuitive type, 61, 62
it's, its, 624
Italics, 136, 621

J

Jargon, 96-98
Job application letters, 536-562
  display knowledge of
          position/company, 550
  display uniqueness, 551
  e-mail application letters, 552, 553
  first paragraphs, 548, 549
  hidden job market (referral
          interviews), 540-543
  information interviews, 540
  information sources, 539, 540
  last paragraph, 552
  length, 555, 556
  organization, 544, 545
  paragraph length/unity, 555
  positive emphasis, 554
  professional appearance, 554
  prospecting letters, 544-549
  résumés, contrasted, 538
  solicited letters, 544-548
  thank-you letters, 544
  writing style, 554
  you-attitude, 555
Job hunting
  follow-up, 576, 578, 579
  information sources, 539-543
  job application letters, 536-562
  job interviews, 565-575
  job offers, 580-582
  résumés, 504-534

salary/benefits, 578, 580
  thank-you letters, 544
Job interviews, 565-575
  appearance, 567, 568
  body, 570
  close, 570
  how to act, 569
  interview strategy, 566, 567
  note-taking, 568, 569
  opening, 569, 570
  rehearsing, 569
  sexist interviews, 571
  stress interviews, 570, 571
  successful vs. unsuccessful
          interviews, 572
  traditional questions, 571-575
  what to bring, 568
Job offers, 580-582
*Job Title Revisions to Eliminate Sex-
     and Age-Referent Language,* 46
Judging type, 61, 62
Judgment, 639
Judgment sample, 389
Junk mail, 279
Justification reports, 366, 417, 421
Justified margins, 136, 137

K

Keywords, 384
Kodansha Encyclopedia of Japan, 380

L

Landscape graphs, 465
Late letters, 237
lay, lie, 624
Layoffs, 204
lectern, podium, 624
Legal concerns, 17
less, fewer, 624
Letter format, 588-597
Letter of transmittal, 428, 429
Letterhead, 592
Letters of recommendation, 239
lie, lay, 624
Light revision checklist, 122
Limitations, 447
Limiter, 652
Line graphs, 462, 464, 465
List of illustrations, 429
List of references, 392-396
Listening, 336-338
Listening errors, 336, 337
loose, lose, 625
Low-context cultures, 315

M

Magazine subscription letter, 290-294
Mail surveys, 389
Mailing lists, 279

Main clause, 615
Make-good reports, 366
Making writing easy to read, 86-112
  active verbs, 98, 99
  e-mail style, 89
  half-truths about style, 91, 92
  improving style, 92, 93
  levels of style, 89
  organizational preferences for
    style, 107
  parallel structure, 104
  put readers in sentences, 105
  readability formulas, 106
  report style, 88
  rules about writing, 92
  sentence length/structure, 102-104
  strong verbs, 100
  technical jargon, 96-98
  tight writing, 100-102
  topic sentences, 105
  transition words/phrases, 106
  word choice, 94-96
Manipulation, 230
Maps, 465, 466
Maslow's hierarchy of needs, 75
Mean, 407
Median, 407
Meetings, 349, 350
Memos, 163, 599-602
Methods, 447
Middle letters, 237, 238
Million Random Digits, A, 389
Minutes, 349
Mirror question, 390
Misplaced modifiers, 613
Mixed abstract, 446
Mixed punctuation, 592
MLA format, 392, 394-396
Mode, 407
Modified block format, 588, 590,
  593, 595
Modifiers, 612
Monochronic cultures, 321
Monologue presentation, 487
moral, morale, 625
Ms., 47
Multiple audiences, 60, 68, 77, 78
Muslims, 316
Myers-Briggs Type Indicator, 61, 62

N

Negative messages, 190-219
  alternate strategies, 202
  alternative/compromise, 199-201
  buffers, 196, 197
  checklist, 208
  customers, to, 197
  disciplinary notices, 204
  e-mail messages, 202, 203

  endings, 201
  giving bad news to
    peers/subordinates, 194-196
  giving bad news to
    supervisors, 193
  humor, 202
  layoffs/firings, 204
  organizing, 193-196
  performance appraisals, 204
  primary purposes, 192
  reasons, 197-199
  recast situation as persuasive
    message, 202
  recast situation as positive
    message, 202
  rejections/refusals, 203, 204
  sample problem, 204-207
  secondary purposes, 192
  subject lines, 192, 193
  tone, 201
Negative performance
  appraisals, 204
Negative words, 40
Netiquette, 89
New Woman's Dress for Success Book,
  The, 568
Newsletters, 140
Noise, 636
Nominative pronouns, 612
Noncompetitive proposals, 369
Nonessential clause, 618
Nonracist/nonagist language, 48, 49
Nonsexist language, 45-48
Nonverbal communication, 4,
  317-322, 344, 345
Noun-pronoun agreement, 611
number, amount, 622
Numbers, 621

O

Objective pronouns, 612
objective, rationale, 625
Observation, 391, 639
Oft-confused words, 622-626
Omnibus motion, 349
One-page memo, 163
Online résumés, 526-531
Online writing labs (OWLs), 121
Open body positions, 344
Open punctuation, 592
Open questions, 386, 387
Openings
  job interviews, 569, 570
  oral presentations, 487-489
  sales and fund-raising letters,
    276-310
Opinion, 639
Optimists, 37
Oral presentations, 482-502

  adapting your ideas to the
    audience, 487
  choose the information, 491, 492
  close, 489
  delivery, 493-497
  eye contact, 494
  fear, 494
  gestures, 496
  group presentations, 498
  involve the audience, 491
  notes, 496, 497
  opening, 487-489
  oral/written messages, compared,
    484, 485
  organize the information, 492, 493
  overview, 493
  patterns of organization, 492, 493
  planning a strategy, 485-491
  purposes, 484
  questions, 497, 498
  signpost, 493
  speaking voice, 494-496
  standing position, 496
  types of presentations, 484, 487
  visuals, 471, 489-491, 497
oral, verbal, 614, 626
Oral vs. written messages, 484, 485
Organ donor cards, 268
Organization culture, 62; *see also*
  Corporate culture
Orientation, 338
our, are, 622
Outsourcing, 13, 14
Overhead transparencies, 489
OWLs, 121

P

P.S., 286, 289
Page design, 132-138
Paired bar charts, 464
Paired graphs, 460, 461
PaperDirect, 140
Parallel structure, 613
Parallelism, 104
Paraphrase, 348
Parentheses, 619
Particular to general, 415
Passive verbs, 36, 98, 99
Patterns of organization, 492, 493
Pay-back reports, 366
pc, 597
Peer pressure, 342
Perceiving type, 61, 62
Perception, 637-639
Performance appraisals, 204, 237-239
Period, 619
Persona, 303
personal, personnel, 625
Personal space, 320

Personality type, 61, 62
Persuasive messages, 220-257; *see also* Difficult persuasive situations
   checklists, 244, 245
   choosing a strategy, 222-225
   collective letters, 236, 237, 241
   cultural contrasts, 326
   direct requests, 225-227, 244
   e-mail messages, 235, 236
   letters of recommendation, 239
   performance appraisals, 237-239
   primary purposes, 222
   problem-solving messages, 228-234
   sample problems, 239-244
   secondary purposes, 222
   tone, 234, 235
Persuasive presentations, 484
Photographs, 465
Phrase, 615
Pictograms, 464
Pie charts, 462, 463
Pitch, 324
Planning, 116
Planning guide, 118, 121
podium, lectern, 624
Point size, 136
Polarization, 642
Politeness, 44
Political direct mail, 302
Polychronic cultures, 321
Population, 389
Positive emphasis, 37-43
Positive message, 156; *see also* Informative and positive messages
Positive words, 40
Possessive pronouns, 612
possible, possibly, 625
Posture, 344
Power implications, 44
PowerPoint, 141, 489, 490
precede, proceed, 625
Prediction errors, 613, 614
Prepositions, 91
prescribe, describe, 623
Presentation slides, 140, 141
Presentations; *see* Oral presentations
Presenting problem, 347
Primary audience, 60
Primary research, 380
principal, principle, 625
Privacy, 17
Pro-and-con pattern, 413, 414
Probes, 390
Problem-solution pattern, 414
Problem-solving messages, 228-234
Problem-solving reports, 366
Procedural messages, 338

Procrastination, 125
Product names, 95
Progress reports, 367, 377-379
Pronouns, 612
Proofreading, 24, 117, 123
Proofreading symbols, 627
Proposals, 368-377
Prospecting letters, 544-549
Psychographic characteristics, 64, 281
Psychological description, 233, 234, 302, 303
Psychological reactance, 200
Punctuation, 614; *see also* Grammar
Purpose statement, 368, 447

Q

Quadrant analysis, 409, 410
Quality analysis, 407
Quarterly reports, 366
Questions for analysis, 22, 23
quiet, quite, 625
Quotation marks, 620

R

Ragged right margins, 136
Random-digit dialing, 388
Random sample, 389
Range, 407
Rapid change, 20
Readability formulas, 106
Reader benefits, 72-77
Reader's Guide to Periodical Literature, The, 281
Rebuttal, 652
Recommendation progress report, 380
Recommendation reports, 366
Recommendations, 447, 448
Reference line, 592
Referral interviews, 540-543
Reflexive pronouns, 612
regulate, relegate, 625
Rejections/refusals, 203, 204
Relating, 345
Release date, 428
Religion, 316
Reply card, 304
Reply envelope, 304
Reports, 365-455
   analyzing numbers, 407-409
   analyzing words, 409
   assumptions, 447
   background (history), 448
   blueprints, 423
   checking the logic, 410, 411
   choosing information, 411, 412
   closure, 416, 417
   conclusions/recommendations, 448

   defining report problems, 367, 368
   definitions (glossary), 447
   documenting sources, 391-396
   executive summary (abstract), 429, 446
   feasibility, 417
   formal vs. informal, 425, 427
   headings, 424, 425
   identify source of data, 406, 407
   informative, 416, 417
   introduction, 446, 447
   justification, 417, 421
   letter of transmittal, 428, 429
   levels of, 366
   limitations, 447
   list of illustrations, 429
   organizing information, 412-421
   patterns for organizing information, 412-416
   presentation, 421-425
   progress, 377-379
   proposals, 368-377
   purpose statement, 368
   putting information in context, 409, 410
   research, 380-391; *see also* Research strategies
   table of contents, 429
   timetable for writing, 406
   title page, 427
   types, 366, 367
   writing style, 422
Requests for proposals (RFPs), 369
Research strategies, 380-391
   electronic sources, 381
   observing customers/users, 391
   print sources, 385
   surveys/interviews, 386-391
   Web sources, 382-386
residence, residents, 625
respectfully, respectively, 625
Respondents, 386
Response rate, 389
Résumés, 504-534
   action verbs, 516
   activities, 521, 522
   career objective, 513
   defined, 506
   details, 509
   difficulties/problems, 523-525
   education, 513-515
   emphasis, 508
   experience, 516, 518
   headings, 518, 521
   honors/awards, 515
   how used, 507
   information sources (Web), 528
   kinds/types, 510
   layout/printing/paper, 509
   length, 508

name/address/phone number, 512
   online, 526-531
   references, 522, 523
   scannable, 528-531
   self-assessment, 506, 507
   Web, 526, 528
   writing style, 509
Reverse chronological résumé, 510
Revising, 117, 119-122
Revision, 24
RFPs, 369
Rhyme, 302
Rhythm, 302
Robert Half and Accountemps Salary
   Guide, 578
Robert's Rules of Order, 349
Robot programs, 165
role, roll, 626
Rule of three, 302
Rules about writing, 92
Run-on sentences, 615

S

Salary information, 260
Sales and fund-raising letters, 276-310
   action close, 286
   body, 285, 286
   direct mail package, 303, 304
   direct mail strategy, 280 282
   ethics, 284, 303
   good direct mail, 278, 279
   junk mail, 279
   opening, 283-285
   organizing, 283-289
   P.S., 286, 289
   political direct mail, 302
   primary purposes, 278
   sample fund-raising letter, 297-301
   sample sales letter (magazine
      subscription letter), 290-294
   secondary purpose, 278
   star-chain-knot pattern, 283-286
   strategy (fund-raising appeals),
      290, 295-297
   strategy (sales letters), 289, 290
   touch, 304
   writing style, 297, 302, 303
Sales proposals, 371
Sales reports, 366
Salutation, 588
Sample problems
   informative and positive
      messages, 171-174
   negative messages, 204-207
   persuasive messages, 239-244
Samples, 304
Sans serif typefaces, 135, 136
Scannable résumés, 528-531
Scope statement, 447

Search engines, 382
Secondary audience, 60
Secondary letters, 304
Secondary research, 380
Segmented bars, 464
Semantic triangle, 643
Semantics, 634, 637
Semicolon, 619
Sense impressions, 233
Sensing type, 61, 62
Sentence fragments, 615, 616
Sentence length/structure, 102-104
Sentence outline, 446
Serif typefaces, 135, 136
Seven Habits of Highly Effective People,
   The (Covey), 313
Sexist generic pronoun, 48
Sexist interviews, 571
Sexist terms/phrases, 46
Short-term memory, 133
sight, site, cite, 623
Signpost, 493
Silence, 324
Simple sentences, 102
simple, simplistic, 626
site, cite, sight, 623
Situational interviews, 576
Six-column grid, 138
Sketches, 465, 466
Skills résumé, 510, 519, 520, 527
Slang, 97
Slides, 489, 490
Smiling, 319
Social Sciences Citation Index, 380
Solicited letters, 544-548
Source Book Profiles, 376
Sources of information
   addresses/facts about companies,
      538, 539
   documenting sources, 391-396
   electronic sources, 381
   observing customers/users, 391
   print sources, 385
   résumés, 528
   surveys/interviews, 386-391
   Web sources, 382-386
Space, 320, 321
Spam, 279
Spatial arrangements, 321
Spatial pattern, 415
Speeches; *see* Oral presentations
Spell checkers, 123
Split infinitives, 614
Spot visuals, 462
Square brackets, 620
Stacked bars, 464
Standard agenda, 340, 341
Star-chain-knot pattern, 283-286
State/province abbreviations,
   603, 606

stationary, stationery, 626
Stereotyping, 641
Stories, 163, 412, 460, 461
Storyboard, 118, 120
Stress, 324
Stress interviews, 570, 571
Strong verbs, 100
Structured interview, 390
Stub, 462
Student groups, 341, 342
Style; *see* Making writing easy
   to read
Subdivided bars, 464
Subject lines, 592
   defined, 666
   direct requests, 226, 227
   informative and positive
      messages, 159-162
   negative messages, 192, 193
   problem-solving messages, 228
Subject-verb agreement, 610
Subjects, 386
Subordinate clauses, 614, 615
Summaries, 169, 170
Summary abstracts, 446
Summary sentence paragraph, 545
Surveys, 386-391

T

Table of contents, 429
Tables, 429, 462, 463
Talking heads, 424
Target audience, 281
Task progress report, 380
Tax-deductibility, 290
Teams, 15; *see also* Groups
Technical jargon, 96-98
Technology, 16, 17
   blind people, and, 50
   writing process, and, 126
Telephone surveys, 388
Term paper style, 89
Thank-you notes, 170, 171
their, there, they're, 626
Think-aloud protocols, 391
Thinking type, 61, 62
Thorough revision checklist, 122
Threats, 261-263, 326
Three Mile Island, 143
Three-column grid, 138
Tight writing, 100-102
Time, 321, 322
Title page, 427
to, too, two, 626
Tone
   defined, 43
   guidelines, 44
   negative messages, 201
   persuasive messages, 234, 235

Tone of voice, 324
Tongue twisters, 496
Topic headings, 424
Topic sentence, 105, 424
Touch, 304, 320, 321
Toulmin logic, 650-656
Trade journals, 540
Traditional term paper style, 89
Transition words/phrases, 106
Transitions, 423
Translators, 325
Transmittals, 168, 169
Transparencies, 489
Trends, 12-20
Trip reports, 367
Truncated code, 384
Truncated visuals, 469, 470
Twelve-column grid, 138
two, to, too, 626
Typefaces, 135, 136
Typos, 123

U

Umbrella paragraph, 169
Underlining, 621
Understatement, 323
Uniform color, 322
unique, unusual, 626
Unisex pronoun, 48
Unjustified margins, 136
Unnecessary words, 100, 101
Unstructured interview, 390

V

VALS profiles, 64
Values and beliefs, 315-317, 326

Values and life styles (VALS)
   profiles, 64
Venting, 347
verbal, oral, 614, 626
Verbal communication, 4
Vested interest, 223
Vicarious participation, 290
Visuals, 456-480
   accuracy, 468-470
   check source of data, 459
   choosing the right visual, 461
   color/decoration, 467, 468
   components, 461, 462
   designing, 459-470
   distortion, 468-470
   drawings, 465
   ethics, 469
   Gannt charts, 465, 467
   integrating, into text, 470, 471
   line graphs, 464, 465
   maps, 465, 466
   photographs, 465
   pie charts, 463
   presentations, and, 471,
      489-491, 497
   sketches, 465, 466
   stories, 460, 461
   tables, 462, 463
   when to use, 458
Voice mail
   getting action, 238
   privacy, and, 17
Voice qualities, 324, 325
Volume, 325

W

Watchdog audience, 60
weather, whether, 626
Web pages, 141, 142
Web research sources; *see also*
   Internet
   evaluating, 384-386
   news sites, 383
   reference collections, 384
   search engines, 382
   subject matter directories, 382, 383
   U.S. government information, 383
Web résumés, 526, 528
well, good, 624
whether, weather, 626
White space, 132
Wild card, 384
WIRMI, 92
Word choice, 94-96
Wordiness, 34, 100-102, 422
Workplace violence, 201
Works Cited, 392-396
Writer's block, 125
Writing, 116
Written vs. oral messages, 484, 485

Y

you, you're, 626
You-attitude, 34-37, 349, 555
Youth, 322

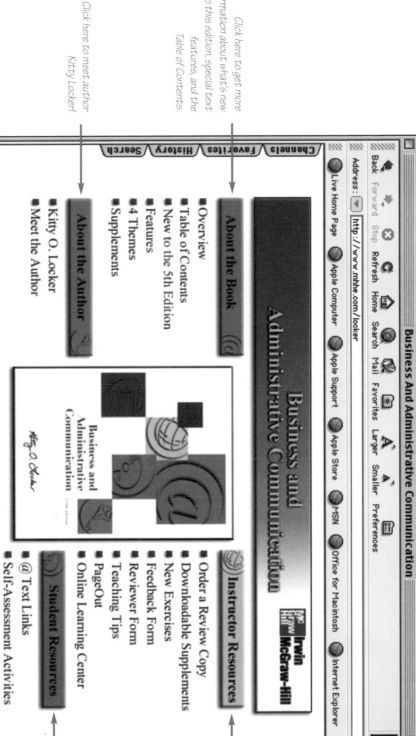

Click here to get more information about what's new to this edition, special text features, and the Table of Contents.

Click here to meet author Kitty Locker!

Business And Administrative Communication

Back | Forward | Stop | Refresh | Home | Search | Mail | Favorites | Larger | Smaller | Preferences

Address: http://www.mhhe.com/locker

Live Home Page | Apple Computer | Apple Support | Apple Store | MSN | Office for Macintosh | Internet Explorer

Channels | Search | History | Favorites

Business and Administrative Communication

McGraw-Hill / Irwin

About the Book
- Overview
- Table of Contents
- New to the 5th Edition
- Features
- 4 Themes
- Supplements

About the Author
- Kitty O. Locker
- Meet the Author

Business and Administrative Communication
Kitty O. Locker

Instructor Resources
- Order a Review Copy
- Downloadable Supplements
- New Exercises
- Feedback Form
- Reviewer Form
- Teaching Tips
- PageOut
- Online Learning Center

Student Resources
- @ Text Links
- Self-Assessment Activities
- Sample Letters, Memos, and Resumes
- Quizzes/Activities/ Review Questions
- Letter Templates
- Online Learning Center

Begin a search: ▶ Catalog ▶ Site ▶ Campus Rep

| DIGITAL SOLUTIONS | GET INVOLVED | AUTHOR MANUAL | ORDER INFO | LEGAL POLICIES & INFO | WHAT'S NEW | SITE MAP | SITE SEARCH |

Internet zone

Instructors: Click here to access downloadable supplements, teaching tips, McGraw-Hill's PageOut, and additional exercises. You'll also have the opportunity to chat with other business communication professors around the world.

Students: Welcome to the Online Learning Center! Click here to find self-assessment activities, additional writing samples, quizzes, review questions, and much more. You'll be able to use our @ links to explore career resources, ethical dilemmas, and organizational culture situations. Come back often for updates!